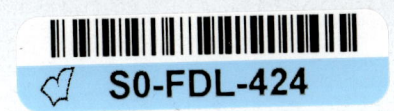

America

The Essential Learning Edition

Fourth Edition

America
The Essential Learning Edition

VOLUME ONE

DAVID EMORY SHI

DAINA RAMEY BERRY

JOSEPH CRESPINO

AMY MURRELL TAYLOR

Fourth Edition

W. W. Norton & Company, Inc.
New York · London

W. W. Norton & Company has been independent since its founding in 1923, when William Warder Norton and Mary D. Herter Norton first published lectures delivered at the People's Institute, the adult education division of New York City's Cooper Union. The firm soon expanded its program beyond the Institute, publishing books by celebrated academics from America and abroad. By midcentury, the two major pillars of Norton's publishing program—trade books and college texts—were firmly established. In the 1950s, the Norton family transferred control of the company to its employees, and today—with a staff of five hundred and hundreds of trade, college, and professional titles published each year—W. W. Norton & Company stands as the largest and oldest publishing house owned wholly by its employees.

Copyright © 2025 by W. W. Norton & Company, Inc.
All rights reserved
Printed in Canada

Editor: Jon Durbin
Project Editors: Jennifer Barnhardt, Elizabeth Coletti
Assistant Editor: Emma Freund
Managing Editors, College: Carla Talmadge and Kim Yi
Associate Director of Production: Benjamin Reynolds
Media Editor: Carson Russell
Associate Media Editor: Caleb Wertz
Assistant Media Editor: Katherine Kopp
Ebook Producer: Emily Schwoyer
Marketing Manager, History: Sarah England Bartley
Design Director: Jillian Burr
Director of College Permissions: Megan Schindel
College Permissions Manager: Elizabeth Trammell
Text Permissions Associate: Patricia Wong
Photo Department Manager: Melinda Patelli
Photo Editor: Amla Sanghvi
Photo Researcher: Julie Tesser
Composition: Graphic World/Project Manager: Gary Clark
Cartography by Mapping Specialists
Manufacturing: Transcontinental—Beauceville, QC

ISBN: 978-1-324-08510-2
Permission to use copyrighted material is included in the back of the book.

W. W. Norton & Company, Inc., 500 Fifth Avenue, New York, NY 10110-0017
wwnorton.com
W. W. Norton & Company Ltd., 15 Carlisle Street, London W1D 3BS
1 2 3 4 5 6 7 8 9 0

For Our Students: Past, Present, and Future

About the Authors

DAVID EMORY SHI is president emeritus at Furman University in Greenville, South Carolina. He is the author of several books focusing on American cultural history, including the award-winning *The Simple Life: Plain Living and High Thinking in American Culture* and *Facing Facts: Realism in American Thought and Culture, 1850–1920*. He remains highly engaged with students and instructors around the country with his many annual "author-in-residence" visits to campuses. Learn more about David Shi at usahistorian.com.

DAINA RAMEY BERRY, Professor of History and Dean of the Humanities and Fine Arts at the University of California, Santa Barbara, is an internationally recognized scholar of gender and slavery in the United States. Her most recent book, *A Black Woman's History of the United States* (co-authored with Kali Nicole Grass), won the 2021 Susan Koppelman Award for the best new book in feminist studies. Berry was also honored with the President's Associates Teaching Excellence Award at the University of Texas, where she served as chair of the history department.

JOSEPH CRESPINO, the Jimmy Carter Professor of History at Emory University in Atlanta and former chair of the history department, is a specialist in twentieth-century political and cultural history. He was the Fulbright Distinguished Lecturer in American Studies at the University of Tubingen in 2014. Among his widely acclaimed books are an award-winning biography, *Strom Thurmond's America*, and most recently, *Atticus Finch: The Biography*. Crespino has received the Excellence in Undergraduate Teaching Award from the Emory University Center for Teaching and Learning.

AMY MURRELL TAYLOR is the T. Marshall Hahn Jr. Professor of History at the University of Kentucky, where she focuses on gender, the Civil War and Reconstruction, and the American South. She has been honored by the university's Provost's Award for Outstanding Teaching and Great Teacher Awards. Her latest book, *Embattled Freedom: Journeys through the Civil War's Slave Refugee Camps*, received several national awards, including the Frederick Douglass Book Prize and the Merle Curti Social History Award.

Contents in Brief

PART ONE	**An Old "New" World**	3
CHAPTER 1	The Collision of Cultures in the Sixteenth Century	7
CHAPTER 2	England and Its American Colonies, 1607–1732	55
CHAPTER 3	Colonial Ways of Life, 1607–1750	103
CHAPTER 4	From Colonies to States, 1607–1776	141
PART TWO	**Building a Nation**	193
CHAPTER 5	The American Revolution, 1775–1783	197
CHAPTER 6	Securing the Constitution and Union, 1783–1800	235
CHAPTER 7	The Early Republic, 1800–1815	283
PART THREE	**An Expanding Nation**	329
CHAPTER 8	The Emergence of a Market Economy, 1815–1860	333
CHAPTER 9	Nationalism and Sectionalism, 1815–1828	367
CHAPTER 10	A New Democratic Era, 1828–1840	395
CHAPTER 11	The South and Slavery, 1800–1860	429
CHAPTER 12	Religion, Romanticism, and Reform, 1800–1860	463
PART FOUR	**A House Divided and Rebuilt**	509
CHAPTER 13	Western Expansion and Southern Secession, 1830–1861	513
CHAPTER 14	The War of the Union, 1861–1865	571
CHAPTER 15	The Era of Reconstruction, 1865–1877	629

Contents

List of **COMPARING PERSPECTIVES** *features*   xx
List of Maps   xxii
List of **THINKING LIKE A HISTORIAN** *features*   xxiv
List of **WHAT'S IT ALL ABOUT?** *features*   xxvi
Preface   xxvii
Acknowledgments   li

PART ONE | An Old "New" World   3

CHAPTER 1 The Collision of Cultures in the Sixteenth Century   7

Early Cultures in the Americas   9
The Age of Exploration and the Rise of Global Trade   18
COMPARING PERSPECTIVES Boundaries in the Age of Exploration and Trade   28
The Spanish Empire   34
The Columbian Exchange   39
The Spanish in North America   41
REVIEWING THE CORE OBJECTIVES   52

CHAPTER 2 England and Its American Colonies, 1607–1732   55

The English Background   56
Settling the American Colonies   60
Indigenous Peoples and English Settlers   89
COMPARING PERSPECTIVES Bacon's Rebellion and the Intersection of Gender, Race, and Class   92
Thriving Colonies   97
REVIEWING THE CORE OBJECTIVES   100

xiv

CHAPTER 3 Colonial Ways of Life, 1607–1750 103

The Demography of the Early Colonies 104
Women in the Colonies 107
Society and Economy in the Colonies 110
Race-Based Chattel Slavery in the Colonies 123
COMPARING PERSPECTIVES Indentured Servants and the Legal System 126
First Stirrings of a Common Colonial Culture 129
REVIEWING THE CORE OBJECTIVES 138

CHAPTER 4 From Colonies to States, 1607–1776 141

French and British Colonies 142
Warfare in the Colonies 150
Tightening of Control over the British Colonies 159
The Road to the American Revolution 166
COMPARING PERSPECTIVES On Coverture, Liberty, and Equality 182
REVIEWING THE CORE OBJECTIVES 186

THINKING LIKE A HISTORIAN: Debating the Origins of the American Revolution 188

PART TWO | Building a Nation 193

CHAPTER 5 The American Revolution, 1775–1783 197

American Society at War 198
Mobilizing for War 199
Setbacks for the British (1777–1781) 208
War as an Engine of Change 221
Equality and Its Limits 225
COMPARING PERSPECTIVES Freedom among the Enslaved in the Revolutionary Era 228
REVIEWING THE CORE OBJECTIVES 232

xv

CHAPTER 6 Securing the Constitution and Union, 1783–1800   235

The Confederation Government   236
The Constitution   243
The Fight for Ratification   251
The Federalist Era   255
COMPARING PERSPECTIVES On Rights and Freedoms   258
Foreign and Domestic Crises   267
REVIEWING THE CORE OBJECTIVES   280

CHAPTER 7 The Early Republic, 1800–1815   283

Jeffersonian Republicanism   284
COMPARING PERSPECTIVES Purchase, Peace, and the Struggle for Land Sovereignty   294
War in the Mediterranean and Europe   300
The War of 1812   305
The Aftermath of War   316
REVIEWING THE CORE OBJECTIVES   322

THINKING LIKE A HISTORIAN: Debating Thomas Jefferson and Slavery   324

PART THREE | An Expanding Nation   329

CHAPTER 8 The Emergence of a Market Economy, 1815–1860   333

The Market Revolution   334
Industrial Development   342
COMPARING PERSPECTIVES Technology and Expansion in the New Nation   346
Immigration   355
Organized Labor and New Professions   359
REVIEWING THE CORE OBJECTIVES   364

CHAPTER 9 Nationalism and Sectionalism, 1815–1828 367

A New Nationalism   368
Debates over the American System   372
"An Era of Good Feelings"   373
COMPARING PERSPECTIVES Slavery and Freedom across Borders   376
Nationalist Diplomacy   379
The Rise of Andrew Jackson   382
REVIEWING THE CORE OBJECTIVES   392

CHAPTER 10 A New Democratic Era, 1828–1840   395

Democratization and the Role of the Federal Government   396
Nullification   401
Jackson's Policy on Indigenous Americans   406
COMPARING PERSPECTIVES The Possession and Dispossession of Native Lands   414
Political Battles   416
Beyond Jackson's Legacy: A New Era   424
REVIEWING THE CORE OBJECTIVES   426

CHAPTER 11 The South and Slavery, 1800–1860   429

Racial Capitalism   430
The Cotton Kingdom   430
Whites in the South   438
Enslaved People in the South   442
COMPARING PERSPECTIVES The Buying and Selling of Enslaved People   448
Forging an Enslaved Community   453
REVIEWING THE CORE OBJECTIVES   460

CHAPTER 12 Religion, Romanticism, and Reform, 1800–1860   463

A More Democratic Religion   464
Romanticism in America   472
The Reform Impulse   480
Anti-Slavery and Women's Rights Movements   487
COMPARING PERSPECTIVES Rights for Women and Enslaved People   496
REVIEWING THE CORE OBJECTIVES   502

THINKING LIKE A HISTORIAN: Debating Separate Spheres   504

PART FOUR | A House Divided and Rebuilt   509

CHAPTER 13 Western Expansion and Southern Secession, 1830–1861   513

Moving West   514
The Mexican-American War   532
Slavery in the Territories   538

COMPARING PERSPECTIVES The Sectional Crisis   546

The Emergence of the Republican Party   552
The Southern Response   565

REVIEWING THE CORE OBJECTIVES   568

CHAPTER 14 The War of the Union, 1861–1865   571

Mobilizing Forces in the North and South   572
Emancipation   589

COMPARING PERSPECTIVES The End of Slavery   598

The War behind the Lines   600
The Faltering Confederacy   607
A Transformational War   622

REVIEWING THE CORE OBJECTIVES   626

CHAPTER 15 The Era of Reconstruction, 1865–1877   629

The War's Aftermath in the South   631
Battles over Political Reconstruction   632

COMPARING PERSPECTIVES Reconstructing Democracy   640

Black Society under Reconstruction   649
The Grant Administration   657
Reconstruction's Significance   671

REVIEWING THE CORE OBJECTIVES   672

THINKING LIKE A HISTORIAN: Debating Reconstruction's Demise   674

xviii

Glossary G-1

Appendix A-1

The Declaration of Independence A-1

Articles of Confederation A-5

The Constitution of the United States A-11

Amendments to the Constitution A-20

Presidential Elections A-30

Admission of States A-36

Population of the United States A-37

Immigration by Region and Selected Country of Last Residence, Fiscal Years 1820–2027 A-38

Legal Immigration to the United States A-50

Presidents, Vice Presidents, and Secretaries of State A-51

Further Readings R-1

Credits C-1

Index I-1

Comparing Perspectives

CHAPTER 1   Boundaries in the Age of Exploration and Trade   28
- From: Treaty of Tordesillas, signed June 7, 1494.
- From: Letter from King Nzinga Mbemba of the Kongo, to King João of Portugal, July 6, 1526.

CHAPTER 2   Bacon's Rebellion and the Intersection of Gender, Race, and Class   92
- From: By the King, A Proclamation for the suppression of a rebellion lately raised within the Plantation of Virginia, October 27, 1676.
- From: The Humble Petition of Sarah Drummond before the Board of Trade and Plantations, November 9, 1677.

CHAPTER 3   Indentured Servants and the Legal System   126
- From: John Punch Court Decision, 1640.
- From: John Reid Jr., Indenture of Apprenticeship with Robert Livingston Jr., November 1, 1742.

CHAPTER 4   On Coverture, Liberty, and Equality   182
- From: William Blackstone, "Chapter the fifteenth, Of Husband and Wife," *Commentaries on the Laws of England*, 1766.
- From: Letter from Abigail Adams to John Adams, March 31, 1776.

CHAPTER 5   Freedom among the Enslaved in the Revolutionary Era   228
- From: "By His Excellency Sir Henry Clinton, K. B. General and Commander in Chief" [Philipsburg Proclamation], June 30, 1779.
- From: "Ran Away" [Runaway Slave Advertisement], *The Georgia Gazette*, January 4, 1781.

CHAPTER 6   On Rights and Freedoms   258
- From: Letter from James Madison to Thomas Jefferson, October 17, 1788.
- From: An Act Respecting Escapees from Justice, and Persons Escaping from the Service of Their Masters, February 12, 1793.

CHAPTER 7   Purchase, Peace, and the Struggle for Land Sovereignty   294
- From: Letter from Thomas Jefferson to Robert Livingston, April 18, 1802.
- From: Speech of Tecumseh to William Henry Harrison, August 20, 1810.

CHAPTER 8   Technology and Expansion in the New Nation   346
- From: Letter from Nemesio Salcedo to Juan Bautista Elguézabal, governor of Texas, January 15, 1805.
- From: Charles Sumner, "Speech for Union Among Men of All Parties Against the Slave Power, and the Extension of Slavery, in a Mass Convention at Worcester," June 28, 1848.

CHAPTER 9   Slavery and Freedom across Borders   376
- From: "Emancipation of Slaves in Texas," *Georgia Messenger*, December 12, 1826.
- From: C. A. Wickliffe, "Fugitive Slaves," *Niles' Register*, June 24, 1826.

CHAPTER 10   The Possession and Dispossession of Native Lands   414
- From: Letter from John Ross to Andrew Jackson, January 23, 1835.
- From: Andrew Jackson, "To the Cherokee Tribe of Indians East of Mississippi River," March 16, 1835.

CHAPTER 11   The Buying and Selling of Enslaved People   448
- From: Auction Announcement, "178 sugar and cotton plantation slaves! In succession of Wm. M. Lambeth and for a partition," March 13–14, 1855.
- From: Receipt of Sale of 58 slaves [Sale by Josiah Brown to A. C. Horton, who was taking them to Texas], July 25, 1860.

CHAPTER 12   Rights for Women and Enslaved People   496
- From: "Declaration of Sentiments," *Report of the Women's Rights Convention Held at Seneca Falls, NY*, July 19–20, 1848.
- From: Frederick Douglass, "What to the Slave Is the Fourth of July?" July 5, 1852.

CHAPTER 13   The Sectional Crisis   546
- From: "The Address of the Hon. Abraham Lincoln, in Vindication of the Policy of the Constitution and the Principles of the Republican Party," February 27, 1860.
- From: "An Address Setting Forth the Declaration of the Immediate Causes Which Induce and Justify the Secession of Mississippi from the Federal Union and the Ordinance of Secession," 1861.

CHAPTER 14   The End of Slavery   598
- From: *The Secret Eye: The Journal of Ella Gertrude Clanton Thomas*, May 29 and June 12, 1865.
- From: "Letter from a Freedman to His Old Master," *Cleveland Daily Leader*, August 28, 1865.

CHAPTER 15   Reconstructing Democracy   640
- From: *Proceedings of the State Convention of Colored Men Held at Lexington, KY*, November 26–28, 1867.
- From: "A Southern Speech: General Wade Hampton on the Crisis," *New York Times*, October 17, 1866.

Maps

CHAPTER 1

Map 1.1 The First Migration   8
Map 1.2 Pre-Columbian Indigenous Civilizations in Central and South America   12
Map 1.3 Pre-Columbian Indigenous Civilizations in North America   16
Map 1.4 The Three West African Kingdoms   21
Map 1.5 Columbus's Voyages   24
Map 1.6 Spanish Explorations of the Americas   42
Map 1.7 English, French, and Dutch Explorations   48

CHAPTER 2

Map 2.1 European Settlements and Indigenous Societies in Seventeenth-Century North America   57
Map 2.2 Early Virginia and Maryland   67
Map 2.3 Early New England Settlements   69
Map 2.4 Early Settlements in the South   77
Map 2.5 The Middle Colonies   81

CHAPTER 3

Map 3.1 Atlantic Trade Routes, 1600–1800   117
Map 3.2 Major Immigrant Groups in Colonial America   118
Map 3.3 The African Slave Trade, 1500–1800   120

CHAPTER 4

Map 4.1 The French in North America   144
Map 4.2 Major Campaigns of the French and Indian War   151
Map 4.3 European Land Claims in North America, 1713   155
Map 4.4 European Land Claims in North America, 1763   156
Map 4.5 Lexington and Concord, April 19, 1775   173

CHAPTER 5

Map 5.1 Major Campaigns in New York and New Jersey, 1776–1777   205
Map 5.2 Major Campaigns in New York and Pennsylvania, 1777   209
Map 5.3 Western Campaigns, 1776–1779   213
Map 5.4 Major Campaigns in the South, 1778–1781   216
Map 5.5 Yorktown, 1781   218
Map 5.6 North America, 1783   219

CHAPTER 6

Map 6.1 Western Land Cessions, 1781–1802   239
Map 6.2 The Northwest Territory, 1785   240
Map 6.3 The Vote on the Constitution, 1787–1790   254
Map 6.4 The Treaty of Greenville, 1795   270
Map 6.5 Pinckney's Treaty, 1795   273
Map 6.6 The Election of 1800   278

CHAPTER 7

Map 7.1 Explorations of the Louisiana Purchase, 1804–1806   298
Map 7.2 Major Northern and Mid-Atlantic Campaigns of the War of 1812   309
Map 7.3 Major Southern Campaigns of the War of 1812   311

CHAPTER 8

Map 8.1 Transportation West, about 1840   336
Map 8.2 The Growth of Railroads, 1850 and 1860   339
Map 8.3 The Growth of Industry in the 1840s   352
Map 8.4 The Growth of Cities, 1820 and 1860   353
Map 8.5 Population Density, 1820 and 1860   356

CHAPTER 9

Map 9.1 The Missouri Compromise, 1820   378
Map 9.2 Boundary Treaties, 1818–1819   381
Map 9.3 The Election of 1828   387

CHAPTER 10

Map 10.1 Indian Removal, 1820–1842   412

CHAPTER 11

Map 11.1 Cotton Production, 1821   433
Map 11.2 Routes of the U.S. Domestic Slave Trade, 1810s–1850s   435
Map 11.3 Population Growth and Cotton Production, 1821–1859   437
Map 11.4 The Enslaved Population, 1820   444
Map 11.5 The Enslaved Population, 1860   445

CHAPTER 12

Map 12.1 Mormon Trek, 1830–1847   471

CHAPTER 13

Map 13.1 Overland Trails   515
Map 13.2 Comanche Empire   517
Map 13.3 The Oregon Dispute, 1818–1846   532
Map 13.4 The Mexican-American War, 1846–1848   534
Map 13.5 The Compromise of 1850   545
Map 13.6 The Kansas-Nebraska Act, 1854   553
Map 13.7 The Election of 1860   564

CHAPTER 14

Map 14.1 Secession, 1860–1861   573
Map 14.2 Campaigns in the West, February–April 1862   585
Map 14.3 The Peninsular Campaign, 1862   588
Map 14.4 Campaigns in Virginia and Maryland, 1862   592
Map 14.5 Campaigns in the East, 1863   608
Map 14.6 Grant in Virginia, 1864–1865   616
Map 14.7 Sherman's Campaigns, 1864–1865   620

CHAPTER 15

Map 15.1 Reconstruction, 1865–1877   646
Map 15.2 The Election of 1876   669

Thinking Like a Historian

PART ONE

Debating the Origins of the American Revolution — 188

Secondary Sources

- Bernard Bailyn, *The Ideological Origins of the American Revolution*, 1992
- Gary Nash, "Social Change and the Growth of Prerevolutionary Urban Radicalism," 1976

Primary Sources

- John Dickinson, "Letter from a Farmer in Pennsylvania," 1767
- Governor Francis Bernard, "Letter to the Lords of Trade," 1765

PART TWO

Debating Thomas Jefferson and Slavery — 324

Secondary Sources

- Douglas L. Wilson, "Thomas Jefferson and the Character Issue," 1992
- Paul Finkelman, "Jefferson and Slavery," 1993

Primary Sources

- Thomas Jefferson, a draft section omitted from the *Declaration of Independence*, 1776
- Thomas Jefferson, *Notes on the State of Virginia*, 1787
- Thomas Jefferson, Letter to M. Warville, 1788
- Thomas Jefferson, Letter to John Holmes, 1820

PART THREE

Debating Separate Spheres — 504

Secondary Sources

- Catherine Clinton, "The Ties that Bind," 1984
- Nancy A. Hewitt, "Beyond the Search for Sisterhood: American Women's History in the 1980s," 1985

Primary Sources

- Lucretia Mott, *Discourse on Women*, 1849
- Sojourner Truth, "And Ar'n't I a Woman?" 1851
- Harriet H. Robinson, *Loom and Spindle, or Life among the Early Mill Girls*, 1898

PART FOUR
Debating Reconstruction's Demise   674

Secondary Sources
- Eric Foner, *Reconstruction: America's Unfinished Revolution*, 1988
- Kidada E. Williams, *I Saw Death Coming: A History of Terror and Survival in the War against Reconstruction*, 2023

Primary Sources
- Mississippi's Republican Governer Adelbert Ames to his wife, Blanche, 1875
- Committee of South Carolina Freedmen to President Andrew Johnson, 1865
- Testimony Before Congress by R. B. Avery, Northern White Carpetbagger, 1880
- Testimony Before Congress by Charlotte Fowler, South Carolina Freedwoman, 1871

What's It All About?
(Available Online)

These unique summary tables provide bullet point review summaries of major developments in each period.

CHAPTER 1	The Columbian Exchange and the Spanish Empire in North America
CHAPTER 2	Different Beginnings, Common Trends: The English Colonies in North America
CHAPTER 3	Comparing the Three English Colonial Regions
CHAPTER 4	The Road to the American Revolution
CHAPTER 5	From Subjects to Citizens
CHAPTER 6	Federalists versus Republicans
CHAPTER 7	Managing Foreign Policy in the Early Republic
CHAPTER 8	Technological Innovation and a National Marketplace
CHAPTER 9	Sectional Conflict and Economic Policies
CHAPTER 10	Creating a Two-Party System: Democrats versus Whigs
CHAPTER 11	Cotton and the Transformation of the South
CHAPTER 12	Abolitionism
CHAPTER 13	Slavery, Territorial Expansion, and Secession
CHAPTER 14	Why Was the North Victorious in the Civil War?
CHAPTER 15	From Slave to Citizen

Preface

For four decades, *America: A Narrative History* has remained among the most popular U.S. history textbooks ever written. Each of its new editions has improved a book celebrated for its compelling narrative prose. Obviously, textbooks are of no use if students do not read them, but a history textbook does not have to be dull and lifeless. A narrative approach, driven by storytelling, can reveal the depth and drama of the past by exposing the textured stories of people—not just the famous and familiar men and women, but also the unknown, unnamed, and forgotten. As a student from Texas recently wrote to author David Shi, "I wanted to tell you how interesting and well-written your history book is! I have found that simply by reading its content, I am personally immersed in the text." More recently, a high school AP history teacher reported, "This was the only textbook I have ever read and enjoyed reading. And, I have read a lot of textbooks in over 40 years of teaching high school."

The testimonials, like many that we have received over the years, confirm that a narrative approach works exceptionally well for students and teachers. Ensuring the continued success of that storytelling emphasis was the most important factor in prompting an important change in this new edition. After having been involved with the *America* textbook since 1986, I (David Shi) realized that it is a good time to collaborate with a new team of co-authors. We looked first for co-authors who have great experience and substantial skill at teaching the undergraduate survey course. At the same time, we wanted three new co-authors who are distinguished scholars, and who are themselves diverse in terms of their own background experiences. And, we found them. All of them share a commitment to narrative history, believing as I do that the stories imbedded in American history are vital to student learning. I am pleased to introduce them here:

- **Daina Ramey Berry, Professor of History and Dean of the Humanities and Fine Arts at the University of California, Santa Barbara,** is an internationally recognized scholar of gender and slavery in the United States. Her most recent book, *A Black Woman's History of the United States* (co-authored with Kali Nicole Gross), won the 2021 Susan Koppelman Award for the best new book in feminist studies. Berry was also honored with the President's Associates Teaching Excellence Award at the University of Texas, where she served as chair of the history department. She offers workshops to educators on innovative ways to teach the U.S. and African American history survey courses and is a Distinguished Lecturer for the Organization of American Historians.
- **Joseph Crespino, the Jimmy Carter Professor of History at Emory University in Atlanta** and former chair of the history department, is a specialist in twentieth-century political and cultural history. He was the

Fulbright Distinguished Lecturer in American Studies at the University of Tubingen in 2014. Among his widely acclaimed books are an award-winning biography, *Strom Thurmond's America*, and most recently, *Atticus Finch: The Biography*. Crespino has received the Excellence in Undergraduate Teaching Award from the Emory University Center for Teaching and Learning.

- **Amy Murrell Taylor is the T. Marshall Hahn Jr. Professor of History at the University of Kentucky,** where she focuses on gender, the Civil War and Reconstruction, and the American South. She has been honored by the university's Provost's Award for Outstanding Teaching and Great Teacher Awards. Her latest book, *Embattled Freedom: Journeys through the Civil War's Slave Refugee Camps*, received several national awards, including the Frederick Douglass Book Prize and the Merle Curti Social History Award.

All three of these distinguished scholar-teachers have frequently taught the U.S. survey course, are skilled at introducing students to the importance of primary sources, write sparkling prose, and are adept at the storytelling art. They have made major contributions to this new edition. As has been the case for forty years, this revision, like its predecessors, has benefited from fresh material we have added across the entire range of historical fields: political, cultural, social, and economic history. Our team of four diverse scholars has added texture, breadth, and vitality to the textbook while maintaining the cohesion of its narrative voice.

The Fourth Edition of *America: The Essential Learning Edition* is designed to be highly teachable and classroom friendly. It shares the same narrative as the Brief Thirteenth Edition of *America* (15% shorter than the Full Edition). Readers will experience the same famous narrative color and style, commitment to inclusiveness, and updated scholarship that have long distinguished the original editions of *America: A Narrative History*, with the added advantage of having a unique guided reading framework that highlights core learning objectives and major developments (more on this below).

Of special emphasis in this new edition is the importance of women's experiences in the American story. The authors took the existing narrative as a starting point and then wove in stories of women who had been hiding in plain sight—present and influential during some of the biggest, most significant political events and economic trends in American history. Their untold stories became the focus of our revisions. In this new edition are women who have not been typically celebrated in history classrooms but whose histories nonetheless have the power to change the way students understand the American past.

Students will learn about women such as Isabel de Olvera, who traveled with explorers in the late sixteenth and early seventeenth centuries to present-day New Mexico. They will also meet Sarah Bradlee Fulton, who boycotted British products to support the quest for American independence in the late eighteenth century. Likewise, when students read about the 1830s Trail of Tears, they will learn about a woman named Nanyehi, who led the Cherokee nation and became the first female voting member of its General Council. Outspoken and fearless, Nanyehi was one of the most effective voices seeking to protect her community from the forces of removal, revealing Cherokee women to be far more than a nameless, suffering mass of people forced from their homes. Students also will read about Matihilde Hennes, an enslaved woman who fled Louisiana for freedom in Mexico in the 1840s, one of many such "freedom seekers" whose courageous escapes inflamed the growing political conflict along the U.S.-Mexico border; and they will meet Catherine Greene, a wealthy southern widow who provided Eli Whitney with funds and workspace, making possible the invention of the cotton gin.

Textured stories like these help students see the past more fully—but also more profoundly. Women's reveal significant historical changes often are stimulated by people living at the margins, from the people living outside the centers of power who exert outsized influence over politics, culture, and economy. Aimee Semple McPherson, for example, was perhaps the most charismatic and influential figure in the Protestant Fundamentalist movement of the 1920s. In the Church of the Foursquare Gospel that she organized in Los Angeles, she preached to tens of thousands of believers every week and reached many more through her pioneering use of radio. She is yet another example of the diverse ways women influenced public life.

At the same time, this new edition recognizes that women's history is full of prominent as well as little-known trailblazers in the continuing fight for rights and equality in the United States. The famous story of how Lucretia Mott and Elizabeth Cady Stanton organized the 1848 Seneca Falls Convention for women's rights is enriched by accounts of lesser-known women such as Maria Miller Stewart, a public speaker and writer who argued that gaining rights for Black women required combating racial prejudice too. It acknowledges that when Stanton's Declaration of Sentiments boldly declared, "We hold these truths to be self-evident: that all men and women are created equal," the National Convention of Colored Citizens in Cleveland, Ohio, also passed a resolution in the same year proclaiming "the equality of the sexes." That assumption of equality inspired decades of women's activism, eventually leading in 1920 to the ratification of the Nineteenth Amendment granting women the right to vote, and to the 1965 Voting Rights Act.

Yet women distinguished themselves in many other ways. Madam C. J. Walker, born Sarah Breedlove in 1867 to Louisiana sharecroppers, became the nation's first female self-made millionaire by developing a line of cosmetics and hair-care products for African American women. Her significance extended well beyond her business success. She became an outspoken champion of social justice for Blacks during the Jim Crow era of racist discrimination. "Don't sit down and wait for the opportunities to come," she told women audiences. "Get up and make them!"

The quest for equality went well beyond voting rights. During both world wars in the twentieth century, millions of women assumed roles traditionally played only by men, including military service. They readily filled the job vacancies created by men leaving for military service, and many of them decided to blaze new trails in what for centuries had been known as "a man's world" of employment, scientific discovery, and political and social leadership. That ongoing story of perseverance and resilience is highlighted in this new edition, along with many other additions that help inform students of the diversity of the American experiment in representative democracy. The enhanced coverage of the women's experience and their many untold stories brings relevance and meaning for many of today's students, while making it possible for them to see political, cultural, social, and economic history through a new lens.

Another exciting development in this edition, which derives from the classroom teaching expertise of the new authorial team, is the inclusion, for the first time, of primary source excerpts in every chapter. The new Comparing Perspectives features use primary sources to pair diverse voices speaking on major subjects in each chapter. Each feature connects to character vignettes and first-person quotations in the main narrative, reinforcing the storytelling strength of the book. In Chapter 3, students will review the case of John Punch, an African American indentured servant who received treatment that was different from what his fellow servants who were White received, contrasted with an indenture contract that outlined the terms of these eighteenth-century agreements. Likewise, the history of the Civil War is enlivened by the writings of two individuals with vastly different points of view on emancipation: Jourdon Anderson, a man newly liberated from slavery in Tennessee who wrote to his former owner requesting payment for years of labor; and Ellen Gertrude Clanton Thomas, a White woman in Georgia who kept a journal documenting her feelings about losing her plantation's enslaved people. Their writings make clear that emancipation was far more than a monumental political issue for the nation—it was also something lived and felt on a daily basis by millions of people.

In Volume 2, the rise of political conservatism in the 1980s is illuminated through two documents that provide different perspectives on freedom and individualism in American life. In Ronald Reagan's famous "Evil Empire Speech" (a term that he never actually used), the president gave a spirited defense of religious liberty, decrying Soviet suppression of religious faith at a time when his presidential successors had tried to turn down the temperature of the Cold War. Reagan's speech is paired with a 1984 article about Apple's new Macintosh computer, which the company trumpeted as a revolutionary product that would make personal computing easier and more accessible for everyday Americans. From the 1980s forward, computer entrepreneurs would tout the liberating possibilities of technology in transforming how Americans worked, played, and lived. Students are asked to point to specific sentences in both texts that provide different ideas about what freedom and individualism meant in the 1980s.

Whether your historical interests are political, social, cultural, or economic, you'll find new coverage, sources, and resources to enhance your teaching with what continues to be the most well-balanced narrative history of America.

When asked what they most wanted in an introductory text, instructors said much the same as their students, but they also asked for a textbook that introduced students to the nature of historical research, analysis, and debate. Many professors also mentioned the growing importance to them and their institutions of *assessing* how well their students met the learning goals established by their department. Accordingly, we have aligned *The Essential Learning Edition* with specific learning outcomes for the introductory American history survey course approved by various state and national organizations, including the American Historical Association. These learning outcomes also inform the accompanying media package, enabling instructors to track students' progress toward mastery of these important learning goals.

These and other suggestions from students and professors have shaped the new Fourth Essential Learning Edition and its unique guided reading framework. Each of the thirty chapters begins with a handful of **Core Objectives**, carefully designed to help students understand—and remember—the major developments and issues in each period. To make it easier for students to grasp the major developments, every chapter aligns the narrative with the learning objectives. Each chapter's Core Objective is highlighted at the beginning. Thereafter, **Core Objective flags** appear in the page margins to reinforce key topics in the narrative that are essential to understanding the broader Core Objectives. The Core Objective flags in the page margins also serve as a reference and review tool for students prior to quizzes and exams. **key terms**, chosen to reinforce the major concepts, are bolded in the text and defined in the margin, helping reinforce their significance. At the end of each chapter, review features continue to reiterate the Core Objectives, including pithy chapter summaries, lists of key terms, and chapter chronologies.

This book continues to be distinctive for its creative efforts to make every component—text, maps, images, and graphs—a learning opportunity and teaching point. Map captions, for example, include lists of questions to help students interpret the data highlighted in them. Select image captions in each chapter also include questions designed to help students interpret a range of images from drawings, prints, photos, historic maps, and political cartoons.

Interactive maps are just one example of the innovative elements in this book designed to get students more *engaged* in the learning dynamic and thereby deepen their learning. Another unique feature, called **Thinking Like a Historian**, helps students better understand—and apply—the research techniques and interpretive skills used by professional historians. Through carefully selected examples, the "Thinking Like a Historian" segments highlight the role of primary and secondary sources as the building blocks of historical research and illustrate the ways in which historians have differed in their interpretations of the past. Within the main text, there is one "Thinking

Like a Historian" feature for each of the seven major periods of American history; each feature takes on a major interpretive issue in that era. In Part I of the activity, students first read excerpts from two original secondary sources that offer competing interpretive views framing that period. In Part II, students then read some of the original primary sources that those same historians used to develop their arguments. Finally, students must answer a series of questions that guide their reading and analysis of the sources.

To strengthen students' history skills, *America: The Essential Learning Edition* offers a collection of online "Thinking Like a Historian" exercises for each chapter. Each exercise highlights the foundational role of primary and secondary sources. For the new Fourth Edition, the Part Four Thinking Like a Historian section on Reconstruction has been completely updated to reflect the current scholarship and now focuses on "Debating Reconstruction's Demise." It pairs excerpts from Eric Foner's *Reconstruction: America's Unfinished Revolution* (1988) and Kidada E. Williams's *I Saw Death Coming: A History of Terror and Survival in the War against Reconstruction* (2023). It also includes all new primary sources.

Among the new coverage in this Fourth Essential Learning Edition are the following:

Chapter 1: The Collision of Cultures in the Sixteenth Century

- New discussions focus on the role that West African kingdoms played in trans-regional trade and how they impacted contact with the Americas.
- New discussions present the global explorations of people of color such as Isabel de Olvera, with her journey to New Mexico, and an African explorer from Spain, Pedro Alonzo Niño ("El Negro"), who piloted one of Columbus's expeditions in 1492.
- New coverage of the Little Ice Age shows how environmental changes impacted global populations.

Chapter 2: England and Its American Colonies, 1607–1732

- The discussion of the Salem witchcraft episode has been moved from Chapter 3, and it has been expanded to explore the social and religious dynamics of colonial New England.
- To centralize the major discussion on slavery and other forms of servitude, there is less focus on those topics in Chapter 2, with the primary discussion nested now in Chapter 3.

Chapter 3: Colonial Ways of Life, 1607–1750

- Major discussions on slavery and servitude have been consolidated in this chapter.
- Expanded discussions on the relationships between masters and indentured servants highlight the differences between slavery and servitude—highlighting the experiences of indentured women.
- New and expanded discussions on Indigenous slavery in the Carolinas focus on how the English fomented wars between Indigenous groups to

increase the number of enslaved people for sale, resulting in the number of enslaved Indigenous people in the Caribbean surpassing that of enslaved Africans in the thirteen colonies during this period.

- Revised coverage on the Tuscarora and Yamasee Wars reveals the interplay of complex relationships among Indigenous groups and English colonists in the Carolinas.
- Increased focus on the complexities of the African slave trade reveals the differing or overlapping roles played by Europeans, Africans, and those in the Americas. New discussions also compare features of the African slave trade with those of the transatlantic slave trade, highlighting the experiences of enslaved people during the Middle Passage.
- New discussions focus on the religious experiences of free and enslaved Blacks during the Enlightenment.

Chapter 4: From Colonies to States, 1607–1776

- Coverage of the North Carolina Regulators and their protests against colonial government has been expanded.
- New discussions cover the forced mass migration of European immigrants and enslaved Africans.
- New coverage introduces the Ethiopian Regiment, in which free and enslaved Blacks fought alongside the British in exchange for their own independence.
- Coverage of the letters on democracy between John and Abigail Adams have been moved to this chapter to support the new Comparing Perspectives feature on their correspondence.

Chapter 5: The American Revolution, 1775–1783

- A new vignette shares Francisco de Miranda's role in the Spanish Alliance.
- New discussions focus on the Continental Army's racially integrated units, with a vignette on the Sixth Connecticut Regiment that explores what patriotism meant to them and why they decided to join the fight for independence.
- New discussions on women and the revolution such as Deborah Sampson, who was promoted to corporal in the Continental Army, and Ann Bailey, who delivered battlefront supplies and fought on the field of battle, for their contributions on the battlefield.

Chapter 6: Securing the Constitution and Union, 1783–1800

- New and expanded discussions cover the origins of the Electoral College and its current significance.
- Expanded discussions relate how enslaved people used the legal system and courts to argue for their freedom—with a new vignette on Elizabeth Freeman ("Mum Bett"), who won her freedom in Massachusetts.
- New discussions on the Fugitive Slave Law of 1793 include a new vignette on Ona Judge, who escaped enslavement from George

Washington's home in Philadelphia, and the president's efforts to return her to slavery.
- New discussions focus on the diverse roles that women played during the early national period. This includes the section entitled "The Absence of Women"—encompassing Eliza Yonge Wilkinson's fight for "liberty of thought" for women and Massachusetts writer Judith Sargent Murray's essay, "On the Equality of the Sexes."

Chapter 7: The Early Republic, 1800–1815

- New discussions frame the War of 1812 not only in terms of expansion but also in terms of the dispossession of Indigenous people and how different Indigenous nations were recruited to fight and were impacted by the war, which greatly reduced their territory and increased the pace of western settlement.
- Expanded discussions of the nation's founders emphasize their contradictory status as both enslavers and American revolutionaries—specifically, Thomas Jefferson's relationship with Sally Hemmings, and the construction of the Capitol building by enslaved people.
- Expanded discussions on Haitian independence reveal how plantation owners in the United States reacted to events in the Caribbean.
- Discussion of the Treaty of Ghent shows how plantation owners in the United States demanded British payment for their "property" losses to the British.

Chapter 8: The Emergence of a Market Economy, 1815–1860

- New material on the intertwining of the northern and southern economies focus on how insurance companies in the North indemnified enslaved people for plantation owners in the South.
- New discussions cover women and the simplification of household tasks with inventions such as the first ice cream freezer.
- New treatments of women's household work with the expectation that working-class women would continue to contribute to the family income through piecemeal cloth work and laundering while staying closer to their children. New discussions explain how Irish women became the primary domestic servants in cities, a role that many native-born White women viewed with contempt.
- A new discussion explains the role that Catherine Littlefield Greene played in supporting Eli Whitney while he perfected the cotton gin.
- New discussions cover the increasing popularity of theatrical performances during this period and the impact that actor Fanny Kemble had on its growth.
- New discussions on the role that women played in early strikes include a new vignette on Louise Mitchell of the New York Tailoresses' Society.

Chapter 9: Nationalism and Sectionalism, 1815–1828

- A new biographical sketch of Rachel Jackson discusses how her marriage to Andrew Jackson impacted his presidential career.
- New material on the rise of Black newspapers in the country includes a vignette on the *Freedom's Journal*, founded in New York City by free Black men.

Chapter 10: A New Democratic Era, 1828–1840

- The chapter title has changed from "The Jacksonian Era" to "A New Democratic Era," reflecting the chapter's widening focus from the impacts of Jackson's presidency to changes in democracy throughout this period.
- Significantly updated material on the federal program of Indigenous removal to the West includes deepened discussions from the Indigenous perspective, with a focus on the experiences of Indigenous women. It also offers updated discussions on the Second Seminole War in Florida.

Chapter 11: The South and Slavery, 1800–1860

- A new chapter introduction reflects the realities and nuances of the American South.
- New discussions and a new map focus on the domestic slave trade routes to the Old Southwest.
- The experiences of families being divided by the forced sale of enslaved people and the creation of maroon communities by freedom-seeking slaves on the slave trade routes.
- Updated discussions cover the role of plantation mistresses and their treatment of enslaved people under their control.
- Fresh treatment of the complex relationship among enslaved Black communities including its impact on the growth in enslaved resistance.

Chapter 12: Religion, Romanticism, and Reform, 1800–1860

- Expanded discussion on transcendentalism addresses its reflective nature as well as a critique of its elitist aspects.
- An expanded vignette on Emerson covers his evolving understanding of gender within the transcendental movement.
- A new vignette presents Frances Ellen Watkins Harper and her work writing and performing protest poetry against slavery and segregation.
- A new vignette presents Charity Bryant, a woman from Massachusetts who was in a romantic relationship with another woman, Sylvia Drake.
- New discussions explore the public school movement and efforts for desegregation in Massachusetts, culminating in the Anti-Segregation Act of 1855.
- New discussions of utopian movements include a new vignette on Scottish immigrant Frances Wright and the contradictions in her

attempt to build a racially integrated society in Nashoba, Tennessee, and her role in the New Harmony community.
- The section titled "Anti-Slavery and Women's Rights Movements" has been reorganized and expanded.

Chapter 13: Western Expansion and Southern Secession, 1830–1861

- The Part Opener expands discussion on conflicts over defining citizenship that arose after the end of the Civil War.
- New discussions on the Comanche Empire explore how they fought against encroaching American settlers in the Southwest.
- New discussions focus on freedom-seeking enslaved people heading to Mexico as a part of the broader story of American expansion.
- New vignettes on powerful women introduce Sarah Polk, who influenced the political ascendancy of her husband, James Polk; and Harriet Scott, who fought for freedom alongside her husband, Dred Scott.

Chapter 14: The War of the Union, 1861–1865

- Expanded discussions of women who fought in the Civil War, including those engaged in espionage, include a new vignette on Rose O'Neal Greenhow, a spy who helped the Confederate Army at the Battle of Bull Run.
- Expanded discussions focus on politically divided families such as that of President Lincoln and Mary Todd Lincoln, whose stance on the war divided their family members, many of whom were Southern sympathizers.
- New discussions cover the mobilization of Blacks into the Union military during the Civil War.
- A new discussion details African Americans' reaction to the Emancipation Proclamation.
- A new discussion focuses on the medical innovations that resulted from the Civil War, such as the triage system.
- New discussions explain efforts by the Women's Loyal National League to end slavery where it was still being practiced at the end of the war.
- A new conclusion evaluates America's place at the end of the war in regard to liberty and equality for all.

Chapter 15: The Era of Reconstruction, 1865–1877

- Fully updated Thinking Like a Historian feature on "Debating Reconstruction's Demise," with new secondary and primary sources that reflect the current scholarship on this heavily researched and discussed topic.
- New discussions focus on how formerly enslaved people demanded payment for work and migrated to find family members and new economic opportunities.
- New discussions relate how formerly enslaved people fought for opportunities for education and the establishment of thousands of Black schools through the Freedmen's Bureau.

- New and expanded discussions on the women's suffrage movement include the emerging role that Black women played in the movement.
- New discussions focus on the phenomenon of convict leasing as a form of coerced labor that was introduced in post–Civil War America, particularly in the South.
- A new vignette introduces Victoria Woodhull, a women's rights activist, stockbroker, and journalist who became the first woman to run for president in 1872.
- A new discussion covers the closure of the Freedman's Bank, which left thousands of Black families without their life's savings and dramatically impeded the development of a Black middle class.

Chapter 16: Business and Labor in the Industrial Era, 1860–1900

- A new vignette introduces Hettie Greene, the richest woman during the Gilded Age.
- New discussions cover differences in wage labor between men and women. A new discussion focuses on women's roles in the Great Railroad Strike of 1877.
- Expanded discussions treat the Knights of Labor and African American men's roles in the organization.
- Expanded discussions explore the role of Asian Americans in the building of the railroads.

Chapter 17: Legends and Realities: The South and the West, 1865–1900

- Updated discussions focus on the Lost Cause legend and the realities of the American South post-Reconstruction.
- Expanded discussions on the disenfranchisement of African American voters include a new vignette on Congressman John R. Lynch, who was the first African American Speaker of the House in the Mississippi State Assembly.
- Updated discussions on the Black response to segregation include a new portrait of the Reverend Benjamin Mays, the eventual president of Morehouse College and an early mentor of Martin Luther King Jr.
- Updated discussions on women working in the West include new profiles of Texas cattle rancher Lizzie Johnson and Black postwoman "Stagecoach Mary" Fields.

Chapter 18: The Gilded Age: Political Stalemate and Rural Revolt, 1865–1900

- Updated discussions explore the impact of social Darwinism in America.
- Expanded discussions focus on the women's suffrage movement.
- New and expanded discussions on rural grassroots politics include the Colored Farmer's National Alliance and women's role in farm alliances.

Chapter 19: Seizing an American Empire, 1865–1913

- A new section explores the motivations and debates surrounding U.S. imperialism.
- New discussions explain how European powers competed to colonize Hawaii and how Indigenous Hawaiian people resisted such efforts.
- New material highlights America's longstanding involvement in the affairs of Cuba as well as the history of U.S. involvement in Puerto Rico.
- Fresh insights illuminate U.S. involvement in Mexican affairs and the borderlands with the United States.

Chapter 20: The Progressive Era, 1890–1920

- A new chapter introduction stresses how the Progressives were a complex mix of people, including many women activists and people of color, who were determined to address political, economic, and social problems that had arisen out of the Industrial Revolution and the dramatic growth of American cities.
- Expanded material on Ida Tarbell shows her not only as a muckraker but also as a pioneering female investigative journalist.
- New discussions highlight the Progressive initiatives at all levels of government, while noting that the dramatic expansion of federal government reform would occur during the New Deal and later.
- More context has been provided on the complicated legacy of *Muller v. Oregon*. It was a triumph in restricting work hours for women. But it was an ambivalent victory for some women who were uncomfortable with the way it established special protections for women, contradicting the argument of equality under the law for women.
- A new section discusses the founding of the NAACP as part of the larger fight to achieve civil rights and to combat the dramatic increases in racial violence during this period.
- The account of the Porvenir Massacre in 1918 has been moved from Chapter 17 to here, where it fits better chronologically. It has also been expanded to include new material on Jose T. Canales, the Hispanic Texas legislator who demanded an investigation into the massacre and who would later play a leading role in forming the League of United Latin American Citizens (LULAC).

Chapter 21: America and the Great War, 1914–1920

- A revised section on the historical context of World War I discusses how it originated from the processes of industrialization, nationalism, imperialism, and militarism throughout Europe.
- Updated discussions focus on the unprecedented nature of German submarine warfare with the sinking of the *Lusitania*; this material helps clarify the U.S. entry into the war.

- Expanded coverage focuses on shifting wartime standards for tolerating dissent and the ensuing dilemma it posed for President Wilson during World War I.
- Expanded discussions on Lenin's background and motivations highlight the brutality of the Bolshevik Revolution as part of the discussions on the expansion of socialism.
- Updated discussions in the section "The Politics of Peace" make clearer Woodrow Wilson's strengths and weaknesses.
- Expanded discussions cover how the Treaty of Versailles was debated within the context of American isolationism.
- Expanded discussions on the Spanish flu epidemic point out its global impact, which was similar to that of the COVID-19 pandemic.

Chapter 22: A Clash of Cultures, 1920–1929

- New discussions detail the origins and history of the radio.
- New discussions on *The Birth of a Nation* explain how it dramatically changed Hollywood filmmaking.
- New discussions of the NAACP's activities focus on its 1925 defense of Ossian Sweet, a Black man who defended himself against a White mob upon moving to a White working-class neighborhood in Detroit.
- New discussions on the rise of religious fundamentalism include a vignette on Aimee Semple McPherson, a female evangelist who used mass media to spread her faith and message and ultimately built a religious empire in Los Angeles.

Chapter 23: The Great Depression and the New Deal, 1933–1939

- The section "From Hooverism to the New Deal" provides more context on why such a capable administrator like Herbert Hoover failed to address the Great Depression quickly and aggressively.
- An expanded biographical vignette on Franklin Delano Roosevelt explores the contradictions between his public and private personalities and how they impacted his success.
- The expanded section "Cultural Life during the Depression" examines the different perspectives emerging from literature and the arts during the Great Depression.
- A new discussion covers the international context and its impact on the creation of Social Security in the United States.
- Expanded discussions focus on Frances Perkins, the first female cabinet member who served under FDR, and her role in developing Social Security.
- New discussions on the court-packing scheme provide more context as to why it seemed threatening to much of the general public.
- More coverage focuses on fears of a Communist-style revolution and how it impacted FDR's policy making.
- An updated and streamlined summary of the New Deal discusses its legacy.

Chapter 24: World War II, 1933–1945

- Expanded explanations of Hitler's and Mussolini's rise to power help students better understand the appeal of fascism.
- New discussions focus on Neville Chamberlain's complicated role at Munich and Winston Churchill's criticisms of Chamberlain.
- New discussions cover FDR's justifications for a third presidential term.
- Updated discussions detail Executive Order 8802 and the creation of the Fair Employment Practices Committee.
- New and expanded discussion focuses on the postwar Nuremberg Trials.
- New coverage of the great 442nd Regimental Combat Team (the all–Japanese American "Go for Broke" unit from Hawaii that became the most highly decorated unit for its size and length of service in U.S. military history).

Chapter 25: The Cold War and the Fair Deal, 1945–1952

- Updated discussions focus on the historiography of the Cold War.
- Updated discussions cover Harry Truman's challenges with postwar inflation and ensuing strikes.
- New and updated discussions explore post–World War II racial violence, Truman's civil rights record, and the integration of baseball with a refreshed vignette on Jackie Robinson.
- A new discussion focuses on the experiences of African American and Hispanic veterans after the war and their impact on civil rights.
- A new section titled "From Civil Rights to Human Rights" details Eleanor Roosevelt's key role in drafting the United Nations' Universal Declaration of Human Rights.
- A new vignette points out how ironic and unexpected it was for Strom Thurmond, a decorated World War II veteran and a moderate in South Carolina politics, ended up heading the Dixiecrats.
- New discussions focus on the partisan divisions impacting Dean Acheson during the Korean conflict and the broader indecision by Truman's State Department regarding U.S. strategic interests on the Korean peninsula.
- Expanded discussions cover the second Red Scare, with updates on the Hiss-Chambers case.

Chapter 26: Affluence and Anxiety in the Atomic Age, 1950–1959

- Expanded discussions on the end of McCarthyism include an updated vignette on Franklin Edward Kameny, an early hero of the gay rights movement.
- Expanded discussions focus on the postwar prosperity and consumption of goods by the middle class that produced mass social anxiety. The section formerly called "Cooling the Suburban Frontier" has been broken into two separate discussions—one on the Sun Belt (and how air conditioning enabled its development), the other on suburban culture—to emphasize that they were different phenomena.

- The discussion on "Operation Wetback" has been moved from a preceding chapter and now appears here under "People of Color on the Move" in the 1950s.
- More context is given for understanding the Cold War and Christian revivalism during the 1950s.
- The discussion of the Beats and their influence has been updated based on recent scholarship.
- A new paragraph in the section on rock 'n' roll more clearly links its cultural impact to the burgeoning civil rights movement.
- In the section "The Early Years of the Civil Rights Movement," a new introductory paragraph frames the Cold War's influence on the early civil rights movement.
- New discussions on the *Brown v. Board of Education* decision explain Earl Warren's role.
- An expanded discussion covers the historical significance of the murder of Emmett Till.
- An expanded vignette on Rosa Parks establishes her long history of activism preceding the bus boycott, focusing on her role in establishing the Committee for Equal Justice and its support for Mrs. Recy Taylor and her work protecting women from domestic violence.
- Expanded discussions focus on Martin Luther King Jr. and nonviolent civil disobedience.
- Refreshed and expanded discussions cover the reception and impact of the 1957 and 1960 Civil Rights Acts.
- Expanded discussions explore the significance of the Korean War.
- Expanded discussions focus on the Hungarian crisis and the Suez War.

Chapter 27: New Frontiers and a Great Society, 1960–1968

- More background, context, and analysis of gender issues is given, including highlights on Black female activists such as Ella Baker, Diane Nash, and Fannie Lou Hamer.
- More coverage focuses on the details and significance of the 1960 presidential election.
- Expanded discussion explores the significance of the murder of four Black girls at the 16th Street Baptist church in Birmingham. An updated discussion focuses on the significance of the 1964 Civil Rights Act.
- An expanded discussion covers Bloody Sunday, the assault on a civil rights march in Selma by Alabama State troopers, and the involvement of John Lewis, who later became a congressman in Georgia.
- More emphasis is provided on the impact of the 1965 Voting Rights Act.
- New discussions offer a broader historical perspective of Lyndon Baines Johnson and the Great Society.
- Updated coverage focuses on Martin Luther King Jr.'s assassination and the broader significance of assassinations in the 1960s.

Chapter 28: Rebellion and Reaction, 1960s and 1970s

- Expanded discussions on Black culture feature Sam Cooke's hit song, "A Change Is Gonna Come" alongside Bob Dylan.
- A new section on Chicano students and the Blowouts that gave voice to issues with underfunded schools in Los Angeles is included as a part of broader Chicano activism in this period.
- Expanded discussions cover Latino/Chicano politics that flowed into the twenty-first century and the history and legacy of La Raza Unida, a party started by Chicanos to promote political involvement.
- New discussions on Title IX focus on the cultural changes regarding women's sports, as seen in Kathrine Switzner's attempts to register and run in the Boston Marathon.
- A new vignette discusses Joan Didion's critique of the counterculture in her classic essay "Slouching Towards Bethlehem."
- New discussions on the characterizations of Nixon highlight his foreign policy accomplishments in spite of the generally negative perception of his presidency.
- A new discussion of Carter's presidential campaign covers how it was helped by revolutions in "Redneck" culture and his revival of the New Deal voting alliance.

Chapter 29: Conservative Revival, 1977–2000

- Expanded discussions on the positive impact of Carter's foreign policy on human rights efforts include a new profile of Patricia Derian, the first Assistant Secretary of State for Human Rights.
- New discussions cover how the 1980 Reagan campaign prolonged the Iranian hostage crisis for political gain.
- Expanded discussions on the computer revolution highlight the leading role played by Steve Jobs and Apple, connecting their impact on society to previous discussions on the counterculture and future discussions of social media.
- New discussions on the 1994 crime bill explore its impact on mass incarceration and people of color in urban areas.
- New discussions recount the controversy around Clarence Thomas's Supreme Court nomination hearings.
- A new discussion covers the Chinese crackdown on democracy protesters in Tiananmen Square.

Chapter 30: Twenty-First Century America, 2000–Present

- This chapter has been strengthened thematically with a new focus on the concept of the "Big Sort" and the impact computers, cable TV, satellite radio, and social media have had on explaining the deep political divisions in this century.
- A refreshed analysis of the Obama presidency includes a discussion of his Supreme Court appointees, Sonia Sotomayor and Elena Kagan—the

third and fourth women to serve on the Court, and Sotomayor as the first Hispanic Supreme Court justice.
- New discussions explore the longer-term structural issues behind rising partisanship, as well as the rise of cable news—especially Fox News and its political influence.
- New discussions focus on social media, how it can stoke partisan outrage, and its role in the 2016 election. Additional coverage includes how President Trump used social media as a political tool.
- Expanded coverage of the George Floyd murder ties it to Eric Garner's death in 2014 and the fact that both were captured by bystanders on cell phone videos, thus linking the resulting protests to the theme of new technology that has widespread social and political ramifications.
- More recent events are discussed in the context of the longer origins of political divisions in our country, especially reinforcing the thematic focus on the nation's ever-deepening politics of polarization over the past eight years.

Finally, a note on terminology. History is a dynamic discipline: as time passes, it benefits not only from the discovery of new evidence and refined interpretations but also from being in conversation with our contemporary culture. We have joined other publishers, magazines, and newspapers in capitalizing group identity terms such as *Black* and *White*. While respecting the various and at times conflicting opinions on this matter, we feel our approach is consistent with the goals of making "a more perfect union" in which all people are treated equally and with dignity, including the language choices many use to identify themselves. In this effort, we have shifted from using the word *slave* in the narrative to *enslaved* and from *fugitive slave* to *freedom seeker*. After all, people did not choose to become slaves; they were instead forcibly *enslaved*. Once enslaved, they yearned to be free again and often risked their lives to liberate themselves. Where the words *slave* and *fugitive slave* are used in historical quotations, we have retained their original form.

No single term can precisely encompass social groups. For example, with references to people with Spanish-speaking ancestors, we use identifying terms that are the most historically accurate and relevant for a given context, region, time period, or group of people—Spanish, Hispanic, Tejano, Californio, Mexican American, Chicano and Chicana, Cuban American, Puerto Rican American, and Latino, Latina, and Latinx. Not only is this approach more historically accurate, but it also better demonstrates the dynamism of group identities in America.

We follow a similar strategy for other significant groups such as African Americans, Native Americans, Asian Americans, immigrants, and LGBTQ Americans. We recognize that there are several ways to deal with these sensitive issues and that the issues of group terminology remain a subject of robust discussion within classrooms, homes, communities, and politics. Our efforts in this edition represent a continuing commitment to remain current in our treatment of such shifting preferences.

Media Resources for Instructors and Students

The new Fourth Essential Learning Edition also makes history an *immersive* experience through its innovative pedagogy and digital resources. In the Norton Illumine Ebook, dynamic new reading support tools, including embedded reading comprehension questions and interactive primary source activities, help students better engage with the reading and practice their history skills. InQuizitive—W. W. Norton's adaptive learning program—helps students better grasp the textbook's key topics and enables instructors to assess learning progress at the individual and classroom levels. Instructors also have access to a library of guided primary sources, plus a series of "Thinking Like a Historian" exercises for every chapter, inviting students to work with both primary and secondary sources. Online activities such as the History Skills Tutorials and "Thinking Like a Historian" exercises support the discipline's efforts to develop students' critical thinking and analytical skills that are applicable to this course as well as a career in virtually any field. An array of valuable support materials ranging from author videos and online document collections to lecture slides and test banks are available for download or integration into a campus learning management system.

America's digital resources are designed to develop successful readers, guiding students through the narrative while simultaneously developing their critical thinking and history skills.

The comprehensive support package features the new interactive Norton Illumine Ebook, an award-winning adaptive learning tool InQuizitive, and the skill-building "Thinking Like a Historian" exercises, available for every chapter of the book, that encourage both primary and secondary source analysis. All of these resources are designed to help students master the Core Objectives in each chapter and continue to nurture their development as historians. To develop the resources, W. W. Norton is committed to partnering exclusively with subject-matter experts who teach the course. As a result, instructors have all the course materials needed to manage their U.S. history survey class, whether they are teaching face-to-face, online, or in a hybrid setting.

Norton Illumine Ebook

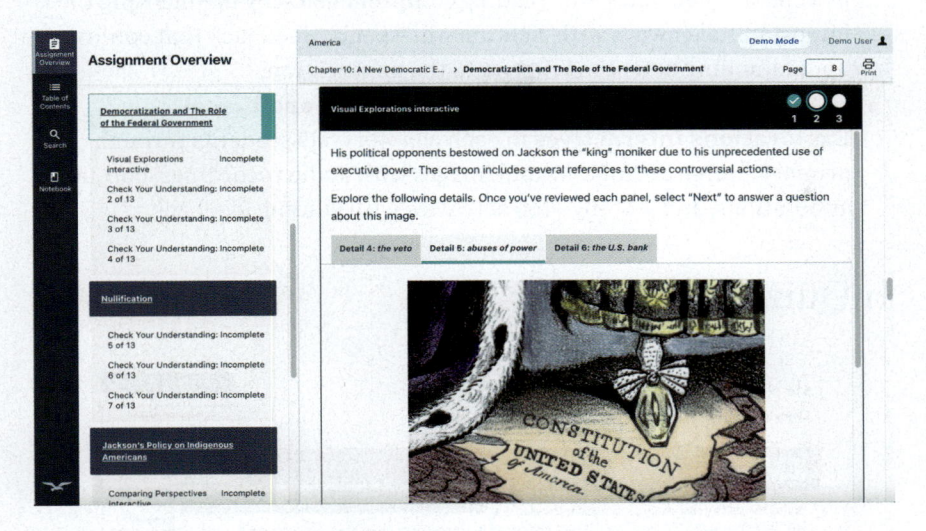

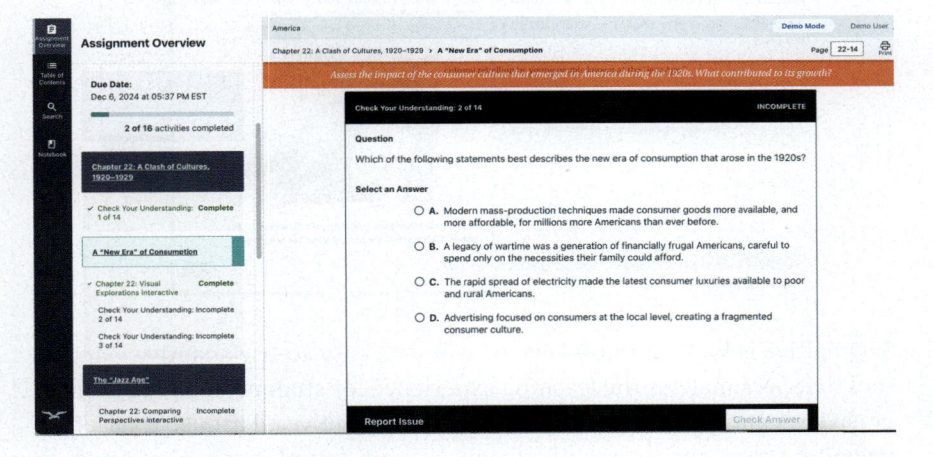

The Norton Illumine Ebook offers an enhanced reading experience at a fraction of the cost of a print textbook. It provides an active reading experience, enabling students to take notes, bookmark, search, highlight, and read offline. Instructors can even add notes that students can see as they are reading the text. The Norton Illumine Ebook can be viewed on all computers and mobile devices. The interactive ebook for *America: The Essential Learning Edition* includes the following interactive features:

- Tool-tip key terms and definitions
- Clickable and zoomable maps and images
- **NEW Author Videos** at the beginning of the chapter give students a closer look at the major chapter themes and preview the important developments to come. These accompany hundreds of additional author videos throughout the text.

- **NEW Check Your Understanding** questions at the end of each section in a chapter help students' reading comprehension by highlighting the important takeaways with rich, answer-specific feedback that confirms understanding before moving on to the next section.
- **NEW Comparing Perspectives interactives and Visual Explorations interactives** in each chapter walk students through primary source documents and images with audio recordings, pop-up annotations, and step-by-step activities with guiding feedback.

InQuizitive

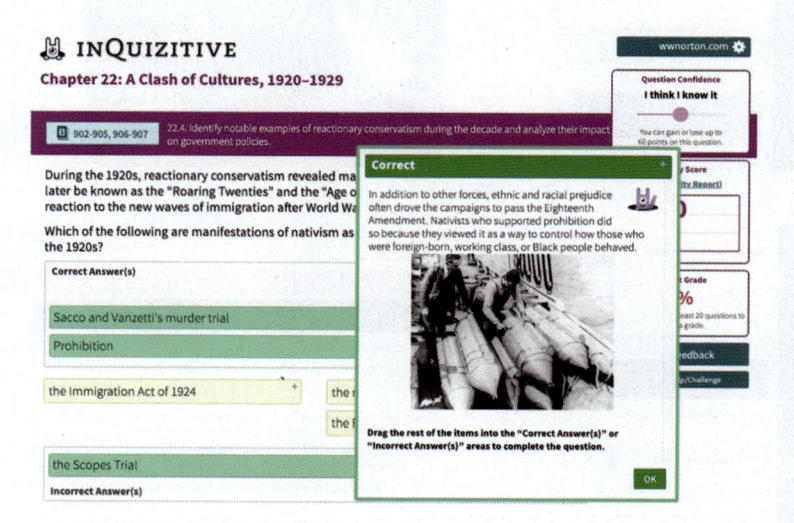

InQuizitive is W. W. Norton's award-winning, easy-to-use adaptive learning tool that personalizes the learning experience for students, helping them to grasp key concepts and achieve key learning objectives. Through a variety of question types, answer-specific feedback, and game-like elements such as the ability to wager points, students are motivated to keep working until they fully comprehend the concepts. As a result, students arrive better prepared for class, giving you more time for discussion and activities. The InQuizitive course for *America* features over 1,500 engaging, interactive questions (approximately 20 percent of which are new or updated) tagged to each chapter's Core Objectives. Each activity ensures thorough coverage of the key concepts within the chapter reading, as well as questions that invite students to dig in and analyze maps, primary source excerpts, and other types of historical evidence such as artifacts, artworks, architecture, photographs, and more.

Thinking Like a Historian Exercises

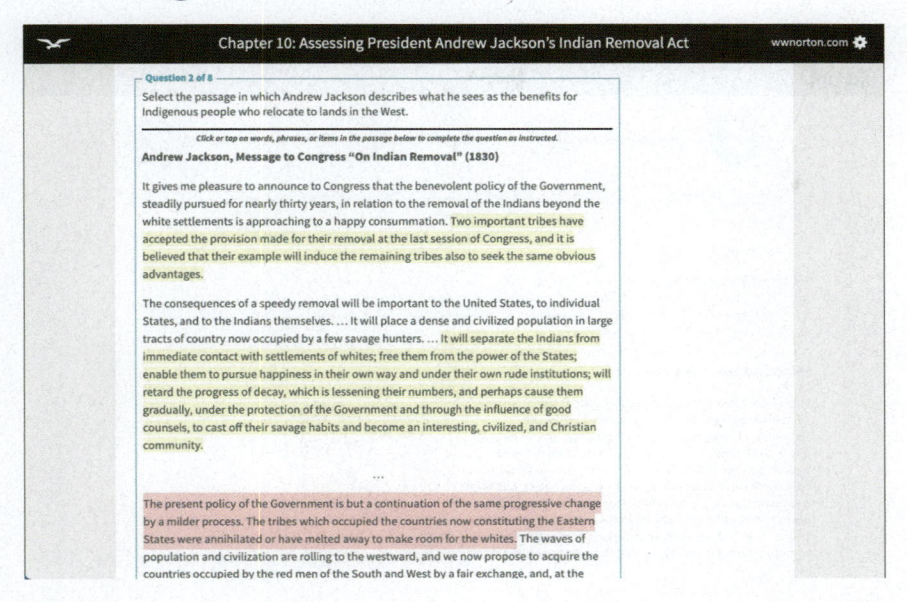

To strengthen students' history skills, *America* offers a collection of assignable "Thinking Like a Historian" exercises for each chapter. Each online exercise highlights the foundational role of primary sources as the building blocks of history. A selection of exercises also includes secondary source document excerpts. Students examine a major historical debate or issue through the lens of primary source evidence and historians' differing interpretations of that evidence. A series of interactive questions with guiding feedback helps students dissect and compare the sources, building historical thinking skills throughout the semester. As a capstone assignment, follow-up short-answer writing prompts, delivered through the learning management system, encourage students to formulate their own interpretations about the historical debate in question.

History Skills Tutorials

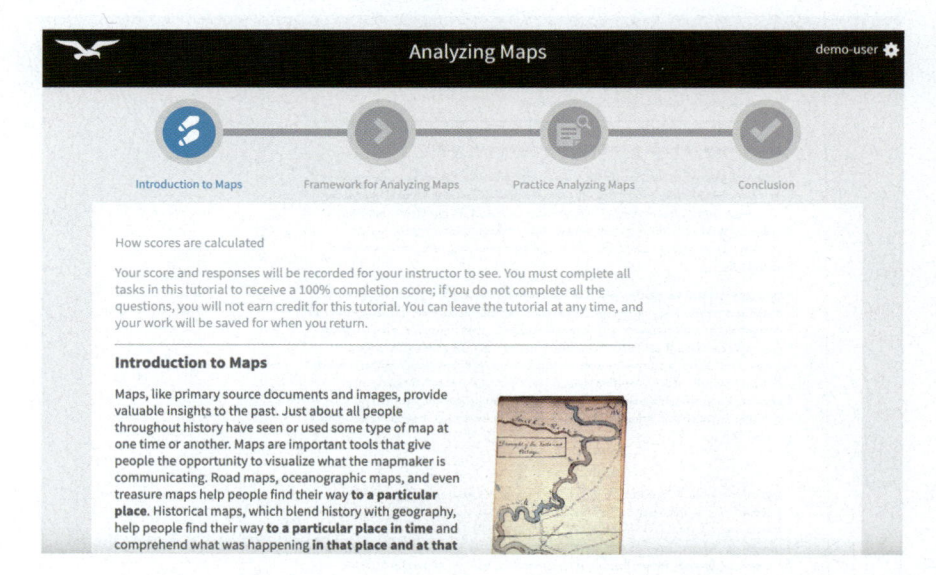

The History Skills Tutorials are interactive, online modules that support student development of the key skills for the American history survey course. The tutorials for *America* focus on the following:

- Analyzing secondary source documents
- Analyzing primary source documents
- Analyzing images
- Analyzing maps

With interactive practice assessments, helpful guiding feedback, and videos with author David Shi, these tutorials teach students the critical analysis skills that they will put to use in their academic and professional careers. These tutorials can be integrated directly into an existing learning management system, making for easy assignability and easy student access.

Additional Content

A collection of additional content offers study and review materials for students to use outside of class. The resources include the following:

- An enhanced **Online Reader** featuring more than one hundred primary source documents and images, each with support materials such as brief headnotes and discussion prompts
- Hundreds of **Author Videos** featuring David Shi, Daina Ramey Berry, Joseph Crespino, and Amy Murrell Taylor to help students understand the essential developments in the American History course
- **Flashcards** inviting students to review the key terms from the textbook
- **Chapter Outlines** giving students a detailed snapshot of the key topics of each chapter

- **"What's It All About?" Infographics** employing the themes of continuity and change to frame visual overviews of important developments, such as the evolution of African Americans' legal status from the Civil War through Reconstruction

Test Bank

The test bank features more than 2,500 questions—including multiple-choice, true/false, and short-answer—aligned to each chapter of the book. Questions are classified according to level of difficulty and Bloom's Taxonomy, providing multiple avenues for comprehension and skill assessment and making it easy to construct tests that are meaningful and diagnostic.

Norton Testmaker brings W. W. Norton's high-quality testing materials online. Create assessments for your course from anywhere with an Internet connection, without downloading files or installing specialized software. Search and filter test bank questions by chapter, type, difficulty, learning objectives, and other criteria. You can also customize test bank questions to fit your course. Easily export your tests or W. W. Norton's ready-to-use quizzes to Microsoft Word or Common Cartridge files for your LMS.

Instructor's Manual

The instructor's manual for *America: The Essential Learning Edition* is designed to help instructors prepare effective lectures. It contains chapter summaries, detailed chapter outlines, lecture ideas, in-class activities, discussion questions, and more.

Resources for Your LMS

High-quality Norton digital media can be easily added to online, hybrid, or lecture courses. Get started building your course with our easy-to-use integrated resources; all activities can be accessed right within your existing learning management system. Graded activities are configured to report to the LMS course grade book. The downloadable file includes integration links to the following resources, organized by chapter:

- Norton Illumine Ebook
- InQuizitive
- History Skills Tutorials
- Thinking Like a Historian exercises
- Thinking Like a Historian writing prompts
- Chapter outlines
- Flashcards

Instructors can also add customizable multiple-choice, true/false, and short-answer questions to their learning management system using Norton Testmaker.

Classroom Presentation Tools

- **Lecture PowerPoint slides**: Available for download, these PowerPoints feature bullet points of key topics, art, and maps—all sequentially arranged to follow the book. The Lecture PowerPoints also include lecture notes in the Notes section of each slide, perfect for use in both in-person and online courses. These slides are customizable in order to meet the needs of both first-time and experienced teachers.
- **Image files**: All images and maps from the book are available separately in JPEG and PowerPoint format for instructor use. Alt-text is provided for each item.

Primary Source Readers To Accompany *America: A Narrative History*

- **NEW!** Ninth Edition of ***For the Record: A Documentary History of America***, by David E. Shi and Holly A. Mayer (Duquesne University), is the perfect companion reader for *America: A Narrative History*. It features over 250 primary source readings from diaries, journals, newspaper articles, speeches, government documents, and novels, including a noteworthy number of readings that highlight the enriched coverage of women's history in this new edition of *America*. If you haven't perused *For the Record* in a while, now would be a good time to take a fresh look.

Acknowledgments

This Fourth Edition of *America: The Essential Learning Edition* has been a team effort. Several professors who have become specialists in teaching the introductory survey course helped create the instructor resources and interactive media:

Media Authors

Keith Altavilla, Lone Star College–CyFair Campus
Seth Bartee, Guilford Technical Community College
Jordan Bauer, University of Alabama at Birmingham
Jerril Burnette, Tyler Junior College
David Cameron, Lone Star College–University Park
Brian Cervantez, Tarrant County College–Northwest Campus
Manar Elkhaldi, University of Central Florida
Laura Farkas, Stevenson University
Christina Gold, El Camino College
Maryellen Harman, North Central Missouri College
Susan Hinely, Stony Brook University
Bettye Hutchins, Vernon College
Justin Liles, Tyler Junior College
David Marsich, Germanna Community College
Brian D. McKnight, University of Virginia's College at Wise
Lise Namikas, Baton Rouge Community College
Jason Newman, Cosumnes River College
Andrea Oliver, Tallahassee Community College
Renee A. Rodriguez, The University of Texas–Rio Grande Valley
Matthew Zembo, Hudson Valley Community College
Carolina Zumaglini, Florida International University

The quality and range of reviews on this project were truly exceptional. The book and its accompanying media components were greatly influenced by the suggestions provided by the following instructors for the current edition:

Future Directions Reviewers

Caitlin Fitz, Northwestern University
Sonia Hernandez, Texas A&M University
Justene Hill Edwards, University of Virginia
Claudio Saunt, University of Georgia

Consulting Reviewers

Andrew Barbero, Pensacola State College
Albert S. Broussard, Texas A&M University–College Station Campus
Stephen Davis, Lonestar College–Kingwood Campus
Kenneth Grubb, Wharton County Junior College
Sandra Harvey, Lonestar College–CyFair Campus

Content Reviewers

Gisela Ables, Houston Community College
LeNie Adolphson, Highland Community College
Jaime Rene Aguila, Midland College
Keith Altavilla, Lone Star College–CyFair Campus
Benjamin Mark Allen, South Texas College
Ralph Angeles, Lone Star College–North Harris
Dominic Aquila, University of St. Thomas–Houston
Patrick Artz, Bellevue University
Philip Baker, Lone Star College/Fulshear High School
Tollie Banker, Hillsborough Community College–SouthShore Campus
Eric Bartels, Norwin High School
Cameron R. Beech, Hinds Community College–Raymond Campus
Donna Belt, Tyler Junior College
Nancy Duke Birkhead, Daytona State College–Daytona Beach Campus
Albert S. Broussard, Texas A&M University–College Station Campus
Christopher Capozzola, Massachusetts Institute of Technology
Alexis Ceaglske, Hawkeye Community College
Ralph Christian Sanchez Angeles, Lone Star College–North Harris Campus
Nicole Coffelt, Dallas College
Nathan Michael Corzine, Coastal Carolina Community College
Aaron Dilday, Palo Alto College
Holger Droessler, Worcester Polytechnic Institute
Kari Frederickson, University of Alabama–Tuscaloosa
Christopher R. Gilson, Northwestern State University
Carl Grady Eades III, Volunteer State Community College
Abbie Grubb, San Jacinto College–South Campus
Stephen Hausmann, University of St. Thomas–Minnesota
David P. Hopkins Jr., Midland College
Theresa Jach, Houston Community College
Andrea Johnson, CSU Dominguez Hills
Theodore Kallman, San Joaquin Delta College
Courtney Kisat, Southeast Missouri State University
Robert Jason Kelly, Holmes Community College–Goodman Campus
Robert H. Lackie, Lincoln Land Community College

Deirdre Lannon, Texas State University
Carmen Lopez, Miami Dade College
James MacDonald, Northwestern State University of Louisiana
Hollie Marquess, Fort Hays State University
David Marsich, Germanna Community College–Fredericksburg Campus
Daniel Matz, Cinnaminson High School
Kent McGaughy, Houston Community College
Sheila McManus, University of Lethbridge–Siksikaitsitapi territory
Christopher Menking, Tarrant County College–Southeast Campus
Sandra Moats, University of Wisconsin–Parkside Campus
Brian Mueller, University of Wisconsin–Milwaukee Campus
Daniel Murphree, University of Central Florida
Melanie Newport, University of Connecticut–Hartford Campus
Andrea Oliver, Tallahassee Community College
John Ratliff, University of Alabama–Tuscaloosa
Renee A. Rodriguez, University of Texas–Rio Grande Valley
Christopher D. Rounds, Augusta University
Michael Schoeppner, University of Maine–Farmington Campus
James Seymour, Lone Star College–CyFair Campus
Scott Stabler, Grand Valley State University–Allendale Campus
Susan Stanfield, University of Texas at El Paso
Sarah Steinbock-Pratt, University of Alabama–Tuscaloosa
Sarah Sullivan, McHenry County College
Christopher C. Thomas, J Sargeant Reynolds Community College–Parham Road Academic Campus
Kenneth Wayne Howell, Blinn College–Bryan Campus
Louis Williams, St. Louis Community College–Forest Park Campus
Rick L. Woten, American Public University

Our colleagues at W. W. Norton shared their dedicated expertise and their poise amid tight deadlines, especially Jon Durbin, Melissa Atkin, Jennifer Barnhardt, Colette Nolan, Elizabeth Coletti, Emma Freund, Carson Russell, Caleb Wertz, Katherine Kopp, Rachel Mayer, Benjamin Reynolds, Patricia Wong, Elizabeth Trammell, Amla Sanghvi, Ted Szczepanski, Debra Morton-Hoyt, Jillian Burr, Lissi Sigillo, Alice Vigliani, Harry Haskell, Nancy Gillan, Letty Mundt, Gerra Goff, Sarah England Bartley, Cynthia Anderson, Julie Sindel, Christina Magoulis, Alicia Jimenez, and Kevin Zambrano.

We want to thank all our past, current, and future students for making us better teachers. Finally, we want to thank our families for their patient support.

David Emory Shi
Daina Ramey Berry
Joseph Crespino
Amy Murrell Taylor

December 2024

America

The Essential Learning Edition

Fourth Edition

JOIN, or DI

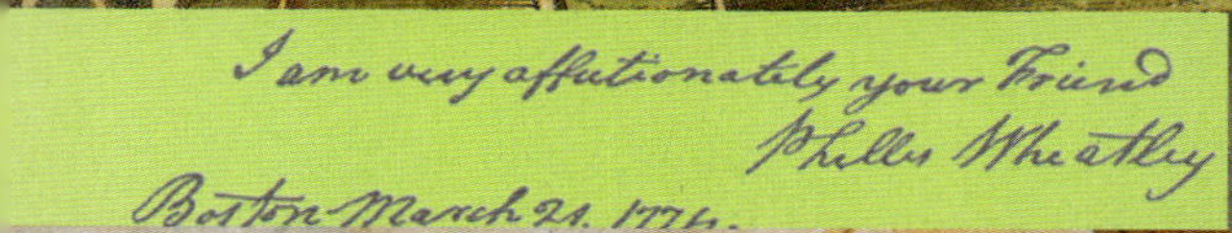
I am very affectionately your Friend
Phillis Wheatley
Boston March 21. 1774.

PART 1

An Old "New" World

History is filled with surprises. Luck and accidents—the unexpected happenings of life—often shape events more than intentions do. Before Christopher Columbus happened upon the Caribbean Sea in an effort to find a westward passage to the Indies (East Asia), the Indigenous peoples he mislabeled Indians had lived in the Americas for thousands of years. The "New World," as Europeans came to call it, was *new* only to the Europeans who began exploring and conquering the region at the end of the fifteenth century.

Over many centuries, ancient peoples in what became known as the Americas—North, Central, and South—had developed hundreds of different societies. Some were rooted in agriculture; others focused on trade or conquest. By the late fifteenth century, many Indigenous people were healthier, were better fed, and lived longer than Europeans, but when the two societies—European and Indigenous—collided, the latter were often infected, enslaved, or exterminated. Yet the familiar story of invasion and conquest oversimplifies the process by which Indigenous people, Europeans, and Africans interacted in the sixteenth and seventeenth centuries. Indigenous people were not simply victims of European expansion; they were also trading partners and military allies of the European newcomers. They became neighbors and advisers, religious converts, and sometimes loving spouses. As such, they participated actively in the creation of America.

The Europeans who risked their lives to colonize the Americas were a diverse lot. They came from Spain, Portugal, France, the British Isles, the Netherlands (Holland), Scandinavia, Italy, and the German states. What they shared was a presumption that Christianity was superior to all religions and that all other peoples were inferior to them and their culture. African peoples came as well to the Americas—most as captives, others as explorers and colonists.

A variety of motives prompted Europeans to make the dangerous voyage to the Americas. Some were fortune seekers lusting for glory and gold, silver, and spices. Others were Christian evangelists eager to create kingdoms of God, or Christian refugees fleeing persecution. Still others were adventurers, convicts, debtors, servants, landless peasants, and political exiles. Most were simply seeking a better way of life. As a Pennsylvania colonist noted, workers "here get three times the wages for their labor than they can in England."

Yet such wages never attracted enough laborers to keep up with the expanding colonial economies, and after attempts to enslave Indigenous peoples, Europeans enslaved Africans and sold them in the Americas. Beginning in 1503, European nations—especially Portugal and Spain—organized the largest forced migration in world history, the transatlantic slave trade. Throughout the sixteenth century, enslaved Africans were forcibly removed to ports as far south as Chile and as far north as Canada. Thereafter, the English and Dutch joined the slave trade. Few Europeans acknowledged the contradiction between the promise of freedom for themselves and the expanding institution of chattel slavery.

Whether voluntary or forced, the intermingling of these diverse peoples and cultures gave colonial American society its distinctive variety. The shared quest for a better life gave America much of its conflict and tragedy.

Even as they sought a better life for themselves, the Europeans unwittingly brought to the Americas infectious diseases that were disastrous for the Indigenous peoples. As much as 90 percent of the Indigenous population would eventually die from European-borne diseases. It was the worst death toll in history, viewed by some as genocide—the deliberate effort by a dominant power to destroy an ethnic or national group.

At the same time, bitter rivalries among the Spanish, French, English, and Dutch triggered costly wars around the world. Amid such conflicts, the monarchs of Europe struggled to manage their often-unruly colonies in the Americas, which, as it turned out, played crucial roles in the monarchs' frequent wars.

The American colonists and their British rulers maintained an uneasy partnership throughout the seventeenth century. By the eighteenth century, many colonists were displaying a feisty independence, which led them to resent government interference in their affairs. In fact, a British official in North Carolina reported that the colonists were "without any Law or Order. Impudence is so very high, as to be past bearing." As royal authorities tightened their control during the mid-eighteenth century, they first met resistance, which in 1775 ignited into revolution.

HERNÁN CORTÉS AND EMPEROR MOCTEZUMA This seventeenth-century oil painting shows the first meeting of Spanish conquistador Hernán Cortés (*center right*) and Emperor Moctezuma of the Mexica (*center left*) in 1519. Just behind Cortés stands Malinche, his mistress and interpreter. Moctezuma's people are not permitted to gaze upon his face, and a servant ensures that his feet do not touch the ground.

CHAPTER 1

The Collision of Cultures

IN THE SIXTEENTH CENTURY

America was born in melting ice. Thousands of years ago, during a period known as the Ice Age, immense glaciers some two miles thick inched southward from the Arctic Circle. The advancing ice crushed hills, rerouted rivers, gouged out lakebeds and waterways, and scraped bare the land in its path.

The glacial ice sheets covered much of North America—including what we now know as Canada, Alaska, the Upper Midwest, New England, Montana, and Washington. Then, as the continent's climate began to warm, the ice slowly melted, eventually opening pathways for the first immigrants from Asia to pass through. Over many centuries, curious people discovered a continent blessed with fertile soils, abundant game animals, and mighty rivers providing passageways throughout the interior.

North and South America were the last continents to be populated by *Homo sapiens*. Debate still rages about when and how humans first arrived in North America.

Until recently, archaeologists had assumed that ancient peoples from northeast Asia were the first humans to arrive in the Americas. Whether curious to explore new lands or attracted by herds of large game animals, they trekked across what is now the Bering Strait, a waterway that connects the Arctic and Pacific Oceans (see Map 1.1). During the Ice Age, however, the Bering Strait was dry—a treeless, frigid tundra (found in arctic and subarctic regions, consisting

CORE OBJECTIVES

1. Explain why there were so many diverse human societies in the Americas before Europeans arrived.
2. Summarize the significant developments in Europe that enabled the Age of Exploration, and the role that West African kingdoms played before the seventeenth century in the rise of early global trade.
3. Describe how the Spanish were able to conquer and colonize the Americas.
4. Assess the impact of the Columbian Exchange between the "Old" and "New" Worlds.
5. Analyze the legacy of the Spanish form of colonization on North American history.

8 | CHAPTER 1 The Collision of Cultures

MAP 1.1 THE FIRST MIGRATION

- Place your finger on the tip of Asia at the top of the map, and follow the migration routes down from North America all the way to South America. What do the branching arrows indicate?
- Did the migrating people always stay on land, or did they sometimes travel by water?
- Based on your reading of the chapter text, why did these peoples migrate to the Americas?

of frozen soil filled with moss, herbs, and small shrubs) known as Beringia that connected eastern Siberia with Alaska. More recent theories suggest that some Asians may have also ventured in boats to the coast of Alaska and then worked their way south along the Pacific coast all the way to South America.

Over thousands of years, nomadic groups (Paleo-Indians) fanned out southward from Alaska and spread across the Americas, forming small communities along the way. Archaeologists studying DNA have found evidence of people from East Asia in western Canada some 25,000 years ago—10,000 years earlier than previously thought.

The Paleo-Indians (also called Ancient Indians) lived in transportable huts with wooden frames covered by animal skins or grasses (thatch). They were skilled hunters and gatherers in search of game animals, whales, seals, fish, berries, nuts, roots, and seeds. As they moved southward, they trekked across prairies and plains, working in groups to kill massive animals unlike any found today: mammoths, mastodons, and giant sloths, wolves, beavers, and bears.

Regardless of when, where, or how humans first arrived in North America, the continent eventually became a dynamic crossroads for adventurous and highly skilled peoples from around the world. They brought with them distinctive backgrounds and motivations that helped form the multicultural society known as America.

Early Cultures in the Americas

Over many centuries, as the climate warmed, days grew so hot that many of the largest mammals—mammoths, mastodons, giant bison—became extinct. Hunters then began stalking smaller, yet more abundant mammals: deer, antelope, elk, moose, and caribou. Over time, the Ancient Indians adapted to their varied environments—coastal forests, grassy plains, southwestern deserts, eastern woodlands. Some continued to hunt and others trapped small game. Some gathered wild plants and herbs, while others farmed. Most did some of each.

By about 5000 BCE (before the Common Era), hunter-gatherer societies began transforming themselves into farming cultures, supplemented by seasonal hunting and gathering. Agriculture provided food that was more nutritious, which accelerated population growth and enabled formerly nomadic people to settle in villages. Indigenous peoples became expert at growing plants that would become the primary food crops of the hemisphere, chiefly **maize (corn)**, beans, and squash.

Maize-based societies viewed corn as the "gift of the gods" because it satisfied many essential needs. For example, Indigenous peoples made hominy by soaking dried kernels of corn in a mixture of water and ashes and then cooking it. They used corn cobs for fuel and the husks to fashion mats, masks, and dolls. They also ground the kernels into cornmeal, which could be mixed with beans to make protein-rich succotash.

The Maya, the Inca, and the Mexica

In *Mesoamerica*, what is now Mexico and Central America, by 5000 BCE agriculture supported the development of sophisticated communities complete with gigantic temple-topped pyramids, palaces, and bridges. Historians and archaeologists know most about the Maya, the Inca, and the Mexica peoples (see Map 1.2).

The Maya

The Maya, who dominated Central America for more than 600 years, worshipped more than a hundred gods and developed a written language

---

> CORE **OBJECTIVE**
> **1.** Explain why there were so many diverse human societies in the Americas before Europeans arrived.

> Agricultural revolution

maize (corn) The primary grain crop in Mesoamerica, yielding small kernels often ground into cornmeal. Easy to grow in a broad range of conditions, it enabled a global population explosion after being brought to Europe, Africa, and Asia.

MAYA SOCIETY A fresco depicting a dressing ceremony of a high priest. He stands in the center garbed in a jaguar skin and an embroidered belt, surrounded by his less elaborately clad attendants. **What does this image reveal about the social hierarchy of Maya society?**

and elaborate works of art and architecture. They used mathematics and astronomy to create a yearly calendar more accurate than the one used by Europeans at the time. Maya civilization featured sprawling cities, terraced farms, and spectacular pyramids.

In about 900 CE (Common Era), however, Maya culture collapsed. Why it disappeared remains a mystery. Was its demise the result of civil wars, or of ecological catastrophe—drought, famine, disease, crop failure? The Maya destroyed much of the rain forest upon whose fragile ecosystem they depended. As an archaeologist has explained, "Too many farmers grew too many crops on too much of the landscape." Deforestation led to hillside erosion and a catastrophic loss of nutrient-rich farmland.

Overpopulation added to the strain on Maya society, prompting civil wars. The Maya eventually succumbed to the Toltec people, who conquered most of the region in the tenth century. Around 1200, however, the Toltec society mysteriously withdrew after a series of droughts, fires, and invasions. The Toltec re-settled at Chapultepec, located on the west bank of Lake Texcoco.

The Inca

Much farther south, many diverse people speaking at least twenty different languages made up the sprawling Inca Empire. By the fifteenth century, the vast Inca realm stretched some 2,500 miles along the Andes Mountains in the western part of South America. It featured irrigated farms, stone buildings, and interconnected networks of roads paved with stones.

The Mexica (Aztec)

During the thirteenth century, the nomadic **Mexica** (me-SHEE-ka), or "people of the sun," began drifting southward from northwest Mexico. (They would later be called Aztecs by European explorers.) The Mexica seized control of the central highlands, where in 1325 they founded the spectacular city of Tenochtitlán (Place of the Stone Cactus) on an island in Lake Texcoco, at the site of present-day Mexico City.

Tenochtitlán would become one of the grandest cities in the world. It served as the capital of a sophisticated **Mexica Empire** ruled by a powerful emperor and divided into two social classes: nobles, warriors, and priests (about 5 percent of the population) comprised one class, with the second consisting of free commoners—merchants, artisans, and farmers.

When the Spanish invaded Mexico in 1519, they found a vast Mexica Empire connected by a network of roads serving 371 city-states organized into 38 provinces. Towering stone temples, paved avenues, thriving marketplaces, and some 70,000 *adobe* (sunbaked mud) huts dominated Tenochtitlán.

> Vast empires and monumental cities

Mexica Otherwise known as the Aztec, a Mesoamerican people of northern Mexico who founded the vast Aztec Empire in the fourteenth century. It was later conquered by the Spanish under Hernán Cortés in 1521.

Mexica Empire The dominion established in the fourteenth century under the imperialistic Mexica, or Aztec, people in the valley of Mexico.

TENOCHTITLÁN This map of the Mexica capital (and the Gulf of Mexico) was published in a 1524 edition of the letters of Hernán Cortés. The capital bloomed in concentric circles, with the Great Temple and political buildings at the center and the residences radiating outward. **What does the map of Tenochtitlán reveal about the people who lived there?**

As their empire expanded across central and southern Mexico, the Mexica people developed sophisticated legal and political systems. Their cities boasted lively markets and featured beautiful gardens and relaxing spas. The Mexica practiced efficient new farming techniques, including the terracing of fields, crop rotation, large-scale irrigation, and other engineering marvels. Their arts and architecture were magnificent.

Mexica rulers claimed godlike qualities, and nobles, priests, and warrior-heroes dominated the social system. The emperor's palace had 100 rooms and baths containing statues, gardens, and a zoo; the aristocracy lived in large stone dwellings, practiced polygamy (having multiple wives), and were exempt from manual labor.

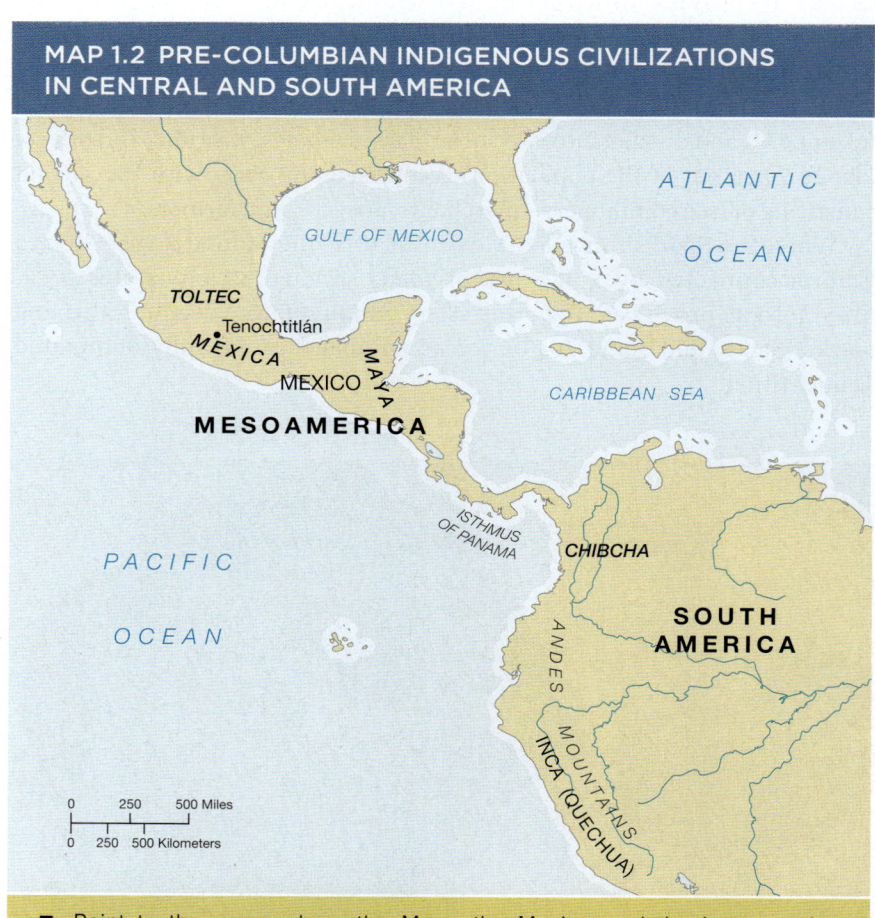

MAP 1.2 PRE-COLUMBIAN INDIGENOUS CIVILIZATIONS IN CENTRAL AND SOUTH AMERICA

- Point to the areas where the Maya, the Mexica, and the Inca peoples flourished. Looking back at Map 1.1, compare these areas to points on the early migration routes shown there.
- Locate the Mexica city of Tenochtitlán. Based on your reading of the chapter text, why was it important?
- What mountain range was home to the Inca peoples? What ocean bordered their communities? How do you suppose these geographic features affected the Inca diet and way of life?

Like most agricultural peoples, the Mexica worshipped multiple gods. Their religious beliefs focused on the interconnection between nature and human life and the sacredness of natural elements—the sun, moon, mountains, and animals. They were obliged to feed the gods human hearts and blood. As a consequence, the Mexica, like most Mesoamerican societies, regularly offered thousands of live human sacrifices to the gods in elaborate weekly rituals. The constant need for human sacrifices fed the Mexica people's relentless warfare against other Indigenous groups. A Mexica song celebrated their warrior code: "Proud of itself is the city of Mexico-Tenochtitlán. Here no one fears to die in war. This is our glory." Warfare, therefore, was a sacred activity. Gradually, the Mexica conquered many neighboring societies, forcing them to make payment of goods and labor to the empire.

> Religion, war, tribute, and trade

North American Societies around 1500

North of Mexico, in what is known as the present-day United States, many Indigenous societies blossomed in the early 1500s. Over the centuries, small kinship groups (*clans*) had coalesced to form larger *bands* involving hundreds of people. The bands evolved into much larger regional groups, or *nations*, whose members spoke the same language. Although few Indigenous societies had an alphabet or written language, they all developed rich oral traditions that passed spiritual myths and social beliefs from generation to generation.

> Diverse regional societies

Similarities and Differences

Like the Mexica, most Indigenous peoples in the Americas believed in godlike spirits. Although their religious practices were diverse, these societies were similar in revering such spirits. To the Sioux, for example, God was Wakan Tanka, the Great Spirit, who ruled over all spirits. The Navajo believed in the Holy People: Sky, Earth, Moon, and Sun. Some believed in ghosts, who acted as their bodyguards in battle.

The importance of hunting to many Indigenous societies helped nurture a warrior ethic in which courage in combat was the highest virtue. Their warfare mostly consisted of small-scale raids intended to enable individual warriors to demonstrate their courage rather than to seize territory or destroy villages. Casualties were minimal. The taking of captives to be sacrificed or enslaved often signaled victory.

For all their similarities, the Indigenous peoples of North America developed markedly different ways of life. In North America alone in 1492, when the first Europeans arrived, there were perhaps 8 million people organized into 240 societies (see Map 1.3). By comparison, Great Britain had about 2 to 3 million people. Many of the Indigenous societies, especially those west of the Appalachian Mountains, would remain vital and dominant long after the United States was created in 1776.

Indigenous peoples practiced diverse customs and developed varied economies. Some wore clothes they wove or made using animal skins, and others decorated themselves with colorful paint, tattoos, and jewelry. Some lived in stone houses, others in circular timber wigwams or bark-roofed longhouses. Still others lived in sod-covered or reed-thatched lodges, or portable tipis made from animal skins. Some cultures built stone pyramids graced by ceremonial plazas, and others constructed enormous *ceremonial mounds* (earthen pyramids used for sacred ceremonies and burials).

Few North American Indigenous societies permitted absolute rulers. Nations had chiefs, but the "power of the chiefs," reported an eighteenth-century British trader, is often "an empty sound. They can only persuade or dissuade the people by the force of good-nature and clear reasoning."

Indigenous Americans owned land in common rather than individually as private property. Men were hunters, warriors, and leaders. Women tended children; made clothes, blankets, jewelry, and pottery; cured and dried animal skins; wove baskets; built and packed tipis; and grew, harvested, and cooked food.

When the men were away hunting or fighting, women took charge of village life. Some nations, like the Cherokee in the Southeast and the Five Nation League of the Iroquois in the Northeast (the League comprised the Mohawk, Oneida, Onondaga, Cayuga, and Seneca Nations), affirmed women's political power. The women "are much respected," a French priest reported on the Iroquois. "The Elders decide no important affair without their advice."

The Southwest

The often hot and dry Southwest (what is now Arizona, New Mexico, Nevada, and Utah) featured a landscape of deep canyons, vast deserts, and snow-covered mountains. The Hopi, Zuni, and other Indigenous groups still live in the multi-story adobe cliffside villages (called *pueblos* by the Spanish) that were erected by their ancient ancestors.

About 500 CE, the Hohokam (meaning "those who have vanished") people migrated from Mexico northward to southern and central Arizona, where they built extensive canals to irrigate crops. They also crafted decorative pottery and turquoise jewelry.

The most widespread of the Southwest pueblo cultures were the Ancestral Pueblo or Anasazi, also called Basketmakers. Unlike the Mexica and Inca peoples, however, Ancestral Pueblo society did *not* have a rigid class structure. The Ancestral Pueblo engaged in warfare only as a means of self-defense, and the religious leaders and warriors worked much as the rest of the people did.

CLIFF DWELLINGS Ruins of Ancestral Pueblo (Anasazi) cliff dwellings in Mesa Verde National Park, Colorado. **Why might the Southwestern societies have built their villages deep into cliff faces?**

The Northwest

Along the narrow strip running up the northwest Pacific coast, sea animals, deer, and edible wild plants were abundant. Here, there was little need to rely on farming. Many of the Pacific Northwest peoples, such as the Haida,

Kwakiutl, and Nootka, needed to work only two days to provide enough food for a week.

The Pacific coast cultures developed intricate religious rituals and sophisticated woodworking skills. They carved towering totem poles featuring symbolic figures, such as the face or spirit animal of a loved one. For shelter, they built large, earthen-floored, cedar-plank houses up to 500 feet long, where groups of families lived together. They also created sturdy, oceangoing canoes made of hollowed-out tree trunks—some large enough to carry fifty people. Socially, they were divided into slaves, commoners, and chiefs.

The Great Plains

The many tribal nations living on the Great Plains, a vast, flat land west of the Mississippi River, included the Arapaho, Blackfeet, Cheyenne, Comanche, Crow, Apache, and Sioux. As nomadic hunter-gatherers, they tracked herds of bison (buffaloes) across a sea of grassland, collecting edible plants as they roamed.

For all their differences, Indigenous societies developed a religious worldview distinctly different from the Christian perspective of Europeans. At the center of most hunter-gatherer religions is the conviction that human beings are related to all living things, among which Indigenous peoples are included. As the Navajo sing, "All my surroundings are blessed as I found it."

> Native Americans' religious beliefs

GREAT SERPENT MOUND Over 1,300 feet in length and three feet high, this snake-shaped burial mound in Adams County, Ohio, is the largest of its kind in the world.

ceremonial mounds A funereal tradition, practiced in the Mississippi and Ohio Valleys by the Adena-Hopewell cultures, of erecting massive mounds of earth over graves, often shaped in the designs of serpents and other animals.

The Mississippians

East of the Great Plains, in the vast woodlands reaching from the Mississippi River to the Atlantic Ocean, several "mound-building" cultures prospered. Between 700 BCE and 200 CE, the Adena and later the Hopewell societies developed communities in the Ohio valley. The Adena-Hopewell cultures grew corn, squash, beans, and sunflowers, as well as tobacco for smoking. They left behind enormous earthworks and elaborate **ceremonial mounds** shaped like snakes, birds, and other animals.

Like the Adena, the Hopewell developed an extensive trading network with other Indigenous societies from the Gulf of Mexico to Canada, exchanging exquisite carvings, metalwork, pearls, seashells, copper ornaments, bear claws, and jewelry. By the sixth century, however, the Hopewell culture disappeared, giving way to the *Mississippian* culture.

The Mississippians were corn-growing peoples who built substantial agricultural towns around central plazas and temples and developed a far-flung trading network that extended to the Rocky Mountains. Their ability to grow large amounts of corn in the fertile floodplains spurred rapid population growth around regional centers.

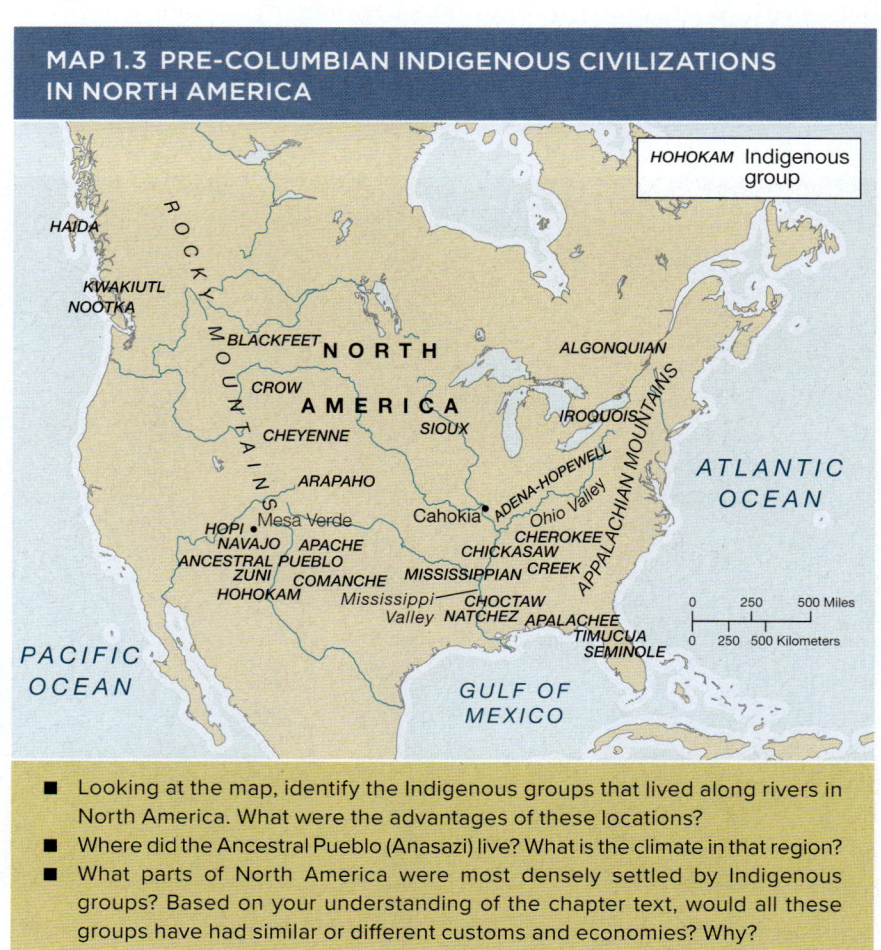

MAP 1.3 PRE-COLUMBIAN INDIGENOUS CIVILIZATIONS IN NORTH AMERICA

- Looking at the map, identify the Indigenous groups that lived along rivers in North America. What were the advantages of these locations?
- Where did the Ancestral Pueblo (Anasazi) live? What is the climate in that region?
- What parts of North America were most densely settled by Indigenous groups? Based on your understanding of the chapter text, would all these groups have had similar or different customs and economies? Why?

The most significant of these advanced regional centers, called *chiefdoms*, was **Cahokia** (600–1300 CE), in southwest Illinois, near the confluence of the Mississippi and Missouri Rivers (across from what is now St. Louis). The Cahokians constructed an enormous farming settlement with monumental public buildings, spacious ceremonial plazas, and more than eighty flat-topped earthen mounds with thatch-roofed temples on top. At the height of its influence, Cahokia hosted 15,000 people on some 3,200 acres.

Cahokia, however, vanished around 1400. Its collapse remains a mystery, but the overcutting of trees to make fortress walls may have set in motion ecological changes that doomed the community when a massive earthquake struck. The loss of trees led to widespread flooding and the erosion of topsoil, which forced residents to seek better land across the Midwest and into what is now the American South.

Cahokia The largest chiefdom of the Mississippian Indian culture located in what is present-day Illinois and the site of a sophisticated farming settlement that supported up to 15,000 inhabitants.

Eastern Woodland peoples Various Native American societies, particularly the Algonquian, Iroquoian, and Muskogean regional groups, who once dominated the Atlantic seaboard from Maine to Louisiana.

Eastern Woodland Peoples

After the collapse of Cahokia, the **Eastern Woodland peoples** spread along the Atlantic seaboard from Maine to Florida and along the Gulf Coast to Louisiana. They included three groups distinguished by their different languages: Algonquian, Iroquoian, and Muskogean. These were the Indigenous societies that Europeans would first encounter when they arrived in North America.

The Algonquian-speaking peoples stretched westward from the New England coast to lands along the Great Lakes and into the Upper Midwest and south to the areas of present-day New Jersey, Virginia, and the Carolinas. They lived in small, round *wigwams* or in multifamily longhouses surrounded by a *palisade*, a tall timber fence to defend against attacks. Their villages typically ranged in size from 500 to 2,000 people.

The Algonquians along the Atlantic coast were skilled at fishing; the inland Algonquians excelled at hunting. All Algonquians foraged for wild food (nuts, berries, and fruits) and practiced agriculture. They annually burned the underbrush in dense forests to improve soil fertility and provide grazing room for deer. In the spring, many Algonquian nations cultivated corn, beans, and squash—plants that they called "the Three Sisters" because they thrived together. The cornstalks provided support for the bean tendrils, and the beans pulled nitrogen out of the air and dispersed it through the soil to benefit all three companion plants. The large leaves generated by the squash provided shade for the corn and bean plants.

West and south of the Algonquians were the powerful Iroquoian-speaking peoples (the Seneca, Onondaga, Mohawk, Oneida, and Cayuga Nations, as well as the Cherokee and Tuscarora). Their lands spread from upstate New York southward through Pennsylvania and into the Carolinas and Georgia. The Iroquois were farmer/hunters who lived in extended family

ALGONQUIAN CHIEF IN WAR PAINT This sketch from the notebook of English settler John White depicts an Indigenous chief.

Gender roles in Iroquoian culture

groups (clans), sharing bark-covered longhouses in towns of 3,000 or more people. The oldest woman in each longhouse served as the "clan mother."

Unlike the Algonquian culture, in which men were dominant, women held the critical leadership roles among the Iroquois. As an elder explained, "In our society, women are the center of all things. Nature, we believe, has given women the ability to create; therefore, it is only natural that women be in positions of power to protect this function." Iroquois men and women operated in separate social domains. No woman could be a chief; no man could head a clan. Women selected the chiefs, controlled the distribution of property, supervised the enslaved, and planted and harvested the crops. They also arranged marriages. After a wedding ceremony, the man moved in with his wife's family. In part, the Iroquoian matriarchy (society led by women) reflected the frequent absence of Iroquois men, who, being skilled hunters and traders, traveled extensively for long periods.

The third major Indigenous group in the Eastern Woodlands population included the peoples along the coast of the Gulf of Mexico who farmed and hunted and spoke the Muskogean language: the Creek, Choctaw, Chickasaw, Seminole, Natchez, Apalachee, and Timucua. Like the Iroquois, they were often matrilineal societies, meaning that ancestry flowed through the mother's line, but they had a more rigid class structure. The Muskogeans lived in towns arranged around a central plaza. Many of their thatch-roofed houses had no walls because of the mild winters and hot, humid summers.

Over thousands of years, the native North Americans had displayed remarkable resilience, adapting to the uncertainties of frequent warfare, changing climates, and varying environments. They would display similar resilience against the challenges created by the arrival of Europeans.

By now, on the eve of European arrival, the Indigenous peoples had developed a range of diverse societies. These were largely the result of geographic and ecological conditions (such as hunting/gathering vs. agricultural); economic needs (such as trade and alliances among groups); and social factors (such as class hierarchy, patriarchy vs. matriarchy, spiritual beliefs, and local languages). Despite these differences, Indigenous societies were independent and strongly rooted in tradition—qualities that would help them meet the challenges brought by the coming Age of Exploration.

CORE OBJECTIVE

2. Summarize the significant developments in Europe that enabled the Age of Exploration, and the role that West African kingdoms played before the seventeenth century in the rise of early global trade.

The Age of Exploration and the Rise of Global Trade

While the Indigenous peoples were flourishing in North America, developments on the European continent led to exploration and change. Ultimately, this increased activity and interconnection among peoples would support the rise of global trade.

The Expansion of Europe

European exploration of the Americas resulted from key developments during the fifteenth century. Dramatic scientific discoveries and technological improvements, along with sustained population growth, fueled European expansion abroad. At this time, Europe's social and political system was structured with a hierarchy governed by land ownership. The three classes included a king, a noble class, and a peasant class.

By the end of the fifteenth century, medieval feudalism's static agrarian social system, in which peasant serfs worked for nobles in exchange for living on and farming the land, began to disintegrate. People were no longer forced to remain in the same area and keep the same social status to which they were born, and a "middle class" emerged that was committed to a more dynamic commercial economy.

> Rise of a middle class

The growing trade-based economy in Europe freed kings from their dependence on feudal nobles. Monarchs unified the scattered cities ruled by princes (principalities) into large, centralized kingdoms. The rise of towns, cities, and a merchant class provided new tax revenues. Over time, the new communities of monarchs, merchants, and bankers displaced the landed nobility as the ruling elite.

> Powerful new nations

The Renaissance

The rediscovery of ancient Greek and Roman texts during the fourteenth and fifteenth centuries spurred the Renaissance (meaning "rebirth"), an intellectual revolution that transformed the arts as well as traditional attitudes toward religion and science. The Renaissance began in Italy and spread across western Europe, bringing with it a more *secular* (non-religious) outlook that took greater interest in humanity than in religion. Rather than emphasizing God's omnipotence (all-powerfulness), Renaissance *humanism* highlighted the power of inventive people to exert command over nature.

The Renaissance was a crucial force in the transition from medievalism to early modernism. From the fifteenth century on, educated people throughout Europe began to challenge prevailing beliefs as well as the absolute authority of rulers and churchmen. They discussed controversial new ideas, engaged in scientific research, and unleashed their artistic creativity. At the same time, the majority of Europeans were uneducated, and some scholars note that they were not affected by the Renaissance in any significant ways.

> Innovations in shipbuilding, navigation, and weaponry led to global revolution in maritime trade

The Renaissance also sparked what came to be called the Age of Exploration. New knowledge and technologies made possible the construction of larger sailing ships capable of oceanic voyages. The Renaissance also brought the invention of gunpowder, cannons, and firearms—and the printing press.

The Rise of Global Trade

By the sixteenth century, trade between western European nations and societies in the Middle East, Africa, and Asia was booming. The Portuguese took the lead, bolstered by expert sailors and fast, three-masted ships called *caravels*.

Portuguese ships traveled along the western coast of Africa collecting grains, gold, ivory, spices, and enslaved human cargo. Eventually, these ships continued around Africa to the Indian Ocean in search of the fabled *Indies* (India and Southeast Asia). They ventured on to China and Japan, where they acquired spices to enliven bland European food, sugar to sweeten food and drink, silk cloth, herbal medicines, and other exotic goods for expanding western markets.

> Factors that facilitated global trade

Global trade flourished because of the emergence of four powerful nations: England, France, Portugal, and especially Spain. The arranged marriage of King Ferdinand II of Aragon and Queen Isabella I of Castile in 1469 unified their two kingdoms into one formidable new nation, Spain. On January 1, 1492, after nearly eight centuries of warfare between Spanish Christians and Muslims, Ferdinand and Isabella declared victory for Catholicism at Granada. The king and queen were eager to spread the Catholic faith.

Religious zeal and other factors—urbanization; world trade; the rise of centralized nations; advances in knowledge, technology, and firepower—combined with natural human curiosity and greed to spur efforts to find western sea routes to the Indies. More immediately, the decision of Turkish rulers to shut off land access to Asia in 1453 forced merchants to focus on seaborne options. For these reasons, Europeans set in motion the events that, as one historian has observed, would bind together "four continents, three races, and a great diversity of regional parts."

West African Cultures and Empires

This great diversity was evident in Africa, even before it became one of the four critical regions involved in the search for seaborne trade routes to the Indies. The African continent is vast, covering 20 percent of the Earth's land area and hosting some 3,000 ethnic groups.

Africa, like Asia and Europe, boasted highly organized societies with empires and dynasties that lasted for centuries. Ancient African societies such as Egypt's developed centralized governments, organized tax systems, early hydraulic engineering and irrigation systems, and a writing system known as hieroglyphs. The pharaohs ruling early Egyptian kingdoms mobilized large armies that conquered adjacent regions, forming an extensive community that lasted approximately 3,000 years, until 332 BCE.

West Africa, which would come to play a vital role in the rise of global trade, had for centuries also been a rich, ancient, and diverse region within the continent. It was characterized by the rise and fall of powerful empires, the growth of widely varied ethnic cultures and societies, and transformational economic and spiritual interactions with other regions of the world.

West Africa emerged from several advanced ancient civilizations, including the Ghana Empire, the Mali Empire, and the Songhai Empire (see Map 1.4). These societies thrived between the fifth and sixteenth centuries and were known for their wealth, dynamic trading networks, and stunning cultural contributions. The region became a vital part of the trade routes between North Africa and sub-Saharan Africa that facilitated the exchange of goods, especially gold, salt, ivory, and enslaved people.

MAP 1.4 THE THREE WEST AFRICAN KINGDOMS

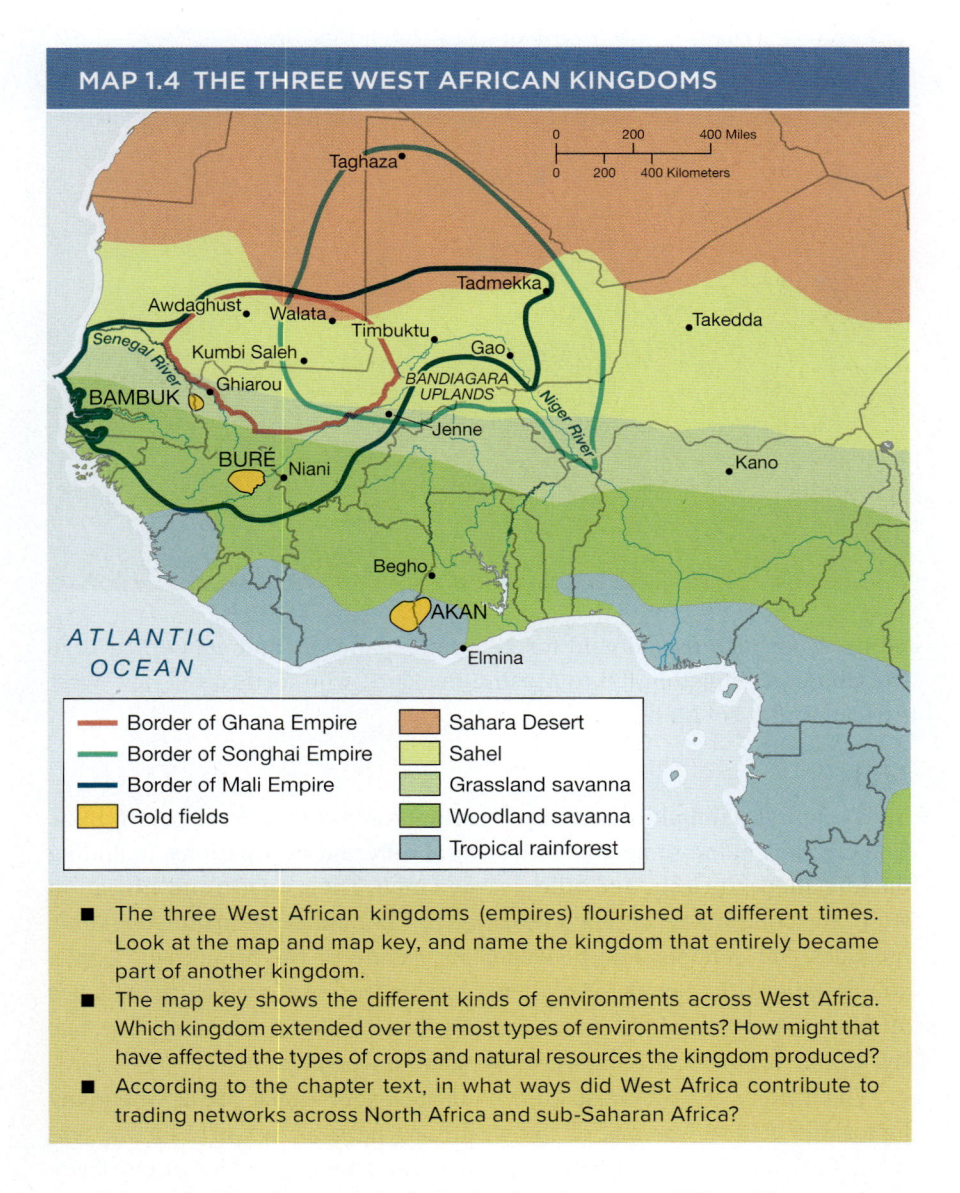

- The three West African kingdoms (empires) flourished at different times. Look at the map and map key, and name the kingdom that entirely became part of another kingdom.
- The map key shows the different kinds of environments across West Africa. Which kingdom extended over the most types of environments? How might that have affected the types of crops and natural resources the kingdom produced?
- According to the chapter text, in what ways did West Africa contribute to trading networks across North Africa and sub-Saharan Africa?

This trade played a crucial role in the development of West African economies and cultures. The Islamic religion was introduced to the region through these trading networks with North Africa and subsequent military invasions that followed the same networks. During this period, Islamic scholarship and culture had a significant influence on West African societies. As Islam became one of the prominent religions in the region, West Africa became home to mosques and other places of higher learning.

Ghana

Ghana occupied a large region, about 500,000 square kilometers, containing small villages and major urban settlements. The kingdom had majestic buildings, intricate sculptures, and a robust military and political system. Vast gold deposits contributed to Ghana's growth, as native traders exchanged gold with Muslim Arabs for ceramics, glass, oil lamps, and salt from Saharan

SANKORE MOSQUE Sankore mosque was built in the fifteenth century and is one of three ancient centers of learning located in Timbuktu, Mali. It is believed to have been established by Mansa Musa, who was the ruler of the Mali Empire, and was the base for the University of Sankore, Timbuktu, Mali

mines. They also traded gold for kola nuts, palm oil, and copper. In 1076 the Ghanaian kingdom fell to Muslim invaders, who formed the new West African Empire of Mali.

Mali

Mali's capital, Timbuktu, became a bustling trade center described in 1526. The city was home to people with several different occupations, including doctors, judges, priests, and other learned men. Their wealth and education led to the creation of centers of learning in Timbuktu that included Islamic mosques, law schools, and book dealers. Home to the Mandingo people, among others, the people of Mali were agriculturalists who cultivated rice and harvested the inland rivers for fish. They added to the long-distance trade and, like urban dwellers, grew wealthy as a result of it.

The Empire of Mali is also known for the leader Mansa Musa, who many historians believe was one of the wealthiest persons in world history. He inherited some of his wealth during his rule, and he added to it through trade (salt and ivory) and taxation. During his reign, he annexed twenty-four cities, including Timbuktu, and established major trading centers throughout the region. He celebrated the arts and encouraged those in his empire to become educated at mosques.

Musa became popular after he made a 3,500-mile pilgrimage in 1324 across the Sahara Desert through Cairo and on to Mecca (a holy city in Saudi Arabia to which devout Muslims made their annual pilgrimage) in the distant Arabian Peninsula. It is said that on his journey he gave out lavish gifts, including bars of gold. He traveled with a caravan of 60,000 men and 12,000 servants and reportedly his royal court, officials, soldiers, griots (entertainers), merchants, camel drivers, and a long train of goats and sheep for nourishment. The empire later declined after it was divided into smaller states and Europeans arrived in the region.

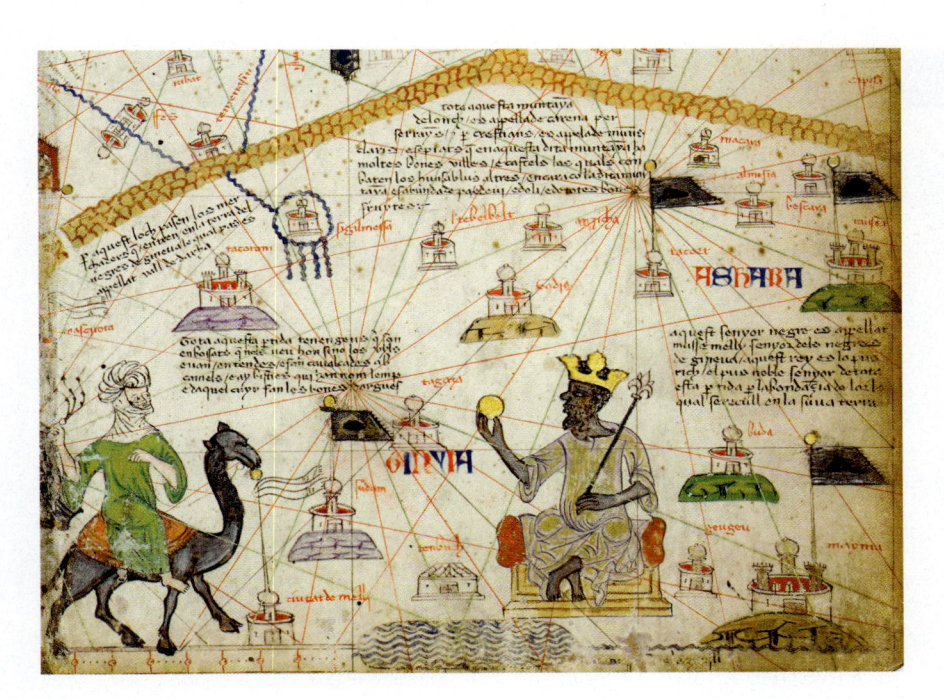

MANSA MUSA'S PILGRIMAGE TO MECCA Detail from the Catalan Atlas showing a map of the Western Sahara and Mansa Musa, 1375. It not only conveys geographical locations but also includes information on ancient and medieval tales, regional politics, astronomy, and astrology.

Songhai

The Empire of Songhai evolved after the decline of Mali and began as a small group of people who lived along the Niger River. Mostly farmers, traders, fishermen, and warriors, Songhai broke away from Mali in 1453. Their practice involved raiding smaller regions of the Mali Empire, until Sonni Ali (1468–1492) became the first of many leaders in the region. He created the only naval fleet in North Africa and was involved in thirty-two wars during his twenty-eight-year reign. The leaders who followed did not achieve the success of Ghana or Mali rulers, largely because they did not have access to the gold fields of the southern coast of West Africa. Additionally, when sea routes to the Mediterranean opened, the trans-Saharan trade faced competition and decline.

The West African empires from the fifth through the sixteenth centuries played an important role in the cultural shift and movement of peoples on the eve of global exploration. European explorers often brought African people on their expeditions as comrades and servants when they traversed new territories. As a result, when global trade emerged, the people from Europe and Africa who populated the Americas were already rich with collaboration, conflict, and innovation.

The Voyages of Columbus

Many factors were in play that prompted Christopher Columbus's efforts to find a faster route to Japan and China. Born in 1451 in the Italian seaport of Genoa, Italy, Columbus took to sea at an early age, teaching himself geography, navigation, and Latin. By the 1480s he was eager to spread Christianity

MAP 1.5 COLUMBUS'S VOYAGES

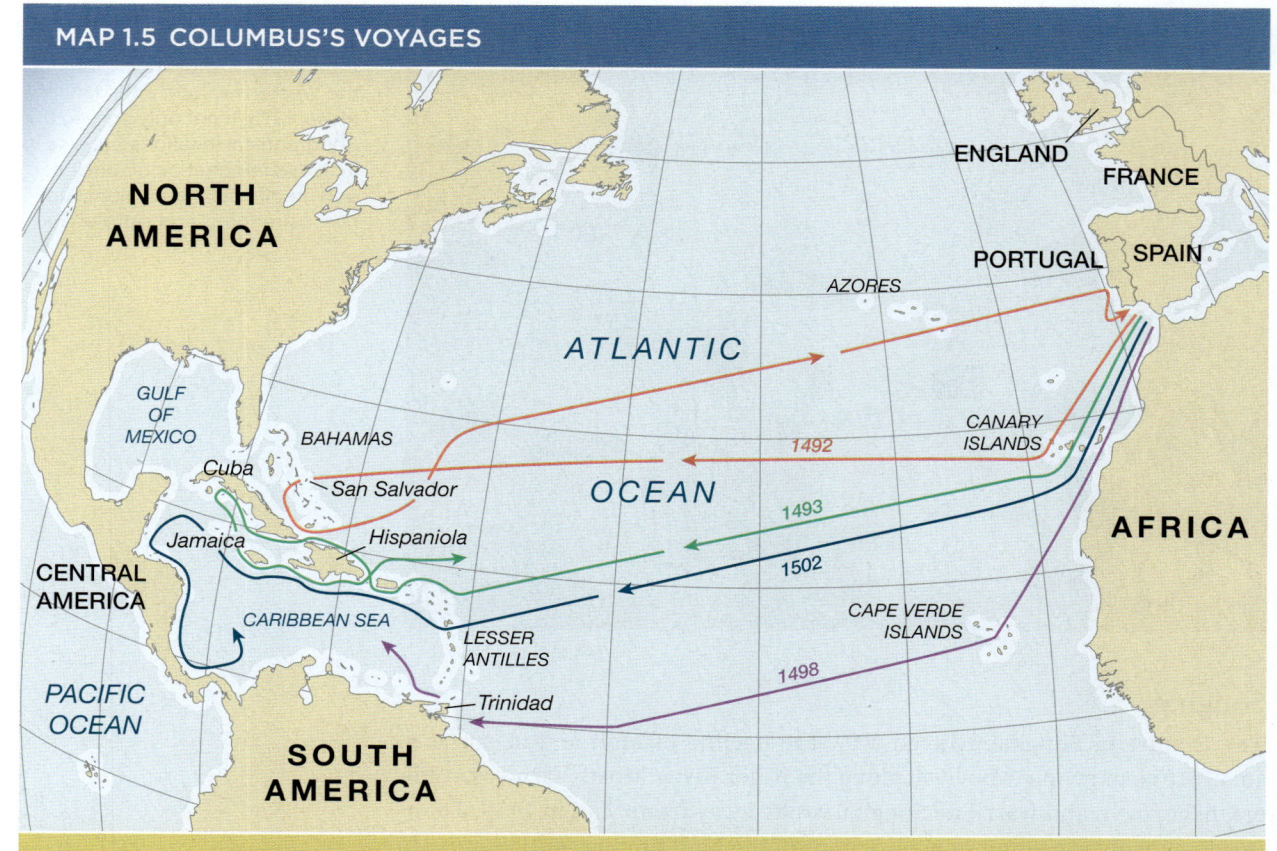

- On the map, point to the country where all of Columbus's voyages began.
- How many years passed between Columbus's first voyage and his fourth?
- Based on your reading of the chapter text, where did Columbus think he had landed on his first voyage? Locate the spot on the map where he did land.

across the globe and win glory and riches for himself. Ultimately, he would undertake four voyages across the Atlantic (see Map 1.5).

Columbus spent a decade trying to convince European monarchs to finance a voyage across the Atlantic. The rulers of England, France, Portugal, and Spain turned him down, but he eventually persuaded the Spanish monarchs Ferdinand and Isabella to fund his voyage. They agreed to award him a one-tenth share of any riches he gathered; they would keep the rest.

Columbus's First Voyage

On August 3, 1492, Columbus and a crew of ninety men and boys, mostly from Spain but from seven other nations as well, set sail on three tiny ships, the *Santa María*, the *Pinta*, and the *Niña*. Relatively unknown in the history of this voyage is the fact that an African explorer from Spain—named Pedro Alonzo Niño but known as El Negro—had the responsibility of piloting the *Santa María*. An experienced sailor from a family of mariners including his father and four brothers, Niño participated in several voyages across the Atlantic, including the first two with Columbus and a third as captain traveling to the region of present-day Venezuela.

As a member of Columbus's first voyage, Niño participated in bartering for pearls on the island of Margarita. The ship traveled first to Lisbon, Portugal, then headed west to the Canary Islands, where the explorers spent a month gathering supplies and making repairs. They then journeyed across the open sea. By early October, the worried sailors—none of whom had ever been away from land so long—rebelled at the "madness" of sailing blindly. They forced Columbus to agree to turn back if land were not sighted within three days.

Finding Land and the Taino. As the ships sailed on, the crew's mood lightened as they saw evidence that land was nearby. At dawn on October 12, a sailor on watch yelled, *"Tierra! Tierra!"* ("Land! Land!"). He had spotted a small island in the Bahamas (east of present-day Florida), known to natives as Guanahani; Columbus would name it San Salvador (Blessed Savior), a name that would not become official until 1925.

After making landfall, and at every encounter with the Indigenous people, known as Taino, Columbus asked if they had gold. If they did, the Europeans seized it; if they did not, they were forced to search for it. Gold was an obsession. As Columbus wrote in his diary, "the best thing in the world is gold; it can even send souls to heaven."

The Taino, unable to understand or repel the visitors, offered gifts of food, water, spears, and parrots. Columbus described them as "well-built, with good bodies, and handsome features." He marveled that they could "easily be made Christians," boasting that "with fifty men we could subjugate them all and make them do whatever we want." He promised to bring six "natives" back to Spain for "his highnesses."

This encounter reflects (and can be said to have started) what would become the typical European attitude toward the Indigenous peoples of the Americas: the belief that they were inferior and therefore could be exploited and enslaved. The Age of Exploration quickly transitioned to the Age of Empire.

Exploring Cuba and Hispaniola. Columbus, excited by Indigenous stories of "rivers of gold" to the west, continued to search for a passage to the Indies. His ships passed through the Bahamas and proceeded westward to the long island of Cuba, which appeared so large that Columbus

COLUMBUS IN THE "NEW WORLD" Christopher Columbus reached the island of San Salvador in 1492, although he was under the impression he had landed in or near the Indies. This woodcut, *Columbus's Landfall*, comes from a 1493 pamphlet describing this voyage—one of several trips he made back and forth across the Atlantic in the decade that followed.

thought it a part of Asia. He went ashore, sword in one hand, cross in the other, exclaiming that it was the "most beautiful land human eyes have ever beheld."

After exploring Cuba for several weeks, the Europeans sailed eastward to the island Columbus called Hispaniola (the Spanish Island), present-day Haiti and the Dominican Republic. He described the island's residents as full "of love and without greed." They had no weapons, wore no clothes, and led a simple life.

Columbus, however, had no interest in simple living. He decided that the Indigenous people were "fitted to be ruled and to be set to work" generating riches for Spain, "for there are great mines of gold and of other metals." He decreed that all members of Indigenous populations over age fourteen must bring him at least a thimbleful of gold dust every three months. But this quota was often unattainable because there was not as much gold in the Caribbean as Columbus imagined. Nevertheless, individuals who failed to supply enough gold had their hands cut off, causing many of them to bleed to death. If Indigenous people fled, fighting dogs hunted them down.

Under Columbus's program of what was essentially forced labor, huge numbers of Indigenous people died from overwork or disease; others committed suicide. Columbus, reported a Spanish priest, was so eager to please King Ferdinand and Queen Isabella "that he committed irreparable crimes against the Indians." In fact, during fifty years of Spanish control the numbers of Indigenous people on Hispaniola were decimated. In their place, the Spanish gradually began importing enslaved Africans because their labor grew to be more valuable than gold.

Columbus's Return and the Treaty of Tordesillas

At the end of 1492, Columbus, still convinced he had reached an outer island of Japan, sailed back to Spain, where he received a hero's welcome for finding the shortcut to Asia. He promised Ferdinand and Isabella that his discoveries would provide them "as much gold as they need . . . and as many slaves as they ask." Thanks to the newly invented printing press, news of Columbus's path-breaking voyage spread rapidly across Europe and helped spur a desire to explore the world.

The excited Spanish monarchs told Columbus to prepare for a second voyage, instructing him to "treat the Indians very well and lovingly and abstain from doing them any injury." Columbus and his men would repeatedly defy this order.

Spanish officials immediately sought to secure their legal claim to the Americas. Rivals Spain and Portugal signed the Treaty of Tordesillas (1494), which divided the non-Christian world by giving most of the Americas to Spain, while Africa and what would become Brazil were granted to Portugal. As a result, while Spain developed its American empire in the sixteenth century, Portugal provided most of its enslaved African laborers.

> Treaty of Tordesillas divides the Americas and Africa between the Spanish and Portuguese empires

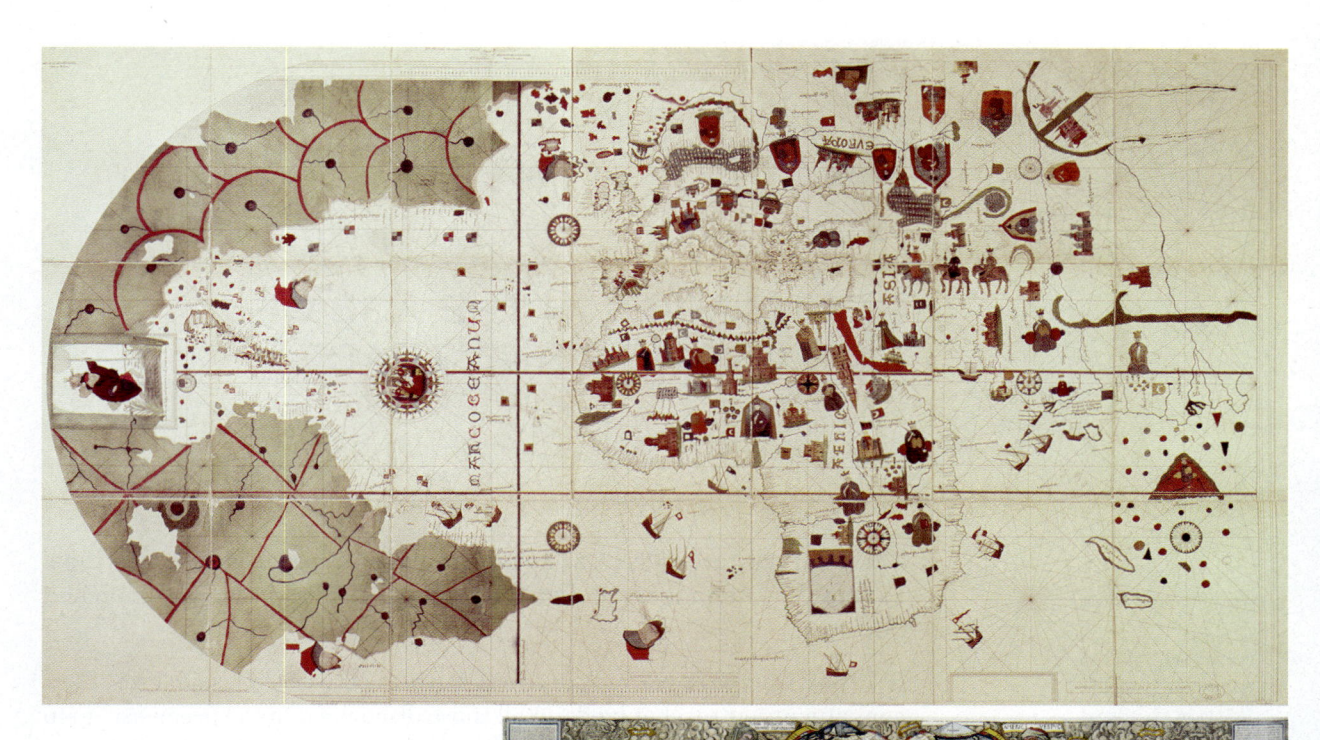

The Age of Exploration and the Rise of Global Trade 27

Columbus's Troubled Second and Third Voyages

In 1493, Columbus returned to the Americas with seventeen ships and 1,400 sailors, soldiers, and colonists—all men. Unfortunately, the Spanish ships also brought infectious germs, including measles, typhus, and smallpox. Also on board were Catholic priests eager to convert the Indigenous people to Christianity. Upon reaching Hispaniola, Columbus discovered that the men he had left behind after his first visit had raped women, robbed villages, and, as Columbus's son later added, committed "a thousand excesses for which they were mortally hated by the Indians."

Columbus proved to be a much better ship captain than a colonizer and governor. His first business venture in the Americas was as a slave trader. When he returned to Spain from his second voyage with 400 enslaved Arawak people, Queen Isabella, who detested slavery, was horrified. "Who is this Columbus who dares to give out my vassals [Indians] as slaves?"

This incident prompted a series of investigations into Columbus's behavior. The queen sent a royal commissioner to Hispaniola, where the first thing he saw were the corpses of six Spanish settlers who had been hanged. The shocked commissioner removed Columbus as governor and forced him back

THE "OLD" AND "NEW" WORLDS (*Top*) The *mappa mundi*, or "map of the world," was drawn by Juan de la Cosa in 1500 and is the first known European map to include the "New World." (*Bottom*) Martin Waldseemüller's 1507 world map was the first to capture the full Western Hemisphere, and to use the name "America." **What do these maps represent and how might they have shaped European worldviews?**

Comparing PERSPECTIVES

BOUNDARIES IN THE AGE OF EXPLORATION AND TRADE

From: Treaty of Tordesillas, signed June 7, 1494.

The Treaty of Tordesillas was an agreement between Spain and Portugal to establish a boundary line that divided lands discovered by Spain and Portugal.

[1.] That, whereas a certain controversy exists between the said lords, their constituents, as to what lands, of all those discovered in the ocean sea up to the present day, the date of this treaty, pertain to each one of the said parts respectively; therefore, for the sake of peace and concord, and for the preservation of the relationship and love of the said King of Portugal for the said King and Queen of Castile, Aragon, etc., it being the pleasure of their Highnesses, they, their said representatives, acting in their name and by virtue of their powers herein described, covenanted and agreed that a boundary or straight line be determined and drawn north and south, from pole to pole, on the said ocean sea, from the Arctic to the Antarctic pole. This boundary or line shall be drawn straight, as aforesaid, at a distance of three hundred and seventy leagues west of the Cape Verde Islands, being calculated by degrees, or by any other manner as may be considered the best and readiest, provided the distance shall be no greater than abovesaid. And all lands, both islands and mainlands, found and discovered already, or to be found and discovered hereafter, by the said King of Portugal and by his vessels on this side of the said line and bound determined as above, toward the east, in either north or south latitude, on the eastern side of the said bound, provided the said bound is not crossed, shall belong to, and remain in the possession of, and pertain forever to, the said King of Portugal and his successors. And all other lands, both islands and mainlands, found or to be found hereafter, discovered or to be discovered hereafter, which have been discovered or shall be discovered by the said King and Queen of Castile, Aragon, etc., and by their vessels, on the western side of the said bound, determined as above, after having passed the said bound toward the west, in either its north or south latitude, shall belong to, and remain in the possession of, and pertain forever to, the said King and Queen of Castile, Leon, etc., and to their successors.

From: Letter from King Nzinga Mbemba of the Kongo, to King João of Portugal, July 6, 1526.

King Nzinga Mbemba wrote this letter to King João of Portugal condemning the slave trade and requesting that Portugal stop sending merchants (slave traders) to his kingdom.

[1526] Sir, Your Highness [of Portugal] should know how our Kingdom is being lost in so many ways that it is convenient to provide for the necessary remedy, since this is caused by the excessive freedom given by your factors and officials to the men and merchants who are allowed to come to this Kingdom to set up shops with goods and many things which have been prohibited by us, and which they spread throughout our Kingdoms and Domains in such an abundance that many of our vassals, whom we had in obedience, do not comply because they have the things in greater abundance than we ourselves; and it was with these things that we had them content and subjected under our vassalage and jurisdiction, so it is doing a great harm not only to the service of God, but [to] the security and peace of our Kingdoms and State as well.

And we cannot reckon how great the damage is, since the mentioned merchants are taking every day our natives, sons of the land and the sons of our noblemen and vassals and our relatives, because the thieves and men of bad conscience grab them wishing to have the things and wares of this Kingdom which they are ambitious of; they grab them and get them to be sold; and so great, Sir, is the corruption and licentiousness that our country is being completely depopulated, and Your Highness should not agree with this nor accept it as in your service.

Questions

1. Given the location of the boundary line it describes, how would the Treaty of Tordesillas have affected Spain and Portugal's commerce in Africa and the Americas?

2. According to King Nzinga Mbemba, what have been the effects of European slave trading on the Kingdom of Kongo?

3. Taken together, what do the Treaty of Tordesillas and the letter by King Nzinga Mbemba indicate about the expansion of the transatlantic slave trade and the demands for African labor in the Americas?

to Spain in 1500. To the end of his life, in 1506, Columbus insisted that he had discovered the outlying parts of Asia. By one of history's greatest ironies, this led Europeans to name the Americas not for Columbus but for another Italian explorer, Amerigo Vespucci.

In 1499, with the support of Portugal's monarchy, Vespucci sailed across the Atlantic, landing first at Brazil and then exploring 3,000 miles of the South American coastline in search of a passage to Asia. In the end, he decided that South America was so extensive and so densely populated that it must be a *new* continent. In 1507, a German mapmaker paid tribute to Amerigo Vespucci by labeling the lands "America."

Vespucci's New World continent

Professional Explorers

Meanwhile, news of the voyages of Columbus and Vespucci stimulated other expeditions. The first professional explorer to sight the North American continent was John Cabot, an Italian sponsored by King Henry VII of England. Cabot's landfall in 1497 in present-day Canada gave England the basis for a later claim to *all* of North America.

The English were unaware that Norsemen (Vikings) from Scandinavia (Norway, Denmark, Sweden) had been the first Europeans to "discover" and attempt to settle areas of North America. As early as the tenth century, Norsemen had landed on the rocky, fogbound shores of Newfoundland and Greenland, a large island off the northeastern coast of North America. There they had established farming settlements, until disappearing after prolonged cold weather forced them back to Scandinavia.

Religious Conflict in Europe

While explorers were crossing the Atlantic, explosive religious conflicts were tearing Europe apart in ways that would shape developments in the Americas. When Columbus sailed west in 1492, all of Europe acknowledged the supremacy of **Roman Catholicism** and its pope in Rome. The pope led a sprawling religious empire, and Catholics were eager to spread their faith around the world.

The Protestant Reformation and Martin Luther

The unity of Catholic Europe began to crack on October 31, 1517, when an obscure, thirty-three-year-old German monk sent his ninety-five "theses" critiquing the "corrupt" Catholic Church to church officials. Martin Luther (1483–1546) could not have known that his explosive charges would ignite history's fiercest spiritual drama, the **Protestant Reformation**.

Martin Luther fractured Christianity by undermining the power of the Catholic Church. He called the pope "the greatest thief and robber that has appeared or can appear on earth." Luther especially criticized the widespread sale of *indulgences,* whereby priests would "forgive" sins in exchange for money. The Catholic Church had forged a profitable business out of forgiving sins, using the revenue to raise massive armies and build lavish

Roman Catholicism The Christian faith and religious practices of the Roman Catholic Church, which exerted great political, economic, and social influence on much of western Europe and, through the Spanish and Portuguese Empires, on the Americas.

Protestant Reformation A sixteenth-century religious movement initiated by Martin Luther, a German monk whose public criticism of corruption in the Roman Catholic Church and whose teaching that Christians can communicate directly with God gained a wide following.

cathedrals. However, Luther insisted that God alone, through the grace and mercy of Christ, offered salvation; people could not purchase it from church officials or earn it through "good works."

Through this simple but revolutionary doctrine of "Protestantism," Luther sought to revitalize Christianity and rid it of priestly corruption. The common people, he declared, represented a "priesthood of all believers." Individuals could seek salvation directly from God rather than through the intervention of priests.

Luther's rebellion spread quickly across Europe thanks to the circulation of thousands of inexpensive pamphlets, which found an ever-increasing number of literate readers. "Every day it rains Luther's pamphlets," sighed a Catholic official. Without printing presses, there may not have been a Protestant Reformation.

Lutheranism. What came to be called Lutheranism began as a religious movement, but it soon developed profound social and political implications. By proclaiming that "all" are equal before God, Lutherans disrupted traditional notions of wealth, class, and monarchical supremacy. Their desire to practice a faith independent of papal or government interference contributed to the ideal of limited government.

MARTIN LUTHER'S BIBLE A page from Martin Luther's translation of the Bible, printed in 1535. A theologian and critic of the Catholic Church, Luther is best remembered for his "ninety-five theses," an incendiary document that served as a catalyst for the Protestant Reformation.

When the pope expelled Luther from the Catholic Church in 1521 and the Holy Roman emperor sentenced him to death, civil war erupted throughout the German principalities where Luther had enthusiastic followers. Luther was now an outlaw, and he survived only because a powerful prince hid him in his castle.

Luther's conflict with the pope plunged Europe into decades of religious warfare during which both sides sought to eliminate dissent by torturing and burning at the stake all those they deemed heretics (people at odds with generally accepted beliefs). A settlement between Lutherans and Catholics did not come until 1555, when the Treaty of Augsburg allowed each German prince to determine the religion of his subjects. Thereafter, southern Europe—France, Spain, and the Italian states—remained mostly Catholic, while most of the northern German states and Scandinavia became Lutheran. By undermining the authority of the Catholic Church, Luther

> Religious wars and upheavals

opened the door for the creation of thousands of new churches representing dozens of new Protestant denominations (religious branches).

John Calvin

If Martin Luther was the lightning that sparked the Reformation, John Calvin provided the thunder. Soon after Luther began his revolt against Catholicism, Swiss Protestants also challenged papal authority. In Geneva, in the Swiss Alps, the movement looked to John Calvin (1509–1564), a brilliant French theologian and preacher.

In his great theological work, *The Institutes of the Christian Religion* (1536), Calvin set forth a stern doctrine. All people, he taught, were damned by Adam's original sin, but the sacrifice of Christ on the cross made possible the redemption of those whom God had "elected" and thus had predestined to salvation from the beginning of time (a doctrine known as predestination). Like Luther, Calvin argued that Christians did not need popes or kings, archbishops, and bishops; each congregation should elect its own elders and ministers to guide their worship and nurture their faith. Calvinists were also expected to live within church authority and follow a strict code of behavior that included the banning of dancing, card-playing, and theater-going.

Calvinism Spreads. For all its harshness, Calvinism spread like wildfire across France, Scotland, the Netherlands, and even into Lutheran Germany. Calvinism formed the basis for the German Reformed Church, the Dutch Reformed Church, the Presbyterians in Scotland, and the Huguenots in France, and it prepared the way for many forms of Protestantism in the English colonies in America, such as Puritan New England.

> Catholic Counter-Reformation

The Catholic Church resisted the emergence of new Protestant faiths by launching a Counter-Reformation. It reaffirmed foundational Catholic beliefs while addressing some of the concerns about priestly abuses raised by Luther, Calvin, and others. In Spain, the monarchy established an Inquisition to root out Protestants and heretics. In 1534, a Spanish soldier, Ignatius of Loyola, organized the Society of Jesus, a militant monastic order created to revitalize Catholicism. Its members, the black-robed Jesuits, fanned out across Europe and the Americas as missionaries and teachers.

Despite Catholic efforts to blunt the appeal of Protestantism, the Reformation succeeded in permanently fragmenting Christianity. Throughout the sixteenth and seventeenth centuries, Catholics and Protestants persecuted, imprisoned, tortured, and killed each other in large numbers.

The Reformation in England

In England, the Reformation followed a unique course. The Church of England (the Anglican Church) emerged through a gradual process of integrating Calvinism with English Catholicism.

The English Reformation originated for purely political reasons. King Henry VIII, who ruled between 1509 and 1547, had won from the pope the title Defender of the Faith for initially refuting Martin Luther's revolutionary ideas. Henry, however, turned against the Catholic Church over the issue of divorce. His marriage to Catherine of Aragon, the youngest daughter of the Spanish monarchs Ferdinand and Isabella, had produced a daughter, Mary, but no son. Henry's obsession for a male heir convinced him that he needed a new wife. First, however, he had to convince the pope to annul, or cancel, his marriage to Catherine, who resisted her husband's plan. When the pope refused to grant an annulment in 1533, Henry VIII responded by severing England's nearly 900-year connection with the Catholic Church.

The pope then excommunicated Henry from the Catholic Church, a move that led Parliament to pass an Act of Supremacy declaring that the king, not the pope, was head of the Church of England. Henry married Anne Boleyn, banned all Catholic "idols" (such as papal authority, convents, and monasteries), required Bibles to be published in English rather than Latin, and confiscated the vast land holdings of the Catholic Church in England.

In one of history's great ironies, Anne Boleyn gave birth not to a male heir but to a daughter, who was named Elizabeth. The disappointed king accused Anne of adultery, had her beheaded, and declared the infant Elizabeth a bastard. (He would marry four more times.) Elizabeth, however, would grow up to be quick-witted and a courageous queen.

In 1547, Henry VIII died and was succeeded by his nine-year-old son Edward VI, who approved efforts to further reform the Church of

QUEEN ELIZABETH The *Armada Portrait*, attributed in 1588 to George Gower, portrays Queen Elizabeth at the height of her reign. A scene in the background features England's victory over the attacking Spanish fleet, the Armada; in the foreground, Elizabeth's right hand rests on a globe, signifying the English expansion into the Americas.

England. Priests were allowed to marry, church services were conducted in English rather than Latin, and new articles of faith were drafted and published.

When Edward grew gravely ill in 1553, he declared that his cousin, Lady Jane Grey, should succeed him. But nine days after his death, his Catholic half-sister, Mary, led an army that deposed Lady Jane and later ordered her beheaded. The following year, Queen Mary shocked many by marrying Philip, the Holy Roman emperor and king of Spain. With his blessing, she restored Catholic supremacy in England, ordering hundreds of Protestants burned at the stake and others exiled.

When "Bloody Mary" died in 1558, her Protestant half-sister, Henry VIII's unwanted daughter Elizabeth, ascended the throne. Over the next forty-five years, despite political turmoil, religious strife, economic crises, and foreign wars, Elizabeth I proved to be one of the greatest rulers in history. An unmarried Protestant in a Catholic- and male-dominated Europe, a monarch who escaped numerous assassination attempts and persecuted and executed Catholics, she helped England prosper. She once told Parliament to remember her as "a Queen, having reigned, lived, and died a virgin." During Elizabeth's long reign, the Church of England again became Protestant while retaining much of the tone and texture of Catholicism.

The turmoil and power struggles in England were just one example of dramatic changes in European society that enabled the Age of Exploration. Other factors included the replacement of the feudal system with a taxable middle class, which led to the rise of powerful new nations; and the development of navigation techniques, improved maps, new weapons, and navies. Rivalries among nations caused by the Protestant Reformation drove the search for gold and silver. At the same time, kingdoms in West Africa that were rich in natural resources were participating in trade networks extending across Africa to Asia and Europe. Soon, Europeans and Africans would find themselves interacting in the Americas as well.

The Spanish Empire

> **CORE OBJECTIVE**
> **3.** Describe how the Spanish were able to conquer and colonize the Americas.

Between 1500 and 1650, some 450,000 Spaniards, most of them poor, single, unskilled men, made their way to the colonies in the Americas. Once there, through a mixture of courage, cruelty, piety, and greed, they shipped 200 tons of gold and 16,000 tons of silver back to Spain. These transactions helped fuel what became known as that nation's Golden Age and triggered the emergence of capitalism in Europe, enabling new avenues for trade and unimagined profits. By plundering, conquering, and colonizing the Americas and enslaving the inhabitants, the Spanish planted Christianity on those continents and gained the financial resources to expand its global empire.

Clash of Cultures

The Caribbean Sea was the gateway through which Spain entered the Americas. After establishing a trading post on Hispaniola, the Spanish proceeded to colonize Puerto Rico (1508), Jamaica (1509), and Cuba (1511–1514). As its colonies multiplied to include Mexico, Peru, and what would become the American Southwest, the monarchy created a name to encompass them: New Spain.

> Spanish foothold in the Caribbean

Many of the Europeans in the first wave of settlement in the Americas died of malnutrition or disease. But the Indigenous Americans suffered far more casualties. Civil disorder, rebellion, and tribal warfare abounded, leaving them vulnerable to division and foreign conquest. Attacks by well-armed soldiers and deadly germs from Europe overwhelmed entire Indigenous societies. More generally, before the colonists' arrival Indigenous Americans had lived in cleaner, less urbanized environments and therefore had been exposed to different microbes than Europeans had. For example, although Europeans had built up resistance to smallpox over several generations, the Indigenous Americans had never been exposed to it—therefore falling victim to widespread epidemics and death.

Cortés's Conquest

The most dramatic European conquest of a formidable Indigenous civilization occurred in Mexico. On February 18, 1519, Hernán Cortés, a Spanish soldier of fortune who went to the Americas "to get rich, not to till the soil like a peasant," sold his Cuban lands to buy ships and supplies, then set sail—without royal authority—for Mexico and its fabled riches. Cortés's eleven ships carried nearly 600 soldiers and sailors, as well as 200 Indigenous Cuban laborers, 16 warhorses, greyhound fighting dogs, and cannons.

> Rivals collaborate against the Mexicas

The Spaniards first stopped on the Yucatan Peninsula, where they defeated a group of Maya (see Map 1.6). To appease his European conqueror, the vanquished chieftain gave Cortés twenty enslaved young women. The Spanish commander distributed them to his captains but kept one of the girls ("La Malinche") for himself and named her Doña Marina. Malinche spoke Mayan as well as Nahuatl, the language of the Mexica people, with whom she had previously lived. She became Cortés's interpreter—and would later bear the married Cortés a son.

After leaving Yucatan, Cortés sailed west and landed at a place he named Veracruz (True Cross). There he convinced the local Totonac people to join his assault against the Mexica, their hated rivals. To prevent his soldiers, called **conquistadores** (conquerors), from deserting, Cortés ordered the Spanish ships burned. He spared only one vessel to carry the expected riches back to Spain. With his small army and thousands of Indian allies, Cortés brashly set out to conquer the sprawling Mexica Empire, which extended from central Mexico to what is today Guatemala. The army's nearly 200-mile march through the mountains to the Mexica capital of Tenochtitlán took almost three months.

conquistadores A term from the Spanish word for "conquerors," applied to Spanish and Portuguese soldiers who conquered lands held by Indigenous peoples in central and southern America as well as in the area that became the current states of Texas, New Mexico, Arizona, and California.

> The Mexica capital Tenochtitlán was larger than London, Paris, and Seville

Spanish Invaders. As the Spanish army marched across Mexico, the conquistadores heard fabulous stories about Tenochtitlán, with its gleaming white buildings and beautiful temples. With some 200,000 inhabitants scattered among twenty neighborhoods, it was larger than London, Paris, and Seville, the capital of Spain. Laid out in a grid pattern on an island in a shallow lake, divided by long cobblestone avenues, crisscrossed by canals, and graced by formidable stone pyramids, the city seemed invincible. The magnificent city, Cortés marveled, contained "all the things to be found under the heavens."

The Mexica viewed themselves as having created the supreme civilization on the planet. "Are we not the masters of the world?" the emperor, Moctezuma II, said to his ruling council when he learned that the Europeans had landed on the coast. Through a combination of threats and deceptions, the Spanish entered Tenochtitlán peacefully. Moctezuma mistook Cortés for the exiled god of the wind and sky, Quetzalcoatl, coming to reclaim his lands. The emperor stared at the newcomers with their long hair, sharp metal swords, gunpowder, and wheeled wagons. He gave the Spaniards a lavish welcome, housing them close to the palace and providing gifts of gold and women.

Within a week, however, Cortés executed a palace coup, taking Moctezuma hostage. The Spanish commander then ordered religious statues destroyed and forced Moctezuma to end the ritual sacrifices of prisoners of war. Cortés explained why the invasion was necessary: "We Spaniards have a disease of the heart that only gold can cure."

CORTÉS IN MEXICO A page from the *Lienzo de Tlaxcala*, a historical narrative from the sixteenth century. The scene, in which Cortés is shown seated on a throne, depicts the arrival of the Spanish in Tlaxcala.

The Mexica Fight Back. For eight months, Cortés tried to convince the Mexica to surrender, but they resolved to resist the invaders. In the spring of 1520, the Spaniards attacked the Mexica and killed many of the ruling elite. The Mexica fought back, however, prompting Cortés to march Moctezuma to the edge of a balcony and force him to order the warriors to lay down their weapons: "We must not fight them," the emperor shouted. "We are not their equals in battle. Put down your shields and arrows." The priests, however, denounced Moctezuma as a traitor and stoned him to death.

For the next seven days, Mexica warriors forced the Spaniards to retreat after suffering heavy losses. The invaders' 20,000 Indigenous allies remained loyal, however, enabling Cortés to regroup his forces. Occasional fighting continued for months. In 1521, having been reinforced with more soldiers and horses from Cuba and thousands more Indigenous warriors eager to defeat the despised Mexica, Cortés surrounded the imperial city for eighty-five days, cut off the city's access to water and food, and watched as a smallpox epidemic devastated the inhabitants, killing 90 percent of them.

The Biological and Military Defeat of Tenochtitlán. The ravages of smallpox and the support of thousands of Indigenous allies help explain how such a small force of well-organized and highly disciplined Spaniards vanquished a proud imperial nation in August 1521. After 15,000 Mexica were slaughtered, the others surrendered. A merciless Cortés ordered the leaders hanged and the priests devoured by dogs, but not before torturing them (literally putting their feet to the fire) in an effort to learn where more gold might be found. A conquistador remembered that the streets "were so filled with sick and dead people that our men walked over nothing but bodies." In two years, Cortés and his army had waged a genocidal war and seized an epic empire that had taken centuries to develop.

Cortés became the first governor-general of New Spain and quickly began replacing the Mexica leaders with Spanish bureaucrats and church officials. Mexico City became the imperial capital of New Spain, and Cortés ordered that a grand Catholic cathedral be built from the stones of Moctezuma's destroyed palace.

Pizzaro's Invasion of the Inca Empire

Cortés's conquest of Mexico established the model for waves of plundering conquistadores to follow. Within fifty years, Spain had established a vast empire (New Spain) in Mexico and Central America, the Caribbean, and South America. The Spanish cemented their control through ruthless violence and enslavement of the Indigenous peoples followed by oppressive rule over them—just as the Mexica had done in forming their empire.

In 1531, Francisco Pizarro led a band of 168 conquistadores and 67 horses down the Pacific coast of South America (see again Map 1.6). They brutally subdued the extensive Inca Empire and its 5 million people living in the area of present-day Ecuador, Peru, Bolivia, Colombia, Chile, and Argentina. The Spanish killed thousands of Inca warriors, seized imperial

> Cortes conquers the Mexicas, and Pizarro invades the Inca

palaces, forced royal women to become their wives, and looted the empire of its gold and silver.

From Peru, Spain extended its control southward through Chile and north to what is present-day Colombia. A government official in Spain reported in 1534 that the amount of gold and silver flowing into the treasury "was incredible."

Spanish America

As the sixteenth century unfolded, the Spanish shifted from looting the Indigenous peoples to enslaving them. To reward the conquistadores, the Spanish government transferred to America a medieval socioeconomic system known as the **encomienda**. Favored soldiers or officials received large parcels of land—and control over the people who lived there. The conquistadores were told to Christianize the Indigenous people and provide them with protection in exchange for "tribute"—a share of their goods and their forced labor.

New Spain thus became a society of extremes: wealthy *encomenderos* and powerful priests at one end, and Indigenous people held in poverty at the other. The Spaniards used brute force to ensure that the Indigenous accepted their role. One governor of a Mexican province loved to watch his massive fighting dog tear apart rebellious Indigenous people. He was equally brutal with colonists. After a Spaniard talked back to him, he had the man nailed to a post by his tongue.

Imposing the Catholic Religion

Once in control of the Americas, the Spanish sought to turn the Indigenous people into obedient Catholics. Hundreds of priests fanned out across New Spain, using force to convert the population. By the end of the sixteenth century, there were more than 300 Catholic monasteries or missions in New Spain.

Some officials criticized the forced religious conversion of Indigenous people and the harsh *encomienda* system. A Catholic priest, Bartolomé de Las Casas, was horrified by the treatment of Indigenous people in Hispaniola and Cuba. The conquistadores behaved like "wild beasts," he reported, "killing, terrorizing, afflicting, torturing, and destroying the native peoples." Las Casas insisted that the role of Spaniards in the Americas was to convert the Indigenous people, "not to rob, to scandalize, to capture, or destroy them, or to lay waste their lands." In 1514, he resolved to devote himself to aiding the Indigenous peoples.

> Bartolomé de Las Casas advocates for the better treatment of Indigenous peoples

Las Casas spent the next fifty years advocating better treatment for Indigenous Americans, earning the title Protector of the Indians. He eventually convinced the monarchy and the Catholic Church to issue new rules calling for improved treatment. Still, the use of "fire and the sword" continued, and angry Spanish colonists on Hispaniola banished Las Casas from the island.

How had the Spanish managed to conquer and colonize the Americas? With advantages in military technology (steel and gunpowder) and the

encomienda A land-grant system under which Spanish army officers (*conquistadores*) were awarded large parcels of land taken from Native Americans.

support of domesticated animals (especially horses), the conquistadores were able to overwhelm Indigenous empires. Even more effective was the deadly effect of European diseases, to which Native Americans had almost no resistance.

The Columbian Exchange

Spain's seizure of empires in the Americas produced unexpected consequences. Most important, the European ships that crossed the Atlantic carried more than human cargo. They also brought plants and animals that set into motion what came to be called the **Columbian Exchange**, a worldwide transfer of plants, animals, and diseases that ultimately worked in favor of the Europeans at the expense of the Indigenous peoples.

Animals, Plants, Diseases

The animals of the two worlds differed even more than the peoples and their ways of life. Europeans had never encountered iguanas, buffaloes, cougars, armadillos, opossums, sloths, tapirs, anacondas, rattlesnakes, catfish, condors, or hummingbirds. Nor had Indigenous Americans ever seen the horses, cattle, pigs, sheep, goats, and chickens brought from Europe to the Americas. Sailing ships also brought stowaway creatures, such as mosquitoes, cockroaches, honeybees, rats, and mice. The animals added new sources of protein to the Indigenous peoples' diets, and the bees provided honey, a natural sweetener. However, the rodents and mosquitos brought destruction and disease.

The exchange of plant life between the Americas and Europe/Africa transformed the diets of both regions. Europeans brought plants never seen in the Americas: sugarcane (originally from New Guinea), wheat (from the Middle East), bananas, and coffee (both from Africa).

Before Columbus's voyage, Europeans did not know about foods such as maize, potatoes (sweet and white), or many kinds of beans (snap, kidney, lima). Other food plants native to the Americas included peanuts, squash, peppers, tomatoes, pumpkins, pineapples, avocados, cacao (the source of chocolate), and chicle (for chewing gum).

The lowly white potato, for example, was transformational. Discovered in South America, it has more calories than an ear of corn, can yield more bushels per acre than wheat, can be stored through the winter, and is easy to cultivate. Explorers brought potatoes back to Europe, where they thrived. The "Irish potato" was eventually transported to North America by Scots-Irish immigrants during the early eighteenth century.

The new crops improved the health of Europeans and spurred a dramatic increase in the population. In turn, the surplus population provided even more of the adventurous young people who would colonize the New World Americas.

> **CORE OBJECTIVE**
> **4.** Assess the impact of the Columbian Exchange between the "Old" and "New" Worlds.

Columbian Exchange The transfer of biological and social elements, such as plants, animals, people, diseases, and cultural practices, among Europe, the Americas, and Africa in the wake of Christopher Columbus's voyages to the Americas.

infectious diseases Also called contagious diseases, illnesses that can pass from one person to another by way of invasive biological organisms able to reproduce in the bodily tissues of their hosts. Europeans unwittingly brought many such diseases to the Americas, devastating the Native American peoples.

The most significant aspect of the Columbian Exchange was the transmission of **infectious diseases**. Europeans and captive Africans brought smallpox, typhus, malaria, mumps, chickenpox, and measles to the Americas. The results were catastrophic. By 1568, just seventy-five years after Columbus's first voyage, infectious diseases had killed 80 to 90 percent of the Indigenous population in the Americas.

Smallpox was an especially ghastly killer; its effects came to be called the Great Dying. In central Mexico alone, some 8 million people, perhaps a third of the Indigenous population, died of smallpox within a decade of the arrival of the Spanish. Unable to explain or cure this or other hideous diseases, Indigenous chieftains and religious leaders often lost their stature—and their lives—as they were usually the first to meet the Spanish and the first infected. The loss of their leaders made the Indigenous peoples more vulnerable to invaders. Many Europeans, however, interpreted such epidemics as diseases sent by God to punish those who resisted conversion to Christianity.

Environmental Changes

> The Little Ice Age stresses North American Indigenous peoples

Some punishment came from environmental changes in specific regions. For example, during one of the coldest periods in recent world history, known as the Little Ice Age, Europe and North America experienced cooler temperatures from about 1300 to 1850. The decreased temperatures stressed the environment, causing crop failures, famines, and pandemics. Although scientists debate the causes, some believe that low sunspot activity and volcanic eruptions impacted the atmospheric wind patterns and caused ocean currents to change. Others say the reverse occurred, that oceanic change led to earthquakes and volcanic eruptions.

> Significant decreases in Indigenous populations contribute to "carbon sink" phenomena

Still others note that the death of Indigenous Americans paved the way for other environmental changes and created the "carbon sink" phenomenon. They suggest that the severe decrease in Indigenous populations allowed for the return of trees and bushes to the land that had been cultivated for generations. Forests grew back, devouring large quantities of carbon dioxide from the earth's atmosphere, which meant that the earth trapped far less of the sun's heat, resulting in cooler and drier temperatures. Regardless of its causes, the Little Ice Age decimated populations and paved the way for starvation, famines, and war.

Overall, the European invasion of the Americas generated a demographic and ecological transformation whose effects are still being felt. In this sense, the Europeans did not so much "discover" a new world as create one.

As a direct result of the Columbian Exchange, the Americas offered Indigenous peoples the benefits of certain European crops and animals; but much more significant, the lasting devastation from infectious disease wiped out entire groups and cultures. At the same time, societies in Europe gained dietary advantages from American food crops and saw irresistible opportunities to establish footholds on American soil.

The Spanish in North America

> **CORE OBJECTIVE**
> **5.** Analyze the legacy of the Spanish form of colonization on North American history.

Throughout the sixteenth century, no European nation other than Spain gained more than a brief foothold in the Americas. While France and England were preoccupied with political disputes and religious conflict at home, Catholic Spain had forged a national and religious unity that enabled it to dominate Europe as well as the Americas. Still, Spanish officials grew increasingly fearful that France and England would threaten their imperial monopoly in the Americas.

For most of the colonial period, Spain governed much of what is now the United States. Spanish culture etched a lasting imprint upon America's future. Hispanic place-names—San Francisco, Santa Barbara, Los Angeles, San Diego, Santa Fe, San Antonio, Pensacola, St. Augustine—survive to this day, as do Hispanic influences in art, architecture, literature, music, law, and food.

> Three centuries of Spanish domination and Hispanic influence

The Spanish Southeast

In 1513, Juan Ponce de León, the Spanish governor of Puerto Rico, made the earliest known European exploration of Florida (Land of Flowers), hoping to find gold and Indian slaves (Map 1.6). Subsequently, other Spanish explorers reached the Southeast and beyond. Pánfilio Narváez traveled to Florida in 1527, and Francisco Vázquez de Coronado explored parts of the present-day Midwest and Southwest during the years 1540–1542.

Some explorers were of African descent, such as Juan Garrido and a man called Estevanico the Moor. Garrido was part of a convoy that arrived on the island of Hispaniola in 1503 and is known as the first person of African descent who set foot in the Americas. Estevanico traveled with Narváez throughout the Caribbean, Florida, the Gulf coast, and later Texas and northern Mexico. Some adventurous Spanish explorers sailed along the Gulf coast from Florida to Mexico, scouted the Atlantic coast to Canada, and even established a short-lived colony on the Carolina coast.

In 1539, Hernando de Soto and some 600 conquistadores landed on the western shore of Florida and set out on horseback to search for riches. Instead of gold, they found "great fields of corn, beans and squash . . . as far as the eye could see." De Soto led the expedition north as far as western North Carolina. The explorers then moved westward across the area of present-day Tennessee, Georgia, and Alabama before happening upon the Mississippi River near what today is Memphis.

After crossing the Mississippi, the conquistadores went up the Arkansas River, looting and destroying Indigenous villages along the way. In the spring of 1542, de Soto died of a fever near Natchez, Mississippi; the next year, the survivors among his party floated down the Mississippi River, and 311 of them made their way to Spanish Mexico.

In 1565, in response to French efforts to colonize north Florida, the Spanish king dispatched Pedro Menendez de Aviles with a ragtag group of

CHAPTER 1 The Collision of Cultures

MAP 1.6 SPANISH EXPLORATIONS OF THE AMERICAS

- Garrido, 1503–1508
- Ponce de León, 1513
- Cortés, 1519
- Narváez (with Estevanico), 1527–1528
- Estevanico, 1527–1539
- Pizarro, 1531–1533
- de Soto, 1539–1542
- Coronado, 1540–1542
- Menendez, 1565

- With your finger, follow each explorer's route on the map.
- Which explorer appears to have spent the most time on land?
- Locate St. Augustine on the map. According to your reading, why did the Spanish establish St. Augustine, the first European settlement in what later became the United States?

1,500 soldiers and colonists to create an outpost on the Atlantic coast of Florida. Named St. Augustine in honor of Augustine of Hippo, it became the first permanent European settlement in the present-day United States.

The Spanish positioned themselves in northern Florida to keep the French out. Throughout the 1560s, French Protestant refugees (Huguenots) established beachhead settlements on the coast of what became South Carolina and Florida. But the settlements did not last long. In one incident, at dawn on September 20, 1565, some 500 Spanish soldiers from

St. Augustine assaulted the French Protestants at Fort Caroline. The Spanish hanged all the men over age fifteen; only women, girls, and young boys were spared. Reflecting the turmoil of the Protestant Reformation back in Europe, the Spanish commander notified his Catholic king that he had killed all the French because "they were scattering the odious Lutheran doctrine in these Provinces." Later, when survivors from a shipwrecked French fleet washed ashore on Florida beaches, the Spanish commander told them they must abandon Protestantism and swear their allegiance to Catholicism. When they refused, his soldiers killed 245 of them.

The Spanish Southwest

The Spanish eventually established other permanent settlements in what are now New Mexico, Arizona, Texas, and California. From the outset, however, the settlements were sparsely populated and inadequately supplied by Spanish colonial officials. The small number of Spanish colonists and the vast size of North America made it impossible for them to impose European-style communities and towns. In fact, throughout the Americas at this time there were only 25,000 Spanish households. By 1650, there were more enslaved Africans than there were Spaniards in the Americas.

Within their colonies, the Spanish exercised virtually absolute power. In New Spain, people were expected to follow orders, no questions asked. There was no freedom of speech, religion, or movement; no local elections; no real self-government. The military officers, bureaucrats, wealthy landowners, and priests appointed by the king regulated every detail of colonial life. Settlers could not travel within the colonies without official permission. And, of course, Indigenous and enslaved people had no rights at all.

> The Spanish exercised absolute authority in New Spain

New Mexico

The land that would later be called **New Mexico** was the first center of Catholic missionary activity in the American Southwest. In 1595, Juan de Oñate, the rich son of a Spanish family in Mexico, received a land grant for *El Norte,* the mostly desert territory north of Mexico above the Rio Grande—what would become Texas, New Mexico, Arizona, California, and parts of Colorado. Over the next three years, he recruited colonists willing to move north with him. In 1598, the caravan of 250 colonists—including women, children, horses, goats, sheep, and 7,000 cattle—began moving north from the mountains above Mexico City. After walking more than 800 miles in seven months, they established the colony of New Mexico, the farthest outpost of New Spain.

Among this group of travelers was a free woman of African and Indigenous descent named Isabel de Olvera. It is believed that in early 1600 she traveled from Querètaro, Mexico, to what is present-day New Mexico after receiving permission from the mayor to join the expedition. The daughter of an African man and an Indigenous woman, she told the court that she wanted to go on the expedition as someone who was "free and not bound by marriage or slavery." After being deposed and confirmed, she received permission to

New Mexico A region in the American Southwest originally established by the Spanish, who settled there in the sixteenth century, founded Catholic missions, and exploited the region's Indigenous peoples.

CULTURAL CONFLICT This Peruvian illustration, from a 1612–1615 manuscript by Felipe Guamán Poma de Ayala, shows a Dominican Catholic friar forcing an Indigenous woman to weave. **What does this image show about the Spanish missionaries' treatment of the Indigenous peoples?**

travel to New Spain. Her story is important because she predates the arrival of the twenty Africans who arrived in the Jamestown settlement in the Virginia colony in 1619.

The Spanish called the local Indigenous people Pueblo (a Spanish word meaning "village") for the city-like aspect of their terraced, multistoried buildings, sometimes chiseled into the steep walls of cliffs.

Oñate, New Mexico's first Spanish governor, told the Pueblo that if they embraced Catholicism and followed his orders, they would receive "an eternal life of great bliss" instead of "cruel and everlasting torment." Assuming Isabel de Olvera made the journey to New Mexico, she would have established herself in this community.

There was, however, little gold or silver in New Mexico. Nor were there enough corn and beans to feed the Spanish invaders, so Oñate forced the Indigenous people to pay tributes to the Spanish authorities in the form of a yard of cloth and a bushel of corn each year.

Once it became evident that New Mexico had little gold, the Spanish focused on religious conversion. Priests required Indigenous people to build and support Catholic missions and to work in the fields they had once owned. They also performed personal tasks for the priests and soldiers—cooking, cleaning, even providing sexual favors. The Indigenous people were herded to church services and whipped if they did not work hard enough. A French visitor reported that it "reminded us of a . . . West Indian [slave] colony." Some Indigenous people welcomed the Spanish as "powerful witches" capable of easing their burdens. Others tried to use the European invaders as allies against rival populations.

Still others rebelled. Before the end of New Mexico's first year of Spanish rule, in December 1598, the Acoma Pueblo people revolted, killing eleven soldiers and two servants. Oñate's response was brutal. Over three days, Spanish soldiers destroyed the entire pueblo, killing 500 Pueblo men and 300 women and children. Survivors were found guilty of treason and enslaved. Children were separated from their parents and moved into a Catholic mission, where, Oñate remarked, "they may attain the knowledge of God and the salvation of their souls." He ordered that every male between the ages of twelve and twenty-five have a hand cut off, and that the left foot of every male over twenty-five be severed to ensure they never again would rebel.

The Mestizo Factor

Few Spanish women journeyed to New Spain in the sixteenth century. Those who did had to be married and accompanied by a husband. However, as noted, Isabel de Olvera received special permission to participate in an expedition and travel to new territory. In her deposition requesting permission, she stated that being of African and Indigenous American descent she believed people in Querètaro would "be annoyed" by her since she was a single woman of mixed race.

In fact, the mixing of races became fairly widespread in the Spanish Southwest, leading to offspring with blended European and Native American heritage—that is, *Mestizos*. Because of the lack of available Spanish women for wives, soldiers and settlers were encouraged to marry Indigenous women, and the practice became common. (Today some three-quarters of Mexicans are Mestizo. In downtown Mexico City, a plaque acknowledging the Spanish takeover in 1521 reads: "This was neither triumph nor defeat. It was the painful birth of the Mestizo nation that is Mexico today.")

By the eighteenth century, Mestizos were a majority in Mexico and New Mexico. As a result of the approved and widespread intermarriage practices, the Spanish adopted an increasingly inclusive social outlook toward Indigenous Americans. (This was a marked contrast to the outlook of later English settlers in their colonies along the Atlantic coast.) However, these interactions and exchanges were complicated. Some Indigenous people falsely claimed to be Mestizo to improve their legal status and avoid paying annual tribute to the Spanish government. Many others experienced hardships and abuse at the hands of the Spaniards.

> Mestizos were a majority in Mexico and New Mexico

Over time, New Spain developed a caste system based on an ethnic hierarchy. At the top were the *Españoles* (Spaniards) followed by the *Criollos* (Spaniards born in the Americas). At the bottom were the *Indegenas* (Indians). In between were enslaved Africans, Mulattoes (people of mixed Black and White ancestry), and Mestizos.

The Pueblo Revolt

In 1608, the Spanish government decided to turn New Mexico into a royal province and moved its capital to Santa Fe (Holy Faith, in Spanish). It became the first permanent seat of government in the present-day United States. By 1630, there were fifty Catholic churches and monasteries in New Mexico as well as some 3,000 Spaniards. Roman Catholic missionaries in New Mexico claimed that 86,000 Pueblo converts had embraced Christianity during the seventeenth century.

> Catholicism in New Spain and the Pueblo Revolt (1680)

However, resentment among the Indigenous people increased as the Spanish stripped them of their ancestral ways of life. "The heathen," reported a Spanish soldier, "have conceived a mortal hatred for our holy faith and enmity [hatred] for the Spanish nation." In 1680, a charismatic Native American named Popé (meaning Ripe Plantings) organized a massive rebellion of warriors from nineteen villages. The Indigenous people burned Catholic churches; tortured, mutilated, and executed 21 priests and 400 Spanish

Pueblo Revolt The Pueblo Revolt of 1680, also known as Popé's Rebellion, was an uprising of most of the Indigenous Pueblo people against the Spanish colonizers in the province of Santa Fe, New Mexico.

Horses and bison

horses The animals that the Spanish introduced to the Americas, eventually transforming many Native American cultures.

settlers; destroyed all relics of Christianity; and forced the 2,400 survivors to flee. The entire province of New Mexico was again in Indigenous hands.

The **Pueblo Revolt** was the most significant defeat that Indigenous people inflicted on European efforts to conquer the Americas. It took twelve years and four military assaults until 1692 for the Spanish to reestablish control over New Mexico.

Horses and the Great Plains

Another important consequence of the Pueblo Revolt was the opportunity it gave Indigenous rebels to acquire Spanish **horses.** Spanish authorities had made it illegal for Indigenous people to own horses, but now the Pueblo people were able to establish a thriving horse trade with other Indigenous populations. By 1690, horses were in Texas. Soon they spread across the Great Plains—the vast, rolling grasslands extending from the Missouri valley in the east to the base of the Rocky Mountains in the west.

Before the arrival of European horses, Indigenous people hunted on foot and used dogs as their beasts of burden. With horses, the Indigenous people in this region gained greater mobility and power. Horses could haul up to seven times as much weight as dogs, and their speed and endurance made the Indigenous groups more effective as hunters and warriors.

Horses grew so valuable that they became a form of Indigenous currency and a sign of wealth and prestige. On the Great Plains, a warrior's status

PLAINS PEOPLES The horse-stealing ride depicted in this hide painting demonstrates the essential role horses played in Plains life.

reflected the number of horses he owned. By the late seventeenth century, horse-riding Indigenous peoples were fighting the Spaniards on more equal terms. This helps explain why the Indigenous populations of the Southwest and Texas, unlike the Indigenous population in Mexico, were able to sustain their cultures for the next 300 years.

Buffalo Hunting

Now the Arapaho, Cheyenne, Comanche, Kiowa, and Sioux reinvented themselves as horse-centered cultures. They left their traditional woodland villages and became nomadic buffalo hunters.

A bull buffalo can weigh more than a ton and stand five feet tall at the shoulder. Indigenous people used virtually every part of the buffalo: meat for food; hides for clothing, shoes, bedding, and shelter; muscles and tendons for thread and bowstrings; intestines for containers; bones for tools; horns for eating utensils; hair for headdresses; and dung for fuel. They used tongues for hairbrushes and tails for flyswatters.

Women and girls butchered and dried the buffalo meat and tanned the hides. As the value of the hides grew, Indigenous hunters began practicing polygamy, because more wives could process more buffalo carcasses. The rising value of wives eventually led Plains peoples to raid other societies in search of women.

While horses brought prosperity and mobility to the Plains peoples, they also triggered more conflicts. Over time, Indigenous hunters on horseback killed more buffaloes than the herds could replace. Further, horses competed with the buffaloes for food, often depleting the prairie grass. Still, the arrival of horses improved the quality of Indigenous life in many ways. By 1800, a White trader in Texas would observe that "this is a delightful country, and were it not for perpetual wars, the natives might be the happiest people on earth."

> Indigenous horseback hunting of buffalo increased competition and conflict

Challenges to the Spanish Empire

Catholic Spain's conquests in the Americas spurred Portugal, France, England, and the Netherlands (Holland) to begin their own explorations and exploitations there (see Map 1.7).

The French and Dutch Exploration of America

The French were the first to pose a serious threat to Spain's monopoly in America. Spanish ships loaded with gold and silver taken from Mexico, Peru, and the Caribbean offered tempting targets for French pirates. At the same time, the French began explorations in North America. In 1524, the French king sent Italian explorer Giovanni da Verrazano across the Atlantic. Upon sighting land (probably at Cape Fear, North Carolina), Verrazano ranged along the coast as far north as Maine. On a second voyage, in 1528, he was killed by Caribbean Indigenous people.

Unlike the Verrazano voyages, those of Jacques Cartier led to the first French effort at colonization in North America. During three voyages, Cartier

> Spanish rivals for New World wealth

MAP 1.7 ENGLISH, FRENCH, AND DUTCH EXPLORATIONS

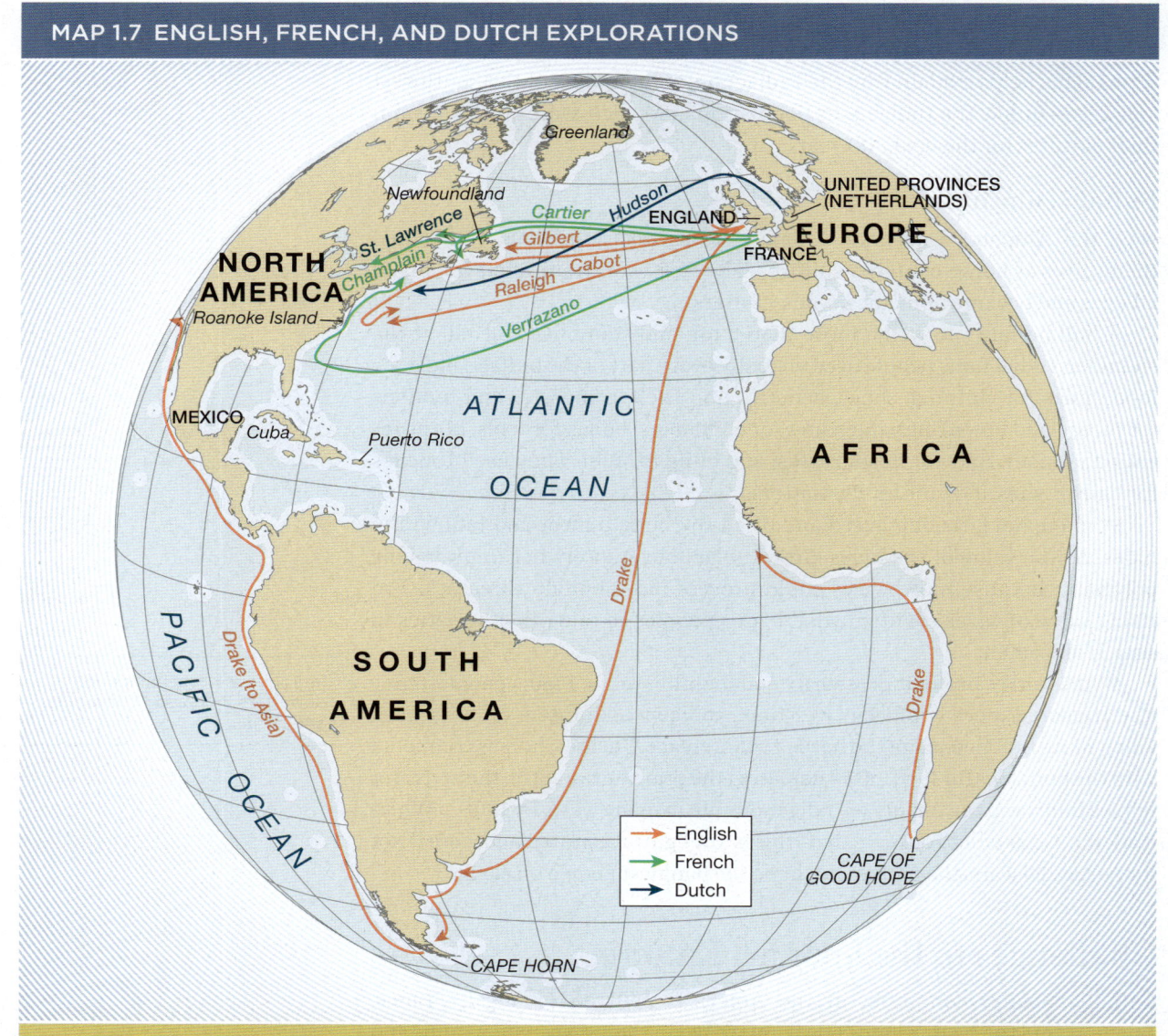

- Name the explorers shown on the map who came from England, France, and the Netherlands.
- Which explorer made the longest voyage?
- According to your reading of the chapter text, why was the defeat of the Spanish Armada important to the history of English exploration in particular

ventured up the St. Lawrence River, which today is the boundary between Canada and New York. Twice he got as far as present-day Montreal, and twice he wintered at Quebec, near which a short-lived French colony appeared in 1541–1542. After midcentury, however, France plunged into religious civil wars, and the colonization of Canada had to await the arrival of Samuel de Champlain, "the Father of New France," after 1600. Over thirty-seven years, Champlain would lead twenty-seven expeditions from France to Canada—and never lose a ship.

The Dutch Revolt

Greater threats to Spanish power in the Americas arose from the Dutch and the English. Back in Europe, in 1566, the Netherlands included seventeen provinces. The fragmented nation had passed by inheritance to the Spanish king in 1555, but the Dutch soon began a series of rebellions against Spanish Catholic rule known as the Dutch revolt.

A long, bloody struggle followed, and although seven provinces agreed to form the Dutch Republic, the Spanish did not officially recognize the independence of the entire Netherlands until 1648.

Almost from the beginning of the Protestant revolt in the Netherlands, the Dutch captured Spanish treasure ships in the Atlantic and conducted illegal trade with Spain's colonies. During this period, England's Queen Elizabeth, who had aided the Dutch, steered a tortuous course to avoid war with Spain while desperately seeking additional resources to defend her island nation. So she encouraged dozens of English privateers to attack Spanish ships in the Americas, leading the Spanish to call her the "pirate queen."

The Defeat of the Spanish Armada

English raids on Spanish ships and settlements continued for some twenty years before war erupted between the two nations. Philip II, the king of Spain, who was Elizabeth's brother-in-law and fiercest opponent, finally began plotting an invasion of England. To do so, he assembled the massive **Spanish Armada**: 132 warships, 7,000 sailors, and 17,000 soldiers. It was the greatest invasion fleet in history to that point.

On May 28, 1588, the Armada set sail for the Netherlands to take on another 17,000 soldiers for the invasion of England. The English navy's 90 warships were waiting as the Spanish fleet moved through the English Channel. As the warships positioned themselves for battle, Queen Elizabeth donned a silver breastplate and told her forces, "I know I have the body of a weak and feeble woman, but I have the heart and stomach of a king, and a King of England too." As the nine-hour battle unfolded, the massive Spanish warships could not compete with the speed and agility of the smaller but more maneuverable English vessels. By the end of the day, the Spanish were forced to flee northward. For two weeks, the English fleet gave chase. Caught up in a mighty "Protestant wind," the Catholic invaders were swept into the North Sea, losing half their ships and a third of their sailors and soldiers.

By mid-August, the wounded Armada was headed south toward home when ferocious storms in the North Atlantic sank more ships than had the English navy. In the end, only sixty of the original warships made it back to Spain, and some 15,000 sailors and soldiers died.

England's stunning victory marked the beginning of the steep decline of Spain's empire, established Queen Elizabeth as an English hero, and cleared the way for colonizing America. By the end of the sixteenth century, Elizabethan England had begun an epic transformation from a poor, humiliated, and isolated nation into a mighty global empire.

Spanish Armada A massive Spanish fleet of 130 warships that was defeated at Plymouth, England, in 1588 by the English navy during the reign of Queen Elizabeth I.

English Exploration of America

English efforts to colonize America began a few years before the battle with the Spanish Armada. In 1584, Queen Elizabeth asked Sir Walter Raleigh to form a colony on the North American coast. His expedition happened upon the Outer Banks of North Carolina and landed at Roanoke Island. Raleigh named the area Virginia, in honor of Elizabeth, the "Virgin Queen." After several false starts, Raleigh in 1587 sponsored another expedition of about 100 colonists, including 26 women and children. They were led by Governor John White, who spent a month helping launch the settlement on Roanoke Island and then returned to England for supplies. White left behind his daughter Elinor and his granddaughter Virginia Dare, the first English child born in the Americas.

White had to delay his journey back to Virginia because of the war with Spain. When he finally returned, in 1590, the Roanoke colony had been abandoned and pillaged. On a post at the entrance to the village, someone had carved the word *CROATOAN*. White concluded that the settlers had set out for the island of that name some fifty miles south, where friendly Indigenous people lived.

The lost Roanoke colony

The English never found the "lost colonists." However, recently discovered evidence indicates that the "Lost Colony" suffered a horrible drought that prevented the settlers from growing enough food to survive. While some may have gone south, most went north, to the southern shores of the Chesapeake Bay, where they lived for years until Indigenous people killed them.

When Queen Elizabeth died in 1603, there were no English settlements in North America. This was about to change, however. Inspired by the success of the Spanish in exploiting the Americas, the English—as well as the French and Dutch—would soon develop American colonial empires of their own.

New Spain in Decline

New Spain's legacy

During the century and a half after 1492, the Spanish developed the most extensive empire the world had ever known. It spanned southern Europe and the Netherlands, much of the Americas, and parts of Asia. Yet the Spanish rulers overreached; the costs of their involvement in the European religious wars of the sixteenth and seventeenth centuries, combined with the administration of a large and complex empire, overtaxed the government's resources.

During the sixteenth century, New Spain gradually developed into a settled society with the same rigid class structure as the home country. New Spain was essentially an extractive empire; its rulers were less interested in creating self-sustaining colonial communities than in extracting gold, silver, and copper while enslaving the Indigenous peoples and converting them to Christianity. Spain never encouraged vast numbers of settlers to populate New Spain.

THE ENGLISH IN VIRGINIA This map depicts the arrival of English explorers on the Outer Banks. Roanoke Island and its colony are on the left.

Spain's colonial system was mostly disastrous for the peoples of Africa and the Americas. For three centuries after Columbus arrived in the Americas, the Spanish explorers, conquistadores, and priests imposed Catholicism on the Indigenous peoples, in many cases destroying generations-long ways of life. Spanish colonization also imposed a cruel system of economic exploitation and dependence. As Bartolomé de Las Casas concluded, "The Spaniards have shown not the slightest consideration for these people, treating them (and I speak from first-hand experience, having been there from the outset) . . . as piles of dung in the middle of the road. They have had as little concern for their souls as for their bodies." In the end, the lust for empire ("God, Glory, and Gold") brought decadence and decline to Spain and much of Europe. It also fueled stronger rivalries among European nations that would ultimately allow England to win dominance in North America.

Reviewing the
CORE OBJECTIVES

■ **Indigenous Societies** Asian hunter-gatherers came across the Bering Strait by foot or, in some cases, arrived by boat and navigated the coastlines in seafaring canoes; and settled the length and breadth of the Americas, forming groups with diverse cultures, languages, and customs. Global warming enabled an agricultural revolution, particularly the growing of *maize*, that allowed former hunter-gatherer peoples such as the *Mexica* to settle and build empires. Some North American peoples, such as the Mississippians, developed an elaborate continental trading network and impressive cities such as *Cahokia*; their *ceremonial mounds* reveal a complex and stratified social organization. The *Eastern Woodland peoples* included both patriarchal and matriarchal societies as well as extensive language-based alliances. The Algonquian, Iroquoian, and Muskogean were among the major Indigenous nations. Warfare was an important cultural component, leading to shifting rivalries and alliances among Indigenous communities and with European settlers.

■ **Age of Exploration and Early Global Trade** By the 1490s, Europeans were experiencing a renewed curiosity about the world. Warfare, plagues, and famine undermined the old agriculture-based system in Europe, and in its place arose a middle class that monarchs could tax. Powerful new nations replaced the landed estates and cities ruled by princes. A revival of interest in antiquity led to the development of modern science and the creation of better maps and navigation techniques, as well as new weapons and ships. Navies became a critical component of global trade and world power.

The empires of West Africa also played a role in the early history of the Americas, as African leaders created highly civilized societies that added to the world economy. Natural resources such as gold, iron, and grains contributed to a trading system among Africa, Asia, and Europe prior to the development of the transatlantic slave trade.

When the Spanish began to colonize the Americas, the conversion of Indigenous peoples to *Roman Catholicism* was important, but the search for gold and silver was primary. The national rivalries sparked by the *Protestant Reformation* in Europe shaped the course of conquest in the Americas.

■ **Conquering and Colonizing the Americas** Spanish *conquistadores* such as Hernán Cortés used their advantages in military technology—including steel, gunpowder, and domesticated animals such as *horses*—in order to conquer the powerful Mexica and Inca Empires. European diseases, first introduced by Columbus's voyages, did even more to ensure Spanish victories. The Spanish *encomienda* system demanded goods and labor from the Indigenous peoples. As the Indigenous population declined, the Portuguese and Spanish began to import enslaved Africans into the Americas.

- **Columbian Exchange** Contact between Europe and the Americas resulted in a tremendous biological exchange, sometimes called the *Columbian Exchange*. Crops such as maize, beans, and potatoes became staples in European countries. Indigenous Americans incorporated into their culture Eurasian animals such as the horse and the pig. But the invaders also carried *infectious diseases* that set off pandemics of smallpox, plague, and other illnesses to which Indigenous people had no immunity. The Americas were depopulated and cultures destroyed.

- **Spanish Legacy** Colonization by the Spanish Empire left a lasting legacy in the borderlands from California to Florida. Spanish horses eventually transformed Indigenous life on the plains. Catholic missionaries contributed to the destruction of the old ways of life by exterminating "heathen" beliefs in the Southwest, a practice that led to open rebellion in *New Mexico* in 1598 and 1680. Spain's rival European nation-states began competing for gold and glory in the Americas. Ultimately, England's defeat of the *Spanish Armada* cleared the path for English dominance in North America.

KEY TERMS

maize (corn) *p. 9*
Mexica *p. 11*
Mexica Empire *p. 11*
ceremonial mounds *p. 16*
Cahokia *p. 17*
Eastern Woodland peoples *p. 17*
Roman Catholicism *p. 30*
Protestant Reformation *p. 30*
conquistadores *p. 35*
encomienda *p. 38*
Columbian Exchange *p. 39*
infectious diseases *p. 40*
New Mexico *p. 43*
Pueblo Revolt *p. 46*
horses *p. 46*
Spanish Armada *p. 49*

CHRONOLOGY

22,000–17,000 BCE	Humans have migrated to the Americas
5000 BCE	The agricultural revolution begins in Mexico
600–1300 CE	The city of Cahokia flourishes in North America
1324	The king of Mali, Mansa Musa, makes a pilgrimage to Mecca
1325	The Mexica (Aztec) Empire is established in Central Mexico
1492	Columbus leads first voyage of discovery in the Americas
1503	Spaniards bring the first enslaved Africans to the Americas
1517	Martin Luther launches the Protestant Reformation
1519	Cortés begins the Spanish conquest of Mexico
1531	Pizarro subdues the Inca Empire in South America for Spain
1565	Spaniards build a settlement at St. Augustine, the first permanent European outpost in what later becomes the United States
1584–1587	Raleigh's Roanoke Island venture
1588	The English navy defeats the Spanish Armada
1600	Isabel de Olvera participates in the Oñate expedition to New Spain
1680	Pueblo Revolt in New Mexico

OLD VIRGINIA As one of the earliest explorers and settlers of the Jamestown colony, John Smith put his intimate knowledge of the region to use by creating this seventeenth-century map of Virginia. In the upper right-hand corner is a Susquehannock, whom Smith called a "G[i]ant-like people."

England and Its American Colonies

1607–1732

CHAPTER 2

For tens of thousands of seekers and adventurers, seventeenth-century America was a vast, unknown land of new beginnings and new opportunities. People came in search of wealth, religious freedom, and new lives. The first European settlers did not arrive to a "virgin land" of uninhabited wilderness, but to a land of Indigenous American societies with established towns, fertile farms, trade networks, a wide variety of governments, and many religions.

Indigenous Americans dealt with the Europeans in different ways. Many resisted, others retreated, and still others developed thriving trade relationships with the newcomers. In some areas, land-hungry colonists quickly decimated the Indigenous population. In others, groups of Indigenous people found ways to live in cooperation with the European settlers—if they were willing (or in some cases forced) to adopt European ways of life.

Soon the settlers became colonists, establishing permanent footholds. After founding the Virginia, Maryland, and New England colonies, the English conquered the Dutch colony of New Netherland and much of the Spanish-controlled Caribbean. They subsequently settled Carolina and eventually established the rest of the thirteen original colonies. The diverse colonies had one element in common: they all took part in the enslavement

CORE OBJECTIVES

1. Identify the economic, political, and religious motivations of English monarchs and investors for the establishment of American colonies.

2. Describe the political, economic, social, and religious characteristics of English colonies in the Chesapeake region, New England, the Carolinas, and the middle colonies—Pennsylvania, New York, New Jersey, and Delaware—before 1700.

3. Analyze the ways in which English colonists and Indigenous Americans responded to each other's presence.

4. Explain how the English colonies became the most populous, prosperous, and powerful region in North America by 1700.

of other peoples, either Indigenous Americans or Africans or both. Slavery, common throughout world history, degraded and decimated Indigenous and African peoples while enriching those who enslaved them.

The English Background

The English colonies differed in important ways from the Spanish colonies in North America. Spanish settlements were the result of royal expeditions undertaken by the Spanish government and managed by its representatives in the colonies. In those areas, most of the wealth seized from Indigenous people became the property of the monarchs who funded the *conquistadores*. English colonization, by contrast, involved individuals seeking freedom from religious persecution at home—Protestants, Catholics, and Jews—and those seeking land and profits. Indigenous peoples' wealth seized by the English colonists became the property of the colonists themselves.

People and Profits

The English colonies were thus private business ventures or religious experiments—or, in some instances, both. Because few people were wealthy enough to finance a colony, those interested in colonization banded together to share the financial risks. Under this strategy, investors purchased shares of stock in a colony to form **joint-stock companies**. They raised large amounts of money and protected individual investors from complete loss if a colony failed. If a colony succeeded, investors would share the profits. Joint-stock companies represented the most important organizational innovation of the Age of Exploration.

The English settlements in America adjoined one another in concentrated geographical areas (see Map 2.1), and so were more compact than those in New Spain. The Indigenous American peoples living along the Atlantic coast had smaller, more scattered populations and were less wealthy than the Mexica and Inca peoples. Also, unlike the French and Spanish colonies, where fur traders and Spanish conquistadores often lived among the Indigenous people and intermarried, most English settlers wanted nothing to do with them. The family-based communities that the settlers created were largely separate from Indigenous villages.

The English settler colonies had far more people than the Spanish, the French, or even the Dutch colonies. In 1660, for example, there were 58,000 colonists in New England, Virginia, and Maryland, compared with 3,000 in New France and 5,000 in Dutch New Netherland. By 1750, English colonists outnumbered the French in North America by nearly 20 to 1—that is, 1.3 million to 70,000. And in the Spanish-controlled areas that later became Texas, New Mexico, Arizona, Florida, and California, there were only 20,000 Spaniards.

Although the English colonies were independent ventures, the English government wanted them to provide raw materials such as timber for shipbuilding, tobacco for smoking, and fur pelts for hats and coats. It also wanted the colonists to buy English-made goods such as textiles, furniture, tea, and other

---

CORE **OBJECTIVE**

1. Identify the economic, political, and religious motivations of English monarchs and investors for the establishment of American colonies.

Joint-stock companies

joint-stock companies Businesses owned by investors, who purchase shares of stock and share the profits and losses.

Economic and social aims of colonization

MAP 2.1 EUROPEAN SETTLEMENTS AND INDIGENOUS SOCIETIES IN SEVENTEENTH-CENTURY NORTH AMERICA

CREEK	Indigenous nations
FLORIDA	Colony area
MAINE	Settlements

- Locate each of the thirteen early colonies. Do they all border on ocean or some other body of water? Why?
- Count the number of Indigenous nations labeled on the map. Are you surprised by this number?
- Based on the proximity of colonies and Indigenous American nations, why do you think settlement by the Europeans caused hostilities with the Indigenous peoples?

luxuries. In this way, the colonies could provide a valuable boost to the English economy, which had suffered as a result of its involvement in European wars.

> Displacement and immigration to America

Moreover, the English monarchs viewed the colonies as a safety valve to relieve social pressures at home. For decades, peasants had been pushed off the land by the *enclosure* movement, in which landlords found it more profitable to raise sheep than to host poor farmworkers and so had evicted many peasants. Doing so generated large numbers of beggars and vagrants, a situation that gave the monarchs a compelling reason to send them to the colonies. In some cases, these emigrants had little to no choice in their relocation and were shipped to America as indentured servants for hire (see Chapter 3). These fixed-term laborers received support for their passage to America in exchange for contracted labor for up to seven years.

The most powerful enticements for prospective colonists were the possibility of acquiring land and the promise of a better life: what later came to be called "the American dream." Land was America's prized treasure—once it was taken from the Indigenous populations.

Political Traditions

At this time, European societies were tightly controlled hierarchies. From birth, people remained in the social order into which they were born. Commoners bowed to priests, priests bowed to bishops, peasants pledged their loyalty to landowners, and nobles knelt before monarchs, who claimed that God had given them absolute power to rule over their domain and its people.

Since the thirteenth century, however, English monarchs had *shared* power with the nobility and with a lesser aristocracy, the *gentry*. England's tradition of limited or constitutional monarchy began with the Magna Carta (Great Charter) of 1215, a statement of fundamental rights that rebellious nobles forced the king to approve. The Magna Carta established that England was to be ruled by laws rather than by tyrants. In theory, everyone was to be equal before the law.

> Parliament, civil rights, and liberties

Subsequently, the people's representatives formed the national legislature known as **Parliament**, which was made up of hereditary and appointed members of the House of Lords and elected members of the House of Commons. Parliament had the authority to impose taxes on the people. By controlling tax revenue, the legislature exercised leverage over the monarchy, which needed tax revenues to sustain its power.

Parliament The legislature of Great Britain, composed of the House of Commons, whose members are elected, and the House of Lords, whose members either hold hereditary positions or are appointed.

Puritans English religious dissenters who sought to "purify" the Church of England of its Catholic practices.

Religious Conflict and War

When Queen Elizabeth, who never married, died in 1603, her cousin, James VI of Scotland, became King James I of England. He called the combined kingdoms of Scotland and England *Great Britain*. Although Elizabeth had ruled through constitutional authority, James claimed to govern by "divine right," which meant he answered only to God.

Puritan Dissenters King James I confronted a divided Church of England, with the reform-minded **Puritans** in one camp and the Anglican archbishop and bishops in the other. The Puritans were theologically conservative dissenters who believed that the Church of England needed further "purifying." They felt that all "papist" (Roman Catholic) rituals must go. This meant no use of holy water, candles, or incense; no "Devil's bagpipes" (pipe organs); no lavish cathedrals, stained-glass windows, or statues of Jesus. Puritans even sought to ban the use of the term *priest*.

The Puritans wanted to simplify religion to its most basic elements: people worshipping God in plain, self-governing congregations without the formal trappings of Catholic and Anglican ceremonies. They had hoped the new king would support their efforts. However, James I, who had been baptized in the Catholic faith, embraced the conservative Anglican Church and sought to imprison or banish the Puritans.

> A divided Church of England and religious persecution

At the same time, the most radical Puritans decided that the Church of England was too corrupt to be reformed. They therefore created congregations separate from the Anglican Church, thus earning the name *Separatists*. Such rebelliousness infuriated Anglican authorities, who required people to attend Anglican church services. In their view, the Separatists were violating the law. During the late sixteenth century, the Separatists (also called *Nonconformists*) were, according to one of them, "hunted and persecuted on every side." Many Puritans left England, and some, who would later be known as Pilgrims (people who travel to foreign lands), sailed to America.

In 1625, King James's son, Charles I, succeeded his father and proved to be an even more stubborn defender of absolute royal power. He raised taxes without consulting Parliament, harassed the Puritans, and even disbanded Parliament from 1629 to 1640. The monarch went too far, however, when he forced Anglican forms of worship on Presbyterian Scotland. In 1638, the Scots rose in revolt; and in 1640, Charles, desperate to save his claim to authority, revived Parliament and ordered its members to raise taxes for the defense of his kingdom. Parliament, led by militant Puritans, refused.

In 1642, when the king tried to arrest five members of Parliament, a civil war erupted in England between Royalists and Parliamentarians. Four years later, parliamentary forces led by Puritan Oliver Cromwell captured Charles and, in a public trial, convicted him of treason, labeling him a "tyrant, traitor, murderer, and public enemy." He was beheaded in 1649. As it turned out, however, the Puritans had killed a king but had not slain the monarchy.

Cromwell ruled like a military dictator, calling himself Lord Protector and outlawing Roman Catholics and Anglicans alike. His Puritanical

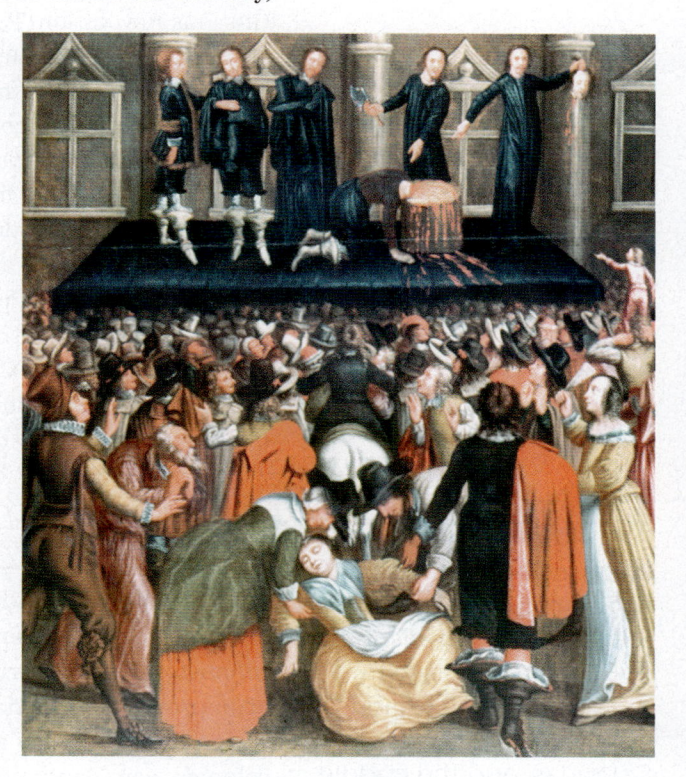

EXECUTION OF CHARLES I
Flemish artist John Weesop witnessed the king's execution and painted this gruesome scene from memory. He was so disgusted by "a country where they cut off their King's head" that he refused to visit England again.

dictatorship, however, fed growing resentment. Many Anglican Royalists, called *Cavaliers*, escaped by sailing to Virginia. After Cromwell's death in 1660, Parliament supported the restoration of the monarchy under Charles II, eldest son of the executed king.

Unlike his father, King Charles II agreed to rule jointly with Parliament. His younger brother, the Duke of York (who became King James II in 1685), was more rigid. James embraced Catholicism, murdered or imprisoned political opponents, appointed Roman Catholics to crucial government posts, and defied Parliament.

The English tolerated James II's rule so long as they expected one of his Protestant daughters, Mary or Anne, to succeed him. In 1688, however, the birth of a royal son who would be raised Roman Catholic stirred a revolt. Political, religious, and military leaders urged the king's daughter Mary and her Protestant husband, William III of Orange (the ruling Dutch prince), to oust her father and assume the English throne as joint monarchs. The willing couple decided to do so. A month after William and his powerful Dutch army landed in England, King James II fled to France.

Amid this dramatic transfer of power, which came to be called the Glorious Revolution, Parliament reasserted its right to counterbalance the authority of the monarchy. Kings and queens saw their authority limited; they could no longer suspend Parliament, create armies, or impose taxes without Parliament's consent.

In retrospect, the political and religious turmoil in England at this time made conditions ripe for establishing colonies in America. The monarchy hoped the colonies would provide raw materials such as timber, tobacco, and fur pelts, as well as money from the colonists' purchases of English-made goods. English kings also wanted to relieve social pressures by sending uprooted peasants and other dissatisfied people across the ocean to America. At the same time, wealthy English investors saw a golden opportunity to establish new and profitable business ventures in America. Founding colonies was an irresistible venture for kings as well as for wealthy profit-seekers.

> CORE **OBJECTIVE**
>
> **2.** Describe the political, economic, social, and religious characteristics of English colonies in the Chesapeake region, New England, the Carolinas, and the middle colonies—Pennsylvania, New York, New Jersey, and Delaware—before 1700.

Settling the American Colonies

During the seventeenth century, all but one of England's North American colonies—Georgia—were founded. The people who founded them—the colonists—were often ruthless individuals willing to risk their lives in hopes of improving them. Many of those who were landless in England found their way to America as indentured servants. Others who populated the colonies were captured Africans forcibly removed from their homelands and brought to America as unpaid laborers.

The Chesapeake Region

In 1606, King James I gave his blessing to a joint-stock enterprise called the Virginia Company. It was owned by merchants seeking to profit from the gold and silver they hoped to find. The king also ordered the Virginia Company to bring the "Christian religion" to the Indigenous Americans, who he believed "live[d] in darkness and miserable ignorance of the true knowledge and worship of God." As was true of many colonial ventures, however, such missionary activities were quickly dropped in favor of making money.

Jamestown

In December 1606, the Virginia Company sent to America three ships carrying 104 colonists, all men and boys. In May 1607, after five storm-tossed months at sea, they reached Chesapeake Bay, which extends 200 miles along the coast of what are today Virginia and Maryland (see Map 2.2). To avoid Spanish raiders, the colonists chose to settle about forty miles inland along a large river. They called it the James, in honor of the king, and named their settlement James Fort, later renamed Jamestown.

On a marshy peninsula fed by salty water and swarming with mosquitos, the colonists built a fort, huts, and a church. They struggled to find enough to eat, for some of them were unfamiliar with farming or were "gentleman" adventurers who despised manual labor. Were it not for the food acquired or stolen from neighboring Indigenous groups, Jamestown would have collapsed.

The Powhatan Confederacy

At this time, the **Powhatan Confederacy** dominated the Indigenous peoples of the Chesapeake region. These peoples shared the same language, religious belief system, cultural traditions, and social structure. Wahunsunacock (called "Chief Powhatan"), the chief of the Powhatan, ruled several hundred villages encompassing 6,000 square miles and 14,000 people in eastern Virginia. The Powhatan people were farmers adept at growing corn. They lived in oval-shaped houses framed with bent saplings and covered with bark or mats.

Wahunsunacock himself lived in a massive lodge on the York River, not far from Jamestown. Forty bodyguards protected him, and a hundred wives bore him several children. The colonist John Smith reported that Wahunsunacock "sat covered with a great robe, made of raccoon skins," flanked by "two rows of men, and behind them as many women, with all their heads and shoulders painted red."

The Powhatan men, Smith stressed, avoided "woman's work." When they were not hunting, fishing, or fighting, they sat watching the "women and children do the rest of the work": gardening, making baskets and pottery, cooking, and "all the rest."

VIRGINIA COMPANY This pamphlet was printed in London in 1609 to promote immigration to Virginia. **What does this advertisement promise its potential settlers, and how does that promise conflict with the reality that greeted them?**

Powhatan Confederacy
An alliance of several powerful Algonquian societies under the leadership of Chief Powhatan, organized into thirty chiefdoms along much of the Atlantic coast in the late sixteenth and early seventeenth centuries.

In fact, Wahunsunacock was as much a dominant ruler as the English or Spanish monarchs. He forced the chieftains he had conquered to give him corn. Upon learning of the English settlement at Jamestown, he planned to impose his will on the "Strangers" as well. When Powhatan scouts discovered seventeen Englishmen stealing corn, they killed the thieves, stuffing their mouths with ears of corn. Only too late would Wahunsunacock realize that the English had come to Virginia not to trade with but rather "to invade my people and possess my country."

Pocahontas

One of the most remarkable Indigenous Americans living near Jamestown was Pocahontas, the favorite daughter of Wahunsunacock. In 1607, then only eleven years old, she figured in what has become perhaps the best-known story of the settlement—her plea for the life of Captain John Smith. After Indigenous men captured Smith and a group of Englishmen trespassing on their land, Wahunsunacock ordered his warriors to kill Smith. As they prepared to smash his skull, young Pocahontas made a dramatic appeal for his life and convinced her father to release him.

WAHUNSUNACOCK Wahunsunacock (Powhatan) holds court in this 1624 line engraving from John Smith's "Generall Historie of Virginia."

Schoolchildren still learn the story of Pocahontas and John Smith, but through the years the story's facts have become distorted or falsified. Pocahontas and John Smith were friends, not lovers. Moreover, she saved Smith on more than one occasion, before she was kidnapped by English settlers eager to extort Wahunsunacock.

Pocahontas, however, surprised her English captors by embracing Christianity. She was baptized and renamed Rebecca, and fell in love with John Rolfe, a twenty-eight-year-old widower who introduced tobacco-growing to Jamestown. After their marriage in 1616, they moved with their infant son, Thomas, to London. This was her second marriage, as she was previously married to Kocoum, an Indigenous man. (The two of them had a son as well.) Her nuptials with Rolfe drew attention from the royal family and curious Londoners. Just months after arriving, however, Lady Rebecca, only twenty years old, contracted a lung disease and died.

Hard Times

Earlier, back in Jamestown, nearly every colonist fell ill within a year of arriving. They experienced disease, drought, starvation, violence, and death. "Our men were destroyed with cruel diseases," a survivor wrote, "but for the most part they died of mere famine."

POCAHONTAS After embracing Christianity, Pocahontas fell in love with John Rolfe, a twenty-eight-year-old widower who had introduced tobacco-growing to Jamestown. After their marriage in 1616, they moved with their infant son, Thomas, to London. She died from a lung infection a few months after their arrival.

Fortunately for the Virginia colonists, they found a bold leader in Pocahontas's friend, Captain John Smith. Previously he had fought in battles across Europe and killed three Turkish officers in duels. At five feet three inches in height, he was a stocky man overflowing with tenacity and confidence. The Virginia Company, impressed by Smith's exploits, appointed him a member of the council to manage the new colony in America.

With the colonists on the verge of starvation, Smith imposed strict military discipline and forced all to work if they wanted to eat. He also bargained effectively with the nearby Indigenous Americans. Through Smith's often brutal efforts, Jamestown survived—but barely.

During the winter of 1609–1610, the food supply again ran out, and most of the colonists died from "the sharp prick of hunger." Desperate settlers consumed their horses, cats, and dogs, and then rats, mice, and snakes. A few dug up "dead corpses out of graves" and ate them. "So great was our famine," Smith wrote, "that a savage we slew and buried, the poorer sort [of colonists] took him up again and ate him." Such stark experiences were also the result of extreme weather changes caused by the Little Ice Age that swept across this region and decimated crops as well as people.

> Starvation and hardship in Jamestown

The Virginia Company continued to recruit more settlers by promising that Virginia would "make them rich." The settlers who came included a few courageous women—such as Anne Burras, who came as a personal maid and was the first settler to marry in Jamestown; and Temperance Flowerdew, who lost her husband during the "starving time" and went back to England, only to return a few years later as the wife of the new governor of Virginia.

In late May 1610, Sir Thomas Gates, a prominent English soldier and sea captain, brought 150 new colonists to Jamestown. They found the settlement in shambles. The fort's walls and settlers' cabins had been used as firewood, and the church was in ruins. Of the original 104 Englishmen, only 38 had survived. They greeted the newcomers by shouting, "We are starved! We are starved!"

After nearly abandoning Jamestown to return to England, Gates rebuilt the Virginia settlements and imposed a strict system of laws. The penalties for running away, for example, included being shot, hanged, or burned. Gates also ordered the colonists to attend church services on Thursdays and Sundays. Religious uniformity became a crucial instrument of public policy and civic duty in colonial Virginia.

Tobacco

Over the next several years, the Jamestown colony limped along until the settlers found a profitable crop: **tobacco**. Smoking had become a widespread habit in Europe, and tobacco plantations were already flourishing on Caribbean islands under Spanish control. In 1612, settlers in Virginia (including John Rolfe) began growing tobacco for export to England, using seeds brought from South America. By 1620, the colony was shipping 50,000 pounds of tobacco to England each year; by 1670, Virginia and Maryland would be exporting 15 *million* pounds annually.

Despite its labor-intensive demands, the growing of tobacco became the most profitable enterprise in colonial Virginia and Maryland. However, large-scale tobacco farming required more land for planting and more laborers to work the fields. Much like sugar and rice, tobacco would become one of the primary crops that ultimately drove the demand for indentured servants and enslaved Africans.

Governance

In 1618, Sir Edwin Sandys, a prominent member of Parliament, became head of the Virginia Company. His crucial innovation was the launching of a new **headright** (land grant) policy: anyone who bought a share in the company and could pay for passage to Virginia could have fifty acres upon arrival and fifty more for each servant he brought along.

The following year, the company promised that the settlers would have all the "rights of Englishmen." Those rights included a legislature elected by the people.

In 1619, the Virginia Company created the first experiment with representative government in the American colonies. The House of Burgesses, modeled after Parliament, would meet at least once a year to make laws and decide on taxes. It included the governor, his four councilors, and twenty-two burgesses elected by free White male property owners over the age of seventeen. (The word *burgess* derived from the medieval *burgh*, meaning a town or community.)

The year 1619 was eventful in other respects as well. The settlement had outgrown James Fort and was formally renamed Jamestown. Also in that year, a ship arrived with ninety young women. Men rushed to claim them

tobacco A "cash crop" grown in the Caribbean as well as the Virginia and Maryland colonies, made increasingly profitable by the rapidly growing popularity of smoking in Europe after the voyages of Columbus.

headright A land-grant policy that promised fifty acres to any colonist who could afford passage to Virginia and fifty more for each accompanying servant. The headright policy was also adopted in other colonies.

as wives by providing the Virginia Company 125–150 pounds of tobacco to cover the cost of each woman's trip.

Slavery in British North America

Still another significant development occurred in 1619, when the English ship *White Lion* stopped at Point Comfort, Virginia, near Jamestown, and unloaded "20 and odd Negars." These were the first Africans known to have reached the British American mainland (not counting African explorers and conquistadores who arrived in New Spain and parts of Spanish Florida). Portuguese slave-traders had captured them in Angola in West Africa. On their way to Mexico, the captured Africans were seized by the marauding *White Lion*, known to raid Portuguese and Spanish ships.

The arrival of Africans in Virginia marked the beginning of two and a half centuries of slavery in British North America. These were the first of roughly 470,000 Africans who would be seized and shipped to the mainland colonies. An additional 10.5 million enslaved Africans would be shipped to South America and the Caribbean.

> The first enslaved Africans

The year 1619 thus witnessed the irony of the Virginia colony establishing the principle of representative government while importing enslaved Africans. From that point on, race-based chattel slavery corroded the ideals of liberty and equality that were evident in the fight for independence.

By 1624, 8,000 English men, women, and children had migrated to Jamestown. Only 1,132 had survived, and many of them were in "a sickly and desperate state." That same year, the Virginia Company declared

ARRIVAL OF THE FIRST AFRICANS IN VIRGINIA
The Dutch, via the Dutch West India Company, brought the first enslaved Africans from Dutch territorial possessions on the West African coast (known as the Guinea coast) to the Virginia plantations in 1619. The effects of the brutality of the voyage are evident on the first twenty enslaved Africans pictured here on the landing in Jamestown.

bankruptcy and Virginia was converted from a joint-stock company to a royal colony, with governors appointed by the king. Governor William Berkeley, who arrived in 1642, presided over the colony's rapid growth for most of the next thirty-five years.

The Jamestown experience did not invent America, but the colonists' will to survive, their mixture of greed and piety, and their exploitation of both Indigenous and African people formed the model for many of the struggles, achievements, and hypocrisies that later defined the American colonies and the nation.

Maryland

> Maryland: The first proprietary colony and a refuge for English Catholics

In 1634, ten years after Virginia became a royal colony, a neighboring settlement appeared on the northern shore of Chesapeake Bay. Named Maryland in honor of Henrietta Maria, the Catholic wife of King Charles I, its 12 million acres were granted to Sir George Calvert, Lord Baltimore (see again Map 2.2). It thereby became the first *proprietary* colony—that is, a colony controlled by an individual—as opposed to a joint-stock company owned by investors.

Calvert, a Roman Catholic, asked the new king, James II, to grant him a charter for a colony north of Virginia. However, Calvert died before the king could act, so the charter went to his son Cecilius, the second Lord Baltimore, who founded the colony and spent the rest of his life making it sustainable.

Cecilius Calvert envisioned Maryland as a refuge for English Catholics. Yet he also wanted the colony to be profitable and to avoid antagonizing Protestants. To that end, he instructed his brother, Leonard, the colony's first governor, to ensure that Catholic colonists worshipped in private and remained "silent" about religious matters.

The St. Mary's Settlement In 1634, the Calverts established the first settlement in coastal Maryland at St. Mary's, near the mouth of the Potomac River, about eighty miles north of Jamestown. Cecilius sought to avoid the mistakes made at Jamestown. He recruited colonists made up of families intending to stay, rather than single men seeking quick profits. He and his brother also wanted to avoid the extremes of wealth and poverty that had developed in Virginia.

Also, to avoid the frequent warfare suffered in Virginia, the Calverts pledged to purchase land from Indigenous people rather than take it by force. Thus, they paid for land and then provided 100 acres to each adult settler and 50 more for each child. The Calverts also promoted the "conversion and civilizing" of the "barbarous heathens"—the Indigenous population.

Still, the early years in the Maryland colony were as difficult as those in Virginia. Nearly half the colonists died before reaching age twenty-one. Some 34,000 colonists arrived between 1634 and 1680, but in 1680 the colony's White population was only 20,000.

Uneasy Governance The Calverts ruled with the consent of the *freemen* (property holders). Yet they could not attract enough Roman Catholics to

MAP 2.2 EARLY VIRGINIA AND MARYLAND

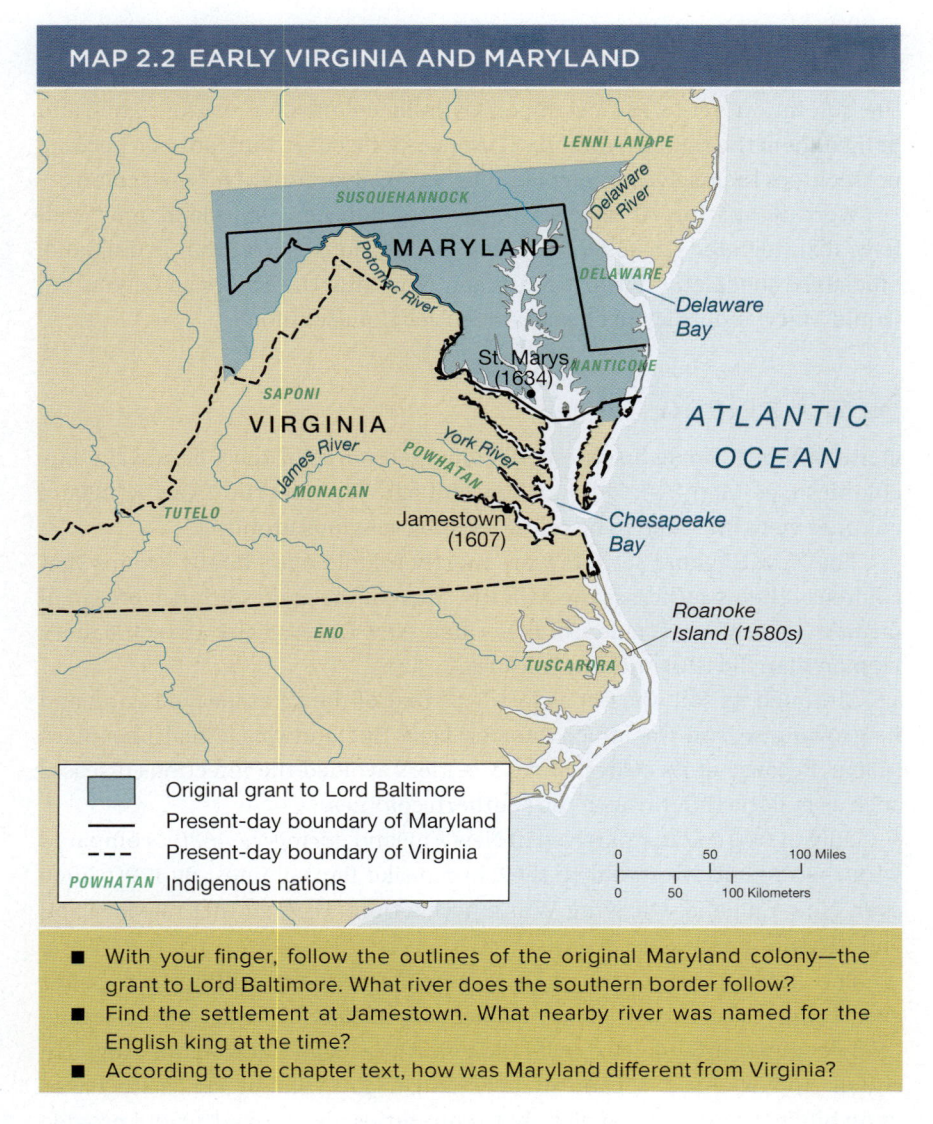

- Original grant to Lord Baltimore
- Present-day boundary of Maryland
- Present-day boundary of Virginia
- POWHATAN Indigenous nations

- With your finger, follow the outlines of the original Maryland colony—the grant to Lord Baltimore. What river does the southern border follow?
- Find the settlement at Jamestown. What nearby river was named for the English king at the time?
- According to the chapter text, how was Maryland different from Virginia?

develop a self-sustaining economy, so they pivoted and offered Protestants "a quiet life sweetened with ease and plenty" on small farms and free from religious persecution. In the end, Maryland succeeded more quickly than Virginia because of its focus from the start on growing tobacco.

Despite the Calverts' caution "concerning matters of religion," Catholics and Protestants feuded as violently as they had in England. When Oliver Cromwell and the Puritans took control in England and executed King Charles I in 1649, Cecilius Calvert feared he might lose his colony. To avoid such a catastrophe, he appointed Protestants to the colony's ruling council. He also issued the Toleration Act (1649), a revolutionary document that welcomed all Christians regardless of their denomination or beliefs. (It also promised to execute anyone who denied the divinity of Jesus.)

Still, Calvert's efforts were not enough to prevent the new government in England from installing Puritans in positions of control in Maryland. In

> Toleration Act (1649)

1650, Puritan colonists revolted and set up a new government that banned both Catholicism and Anglicanism. The Puritans then, in 1654, rescinded the Toleration Act of 1649, stripped Catholic colonists of voting rights, and denied them the right to worship. The once-persecuted Puritans had become persecutors themselves, at one point driving Calvert out of his own colony.

Were it not for its success in growing tobacco, Maryland may well have disintegrated. In 1692, following the Glorious Revolution in England, officials banned Catholicism in Maryland. Only after the American Revolution would Marylanders again be guaranteed religious freedom.

New England

Quite different English settlements emerged north of the Chesapeake Bay colonies (see Map 2.3). Unlike Maryland and Virginia, the "New" England colonies were intended to be self-governing religious utopias.

The New England settlers were mostly middle-class family groups that could pay their way across the Atlantic. Most of the male settlers were small farmers, merchants, seamen, or fishermen. New England also attracted more women than did the southern colonies.

Although its soil was not as fertile as that of the Chesapeake region and its growing season was much shorter, New England was a healthier place to live. Because of its colder climate, settlers avoided the infectious diseases such as malaria that ravaged the southern colonies.

Only 21,000 colonists arrived in New England during the 1630s, compared with the 120,000 who went to the Chesapeake Bay colonies. By 1700, however, New England's thriving White population *exceeded* that of Maryland and Virginia combined.

The Puritans who arrived in Massachusetts were willing to sacrifice everything to create a model Christian society. These self-described "visible saints" intended to purify their churches of *all* Catholic and Anglican rituals and to enact a code of laws and a government structure based upon biblical principles. Such holy communities, they hoped, would provide a beacon of righteousness for a wicked England to emulate.

Plymouth

The first permanent English settlement in New England was established by the Plymouth Company, a group of seventy British investors. Eager to make money by exporting the colony's abundant natural resources, the joint-stock company agreed to finance settlements in exchange for the furs, timber, and fish the colonists would ship back to England for sale.

Among the first to accept the company's offer were Puritan Separatists, who had been forced to leave England because they refused to worship in Anglican churches. The Separatist "saints" demanded that each congregation govern itself rather than be ruled by a corrupt bureaucracy of bishops and archbishops. The Separatists expressed their spiritual devotion in the naming of their children. Mary Brewster, for instance, called her

MAP 2.3 EARLY NEW ENGLAND SETTLEMENTS

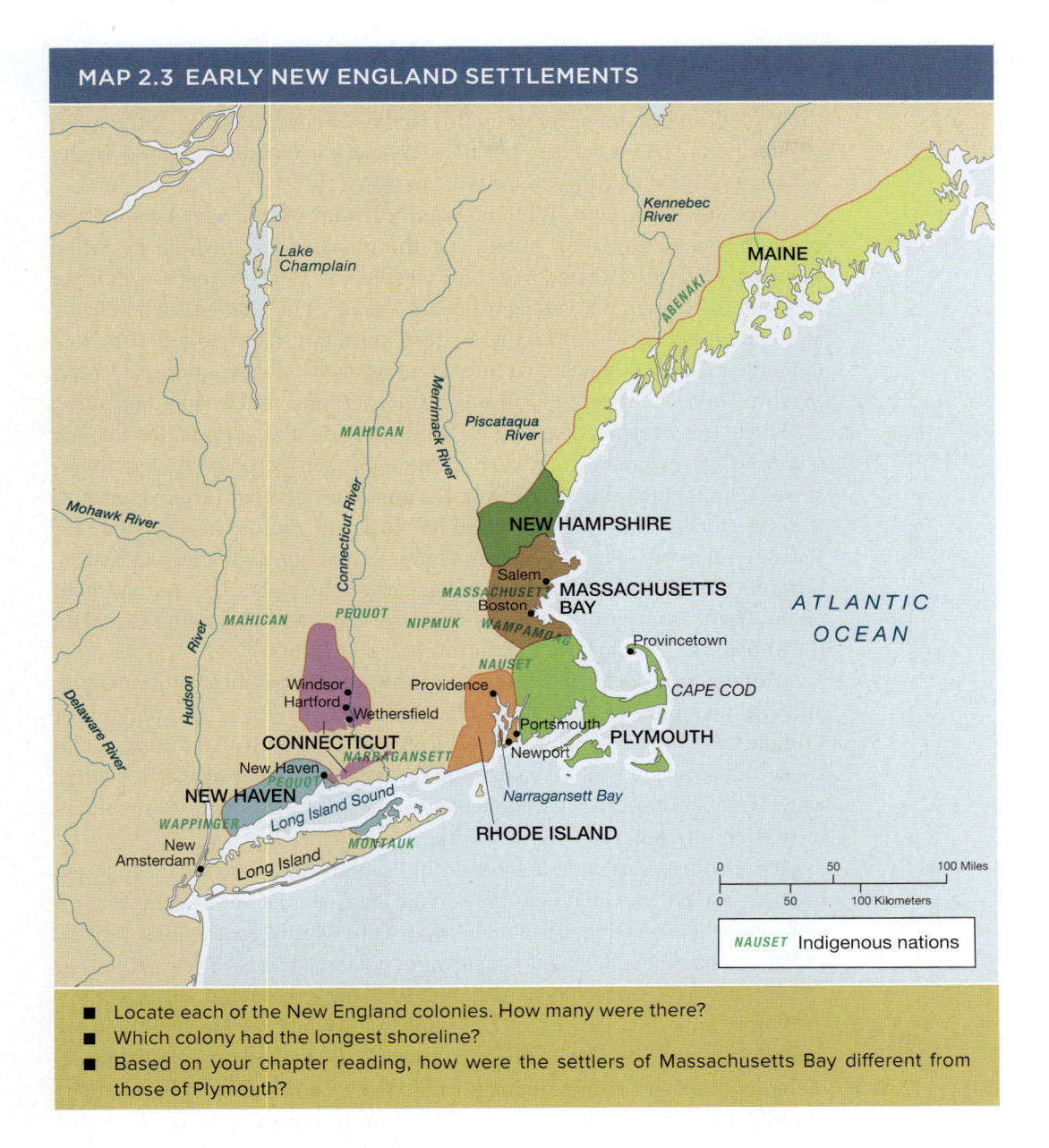

- Locate each of the New England colonies. How many were there?
- Which colony had the longest shoreline?
- Based on your chapter reading, how were the settlers of Massachusetts Bay different from those of Plymouth?

two youngest children Wrestling (with the Devil) and Love (of God). Two daughters were named Fear (of persecution) and Patience.

Separatists, mostly simple farm folk, were tired of being, as they said, "clapped up in prison," so they made the difficult choice to leave England for Holland. There, over time, they worried that their children were embracing urban ways of life in Dutch Amsterdam. Such concerns led them to create a holy community in America.

In September 1620, a group of 102 women, men, and children crammed aboard the tiny *Mayflower*, a leaky, three-masted vessel barely 100 feet long, and headed across the Atlantic. They were bound for the Virginia colony, where they had obtained permission to settle. It was hurricane season, however, and violent storms blew the ship off course to Cape Cod, southeast of what later became Boston, Massachusetts. Having exhausted most of their food and water after spending sixty-six days crossing 2,812 miles of ocean, they had no choice but to settle there in "a hideous and desolate wilderness full of wild beasts and wild men."

Once safely on land, William Bradford, who would later become the colony's second governor, noted that the pious settlers, whom he called Pilgrims, "fell upon their knees and blessed the God of Heaven who had brought them over the vast and furious ocean." They called their hillside settlement Plymouth, after the English port city from which they had embarked. Like the Jamestown colonists, they too would experience a "starving time" of drought, famine, bitter cold, desperation, and frequent deaths.

> The Mayflower Compact (1620)

Since the *Mayflower* colonists were outside the jurisdiction of any organized government, forty-one of them, all men, resolved to rule themselves. They signed the **Mayflower Compact**, a covenant (group contract) to form "a civil body politic" based on "just and civil laws" designed "for the general good." The Mayflower Compact was not democracy in action, however. The saints granted only themselves the rights to vote and hold office. Their "inferiors"—"strangers" and servants who also had traveled on the *Mayflower*—would have to wait for their civil rights.

At Plymouth, the civil government grew out of the church government, and the members of each were identical. The signers of the Mayflower Compact at first met as the General Court of Plymouth Plantation, which chose the governor and his assistants (or council). Other property owners were later admitted as members, or *freemen*; but only church members were eligible to join the General Court.

The colonists settled in a deserted Indigenous American village that had been devastated by smallpox. Those who had qualms about squatting on Indigenous lands rationalized them away. One Pilgrim soothed his guilt by explaining that the Indigenous people were "not industrious." They had neither "art, science, skill nor faculty to use either the land or the commodities of it."

Before long the Pilgrims experienced a "starving time," as had the early Jamestown colonists. During their first winter, almost half the colonists died, including fourteen of the nineteen women and six children. Only the theft of Indigenous corn enabled the English colony to survive. Eventually, a local Indigenous man named Squanto (Tisquantum) taught the colonists to grow corn, catch fish, gather nuts and berries, and negotiate with the Wampanoag people. Still, when another shipload of colonists arrived in 1623, they "fell a-weeping" as they found the original Pilgrims in such a "low and poor condition." By the 1630s, Governor Bradford was lamenting the failure of Plymouth to become a thriving holy community.

Massachusetts Bay

The Plymouth colony's population never rose above 7,000, and after ten years it was overshadowed by its much larger neighbor, the **Massachusetts Bay Colony**. Like Plymouth, the new colony was also intended to be a holy

Mayflower Compact (1620)
A formal agreement signed by the Separatist colonists aboard the *Mayflower* to abide by laws made by leaders of their choosing.

Massachusetts Bay Colony
The English colony founded by Puritans in 1630 as a haven for persecuted Congregationalists.

commonwealth for Puritans, but the Massachusetts Bay Puritans were different from the Pilgrims. They remained Anglicans—they wanted to purify the Church of England from within. They were called non-separating *Congregationalists* because their churches were governed by their independent congregations rather than by an Anglican bishop in England. The Puritans believed they were God's "chosen people." They limited church membership to "visible saints"—that is, those who could demonstrate that they had received God's grace.

In 1629, King Charles I gave a royal charter to the Massachusetts Bay Company, a group of Calvinist Puritans making up a joint-stock company. They were led by John Winthrop, a lawyer with twelve children, intense religious convictions, and mounting debts. Winthrop wanted the new colony to be a haven for Puritans where faith would flourish. This group sought to create "a City upon a Hill," as Winthrop declared, borrowing the phrase from Jesus's Sermon on the Mount. "The eyes of all people are on us," he said, so the Puritans must live up to their sacred destiny.

In 1630, Winthrop, his wife, three of his sons, and eight servants joined some 700 Puritan settlers on 11 ships loaded with cows, horses, supplies, and 42 tons of beer, which remained safely drinkable much longer than did water. Unlike the first colonists in Virginia, most of the Puritans in Massachusetts arrived as family groups. They landed near the mouth of the Charles River, where they built a village and called it Boston, after the English town of that name. Winthrop was delighted to discover that the local Indigenous people had been "swept away by the smallpox . . . so God hath hereby cleared our title to this place."

Disease knew no boundaries, however. Within eight months, 200 Puritans had died of various illnesses, and many others had returned to England. What eventually allowed the Massachusetts Bay Colony to thrive was a flood of additional colonists after 1633.

John Winthrop had cleverly taken the royal charter for the colony with him to America, thereby transferring government authority from London to Massachusetts, where he hoped to govern the godly colony with little oversight by the monarchy.

Winthrop and other Puritan leaders prized stability and hated the idea of democracy—the people ruling themselves. As the Reverend John Cotton explained, "If the people be governors, who shall be governed?" For his part, Winthrop claimed that a democracy was "the worst of all forms of government." Puritan leaders never embraced religious toleration, political freedom, social equality, or cultural diversity. They believed that the role of government should be to enforce religious beliefs and ensure social stability.

Ironically, the same Puritans who had fled persecution in England did not hesitate to persecute people of other religious views in New England. In

JOHN WINTHROP The first governor of the Massachusetts Bay Colony, Winthrop envisioned a community that would be "a City upon a Hill."

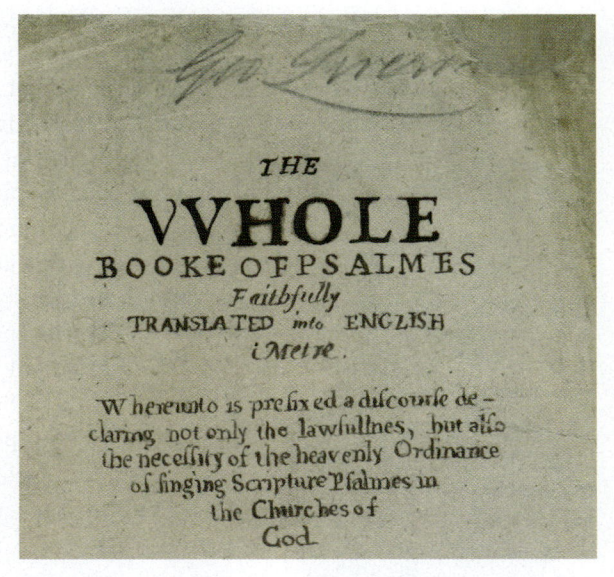

PURITAN WORSHIP A detail of the title page of *The Whole Book of Psalmes Faithfully Translated into English Metre* (Massachusetts, 1640), the first book printed in the English mainland colonies. Puritan worshippers sang psalms from its pages, sans musical accompaniment.

the Puritans' eyes, Catholics, Anglicans, Quakers, and Baptists had no rights; they were punished, imprisoned, banished, tortured, or executed.

Unlike "Old" England, New England had no powerful lords or bishops, kings or queens. The Massachusetts General Court, in which power rested under the royal charter, consisted of all the shareholders, called freemen. At first, the freemen had no power except to choose "assistants," who in turn elected the governor and deputy governor. In 1634, however, the freemen turned themselves into the General Court, with two or three deputies to represent each town.

A final stage in the democratization of the government came in 1644. At that time, the General Court organized itself into a House of Assistants, corresponding roughly to Parliament's House of Lords; and a House of Deputies, corresponding to the House of Commons. From that point forward, all decisions had to be ratified by a majority in each house.

> Rights and representation in New England

Thus, over fourteen years, the joint-stock Massachusetts Bay Company evolved into the governing body of a holy commonwealth in which freemen exercised increasing power. Puritans had fled not only religious persecution but also political repression, and they ensured that their liberties in New England were spelled out and protected.

Rhode Island

> Roger Williams challenges Puritan control

More by accident than design, the Massachusetts Bay Colony became the staging area for other New England colonies created by people dissatisfied with Puritan control. Young Roger Williams, who had arrived from England in 1631, was among the first to cause problems, precisely because he was the purest of Puritans—a Separatist. He criticized Puritans for not completely cutting their ties to the "whorish" Church of England. Williams also claimed that the charter of the Massachusetts Bay Company was itself invalid because the king of England had no right to grant Puritans the ancestral lands of Indigenous Americans. Whereas John Winthrop cherished strict governmental and clerical (church) authority, Williams championed individual liberty and criticized the way colonists were mistreating the Indigenous people.

Williams held a brief pastorate in Salem, north of Boston, and then moved south to Separatist Plymouth. There he learned the languages of local Indigenous populations and continued to question the right of English settlers to confiscate those peoples' lands. He then returned to Salem.

Williams posed a radical question: If one's salvation depends solely upon God's grace, as John Calvin had argued, why bother to have churches at all? Why not give individuals the right to worship God directly, in their own way? In Williams's view, true *Puritanism* required complete separation of church and government. "Forced worship," he declared, "stinks in God's nostrils."

ROGER WILLIAMS An outspoken Separatist, Williams challenged John Winthrop's strict authority and brutal treatment of Indigenous Americans.

Such "dangerous opinions" threatened the very foundations of New England Puritanism and led Governor Winthrop and the General Court to banish Williams to England. Before he could be deported, however, he and his wife slipped away during a blizzard and found shelter among the Narragansett people. He studied their language, defended their rights as human beings, and in 1636 bought land from them and established the town of Providence at the head of Narragansett Bay.

From the beginning, the Colony of Rhode Island and Providence Plantations was the most democratic of the colonies, governed by the heads of households rather than by church members. Newcomers could be admitted to full citizenship by a majority vote, and all who fled religious persecution were welcomed. For their part, the Massachusetts Puritans came to view Rhode Island as a refuge for rogues. A Dutch visitor reported that Rhode Island was "the sewer of New England. All the cranks of New England retire there."

Anne Hutchinson

Roger Williams was only one of several prominent Puritans who clashed with Governor John Winthrop's stern, unyielding governance of the Massachusetts Bay Colony. Another, Anne Hutchinson, quarreled with Puritan leaders for different reasons. The strong-willed wife of a prominent merchant, Hutchinson raised thirteen children, served as a midwife helping deliver neighbors' babies, and hosted meetings in her Boston home to discuss sermons. Soon, however, the discussions became large, twice-weekly gatherings (of both men and women) at which Hutchinson discussed religious matters.

Blessed with extensive biblical knowledge and a quick wit, Hutchinson criticized mandatory church attendance and the absolute power of ministers and magistrates. Most controversial of all, she claimed to know which of her neighbors had gained salvation and which were damned, including ministers. Puritan authorities saw her as a "dangerous" woman, a devout anarchist who threatened their authority.

In 1637, the pregnant Hutchinson was hauled before the all-male General Court in 1637 for trying to "undermine the Kingdom of Christ." For two days she sparred with the Puritan leaders, steadfastly refusing to acknowledge any wrongdoing. Hutchinson's ability to cite chapter-and-verse biblical defenses of her actions led an exasperated Governor Winthrop to explode: "We are your judges, and not you ours. . . . We do not mean to discourse [debate] with those of your sex."

As the trial continued, the Court lured Hutchinson into convicting herself when she claimed to have received direct revelations from God. This was blasphemy in the eyes of Puritans, for if God were speaking directly to her, there was no need for ministers or churches. In 1638, the General Court excommunicated Hutchinson from the church and banished her for having behaved like a "leper" not fit for "our society." She initially settled with her family

THE TRIAL OF ANNE HUTCHINSON In this nineteenth-century wood engraving, Anne Hutchinson stands her ground against charges of heresy from the all-male leaders of Puritan Boston.

witchcraft hysteria Cases of mass hysteria in early modern Europe and colonial America in which thousands of people were accused of being witches, many of whom were put on trial, tortured, and executed.

and followers on an island in Rhode Island's Narragansett Bay. The hard journey took its toll, however. Hutchinson grew sick, and her fourteenth baby was stillborn.

Hutchinson's spirits never recovered. After her husband's death in 1642, she moved near New Amsterdam (New York City), which was then under Dutch control. The following year, a group of Indigenous Americans massacred Hutchinson and six of her children. Her fate, wrote a spiteful John Winthrop, was "a special manifestation of divine justice."

Witches in Salem

Women accused of witchcraft

The trial and persecution of Anne Hutchinson resembled the hearings of other women that took place in Salem nearly fifty years later.

In 1692–1693, the growing social and religious strains within the Massachusetts Bay Colony reached a climax in the **witchcraft hysteria** at Salem Village (now called Danvers). The community was located on the northern edge of Salem Town, a flourishing port fifteen miles north of Boston. Prior to this dramatic episode, belief in witchcraft had been widespread throughout Europe, and almost 300 New Englanders (mostly middle-aged women) had been accused of practicing witchcraft. More than 30 of them had been hanged.

Tituba The Salem outbreak, however, was unique in its scope and intensity. During the brutally cold winter of 1692, several girls became fascinated with a fortune teller named Tituba, an enslaved woman of the Arawak tribe

TITUBA Tituba, an enslaved housekeeper and fortune teller in Salem, was wrongfully imprisoned after several young girls accused her of being a witch. She was later released but returned to slavery until she disappeared from the historical record altogether.

in Venezuela, sold into slavery in Barbados. Two of the girls, nine-year-old Betty Parris and eleven-year-old Abigail Williams—the daughter and niece, respectively, of the controversial village minister, Samuel Parris—began to behave oddly. They thrashed, shouted, barked, sobbed hysterically, and flapped their arms as if to fly. When asked who was tormenting them, they replied that three women—Tituba, Sarah Good, and Sarah Osborne—were Satan's servants.

Upon hearing this, Parris beat Tituba, his enslaved housekeeper, until she confessed to doing Satan's bidding. (Under the rules of the era, those who confessed were jailed; those who denied the charges were hanged.) Authorities arrested Tituba and the other accused women. Two of them were hanged, but not before they named other supposed witches and more young girls experienced convulsive fits. The mass hysteria extended to surrounding towns, and within a few months the Salem Village jail was filled with more than 150 men, women, and children—and two dogs—all accused of practicing witchcraft. Tituba remained in prison for thirteen months and was eventually released, sold to a new enslaver and then vanished from the historical record.

Mary Easty Another accused witch was Mary Easty, whose sister, Rebecca Nurse, had been hanged previously for witchcraft. Easty, a mother of seven, was a widely respected woman who lived on a prosperous farm. Nevertheless, young girls insisted in 1692 that she was bewitching them.

At Easty's trial, the judge urged her to confess. "How far have you complied with Satan?" he asked. She responded: "Sir, I never complied with him, but pray against him all my days." Unconvinced, the judge again demanded that she admit her guilt. Easty continued to profess her innocence: "I will say it, if it was my last time, I am clear of this sin."

Easty was not convincing, however. On September 22, 1692, she and seven others—Martha Corey, Alice Parker, Ann Pudeator, Margaret Scott, Wilmot Reed, Samuel Wardwell, and Mary Parker—were carted to Gallows Hill and hanged. Almost twenty years later, the government awarded Easty's family £20 (British pounds) for her wrongful execution.

As the allegations and executions multiplied and spread beyond Salem, leaders of the Massachusetts Bay Colony began to worry that the witch hunts were spinning out of control. The governor finally intervened when his own wife was accused of serving the devil. He disbanded the special court in Salem and ordered the remaining suspects released.

By then, nineteen people (fourteen women and five men, including a former minister) had been hanged—all justified by the biblical verse that tells

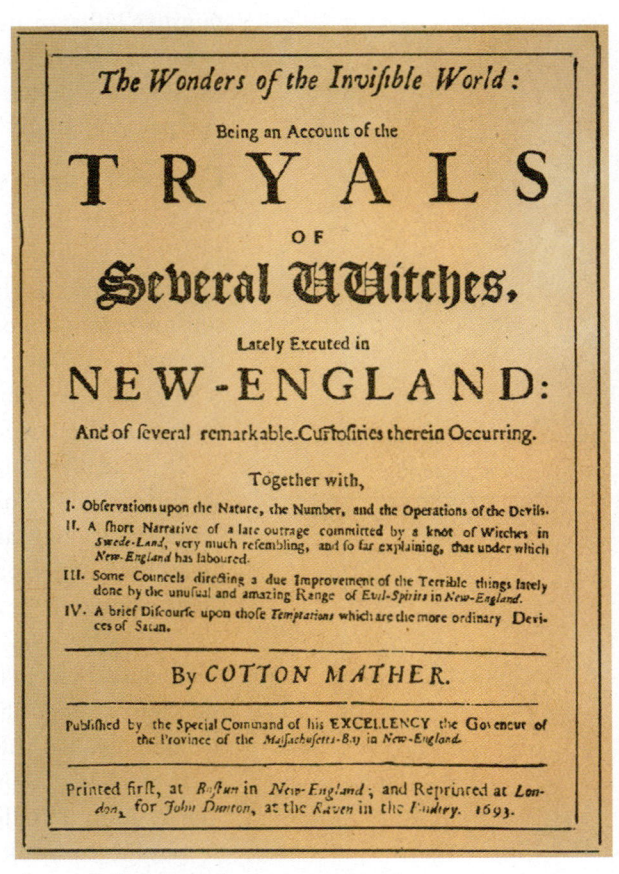

SALEM WITCHCRAFT TRIALS
Title page of the 1693 London edition of Cotton Mather's account of the Salem witchcraft trials. Mather, a prominent Boston minister, warned his congregation that the devil's legions were assaulting New England.

believers not to "suffer a witch to live." A little over a year after it had begun, the witchcraft frenzy was finally over.

Explaining the Hysteria What explains Salem's mass hysteria? It may have represented nothing more than imaginative adolescents eager to enliven the routine of everyday life. Alternatively, community tensions may have led people to accuse neighbors, masters, relatives, or rivals as an act of spite or vengeance. Some historians have stressed that most of the accused witches were women, many of whom had in some way defied the traditional roles assigned to females.

Still another interpretation suggests that the accusations may have reflected the psychological strains caused by frequent attacks by Indigenous people just north of Salem, along New England's northern frontier. Some of the convulsing girls were survivors of that violence; they had seen their families killed or mutilated by Indigenous warriors and suffered from what today is called post-traumatic stress disorder. Regardless of the actual causes, the witchcraft controversy also reflected the peculiar social tensions and personal feuds in Salem Village.

Connecticut, New Hampshire, and Maine

Connecticut had a more conventional beginning than did Rhode Island. In 1636, the Reverend Thomas Hooker led three congregations from Massachusetts Bay to the Connecticut Valley, where they organized the self-governing colony of Connecticut. Three years later, the Connecticut General Court adopted the Fundamental Orders, laws that provided for a "Christian Commonwealth" like that of Massachusetts, except that voting was not limited to church members.

> New England expands

In 1622, the king had given to Sir Ferdinando Gorges and Captain John Mason a vast tract of land that would ultimately encompass the states of New Hampshire and Maine. In 1629, the two men divided their territory. Mason took the southern part, which he named the Province of New Hampshire, and Gorges opted for the northern region, which became the Province of Maine (see again Map 2.3). During the early 1640s, Massachusetts took over New Hampshire; and in the 1650s, extended its authority to the scattered settlements in Maine. The land grab led to lawsuits; and in 1678, English judges decided against Massachusetts. New Hampshire became a royal colony in 1679, but Massachusetts continued to control Maine. A new Massachusetts charter in 1691 finally incorporated Maine into Massachusetts.

Similar to Hooker, John Davenport established the New Haven Colony around the same time. He too was a Puritan minister fleeing religious persecution by the Church of England, and he ended up in Boston as well. However, dissatisfied with Boston, he and his fellow colonists sailed to New Haven and established the colony in 1638.

The New England colonies thus began as holy commonwealths committed to planting Christian values in America. Only later did Puritan leaders realize that not everyone was equally committed to the community of faith.

MAP 2.4 EARLY SETTLEMENTS IN THE SOUTH

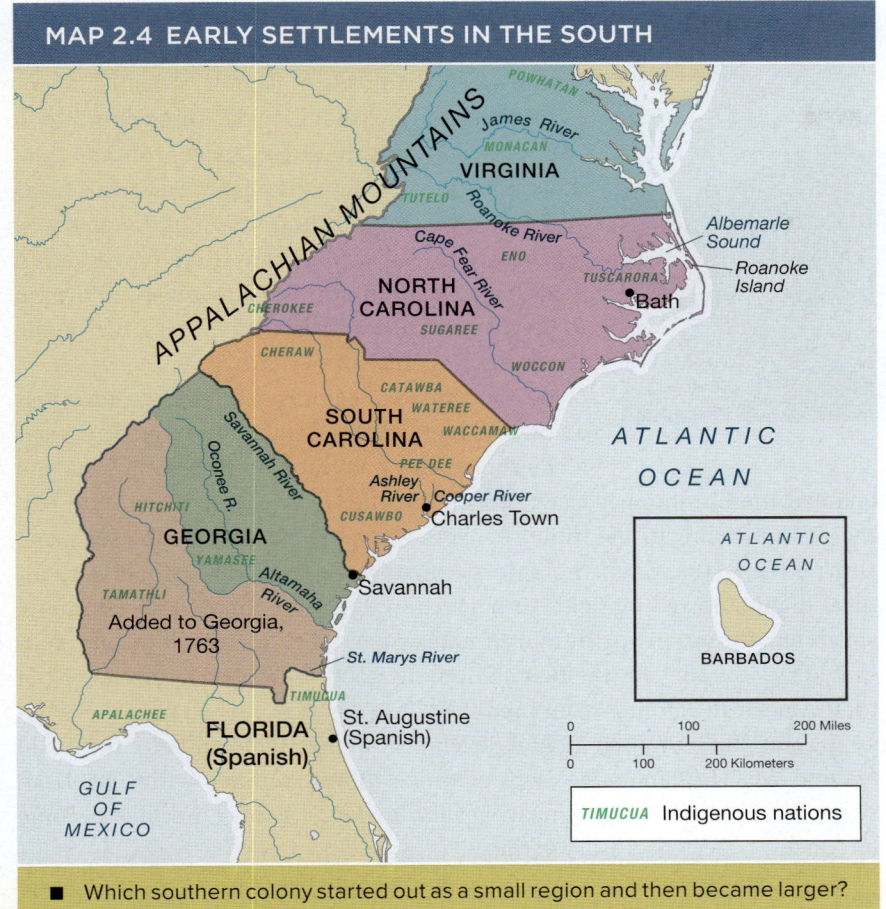

- Which southern colony started out as a small region and then became larger?
- Which two southern colonies were originally part of one larger settlement?
- According to your chapter reading, how were the Carolina colonies created?

With each passing year, new colonists arrived who had no interest in creating a holy "City upon a Hill," and the tensions between those pursuing profits and those preaching piety would eventually fracture the Puritan utopia.

The Carolinas

Carolina, the southernmost mainland British American colony in the seventeenth century, began as two widely separated areas that officially became **North and South Carolina** in 1712. The northernmost part, long called Albemarle, had been settled in the 1650s by colonists who drifted southward from Virginia. For a half-century, Albemarle remained a remote scattering of farms along the shores of Albemarle Sound (see Map 2.4).

The Barbados Connection

The eight prominent nobles, called lords proprietors, to whom the king had given Carolina, neglected Albemarle and instead focused on sites to the south that were more promising. To speed their efforts to generate profits from

North and South Carolina English proprietary colonies, originally formed as the Carolina colonies, that were officially separated into the colonies of North and South Carolina in 1712. Their semitropical climate made them profitable centers of rice, timber, and tar production.

Ties to Caribbean colonies

CARIBBEAN SUGAR Enslaved Africans plant sugarcane cuttings on a sugar plantation in Antigua in this 1823 engraving. The windmill (in the background) powers the grinding mill.

growing sugarcane, they recruited established English planters from Barbados, the most easterly of the Caribbean "sugar islands," located about 1,700 miles southeast of Florida. First colonized in 1627, Barbados was the oldest, most profitable, and most notorious colony in English America. It was widely known for its brutal treatment of enslaved laborers, many of whom were literally worked to death on sugar plantations. Following their arrival in Barbados, these enslaved laborers had a life expectancy of only seven years.

To seventeenth-century Europeans, sugar was a new and highly treasured luxury item. The sugar trade fueled the wealth of European nations and enabled them to finance their colonies in the Americas. By the 1720s, half the ships traveling to and from New York City were carrying Caribbean sugar. During the 1640s, English planters transformed Barbados into an agricultural engine dotted by fields of sugarcane. Like the bamboo it resembles, sugarcane thrives in hot, humid climates. Sugar, then called white gold, generated more money for the British than the goods produced by all the rest of their American colonies combined.

By this time, the British had developed an insatiable appetite for Asian tea and West Indian coffee, both of which they sweetened with Caribbean sugar. As a planter noted, sugar was no longer "a luxury; but has become by constant use, a necessary of life."

Sugar was hard to produce. Enslaved people used machetes to harvest the canes and then hauled them to wind-powered grinding mills where they were crushed to extract the sap. The sap was boiled, and the hot "juice"—liquid sugar—was poured into troughs to granulate before being shoveled into barrels. These barrels were stored in a curing house to allow the molasses to drain off. The resulting granular brown sugar, called *muscovado*, was shipped to refiners to be prepared for sale. The molasses was distilled into rum, the most popular drink in the colonies. By the early seventeenth century, the British sugar colonies—Barbados, St. Kitts, Nevis, Antigua, and Jamaica—were sending tons of molasses and sugar to Europe and British America.

Barbados was dominated by a few wealthy planters who depended on enslaved Africans to do the work. An Englishman pointed out in 1666 that Barbados and the other "sugar colonies" thrived because of enslaved "Negroes" and "without constant supplies of them cannot subsist." In fact, so many of the enslaved laborers in Barbados died from overwork, poor nutrition, and disease that the sugar planters capitalized on the **transatlantic slave trade** to regularly replace them with newly imported enslaved people.

Because all available land on the island was under cultivation, the sons and grandsons of the planter elite had to look elsewhere to find plantations of their own. Many seized the chance to settle Carolina and bring with them the Barbadian plantation system.

transatlantic slave trade The oceanic trade in captured African men, women, and children across the Atlantic to the Americas that took place from the sixteenth through the nineteenth centuries. It is estimated that 10 to 12 million enslaved Africans were brought to the Americas through this global system of forced removal and captivity.

Charles Town

The first 145 English colonists in South Carolina arrived in 1669 at Charles Town (later Charleston), on the west bank of the Ashley River. They brought three enslaved Africans with them. Over the next twenty years, half the colonists came from Barbados and other Caribbean colonies.

The Carolina coastal plain so impressed settlers with its flatness that they called it the "low country." Planters from the Caribbean brought to Carolina enormous numbers of enslaved Africans to clear land, plant crops, herd cattle, and slaughter pigs and chickens. Carolina, a Swiss immigrant said, "looks more like a negro country than like a country settled by white people."

Governance and Immigrants The government of Carolina grew out of a unique document, the Fundamental Constitutions of Carolina, drafted by Lord Anthony Ashley Cooper, one of the eight proprietors, with the help of his secretary John Locke. The Constitutions called for a royal governor, a council, and a Commons House of Assembly. In practice, however, what became South Carolina was dominated by a group of prominent Englishmen who were awarded large land grants.

To generate an agricultural economy, the Carolina proprietors awarded land grants (*headrights*) to every male immigrant who could pay for passage across the Atlantic. The Fundamental Constitutions granted religious toleration, which gave Carolina a higher degree of religious freedom (extending to Jews and "heathens") than was allowed in England or any other colony except Rhode Island.

In 1685, the Carolina colony received an unexpected surge of immigrants after France's Catholic king revoked the Edict of Nantes, which had guaranteed the civil rights of the Huguenots (French Protestants). Subsequently, hundreds of Huguenots left their homes in France and settled in Carolina to avoid religious persecution.

The early settlers in Carolina experienced morale-crushing hardships. "I have been here for six months," twenty-three-year-old Judith Manigault, a Huguenot refugee working as a servant, wrote to her brother in Europe. She reported that she had been "working the ground like a slave" and had "suffered all sorts of evils," but "God surely gave us good grace to have been able to withstand all sorts of trials." Her son Gabriel benefited from her perseverance; he later became one of the richest men in the province.

In 1712, the proprietors divided the Carolina colony into North and South; and seven years later, South Carolina became a royal colony. North Carolina remained under the proprietors' rule until 1729, when it too became a royal colony.

Profitable Colonies

The two Carolinas proved to be wise investments. Both colonies had vast forests of pine trees that provided lumber and other materials for shipbuilding. The sticky pine resin could be boiled to make tar, which was used to waterproof the seams of wooden ships. (This is why North Carolinians came to be called Tar Heels.)

Rice rather than sugar became the dominant crop in South Carolina because it was perfectly suited to the hot, humid growing conditions. Rice, like sugarcane and tobacco, is a labor-intensive crop. Enslavers used Africans to work their fields not only because the enslaved labor was cheaper but also because of the Africans' knowledge of rice production and irrigation. Indeed, West Africans had been growing rice for generations.

By the start of the American Revolution in 1775, South Carolina had become the most profitable of the thirteen colonies, and some of its rice planters were among the wealthiest men in the world. The colony also hosted the most enslaved Black people—over 100,000, compared with only 70,000 Whites. In 1737, the lieutenant governor warned, "Our negroes are very numerous and more dreadful to our safety than any Spanish invaders."

The Middle Colonies and Georgia

The area between New England and the Chesapeake—Maryland and Virginia—included the "middle colonies" of New York, New Jersey, Delaware, and Pennsylvania, which were initially controlled by the Dutch (see Map 2.5). Farther to the south, Georgia, the last colony to be founded, encompassed the borderlands between Carolina and Spanish Florida.

Once they were well established, the middle colonies produced surpluses of foodstuffs for export to the slave-based plantations of the South and the West Indies: wheat, barley, oats and other grains, flour, and livestock. Three great rivers—the Hudson, Delaware, and Susquehanna—and their tributaries provided access to the backcountry of Pennsylvania and New York, and to a rich fur trade with Indigenous people. The region's bustling commerce thus grew to rival that of New England.

The Dutch Republic and Trade

At this time in Europe, the Dutch Republic was a coalition of seven provinces also called the Netherlands or Holland. It encompassed 2 million people of varied backgrounds who gained their independence from Spanish control in 1581.

By 1670, the mostly Protestant Dutch had the largest fleet of merchant ships in the world and controlled northern European trade. They had become one of the most diverse and tolerant societies in Europe—and England's fiercest competitor in international commerce.

In the early 1600s, the Dutch East India Company (organized in 1602) hired English sea captain Henry Hudson to explore America in hopes of finding a northwest passage to the Indies. Sailing along the coast of North America in 1609, Hudson crossed Delaware Bay and then sailed ninety miles up the "wide and deep" river that eventually would be named for him. Upriver, a group of Indigenous people invited Hudson and his crew ashore.

MAP 2.5 THE MIDDLE COLONIES

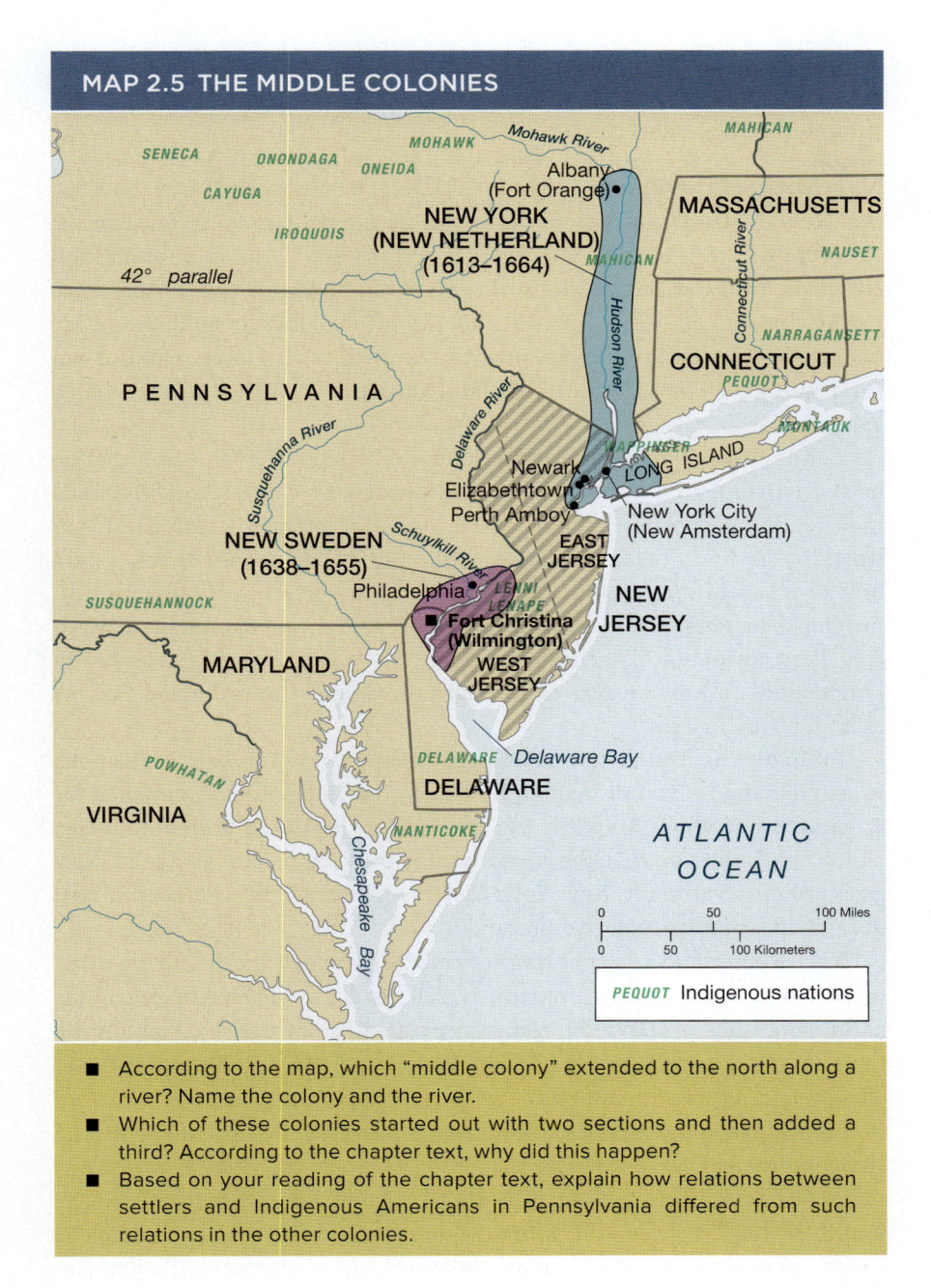

- According to the map, which "middle colony" extended to the north along a river? Name the colony and the river.
- Which of these colonies started out with two sections and then added a third? According to the chapter text, why did this happen?
- Based on your reading of the chapter text, explain how relations between settlers and Indigenous Americans in Pennsylvania differed from such relations in the other colonies.

Hudson said the Indigenous people's farmland "was the finest for cultivation that I ever in my life set foot upon."

The rivers along the Atlantic Seaboard became the first highways in colonial America. The Hudson River ultimately became one of the most strategically important. It was wide and deep enough for oceangoing vessels to travel far north into the interior, where the Dutch acquired thousands of beaver and otter pelts harvested by Indigenous people. In 1625, for example, Dutch traders acquired 5,295 beaver pelts and 463 otter skins, which they shipped to the Netherlands. By 1632, those numbers had tripled. In exchange, the Indigenous people received iron kettles, axes, knives, weapons, rum, cloth, and various trinkets.

> **The Dutch in North America**

New Netherland Becomes New York Like Virginia and Massachusetts, the **New Netherland** colony emerged as a profit-making enterprise. "Everyone here is a trader," explained one resident. And like the French colonists in Canada and along the Mississippi River, the Dutch were mainly interested in the fur trade, as the intense European demand for beaver hats generated huge profits. In 1610, the Dutch established fur-trading posts on Manhattan Island and upriver at Fort Orange (later called Albany).

Land policies in New Netherland continued the Dutch practice of the patroonship—that is, the granting of vast estates to influential men (called patroons). Like a feudal lord, the *patroon* (from the Latin word for "father") provided cattle, tools, and buildings. His tenants paid him rent, used his gristmill for grinding flour, gave him first option to purchase surplus crops, and submitted to a court he established. With free land available elsewhere, however, New Netherland's population languished, and new waves of immigrants sought the promised land of Pennsylvania instead.

In 1626, the Dutch governor purchased Manhattan (an Indigenous word meaning "island of many hills") from the Indigenous Americans for 60 guilders, or about $1,000 in current value. The Dutch then built a fort and a fur-trading post at the lower end of the island. The village of New Amsterdam (eventually New York City), which grew up around the fort, became the capital of New Netherland.

New Netherland was a corporate colony governed by the newly organized Dutch West India Company, which issued a Charter of Freedoms and Exemptions in 1629. The company controlled political life, appointing the colony's governor and advisory council and prohibiting any form of elected legislature. All commerce with the Netherlands had to be carried in the company's ships, and the company controlled the fur trade with the Indigenous people.

Dutch settlements gradually emerged wherever fur pelts might be found. In 1638, a Swedish trading company established Fort Christina at the site of present-day Wilmington, Delaware, and scattered settlements up and down the Delaware River (see again Map 2.5).

A Tolerant Society, with Limitations Unlike most other European nations with colonies in the Americas, the Dutch embraced ethnic and religious diversity. In 1579, the treaty creating the Dutch Republic declared that "everyone shall remain free in religion and . . . no one may be persecuted or investigated because of religion." Reflecting this outlook, both the Dutch Republic and New Netherland welcomed exiles from across Europe: Spanish and German Jews, French Protestants (Huguenots), English Puritans, and

New Netherland A Dutch colony conquered by the English in 1667, out of which four new colonies were created—New York, New Jersey, Pennsylvania, and Delaware.

CASTELLO PLAN OF NEW AMSTERDAM A map of New Amsterdam in 1660, shortly before the English took the colony from the Dutch and christened it New York City.

Catholics. As a result, barely half the residents in the Dutch colony were Dutch. There were even Muslims in New Amsterdam, where in the 1640s the 500 residents communicated in eighteen different languages. From its inception, New York City was America's first multiethnic community—immigrants dominated its population.

The Dutch did not show the same tolerance for Indigenous people, however. Soldiers regularly massacred neighboring Indigenous Americans. At Pound Ridge, Anglo-Dutch soldiers surrounded an Indigenous village, set it ablaze, and killed all 180 residents who tried to escape. Such violent acts only led the Indigenous people to respond in kind.

Dutch tolerance had other limitations, too. In 1654, a French ship arrived in New Amsterdam harbor carrying twenty-three *Sephardim*— that is, Jews of Spanish-Portuguese descent. They had come seeking refuge from Portuguese-controlled Brazil and were the first Jewish settlers to arrive in North America. However, the colonial governor, Peter Stuyvesant, the grim son of a Calvinist minister, refused to accept them. A short-tempered leader who had earlier lost a leg to a Spanish cannonball,

> The first Jewish settlers

JEWISH CEMETERY
A seventeenth-century Jewish cemetery in New York City shows the legacy of religious diversity in New Amsterdam, enduring even as the city developed around it.

he dismissed Jews as a "deceitful race" and "hateful enemies." Dutch officials in Amsterdam overruled him, however, pointing out that it would be "unreasonable and unfair" to refuse to provide the Jews a haven. They told the stubborn governor that they wanted to "allow everyone to have his own belief, as long as he behaves quietly and legally, gives no offense to his neighbor, and does not oppose the government."

Not until the late seventeenth century could Jews worship in public, however. Such restrictions help explain why the American Jewish community grew so slowly. In 1773, more than 100 years after the first refugees arrived, Jews represented only one-tenth of 1 percent of the entire colonial population. Only in the nineteenth century would the Jewish community in the United States witness dramatic growth.

The Dutch West India Company tolerated Jews and other ethnic minorities, yet supported slavery. In 1626, the company began importing enslaved Africans to meet its labor shortage. By the 1650s, New Amsterdam had one of the largest slave markets in America.

Tensions with English Settlers and the King The extraordinary success of the Dutch economy, however, also proved to be its downfall. Like imperial Spain, the Dutch Empire expanded too rapidly. The Dutch dominated the European trade with China, India, Africa, Brazil, and the Caribbean, but they could not control their far-flung possessions. As a result, it did not take long for European rivals to exploit the sprawling empire's weak points.

The Dutch in North America especially distrusted the English. One New Netherlander complained that the English were a people "of so proud a nature that they thought everything belonged to them."

England seizes New Netherland

In London, King Charles II decided to seize New Netherland in an effort to dominate naval power, trade, and colonization. In 1664, the residents of New Amsterdam, many of whom were not Dutch, balked when Governor Stuyvesant called on them to defend the colony against an English invasion fleet. After the English surrounded New Amsterdam and threatened the "absolute ruin and destruction of fifteen hundred innocent souls," Stuyvesant surrendered the colony without firing a shot.

The Dutch negotiated an unusual surrender agreement that allowed New Netherlanders to retain their property, churches, language, and local officials. The English renamed the harbor city of New Amsterdam as

New York, in honor of James Stuart, the Duke of York and the king's brother, who had led the successful invasion. As a reward, the king also granted his sibling the entire Dutch region of New Netherland.

New Jersey

Shortly after the conquest of New Netherland, the Duke of York granted the lands between the Hudson and Delaware Rivers to Sir George Carteret and Lord John Berkeley (brother of Virginia's governor). The duke named the territory for Carteret's native Jersey, an island in the English Channel. In 1676, by mutual agreement, New Jersey was divided into East and West Jersey (Map 2.5), with Carteret taking the east, Berkeley the west.

New settlements arose in East Jersey. Disaffected Puritans from the New Haven colony in Connecticut founded Newark, Carteret's brother brought a group to found Elizabethtown, and a group of Scots founded Perth Amboy. In the west, a scattering of Swedes, Finns, and Dutch remained; but they were soon overwhelmed by large groups of English and Welsh Quakers, as well as German and Scots-Irish settlers.

The Scots-Irish were mostly Presbyterian Scots recruited by the English government during the first half of the seventeenth century to migrate to Ulster, in northern Ireland, and thereby dilute the appeal of Catholicism and anti-English rebellions. Many of them struggled to make a living in Ulster. In contrast, one of them highlighted the benefits of life in America: "The price of land [here] is so low . . . forty or fifty pounds will purchase as much ground [in America] as one thousand pounds [would buy in Ireland]."

In 1702, East and West Jersey were united as the single royal colony of New Jersey. Unlike the Puritan New England colonies, New Jersey promoted religious tolerance, welcoming Catholics, Jews, Lutherans, and Quakers.

Pennsylvania

Pennsylvania was founded as a Quaker commonwealth. Earlier, in England, the Society of Friends—known as Quakers because they were supposed to "tremble at the word of the Lord"—became the most influential of several new religious groups that emerged from the English civil war that raged from 1642 to 1651. Founded in 1647 by George Fox, the Society of Friends rebelled against *all* forms of political and religious authority, including salaried ministers, military service, and taxes. The Quakers insisted that everyone, not just a select few, could experience a personal revelation from God—what they called the "Inner Light" of the Holy Spirit.

Quaker Beliefs and Resilience Quakers believed that each individual could achieve salvation through a personal communion with God. They demanded complete religious freedom for everyone, promoted equality of the sexes (including the full participation of women in religious affairs), and discarded all formal religious creeds and rituals, including an ordained priesthood. When gathered for worship, they kept silent until the Inner Light moved them to say what was fitting at the right moment.

> The Quakers and women's equality

The Quakers were also fierce pacifists who stressed the need to lead lives of service to society. Like Fox, some early Quakers went barefoot, others wore rags, and a few went naked to demonstrate their "primitive" commitment to Christ.

> **Persecution of Quakers**

The Quakers often suffered violent abuse because their behavior seemed threatening to the social and religious order. Authorities accused them of disrupting "peace and order" and undermining "religion, Church order, and the state." Quakers were especially hated because they refused to acknowledge the supremacy of Puritanism. New England Puritans first banned Quakers, then lopped off their ears if they returned. When that did not stop them, authorities pierced their tongues with a red-hot rod.

Still, the Quakers kept coming. In fact, they often sought out abuse and martyrdom as proof of their convictions. Mary Dyer, a follower of Anne Hutchinson who also was banned from Massachusetts, later became a Quaker and returned to the colony to visit jailed Quakers. She was eventually arrested and sentenced to death. At the last minute, however, her son convinced the court to release her—against her wishes—on the condition that she relocate to Rhode Island.

In April 1660, however, a defiant Dyer went back to Massachusetts to protest the "wicked [anti-Quaker] law against God's people and offer up her life there." The mother of six was again sentenced to death. "The will of the Lord be done," she said. "Yea, joyfully shall I go." And go she did—to martyrdom. She was hanged.

William Penn The settling of English Quakers in West Jersey encouraged other Friends to migrate, especially to the Delaware River side of the colony, where William Penn founded a Quaker commonwealth, the colony of Pennsylvania. Penn, the son of the celebrated admiral Sir William Penn, was one of the most improbable of colonial leaders. While a student at Oxford University, he was expelled for criticizing the requirement that students attend daily chapel services in the Anglican Church. His furious father banished his son from their home. The younger Penn lived in France for two years, then studied law before moving to Ireland to manage the family's estates. While he was there, officials arrested him in 1666 for attending a Quaker meeting. Much to the chagrin of his parents, Penn became a Quaker and was arrested several more times for his religious convictions.

> **Quaker-controlled Pennsylvania**

Upon his father's death, William Penn inherited a substantial fortune, including a sprawling tract of land in America, which the king urged him to settle as a means of ridding England of Quakers. The king insisted that the land be named in honor of Penn's father—Pennsylvania (literally, Penn's Woods).

The new colony was larger than England itself. Unlike John Winthrop in Massachusetts, Penn encouraged people of different religions from different countries to settle in Pennsylvania. He considered it a "holy experiment" where people of *all* faiths, nations, and social classes could live together in harmony. By the end of 1681, thousands of immigrants had responded to Penn's offer, and a bustling town was emerging at the junction of the Schuylkill and Delaware Rivers. Penn called it Philadelphia (meaning City of Brotherly Love).

The relations between the Indigenous Americans and the Pennsylvania Quakers were unusually peaceful because of the Quakers' friendliness and Penn's policy of purchasing land titles from Indigenous Americans. Penn told representatives of the Delaware Nation that he wanted to enjoy the land "with your love and consent, that way we may always live together as neighbors and friends."

The colony's government, which rested on three Frames of Government drafted by Penn, resembled that of other proprietary colonies except that the freemen (owners of at least fifty acres) elected the council members as well as the assembly. The governor had no veto, although Penn, as proprietor, did. Penn hoped to show that a colonial government could abide by Quaker principles. It could maintain peace and order, while demonstrating that religion could flourish without government support and with absolute freedom of conscience.

Over time, however, the Quakers struggled to forge a harmonious colony. In Pennsylvania's first ten years, it had six governors. A disappointed Penn, who only visited his colony twice, wrote from London: "Pray [please] stop those scurvy quarrels that break out to the disgrace of the province." Ironically, as Penn's colony began to flourish, he slid into poverty, eventually landing in debtor's prison.

Delaware

In 1682, the Duke of York granted William Penn the area known as Delaware. Situated along the Middle Atlantic seaboard, it was founded by Swedish settlers who cultivated wheat, barley, corn, and peas there. It was another part of the former Dutch territory (which had been New Sweden before being acquired by the Dutch in 1655). Delaware took its name from the Delaware River (Map 2.5), which had been named to honor Thomas West (Baron De La Warr), Virginia's first colonial governor. Although initially part of Pennsylvania, it was granted the right to choose its own legislative assembly in 1704 because of conflict between the representatives from the two sets of county governments. The point of contention was the Delaware county economies, which were more like the Chesapeake colonies and based on tobacco plantations and the labor of enslaved workers. From then until the American Revolution, Delaware had a separate assembly but shared Pennsylvania's governor.

Georgia

The last English colony to be founded, Georgia emerged a half century after Pennsylvania. During the seventeenth century, it was populated by settlers who moved southward into the region between South Carolina and Spanish Florida. The only colony to ban slavery from its inception, Georgia settlers feared "white idleness." Thus from 1733 to 1751, the thirteenth colony prohibited enslaved labor.

SAVANNAH, GEORGIA The earliest known view of Savannah, Georgia (1734). The town's layout was carefully planned to incorporate parks and public spaces.

> Georgia established for the "worthy poor"

In 1732, King George II gave the land between the Savannah and Altamaha Rivers to twenty-one trustees appointed to govern the Province of Georgia, named in honor of the king. Georgia provided a military buffer against Spanish Florida. It also served as a social experiment by bringing together settlers from different countries and religions, many of them refugees, debtors, or members of the "worthy poor." General James E. Oglethorpe, a prominent member of Parliament, was appointed to head the colony.

In 1733, about 120 colonists established Savannah on the Atlantic coast near the Savannah River. Carefully laid out by Oglethorpe, the town, with its geometric pattern of crisscrossing roads graced by numerous parks, remains a splendid example of city planning. Protestant refugees from Austria began to arrive in 1734, followed by Germans and German-speaking Moravians and Swiss, who for a time made the colony more German than English. The addition of Welsh, Highland Scots, Sephardic Jews, and others gave the early colony a diverse ethnic character like that of Charleston, South Carolina.

In 1752, Georgia became a royal colony. As a buffer against Spanish Florida, the colony succeeded; but as a social experiment creating a "common

> *Therefore be it enacted,* That all negroes, Indians, mulattoes, or mestizoes, who now are, or hereafter shall be in this province, (free Indians in amity with this government, and negroes, mulattoes, or mestizoes, who now are or hereafter shall become free, excepted) and all their issue and offspring born, or to be born, shall be, and they are hereby declared to be and remain for ever hereafter absolute slaves, and shall follow

THE COLONIAL LAW OF 1755 Georgia was the only colony that banned slavery at its founding. As the colony became more self-sufficient and grew over its early decades, it began to resemble the other southern colonies and eventually legalized slavery in 1755.

man's utopia," Georgia failed. Initially, landholdings were limited to 500 acres to promote economic equality. Rum was banned, and the importation of enslaved people was forbidden. The idealistic rules soon collapsed, however, as the colony struggled to become self-sufficient. The regulations against rum and slavery were widely disregarded and finally abandoned. By 1755, the ban on slavery had been lifted; by 1759, all restrictions on landholding had been removed.

Georgia boomed in population and wealth after 1763, when it came to resemble the plantation society in South Carolina. Georgians exported rice, lumber, beef, and pork, and they carried on a lively trade with the islands in the West Indies.

Overall, in reviewing the English colonies' development throughout the seventeenth century, it is possible to say that their characteristics were as diverse as the types of people who settled them—their social class and ethnic background; their religious beliefs; their status as free, indentured, or enslaved. Also diverse were the types of governance and economies that developed, and the geography and climate of each area.

Life in the earliest settlements was challenging, as the first colonists struggled against harsh weather and insufficient supplies. Conditions improved under land grants and proprietary governance, as well as the development of trading economies. In southern areas, strengthening economies based on tobacco, sugar, and rice brought wealth for enslavers but oppressive—sometimes lethal—working conditions for laborers, especially enslaved Africans. Parts of New England and the middle colonies were active sites for religious groups, especially Puritans, Catholics, and Quakers. In all these areas, settlers interacted with Indigenous people in ways both peaceful and violent.

Indigenous Peoples and English Settlers

The process of establishing English colonies in America did not occur in a vacuum: Indigenous Americans played a crucial role in the development of British America. Initially, the thriving commerce in animal skins—especially beaver, otter, and deer—helped spur exploration of the

> **CORE OBJECTIVE**
> **3.** Analyze the ways in which English colonists and Indigenous Americans responded to each other's presence.

vast American continent. Yet it both enriched and devastated the lives of Indigenous peoples.

To acquire pelts from the Indigenous Americans, French and Dutch merchants built trading outposts in upper New York and along the Great Lakes. There they established friendly relations with the Huron, Algonquian, and other Indigenous nations, who greatly outnumbered them. The Huron and Algonquian also sought French support in their ongoing wars with the Iroquois nations.

Most of the English colonists adopted a different strategy for dealing with the Indigenous people. The English were more interested in pursuing their "God-given" right to hunt and farm on Indigenous American lands and to fish in Indigenous American waters.

Food and Land

The English settled along the Atlantic Seaboard, where Indigenous populations were much smaller than those in Mexico or on the islands in the Caribbean. Moreover, the Indigenous peoples of North America were fragmented, often fighting among themselves over disputed lands.

> **Battles over Indigenous lands**

Jamestown's earliest settlers had already learned that land was essential to their survival—to growing corn and other food sources. By 1616, the discovery that tobacco flourished in Virginia intensified the settlers' lust for even more land. English tobacco planters desired the Indigenous people's fields because they had been cleared and were ready to be planted. In 1622, the Indigenous Americans tried to repel the land-grabbing English. Captain Smith reported that the "wild, naked natives" attacked twenty-eight farms and plantations along the James River, "not sparing either age or sex, man, woman, or child," killing one-fourth of the settlers. The English retaliated by decimating the Indigenous American populations of Virginia. Smith said the colonists were determined to "force the Savages to leave their Country."

Bacon's Rebellion

> **Intensified conflict with Indigenous peoples**

The relentless stream of settlers into Virginia exerted constant pressure on Indigenous lands and created growing social tensions among Whites. The largest planters in the colony sought to live like the wealthy "English gentlemen" who owned huge estates in the English countryside. In Virginia, these planters seized the most fertile land along the coast and rivers, leaving very little land for freed servants to acquire for themselves. By 1676, one-fourth of the free White men were landless. They were forced to roam the countryside, squatting on private property, working at odd jobs, poaching game, or committing other petty crimes to survive.

In the mid-1670s, simmering tensions caused by falling tobacco prices (stemming from overproduction), rising taxes, and crowds of landless freed servants sparked what came to be called **Bacon's Rebellion**. The discontent erupted when a squabble between a White planter and Indigenous Americans on the Potomac River led to the murder of the planter's herdsman. Frontier vigilantes retaliated by killing two dozen Indigenous people.

Bacon's Rebellion (1676) An unsuccessful revolt led by planter Nathaniel Bacon against Virginia governor William Berkeley's administration, which, Bacon charged, had failed to protect settlers from raids by Indigenous Americans.

Scattered attacks continued southward to the James River, where a group of Indigenous Americans killed Nathaniel Bacon's farm manager. In 1676, when Governor William Berkeley refused to attack the raiders, Bacon organized a rebel group to terrorize the "protected and darling Indians." He pledged to kill all the Indigenous people in Virginia and promised to free any servants and enslaved individuals who joined him.

The rebellion became a battle of landless servants, small farmers, and even enslaved Africans against Virginia's wealthiest planters and political leaders. Bacon, however, was also the spoiled son of a wealthy family and had a talent for trouble. The vicious assaults by his followers against peaceful Indigenous Americans, along with his greed for power and land, sparked the conflict with the governing authorities and the planter elite.

Governor Berkeley declared Bacon a rebel, ordered him arrested, and challenged him to a duel with swords. Bacon declined. Thereafter, the colony plunged into civil war. Berkeley opposed Bacon's plan to destroy the Indigenous people, not because he liked them but because he did not want to disrupt the profitable deerskin trade. Bacon, whose ragtag "army" now numbered in the hundreds, issued a "Declaration of the People of Virginia" accusing Berkeley of corruption and attempted to take the governor into custody. Berkeley's forces resisted—feebly—and Bacon's men burned Jamestown in frustration.

Bacon, however, fell ill from dysentery and died a month later, after which the rebellion disintegrated. Berkeley, disappointed that Bacon had died before he could be executed, satisfied his wrath by having twenty-three of Bacon's lieutenants hanged. For such severity, King Charles II denounced Berkeley and recalled him to England, where he died within a year.

NEWS OF THE REBELLION
A pamphlet printed in London provided details about Bacon's Rebellion to the British public, curious to hear the "strange news from Virginia."

Indigenous Americans and Christianity

The New England Puritans aggressively tried to convert Indigenous people to Christianity and "civilized" living. They believed conversion would save the souls of Indigenous people. They also insisted that the converts abandon their traditional religions and languages, their clothes, long hair, Indigenous names, and villages, and forced them to move to so-called "praying towns" to separate them from their "heathen" brethren.

> Religious conversion and land confiscation

This was met with great resistance among the many Algonquian people who lived in the region. Indigenous people saw the presence of Europeans as invasive to their way of life. After all, they had lived for centuries in harmony with the land, not in possession of it.

The Pequot War

Most of the New England Puritans, like the colonists in Virginia, viewed Indigenous peoples as demonic savages, "barbarous creatures," "merciless

Comparing PERSPECTIVES

BACON'S REBELLION AND THE INTERSECTION OF GENDER, RACE, AND CLASS

From: By the King, A Proclamation for the suppression of a rebellion lately raised within the Plantation of Virginia, October 27, 1676.

This proclamation was issued by King Charles II following Bacon's Rebellion. It called for an end to the rebellion offering those involved to take oaths to be pardoned within 20 days of the proclamation. It also called for slaves to render themselves to the Royal Governor to claim their liberty.

Whereas Nathaniel Bacon of the Plantation of Virginia, and others his Adherents and Complices have lately in a Traitorous and Rebellious manner levyed War within the said Plantation, against the Kings most Excellent Majesty, and more particularly being Assembled in a Warlike manner to the number of about Five Hundred Persons, did in the Month of June last past . . . Besiege the Governor and Assembly of the said Plantation . . . and did by Menaces and Threats of present Death compel the said Governor and Assembly to pass divers pretended Acts.

His Majesty doth hereby Declare, That such Person or Persons as shall Apprehend the said Nathaniel Bacon, and him shall bring before His Majesties Governor . . . shall have as a Reward from His Majesties Royal Bounty, the sum of Three Hundred Pounds Sterling. His Majesty out of His Royal Pity and Compassion to his seduced Subjects, doth hereby Declare, That if any of His Subjects who have or shall have engaged with, or adhered to the said Nathaniel Bacon in the said Rebellion, shall within the space of Twenty days after the publishing of this His Royal Proclamation, submit himself to His Majesties Government . . . That then such Person so submitting, taking such Oath, and giving such Security, is hereby pardoned and forgiven the Rebellion and Treason by him committed, and shall be free from all punishments and forfeitures for or by reason of the same. And His Majesty doth hereby further Declare, That if any of His Subjects who have engaged, or shall engage with, or have adhered, or shall adhere to the said Nathaniel Bacon in the said Rebellion, shall not accept of this His Majesties gracious offer of Pardon, but shall after the said

Twenty days expired, persist and continue in the said Rebellion, That then such of the Servants or Slaves of such persons so persisting and continuing such Rebellion, as shall render themselves to, and take up Arms under His Majesties Governor, Deputy Governor, or other Commander in Chief of His Majesties Forces within the said Plantation, shall have their Liberty, and be for ever Discharged and Free from the Service of the said Offenders.

From: The Humble Petition of Sarah Drummond before the Board of Trade and Plantations, November 9, 1677.

Sarah Drummond petitioned the Board of Trade and Plantations to restore her late husband's property, William Drummond, who had been executed for his role in Bacon's Rebellion. She asked that her husband's "estate may bee entirely restored and confirmed to her and her Children for their future support and maintenance."

That your petitioner's said husband was, after the Late Rebellion there, taken, stript, and brought before Sir William Berkley his Maty's then Governor there, who immediately (though in the time of peace) was, without laying anything to his charge, sentenced to dye by Martial Law (although he never bore armes or any military Office) not being permitted to answer for himselfe, or reserved for tryal, according to the known Laws of this his Majestie's Kingdome, as others were; and, within four hours after sentence, hurried away to execution by the Governor's particular order who before that time (upon some private pique) had vow'd that yor petitioner's husband should not live one hour after hee was in his power. That although the said Sir William Berkley did invest the Widdows of all the Rebells that were either killed, or executed, in their husbands Estates, nay even the Widdow of that Grand Rebell Nathaniel Bacon (the only person excepted by his Maty's gracious pardon) yet soe great was the said Governor's inveteracy against your petitioners husband, that hee not only took away his life, but caused his small Plantation to bee seized and given to himselfe by the Council; his goods to bee removed and imbezled, and forced Your petr, with her five poor Children, to fly from their habitation, and wander in the Deserts and Woods, till they were ready to starve.

Questions

1. What methods does the King of England utilize to quell Bacon's Rebellion? According to the chapter text, were these methods effective?
2. What does Sarah Drummond's petition reveal about gender roles in Early America?
3. What do these documents reveal about various groups of people such as women, the poor, and enslaved people during the Rebellion?

ALGONQUIAN CEREMONY
As with most Indigenous Americans, Algonquians' religious beliefs were shaped by their dependence on nature for survival, as illustrated in this celebration of the harvest.

> Bloody war between Puritans and Pequots

and cruel heathens." As one colonist asserted, they had no place in a "new England."

In 1636, settlers in Massachusetts accused a Pequot man of murdering a colonist; they took revenge by setting fire to a Pequot village. (The Pequot were an Algonquian-speaking nation.) As the residents fled the flames, the Puritans killed them—men, women, and children. William Bradford, the governor of Plymouth, acknowledged that it was "a fearful sight to see them thus frying in the fire," but "the victory seemed a sweet sacrifice" provided by God.

Sassacus, the Pequot chief, organized the survivors and counterattacked. During the ensuing Pequot War of 1636–1637, the colonists and their Mohegan and Narragansett allies killed hundreds of Pequot people, including unarmed women and children, in their village near West Mystic in the Connecticut River valley.

By the end of the conflict, some 900 Indigenous people had been killed and the rest taken prisoner. Under the terms of the 1638 Treaty of Hartford, the Pequot Nation was dissolved. Captured warriors and boys were sold to plantations in Barbados and Jamaica in exchange for enslaved Africans brought to New England. Pequot women were forced to work as house servants in New England. In 1641, the Massachusetts Bay Colony issued its first written law regulating enslaved Indigenous Americans, allowing that "those lawful captives taken in just wars" could be enslaved for life.

A few Pequots escaped. Sassacus himself sought refuge with the Mohawk people in New York. He pleaded with them to spare his life. They did not. In fact, they sent his scalp to the English as a peace offering.

King Philip's War

After the Pequot War, relations between colonists and Indigenous people improved, but the continuing influx of English settlers in the last quarter of the seventeenth century brought the era of peaceful coexistence to a bloody end.

Indigenous American leaders—especially the chief of the Wampanoag Nation, Metacom (known to the colonists as King Philip)—as well as Nipmuc, Pocumtuck, and Narragansett people resented English efforts to take their lands and to convert their people to Christianity. In the fall of 1674, John Sassamon, an Indigenous American Christian who had graduated from Harvard College, warned the English that the Wampanoag people and their allies were preparing for war. He was right. Soon, Indigenous people throughout eastern New England participated in a coordinated attack on the colonies and their enemies. Women leaders like Weetamoo (Metacom's sister-in-law) emerged from this conflict as diplomats who helped negotiate treaties to protect tribal land and who assisted their people in finding safe places in the swamps of central Massachusetts.

A few months later, Sassamon was found dead in a frozen pond. With little evidence, colonial authorities convicted three Wampanoags of murder and hanged them. Enraged Wampanoag warriors then burned Puritan farms on June 20, 1675. Three days later, an Englishman shot a Wampanoag warrior, and the Wampanoags retaliated by ambushing and beheading a group of Puritans. (One colonist had his stomach ripped open and a Bible stuffed inside.)

The gruesome violence spun out of control in what came to be called **King Philip's War (1675–1678)**, or Metacom's War. The fighting killed more people in proportion to the population than any American conflict since. Vengeful bands of warriors destroyed fifty colonial towns. Rival Indigenous groups fought on both sides.

Within a year, the colonists launched a surprise attack, killing 300 Narragansett warriors and 400 women and children. The Narragansetts retaliated by destroying Providence, Rhode Island, and threatening Boston itself. The situation grew so desperate that the colonies passed America's first conscription laws, drafting into the militia all males between the ages of sixteen and sixty. In the summer of 1676, Metacom's wife and only son were captured, leading the chieftain to cry: "My heart breaks; now I am ready to die."

In the end, 600 colonists—5 percent of the colony's male English population—died during the war. Some 1,200 homes were burned and 8,000 cattle killed. The Wampanoag people and their allies suffered even higher casualty rates, with perhaps as many as 4,000 dead. Colonists destroyed villages and shipped off hundreds of captives as slaves to the Caribbean islands.

King Philip's War (1675–1678) A war in New England resulting from the escalation of tensions between Indigenous Americans and English settlers; the defeat of the Indigenous Americans led to broadened freedoms for the settlers and their dispossessing the region's Indigenous Americans of most of their land.

KING PHILIP'S WAR A 1772 engraving by Paul Revere depicts Metacom (King Philip), leader of the Wampanoags. How does this representation of King Philip compare with John White's sketch of an Indigenous American chief on p. 17?

CHEROKEE CHIEFS A print depicting seven Cherokee chiefs who had been taken from Carolina to England in 1730.

The war slashed New England's Indigenous population in half, dropping it to fewer than 9,000. Those who remained were forced to move to villages supervised by English officials. Metacom escaped, only to be hunted down and killed by an Indigenous warrior who was fighting with the colonists. The victorious New Englanders marched Metacom's severed head to Plymouth, where it sat atop a pole for twenty years—a grisly reminder of the English determination to ensure their dominance over Indigenous Americans.

The Iroquois League

> Iroquois relations with French and English

The various Indigenous groups' inability to unite against the Europeans, as well as their vulnerability to infectious diseases, doomed them to conquest and exploitation. Yet Indigenous peoples throughout the colonies, drawing upon their own spiritual traditions in the face of unrelenting suffering, came together to reconstruct communities devastated by disease, war, and displacement.

In the interior of New York, however, a different situation arose. There, sometime before 1600, the Iroquois Nations had forged an alliance so strong that the outnumbered Dutch and, later, English traders were forced to work with them to acquire beaver pelts. By the early seventeenth century, some fifty sachems (chiefs) governed the 12,000 members of the **Iroquois League**, known to its members as the *Haudenosaunee,* or Great Peace. Its capital was Onondaga, a bustling town a few miles south of what later became Syracuse, New York.

The league was governed by a remarkable constitution, called the Great Law of Peace, which had three main principles: peace, equity, and justice. Each person was to be a shareholder in the tribe's wealth or poverty. The constitution established a Great Council of fifty male *royaneh* (religious-political leaders), each representing one of the female-led clans of the Iroquois Nations. The Great Law of Peace gave power to the people. It insisted that every time the royaneh dealt with "an especially important matter

Iroquois League An alliance of the Iroquois Nations, originally formed sometime between 1450 and 1600, that used their combined strength to pressure Europeans to work with them in the fur trade and to wage war across what is today eastern North America. The League's unique constitution, the Great Law of Peace, was based on principles of peace, equity, and justice, and it gave power to all the people.

or a great emergency," they had to "submit the matter to the decision of their people," both men and women.

The search for furs and captives led Iroquois war parties to range widely across eastern North America. They gained control over an extensive area reaching from the St. Lawrence River to Tennessee and from Maine to Michigan. For more than twenty years, warfare raged across the Great Lakes region between the Iroquois (supported by Dutch and English fur traders) and the Algonquian and Huron (and their French allies). In the 1690s, the French and their Indigenous American allies destroyed Iroquois crops and villages, infected them with smallpox and other diseases, and reduced the male population by more than a third. Facing extermination, the Iroquois made peace with the French in 1701. During the first half of the eighteenth century, they stayed out of the almost constant wars between the English and French, which enabled them to play the two European powers against each other while creating a thriving fur trade for themselves.

WAMPUM BELT Woven to certify treaties or record transactions, the white squares on this belt likely denote nations and alliances, while the purple likely conveys apprehension.

The Iroquois experience reflects just one of the ways Indigenous peoples and colonists interacted and adapted to each other's presence in America. For example, early English settlers at Jamestown were able to establish trading relations, while later settlers who invaded Indigenous lands sparked armed conflicts and, on both sides, retaliatory wars. Only two colonial leaders treated the Indigenous people as equals. In some cases, when certain Indigenous nations allied with colonists, tensions grew between those nations and other Indigenous peoples. Overall, the process of adapting to the mix of population was as complex as the varied population itself.

Thriving Colonies

By the early eighteenth century, England's colonies had outstripped those of both the French and the Spanish as tensions among the three major European powers grew. English America, both the mainland colonies and those in the Caribbean, had become the most populous, prosperous, and powerful of the European empires' colonial holdings. Although some settlers found hard labor, desperation, and an early death in America, others flourished only because they were able to exploit Indigenous people, indentured servants, or Africans.

The English colonists enjoyed crucial advantages over their European rivals. The tightly controlled colonial empires created by the monarchs of

> **CORE OBJECTIVE**
> **4.** Explain how the English colonies became the most populous, prosperous, and powerful region in North America by 1700.

Spain and France stifled innovation. By contrast, the English and Dutch organized colonies as profit-making enterprises with a minimum of royal control. Where New Spain was dominated by wealthy men, many of whom intended to return to Spain, many English colonists ventured to America because life in England had grown intolerable for them. Leaders of the Dutch and non-Puritan English colonies, unlike the Spanish and French, welcomed people of many nationalities and religions who came in search of a new life. Perhaps most important, the English colonies enjoyed a greater degree of self-government, which made them more dynamic and innovative than their French and Spanish counterparts.

Throughout the seventeenth century, geography reinforced England's emphasis on concentrated settlements in America. No single great river offered a highway to the interior. The farthest westward expansion of English settlement stopped at the eastern slopes of the Appalachian Mountains. To the east of the mainland colonies lay the Atlantic Ocean, which served as a highway for the transport of people, ideas, commerce, and ways of life from Europe to America. The Atlantic, however, also provided a barrier separating old ideas from new, allowing the English colonies to evolve in new ways while developing new ideas about economic freedom and political liberties that would flower in the eighteenth century.

Reviewing the
CORE OBJECTIVES

- **English Background** England's colonization of North America differed from that of its European rivals. Although chartered by the Royal Crown, English colonization was funded by *joint-stock companies,* groups of proprietors eager for profits. The colonial governments reflected the English model of a two-house *Parliament* and long-held English views on civil liberties and representative institutions. The colonization of the eastern seaboard of North America occurred at a time of religious and political turmoil in England, strongly affecting colonial culture and development.

- **Settling the American Colonies** The early years of Jamestown and Plymouth were grim. The Virginia and Plymouth companies enticed colonists with headrights, or land grants. The *tobacco* economy flourished, but success also initiated a slave-based economy in the South. Sugar and rice plantations developed in the proprietary Carolina colonies, which operated with minimal royal intrusion. Family farms and a mixed economy characterized the middle and New England colonies. Religion was the primary motivation for the founding of several colonies. *Puritans* drafted the *Mayflower Compact* and founded *Massachusetts Bay Colony* as a Christian commonwealth. Rhode Island was established by Roger Williams, a religious dissenter from Massachusetts. Maryland was founded as a refuge for English Catholics. William Penn, a Quaker, founded Pennsylvania and invited Europe's persecuted religious sects to his colony. The Dutch allowed members of all faiths to settle in *New Netherland*, which was surrendered to the English in 1664.

- **Indigenous Relations** Trade with the *Powhatan Confederacy* enabled residents of Jamestown to survive its early years, but armed conflicts such as *Bacon's Rebellion* occurred as settlers invaded Indigenous American lands. Puritans retaliated in the Pequot War of 1636–1637 and *King Philip's War* (1675–1678). Among the chief colonial leaders, only Roger Williams and William Penn treated Indigenous Americans as equals. The powerful *Iroquois League* played the European powers against each other to control territories.

- **Thriving English Colonies** By 1700, English America was the most populous and prosperous region of North America. This prosperity in part was based on its use of, and involvement in the trade of, enslaved workers and indentured servants. Minimal royal interference in the proprietary for-profit colonies, widespread landownership, and religious diversity attracted a variety of investors and settlers.

KEY TERMS

joint-stock companies *p. 56*

Parliament *p. 58*

Puritans *p. 58*

Powhatan Confederacy *p. 61*

tobacco *p. 64*

headright *p. 64*

Mayflower Compact (1620) *p. 70*

Massachusetts Bay Colony *p. 70*

witchcraft hysteria *p. 74*

North and South Carolina *p. 77*

transatlantic slave trade *p. 78*

New Netherland *p. 82*

Bacon's Rebellion (1676) *p. 90*

King Philip's War (1675–1678) *p. 95*

Iroquois League *p. 96*

CHRONOLOGY

1603	James I becomes king of England
1607	Jamestown is established, the first permanent English colony
1612	John Rolfe begins growing tobacco for export
1619	The first enslaved Africans arrive in English America
1620	Plymouth colony is founded by Pilgrims; Mayflower Compact
1622	War between Indigenous people and colonists begins
1630	Massachusetts Bay Colony is founded
1634	The settlement of Maryland begins
1636–1637	Pequot War in New England
1642–1651	English Civil War (Puritans vs. Royalists)
1649	Toleration Act in Maryland
1660	Restoration of English monarchy
1669	Charles Town is founded in the Carolina colony
1675–1678	King Philip's War in New England
1676	Bacon's Rebellion erupts in Virginia
1681	Pennsylvania is established
1692–1693	Salem witch trials
1733	Georgia is founded

InQuizitive

Go to InQuizitive to see what you've learned—and learn what you've missed—with personalized feedback along the way.

THE ARTISANS OF BOSTON (1766) While fishing, shipbuilding, and maritime trade dominated New England economies, many young men entered apprenticeships, learning trades from master craftsmen in the hopes of becoming blacksmiths, carpenters, gunsmiths, printers, candlemakers, leather tanners, and more.

CHAPTER 3

Colonial Ways of Life

1607–1750

The process of establishing a new society on the North American continent involved often-violent encounters among European, African, and Indigenous cultures. War, duplicity, conquest, displacement, and enslavement were the tragic results. On another level, however, the process of transforming the continent was a story of blending and accommodation as well as force and greed; of diverse peoples and cultures engaged in the everyday tasks of building homes, planting crops, trading goods, raising families, enforcing laws, and worshipping their gods. Those who colonized America during the seventeenth and eighteenth centuries were part of a massive social migration occurring throughout Europe and Africa. Everywhere, it seemed, people were in motion—moving from farms to villages; from villages to cities; and from homelands to colonies, plantations, and farms. Some of these people were moving against their will, being transported as captives from Africa to North America or being displaced from their native lands, as the Indigenous Americans were by the colonists.

Most of the Europeans who migrated to America were responding to powerful social and economic forces. Rapid population growth and the rise of commercial agriculture in their home countries squeezed poor farmworkers off the land and into cities, where they struggled to survive. The fact that most Europeans in the seventeenth and eighteenth centuries were desperately

CORE OBJECTIVES

1. Explain the major factors that contributed to the demographic changes in the British American colonies during the eighteenth century.

2. Describe the various roles of White and enslaved women in the British American colonies.

3. Compare the societies and economies of the southern, New England, and middle colonies, and describe the roles of indentured servants, enslaved Indigenous people, and enslaved Africans.

4. Describe the creation of race-based chattel slavery during the seventeenth century and its impact on the social and economic development of colonial America.

5. Analyze the impact of the Enlightenment and Great Awakening on American religious thought during the colonial period.

poor helps explain why so many were willing to risk their lives by journeying to the British American colonies. Others sought political security or religious freedom.

Those who initially settled in colonial America were mostly young (more than half were under age twenty-five), male, and poor, and almost half were indentured servants or enslaved people. During the eighteenth century, England transported some 50,000 convicts to the British colonies to relieve its own overcrowded jails and to address the constant demand for more workers in North America. Once in America, many of the newcomers kept moving in search of better lands or new business opportunities. This extraordinary mosaic of people created America's enduring institutions and values as well as its distinctive spirit and restless energy. It also led to deep conflicts and division.

> CORE **OBJECTIVE**
> 1. Explain the major factors that contributed to the demographic changes in the British American colonies during the eighteenth century.

The Demography of the Early Colonies

The early British American colonial population encompassed several dynamic groups of people. They arrived with different dreams and aspirations, and those who were already there had to make sense of the newcomers. As the population grew, people found ways to interact with one another through social, labor, and prescribed gender roles. Their roles shifted as it became necessary to adapt to an expanding economy and to accommodate new arrivals.

Population Growth

> Rapid population growth

Life in British America was hard. Many of the first colonists died of disease or starvation; others were killed by Indigenous Americans defending their native lands. The average **death rate** was 50 percent. Once colonial life became more settled, however, the population grew rapidly. On average, it doubled every twenty-five years. By 1750, the number of colonists had passed 1 million; by 1775, it approached 2.5 million. In comparison, the combined population of England, Scotland, and Ireland in 1750 was 6.5 million. An English visitor reported in 1766 that America would surely become "the most prosperous empire the world had ever seen." But that would mean trouble for Britain: "How are we to rule them?"

> Scarce laborers and better living conditions

Benjamin Franklin, a keen observer of life in British America, said that the colonial population grew so rapidly because land was plentiful and cheap, and laborers were scarce and costly. In contrast, Europe suffered from overpopulation and expensive farmland. From this reversal of conditions flowed many of the changes that European culture underwent during the colonization of America—not the least being that land and good fortune lured enterprising immigrants and led the colonists to have large families, in part because farm children could help work in the fields.

death rate The proportion of deaths per 1,000 of the total population; also called *mortality rate*.

Birth and Death Rates

Colonists tended to marry and start families at an earlier age than was common in Europe. In England, the average age at marriage for women was twenty-five or twenty-six; in America, it was twenty. The **birth rate** rose accordingly, since women who married earlier had time for about two additional pregnancies during their childbearing years. On average, a married woman had a child every two to three years before menopause. Some women had as many as twenty pregnancies. Abiah Folger, Benjamin Franklin's mother, for example, bore sixteen children; his grandmother Mary Folger had seventeen.

Birthing children was dangerous, however, since most babies were delivered at home—and often in unsanitary conditions. Miscarriages were common. Between 25 and 50 percent of women died during childbirth or soon thereafter, and almost a quarter of all babies did not survive infancy, especially during the early stages of a colonial settlement.

Disease and epidemics were common. Half of the children born in Virginia and Maryland died before reaching age twenty. Boston minister Cotton Mather lost eight of fifteen children in their first year of life. Martha Custis, the Virginia widow who married George Washington, had four children during her first marriage. They all died young, at ages two, three, sixteen, and seventeen. Over time, however, infants and adults began to live longer in the colonies than in Europe.

Lower mortality rates resulted from several factors. Because fertile land was plentiful, famine seldom occurred after the early years of colonization; and although American winters were more severe than those in England, firewood was abundant. Being younger (the average age in 1790 was sixteen), Americans were less susceptible to disease than were Europeans. The fact that people in America were more scattered than people in Europe also meant they were less exposed to infectious diseases. That fact of life began to change as colonial cities grew larger and more densely populated. By the mid-eighteenth century, the colonies experienced levels of disease much like that in Europe.

Immigrants and Citizenship

High rates of immigration from Europe to the British American colonies across the eighteenth century continued to drive the overall population upward. To sustain high levels of immigration, in 1740 Parliament passed the Naturalization Act. It announced that immigrants living in America for

COLONIAL FARM This plan of a newly cleared farm shows how trees were cut and the stumps left to rot.

birth rate The proportion of births per 1,000 of the total population.

Naturalization Act (1740)

MARTHA CUSTIS WASHINGTON AND ABIAH FOLGER FRANKLIN Children's birth rates were high in British America, as were infant death rates. Many women also died during childbirth or due to complications from it. Martha Custis Washington (*pictured right*) gave birth to four children during her first marriage, all four of whom died before the age of twenty. Abiah Folger Franklin (*pictured left*), the mother of Benjamin Franklin, bore sixteen children.

seven years would become subjects of the British Empire after swearing a loyalty oath and providing proof that they were Protestants. While excluding "papists" (a disparaging term for Roman Catholics), the law did make exceptions for Jews.

Nativism

Nativism—a prejudice against particular groups of immigrants—emerged in the colonies as the population grew. For example, as the number of desperately poor Irish immigrants soared, so, too, did prejudice against them. In 1726, Benjamin Franklin, then twenty years old, watched as a shipload of Irish immigrants disembarked in New York City. He wondered how the more affluent passengers could have put up with being "confined and stifled up with such a lousy, stinking rabble."

Still, the Irish and Scots-Irish kept coming. An Irish immigrant in New York wrote home to his minister, urging him to "tell all the poor folk . . . that God has opened a door for their deliverance" in America. (*Scotch-Irish* is the more common but inaccurate name for the Scots-Irish, the mostly Presbyterian population that the British government transplanted from Scotland to the northern Ireland province of Ulster to "protestant-ize" Catholic Ireland.)

As another example, although Pennsylvania was founded as a haven for all European people, by the mid-eighteenth century concerns arose about the influx of Germans. Franklin feared that they would "soon outnumber us" and be a source of constant tension. Why, he asked, "should Pennsylvania, founded by the English, become a Colony of Aliens?" He was "not against the admission of Germans in general, for they have their Virtues," but he urged that they be spread across the colonies so as not to become a majority anywhere.

Overall, the demographic changes in the colonies during the eighteenth century reflected a combination of factors. Population growth increased through the lure of cheap land, which attracted more immigrants, and through a high birth rate. At the same time, the death rate gradually dropped, a result of fewer famines and the robustness of the mostly young colonists, who were less susceptible to disease. As the population expanded with many poor immigrants seeking better opportunities, colonists developed prejudice against some groups.

Women in the Colonies

In comparison to New Spain and New France, British America had far more women. But more women did not mean greater equality. As a New England minister argued, "The woman is a weak creature not endowed with [the] strength and constancy of mind [of men]."

White women, as had been true for centuries, were expected to focus on "housewifery," or the "domestic sphere." They were to obey and serve their husbands, nurture their children, and maintain their households. Governor John Winthrop of the Massachusetts Bay Colony insisted that a "true wife" would find contentment only "in subjection to her husband's authority."

Women in most colonies could not vote, own property, hold office, attend schools or colleges, bring lawsuits, sign contracts, or become ministers. Divorces were allowed only for desertion or "cruel and barbarous treatment." No matter who was named the "guilty party," the father received custody of the children.

An overall shortage of women in the early years of colonial settlement made them more highly valued in British America than in Europe. The Puritan emphasis on a well-ordered family life led to laws protecting wives from physical abuse and—in some cases—allowing for divorce. Yet the age-old notion of female subordination and domesticity remained firmly entrenched. In fact, any money earned by a married woman became the legal property of her husband.

> **CORE OBJECTIVE**
> **2.** Describe the various roles of White and enslaved women in the British American colonies.

"Women's Work"

Virtually every member of a colonial household worked, and the expectations for women—especially enslaved women—were extensive. As John Cotton, a Boston minister, admitted in 1699, "Women are creatures without which there is no Comfortable living for a man."

In the eighteenth century, **women's work** typically centered on activities in the house, garden, and fields. Farm women usually rose by sunrise. They fed and watered the livestock, cared for the children, tended the garden, prepared lunch (the main meal) and dinner, milked the cows, and cleaned the kitchen before retiring soon after dark. (In fact, the greatest accidental killer of women was the open-hearth kitchen fires that ignited long dresses.) Most colonial women—not just farm women—also spun wool for clothing, knitted linen and cotton, pieced quilts, made candles and soap, chopped wood, mopped floors, and washed clothes.

women's work A traditional term referring to labor in the house, garden, and fields performed by women; eventually expanded in the colonies to include medicine, shopkeeping, upholstering, and the operation of inns and taverns.

THE FIRST, SECOND, AND LAST SCENE OF MORTALITY Prudence Punderson's needlework (ca. 1776) shows the domestic path, from cradle to coffin, followed by most colonial women. Her needlework depicts an affluent home with elaborate furniture and an enslaved laborer.

Many unmarried White women moved into other households to help with children or to make clothes. Others took in children or spun thread into yarn to exchange for cloth. Still others hired themselves out as apprentices to learn a skilled trade or craft, or operated laundries or bakeries. White women who failed to perform household work were punished as if they were servants or enslaved. According to town records of Salem, Massachusetts, in 1643 a woman named Margaret Page was jailed "for being a lazy, idle, loitering person." In Virginia, a female indentured servant was forced to work in the tobacco fields even though she was ill. She died in a furrow, with a hoe still in her hands.

Prostitution was one of the most lucrative businesses among colonial women who could not find other work. Port cities had thriving brothels. They catered to sailors and soldiers, but men from all walks of life frequented what were called "bawdy houses," or, in Puritan Boston, "disorderly houses." Local authorities frowned on these "loose women." In Massachusetts, convicted prostitutes were stripped to the waist, tied to the back of a horse-drawn cart, and whipped as it moved through town.

Some enslaved women whose owners expected sexual favors turned the tables by demanding compensation. The sexual exploitation of enslaved women was extensive, yet there were no legal protections for them.

Enslaved Women Enslaved women worked from before sunrise to after dark. Depending on the location, season, and labor setting, some were on call twenty-four hours per day. In domestic settings, they attended to every aspect of their enslavers' lives: cooking; housekeeping; running errands; tending to gardens; and serving as seamstresses, ironers, and laundresses. As body servants, they tied women's corsets, brushed their hair, gave them baths, and nursed their children. Enslaved women's work did not end at bedtime. Some were expected to sleep in their enslaver's rooms at the foot of their beds. In the middle of the night enslaved women and girls fanned flies, provided fresh glasses of water or hot cups of tea, and were at their enslaver's beck and call.

Ona Judge, the enslaved seamstress to Martha Washington, served the first president and his wife in these capacities. In an interview given years after she escaped, she stated that she'd left the Washingtons while they were eating dinner. She claimed that she'd had to leave; otherwise, she would "never get my liberty." Thus, even enslaved women who worked in the president's residence, those who dressed in fine clothing and labored indoors, desired liberty in early America.

Enslaved women in agricultural settings cultivated crops such as tobacco, cotton, sugar, wheat, corn, potatoes, and other vegetables. Their days began in the dark, as they went to the fields between 4:00 and 5:00 A.M. They worked until about 9:00 P.M. during the summer months and about 7:00 P.M. in the winter months. Some of this was backbreaking labor in challenging climates. Their labor supported White families, particularly those wealthy enough to afford enslaved laborers.

Eliza Lucas Pinckney and Plantation Management On occasion, circumstances forced women to exercise leadership outside the home. Such was the case with South Carolinian Elizabeth ("Eliza") Lucas Pinckney (1722–1793). Born in the West Indies, raised on the island of Antigua, and educated in England, Eliza moved to Charles Town (later renamed Charleston), South Carolina, when her father, George Lucas, a British army officer, inherited three plantations. The following year, however, he was called back to Antigua, leaving Eliza to manage three plantations with about eighty-six enslaved people.

Eliza loved the "vegetable world" and focused on growing *indigo*, a West Indian weed that produced a blue dye that was highly desired for coloring fabric, especially military uniforms. Indigo made Eliza's family a fortune, as it did for many other Carolina plantation owners. Enslaved people on her family's estates were responsible for every phase of indigo production, from planting to harvesting, and building and maintaining the vats used during the harvesting process. They picked the plants three times during the year; soaked the harvest in vats with boiling water; then beat the water until the grains thickened, producing a beautiful blue hue that stained the hands of every worker.

In 1744, Eliza married Charles Pinckney, a wealthy widower, who was a leader of the South Carolina Assembly. She vowed that she would continue to manage her plantations. Fourteen years later, Charles died of malaria. Now a thirty-six-year-old widow, Eliza responded by adding her husband's plantations to her responsibilities. Eliza Pinckney demonstrated the possibility of White women breaking out of the confining tradition of housewifery and subordination and assuming roles of social prominence and economic leadership—work that was accomplished with the help of an enslaved workforce.

Women and Religion

During the colonial era, no religious denomination allowed women to be ordained as ministers. Puritans cited biblical passages claiming that God required "virtuous" women to submit to male authority and remain silent in congregational matters. Women who challenged ministerial authority were usually punished. Yet by the eighteenth century, as is true today, most church members were women.

In the British American colonies, the religious roles of Black women were different from those of their White counterparts. In most West African societies, women served as priestesses and religious practitioners. Although some enslaved Africans came from societies that practiced Christianity well before European colonization, others practiced Orthodox Islam. Many sustained their African religious traditions after arriving in the colonies, even when they were often prohibited from doing so. In America, Black women (and men) were generally excluded from church membership for fear that Christianized enslaved people might seek to gain their freedom by citing and quoting religious doctrine.

In sum, despite the early settlers' beliefs about women's unequal status, the role that women played contributed to the stability of family life and social relations in the colonies. Women's work primarily involved doing household tasks, though some women took on other roles when necessary—as when a husband died. Enslaved women provided labor for wealthy families and preserved their African religious traditions by supporting their own families to the extent that their forced labor allowed.

ELIZABETH LUCAS PINCKNEY'S DRESS This rare sack-back gown made of eighteenth-century silk has been restored and is displayed at the Charleston Museum in South Carolina. *(Courtesy of The Charleston Museum, Charleston, South Carolina, www.charlestonmuseum.org)*

CORE OBJECTIVE

3. Compare the societies and economies of the southern, New England, and middle colonies, and describe the roles of indentured servants, enslaved Indigenous people, and enslaved Africans.

Society and Economy in the Colonies

The British American colonies were part of a complex North Atlantic commercial network. Companies, merchants, and farmers traded sugar, wheat, tobacco, rum, rice, and many other commodities, including enslaved Africans and Native Americans, with Great Britain and its highly profitable island colonies in the West Indies—Bermuda, Barbados, and Jamaica.

In addition, American merchants traded (smuggled) with Spain, France, Portugal, Holland, and their colonies, which were often at war with Britain and therefore officially off-limits. Out of necessity, the colonists were dependent on Britain and Europe for manufactured goods and luxury items such as wine, glass, and jewelry.

The early British American colonies needed to produce a steady output of goods to sustain their role in the commercial exchanges. Environmental, social, and economic factors contributed to the diversity of commodities they were able to trade. So did the availability of labor.

indentured servants Settlers who signed on for a temporary period of servitude to a master in exchange for passage to the New World.

Indentured Servitude and Indigenous Slavery

During the seventeenth century, the English colonies and their trade networks grew so fast that they needed many more workers than there were settlers.

Indentured Servitude

To solve the labor shortage, the planters first recruited **indentured servants** from England, Ireland, Scotland, and continental Europe. The term derived from the *indenture*, or contract, that enabled a person to pay for passage to America by promising to work for a fixed number of years (usually between three and seven).

> Rising inequality and a slave-based economy in the South

Of the 500,000 English immigrants to America from 1610 to 1775, some 350,000 came as indentured servants. However, not all servants came voluntarily. Many homeless children in London were "kid-napped" and sold into servitude in America. Also, Parliament decided it could save money on prisons by shipping felons to the colonies, and as a result some 50,000 were transported to North America.

Once in the colonies, servants were provided with food and a bed, but life was harsh. Many of them died before their term of indenture ended. Servants also had few rights. As a Pennsylvania judge explained in 1793, indentured servants occupied "a middle rank between slaves and free men." They could own property but could not engage in trade. Marriage required the master's permission. Masters could whip servants and extend their length of service as punishment for bad behavior. Elizabeth Sprigs, a servant in Maryland, told of her "toiling day and night, and then [being] tied up and whipped to that degree you would not beat an animal." Servants, unlike enslaved Africans, could file a complaint with the local court.

INDENTURED SERVANTS An advertisement from the *Virginia Gazette*, October 4, 1779, publicizing the upcoming sale of indentured servants. *(Earl Gregg Swem Library, Special Collections Research Center, William & Mary Libraries)*

The most important difference between servanthood and slavery was that the former did not last a lifetime. Once the indenture ended, the servant could claim the "freedom dues" set by custom and law: a little money, a few tools, some clothing and food, and—in some cases—small tracts of land. Some former servants did very well. In 1629, the Virginia legislature included seven members who had arrived in America as indentured servants; by 1637, fifteen former indentured servants were serving in the Maryland Assembly. Such opportunities were much less common in Europe, giving people even more reason to travel to America.

The Trade in Enslaved Native Americans

At the same time that they benefited from contractual arrangements with indentured servants, English colonists in Carolina developed a profitable trade with—and in—Indigenous people.

> Enslavement of Indigenous Peoples

By 1690, traders from Charles Town had made their way up the Savannah River to arrange deals with the Cherokee, Creek, and Chickasaw. Between 1699 and 1712, when Carolina was divided into two colonies, North and South, traders exported to England an average of 54,000 deerskins per year. The valuable hides were transformed into leather gloves, belts, hats, work aprons, and book bindings.

The growing trade in deerskins entwined Indigenous people in a dependent relationship with Europeans that would ultimately prove disastrous to the traditional Indigenous way of life. Beyond seizing and enslaving Indigenous people, English traders provided firearms and rum as payment to Indigenous leaders who sold into slavery any people they captured during wars with rival nations.

The profitability of captive Native Americans prompted a frenzy of slaving activity among English settlers. In Carolina, as many as 50,000 Indigenous people, mostly women and children, were sold into slavery in Charles Town between 1670 and 1715. Thousands more were sold to "slavers" who took them to Caribbean islands.

The growing trade in enslaved Native Americans triggered bitter struggles between rival Indigenous nations and generated massive internal migrations across the southern colonies.

Yamasee Warfare

The Yamasee peoples in Carolina felt betrayed when White traders paid them less than they wanted for the Tuscarora that were captured during recent warfare. What made this shortfall so acute was that the Yamasee owed debts to traders totaling 100,000 deerskins. To recover their debts, White traders cheated the Yamasee, confiscated their lands, and began enslaving their women and children. In April 1715, the Yamasee attacked coastal plantations and killed more than 100 Whites.

> Yamasee peoples resist colonial slave traders

Subsequently, the governor mobilized all White and Black men to defend the colony; other colonies supplied weapons. But it wasn't until the governor bribed the Cherokee to join them that the Yamasee War ended—in 1717. The defeated Yamasee fled to Spanish-controlled Florida. By then, hundreds of Whites had been killed and dozens of plantations destroyed and abandoned. To prevent another conflict, the colonial government outlawed all private trading with Native Americans.

By the early eighteenth century, however, traders in the Carolinas would come to prefer enslaved Africans over enslaved Native Americans.

staple crops Profitable market crops, such as cotton, tobacco, and rice, that predominate in a region.

Similarities and Differences among the British Colonies

As the British colonies in North America began to mature, they developed cultures that shared some features in common—but also reflected substantial differences.

The Southern Colonies

In the southern colonies, inequalities of wealth and status became more visible. The use of enslaved Indigenous and African people to grow tobacco, sugar cane, rice, and indigo generated enormous wealth for a few landowners. Socially, the planters and merchants became a class apart from the "common folk"—dominating the legislatures, buying luxury goods from London and Paris, and building brick mansions with formal gardens.

> Inequalities of wealth in southern colonies

Warm weather and plentiful rainfall helped the southern colonies grow the profitable **staple crops** valued by Great Britain. Tobacco production soared. "In Virginia and Maryland," wrote a royal official in 1629, "tobacco . . . is our All, and indeed leaves no room for anything else." So much tobacco was grown in Virginia that the royal governor in 1616 passed Dale's Laws (named for Virginia's first governor, Thomas Dale) requiring every farmer to plant at least two acres of corn to ensure an adequate food supply.

The growing of rice also expanded dramatically. By 1700, South Carolina was exporting 400,000 pounds of rice each year; by 1768, some 66 *million* pounds of rice were shipped to Great Britain and northern Europe. Rice accounted for more than half of the colony's exports during the eighteenth century.

Over time, South Carolina rice planters became the wealthiest group in the British colonies. They situated their plantations along coastal rivers so they could use barges to transport rice to nearby ports for shipment to Europe. As rice plantations grew, the demand for enslaved laborers rose dramatically, for White colonists balked at working long hours in "mud and water." Almost 90 percent of the enslaved Africans transported to America were sold into the southern colonies. South Carolina had a majority Black population.

VIRGINIA PLANTATION WHARF Southern colonial plantations were often constructed along rivers, with easy access to ocean-going vessels, as shown on this 1730 tobacco label. **How does this illustration represent the rigid race and class system of the southern colonies?**

New England

> New England townships

New England was quite different from the southern and middle Atlantic regions. Religious concerns outweighed all else. Commercial agriculture was almost nonexistent because of the rocky soil and frigid climate, so traders and shopkeepers predominated. Village and town life was much less reliant on plantation slavery, yet local economies grew profitable from participating in the transatlantic slave trade and producing goods such as the shoes and clothing worn by the enslaved. The New England economy thrived off of slavery in different ways than their southern counterparts did.

Puritan Religion Whenever Puritans founded towns, the first public structure to be built was usually a church. The Puritans believed that God had created a *covenant*, or contract, through which people formed a congregation for common worship. This led to the idea of people joining together to form governments. Puritan leaders, however, also sought to do the will of God, and the ultimate source of authority for them was not majority rule of the members but rather the Bible, as interpreted by ministers and magistrates (political leaders).

> Close relationship between church and state

By law, every town had to collect taxes to support a church, and every resident—church member or not—was required to attend midweek and Sunday religious services. The average New Englander heard more than 7,000 sermons in a lifetime.

Although the Puritans had left England and sailed to America with the goal of creating pious, prosperous communities, the traditional caricature of dour, black-clothed Puritans is false. Yes, they banned card-playing, dancing in taverns, swearing, and bowling. They fined people for celebrating Christmas, for in their view only pagans marked the birth date of their rulers with merrymaking. Puritans also frowned on hurling insults, disobeying parents, and disrespecting civil and religious officials. In 1631, a servant named Phillip Ratcliffe had both of his ears cut off for making scandalous comments about the governor and the church in Salem.

Yet Puritans also wore colorful clothing, enjoyed secular music, and consumed prodigious quantities of beer and rum. "Drink is in itself a good creature of God," said the Reverend Increase Mather, "but the abuse of drink is from Satan." Drunks were arrested, and repeat offenders were forced to wear the letter *D* in public.

Moderation was the Puritan guideline, and it applied to sexual life as well. Although sexual activity outside of marriage was strictly

HOUSING IN COLONIAL NEW ENGLAND This frame house, built in the 1670s, belonged to Rebecca Nurse, one of the women hanged as a witch in Salem Village in 1692.

forbidden, New England courts overflowed with cases of adultery and illicit sex. A man found guilty of sleeping with an unwed woman could be jailed, whipped, fined, and forced to marry the woman. Female offenders were also punished, and judges required adulterers to wear the letter *A*.

Over time, growing numbers of children and grandchildren of the original members drifted away from Puritanism and could not give the required testimony of spiritual conversion. Another blow to Puritan ideals came with the Massachusetts royal charter of 1691, which required the Puritan colony to "tolerate" religious dissenters (such as Quakers; see chapter 2).

Dwellings and Daily Life The first colonists in New England built simple wood-frame houses, with steeply pitched roofs to reduce the buildup of snow. Not until the eighteenth century were the exteriors of most houses painted, usually a deep "Indian" red, as the colonists called it. The interiors were dark and illuminated by candles or oil lamps, both of which were expensive; most people usually went to sleep soon after sunset.

There were no bathrooms (called privies at the time). Family life revolved around the main room on the ground floor, called the hall, where meals were cooked in a fireplace and where the family spent most of their time.

Food was served at a table of rough-hewn planks, called the board, and the only eating utensils were spoons and fingers. The father was sometimes referred to as the "chair man" because he sat in the only chair (the origin of the term *chairman of the board*). The rest of the family usually stood, or sat on stools or benches. A typical meal consisted of corn, boiled meat, and vegetables washed down with beer, cider, rum, or milk. Cornbread was a daily favorite.

Economy In 1630, as John Winthrop and the Puritans had prepared to embark for New England, he had stressed that God made some people powerful and rich and others helpless and poor—so that the elite would show mercy and the masses would offer obedience. He reminded the Puritans that all were given a noble "calling" by God to work hard and ensure that material pursuits never diminished the importance of spiritual devotion. This was the perspective under which New England colonial society was established.

Early New England farmers and their families led hard lives. The growing season was short, and the crops and livestock were those familiar to the English countryside: wheat, barley, oats; with some cattle, pigs, and sheep.

Many New Englanders turned to the sea for their livelihood: the waters off the New England coast had the heaviest concentrations of cod in the world. Whales supplied ambergris, a waxy substance used in the

PROFITABLE FISHERIES The rich fishing grounds of the North Atlantic provided New Englanders with a prosperous industry for centuries. Pictured here are scenes of fishing for, curing, and drying cod in Newfoundland in the early 1700s. **Who provided the labor for northern fisheries?**

triangular trade A network of trade in which exports from one region were sold to a second region; the second sent its exports to a third region, which exported its own goods back to the first country or colony. The term most often applies to the transatlantic slave trade of the seventeenth and early eighteenth centuries.

"Triangular" trade networks

manufacture of perfumes and lubrications; the colonists also burned it as lamp oil. New Englanders exported dried fish to Europe, with lesser grades going to the West Indies as food for enslaved laborers. The thriving fishing industry encouraged the development of shipbuilding and spurred transatlantic commerce. Rising incomes and a booming trade with Britain and Europe soon brought a taste for luxury goods that clashed with the Puritan ideal of plain living and spiritual thinking.

Trade in New England differed from that in the South in one important respect—the lack of agricultural staple crops to exchange for English goods put the northern region at a relative disadvantage (though the success of shipping and commercial enterprises worked in their favor). Between 1698 and 1717, New England and New York bought more from England than they exported to it, thereby creating an unfavorable balance of trade.

These circumstances gave rise to the **triangular trade.** New England merchants shipped rum to the western coast of Africa, where it was exchanged for captured and enslaved Africans. Ships then took the captive Africans to profitable Caribbean islands to sell. (The islands were profitable because of their sugar plantations, which produced highly desired raw sugar and molasses.) The ships returned home with various commodities, including molasses, from which New Englanders manufactured rum. In another version of the triangular trade, shippers sent foodstuffs to the Caribbean islands, carried sugar and molasses to England, and returned with goods manufactured in Europe (see Map 3.1).

The Middle Colonies

Both geographically and culturally, the middle colonies (New York, New Jersey, Pennsylvania, Delaware, and Maryland) stood between New England and the South. As such, they more completely reflected the diversity of colonial life and more fully foreshadowed the pluralism of America.

In the makeup of their population, the middle colonies differed from New England's Puritan settlements and the plantation colonies in the South. In New York and New Jersey, Dutch culture and language lingered. Along the Delaware River near Philadelphia, the first settlers—Swedes and Finns—were overwhelmed by an influx of Europeans. By the mid-eighteenth century, the middle colonies were the fastest-growing region in North America. Pennsylvania became the great distribution point for the ethnic groups of European origin. Germans came to America (primarily to Pennsylvania) mainly from the Rhineland region of Europe, where brutal religious wars had pitted Protestants against Catholics. William Penn's recruiting brochures circulated throughout central Europe, and his promise of religious freedom

WILLIAM PENN In this eighteenth-century engraving, William Penn welcomes a German immigrant to Philadelphia. **What factors in Europe brought so many Germans to Pennsylvania in the eighteenth century?**

MAP 3.1 ATLANTIC TRADE ROUTES, 1600–1800

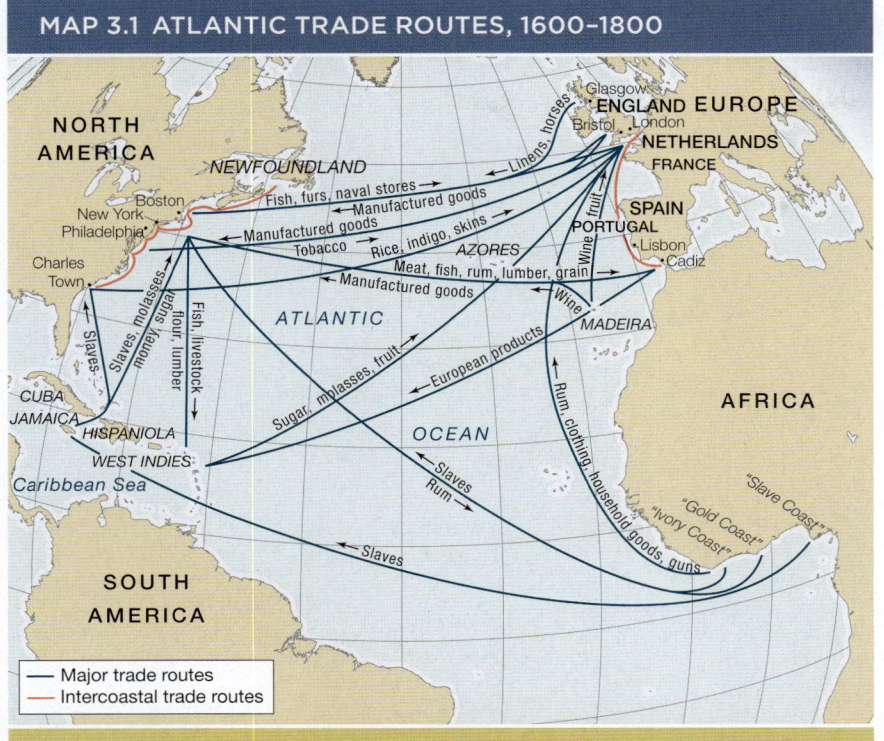

- Count the number of major trade routes shown on the map. Where do they cluster most densely? Why?
- Make a list of every commodity shipped along the trade routes. Which three commodities are listed most often? Where do they originate, and where do they go?
- Based on your understanding of the chapter text, what made this trade triangular and what were the three parts of the trade?

appealed to members of many persecuted sects—especially the Mennonites, German Baptists whose beliefs resembled those of the Quakers.

Throughout the eighteenth century, a quarter-million Scots-Irish immigrants moved still farther out into the Pennsylvania backcountry. Plentiful land in America was the great magnet for the cash-poor Scots-Irish, most of whom were farmworkers eager "to have land for nothing" and "unwilling to be disappointed." In most cases, the lands they "squatted on" were the ancestral grounds claimed by Native Americans. In 1741, for example, a group of Delaware people protested that the Scots-Irish were taking "our land" without giving "us anything for it." If the colonial government did not stop the flow of Whites, the Delaware people threatened, they would "drive them off." In the end, the Scots-Irish continued to migrate to this region.

The Scots-Irish and Germans became the largest non-English ethnic groups in the colonies (see Map 3.2). Other ethnic minorities also enriched the population: Huguenots (French Protestants whose religious freedom had been revoked in 1685, forcing many to leave France), Irish, Welsh, Swiss, and Jews. New York had inherited from the Dutch a tradition of ethnic and

> Ethnic diversity in the middle colonies

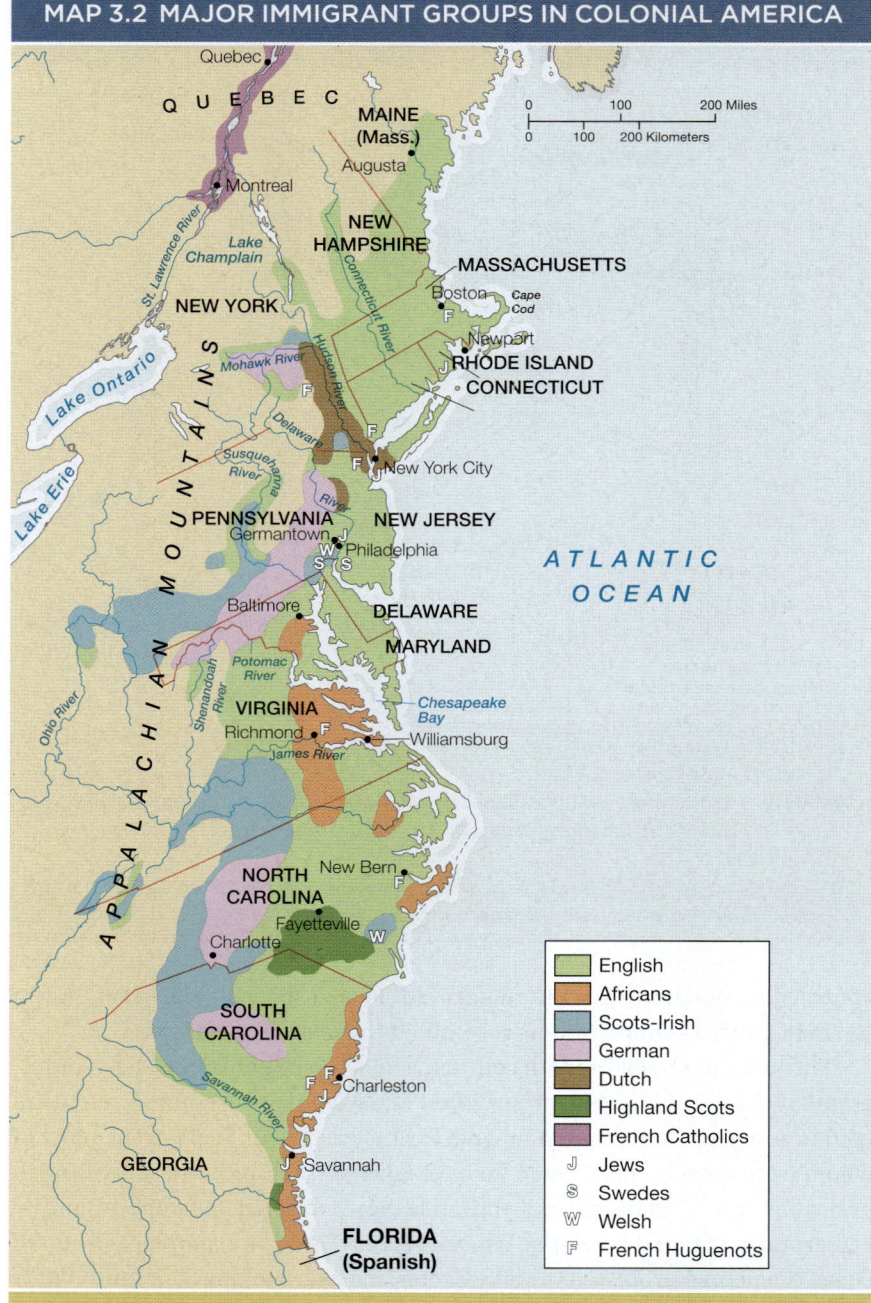

MAP 3.2 MAJOR IMMIGRANT GROUPS IN COLONIAL AMERICA

- Judging from the map, what geographical feature kept most immigrant groups from settling far from coastal areas? Which group settled the farthest west?
- After examining the map key, name the one group that would not be considered willing immigrants. Identify its locations on the map. Within which other immigrant group's settlements was it located? Explain why.
- According to this map and the chapter text, in what ways did the middle colonies foreshadow the diversity of the future nation?

religious tolerance, which had given the colony a diverse population: French-speaking Walloons (a Celtic people of southern Belgium), French, Germans, Danes, Portuguese, Spaniards, Italians, Bohemians, Poles, and others, including some New England Puritans.

Before the mid-eighteenth century, White settlers in the Pennsylvania backcountry had reached the Appalachian Mountains. A British official described these colonists as natural wanderers who "forever imagine the lands further off are still better than those upon which they are already settled." Rather than crossing the steep mountain ridges, the Scots-Irish and Germans filtered southward. Germans were the first White settlers in the Upper Shenandoah Valley in southern Pennsylvania, western Maryland, and northern Virginia, and the Scots-Irish filled the lower valley in western Virginia and North Carolina (see again Map 3.2).

In the eighteenth century, the population in British North America soared and the colonies grew more diverse. In 1790, the White population was 61 percent English; 14 percent Scottish and Scots-Irish; 9 percent German; 5 percent Dutch, French, and Swedish; 4 percent Irish; and 7 percent "unidentifiable"—a category that included people of mixed origins as well as free Blacks. If one adds to the 3,172,444 Whites in the 1790 census the 756,770 non-Whites (without even considering the almost 100,000 Native Americans who went uncounted), only about half of the nation's inhabitants, and perhaps fewer, could trace their origins to England—thus revealing the increasing ethnic and cultural diversity of the British North American colonies.

Colonial Society: A Slave Society

The transport of African captives, mostly young men, across the Atlantic to the Americas was the largest forced migration in world history. Overall, Europeans transported 12.5 million enslaved Africans to communities in North and South America and the Caribbean (see Map 3.3). Of these, at least 15 percent died in transit. The majority were delivered to Portuguese Brazil (5.5 million) and the Caribbean "sugar" islands—Barbados, Cuba, Jamaica, and others (5 million). There the heat, humidity, and rigorous labor shortened the life expectancy of enslaved workers.

By 1700, there were enslaved Africans in every colony, and they made up 11 percent of the total population (20 percent by 1770). Slavery in English North America differed significantly from region to region, however. Africans were a tiny minority in New England (about 2 percent). Because the soil was not as fertile as in the South and could not sustain large plantations, slavery in New England prevailed in small settings where both enslavers and the enslaved often lived under the same roof.

Slavery was much more common in the Chesapeake colonies and the Carolinas, where large plantations dominated. By 1750, for example,

MAP 3.3 THE AFRICAN SLAVE TRADE, 1500–1800

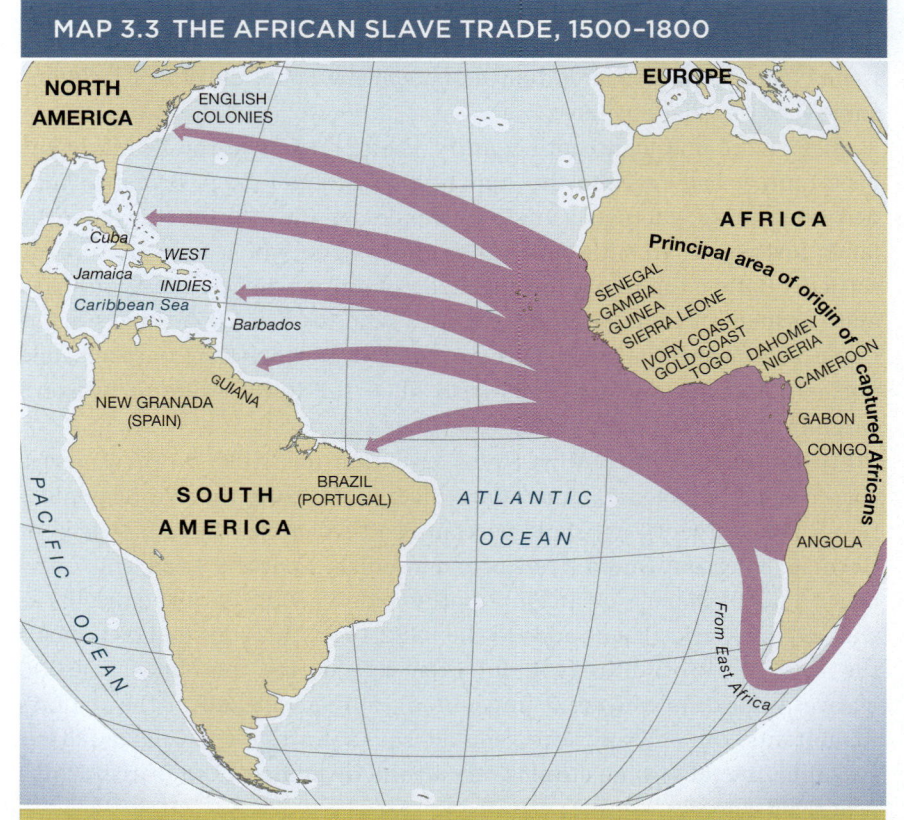

- Looking at the map of Africa, locate the principal area where captured Africans originated. Was it along the coast or farther inland?
- Based on the chapter text, explain how Africans were captured and enslaved, and describe the conditions they endured on the Middle Passage.
- Looking at the map, identify the destinations of the enslaved Africans. According to the chapter text, why did those areas want their forced labor?

about 80 percent of the enslaved Black people in the Chesapeake region had been born there.

African Roots and the Middle Passage

Enslaved Africans came from all over the African continent (see again Map 3.3), spoke as many as fifty distinct languages, and worshipped diverse gods. Some came from large kingdoms such as Ghana, Songhai, and Mali; while others came from smaller, dispersed villages. In their homelands, warfare was as common as it was in Europe: rival nations conquered, kidnapped, and traded their prisoners of war.

Slavery in Africa, however, did not involve treating humans as a form of property. Rather, captured people lived with their captors, and their children were not automatically enslaved. The involvement of Europeans in transatlantic slavery, whereby captives were sold and shipped to other nations, is a different and more complex story. And it is a story that involved many European nations: Sweden, Denmark, France, Great Britain, the Netherlands, Spain, and Portugal.

During the seventeenth and eighteenth centuries, Europeans worked with African slave traders to bring captives to fortifications built along the West African coast. Few of the captives had ever seen the ocean, a sailing ship, or a White person. After languishing as prisoners for weeks or months, the captured Africans would be led to waiting ships owned by European slave traders. As one of them remembered, "it was a most horrible scene; there was nothing to be heard but rattling of chains, smacking of whips, and groans and cries of our fellow men."

Once purchased, the millions destined for slavery in the Americas and the Caribbean islands were branded on the back, buttocks, or shoulder with a company mark, put in chains, and loaded onto mostly British-owned ships. Forced to stay below deck in constant darkness, they were chained together on top of one another with no room to move or stand. They slept in their own and others' urine and excrement. Only occasionally were they allowed to go above deck for fresh air.

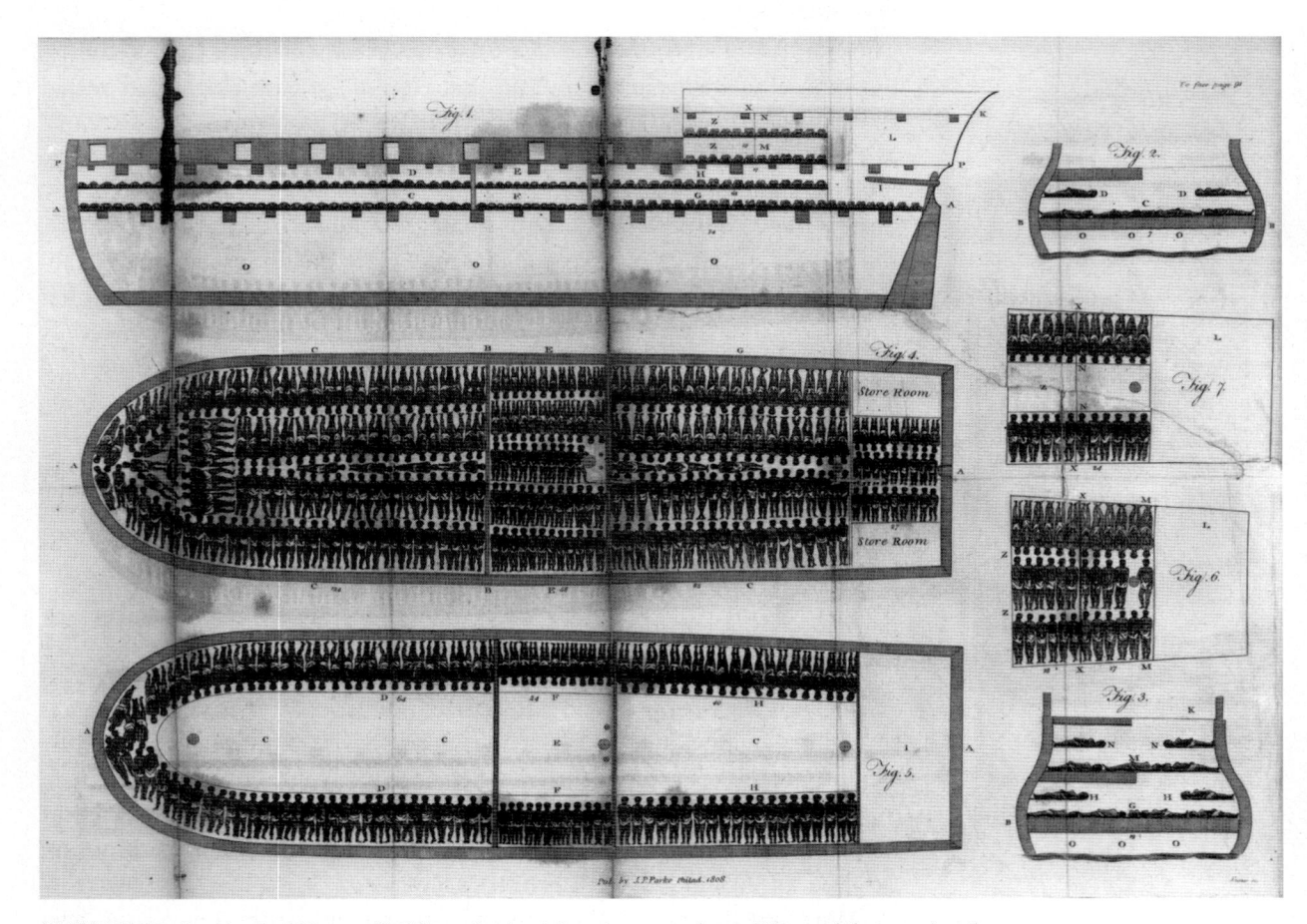

SLAVE SHIP One in six Africans died from the brutal and cramped conditions while crossing the Atlantic in ships like this one, from an American diagram ca. 1808.

Middle Passage The hellish and often deadly middle leg of the transatlantic "triangular trade" in which European ships carried manufactured goods to Africa, then transported enslaved Africans to the Americas and the Caribbean islands, and finally conveyed American agricultural products back to Europe.

The transatlantic voyage of the slave ships, which could last up to six months, was known as the **Middle Passage** because it served as the middle leg of the triangular trade. On the first leg, European ships carried rum, clothing, household goods, and guns to Africa, which they exchanged for enslaved Africans. The captives then were taken on the second (or "middle") leg of the triangular trade to the Americas. Once the human cargo was unloaded, the ships were filled with lumber, tobacco, rice, sugar, rum, and other products for the third voyage to English and European ports (see again Map 3.1).

The Middle Passage was horrific. One in six African captives died along the way. Almost one in ten of these floating prisons (as contemporary historians describe them) experienced a slave revolt. Some captives committed suicide by jumping off the ships; others starved themselves and refused to eat. Yet many of the English businessmen involved in human trafficking considered their work highly respectable. "What a glorious and advantageous trade this is," wrote slave trader James Houston. "It is the hinge on which all the trade of this globe moves."

Africans as Property

Those in the business of trading enslaved Africans justified their activities by embracing a widespread racism that viewed Africans as animals rather than human beings. Once they arrived in America, Africans were treated as property (chattel), herded in chains to public auctions, and sold to the highest bidder.

On large southern plantations that grew tobacco, sugarcane, or rice, the enslaved laborers worked in gangs and were often housed in crude cabins, fed like livestock out of horse troughs, and issued poor-quality clothes and shoes. To ensure that they worked hard and did not cause trouble, they were whipped, branded, shackled, castrated, sexually abused, or sold away, often to the Caribbean islands where few survived the harsh working conditions.

> Resistance of enslaved Africans

Enslaved Africans, however, found ways to resist. Some rebelled by refusing work orders, sabotaging crops, stealing tools, faking illness or injury, or running away. If caught, the freedom seekers faced certain punishment. But if successful, runaways also faced uncertain freedom. Where would they run *to* in a society ruled by Whites and permeated by racism?

Slave Culture

In the process of being forced into lives of bondage in a new world, Africans from diverse homelands forged a new identity as African Americans. At the same time, they wove into American culture many strands of their African heritage. These included new words that entered the language, such as *tabby, tote, goober, yam,* and *banana,* as well as the names of the Coosaw, Pee Dee, and Wando Rivers in South Carolina.

More significant are their lasting African influences upon American music, folklore, and religious practices. Enslaved men and women often used songs, stories, and religious preaching to circulate coded messages expressing their distaste for their owners. The fundamental theme of their hybrid religion, adapted from the Christianity they were forced to embrace, was deliverance. God, many of them believed, would eventually open the gates to heaven's promised land.

No matter where in the colonies enslaved Africans lived, their labor—and that of indentured servants—contributed to a thriving trading economy that characterized this period. The demand for forced labor on Caribbean sugar plantations, as well as on rice, tobacco, and indigo plantations in the Carolinas, led European traders to develop a system of transporting millions of captured Africans across the Atlantic via the brutal Middle Passage. The period's economic success, based largely on the labor of these groups as well as enslaved Indigenous people, attracted European immigrants from many different ethnic and religious backgrounds. All these elements combined to make colonial society increasingly diverse.

AFRICAN HERITAGE IN THE SOUTH The survival of African culture among enslaved people in America is evident in this late eighteenth-century painting of a South Carolina plantation. The musical instruments and pottery are of African (probably Yoruba) origin.

Race-Based Chattel Slavery in the Colonies

The profound economic, political, and cultural effects of African slavery in the Americas would be felt far into the future. Most Europeans during the colonial period viewed **chattel slavery** (the idea that people of African descent were moveable forms of property) as a normal aspect of everyday life; few considered it a moral issue. They believed that slavery was a personal misfortune determined by God rather than a social evil.

Differing Treatment of Enslaved Africans

The first Africans in North America had been transported to New Spain in the sixteenth century, long before British colonists arrived in Virginia. In 1539, the Spanish explorer Hernando DeSoto transported some fifty enslaved Africans to help establish a settlement in what is now Florida. Thereafter, hundreds more enslaved Africans were taken to Florida.

The main difference in how enslaved Africans were treated in Spanish Florida compared with the British colonies centered on religion: the Spanish monarchy said enslaved people might be freed if they converted to Roman Catholicism. During the seventeenth century, growing numbers of enslaved people in the British colonies escaped and made their way to

CORE **OBJECTIVE**
4. Describe the creation of race-based chattel slavery during the seventeenth century and its impact on the social and economic development of colonial America.

chattel slavery The system of slavery that considered people a legal form of movable property. This type of enslavement included being bought and sold and forced to perform unpaid labor for life. Chattel slavery is most associated with slavery in the Americas and people of African descent.

Florida, where Spanish authorities in 1623 announced that enslaved people who touched Spanish-controlled soil and converted to Catholicism could become free Spanish citizens.

> Enslaved Africans in Spanish Florida vs. the British colonies

Members of the Creek and Seminole nations in Florida also provided refuge for enslaved people who escaped from British colonies. In the eighteenth century, a British official reported that for decades freedom seekers from Georgia and South Carolina had made their way to "Indian towns, from whence it proved very difficult to get them back."

Slave Codes In the Chesapeake colonies of Virginia and Maryland, Africans were initially treated much like indentured servants—with a limited term of service, after which they gained their freedom (but not equality). By the 1640s, however, slavery had become a permanent and hereditary condition determined by race.

The case of John Punch (1641) marked one of the origins of racial slavery. Punch, an indentured servant from Africa, ran away with two other servants—a Scotsman named James Gregory and a Dutchman named Victor. All three worked for Hugh Gwyn, and they escaped together. However, when caught, James and Victor received an extension of their indentured service for a few extra years. Punch, because he was African, was punished with slavery for the rest of his "natural life." This case revealed how colonial legislatures formalized the institution of race-based chattel slavery, with detailed **slave codes** regulating most aspects of enslaved people's lives. The South Carolina code, for example, defined all "Negroes, Mulattoes, and Indians" sold into bondage as having become enslaved *for life*, as were the children born of enslaved mothers.

In 1667, the Virginia legislature declared that enslaved individuals could not serve on juries, travel without permission, or gather in groups of more than two or three. Some colonies even prohibited manumission, the practice whereby owners could free their enslaved people. The codes allowed owners to punish enslaved people by whipping and other forms of physical abuse. In 1713, a South Carolina planter punished one of his enslaved men by closing him up in a coffin to die, only to have the trapped man's son slip in a knife so that he could kill himself rather than suffocate.

More Africans, Fewer Indentured Servants During the seventeenth and eighteenth centuries, the sugar-based economies of the French and British West Indies and Portuguese Brazil sparked greater demand for enslaved Africans. By 1675, the island colonies in the Caribbean had more than 100,000 enslaved people, while the colonies on the North American mainland had about 5,000.

As tobacco, rice, and indigo crops became more established in Maryland, Virginia, and the Carolinas, however, the number of enslaved Africans in those colonies grew substantially, while the flow of White indentured servants from Britain and Europe to America slowed. After 1700, the largest number of new arrivals were enslaved Africans, who totaled five times more

slave codes Laws passed by each colony, and later by states, governing the treatment of enslaved people; designed to deter freedom seekers and rebellions, slave codes often included severe punishments for infractions.

than all European immigrants combined. While most of the enslaved people were in the southern colonies, all thirteen colonies embraced slavery.

During the late seventeenth century, the profitability of African slavery led to the emergence of dozens of slave-trading companies, in both Europe and America, thus expanding the availability of enslaved Africans and lowering the price. Colonists favored enslaved people over indentured servants because enslaved people were viewed as property with no civil rights, and they were enslaved for life. As Jedidiah Morse, a prominent minister in Charles Town, admitted in the late eighteenth century, "No white man, to speak generally, ever thinks of settling a farm, and improving it for himself, without negroes."

Slavery in New York City In contrast to their experience in the southern colonies, most of the enslaved people in the northern colonies lived in towns or cities. Ethnically diverse New York City had more enslaved people than any other American city; and by 1740, it was second only to Charles Town, South Carolina, in the percentage of enslaved people in its population.

As the number of Africans increased in the city, fears and tensions mounted—and occasionally exploded. In 1712, several dozen enslaved people revolted; they started fires, then killed Whites trying to fight the blaze. Called out to suppress the "Negro plot," the militia captured twenty-seven enslaved people, six of whom committed suicide. The rest were executed. New York officials thereafter passed a citywide *black code* that strictly regulated the behavior of both free and enslaved Blacks.

However, the harsh regulations did not prevent other acts of resistance. In March 1741, city dwellers worried that enslaved people were setting a series of suspicious fires, including one at the governor's house. "The Negroes are rising!" shouted terrified Whites.

Mary Burton, a sixteen-year-old White indentured servant, told authorities that enslaved people and poor Whites were plotting to "burn the whole town" and kill the White men. The plotters were supposedly led by John Hughson, a White trafficker in stolen goods. His wife, two enslaved people, and a prostitute were charged as co-conspirators. Despite their denials, all were convicted and hanged. Within weeks, more than half of the adult enslaved males in the city were in jail.

What came to be called the Conspiracy of 1741 ended after seventeen enslaved people and four Whites were hanged. Thirteen more Blacks were burned at the stake, while many others were deported to the Caribbean colonies.

SLAVERY IN NEW AMSTERDAM (1642) This engraving of the Dutch colony of New Amsterdam, later known as New York City, reveals the significance of race-based chattel slavery to the colonial economy.

Slave rebellion in New York

Comparing PERSPECTIVES

INDENTURED SERVANTS AND THE LEGAL SYSTEM

From: John Punch Court Decision, 1640.

In the summer of 1640, the General Court punished three indentured servants, a Dutchman, a Scotsman, and an African. All three ran away to break their contract, however the court response showed different treatment.

Whereas Hugh Gwyn hath by order from this Board Brought back from Maryland three servants formerly run away from the said Gwyn, the court doth therefore order that the said three servants shall receive the punishment of whipping and to have thirty stripes apiece one called Victor, a Dutchman, the other a Scotchman James Gregory, shall first serve out their times with their master according to their Indentures, and one whole year apiece after the time of their service is Expired. By their said Indentures in recompense of his Loss sustained by their absence and after that service to their said master is Expired to serve the colony for three whole years apiece, and that the third being a negro named John Punch shall serve his said master or his assigns for the time of his natural Life here or elsewhere.

From: John Reid Jr., Indenture of Apprenticeship with Robert Livingston Jr., November 1, 1742.

Indentureship took many forms in the British American Colonies. In the case of John Reid Jr., from New Jersey, his parents signed an indenture agreement with Robert Livingston Jr., from a prominent New York family, so that he could learn the merchant trade.

This *Indenture* Witnesseth, that John Reid of freedhold in the County of Monnmouth Jersey by and with the Consent of his father John Reid of S^d place hath put himself, and by these Presents doth voluntarily, and of his own free Will and Accord put himself an Apprentice to Robert Livingston Jun of New York with him to live, and (after the Manner of an Apprentice) to Serve from the first Day of November: *Anno Domini*, One Thousand Seven Hundred and Forty two till the full Term of five years be complete and ended. During all which Term the said Apprentice his said Master faithfully shall serve, his Secrets keep, his lawfull Commands gladly every where obey: he shall do no Damage to His said Master nor see to be done by others without letting or giving Notice to his said master he shall not waste his said Masters Goods, nor lend them unlawfully to any, he shall not commit Fornication, nor contract Matrimony within the said Term. At Cards, Dice or any other unlawful Game, he shall not play, whereby his said Master may have Damage with his own Goods, nor the Goods of others within the said Term, without Lisence [sic] from his said Master, he shall neither buy not [sic] sell, he shall not absent himself Day nor Night from his said Masters Service without his Leave, nor haunt Ale-Houses, Taverns or Play-Houses; but in all Things as a faithful Apprentice he shall behave himself to his said Master and all his during the said Term. And the said Master during the said Term shall by the best Means or Method that he can, Teach or cause the said Apprentice to be Taught the Art and Mystery of a Marchent [sic] And also shall find and provide unto the said Apprentice sufficient meat Drink and Lodging.

For the true Perfomance of all and every the said Covenants and Agreements, either of the said Parties bind themselves unto the other by these Presents. *In Witness* whereof they have hereunto interchangeably put their Hands and Seals this first Day of November in the Sixteenth Year of His Majesty's Reign *Annoq*; [sic] *Domini*, One Thousand Seven Hundred and Forty Two, *Sealed and delivered in the Presence of* John Reid John Carpenter John Reid J^{nr}: Richard Smith.

Questions

1. Why did John Punch receive a different sentence?
2. What kinds of restrictions did indentured servants have in their contracts?
3. What can one learn from the legal treatment of indentured servants?

THE CONSPIRACY OF 1741 The title page of *A Journal of the Proceedings in the Detection of the Conspiracy* (1741), which summarizes the alleged plot by enslaved people and poor Whites to set a series of fires in New York City.

Freedom Seekers and Slave Rebellions Many enslaved people who ran away (freedom seekers) in colonial America faced severe punishments when caught. For example, a West African man named Antonio tried to escape several times. After his last attempt, in 1656, his owner, a young Dutch planter named Syman Overzee, tortured and killed him. Authorities charged Overzee with murder—only to have an all-White jury acquit him.

As in New York City, enslaved people organized rebellions in which they stole weapons, burned and looted plantations, and killed their captors. On Sunday morning, September 9, 1739, while White families were attending church, some twenty African-born enslaved people attacked a store in Stono, South Carolina, twenty miles southwest of Charles Town. The rebels seized weapons, killed and decapitated two shopkeepers, and fled south toward Spanish Florida. Along the way, they gathered more recruits.

Within a few days, the Stono rebels had burned six plantations and killed about two dozen Whites. They spared one innkeeper because he was "kind to his slaves." The rebels continued to free enslaved people as they moved southward. Then well-armed militiamen on horseback caught up with them. Most of the rebels were killed, and sixty of those captured were decapitated by enraged planters.

The **Stono Rebellion,** the largest uprising of the colonial period, so frightened White planters that they convinced the South Carolina assembly to ban the importation of enslaved Africans for ten years. They also convinced the assembly to pass the Negro Act of 1740, which called for more oversight of enslaved people's activities and harsher punishments for rebellious behavior. Enslaved people could no longer grow their own food, gather in groups, learn to read or write, or earn money on the side. Those leaving their owner's supervision were required to have a pass documenting their whereabouts. The law also reduced the penalty for a White killing an enslaved person to a minor offense, and it banned enslaved people from testifying in courts.

By the time of the American Revolution, slavery in North America was a rapidly growing system. The colonists believed they were entitled to enslave Africans and Native Americans because, in their view, these were people in need of civilizing. But at the same time, the colonists benefited from the diverse skills of enslaved laborers in helping to produce crops and goods that improved the colonists' quality of life and sustained their dynamic economy.

Stono Rebellion A 1739 slave uprising in South Carolina that was brutally quashed, leading to executions as well as a severe tightening of the slave codes.

As the enslaved population expanded, worsening race relations and slave rebellions in the North and South prompted the issuing of slave codes to regulate the movement of all enslaved people. They were regarded merely as chattel—that is, as property.

First Stirrings of a Common Colonial Culture

By the middle of the eighteenth century, the thirteen colonies were growing and maturing. Schools and colleges were springing up, and the standard of living was rising. More and more colonists were able to read about the latest ideas circulating in London and Paris while purchasing the latest consumer goods from Europe.

The rage for luxury goods—especially jewelry, fine clothing, and beaver hats—heightened the visibility of social inequality, particularly in the cities. In 1714, a Bostonian regretted the "great extravagance that people are fallen into, far beyond their circumstances, in their purchases, buildings, families, expenses, apparel—generally in their whole way of living."

> **CORE OBJECTIVE**
> **5.** Analyze the impact of the Enlightenment and Great Awakening on American thought during the colonial period.

Commerce and culture

Colonial Cities

Throughout the seventeenth and eighteenth centuries, the colonies were mostly populated by farmers or farmworkers. However, a handful of cities blossomed into dynamic centers of political and social life. Economic opportunity drove most city dwellers. In New York City, for example, a visitor said the "art of getting money" dominated everything the residents did.

Colonial cities hugged the coastline or, like Philadelphia, sprang up on rivers large enough to handle oceangoing vessels. Never accounting for more than 10 percent of the colonial population, the large coastal cities had a disproportionate influence on commerce, politics, society, and culture. By the end of the colonial period, Philadelphia, with some 30,000 people, was the largest city in the colonies; New York City, with about 25,000, ranked second. Boston numbered 16,000; Charleston, South Carolina, 12,000; and Newport, Rhode Island, 11,000.

THE RAPALJE CHILDREN (1768)
John Durand painted the children of a wealthy Brooklyn merchant wearing clothing typical of upper-crust urban society.

The Social and Political Order

The urban social elite was dominated by wealthy merchants and property owners served by a middle class of shop owners, innkeepers, and skilled craftsmen. Almost two-thirds of urban male workers were artisans—carpenters and coopers (barrel makers), shoemakers and tailors, silversmiths and blacksmiths, sailmakers, stonemasons, weavers, and potters. At the bottom of the social order were sailors, manual laborers, servants, and enslaved laborers.

> Urban problems and social support

Colonial cities were busy and crowded, and lethal epidemics such as cholera, malaria, and yellow fever were common. Frequent fires led to the development of firefighting companies. Rising rates of crime and violence required increased policing by sheriffs and local militias. At the same time, urban elites grew concerned about the poor and homeless. The number of Boston's poor receiving aid rose from 500 in 1700 to 4,000 in 1736. People designated as "helpless" were often provided money, food, clothing, and fuel. In some towns, poorhouses were built to house the homeless and provide them with jobs.

The Urban Web

The first American roads were Native American trails widened with frequent travel. "The roads all along this way are very bad," wrote Sarah Kemble Knight in 1704 after a harrowing five-day trip from Boston to New Haven, Connecticut. The route was "encumbered with rocks and mountainous passages, which were very disagreeable to my tired carcass."

Travel and Taverns Overland travel was initially by horse or on foot. Eventually wagons and coaches came into use. Inns and taverns (also called public houses, or pubs) were essential social institutions, since travel at night was treacherous—and colonial Americans loved to drink.

> Travel and taverns: The circulation of new ideas

Taverns and inns were places to eat, relax, read a newspaper, play cards, gossip, and conduct business; and to enjoy beer, hard cider, and rum. But

TAVERN CULTURE A tobacconist's business card from 1770 depicts men talking in a Philadelphia tavern while they drink ale and smoke pipes.,

ministers and magistrates began to worry that the pubs were promoting drunkenness and social rebelliousness. Not only were poor Whites drinking heavily but so too were Indigenous people, which, one governor told the assembly, would have "fatal consequences to the Government." By the end of the seventeenth century, taverns had become the most important social institutions in the colonies—and the most democratic. They were places where rich and poor intermingled, and by the mid-eighteenth century they would become gathering spots for people protesting British rule.

Mail Delivery Long-distance communication was a more complicated matter. Postal service was almost nonexistent—people gave letters to travelers or sea captains in hopes that they would be delivered. Under a parliamentary law of 1710, the postmaster of London named a deputy in charge of the colonies. Eventually, a postal system emerged along the Atlantic Seaboard, providing the colonies with an effective means of communication that would prove crucial in the growing controversy with Great Britain. More reliable mail delivery also spurred the popularity of newspapers.

The Enlightenment

The most significant of the new European ideas circulating in eighteenth-century America grew out of a burst of intellectual activity known as the **Enlightenment**. The Enlightenment celebrated rational inquiry, scientific research, and individual freedom. Enlightened thinkers sought the truth, wherever it might lead. Immanuel Kant, an eighteenth-century German philosopher, summed up the Enlightenment point of view: "Dare to know! Have the courage to use your own understanding." He and others applied the power of reason to analyze the workings of nature, and they employed new tools such as microscopes and telescopes to engage in close observation, scientific experimentation, and precise mathematical calculation.

Often called the Age of Reason, the Enlightenment was triggered by a scientific revolution in the sixteenth century that transformed the way educated people observed and understood the world. Just as explorers alerted Europeans to the excitement of new geographical discoveries, early modern scientists began to realize that social "progress" could occur through new intellectual and technological discoveries.

The ancient Christian view that the God-created earth was at the center of the universe, with the sun revolving around it, was overthrown by the controversial solar system described by Nicolaus Copernicus, a Polish astronomer and Catholic priest. In 1533, Copernicus asserted that the earth and other planets orbit the sun. Catholic officials scorned his theory until it was later confirmed by other scientists using telescopes.

Newton and the Deists In 1687, Englishman Isaac Newton announced his transformational theory of the earth's gravitational pull. He challenged biblical notions of the world's workings by depicting a changing, dynamic universe moving in accordance with "natural laws" that could be grasped by

> The scientific revolution

Enlightenment A revolution in thought begun in Europe in the seventeenth century that emphasized reason and science over the authority and myths of traditional religion.

BENJAMIN FRANKLIN A champion of rational thinking and commonsense behavior, Franklin was an inventor, a philosopher, an entrepreneur, a slaveholder, and a statesman. This depiction of him, by Benjamin West, emphasizes his scientific achievements, one of which was his demonstration of the electrical nature of lightning in 1752.

human reason and explained by mathematics. He implied that natural laws (rather than God) govern all things, from the orbits of the planets to the effects of gravity to the science of human relations: politics, economics, and society.

Some enlightened people, called **Deists**, carried Newton's scientific outlook to its logical conclusion, claiming that God created the world and designed its natural laws, which governed the operation of the universe. In other words, God planned the universe and set it in motion, but no longer interacted directly with the earth and its people. Therefore, the best way to improve society and human nature, according to Deists such as Thomas Jefferson and Benjamin Franklin, was by cultivating Reason, which was the highest Virtue (Enlightenment thinkers often capitalized both words).

Faith in the possibility of human progress was one of the most important beliefs of the Enlightenment. Equally important was the notion of political freedom. Both Thomas Jefferson and Benjamin Franklin were intrigued by the writings of English political philosopher John Locke, who maintained that "natural law" called for a government that rested on the consent of the governed and respected the "natural rights" of all. Those rights included the basic civic principles of the Enlightenment—human rights, political liberty, religious toleration—that would later influence colonial leaders' efforts to justify a revolution.

In this sense, the Enlightenment was a disruptive force that spawned not just revolutionary ideas but revolutionary movements.

Benjamin Franklin: Child of the Enlightenment The American version of the Enlightenment was best exemplified by Benjamin Franklin. Born in Boston in 1706, he left home at the age of sixteen, bound for Philadelphia. Six years later, he bought a print shop and began editing and publishing the *Pennsylvania Gazette* newspaper. As his printing business prospered, his reputation grew.

Franklin celebrated the virtues and benefits of self-reliance, hard work, and public service. He taught himself to read in four languages. Before he retired from business at the age of forty-two, Franklin had founded a public library, started a firefighting company, helped create what became the University of Pennsylvania, and organized a debating club that grew into the American Philosophical Society.

Deists Those who applied Enlightenment thought to religion, emphasizing reason, morality, and natural law rather than scriptural authority or an ever-present god intervening in the daily life of humans.

Franklin was an inventive genius devoted to scientific investigation. His wide-ranging experiments extended to the fields of medicine, meteorology, geology, astronomy, and physics. He developed the Franklin stove, the lightning rod, bifocal spectacles, and a musical instrument known as a glass harmonica.

The Great Awakening

The growing popularity of Enlightenment rationalism posed a direct threat to traditional religious life. But in the early eighteenth century, the American colonies experienced a revival of spiritual zeal designed to restore the primacy of emotion in the religious realm. Between 1700 and 1750, when the controversial ideas of the Enlightenment were circulating among the colonists, hundreds of new Christian congregations were founded.

Most Americans (85 percent) lived in colonies with an "established" church, meaning that a colony's government endorsed—and collected taxes to support—a single official denomination.

The Church of England was the established church in Virginia, Maryland, Delaware, and the Carolinas. Puritan Congregationalism was the official faith in most of New England. In New York, Anglicanism vied with the Dutch Reformed Church for control. Pennsylvania had no state-supported church, but Quakers dominated the legislative assembly. New Jersey and Rhode Island had no official denomination, and hosted numerous Christian splinter groups.

Most of the colonies organized religious life around local parishes. In colonies with official tax-supported religions, people of other faiths could not preach without the permission of the parish. In the 1730s and 1740s, the parish system was thrown into turmoil by the arrival of traveling evangelists, called *itinerants*, who worried about the erosion of religious fervor and claimed that most local parish ministers were incompetent. In their emotionally charged sermons, the itinerants—several of whom were White women and African Americans—insisted that Christians must be "reborn" in their convictions and behavior.

During the early 1730s, these itinerant preachers helped spark a series of revivals known as the **Great Awakening**. The revivals spread up and down the Atlantic coast. The highly emotional gatherings divided congregations, towns, and families; they even fueled popular new denominations, especially Baptists and Methodists. A skeptical Benjamin Franklin admitted that the Awakening was having a profound effect on social life: "Never did the people show so great a willingness to attend sermons."

Jonathan Edwards In 1734–1735, a remarkable spiritual transformation occurred in the congregation of Jonathan Edwards, a prominent Congregationalist minister in the Massachusetts town of Northampton. A brilliant philosopher and theologian, Edwards had entered Yale College in 1716, at age thirteen, and graduated at the top of his class four years later.

Great Awakening An emotional religious revival movement that swept through the thirteen colonies from the 1730s through the 1740s.

> Religious response to the Enlightenment

> Traveling evangelists and intense revivals

JONATHAN EDWARDS One of the foremost preachers of the Great Awakening, Edwards dramatically described the torments that awaited sinners in the afterlife.

GEORGE WHITEFIELD PREACHING Another influential figure of the Great Awakening was George Whitefield, a British Anglican preacher who made several trips to America to spread his religious sentiments. This painting by Englishman John Collet does not depict the massive crowds Whitefield was known to attract, but it does represent their diversity of age, sex, and class. **Why did the message of the Great Awakening appeal to such a wide range of people?**

When Edwards arrived in Northampton in 1727, the town's lack of religious conviction shocked him. He claimed that the young people indulged in "lewd practices" that "corrupted others." He warned that Christians had become obsessed with making and spending money, and that the rage for controversial ideas associated with the Enlightenment were eroding the importance of religious life. Edwards rushed to restore the emotional side of religion. "Our people," he said, "do not so much need to have their heads stored [with new scientific knowledge] as to have their hearts touched [with spiritual intensity]."

The fiery Edwards used vivid descriptions of the torments of hell and the delights of heaven to rekindle spiritual intensity among his congregants.

In 1741, he delivered his most famous sermon, "Sinners in the Hands of an Angry God," in which he reminded the congregation that hell is real and that God "holds you over the pit of hell, much as one holds a spider, or some loathsome insect, over the fire. . . . He looks upon you as worthy of nothing else, but to be cast into the fire." When he finished, Edwards had to wait several minutes for the thoroughly moved congregants to quiet down before he could lead them in a closing hymn.

George Whitefield The most celebrated promoter of the Great Awakening was a young English minister, George Whitefield, who visited the colonies seven times between 1738 and 1748. Whitefield set out to restore the fires of religious intensity in America.

Starting in Georgia in 1738, the young evangelist began a fourteen-month tour of the colonies, preaching a fiery gospel of redemption to huge crowds gathered in barns, open fields, and cemeteries. He rejected the Calvinist assumption that people must prepare for salvation. In his view, the grace of God arrived suddenly and without warning, like the dawn.

A Connecticut farmer who attended one of Whitefield's open-air sermons described the blond-haired evangelist, often dressed in sparkling white robes, as "almost angelical" in appearance. Another participant reported that Whitefield's theatrical performance entranced the crowd: "He exceedingly wept, stamped loudly and passionately and was frequently so overcome that, for a few seconds, you would suspect he would never recover."

Yet Whitefield's critics were as fervent as his admirers. Anglican ministers dismissed him as being preoccupied with converting commoners and "the ignorant." A disgusted Bostonian described a revival meeting's theatrics: "The meeting was carried on with . . . some screaming out in Distress and Anguish . . . some again jumping up and down . . . some lying along on the floor." Whitefield enthralled audiences with his golden voice, flamboyant style, and unparalleled eloquence. Even Benjamin Franklin, a confirmed rationalist who saw Whitefield preach in Philadelphia, was so excited by the sermon that he emptied his pockets into the collection plate.

As the call to Christ reverberated throughout the colonies, the Great Awakening reached the enslaved and free Blacks of Savannah, Georgia. Members of the First African Baptist Church, one of the oldest African American churches in North America, followed the leadership of George Liele and later Andrew Bryan. Liele, born enslaved in Virginia and brought to Georgia by his enslaver, was the first ordained African American missionary and tended to the spiritual lives of Savannah's Black population. Bryan, born enslaved in South Carolina and transported to Georgia, experienced conversion after being influenced by Liele's ministry. Bryan helped found the First Baptist church in Savannah. Congregants worshipped in a rice barn until 1794, when Bryan purchased the land on which the church currently stands as a historic site and contemporary place of worship.

ANDREW BRYAN The Great Awakening also reached enslaved and freed Black people. Andrew Bryan and George Liele co-created the First African Baptist Church in Savannah, Georgia, with hundreds of parishioners. Bryan was twice imprisoned for preaching to enslaved people.

Women and Revivals The Great Awakening's most controversial element was the emergence of women who defied convention by speaking at religious services. Among them was Sarah Haggar Osborne, a Rhode Island schoolteacher who organized prayer meetings that eventually included men and women, Black and White. When concerned ministers told her to stop, she refused to "shut my mouth and doors and creep into obscurity."

Similarly, in western Massachusetts, Bathsheba Kingsley spread the gospel because she had received "immediate revelations from heaven." When her husband tried to intervene, she pummeled him with "hard words and blows," praying loudly that he "go quick to hell." For all the turbulence created by the revivals, however, churches remained male bastions of political authority.

The Heart versus the Head The Great Awakening subsided by 1750. Like the Enlightenment, it influenced the forces leading to the revolution against Great Britain and set in motion powerful currents that still flow in American life.

The Awakening implanted in American culture the evangelical impulse and the emotional appeal of revivalism, weakened the status of the entrenched clergy and state-supported churches, and encouraged believers to exercise their own individual judgment. By promoting the proliferation of denominations, it heightened the need for toleration of dissent.

In some respects, however, the Awakening and the Enlightenment led by different roads to similar ends—one stressing the urgings of the spirit, and the other celebrating the cold logic of reason. Both movements spread across the mainland colonies and thereby helped bind the regions together. Both emphasized the power and right of individual decision-making, and both aroused hopes that America would become the promised land in which people might attain the perfection of piety or reason, if not both.

By urging believers to exercise their own spiritual judgment, revivals weakened the authority of the established churches and their ministers, just as resentment of British economic regulations would later weaken colonial loyalty to the king. As such, the Great Awakening and the Enlightenment helped nurture a growing commitment to individual freedom and resistance to authority that would play a key role in what the colonists saw as the rebellion against British "tyranny" in 1776.

Reviewing the
CORE OBJECTIVES

- **Demography of the Early Colonies** Cheap land lured poor immigrants to America. The initial shortage of women eventually gave way to earlier marriage than in Europe, leading to higher *birth rates* and larger families. After the first years of settlement, *death rates* were lower in the colonies than in Europe, which led to rapid population growth in the colonies.

- **Women in the Colonies** English colonists brought their beliefs and prejudices with them to America, including convictions about the lower status and limited roles of White women. Colonial women remained largely confined to *women's work* in the house, yard, and field. Over time, though, necessity created opportunities for women outside their traditional roles. Enslaved African women, by contrast, were forced to take on the most difficult physical labor inside White homes and in agricultural fields, encouraging some to resist by escaping.

- **Society and Economy in the Colonies** A thriving colonial *triangular trading* economy sent raw materials such as fish, lumber, and furs to England in return for manufactured goods. The expanding economy created new wealth and a rise in consumption of European goods. The colonies increasingly relied on *indentured servants* for their labor supply. By the end of the seventeenth century, however, the enslavement of Indigenous and African people had replaced indentured servants as the primary source of labor in the Chesapeake region. The demand for forced labor in the sugar plantations of the West Indies drove European slave traders to organize the transport of captured Africans via the *Middle Passage* across the Atlantic. Planters in the Carolinas also adopted African slavery as the preferred labor system. African cultures fused with others in the Americas to create a hybrid African American culture. Economic success led to increased European immigration, and by 1790 there were German, Scots-Irish, Welsh, and Irish immigrants, as well as other European ethnic groups, settling in the middle colonies, along with Quakers, Jews, Huguenots, and Mennonites.

- **Race-Based Chattel Slavery in the Colonies** Deeply rooted prejudice led to race-based *chattel slavery*. Africans were considered "heathens" whose supposed inferiority entitled White Americans to enslave them, yet they brought diverse skills to help build America's economy with their forced labor. The use of enslaved Africans was concentrated in the South, where landowners used them to produce lucrative *staple crops*, such as tobacco, rice, and indigo. But enslaved people lived in cities, too, especially New York. As the enslaved population increased, race relations grew tense, and *slave codes* were created to regulate the movement of enslaved people. Sporadic slave uprisings, such as the *Stono Rebellion*, occurred in both the North and the South.

- **The Enlightenment** Printing presses, education, and city life generated a flow of new ideas that circulated via long-distance travel, tavern life, the postal service, and newspapers. The attitudes of the *Enlightenment* were transported along international trade routes. Sir Isaac Newton's scientific discoveries culminated in the belief that reason could improve society. Benjamin Franklin, who believed that people could shape their own destinies, became the face of the Enlightenment in America. *Deists* espoused the religious views of the Age of Reason. By the 1730s, a revival of faith, the *Great Awakening*, swept through the colonies. New congregations formed as evangelists insisted that Christians be "reborn." Individualism, not orthodoxy, was stressed in this first popular religious movement in America's history.

KEY TERMS

death rate *p. 104*
birth rate *p. 105*
women's work *p. 107*
indentured servants *p. 111*
staple crops *p. 113*
triangular trade *p. 116*
Middle Passage *p. 122*
chattel slavery *p. 123*
slave codes *p. 124*
Stono Rebellion *p. 128*
Enlightenment *p. 131*
Deists *p. 132*
Great Awakening *p. 133*

CHRONOLOGY

1683	German Mennonites arrive in Pennsylvania
1687	Sir Isaac Newton publishes his theory of universal gravitation
1691	South Carolina passes the first slave codes; other colonies follow
1712	Revolt of enslaved people in New York City; New York passes stricter laws governing those enslaved
1730s–1740s	The Great Awakening
1738	George Whitefield preaches his first sermon in America
1739	Stono Rebellion
1740	British Parliament passes the Naturalization Act
1741	Jonathan Edwards preaches "Sinners in the Hands of an Angry God"
	The Conspiracy of 1741
1750	Colonial population passes 1 million
1775	Colonial population passes 2.5 million

InQuizitive

Go to InQuizitive to see what you've learned—and learn what you've missed—with personalized feedback along the way.

BOSTON TEA PARTY In one of the most famous insurrections that contributed to the colonists' anti-British fervor, a swarm of Patriots disguised as Mohawk warriors seized three British ships and dumped more than 300 chests of East India Company tea into Boston Harbor.

CHAPTER 4

From Colonies to States

1607–1776

Four great competing European powers—Spain, France, England, and the Netherlands (Holland)—created colonies in North America during the sixteenth and seventeenth centuries. Throughout the eighteenth century, wars raged across Europe, mostly pitting the Catholic nations of France and Spain against Protestant Great Britain and the Netherlands. Those conflicts spread to North America, which became a primary battleground involving both colonists and Indigenous people allied with different European powers.

Spain's sparsely populated settlements in the Americas included regions such as Mexico, Central America, what became known as the southwestern United States, Florida, and parts of the West Indies. The Spanish Empire displaced Indigenous people and emphasized their conversion to Catholicism. It also prohibited manufacturing within its colonies, strictly limited trade with Indigenous people, and searched—mostly in vain—for gold.

The French and British colonies developed thriving trade relations with Indigenous people at the same time that the bitter rivalry between Great Britain and France gradually shifted the balance of power in Europe. By the end of the eighteenth century, Spain and the Netherlands were in decline, leaving France and Great Britain to fight for dominance. Their nearly constant warfare led Protestant Great Britain to tighten its control

CORE OBJECTIVES

1. Compare how the British and French Empires administered their colonies before 1763.
2. Analyze how the French and Indian War changed relations among the European powers in North America.
3. Describe how, after the French and Indian War, the British tightened their control over the colonies, and summarize the colonial responses.
4. Explain the underlying factors amid the events in the 1770s that led the colonists to declare their independence from Britain.

over the American colonies to raise the funds needed to combat Catholic France and Spain. Tensions over these British efforts to preserve their empire at the expense of the American colonists' freedoms would lead to rebellion and eventually to revolution.

> CORE **OBJECTIVE**
> **1.** Compare how the British and French Empires administered their colonies before 1763.

French and British Colonies

The British colonies spanning the Atlantic coast from what is now Maine to Georgia were populated by settlers and immigrants from the European mainland who were determined to thrive through farming and trade. Many had come seeking religious freedom, with the result that the colonies comprised a multifaceted patchwork of largely Protestant denominations. The settlers were devoted to hard work, and their labor supported an active trade with England that benefited both the colonies and the motherland. Their success was based partly on the growing prevalence of enslaved Africans who dramatically increased productivity, and partly on efforts to push Indigenous peoples further west to open up the land for use.

The French challenged the English presence in the Americas by establishing Catholic colonies in the Caribbean, Canada, and the Mississippi Valley west of the Appalachian Mountains. Yet the French never invested enough people or resources in North America. By the mid-eighteenth century, the French residents of New France numbered less than 5 percent of the population in British America, and the relatively small French investment in Canada and Louisiana never turned a profit. In fact, New France became an enormous financial drain on the French economy, but imperial pride kept the monarchy from abandoning its North American colonies.

New France

> French fur-trading companies, forging alliances with indigenous peoples

The actual settlement of New France began in 1605, when the soldier-explorer Samuel de Champlain founded Port-Royal in Acadia, along the Atlantic coast of Canada. Three years later, Champlain established Quebec, to the west, along the St. Lawrence River (see Map 4.1). Until his death in 1635, Champlain, "the Father of New France," governed Canada on behalf of trading companies eager to create a prosperous commercial colony tied to the robust fur trade with Indigenous nations and plentiful fishing opportunities off the Atlantic coast.

In 1627, the French monarchy announced that only French Catholics could live in New France. This restriction stunted the settlement's growth—as did the harsh winter climate. As a consequence, the number of French colonists in Canada was *much* smaller than the number of British, Dutch, and Spanish settlers in other North American colonies.

CHAMPLAIN IN NEW FRANCE This sketch shows Samuel de Champlain firing at a group of Iroquois, killing two chieftains, in 1609.

Relations with Indigenous Societies

From the beginning, the French sought to work with the Indigenous people. Champlain recruited Huron and Algonquian warriors to help conquer the feared Iroquois, their historic enemies. In his first confrontation with the Iroquois, the French commander fired his *arquebus* (forerunner to the rifle) at the Iroquois chiefs, killing two and wounding another. He then "pursued them and laid low still more of them." It was the Iroquois people's first encounter with a firearm. They dropped their weapons and fled.

Champlain knew that the French could survive only by befriending the Indigenous peoples. To that end, he dispatched trappers and traders to live with them, learn their languages and customs, and marry their women. Many of these woodsmen pushed into the forested regions around the Great Lakes and developed a flourishing fur trade with the Indigenous people.

The most successful and long-lasting business that developed from this trade arose to satisfy European demand for felt hats made from beaver fur. Two French traders sought to establish trading posts deep within the continent's interior that would enable Indigenous trappers to exchange valuable pelts for European manufactured goods, such as metal tools, guns, and textiles. Failing to gain support from the French government, however, in 1665 the men obtained backing from the English king and other investors.

Five years later, the Hudson's Bay Company was chartered by the English. Its success was built on mutually beneficial exchanges between Indigenous fur traders and French trappers and businessmen, overseen by British administrators. Despite originating in northern New France, the company's

MAP 4.1 THE FRENCH IN NORTH AMERICA

Legend:
- English possessions
- French possessions
- Spanish possessions
- Disputed territory
- → Marquette and Jolliet's route, 1673
- → La Salle's route, 1682

- After consulting the map key, name the southernmost point of French possessions in North America. What river leads to this point?
- Find New France on the map. What geographic features enabled the French explorers to travel so far from this territory?
- According to the chapter text, how were the French settlements in North America different from the Spanish and English colonies?

reach gave Britain a foothold in vast areas of the North American interior (see again Map 4.1).

Catholicism and Jesuit Missionaries

The fur trade enticed the French to settle in Canada, but the activities of Catholic missionaries gave New France its dynamism. Like Spain, France aggressively sought to convert the Native Americans to Catholicism, in part because it was expected that Christian Indigenous people would become more reliable trading partners and military allies.

Jesuit missionaries led the way. The Society of Jesus (the Jesuits) had been founded in 1534, when Ignatius of Loyola, a Spanish soldier and nobleman, and six companions pledged to lead lives of poverty and chastity—and to defend the Roman Catholic Church. A year later, the Pope officially recognized the Jesuits and urged them to convert "pagan people" around the world. The Jesuits became famous for their religious fervor, missionary zeal, and personal courage. They served as the front line of the Catholic Counter-Reformation, fighting the spread of Protestantism and traversing the globe as earnest missionaries. Some 3,500 Jesuits served in New Spain and New France.

French Jesuits in distinctive black robes fanned out from Quebec, traveling across the Great Lakes region and even down the Mississippi River. Known as the Black Robes, they carried with them smallpox and other infectious diseases that killed far more Indigenous people than were converted to Christianity.

Unlike their Spanish counterparts, the Jesuits in French Canada were rarely accompanied by soldiers. Most of them lived among the people of the Huroń Nation. Jesuits and Indigenous people learned from each other's belief systems, but the Indigenous Americans never fully abandoned their own folkways. Yet this relationship was not always harmonious. By befriending the Huron and Algonquian peoples, the French outraged other Indigenous nations. The tribes that made up the Iroquois Confederacy (the Mohawk, Oneida, Onondaga, Cayuga, and Seneca) had long warred against the Huron.

Exploring to the South

New France always had far fewer colonists than British America. The French colony, however, had one important advantage over the British colonies: access to the great inland rivers that teemed with fur-bearing animals such as beaver, otter, and mink.

JESUITS IN NEW FRANCE Founded in 1539, the Jesuits sent missionaries to North America with the goal of converting Indigenous people to Catholicism, which they believed would make them more reliable trading and military partners.

> French geographical advantage over the British

From their Canadian outposts along the Great Lakes, French explorers in the early 1670s moved down the Mississippi River to the Gulf of Mexico. Louis Jolliet, a fur trader born in Quebec, teamed with Father Jacques Marquette, a Jesuit priest fluent in Indigenous languages, to explore the Wisconsin River south to the Mississippi. Traveling in canoes, they paddled to within 400 miles of the Gulf of Mexico (Map 4.1).

Other French explorers followed. In 1682, René-Robert Cavelier, sieur de La Salle, organized an expedition that started in Montreal, crossed the Great Lakes, and then went down the Mississippi to the Gulf of Mexico—the first European to do so. La Salle claimed for France the vast Ohio and Mississippi valleys all the way to the Rocky Mountains. He named the region Louisiana, after King Louis XIV.

New Orleans became the capital of the sprawling Louisiana Territory that encompassed much of the interior of the North American continent.

That same year, the Spanish, concerned about the French presence in Louisiana, founded San Antonio in the Texas province of New Spain. They built a Catholic mission (later called the Alamo) and a fort (*presidio*) to convert the Indigenous people and fend off efforts by the French to expand into Texas. Some early explorers, such as Juan Garrido and Estevanico, had come to this region in the late sixteenth century (see Chapter 1); the travels of these two men indicate that people of African descent were present in the region prior to 1619.

Throughout the eighteenth century, New France remained a vast region traversed by a mobile population of traders, trappers, missionaries, and mainly Indigenous people. By building closer bonds and encroaching far less upon Indigenous lands, the French won Indigenous allies against the more numerous British Americans. For well over a century, in fact, Indigenous people would determine the military balance of power within North America, protecting and defending their native land.

The British Colonial System

The diverse British colonies of North America were quite different from those of New France. British colonial governments were typically headed by a royal governor or proprietor (owner) who could appoint and remove officials, command the militia, and grant pardons to people convicted of crimes.

Yet the British colonists enjoyed rights and powers absent in Britain and in New France. In particular, they had *elected* legislatures.

The Habit of Self-Government

> Growing influence of legislative assemblies

The most important political trend in eighteenth-century British America was the expanding power and influence of the colonial legislatures. Like Parliament, the colonial assemblies controlled the budget and could pass laws and regulations. Most assemblies exercised influence over the royal governors by paying their salaries.

Throughout the eighteenth century, the colonial assemblies acquired new powers—particularly with respect to government appointments—that Parliament had yet to exercise itself. Self-government in British America became first a habit, then a cherished "right."

Mercantilism

The English Civil War during the 1640s sharply reduced the flow of money and people to America and forced colonists to take sides in the conflict between Royalists and Puritans (see Chapter 2). Oliver Cromwell's victory over the monarchy in 1651 had direct effects in the colonies. As England's new ruler, Cromwell sought to enforce **mercantilism**—a political and economic policy in which the government controlled economic activities. Key industries were regulated, taxed, or subsidized (supported by payments from the government), and people with specialized skills or knowledge of new technologies, such as textile machinery, were not allowed to leave the country.

Mercantilism also supported the creation of global empires. Colonies, it was assumed, enriched the mother country in several ways: (*1*) by providing silver, gold, and crucial raw materials such as furs, fish, and timber; (*2*) by creating a captive market of consumers who were forced to buy goods produced in the home country; and (*3*) by relieving social tensions and political unrest in the home country, because colonies could become a haven for the poor, the unemployed, and the imprisoned.

Navigation Acts

Such mercantilist assumptions prompted Oliver Cromwell to adopt the first in a series of **Navigation Acts** intended to increase control over the colonial economies. The Navigation Act of 1651 required that all goods going to and from the colonies be transported in English-owned ships. The law was intended to hurt the Dutch, who had developed a thriving shipping business between America and Europe. Dutch shipowners charged much less to transport goods than did the English, and after 1651 they encouraged smuggling in the colonies as a means of defying the Navigation Acts.

After the monarchy was restored to power in England in 1660, the Royalist Parliament passed the Navigation Act of 1660, which specified that certain colonial products (such as tobacco) were to be shipped *only* to England. Subsequently, the Navigation Act of 1663, called the Staples Act, required that *all* shipments from Europe to America first stop in Britain to be offloaded and taxed before being sent to the colonies.

By this point, England and the Netherlands were embroiled in war. In 1664, English warships conquered New Netherland, ending Dutch colonial activity in North America. By 1700, the English had surpassed the Dutch as the world's leading maritime power, and most products sent to and from America via Europe and Africa were carried in English ships.

---

mercantilism The policy, practiced by England and other imperial powers, of regulating colonial economies to benefit the mother country.

Navigation Acts (1651–1775) Restrictions passed by Parliament to control colonial trade and bolster the mercantile system.

> Navigation Acts target the Dutch

BOSTON FROM THE SOUTHEAST This view of eighteenth-century Boston shows the importance of shipping and its regulation in the colonies, especially in Massachusetts Bay.

Resentment in the Colonies

Dominion of New England

Colonial merchants and shippers resented the Navigation Acts, but the English government refused to lift the restrictions. The New England colonies were particularly hard-hit. In 1678, a defiant Massachusetts legislature declared that the Navigation Acts had no legal standing. In 1684, King Charles II responded by revoking the royal charter for Massachusetts. The following year, Charles died and his brother, King James II, succeeded him, becoming the first Catholic monarch in more than 100 years. The new king reorganized the New England colonies into a single entity called the Dominion of New England.

In 1686, a new royal governor of the Dominion, Sir Edmund Andros, arrived in Boston. Andros quickly angered the colonists when he stripped New Englanders of their civil rights, imposed new taxes, ignored town governments, strictly enforced the Navigation Acts, and punished smugglers.

The Glorious Revolution

In 1688, the Dominion of New England added the former Dutch provinces of New York, East Jersey, and West Jersey to its control, just a few months before the **Glorious Revolution** erupted in England. People called the revolution "glorious" because it took place with little bloodshed. The Catholic king, James II, fearing imprisonment, fled to France and was replaced by his daughter Mary and her husband William III, the ruling Dutch Prince (and the king's nephew). Both William and Mary were Protestants.

Glorious Revolution (1688) A successful coup, instigated by a group of English aristocrats, that overthrew King James II and instated William of Orange and Mary, his English wife, to the English throne.

William III and Mary II went on to govern England as joint constitutional monarchs, their powers limited by Parliament. Both rulers signed the Declaration of Rights, which became known in England as the Bill of Rights. This document affirmed several constitutional principles, including the right for Parliament to meet regularly. It also mandated that elections be free from monarchical intervention and that freedom of speech in Parliament be protected.

The monarchy in England would never again exercise absolute power. In addition, the long-standing geographical designation "Great Britain" for the united kingdoms of England, Scotland, and Wales was revived as the nation's official name.

Also in 1689, colonists in Boston staged a revolt against the monarchy when a group of merchants, ministers, and militiamen (citizen-soldiers) arrested Governor Andros and his aides and removed the Massachusetts Bay Colony from the new Dominion of New England. Within a few weeks, the other colonies that had been absorbed into the Dominion also restored their independence.

William and Mary, however, had no patience with the colonists' rebelliousness. In response, they appointed new royal governors in Massachusetts, New York, and Maryland. In Massachusetts, the governor vetoed acts of the colonial assembly and removed the requirement that only church members could vote in elections.

Amid the continuing tension between colonies and monarchy over governance issues, a powerful justification for revolution appeared in 1690 when English philosopher John Locke published *Two Treatises on Government*. This work had an enormous impact on political thought in the colonies. Locke rejected the "divine" right of monarchs to govern with absolute power, and insisted that all people are endowed with **natural rights** to life, liberty, and property. When monarchs failed to protect the property and lives of their subjects, Locke argued, the people had the right to overthrow the monarchs.

A New Emerging Colonial System

While the new monarchs had rid the colonies of the much-hated Dominion of New England, many colonists were disappointed when the king took steps to stop American smugglers from evading royal taxes and to enforce the Navigation Acts. The Act to Prevent Frauds and Abuses of 1696 allowed customs officials in America to use "writs of assistance" (search warrants that did not have to specify the place to be searched), and ordered that accused smugglers be tried in *royal admiralty courts* (because juries in colonial courts rarely convicted their peers).

Soon, however, British efforts to enforce the Navigation Acts waned. Kings George I and George II, German princes who were descendants of James I, showed much less interest in enforcing colonial trade laws. Robert Walpole, the long-serving prime minister (1721–1742) and lord of the Treasury, initiated a policy of **salutary neglect**. He did so in large part because rigid

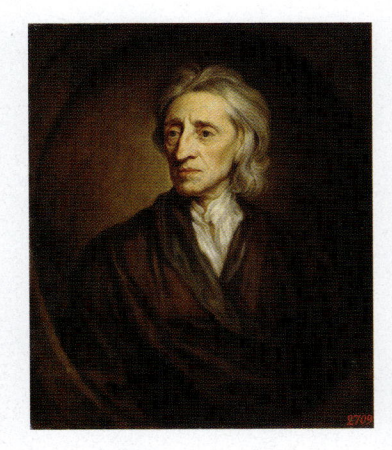

JOHN LOCKE An English philosopher and a strong believer in natural rights, Locke in his writings rationalized revolutionary movements to overthrow unsatisfactory governments.

natural rights An individual's basic rights (to life, liberty, and property) that should not be violated by any government or community.

salutary neglect An informal British policy during the first half of the eighteenth century that allowed the American colonies freedom to pursue their economic and political interests in exchange for colonial obedience to the Crown.

enforcement would have been too expensive. What Walpole did not realize was that his policy of salutary neglect would lead many colonists to develop an independent attitude that would ultimately blossom into revolution.

By now, the American colonies reflected the evolution in British policy. Initially allowed to enjoy significant self-government, the colonies grew to resent the more-restrictive policies and governance that the monarchy imposed. In contrast, France had initially applied a strict policy of absolute power over its North American colonies but it also cultivated better relations with Indigenous Americans, especially through a lucrative fur trade. As these differing approaches to colonial administration unfolded, new political philosophies in England began to challenge the divine right of monarchs.

> CORE **OBJECTIVE**
> **2.** Analyze how the French and Indian War changed relations among the European powers in North America.

Warfare in the Colonies

The Glorious Revolution of 1688 had transformed relations among the great powers of Europe. Great Britain's Protestant rulers William and Mary, passionate foes of Catholic France's Louis XIV, organized an alliance of European nations against the French in a transatlantic war known in the American colonies as King William's War (1689–1697). It would be the first of four major wars fought over the next seventy-four years that would shift the balance of power in Europe—and in North America.

The prolonged warfare between the British and French and their Indigenous allies reshaped the relationship between the colonies and Great Britain, which emerged from the wars as the most powerful nation in the world. Thereafter, international commerce became increasingly essential to the expanding British Empire, thus making the American colonies even more important to Great Britain

The French and Indian War

The most important conflict between Britain and France (and its Catholic ally, Spain) in North America was the **French and Indian War** (1756–1763), globally known as the **Seven Years' War**. The conflict started with frontier clashes in America in 1754, sparked by French and British competition for the Indigenous lands in the vast Ohio valley. Whoever controlled the Ohio Country would control the entire continent because of the strategic importance of the Ohio and Mississippi Rivers.

To defend their interests, the French built forts in the Ohio Country. When Virginia's governor learned of the forts, he sent an ambitious twenty-two-year-old militia officer, Major George Washington, to warn the French to leave. The French, however, rebuffed him in late 1753.

A few months later, in the spring of 1754, Washington went back to the Ohio Country with 150 untrained volunteer soldiers and Indigenous

French and Indian War (Seven Years' War) (1756–1763) The last and most important of four colonial wars between England and France for control of lands in North America east of the Mississippi River.

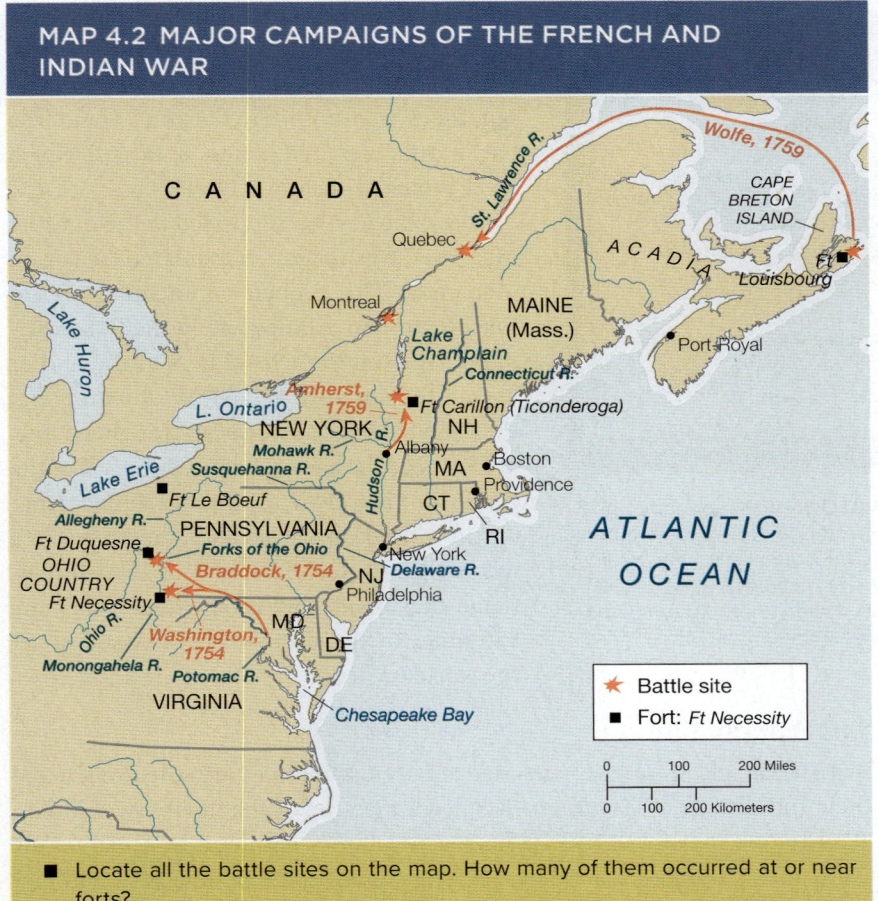

MAP 4.2 MAJOR CAMPAIGNS OF THE FRENCH AND INDIAN WAR

- Locate all the battle sites on the map. How many of them occurred at or near forts?
- Find Fort Necessity. What was the significance of the siege that took place there?
- Look back at Map 2.1. Compare the territories of Indigenous societies shown on that map with the location of forts on this map. During the campaigns of the French and Indian War, why would it have been important for the attacking military troops to have Indigenous allies?

allies. They planned to build a fort where the Allegheny, Monongahela, and Ohio Rivers converged (where the city of Pittsburgh later developed; see Map 4.2). The so-called Forks of the Ohio was the key strategic gateway to the vast territory west of the Appalachian Mountains, and both sides were determined to control it.

After traveling for two months through dense forests and treacherous mountain passes, Washington learned that French soldiers had beaten him to the site and had built Fort Duquesne in western Pennsylvania. Washington decided to camp his men about forty miles away. The next day, the Virginians ambushed a French scouting party, killing ten—the first fatalities in what would become the French and Indian War.

Reinforced by more Virginians and British soldiers dispatched from South Carolina, Washington and his troops hastily constructed a tiny,

THE FIRST AMERICAN POLITICAL CARTOON First appearing on May 9, 1754, in the *Pennsylvania Gazette*, this widely circulated political cartoon by Benjamin Franklin urged the colonies to unite against the French. Twenty years later, when the French became an ally of the colonies and the British became the primary threat to American liberty, the cartoon was revived with new meaning.

circular stockade, calling it Fort Necessity. Washington remarked that the valley provided "a charming field for an encounter," but there was nothing charming about the battle that erupted when a large French force attacked on July 3, 1754.

After the day-long, lopsided Battle of Great Meadows, Washington surrendered (see again Map 4.2). The French commander forced Washington to admit that he had "assassinated" the ten French soldiers at the earlier encounter. On July 4, 1754, Washington and the defeated Virginians began trudging home.

France now had undisputed control of the Ohio Country. Yet Washington's failed expedition wound up triggering a massive world war nearly two years later. As a British politician exclaimed, "the volley fired by a young Virginian in the backwoods of America set the world on fire."

The Albany Plan

British officials in America, worried about possible war with the French and their Indigenous allies, urgently called a meeting of the northern colonies. Twenty-one representatives from seven colonies gathered in Albany, New York. It was the first time that a large group of colonial delegates had met to take joint action.

At the urging of Pennsylvania's Benjamin Franklin, the Albany Congress (June 19–July 11, 1754) approved the **Albany Plan of Union**. It called for the colonies to band together, headed by a president appointed by the king. Each colonial assembly would send two to seven delegates to a "grand council," which would have legislative powers. The Union would have jurisdiction over Indigenous affairs.

The Albany Plan of Union, however, was too radical. British officials and the colonial legislatures, eager to maintain their individual powers, simply wanted a military alliance against Indigenous attacks, so they rejected the plan. Benjamin Franklin later maintained that the Plan of Union, had it been approved, might have postponed or avoided the Revolutionary War. It would, however, become a model of governance for the new American nation in 1777.

Albany Plan of Union (1754) A failed proposal by the seven northern colonies in anticipation of the French and Indian War, urging the unification of the colonies under one Crown-appointed president.

War in North America

The British decided to force a showdown with the French. In June 1755, a British fleet captured the forts protecting French Acadia, along the Atlantic coast of Canada. The British then expelled 11,500 Acadians, the Catholic French residents. Hundreds of Acadians eventually found their way to French Louisiana, where they became known as Cajuns.

Also in 1755, the British government sent 1,000 red-coated soldiers from Great Britain to dislodge the French from the Ohio Country. Their arrival on American soil would change the dynamics of British North America. Although the colonists endorsed the use of force against the French, they later would oppose the use of British soldiers to enforce colonial regulations.

Braddock's Defeat The British commander-in-chief in America, General Edward Braddock, had no experience with frontier combat and little knowledge of American geography. He also failed to recruit large numbers of Indigenous allies. Braddock viewed Indigenous people with contempt, telling eight Indigenous scouts who assisted his forces that he would not reward them with land as the French did, for "No savage should inherit the land." His dismissal of Indigenous people and his ignorance of unconventional warfare would prove fatal.

With the addition of some American militiamen, including George Washington as a volunteer officer, Braddock's force left northern Virginia to confront the French, hacking a 125-mile-long road west through the Allegheny Mountains toward Fort Duquesne.

On July 9, 1755, as the British neared the fort, they were ambushed by French soldiers, Canadian militiamen, and Indigenous people; the British suffered shocking losses. Braddock was shot; he died three days later. Washington led a hasty retreat, despite having two horses shot dead under him and his coat and pants riddled by bullets. A British officer wrote that "the whole time," George Washington behaved "with the greatest courage."

What came to be called the Battle of Monongahela (Map 4.2) was one of the worst British defeats in history. The French and their Indigenous allies killed 63 of 86 British officers and 914 of 1,373 soldiers. A devastated Washington wrote to his brother that the vaunted British redcoats had "broke & run as sheep pursued by hounds." The Virginians, he noted in contrast, "behaved like Men and died like Soldiers."

A World War

General Braddock's shocking defeat showed that the British army could be beaten. It also emboldened Indigenous people who were allied with the French to attack English settlements throughout western Pennsylvania, Maryland, and Virginia. Desperate to respond, the Pennsylvania colonial government offered rewards for each Indigenous person's scalp.

Indigenous people and the colonists fought mercilessly throughout 1755 and 1756. The first true "world war," the Seven Years' War in

AN IROQUOIS WARRIOR This eighteenth-century French engraving shows an Iroquois warrior in full battle dress. **How does the artist's representation of this Iroquois warrior differ from Braddock's view of the Native Americans?**

> The French and Indian War becomes the Seven Years' War

GEORGE III In 1760, the young George III became king of Great Britain and soon governed the most powerful empire in the world.

Europe (the battles in North America were called the French and Indian War) would eventually be fought on parts of five continents and three oceans. In the end, it would redraw the political map of North America.

In 1759, the French and Indian War reached its climax in North America with a series of British triumphs. The most decisive victory was at Quebec, the hilltop fortress city and capital of French Canada. During the dark of night, some 4,500 British troops scaled the cliffs above the St. Lawrence River and at dawn surprised the French defenders in a battle that lasted only ten minutes (Map 4.2). The French surrendered four days later.

The Battle of Quebec marked the turning point in the war. By 1761, France, governed by Louis XV, had lost Canada; its armies were bogged down in Germany; and its government was bankrupt and humiliated. Thereafter, the conflict in North America ebbed, although sporadic combat continued until 1763.

A New British King

On October 25, 1760, the ailing British king George II arose at 6:00 A.M., drank his usual chocolate milk, and adjourned to his toilet closet. A few minutes later, a servant heard a strange noise, opened the door, and found the king dead, the result of a ruptured artery. His death brought an untested new king—George's twenty-two-year-old grandson—to the throne. Although initially shy and insecure, King George III would become a strong-willed leader who would oversee the military defeat of France and Spain in the Seven Years' War.

The Treaty of Paris (1763)

> The British gain most of North America; the Spanish gain the Louisiana Territory

The **Treaty of Paris**, signed in February 1763, gave Britain control of France's territories east of the Mississippi River. This encompassed all of Canada, what was then called Spanish Florida (including much of present-day Alabama and Mississippi), and several sugar-growing islands in the West Indies. As compensation, France's ally Spain received the vast Louisiana Territory, including the strategic port of New Orleans and all French land west of the Mississippi. France itself was left with no territory on the North American continent, while Great Britain dramatically increased its imperial holdings and emerged as the greatest empire in the world (see Maps 4.3 and 4.4).

British Americans were delighted. The French menace had been removed from the Ohio valley; and, as a New England minister declared, Great Britain had reached the "summit of earthly grandeur and glory."

Treaty of Paris (1763) The settlement between Great Britain and France that ended the French and Indian War.

Warfare in the Colonies | 155

MAP 4.3 EUROPEAN LAND CLAIMS IN NORTH AMERICA, 1713

- Consult the map key, and then name the imperial power that claimed territory in two different areas of North America before 1763. Which imperial power claimed land between those areas?
- Name the northernmost and southernmost areas claimed by England along the Atlantic coast.
- Now look at Map 4.4 on the next page. Comparing Maps 4.3 and 4.4, name the additional territories England acquired by 1763. Which imperial power no longer claimed lands in North America at that time?

Yet Britain's military success created massive challenges. New territories had to be managed and funded. The staggering cost of maintaining the sprawling North American empire, including the permanent stationing of 10,000 British soldiers in the colonies, strained the imperial budget.

Managing a New Empire

No sooner was the Treaty of Paris signed than King George III and his cabinet, working through Parliament, began regulating the colonies in new ways.

The king ordered stiffer enforcement of economic regulations on the colonies to help reduce the crushing national debt caused by the war. In 1763,

> Colonists taxed to pay staggering British war debts

MAP 4.4 EUROPEAN LAND CLAIMS IN NORTH AMERICA, 1763

- Find the Proclamation Line of 1763. According to the chapter text, who was not supposed to cross it, and why?
- Referring to the map key, name the imperial power that claimed all the land east of the Mississippi River in 1763. According to the chapter text, what were the consequences of claiming all this land?
- Looking at Maps 4.3 and 4.4 together, identify three ways in which the map of North America changed between 1713 and 1763.

the average British citizen paid twenty-six times as much in annual taxes as did the average American colonist. British leaders thought it only fair that Americans should pay more of the expenses for administering and defending the colonies.

Many Americans disagreed, however, arguing that the various Navigation Acts restricting their economic activity were already a form of taxation. "It is truly a miserable thing," said a Connecticut minister, "that we no sooner leave fighting our neighbors, the French, but we must fall to quarreling among ourselves." The resulting tension set in motion a chain of events that would lead to revolution and independence.

Pontiac's Rebellion

After the war, colonists grew eager to take ownership of Indigenous lands west of the Appalachian Mountains that the French had ceded to the British in the Treaty of Paris. Indigenous leaders, who had not been invited to participate in the treaty negotiations, were shocked to learn that the French had "given" their ancestral lands to the British, who were intent upon imposing a harsh settlement on those Indigenous people who had been allies of the French. Indigenous nations in Ohio such as the Shawnee, Iroquois, Algonquian, and Sioux complained to British army officers that "as soon as you conquered the French, you did not care how you treated us."

Frustrated Shawnees led by Chief Cornstalk fought back in the spring of 1763, capturing most of the British forts around the Great Lakes and in the Ohio valley. "Never was panic more general," reported the *Pennsylvania Gazette*, "than that of the Back[woods] Inhabitants, whose terrors at this time exceed that followed on the defeat of General Braddock." At Fort Pitt, formerly Fort Duquesne, the British commander instituted germ warfare when he ordered that blankets infected with smallpox be circulated among the Indigenous people.

The widespread Indigenous attacks came to be called **Pontiac's Rebellion** because of the prominent role played by the Ottawa chieftain in recruiting other tribes to help stop British expansion into their native lands. Pontiac told a British official that the "French never conquered us, neither did they purchase a foot of our Country, nor have they a right to give it to you."

British officials hoped to negotiate with Pontiac an arrangement whereby the two sides would trade generously with one another, but not fight each other. Colonists, however, had other goals, most notably revenge.

In December 1763, frontier ruffians in Pennsylvania took the law into their own hands. Outraged at the unwillingness of the Pennsylvania assembly, dominated by pacifist Quakers, to protect them from marauding Indigenous people, a group called the Paxton Boys (Scots-Irish farmers from Paxton, a cluster of log cabins near Harrisburg) massacred twenty peaceful Conestoga men, women, and children. Then they threatened to kill the so-called Moravians, a group of Christian converts living near Bethlehem. When the Indigenous people took refuge in Philadelphia, some 1,500 Paxton Boys marched on the capital, where Benjamin Franklin helped persuade them to return home.

Pontiac's Rebellion (1763) A series of Indigenous American attacks on British forts and settlements after France ceded to the British its territory east of the Mississippi River as part of the Treaty of Paris without consulting France's Native American allies.

PONTIAC'S REBELLION A hand-colored woodcut depicts Pontiac and allies meeting with British officials during the rebellion. No authentic portrait of Pontiac is known to exist. **What were the results of the Ottawa chieftain's resistance to British occupation of Native American land?**

Proclamation Act of 1763 The proclamation drawing a boundary along the Appalachian Mountains from Canada to Georgia in order to minimize occurrences of violence between settlers and Native Americans; colonists were forbidden to go west of the line.

The Proclamation Line

To help keep peace with the Indigenous nations, King George III issued the **Proclamation Act of 1763**, which drew an imaginary line along the crest of the Appalachian Mountains from Canada to Georgia (see again Map 4.4). American settlers ("our loving subjects") were forbidden to go west of the line to ensure that the Indigenous peoples would not be "molested or disturbed" on their ancestral lands. Settlers already living west of the Appalachians were told to leave.

For the first time, royal officials were curtailing territorial expansion, and American colonists did not like it. George Washington was among those who objected. Like thousands of other British Americans, he was land-hungry; he wanted "to secure some of the most valuable lands in the King's part" even if it meant defying "the Proclamation that restrains it at present."

In practice, the Proclamation Line ended the activities of speculators to buy huge tracts of Indigenous lands but did not keep settlers from pushing into the Indigenous territory in the Ohio valley. By 1767, an Indigenous chief was complaining that White settlers were "making more encroachments on their Country than ever they had before."

Immigration and Forced Migration Soar

Two unexpected results were a surge in European immigration to the American colonies and the growth and expansion of the transatlantic slave trade to the Americas. Between 1763 and 1775, more than 30,000 English, 55,000 Protestant Irish, and 40,000 Scottish immigrants arrived in the colonies, along with 12,000 German and Swiss settlers. At the same time, some 85,000 Africans were brought by force to the southern colonies. It was the greatest mass and forced migration in history to that point, and it provided the impetus for much of America's development thereafter.

Captive Africans Captive men, women, and children disembarked at ports in New England, the Chesapeake, and the southern colonies. From 1700 to 1780, approximately 256,000 captured Africans arrived in Savannah, Charles Town (later Charleston), Philadelphia, New York, Newport, and Boston. They were enslaved upon arrival and put to work in a variety of agricultural, industrial, and nonagricultural settings. Their presence in the colonies led to a Black majority in places such as South Carolina as early as 1720. As a result, slavery, and the trade itself, served as the backbone of the northern and southern economies.

The New England colonies dominated the slave trade by outfitting ships to parts of West Africa and by serving as a major point of entry for those arriving from the continent. Northern communities were complicit with the institution of slavery and also produced clothing and shoes for the enslaved Africans in the southern colonies. While it was still legal to trade in human beings, southern planters eventually moved toward creating a self-sustaining system by the early nineteenth century. This system exploited enslaved women to keep the enslaved population growing by natural reproduction,

AN EAST PROSPECT OF THE CITY OF PHILADELPHIA A detail of an engraving from 1771 showcases the religious diversity among European immigrants in the city of Philadelphia, as seen from across the Delaware River. An Anglican church, a Presbyterian church, a Dutch Calvinist church, and a Quaker meetinghouse—among others—punctuate the Philadelphia skyline.

rather than by direct imports of more captives from Africa. On the eve of American independence, there were approximately 500,000 enslaved people in the colonies. This number would grow even larger after independence.

European Immigrants Most of the new European arrivals were young males who had served as apprentices to learn a craft or trade. Many others were poor farm families who emigrated as a group. Half of them could not afford to pay the cost of crossing the Atlantic and therefore arrived as indentured servants.

The settlers were entering a new society that had no rigid aristocracy. A young English farmer wrote home to say that he missed his friends but valued more his chance to become "independent" in ways unavailable in England. This independence was reserved for European immigrants, as enslaved Africans arrived to a much different America.

The America that all new arrivals landed in had been transformed by the outcomes of the French and Indian War, which redistributed control over vast stretches of land. The war in North America had been part of a larger series of wars (the Seven Years' War) between Britain and its European allies against France or Spain and their allies. Under the treaty that ended the conflict, France lost all its territory in North America, Britain gained Florida and Canada, and Spain gained the Louisiana Territory. In addition to shifting the international balance of power in Europe, the war's outcome left Britain in control of desirable Indigenous lands in the Ohio valley.

Tightening of Control over the British Colonies

As Britain tightened its hold over the colonies—and over the Indigenous peoples and enslaved Africans—after 1763, American colonists reminded Parliament that their original charters guaranteed that they should have all

> **CORE OBJECTIVE**
> **3.** Describe how, after the French and Indian War, the British tightened their control over the colonies, and summarize the colonial responses.

the rights and liberties of English citizens. Why should they be governed by a distant legislature in which they had no elected representatives? Such arguments, however, fell on deaf ears in Parliament.

Grenville's Colonial Policy

British government insists that colonists pay war debt

A new British government, led by Prime Minister George Grenville, continued to grapple with the huge debts accumulated during the Seven Years' War, along with the added expenses of maintaining troops in America. Grenville insisted that American settlers pay for the British soldiers defending them. He resented the large number of American smugglers who avoided British taxes on imported goods, and ordered colonial officials to tighten enforcement of the Navigation Acts.

The Sugar Act (1764)

George Grenville's crackdowns posed a serious threat to New England's prosperity. Distilling rum out of molasses, a sweet syrup made from sugarcane, had become quite profitable, especially if the molasses could be smuggled in from Caribbean islands still controlled by the French.

New taxes and regulations

To raise more money from the colonies, Grenville put through the American Revenue Act of 1764, commonly known as the Sugar Act, which cut the tax on molasses in half. Doing so, he believed, would reduce the temptation to smuggle French molasses. The Sugar Act, however, also added *duties* (taxes) on other goods (sugar, wines, coffee, spices) imported into America. The new tax revenues, Grenville believed, would help pay for "the necessary expenses of defending, protecting, and securing, the said colonies."

With the Sugar Act, Parliament sought to *raise revenues* from the colonies and not merely to *regulate* their trade with other nations, as had been the case up to that point. Colonists claimed that the Sugar Act taxed them without their consent, since they had no elected representatives in Parliament. British officials argued, however, that Parliament's power over the colonies was absolute and indivisible. If the American colonists accepted parliamentary authority in *any* area, they had to accept it in *every* area, including taxation.

THE GREAT FINANCIER A British cartoon from 1765 depicts the struggling British economy. George Grenville stands in the center holding up a scale to measure British "Debts" and "Savings," with the debts far outweighing the savings. On the left, an Indigenous woman wearing a yoke represents America, burdened by taxes without representation. **Why was Britain in such financial straits in the early 1760s, and how did Grenville attempt to pay off Britain's debts?**

The Quartering Act (1765)

Then in March 1765, Grenville persuaded Parliament to pass the Quartering Act as part of his new system of colonial regulations. The Quartering Act required the colonies to feed and house many of the 10,000 British troops stationed in the colonies. Such a step seemed perfectly appropriate to Grenville, since he and many others in Britain believed that the American settlers should contribute to the expense of defending their colonies. Many colonists, however, viewed the Quartering Act as yet another form of tax as well as another form of repression against the colonists. Why, they asked, were so many British soldiers needed in colonial cities? If the British troops were there to defend against Indigenous people, why were they based in cities rather than along the frontier?

The Stamp Act (1765)

Later in March 1765, Grenville pushed through an even more controversial measure. The **Stamp Act** required colonists to purchase paper from London embossed with a government revenue stamp. Only British currency could be used to purchase the stamped paper. This law affected all colonists because it applied to paper for virtually every possible use: newspapers, pamphlets, deeds, licenses, insurance policies, college diplomas, even playing cards. The requirement was to go into effect on November 1.

The Stamp Act was the first effort by Parliament to place a tax directly on American goods and services rather than levying an "external" tax on imports and exports, and it offended just about everyone. Benjamin Franklin's daughter Sarah ("Sally") wrote to her father while he visited London, reporting that the only subject of conversation in America was the Stamp Act, "and nothing else is talked of.... Everybody has something to say" about the hated tax, in part because, when combined with the Sugar Act, it promised to bring American economic activity in the colonies to a halt. It also showed that Parliament was determined to deny American colonists their rights to representation in Parliament.

Stamp Act (1765) An act of Parliament requiring that all printed materials in the American colonies use paper with an official tax stamp in order to pay for British military protection of the colonies.

OPPOSITION TO THE STAMP ACT On October 31, 1765, the *Pennsylvania Journal* printed a skull and crossbones on its masthead in protest of the Stamp Act, which was to take effect the next day. **Why was the Stamp Act met with such opposition by the colonists?**

Boston lawyer John Adams led the opposition to the Stamp Act. In doing so, he unwittingly exposed the contradiction between the colonists' efforts to protect their own civil liberties and their enslavement of hundreds of thousands of Africans and Indigenous people. Adams expressed his defiance of the Stamp Act, for example, by pledging, "We will not be their negroes." But another Boston agitator, James Otis Jr., saw a problem in statements like Adams's. Yes, "the colonists are by the law of nature free born," Otis acknowledged, but "indeed all men are, white or black." It was therefore absurd to "enslave a man [simply] because he is black."

The British controlled thirty colonies in the Western Hemisphere, but only the thirteen mainland colonies rose up against the new taxes. To American settlers, the "engine" of British tyranny was a threat to their very existence.

The Whig Point of View

George Grenville's colonial policies ignited an intense debate about the proper relationship between Great Britain and its colonies. American colonists who opposed British policies began to call themselves Patriots, or *Whigs*, a name earlier applied to British critics of royal power. In turn, Whigs labeled the king and his "corrupt" government ministers and Parliamentary supporters *Tories*, a term of abuse meaning "friends of the king."

In 1764 and 1765, colonial Whigs felt that Grenville was violating their rights in several ways. Although the French had been defeated and Canada was solidly under British control, thousands of British soldiers remained in America. Were the troops there to protect the colonists or scare them into obedience?

Whigs also argued that although British citizens had the right to be taxed only by their elected representatives in Parliament, American colonists had no such representatives. British leaders countered that the colonists enjoyed **virtual representation** by all members of Parliament; but William Pitt, a staunch supporter of American rights in Parliament, dismissed virtual representation as "the most contemptible idea that ever entered into the head of a man." Many others, in both Britain and America, agreed. Sir Francis Bernard, the royal governor of Massachusetts, correctly predicted that the stamp tax "would cause a great Alarm & meet much Opposition."

Protests in the Colonies

The Stamp Act did arouse intense resentment and resistance. In a flood of pamphlets, speeches, resolutions, and street protests, critics repeated a slogan familiar to American colonists: "No taxation without representation [in Parliament]."

Rebels, calling themselves **Sons of Liberty**, emerged in every colony to organize protests, often meeting beneath "liberty trees"—in Boston, a great elm; in Charles Town, a live oak; in New York, they met under the "liberty

---

virtual representation The idea that the American colonies, although they had no actual representative in Parliament, were "virtually" represented by all members of Parliament.

Sons of Liberty First organized by Samuel Adams in the 1770s, groups of colonists dedicated to militant resistance against British control of the colonies.

THE LIBERTY TREE At this meeting of the Sons of Liberty, angry colonists hang effigies of two tax collectors from the branches of a Liberty Tree.

pole." These men represented all walks of life and were a well-organized, militant political organization created in a clandestine fashion.

The Nonimportation Movement

Since the mid-seventeenth century, colonial consumers had become dependent on imported British manufactured goods—textiles, ceramics, glassware, and printed products. Now, however, patriots by the thousands signed nonimportation (boycott) agreements pledging not to buy British goods.

The nonimportation movement united Whigs from different communities and different colonies. Women played a key role in the resistance. Calling themselves **Daughters of Liberty**, women such as Sarah Bradlee Fulton stopped buying imported British clothes and quit drinking British tea to "save this abused Country from Ruin and Slavery." Using herbs and flowers, they made "Liberty Tea" instead. The Daughters of Liberty also participated in public "spinning bees," whereby they gathered in town squares to spin yarn and wool into fabric, known as homespun. In 1769, the *Boston Evening Post* reported that the "industry and frugality of American ladies" were enabling "the political salvation of a whole continent."

Colonial Unity

The boycotts worked. Imports of British goods fell by 40 percent, and thousands of English workers lost their jobs as a result. At the same time, the Virginia House of Burgesses struck the first official blow against the Stamp Act with the Virginia Resolves (1765), a series of resolutions inspired by

> Boycotts of British goods

Daughters of Liberty Colonial women who protested the British government's tax policies by boycotting British products, such as clothing, and who wove their own fabric, or "homespun."

> Virginia Resolves and the Declaration of Rights and Grievances

REPEAL OF THE STAMP ACT This 1766 cartoon shows George Grenville carrying the dead Stamp Act in its coffin. In the background, trade with America starts up again.

Patrick Henry. Virginians, Henry asserted, could be taxed only by their elected legislature, not by Parliament.

That same year, the Massachusetts House of Representatives invited the other colonial assemblies to send delegates to New York City to discuss opposition to the Stamp Act. Over two weeks in October, the men attending the Stamp Act Congress formulated a Declaration of the Rights and Grievances of the Colonies. The delegates insisted that they would accept no taxes being "imposed on them" without "their own consent, given personally, or by their representatives."

Repeal of the Stamp Act

George Grenville, having lost the confidence of King George III, was replaced by Lord Rockingham in July 1765. The growing rebellion in America convinced Rockingham that the Stamp Act was a mistake, and Parliament repealed it in February 1766. To save face, Parliament also passed the Declaratory Act, which asserted its power to govern the colonies "in all cases whatsoever."

The repeal of the Stamp Act set off excited celebrations throughout the colonies. A British newspaper reported that the debate over the stamp tax had led some colonists to express a desire for "independence." The editor predicted that eventually the colonies would "shake off all subjection. If we yield to them . . . by repealing the Stamp Act, it is all over."

The Townshend Acts Fan the Flames

More taxes under Townshend

In July 1766, George III replaced Lord Rockingham with William Pitt, the former prime minister who had exercised leadership during the Seven Years'

War. For a time, the guiding force in the Pitt ministry was Charles Townshend, the Treasury chief whose "abilities were superior to those of all men," said a colleague, "and his judgment [common sense] below that of any man."

In 1767, Townshend pushed through Parliament a plan to generate more colonial revenue. The Revenue Act of 1767, which taxed colonial imports of glass, lead, paint, paper, and tea, was the most hated of the so-called **Townshend Acts**. It posed an even more severe threat than George Grenville's taxes had, for Townshend planned to use the new tax revenues to pay the salaries of the royal governors in the colonies. Until that point, the colonial assemblies had paid the salaries, thus giving them leverage over the governors. John Adams observed that Townshend's plan would make the royal governors "independent of the people." Writing in the *Boston Gazette,* Adams insisted that such "an INDEPENDENT ruler, [is] a MONSTER in a free state."

Townshend Acts (1767)
Parliamentary measures to extract more revenue from the colonies; the Revenue Act of 1767, which taxed tea, paper, and other colonial imports, was one of the most notorious of these policies.

Discontent on the Frontier

While the disputes over British policies raged along the seaboard, the backcountry stirred with internal colonial quarrels that had nothing to do with the Stamp and Townshend Acts. Rival claims to lands east of Lake Champlain pitted New York against New Hampshire. Eventually, the residents of the disputed area formed their own state of Vermont, which would be recognized as a state in 1791.

In North Carolina, farmers felt especially oppressed by the government's refusal to issue paper money or accept produce in payment of taxes, and by 1766 they resisted. Calling themselves Regulators, they refused to pay taxes, challenged public officials, and disobeyed the law.

NORTH CAROLINA REGULATORS The North Carolina Regulators were a group of frontier colonists who opposed political corruption, excessive taxes, and mistreatment. They mobilized themselves to administer vigilante justice and to block tax collection efforts.

Loyalists Colonists who remained loyal to Britain before and during the Revolutionary War.

Patriots Colonists who rebelled against British authority before and during the Revolutionary War.

In 1771, William Tryon, the royal governor of North Carolina, led 1,200 militiamen to victory over some 2,000 poorly organized Regulators in the Battle of Alamance. Tryon's men then ranged through the western backcountry, forcing some 6,500 farmers to sign an oath of allegiance to the king in order to be pardoned.

These disputes and revolts illustrated the diversity of opinion among American colonists on the eve of the Revolution. Britain's efforts to tighten control over the colonies after the French and Indian War had brought them to this point. Facing extensive debt, the British imposed various taxes on the colonies to pay for their defense by imperial troops. Claiming "No taxation without representation," the colonists resisted and, in many cases, refused to pay the taxes and challenged public officials. Although some colonists remained loyal to the Crown, rebel coalitions such as the Sons of Liberty and Daughters of Liberty united differing factions of dissatisfied colonists in protest against the British government.

> **CORE OBJECTIVE**
> **4.** Explain the underlying factors amid the events in the 1770s that led the colonists to declare their independence from Britain.

The Road to the American Revolution

The Townshend Acts surprised and angered many colonists, including Samuel ("Sam") Adams of Boston. A failed beer brewer and tax collector, he had become one of the most radical rebels and a driving force behind the Sons of Liberty. He decided that a small group of determined Whigs could generate a mass movement. "It does not take a majority to prevail," Adams insisted, "but rather an irate, tireless minority, keen on setting brushfires of freedom in the minds of men."

American Patriots

Early in 1768, Adams and James Otis Jr. convinced the Massachusetts Assembly to circulate a letter that restated the illegality of taxation without representation. British officials ordered the Massachusetts Assembly to withdraw the letter. The delegates refused, and the king ordered the Massachusetts legislature dissolved.

In October 1768, in response to an appeal by the royal governor, 4,000 British troops arrived in Boston. They disembarked with great ceremony, marching through the streets behind a brass band. **Loyalists**, as the Americans who supported the king and Parliament had begun to be called, welcomed the soldiers; **Patriots**, those rebelling against British authority, viewed the troops as an occupation force. Sam Adams growled that the king had "no right to send troops here . . . and I look upon them as foreign enemies." He then threatened violence: "We will destroy every soldier that dares put his foot on shore."

SAMUEL ADAMS Adams was an organizer of the Sons of Liberty, the secret society that was formed to preserve the rights of American Patriots.

THE BLOODY MASSACRE Paul Revere created this engraving of the Boston Massacre about three weeks after the event, and it was one of the most effective pieces of political propaganda of the Revolutionary period. It shows an organized row of British soldiers shooting down an unarmed cluster of colonists, richly dressed and putting themselves in the line of fire as they carry their wounded compatriots to safety. Some historians, however, question the accuracy of this engraving. **What would a more accurate representation of the Boston Massacre show?**

Meanwhile, in London, the king appointed still another new chief minister, Lord Frederick North, and told him to crack down on the rebellious colonists. "America must fear you—before she can love you," North told Parliament.

The Boston Massacre (1770)

In Boston, the presence of British soldiers had become a constant source of irritation. Crowds frequently heckled the soldiers, many of whom had earned the abuse by harassing the colonists.

On the evening of March 5, 1770, two dozen Boston rowdies—teens, Irishmen, and sailors—began throwing icicles and oyster shells at Hugh White, a young soldier guarding the Customs House. Someone rang the town fire bell, drawing a larger crowd to the scene, as the taunting continued: "Kill him, kill him, knock him down!"

A squad of soldiers arrived to help White, but the crowd surrounded them. When someone knocked a soldier down, he arose and fired his musket. Others joined in. After the smoke had cleared, five men lay dead or dying on the cobblestone street, and eight more were wounded. The first one killed was Crispus Attucks, a formerly enslaved man who worked at the docks. He is known as the first person to die for American independence. The *Boston Gazette* called it a "horrid massacre." More than 10,000 people attended the funerals of the murdered colonists.

Nine British soldiers were arrested and jailed. Never in Massachusetts had a trial generated such passion and excitement. Sam Adams and other firebrands demanded quick justice, but six months passed before the trial convened. Finally, in late October, two of the British soldiers, convicted of manslaughter, were branded on the thumb with a hot iron.

Impact of the Boston Massacre

The so-called **Boston Massacre** sent shock waves throughout the colonies and all the way to London. Only the decision to postpone the trial allowed tensions to ease. At the same time, the impact of the colonial boycott of British products persuaded Lord North to modify the Townshend Acts.

Late in April 1770, Parliament repealed all the Townshend duties except for the tea tax, which the king wanted to keep as a symbol of Parliament's authority. Colonial discontent subsided. The redcoats left Boston but remained in Canada, and the British navy continued to patrol the New England coast looking for smugglers.

The *Gaspée* Incident (1772)

The Gaspée incident

Two months later, a naval incident further eroded the colonies' fragile relationship with the mother country. Near Warwick, Rhode Island, the British warship *Gaspée* ran aground while chasing smugglers. Its hungry crew seized local sheep, hogs, and chickens. A crowd of enraged colonists then boarded the *Gaspée*, shot the captain, removed the crew, and looted and burned the ship.

In response to the *Gaspée* incident, Sam Adams organized in Boston the first **Committee of Correspondence**, which issued a statement of the American colonies' rights and grievances and invited other towns to do the same. Similar committees sprang up across the colonies, forming a unified network of communication and resistance.

By 1772, Thomas Hutchinson, the royal governor of Massachusetts, could tell the colonial assembly that the choice facing American colonists was stark: They must choose between obeying "the supreme authority of Parliament" and "total independence." Privately, Hutchinson grew convinced that colonial rebelliousness resulted from too much "democracy" in America. In England, fewer than one in five men could vote; but two-thirds of American colonists voted. The result of such widespread participation, he complained, was constant disobedience.

Boston Massacre (1770) A violent confrontation between British soldiers and a Boston mob on March 5, 1770, in which five colonists were killed.

Committee of Correspondence A group of Boston colonists organized by Samuel Adams to address American grievances, assert American rights, and form a network of rebellion.

The Boston Tea Party (1773)

The British prime minister, Lord North, soon provided the spark to transform American resentment into rebellion. In 1773, he tried to bail out the struggling East India Company, which had in its London warehouses some 17 million pounds of Asian tea that it desperately needed to sell before the tea rotted. Under North's leadership, Parliament passed the Tea Act of 1773 to allow the company to send its tea directly to America without paying taxes. British tea merchants could thereby undercut the prices charged by their American competitors, most of whom were smugglers who bought tea from the Dutch.

In Massachusetts, the Committees of Correspondence alerted colonists that the British government was trying to purchase colonial submission with cheap tea. ("Tea stands for Tyranny!") The reduction in the price of tea was a clever trick to make colonists accept taxation without consent. In Boston, furious citizens decided that their passion for liberty outweighed their love for tea.

On December 16, 1773, scores of Patriots boarded three British cargo ships in Boston Harbor and dumped 342 chests filled with 46 tons of East India Company tea into the icy water. The Patriots disguised themselves as Mohawk warriors to protect their identities and make a political statement against British authority.

The **Boston Tea Party** was, according to John Adams, "so bold, so daring" that it represented a turning point in relations with the monarchy. The destruction of so much valuable tea convinced George III that a forceful response was required. "The die is now cast. The colonists must either submit or triumph. We must not retreat," he wrote to Lord North, who decided

Boston Tea Party (1773) A demonstration against the Tea Act of 1773 in which the Sons of Liberty, dressed as Native Americans, dumped hundreds of chests of British-owned tea into Boston Harbor.

Boston Tea Party

THE ABLE DOCTOR, OR AMERICA SWALLOWING THE BITTER DRAUGHT This 1774 engraving shows Lord Frederick North, the Boston Port Bill in his pocket, pouring tea down America's throat and America spitting it back.

to make Boston an example to the rest of the colonies. In the end, the king's efforts to reassert royal control helped turn a rebellion into a revolution that would cost Britain far more than three shiploads of tea.

The Coercive Acts

In 1774, as a result of the Tea Party, Lord North convinced Parliament to punish Boston and the province of Massachusetts by passing a cluster of harsh laws, called the **Coercive Acts**. (Colonists renamed them the "Intolerable Acts.")

The Port Act closed Boston Harbor until the city paid for the lost tea. (It never did.) The closing of the port meant the loss of many jobs, and the cost of consumer goods skyrocketed as trade ceased. A new Quartering Act ordered colonists to provide lodging and supplies for British soldiers.

Finally, the Massachusetts Government Act undermined self-government by giving the royal governor the authority to appoint the colony's legislative council (which until then had been elected by the people), as well as local judges and sheriffs. It also banned town meetings. Collectively, the Intolerable Acts outraged colonists and transformed scattered resistance into widespread rebellion.

By August 1774, Patriots across Massachusetts were taking control of local governments. They also began stockpiling weapons and gunpowder in anticipation of an eventual clash with British troops.

Elsewhere, colonists rallied to help Boston by boycotting, burning, or dumping British tea. In Edenton, North Carolina, fifty-one women, led by Penelope Barker, met in October 1774 and staged the Edenton Tea party. They resolved to stop buying British tea and other imports "until such time that all acts which tend to enslave our Native country shall be repealed." Barker sent a copy of their resolution to London newspapers to let the British government know that American women were as upset by George III's harsh policies as were the men. "Maybe it has only been men who have protested the king up to now," Barker explained. "That only means we women have taken too long to let our voices be heard. We are signing our names to a document, not hiding ourselves behind [Indigenous] costumes like the men in Boston did at their tea party. The British will know who we are."

In Virginia, George Washington found himself in a debate with Bryan Fairfax, an old friend and a self-described Royalist. Fairfax blamed the Boston rebels for the tensions with London. Washington disagreed, defending the "quiet and steady conduct of the people of the Massachusetts Bay." It was time, he added, for the American colonists to stand up for their rights or submit to being treated like "abject slaves."

Earlier, in Williamsburg, when the Virginia assembly (House of Burgesses) met in May, Thomas Jefferson suggested that June 1, 1774—the effective date of the Boston Port Act—become an official day of fasting and prayer throughout the colony.

> Women organize boycotts of British tea and other goods

Coercive Acts (1774) Four parliamentary measures that required the colonies to pay for damages caused by the Boston Tea Party. The Acts closed the port of Boston, imposed a military government, disallowed colonial trials of British soldiers, and forced the quartering of troops in private homes.

The royal governor responded by dissolving the assembly, whose members then decided to form a Continental Congress to represent all the colonies in the growing dispute with the mother country. As Samuel Savage, a Connecticut colonist, wrote in May 1774, the conflict had come down to a single question: "Whether we shall or shall not be governed by a British Parliament."

The First Continental Congress (1774)

On September 5, 1774, fifty-five delegates from twelve colonies (Georgia was absent), making up the First Continental Congress, assembled in Philadelphia, the largest American city. The gathering was unprecedented. Never had representatives from so many colonies met to coordinate joint resistance to British policies. John Adams wrote to his wife, Abigail, that every delegate "is a great man—an orator, a critic, a statesman," and they were beginning to imagine themselves as a nation rather than as individual colonies: "The distinctions between Virginians, Pennsylvanians, New Yorkers, and New Englanders are no more."

The Continental Congress stressed their "allegiance and submission" to the king while pledging to resist British tyranny with force. The delegates adopted a Declaration of American Rights, which proclaimed once again the rights of colonists as British citizens and denied Parliament's authority to regulate internal colonial affairs. "We demand no new rights," said the Congress. "We ask only for peace, liberty, and security."

Boycotting British Goods

The Congress also adopted the Continental Association of 1774, which recommended that every colony organize committees to enforce a complete boycott of all imported British goods—a dramatic step that would be followed by a refusal to export American goods to Britain. The county and city committees forming the Continental Association became the organizational network for the resistance movement. Seven thousand men across the colonies served on the local committees, and many more women helped put the boycotts into practice. The committees required colonists to sign an oath refusing to purchase British goods.

Thousands of common people—men and women—participated in the boycott of British goods, volunteered in Patriot militia units, attended town meetings, and ousted royal officials. As the residents of Pittsfield, Massachusetts, affirmed in a petition, "We have always believed that the people are the fountain of power." The Loyalist Thomas Hutchinson, however, assured the king that the American colonists could not remain united because "the people were greatly divided among themselves in every colony." Hutchinson had no doubt "that all America would *submit*, and that they *must*, and moreover would, *soon*."

Hutchinson could not have been more wrong. The rebellion now extended well beyond simple grievances over taxation. Patriots decided that Parliament, the king, and his prime minister were engaged in a *conspiracy* against their liberties. By the end of 1774, more and more colonists were rejecting the authority of Parliament over their lives. Militant Patriots replaced royal governors with "committees of safety" that began secretly purchasing weapons and gunpowder from European nations. The colonies were mobilizing for war. In Boston, an increasingly nervous General Thomas Gage, the commander-in-chief of British forces in North America and newly appointed military governor, requested more troops to suppress the growing "flames of sedition." He reported that "civil government is near its end." Gage even tried to bribe Sam Adams to switch sides, but Adams refused.

Last-Minute Compromise

In London, King George fumed over his failure to control the colonies. He wrote to Lord North that the colonists were displaying a "most daring spirit of resistance and disobedience" and that "blows must decide" whether the colonists "are to be subject to this country or independent."

In early 1775, Parliament announced that Massachusetts was officially "in rebellion." London officials hired Samuel Johnson to write a pamphlet called *Taxation No Tyranny* (1775), expressing the British government's perspective on the colonists and their slogan, "No Taxation without Representation." However much the American colonists might complain about taxes, he insisted, they remained British subjects who should obey government actions. If the colonists wanted to participate in Parliament, Johnson suggested, they could move to England. Whatever the case, Johnson expressed confidence that the dispute between England and America would be resolved through "English superiority and American obedience."

Bold Talk of War

Patriots, however, were not in an obedient mood. Patrick Henry, soon to be governor of Virginia, announced that war with England had become unavoidable. The twenty-nine-year-old Henry, a farmer and storekeeper turned self-taught lawyer, claimed that the colonies had "done everything that could be done to avert the storm which is now coming on," but their protests had been met only by "violence and insult." Freedom, Henry shouted, could now be bought only with blood: "We must fight!" If forced to choose, he supposedly exclaimed, "Give me liberty"—he then paused dramatically, clenched his fist as if it held a dagger, and plunged it into his chest—"or give me death."

As Henry predicted, events quickly moved toward armed conflict. By mid-1775, the king and Parliament had lost control of the colonies; they could neither persuade nor force the Patriots to accept new regulations and taxes. Reporting from Boston, General Gage warned his superiors in London that armed conflict would unleash "civil war." But John Montagu, Lord Sandwich, head of the British navy, dismissed the rebels as "raw, undisciplined, cowardly men" without an army or navy. The assumption in London

PATRICK HENRY OF VIRGINIA Henry was a longtime advocate of colonial rights, fighting for the Stamp Act Resolutions to be passed in Virginia in 1765. A decade later, in a speech to Virginia's Revolutionary Convention, he made the famous declaration, "Give me liberty, or give me death!"

that the colonists would back down infuriated Joseph Warren, a Boston physician. "These fellows say we won't fight. By heavens, I hope I shall die up to my knees in blood."

Fighting Begins: Lexington and Concord

On April 14, 1775, the British army received orders to stop the "open rebellion" in Massachusetts. General Gage decided to arrest rebel leaders such as Sam Adams and seize the militia's gunpowder stored at Concord, a village of 265 families sixteen miles northwest of Boston. Adams, however, had been alerted to the danger by none other than Gage's American-born wife, Margaret Kemble. The British governor-general was so humiliated by his wife's treason that he shipped her off to his estate in England.

Lexington After dark on April 18, some 800 British soldiers converged near the Boston Common. Under a moonlit sky, the redcoats quietly boarded boats and crossed the Charles River to Cambridge, then set out on foot for Lexington, about eleven miles away (see Map 4.5). When Patriots got wind of the plan, Paul Revere and William Dawes mounted their horses for their famous "midnight ride" to warn rebel leaders that the British were coming. In Lexington, the church bell began to ring, and bonfires were lit across the countryside, alerting militiamen to grab their weapons and rush to the town square. Other riders fanned out to alert the militias in towns near Lexington.

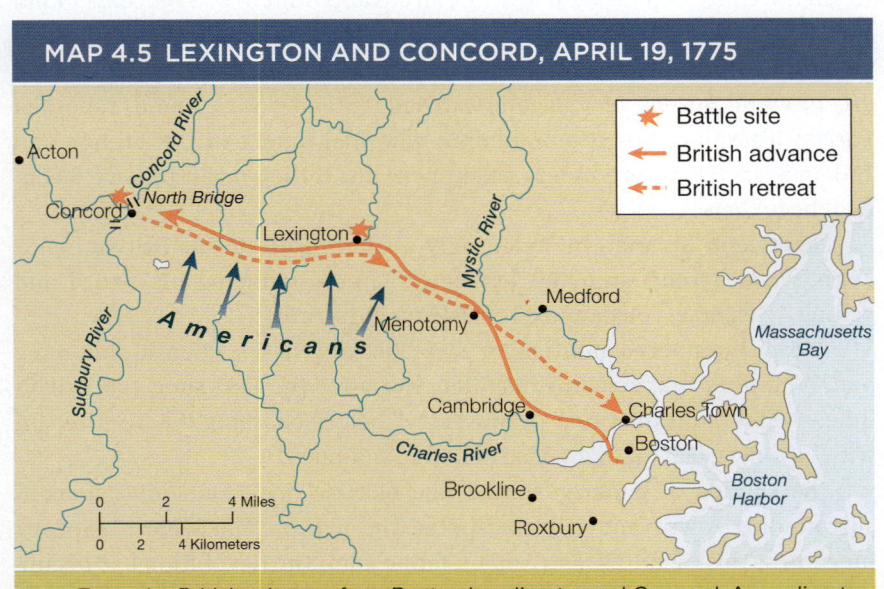

MAP 4.5 LEXINGTON AND CONCORD, APRIL 19, 1775

- Trace the British advance from Boston heading toward Concord. According to the chapter text, why were they going there?
- Trace the British retreat from Concord back to Charles Town. What do the blue arrows labeled "Americans" represent?
- According to the chapter text, why did the Americans' tactics along the road between Concord and Lexington succeed?

THE BATTLE OF LEXINGTON (1775) Pictured here is Amos Doolittle's impression of the Battle of Lexington as combat begins between the Royal Marines and the Minutemen.

> Shots fired at Lexington and Concord

In the chilly gray dawn of April 19, an advance unit of 238 redcoats found American captain John Parker and seventy-six Minutemen (Patriot militia who could assemble "at a minute's notice") lined up on the Lexington town green, while dozens of villagers watched. "Stand your ground," shouted Parker, a farmer with seven children who had fought in the French and Indian War. "Don't fire unless fired upon; but if they mean to have a war, let it begin here!"

Parker and his men intended only a silent protest, but British major John Pitcairn rode onto the Lexington Green, swinging his sword and yelling, "Disperse, you damned rebels! You dogs, run!"

The outnumbered militiamen were backing away when a shot rang out. Who fired first remains disputed; but after the first shot, the British unleashed a "continual roar of musketry" before charging the Minutemen with bayonets, leaving eight dead and nine wounded.

The sounds of gunfire "spread like electric fire," and militiamen in surrounding towns and villages spread the alarm. "Oh, what a glorious morning is this!" exulted Sam Adams, for he knew the Revolution had begun.

Concord The British officers next led their men west to Concord, where they destroyed hidden military supplies, killed livestock, and burned Patriot houses. They shot or bayoneted those who resisted. More than a hundred bullet holes pockmarked a tavern where the owner, his wife, and two villagers were found bayoneted, their skulls crushed. A young boy was so enraged at British atrocities that he used a hatchet to scalp a wounded redcoat and hack off his ears.

While marching out of Concord, the British encountered swarms of American riflemen. Shots were fired, and a dozen or so British soldiers were killed or wounded. More important, the short skirmish and ringing church bells alerted nearby rebel farmers, ministers, craftsmen, and merchants to grab their muskets. They were, as one of them said, determined to "be free or die."

By noon, the exhausted redcoats began a twenty-mile retreat that soon turned into a living hell. Less than a mile out of Concord, they suffered the first of many ambushes (see again Map 4.5). The narrow road became a gauntlet of death as rebel marksmen fired from every direction, hidden behind stone walls, trees, barns, and houses. "It was a day full of horror," one of the soldiers recalled. The redcoats were no longer marching; they were fleeing. "We began to run rather than retreat," one of them said.

By nightfall, the redcoats were safely back in Boston, having marched some forty miles and suffered three times as many dead and wounded as the Americans. A British general reported that the colonists had earned his respect: "Whoever looks upon them as an irregular mob will find himself much mistaken."

Until the Battles of Lexington and Concord, both sides had assumed that the other would back down. Instead, the clash of redcoats and rebels in the two villages had turned a resistance movement into a war of rebellion. Thousands of New England militiamen, having heard that the redcoats had "engaged in butchering and destroying our brethren," began to converge on Boston, eager for revenge. In Virginia, Thomas Jefferson noted that "a frenzy of revenge" had been unleashed among "all ranks of people." In Georgia, the royal governor noted that "a general rebellion throughout America is coming on suddenly and swiftly." In London, a British government official said, "The news from America is as bad as possible."

Rebellion Turns into War

The Revolutionary War had begun. Patriots seized control of local governments and rooted out Loyalists. A British supporter of the rebellion told Admiral Richard Howe, the commander of the Royal Navy's North American fleet, "In all the wars which you have formerly been concerned in, you had only armies to contend with. In this case, you have both an army and a country to combat."

General George Washington

In mid-June 1775, the Second Continental Congress unanimously selected forty-three-year-old George Washington to lead the new Continental Army. It was, he said, "an honor he wished to avoid," but he could not refuse it once offered.

Washington had earned his new role. Having lost his father at an early age, he had hoped to serve in the British navy, until his mother implored him to manage the family farm instead. His service in the French and Indian War had made him one of the few experienced American army officers. He was admired for his success as a planter, surveyor, and land speculator, as well as for his service in the Virginia legislature and the Continental Congress. Washington also married well: his wife, Martha Custis, had been the wealthiest widow in Virginia.

Perhaps most important to the Revolutionary cause, George Washington *looked* like a leader. Weighing 200 pounds and standing almost six feet four, he was an imposing figure, both powerful and graceful. His courage in battle, perseverance after defeat, and integrity in judgment would earn him the respect of his troops and the nation.

Washington refused to be paid for his service. His first act as commander was to draft a will and write to his wife, explaining that he had done his best to avoid being considered for the position but that in the end it seemed his "destiny" to lead the Revolution.

The Battle of Bunker Hill

The first major battle: Bunker Hill

On Saturday, June 17, the day that George Washington was named commander-in-chief, Patriot militiamen engaged British forces in their first major clash, the Battle of Bunker Hill (nearby Breed's Hill was the battle's actual location).

To strengthen their control over the area around Boston, some 2,400 British troops boarded barges and crossed the Charles River to the Charlestown Peninsula. With drums beating and bayonets glistening, they marched up Breed's Hill in tight formation through waist-high grass, boosting themselves over fences and low stone walls as the American defenders watched from behind their earthworks.

The militiamen—mostly farmers—waited until the redcoats ventured within thirty paces, then loosed a volley of lead that crumpled the first three rows of England's finest warriors and sent the attackers retreating in disarray. A Patriot said the British fell like "grass when mowed."

The British regrouped and attacked again, but the Patriot riflemen forced them back a second time. General William Howe could not believe his eyes. All his aides had been killed or wounded, and his professional soldiers were being stymied by what he'd considered to be a "rabble" of untrained farmers. It was, he said, "a moment that I never felt before." During the third British assault, the colonists ran out of gunpowder and retreated, but the British were too tired to follow. In less than an hour, the Loyalists had suffered 1,054 casualties (killed or wounded), more than twice the Patriot losses. A British officer reported to London that "we have lost a thousand of our best men and officers" because of "an absurd and destructive confidence, carelessness, or ignorance."

"Open and Avowed" Enemies

Three weeks after the Battle of Bunker Hill, in July 1775, the Continental Congress sent King George the Olive Branch Petition, urging him to negotiate. When the petition reached London, however, the king refused to read it. Instead, in a Proclamation of Rebellion, he denounced the "traitorous" Americans as "open and avowed" enemies trying to establish their own "independent empire."

Few Patriots were ready to call for independence, however. When the Continental Congress had convened at Philadelphia in May 1775, most of the delegates still wanted Parliament to restore their rights so that they could resume being loyal British colonists.

Independence

The Revolutionary War was well under way when Thomas Paine, a thirty-nine-year-old English tax collector who had lost his job, fallen deeply in debt, separated from his second wife, and immigrated to America in 1774, helped transform a rebellion into a revolution. He had arrived in America penniless and unknown but soon found work as a journalist writing for the *Pennsylvania Magazine* in Philadelphia.

In January 1776, Paine published a stirring fifty-page pamphlet titled **Common Sense**, in which he urged Americans to seize their independence. Nothing was more absurd, he maintained, than the notion that God had given

> Olive Branch Petition rejected

Common Sense (1776) A popular pamphlet written by Thomas Paine attacking British principles of hereditary rule and monarchical government and advocating a declaration of American independence.

THE COMING REVOLUTION The Continental Congress votes for independence, July 2, 1776.

kings the right to rule with absolute power or that an island nation (England) should exercise dominance over an entire continent (North America).

Until *Common Sense* appeared, most Patriots had directed their grievances at Parliament. Paine, however, directly attacked the king. The "common sense" of the matter, he stressed, was that George III, "the royal brute unfit to be the ruler of a free people," had caused the rebellion and had ordered the violation of American rights. Paine urged Americans to abandon the monarchy and proclaim their independence: "The blood of the slain, the weeping voice of nature cries, 'TIS TIME TO PART.'"

> Paine's *Common Sense* musters public support for independence

Within three months of the pamphlet's appearance, more than 150,000 copies were circulating throughout the colonies and around the world. It convinced many anxious American rebels that independence was necessary and inevitable. "*Common Sense* is working a powerful change in the minds of men," George Washington observed. Having received correspondence from associates in Europe, John Adams reported that the French and other Europeans were also enraptured by their reading of *Common Sense*. "Without the pen of the author of *Common Sense*," Adams later maintained, "the sword of Washington would have been raised in vain."

The Battle of Moore's Creek Bridge

Thomas Paine's words boosted the Patriots' morale, but what they needed most was a true battlefield victory. It came near Wilmington, North Carolina, in late February 1776. The royal governor of North Carolina ordered the Tory (Loyalist) militia—mostly Scottish Highlanders who had served in the British army and were now promised 200 acres in exchange for their service—to don their kilts, sharpen their swords, sound their bagpipes, and head toward the coast to link up with British forces landing by sea. The governor, expecting a Loyalist victory, announced: "This is the moment when this country may be delivered from anarchy." The Patriots rushed to stop them.

On February 27, the two forces clashed at Moore's Creek Bridge, near the Cape Fear River. The battle was intense but brief, lasting three minutes. About 50 Tories were killed and 20 more wounded, while the victorious Patriots suffered only two casualties. Some 850 Loyalists were taken prisoner. The battle ended royal authority in North Carolina and revealed that the Revolution would be as much a civil war as a conflict between American and British forces, as only North Carolina Patriots and Loyalists fought at Moore's Creek Bridge; no British soldiers participated. Within two months of the American victory, on April 12, 1776, North Carolina became the first colony to vote in favor of independence from Britain.

Breaking the Bonds of Empire (1776)

In June 1776, one by one, the colonies authorized their delegates in the Continental Congress to take the final step. On June 7, Richard Henry Lee of Virginia moved "that these United Colonies are, and of right ought to be, free and independent states." At first, six colonies were not ready to take such a dangerous step; but Lee's resolution finally passed on July 2, a date that John Adams predicted would "be the most memorable" in the history of America.

The more memorable date, however, became July 4, 1776, when fifty-six members of Congress formally adopted the **Declaration of Independence** creating the "United States of America." The stakes could not have been higher. The delegates knew that they were likely to be hanged if captured by British troops. "Well, Gentlemen," Benjamin Franklin told the Congress, "we must now hang together, or we shall most assuredly hang separately." Benjamin Harrison injected needed wit at that point, noting that when it was his turn to try on a British noose, his plentiful weight would bring him a mercifully swift death.

Declaration of Independence (1776) The formal statement, principally drafted by Thomas Jefferson and adopted by the Second Continental Congress on July 4, 1776, that officially announced the thirteen colonies' break with Great Britain.

Jefferson's Declaration

The risky decision to declare independence embodied a carefully reasoned political philosophy. A quest for freedom, for liberty from tyranny, animated the drama of American independence. Patriots wholeheartedly believed that the people should govern themselves and that they should enjoy both individual freedom and equal rights.

The formal rationale for independence was developed by thirty-three-year-old Thomas Jefferson, a Virginia planter and attorney serving in the Continental Congress. In Philadelphia, he drafted a justification for independence that John Adams and Benjamin Franklin then edited.

The Declaration of Independence was crucially important not simply because it marked the creation of a new nation (although the word *nation* was nowhere in the document), but because of the political ideals it expressed. Jefferson explained, "We hold these truths to be sacred & undeniable":

> That all men are created equal & independent, that from that creation they derive rights inherent & inalienable, among which are the preservation of life, liberty, & the pursuit of happiness; that to secure these ends, governments are instituted among men, deriving their just powers from the consent of the governed.

These were to be the new nation's founding principles. After reading Jefferson's draft, Benjamin Franklin saw fit to change the phrase "sacred & undeniable" to "self-evident" so as not to imply that the Declaration of Independence came from God.

Once Jefferson had established America's foundational principles, he listed the most acute grievances against British rule. Over the previous ten years, colonists had deplored acts of Parliament that impinged on their freedoms, especially efforts to impose "taxes on us without our consent." Now, Jefferson directed colonial resentment at King George III himself, arguing that the monarch should have reined in Parliament's efforts to "tyrannize" the colonies.

Jefferson, an enslaver, then charged that the king had *imposed* slavery on Americans by stripping a "distant people who never offended him" (Africans) of their "most sacred right of life & liberty." In fact, however, as Jefferson knew full well, the British monarchy had not forced the system of race-based slavery on colonists; they had been enslaving Africans since 1619, long before George III assumed the throne.

After listing the "repeated injuries and usurpations" committed against the thirteen colonies by the king and Parliament, Jefferson asserted that Americans had the fundamental right to create governments of their own choosing. The people, he explained, give governments their legitimacy, and are entitled to "alter or abolish" those governments when denied their rights. Because George III was trying to impose "an absolute tyranny over these states," the "Representatives of the United States of America" declared the thirteen "United Colonies" of British America to be "Free and Independent States."

The Contradictions of Freedom and Slavery

Once the Continental Congress chose independence, its members revised Jefferson's draft declaration before sending it to London. Southern representatives insisted on deleting Jefferson's passage criticizing George III for imposing slavery on the colonies. In doing so, they revealed the major paradox at work in the movement for independence: the rhetoric of freedom ("all men are created equal and independent") did not apply to the widespread system of slavery that fueled the colonial economy. Slavery was the absence of liberty, yet few Revolutionaries confronted the hypocrisy of their protests in defense of freedom—for Whites only.

In 1764, a group of enslaved people in Charleston watching a demonstration against British tyranny by White Sons of Liberty got caught up in the moment and began chanting, "Freedom, freedom, freedom." But that was not what southern planters wanted for African Americans. In 1774, when a group of freedom seekers killed four Whites in a desperate attempt to gain their freedom, Georgia planters captured the rebels and burned them alive.

Harvard-educated attorney James Otis Jr. was one of the few Patriots who demanded freedom for Black people and women as well as for the colonies. In 1764, he had argued that "the colonists, black and white, born here, are free British subjects, and entitled to all the essential civil rights of such." Otis went so far as to suggest that slavery itself should be ended, since "all men . . . White or black" were "by the law of nature freeborn."

Otis also asked, "Are not women born as free as men? Would it not be infamous to assert that the ladies are all slaves by nature?" His sister, Mercy Otis Warren, became a tireless advocate of American resistance to British "tyranny" through her poems, pamphlets, and plays. In a letter to a friend, she noted that British officials needed to realize that America's "daughters are politicians and patriots and will aid the good work [of resistance] with their female efforts."

ETHIOPIA REGIMENT Formed in 1775 by Lord Dunmore, the Ethiopia Regiment was a military unit made up of free and enslaved people. This unit was important because it gave Blacks the opportunity to show themselves as loyal to the British in exchange for their freedom.

Enslaved people insisted on independence, too. In 1773, a group of four enslaved Bostonians addressed a public letter to the town government in which they referred to the hypocrisy of enslavers who protested against British regulations and taxes. "We expect great things from men who have made such a noble stand against the designs of their fellow-men to enslave them," they noted. But freedom in 1776 was a celebration to which enslaved people were not invited.

Blacks fought on both sides of the war. Some chose the British after hearing that Lord Dunmore, the royal governor of Virginia, issued a proclamation to free all enslaved persons who aligned themselves with the British cause (see Chapter 5). Dunmore created the Ethiopia Regiment, consisting of free and formerly enslaved people of African descent. They fought in several battles and contributed to the British war effort.

George Washington acknowledged the contradictory aspects of the Revolutionary movement when he warned that the alternative to declaring independence was to become "tame and abject slaves, as the blacks we rule over with such arbitrary sway [absolute power]." Washington and other enslavers at the head of the Revolutionary movement were in part so resistant to "British tyranny" because they witnessed every day what actual slavery was like.

Phillis Wheatley, the first African writer to publish her poetry in America, highlighted the "absurdity" of White colonists claiming their freedom while continuing to exercise "oppressive power" over enslaved Africans. Wheatley, born in West Africa and brought to America on a slave ship, was enslaved by John Wheatley of Boston. She was recognized for her intelligence, and the Wheatleys supported her educational journey through subjects including English literature, classical literature, history, and religious studies. She went on to publish a collection of thirty-nine poems.

PHILLIS WHEATLEY A portrait of America's first celebrated African American poet.

The Status of Women

The ideal of freedom applied to the status of women as much as to that of African Americans. The legal status of women was governed by British common law, which essentially limited their roles to child rearing and maintaining the household. Women could not vote or hold office, and few had access to formal education. Boys were taught to read and write; girls were taught to read and sew. Until married, women were subject to the dictates of their fathers.

However, once a woman married, she then became the possession of her husband, and all property she brought to the marriage became his. A married woman had no right to buy, sell, or manage property. Technically, any wages a wife earned belonged to the husband. Women could not sign

Comparing PERSPECTIVES

ON COVERTURE, LIBERTY, AND EQUALITY

From: William Blackstone, "Chapter the fifteenth, Of Husband and Wife," *Commentaries on the Laws of England*, **1766.**

William Blackstone, a prominent English jurist, in his authoritative *Commentaries on the Laws of England*, commented on the laws of coverture that shaped relations between women and men in colonial life. He included legal definitions of women's roles in marriage and society.

By marriage, the husband and wife are one person in law: that is, the very being or legal existence of the woman is suspended during the marriage, or at least is incorporated and consolidated into that of the husband; under whose wing, protection, and *cover*, she performs every thing; and is therefore called in our law-French a *feme-covert* . . . is said to be *covert-baron*, or under the protection and influence of her husband, her *baron*, or lord; and her condition during her marriage is called her *coverture*.

Upon this principle, of a union of person in husband and wife, depend almost all the legal rights, duties, and disabilities, that either of them acquire by the marriage. I speak not at present of the rights of property, but of such as are merely *personal*. For this reason, a man cannot grant any thing to his wife, or enter into covenant with her: for the grant would be to suppose her separate existence; and to covenant with her, would be only to covenant with himself: and therefore it is also generally true, that all compacts made between husband and wife, when single, are voided by the intermarriage.
. . .

The husband also (by the old law) might give his wife moderate correction. For, as he is to answer for her misbehaviour, the law thought it reasonable to intrust him with this power of restraining her, by domestic chastisement, in the same moderation that a man is allowed to correct his servants or children; for whom the master or parent is also liable in some cases to answer.

From: Letter from Abigail Adams to John Adams, March 31, 1776.

In a letter to her husband, John Adams, written in 1776, Abigail Adams rejected coverture and expressed her dissatisfaction with the law.

I wish you would ever write me a letter half as long as I write you; and tell me if you may where your fleet are gone? What sort of defence Virginia can make against our common enemy? Whether it is so situated as to make an able defence? …

…

    I have sometimes been ready to think that the passion for Liberty cannot be equally strong in the breasts of those who have been accustomed to deprive their fellow creatures of theirs. Of this I am certain that it is not founded upon that generous and Christian principal of doing to others as we would that others should do unto us.

…

    … I long to hear that you have declared an independency—and by the way in the new Code of Laws which I suppose it will be necessary for you to make I desire you would remember the ladies and be more generous & favorable to them than your ancestors. Do not put such unlimited power in the hands of the husbands. Remember all men would be tyrants if they could. If particular care and attention is not paid to the ladies, we are determined to foment a rebellion, and will not hold ourselves bound by any laws in which we have no voice or representation—that your sex are naturally tyrannical is a truth so thoroughly established as to admit of no dispute, but such of you as wish to be happy willingly give up the harsh title of master for the more tender and endearing one of friend. Why then, not put it out of the power of the vicious and the lawless to use us with cruelty and indignity with impunity. Men of sense in all ages abhor those customs which treat us only as the vassals of your sex. Regard us then as beings placed by providence under your protection & in imitation of the Supreme Being make use of that power only for our happiness.

Questions

1. According to Blackstone's commentaries, how does the law of coverture restrict women's rights?

2. What does Abigail Adams's letter to her husband reveal about gender and power in colonial marriage?

3. How did marriage suppress or restrict women's independence and expression during the colonial period?

contracts, file lawsuits, or testify in court. A husband could beat and even rape his wife without fearing legal action. Divorces were extremely difficult to obtain.

Given their limited status, America's struggle for independence from Great Britain led some women to demand their own independence. Early in the struggle, Abigail Adams, one of the most learned and spirited women of the time, wrote to her husband, John, while he served in the Continental Congress: "In the new Code of Laws which I suppose it will be necessary for you to make I desire you would remember the Ladies," she wrote. Otherwise, "if particular care and attention is not paid to the ladies, we are determined to foment a rebellion."

John Adams laughed at his wife's radical proposals. He insisted on retaining the traditional privileges enjoyed by males: "Depend upon it, we know better than to repeal our Masculine systems." If women were to be granted equality, he warned, then "children and apprentices" and "Indians and Negroes" would also demand equal rights and freedoms.

ABIGAIL ADAMS A 1766 portrait of Abigail Adams, the wife of John Adams. Though an ardent Patriot, she and other women like her saw few changes in women's rights emerging in the new United States.

Thomas Jefferson shared Adams's stance. In his view, there was no place for female political participation in the struggle for independence. Women should not "wrinkle their foreheads with politics" but instead should "soothe and calm the minds of their husbands." Improvements in the status of women would have to wait.

"We Always Had Governed Ourselves"

Americans in 1775–1776 probably enjoyed a higher standard of living than most other societies. Their diet was better than that of Europeans, and their average life span was longer. In addition, the percentage of property owners in the thirteen colonies was higher than that in Britain or Europe. At the same time, the taxes forced on Americans after 1763 were not as great as those imposed on the British people. And many colonists, perhaps as many as half, were indifferent, hesitant, or actively opposed to rebellion.

Reasons for the Revolt So why did so many Americans revolt? Historians have highlighted many factors: the British efforts to tighten their regulation of colonial trade, the restrictions on colonists eager to acquire western lands, the growing tax burden, the mounting debts to British merchants, the lack of American representation in Parliament, and the role of radicals such as Samuel Adams and Patrick Henry in arousing anti-British feelings.

Yet other reasons were more immediate and personal. Many wealthy New Englanders and New Yorkers most critical of tighter British regulations, such as Boston merchant John Hancock, were smugglers; paying more British taxes would have cost them a fortune. Likewise, South Carolina's Henry Laurens and Virginia's Landon Carter, both prosperous planters, worried that the British might abolish slavery.

Indigenous groups such as the Oneida, Mohawk, and Cayuga also participated in the war. Some chose to side with the British; others aided the American colonists. African Americans also weighed in by joining the military, running away, and protesting.

Overall, however, what Americans collectively resented most were the British efforts to constrict colonists' civil liberties, thereby denying their rights as British citizens. As Hugh Williamson, a Pennsylvania physician, explained, the Revolution resulted not from "trifling or imaginary" injustices but from "gross and palpable" violations of American rights that had thrown "the miserable colonists" into the "pit of despotism."

Unified Resistance Yet how did the diverse colonies develop such a unified resistance? Although most Patriots were of English heritage, people of many other backgrounds were represented: Scots, Irish, Scots-Irish, Welsh, Germans, Dutch, Swedes, Finns, Swiss, French, and Jews, as well as growing numbers of Africans and diminishing numbers of Native Americans.

What most Americans—regardless of their backgrounds—had come to share by 1775 was a defiant attachment to the civil rights and legal processes guaranteed by the English constitutional tradition. This outlook, rooted in the defense of sacred constitutional principles, made the Revolution conceivable. Armed resistance made it possible, and independence, ultimately, made it achievable for some. Others would continue to fight for freedom, liberty, and justice against insurmountable odds for decades to come.

The Revolution would invent a new kind of nation: a large republic based on the shared political notion that all *citizens* were equal and independent, and that all governmental authority had to be based on long-standing constitutional principles and the consent of the governed. This vision transformed a prolonged effort to preserve rights and liberties enjoyed by British citizens into a movement to create an independent nation. With their Declaration of Independence, the Revolutionaries—men and women, farmers, artisans, mechanics, sailors, merchants, tavern owners, and shopkeepers—had become determined to develop their own society. Americans wanted to trade freely with the world and to expand what Jefferson called their "empire of liberty" westward, across the Appalachian Mountains and into ancestral Indigenous lands.

The Revolutionaries knew the significance of what they were attempting. They were committing themselves, stressed John Adams, to "a Revolution, the most complete, unexpected, and remarkable of any in the history of nations."

Reviewing the
CORE OBJECTIVES

- **British and French Colonies**
France followed the model of absolute power in governing its far-flung trading outposts in Canada and the Louisiana Territory, but good relations with Native Americans and a profitable fur trade kept the balance of power in North America. The British policy of *salutary neglect* allowed its colonies a large degree of self-government, until its decision to enforce more rigidly its policy of *mercantilism*—as seen in such measures as the *Navigation Acts* (1651–1775)—became a means to enrich its global empire. The *Glorious Revolution* (1688) in Great Britain inspired new political philosophies that challenged the divine right of kings with the *natural rights* of free men.

- **Warfare in the Colonies** The *Seven Years' War* (1756–1763), known as the *French and Indian War* in the American colonies, was the first world war, eventually won by the British. Worried colonists created the *Albany Plan of Union*, which was ultimately rejected but which formed an early blueprint for an independent American government. In the *Treaty of Paris* in 1763, France lost all its North American possessions, Britain gained Canada and Florida, and Spain acquired the vast Louisiana Territory. With the war's end, Indigenous people fought to regain control of their land in *Pontiac's Rebellion* (1763). Great Britain negotiated peace in the *Proclamation Act of 1763*, but land-hungry settlers ignored the Proclamation Line.

- **British Colonial Policy** After the French and Indian War, the British government was saddled with an enormous national debt. To reduce that burden, George Grenville's colonial policy imposed various taxes to compel colonists to pay for their own defense. Colonists resisted, claiming that they could not be taxed by Parliament because they were not represented in Parliament. Colonial reaction to the *Stamp Act* of 1765 was the first sign of real trouble for British authorities. British officials tried to appease colonists with the argument that they were duly represented in Parliament through *virtual representation*, since parliamentarians were sworn to represent the entire nation as well as their particular district. Conflicts between Whigs and Tories intensified when the *Townshend Acts* (1767) imposed additional taxes. The *Sons of Liberty* and *Daughters of Liberty* mobilized resistance with successful boycotts of British goods, helping convince Parliament to repeal the Stamp Act in 1766.

- **The Road to the American Revolution** But the crisis worsened. Conflicts between *Loyalists* and *Patriots* escalated. Spontaneous resistance led to the *Boston Massacre* (1770), and the First Continental Congress formed *Committees of Correspondence* to organize and spread resistance further. Organized protesters later staged the *Boston Tea Party* (1773). The British response, called the *Coercive Acts* (1774), sparked further violence. Thomas Paine's pamphlet *Common Sense* (1776) helped kindle Revolutionary fervor as well as plant the seed of independence; and conflicts over trade regulations, taxes, and expansion now erupted into war. In the heat of battle, compromise became less likely, and finally impossible, and the Continental Congress delivered its *Declaration of Independence* (1776).

KEY TERMS

mercantilism *p. 147*
Navigation Acts (1651–1775) *p. 147*
Glorious Revolution (1688) *p. 148*
natural rights *p. 149*
salutary neglect *p. 149*
French and Indian War (Seven Years' War) (1756–1763) *p. 150*
Albany Plan of Union (1754) *p. 152*
Treaty of Paris (1763) *p. 154*
Pontiac's Rebellion (1763) *p. 157*
Proclamation Act of 1763 *p. 158*
Stamp Act (1765) *p. 161*
virtual representation *p. 162*
Sons of Liberty *p. 162*
Daughters of Liberty *p. 163*
Townshend Acts (1767) *p. 165*
Loyalists *p. 166*
Patriots *p. 166*
Boston Massacre (1770) *p. 168*
Committees of Correspondence *p. 168*
Boston Tea Party (1773) *p. 169*
Coercive Acts (1774) *p. 170*
Common Sense (1776) *p. 177*
Declaration of Independence (1776) *p. 179*

CHRONOLOGY

1651	First Navigation Act is passed by Parliament
1688–1689	Glorious Revolution
1754	Albany Plan of Union
1756–1763	Seven Years' War (French and Indian War)
1763	Treaty of Paris ends Seven Years' War
	Pontiac's Rebellion begins
	King George issues Proclamation Act
1764–1765	Sugar Act and Stamp Act
1765	Stamp Act Congress
1766	Repeal of the Stamp Act
1767	Townshend Acts
1770	Boston Massacre
1773	Tea Act and Boston Tea Party
1774	Coercive Acts
	First meeting of Continental Congress
1775	Military conflict at Lexington and Concord
	The Continental Congress creates an army
1776	Thomas Paine publishes *Common Sense*
	The Continental Congress declares independence

InQuizitive

Go to InQuizitive to see what you've learned—and learn what you've missed—with personalized feedback along the way.

> **THINKING LIKE A HISTORIAN**

DEBATING the Origins of the American Revolution

History is more than just the memorization of *what* happened. It also involves interpreting *why* the past unfolded as it did. In seeking to understand *why*, historians often find themselves disagreeing. This happens for many reasons. Historians themselves are influenced by their own outlook and the society they live in. Historians can revise their thinking in light of fresh information from newly discovered *primary sources*. They can also interpret previously examined sources in new ways by applying new methodologies and theories. The study of how interpretations of history have changed is called *historiography*. It is the history of the field of history! For Part 1, "An Old 'New' World," the case study of the origins of the American Revolution demonstrates how historians can disagree because they use different types of sources. Thus, it is an excellent topic for sharpening your historiographical skills.

For this exercise you have two tasks:

PART I: Compare the two secondary sources on the American Revolution.
PART II: Using primary sources, evaluate the arguments of the two secondary sources.

PART I Comparing and Contrasting Secondary Sources

Below are excerpts from two prominent historians of the American Revolution whose work is at odds over its origins. The first piece comes from the late Bernard Bailyn of Harvard University, who explored how *ideology* shaped the American Revolution—the system of ideas, ideals, and beliefs that undergird political and economic theory and practice. Bailyn focused on the way that ideas from the English Whigs, who argued that the English constitution limited the power of the king, influenced American Revolutionaries. The author of the second excerpt, the late Gary Nash of the University of California, Los Angeles, studied the role that common people, as well as the economic forces that affected their lives, played in the American Revolution. Nash sought to uncover not just the Whig ideology that is the focus of Bailyn's work but also the ideas and forces that motivated people to participate in this great struggle. While the writings of Bailyn and Nash agree on much, they also illustrate how different methodologies lead to different historical interpretations. On one hand, Bailyn looked at the ideas and writings of the Revolutionary elite—their ideas and arguments—to explain what people actually did. On the other hand, Nash examined the actions and economic circumstances of Revolutionaries who produced no written records in order to understand their motivations. So while Bailyn sought to understand the causes of the Revolution through the writing of the colonial elite, Nash looked at the actions of common people to understand why they participated in this struggle.

Compare the views of these two historians by answering the following questions. Be sure to find specific examples in the text to support your answers.

- What is the topic of each excerpt?
- Are there any similarities between these two excerpts?
- According to each author, what role did ideology play in the origins of the American Revolution?
- According to each author, what role did economics and material conditions play in the origins of the Revolution?
- What type of primary sources does each author mention?
- What might account for the differences (if any) in interpretation between the authors?

188

Secondary Source 1
Bernard Bailyn, *The Ideological Origins of the American Revolution*, 1992

Study of the pamphlets [thin booklets] confirmed my rather old-fashioned view that the American Revolution was above all else an ideological, constitutional, political struggle and not primarily a controversy between social groups undertaken to force changes in the organization of the society or the economy. It confirmed too my belief that intellectual developments in the decade before Independence led to a radical idealization and conceptualization of the previous century and a half of American experience, and that it was this intimate relationship between Revolutionary thought and the circumstances of life in eighteenth-century America that endowed the Revolution with its peculiar force and made it so profoundly a transforming event. But if the pamphlets confirmed this belief, they filled it with unexpected details and gave it new meaning.

. . . I began to see a new meaning in phrases that I, like most historians, had readily dismissed as mere rhetoric and propaganda: "slavery," "corruption," "conspiracy." These inflammatory words were used so forcefully by writers of so great a variety of social statuses, political positions, and religious persuasions; they fitted so logically into the pattern of radical and opposition thought; and they reflected so clearly the realities of life in an age in which monarchical autocracy flourished, in which the stability and freedom of England's "mixed" constitution was a recent and remarkable achievement, and in which the fear of conspiracy against constituted authority was built into the very structure of politics, that I began to suspect that they meant something very real to both the writers and their readers: that there were real fears, real anxieties, a sense of real danger behind these phrases, and not merely the desire to influence by rhetoric and propaganda the inert minds of an otherwise passive populace. The more I read, the less useful, it seemed to me, was the whole idea of propaganda in its modern meaning when applied to the writings of the American Revolution. . . . In the end I was convinced that the fear of a comprehensive conspiracy against liberty throughout the English speaking world—a conspiracy believed to have been nourished in corruption, and of which, it was felt, oppression in America was only the most immediately visible part—lay at the heart of the Revolutionary movement.

Source: Bailyn, Bernard. *The Ideological Origins of the American Revolution*. Cambridge, Mass.: Belknap Press of Harvard University Press, 1992. xx–xxiii.

Secondary Source 2
Gary Nash, "Social Change and the Growth of Prerevolutionary Urban Radicalism," 1976

One of the purposes of this essay is to challenge these widely accepted notions that the "predicament of poverty" was unknown in colonial America, that the conditions of everyday life among "the inarticulate" had not changed in ways that led toward a revolutionary predisposition, and that "social discontent," "economic disturbances," and "social strains" can generally be ignored in searching for the roots of the Revolution. I do not suggest that we replace an ideological construction with a mechanistic economic interpretation, but argue that a popular ideology, affected by rapidly changing economic conditions in American cities, dynamically interacted with the more abstract Whig ideology borrowed from England. These two ideologies had their primary appeal within different parts of the social structure, were derived from different sensibilities concerning social equity, and thus had somewhat different goals. The Whig ideology, about which we know a great deal through recent studies, was drawn from English sources, had its main appeal within upper levels of colonial society, was limited to a defense of constitutional rights and political liberties, and had little to say about changing social and economic conditions in America or the need for change in the future. The popular ideology, about which we know very little, also had deep roots in English culture, but it resonated most strongly within the middle and lower strata of society and went far beyond constitutional rights to a discussion of the proper distribution of wealth and power in the social system. It was this popular ideology that undergirded the politicization of the artisan and laboring classes in the cities and justified the dynamic role they assumed in the urban political process in the closing decades of the colonial period.

To understand how this popular ideology swelled into revolutionary commitment within the middle and lower ranks of colonial society, we must first comprehend how the material conditions of life were changing for city dwellers during the colonial period and how people at different levels of society were affected by these alterations. We cannot fathom this process by consulting the writings of merchants, lawyers, and upper-class politicians, because their business and political correspondence and the tracts they wrote tell us almost nothing about those below them in the social hierarchy. But buried in more obscure documents are glimpses of the lives of both ordinary and important people—shoemakers and tailors as well as lawyers and merchants. The story of changing conditions and how life in New York, Philadelphia, and Boston was experienced can be discerned, not with perfect clarity but in general form, from tax, poor relief, and probate records.

The crescendo of urban protest and extralegal activity in the prerevolutionary decades cannot be separated from the condition of people's lives.... The willingness of broad segments of urban society to participate in attacks on narrowly concentrated wealth and power—both at the polls where the poor and propertyless were excluded, and in the streets where everyone, including women, apprentices, indentured servants, and slaves, could engage in action—should remind us that a rising tide of class antagonism and political consciousness, paralleling important economic changes, was a distinguishing feature of the cities at the end of the colonial period. It is this organic link between the circumstances of people's lives and their political thought and action that has been overlooked by historians who concentrate on Whig ideology, which had its strongest appeal among the educated and well-to-do.

Source: Nash, Gary. "Social Change and the Growth of Prerevolutionary Urban Radicalism." *The American Revolution: Explorations in the History of American Radicalism*, edited by Alfred F. Young, 6–7. DeKalb: Northern Illinois University Press, 1976.

PART II Using Primary Sources to Evaluate Secondary Sources

When historians are faced with competing interpretations of the past, they often look at *primary* source material as part of the process of evaluating the different arguments. Below is a selection of primary source materials relating to the origins of the American Revolution.

The first document is an excerpt from a series of letters by Pennsylvania Quaker John Dickinson that he published anonymously under the pen name "A Farmer." Dickinson wrote the first letter in 1767, following Parliament's suspension of the New York Assembly for failure to comply with the Quartering Act of 1765, which required the colonies to provide British troops with food and shelter.

The second document is an excerpt from a letter sent by Massachusetts Bay governor Francis Bernard to British officials in London following the Stamp Act Riots in Boston during August of 1765. The riots began on August 13 with an attack upon the house of Andrew Oliver, who was responsible for the collection of the tax. This act of destruction was widely celebrated by Samuel Adams and other Sons of Liberty. A few days later a mob ransacked and looted the house of the lieutenant-governor, Thomas Hutchinson. This mob acted without the support of Adams or other elite leaders.

Carefully read the primary sources and answer the following questions. Decide which of the primary source documents support or refute Bailyn's and Nash's arguments about this period. You may find that the documents do both but for different parts of each historian's interpretation. Be sure to identify which specific components of each historian's argument the documents support or refute.

■ Which of the two historians' *arguments* is best supported by the *primary source* documents? If you find that both arguments are well supported by the evidence, why do you think the two historians had such different interpretations about the period?

■ Based on your comparison of the two historians' arguments and your analysis of the primary sources, what have you learned about historiography and the ways historians interpret the past?

Primary Source 1

John Dickinson, "Letter from a Farmer in Pennsylvania," 1767

My dear COUNTRYMEN,

I am a FARMER settled after a variety of fortunes, near the banks of the river *Delaware* in the province of *Pennsylvania*.... Being master of my time, I spend a good deal of it in a library.... I believe I have acquired a greater share of knowledge in history, and the laws and constitution of my country, than is generally attained by men of my class.... From my infancy I was taught to love humanity and liberty. Inquiry and experience have since confirmed my reverence for the lessons then given me, by convincing me more fully of their truth and excellence. ... With a good deal of surprise I have observed, that little notice has been taken of an act of Parliament, as injurious in its principle to the liberties of these colonies, as the STAMP ACT was: I mean the act for suspending the legislation of New-York.... It [the Act] is a parliamentary assertion of the *supreme authority* of *the British legislature* over these colonies in *the part of taxation*; and is intended to COMPEL *New-York* into a submission to that authority. It seems therefore to me as much a violation of the liberty of the people of that province, and consequently of all these colonies, as if the parliament had sent a number of regiments to be quartered upon them till they should comply. For it is evident, that the suspension is meant as a compulsion; and the *method* of compelling is totally indifferent. It is indeed probable that the sight of red coats, and the beating of drums would have been most alarming, because people are generally more influenced by their eyes and ears than by their reason: But whoever seriously considers the matter, must perceive, that a dreadful stroke is aimed at the liberty of these colonies: For the cause of *one* is the cause of *all*. If the parliament may lawfully deprive *New-York* of any of its rights, it may deprive any, or all the other colonies of their rights; and nothing can possibly so much encourage such attempts, as a mutual inattention to the interests of each other. *To divide, and thus to destroy*, is the first political maxim in attacking those who are powerful by their union. He certainly is not a wise man, who folds his arms and reposes himself at home, viewing with unconcern the flames that have invaded his neighbour's house, without any endeavours to extinguish them.

Source: Dickinson, John. "Letters from a Farmer." *Letters from a Farmer in Pennsylvania, to the Inhabitants of the British Colonies*. Edited by R. T. H. Halsey, 6–12. New York: The Outlook Company, 1903.

Primary Source 2

Governor Francis Bernard, "Letter to the Lords of Trade," 1765

The disorders of the town having been carried to much greater lengths than what I have informed your lordships of. After the demolition of Mr. Oliver's house was found so practicable and easy, and that the government was obliged to look on, without being able to take any one step to prevent it, and the principal people of the town publicly avowed and justified the act; the mob, both great and small, became highly elated, and all kinds of ill-humours were set on foot; everything that, for years past, had been the cause of any unpopular discontent, was revived; and private resentments against persons in office worked themselves in, and endeavoured to exert themselves under the mask of the public cause.... Towards evening, some boys began to light a bonfire before the town-house, which is an usual signal for a mob. Before it was quite dark, a great company of people gathered together, crying 'Liberty and Property;' which is their usual notice of their intention to plunder and pull down a house.

...

The lieutenant-governor [Thomas Hutchinson] ... was at supper with his family when he received advice that the mob was coming to him.... As soon as the mob had got into the house, with a most irresistible fury, they immediately looked about for him, to murder him, and even made diligent enquiry whither he was gone. They went to work with a rage scarce to be exemplified by the most savage people. Every thing moveable was destroyed in the most minute manner, except such things of value as were worth carrying off.... It was now becoming a war of plunder, of general leveling, and taking away the distinction of rich and poor: so that those gentlemen, who had promoted and approved the cruel treatment of Mr. Oliver, became now as fearful for themselves as the most loyal person in the town could be. When first the town took this new turn, I was in hopes that they would have disavowed all the riotous proceedings; that of the first night, as well as the last. But it is no such thing; great pains are taken to separate the two riots: what was done against Mr. Oliver is still approved of, as a necessary declaration of their resolution not to submit to the Stamp Act.

Source: Bernard, Francis. "Extract from a Letter to the Lords of Trade, dated August 31, 1765." *The Parliamentary History of England, from the Earliest Period to the Year 1803. From which Last-Mentioned Epoch It Is Continued Downwards in the Work Entitled, "The Parliamentary Debates."* Vol. 16, A. D. 1765–1771. London: Printed by T. C. Hansard, Peterborough-Court, Fleet-Street: for Longman, Hurst, Rees, Orme, & Brown; J. Richardson; Black, Parry, & Co.; J. Hatchard; J. Ridgway; E. Jeffery; J. Booker; J. Rodwell; Cardock & Joy; R. H. Evans; E. Budd; J. Booth; and T. C. Hansard, 1813. 129–131.

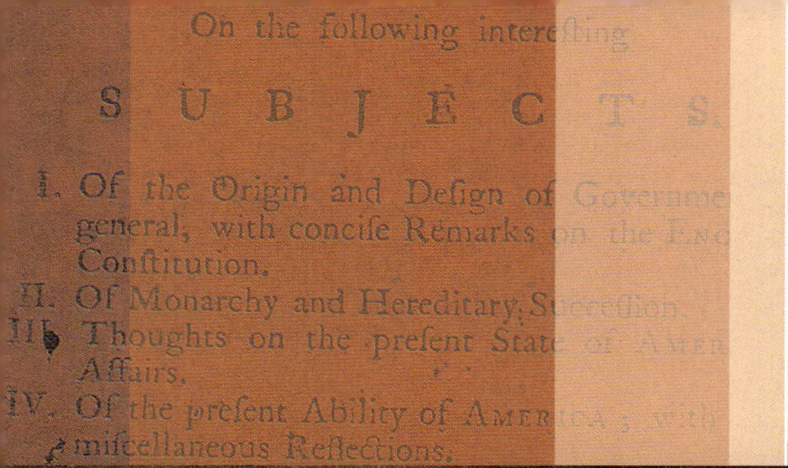

On the following interesting
SUBJECTS.
I. Of the Origin and Design of Government in general, with concise Remarks on the English Constitution.
II. Of Monarchy and Hereditary Succession.
III. Thoughts on the present State of American Affairs.
IV. Of the present Ability of AMERICA, with miscellaneous Reflections.

BURNING of the FRIGATE PHILADELPHIA in the HARBOUR of TRIPOLI, 16th Feb. 1804.

INHABITANTS OF AMERICA,

Building a Nation

PART 2

In August 1776, Benjamin Rush, a Philadelphia physician, recognized that the thirteen American colonies needed to function like a united nation. Yet it was one thing for Patriot leaders to declare independence and quite another to win it on the battlefield. The odds greatly favored Great Britain, the richest nation in Europe, with its population of some 11 million people. Fewer than half of the 2.5 million colonists were Patriots who actively supported the Revolution, and many others—the Loyalists (or Tories, as the Patriots mockingly called them)—fought against it.

Still others sought just to stay alive, often by changing sides.

Many Americans were suspicious of both sides and hesitant to embrace an uncertain cause. The thirteen independent states had new, untested governments; the Continental Congress struggled to serve as a national government with few powers; and General George Washington found himself in charge of an inexperienced and poorly equipped army facing the world's greatest military power.

Nevertheless, the Revolutionaries persevered. As a military leader, Washington was more than able but did not have strategic knowledge for the conditions he would face; some say he was more determined than brilliant. His soldiers may have lacked the experience and equipment of their British counterparts, but they had extensive knowledge of the new nation's geography and used it to their advantage. Washington chose excellent officers, inspired loyalty, and quickly perceived that dealing with the Continental Congress was as crucial to victory as was gunpowder.

Equally important to the Revolutionary cause was the decision by the French (and later the Spanish and Dutch) to join the fight against Britain. The Franco-American alliance, negotiated in 1778, was a vital turning point in the war. In 1783, after eight years of sporadic fighting and heavy human and financial losses, the British relinquished the American colonies.

While fighting the British, the Patriots also had to create new governments for themselves. Their deeply ingrained resentment of British imperial rule led Americans to give more power to the individual states than to the *Confederation*—the new national government.

Such powerful local ties help explain why the Articles of Confederation, the original constitution organizing the league of thirteen independent states, provided only minimal national authority. In fact, the Articles were not officially ratified by the states until 1781. And even then, it remained unclear whether the American states would unite as a new nation or whether their coalition would fragment at any moment. It often seemed that all they had in common was a desire for independence from British rule.

After the Revolutionary War, the tenuous political bonds authorized by the Articles of Confederation could not meet the needs of the new nation. This realization led to the calling of the Constitutional Convention in 1787. The process of drafting and approving the new constitution generated heated debate about the respective powers granted to the states and the national government, a debate that became the central theme of American political thought.

The Revolution also unleashed social forces that reshaped American culture in terms of the roles of women, African Americans, Hispanics, and Indigenous Americans. Sectionalism among the different regions of the country, westward expansion into ancestral Indigenous lands, and foreign relations presented major challenges.

These critical issues spawned the first national political parties. During the 1790s, the Federalist Party (led by George Washington, John Adams, and Alexander Hamilton) and the Democratic-Republican Party (led by Thomas Jefferson and James Madison) furiously debated the political and economic future of the republic.

With Jefferson's election as president in 1800, the Democratic-Republicans remained dominant for the next quarter century. In the process, they presided over a maturing republic that expanded westward at the expense of Indigenous Americans, embraced industrial development, engaged in a second war with Great Britain, and witnessed growing tensions between North and South over the institution of slavery.

THE DEATH OF GENERAL MERCER AT THE BATTLE OF PRINCETON (ca. 1789–1831) Soon after the American victory in Trenton, New Jersey, George Washington (*center, on horseback*) and his men had another unexpected win at the Battle of Princeton. One of the casualties, however, was Washington's close friend General Hugh Mercer (*bottom*), whose death became a rallying symbol for the Revolution.

CHAPTER 5

The American Revolution

1775–1783

Few Europeans thought the untested Americans could win against the world's most powerful empire. Although the British triumphed in most of the major battles, the Patriots outlasted them and eventually forced King George III to grant independence to the upstart United States of America. This stunning result reflected the tenacity of the Patriots as well as the difficulties the British faced in fighting a prolonged war 3,000 miles from home and in adjusting to the unorthodox American ways of warfare.

What began as a war for independence became both a *civil war* between Americans (Patriots versus Loyalists, each side joined by Indigenous allies) and a *world war* involving numerous European nations. The crucial development in the war enabled the United States to forge military alliances with France, Spain, and the Netherlands, all of which were eager to humble Great Britain. They provided the Revolutionaries with money, weapons, soldiers, and warships.

The Revolutionary War unleashed social and political changes, as it required ordinary people to take a more active role in government—local, state, and national. In Virginia, voters in 1776 elected a new state legislature that, an observer noted, "was composed of men not quite so well dressed, nor so politely educated, nor so highly born" as in the past. The war sparked larger conversations about liberty and justice, but these

CORE OBJECTIVES

1. Describe the ways in which the American Revolution was also a civil war.
2. Explain the challenges faced by both British and American military leaders in fighting the Revolutionary War.
3. Identify key turning points in the Revolutionary War, and explain how they changed the direction of the war.
4. Examine how the Revolutionary War was an "engine" for political and social change.
5. Compare the impact of the Revolutionary War on people of African descent, women, people of Hispanic descent, and Indigenous Americans.

freedoms benefited White men only and excluded women, African Americans, Indigenous Americans, and Hispanic Americans.

American Society at War

> **CORE OBJECTIVE**
> 1. Describe the ways in which the American Revolution was also a civil war.

The Revolution was as much a deeply divisive civil war among bitterly opposed American factions (including the Indigenous peoples allied with both sides) as it was a struggle against Great Britain. It sundered families and friends, towns and cities.

Benjamin Franklin's son, William, for example, was the royal governor of New Jersey and a Loyalist. His Patriot father removed William from his will and cut off communication. Similarly, eighteen-year-old Bostonian Lucy Flucker defied her Loyalist father's wishes and married bookseller Henry Knox in 1774. (Knox would become a distinguished American general.) Lucy's estranged family fled Boston with the British army in 1776, and she never saw them again. "I have lost my father, mother, brother, and sister, entirely lost them," she wrote.

> Colonists divided

The colonists were divided into three groups: (1) Patriots, who formed the Continental Army and fought in state militias; (2) Loyalists, or Tories, siding with Britain; and (3) a middle group that sought to remain neutral but were eventually swayed by the Patriots. Americans also switched sides during the war, some as many as four or five times.

Loyalists

The Loyalists viewed the Revolution as an act of treason. They were most numerous in the seaport cities and the Carolinas, and they came from

FOUR SOLDIERS (ca. 1781) This illustration by a French lieutenant captures the varied appearances of Patriot forces in the war (*left to right*): a Black soldier (freed for joining the First Rhode Island Regiment), a New England militiaman, a frontiersman, and a French soldier. **What does this illustration show about the Patriot forces?**

all walks of life. Governors, judges, and other royal officials were almost all Loyalists; most Anglican ministers also preferred the "mother country." Many small farmers who had largely been unaffected by the controversies over British colonial regulations rallied to the British side. More New York men joined Loyalist regiments than enlisted in the Continental Army.

Yet the British were repeatedly frustrated by the failure of both Loyalists and Loyalist militias to materialize in strength and resist the Patriots whenever the British left an area. The Loyalists faced a difficult choice: either leave their property behind and accompany the British, or stay and face the wrath of the Patriots. Another problem was what one British officer called "the licentiousness of the [Loyalist] troops, who committed every species of rapine and plunder" and thereby pushed potential friends to the Patriot side.

Patriots

The Patriots supported the war because they realized that the only way to protect their liberty was to separate themselves from British control. They also wanted to establish an American republic that would convert them from being *subjects* of a king to being *citizens* with the power to elect their own government and pursue their own interests. "We have it in our power," wrote Thomas Paine, "to begin the world over again. . . . The birthday of a new world is at hand."

That birthday, however, would come at the bitter cost of families and communities divided over their loyalties. As the American Revolution unfolded, a civil war did too. Members of all social classes—from wealthy elites to recent immigrants, enslaved Africans, and Indigenous Americans—would be pulled into the conflict. Even most of those who tried to stay neutral were eventually forced to choose between the British and the Americans.

Mobilizing for War

The British and the Americans would face substantial challenges in fighting the war. First and foremost for each side was to figure out how to put into the field an army that was capable of winning the war. Second was to develop successful strategies for winning.

British Military Power

The British Empire sent 35,000 soldiers and half of its huge navy to suppress the American rebellion. The British also hired foreign soldiers (mercenaries), as evidenced by the 30,000 German soldiers who served in the British armies. Most were from the German state of Hesse-Cassel; thus, Americans called them **Hessians**.

The British also recruited Loyalists, Indigenous Americans, and people of African and Hispanic descent, but never had as many enlistments as they had hoped. Further, the British initially assumed that there would be enough

> **CORE OBJECTIVE**
> **2.** Explain the challenges faced by both British and American military leaders in fighting the Revolutionary War.

American challenges: Massive British forces

Hessians German mercenary soldiers who were paid by the British royal government to fight alongside the British army during the American Revolution.

food for their troops and forage for their horses in America. As the war ground on, however, most of their supplies had to be shipped from Britain. The war's increasing costs—in human lives and war debt—demoralized the British.

Another problem facing the British was that its government in the colonies under Lord Frederick North lacked a consistent war strategy. At first, the British tried to use their naval superiority to blockade New England's seaports and strangle American commerce. When that failed, they sought to destroy George Washington's troops in New York. Despite early success, the British commanders failed to pursue the retreating American rebels. Next, the British tried to drive a wedge between New England and New York, splitting the colonies in two. That too would fail, leading to the final British strategy: moving the main army into the southern colonies in hopes of rallying Loyalists in the region.

The Continental Army

While the Patriots had the advantage of fighting on their home ground, they also had to create an army and a navy from scratch. Before the war, **citizen-soldiers** (militiamen) were civilians summoned as needed from their farms and shops. During the Revolution, however, militiamen were at times unreliable and ungovernable. They were, reported General Washington, "nasty, dirty, and disobedient."

GEORGE WASHINGTON AT PRINCETON Commissioned for Independence Hall in Philadelphia, this 1779 painting by Charles Willson Peale portrays Washington as the hero of the Battle of Princeton.

Washington knew that militiamen alone could not win the war. He therefore convinced the Continental Congress to create a **Continental Army** with full-time, well-trained soldiers. About half of the 200,000 Americans who served in the war were militiamen (Minutemen) and half were in the Continental Army. Most of the Continental Army recruits came from the margins of colonial society: poor farmers, unskilled laborers, or recently arrived immigrants. Most were young and single. Some 5,000 people of African descent, virtually all formerly enslaved, also served.

What the Continental Army needed most were capable officers, intensive training, modern weapons, and multiyear enlistment contracts. Its soldiers also needed strict discipline. As Washington and his officers began organizing and training the army, those who violated the rules were jailed, flogged, sent packing, or even hanged as an example to others.

Many Patriots found army life unbearable and combat horrifying. General Nathanael Greene, a Rhode Island Quaker who abandoned pacifism for the war effort and became Washington's ablest commander, remarked that few Patriots could "stand the shocking scenes of war, to march over dead men, to hear without concern the groans of the wounded."

> American challenges: Finance and supply for the military, citizen-soldiers

citizen-soldiers Part-time non-professional soldiers, mostly poor farmers or recent immigrants who had been indentured servants, who played an important role in the Revolutionary War.

Continental Army The army authorized by the Continental Congress, 1755–1784, to fight the British; commanded by George Washington.

Desertions grew as the war dragged on. At times, General Washington could put only a few thousand men in the field. Eventually, Congress provided more generous enticements, such as land grants and cash bonuses, to encourage recruits to serve in the army.

Some 18,000 Americans died as prisoners of the British—almost three times as many as died in combat. The British treated captured Patriot soldiers as traitors, which meant they could be as brutal to the captives as they wanted. Beatings and whippings were commonplace, as was the practice of denying food and water to prisoners deemed "rowdy."

> British maltreatment of prisoners of war

As word seeped out about the horrific treatment of Patriot prisoners, outraged Americans deepened their resolve to gain independence. In 1777, Benjamin Franklin wrote to a British friend: "As to our submitting again to the government of Britain, 'tis vain to think of it. She has given us by her numberless barbarities, in the prosecution of the war and in the treatment of prisoners . . . that we can never again trust her in the management of our affairs."

Problems of Finance and Supply

Financing the Revolution was much harder for the Americans than it was for Great Britain. Lacking the power to impose taxes, Congress could only *ask* the states to provide funds for the national government. Yet the states rarely provided their expected share of the war's expenses, and Congress reluctantly had to allow Patriot armies to take supplies directly from farmers in return for promises of future payment.

In a predominantly agricultural society such as America, turning farmers into soldiers hurt the economy. William Hooper, a North Carolinian who signed the Declaration of Independence, grumbled that "a soldier made is a farmer lost."

Many states found a source of revenue in the sale of abandoned Loyalist homes and land. Nevertheless, Congress and the states still fell short of funding the war's cost and were forced to print more and more paper money, which eroded its value.

Indigenous Americans and the Revolution

Both the British and the Americans recruited Indigenous people to fight. But the British were far more successful at it, largely because they had long-standing relationships with chieftains and promised to protect ancestral Indigenous lands. The tribes making up the Iroquois Confederacy split their allegiances, with most Mohawk, Onondaga, Cayuga, and Seneca people joining the British, and most Oneida and Tuscarora supporting the Patriots. In the Carolinas, the Cherokee joined the British in hopes of driving out Americans who had taken their lands. Most of the Indigenous people in New England either tried to remain neutral or sided with the Patriots.

> American and British challenges: Recruiting Indigenous Americans

Disaster in Canada

In July 1775, the Continental Congress authorized an expedition into British Canada to attack Quebec in the hope of convincing the French Canadians to become allies.

Two months later, the Americans—after spending six weeks struggling through dense forests, crossing roaring rapids, and wading through frost-covered marshes—arrived outside Quebec, tired, freezing, and hungry. A silent killer then ambushed them: smallpox.

As the virus raced through the American camp, General Richard Montgomery faced an impossible dilemma. Most of his soldiers had signed up for short tours of duty, and many were scheduled for discharge at the end of the year. Because of the impending departure of his men, Montgomery could not afford to wait until spring for the smallpox to subside. Seeing little choice but to fight, on December 31, 1775, he ordered an attack on the British forces defending Quebec.

The assault was a disaster. More than 400 Americans were taken prisoner; the rest of the Patriot force retreated to their camp outside the walled city. The British, sensing weakness, attacked and sent the Patriots on a frantic retreat up the St. Lawrence River to the American-held city of Montreal and eventually back to New York and New England.

By the summer of 1776, the Patriots had come to realize that their quest for independence would be neither short nor easy. George Washington confessed to his brother that his efforts to form an effective army out of "the great mixture of troops" were filled with "difficulties and distresses."

Washington's Narrow Escape

During the summer of 1776, the British invaded New York City, the young nation's leading commercial seaport. So many Loyalists lived there that it was called Tory Town. By the end of the summer, two-thirds of the British army were camped on Staten Island preparing to invade the city.

New York City under threat

The British commanders, General William Howe and his brother, Admiral Richard Howe, met with Patriot leaders to negotiate a settlement. After the negotiations failed, a British fleet of 427 ships began offloading 32,000 troops on Long Island near New York City (see Map 5.1). It was the largest seaborne military expedition in history.

Although George Washington's nearly 10,000 men were too few to protect New York, Congress insisted that the city be defended at all costs. As John Adams explained, New York was the "key to the whole continent."

In late August 1776, as the Americans who were entrenched on Long Island waited for the British attack, General Washington walked back and forth behind his greatly outnumbered men with two loaded pistols, warning them that he would shoot anyone who ran. He assured them that he would "fight as long as I have a leg or an arm."

Yet it would not be enough. As the Battles of Long Island and White Plains unfolded, the outgunned Americans were decimated. A Marylander reported that a British cannonball careened through the American lines. It "first took the head off a stout heavy man; then took off Chilson's arm, which was amputated. It then struck Sergeant Garret on the hip. What a sight that was to see men with legs and arms and packs all in a heap." It was

LORD STIRLING AT THE BATTLE OF LONG ISLAND The Battle of Long Island was a devastating loss for George Washington, his troops, and American morale. In this dramatic painting by Alonzo Chappel, Patriot soldiers attack the British to enable the retreat of other units to Manhattan.

impossible "to describe the confusion and horror," a soldier said of the panicked Patriot retreat across swampy marshes.

Over the course of six hours, the inexperienced American army suffered a humiliating defeat. The smoke and chaos of battle disoriented the untested Americans. They steadily gave ground, leading British commanders to assume that the Revolution was about to end. The lopsided British victory caused faith in General Washington to plummet. As John Adams lamented, "In general, our generals were outgeneraled."

Washington realized that the only hope for his battered army was to organize a hasty retreat to Manhattan. Thanks to a timely rainstorm and the heroic efforts of experienced New England boatmen, the 9,500 Americans and their horses and equipment were rowed across the East River throughout the night of August 29. A thick early-morning fog cloaked the American retreat. General Washington was in the last boat to leave.

American army retreats from New York

When the fog lifted, British scouts reported startling news: the American army was gone. Admiral Howe's hopes for a quick end to the Revolution were dashed. Had the British army moved faster, it could have trapped Washington's entire force. But instead, the British rested as the main American army made an astonishing escape from New York. The Patriot troops then crossed the Hudson River, retreated into New Jersey, and crossed over the Delaware River into Pennsylvania (see again Map 5.1).

New York City became the headquarters of both the Royal Navy and the British army. The large Loyalist population in the city excitedly welcomed the British occupation. "Hundreds in this colony are against us," a New York City Patriot reported to John Adams. "Tories openly express their sentiments in favor of the enemy."

Thomas Paine: "The Times That Try Men's Souls"

By December 1776, the Revolution was near collapse. Washington had only 3,000 soldiers left. In a candid letter to his cousin, he confessed that his army was decimated by sickness and desertions. Unless he could organize "the speedy enlistment of a new army," the "game will be pretty well up."

Then help emerged from an unexpected source: the English-born war correspondent Thomas Paine. Having opened 1776 with his inspiring pamphlet *Common Sense*, Paine now composed *The American Crisis*, in which he gave voice to the desperate struggle for independence:

> These are the times that try men's souls: The summer soldier and the sunshine patriot will, in this crisis, shrink from the service of his country; but he that stands it NOW deserves the love and thanks of man and woman. Tyranny, like Hell, is not easily conquered. Yet we have this consolation with us, that the harder the conflict, the more glorious the triumph.

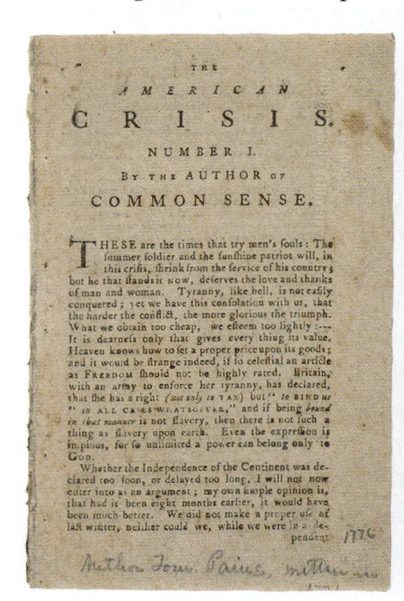

THOMAS PAINE'S *THE AMERICAN CRISIS* Thomas Paine's inspiring pamphlet was originally published anonymously "by the author of *Common Sense*," because the British viewed its content as evidence of treason. **What was the immediate impact of Paine's *The American Crisis*?**

MAP 5.1 MAJOR CAMPAIGNS IN NEW YORK AND NEW JERSEY, 1776–1777

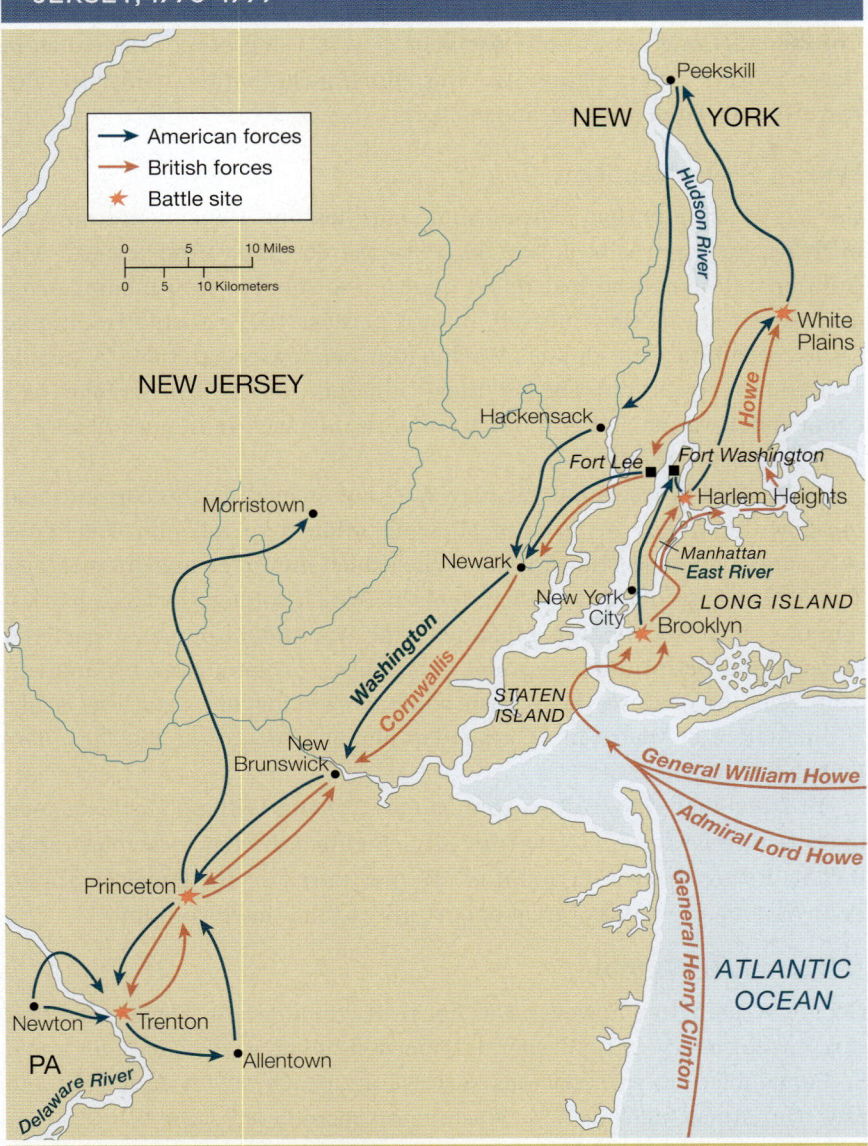

- Locate the British fleets arriving along the Atlantic coast. Who was commanding them, and where did they first land?
- Starting at Brooklyn, trace the movements of American forces north to Peekskill, then south to Newton, and back north via Allentown to Morristown. Using the distance key, estimate how far the troops traveled. What conditions did they face during this time?
- Based on your understanding of the chapter text, what was the significance of the Battle of Trenton?

Paine's rousing pamphlet boosted the Patriots' flagging spirits. Washington ordered that *The American Crisis* be read aloud to small groups of his dwindling army. Paine's stirring words also emboldened members of the Continental Congress; and on December 27, 1776, Congress gave Washington "large powers" to strengthen the war effort, including the ability to offer recruits cash, land, clothing, and blankets.

War: A Stern Teacher

George Washington had learned some hard lessons. Dependence on state **militias**, he now realized, "would prove the downfall of our cause." The frontier militiamen he had relied upon to bolster the Continental Army came and went as they pleased, in part because they resisted traditional forms of military discipline. Washington acknowledged that "a people unused to restraint must be led; they will not be driven." His strength as a commander was an ability to learn from his mistakes and to use resilience and flexibility as weapons.

> American forces adapt: Launching hit-and-run campaigns

With soldiers deserting every day, Washington modified his conventional top-down approach in favor of allowing soldiers to tell him their concerns and offer suggestions. What he heard led him to change his strategy. The Americans could not defeat veteran British soldiers in large battles. "On our side," Washington explained, "the war should be defensive." His focus would be on quickness and elusiveness, on launching hit-and-run campaigns to confuse the British while preserving his struggling army. Ultimately, the American commander planned to outlast his foes. The British fell into his trap.

In December 1776, British commander General William Howe decided to wait out the winter in New York City. (Eighteenth-century armies rarely fought during the winter months.) By not pursuing the Americans into Pennsylvania, Howe lost a great opportunity to end the Revolution.

A Desperate Gamble

George Washington, however, was not ready to hibernate. He decided that the Revolutionary cause desperately needed "some stroke" of good news. So he gambled on an audacious surprise attack. On a "fearfully cold and raw" Christmas night in 1776, Washington secretly led some 2,400 men—including ten men of African descent—packed into forty-foot-long boats and maintaining a "profound silence," across the ice-clogged Delaware River into New Jersey. Near sunrise at Trenton, the Americans surprised 1,500 sleeping Hessians. The **Battle of Trenton** (Map 5.1) was a total rout. Just two of Washington's men were killed, and only four wounded. The Americans captured 1,000 prisoners, 40 horses, 6 cannons, 1,000 muskets, and 40 barrels of rum, some of which was consumed immediately.

After the battle, Washington hurried his men and their German captives back across the river, urging his troops to treat the prisoners "with humanity, and let them have no reason to complain of our copying the brutal example of the British army."

militias Part-time "citizen-soldiers" called out to protect their towns from foreign invasion and ravages during the American Revolution.

Battle of Trenton (1776) The first decisive American victory in the Revolutionary War that proved pivotal in reviving morale and demonstrating General Washington's abilities.

Four days later, the Americans again crossed the Delaware River and attacked British forces around Princeton, before taking shelter in winter quarters at Morristown, New Jersey (Map 5.1). A British officer complained that the Americans had "become a formidable enemy."

Among the formidable forces that battled at Trenton were racially integrated units. This typically happened when local militias from the colonies were integrated into the regular Continental Army. One such example was the Sixth Connecticut Regiment, which included three men of African descent: Pomp Liberty, Cuff Freedom, and Jube Freedom, whose names confirmed their acts of patriotism and indicated why they decided to join the fight.

The victories at Princeton and Trenton saved the cause of independence and shifted the war's momentum. A fresh wave of Patriots signed up to serve in the army, and Washington regained the confidence of his men. However, although the "dark days" of late 1776 were over, unexpected challenges quickly chilled the Patriots' excitement.

Winter in Morristown

During the record-cold winter in early 1777, George Washington's ragged army was again much diminished, as six-month enlistment contracts expired and deserters fled the hardships caused by the brutal weather and widespread disease. One soldier recalled that "we were absolutely, literally starved. . . . I saw several of the men roast their old shoes and eat them."

Smallpox and other infectious diseases caused more casualties than did combat. By 1777, Washington had come to dread smallpox more than "the Sword of the Enemy." On any given day, one-fourth of American troops were deemed unfit for duty. The threat was so great that Washington ordered a mass inoculation of the entire army—a risky undertaking that, in the end, paid off and was one of Washington's greatest strategic accomplishments.

Only about 1,000 Patriots stayed through the brutal New Jersey winter. With the spring thaw, however, new recruits began claiming the $20 bounty and 100 acres of land offered by Congress to those who enlisted for three years or for the duration of the conflict, if less. Having cobbled together some 9,000 regular troops, Washington began skirmishing with the British forces in northern New Jersey.

By this point in the war, the challenges facing the British and American military leaders had become clear. Despite their well-trained military and naval forces, the British lacked a consistent war strategy, were fighting far from home in unfamiliar territory, and faced mounting costs as basically all supplies had to come from Britain. The Americans, despite fighting on home ground, had to build an army from untrained and poorly equipped

FREE BLACK MEMBERS OF THE SIXTH CONNECTICUT REGIMENT A watercolor painting of a free Black soldier of the Sixth Connecticut Regiment. Notice the uniform, the weaponry, and the supplies on his left shoulder. Black Patriots such as Pomp Liberty, Cuff Freedom, and Jube Freedom contributed to the war effort.

American challenges: Demoralized troops, disease

citizen-soldiers, and relied on a costly series of attacks that exhausted and demoralized the troops. As both sides made gains and suffered losses, victory would be won by the army that fought the longest, and with each passing year it became more difficult—and expensive—for the British to supply its large army and navy in America.

Setbacks for the British (1777–1781)

CORE OBJECTIVE
3. Identify key turning points in the Revolutionary War, and explain how they changed the direction of the war.

In 1777, the British devised a fresh plan to defeat the "American rebellion." It centered on a three-pronged assault on the state of New York (see Map 5.2). The complicated plan called for an army, based in Canada and led by General John Burgoyne, to advance southward from Quebec via Lake Champlain to the Hudson River. At the same time, another British force would move eastward from Oswego, in western New York. General William Howe would lead a third army up the Hudson River from New York City. All three armies would eventually converge in central New York and strangle any remaining Patriot resistance. By gaining control of New York, the British would cut off New England from the rest of the colonies.

British forces converge in central New York

The Campaign of 1777

The British armies, however, failed in their execution. At the last minute, Howe changed his mind and decided to move south from New York City to attack the Patriot capital, Philadelphia. General Washington withdrew most of his men from New Jersey to meet Howe's threat, while other American units banded together in upstate New York to deal with the British there.

On September 11, 1777, at Brandywine Creek, southwest of Philadelphia, the British overpowered Washington's army and occupied Philadelphia, then the largest and wealthiest American city. The members of the Continental Congress fled. Washington and his army withdrew to primitive winter quarters twenty miles away at the rural hamlet of Valley Forge, while Howe and his men remained in the comfortable confines of Philadelphia.

Meanwhile, an overconfident General Burgoyne (nicknamed "General Swagger") led his army southward from Canada, eventually reaching Lake Champlain in June 1777. The British then pushed south through dense forests and rugged terrain toward the Hudson River. Their advance, however, was slowed by growing numbers of Patriot soldiers.

GENERAL JOHN BURGOYNE After three weeks of fighting, Burgoyne, commander of Britain's northern forces, surrendered to the Americans at Saratoga on October 17, 1777.

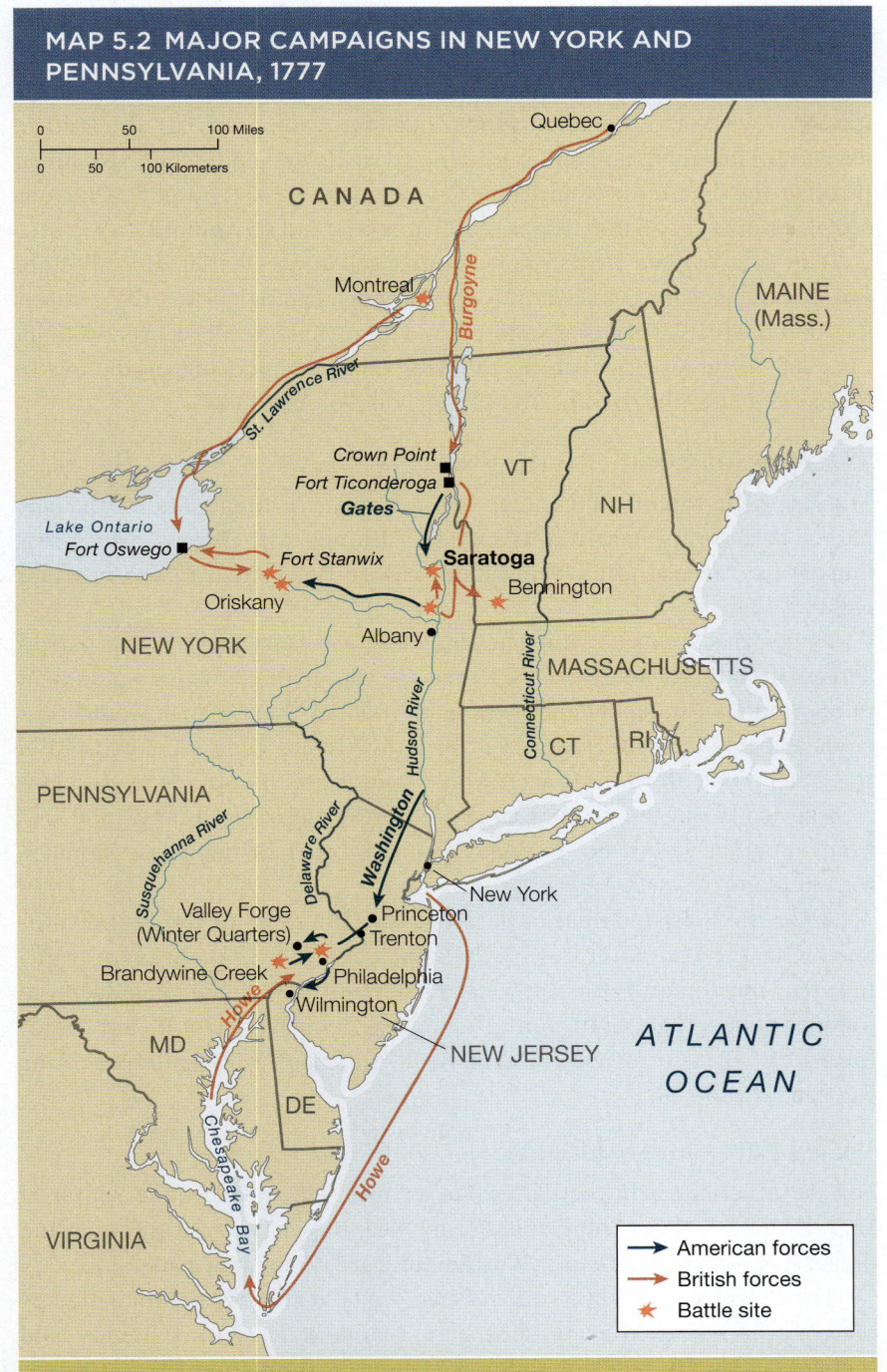

MAP 5.2 MAJOR CAMPAIGNS IN NEW YORK AND PENNSYLVANIA, 1777

- Follow the movements of American forces under General George Washington and British forces under Generals William Howe and John Burgoyne. Which army made more use of waterways?
- Notice the action between the warring forces in two different areas on the map. Which colonies were involved in each area? Whose military strategy is reflected here?
- According to the chapter text, why were the Battles of Saratoga a turning point in the Revolution?

Battles of Saratoga (1777) The decisive defeat of almost 6,000 British troops under General John Burgoyne in several battles near Saratoga, New York, in October 1777; the American victory helped convince France to enter the war on the side of the Patriots.

Treaty of Alliance (1778) A critical diplomatic, military, and economic alliance between France and the newly independent United States.

Valley Forge (1777–1778) During the Revolutionary War, the American military encampment near Philadelphia where more than 3,500 soldiers deserted or died from cold and hunger in the winter.

As Patriot militiamen converged from across central New York, Burgoyne pulled his forces back to the village of Saratoga (now called Schuylerville), where the reinforced American army surrounded the British. In the ensuing three-week-long **Battles of Saratoga** (see again Map 5.2), the British, desperate for food and ammunition, twice tried—and failed—to break through the encircling Americans. On October 17, 1777, Burgoyne surrendered, turning over 5,800 troops, 7,000 muskets, and 42 cannons.

The catastrophic British defeat unhinged King George. He fell "into agonies on hearing the account." The Saratoga campaign was the greatest loss that the British had ever suffered, and they would never recover. William Pitt, the former British prime minister, made a shocking prediction to Parliament after the defeat: "You cannot conquer America."

The Crucial Alliance with France

The surprising victory at Saratoga was a strategic turning point for the new nation because it enabled a **Treaty of Alliance** with France, which was hungry for revenge after losing four wars to the British in the previous eighty years.

Under the Treaty of Alliance, signed on February 6, 1778, the parties agreed: first, that when France entered the war, both countries would fight until American independence was won; second, that neither would conclude a "truce or peace" with Great Britain without "the formal consent of the other"; and third, that each would guarantee the other's possessions in America "from the present time and forever against all other powers." France further agreed not to seek Canada or other British possessions on the mainland of North America.

After the British defeat at Saratoga and the news of the French alliance with the United States, Parliament tried to end the war by granting all of the demands the Americans had made before they had declared independence. The Continental Congress, however, would not negotiate until Britain officially recognized American independence. King George III refused.

Valley Forge and Stalemate

Winter of 1777–1778 at Valley Forge

For the American army at **Valley Forge**, near Philadelphia, the winter of 1777–1778 was a time of intense suffering. Keeping his ragtag army intact and preserving morale was George Washington's greatest test of leadership.

The Patriots—including some twelve-year-old soldiers accompanied by their mothers—lacked coats, shoes, and blankets. They were hungry, and their 900 log-and-mud huts offered little protection from the icy winds. Bare feet froze, turned black, and were amputated.

By February 1778, some 7,000 troops were too ill for duty, and horses were dying from starvation. The first soldier to die at Valley Forge, known only as Jethro, was one of hundreds of free Black men who served in the conflict. More than 2,500 soldiers died at Valley Forge, another 1,000 deserted, and several hundred officers resigned or left before winter's end. Washington warned Congress that if fresh food and supplies were not provided, the army would be forced "to starve, dissolve, or disperse."

In the early spring of 1778, Washington sought to boost morale by directing his men to confiscate livestock from surrounding farms as a food source—and by organizing a rigorous training program. For that he turned to an energetic Prussian soldier of fortune, Friedrich Wilhelm, Baron von Steuben, who taught the Americans how to march, shoot, and attack in formation, and educated them on basic hygiene.

Another foreign volunteer who joined the American army at Valley Forge was a nineteen-year-old, red-haired French orphan named Gilbert du Motier, the Marquis de Lafayette. A wealthy young idealist excited by the American cause, Lafayette offered to serve in the Continental Army for no pay in exchange for being named a major general. "It is not to teach but to learn that I have come hither," he explained. He gave $200,000 to the war effort, outfitted a ship, recruited other French volunteers, and left behind his pregnant wife and year-old daughter to join the "grand adventure."

George Washington was initially skeptical of the French aristocrat, not yet twenty years old, but Lafayette soon became the commander-in-chief's most trusted aide. "I do not know a nobler, finer soul, and I love him as my own," Washington told a French diplomat. The precocious French general helped forge the Americans' military alliance with France.

By the spring of 1778, British forces withdrew from Pennsylvania to New York City, with the American army in hot pursuit. From that time on, the combat in the north settled into a long stalemate.

BARON VON STEUBEN George Washington leads Baron von Steuben on a tour through Valley Forge, where Steuben would embark on a rigorous training program to bring the American soldiers up to caliber. **What conditions did Steuben find when he arrived at Valley Forge?**

War in the West

The Revolution had created two wars. In addition to the main conflict in the East, a frontier guerrilla war pitted Indigenous people and Loyalists against isolated Patriot settlers living along the northern and western frontiers. In the Ohio valley, as well as in western New York and Pennsylvania, the British urged Loyalists and their Indigenous allies to raid settlements and offered to pay bounties for American scalps.

To end the British-led attacks, early in 1778 George Rogers Clark took 175 Patriot frontiersmen down the Ohio River. On the evening of July 4, the Americans captured British-controlled Kaskaskia, in present-day Illinois. Then, without bloodshed, Clark took Cahokia (in Illinois, across the Mississippi River from St. Louis) and Vincennes (in present-day Indiana) (see Map 5.3).

> Terror tactics on the western frontier

IROQUOIS AND LOYALISTS American Revolutionary General Nicholas Herkimer and the Americans battle British soldiers and Mohawk (Iroquois) forces led by Chief Joseph Brant and Loyalist John Butler at Oriskany in western New York State (1777).

While Clark's Rangers were in Indiana, a much larger U.S. force moved against Iroquois strongholds in western New York. Loyalists and their Indigenous allies had already killed hundreds of Patriot militiamen in the region. In response, George Washington sent 4,000 men, under General John Sullivan, to crush "the hostile tribes" and "the most mischievous of the Tories." At Newtown, New York, on August 29, 1779, Sullivan's soldiers destroyed about forty Seneca and Cayuga villages, which broke the power of the Iroquois Confederacy (see again Map 5.3).

In early 1776, a delegation of northern Indigenous peoples—Shawnee, Delaware, and Mohawk—talked the Cherokee into attacking frontier settlements in Virginia and the Carolinas. Swift retaliation followed as Carolina militiamen, led by Andrew Pickens, burned dozens of Cherokee villages. By weakening the major Indigenous nations along the frontier, the American Revolution cleared the way for White settlers to seize Indigenous lands after the war.

The War Moves South

The British "southern strategy"

In late 1778, the British military leaders changed tactics and launched their "southern strategy," built on the assumption that large numbers of Loyalists in the Carolinas, Virginia, and Georgia would join their cause. Once the British gained control of the southern colonies, they would have the shrinking United States trapped between Canada and the South.

In December 1778, General Henry Clinton, the new commander-in-chief of British forces, sent 3,500 redcoats, Hessians, and Loyalists to take the

MAP 5.3 WESTERN CAMPAIGNS, 1776–1779

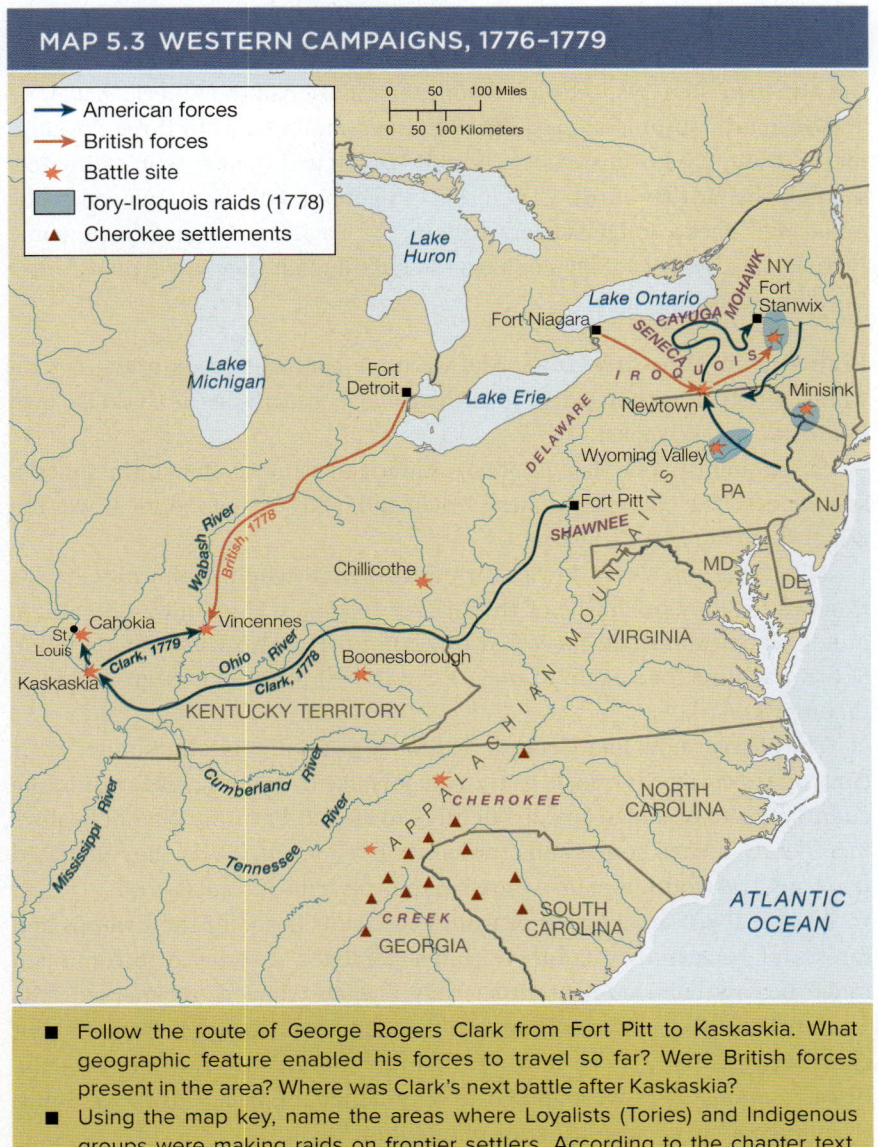

- Follow the route of George Rogers Clark from Fort Pitt to Kaskaskia. What geographic feature enabled his forces to travel so far? Were British forces present in the area? Where was Clark's next battle after Kaskaskia?
- Using the map key, name the areas where Loyalists (Tories) and Indigenous groups were making raids on frontier settlers. According to the chapter text, how did American forces respond?
- Point to the Indigenous nations (in purple) and related battle sites shown on this map, and explain why the outcomes of conflicts between settlers and Indigenous people at these sites were significant for the future of the frontier along the Appalachians.

poorly defended port city of Savannah, on the southeast Georgia coast, and roll northeastward from there. He solicited support from local Loyalists and the Cherokee.

Initially, General Clinton's southern strategy worked. Within two years, the British and their allies would defeat three American armies; occupy Georgia and much of South Carolina; and kill, wound, or capture some 7,000 American soldiers (see Map 5.4). Hundreds of Americans in the cities captured by the British suddenly announced that they were Loyalists. The British success led Lord George Germain, the official in London overseeing the war, to predict a "speedy and happy termination of the American war."

Germain's optimistic prediction, however, fell victim to three developments. First, the Loyalist strength in the South was weaker than estimated; second, the British effort to unleash Indigenous attacks convinced many undecided backcountry settlers to join the Patriot side; and third, some British and Loyalist soldiers behaved so harshly that they drove many other Loyalists to switch sides.

Fighting in the Carolinas The Carolina campaign took a major turn when British forces bottled up an entire American army on the Charles Town Peninsula for six weeks.

Subsequently, on May 12, 1780, American general Benjamin Lincoln surrendered the encircled Charles Town and its 5,500 defenders. It was the greatest Patriot loss of the war.

More bad news followed in mid-August when General Charles Cornwallis, now in charge of the British troops in the South, defeated a much larger American force led by General Horatio Gates at Camden, South Carolina (see again Map 5.4). Some 700 Americans were killed or taken prisoner.

> The British and Loyalists alienate neutral frontiersmen

The British now had Georgia and most of South Carolina under their control. However, they made a strategic mistake by sending officers into the countryside to organize Loyalist fighters to assault Patriots. When Loyalists mercilessly burned homes and murdered surrendering rebels, they alienated many neutral frontiersmen—who then took up arms for the Patriots.

In mid-1780, small bands of frontier Patriots based in the swamps and forests of backcountry South Carolina launched a series of hit-and-run raids. Led by colorful fighters such as Francis Marion, nicknamed "the Swamp Fox," and Thomas Sumter, "the Carolina Gamecock," the Patriot guerrillas gradually wore down British confidence. By August 1780, the British commanders were forced to admit that the backcountry of South Carolina was "in an absolute state of rebellion."

> The Battle of King's Mountain (1780)

The Battle of King's Mountain Cornwallis's cavalry officers sought revenge. They included Scotsman Major Patrick Ferguson, who threatened to march over the Blue Ridge Mountains and hang the mostly Scots-Irish Presbyterian Patriot leaders ("backwater barbarians"). Instead, however, Patriot men from southwestern Virginia and western North and South Carolina—all experienced hunters and riflemen who had often fought Cherokees—went hunting for Ferguson and his army of Loyalists in late September 1780.

After nearly two weeks in the saddle, in early October 1780 the Patriots found Major Ferguson and his Loyalist army camped near King's Mountain along the border between North and South Carolina (Map 5.4). By the end of the hour-long battle, Ferguson's lifeless body was pocked with seven bullet holes and both of his arms were broken. Surrounding him were 157 dead Tories, with 163 others too badly wounded to be moved. Seven hundred Loyalists were captured. Nine of them were hanged and many others brutalized during their long march to a North Carolina prison.

As with so many confrontations in the South, the Battle of King's Mountain resembled an extended family feud. Seventy-four sets of brothers fought on opposite sides, as did twenty-nine sets of fathers and sons. Five brothers in the Goforth family from Rutherford County, North Carolina, fought at King's Mountain; three were Loyalists, and two were Patriots. Only one of them survived. Two of the Goforth brothers, Preston and John Preston, fighting on opposite sides, recognized each other during the battle, took deadly aim as if in a duel, and fired simultaneously, killing each other.

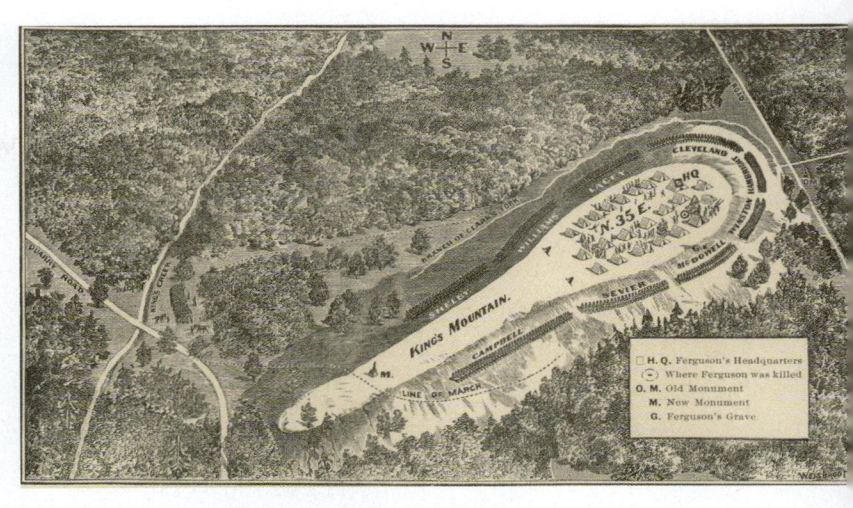

VICTORY AT KING'S MOUNTAIN A diagram of the Battle of King's Mountain by historian Benson John Lossing shows how detachments of Patriots surrounded Major Ferguson and his encampment of Loyalists, taking them by surprise.

The victory at King's Mountain boosted American morale and undermined the British strategy in the South. Thomas Jefferson called the Patriot victory "the turn of the tide of success." General Cornwallis's forces retreated from Charlotte, North Carolina, to South Carolina.

Patriots Gain Momentum in the South In late 1780, George Washington chose a new commander for the American army in the South: General Nathanael Greene, "the fighting Quaker" of Rhode Island. Greene was bold and daring, and well suited to a drawn-out war. He arrived in Charlotte to find that his troops lacked everything "necessary either for the Comfort or Convenience of Soldiers." Yet he also knew that if his army failed, the South would be "re-annexed" to Britain.

American victory at Cowpens

Like General Washington, Greene adopted a hit-and-run strategy. From Charlotte, he moved his army eastward while sending General Daniel Morgan and about 700 riflemen on a sweep to the west of Cornwallis's headquarters at Winnsboro, South Carolina (Map 5.4). Their assignment was to "annoy the enemy."

On a bitterly cold Wednesday, January 17, 1781, Morgan's force took up positions in a meadow called Cowpens in northern South Carolina. There, Morgan lured Sir Banastre Tarleton's horsemen into an elaborate trap. Tarleton rushed his men forward, only to be ambushed by Morgan's cavalry. Tarleton escaped; but 110 British soldiers died and more than 700 were taken prisoner, along with their horses and weapons.

Morgan's army then moved into North Carolina and joined Greene's troops. Greene lured the starving British army north, then attacked at

MAP 5.4 MAJOR CAMPAIGNS IN THE SOUTH, 1778–1781

- Name the southern colonies that saw major campaigns during the years 1778–1781. Identify the British and American generals involved. Which campaigns involved a Spanish general?
- Locate King's Mountain. By looking at the red and blue arrows denoting British and American forces in that area, who would you expect to win the battle there? Who actually did, and why?
- Point to Savannah and Charles Town. According to the chapter text, why were the battles here major victories for the British?

FRANCISCO DE MIRANDA This Venezuelan-born revolutionary fought against the British in order to support the independence of Spanish American colonies.

Guilford Courthouse (near what became Greensboro, North Carolina) on March 15, 1781 (Map 5.4). In the end, the Americans lost the battle of Guilford Courthouse but inflicted such heavy losses that Cornwallis left behind his wounded and marched his weary men toward Wilmington, on the North Carolina coast, to rest and figure out their next steps.

Cornwallis decided to abandon the Carolinas and move into Virginia, telling General Clinton in New York that he should march southward so that the two armies could merge and end the war in Virginia with a climactic victory that will "give us America."

The Spanish Alliance

In 1779, Spain, like France, had forged an alliance with the United States. The Spanish had no great love for the Americans, but they were eager to deal a blow to Great Britain. Although the support provided by Spain was much less than the French effort, George Washington would later claim that the Spanish assistance was essential to the American victory.

Bernardo de Gálvez, a Spanish army general who was the new governor of the Spanish-controlled Louisiana Territory, provided weapons and supplies to the American Revolutionaries. He then organized a multicultural force of Spanish soldiers, including Creole militiamen, Indigenous Americans, free Blacks, American volunteers—and a Venezuelan revolutionary named Francisco de Miranda, who opposed the British and supported independence in the Spanish American colonies. Once Gálvez's soldiers were equipped and trained, they attacked British forts along the Mississippi River, capturing over a thousand British and German troops, three forts, eight substantial ships, and vast acres of farmland on the east bank of the river (Map 5.4).

In early 1780, Gálvez forced the surrender of British forces protecting the port city of Mobile, Alabama. The following year, with Miranda's assistance, Gálvez and his Spanish forces captured Pensacola, on the Gulf of Mexico. His success forced the British to divert scarce military resources from fighting the Americans and played a little-known but crucial role in pressuring Great Britain to negotiate for peace. Miranda later became the governor of Cuba, and in that position would help supply French forces fighting at Yorktown, Virginia.

Yorktown and the Final Campaigns

Meanwhile, the war in America ground on. By September 1781, the Americans had narrowed British control in the South to Charles Town and Savannah, although Patriots and Loyalists would continue to battle each other for more than a year in the backcountry.

Cornwallis in Virginia General Cornwallis decided that Virginia must be eliminated as a source of American reinforcements and supplies. As his base, he picked Yorktown, a small tobacco port between the York and James Rivers on the Chesapeake Bay (see Map 5.5). He was not worried about an American attack, because he assumed General Washington's main force would remain 400 miles away in New York.

As Cornwallis's army moved into Virginia, however, George Washington led an ambitious plan of attack that required extensive coordination with the French. The French had finally managed to land 6,000 soldiers at Newport, Rhode Island, by July 1780, but they had been stranded there for a year, blockaded by British warships. By May 1781, however, the elements for a combined French-American action suddenly fell into place.

De Grasse and the French Fleet Washington first persuaded the commander of the French army in Rhode Island to join an attack on the British in New York City. Before they could strike, however, word came from the Caribbean that Admiral François Joseph Paul de Grasse was headed for the Chesapeake Bay with his fleet of French warships and some 3,000 soldiers.

This unexpected news from the French led Washington to change his strategy. He immediately began moving his army in New York south toward Yorktown. At the same time, French ships slipped out of the British blockade at Newport and also headed south.

On August 30, Admiral de Grasse's twenty-four warships reached Yorktown, and French troops joined the Americans confronting Cornwallis's army. On September 6, the day after a British fleet appeared, de Grasse's warships attacked and forced the British navy to abandon Cornwallis's surrounded army, leaving the redcoats with no access to fresh food and supplies. De Grasse then sent ships up Chesapeake Bay to ferry down the soldiers who had marched south from New York, bringing the combined American and French forces to 19,000 men—more than double the size of Cornwallis's besieged army.

The climactic **Battle of Yorktown** (see again Map 5.5) began on September 28, 1781. The American and French troops closed off Cornwallis's last escape route and began bombarding the British with cannons. Cornwallis

GENERAL BERNARDO DE GÁLVEZ An eighteenth-century portrait of the Spanish general and statesman who spearheaded the capture of British-held Pensacola, Florida, in 1781.

> Yorktown: French forces tip the balance, and British surrender

Battle of Yorktown (1781)
The last major battle of the Revolutionary War; General Cornwallis, along with over 7,000 British troops, surrendered to George Washington at Yorktown, Virginia, on October 17, 1781.

held out for three weeks, but on October 17, 1781—the anniversary of the American victory at Saratoga—he surrendered. Two days later, some 7,000 British soldiers laid down their weapons as the military band played "The World Turned Upside Down."

Claiming to be ill, but sick only with humiliation, a sullen General Cornwallis sent a painfully brief report to the British commander-in-chief in New York: "I have the mortification to inform your Excellency that I have been forced to surrender the troops under my command."

Interspersed among the surrendering British soldiers were hundreds of formerly enslaved people who had fled their southern masters and found refuge among the redcoats. Within days, American slave owners rushed to Yorktown in hopes of retrieving their freedom seekers. Among those eventually restored to captivity were seven freedom seekers from George Washington's Mount Vernon plantation and nine from Thomas Jefferson's Monticello.

The Treaty of Paris (1783)

Although Cornwallis had surrendered his army, the war was not yet over; it would officially last for another fifteen months. The British still had more than 20,000 troops in America. They controlled New York City, Charles Town, and Savannah, and their warships still blockaded several American ports. Fighting continued, especially in the southern states, yet any lingering British hopes vanished at Yorktown.

In December 1781, King George decided against sending more troops to America. Early in 1782, British officials contacted Benjamin Franklin in Paris to ask if the Americans would be willing to sign a peace treaty without involving the French. Franklin replied that the United States had no intention of deserting its "noble" French ally to sign a treaty with "an unjust and cruel Enemy."

In February 1782, Parliament voted to begin negotiations to end the war, and on March 20, Prime Minister North resigned.

In part, the British leaders chose peace in America so that they could concentrate on their continuing global war with France and Spain. At the same time, France let Franklin know that it was willing to let the United States negotiate its own treaty with Great Britain.

Upon learning of the British decision to negotiate, Congress named a group of prominent Americans to go to Paris to discuss terms. They included

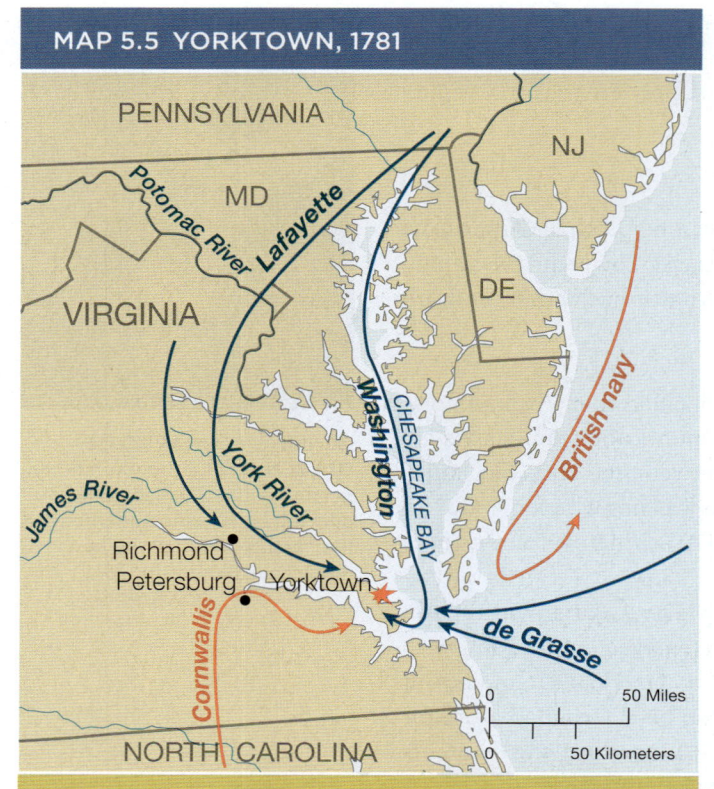

MAP 5.5 YORKTOWN, 1781

- Locate Yorktown. What geographic features made it an advantageous base for the British?
- Looking at Yorktown, study the positions of British forces compared to American forces. How did the arrival of French forces under de Grasse cut off an escape route for the British?
- Based on your understanding of the chapter text, explain what made the Battle of Yorktown the final, decisive battle of the Revolution.

Setbacks for the British (1777–1781) | 219

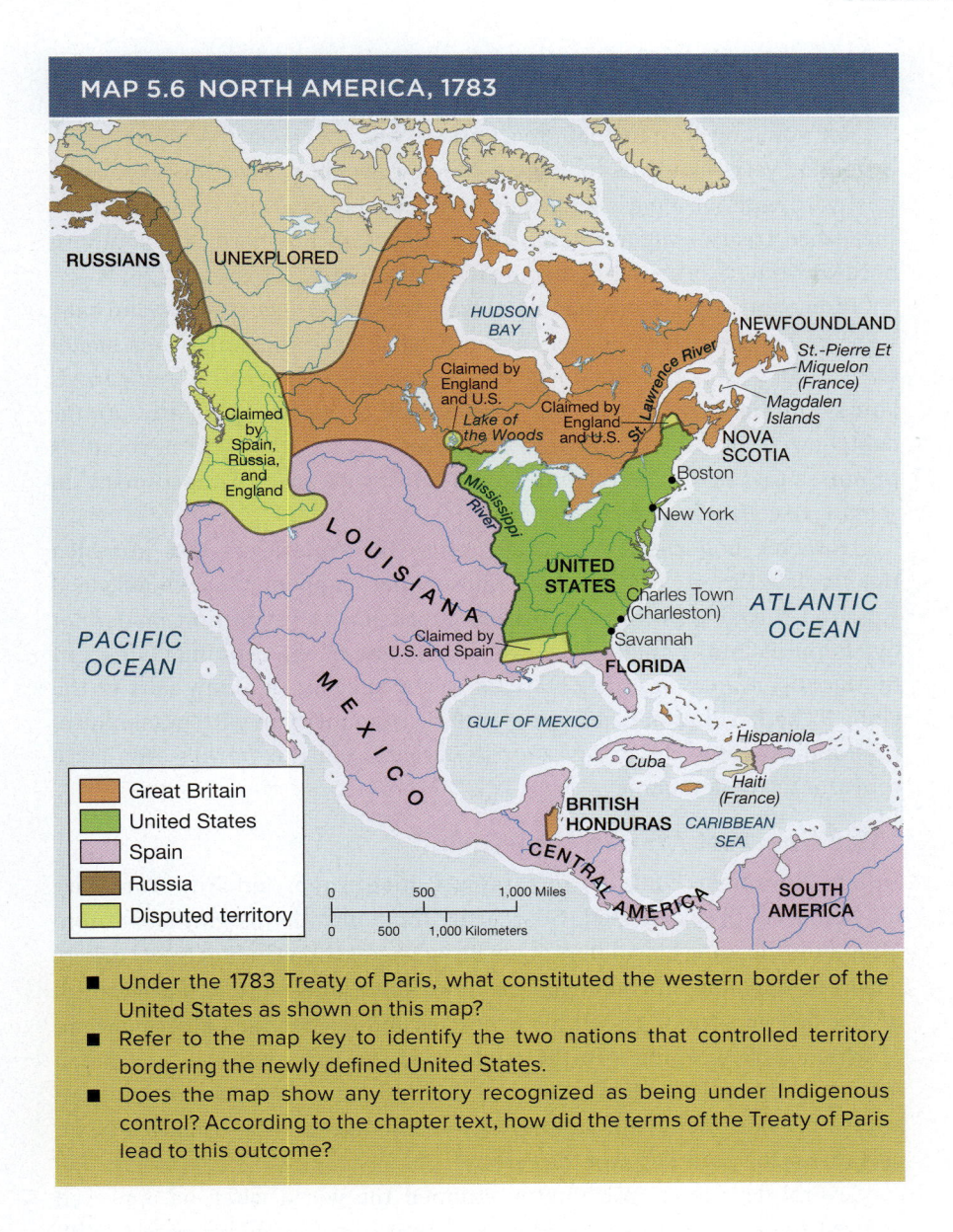

MAP 5.6 NORTH AMERICA, 1783

Legend:
- Great Britain
- United States
- Spain
- Russia
- Disputed territory

- Under the 1783 Treaty of Paris, what constituted the western border of the United States as shown on this map?
- Refer to the map key to identify the two nations that controlled territory bordering the newly defined United States.
- Does the map show any territory recognized as being under Indigenous control? According to the chapter text, how did the terms of the Treaty of Paris lead to this outcome?

John Adams, who was then representing the United States in the Netherlands; John Jay, minister (ambassador) to Spain; and Benjamin Franklin, already in France. On April 19, 1783, eight years to the day since the British had attacked American militiamen on Lexington Green, a permanent ceasefire began so that diplomats could agree to a peace treaty.

Those negotiations took almost six months. On September 3, 1783, the warring nations signed the **Treaty of Paris**. Its provisions were surprisingly favorable to the United States. Great Britain recognized the independence of the thirteen former colonies and agreed that the Mississippi River was America's western boundary, making the new United States larger in size than any European nation (see Map 5.6). At a banquet celebrating the signing of the treaty, a French diplomat proposed a toast to "the growing

Treaty of Paris (1783)
The treaty that ended the Revolutionary War, recognized American independence from Britain, created the border between Canada and the United States, set the western border at the Mississippi River, and ceded Florida to Spain.

greatness of America," now destined to become "the greatest empire in the world."

For now, however, the path to greatness was not so clear. A primary task in coming years would be to manage the new republic's ceaseless expansion westward without a national government capable of doing so. In addition, the peace treaty's vague references to America's northern and southern borders would be a source of dispute for years.

Indigenous Americans had no role in the peace negotiations, and they were by far the biggest losers, as the English gave the Americans something that was not theirs to give: vast parcels of ancestral Indigenous lands. Florida, as it turned out, passed back to Spain. As for the prewar debts owed by Americans to British merchants, the U.S. negotiators promised that British merchants should "meet with no legal impediment" in seeking to collect money owed them.

However imperfect the peace treaty, the Americans had humbled the British Empire. "A great revolution has happened," acknowledged Edmund Burke, a prominent British politician. "A revolution made, not by chopping and changing of power in any one of the existing states, but by the appearance of a new state, of a new species, in a new part of the globe." The Revolution had severed America's connection with monarchical rule and provided the catalyst for the creation of the world's only large representative democracy.

"The Greatest Man in the World"

In late November 1783, the remaining British troops left New York City for home. As they departed, George Washington rode his gray horse into Manhattan, leading his soldiers down Broadway as thousands of New Yorkers cheered. At a noon luncheon on December 4, Washington, "with a heart full of love and gratitude," raised his wineglass and toasted his officers, several of whom were weeping: "To the memory of those heroes who have fallen for our freedom!" He then expressed the hope that his new nation would always provide shelter for immigrants and refugees: "May America be an asylum for the persecuted of the earth!"

Several days later, Washington stunned the world when he appeared before Congress in Annapolis, Maryland, and surrendered his sword. With trembling hands and a rasping voice, he asked the members to accept his retirement so that he could return to managing his Mount Vernon plantation. "Having now finished the work assigned to me, I retire from the great theater of Action . . . and take my leave of all employments of public life."

General Washington's resignation was extraordinary: he was so revered that he could have seized political power. His devotion to his new country outweighed his personal ambition, however, and his willingness to give up power only enhanced his prestige and moral authority. Even King George III called him "the greatest man in the world."

Under Washington's direction, the young nation had successfully navigated through several turning points in its battle for independence.

After early British victories, the successful Battle of Trenton had boosted American morale and enlistments in Washington's army. After the wins at Saratoga, a strategic alliance with France was key for the Americans and a blow to the British. Equally key was Washington's success in maintaining his army during two harsh winters. Subsequent British losses in the South, combined with new supplies and the arrival of the French fleet, had enabled the Patriots' victory at Yorktown, which triggered negotiations to end the war.

War as an Engine of Change

Like all major wars, the American fight for independence had unexpected effects on political, economic, and social life. It upset traditional social relationships and affected the lives of people who had long been discriminated against—African Americans, women, and Indigenous Americans. The United States had gained its liberty from British tyranny, but which Americans were to enjoy the blessings of that freedom? In important ways, then, the Revolution was an engine for political experimentation and social change, and it ignited a prolonged debate about what new forms of government would best serve the new American republic.

> **CORE OBJECTIVE**
> **4.** Examine how the Revolutionary War was an "engine" for political and social change.

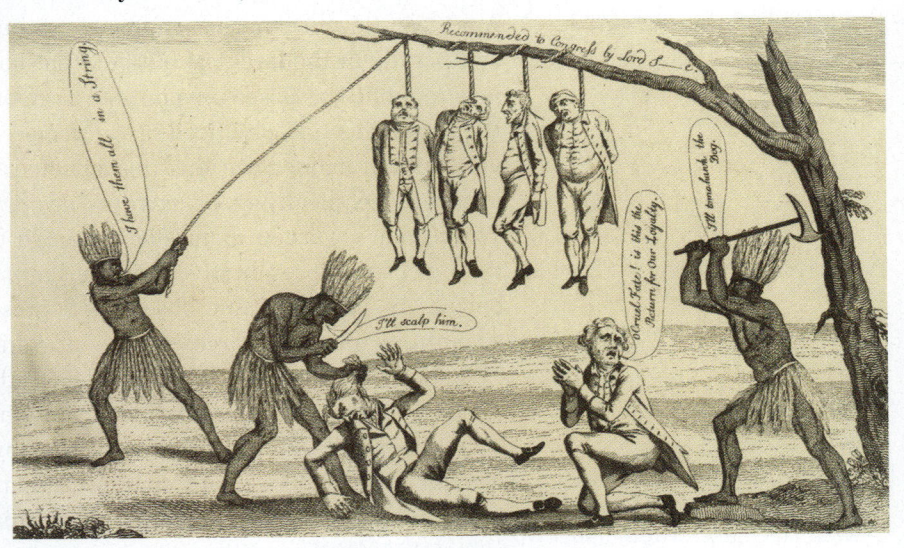

The Loyalists Flee

The Loyalists suffered for their support of King George III and their refusal to pledge allegiance to the new United States. During and after the Revolution, their property was confiscated or destroyed, and many Loyalists were assaulted, brutalized, and executed by Patriots (and vice versa).

After the American victory at Yorktown, tens of thousands of panicked Loyalists made their way to seaports to board British ships and flee the United States. Thousands of African Americans, mostly freedom seekers, also flocked to New York City, Charles Town, and Savannah, with many of their owners in hot pursuit. Boston King, one of the freedom seekers, said he saw White slave owners grabbing their escaped enslaved "property" "in the streets of New York, or even dragging them out of their beds."

"THE CRUEL FATE OF THE LOYALISTS" (1783) After the Revolution, many Loyalists fled to British colonies in the Caribbean and Canada. This British cartoon shows Patriots, depicted as "savages let[ting] loose," mercilessly hanging and scalping Loyalists.

Some 80,000 refugees—White Loyalists, free Blacks, freed enslaved people, and Indigenous Americans who had allied with the British—dispersed throughout the British Empire. Among those who resettled in Canada were 3,500 formerly enslaved people who had been freed in exchange for joining the British army. Some 2,000 freed Black people chose to go to Sierra Leone, in Africa, where British abolitionists helped them establish an experimental colony called Freetown.

About 12,000 Georgia and South Carolina Loyalists, including thousands of their enslaved people, went to British-controlled East Florida, only to see their new home handed over to Spain in 1783. Spanish authorities gave them a hard choice: swear allegiance to the Spanish king and convert to Catholicism or leave. Most of them left.

Some of the doubly displaced Loyalists sneaked back into the United States, but most went to British islands in the Caribbean. The departure of so many Loyalists was one of the most important social consequences of the Revolution. Their confiscated homes and lands and vacated jobs created new social, economic, and political opportunities for Patriots.

A Political Revolution

The Americans had won their independence. Had they experienced a political revolution as well? Years later, President John Adams insisted that the Revolution had begun long before the shooting started. "The Revolution was in the minds and hearts of the people. . . . This radical change in the principles, opinions, sentiments, and affections of the people was the real American Revolution."

Republican Ideology

American Revolutionaries embraced a **republican ideology** instead of the aristocratic or monarchical outlook that had long dominated Europe. The new republic was based on a limited form of democracy. In ancient Greece, the Athenians had practiced *direct democracy*, which meant that citizens voted on all major decisions that affected them. The United States, however, was technically a *representative democracy*, in which property-holding White men governed themselves through the concept of republicanism—they elected representatives, or legislators, to make decisions on their behalf. As Thomas Paine observed, representative democracy had many advantages over monarchies, one of which was greater transparency: "Whatever are its excellencies and defects, they are visible to all."

Revolutionary leaders believed that they must protect the rights of individuals and states from being violated by the national government. The war for independence thus sparked the crafting of **state constitutions** to support the new governments, all of which were designed to reflect the principles of the republican ideology and protect the rights of the people.

The first state constitutions created governments during the War of Independence much like the colonial governments, but with *elected*

> Representative democracy and individuals' rights

republican ideology A political belief in representative democracy in which citizens govern themselves by electing representatives, or legislators, to make key decisions on the citizens' behalf.

state constitutions Charters that define the relationship between the state government and local governments and individuals, while also protecting individual rights and freedoms.

governors and senates instead of royally *appointed* governors and councils. Most of the constitutions also included a bill of rights that protected freedom of speech, trial by jury, and freedom from self-incrimination, while limiting the powers of governors and strengthening the powers of the legislatures.

The Articles of Confederation

Once the colonies had declared their independence in 1776, the new thirteen states needed some form of national government. Before March 1781, the Continental Congress had exercised emergency powers without any legal or official authority.

Plans for a permanent form of government emerged as early as July 1776, when a committee appointed by Congress produced a draft constitution called the *Articles of Confederation and Perpetual Union*. But it took five years for the squabbling states to ratify the **Articles of Confederation** (March 1781), partly because there was a war to wage and partly because local and state concerns trumped national needs. The Articles essentially legalized the way the government had been operating since independence was declared, although the Continental Congress was renamed the Confederation Congress in 1781.

The Confederation revealed that developing a sense of *nationhood* would be as difficult for the thirteen states as achieving independence had been on the battlefields. The Articles reflected the long-standing fears of monarchy by not allowing for a president or chief executive. The Confederation government also had no national courts and no power to enforce its resolutions and ordinances. The Congress had full power over foreign affairs and disputes between the states; but it could not levy taxes, and its budgetary needs depended on requisitions from the states, which state legislatures often ignored.

The states were in no mood to create a strong central government. The Confederation Congress, in fact, was granted less power than the colonists had once accepted in the British Parliament, since it could not regulate interstate and foreign commerce. A "special majority" in the Confederation Congress, or nine of the thirteen states, had to approve measures dealing with war, treaties, coinage, finances, and the military. Unanimous approval from the states was needed to impose tariffs (often called "duties," or taxes) on imports and to amend the Articles.

For all its weaknesses, however, the Confederation government represented the most practical structure for the new nation. After all, the Revolution had yet to be won, and an America besieged by British armies and warships could not risk divisive debates over the distribution of government power.

> Limited central government and state power

Articles of Confederation The first form of government for the United States, ratified by the original thirteen states in 1781; weak in central authority, it was replaced by the U.S. Constitution drafted in 1787.

Expansion of Political Participation

The new state governments enabled more citizens to participate in self-governance than ever before. Property qualifications for voting, which already allowed an overwhelming majority of White men to vote, were lowered after 1776. As a group of farmers explained, "No man can be free and independent" unless he possesses "a voice . . . in the most important offices in the legislature." In Pennsylvania, Delaware, North Carolina, and Georgia, any male taxpayer could vote, regardless of how much—if any—property he owned. A higher percentage of American males could vote in the late eighteenth and early nineteenth centuries than could their counterparts in Great Britain. As broader voting rights led to a more representative group of government officials, farmers, tradesmen, and shopkeepers were elected to state legislatures. Their inclusion, however, also coincided with social upheaval and disenfranchisement for other groups of people.

A Social Revolution

The American Revolution was fought in the name of liberty, a virtuous ideal that proved elusive even in victory. What did the Revolution's promise of liberty mean to the "poor and middling sort" (according to one general) who populated the Patriot army and navy—mechanics, artisans, apprentices, dock workers, servants, farmers, and those now free?

In the end, the new republic's social fabric and political culture were visibly different after the war, and the energy created by the concepts of liberty, equality, and dignity for all changed the dynamics of social and political life.

Freedom of Religion

The Revolution tested traditional religious loyalties and triggered important changes in the relationship between churches and governments. Before the Revolution, Americans *tolerated* religious dissent; after the Revolution, they insisted on complete *freedom* of religion as embodied in the principle of separation of church and state.

The Anglican Church, established as the official religion in five colonies and parts of two others, was especially vulnerable to changes prompted by the war. Anglicans tended to be pro-British, and non-Anglicans—notably Baptists and Methodists—outnumbered Anglicans in all states except Virginia. All but Virginia eliminated tax support for the church before the fighting was over, and Virginia did so soon afterward. Although Anglicanism survived in the form of the new Episcopal Church, it never regained its pre-Revolutionary stature.

In 1776, the Virginia Declaration of Rights had guaranteed the free exercise of religion.

RELIGIOUS DEVELOPMENT The Congregational Church developed a national presence in the early nineteenth century. Lemuel Haynes, depicted here, was its first African American preacher. **What was the relationship between the American Revolution and religious freedom?**

Ten years later, the **Virginia Statute of Religious Freedom** (written by Thomas Jefferson) declared that "no man shall be compelled to frequent or support any religious worship, place or ministry whatsoever" and "that all men shall be free to profess, and by argument to maintain, their opinions in matters of religion." These statutes, and the Revolutionary ideology that justified them, helped shape the course that religious life would take in the United States: diverse and voluntary rather than monolithic and enforced by the government.

> Religious freedom

Religious freedom, representative democracy, an expanded franchise for White men—the Revolution had produced dramatic changes in the nation's social and political life. The new system of representative democracy, as instituted in the new state constitutions, enabled more men to participate in governance. The war did not, however, significantly alter the social or political status of enslaved Blacks or of Indigenous Americans.

Equality and Its Limits

The war created new relationships to society and led marginalized groups like African Americans, women, Hispanics, and Indigenous Americans to challenge notions of liberty. What did it mean to fight in the army and experience disenfranchisement at the same time? The limits of equality became even more evident after the war.

> **CORE OBJECTIVE**
> **5.** Compare the impact of the Revolutionary War on people of African descent, women, people of Hispanic descent, and Indigenous Americans.

The Paradox of Slavery

The sharpest irony of the American Revolution was that Great Britain offered enslaved people more opportunities for freedom than did the United States. In November 1775, the royal governor of Virginia, John Murray (Lord Dunmore), himself the owner of fifty-seven enslaved people, announced that all enslaved people and indentured servants would gain their freedom if they joined "Her Majesty's troops." Within a month, the British army had attracted more than 300 freedom seekers to what came to be called the Ethiopian Regiment. The number soon grew to almost 1,000 males and twice as many women and children.

The British recruitment of enslaved people outraged George Washington, Thomas Jefferson, and other plantation owners in Virginia. Washington knew that the British offer would entice many enslaved people to escape. Dozens of his own enslaved people had fled his control since 1760. Jefferson expressed the same concerns after twenty-three enslaved people escaped from his plantation outside Charlottesville. He eventually reclaimed six of them, only to sell them for their "disloyalty."

In 1775, authorities in Charles Town, South Carolina, executed Thomas "Jerry" Jeremiah, a free man of color who was the wealthiest Black man in North America. A harbor pilot, Jeremiah owned enslaved people himself. His crime? He supposedly incited a rebellion by telling enslaved people that British troops were coming "to help the poor Negroes," and that he intended to side with the British.

Virginia Statute of Religious Freedom (1786) A Virginia law, drafted by Thomas Jefferson in 1777 and enacted in 1786, that guarantees freedom of, and from, religion.

At Jeremiah's "trial"—which had no judge, jury, or attorneys—Henry Laurens, a planter and former slave trader who would later be elected president of the Continental Congress, charged that Jeremiah "was a forward fellow, puffed up by prosperity, ruined by Luxury & debauchery" and prone to "vanity & ambition." Laurens demanded that "nothing less than Death Should be the Sentence." On August 18, 1775, authorities hanged Jeremiah and burned his body to ashes.

Such brutalities led a British abolitionist to remark that America was "the land of the brave and the land of the slave." Many southern Revolutionaries were fighting less for independence from "British tyranny" than to retain their slave-labor system. The fact that nearly 20 percent of American enslaved people risked death by joining British armies demonstrated how steadfast they were in obtaining their freedom.

AFRICAN AMERICANS AT WAR Although many enslaved men were recruited to join the British forces, some fought on the Patriot side. Peter Salem, formerly owned by a Massachusetts family, was freed so that he could join the American militia; he is depicted here fighting in the Battle of Bunker Hill. **How did the British, the southerners, and the northerners differ in their approach to African Americans' involvement in the war?**

Americans debate the enlistment of Black men

Southern Backlash

In the end, the British policy of recruiting enslaved people backfired and only persuaded more fence-straddling White southerners to join the Patriot cause. Edward Rutledge of South Carolina said that the British decision to arm enslaved people did more to create "an eternal separation between Great Britain and the colonies than any other expedient."

The Southern Colonies' commitment to slavery and its underlying prejudice significantly fueled the Revolutionary rebellion. What South Carolinians wanted from the Revolutionary War, explained Pierce Butler, "is that their slaves not be taken from them" by British armies.

In response to the British recruitment of enslaved African Americans, General Washington authorized the enlistment of free Blacks—not enslaved people—into the American army. Indigenous groups, such as the Catawba in South Carolina, fought with the Continental Army as well. In February 1776, however, southern representatives convinced the Continental Congress to instruct Washington to enlist no more African Americans, free or enslaved. Two states, South Carolina and Georgia, refused to allow *any* Blacks to serve. As the American war effort struggled, however, Massachusetts organized two all-Black army units, and Rhode Island organized one, which also included Indigenous Americans. About 5,000 African Americans fought on the Patriot side, while the British and their allies had 15,000 to 20,000 people of African descent.

While thousands of free Blacks and freedom seekers fought in the war, the vast majority of African Americans did not choose sides so much as they

WOMEN AND THE REVOLUTION Women such as Deborah Sampson (*left*) and Ann Bailey (*right*) contributed to the American Revolution. Legend suggests that Bailey provided supplies at Fort Lee in South Carolina, killed members of the Shawnee Nation, and tried to avenge the death of her first husband, Richard Trotter. Afterward, she was referred to as "Mad Ann" or "Mad Ann Bailey."

chose freedom, equality, and justice. Several hundred thousand enslaved Blacks, mostly in the southern states, took advantage of the disruptions caused by the war to seize their freedom.

In the North, which had far fewer enslaved people than the South, the ideals of liberty and freedom led most states to legally abolish slavery, either during the war or shortly afterward (see Chapter 6). But those same ideals had little impact in the southern states.

The Status of Women

The ideal of liberty spawned by the Revolution applied to the status of White women as much as to that of African Americans. The legal status of women was governed by British common law, which essentially limited their roles to child-rearing and maintaining the household. Women could not vote or hold office, and few had access to formal education. Boys were taught to read and write; girls were taught to read and sew. Until married, women were subject to the dictates of their fathers.

However, once a woman married, she became the possession of her husband, and all property she brought to the marriage became his. A married woman had no legal right to buy, sell, or manage property. Technically, any wages a wife earned belonged to the husband. Women could not sign contracts, file lawsuits, or testify in court. A husband could beat and even rape his wife without fearing legal action. Divorces were extremely difficult to obtain.

Yet the Revolution allowed all women, free and enslaved, opportunities to broaden their social roles and to support the armies in various ways. They handled supplies, served as messengers or spies, and worked as "camp followers" who supported soldiers in exchange for daily rations. Some officers paid women to be their personal servants.

> Women in war

White women in particular experienced these changes. They responded to wartime needs by managing farms; publishing newspapers; and serving as soldiers, sometimes as spies. Women such as Anna Strong of New York spied for the Patriots; she used a clothesline to hang her black petticoat as a signal to Patriot forces. White women also aided the war efforts by boycotting British products.

Comparing PERSPECTIVES

FREEDOM AMONG THE ENSLAVED IN THE REVOLUTIONARY ERA

From: "By His Excellency Sir Henry Clinton, K. B. General and Commander in Chief" [Philipsburg Proclamation], June 30, 1779.

The Philipsburg Proclamation, issued by the British general Sir Henry Clinton on June 30, 1779, offered avenues to freedom for enslaved people in the South Carolina and Georgia regions. The proclamation was a military tactic aimed to hinder the Patriots' cause. Despite the proclamation's promises, by 1780 Clinton had returned nearly 100 formerly enslaved individuals to their previous owners.

Whereas the Enemy have adopted a practice of enrolling Negroes among their Troops, I do hereby give notice That all Negroes taken in Arms, or upon any Military duty, shall be purchased for the public service at a stated Price; the money to be paid to the Captors.

But I do most strictly forbid any Person to sell or claim right over any Negroe the property of a Rebel who may take Refuge with any part of His Majesty's Army: And I do promise to every Negroe who shall desert the Rebel Standard, full Security to follow within these Lines, any Occupation which he shall think proper.

Given under my Hand, at Head Quarters,
Philipsburgh the 30th Day of June 1779.
H CLINTON

From: "Ran Away" [Runaway Slave Advertisement], *The Georgia Gazette*, January 4, 1781.

This is a runaway slave advertisement declaring that fifty-six-year-old Rose, an Ibo woman, and her entire family are at large. Her enslaver, Mrs. Thomas, advertises a "handsome" reward for the return of Rose and her family, who fled Charles Town following the city's siege by the British in 1780.

RAN AWAY some time ago from Mrs. Mary Thomas's plantation in South Carolina, the following

Negroes:

    O'd Rose, a short black Ebo wench, about 56 years old;—Celia, a short wench, (daughter to the above Old Rose) about 36 years old;—Elsey, thick and chubbed, (a grand daughter of said Rose) about six years old;—Cato, an elderly fellow, of a yellow complexion, and husband of the above Celia, but perhaps changed;—Kate, a middle sized wench, with her country marks about her face, speaks bad English, of the Angola country;—Scipio, a middle sized well set fellow, 36 years old;—Dick, a middle sized well set fellow, and son to Old Rose, he is above 22 years old;—Town Sue, a short wench with a cast in one eye, speaks very good English, is smart and sensible, and about 35 years old;— Will, a smart waiting boy, tall, long visaged, with two large fore teeth, which are continually shewn by his mouth being seldom shut, had on a green coat trimmed with lively lace, which was his waiting dress;—Country Sue, a middle sized wench, but rather inclined to tall, a sister to Celia, and daughter of Old Rose, 32 years old.

    Whoever delivers the above Negroes to Mrs. Thomas in Charlestown, or the subscriber in Savannah, shall be handsomely rewarded; and whoever harbours, conceals, or carries them off, may depend upon being prosecuted to the utmost rigour of the law.

D. ZUBLY jun.

Questions

1. What freedoms did General Clinton offer to enslaved people?
2. What can be learned about the nativity (or birth places) of various members of enslaved families?
3. Based on your reading of both the documents and the chapter text, how were enslaved people granted and denied freedom from both sides during the Revolutionary War?

WOMEN AT WAR An 1856 Currier & Ives print celebrates "Molly Pitcher," the heroine of Monmouth, who loaded cannons in her husband's place after he fell in battle.

In military camps, White and Black women alike cleaned, cooked, washed clothes, and tended to the sick and wounded. Some worked as prostitutes. Female soldiers gave their services to the war effort, too. Some dressed in their husbands' clothes to mask their gender and officially enlist. Ann Bailey cut her hair, dressed like a man, and used a husky voice to join the Patriot army in New York as "Samuel Gay." (Bailey performed so well that she was promoted to corporal, only to be discovered as a woman, dismissed, jailed, and fined.)

White soldiers' wives who were camp followers sometimes brought along their children. Washington was forced to accept them because he was afraid to lose "a number of men, who very probably would have followed their wives" home.

On occasion, wives took the place of their soldier-husbands. In 1777, some 400 armed women mobilized to defend Pittsfield, Vermont. The men of the town had gone off to fight in the war, so when a band of Loyalists and Indigenous people approached the village, the women held off the attackers until additional support arrived.

Indigenous Americans Are Besieged

Most Indigenous people sought to remain neutral in the war, but both British and American agents urged Indigenous peoples to fight on their side. The result was chaos. On both sides, they attacked villages, burned crops, and killed civilians. Americans, both frontiersmen and soldiers, exacted ruthless revenge.

During and after the war, the new U.S. government assured its Indigenous allies that it would respect their lands and their rights. But many White Americans used the disruptions of war to destroy and displace Indigenous people. Once the war ended and independence was secured, there was no peace for the Indigenous people and their lands were given away by the Treaty of Paris. By the end of the eighteenth century, land-hungry Americans were again pushing into traditional Indigenous territories on the western frontier.

> Displacement and destruction of Indigenous Americans

The Emergence of Nationalism

On July 2, 1776, when the Second Continental Congress resolved "that these United Colonies are, and of right ought to be, free and independent states," John Adams had written his wife, Abigail, that future generations would remember that date as their "day of deliverance." Adams got everything right but the date. As luck would have it, July 4, the date the Declaration of Independence was approved, became Independence Day rather than July 2, when independence was formally declared.

The celebration of Independence Day quickly became the most important public ritual in the United States. People suspended their normal routines to devote a day to parades, patriotic speeches, and fireworks. In the process, the infant republic began to create its own myth of national identity.

George Washington acknowledged that important work remained. While retiring from military service, he penned a letter to the thirteen states in which he told the American people it would be "their choice . . . and conduct" that would determine whether the United States would become "respectable and prosperous, or contemptible and miserable as a Nation." Yet he remained hopeful, for Americans had already done the impossible by winning their independence on the battlefield. In closing, he urged the citizenry to rejoice and be grateful as they set about demonstrating to a skeptical world that a large and unruly republic could survive and flourish—forever.

Reviewing the
CORE OBJECTIVES

- **Civil War** The American Revolution was also a civil war, dividing families and communities. There were at least 100,000 Loyalists in the colonies, including royal officials, Anglican ministers, and recent immigrants. After the hostilities ended, many Loyalists—including enslaved people who had fled plantations to support the British cause—left for Canada, the West Indies, or Great Britain.

- **Military Challenges** In 1776, the British had the mightiest army and navy in the world, and their ranks included thousands of *Hessians* (German mercenaries). The Americans had to create an army—the *Continental Army*—and sustain it. To defeat the British, George Washington realized that the Americans had to turn unreliable *citizen-soldiers* into a disciplined fighting force and draw on state *militias* for support. He decided to wage a long and costly hit-and-run war, wagering that since the British army was fighting thousands of miles from its home base, King George would eventually give up in order to cut the nation's mounting losses.

- **Turning Points** After forcing the British to evacuate Boston, the American army suffered a string of defeats before George Washington surprised the Hessians at the *Battle of Trenton* at the end of 1776. The victory bolstered American morale and prompted more enlistments in the Continental Army. The French were likely allies for the colonies from the beginning of the conflict because they resented their losses to Britain in the Seven Years' War. After the British defeat at the *Battles of Saratoga* (1777), the colonies negotiated the *Treaty of Alliance* (1778) with France. Washington was able to hold his ragged forces together despite daily desertions and two especially difficult winters in Morristown and *Valley Forge* (1777–1778), the second and third major turning points. The British lost support on the frontier and in their southern colonies when terrorist tactics backfired. The Battle of King's Mountain (1780) drove southern Loyalists into retreat, and French supplies and the French fleet helped tip the balance and ensure the American victory at the *Battle of Yorktown* (1781), the final turning point that triggered negotiations leading to the *Treaty of Paris* (1783) which ended the war and acknowledged America's independence.

- **A Political and Social Revolution** The American Revolution disrupted and transformed traditional social relationships. American Revolutionaries embraced a *republican ideology* in contrast to a monarchy, and more White men gained the right to vote in the new nation as property requirements were lowered or removed entirely. But fears of a monarchy being reestablished led colonists to vest power in the states, rather than in a powerful national government, under the *Articles of Confederation*. The states wrote new *state constitutions* that instituted more elected positions. The *Virginia Statute of*

Religious Freedom (1786) led the way in guaranteeing the separation of church and state, and religious toleration was transformed into religious freedom for all, including Roman Catholics and Jews.

■ **People of African Descent, Women, and Indigenous Americans** In one of the Revolution's ironies, as many as 20 percent of enslaved people in the colonies sought liberty by fleeing to the British forces. Although many women had undertaken nontraditional roles during the war, afterward they remained largely confined to the domestic sphere, with no changes broadening their legal or political status. The Revolution had catastrophic effects on Indigenous people, regardless of which side they had supported during the war. During and after the Revolution, American settlers seized Indigenous land, often in violation of existing treaties.

KEY TERMS

Hessians *p. 199*
citizen-soldiers *p. 200*
Continental Army *p. 200*
militias *p. 206*
Battle of Trenton (1776) *p. 206*
Battles of Saratoga (1777) *p. 210*
Treaty of Alliance (1778) *p. 210*
Valley Forge (1777–1778) *p. 210*
Battle of Yorktown (1781) *p. 217*
Treaty of Paris (1783) *p. 219*
republican ideology *p. 222*
state constitutions *p. 222*
Articles of Confederation *p. 223*
Virginia Statute of Religious Freedom (1786) *p. 225*

CHRONOLOGY

1776 British forces seize New York City
General Washington's troops defeat British forces at the Battle of Trenton
States begin writing new constitutions

1777 American forces defeat the British in a series of battles at Saratoga, New York

1778 Americans and French sign the crucial Treaty of Alliance
George Rogers Clark's militia defeats British troops in the Mississippi Valley
British seize Savannah and Charles Town

1779 American forces defeat the Iroquois Confederacy at Newtown, New York

1780 Patriots defeat Loyalists at the Battle of King's Mountain

1781 British invasion of southern colonies is turned back at the Battles of Cowpens and Guilford Courthouse
American and French forces defeat British troops at Yorktown, Virginia

1783 Treaty of Paris is signed, formally ending the Revolutionary War

1786 Virginia adopts the Statute of Religious Freedom

InQuizitive

Go to InQuizitive to see what you've learned—and learn what you've missed—with personalized feedback along the way.

WASHINGTON AS A STATESMAN AT THE CONSTITUTIONAL CONVENTION (1856) This painting by Junius Brutus Stearns is one of the earliest depictions of the drafting of the Constitution. It captures the moment after the Convention members, including George Washington (*right*), completed the final draft.

Securing the Constitution and Union

1783–1800

CHAPTER 6

During the 1780s, the United States of America was rapidly emerging as the lone large republic in an unstable world dominated by monarchies. The new nation was distinctive in that it was born out of a conflict over ideas, principles, and ideals rather than from centuries-old racial or ancestral bonds, as was the case in Europe and elsewhere.

Yet Americans had little time to celebrate their victory in the Revolutionary War. As Alexander Hamilton, an army officer turned congressman, warned in 1783, "We have now happily concluded the great work of independence, but much remains to be done to reach the fruits of it." America was independent, but it was not yet a self-sustaining nation.

CORE OBJECTIVES

1. Identify the strengths and weaknesses of the Articles of Confederation and explain how they prompted the creation of a new U.S. constitution in 1787.

2. Describe the political innovations that the 1787 Constitutional Convention developed for the new nation.

3. Summarize the major debates surrounding the ratification of the Constitution. Explain why they arose and how they were resolved.

4. Compare the Federalists' vision for the United States with that of their Republican opponents during the 1790s.

5. Assess how attitudes toward Great Britain and France shaped American politics in the late eighteenth century.

CORE OBJECTIVE

1. Identify the strengths and weaknesses of the Articles of Confederation and explain how they prompted the creation of a new U.S. constitution in 1787.

A deliberately weak central government

The Confederation Government

Forging a new *nation* out of a *confederation* of thirteen rebellious colonies that had become "free and independent" states posed huge challenges, not the least of which was managing what George Washington called a "deranged" economy suffocating in war-related debts. The Confederation Congress had no cash and could not impose taxes to raise needed funds.

A Loose Alliance of States

The Articles of Confederation, formally approved in 1781, had created a loose alliance (or confederation) of thirteen independent states that were united only in theory. In practice, each state government acted mostly on its own.

The weak national government under the Articles had only one component, a one-house legislature. There was no executive branch, no national judiciary (court system). State legislatures, not voters, appointed the members of the Confederation Congress, in which each state, regardless of size or population, had one vote. This meant that Rhode Island, with 68,000 people, had the same voting power as Virginia, with more than 747,000 inhabitants.

George Washington called the Confederation "a half-starved, limping government." It could neither regulate trade nor create taxes to pay off the country's war debts. It could approve treaties but had no power to enforce their terms. It could call for raising an army but could not force men to serve.

The Congress, in short, could not enforce its own laws, and its budget relied on "voluntary" contributions from the states. In 1782, for example, the Confederation asked the states to provide $8 million for the national government; they sent $420,000. The lack of state support forced the Congress to print paper money, called Continentals, whose value plummeted to 2 cents on the dollar as more and more were printed. Virtually no gold and silver coins remained in circulation; they had all gone abroad to purchase war supplies.

It was hard to find people to serve in such a weak Congress, and many openly doubted the stability of the new republic. As John Adams wrote to Thomas Jefferson, "The Union is still to me an Object of as much Anxiety as ever independence was."

The Newburgh Conspiracy To garner support for their plan to finance the Confederation government, Superintendent of Finance Robert Morris and his nationalist friends in 1783 took a dangerous gamble. George Washington's army, encamped at Newburgh, New York, on the Hudson River, had grown restless after the Battle of Yorktown. The soldiers' pay was late, as usual, and the officers feared that the land grants promised to them by the government might never be honored once their service was no longer needed. In this atmosphere of dissatisfaction, Morris and his friends saw an opportunity.

A delegation of concerned officers traveled to Philadelphia, where they hatched a scheme to confront the states with the threat of a *coup d'état* (violent overthrowing of the existing government) unless the national government was given more power. New York congressman Alexander Hamilton even sought to bring George Washington, his former commander, into the plan.

> Hamilton's *coup d'etat*

Washington sympathized with the basic purpose of Hamilton's scheme, but he was also convinced that a military coup would be both dishonorable and dangerous. In March 1783, he confronted the plotting officers and expressed his "horror and detestation" of any effort to assume dictatorial powers. A military revolt would open "the flood-gates of civil discord" and "deluge our rising empire in blood." When he finished his argument, his officers adopted resolutions denouncing the "infamous propositions," and the so-called Newburgh Conspiracy evaporated.

A Struggling but Necessary Confederation Yet in spite of its limitations, the Confederation Congress did lay important foundations for the new national government. The Articles of Confederation were crucially important in supporting the political concept of *republicanism* (representative democracy and majority rule), which meant that America would be governed not by monarchs or aristocrats but "by the authority of the people," whose elected representatives would make decisions on their behalf. The Congress also formulated the basic principles of land distribution and territorial government that would guide America's westward expansion.

> Support of republicanism

Land Policy

In ending the Revolutionary War, the 1783 Treaty of Paris more than doubled the size of the United States, extending the nation's western boundary to the Mississippi River. Under the Articles of Confederation, land outside the boundaries of the thirteen original states became *public domain*, owned and administered by the national government.

In 1784, George Washington, now a civilian, traveled west to lands he owned in the Ohio valley. Along the way, he saw American settlers streaming westward. "The spirit of emigration is great," he wrote to the president of the Confederation Congress. But chaos would ensue unless some orderly process for western settlement were devised.

Between 1784 and 1787, the Confederation Congress responded to such concerns by creating three major ordinances (policies) detailing how western lands would be surveyed, sold, and developed by the national government. These ordinances provided the framework for western settlement that would shape much of the nation's development during the nineteenth century.

> Creation of land ordinances

Land Ordinances of 1784 and 1785 Thomas Jefferson drafted the Land Ordinance Act of 1784, which established a system for dividing the vast,

LAND ORDINANCE OF 1785
A map of the Northwest Territory of the United States in 1785. The land was divided into a series of townships, which were split up into farms for auction.

Northwest Ordinance (1787)
The land policy for new western territories in the Ohio Valley that established the terms and conditions for self-government and statehood while also banning slavery from the region.

unmapped area west of the Appalachian Mountains into as many as fourteen self-governing territories of equal size (see Map 6.1). In the new territories, all White males would be eligible to vote, hold office, and write constitutions for their territorial governments. When a territory's population equaled that of the smallest existing state (Rhode Island), it would be eligible for statehood.

Before Jefferson's plan could take effect, the Confederation Congress created the Land Ordinance of 1785. It called for organizing the Northwest Territory—what would become the states of Ohio, Michigan, Indiana, Illinois, Minnesota, and Wisconsin (see Map 6.2)—into townships of thirty-six square miles each that would be surveyed, sold for less than a dollar an acre, and settled. Then the surveyors would keep moving westward, laying out more townships for settlement.

Wherever Indigenous homelands were purchased—or taken—they were surveyed and divided into six-mile-square townships laid out along a grid running east–west and north–south. Each township was in turn divided into thirty-six sections one mile square (640 acres), with each section divided into four farms. The 640-acre sections of "public lands" were to be sold at auctions, the proceeds of which would go to the national Treasury.

The Northwest Ordinance

Two years after passage of the Land Ordinance of 1785, the Confederation Congress passed the third major land policy: the **Northwest Ordinance** of 1787, which set forth two key principles. First, the new territories would eventually become coequal states, as Jefferson had proposed. Second, slavery would be banned from the region north of the Ohio River. (But enslaved people already living there would remain in bondage.) The Northwest Ordinance also included a promise, which would be repeatedly broken, that Indigenous lands "shall never be taken from them without their consent."

For a new territory to become a state, the Ordinance specified a three-stage process. First, Congress would appoint a territorial governor and other officials to create a legal code and administer justice. Second, when the population of adult males reached 5,000, they could elect a territorial legislature. Third, when a territory's population reached 60,000 "free inhabitants," the males could draft a constitution and apply to Congress for statehood.

Foreign Tensions

At the same time that land policy was being addressed, relations with Great Britain and Spain continued to fester because both nations retained trading posts, forts, and soldiers on American soil, and both encouraged Indigenous people to resist American efforts to settle on tribal lands.

MAP 6.1 WESTERN LAND CESSIONS, 1781–1802

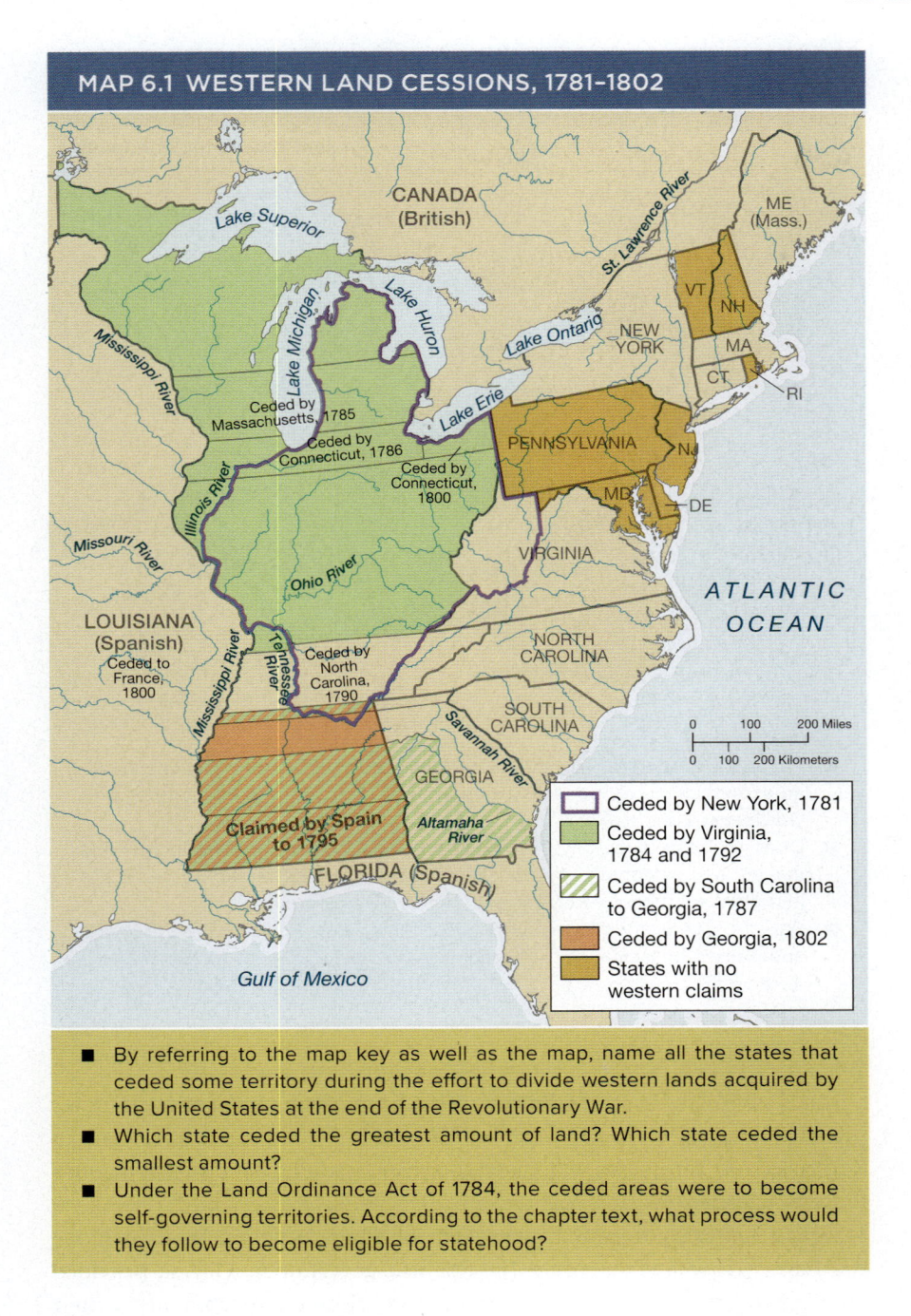

- By referring to the map key as well as the map, name all the states that ceded some territory during the effort to divide western lands acquired by the United States at the end of the Revolutionary War.
- Which state ceded the greatest amount of land? Which state ceded the smallest amount?
- Under the Land Ordinance Act of 1784, the ceded areas were to become self-governing territories. According to the chapter text, what process would they follow to become eligible for statehood?

The British refused to remove troops stationed south of the Canadian border in protest of the Americans' failure to pay debts owed from before the war and of the American seizure of Loyalist property during and after.

The Spanish disputed both the location of the southern boundary of the United States and the Americans' right to send boats down the Mississippi River. Having acquired the Louisiana Territory—including the port of New Orleans and all the area west to the Rocky Mountains—after the

MAP 6.2 THE NORTHWEST TERRITORY, 1785

- Within the green area labeled Northwest Territory, boundary lines delineate areas that ultimately became six new states. According to the chapter text, which states are they?
- Does the map show any of the territory being designated as Indigenous lands? What might that indicate about the Confederation Congress's intentions for the future of lands in the Northwest Territory?
- Based on your understanding of the chapter text, how did the surveying and selling of land within townships promote settlement in the western territories?

Seven Years' War, Spain closed the river to American use in order to deter American expansion to the west and the south. This infuriated settlers in Kentucky and Tennessee, who used the river to send their crops and goods to New Orleans.

Spain had also regained ownership of Florida, which then included southern Alabama. Thereafter, the Spanish governor in Florida provided firearms to Creek warriors, who resisted American encroachment on their native lands in southern Georgia.

Trade and the Economy

Great Britain also contributed to the fragile state of the American economy. Seven years of warfare had nearly bankrupted the new nation.

The British now treated the United States as an enemy nation. British warships began stopping American ships in the Atlantic, kidnapping

English-born American sailors, and "impressing" them into service in the Royal Navy. The British also closed their Caribbean colonies to American commerce. New England shipowners and southern planters were especially hard hit by this move, as exports of tobacco, rice, rum, and other commodities remained far below what they had been before the war.

To punish Britain for banning U.S. trade with the British West Indies, many state governments imposed special taxes (called tonnage fees) on British vessels arriving in American ports and levied tariffs (taxes) on British goods brought to the United States. The British responded by sending their ships to ports in states whose tariff rates were the lowest. By charging different tariffs on the same products, the states waged commercial war with one another. The result was economic chaos. By 1787, it was evident that the national government needed to regulate both interstate trade and foreign relations.

> Need to regulate interstate commerce and foreign relations

Money

Complex financial issues had also hampered economic activity after the war. There were few gold and silver coins and no national paper currency. The nation had only three banks—in Philadelphia, New York City, and Boston—all of which had been chartered by state governments and were therefore limited to operating within a single state. At the same time, farmers found themselves squeezed by lower crop prices, mounting debts, and soaring state taxes.

> High taxes and no national currency

The widespread shortage of "hard money" (gold and silver coins) was causing people to postpone paying their tax bills. By 1785, citizens deep in debt were urging their state governments to increase the money supply by printing new paper currency. Militiamen and farmers launched the loudest protests seeking relief. In 1785–1786, seven states began issuing paper money to help indebted farmers and to pay the cash bonuses promised to military veterans.

Economic and political elites, however, feared that the printing of more money would inflate the money supply and thereby reduce the purchasing power of currency.

Shays's Rebellion

Concerns about a taxpayer "revolt" became all too real in western Massachusetts when struggling farmers demanded that the state issue more paper money and give them additional time to pay what they claimed were "unjust" state and local taxes. Farmers also resented the new state constitution because it raised the property qualifications for voting and holding elected office, thus stripping poorer men of any voice in the political process.

> Shays's Rebellion against taxes

In 1786, when the merchant-dominated Massachusetts legislature refused to lower taxes or issue more paper money, three rural counties revolted. Armed groups of angry farmers, calling themselves Regulators, or "the voice of the people," banded together to force judges and sheriffs to stop seizing the cattle and farms of "debtors" who could not pay their taxes. These Regulators, like their South Carolina and North Carolina predecessors (see Chapter 4), took matters into their own hands and challenged local authorities. The insurgents were convinced that the state's political leaders were creating policies designed to make the wealthiest people even wealthier—at the expense of the poorest residents.

The situation worsened in the winter of early 1787 when a group of dissatisfied farmers led by thirty-nine-year-old Daniel Shays, a distinguished war veteran, marched on the federal arsenal at Springfield. The state government responded by sending 4,400 militiamen, who scattered the debtor army with a single cannon blast that left four farmers dead and many wounded. Shays fled to Vermont. Several rebels were arrested, and two were hanged. The rebels nevertheless earned a victory of sorts, as the legislature agreed to eliminate some of the burdensome taxes and fees.

News of **Shays's Rebellion** sent shock waves across the nation. In Massachusetts, Abigail Adams dismissed the rebel farmers as "ignorant, restless desperadoes, without conscience or principles." George Washington was equally concerned. America, he said, needed a stronger national "government by which our lives, liberty, and properties will be secured."

The Revolutionary elite resolved to create barriers to the unruly democracy spawned by the Revolution. Thomas Jefferson, however, urged state officials to be lenient with the rebels. He wrote to James Madison that "a little rebellion now and then is a good thing" in a republic, where the people rule. Grassroots rebellions were "a medicine necessary for the sound health of government."

The new American republic had reached this point because the Articles of Confederation were not strong enough to effectively govern and unify the newly "free and independent" states. Among the Confederation government's weaknesses was its inability to regulate trade or to impose taxes to fund the crushing Revolutionary War debt. Nonetheless, the Articles had been successful in supporting the foundational concepts of representative democracy and majority rule; they had also helped define the process by which new western territories would be organized and governed. But when uprisings by farmers protesting high taxes persisted, it became clear that without a stronger form of national government there would be no economic or social stability in the young republic.

SHAYS'S REBELLION In this engraving, a line of militiamen fire at Shays and his followers while the surviving rebels turn and flee. Shays demanded a more flexible monetary policy and the right to postpone paying taxes until the postwar agricultural depression lifted. **Why, given the rebels' defeat in combat, might the state legislature have decided to grant some of their demands?**

Shays's Rebellion (1786–1787) The storming of the Massachusetts federal arsenal in 1787 by Daniel Shays and 1,200 armed farmers seeking debt relief from the state legislature through the issuance of paper currency and lower taxes.

The Constitution

In the wake of Shays's Rebellion, what John Jay called "the better kind of people" sought to empower the national government to bring social order and provide economic stability. "Our present federal government," said Henry Knox, a Boston bookseller and Revolutionary War general, "is a name, a shadow, without power, or effect."

It was essential, said James Madison, to create a federal constitution that would repair the "vices of the political system" and "decide forever the fate of republican government." Alexander Hamilton urged that a national gathering of delegates be given "full powers" to revise the Articles of Confederation so as to suppress "the amazing violence and turbulence of the democratic spirit" infecting the nation.

> **CORE OBJECTIVE**
> **2.** Describe the political innovations that the 1787 Constitutional Convention developed for the new nation.

The Constitutional Convention

In 1787, the Confederation Congress responded to the unrest by calling for a special "federal" convention to gather in Philadelphia's State House (now known as Independence Hall) for the "purpose of revising the Articles of Confederation." Only Rhode Island refused to participate.

The delegates began work on May 25, 1787. Although the states appointed fifty-five delegates, some quit in disgust and others were distracted by other

> Revising the Articles of Confederation

SIGNING OF THE CONSTITUTION Thomas Pritchard Rossiter's painting shows George Washington presiding over what Thomas Jefferson called "an assembly of demi-gods" in Philadelphia.

JAMES MADISON This 1783 miniature shows Madison at thirty-two years old, just four years before he would assume a major role in drafting the Constitution.

priorities. Yet after fifteen weeks of deliberations, thirty-nine delegates signed the new federal Constitution on September 17.

The Constitution reflected the individuals who created it. Their average age was forty-two, with the youngest being twenty-six. Most were members of the political and economic elite. Twenty-six were college graduates, two were college presidents, and thirty-four were lawyers. Others were planters, merchants, bankers, and clergymen. They were all White and male, and two dozen of them—including George Washington, Thomas Jefferson, and James Madison—owned enslaved people.

These men (who became known as the founding fathers, the founders, or the framers) were also practical men of experience. Twenty-two had fought in the Revolutionary War. Eight of the framers had immigrated from countries other than Britain. Seven had been state governors, and eight had helped write their state constitutions. Most had been members of Congress, and eight had signed the Declaration of Independence.

Drafting the Constitution

George Washington was unanimously elected as the presiding officer at the Federal Convention (later renamed the Constitutional Convention). He attended every session but participated little in the debates, for fear that people would take his opinions too seriously.

Most active was James Madison of Virginia, the ablest political theorist in the group. Madison was a thirty-six-year-old attorney who owned a huge tobacco plantation called Montpelier. Barely five feet tall and weighing only 130 pounds, Madison was too frail to serve in the Revolutionary army.

Madison is "a good and able man," remarked Fisher Ames of Massachusetts, but he "speaks low, his person [body] is little and ordinary," and he is "too timid in his politics." Although shy and soft-spoken, Madison had an agile mind and a commitment to public service. He had served in the Continental Congress, where he had become a nationalist. Now he resolved to ensure the "supremacy of national authority." The logic of his arguments—and his willingness to compromise—proved decisive in shaping the new constitution. "Every person seems to acknowledge his greatness," said a Georgia delegate.

Most of the delegates agreed with Madison that the republic needed a stronger national government, weaker state legislatures, and the power to restrain the "dangerous" democratic impulses unleashed by the Revolution. "The evils we experience," said Elbridge Gerry of Massachusetts, "flow from the excess of democracy."

Legitimacy derived from "the people"

Guiding Assumptions Two interrelated assumptions guided the Constitutional Convention: that the national government must have direct authority over the citizenry rather than governing through the state governments, and that it must derive its legitimacy from the "genius of the people." Thus, the final draft of the Constitution begins: "We the people of the United States, in Order to form a more perfect Union, . . . do ordain and establish this Constitution for the United States of America."

The insistence that the voters were "the legitimate source of all authority," as James Wilson of Pennsylvania stressed, was the most important political innovation since the Declaration of Independence. No other nation in the world had endowed "the people" with such authority. By declaring the Constitution to be the voice of the people, the founders authorized the federal government to limit the powers of the states.

The delegates realized, too, that an effective national government needed authority to collect taxes, borrow and issue money, regulate commerce, fund an army and navy, and make laws. This meant that the states must be stripped of the power to print paper money, make treaties, wage war, and levy taxes and tariffs on imported goods. This concept of dividing authority between the national government and the states came to be called **federalism**.

federalism The concept of dividing governmental authority between the national government and the states.

The Virginia and New Jersey Plans James Madison drafted the framework for the initial discussions at the Constitutional Convention. His proposals, called the Virginia Plan, started with a radical suggestion: that the delegates scrap their original instructions to *revise* the Articles of Confederation and instead create a *new* constitution.

Madison's Virginia Plan called for a "national government [with] a supreme legislative, executive, and judiciary." It proposed a bicameral Congress, meaning that Congress would be divided into two houses: a lower House of Representatives chosen by the "people of the several states," and an upper house of senators elected by the state legislatures. The more populous states would have more representatives in Congress than the smaller states. Madison also wanted to give Congress the power to veto state laws. Overall, the Virginia Plan sparked furious disagreements. When asked why the small states were so suspicious of the plan, Gunning Bedford of Delaware replied: "I do not, gentlemen, trust you."

The Virginia Plan

On June 15, Bedford and other delegates submitted an alternative proposal called the New Jersey Plan, developed by William Paterson of New Jersey. It sought to keep the existing equal representation of the states in a unicameral (one-house) national legislature. It also gave Congress newly expanded powers, but not the right to veto state laws.

The New Jersey Plan

The Structure of the Federal Government

An intense debate over congressional representation was resolved in mid-July by the so-called Great Compromise, which incorporated elements of both plans. Roger Sherman of Connecticut suggested that one chamber of the proposed Congress have its seats allotted according to population, with the other preserving the principle of one vote for each state. And that is what happened. Larger states won apportionment (the allocation of delegates to each state) by population in the proposed House of Representatives, while the delegates of smaller states won equality of representation in the Senate, where each state would have two members elected by the legislatures.

The Great Compromise

separation of powers The strict division of the powers of government among three separate branches (executive, legislative, and judicial), which in turn check and balance one another.

> A bicameral Congress with a separation of powers

The Legislature (Congress) The Great Compromise embedded the innovative concept of **separation of powers** into the new Congress. While James Madison believed that in "a republican government, the legislative authority necessarily predominates," he and others also sought to keep the Congress from becoming too dominant.

The members of the House of Representatives would be elected by voters every two years. (Under the Articles of Confederation, members of Congress had been chosen by state legislatures.) Madison argued that allowing individual citizens to elect the people's House was "essential to every plan of free government." Indeed, such representative democracy centered on majority rule was the essence of a republican form of government.

The framers viewed the upper house, or Senate, as a check on the excesses of democracy that might emerge in the lower house, or the House of Representatives. John Adams, for example, argued that the Senate should be made up of "illustrious" and well-educated members elected for six-year terms so as to counterbalance those in the House of Representatives elected every two years by what he feared would be gullible and uninformed voters. The Senate could overrule the House or the president. Madison explained that the Senate would help "protect the minority of the opulent against the majority." Finally, the delegates decided that members of both the House and the Senate would be paid so that even those who were not wealthy could run for office.

The Executive (the President) The Constitutional Convention also struggled over issues related to the executive branch. Some delegates wanted a powerful president who could veto acts of Congress. Others felt that the president should simply "execute" the laws as passed by Congress. Still others, including Benjamin Franklin, wanted a "plural executive" rather than a single man governing the nation. The eventual decision to have a single chief executive, a "natural born Citizen" at least thirty-five years old of any or no religion, worried many delegates. George Mason of Virginia feared that a single president might start behaving like a king.

> Presidential powers

In the end, several compromises ensured that the president would be powerful enough to counterbalance the Congress. The president, to be elected for four-year terms, could veto acts of Congress; but the vetoes would then be subject to overruling by a two-thirds vote in each house. The president became the nation's chief diplomat and commander-in-chief of the armed forces, and was responsible for implementing the laws made by Congress.

> Checks on presidential power

Yet the president's powers were also limited. The chief executive could neither declare war nor make peace; only Congress could do that. Moreover, the president could be removed from office. The House of Representatives could impeach (that is, bring to trial) the chief executive—and other civil officers—on charges of treason, bribery, or "other high crimes and misdemeanors," but an impeached president would have to leave office only if two-thirds of the Senate voted for conviction.

The Electoral College To preserve the separation of the three branches of government, the president would be elected every four years by the **Electoral College**—a group of highly qualified "electors" chosen by "the people" in local elections. The number of each state's electors would equal the number of its congressional representatives and senators. At this time, there were 55 delegates representing 12 states. In order to pass a resolution at the Convention, 7 states were needed for a majority. Today, these numbers have changed: a presidential candidate has a possible total of 538 electoral votes and needs more than 270 to win the majority and secure the election.

Establishing the Electoral College was a compromise between those wanting the president to be elected by Congress and those preferring a direct vote of qualified citizens. However, it also meant that presidential candidates would often focus their campaigns on winning the states that generated the most electoral votes. Moreover, a candidate who won the popular vote could still lose the election if they had fewer electoral votes. This system continues to apply today.

The Judiciary The third proposed branch of government, the judiciary, sparked little debate. The new constitution called for a supreme national court headed by a chief justice. The court's role was not to make laws (a power reserved to Congress) or to execute and enforce the laws (reserved to the presidency), but to *interpret* the laws and to ensure that every citizen received *equal justice* under the law.

The U.S. Supreme Court had final authority in interpreting the Constitution and in settling constitutional disputes between states. Article VI of the Constitution declared that the federal constitution, federal laws, and treaties were "the supreme Law of the Land."

> **Electoral College (1787)** An electoral system established in Article II, Section I, of the U.S. Constitution to determine the presidential and vice-presidential selection process. Presidential candidates must win the majority of the electoral votes in order to secure the presidency.

> Powers of the U.S. Supreme Court

The Limits of the Constitution

The men who drafted the Constitution claimed to be representing all Americans. However, as Senator Stephen Douglas of Illinois would note seventy years later, the Constitution was in fact "made by white men, for the benefit of white men and their posterity [descendants] forever." Important groups were left out of the Constitution's protections. Among these were Indigenous Americans, enslaved people, and women.

Indigenous Exclusion

Although the Constitution offered protection for its citizens, many people were excluded from citizenship. Indigenous Americans, for example, could not be citizens unless they paid taxes, which few did. The Constitution also declared that Native American "tribes" were not part of the United States but were separate "nations."

Indigenous people were not willing to concede their ancestral lands and sign on to becoming citizens of a nation that was destroying theirs. They also did not consent to the Commerce Clause of the U.S. Constitution, Article 1, Section 8, which sought to regulate trade with Indigenous nations and gave the new government power and control over such treaties.

Addressing Slavery

The population of enslaved people were also denied citizenship rights. Of all the issues that emerged during the Constitutional Convention of 1787, none was more explosive than slavery. As James Madison stressed, "the great division of interest" among the delegates "did not lie between the large & small states: it lay between the Northern & Southern," primarily from "their having or not having slaves."

Northern states begin abolishing slavery

When the Patriots declared independence in 1776, slavery existed in every state. However, over the next two decades, beginning with Pennsylvania in 1780, all states north of Maryland abolished slavery through various forms of emancipation—by liberating people at a specific age, upon the death of the enslaver, or according to other region-specific stipulations. This meant that, for the first time, a geographic line was being drawn in the United States between the "free" states in the North and the "slave" states in the South.

Suing for Freedom in Massachusetts Some enslaved people pushed for emancipation by taking legal action. In Massachusetts, for example, the state's 1780 constitution contained this clause: "All men are born free and equal." This led enslaved people such as Quock Walker and Elizabeth Freeman to sue for their freedom, following the example of nearly thirty other enslaved people in Massachusetts who had sued their enslavers prior to 1780. Many of them had done so on the basis of broken promises from their enslavers, or because of the questionable status of their mothers. (By the early 1660s, the status of an enslaved individual was defined by that of their mother. If the mother was free, then so too were her offspring.)

ELIZABETH FREEMAN Also known as "Mum Bett" Freeman sued for her freedom through the courts in Massachusetts and won on the grounds that the state had abolished slavery. Her victory led to many similar successful suits in the years that followed, and helped make slavery a major topic during the Constitutional Convention of 1787.

Freeman, also known as Mum Bett, went to the courts in search of her freedom in 1781 on different grounds. Likely born in the mid-1740s, she would have heard conversations about freedom, liberty, and independence from her enslavers. She and an enslaved man named Brom worked with an attorney to sue for their freedom on the grounds that the Massachusetts state constitution had outlawed slavery by declaring that all people were born free. In 1781, they won their case (*Brom and Bett v. Ashley*) and received their freedom, setting the stage for other enslaved people to do the same. In fact, a man named Quock Walker cited *Brom and Bett* shortly thereafter, and he too was granted his freedom. These cases spelled doom for slavery in Massachusetts.

Competing Viewpoints At the same time, as enslaved people were taking the initiative to seek freedom through the courts, slavery was becoming a key topic during the Constitutional Convention.

Some delegates viewed slavery as an embarrassing contradiction to the principles of liberty and equality embodied in the Declaration of Independence ("all men are created equal") and the new constitution. Luther Martin, whom some considered Maryland's most brilliant attorney, pointed out that owning human beings was "inconsistent with the principles of the revolution and dishonorable to the American character."

Most of the southern delegates strongly disagreed. Many were planters who had grown dependent on enslaved people. (It is estimated that about twenty-five of the fifty-five delegates at the convention were enslavers.) South Carolinian Charles Pinckney stressed the practical reality in the southern states: "South Carolina and Georgia cannot do without slaves." Delegates owning enslaved people would have walked out of the negotiations had there been an attempt to abolish slavery. The framers therefore decided not to include a plan for limiting or ending slavery, nor did the founding document treat the enslaved population as human beings with civil rights.

CHARLES CALVERT AND HIS SLAVE (1761) This image of Charles Calvert (direct descendant of Lord Baltimore) at age five, dressed in full military attire and towering over the kneeling enslaved boy, who is dressed as a military drummer, clearly establishes their roles and status within the elite colonial families of the Chesapeake region.

The Three-Fifths Compromise The fact that the Constitution denied freedom and rights to enslaved people raised questions about how the 700,000 of them currently residing in the new nation would be counted for the purposes of representation. Southerners supported counting enslaved people as part of their states' population because the size of state delegations in the proposed House of Representatives would be based on population. Northerners maintained that it made no sense to count enslaved people when they were treated as property, not human beings.

The delegates agreed to a compromise in which three-fifths of "all other persons" (that is, the enslaved) would be included in population counts as a basis for apportioning a state's congressional representatives. In a constitution intended to "secure the blessings of liberty to ourselves and our posterity," the three-fifths clause was an example of compromise being divorced from principle. The bargain over slavery would bedevil the nation for the next seventy-five years.

The three-fifths compromise

Other Slavery Compromises Another concession to Southern delegates appeared in a section about the African slave trade (Middle Passage). The Constitution's Article 1, Section 9, stipulated that "the Migration or Importation of such Persons . . . shall not be prohibited by the Congress prior to the Year one thousand eight hundred and eight." This extended the life of the slave trade for at least two more decades.

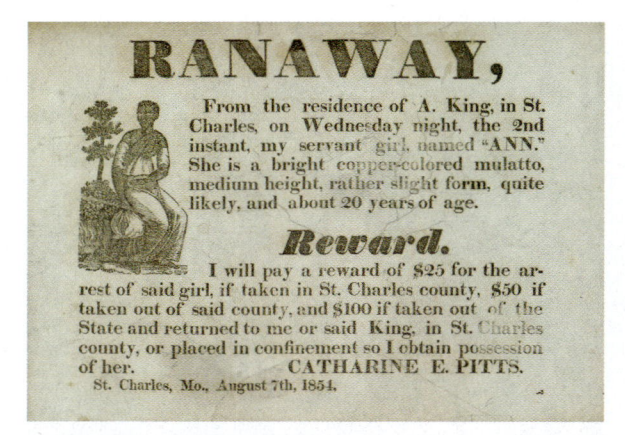

REWARD ADVERTISEMENT
Broadside and newspaper advertisements taken out by slaveholders seeking the return of freedom-seeking enslaved people were widely used from the late eighteenth century through the middle of the nineteenth century.

The framers also sought to prevent enslaved people in Southern states from escaping to the North, now that those northern states were abolishing slavery. First with the Constitution's Fugitive Slave Clause, and then with the 1793 Fugitive Slave Act, new restrictions greeted enslaved people who tried to liberate themselves. The act authorized local governments to capture and return freedom seekers to their enslavers, and imposed penalties on anyone who helped freedom seekers.

The act empowered slave owners in the South to hunt down and punish anyone who fled their plantations. The owners placed advertisements in newspapers seeking information about the whereabouts of fugitives; they also hired professional slave catchers to roam the northern states and violently kidnap anyone suspected of running away.

The life of Ona Judge reveals how the Fugitive Slave Act impacted freedom-seeking enslaved people. Judge was born at Mount Vernon in 1773 into a family of enslaved people whom Martha Custis brought to her marriage with George Washington. Ona's mother married a White indentured servant at Mount Vernon, which meant that Ona was of biracial ancestry and also legally an enslaved person, since her mother was enslaved.

Ona traveled with the Washingtons to serve them in the Presidential House in Philadelphia. But upon learning that Martha Washington planned to give her as a wedding present to Martha's granddaughter, Ona escaped and fled north to New Hampshire, where she married a seaman and raised a family. George Washington used the 1793 Fugitive Slave Act to pursue bringing Ona back to Mount Vernon, and Philadelphia newspapers ran articles on her escape announcing that a $10 bounty would be paid for her return. Ultimately, Washington's efforts were to no avail.

In a concession to delegates who were opposed to slavery, the original Constitution also never mentions the word *slavery*. As slaveholder James Madison explained, it would be "wrong to admit in the Constitution the idea that there could be property in men." Instead, the document speaks of "free persons" and "all other persons" and of persons "held to service of labor." The word *slavery* would not appear in the Constitution until the Thirteenth Amendment abolished it in 1865.

The Absence of Women's Rights

The delegates at the Constitutional Convention refused even to discuss political rights for women. In the new United States, women could not vote, hold elected office, or own property. Gaining a divorce also remained extraordinarily difficult for them. "Every man, by the Constitution, is born with an equal right to be elected to the highest office," asserted Reverend John Ogden of Portsmouth, New Hampshire, in *The Female Guide* (1793). "And every woman is born with an equal right to be the wife of the most eminent man."

Yet not all women were willing to maintain their subordinate role. Just as the Revolutionary War enabled many African Americans to seize their freedom, it also inspired some women to demand political equality. Judith Sargent Murray, a Massachusetts writer, argued that the rights and liberties fought for by Patriots belonged not just to men but to women as well. In her essay "On the Equality of the Sexes," published in 1790, she challenged the prevailing view that men had greater intellectual capacities than women. She insisted that any differences resulted from prejudice and discrimination that prevented women from having access to formal education and worldly experience.

The arguments for gender equality, however, fell mostly on deaf ears. Nowhere does the Constitution include the word *women*. Writing from Paris, Thomas Jefferson expressed the hope that American "ladies" would forget about political participation and be "contented to soothe and calm the minds of their husbands returning ruffled from political debate."

Many women instead sought new meaning in their roles as wives and mothers. White women like Martha Washington and Abigail Adams tried to fulfill an emerging ideal of republican motherhood, which encouraged women to raise their children—especially their sons—to be good citizens with sound moral values and discernment. The future of the republic would depend on it.

Enslaved women, however, could not aspire to republican motherhood because their children were considered someone else's property. Instead, they did all they could to teach their children how to interact with their enslavers and protect themselves from physical and sexual abuse.

The Constitutional Convention may not have protected the rights of all people living in the new republic, but it did develop significant political innovations. The delegates crafted a federalist system of national governance based on clear separation of powers among executive, legislative, and judicial branches working alongside state governments. Issues surrounding the protection of state power and the representation of "the people" were resolved by creating a Senate with equal representation for each state, and a House of Representatives with each state's delegate numbers based on population counts—including a compromise to count three-fifths of the enslaved people in Southern states. The next challenge would involve winning approval for the new constitution at each state's ratification convention.

> Advocates and arguments for gender equality

The Fight for Ratification

On September 17, 1787, the Federal Convention reported that it had completed the new constitution. The Confederation Congress sent the final draft to thirteen special state conventions for official approval (ratification). "Gentlemen," announced Benjamin Franklin, "you have a republic, if you can keep it."

Over the next ten months, people from all walks of life debated the new constitution's merits—on street corners and in taverns, at churches, in newspapers, in workplaces, and in the state conventions. Gilbert Livingston, a

> CORE **OBJECTIVE**
> **3.** Summarize the major debates surrounding the ratification of the Constitution. Explain why they arose and how they were resolved.

anti-Federalists Opponents of the Constitution as an infringement on individual and states' rights, whose criticism led to the addition of a Bill of Rights to the document. Many anti-Federalists later joined Thomas Jefferson's Democratic-Republican Party.

delegate to the New York ratifying convention, viewed his participation in the debate as the "greatest transaction of his life." Richmond, the new state capital of Virginia, according to one observer, had trouble hosting the "prodigious number of People from all parts of the Country" who wanted to witness the debates.

Choosing Sides: Anti-Federalists versus Federalists

Advocates for the new constitution took the name Federalists; opponents were called **anti-Federalists**. The two sides formed the seeds for America's first two-party political system.

The Federalists, led by James Madison and Alexander Hamilton, had several advantages. First, they had a concrete proposal—the draft constitution itself; their opponents had nothing to offer but criticism. Second, many Federalists had been members of the Constitutional Convention and were familiar with the disputed issues in the document. Third, Federalists were more unified and better organized.

The anti-Federalist leaders—Virginians Patrick Henry, George Mason, Richard Henry Lee, and future president James Monroe; George Clinton of New York; Samuel Adams, Elbridge Gerry, and Mercy Otis Warren of Massachusetts; Luther Martin and Samuel Chase of Maryland—raised valid concerns. Some wanted to retain the Confederation. Others wanted to start over. Still others wanted to revise the proposed constitution.

Anti-Federalists feared that the new national government would eventually grow corrupt and tyrannical. George Mason of Virginia spoke for many in vowing that he would "sooner chop off my right hand" than approve the new constitution. Mason and the other anti-Federalists especially criticized

FEDERALISTS VERSUS ANTI-FEDERALISTS This satirical engraving by Amos Doolittle portrays the conflicts that arose over ratification of the Constitution. In the center, stuck in the mud, is a wagon that represents Connecticut, laden with debt. On either side, the Federalists *(right)* and anti-Federalists *(left)* engage in a tug-of-war, pulling Connecticut in opposite directions. The three merchant ships *at the bottom* are carrying goods from Connecticut to New York, and the phrase *below* criticizes the tariffs that states imposed on such interstate imports. **With whom does Doolittle appear to agree, the Federalists or the anti-Federalists?**

the absence of a "bill of rights" to protect individuals and states from the power of the national government. Other than mentioning a bill of rights, however, the anti-Federalists had no comprehensive alternative to the draft constitution.

The Federalist Papers

Among the legacies of the debate over the Constitution is what came to be called **The Federalist Papers**, a collection of eighty-five essays published in New York newspapers in 1787 and 1788. Written by James Madison, Alexander Hamilton, and John Jay, the essays were intended to convince New Yorkers to ratify the new constitution.

The United States, according to *The Federalist Papers*, was to be a republic grounded in radically new notions: the people, not a king or queen, would be sovereign, and the rule of law would ensure that tyrants could never violate the civil rights protecting the citizenry.

In the most famous of the *Federalist* essays, No. 10, Madison turned the conventional wisdom about republics on its head. From ancient times, he wrote, it had been assumed that republics ("representative democracies") survived only if they were small and homogeneous. Madison, however, argued that small republics usually fell victim to warring factions. In the United States, he explained, the size and diversity of the expanding nation would make it impossible for any single faction to form a majority that could corrupt the federal government—or society at large.

The Federalist Papers
A collection of eighty-five essays, published widely in newspapers in 1787 and 1788, written by Alexander Hamilton, James Madison, and John Jay in support of adopting the proposed U.S. Constitution.

The States Decide

The heated debate over ratification of the new constitution at times boiled over into violence. Riots erupted in several cities. Newspapers took sides, leading one New Englander to remark that the papers were being "read more than the Bible."

Amid the intense discussions, ratification of the new constitution gained momentum at the end of 1787 (see Map 6.3). Delaware, New Jersey, and Georgia were among the first states to ratify the Constitution. Massachusetts, still sharply divided in the aftermath of Shays's Rebellion, was the first state in which the outcome was close, approving the Constitution by a vote of 187 to 168.

On June 21, 1788, New Hampshire became the ninth state to ratify the Constitution, thereby reaching the minimum number of states needed for approval. The Constitution, however, could hardly succeed without the approval of Virginia, the largest, wealthiest, and most populous state; or of New York, which had the third-highest population and occupied a key position geographically. Both states included strong opposition groups that were eventually won over by an agreement to add a bill of rights.

RATIFICATION OF THE CONSTITUTION

Order of Ratification	State	Date of Ratification
1	Delaware	December 7, 1787
2	Pennsylvania	December 12, 1787
3	New Jersey	December 18, 1787
4	Georgia	January 2, 1788
5	Connecticut	January 9, 1788
6	Massachusetts	February 6, 1788
7	Maryland	April 28, 1788
8	South Carolina	May 23, 1788
9	New Hampshire	June 21, 1788
10	Virginia	June 25, 1788
11	New York	July 26, 1788
12	North Carolina	November 21, 1789 (rejected during the first convention, in 1788)
13	Rhode Island	May 29, 1790

MAP 6.3 THE VOTE ON THE CONSTITUTION, 1787–1790

- Federalist majority
- Anti-Federalist majority
- Evenly divided

- According to the map, which two groups were involved in debating ratification of the Constitution? Based on the color-coded areas reflecting these groups' majorities, does it look like one was more influential than the other?
- Which states had 100 percent majority support by one group only? Which states had some areas in which the opposing groups were evenly divided over the ratification issue?
- According to the chapter text, who were the leading Federalists and anti-Federalists? Why were the anti-Federalists opposed to ratifying the Constitution?

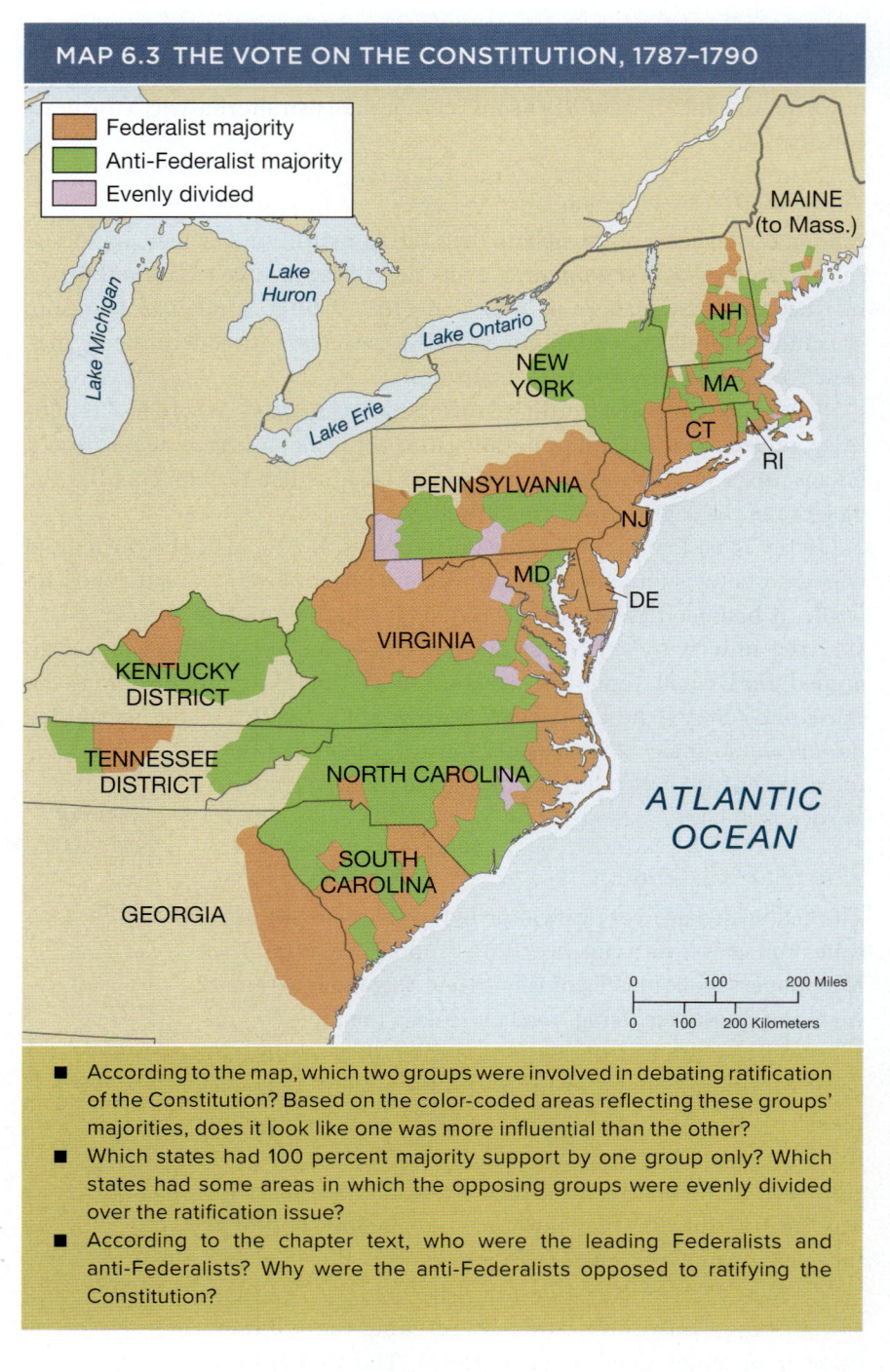

Upon notification of New Hampshire's decision to ratify the Constitution, the Confederation Congress chose New York City as the national capital and called for the new government to assume power in 1789. "Our Constitution is in actual operation," Benjamin Franklin wrote to a friend. "Everything appears to promise that it will last; but in this world nothing is certain but death and taxes."

The Constitution was by no means perfect (after all, it has been amended twenty-seven times); it was a bundle of compromises and concessions that left many issues, notably slavery, undecided or ignored. But most of its supporters believed that it was the best frame of government obtainable and that it would continue to evolve and improve.

The major debates surrounding the Constitution's ratification had arisen from a shared desire to build a government that would never become as imperious as Great Britain's tyrannical rule over the colonies. The Federalists argued that by making "the people" sovereign and the rule of law paramount, the new constitution would protect the nation from tyranny. The anti-Federalists, however, feared that a too-powerful presidency and national government might become overbearing and trample on the rights of individuals and the states. The Constitution was adopted, but the resistance to it would help convince the new Congress to propose the first ten amendments to the Constitution, now known as the Bill of Rights.

The Federalist Era

The Constitution promised to create a more powerful national government better capable of managing a rapidly growing republic. Yet it was one thing to ratify a new constitution and quite another to make the new government run smoothly.

With each passing year, political groups within the United States debated how to interpret and apply the provisions of the new constitution. During the 1790s, the federal government would confront rebellions, states threatening to secede, staggering debt, and foreign wars, as well as the formation of competing political parties—Federalists and Democratic Republicans, more commonly known as **Jeffersonian Republicans**, or simply as Republicans.

The Republicans were mostly southerners, like Virginians Thomas Jefferson and James Madison, who wanted the country to remain a rural nation of small farmers dedicated to republican values. The Federalists, led by Alexander Hamilton and John Adams, were clustered in New York and New England. They embraced urban culture, industrial development, and commercial growth.

The First President

On March 4, 1789, the new Congress convened in New York City. A few weeks later, the presiding officer of the Senate certified that George Washington, with 69 Electoral College votes, was the nation's unanimous choice for president. John Adams of Massachusetts, with 34 votes, became vice president. (At this time, no candidates ran specifically for the vice presidency; the presidential candidate who came in second, regardless of party affiliation, became vice president.)

Washington greeted the news of his election with a "heart filled with distress," likening himself to "a culprit who is going to the place of his

> **CORE OBJECTIVE**
> **4.** Compare the Federalists' vision for the United States with that of their Republican opponents during the 1790s.

Jeffersonian Republicans A political party founded by Thomas Jefferson in opposition to the Federalist Party led by Alexander Hamilton and John Adams; also known as the Democratic-Republican Party.

execution." He would have preferred to stay in retirement at Mount Vernon, his Virginia plantation, but agreed to serve because he had been "summoned by [his] country."

Some complained that Washington's personality was too cold and aloof, and that he lacked sophistication. He had never attended a college, and John Adams groused that Washington was "too illiterate, unlearned, [and] unread" to be president. As a French diplomat observed, however, Washington had "the soul, look, and figure of a hero in action."

Born in Virginia in 1732, Washington was a largely self-educated former surveyor, land speculator, and soldier whose father had died when he was eleven years old. In 1759, he married Martha Dandridge Custis, a young widow with two small children and one of the largest fortunes in Virginia. She brought about eighty-four enslaved people to their union. In the years that followed, he became a prosperous tobacco planter, land speculator, and slave owner. Washington loved riding horses, hunting foxes, playing cards or billiards, fishing, hosting oyster roasts, and drinking wine.

WASHINGTON'S INAUGURATION This portrayal of George Washington as he arrived at the Battery in New York for his 1789 inauguration was intended to enhance his legend as the nation's founding father and to signify the importance that he was elected to become the first president of the United States. **Note the presence of the Indigenous Americans in the *lower right* and the foreign flags in the distance—in what ways does this painting exaggerate Washington's support, and in what ways is it an accurate representation of the sentiment at the time?**

Now, at age fifty-seven, Washington brought to the presidency both a detached reserve and a deep capacity for leadership. Few doubted that he was the best person to lead the new nation. People were already calling him the "father of his country."

In his inaugural address, written by Alexander Hamilton, Washington appealed for unity, pleading with Congress to abandon "local prejudices" and "party animosities" to create the "national" outlook that was necessary for the fledgling republic to thrive. Within a few months, he would see his hopes dashed. Personal rivalries, sectional tensions, and partisan infighting would dominate political life in the 1790s.

Washington's Cabinet

President Washington faced massive challenges, and he knew that his every decision would have special significance because he was the first president. "The eyes of America—perhaps of the world—are turned to this Government," he said. He was entering "untrodden ground" and therefore must ensure that his actions were based on "true principles."

During the summer of 1789, Congress created executive departments corresponding to those formed under the Confederation. To head the Department of State, Washington named Thomas Jefferson. To lead the Department of the Treasury, he appointed Alexander Hamilton, who was widely read in matters of government finance. Henry Knox was secretary of war; and John Jay became the first chief justice of the Supreme Court.

Washington routinely called his chief staff members together to discuss matters of policy. This was the origin of the president's *cabinet*, an unofficial advisory body. The office of vice president, said its first occupant, John Adams, was the most "insignificant office . . . ever . . . contrived."

The Bill of Rights

To address concerns raised by opponents of the new federal government, James Madison, now a congressman, presented to Congress a set of constitutional amendments intended to protect individual rights. After considerable debate, Congress approved twelve amendments in September 1789. By the end of 1791, the necessary three-fourths of the states had approved *ten* of the twelve proposed amendments, now known as the **Bill of Rights**.

> Protecting individual rights vs. the power of the government

The Bill of Rights provided safeguards for individual rights of speech, assembly, religion, and the press; the right to own firearms; the right to refuse to house soldiers; protection against unreasonable searches and seizures; the right to refuse to testify against oneself; the right to a speedy public trial, with an attorney present, before an impartial jury; and protection against "cruel and unusual" punishments. The Tenth Amendment addressed the widespread demand that powers not delegated to the national government "are reserved to the States respectively, or to the people."

The amendments were written in broad language that seemed to exclude no one. In fact, however, they technically applied only to property-owning White men. And, like the Constitution itself, the Bill of Rights gave

Bill of Rights (1791) The first ten amendments to the U.S. Constitution, adopted in 1791 to guarantee individual rights and to help secure ratification of the Constitution by the states.

Comparing PERSPECTIVES

ON RIGHTS AND FREEDOMS

From: Letter from James Madison to Thomas Jefferson, October 17, 1788.

In this letter from James Madison to Thomas Jefferson, Madison shares his views on the Bill of Rights. He discusses the strengths and weaknesses of it and the importance of establishing a set of common principles.

. . . The articles relating to Treaties, to paper money, and to contracts, created more enemies than all the errors in the System positive & negative put together. It is true nevertheless that not a few, particularly in Virginia have contended for the proposed alterations from the most honorable & patriotic motives; and that among the advocates for the Constitution there are some who wish for further guards to public liberty & individual rights. As far as these may consist of a constitutional declaration of the most essential rights, it is probable they will be added; though there are many who think such addition unnecessary, and not a few who think it misplaced in such a Constitution. There is scarce any point on which the party in opposition is so much divided as to its importance and its propriety. My own opinion has always been in favor of a bill of rights; provided it be so framed as not to imply powers not meant to be included in the enumeration. At the same time I have never thought the omission a material defect, nor been anxious to supply it even by *subsequent* amendment, for any other reason than that it is anxiously desired by others. I have favored it because I supposed it might be of use, and if properly executed could not be of disservice. . . .

I am sure that the rights of conscience in particular, if submitted to public definition would be narrowed much more than they are likely ever to be by an assumed power. One of the objections in New England was that the Constitution by prohibiting religious tests, opened a door for Jews Turks & infidels.

From: An Act Respecting Escapees from Justice, and Persons Escaping from the Service of Their Masters, February 12, 1793.

The Fugitive Slave Act, passed by the U.S. Congress and signed into law by President George Washington, helped enforce the fugitive slave clause of the U.S. Constitution. It created a system by which enslaved people who fled slavery and crossed state lines could be apprehended and returned to their enslavers.

Sec. 1. Be it enacted by the Senate and House of Representatives of the United States of America in Congress assembled, That whenever the executive authority of any State in the Union, or of either of the territories northwest or south of the river Ohio, shall demand any person as a fugitive from justice, of the executive authority of any such state or territory to which such person shall have fled, and shall moreover produce the copy of an indictment found, or an affidavit made before a magistrate of any state or territory as aforesaid, charging the person so demanded, with having committed treason, felony or other crime, certified as authentic by the governor or chief magistrate of the state or territory from whence the person so charged, fled, it shall be the duty of the executive authority of the state or territory to which such person shall have fled, to cause him or her to be arrested and secured, and notice of the arrest to be given to the executive authority making such demand, or to the agent of such authority appointed to receive the fugitive, and to cause the fugitive to be delivered to such agent when he shall appear: But if no such agent shall appear within six months from the time of the arrest, the prisoner may be discharged. And all costs or expenses incurred in the apprehending, securing, and transmitting such fugitive to the state or territory making such demand, shall be paid by such state or territory.

Questions

1. What concerns cause Madison to weigh the pros and cons of having a Bill of Rights?

2. According to the excerpt given here, if an enslaved person who escaped were to be caught, what would be the responsibilities of the "executive authorities" of the states to which and from which the person fled?

3. Do these two documents relating to individual rights and freedoms reflect attitudes and practices that treat all people equally? Explain why or why not.

no protections or civil rights to enslaved or Indigenous Americans. Similar restrictions applied to women, who could not vote in most state and national elections. Equally important, the Bill of Rights did not prevent *states* from violating the civil rights of citizens.

Still, the United States was the first nation to put such safeguards into its government charter. While the Constitution had designed a vigorous federal government binding together the thirteen states, the Bill of Rights accomplished something just as necessary: codifying the individual rights and freedoms of its citizens.

Religious Freedom

> Separation of church and state

The debates over the Constitution and the Bill of Rights generated a religious revolution. Unlike the New England Puritans, whose colonial governments enforced their religious beliefs, the Christian men who crafted the Constitution were determined to protect religious life from government interference and coercion. The Constitution, therefore, never mentions God. In contrast to the monarchies of Europe, the United States would keep the institutions of church and government separate and allow people to choose their own religions (expressed as "freedom of conscience"). To that end, the First Amendment declared that "Congress shall make no law respecting an establishment of [a single] religion or prohibiting the free exercise thereof." This statement has since become one of the most important—and controversial—principles of American government.

The First Amendment created a framework within which people of all religious persuasions could flourish, and prohibited the federal government from endorsing or supporting any particular denomination or interfering with the religious choices that people make. As Thomas Jefferson later explained, the First Amendment erected a "wall of separation between church and State."

Immigration and Naturalization

In the list of grievances against King George III in the Declaration of Independence, Thomas Jefferson had charged that the monarch had "endeavored to prevent the population of these States" by "obstructing the laws for naturalization of foreigners, [and] refusing to pass others to encourage their migration hither."

> The Naturalization Act

To ensure that America continued to share what the Declaration of Independence called its "blessings of liberty," the Constitution called upon Congress to create policies to accommodate the continuing stream of immigrants from around the world. George Washington had strong feelings on the matter. He viewed America's open embrace of refugees and immigrants as one of the nation's most important values. The United States, he believed, should always serve as a refuge for the world's oppressed people. This view, however, did not acknowledge the reality that he and many of the founding fathers owned some of those oppressed people (the enslaved) and waged war on others (the Indigenous).

In his first address to Congress in 1790, President Washington urged legislators to craft a "liberal" naturalization law to attract immigrants. Congress responded with the Naturalization Act of 1790, which specified that any "free white person" could gain citizenship (that is, become naturalized) after living at least two years in the United States. (In 1795, Congress increased the residency requirement to five years.) The Naturalization Act established an important principle: immigrants were free to renounce their original citizenship to become American citizens.

During the 1790s, some 100,000 European immigrants arrived in the United States, beginning a process that would grow with time. Because of its openness to immigrants and its liberal naturalization policy, the United States has admitted more people from more places than any other nation in the world.

Hamilton's Vision of a Prosperous America

In 1776, the same year that Americans were declaring their independence, Adam Smith, a Scottish philosopher, published a revolutionary book titled *An Inquiry into the Nature and Causes of the Wealth of Nations*. It provided the first full description of what would come to be called a *capitalist* economy. (The term *capitalism* would not appear until 1850.)

Capitalism versus Mercantilism *The Wealth of Nations* was a declaration of independence from Great Britain's mercantilist system. Under *mercantilism*, national governments had exercised tight control over economic life. Smith argued that instead of controlling economic activity, governments should allow individuals and businesses to compete freely for profits in the marketplace. By liberating individual self-interest and entrepreneurial innovation from the constraints of government authority, he insisted, the public welfare would be enhanced. The poverty that had entrapped the masses of Europe for centuries would end to the extent that governments allowed for "free enterprise," by which individuals, through their hard work and ingenuity, could become prosperous. Smith also explained that the strongest national economies would be those in which *all* the major sectors were flourishing—agriculture, trade, banking, finance, and manufacturing.

Alexander Hamilton read *The Wealth of Nations*; and, as secretary of the Treasury, he took charge of the nation's financial affairs. Hamilton envisioned what America would become: the world's most prosperous capitalist nation. But along the way he departed from some of Smith's ideas and believed the federal government needed to take an active role in leading the nation's capitalist development.

Hamilton's Background Hamilton was a self-made and self-educated aristocrat—and an immigrant. Born in the West Indies in 1755, he was deserted at age ten by his Scottish father and left an orphan at thirteen by the death of his mother. With the help of friends and relatives, he found his way to New Jersey in late 1772 before moving a year later to New York City. There he entered King's College (now Columbia University).

Adam Smith's *The Wealth of Nations*

ALEXANDER HAMILTON A fervent Federalist and a prolific contributor to *The Federalist Papers*, Hamilton served as George Washington's secretary of the Treasury from 1789 to 1795. Faced with the daunting challenge of repaying the national debt, Hamilton promoted an economic system that established federal taxes and a national bank.

When the war with Britain erupted, Hamilton joined the Continental Army as a captain at age nineteen. He distinguished himself in battle and became one of General Washington's favorite aides. After the war, he established a thriving legal practice in New York City, married into a prominent family, and served as a member of the Confederation Congress.

Hamilton became the foremost advocate for an "energetic government" promoting vibrant economic development. The United States, he argued, was too dependent on agriculture. He therefore championed trade, banking, finance, investment, and manufacturing, as well as bustling commercial cities, as the most essential elements of America's future.

Paying Debts

Hamilton's economic reforms

Underlying Alexander Hamilton's policies was the fact that the United States had been born in debt. To fight the British, the colonial governments had borrowed heavily from the Dutch and the French. After the war, the new nation had to find a way to pay off those debts. Yet there were no national bank and no national currency. In essence, the republic was bankrupt.

It fell to Alexander Hamilton to determine how the debts should be repaid and how the new government could balance its budget. Governments have four basic ways to pay their bills: (1) impose taxes or fees on individuals and businesses, (2) levy tariffs (that is, taxes on imported goods), (3) borrow money by selling interest-paying government bonds to investors, and (4) print money.

Under Hamilton's leadership, the United States did all these things—and more. To raise funds, Congress enacted tariffs (taxes) on a variety of imported items, which enabled American manufacturers to charge higher prices for their products sold in the United States. This penalized consumers, however,

DOMESTIC INDUSTRY American craftsmen, such as these letterpress printers, favored tariffs on foreign goods that competed with their own products.

particularly those in the southern states that were most dependent upon imported goods.

In essence, tariffs benefited the nation's young manufacturing sector, most of which was in New England, at the expense of the agricultural sector, which feared that foreign nations might respond by reducing imports of products grown on U.S. farms. Tariff policy soon became an explosive political issue.

Raising Federal Revenue

The levying of tariffs marked but one element in Alexander Hamilton's plan to put the new republic on sound financial footing. In a series of reports submitted to Congress, he outlined a visionary program for the nation's economic development.

The first report dealt with how the federal government should refinance the massive debt the states and the Confederation government had accumulated. Selling government bonds to pay the interest due on the war-related debts, Hamilton argued, would provide investors ("the monied interest") a direct stake in the success of the new government.

Nationalizing states' debts

Hamilton also insisted that the federal government should pay ("assume") the states' debts from the Revolutionary War because they were a *national* responsibility; *all* Americans had benefited from the war for independence. A well-managed federal debt that absorbed the states' debts, he claimed, would be a "national blessing," provide a "mechanism for national unity," and promote long-term prosperity by showing the world that America honored its obligations.

Settling Sectional Differences

Hamilton's farsighted proposals created a storm of controversy. James Madison, Hamilton's close ally in the fight for the new constitution, broke with him over the federal government "assuming" the states' debts. Madison was troubled that northern states owed far more than southern states. Four states (Virginia, North Carolina, Georgia, and Maryland) had already paid off most of their war debts. The other states had not. Why should the southern states, Madison asked, subsidize the debts of the northern states?

Madison's opposition to Hamilton's debt-assumption plan ignited debate in Congress. In April 1790, the House of Representatives voted down the "assumption" plan, 32–29.

Hamilton, however, did not give up. After failing to get members of Congress to switch their votes, he asked Thomas Jefferson to help break the impasse. In June 1790, Jefferson invited Hamilton and Madison to join him for dinner in New York City. By the end of the evening, they had reached a famous compromise. First, they agreed that the national capital should move from New York City to Philadelphia for the next ten years, and then move to a new city to be built in a ten-mile-square "federal district" astride the Potomac River, sandwiched between the slave states of Maryland and Virginia.

The Compromise of 1790

Hamilton agreed to find the votes in Congress to approve the move in exchange for Madison pledging to find the two votes needed to pass the debt-assumption plan.

The Compromise of 1790 went as planned. Congress voted as hoped, and in late 1790 the federal government moved to Philadelphia. Ten years later, the nation's capital moved again, this time to the new city of Washington, in the federal District of Columbia.

Hamilton's debt-funding scheme proved a success. Investors purchased the bonds issued by the federal government in 1790, providing money to begin paying off the war debts. In addition, Hamilton obtained new loans from European governments. Within a few years, the nation had a higher financial credit rating than all the nations of Europe.

A National Bank

The fact that Alexander Hamilton's Department of the Treasury had *forty* staff members while Thomas Jefferson's Department of State had *five* demonstrated the priority that George Washington gave to the nation's financial situation.

Hamilton's national bank

After securing congressional approval of his debt-funding plan, Hamilton called for a national bank modeled after the Bank of England. Such a bank, Hamilton believed, would foster greater "commerce among individuals" and provide a safe place for the federal government's revenues. A national bank, he explained, would increase the nation's money supply by issuing paper currency in amounts greater than the actual "reserve" (gold and silver coins and government bonds) in its vaults. By issuing loans and thereby increasing the amount of money in circulation, a national bank and its branches would serve as the engines of prosperity.

Once again, James Madison and Thomas Jefferson led the opposition to Hamilton's banking scheme. They maintained that the Constitution said nothing about creating a national bank, so the government could not start one. Jefferson also believed that Hamilton's proposed bank would not help most Americans. Instead, Jefferson argued, an inner circle of financiers and investors would, over time, exercise too much control over the bank and Congress.

Hamilton, however, had the better of the argument. Representatives from the northern states voted 33–1 in favor of the national bank; southern congressmen opposed it 19–6. The lopsided vote illustrated the growing political division between North and South.

Before signing the bill, President Washington sought the advice of his cabinet,

BANK OF THE UNITED STATES Proposed by Alexander Hamilton, the Bank of the United States opened in 1791 in Philadelphia, the nation's temporary capital.

where he found an equal division of opinion. The result was the first great debate on constitutional interpretation. Were the powers of Congress only those *explicitly* stated in the Constitution, or were other powers *implied*? The argument turned chiefly on Article I, Section 8, which authorized Congress to "make all Laws which shall be necessary and proper for carrying into Execution the foregoing Powers."

Such language left lots of room for disagreement and led to a savage confrontation between Jefferson and Hamilton. The Treasury secretary had come to view Jefferson as a "contemptible hypocrite" guided by an "unsound & dangerous" agrarian economic philosophy. Jefferson hated commerce, speculators, factories, banks, and bankers—almost as much as he hated Hamilton.

To thwart the proposed national bank, Jefferson argued that a bank might be convenient, but it was not *necessary*, as Article I, Section 8 specified. In a 16,000-word report to the president, Hamilton countered that the power to charter corporations was an "implied" power of any government. As he pointed out, the three banks already in existence had been chartered by states, none of whose constitutions specifically mentioned the authority to incorporate banks. Hamilton eventually convinced Washington to sign the bank bill.

The new **Bank of the United States** (B.U.S.) created in 1791, had three primary responsibilities: (1) to hold the government's revenues and pay its bills, (2) to provide loans to the federal government and to state-chartered banks to promote economic development, and (3) to manage the nation's money supply by regulating the power of state-chartered banks to issue paper currency or banknotes. The B.U.S. could issue national banknotes as needed to address the chronic shortage of gold and silver coins. Within a few years, the B.U.S. had added eight branches in the nation's major cities.

Encouraging Manufacturing

In the last of his reports to Congress, the "Report on Manufactures," Alexander Hamilton set in place the capstone of his design for a modern capitalist economy: the active governmental promotion of new manufacturing and industrial enterprises (mills, mines, and factories).

Industrialization, Hamilton believed, would diversify an economy that was dominated by agriculture and dependent on imported British goods; improve productivity through greater use of machinery; provide work for those not ordinarily employed outside the home, such as women and children; and encourage immigration of skilled industrial workers from other nations.

To foster industrial development, Hamilton recommended that in addition to increasing tariffs on imports, the federal government should provide financial incentives (called bounties) to industries making crucial products such as wool, cotton cloth, and window glass. Such government support, he claimed, would enable new industries to compete "on equal terms" with long-standing British enterprises. Finally, Hamilton asked Congress to fund

Bank of the United States
National bank responsible for holding and transferring federal government funds, making business loans, and issuing a national currency.

Disagreement over the federal government's explicit and implied powers

Hamilton's "Report on Manufactures"

THOMAS JEFFERSON Jefferson, Alexander Hamilton's chief rival, fought against New Yorker Hamilton's emphasis on industrial development. Jefferson pushed for an agrarian America instead.

major transportation improvements, including the development of roads, canals, and harbors.

In the end, however, few of Hamilton's pro-industry ideas were enacted because of strong opposition from Thomas Jefferson, James Madison, and other southerners. Hamilton's proposals, however, provided arguments for future advocates of manufacturing and federally funded transportation projects (called internal improvements).

Hamilton's Leadership

Alexander Hamilton's leadership was important. During the 1790s, as the Treasury Department began to pay off the nation's war debts, foreigners invested heavily in the American economy, and European nations as well as China began a growing trade with the United States. Economic growth, so elusive in the 1780s, blossomed. A Bostonian reported that the nation had never "had a brighter sunshine of prosperity. . . . Our agricultural interest smiles, our commerce is blessed, our manufactures flourish."

All was not well, however. Hamilton had upset many people, especially in the agricultural South and along the western frontier.

The Beginnings of Political Parties

Thomas Jefferson and James Madison were increasingly concerned that Hamilton's urban-industrial economic vision and his political deal-making threatened precious liberties. Jefferson's intensifying opposition to Hamilton's politics and policies fractured Washington's cabinet. Jefferson wrote that he and Hamilton "daily pitted in the cabinet like two cocks [roosters]." Washington urged them to rise above their toxic "dissensions," but it was too late. They had become enemies, as well as the leaders of the first loosely organized political parties, the Federalists and the Democratic Republicans.

Federalists and Democratic Republicans The Federalists were most numerous in New York and New England and were also powerful among the planter elite in South Carolina. Generally, they feared the excesses of democracy; distrusted what they considered to be the "common people"; and wanted a strong central government led by the wisest leaders, who would be committed to economic growth, social stability, and national defense.

What most worried the Federalists, as Alexander Hamilton said, was the "poison" of "DEMOCRACY." The people, he stressed, were "turbulent and changing; they seldom judge or determine right [wisely]."

By contrast, the Democratic Republicans, led by Thomas Jefferson and James Madison, were most concerned about threats to individual freedoms and states' rights that would be posed by a strong national government. They trusted the people. "The will of the majority, the natural law of every society," Jefferson insisted, "is the only sure guardian of the rights of men."

Soon, unexpected events in Europe influenced the two political parties. In July 1789, violence erupted in France when masses of the working poor, enraged over soaring prices for bread and partly inspired by the American Revolution, revolted against King Louis XVI.

The **French Revolution** captured the imagination of many Americans, especially Jefferson and the Democratic Republicans, as France saw royal tyranny being displaced by a democratic republic that gave voting rights to all adult men regardless of how much property they owned. In solidarity with the rebelling French masses, Americans formed forty-two Democratic-Republican clubs that hosted rallies on behalf of the French Revolution.

Yet that revolution would also pull this nation's first political parties even further apart. The Federalists were less enthusiastic about the revolt in France and remained committed to building a strong national government in the United States led by an educated elite. During Washington's administration the Federalists supported industrial development and commercial growth, funded the national debt through tariffs and taxes, and created the first national bank. They also sought a more diverse economy that balanced trade, finance, and manufacturing along with agriculture. Democratic Republicans, however, opposed policies such as these, which they believed hurt the interests of farmers and planters, particularly in the South; and pushed back against what they believed was an excessive assertion of federal power over the states. Like the rebels in France, they envisioned a nation led by ordinary people. By now, however, these party differences had begun to complicate the governing of the young nation.

French Revolution (1789–1799)
The revolutionary movement beginning in 1789 that overthrew the monarchy and transformed France into an unstable republic before Napoléon Bonaparte assumed power in 1799.

Foreign and Domestic Crises

During the nation's fragile infancy, George Washington tried to rise above party differences. In 1792, he was unanimously reelected to a second presidential term—and quickly found himself embroiled in the cascading consequences of the French Revolution.

In 1791, the monarchies of Prussia and Austria had invaded France to stop the revolutionary movement from infecting their own absolutist societies. The invaders, however, only inspired the French revolutionaries to greater efforts.

By early 1793, the most radical of the French revolutionaries, called *Jacobins*, had executed the king and queen as well as hundreds of aristocrats and priests. The Jacobins not only promoted democracy, religious toleration, and human rights, but also called for social, racial, and sexual equality.

Then, on February 1, 1793, the French revolutionary government declared war on Great Britain, Spain, and the Netherlands, thus beginning a conflict that spanned Europe and would last for twenty-two years.

> **CORE OBJECTIVE**
> **5.** Assess how attitudes toward Great Britain and France shaped American politics in the late eighteenth century.

Effects of the French Revolution

As the French republic plunged into warfare, the French Revolution (1789–1799) entered its vicious phase, the so-called Reign of Terror. In

1793–1794, Jacobins executed thousands of "counterrevolutionary" political prisoners and Catholic priests, along with many revolutionary leaders.

Meanwhile, the Revolution's effects were felt on the Caribbean island of Saint-Domingue (later Haiti), where a rebellion led by Toussaint L'Ouverture began in 1791 and lasted until 1804. In a violent uprising, enslaved people overthrew the French government there and established the first independent Black nation. Referred to as the Haitian Revolution, reports of this extended conflict reached enslaved communities in the new American nation and caused conflict and tensions between enslaved people and their enslavers.

Observing from a distance in the United States, Secretary of State Thomas Jefferson, who loved French culture and democratic ideals, wholeheartedly endorsed the French Revolution. He even justified the Reign of Terror by asserting that the "tree of liberty must be refreshed from time to time with the blood of patriots and tyrants."

By contrast, Alexander Hamilton and John Adams saw the French Revolution as vicious and godless, and they sided with Great Britain and its allies. Such conflicting attitudes transformed the first decade of American politics into one of the most fractious periods in the nation's history—an "age of passion."

The European war tested the ability of the United States to remain neutral in world affairs. France and Britain each sought to stop the other from trading with the United States, even if it meant attacking U.S. merchant ships.

As George Washington began his second presidential term in 1793, he faced an awkward decision. According to the 1778 Treaty of Alliance, the United States was deemed a *perpetual* ally of France. Americans, however, wanted no part of the war between France and Great Britain. Hamilton and Jefferson agreed that entering the conflict would be foolish but differed on how best to stay out. Hamilton wanted to declare the military alliance formed with the French during the American Revolution invalid because it had been made with a monarchy that no longer existed. Jefferson preferred to use the alliance with France as a bargaining point with the British.

In the end, Washington chose a middle course. On April 22, 1793, he issued a neutrality proclamation that declared the United States "friendly and impartial toward the belligerent powers" and warned U.S. citizens to remain neutral.

Instead of settling matters, however, the neutrality proclamation brought to a boil the feud between Jefferson and Hamilton.

> The French Revolution divides Federalists and Republicans

Citizen Genêt

At the same time that President Washington issued the neutrality proclamation, he accepted Thomas Jefferson's argument that the United States should officially recognize the French revolutionary government and welcome its ambassador to the United States. Serving in this position was twenty-nine-year-old Edmond-Charles Genêt.

CITIZEN GENÊT The French ambassador, known as Citizen Genêt, meets George Washington after the French official had violated American neutrality laws.

In April 1793, Citizen Genêt, as he became known, landed at Charleston, South Carolina. He then openly violated U.S. neutrality by recruiting four American privateers (that is, privately owned warships) to capture English and Spanish merchant vessels.

After five weeks in South Carolina, Genêt traveled to Philadelphia, where his efforts to draw America into the war on France's side embarrassed his friends in the Republican Party. When Genêt threatened to go around President Washington and appeal directly to the American people, even Jefferson disavowed "the French monkey." In August, Washington—at Hamilton's urging—demanded that the French government replace Genêt.

Meanwhile, the growing excesses of the radicals in France were quickly cooling U.S. support for the French Revolution. Jefferson, however, was so disgusted by Hamilton and Washington's refusal to support the French that he resigned as secretary of state and returned to his Virginia home.

Vice President John Adams greeted Jefferson's departure by saying "good riddance." President Washington felt the same way. He never forgave Jefferson and Madison for organizing Democratic-Republican clubs to oppose his policies. After accepting Jefferson's resignation, Washington never spoke to him again.

Frontier Tensions

Meanwhile, new conflicts erupted in the Ohio valley between settlers and Indigenous Americans. In the fall of 1793, General "Mad Anthony" Wayne led a military expedition into the Northwest Territory's so-called Indian Country that sparked what became known as the Northwest Indian War. This conflict arose after the British transferred the Ohio Country to the United States.

Indigenous people living in the region insisted that the British had no right to give away ancestral tribal lands, and formed the Western Confederacy to resist American settlement.

In August 1794, the Western Confederacy of some 2,000 Shawnee, Ottawa, Chippewa, Delaware, and Potawatomi warriors, supported by the British, attacked General Wayne's troops and their Indian allies in the Battle of Fallen Timbers, along the border between the Michigan and Ohio territories.

The American soldiers defeated the Indigenous people, however, destroying their crops and villages and building a line of forts in the northern Ohio and Indiana territories. The Indigenous Americans then signed the Treaty of Greenville (see Map 6.4) in August 1795, by which the United States bought for $20,000 most of the territory that would form the state of Ohio and the cities of Detroit and Chicago.

Jay's Treaty

During 1794, the British efforts to incite Indigenous people's attacks on American settlements along the western frontier threatened to renew warfare between the old enemies. In addition, as England and France engaged in warfare on land and sea, British warships violated international law by

MAP 6.4 THE TREATY OF GREENVILLE, 1795

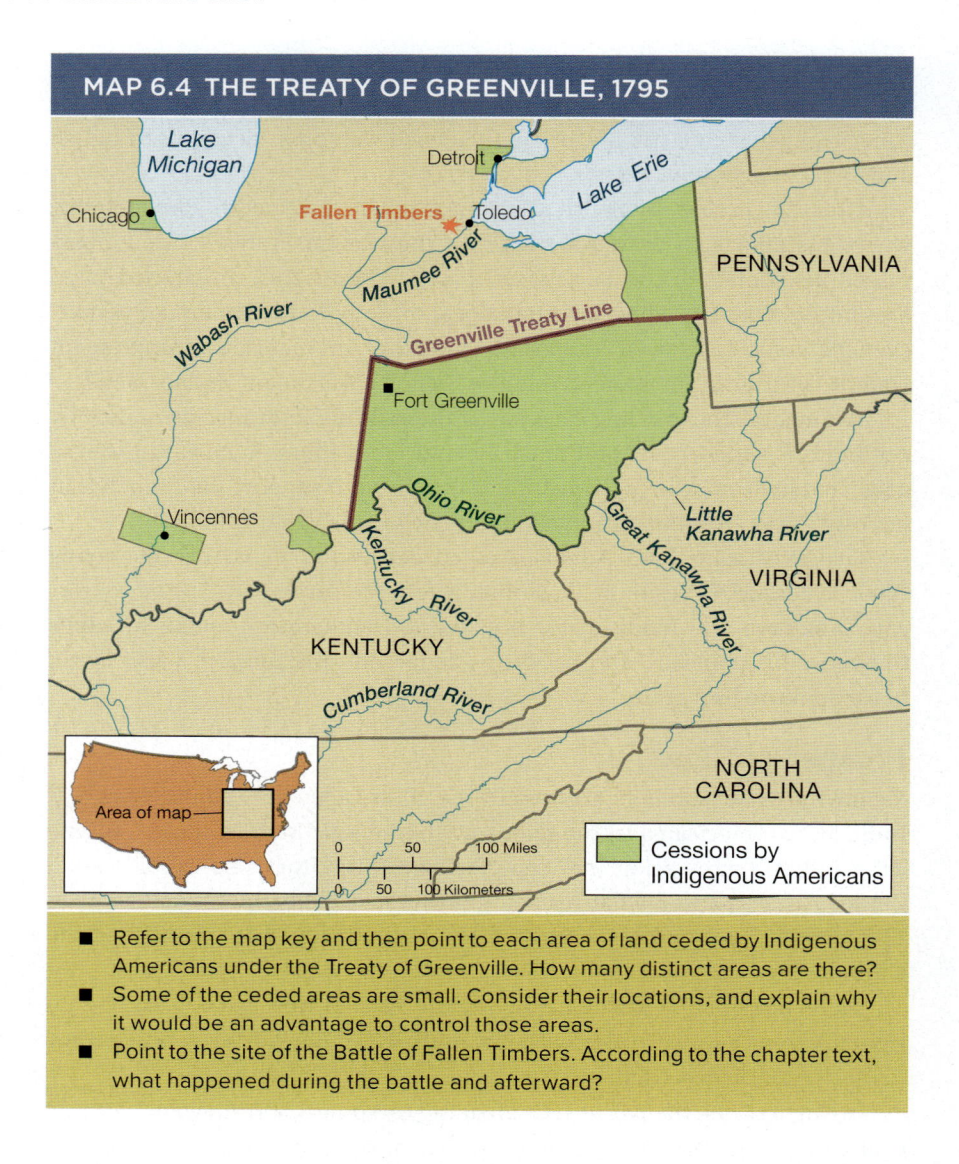

- Refer to the map key and then point to each area of land ceded by Indigenous Americans under the Treaty of Greenville. How many distinct areas are there?
- Some of the ceded areas are small. Consider their locations, and explain why it would be an advantage to control those areas.
- Point to the site of the Battle of Fallen Timbers. According to the chapter text, what happened during the battle and afterward?

seizing hundreds of U.S. merchant ships sailing for French ports. Their crews were given the choice between joining the British navy, a process called impressment, or being imprisoned.

On April 16, 1794, President Washington sent John Jay to London to settle the major issues between the two nations. After prolonged negotiations, Jay agreed to the British demand that America not sell products to France for the construction of warships. The British refused, however, to stop intercepting American merchant ships headed to France and "impressing" their sailors. Jay also conceded that the British need not compensate U.S. citizens for the enslaved African Americans who had escaped to British armies during the Revolutionary War.

In return for such concessions, Jay won three important promises. The British would (1) evacuate their six forts along the northwest frontier by 1796, (2) reimburse Americans for the seizures of ships and cargo in

1793–1794, and (3) grant U.S. merchants a limited right to trade again with the island colonies of the British West Indies.

When the terms of **Jay's Treaty** were disclosed, many Americans, especially Republicans, were outraged. In Philadelphia, an angry crowd burned a copy of the treaty and an effigy of John Jay, shouting, "Kick this damned treaty to hell!" Even President Washington could not avoid abuse. "To follow Washington now is to be a Tory," wrote a newspaper editor, "and to deserve tar and feathers." The criticism stunned the president.

The wildly unpopular treaty created the most serious crisis of Washington's presidency. Some called for his impeachment. The president, however, decided that the proposed agreement was the only way to avoid another war with Britain—one that the United States was bound to lose.

In 1795, with Washington's support, Jay's Treaty barely won the necessary two-thirds majority in the Senate. The majority of those who opposed it were southerners, most of them Jeffersonian Republicans. While weary of partisan squabbles, Washington had given the young nation a precious gift—the gift of peace.

The Whiskey Rebellion

During these turbulent years, the Washington administration faced another challenge in the backcountry when frontier farmers launched the so-called **Whiskey Rebellion** (1794). Alexander Hamilton's 1791 tax on distilled spirits had ignited resistance among cash-poor farmers throughout the western frontier. Liquor made from grain or fruit was the region's most valuable product; it was even used as a form of currency. Americans—men, women, and children—drank whiskey day and night.

When efforts to repeal the tax failed, many of its opponents turned to violence. Beginning in September 1791, angry groups of farmers, militiamen, and laborers attacked federal tax collectors and marshals. In the summer of 1794, the discontent exploded into rebellion in western Pennsylvania, home to one-fourth of the nation's whiskey stills. An upset mob of farmers threatened to assault nearby Pittsburgh, loot the homes of the rich, and set the town ablaze.

The Whiskey Rebellion was the first great domestic challenge to the federal government, and George Washington responded decisively. At Hamilton's

JAY'S TREATY A firestorm of controversy greeted Jay's Treaty in America. As depicted here, opponents of the treaty rioted and burned Jay in effigy.

Jay's Treaty (1794) A controversial agreement between Britain and the United States, negotiated by Chief Justice John Jay, that settled disputes over trade, prewar debts owed to British merchants, British-occupied forts in American territory, and the seizure of American ships and cargo.

Whiskey Rebellion (1794) A violent protest by western Pennsylvania farmers against the federal excise tax on corn whiskey; the protest was put down by a federal army.

THE WHISKEY REBELLION
George Washington as commander-in-chief reviews the troops that were mobilized to quell the Whiskey Rebellion in 1794.

urging, Washington ordered the whiskey rebels to disperse by September 1 or he would send in the militia.

When the rebels failed to respond, 13,000 militiamen began marching to western Pennsylvania. Washington donned his military uniform and rode on horseback to greet the soldiers.

The huge army, commanded by Virginia's governor, Henry "Lighthorse Harry" Lee, panicked the rebels, who vanished into the hills. Two were sentenced to hang, only to be pardoned by President Washington. The show of force led the rebels and their sympathizers to change their tactics. Rather than openly defying federal laws, they voted for Republicans, who won decisively in the next Pennsylvania elections.

Pinckney's Treaty

While events were unfolding in Pennsylvania, the Spanish began negotiations over control of the Mississippi River and the disputed northern boundary of their Florida colony. Thomas Pinckney, the negotiator for the United States, pulled off a diplomatic triumph in 1795 when he convinced the Spanish to accept a southern American boundary in west Florida along the northern coast of the Gulf of Mexico (the current boundary between Florida and Georgia). The Spanish also agreed to allow Americans to ship goods, grains, and livestock down the Mississippi River to Spanish-controlled New Orleans. Senate ratification of Pinckney's Treaty (also called the Treaty of San Lorenzo) came quickly, for westerners were eager to transport their crops and livestock to New Orleans (see Map 6.5).

Western Settlement

The treaties signed by John Jay and Thomas Pinckney spurred a new wave of settlers into the western territories. Their lust for land aroused a raging debate in Congress over what the federal government should do with the vast areas it had acquired or taken from the British, the Spanish, and the Indigenous Americans.

Land Policy Federalists wanted the government to charge high prices for western lands to keep the East from losing both political influence and a labor force important to the growth of manufacture. They also preferred that government-owned lands be sold in large parcels to speculators, rather than in small plots to settlers. Thomas Jefferson and James Madison were reluctantly prepared to go along with these policies for the sake of reducing

MAP 6.5 PINCKNEY'S TREATY, 1795

- Refer to the map key, then locate the territory claimed by Spain after 1793 (before Pinckney's Treaty was signed). What geographic feature marks its western boundary?
- Now locate the line of Pinckney's Treaty showing the new southern boundary of U.S. territory in the area. Why would the Americans have wanted to acquire all that territory above the treaty line?
- According to the chapter text, why was the treaty popular with western settlers? What geographic features played a role in the treaty terms and its popularity?

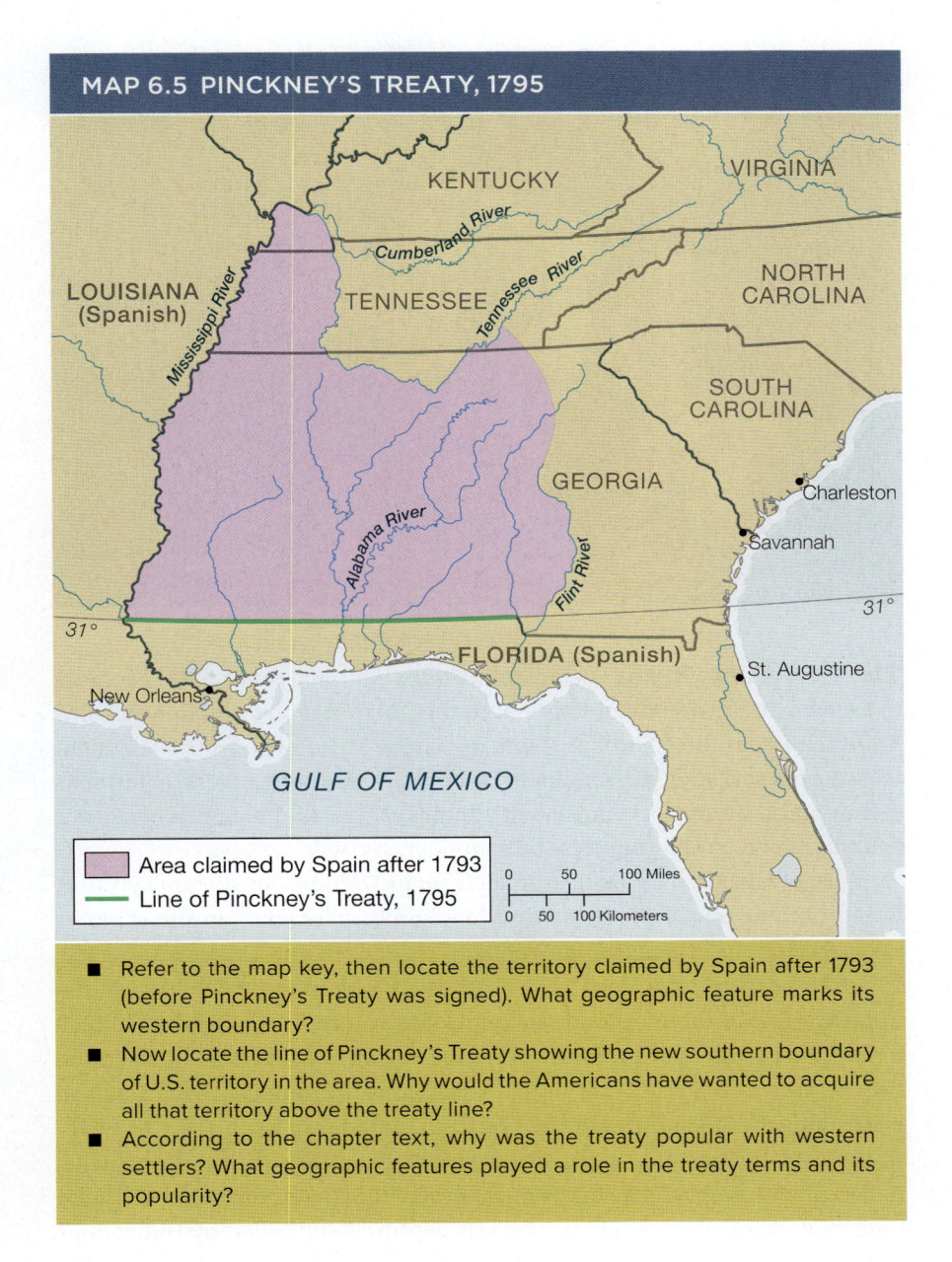

the national debt, but Jefferson preferred that government-owned land be sold to small farmers rather than speculators.

For the time being, the Federalists prevailed. With the Land Act of 1796, Congress doubled the price of federal land and required that much of it be sold in 640-acre sections, making the minimum cost well beyond the means of ordinary settlers.

Criticism of the policies led to the Land Act of 1800, which reduced the minimum parcel size to 320 acres and allowed payments to be spread over four years.

DANIEL BOONE ESCORTING SETTLERS THROUGH CUMBERLAND GAP In this 1851 painting by George Caleb Bingham, a Missouri artist known for his mythologizing portraits of frontier life, Daniel Boone leads a group of settlers westward through the Appalachian Mountains. **How does Bingham's portrayal of the settlers reveal his vision of westward expansion and the spirit of those who made the difficult journey?**

The Wilderness Road The lure of western lands led thousands of settlers to follow pathfinder Daniel Boone into the territory known as Kentucky, or Kaintuck (from the Cherokee *Kentake*, "Great Meadow"). In the late eighteenth century, the Indigenous-held lands in Kentucky were a farmer's dream and a hunter's paradise, with their fertile soil, bluegrass meadows, abundant forests, and countless buffalo, deer, and wild turkeys.

Born of Quaker parents on a small farm in 1734 in central Pennsylvania, Boone became one of America's first folk heroes, a larger-than-life explorer known as the "Columbus of the Woods."

After hearing numerous reports about the wonderful lands over the Appalachian Mountains, Boone set out from western North Carolina in 1769 to find a trail into Kentucky. He discovered what was called the Warriors' Path, a narrow footpath that buffalo, deer, and Indigenous Americans had worn along the steep ridges of the Appalachian Mountains.

In 1773, Boone led a group of settlers into Kentucky, including his wife, Rebecca, and their eight children. However, they were forced to abandon their migration after his eldest son was captured and killed by Indigenous people. Two years later, he and thirty woodsmen used axes to widen the 208-mile-long Warriors' Path into what became the Wilderness Road, a passageway through the Cumberland Gap that more than 300,000 settlers would use over the next twenty-five years.

Transfer of Power

In 1796, George Washington decided that two presidential terms in office were enough. He was eager to retire to Mount Vernon. He would leave behind a formidable record of achievement, including the organization of a new national government, a prosperous economy, the recovery of territory from Britain and Spain, a stable northwestern frontier, and the admission of three new states: Vermont (1791), Kentucky (1792), and Tennessee (1796).

Washington's Farewell On September 17, 1796, George Washington delivered a farewell address in which he criticized the rising spirit of political partisanship and the emergence of political parties. They endangered the republic, he felt, by putting the narrow interests of a few before the good of the nation. In foreign relations, Washington advised, the United States should stay away from Europe's quarrels by avoiding "permanent alliances with any portion of the foreign world." His warning would serve as a fundamental principle in U.S. foreign policy until the early twentieth century.

> Washington's farewell address warns against partisanship

The Election of 1796

With George Washington out of the race, the United States had its first contested election for president. The Federalists chose Vice President John Adams as their candidate. The Republicans nominated Thomas Jefferson. Aaron Burr, a young New York attorney and senator, also ran as a Republican.

The campaign was nasty. The Federalists were attacked for unpopular taxes, excessive spending, and abuses of power. Republicans called John Adams "His Rotundity" and labeled him a monarchist who despised "the people." Federalists countered that Jefferson was a French-loving atheist eager for another war with Great Britain. Adams won the election with seventy-one electoral votes; but in an odd twist, Jefferson, who received sixty-eight electoral votes, became vice president. The Federalists won control of both houses of Congress.

> Adams elected president; Jefferson elected vice president (1796)

The Adams Administration

John Adams viewed everyone as less talented and less deserving than he believed himself to be—and he told them so. Popularity, he admitted, "had never been his mistress." An independent thinker with a combative spirit and volcanic temper, he fought as often with his fellow Federalists as with Republicans. Benjamin Franklin said Adams was "always an honest man, often a wise one, but sometimes... absolutely out of his senses."

John Adams feared democracy and despised social equality. He once referred to ordinary Americans as the "common herd of mankind." On the most essential issue of his presidency, war and peace, he held firm to his beliefs in keeping the new country out of war—probably at the cost of his reelection.

War with France

As America's second president, John Adams inherited an undeclared conflict with France, a by-product of French anger over Jay's Treaty between the United States and Great Britain. The navies of both nations were capturing U.S. ships headed for the other's ports. By the time of Adams's inauguration in 1797, the French had plundered some 300 American vessels and broken diplomatic relations with the United States.

JOHN ADAMS A political philosopher and politician, Adams won the election of 1796 by a thin margin, becoming the second president of the United States. He was the first president to take up residence in the White House, in early 1801.

CONFLICT WITH FRANCE
A cartoon indicating the anti-French sentiment generated by the XYZ Affair. In the *background*, a savage-looking figure bearing the French flag operates the guillotine, while on the *left* the three American negotiators reject the "Paris Monster's" demand for money.

The XYZ Affair

Adams sought to ease tensions by sending three prominent Americans to Paris to negotiate. Upon their arrival, however, they were confronted by three French officials (labeled X, Y, and Z by Adams in his report to Congress) who announced that negotiations could begin only if the United States paid a bribe of $250,000 and loaned France $12 million.

Such bribes were common in the eighteenth century. When the so-called XYZ Affair became public, hostility toward France soared. Many Republicans joined with Federalists in calling for war.

Soon, Federalists in Congress voted to construct warships and triple the size of the U.S. Army. By the end of 1798, French and American ships were engaged in an undeclared naval war in the Caribbean Sea.

War at Home

At the same time, Federalists worried that immigrants from France, especially, would bring social and political radicalism to the United States. Ultimately, the **Alien and Sedition Acts of 1798**, passed amid a wave of patriotic war fervor, gave the president extraordinary powers to limit the freedom of "aliens" (immigrants who had not yet gained citizenship). The acts also violated the Bill of Rights, including freedom of speech and of the press, by making it a crime to publicly criticize the government. That part was aimed at the Federalists' critics, the Republicans.

To counter the Alien and Sedition Acts, James Madison and Thomas Jefferson drafted the Kentucky and Virginia Resolutions, which were passed by the two state legislatures in late 1798. Jefferson threatened disunion in claiming that state legislatures should nullify (that is, reject and ignore) acts of Congress that violated the constitutional guarantee of free speech.

Meanwhile, President Adams was seeking peace. In 1799, he dispatched another team of diplomats to negotiate with a new French government

Alien and Sedition Acts of 1798 Four measures passed during the undeclared war with France that limited the freedoms of speech and press and restricted the liberty of immigrants.

"THE CONGRESSIONAL PUGILISTS" An infamous print of the fight between Roger Griswold and Matthew Lyon on the floor of the House of Representatives portrays the degree of conflict between the Federalists and Republicans over the Alien and Sedition Acts. After a volley of verbal abuse, Lyon spat tobacco juice at Griswold, who retaliated by attacking Lyon with a wooden cane; in turn, Lyon took up a pair of fire tongs.

under Napoléon Bonaparte. In a treaty called the Convention of 1800, the Americans dropped their demands to be repaid for ships taken by the French, and the French agreed to end the military alliance with the United States that dated to the Revolutionary War. The Senate quickly ratified the agreement.

Republican Victory in 1800

The furor over the Alien and Sedition Acts influenced the pivotal—and polarized—presidential election of 1800. The Federalists renominated John Adams, although Alexander Hamilton publicly questioned Adams's fitness to be president, citing his "disgusting egotism."

Thomas Jefferson and Aaron Burr, the Republican candidates, once again represented the alliance of the two most powerful states, Virginia and New York. A Federalist newspaper predicted that if the "godless" Jefferson were elected, "murder, robbery, rape, adultery, and incest will be openly taught and practiced."

In the **election of 1800**, Jefferson and Burr emerged with 73 electoral votes each. Adams received 65. When Burr refused to withdraw in favor of Jefferson, the tie vote in the Electoral College required a deciding vote in the House of Representatives. After thirty-six ballots, a majority of House members chose Jefferson over Burr (see Map 6.6).

Before the Federalists turned over power on March 4, 1801, President Adams and Congress passed the Judiciary Act of 1801, an effort to ensure Federalist control of the judicial system by creating sixteen federal circuit courts, with a new judge for each. It also reduced the number of Supreme Court justices from six to five in an effort to keep Jefferson from appointing a new member. Before he left office, Adams appointed Federalists to all the new positions. The Federalists, quipped Jefferson, had "retired into

> Jefferson wins presidency

election of 1800 The presidential election involving Thomas Jefferson and John Adams that resulted in the first Democratic-Republican victory after the Federalist administrations of George Washington and John Adams.

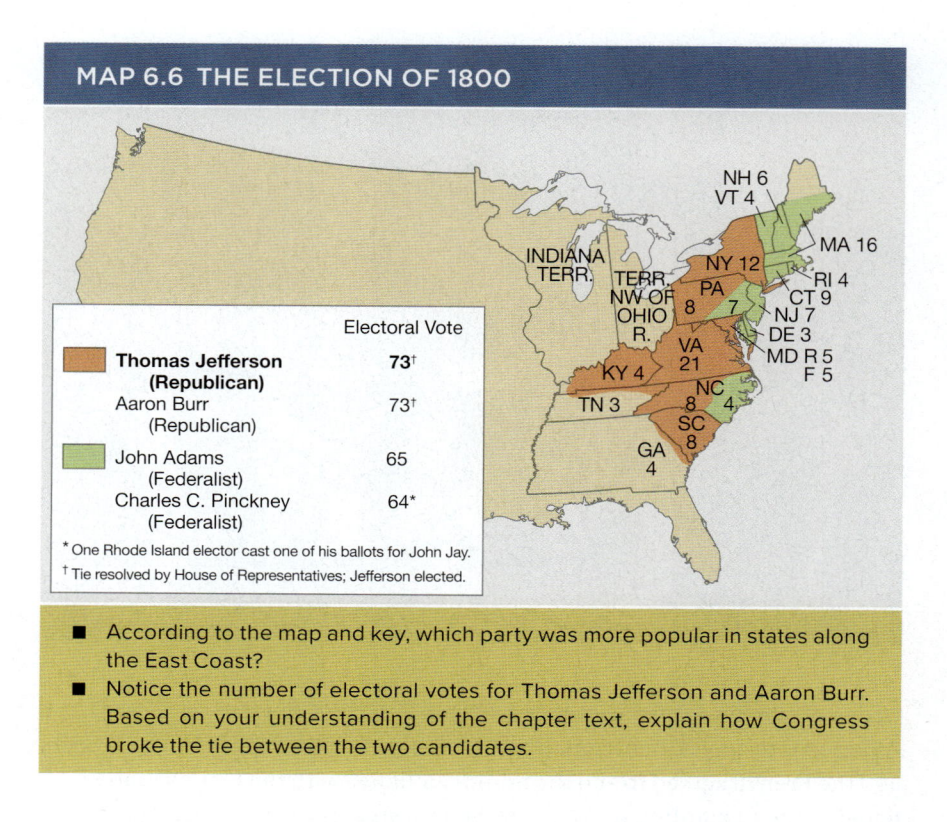

MAP 6.6 THE ELECTION OF 1800

	Electoral Vote
Thomas Jefferson (Republican)	73†
Aaron Burr (Republican)	73†
John Adams (Federalist)	65
Charles C. Pinckney (Federalist)	64*

*One Rhode Island elector cast one of his ballots for John Jay.
†Tie resolved by House of Representatives; Jefferson elected.

State electoral votes: NH 6, VT 4, MA 16, NY 12, RI 4, CT 9, NJ 7, PA 8, DE 3, MD R 5 F 5, VA 21, KY 4, NC 8 4, TN 3, SC 8, GA 4

- According to the map and key, which party was more popular in states along the East Coast?
- Notice the number of electoral votes for Thomas Jefferson and Aaron Burr. Based on your understanding of the chapter text, explain how Congress broke the tie between the two candidates.

---

the judiciary as a stronghold." They never again would exercise significant political power.

Jefferson's win can be partly attributed to the new nation's struggle with foreign relations—and with events surrounding France and Great Britain in particular. Americans found themselves divided over President Washington's policy of neutrality during the French Revolution and debated who was more threatening to the nation's well-being—France, or its enemy Great Britain. Both posed a threat to U.S. merchant ships. Great Britain also supported Indigenous attacks on the western frontier, leading to the controversial Jay's Treaty that Republicans believed gave too much to the British. An undeclared naval war with France (the Quasi War) continued during the presidency of John Adams, leading to the controversial Alien and Sedition Acts that further angered the Republicans. In this atmosphere, Jefferson won the election but would soon learn that domestic and foreign policy challenges still haunted the young nation.

A New Era

The election of 1800 further divided the young republic into warring political factions and marked a major turning point in the nation's history. It was the first time one party had relinquished presidential power to the opposition, and it was the only election that pitted a sitting president (Adams) against his own vice president (Jefferson).

Jefferson's hard-fought victory signaled the emergence of a new, more democratic political culture dominated by bitterly divided parties and wider public participation. With the gradual elimination of the requirement that citizens must own property in order to be able to vote, the electorate expanded enormously in the early nineteenth century.

Jefferson called his election the "Revolution of 1800," for it marked the triumph of the Republican Party and the slaveholding South. Three Republican slaveholders from Virginia—Jefferson, James Madison, and James Monroe—would hold the presidency for the next twenty-four years.

John Adams was so upset by his defeat that he refused to participate in Jefferson's inauguration in the new federal capital in Washington, D.C. Instead, Adams boarded a stagecoach at 4:00 A.M. for the 500-mile trip to his home in Massachusetts. He and Jefferson would not communicate for the next twelve years. As Adams returned to work on his Massachusetts farm, he told his eldest son, John Quincy, that anyone governing the United States "has a hard, laborious, and unhappy life." Thomas Jefferson would soon feel the same way.

Reviewing the
CORE OBJECTIVES

- **Confederation Government** Despite the weak form of government organized under the Articles of Confederation, the Confederation government managed to construct important alliances during the Revolutionary War, help win the War of Independence, and negotiate the Treaty of Paris (1783). It created executive departments and, through the *Northwest Ordinance*, established the process by which new western territories would be organized and governments formed before they applied for statehood. The Articles of Confederation, however, did not allow the national government to raise taxes to fund its debts. *Shays's Rebellion* made many Americans fear that such uprisings would eventually destroy the new republic unless the United States formed a stronger national government.

- **Constitutional Convention** When delegates gathered at the convention in Philadelphia in 1787 to revise the existing government, they decided to scrap the Articles of Confederation and start over. An entirely new document emerged, which created a system called *federalism* in which a strong national government with clear *separation of powers* among executive, legislative, and judicial branches functioned alongside state governments. Arguments about how best to ensure that the rights of individual states were protected and also that "the people" were represented in the new Congress were resolved by establishing a Senate, with equal representation for each state; and a House of Representatives, with each state's number of delegates determined by population counts that included enslaved people through the three-fifths clause. The establishment of the *Electoral College* settled the debate over whether the president should be elected by Congress or by the people.

- **Ratification of the Constitution** Ratification of the Constitution was hotly contested. *Anti-Federalists* such as Virginia's Patrick Henry opposed the new structure of government because it lacked a bill of rights. To sway New York State toward ratification, Alexander Hamilton, James Madison, and John Jay wrote *The Federalist Papers*. Ratification became possible only when Federalists promised to add what came to be called the *Bill of Rights*.

- **Federalists versus Republicans** Strengthening the economy was the highest priority of the Washington administration. Alexander Hamilton and the Federalists wanted to create a diverse economy in which agriculture was balanced by trade, finance, and manufacturing.

  Thomas Jefferson and others, known as the *Jeffersonian Republicans*, worried that Hamilton's plans violated the Constitution and made the federal government too powerful. They envisioned a nation dominated by farmers and planters in which the rights of states would be protected against federal power.

  As part of Alexander Hamilton's economic reforms, he crafted a federal budget that funded the national debt through tax revenues and tariffs on imports; and he created a national bank, the first *Bank of the United States.*

■ **Trouble Abroad** President Washington faced his first domestic crisis when rebellious farmers and moonshiners in Pennsylvania refused to pay the federal tax on whiskey. In response, Washington organized a formidable force to suppress the *Whiskey Rebellion* (1794). With the outbreak of war throughout much of Europe during the *French Revolution,* George Washington's policy of neutrality violated the terms of America's 1778 treaty with France. At the same time, Americans sharply criticized *Jay's Treaty* with the British for giving too much away. French warships began seizing British and American ships in an undeclared naval war. Federalists supported Washington's approach; Republicans were more supportive of France. During the presidency of John Adams, this undeclared naval war continued, which led to the controversial *Alien and Sedition Acts of 1798.* Criticism of the Adams administration spilled over into the hotly contested presidential *election of 1800,* in which Thomas Jefferson defeated Adams.

KEY TERMS

Northwest Ordinance (1787) *p. 238*

Shays's Rebellion (1786–1787) *p. 242*

federalism *p. 245*

separation of powers *p. 246*

Electoral College (1787) *p. 247*

anti-Federalists *p. 252*

The Federalist Papers *p. 253*

Jeffersonian Republicans *p. 255*

Bill of Rights (1791) *p. 257*

Bank of the United States *p. 265*

French Revolution (1789–1799) *p. 267*

Jay's Treaty (1794) *p. 271*

Whiskey Rebellion (1794) *p. 271*

Alien and Sedition Acts of 1798 *p. 276*

election of 1800 *p. 277*

CHRONOLOGY

1781	Articles of Confederation take effect
	Brom and Bett v. Ashley
1783	Newburgh Conspiracy
	Treaty of Paris ends the War of Independence
1784–1785	Land Ordinances
1787	Shays's Rebellion
	Northwest Ordinance
	The Constitutional Convention is held in Philadelphia
1787–1788	*The Federalist Papers* are published
1789	President George Washington is inaugurated
1791	Bill of Rights is ratified
	Bank of the United States is created
1793	Washington issues a proclamation of neutrality
	Fugitive Slave Act
1794	Jay's Treaty is negotiated with England
	Whiskey Rebellion in Pennsylvania
	U.S. Army defeats Western Confederacy of Indigenous nations in the Battle of Fallen Timbers
1796	John Adams is elected president
1798–1800	"Quasi war" with France
1798	Alien and Sedition Acts are passed
1800	Thomas Jefferson is elected president

WE OWE ALLEGIANCE TO NO CROWN The War of 1812 generated a renewed spirit of nationalism, inspiring Philadelphia sign painter John Archibald Woodside to create this patriotic ca. 1814 painting.

CHAPTER 7

The Early Republic

1800–1815

When President Thomas Jefferson took office in 1801, the United States and its western territories reached from the Atlantic Ocean to the Mississippi River. Nine of ten Americans lived on farms, and land-hungry settlers were rushing westward across the Appalachian Mountains to snatch up the ancestral hunting grounds of Indigenous people in Tennessee and Kentucky. Everywhere, people were on the move. Restless mobility and impatient striving soon came to define the American way of life.

Former president John Adams observed that "there is no people on earth so ambitious as the people of America . . . because the lowest can aspire as freely as the highest." Adams's statement, however, largely applied to White men. Other groups—such as women, Indigenous nations, African Americans, and other underrepresented communities—experienced continued subjugation and, in some cases, dispossession. Nevertheless, they all felt the effects of the young country's expansionist impulses.

In 1800, White people eager to own their own farms bought 67,000 acres of government-owned land; the next year, they bought 498,000 acres. Indigenous Americans, including the Shawnee, the Miami, and the Potawatomi, long resisted this invasion, even siding with the British during the War of 1812 in a determined effort to protect their ancestral lands. But most of the White settlers were more concerned with seizing their own economic opportunities through slavery

CORE OBJECTIVES

1. Summarize the major domestic political developments that took place during Thomas Jefferson's administration.

2. Describe how foreign events affected the United States during the Jefferson and Madison administrations.

3. Explain the primary causes of the American decision to declare war on Great Britain in 1812 and how the conflict played out in different areas of the country.

4. Analyze the most significant outcomes of the War of 1812 on the United States, and their importance.

and therefore had little concern for the plight of Indigenous people. The forced relocation of Indigenous people in the nineteenth century would thus facilitate the expansion of slavery into western territories.

Ultimately, these early years of the young republic were a time of contrasts between ambitious efforts for self-improvement by some and frustration over the impacts of settlement, dispossession, and enslavement by others, all playing out against a backdrop of increasingly regional politics.

> CORE **OBJECTIVE**
>
> **1.** Summarize the major domestic political developments that took place during Thomas Jefferson's administration.

Jeffersonian Republicanism

The 1800 presidential campaign between Federalists and Jeffersonian Republicans had been so fiercely contested that some observers predicted civil war as the House of Representatives decided the outcome of the election. On March 4, 1801, however, fifty-seven-year-old Thomas Jefferson was inaugurated without incident.

Jefferson's inauguration marked the emerging dominance of the nation's political life by Republicans—and Virginians. The most populous state, Virginia supplied one-fourth of the Republican congressmen in the House of Representatives that convened in early 1801, many of whom owned enslaved people.

THE CAPITOL BUILDING This 1806 watercolor of the Capitol Building was painted by Benjamin Henry Latrobe, its architect, and was inscribed to Thomas Jefferson. A tall dome would be added later, after the building was damaged in the War of 1812.

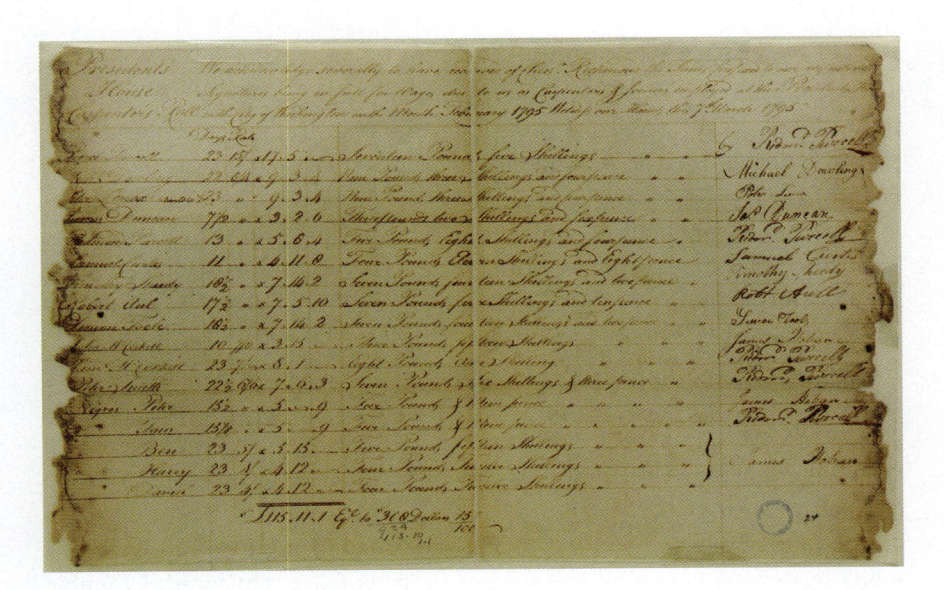

THE PAYROLL LIST The payroll list of enslavers who rented their carpenters to help build the Executive Mansion and the U.S. Capitol. Peter, Ben, Harry, and Daniel are listed as carpenters owned by James Hoban.

Former secretary of state Timothy Pickering of Massachusetts acknowledged that the northeastern states, where federalism was centered, could no longer "reconcile their habits, views, and interests with those of the South and West."

Jefferson was the first president to be inaugurated in the new national capital of Washington, District of Columbia. The unfinished city consisted of a few buildings clustered around two unfinished centers, Capitol Hill and the "Executive Mansion." (It would not be called the White House until 1901.) Cattle grazed along the Mall, while pigs and geese prowled the unpaved streets. Workers, many of them enslaved carpenters and bricklayers, had barely completed building the Capitol and the Executive Mansion before Jefferson was sworn in. According to a payroll list, 122 enslaved laborers worked on the Capitol and the Executive Mansion—including Peter, Ben, Harry, and Daniel, carpenters enslaved by architect James Hoban.

The "People's President"

During his inauguration, Jefferson emphasized his connection to the "plain and simple" ways of the "common" people. Instead of wearing a ceremonial sword and riding in a horse-drawn carriage, as George Washington and John Adams had done, Jefferson walked to the Capitol Building. Jefferson's deliberate display of **republican simplicity** set the tone for his administration. He wanted Americans to notice the difference between the monarchical style of the Federalists and the plain manners of the Republicans. His visible humility, however, did not stop Jefferson from owning enslaved people and putting them to work in the Executive Mansion.

Jefferson's inaugural appeal for unity proved illusory. In a letter to a British friend, the Republican president said he feared that Federalists, a "herd of traitors," wanted to destroy "the liberties of the people" and convert the republic into a monarchy.

republican simplicity A deliberate attitude of humility and frugality, as opposed to monarchical pomp and ceremony, adopted by Thomas Jefferson during his presidency.

A More Democratic Society

Expanded political participation

Jefferson wanted certain groups of common people to play a larger role in politics and social life than in previous administrations. During and after the Revolutionary War, an increasing proportion of White males, especially small farmers, wage laborers, artisans, mechanics, and apprentices—long excluded from politics—gained the right to vote or hold office as states reduced or eliminated requirements that voters own property. Thereafter, widespread public participation in the political process became a distinguishing feature of American life.

Democracy expanded for White men at the expense of other groups, however. Women, African Americans, Indigenous people, and others all struggled with the denial of their rights and liberties. The constraints on their experiences overshadowed their view of life and its possibilities in the democratizing nation.

As more of the common White men participated in the political process, many leaders in both political parties grew worried that men of humble origins—some of whom were uneducated and even illiterate—were replacing the social and political elite (referred to as the natural aristocracy) in the state legislatures. More than half of the members of the Republican-controlled Congress elected in 1800 were first-time legislators. Federalist John Adams so detested the democratic forces that were transforming politics and social life that he despaired for the nation's future: "Oh my Country," he moaned, "how I mourn over" its "overweening admiration of fools and knaves! the never failing effects of *democracy!*" These sentiments reflected the seemingly contradictory aspects of the young nation's desire to be more democratic and inclusive at the same time that it continued to declare large segments of the population unfit to participate in politics.

A Contradictory Leader

Jefferson's contradictions

President Jefferson, who owned hundreds of enslaved people, displayed political and personal contradictions. He was progressive and enlightened in some areas, self-serving and hypocritical in others. He loathed political maneuvering, yet he was a master at it. He championed government frugality; yet he nearly bankrupted himself buying expensive wines, paintings, silverware, and furniture. The same Jefferson who had written in the Declaration of Independence that "all men are created equal," also bought, bred, flogged, and sold enslaved people while calling slavery "an abominable crime" and a "hideous blot" on civilization. He was not alone in this contradictory behavior, as White people of means had purchased enslaved people while claiming liberty and freedom from Great Britain a generation earlier.

Jefferson highlighted the evils of racial mixing because of what he considered to be the "inferior" attributes of African Americans; yet after his wife, Martha, died, her half-sister, an enslaved woman named Sarah "Sally" Hemings, gave birth to six of his children. For Jefferson, Hemings became

SALLY HEMINGS'S ROOM AT MONTICELLO This photo of Sally Hemings's room at Jefferson's estate, Monticello, shows a silhouette of Hemings on the wall that is part of a recently established exhibit. Because there are no known likenesses of Hemings, this technique was used to represent her presence.

what a friend called his "substitute for a wife" in a plantation world where a veil of silence cloaked the contradictory nature of those who celebrated the ideals of liberty and equality while benefiting from the coerced labor and sexuality of enslaved people such as Hemings.

At age fourteen, Hemings accompanied Jefferson's daughter Maria to Paris, where Jefferson was serving as U.S. ambassador. Two years later while still in France, Jefferson, thirty years her senior, impregnated Hemings with their first child. Before returning to Virginia in 1789, a pregnant Sally made a deal with Jefferson: rather than remain in France, where she was legally free, she would return to Jefferson's Virginia plantation if he agreed to free any children they had together. True to his word, Jefferson eventually freed four of Hemings's six children who reached age twenty-one—the only enslaved people he ever liberated. Today, visitors to Jefferson's mountaintop estate near Charlottesville, Monticello (Little Mountain), can view a replica of Sally Hemings's room.

Jefferson was an inventive man of staggering abilities. As a self-trained architect, he designed the state capitol in Richmond, Virginia, as well as his thirty-three-room Monticello mansion. He was an expert in constitutional law and political philosophy; religion and ethics; classical history; natural science, paleontology, and mathematics; music and linguistics; and farming, cooking, and wine. He was also an introvert who disliked speaking in public.

Jefferson in Office

For all his shyness and admitted weakness as a speaker, Thomas Jefferson was the first president to pursue the role of party leader, and he openly cultivated congressional support. In his cabinet, the leading figures were

> President as party leader

AT LEISURE AT MONTICELLO
This scene of Jefferson's Monticello estate shows his descendants playing in the garden. Designed by Jefferson himself after the sixteenth-century Italian architect Andrea Palladio, Monticello stands as a testament to Jefferson's classical tastes. **How did Jefferson's aristocratic lifestyle conflict with his persona as the "people's president"?**

Secretary of State James Madison, his best friend and political ally; and Secretary of the Treasury Albert Gallatin, a Pennsylvania Republican whose financial skills had won him the respect of Federalists and Republicans alike.

In filling lesser offices, however, Jefferson often succumbed to pressure from Republicans to remove Federalists, only to discover that there were few qualified candidates to replace them. And when Gallatin asked if he might appoint women to some posts, Jefferson revealed the limits of his democratic principles: "The appointment of a woman to office is an innovation for which the public is not prepared, nor am I."

Marbury v. Madison (1803)

In one area—the federal judiciary—the new president decided to remove most of the offices altogether, partly because the court system was the only branch of the government still controlled by Federalists. In 1802, at Jefferson's urging, the Republican-controlled Congress repealed the Judiciary Act of 1801, which the Federalists had passed just before the transfer of power to the Jeffersonian Republicans. The Judiciary Act had ensured Federalist control of the judicial system by creating sixteen federal circuit courts and appointing—for life—a Federalist judge for each. The controversial effort to repeal these judgeships sparked the landmark case of ***Marbury v. Madison* (1803)**.

Chief Justice John Marshall The case went to the Supreme Court, which at the time was presided over by Chief Justice John Marshall. A Virginia Federalist, he had served in the army during the Revolutionary War, attended law school at the College of William and Mary, and become a respected Richmond attorney.

Marshall later served in Congress and became secretary of state under President John Adams, who appointed him chief justice of the Supreme

Marbury v. Madison (1803)

***Marbury v. Madison* (1803)**
The first Supreme Court decision to declare a federal law—the Judiciary Act of 1789—unconstitutional ("judicial review").

Court early in 1801. Blessed with a keen intellect and an analytical mind, Marshall was a lifelong critic of Jefferson, whom he considered a war-shirking aristocrat who prized the authority of states over the national government.

As the new president, Jefferson preferred a weak Supreme Court. John Marshall, however, set out to infuse the Court with power sufficient to constrain the president and the Congress. He wanted to ensure that the national government, rather than the states, remained supreme. He succeeded beyond everyone's expectations.

By the time Marshall completed thirty-four years on the Supreme Court (1801–1835), he would leave a record of issuing landmark decisions that made it the most powerful court in the world, distinctive for its emphasis on protecting individual rights while insisting upon the supremacy of the national government over the states. "Our Constitution is not a compact" of states, Marshall affirmed. "It is the act of [the] people of the United States."

The Court's Ruling The *Marbury* case involved the appointment of Maryland Federalist William Marbury as justice of the peace in the District of Columbia. Marbury's letter of appointment (called a commission), signed by President John Adams two days before he left office, was still undelivered when James Madison took office as secretary of state, and President Jefferson directed Madison to withhold it. Marbury then sued for a court order directing Madison to deliver his commission.

In the unanimous ruling, Marshall and the other Supreme Court justices held that Marbury deserved his judgeship. At the same time, however, the Court also ruled that the Federal Judiciary Act of 1789, which had given the Court authority in such proceedings, was unconstitutional, which meant that the Court could issue no order to Madison in the case.

In this ruling, with one bold stroke, Marshall elevated the stature of the Court by reprimanding Jefferson while avoiding an awkward confrontation with an administration that might have defied his order. Marshall stressed that the Supreme Court was "emphatically" empowered "to say what the law is," even if it meant overruling both Congress and the president.

The *Marbury* decision granted the Supreme Court a power not mentioned in the Constitution: the right of what came to be called *judicial review*, whereby the Court determines whether acts of Congress (and the presidency) are constitutional. Marshall established that the Supreme Court was the final authority in all constitutional interpretations.

<!-- margin note: Judicial review -->

Although the Court did not declare another federal law unconstitutional for fifty-four years, it has since struck down more than 150 acts of Congress and more than 1,100 "unconstitutional" acts of state legislatures, all in an effort to protect individual liberties and civil rights. Marshall essentially created American constitutional law, making the unelected, life-tenured justices of the Supreme Court more effective allies of a strong national government than even the framers had imagined.

Jefferson's Economic Policies

Despite the outcome of the *Marbury* case, President Jefferson's first term did include some triumphs. Surprisingly, he did not dismantle Alexander Hamilton's Federalist economic program, and he learned to accept the national bank as essential to economic growth.

> Paying down the national debt

Jefferson, however, did reject Hamilton's argument that a federal debt was a national "blessing," arguing that it should be eliminated to reduce the potential for corruption. To pay down the debt, Jefferson slashed the federal budget. He fired all federal tax collectors and cut the military budget in half, saying that state militias provided adequate protection against foreign enemies. Jefferson's was the first national government in history to *reduce* its own scope and power.

Jefferson also repealed the whiskey taxes that Hamilton and George Washington had implemented in 1791. Fortunately, the nation's prosperous economy helped the federal budget absorb the loss of the whiskey tax. In addition, revenues from federal tariffs on imports rose with the growing European trade, and the sale of government-owned western lands soared as Americans streamed westward.

Western Expansion

> Jefferson's focus on western expansion

Where Alexander Hamilton always faced east, looking to Great Britain for his model of national greatness, Thomas Jefferson looked to the west for his inspiration. Only by expanding westward, he believed, could America avoid the social turmoil and misery common in the cities of Europe—and remain a nation of self-sufficient farmers. Under Jefferson's administration, government land sales west of the Appalachian Mountains skyrocketed as settlers dispossessed Indigenous people from their native lands and established permanent homes for themselves. Jefferson, however, wanted even more western territory; and in 1803, after Napoléon Bonaparte's defeat in Haiti, Jefferson made a land purchase that more than doubled the size of the nation.

The Louisiana Purchase

Back in 1801, American diplomats in Europe heard rumors that Spain had transferred its huge Louisiana province back to France, now led by Napoléon Bonaparte. Short of stature but aggressive on the battlefield, Napoléon was one of the most feared rulers in the world. After taking control of the French government in 1799, Napoléon set out to restore his country's North American empire (Canada and Louisiana) that had been lost to Great Britain in 1763. Napoléon left no doubt about his ultimate goal. He wanted, he boasted, "to rule the world."

> The threat of Napoleonic France

President Jefferson labeled Napoléon a "scoundrel" who would become "a gigantic force" threatening the United States. Napoleonic France being in control of the Mississippi Valley would lead to "eternal friction" and, eventually, war.

Negotiations with Napoléon To prevent France from seizing the Mississippi River, Jefferson sent New Yorker Robert R. Livingston to Paris in 1801 as ambassador to France. Livingston's primary objective was to negotiate the acquisition of the strategic port city of New Orleans, situated at the mouth of the Mississippi River.

Over the years, New Orleans had become a dynamic crossroads where some 50,000 people of different nationalities intermingled, garnering huge profits from the vast amount of goods traded up and down the Mississippi. For years, Americans living in Tennessee and Kentucky had threatened to secede if the federal government did not ensure that they could send their crops and goods downriver to New Orleans.

By early 1803, when negotiations in Paris had stalled, Jefferson grew so concerned that he sent Virginian James Monroe, his trusted friend, to assist the sixty-six-year-old Livingston. No sooner had Monroe arrived than Napoléon surprisingly offered to sell not just New Orleans but *all* of the immense, unmapped Louisiana Territory—from the Mississippi River west to the Rocky Mountains, and from the Canadian border south to the Gulf of Mexico. Napoléon's belief that he could sell the territory ignored the centuries-long existence of Indigenous people in the region who claimed the lands as their own.

Napoléon and the Haitian Revolution The unpredictable Napoléon moved to sell Louisiana because of events in Saint-Domingue (Haiti). The French colony was in the middle of a slave rebellion led by Toussaint L'Ouverture, a charismatic revolutionary who had proclaimed both independence from France and the creation of the Republic of Haiti in 1791. Known as the **Haitian Revolution**, the rebellion lasted from 1791 to 1804, when Haiti gained its independence and became the first independent Black nation.

It was the first successful rebellion by enslaved people in history, and—although it occurred on Haiti in the Caribbean—the event panicked enslavers in the southern U.S. states, who feared that news of the revolt would spread to America. Between 1791 and 1804, southern planters sent arms, ammunition, and money to Haiti to help French forces put down the insurrection. Amid the turmoil, some 16,000 Black refugees from Haiti fled to the United States, and their arrival stoked fears of anti-slavery uprisings led by "French negroes" serving as "agents of rebellion." Those who remained on the island celebrated their independence. As a result of this

> **Haitian Revolution (1791–1804)**
> A slave rebellion on the Caribbean island of Saint-Domingue, a French colony, led by Toussaint L'Ouverture. Renamed the Republic of Haiti by the revolutionaries, it won independence from France and became the first independent Black nation.

Toussaint L'Ouverture and his successful slave rebellion

TOUSSAINT L'OUVERTURE This image by artist Jacob Lawrence depicts L'Ouverture, the charismatic revolutionary who led a rebellion of enslaved and freed people of color on the French island of Saint-Domingue, while declaring their independence and the creation of the Republic of Haiti 1791.

THE CESSION OF NEW ORLEANS The United States purchased the Louisiana Territory from Napoléon in 1803, effectively doubling the nation's size. In this contemporary watercolor, the French flag is raised over the city of New Orleans one final time, soon to be replaced with the American flag. **Why was the city of New Orleans an important acquisition for the United States?**

insurrection, the U.S. government refused to allow Americans to do business in Haiti and did not even recognize Haitian independence until 1862.

The Louisiana Purchase

Napoléon's Decision to Sell After losing more than 24,000 soldiers to the conflict, Napoléon decided to cut his losses by selling the entire Louisiana Territory to the United States and using the proceeds to finance his "inevitable" next war with Great Britain.

On May 2, 1803, the United States agreed to pay $15 million (3¢ an acre) for the entire Louisiana Territory. However, scholars confirm that France did not really own the land to begin with; rather, France sold the colonial rights to the land, which the Americans would then exercise in order to dispossess Indigenous people who had lived on this land for generations. As a result, Indigenous groups in subsequent years paid a heavy price in warfare as well as in legal and financial battles in attempts to retain their ancestral lands. Yet a delighted Livingston said that "from this day the United States take their place among the powers of the first rank." He called the land transfer the "noblest work of our whole lives."

The arrival of the signed treaty in Washington, D.C., presented President Jefferson with a political dilemma. Nowhere did the Constitution mention the purchase of territory. Was such an action legal?

In the end, Jefferson's desire to double the size of the republic trumped his concerns about an unconstitutional exercise of executive power.

Louisiana Purchase (1803) President Thomas Jefferson's purchase of the Louisiana Territory from France for $15 million, doubling the size of U.S. territory.

Lewis and Clark expedition (1804–1806) Led by Meriwether Lewis and William Clark, a mission to the Pacific coast commissioned for the purposes of scientific and geographical exploration.

Acquiring the Louisiana Territory, the president explained, would promote "the peace and security of the nation in general" by removing the French threat and creating a protective buffer separating the United States from the rest of the world.

Disagreement over the Purchase New England Federalists strongly opposed the purchase. They feared that adding the vast territory would weaken New England and the Federalist Party, since the new western states were likely to be settled by wage laborers from New England seeking cheap land and by southern slaveholders, all of whom were Jeffersonian Republicans. As a newspaper editorialized, "Will [Jefferson and the] Republicans, who glory in their sacred regard to the rights of human nature, purchase an *immense wilderness* for the purpose of cultivating it with the labor of slaves?"

> Opposition from the Federalists

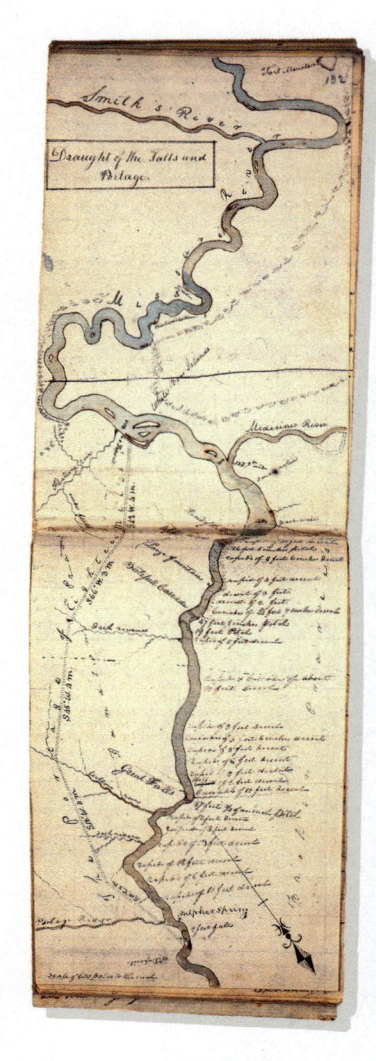

In a reversal of traditional stances, Federalists found themselves arguing for strict interpretation of the Constitution in opposing the Louisiana Purchase. Many believed that doing so was a violation of the Constitution, claiming that the founding document did not authorize the president to make large land purchases. "We are to give money of which we have too little for land of which we already have too much," argued a Bostonian in the *Columbian Centinel*.

Eager to close the deal, Jefferson called a special session of Congress in October 1803, at which the Senate ratified the treaty by a vote of 26–6. In December, U.S. officials took formal possession of the Louisiana Territory. The purchase included 875,000 square miles of land (529,402,880 acres). Six states in their entirety, and most or part of nine more, would be carved out of the Louisiana Purchase, from Louisiana north to Minnesota and west to Montana.

Some historians consider the **Louisiana Purchase** the most significant event of Jefferson's presidency and one of the most important developments in American history. It spurred western exploration and expansion, and it enticed cotton growers to settle in the Old Southwest—Alabama, Mississippi, and Louisiana.

The Lewis and Clark Expedition (1804–1806)

To learn more about the Louisiana Territory and its prospects for trade and agriculture, Jefferson asked Congress to fund an expedition to find the most "practicable water communication across this continent." The president then appointed army captains Meriwether Lewis and William Clark to lead what came to be known as the **Lewis and Clark expedition**. The twenty-nine-year-old Lewis was Jefferson's private secretary. Jefferson admired his "boldness, enterprise, and discretion." The thirty-three-year-old Clark, from Louisville, Kentucky, was an accomplished frontiersman and "as brave as Caesar."

On a rainy May morning in 1804, Lewis and Clark's Corps of Discovery, numbering about thirty "stout" men, set out from Wood River, a village near

A MAP OF LEWIS AND CLARK'S JOURNEY In their journals, Meriwether Lewis and William Clark sketched detailed maps of previously unexplored regions, such as this one. However, these regions had long been home to Indigenous nations such as the Mandan, the Hidatsa, the Shoshone, the Sioux, and the Blackfeet.

Comparing PERSPECTIVES

PURCHASE, PEACE, AND THE STRUGGLE FOR LAND SOVEREIGNTY

From: Letter from Thomas Jefferson to Robert Livingston, April 18, 1802.

Thomas Jefferson stresses the importance of the acquisition of the Louisiana Territory in this 1802 letter to Robert Livingston, the U.S. ambassador to France.

The cession of Louisiana & the Floridas by Spain to France . . . compleatly reverses all the political relations of the US. . . . [O]f all nations of any consideration France is the one which hitherto has offered . . . the most points of a communion of interests. [F]rom these causes we have ever looked to her as our natural friend . . . with which we never could have an occasion of difference. . . . [T]here is on the globe one single spot, the possessor of which is our natural & habitual enemy. [I]t is New Orleans, through which the produce of three eighths of our territory must pass to market, and from its fertility it will ere long yield more than half of our whole produce and contain more than half our inhabitants. . . .

. . .

The day that France takes possession of N. Orleans . . . seals the union of two nations who in conjunction can maintain exclusive possession of the ocean. [F]rom that moment we must marry ourselves to the British fleet & nation. [W]e must turn all our attentions to a maritime force . . . and having . . . cemented together a power which may render reinforcement of her settlements here impossible to France, make the first cannon which shall be fired in Europe the signal for tearing up any settlement she may have made, and for holding the two continents of America in sequestration for the common purposes of the United British & American nations. [T]his is not a state of things we seek or desire. [I]t is one which this measure, if adopted by France, forces on us. . . . [I]t is not from a fear of France that we deprecate this measure proposed by her.

From: Speech of Tecumseh to William Henry Harrison, August 20, 1810.

Tecumseh demands that the United States end the purchasing of native lands, stressing that the land already sold was done through the "mischief" of a few village chiefs and, later, through threats.

Brother, since the peace was made, you have killed some of the Shawnees, Winnebagoes, Delawares, and Miamis, and you have taken our land . . . and I do not see how we can remain at peace if you continue to do so. . . .

You . . . force the red people to do some injury. It is you that are pushing them on. . . .

. . .

Brother, you ought to know what you are doing with the Indians. Perhaps it is by direction of the President to make those distinctions. It is a very bad thing, and we do not like it. Since my residence at Tippecanoe we have endeavored to level all distinctions—to destroy village chiefs, by whom all mischief is done. It is they who sell our lands to the Americans. . . .

Brother, this land that was sold and the goods that were given for it were only done by a few. The treaty was afterwards brought here, and the Weas were induced to give their consent because of their small numbers. The treaty at [Fort] Wayne was made through the threats of Winnemac; but in future we are prepared to punish those chiefs who may come forward to propose to sell the land. If you continue to purchase of them it will produce war among the different tribes, and . . . I do not know what will be the consequence to the white people.

. . .

Brother, . . . take pity on the red people and do what I have requested. If you will not give up the land and do cross the boundary of your present settlement, it will . . . produce great troubles among us.

How can we have confidence in the white people? When Jesus Christ came on earth, you killed him and nailed him on a cross. You thought he was dead, but you were mistaken.

Questions

1. What is the significance of the land acquisitions in Louisiana and Florida, according to Thomas Jefferson?

2. How does Tecumseh describe the impact of "peace" on Indigenous people?

3. In what ways did the War of 1812 bring peace and chaos to American settlers and to Indigenous people?

BRONZE STATUE OF YORK IN LOUISVILLE, KENTUCKY
This eight-foot sculpture of York, the enslaved man who accompanied Meriwether Lewis and William Clark on their expedition to the Pacific Northwest, stands near the riverfront in Louisville, Kentucky. It was created by sculptor Ed Hamilton for the 200th anniversary of the historic expedition, and was dedicated in October 2003.

the former French town of St. Louis. Among the original thirty men was Clark's enslaved man York, who would make significant contributions on the trip and become the first African American to cross the continent and see the Pacific Ocean. The group traveled in two large dugout canoes (called *pirogues*) and one large, flat-bottomed, single-masted keelboat filled with food, weapons, medicine, and gifts for the Indigenous people they were sure to encounter. They headed up the Mississippi to the mouth of the Missouri River, where they added a dozen more men before proceeding. Unsure of where they were going and what or whom they might encounter, they were eager to discover if the Missouri made its way to the Pacific Ocean.

Six months later, near the Mandan Sioux villages in what would become Bismarck, North Dakota, the Corps of Discovery built Fort Mandan (see Map 7.1). There they wintered in relative comfort, sending downriver a barge loaded with maps and soil samples; the skins and skeletons of weasels, wolves, and antelope; and live specimens of prairie dogs and magpies, previously unknown in America.

In the spring of 1805, the Corps of Discovery added two guides: a French fur trader and his remarkable wife, a Shoshone woman named Sacagawea (Bird Woman), barely sixteen years old. In appreciation for Lewis and Clark's help in delivering her baby boy, Baptiste, Sacagawea provided crucial assistance as a guide, translator, and negotiator as they explored the Upper Missouri and encountered various Indigenous people, most of whom, Lewis wrote, were "hospitable, honest, and sincere people."

From Fort Mandan, the adventurers crossed the Rocky Mountains and descended the Snake and Columbia Rivers to the Pacific Ocean, where they arrived in November. Near the future site of Astoria, Oregon, at the mouth of the Columbia River, they built Fort Clatsop, where they spent a cold, rainy winter (see again Map 7.1).

In 1806 they headed back to St. Louis, having weathered blizzards, broiling sun, fierce rapids, pelting hail, grizzly bears, illnesses, and swarms of mosquitos. "I have been wet and as cold in every part as I ever was in my life," Clark noted. "Indeed I was at one time fearful my feet would freeze in the thin moccasins which I wore." Despite the physical hardships, only one member of the group died, and that was because of a ruptured appendix.

The expedition, which lasted twenty-eight months and covered some 8,000 miles, returned with extensive journals that described their experiences and observations while detailing some 180 plants and 125 animals. Their maps attracted traders and trappers to the region and led the United States to claim the Oregon Country (the entire Pacific Northwest) by right of discovery and exploration. Based on the judgments of Lewis and Clark as well as other reports, Jefferson decided that the Indigenous people living in the Louisiana Territory were as "incapable of self-government as children." Therefore, rather than follow the steps outlined in the Northwest Ordinance (see Chapter 6), Jefferson created a military government to rule the region until enough White Americans had arrived to govern for themselves.

Political Schemes

The Lewis and Clark expedition and the Louisiana Purchase strengthened Thomas Jefferson's already solid support in the South and West. In New England, however, Federalists panicked because they assumed that the new states carved out of the Louisiana Territory would be dominated by Jeffersonian Republicans.

To protect their interests, the Federalists hatched a scheme to link New York politically to New England by trying to elect Vice President Aaron Burr, Jefferson's ambitious Republican rival, as governor of New York. Burr chose to drop his Republican affiliation and run as an independent candidate.

Several leading Federalists opposed the scheme, however. Alexander Hamilton urged Federalists not to vote for Burr, calling him a "dangerous" and "unprincipled" man "who ought not to be trusted with the reins of government."

Burr ended up losing to the Republican candidate. A furious Burr blamed Hamilton for his defeat and challenged him to a duel. Burr had already been involved in three duels, while Hamilton had been to the brink of dueling ten times. This time, however, would prove different.

At dawn on July 11, 1804, the men met near Weehawken, New Jersey, on a ledge overlooking the Hudson River above New York City. Hamilton, whose oldest son, Philip, just nineteen, had been killed in a duel at the same location, fired first but intentionally missed as a demonstration of his religious and moral principles.

Vice President Burr showed no such scruples. His shot struck Hamilton four inches above the hip; the bullet ripped through his ribs and liver before

SACAGAWEA This ca. 1810 drawing depicts Sacagawea, the Shoshone woman who accompanied American explorers Meriwether Lewis and William Clark as an interpreter and guide on their western expedition.

The Burr–Hamilton duel

MAP 7.1 EXPLORATIONS OF THE LOUISIANA PURCHASE, 1804–1806

- Trace the route of Meriwether Lewis and William Clark from near St. Louis to Fort Clatsop and back. Where did they split up and explore separately?
- Considering the men's route, identify the geographic features that would have affected their travel the most. What was likely the highest-elevation area they crossed?
- According to the chapter text, what were the consequences of Lewis and Clark's reports about the western territory?

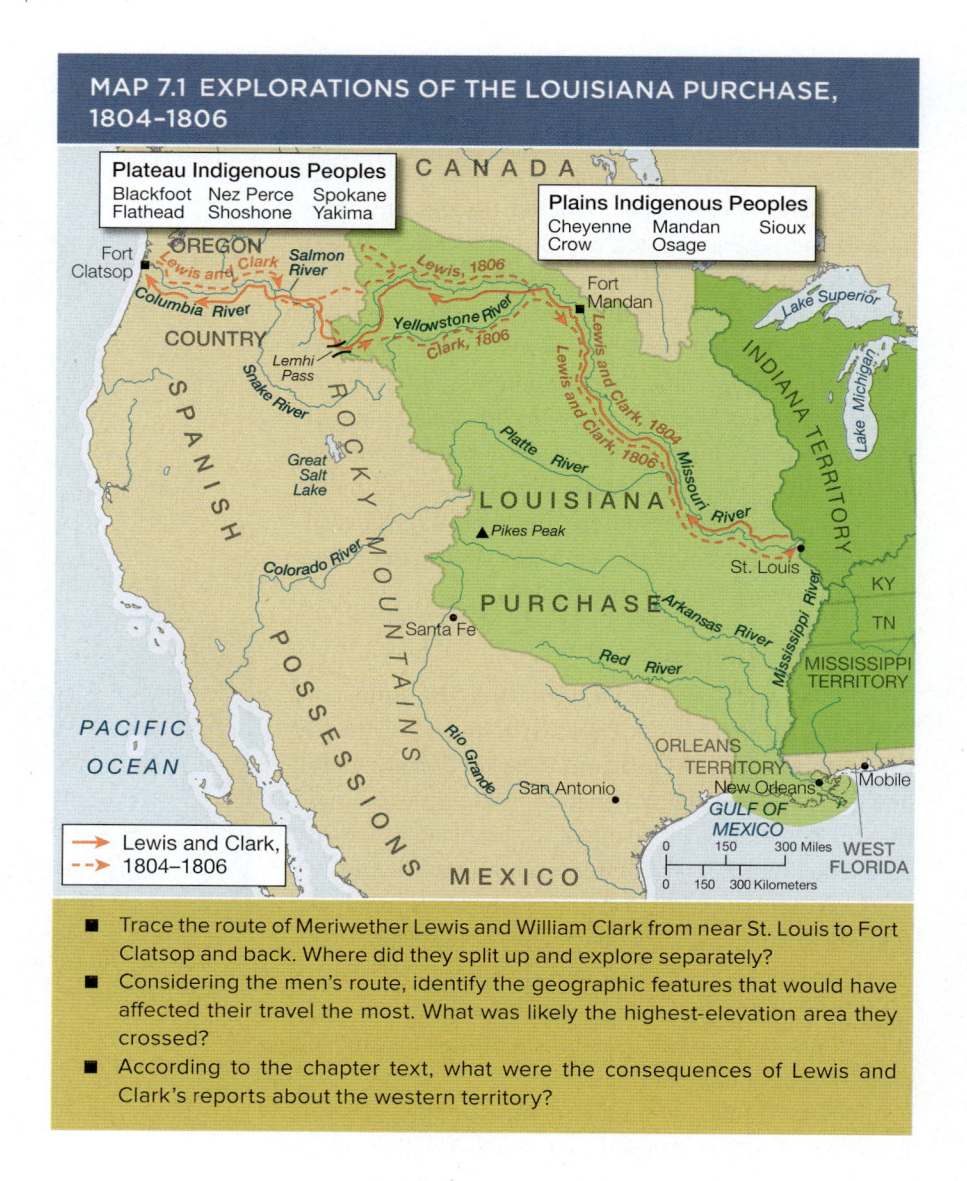

lodging in his spine. He died the next day, in his forty-seventh year. Charged but never convicted of murder, Burr fled to South Carolina. He later returned to Washington, D.C., to finish out his term as vice president.

Jefferson Reelected

In the meantime, the presidential campaign of 1804 began. To avoid the problems associated with parties running multiple candidates for the presidency, Congress had passed the Twelfth Amendment to the Constitution (ratified in June 1804), stipulating that the members of the Electoral College must use separate ballots to vote for the president and vice president.

A congressional caucus of Republicans renominated Jefferson and chose George Clinton of New York as the vice presidential candidate. Jefferson had accomplished much during his first term: the Louisiana

Purchase, a prosperous economy, and reductions of both the federal government and the national debt. One Massachusetts Republican claimed that the United States was "never more respected abroad. The people were never more happy at home." Given Jefferson's achievements, the Federalist candidate, South Carolinian Charles C. Pinckney, never had a chance. Jefferson won 162 of 176 electoral votes.

The Burr Conspiracy

Meanwhile, Aaron Burr continued to connive and scheme. After the controversy over his duel with Alexander Hamilton subsided, he tried to carve out his own personal empire in the West. What came to be known as the Burr Conspiracy was hatched when Burr and General James Wilkinson—an old friend then serving as senior general of the U.S. Army; and the self-serving, conniving governor of the Louisiana Territory—plotted to use a well-armed force of volunteers to separate part of the lower Mississippi Valley from the Union. They then planned to declare it an independent republic, with New Orleans as its capital and Burr as its ruler. Burr claimed that "the people of the western country were ready for revolt."

In late 1806, Burr traveled down the Ohio and Mississippi Rivers toward New Orleans with 100 volunteers, only to have Wilkinson turn on him and alert Jefferson to the scheme. (Burr and Wilkinson had a contentious relationship, and Wilkinson now used this opportunity to advance his own interests in the West.) Upon being alerted, the president ordered that Burr be arrested. He was hellbent on seeing Burr hanged.

In August 1807, Burr was tried for treason before Supreme Court Chief Justice John Marshall but acquitted because of a lack of evidence.

Jefferson was disgusted. He charged that Chief Justice John Marshall had bent the law "to twist Burr's neck out of the halter of treason." The president even considered asking Congress to impeach Marshall, but in the end he did nothing. With further charges pending, Burr skipped bail and sought refuge in Europe. He returned to America in 1812 and resumed practicing law in New York.

Ending the Transatlantic Slave Trade

In addition to shrinking the federal budget and reducing the national debt, Jefferson signed a landmark bill in 1808 that outlawed the importation of African captives into the United States. This came about partly because southerners had come to believe that captive African-born enslaved laborers were more prone to revolt than those born in the United States. The new law took effect on January 1, 1808, the earliest date possible under the Constitution. For years to come, however, illegal global trafficking in African people continued—until the eve of the Civil War.

The bill ending the transatlantic slave trade was just one of several major political developments that occurred during Jefferson's presidency. His administration also repealed the whiskey tax, reduced government expenditures, and promoted smaller government along with economic and

SLAVERY'S ENDURANCE IN SOUTH CAROLINA Enslaved men, women, and children on a South Carolina plantation gathered for a photograph in 1862—a reminder of slavery's persistence in some parts of the United States decades after the bill outlawing the importation of enslaved people.

population growth. Commercial agriculture and exports to Europe increased. The Louisiana Purchase greatly expanded the nation's boundaries. Back in the nation's capital, the *Marbury v. Madison* decision established both the Supreme Court's right of judicial review over acts of Congress and the federal government's supremacy over state governments. Soon, these domestic changes would be matched by developments on the international scene.

CORE **OBJECTIVE**
2. Describe how foreign events affected the United States during the Jefferson and Madison administrations.

War in the Mediterranean and Europe

Upon assuming the presidency in 1801, Jefferson had promised "peace, commerce, and honest friendship with all nations." By the spring of 1803, however, soon after completing the sale of Louisiana to America, Napoléon Bonaparte declared war on Great Britain. The conflict would last for eleven years and eventually involve all of Europe. Most Americans wanted to remain neutral and trade with both sides, but other countries were determined to keep that from happening.

The Barbary Pirates

On the Barbary coast of North Africa, the Islamic rulers of Morocco, Algiers, Tunis, and Tripoli had for centuries preyed upon unarmed European and American merchant ships. The U.S. government made numerous blackmail payments to these **Barbary pirates** in exchange for captured American merchant ships and crews.

Barbary pirates North Africans who waged war (1801–1805) on the United States after Jefferson refused to pay tribute (a bribe) to protect American ships.

In 1801, however, the ruler of Tripoli upped his blackmail demands and declared war on the United States. In response, Jefferson sent warships to blockade Tripoli, and a sporadic naval war dragged on until 1805.

Meanwhile, a force of U.S. Marines marched 500 miles across the desert to assault Derna, Tripoli's second largest town—a feat highlighted in the Marine Corps hymn still sung today ("to the shores of Tripoli"). The Tripoli ruler finally agreed to a $60,000 ransom and released the crew of the captured ship *Philadelphia*. The agreement was still considered blackmail (called tribute in the nineteenth century), but the sum was markedly less than the $300,000 the pirates had demanded and much less than the cost of an outright war.

BURNING OF THE FRIGATE PHILADELPHIA U.S. Navy Lieutenant Stephen Decatur set fire to the captured U.S. ship *Philadelphia* during the U.S. government's standoff with Tripoli over the impressment of American sailors. **Why was the United States at war with Tripoli?**

Naval Harassment by Britain and France

Issues involving shipping to France and Britain were harder to resolve than those involving the Barbary pirates. During 1805, the European war reached a stalemate: the French army controlled most of Europe, and the British navy dominated the seas.

In 1806, Britain imposed a naval blockade of the European coast to prevent merchant ships from other nations, including the United States, from making port in France. Soon, British warships began seizing American merchant ships bound for France. The U.S. Congress responded by passing the Non-Importation Act, which banned the importation of British goods.

Then, in early 1807, Napoléon announced that French warships would blockade the ports of Great Britain. The British responded that they would no longer allow foreign ships to trade with the French-controlled islands in the Caribbean. Soon thereafter, British warships appeared along the American coast and began searching U.S. merchant vessels as they headed for the Caribbean or Europe.

The tense situation posed a dilemma for American shippers. If they agreed to British demands to stop trading with the French, the French would retaliate by seizing U.S. vessels headed to and from Great Britain. If they agreed to French demands that they stop trading with the British, the British would seize American ships headed to and from France. Some American merchants decided to risk becoming victims of the Anglo-French war—but British and French warships captured hundreds of their ships throughout 1807.

American merchant ships caught in the crossfire of French and British war

PREPARATION FOR WAR TO DEFEND COMMERCE Shipbuilders, such as those pictured here constructing the *Philadelphia*, played an important role in the war efforts against America's many rivals.

Impressment

For American sailors, the danger on the high seas was heightened by the practice of *impressment*, whereby British warships stopped U.S. vessels, boarded them, and kidnapped sailors they claimed were British citizens. Fully half of the sailors on American ships, about 9,000 men, had been born in Britain and later deserted the Royal Navy to seek higher pay on U.S. ships. However, the British often did not bother to determine the citizenship of those they impressed into service, which meant that 6,200 American sailors were forced into the British navy between 1803 and 1811.

The *Chesapeake* Incident (1807)

The crisis boiled over in June 1807, when the British warship HMS *Leopard* stopped a smaller U.S. vessel, the *Chesapeake*, eight miles off the Virginia coast. After the *Chesapeake*'s captain refused to allow the British to search his ship for English deserters, the *Leopard* opened fire without warning, killing three Americans and wounding eighteen.

The attack was both an act of war and a national insult. "We have never, on any occasion, witnessed . . . such a thirst for revenge," the *Washington Federalist* reported. In early July, Jefferson banned all British warships from American waters. He also called on state governors to mobilize their militias. Like John Adams before him, however, Jefferson resisted war fever, in part because the undersized U.S. Army and Navy were not prepared to fight. Jefferson's caution outraged his critics.

The Embargo Act (1807)

Unwilling to ignite a war, President Jefferson decided to use "peaceable coercion" to force Britain and France to stop violating American rights. Late in 1807, he convinced enough Republicans in Congress to cut off *all* American foreign trade. As Jefferson said, his choices were "war, embargo, or nothing."

The unprecedented **Embargo Act** (December 1807) stopped all American exports by prohibiting U.S. ships from sailing to foreign ports in order to "keep our ships and seamen out of harm's way." Jefferson and his secretary of state, James Madison, expected that the embargo would force the warring European nations to quit violating American rights. But neither the French nor the British were intimidated by the loss of trade with America.

What the embargo did achieve was the destruction of the U.S. economy. With each passing month, the loss of foreign markets sent U.S. exports plummeting from $48 million in 1807 to $9 million a year later. Federal revenue from tariffs plunged from $18 million to $8 million. Shipbuilding declined by

Embargo Act (1807) A law promoted by President Thomas Jefferson prohibiting American ships from leaving for foreign ports, in order to safeguard them from British and French attacks. This ban on American exports proved disastrous to the U.S. economy.

two-thirds, and farmers and planters in the South and West saw prices for their exported crops cut in half.

New England's thriving port cities became ghost towns; thousands of ships and sailors were out of work. Meanwhile, smuggling soared, especially along the border with British Canada. Americans raged at what critics called "Jefferson's embargo." One letter writer told the president that he had paid four friends "to shoot you if you don't take off the embargo."

The embargo turned American politics upside down. To enforce it, Jefferson, once the leading advocate for *reducing* the power of the federal government, now found himself *expanding* federal power. In effect, the United States used its own warships to blockade its own ports.

Congress finally voted 70–0 to end the embargo on March 4, 1809, the day the "splendid misery" of Jefferson's second presidential term ended. The president left the Executive Mansion defeated. One of his stern critics, Virginia congressman John Randolph, declared that never had a president "left the nation in a state so deplorable and calamitous."

In the election of 1808, the presidency passed to another prominent Virginian—Jefferson's secretary of state, James Madison. The Federalists, again backing Charles C. Pinckney of South Carolina and Rufus King of New York, won only 47 electoral votes to Madison's 122.

James Madison and the Drift to War

President Madison soon made things worse. Although he had been a talented legislator and was called the Father of the Constitution, he proved to be a weak, indecisive chief executive. He was a persuader, not a commander.

Madison's wife, Dolley, was a member of the president's inner circle. Seventeen years younger than her husband, she was a respected First Lady who excelled at entertaining political leaders and foreign dignitaries. Journalists called her the Queen of Washington City.

From the beginning, Madison's presidency became entangled in foreign affairs and was disrupted by his lack of executive experience. Madison and his advisers repeatedly overestimated the young republic's diplomatic leverage and military strength. The result was international humiliation.

Madison continued the Jeffersonian policy of "peaceable coercion" against the European nations, which was as ineffective for him as it had been for Jefferson. In place of the disastrous embargo, Congress passed the Non-Intercourse Act (1809), which reopened trade with all countries *except* France and Great Britain and their colonies. It authorized the president

"OGRABME, OR, THE AMERICAN SNAPPING-TURTLE" A merchant trying to trade with the British is held back by a so-called Ograbme (*embargo* spelled backward) in this political cartoon from 1807. **Why was Jefferson's Embargo Act so unpopular?**

The Embargo Act's toll on the U.S. economy

The Non-Intercourse Act (1809)

ANTI-JEFFERSON SENTIMENT
This 1807 Federalist cartoon compares Washington (*left*, flanked by a British lion and an American eagle) and Jefferson (*right*, with a snake and a lizard). Below Jefferson are volumes of French philosophy, while Washington's volumes simply read: *Law*, *Order*, and *Religion*.

to reopen trade with France or Great Britain if either should stop violating American rights on the high seas. In December 1810, France issued a vague promise to restore America's neutral rights, whereupon Madison gave Great Britain three months to do the same. The British refused, and the Royal Navy continued to seize American vessels.

On June 1, 1812, a reluctant Madison asked Congress to declare war against the United Kingdom of Great Britain and Ireland. If the United States did not defend its maritime rights, he explained, then Americans were "not independent people, but colonists and vassals."

> America declares war on Great Britain (1812)

The House of Representatives voted to declare war by a margin of 79–49. Two weeks later, the Senate followed suit, 19–13. Every Federalist in Congress opposed "Mr. Madison's War," while 80 percent of Republicans supported it. The southern and western states wanted war; the New England states opposed it.

By declaring war, Madison and the Republicans hoped to unite the nation and discredit the Federalists. They also planned to end Indigenous-led attacks along the Great Lakes and in the Ohio valley by invading British Canada, which had lent support to Indigenous forces. Jefferson presumed that the French Canadians would be eager to rise up against their British rulers and help American armies conquer Britain's vast northern colony. It did not work out that way.

Foreign events troubled the administrations of both James Madison and Thomas Jefferson. From sending warships to subdue the Barbary pirates to instituting the Embargo Act in order to stop the warring British and French forces from interfering with American commerce, Jefferson ended up exerting the power of the federal government more strongly than he originally intended. Madison, his successor, lifted the embargo on all foreign powers except Britain and France—with an option to reopen trade with those two countries if they stopped violating American maritime rights. France acquiesced. But Britain's continued impressment of sailors on American ships, as well as its support of Indigenous attacks on the western frontier, led Madison to seek a declaration of war against Britain. Congress voted for war in June 1812.

War of 1812 (1812–1815) A conflict fought in North America and at sea between Great Britain and the United States over American shipping rights and British-inspired attacks on American settlements by Indigenous groups. Canadians and Indigenous Americans also fought in the war on each side.

The War of 1812

The **War of 1812** marked the first time that Congress declared war. Great Britain was preoccupied with defeating Napoléon in Europe; and in fact, in June 1812, it had promised to quit interfering with American shipping. President Madison and the Republicans, however, believed that only war would end the practice of impressment and stop the attacks by Indigenous groups along the western frontier.

This war was therefore more than an American war for a second independence. It was also a war fought by Indigenous groups who chose (or were forced) to side with either the American colonists or the British government. Members of the Shawnee, along with the Chippewa, Ottawa, and Potawatomi of the Great Lakes region, supported the British. Members of the Creek Nation in the Southeast fought on both sides of the conflict as well as against their own Creek factions; and the Seneca, Mohawk, and other Iroquois nations were similarly divided between Americans and British loyalties. The Choctaw supported the American settlers.

Conflicts with Indigenous Groups

In the years leading up to the war, Indigenous forces supported by the British strenuously resisted the American presence in the Ohio valley. The long-running conflict then took a turn with the rise of two Shawnee leaders, brothers Tecumseh and Tenskwatawa, who lived in a large village called Prophetstown on the Tippecanoe River in northern Indiana.

> **CORE OBJECTIVE**
>
> **3.** Explain the primary causes of the American decision to declare war on Great Britain in 1812 and how the conflict played out in different areas of the country.

BRITISH IMPRESSMENT Three American sailors are forced to abandon their ship and join the British forces in this contemporary print. This humiliating practice was common in the years before the War of 1812, and it put merchant sailors at great risk. **How did Congress use impressment as one of its justifications for the war?**

TECUMSEH A leader of the Shawnee, Tecumseh tried to unite Indigenous American nations in opposition to European culture and in defense of their ancestral lands; he was killed in 1813 at the Battle of the Thames.

Born in 1768, Tecumseh (Shooting Star) and his family had been forced to flee from invading armies five times between 1774 and 1782. By the 1790s, when Tecumseh became chief, his father and two of his brothers had been killed in battle and his nation was perennially threatened by starvation as the game animals in the Shawnees' ever-shrinking hunting grounds declined in number.

Chief Tecumseh decided that the fate of the Indigenous Americans depended on their diverse nations being unified. He hoped to create a single alliance powerful enough, with British assistance, to fend off further American expansion.

Tenskwatawa (The Open Door), who was known as the Prophet, gained a large following for his predictions that White Americans ("children of the devil") were on the verge of collapse. As a young man, Tenskwatawa had experienced a spiritual rebirth and become a charismatic spokesman for Indigenous resistance to the intrusion of the Americans. Indigenous peoples must, he stressed, abandon all things American: clothing, customs, Christianity, and especially liquor. If they did so, the Great Spirit would reward them by turning the Whites' gunpowder to sand.

Inspired by his brother's spiritual message, Tecumseh traveled in 1811 from Wisconsin to Alabama to form alliances with other Indigenous American nations. In Alabama, he told a gathering of 5,000 Indigenous people that they should "let the white race perish" because "they seize your land; they corrupt your women; they trample on the ashes of your dead!"

William Henry Harrison, governor of the Indiana Territory, met with Tecumseh twice and described him as "one of those uncommon geniuses who spring up occasionally to produce revolutions and overturn the established order of things." Yet in the fall of 1811, Harrison gathered 1,000 troops and advanced on Prophetstown.

What became the **Battle of Tippecanoe** was a disastrous defeat for the Indigenous people, as Harrison's troops burned the village and destroyed its supplies. **Tecumseh's Indian Confederacy** went up in smoke, and he fled to Canada.

The Lust for Canada and Florida

Some Americans demanded war with Great Britain because they wanted to seize British Canada. The fact that there were nearly 8 million Americans and only 300,000 Canadians led many Americans to believe that doing so would be quick and easy.

The British were also vulnerable far to the south. East Florida, which had returned to Spain's control in 1783, posed a threat because Spain was too weak—or too unwilling—to prevent attacks by Indigenous groups across the border with Georgia. In the absence of a strong Spanish presence, British agents and traders remained in East Florida, smuggling goods

Battle of Tippecanoe (1811) A battle in northern Indiana between U.S. troops and Indigenous American warriors led by prophet Tenskwatawa, the half-brother of Tecumseh.

Tecumseh's Indian Confederacy A group of Indigenous American nations under the leadership of Shawnees Tecumseh and Tenskwatawa; its mission of fighting off American expansion was thwarted at the Battle of Tippecanoe (1811), when the Indian Confederacy fell apart.

and conspiring with Indigenous people against the Americans. Spanish Florida had also long been a haven for freedom-seeking enslaved people who had managed to flee enslavement in Georgia and South Carolina. Many Americans living along the Florida–Georgia border hoped that war would enable them to oust both the British and the Spanish from Florida.

War Fever

In the Congress that assembled in late 1811, the most vocal "war hawks" were Henry Clay of Kentucky and John C. Calhoun of South Carolina. Clay, the brash young Speaker of the House, was "for resistance by the *sword*." His bravado inspired others. "I don't like Henry Clay," Calhoun said. "He is a bad man, an imposter, a creator of wicked schemes. I wouldn't speak to him, but, by God, I love him" for wanting war against Britain. When Calhoun learned that President Madison had finally decided on war, he threw his arms around Clay's neck and led his colleagues in a mock Indigenous American war dance.

> The "war hawks" defend the war and America's national honor

In New England and much of New York, however, there was little enthusiasm for war because military conflict threatened to cripple the region's shipping industry. Both Massachusetts and Connecticut refused to send soldiers to fight, and merchants openly sold supplies to British troops in Canada.

War Preparations

One thing was certain: the United States was unprepared for war, both financially and militarily, and James Madison failed to inspire public confidence and military resolve.

The war did not go well at the beginning. The British navy blockaded American ports, which caused federal tariff revenues to tumble. In March 1813, Treasury Secretary Albert Gallatin warned Madison that the United States had "hardly enough money to last till the end of the month." Furthermore, Republicans in Congress delayed approving tax increases needed to finance the war.

> Problems financing the war

The military situation was almost as bad. In 1812, the British had 250,000 professional soldiers and the most powerful navy in the world. By contrast, the U.S. Army numbered only 3,287 ill-trained and poorly equipped men, led by officers with little combat experience. In January 1812, Congress authorized an army of 35,000 men; but a year later, just 18,500 had been recruited—many of them Irish American immigrants who hated the English and were enticed to enlist by congressional promises of cash and land.

> Problems with army recruitment

Madison, who refused to allow free Black or enslaved people to serve in the army, had to plead with state governors to provide militiamen, only to have the Federalist governors in anti-war New England decline. The British, on the other hand, had thousands of soldiers stationed in Canada and the West Indies, and they recruited more Indigenous allies than did the Americans.

U.S. NAVAL VICTORIES In this cartoon, John Bull (the personification of England) is "stung to agony" by *Wasp* and *Hornet*, two American ships that clinched early victories in the War of 1812.

The U.S. Navy was in better shape than the army, but it had only 16 warships compared with Britain's 600. The lopsided military strength of the British led Madison to mutter that the United States was in "an embarrassing situation."

A Continental War

For these reasons and more, the War of 1812 was an unusual conflict. It was three wars fought on three fronts. One theater was the Chesapeake Bay along the coast of Maryland and Virginia, including Washington, D.C. The second was in the South—Alabama, Mississippi, and West and East Florida—where American forces led by Andrew Jackson invaded lands owned by the Creek and the Spanish. The third front might be more accurately called the Canadian-American War. It began in what is now northern Indiana and Ohio and southeastern Michigan, and in the contested border regions around the Great Lakes. The fighting raged back and forth across the border as the United States repeatedly invaded British Canada, only to be repulsed.

The War in the North

The War of 1812 was a civil war. Canadians, thousands of whom were former American Loyalists who had fled north after the Revolutionary War, remained loyal to the British Empire, while Americans and a few French Canadians and Irish Canadians sought to push Britain out of North America and annex Canada. In some cases, Americans fought former Americans, including families that were divided in their allegiances. Siblings even shot each other.

Indigenous people dominated the borderlands around the Great Lakes. Michigan's governor recognized that "the British cannot hold Upper Canada [Ontario] without the assistance of the Indians," but the "Indians cannot conduct a war without the assistance of a civilized nation [Great Britain]." So the American assault on Canada involved attacking Indigenous people, Canadians, and British soldiers.

Invading Canada

President Madison approved a three-pronged plan for the invasion of British Canada. It called for one army to move north through upstate New York, along Lake Champlain, to take Montreal, while another was to advance into Upper Canada by crossing the Niagara River between Lakes Ontario and Erie. The third attack would come from the west, with an American force moving east into Upper Canada from Detroit, Michigan (see Map 7.2). The plan was to have all three attacks begin at the same time to force the British troops in Canada to split up.

Initial failures in the invasion of Canada

The plan, however, was a disaster. The underfunded and undermanned Americans could barely field one army, much less three, and communication was spotty at best. In July 1812, General William Hull, a Revolutionary War

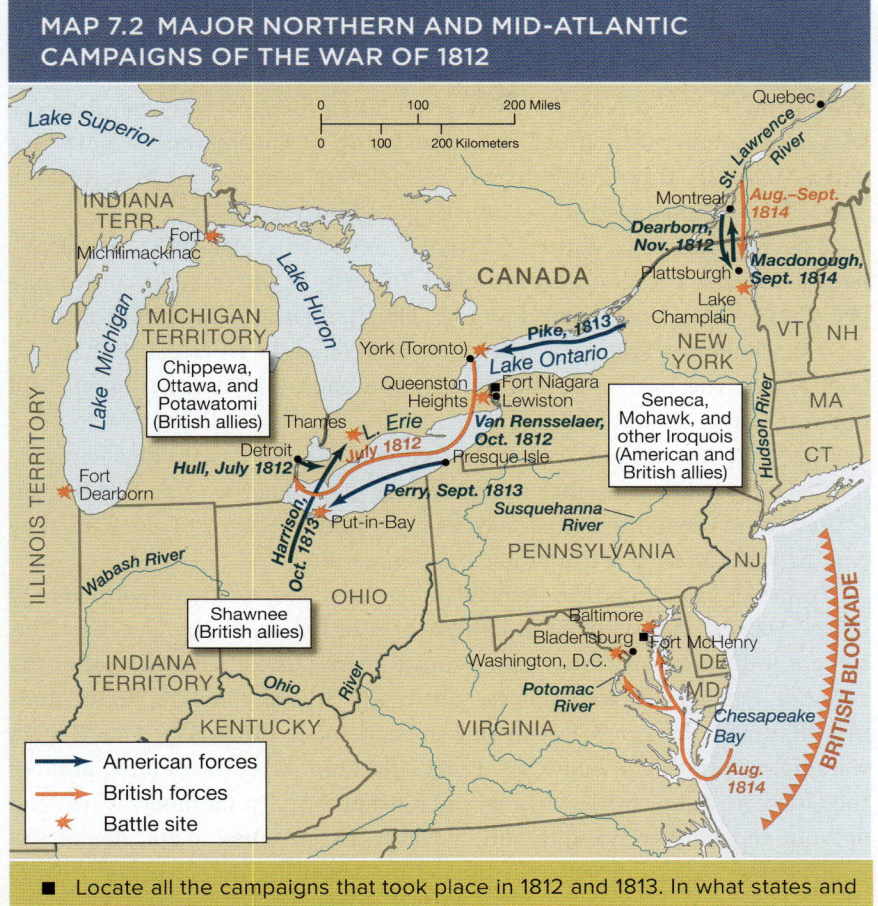

MAP 7.2 MAJOR NORTHERN AND MID-ATLANTIC CAMPAIGNS OF THE WAR OF 1812

- Locate all the campaigns that took place in 1812 and 1813. In what states and territories did they occur?
- Locate all the 1814 campaigns. Judging by the color of the arrows (see the map key), which nation's forces were more active in these campaigns?
- Based on your understanding of the chapter text, explain the American strategy in regard to Canada. How does this map reflect it?

veteran and governor of the Michigan Territory, marched his ragtag army across the Detroit River into Canada. He told the Canadians that he had come to free them from British "tyranny and oppression."

The Canadians, however, did not want to be liberated, and the Americans were soon pushed back to Detroit by British troops, Canadian militiamen, and their Indigenous American allies.

Hull, tricked by the British commander's threats to unleash thousands of Indian warriors, did the unthinkable: he surrendered his entire force of 2,500 troops without firing a shot. His capitulation opened the western frontier to raids by British troops and their Canadian and Indigenous American allies. President Madison felt humiliated. Hull was dismissed from the army for his cowardice.

The second prong of the American plan, the assault on Montreal, simply never happened. The third prong began at dawn on October 13, 1812, when U.S. troops led by General Stephen Van Rensselaer rowed across the Niagara River from Lewiston, New York, to the Canadian village of Queenston, where they suffered a crushing defeat in the Battle of Queenston Heights (see again Map 7.2). Almost a thousand U.S. soldiers were forced to surrender. The losses in Canada led many Americans to lose hope.

Then there was a glimmer of good news. In April 1813, Americans led by General Zebulon Pike attacked York (later renamed Toronto), the provincial capital of Upper Canada. The British and Canadian militiamen surrendered; and over the next several days, partly because Pike had been killed, the U.S. soldiers went on a rampage, plundering the city and burning government buildings.

After the torching of York, the Americans sought to gain naval control of the Great Lakes and other inland waterways along the Canadian border. If they could break the British naval supply line and secure Lake Erie, they could divide the British from their Indigenous allies.

> Perry turns the tides in the north

In 1813, at Presque Isle, Pennsylvania, near Erie, twenty-eight-year-old Oliver Hazard Perry, the commander of U.S. forces, supervised the construction of warships from timber cut in nearby forests. By the end of the summer, Perry's new warships set out in search of the British, finally finding them at Lake Erie's Put-in-Bay in September (Map 7.2). Two British warships pounded the *Lawrence*, Perry's flagship. After four hours, none of the *Lawrence*'s guns were working, and most of the crew members were dead or wounded. Perry refused to quit, however. He switched to another vessel, kept fighting, and, miraculously, ended up accepting the surrender of the entire British squadron. Hatless and bloodied, Perry famously reported, "We have met the enemy and they are ours."

The British were forced to evacuate Upper Canada. They gave up Detroit and were defeated at the Battle of the Thames in southern Canada in October 1813. During the battle, the British fled, leaving the great chief Tecumseh and 500 warriors to face the wrath of the Americans. When Tecumseh was killed, the remaining Indigenous fighters retreated. Perry's victory and the defeat of Tecumseh enabled the Americans to recover control of most of Michigan and seize the Western District of Upper Canada. Thereafter, the war in the North lapsed into a military stalemate.

The Creek War

War also flared in the South in 1813. The Creek Nation consisted of several groups with different languages and customs. In the early nineteenth century, Creeks in western Georgia and what is now Alabama had split into two factions: the Upper Creeks (called Red Sticks because of their bright-red war clubs), who opposed American expansion and sided with the British; and the Lower Creeks, who wanted to remain on good terms with the Americans. On August 30, Red Sticks attacked Fort Mims on the

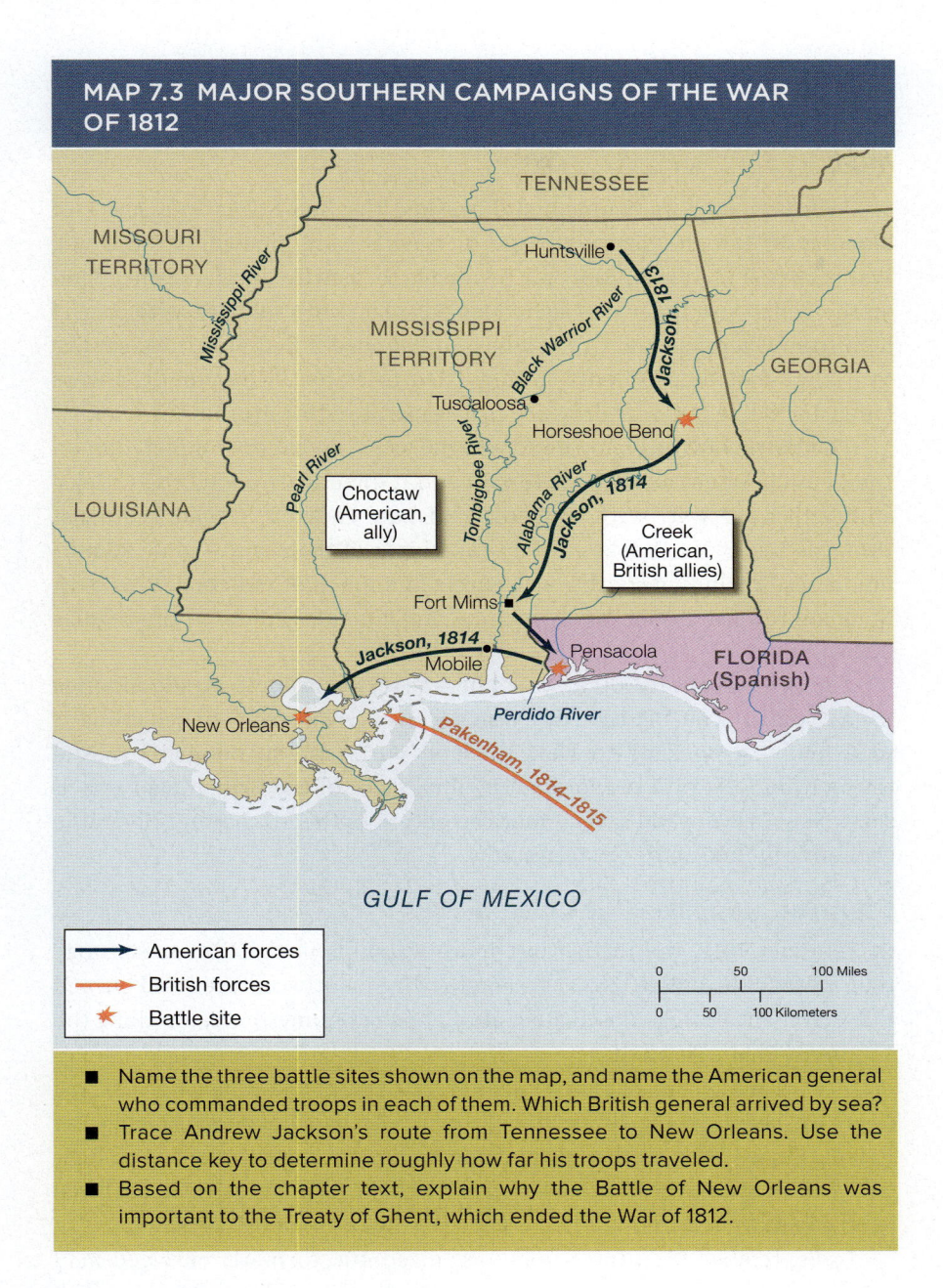

MAP 7.3 MAJOR SOUTHERN CAMPAIGNS OF THE WAR OF 1812

- Name the three battle sites shown on the map, and name the American general who commanded troops in each of them. Which British general arrived by sea?
- Trace Andrew Jackson's route from Tennessee to New Orleans. Use the distance key to determine roughly how far his troops traveled.
- Based on the chapter text, explain why the Battle of New Orleans was important to the Treaty of Ghent, which ended the War of 1812.

Alabama River and massacred hundreds of White and African American men, women, and children, as well as Lower Creeks (see Map 7.3).

Thirsting for revenge, Andrew Jackson, commanding general of the Army of West Tennessee, recruited about 2,500 volunteer militiamen and headed south. With him were David Crockett, a famous sharpshooter; and Sam Houston, a nineteen-year-old Virginia frontiersman who would later lead the Texas War for Independence against Mexico.

> Andrew Jackson's campaign in the south

From a young age, Jackson had gloried in violence and prospered by it. His soldiers later nicknamed him "Old Hickory" in recognition of his toughness. Jackson told all "brave Tennesseans" that their "frontier [was] threatened with invasion by the savage foe" and that the Indigenous Americans were advancing "with scalping knives unsheathed, to butcher your wives, your children, and your helpless babes."

Jackson's soldiers listened, and crushed the Red Sticks in a series of bloodbaths. But the decisive battle in what became known as the Creek War occurred in March 1814, on a peninsula formed by the Horseshoe Bend on the Tallapoosa River (see again Map 7.3). Jackson's soldiers, with crucial help from Cherokee and Creek allies, surrounded a Red Stick fort, set fire to it, and shot the residents as they tried to escape. Nine hundred were killed, including 300 who drowned in a desperate effort to cross the river.

The Battle of Horseshoe Bend was the worst defeat ever inflicted upon Indigenous Americans by U.S. forces, and it effectively ended the Creeks' ability to wage war. With the Treaty of Fort Jackson, signed in August 1814, the Red Stick Creeks gave up two-thirds of their land—some 23 million acres—including southwest Georgia and much of Alabama. President Madison rewarded Jackson by naming him a major general in the regular U.S. Army.

The British sent 16,000 more soldiers to try yet again to invade America from Canada. The British navy also received reinforcement, enabling it to extend its blockade to New England ports and to bombard coastal towns from Delaware to Florida. The final piece of the British plan was to seize New Orleans and sever American access to the Mississippi River, the economic lifeline of the western states.

Fighting along the Chesapeake Bay

In February 1813, the British had more warships in the Chesapeake Bay than were in the entire U.S. Navy, and they frequently captured and burned U.S. merchant vessels. The British also launched numerous raids along the Virginia and Maryland shore.

The presence of British ships on the coast and inland rivers led many enslaved people to escape or revolt. As had happened during the Revolutionary War, British naval commanders promised freedom to fugitives from slavery who aided or fought with them. As many as 4,000 enslaved people in Maryland and Virginia escaped to the safety of British ships.

> The British organize a Black military unit

In September 1813, the British organized 400 formerly enslaved men into an all–African American military unit called the Colonial Marines. The recruits were provided uniforms, meals, $6 a month in wages, and the promise of a gift of land after their service. News of the Colonial Marines panicked White residents along the Chesapeake Bay; they feared that the freed men would "have no mercy on them."

The Burning of Washington, D.C.

During the late summer of 1814, U.S. forces suffered their most humiliating experience of the war when British troops captured and burned Washington, D.C. In August, a group of 4,500 British soldiers landed at

THE BURNING OF THE CAPITAL In this illustration by Joseph Boggs Beale, residents of Washington, D.C., evacuate the city as the White House and the Capitol blaze with flames in the background.

Benedict, Maryland, routed the American militia at Bladensburg (Map 7.2), and headed for the nation's capital just six miles away.

President Madison called an emergency meeting of his cabinet. The secretary of war, John Armstrong, insisted that the British were not interested in the insignificant American capital. "They certainly will not come here," he told the president. "What the devil will they do here? No! No! Baltimore is the place, sir. That is of so much more consequence."

The Undefended Capital But the British were indeed headed for the American capital. Thousands fled the city. Madison strapped two pistols onto his waist, called out the poorly led and untrained militia, then left the capital to help rally the troops for the battle at Bladensburg. His efforts failed, however, as the American defense disintegrated. Many militiamen fled.

On August 24, British redcoats marched unopposed into the defenseless American capital. Madison and his wife, Dolley, fled just in time—after first saving a portrait of George Washington and a copy of the Declaration of Independence.

> The British march on the capital

The vengeful British, aware that American troops had burned York, the Canadian capital, torched the White House (then called the Executive Mansion), the Capitol, the Library of Congress, and other government buildings before heading north to assault Baltimore (Map 7.2).

The destruction of Washington, D.C., embarrassed and infuriated Americans. Even worse, people had lost confidence in the government and the military. David Campbell, a Virginia congressman, told his brother that America was "ruled by fools and the administration opposed by knaves." The secretary of war resigned; Madison, after escaping to Virginia, replaced him with James Monroe, who was also secretary of state. A desperate Monroe soon proposed enlisting free Blacks into the army. But many worried that such changes were too few and too late.

Expelling the British President Madison called an emergency session of Congress and appealed to Americans to "expel the invaders." A Baltimore newspaper reported that the "spirit of the nation is roused." That determination showed itself when fifty British warships sailed into Baltimore Harbor on September 13, while 4,200 British soldiers, including the all-Black Colonial Marines, assaulted the city by land. About 1,000 Americans held Fort McHenry, located on an island in the harbor.

> Baltimore holds out against British warships

Throughout the night, the British bombarded Fort McHenry. Yet the Americans refused to surrender. At daybreak, the soldiers in the battered fort stood defiant, guns at the ready. The frustrated British sailed away.

Francis Scott Key, a slaveholding lawyer from a Maryland plantation family who later would become a district attorney for Washington, D.C., watched the assault from a British warship, having been sent to negotiate the release of a captured American. The sight of the massive U.S. flag still flying over Fort McHenry at dawn inspired Key to scribble down the verses of what came to be called "The Star-Spangled Banner," which began, "Oh, say can you see, by the dawn's early light?"

Later revised and set to the tune of an English drinking song, it became America's national anthem in 1931. Less well known is that Key declared that Africans in America were "a distinct and inferior race of people, which all experience proves to be the greatest evil that afflicts a community." The lesser-known third stanza of "The Star-Spangled Banner" refers to the killing of enslaved men who had joined the British army in exchange for their freedom:

> No refuge could save the hireling and the slave
> From the terror of night or the gloom of the grave
> And the star-spangled banner in triumph doth wave
> O'er the land of the free and the home of the brave.

Antislavery critics later mocked Key's celebration of America as being "the land of the free, [and] home of the oppressed."

A LESSER-KNOWN STANZA The third stanza of Francis Scott Key's "Star-Spangled Banner" celebrated the triumph of the "broad stripes and bright stars" over enslaved Africans who had aligned with the British in the course of seeking their freedom.

The Battle of Lake Champlain

The British failure to conquer Baltimore gave Americans a desperately needed morale boost. More good news arrived from upstate New York, where the outnumbered Americans at Plattsburgh, along Lake Champlain, were saved by the heroics of Commodore Thomas Macdonough, commander of the U.S. naval squadron.

On September 11, 1814, just days after the burning of Washington, D.C., British soldiers attacked at Plattsburgh while their navy engaged Macdonough's warships in a battle that ended with the entire British fleet either destroyed or captured. The Battle of Lake Champlain (also called the Battle of Plattsburgh) forced the British to abandon the northern campaign and retreat into Canada (Map 7.2).

> Victories reinvigorate American morale

In November, an army led by Andrew Jackson in Florida seized Spanish-controlled Pensacola, on the Gulf coast, preventing another British army from landing and pushing northward into the southern states (Map 7.3). The American victories in New York and Florida convinced Congress not to abandon Washington, D.C. Instead, the members voted to rebuild the Capitol and the Executive Mansion.

What had brought the nation to this point? The war had been raging on three fronts: along the Great Lakes and Canada to the North; in the Creek War to the South; and along the Chesapeake Bay, especially around the capital in Washington, D.C. In the North, American forces were pushed back by British troops and Canadian and Indigenous American allies; the Americans did, however, gain firm control of most of Michigan and part of Upper Canada. In the South, defeated Creeks surrendered millions of acres of land. And in the Chesapeake, the burning of Washington, D.C., spurred American forces to defeat the British in northern New York and abandon their main military goals.

The Aftermath of War

> CORE **OBJECTIVE**
> 4. Analyze the most significant outcomes of the War of 1812 on the United States, and their importance.

While the fighting raged, U.S. diplomats, including Henry Clay and John Quincy Adams, son of the former president, had begun meeting with British officials in Ghent, near Brussels in present-day Belgium, to discuss ending the war. Negotiations dragged on for weeks, but on Christmas Eve 1814, the diplomats finally reached an agreement.

The Treaty of Ghent (1814)

In the **Treaty of Ghent (1814)**, the two countries agreed to return each side's prisoners and restore the previous boundaries. This was a godsend for the Americans, since British forces at the time controlled eastern Maine, northern Michigan, a portion of western New York, and several islands off the coast of Georgia. The British also pledged to stop supporting attacks by Indigenous people along the Great Lakes.

What had begun as an American effort to protect its honor, end British impressment, and conquer Canada had turned into a second war of independence. At the end of the negotiations, John Quincy Adams wrote to his wife that he had had the honor of "redeeming our union." Although the Americans lost the war for Canada and saw their own national capital destroyed, they won the southern war, defeating the Indigenous Americans and taking their lands. More important, the Treaty of Ghent saved the splintered republic from possible civil war and financial ruin.

Treaty of Ghent (1814) The agreement between Great Britain and the United States that ended the War of 1812.

It took longer to address the war's effect on slavery. Enslavers in the South looked to the federal government to compensate them financially for the enslaved labor they had lost to the British forces. They wrote to Secretary of State John Quincy Adams declaring their losses and negotiating the value of enslaved people. After fourteen years of negotiations, southern planters in Maryland, Virginia, Georgia, and South Carolina, received a fixed value for each enslaved person lost to the British in 1828. Some historians argue that these actions represent the first form of reparations—reparations for enslavers, not for the enslaved.

The Battle of New Orleans (1814–1815)

Because it took six weeks for news of the Treaty of Ghent to reach the United States, fighting continued at the end of 1814. On December 1, Andrew Jackson arrived in New Orleans after hearing of the British plan to seize the city. "I will smash them, so help me God!" he vowed. Jackson declared martial law and prepared the defense of New Orleans.

Preparations and Assault On December 12, a British fleet with sixty ships and thousands of soldiers took up positions on the coast of Louisiana, hoping to capture New Orleans and thereby gain control of the Mississippi River. But British general Sir Edward Pakenham's painfully careful preparation for an assault gave Jackson time to organize hundreds of enslaved people "loaned" by planters. They dug trenches, built ramparts bristling with cannons, stacked cotton bales and barrels of sugar, and dug a ten-foot-wide moat for protection.

The 4,500 Americans—including militiamen, Choctaws, African Americans, Tennessee and Kentucky sharpshooters, and Creole pirates—built an almost-invulnerable position at Chalmette Plantation, seven miles south of New Orleans. On one side of their lines was a swamp and on the other was the Mississippi River.

> Jackson organizes American forces to defend New Orleans

Sporadic fighting occurred for more than three weeks before General Pakenham ordered a frontal assault on the entrenched American defenders at dawn on Sunday, January 8, 1815 (Map 7.3). Andrew Jackson was inside a home in New Orleans and could only watch as a cannonball passed through the room. "Come on," he yelled to his staff, "we shall have a warm day."

The 5,300 British soldiers assaulted the Americans with a murderous hail of artillery shells and rifle fire. They kept coming, only to discover that an officer had forgotten the ladders needed to scale the American ramparts.

When the smoke cleared, a Kentucky militiaman said that the battlefield looked at first like "a sea of blood. It was not blood itself, but the red coats in which the British soldiers were dressed. The field was entirely covered in prostrate bodies."

In just twenty-five minutes, the British had lost some 2,100 men in the **Battle of New Orleans**, including General Pakenham and his second in command. (The British stored Pakenham's corpse in a barrel of rum for burial in Britain.)

Battle of New Orleans (1814–1815) The final major battle in the War of 1812, in which the Americans under General Andrew Jackson unexpectedly and decisively countered the British attempt to seize the port of New Orleans, Louisiana.

Hartford Convention (1814–1815) A series of secret meetings in December 1814 and January 1815 at which New England Federalists protested American involvement in the War of 1812 and discussed several constitutional amendments, including limiting each president to one term, designed to weaken the dominant Republican Party.

Jackson and the Americans forced the remnants of the defeated British army to retreat and sail away empty-handed. The Americans suffered only seventy-one killed or wounded.

With New Orleans and the Mississippi Valley liberated from British authority, it opened the way for more American settlement of western lands.

A Military and Psychological Victory Although the Battle of New Orleans occurred after the Treaty of Ghent had been signed, it was vitally important psychologically. Had the British won, they might have tried to revise the treaty in their favor. Jackson's victory ensured that both governments would act quickly to approve the treaty.

The surprising American triumph generated a wave of patriotism. The young nation had displayed its strength and proved to the world that it was becoming a great power. As a Washington, D.C., newspaper crowed, "ALMOST INCREDIBLE VICTORY!"

Such pride in the Battle of New Orleans would later help transform General Jackson into a presidential candidate. Jackson, wrote a southerner in April 1815, "is everywhere hailed as the savior of the country. . . . He has been feasted, caressed, & I may say idolized."

The Hartford Convention

The war also weakened the Federalist Party. A few weeks before the Battle of New Orleans, the New England Federalists, frustrated by the rising expense of "Mr. Madison's War," which they opposed, had taken matters into their own hands at the **Hartford Convention** in Hartford, Connecticut.

JACKSON'S ARMY DEFENDS NEW ORLEANS Unaware that the war was over, in January 1815 Andrew Jackson led his troops and the enslaved people on loan from southern planters to a decisive victory over the British at New Orleans. **What was the diplomatic and symbolic importance of Jackson's victory?**

At the convention, the Federalist delegates proposed new constitutional amendments designed to limit Republican (and southern) political power. The amendments included abolishing the counting of enslaved people in determining a state's representation in Congress, requiring a two-thirds supermajority rather than a simple majority vote to declare war or admit new states, and barring successive presidents from the same state (a provision clearly directed at Virginia).

The delegates also threatened that some New England states might "secede" from the Union if their demands were dismissed. Yet that threat quickly evaporated. In February 1815, when messengers from the convention reached Washington, D.C., they found the capital celebrating the great American victory at New Orleans.

Ignored by Congress and the president, the Federalist delegates went home. The episode proved fatal to the Federalist Party, which never recovered from the shame of disloyalty stamped on it by the Hartford Convention. The victory at New Orleans and the arrival of the peace treaty from Europe transformed the national mood and turned President Madison into a national hero.

The War's Legacies

There was no clear military victor in the War of 1812, nor much clarification about the issues that had ignited the war. For all the clumsiness with which the war was managed, however, it had secured the young republic from British or European threats. As James Monroe said, "we have acquired a character and a rank among the other nations, which we did not enjoy before."

Increasing Economic Independence Most Americans viewed the war as a glorious triumph. It also propelled the United States toward economic independence, as the interruption of trade with Europe forced America to expand its industrial sector and become more self-sufficient.

> Economic independence

The British blockade of U.S. ports had caused a shortage of cotton cloth in the United States, leading to the creation of the nation's first cotton-manufacturing industry, in Waltham, Massachusetts. By the end of the war, there were more than 100 cotton mills in New England and 64 more in Pennsylvania. Even Thomas Jefferson admitted in 1815 that his beloved agricultural republic had been transformed: "We must now place the manufacturer by the agriculturalist." The new American republic was emerging as an agricultural, commercial, and industrial world power.

Perhaps the most noteworthy result of the War of 1812 was the reversal of positions among Republicans and Federalists regarding the balance of state and federal power.

> Reversal of political roles for Republicans and Federalists

The British invasion of Washington, D.C., convinced President Madison of the necessity of a stronger army and navy. In addition, the lack of a national bank had hurt the federal government's efforts to finance the war; state and local banks were so unstable that it was difficult to raise the funds needed to pay military expenses. In 1816, Madison created the Second Bank of the

United States (B.U.S.) to exercise a regulating influence over the many state banks that were issuing their own paper currency.

While business leaders appreciated the centralized control provided by the B.U.S., many working-class people, especially in the new western states, distrusted the national bank in Philadelphia. At the same time, the rise of new industries prompted manufacturers to call for increased tariffs on imports to protect American industries from unfair foreign competition. Madison went along, despite his criticism of tariffs in the 1790s.

While Madison reversed himself by embracing nationalism and a broader interpretation of the Constitution, the Federalists reversed themselves and adopted Madison's and Jefferson's original emphasis on states' rights and strict interpretation of the Constitution to defend the special interests of their regional stronghold, New England. It was the first great reversal of partisan political positions. It would not be the last.

> Westward expansion and occupation of Indigenous American lands

Dispossession of Indigenous Lands The War of 1812 proved devastating to the eastern Indigenous nations, most of which had fought with the British. The war accelerated westward settlement, and Indigenous American resistance was greatly diminished after the death of Tecumseh and his Confederacy. The British essentially abandoned their Indigenous allies, and none of their former lands were returned to them.

Lakota chief Little Crow expressed the betrayal felt by Indigenous Americans when he rejected the consolation gifts from the local British commander: "After we have fought for you, endured many hardships, lost some of our people, and awakened the vengeance of our powerful neighbors, you make peace for yourselves. . . . You no longer need our service; you offer us these goods to pay us for [your] having deserted us. But no, we will not take them; we hold them and yourselves in equal contempt."

As the Indigenous people were pushed out, tens of thousands of Americans moved into the Great Lakes region and into Georgia, Alabama, and Mississippi, occupying more territory in a single generation than had been settled in the 150 years of colonial history. The federal government hastened western migration by giving war veterans 160 acres of land between the Illinois and Mississippi Rivers.

In this atmosphere, the trans-Appalachian population soared from 300,000 to 2 million between 1800 and 1820. By 1840, more than 40 percent of Americans lived west of the Appalachians in eight new states. The number of free Blacks tripled, from 59,000 in 1790 to more than 174,000 by 1810, while the number of enslaved people doubled to 1,191,364. At the same time, the growing dispute over slavery and its westward expansion into new territories set in motion an explosive debate that would once again test the grand experiment in republican government.

Reviewing the
CORE OBJECTIVES

- **Jefferson's Administration** The Jeffersonian Republicans did not dismantle much of Hamilton's Federalist economic program, but they did repeal the whiskey tax, reduce government expenditures, and promote what was called *republican simplicity*—smaller government and plain living.

While Republicans idealized the agricultural world that had existed prior to 1800, the first decades of the 1800s were a period of explosive economic and population growth in the United States, transforming the nation. Large-scale commercial agriculture and exports to Europe flourished; Americans moved west in huge numbers. The *Louisiana Purchase* (1803), in some ways a result of France's preoccupation with the *Haitian Revolution* (1791–1804), dramatically expanded the boundaries of the United States. The *Lewis and Clark expedition* (1804–1806) explored the new region and published reports that excited interest in the Far West. In *Marbury v. Madison* (1803), the Federalist chief justice of the Supreme Court, John Marshall, declared a federal act unconstitutional for the first time. With that decision, the Court assumed the right of judicial review over acts of Congress and established the constitutional supremacy of the federal government over state governments.

- **War in the Mediterranean and Europe** Thomas Jefferson sent warships to subdue the *Barbary pirates* on the coast of North Africa and negotiated with the Spanish and French to ensure that the Mississippi River remained open to American commerce. Renewal of war between Britain and France in 1803 complicated matters for American commerce with Europe. Neither country wanted its enemy to purchase U.S. goods, so both blockaded each other's ports. In retaliation, at the end of 1807 Jefferson convinced Congress to pass the *Embargo Act*, which prohibited all foreign trade.

- **The War of 1812** Renewal of the European war in 1803 created naval conflicts with Britain and France. President James Madison ultimately declared war against Great Britain over the issue of neutral shipping rights and the fear that the British were inciting Indigenous Americans to attack frontier settlements. Indigenous nations took sides in the war. Tecumseh led the Confederacy against the Americans during the *War of 1812*. Earlier, at the *Battle of Tippecanoe* (1811), U.S. troops had defeated elements of *Tecumseh's Indian Confederacy*, an alliance of Indigenous nations determined to protect their ancestral lands. At the Battle of the Thames (1813), Tecumseh was killed and the Confederacy disintegrated soon thereafter.

- **Aftermath of the War of 1812** The *Treaty of Ghent* (1814) ended the war by essentially declaring it a draw. A smashing American victory in January 1815 at the *Battle of New Orleans* occurred before news of the peace treaty had reached the continent, but the lopsided American triumph helped ensure that the treaty would be ratified and enforced. Eastern Indigenous nations, many of whom had sided with the British, were devastated after the war and were steadily pushed and removed westward across the Mississippi River by the onslaught of White settlers taking over ancestral Indigenous lands. One effect of the conflict was to establish the economic independence of the United States, as goods previously purchased from Great Britain were now manufactured at home. During and after the war, Federalists and Republicans seemed to exchange roles: delegates from the waning Federalist party met at the *Hartford Convention* (1814–1815) to defend states' rights and threaten secession, while Republicans now promoted nationalism and a broad interpretation of the Constitution.

KEY TERMS

republican simplicity *p. 285*

Marbury v. Madison (1803) *p. 288*

Haitian Revolution (1791–1804) *p. 291*

Louisiana Purchase (1803) *p. 293*

Lewis and Clark expedition (1804–1806) *p. 293*

Barbary pirates *p. 300*

Embargo Act (1807) *p. 302*

War of 1812 (1812–1815) *p. 305*

Battle of Tippecanoe (1811) *p. 306*

Tecumseh's Indian Confederacy *p. 306*

Treaty of Ghent (1814) *p. 316*

Battle of New Orleans (1814–1815) *p. 317*

Hartford Convention (1814–1815) *p. 318*

CHRONOLOGY

1801 Thomas Jefferson is inaugurated as president

Barbary pirates harass U.S. shipping in North Africa and capture American sailors

The pasha of Tripoli declares war on the United States

1803 Supreme Court issues *Marbury v. Madison* decision

Louisiana Purchase

1804–1806 Lewis and Clark expedition

1804 Jefferson is overwhelmingly reelected; Haitian Revolution ends

1807 British interference with U.S. shipping increases, prompting President Jefferson to announce Embargo Act

1808 International slave trade is outlawed in the United States

1811 Defeat of Tecumseh's Indian Confederacy at the Battle of Tippecanoe

1812 Congress declares war on Britain

U.S. invasion of Canada

1813–1814 Creek War

1814 British capture and burn Washington, D.C.

Hartford Convention begins

1815 Battle of New Orleans

News of the Treaty of Ghent reaches the United States

InQuizitive

Go to InQuizitive to see what you've learned—and learn what you've missed—with personalized feedback along the way.

THINKING LIKE A HISTORIAN

DEBATING Thomas Jefferson and Slavery

One of the more difficult tasks that historians face is assessing the actions of historical figures within an ethical framework. Should people in the past be assessed by the standards of their time or by those of today? Should we hold celebrated historical figures to a higher ethical standard? For Part 2, *"Building a Nation,"* the complex relationship of Thomas Jefferson to slavery demonstrates how historians can disagree when they evaluate historic individuals from an ethical perspective.

This exercise involves two tasks:

PART 1: Compare the two secondary sources on Thomas Jefferson and slavery.
PART 2: Using primary sources, evaluate the arguments of the two secondary sources.

PART I Comparing and Contrasting Secondary Sources

Following are two secondary sources focused on the question of Jefferson and his relationship with slavery. The first is from Douglas L. Wilson, professor emeritus of English and codirector of the Lincoln Studies Center at Knox College; the second is written by Paul Finkelman, professor of law at Marquette University. In these selections, Wilson and Finkelman explore one of the great contradictions in early American history: that Thomas Jefferson, the author of the Declaration of Independence, was a slave owner. Further complicating the matter was Jefferson's relationship with Sally Hemings, an enslaved woman with whom he had several children. Both passages grapple with the issue of *presentism*, the application of present-day ideas and beliefs onto the past.

Compare the views of these two scholars by answering the following questions. Be sure to find specific examples in the selections to support your answers.

- How does each author address the issue of presentism?
- What ethical standards do the authors use to evaluate Jefferson?
- What evidence do they offer when evaluating Jefferson?
- How does each author assess Jefferson's ethical standards?
- What ethical standard would you use?

Secondary Source 1

Douglas L. Wilson, "Thomas Jefferson and the Character Issue," 1992

How could the man who wrote that "All men are created equal" own slaves? This, in essence, is the question most persistently asked of those who write about Thomas Jefferson, and by all indications it is the thing that contemporary Americans find most vexing about him.... The question carries a silent assumption that because he practiced slave holding, Jefferson must have somehow believed in it, and must therefore have been a hypocrite. My belief is that this way of asking the question . . . reflects the pervasive presentism of our time. Consider, for example, how different the question appears when inverted and framed in more historical terms: How did a man who was born into a slave holding society, whose family and admired friends owned slaves, who inherited a fortune that was dependent on slaves and slave labor, decide at an early age that slavery was morally wrong and forcefully declare that it ought to be abolished?

But when the question is explained in this way, another invariably follows: If Jefferson came to believe that holding slaves was wrong, why did he continue to hold them? . . . Obstacles to emancipation in Jefferson's Virginia were formidable, and the risk was demonstrably great that emancipated slaves would enjoy little, if any, real freedom and would, unless they could pass as white, be more likely to come to grief in a hostile environment. In short, the master whose concern extended beyond his own morality to the well-being of his slaves was caught on the horns of a dilemma. Thus the question of why Jefferson didn't free his slaves only serves to illustrate how presentism involves us in mistaken assumptions about historical conditions—in this case that an eighteenth-century slave holder wanting to get out from under the moral stigma of slavery and improve the lot of his slaves had only to set them free.

Although we may find Jefferson guilty of failing to make adequate allowance for the conditions in which blacks were forced to live, Jefferson did not take the next step of concluding that blacks were fit only for slavery. This rationalization of slavery was indeed the common coin of slave holders and other whites who condoned or tolerated the "peculiar" institution, but it formed no part of Jefferson's thinking. In fact, he took the opposite position: that having imposed the depredations of slavery on blacks, white Americans should not only emancipate them but also educate and train them to be self-sufficient, provide them with necessary materials, and establish a colony in which they could live as free and independent people.

Source: Wilson, Douglas L. "Thomas Jefferson and the Character Issue." *Atlantic Monthly* November 1992, pp. 57–74.

Secondary Source 2

Paul Finkelman, "Jefferson and Slavery," 1993

An understanding of Jefferson's relationship to slavery requires analysis of his statements on and beliefs about the institution and an account of his actions as a public leader and a private individual. Scrutinizing the contradictions between Jefferson's professions and his actions does not impose twentieth-century values on an eighteenth-century man. Because he was the author of the Declaration of Independence and a leader of the American Enlightenment, the test of Jefferson's position on slavery is not whether he was better than the worst of his generation, but whether he was the leader of the best; not whether he responded as a southerner and a planter, but whether he was able to transcend his economic interests and his sectional background to implement the ideals he articulated. Jefferson fails the test. When Jefferson wrote the Declaration, he owned over 175 slaves. While many of his contemporaries freed their slaves during and after the Revolution, Jefferson did not.

In the fifty years from 1776 until his death in 1826, a period of extraordinary public service, he did little to end slavery or to dissociate himself from his role as the master of Monticello. To the contrary, as he accumulated more slaves he worked assiduously to increase the productivity and the property values of his labor force. Nor did he encourage his countrymen to liberate their slaves, even when they sought his blessing. Even at his death Jefferson failed to fulfill the promise of his rhetoric. In his will he emancipated only five bondsmen, condemning nearly two hundred others to the auction block....

... He knew slavery was wrong. It could not have been otherwise for an eighteenth-century natural law theorist. Many of his closest European and American friends and colleagues were leaders of the new abolition societies. Jefferson was part of a cosmopolitan "republic of letters" that was overwhelmingly hostile to slavery. But, for the most part, he suppressed his doubts, while doing virtually nothing to challenge the institution. On this issue Jefferson's genius failed him. As David Brion Davis observes, "Jefferson had only a theoretical interest in promoting the cause of abolition."

Jefferson could not live without slaves. They built his house, cooked his meals, and tilled his fields. In contrast to George Washington, Jefferson carelessly managed his lands and finances and lived beyond his means. Washington refused to traffic in slaves. Chronically in debt, Jefferson overcame his professed "scruples about selling negroes but for delinquency or on their own request," selling scores of slaves in order to make ends meet. Jefferson could not maintain his extravagant life style without his slaves and, to judge from his lifelong behavior, his grand style was far more important than the natural rights of his slaves....

Throughout his life, as he condemned slavery, Jefferson implied that, however bad it was for slaves, the institution was somehow worse for whites. His concerns about the institution had more to do with its effect on whites and white society than on its true victims.... Jefferson's concerns were solely with the "morals and manners" of the master class. He was concerned that slavery leads to despotism by the masters; but he never expressed regret for the mistreatment of the slave. Similarly, throughout his life Jefferson expressed his fears of miscegenation and a weakening of white society through contact with blacks. He favored some form of colonization that would put blacks "beyond the reach of mixture."

Source: Finkelman, Paul. "Jefferson and Slavery: 'Treason against the Hopes of the World.'" In *Jeffersonian Legacies*, edited by Peter S. Onuf, 181–221. Charlottesville: University Press of Virginia, 1993.

PART II Using Primary Sources to Evaluate Secondary Sources

When historians are faced with competing interpretations of the past, they often look at primary source material as part of the process of evaluating the different arguments. Below are primary source materials relating to Thomas Jefferson's relationship with slavery. The first document is an excerpt from a draft of the Declaration of Independence largely written by Thomas Jefferson. This excerpt was removed from the final version of the declaration. The second document is a selection from Jefferson's 1785 book on the state of Virginia, relating to slaves and slavery. The third document is a letter Jefferson wrote while serving in Paris as the U.S. minister (ambassador) to France in 1788; and the fourth is a letter from April 1820 expressing his feelings regarding the Missouri Compromise, which admitted Missouri as a slave state and created a northern boundary for slavery in the western territories.

Carefully read the primary sources and answer the following questions. Decide which of the primary source documents support or refute Wilson's and Finkelman's arguments about Jefferson. You may find that some documents do both but for different parts of each historian's interpretation. Be sure to identify which specific components of each historian's argument the documents support or refute.

- Which of the two historians' *arguments* is best supported by the *primary source* documents? If you find that both arguments are well supported by the evidence, why do you think the two historians had such different interpretations about Jefferson?

- Based on the ethical standard you choose in Part I and these documents, how would *you* assess Jefferson's relationship with slavery? You may consider how Jefferson's views change over time.

- What has using primary sources to evaluate the Wilson and Finkelman arguments taught you about making ethical assessments of historical figures?

Primary Source 1

Thomas Jefferson, a draft section removed from the *Declaration of Independence*, 1776

He [King George III] has waged cruel war against human nature itself, violating its most sacred rights of life & liberty in the persons of a distant people [Africans] who never offended him, captivating & carrying them into slavery in another hemisphere, or to incur miserable death in their transportation thither. This piratical warfare, the opprobrium of infidel powers, is the warfare of the Christian king of Great Britain. Determined to keep open a market where men should be bought & sold, he has prostituted his negative for suppressing every legislative attempt to prohibit or to restrain this execrable [disgusting] commerce: and that this assemblage of horrors might want no fact of distinguished die [has become officially sanctioned], he is now exciting those very people to rise in arms among us, and to purchase that liberty of which he has deprived them, & murdering the people upon whom he also obtruded them; thus paying off former crimes committed against the liberties of one people, with crimes which he urges them to commit against the lives of another.

Source: Jefferson, Thomas. "Thomas Jefferson, June 1776, Rough Draft of the Declaration of Independence," 1776. *The Thomas Jefferson Papers Series 1. General Correspondence. 1651–1827.* American Memory, Library of Congress, Washington, D.C.

Primary Source 2

Thomas Jefferson, *Notes on the State of Virginia*, 1787

It will probably be asked, Why not retain and incorporate the Blacks into the State [after emancipation], and thus save the expense of supplying, by importation of white settlers, the vacancies they will leave? Deep-rooted prejudices entertained by the Whites; ten thousand recollections by the Blacks, of the injuries they have sustained; new provocations; the real distinctions which nature has made; and many other circumstances, will divide us into parties, and produce convulsions, which will probably never end but in the extermination of the one or the other race. To these objections, which are political, may be added others, which are physical and moral. . . . Comparing them by their faculties of memory, reason, and imagination, it appears to me, that in memory they are equal to the Whites; in reason much inferior, . . . and that in imagination they are dull, tasteless and anomalous. . . .

To our reproach it must be said, that though for a century and a half we have had under our eyes the races of Black and of Red men, they have never yet been viewed by us as subjects of natural history. I advance it therefore as a suspicion only, that the Blacks, whether originally a distinct race, or made distinct by time and circumstances, are inferior to the Whites in the endowments both of body and mind. It is not against experience to suppose, that different species of the same genus, or varieties of the same species, may possess different qualifications. Will not a lover of natural history then, one who views the gradations in all the races of animals with the eye of philosophy, excuse an effort to keep those in the department of man as distinct as nature has formed them? This unfortunate difference of colour, and perhaps of faculty, is a powerful obstacle to the emancipation of these people. Many of their advocates, while they wish to vindicate the liberty of human nature, are anxious also to preserve its dignity and beauty. Some of these, embarrassed by the question 'What further is to be done with them?' join themselves in opposition with those who are actuated by sordid avarice [greed] only. Among the Romans emancipation required but one effort. The slave, when made free, might mix with, without staining the blood of his master. But with us a second is necessary, unknown to history. When freed, he is to be removed beyond the reach of mixture. . . . There must, doubtless, be an unhappy influence on the manners of our people, produced by the existence of slavery among us. The whole commerce between master and slave is a perpetual exercise of the most boisterous passions, the most unremitting despotism on the one part, and degrading. . . . For if a slave can have a country in this world, it must be any other in preference to that in which he is born to live and labor for another.

Source: Jefferson, Thomas. "Laws, Query XIV." *Notes on the State of Virginia*. London: Printed for John Stockdale, Opposite Burlington-House, Piccadilly, 1787. 229–271.

Primary Source 3

Thomas Jefferson, Letter to M. Warville [a Frenchman], February 11, 1788

Sir,

I am very sensible of the honor you propose to me, of becoming a member of the society for the abolition of the slave-trade. You know that nobody wishes more ardently, to see an abolition, not only of the trade, but of the condition of slavery: and certainly nobody will be more willing to encounter every sacrifice for that object. But the influence and information of the friends to this proposition in France will be far above the need of my association. I am here as a public servant, and those whom I serve, having never yet been able to give their voice against the practice, it is decent for me to avoid too public a demonstration of my wishes to see it abolished. Without serving the cause here, it might render me less able to serve it beyond the water. I trust you will be sensible of the prudence of those motives, therefore, which govern my conduct on this occasion, and be assured of my wishes for the success of your undertaking, and the sentiments of esteem and respect, with which I have the honor to be, Sir, your most obedient, humble servant,

Th: Jefferson.

Source: Jefferson, Thomas. "Thomas Jefferson to Jean Plumard Brissot de Warville, February 11, 1788," 1788. *The Thomas Jefferson Papers*. Series 1: General Correspondence, 1651–1827. American Memory, Library of Congress, Washington, D.C.

Primary Source 4

Thomas Jefferson, Letter to John Holmes, April 22, 1820

I thank you, dear Sir, for the copy you have been so kind as to send me of the letter to your constituents on the Missouri question [the admission of Missouri as slave state]. . . . The cession of that kind of property [slaves] (for so it is misnamed) . . . would not cost me a second thought, if, in that way, a general emancipation and expatriation could be effected: and, gradually, and with due sacrifices, I think it might be. But as it is, we have the wolf by the ears, and we can neither hold him, nor safely let him go. Justice is in one scale, and self-preservation in the other. Of one thing I am certain, that as the passage of slaves from one State to another, would not make a slave of a single human being who would not be so without it, so their diffusion over a greater surface would make them individually happier, and proportionally facilitate the accomplishment of their emancipation. . . .

Th: Jefferson.

Source: Jefferson, Thomas. "Thomas Jefferson to John Holmes, April 22, 1820," 1820. *The Thomas Jefferson Papers*, Series 1: General Correspondence, 1651–1827. American Memory, Library of Congress, Washington, D.C.

A CARD.

BLOUNT & DAWSON,
GENERAL BROKERS

the Purchase and Sale of Negroes and Other Property.

SAVANNAH, GEORGIA.

When the Office and New Jail completed by Wm. Wright, Esq., we are prepared secure and good accommodations for all negroes left with us for Sale or keeping, would respectfully solicit a share of public patronage.

Two Doors East of J. Bryan & Co., opposite the State Bank.

BLOUNT.   W. C. DAWSON.

Having leased the above gentlemen my office and jail, would take pleasure in recommending them to my patrons and the public generally.

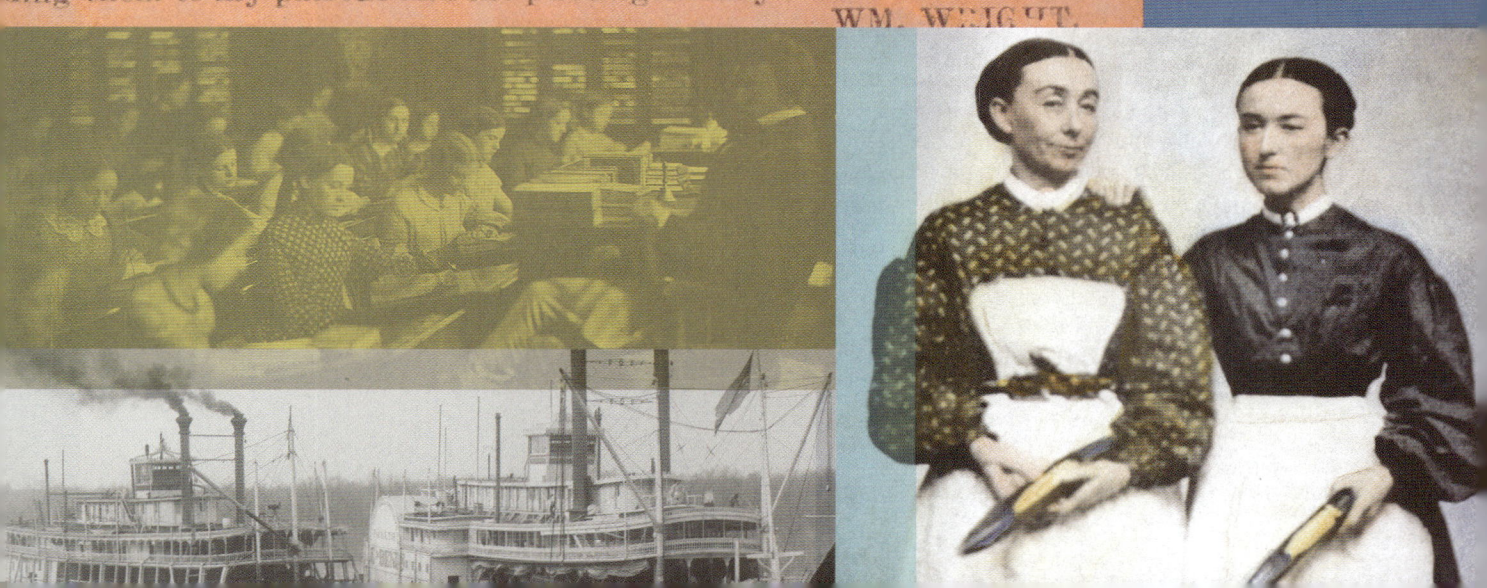

WM. WRIGHT.

An Expanding Nation

PART 3

During the nineteenth century, the United States experienced wrenching changes. With each passing decade, its predominantly agrarian society developed a more diverse economy, with factories and cities emerging alongside farms and towns. The pace of life quickened, and ambitions soared. A visiting Frenchman noted in 1831 that he knew "of no country where wealth has taken a stronger hold on the affections of men" than in America.

The nation's boundaries expanded and its rate of population growth was greater than anything known in Europe. By the early 1820s, thanks to the rapidly expanding system of slavery, the total number of enslaved Americans was more than two and a half times greater than in 1790, and the number of all Black people had doubled. The White population increased just as rapidly.

Other nations became worried about America's growing power. Spain's governor in New Orleans warned officials in Spain that the greatest threat to their possessions in North America was "not military but demographic." The rapid population increase in the United States would eventually drive the Spanish out of the continent.

Americans began uprooting themselves in a relentless pursuit of westward expansion. The West provided the key to the nation's nineteenth-century development, and millions migrated across the Allegheny and Appalachian Mountains into the Midwest, then crossed the Mississippi River and spread out across the Great Plains. By the 1840s, Americans had reached the Pacific Ocean.

This feverish expansion drew White American settlers into conflict with the Indigenous, Mexican, British, and Spanish people who already claimed lands in the West. But most White Americans believed it was their God-given destiny to spread across the continent—even if doing so required violent force.

In 1845, an editorial in the *United States Journal* claimed that "we, the American people, are the most independent, intelligent, moral, and happy people on the face of the earth." The constitutional republic governed by "natural aristocrats" such as Thomas Jefferson, James Madison, James Monroe, and John Quincy Adams gave way to the frontier democracy promoted by men like Andrew Jackson. Americans began to demand government of, by, and for the people.

They also began identifying by region and believed that stark differences separated the societies of the North and the South. Northerners embraced the Industrial Revolution, large cities, foreign immigrants, and the ideal of "free laborers" rather than enslaved workers. Southerners remained rural, agricultural, and increasingly committed to enslaved labor as the backbone of their cotton-centered economy.

Though these regional economies were joined in one emerging system of American capitalism, Americans still grew suspicious of one another. Southerners, in particular, feared the growing possibility that a northern-controlled Congress might abolish slavery. The planter elite's aggressive efforts to preserve and expand slavery ignited a prolonged political controversy with the North that would eventually lead to civil war.

The so-called Jacksonian era during the first half of the nineteenth century celebrated individual freedom and self-expression for White men. Religious life experienced another wave of revival centered on the power of individuals to embrace Christ and attain salvation on their own. This emphasis on individualism and freedom of expression shaped cultural life in general.

The Romantic movement applied democratic ideals to virtually every field: philosophy, religion, literature, and the fine arts. In New England, Ralph Waldo Emerson and Henry David Thoreau joined other "transcendentalists" in promoting a radical individualism. At the same time, activists fanned out to reform and even perfect society by creating public schools accessible to all children; working to abolish slavery and promote women's rights; combating the consumption of alcohol; and striving to improve living conditions for the disabled, the mentally ill, the poor, and the imprisoned.

During the first half of the nineteenth century, these and other developments combined to shape the America we live in today. Social reform, religious fervor, soaring immigration and nativist prejudices, unpopular wars triggered by presidential actions, racial prejudice and injustice, and violent swings in the business cycle resemble many of the pressing issues that have persisted for generations.

LACKAWANNA VALLEY (1855) Often hailed as the father of American landscape painting, George Inness was commissioned by a railroad company to capture its trains coursing through the lush Lackawanna Valley in northeastern Pennsylvania. New inventions and rapid industrial growth would continue to change the American landscape.

The Emergence of a Market Economy

1815–1860

CHAPTER 8

Amid the postwar celebrations in 1815, Americans set about transforming their victorious young nation. Prosperity returned as British and European markets again welcomed American ships and commerce. During the war, the loss of trade with Britain and Europe had forced the United States to develop more factories and mills, spurring the development of the more diverse economy that Alexander Hamilton had championed in the 1790s.

Between 1815 and 1860, the United States became a transcontinental power, expanding to the Pacific coast. Swarms of land-hungry people streamed westward. Between 1815 and 1821 alone, six new states joined the Union (Alabama, Illinois, Indiana, Mississippi, Missouri, and Maine).

Nineteenth-century Americans were a restless, ambitious people. A Boston newspaper commented that the entire American "population is in motion." Everywhere, it seemed, people were moving to the next town, the next farm, the next opportunity. In many cities, half the population moved every ten years. In 1826, a newspaper editor in Rochester, New York, reported that 120 people left the city every day while 130 moved in.

The lure of cheap land and plentiful jobs, as well as the promise of political and religious freedom, attracted millions of immigrants. This great wave of humanity was not always welcomed, however. Ethnic prejudices, anti-Catholicism, and language barriers made it difficult for many

CORE OBJECTIVES

1. Describe how changes in transportation and communications altered the economic landscape during the first half of the nineteenth century.
2. Explain the impact of the Industrial Revolution on the way people worked and lived.
3. Analyze how immigration altered the nation's population and shaped its politics.
4. Evaluate the impact of the expanding capitalist "market economy" on workers, professionals, and women.

market economy Large-scale manufacturing and commercial agriculture that emerged in America during the first half of the nineteenth century, displacing much of the premarket subsistence and barter-based economy and producing boom-and-bust cycles while raising the American standard of living.

immigrants—mostly from Ireland, Germany, and China—to find acceptance in American culture.

In the Midwest, large-scale commercial agriculture emerged as big farms grew corn and wheat and raised pigs and cattle to be sold in distant markets. In the South, cotton became so profitable that it increasingly dominated the region's economy, luring farmers and planters (wealthy farmers with extensive acreage worked by enslaved people) into the new states of Alabama, Mississippi, Louisiana, and Arkansas.

Not everyone moved freely. Indigenous people in the Southeast—the Cherokee, Choctaw, Chickasaw, Creek, and Seminole—were violently uprooted and removed to Indian Territory (present-day Oklahoma) to open up vast acres of land for cotton cultivation, while slave traders forced enslaved people from Virginia and the Carolinas into the cotton-growing states.

Meanwhile, the Northeast experienced a surge of industrial development. Water- and steam-powered industries reshaped the region's economic and social life. Mills and factories transformed the way people labored, dressed, and lived. With the rise of the factory system, more and more economic activity occurred outside the home and off the farm. An urban middle class began to emerge as Americans—including young women—moved to towns and cities, lured by jobs in new factories, stores, and banks.

By 1850, the United States boasted the world's fastest-growing economy. Dramatic technological innovations transformed the economy into an interconnected national marketplace. The railroad, the steamboat, the telegraph, the clipper ship, and the photograph combined to shrink time and distance. Newly elected President Andrew Jackson, for example, arrived in Washington, D.C., in 1829 riding in a horse-drawn carriage. Eight years later, he left the presidency and returned to Tennessee in a railroad car.

Amid such dramatic changes, the nation began to divide into three powerful regional political blocs—North, South, and West—whose shifting alliances would shape political life until the Civil War.

CORE **OBJECTIVE**

1. Describe how changes in transportation and communications altered the economic landscape during the first half of the nineteenth century.

The Market Revolution

In the eighteenth century, most White Americans were farm folk who operated within a "household economy." That is, they produced enough food, livestock, and clothing for their own family's needs and perhaps a little more to barter (exchange) with their neighbors. During the nineteenth century, however, farm families began producing surplus crops and livestock to sell, for cash, in distant markets. They were then able to buy more land, better equipment, and the latest manufactured household goods.

Such large-scale commercial agriculture, the first stage of a **market economy**, produced boom-and-bust cycles; and was often built upon the backs of enslaved laborers, immigrant workers, and displaced Mexicans. It was their labor, in large part, that enabled White Americans to enjoy unprecedented opportunities for economic gain and geographic mobility.

What the market economy needed most were "internal improvements"—deeper harbors, lighthouses, and a national network of canals, bridges, roads, and railroads—to facilitate the flow of goods across states. In 1817, for example, South Carolina congressman John C. Calhoun expressed his desire to "bind the Republic together with a perfect system of roads and canals." As the world's largest republic, the United States desperately needed a national transportation system.

> The need for internal improvements

Calhoun's idea sparked a fierce debate over how to fund such improvements (what today is called infrastructure): Should it be the responsibility of the federal government, the individual states, or private corporations? Since the Constitution said nothing about the federal government's role in funding transportation improvements, many people argued that such projects must be initiated by state and local governments. Others insisted that the Constitution gave the federal government broad powers to promote the "general welfare," which included enhancing transportation and communication. The debate over the funding of internal improvements would continue throughout the nineteenth century.

Transportation Improvements

An array of transportation innovations—larger horse-drawn wagons (called Conestogas), new roads, canals, steamboats, and the first railroads—knitted together the expanding national market for goods and services and greatly accelerated the pace of life.

> New means of transportation

Overland Transportation

Until the nineteenth century, travel had been slow, uncomfortable, and expensive. For example, it took a stagecoach four days to get from New York City to Boston. Because of long travel times, many farm products could only be sold locally before they spoiled.

That soon changed, as coach lines began using continual relays, or "stages," of fresh horses made available every forty or so miles. These "stagecoaches" made travel less expensive and more accessible and increased their speed as the quality of roads improved (see Map 8.1).

A New National Road

As settlers moved west, people demanded better roads. In 1803, when Ohio became a state, Congress ordered that 5 percent of the money from the sale of federally owned land in the state should go toward building a National Road from the Atlantic coast across Ohio and westward. Construction finally began in 1811. Originally called the Cumberland Road, it was the first interstate roadway financed by the federal government. By 1818, the road was open and extended from Cumberland, Maryland, to Vandalia, Illinois.

MAP 8.1 TRANSPORTATION WEST, ABOUT 1840

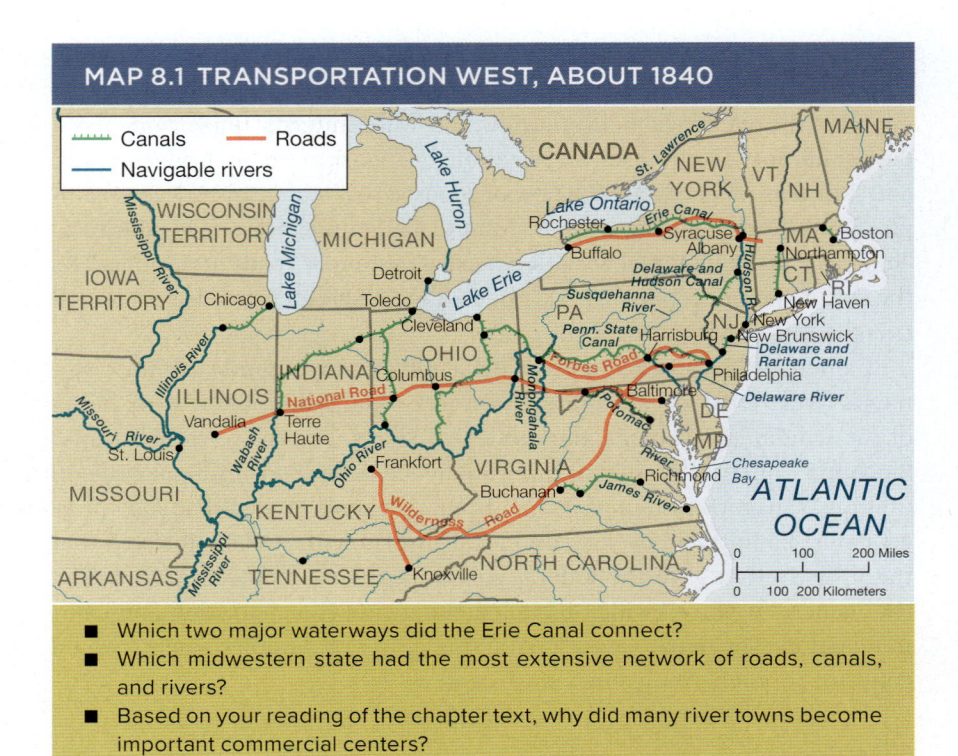

- Which two major waterways did the Erie Canal connect?
- Which midwestern state had the most extensive network of roads, canals, and rivers?
- Based on your reading of the chapter text, why did many river towns become important commercial centers?

The National Road quickened the settlement of the West and the emergence of a national market economy by reducing transportation costs, creating new markets, and stimulating the growth of towns.

Water Transportation

By the early 1820s, the turnpike boom was giving way to advances in water transportation. Steamboats, flatboats (barges propelled by men using long poles), and canal barges carried people and goods far more cheaply than did horse-drawn wagons.

Flatboats, however, went only downstream. Once unloaded at southern ports such as Natchez, Mississippi, or New Orleans, Louisiana, flatboats that had traveled down the Ohio and Mississippi Rivers were sold and dismantled to provide lumber for construction.

The difficulties of getting back upriver were solved when Robert Fulton and Robert R. Livingston sent the *Clermont*, the first commercial steamboat, up the Hudson River from New York City to Albany in 1807. The 150-mile trip took thirty hours.

Thereafter, the use of wood-fired **steamboats** spread rapidly. By bringing two-way travel to the rivers in the Mississippi Valley, steamboats created a transcontinental market and a commercial agricultural empire that produced much of the nation's cotton, timber, wheat, corn, cattle, and hogs. By 1836, 750 steamboats operated on American rivers.

> Water transportation: Steamboats

steamboats Ships and boats powered by wood-fired steam engines that made two-way traffic possible in eastern river systems, creating a transcontinental market and an agricultural empire.

TRAVELING THE WESTERN WATERS Steamboats traveling both ways on the Mississippi River created a transcontinental market and a commercial agricultural empire. Pictured here are steamboats docked on a levee on the Mississippi River.

The use of steamboats transformed St. Louis, Missouri, into a booming river port. New Orleans developed even faster. By 1840, it was perhaps the wealthiest American city, having generated a thriving trade with the Caribbean islands and the new Latin American republics that had overthrown Spanish rule. The annual amount of trade shipped through the river city doubled that of New York City by 1843, in large part because of the explosion in cotton production.

Wood-burning steamboats were a risky form of transportation, however. Accidents, explosions, and fires were common, and sanitation was poor. Passengers crowded on board along with pigs and cattle. There were no toilets on steamboats until the 1850s; passengers shared the same two washbasins and towels. Despite the inconveniences, however, steamboats were the fastest form of transportation in the first few decades of the nineteenth century.

Canals also sped the market revolution. The **Erie Canal** in central New York connected the Great Lakes and the Midwest to the Hudson River and New York City. New York governor DeWitt Clinton took the lead in promoting the risky project, boasting that New York had the opportunity to "create

> Water transportation: Canal systems

Erie Canal (1825) Most important and profitable of the many barge canals built in the early nineteenth century, connecting the Great Lakes to the Hudson River and making New York City the nation's largest port.

a new era in history, and to erect a work more stupendous, more magnificent, and more beneficial, than has hitherto been achieved by the human race."

It was not an idle boast. A "river of gold" flowed along the Erie Canal after it opened in 1825. It drew eastward much of the midwestern trade (furs, lumber, textiles) that earlier had been forced to go to Canada or make the long journey down the Ohio and Mississippi Rivers to New Orleans and the Gulf of Mexico. Thanks to the Erie Canal, the backwoods village of Chicago developed into a bustling city because of its commercial connection via the Great Lakes to New York City, and eventually to Europe.

The Erie Canal was an engineering triumph. Forty feet wide and four feet deep, it was the longest canal in the world, extending 363 miles across New York from Albany in the east to Buffalo and Lake Erie in the west, and rising some 675 feet in elevation. It crossed rivers and valleys, marshes and forests.

Thousands of laborers built the canal. They were mostly German and Irish immigrants who were paid less than a dollar a day to drain swamps, clear forests, build stone bridges and aqueducts (channels for carrying water), and blast through solid rock.

The canal unlocked the floodgates of western settlement and tied together the regional economies of the Midwest and the East while further isolating the Deep South. Transporting goods from Buffalo to New York City previously took three weeks; now it took only eight days. The canal also reduced the cost of moving a ton of freight from $100 to $5. It was so profitable that it paid off its construction costs in just seven years.

The success of the Erie Canal and the New York canal system inspired other states to build some 3,000 miles of waterways by 1837.

Railroads

> Railroads connect the continent

The canal era, however, was short-lived. During the second quarter of the nineteenth century, a more versatile and powerful form of transportation emerged: **railroads**. In 1825, the year the Erie Canal was completed, the world's first steam-powered railway began operating in England. Soon thereafter, a railroad-building craze struck the United States. In 1830, the nation had only 23 miles of railroad track. Over the next few decades, railroad coverage grew to 9,021 miles by 1850 and to 30,626 miles by 1860 (see Map 8.2).

The railroad quickly surpassed other forms of transportation because trains could carry more people and freight faster, farther, and more cheaply. The early railroads averaged 10 miles per hour, more than twice the speed of stagecoaches and up to four times that of boats and barges. Railroads could also operate year-round, which gave them a huge advantage over canals that froze over in winter and dirt roads that became rivers of mud during rainy seasons.

The building of railroads stimulated the national economy not only by improving transportation but also by creating a huge demand for iron, wooden cross-ties, bridges, locomotives, freight cars, and other equipment. Railroads also gave rise to new villages along their lines. The rail station became the central building in every town, a public place where people from all walks of life converged.

railroads Steam-powered vehicles that improved passenger transportation, quickened western settlement, and enabled commercial agriculture in the nineteenth century.

MAP 8.2 THE GROWTH OF RAILROADS, 1850 AND 1860

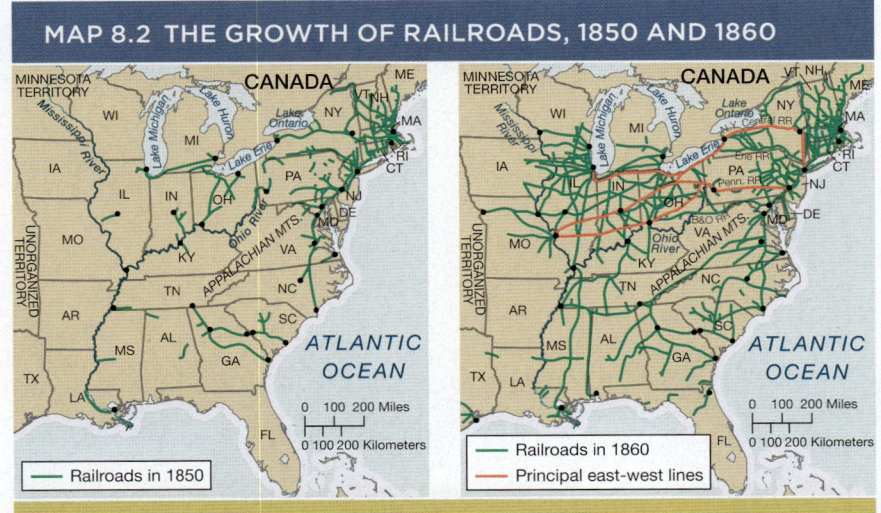

- Which section of the country experienced the most dramatic growth in railroad construction in the 1850s?
- Referring to Map 8.1, explain how railroads replaced canals as the principal mode of overland transportation.
- According to the chapter text, what role did railroads play in the economic and social development of the nation?

Perhaps most important, railroads expanded the geography of American capitalism, making possible larger industrial and commercial enterprises from coast to coast. Railroads were the first "big" businesses—huge corporations employing thousands of people while exercising extraordinary influence over the regions they served.

Railroad mania, however, had negative effects as well. Its quick profits frequently led to political corruption. Railroad titans often bribed legislators. By facilitating White Americans' access to the trans-Appalachian West, the railroads also threatened Indigenous American cultures.

Ocean Transportation

The year 1845 brought a great innovation in ocean transport with the launching of the first clipper ship, the *Rainbow*. Built for speed, **clipper ships** were the nineteenth-century equivalent of supersonic jetliners. The three-masted schooners were twice as fast as the older merchant ships. Long and lean, with sleek hulls, flat bottoms, taller masts, and more sails, they cut dashing figures during their brief but colorful career, which lasted less than two decades.

The American thirst for Chinese tea prompted the clipper boom. Asian tea leaves had to reach the market quickly after harvest, and fast clipper ships made this possible. Even more important, the discovery of gold in California in 1848 lured thousands of prospectors and entrepreneurs from the East on ships that sailed around South America's dangerous southern tip, Cape Horn. A clipper ship could make the trip in 123 days, some 80 days faster than a conventional ship. After the Civil War, however, the clipper ship—which lacked

> Ocean transportation: Clipper ships enable high-speed ocean travel

clipper ships Tall, slender ships favored over older merchant ships for their speed; ultimately gave way to steamships because clipper ships lacked cargo space.

BUILDING A CLIPPER SHIP This 1833 oil painting captures the Messrs. Smith & Co. Ship Yard in Manhattan, where shipbuilders are busy shaping timbers to construct a clipper ship.

ample cargo space—would give way to the steamship and the transcontinental railroad (see Chapter 16).

Communications

Innovations in transportation also helped spark improvements in communications, which knitted the nation even closer together. At the beginning of the nineteenth century, it took days—often weeks—for news to travel along the Atlantic seaboard. For example, after George Washington died in 1799 in Virginia, the news did not appear in New York City newspapers until a week later. By 1829, however, relay horse riders delivered President Andrew Jackson's inaugural address from Washington, D.C., to New York City in fewer than twenty hours.

Growth of newspapers

The number of newspapers soared. In 1790, there were 92 weekly newspapers; by 1810, there were 371, and many newspapers had become dailies. Most were affiliated with particular religious, political, or social groups. The first African American newspaper, *Freedom's Journal*, was founded in 1827 in New York as a platform for abolition and equal rights for Black people; while the first Indigenous newspaper, the *Cherokee Phoenix*, appeared the following year. In addition, new steam-powered printing presses reduced the cost of newspapers from 6¢ to a penny each, enabling virtually everyone to benefit from the news contained in the "penny press."

America published more newspapers than other nations—twice as many as Great Britain alone. When a British traveler asked a milkman in Cincinnati

PONY EXPRESS Founded in 1860, the Pony Express Company pledged speedy delivery of mail from Missouri to as far west as California, relying on a relay team of 400 horses. In this hand-colored woodcut based on Frederic Remington's oil painting, Pony Express riders are shown changing horses.

why Americans spent so much time reading newspapers, he quickly replied: "How should freemen spend their time, but looking after their government, and watching that them fellers as we give offices to, does their duty?"

Mail deliveries also improved. The number of U.S. post offices soared from 75 in 1790 to 3,459 in 1817. In the new western states and territories, however, postal service was scarce and slow. To address the problem, two 1852 entrepreneurs, Henry Wells and William G. Fargo, formed an express delivery service called Wells Fargo & Company that was powered by horse-drawn stagecoaches. By 1857, Wells Fargo formed the Overland Mail Company, establishing regular twice-a-week mail service between St. Louis and San Francisco. Prior to that innovation, mail service was twice a month by steamship.

> Expansion of the postal service

Still, people sought even faster delivery. In 1860, Alexander Majors, William Russell, and William B. Waddell founded the Pony Express Company to deliver mail cross-country between St. Joseph, Missouri, and Sacramento, California—a distance of more than 1,800 miles—by horse rather than by wagon. Majors, Russell, and Waddell acquired 400 fast horses and established 184 relay stations from Missouri west to California, enabling their 120 riders to change horses every ten to fifteen miles. The Pony Express riders set their fastest time delivering Abraham Lincoln's presidential inaugural address in 1861, which arrived in California in eight days. Riding alone, day and night, across western prairies, deserts, and snow-covered mountains was a dangerous enterprise for riders and horses alike. They also became targets for Indigenous raiders trying to halt the expansion of White Americans into western lands.

> The Pony Express

The Pony Express Company, however, lasted only eighteen months. It was driven out of business by the most important advance in communications: the creation of a national electromagnetic **telegraph system**. Samuel F. B. Morse, its portrait-painter-turned-inventor, sent the first intercity

telegraph system System of electronic communication invented by Samuel F. B. Morse that could transmit messages instantaneously across great distances.

telegraph message from Washington, D.C., to Baltimore, Maryland in May 1844. It read: "What hath God wrought?"

> **New telegraph lines span the continent**

By the end of the 1840s, most major cities benefited from telegraph lines; by 1861 the telegraph spanned the continent, connecting the Pacific Coast to cities in the East. A New Orleans newspaper claimed that with the invention of the telegraph, "scarcely anything now will appear to be impossible."

The Role of Government

> **Government financing for internal improvements**

Between 1800 and 1860, an undeveloped nation of scattered farms, primitive roads, and modest local markets became an engine of capitalist expansion, urban energy, and global reach.

The transportation improvements that made all this growth possible were financed by both state governments and private investors. The national government bought stock in turnpike and canal companies and, after the success of the Erie Canal, awarded land grants to western states to support canal and railroad projects. In 1850, Stephen A. Douglas, a powerful Democratic senator from Illinois, convinced Congress to provide a major land grant to support a north–south rail line connecting Chicago and Mobile, Alabama. The 1850 congressional land grant set a precedent for other bounties that totaled about 20 million acres by 1860.

All of this investment transformed the nation's capitalist economy in the first half of the nineteenth century. The agrarian nation of independent small farmers once envisioned by Thomas Jefferson had given way to a network of paved roads, navigable rivers, canals, and railroads that facilitated the movement of people and goods from the old Northeast to the more sparsely settled regions of the West. Self-sufficient households were now connected to far-flung markets; and with new innovations in transportation, communications, and manufacturing, the nation was quickly evolving into an industrial powerhouse.

Industrial Development

> **CORE OBJECTIVE**
> **2.** Explain the impact of the Industrial Revolution on the way people worked and lived.

The concentration of huge numbers of people in cities, coupled with the transportation and communication revolutions, greatly increased the number of potential customers for a given product. This in turn gave rise to *mass production*, whereby companies used new technologies (labor-saving machines) to produce greater quantities of products, which could thereby be sold at lower prices while generating higher profits. The innovation of water-powered mills and coal-powered steam engines sparked an Industrial Revolution in Europe and America from the mid-eighteenth century to the late nineteenth century.

Industrial Revolution Major shift in the nineteenth century from handmade manufacturing to mass production in mills and factories using water-, coal-, and steam-powered machinery.

The **Industrial Revolution**, centered on the invention of the steam engine, was the most important economic development in human history since the advent of agriculture. Prior to 1800, most products were handmade by skilled artisans.

Now, factories, mills, mines, and industrial plants emerged to replace the artisans and craftspeople making clothing, shoes, clocks and watches, furniture, firearms, and an array of other items. "It is an extraordinary era in which we live," reported Daniel Webster in 1847. "It is altogether new. The world has seen nothing like it before."

American Technology

During the nineteenth century, Americans became known for their "practical" inventiveness. Between 1790 and 1811, the U.S. Patent Office approved an annual average of seventy-seven patents certifying new inventions; by the 1850s, the Patent Office was approving more than 28,000 new inventions each year.

"Practical" inventiveness

Many inventions generated dramatic changes. In 1844, for example, Charles Goodyear patented a process for "vulcanizing" rubber, which made the product stronger, more elastic, waterproof, and winter-proof. Vulcanized rubber was used for a variety of products, from shoes and boots to seals, gaskets, hoses, and eventually tires.

In 1846, Elias Howe patented his design of the sewing machine. It was soon improved upon by Isaac Merritt Singer, who founded the Singer Sewing Machine Company, which initially produced only industrial sewing machines for use in textile mills but eventually offered portable machines for home use. Sewing machines helped transform everyday life for many women by dramatically reducing the time needed to make clothes at home.

The promise of simplifying basic household tasks turned women into inventors too. In the first half of the nineteenth century, women earned patents for spinning-wheel parts and corset designs, as well as a machine that wove straw into hats. The problem of making ice cream set Nancy Johnson to work at her home in Philadelphia. Realizing that only elite households could make ice cream—since one had to own a separate building for storing ice (an icehouse) in order to do so—Johnson designed a small, hand-cranked freezer that enabled ordinary families to make ice cream for generations to come.

Technological advances improved living conditions because houses could be better heated and better illuminated. The first sewer systems also helped clean up cities by ridding streets of human and animal waste.

The Cotton Gin

One invention launched an economic revolution. In 1792, Eli Whitney, a recent Yale graduate from New England, spent several months at Mulberry Grove Plantation on the Georgia coast, where he "heard much said of the difficulty of ginning cotton." Cotton had been used for clothing and bedding from ancient times, but cotton cloth

NANCY JOHNSON Nancy Marie Donaldson Johnson patented the first hand-cranked ice cream freezer in 1843. In addition to being an inventor, she was also a teacher; during the Civil War, she moved from Philadelphia to Port Royal, South Carolina, to work at a school for people newly freed from slavery.

was rare and expensive because it took so long to "gin"—that is, to separate the lint (cotton fibers) from the sticky seeds. One person working all day could process barely one pound by hand.

The owner of Mulberry Grove was a woman named Catherine Greene, a Rhode Island native and widow of the general Nathanael Greene, who had been granted their Georgia land as compensation for his military service in the Revolutionary War. Catherine Greene encouraged Whitney to find another way of extracting the seeds and gave him the space and tools he needed to begin tinkering. It is also believed that the plantation's enslaved people gave him ideas for designing a new machine. Within a year, Whitney produced what he called "an absurdly simple contrivance" that used nails attached to a roller to remove the seeds from cotton bolls. Completed in 1793, the **cotton gin** (short for engine) proved to be fifty times more productive than a hand laborer.

Almost overnight, Whitney's gin transformed cotton from simply a local crop to a global industry led by the American South. Whitney, however, never made a fortune from it, despite patenting the design in 1794. Others imitated his invention, and a series of lawsuits funded by Greene failed and left Whitney with next to nothing. "My situation," he wrote, "makes me perfectly miserable."

King Cotton

During the first half of the nineteenth century, southern-grown **cotton** became the dominant force driving both the national economy and the controversial efforts to expand slavery into the western territories. People called it "white gold" for the enormous wealth that cotton generated.

Slavery expanded accordingly. The number of enslaved people increased from just under 700,000 in 1790 to nearly 4 million on the eve of the American Civil War; approximately 70 percent were involved in some way with cotton production. So closely tied were cotton and slavery that the price of an enslaved person directly correlated to the price of cotton. The commercial growing of cotton spread plantation slavery across the South, especially the Carolinas, Georgia, Tennessee, Alabama, Mississippi, Louisiana, Arkansas, and Texas.

By the mid-nineteenth century, people worldwide were wearing more-comfortable and easier-to-clean cotton clothing. When British textile manufacturers chose the less brittle American cotton over the varieties grown in the Caribbean, Brazil, and India, the demand for southern cotton skyrocketed, as did its price. By 1860, British textile mills were processing a billion pounds of cotton a year, 77 percent of which came from the southern states. On the eve of the Civil War, cotton represented 60 percent of America's exports.

People from all across the nation—and the world—became invested in the southern cotton boom. Cotton spurred the development of textile mills in New England; expanded the shipping fleets of New York City; and made the ports of New Orleans, Mobile, Savannah, and Charleston sources

CATHERINE LITTLEFIELD GREENE The wife of revolutionary war hero General Nathanael Greene, she played a significant role in managing their southern plantation after the war. She also established a workshop for inventor Eli Whitney and helped him perfect the final features of the cotton gin.

> American cotton becomes an international commodity

cotton gin Hand-operated machine invented by Eli Whitney that quickly removed seeds from cotton bolls, enabling the mass production of cotton in nineteenth-century America.

cotton White fibers harvested from plants that made comfortable, easy-to-clean products, especially clothing; the most valuable cash crop driving the economy in nineteenth-century United States and Great Britain.

of enormous profits for the regional and national economies. The South harvested raw cotton; and northern buyers and shipowners carried it to New England, Great Britain, and France, where textile mills spun the fiber into thread and fabric. Some of that fabric, sewn into clothing and hats, then returned to the South to clothe the enslaved people who had cultivated its cotton fiber.

The seemingly distinct economic systems of the North and South—industrial and agricultural—were in fact deeply interconnected in the expanding system of cotton capitalism. Northern insurance companies, such as Aetna Insurance Company, issued life insurance policies to protect Southern slave owners in the case of an enslaved person's death. Northern banks issued loans to southern planters that, in the case of a planter's default, gave the banks ownership of enslaved people. The capital flowing out of northern, as well as European, institutions financed the growth of global cotton capitalism.

The Expansion of Slavery

Cotton remained a labor-intensive crop, even with the invention of the cotton gin, and growers were convinced that only enslaved people could make their farms and plantations profitable. They purchased enslaved people who had been forced into the cotton-growing regions of Georgia, Alabama, and Mississippi by slave traders, who took them from Virginia, Maryland, and Kentucky. By 1860, close to a million enslaved people had been "sold south" in what is known as the domestic slave trade (see Chapter 11).

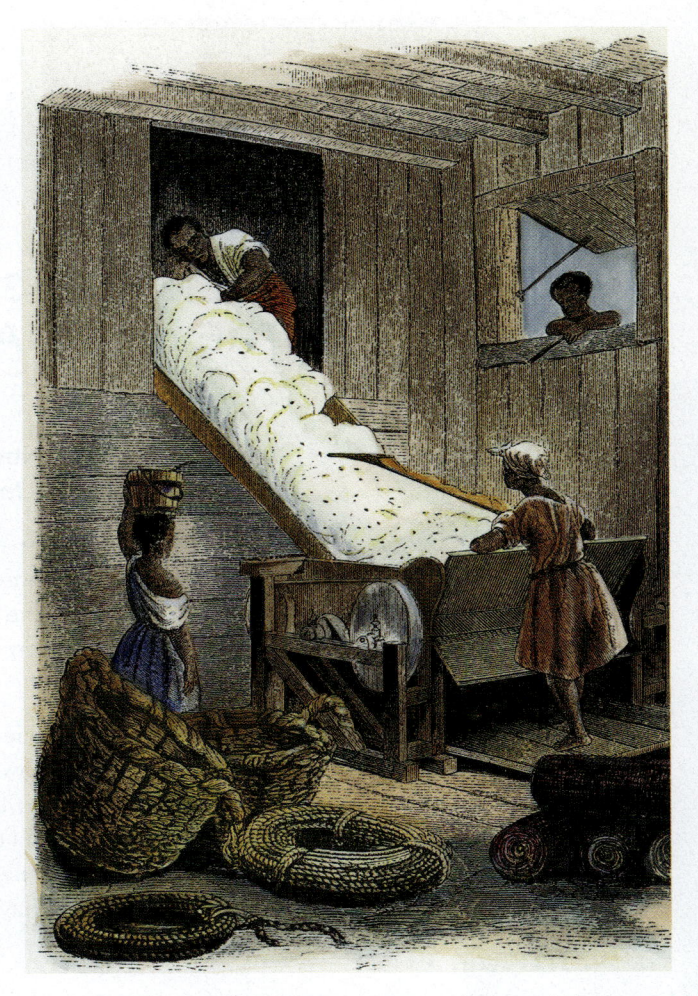

COTTON GIN Before Eli Whitney's cotton gin, it would have taken days for the four enslaved people in this engraving to pick through the avalanche of cotton depicted here and separate the cotton seeds from the fibers. **How did the cotton gin affect the economy of the South and, more broadly, the nation?**

Enslaved peoples' arrival in the cotton-growing states created boom times in the Deep South, where land was also cheaper than it was in the East. A cotton farmer in Mississippi urged a friend in Kentucky to sell his farm and join him: "If you could reconcile it to yourself to bring your negroes to the Mississippi Territory, they would certainly make you a handsome fortune in ten years by the cultivation of Cotton." Enslaved people became so valuable that stealing them became a common problem. Slave owners also resorted to violent coercion—whippings, sexual assaults, separating children from their mothers—to make sure they extracted as much profit as possible from each individual.

Farming the Midwest

By 1860, more than half of Americans lived west of the Appalachian Mountains. The fertile farmlands in the Midwest—Ohio, Michigan, Indiana,

Comparing PERSPECTIVES

TECHNOLOGY AND EXPANSION IN THE NEW NATION

From: Letter from Nemesio Salcedo to Juan Bautista Elguézabal, governor of Texas, January 15, 1805.

This letter marks the introduction of the cotton gin to the Spanish province of Texas. Nemesio Salcedo, commandant of Mexico's northern provinces, writes to the governor of Texas seeking assistance in importing the machinery from the United States and ushering in a new era of cotton cultivation.

I remit to you the attached petition in which Don Geronimo Maceyra solicits a license so that on his own account he can introduce, from Louisiana, twelve pairs of cotton gins; so that through the utility that the establishment of said machines for which they are destined will provide this country, you are able to not only make the commandant at Nacogdoches aware to allow their introduction but also have him endorse their remittance, from that town to this capital.

From: Charles Sumner, "Speech for Union Among Men of All Parties Against the Slave Power, and the Extension of Slavery, in a Mass Convention at Worcester," June 28, 1848.

Charles Sumner chastises the "Slave Power" (proslavery political leaders) at a political convention in Worchester, Massachusetts, in 1848. Sumner—a leading abolitionist and future U.S. senator—tells his audience that the institution of slavery has laid a curse on their land and threatens the nation's expansion to the Pacific Ocean. Texas, formerly a province of New Spain, was an independent republic from 1836 to 1845, when it was annexed by the United States, leading to the Mexican-American War (1846–1848).

. . . It is during late years, that the Slave Power has introduced a new test for office—a test which would have excluded Washington, Jefferson, and Franklin. It applies an arrogant and unrelenting ostracism to all who express themselves against Slavery. And now . . . it proposes to extend this curse to new soils not darkened by its presence. It seeks to make the flag of our country the carrier of Slavery into distant lands; to scale the mountain fastnesses of Oregon, and descend with its prey upon the shores of the Pacific; to cross the Rio Grande, and there, in broad territories, recently obtained by robber hands from Mexico, to plant a shameful institution, which that republic has expressly abolished.

. . . [I]t was the secret influence which went forth from among ourselves, that contributed powerfully to this consummation. Yes! It was brought about by an unhallowed union—conspiracy, rather let it be called—between two remote sections of the country—between the politicians of the South-West and the politicians of the North-East; between the cotton planters and flesh-mongers of Louisiana and Mississippi, and the cotton spinners and traffickers of New England; between the lords of the lash and the lords of the loom.

And now the question occurs, What is the true line of duty with regard to these two candidates? Though nominated by different parties, they represent, as I have said, substantially the same interest—the Slave Power. The election of either would be a triumph of the Slave Power, and entail upon the country, in all probability, the sin of extending slavery. . . .

Questions

1. How does Maceyra's petition reflect the technological edge that the United States enjoyed over Spain?

2. According to Sumner, why does the economy of the North-East, in addition to the Southwest, stand to benefit from the extension of slavery in the West?

3. What do the two documents say about the relationship between slavery and technology?

Illinois, and Iowa—drew farmers from the rocky hillsides of New England and the exhausted soils of Virginia. They were eager to make a fresh start on their *own* land made available by the government.

> **Squatters' claims on western farmland**

A national land law of 1820 reduced the price of federal land. However, even that was not enough for westerners. They demanded "preemption," the right of squatters (people who simply built a cabin and started farming without actually purchasing government land) to buy land at the minimum price; and "graduation," the progressive reduction of the price of land that did not sell immediately. Congress eventually responded with two bills. Under the Preemption Act of 1830, squatters could get 160 acres at the minimum price of $1.25 per acre. Under the Graduation Act of 1854, prices of unsold lands were to be lowered in stages over thirty years.

> **New technologies drive commercial agriculture**

Technology also enabled greater agricultural productivity. The development of durable iron plows (rather than wooden plows) eased the backbreaking job of tilling the soil. Vermonter John Deere's steel plow (1837) improved on that basic design with sharp edges that could cut through the tough prairie grass in the Midwest and the Great Plains. By 1845, Massachusetts alone had seventy-three plants making more than 60,000 plows per year. Most were sold to western farmers, illustrating the emergence of a national marketplace for goods and services.

Other technological improvements quickened the growth of large-scale commercial agriculture. By the 1840s, new mechanical seeders had replaced the process of sowing seed by hand. In 1831, twenty-two-year-old Virginian Cyrus Hall McCormick invented a horse-pulled mechanical reaper to harvest wheat, a development as significant to the agricultural economy of the Midwest, Old Northwest, and Great Plains as the cotton gin was to the South.

McCORMICK'S REAPING MACHINE This illustration appeared in the catalog of the Great Exhibition held at the Crystal Palace in London in 1851. The plow eased the transformation of rough plains into fertile farmland, and the reaping machine accelerated the harvesting of hay, wheat, and other grains.

In 1847, **McCormick reapers** were selling so fast that its inventor moved to Chicago and built a manufacturing plant that produced 4,000 machines a year. McCormick reapers transformed the scale of commercial agriculture. Using a handheld sickle, a farmer could harvest a half-acre of wheat a day; with a McCormick reaper, two people could cut twelve acres a day.

McCormick reapers Mechanical reapers invented by Cyrus Hall McCormick in 1831 that dramatically increased the production of wheat.

Early Textile Manufacturers

While technological breakthroughs such as the cotton gin, mechanical harvester, and railroads accelerated agricultural development and enabled a national economy, other technologies altered the economic landscape even more profoundly.

Industrial capitalists who financed and built the first factories transformed the nature of work. People had never before labored for twelve-hour shifts in large windowless buildings filled with deafening machines and hundreds of sweating workers. The informal routine of farmwork was replaced by the close supervision of managers and the regimentation signaled by the factory whistle and the time clock.

Mills and factories were powered initially by water wheels and later by coal-fired steam engines. The shift from river water to coal sped the growth rate of the textile industry (and industries of all types) and initiated an Industrial Revolution destined to end Great Britain's domination of the world economy.

Rise of the factory system: Steam-powered mills

By 1815, hundreds of textile mills in New England, New York, and Pennsylvania were producing thread, cloth, and clothing. By 1860, the output of America's mills and factories would be one-third, and by 1880 two-thirds, that of Great Britain.

Promoting Industry through Tariffs

New government protections supported this growth. New England mill owners, concerned about cheap British cloth flooding into American markets after the War of 1812, pressed Congress to impose a federal tariff (tax) on imported cloth. This would deter the British from selling their cloth in the United States for less than the prices charged by American manufacturers.

Import tariffs to promote American-made textiles

The mill owners neglected to admit that tariffs hurt consumers by forcing them to pay higher prices for imported goods. Over time, as Scotsman Adam Smith explained in his pathbreaking book on capitalism, *The Wealth of Nations* (1776), consumers not only pay higher prices for imported goods as a result of tariffs but also pay higher prices for domestic goods, since businesses invariably take advantage of opportunities to raise the prices charged for their products.

Tariffs helped protect American industries from foreign competition. But New England shipping companies opposed higher tariffs because they would reduce the amount of goods sent from Britain and Europe. Many southerners opposed tariffs because of fears that Britain and France would retaliate with tariffs on American cotton and tobacco shipped to their ports.

In the end, Congress passed the Tariff of 1816, which placed a tax on imported cloth. Such tariffs were a major factor in spurring industrialization.

MILL GIRLS Massachusetts mill workers of the mid-nineteenth century, photographed holding the shuttles needed to weave thread into fabric using a power loom. *What sort of working conditions would these and other Lowell girls have experienced?*

Tolerable living conditions

Lowell system Model New England factory communities that provided employees—mostly young women—with meals, a boardinghouse, moral discipline, and educational opportunities.

By impeding foreign competition, they enabled American manufacturers to dominate the national marketplace.

The Lowell System

The factory system first emerged at Waltham, Massachusetts, in 1813, when a group known as the Boston Associates constructed the first textile mill in which the mechanized processes of spinning yarn and weaving cloth (copied from English mills) were brought together under one roof. In 1822, the Boston Associates, led by Francis Cabot Lowell, developed another cotton mill at a village along the Merrimack River twenty-eight miles north of Boston, which they renamed Lowell. It soon became the model for mill towns throughout New England, often referred to as the **Lowell system**.

The founders of the Lowell system sought to develop ideal industrial communities. To avoid the wretched conditions of the overcrowded English textile-mill villages, they located their four- and five-story brick-built mills along rivers in the countryside and lined the streets with trees and tidy flower beds.

Women—mostly young women from farm families—became the first factory workers in the nation. Mill owners preferred women because of their dexterity in operating machines and their willingness to endure the mind-numbing boredom of operating spinning machines and looms for a wage of $2.50 per week—a wage lower than that paid to men for the same work. Many, perhaps most, of the young women viewed their work in mills as temporary. "There are few who look upon factory labor as a pursuit for life," one of them reported. "It is but a temporary vocation; and most of the girls resolve to quit the Mill. . . . Money is their object."

Whatever their motives, in the early 1820s a steady stream of young girls and single women began flocking to Lowell. To reassure worried parents, mill owners promised to provide the "Lowell girls" with tolerable work, competitive wages, comfortable boardinghouses (four girls to a room), moral discipline, and educational opportunities.

Initially the "Lowell idea" worked. Visitors commented on the well-designed mills, with their lecture halls and libraries. The "Lowell girls" were "neatly dressed" and appeared "healthy and happy." They lived in dormitories staffed by "virtuous" matrons who enforced strict rules regarding contact with men, evening curfews, and mandatory church attendance. Despite thirteen-hour workdays and five-and-a-half-day workweeks, some women still found the time and energy to form study groups, write poetry, publish a literary magazine, and attend lectures.

Lowell lost its innocence, however, as it grew more profitable. By 1832, some 500 cotton mills were operating in New England. Eight years later, Lowell had come to house 8,000 textile workers. The once clean and tidy rural village had become a grimy industrial city, and the repetitive routine of tending a spinning machine or a loom all day led to boredom and fatigue. Greed prompted mill owners to produce too much cloth, which depressed prices. The owners slashed wages and quickened the pace of work. One worker described the situation as constituting "factory tyranny."

Protests by Lowell Women

In 1834, the Lowell women went on strike to protest wage cuts and deteriorating working and living conditions. The angry mill owners labeled the hundreds of striking women "ungrateful" and "unfeminine"—and tried to get rid of the strike's leaders. One mill manager reported that "we have paid off several of these Amazons [female warriors in ancient Greece] & presume that they will leave town on Monday."

The workers lost the strike. Two years later, however, the Lowell women again walked out to protest rent increases in company-owned boardinghouses. This time the owners backed down. Over time, however, the owners began hiring Irish immigrants who were so desperate for jobs that they rarely complained about the working conditions. By 1850, some 40 percent of the mill workers were Irish, and the mill owners also started hiring boys for jobs once reserved for girls.

Women's Work and the Household

Industrialization brought other changes to the ways in which women worked, especially in northern cities.

Now that men had more opportunities to earn a living outside the home—in a factory or business—the household no longer had to be a place where men and women worked side by side, as they had on a farm. The home could now become a woman's "sphere," a place where she could focus her attention on nurturing children rather than on making money. The belief that this private sphere should remain distinct from the public, male-dominated world of work and politics was known as *separate spheres* (see also Chapter 12).

Only the middle and upper classes could aspire to this ideal, however. Working-class women still had to work to support their families financially, though some factory owners increasingly insisted that they work at home. Through the "putting-out" or "piecework" system, employers gave seamstresses unfinished garments to finish in their homes, on their own sewing machines, and then paid the women for each "piece" completed. Piecework was particularly common among immigrant women in New York. It kept them close to their children, but at a cost: They usually worked fifteen-to-eighteen-hour days in dark and crowded tenement housing, bending over machines that left them with strained arms and chronic pain.

> Working-class women support families through piecework

Free Black women in cities such as Baltimore developed a similar labor system while working as laundresses. Though some had been forced to launder clothes while enslaved, now, as free women, they turned that skill into a business and brought laundry into their homes. It was difficult and often

MAP 8.3 THE GROWTH OF INDUSTRY IN THE 1840S

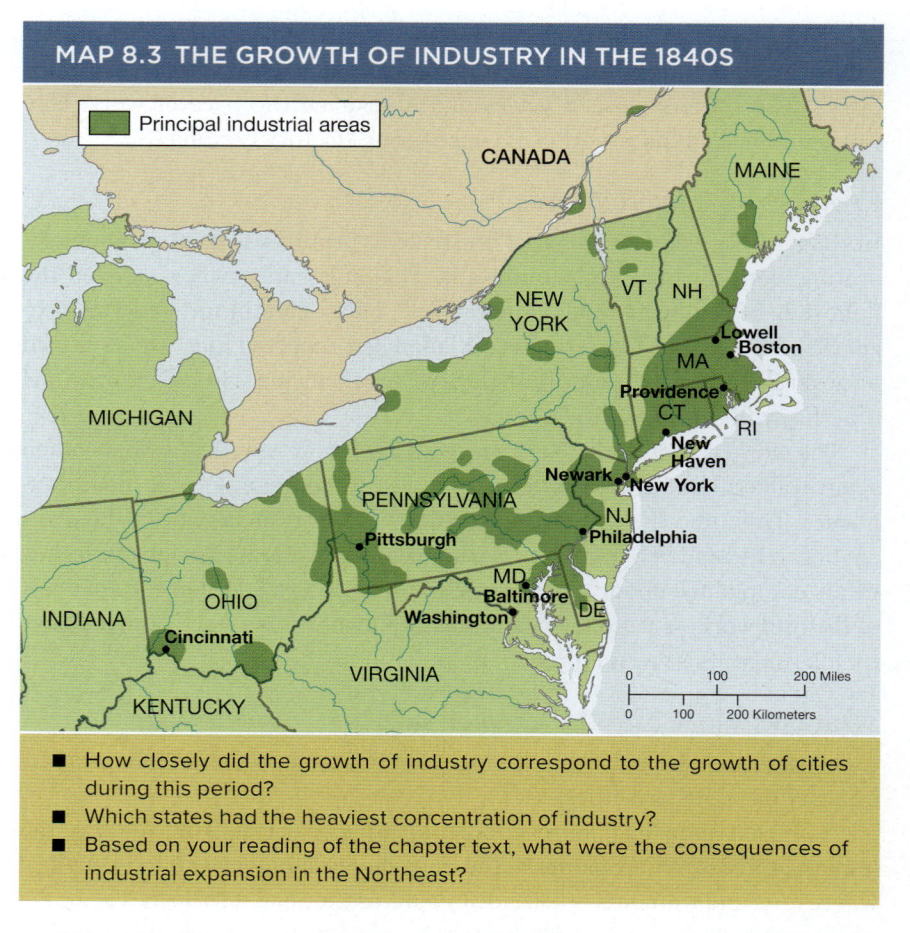

- How closely did the growth of industry correspond to the growth of cities during this period?
- Which states had the heaviest concentration of industry?
- Based on your reading of the chapter text, what were the consequences of industrial expansion in the Northeast?

backbreaking physical labor, but it also brought some measure of relief to work independently without the direct supervision of an employer.

Industrialization, Cities, and the Environment

Urban growth

The rapid growth of commerce and industry spurred the growth of cities and mill villages. Lowell's population in 1820 was 200. By 1830, it was 6,500, and ten years later it had soared to 21,000. Other factory centers sprouted up across New England and into other northern and midwestern states, displacing forests, farms, and villages while filling the air with smoke, noise, and stench (see Map 8.3). Between 1820 and 1840, the number of city dwellers more than doubled.

The Atlantic seaports—including New York City, Philadelphia, Baltimore, and Boston—remained the largest cities. New Orleans became the nation's fifth largest because of its role in shipping goods down the Mississippi River to the East Coast and to Europe. New York, however, outpaced all its competitors in growth. By 1860, it was the first city whose population surpassed more than 1 million, largely because of its superior harbor and its access to the commerce floating down the Hudson River from the Erie Canal (see Map 8.4).

MAP 8.4 THE GROWTH OF CITIES, 1820 AND 1860

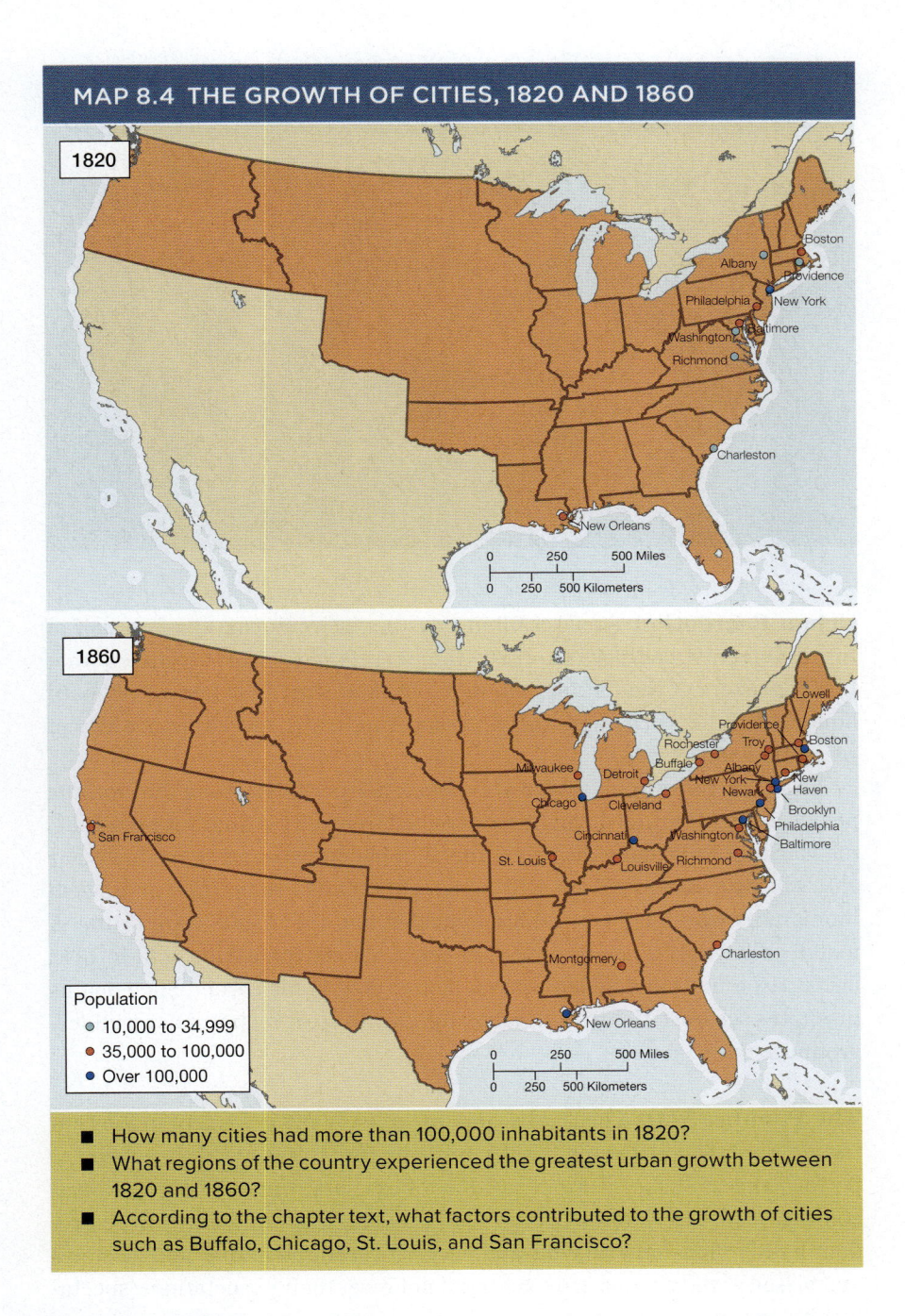

- How many cities had more than 100,000 inhabitants in 1820?
- What regions of the country experienced the greatest urban growth between 1820 and 1860?
- According to the chapter text, what factors contributed to the growth of cities such as Buffalo, Chicago, St. Louis, and San Francisco?

Popular Culture

During the colonial era, working-class Americans had little time for amusement. Most adults worked from dawn to dusk six days a week. In rural areas, free time was often spent in communal activities, such as barn raisings, shooting matches, and footraces. By the early nineteenth century, however, an increasingly urban society enjoyed more diverse forms of recreation.

BARE-KNUCKLE BOXING Blood sports such as "bare-knuckle boxing," portrayed here in a contemporary painting by George A. Hayes, emerged as popular urban entertainment for men of all social classes, but especially among the working poor.

Urban Recreation Social drinking was pervasive during the first half of the nineteenth century. In 1829, the secretary of war estimated that three-quarters of the nation's laborers drank at least four ounces of "hard liquor" daily. Taverns and social or sporting clubs served as centers of recreation and leisure.

So-called blood sports were also popular, especially among the working poor. Cockfighting and dogfighting attracted frenzied betting, but prizefighting (boxing) eventually displaced the animal contests and proved popular with all social classes. The early contestants tended to be Irish or English immigrants who fought with bare knuckles, and the results were brutal. A match ended only when a contestant could not continue. One bout in 1842 lasted 119 rounds and ended when a fighter died in his corner. Such deaths prompted several cities to outlaw boxing, only to see it reappear as an underground activity.

The Popular Arts Theater became the most popular form of indoor entertainment. People from all walks of life flocked to see a wide spectrum of performances: Shakespeare's tragedies, "blood and thunder" melodramas, comedies, minstrel shows, operas, and local pageants. Audiences were predominantly men—and raucous audiences cheered the heroes and heroines and hissed at the villains. If an actor did not meet their expectations, spectators hurled curses, nuts, eggs, fruit, shoes, or chairs.

By the 1830s, theater transformed itself into a more respectable artistic pursuit, and women and girls increasingly sat in audiences—and appeared on stage. Fanny Kemble, born into a prominent British theater family, rose to American stardom after performing on a theatrical tour of the United States in 1832. Adoring fans quickly began styling their hair in "Fanny Kemble curls" and were willing to accept her pursuit of a visible career outside of the home.

The 1830s also brought the first uniquely American form of mass entertainment: "blackface" minstrel shows, featuring White performers who put black paint on their faces and mocked Black people. "Minstrelsy" featured banjo and fiddle music, "shuffle" dances, and lowbrow humor. Between the 1830s and the 1870s, minstrel shows were popular among northern working-class ethnic groups and southern Whites.

The most popular minstrel songs were written by a White composer named Stephen Foster. In 1846, he composed "Oh! Susanna," which became so popular that it catapulted Foster into the limelight. He responded with other tunes such as "Old Folks at Home" (popularly known as "Way Down upon the Swanee River"), "My Old Kentucky Home," and "Old Black Joe," all of which perpetuated sentimental, racist myths of happy enslaved people who were loyal to their owners.

American society was transformed by the Industrial Revolution that also turned the United States into a global economic force. An array of technological innovations, from the cotton gin to home ice-cream freezers, revolutionized life both on the nation's farms and in its mushrooming cities. Meanwhile, the importance of the southern cotton crop to the global economy, and the related expansion of New England's textile industry, led to the dramatic growth of slavery and the increasing participation of women in the workforce. Urbanization and the proliferation of factories thus brought widespread prosperity, but at significant social and environmental cost.

FANNY KEMBLE Fanny Kemble (1809–1893) stepped away from acting in 1834 to marry a South Carolina planter, Pierce Butler. But problems in the marriage, along with her opposition to her husband's dependence on slavery, led Kemble to divorce him and return to England as an abolitionist.

Immigration

> **CORE OBJECTIVE**
> **3.** Analyze how immigration altered the nation's population and shaped its politics.

During the forty years between the outbreak of the American Revolution and the end of the War of 1812, immigration to America had slowed to a trickle. The French Revolution and the Napoleonic Wars restricted travel to and from Europe until 1815. Thereafter, however, the number of immigrants rose steadily. They were eager to experience the so-called American dream—the seductive promise that in the United States, every person had the chance to improve their life.

After 1837, a worldwide financial panic and economic slump accelerated the pace of immigration. American employers, especially those in free states who did not rely on enslaved labor, aggressively recruited foreigners, believing they would work for lower wages than native-born Americans would. The *Chicago Daily Tribune* observed that the tide of German immigrants was perfect for the "cheap and ingenious labor of the country."

MAP 8.5 POPULATION DENSITY, 1820 AND 1860

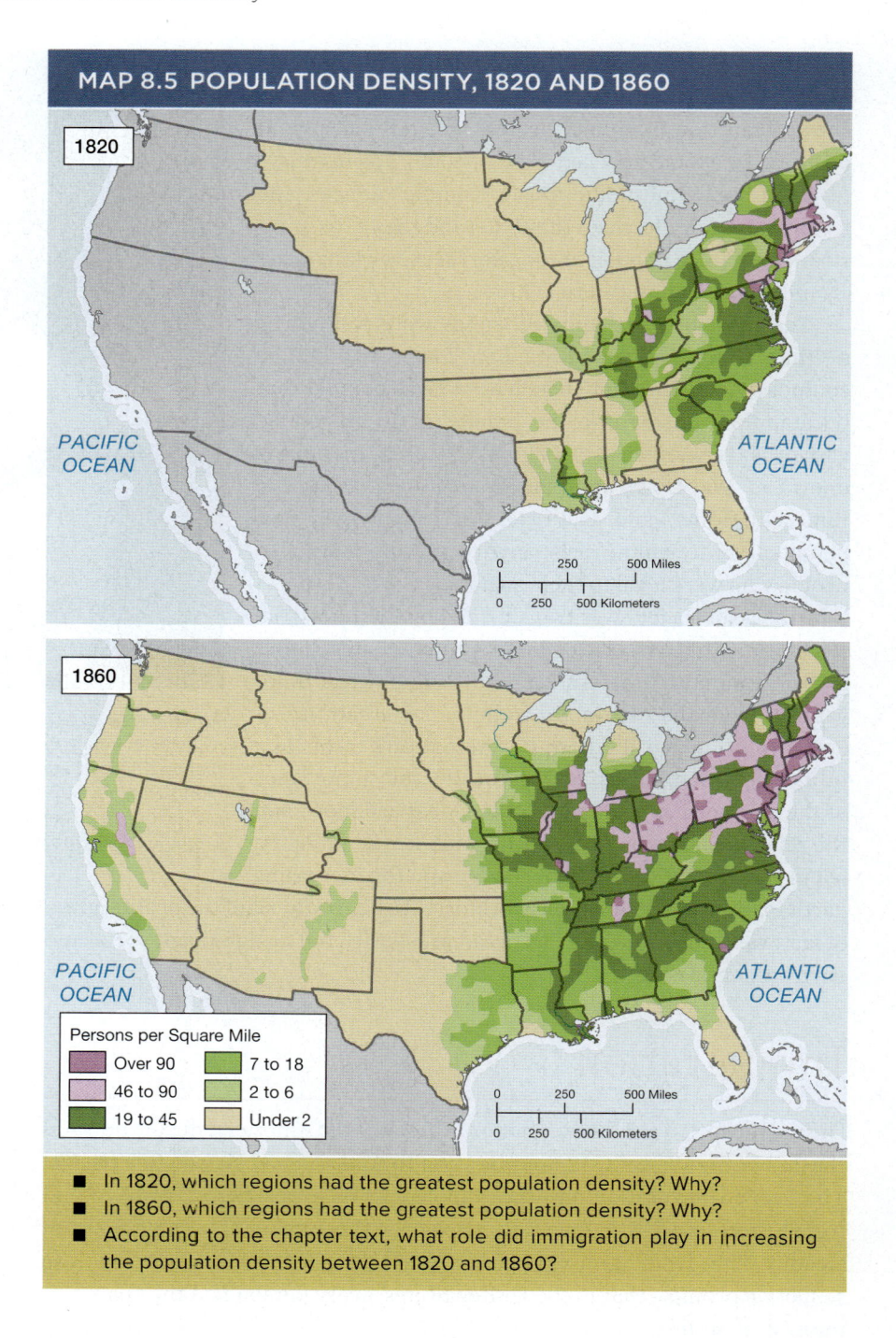

Persons per Square Mile
- Over 90
- 46 to 90
- 19 to 45
- 7 to 18
- 2 to 6
- Under 2

- In 1820, which regions had the greatest population density? Why?
- In 1860, which regions had the greatest population density? Why?
- According to the chapter text, what role did immigration play in increasing the population density between 1820 and 1860?

The rapid development of California lured Chinese immigrants in significant numbers; while Scandinavians settled mostly in Wisconsin and Minnesota, where the climate and woodlands reminded them of home. By 1860, more than one of every eight Americans was foreign-born (see Map 8.5).

The Irish

No nation proportionately sent more of its people to America than Ireland. They first arrived in British America in significant numbers during the 1720s. By the mid-nineteenth century, however, their numbers soared. A prolonged agricultural crisis that brought immense social hardships caused many Irish to flee their homeland.

Irish farmers primarily grew potatoes; the average Irishman ate five pounds of potatoes a day. In 1845, a fungus destroyed the potato crop and triggered the potato famine. More than a million people died, and almost 2 million more left Ireland, whose total population was only 8 million.

Most Irish immigrants—almost all of them Roman Catholics—traveled to Canada and the United States. In just one year, Boston's Irish population jumped from 30,000 to 100,000. As one group of immigrants explained, "All we want to do is get out of Ireland; we must be better anywhere but here." America, they knew, had paying jobs and plenty to eat.

By the 1850s, Irish people made up more than half the population of Boston and New York City, and were almost as dominant in Philadelphia. Most were desperately poor and crowded into filthy tenement houses. Irish neighborhoods were plagued by diseases, alcoholism, and crime. Almost 80 percent of infants born to Irish immigrants died.

The Irish often took on the hardest and most dangerous jobs. A visiting Irish journalist wrote that there were "several sorts of power working at the fabric of the Republic: water-power, steam-power, horse-power, and Irish power. The last works hardest of them all." It was mostly Irish men who built the canals and railroads, and mostly Irish women who worked as live-in household servants for middle- and upper-class families.

> Irish immigration: Unskilled and dangerous labor

Rise of Anti-Immigrant Prejudice

Irish immigrants confronted humiliating stereotypes and intense anti-Catholic prejudice. Many employers posted signs reading "No Irish Need Apply." Anti-Catholic and anti-Irish newspapers and magazines emerged in every major city. A New England magazine called the thousands of Irish immigrants pouring into the region "the most corrupt, debased, and the most brutally ignorant" race in America.

Irish Americans, however, could be equally prejudiced toward other groups in the United States, such as free African Americans, who competed with them for low-wage jobs. In 1850, the *New York Tribune* expressed concern that the Irish, having escaped from "a galling, degrading bondage" in their homeland, voted against proposals for equal rights for Blacks and frequently arrived at the polls shouting, "Down with the Colored people!"

Many African Americans viewed the Irish with similar contempt. Irish immigrants in large cities often took jobs as waiters, dock workers, and deliverymen that had long been held by African Americans. The Irish, said one free Black person, were "crowding themselves into every place of business and labor and driving the poor colored American citizen out."

Impact of Irish Immigration

Some enterprising Irish immigrants, however, did forge remarkable careers in America. Twenty years after arriving in New York, Alexander T. Stewart became the owner of the nation's largest department store, A. T. Stewart & Company, and accumulated vast real-estate holdings. Dublin-born Victor Herbert emerged as one of America's most revered composers, and Irish dancers and playwrights came to dominate the stage.

The growth of Roman Catholicism

By the start of the Civil War, the Irish had energized trade unions and made the Roman Catholic Church the nation's largest religious denomination. Years of persecution had instilled in Irish Catholics a fierce loyalty to the church as "the supreme authority over all the affairs of the world." Such passion for Catholicism generated unity among Irish Americans. Most of them settled in all-Irish neighborhoods in the nation's largest cities. They also formed powerful Democratic political organizations—such as Tammany Hall in New York City—that would dominate political life during the second half of the nineteenth century.

The Germans

German immigration: Skilled and diverse workers

German immigrants were almost as numerous as the Irish. Unlike the Irish, however, the German arrivals included a large number of skilled craftspeople and well-educated professional people—doctors, lawyers, teachers, engineers—some of whom were refugees from the failed German revolution of 1848. Among those who prospered in the United States was Heinrich Steinweg, a piano maker who in America changed his name to Steinway and became famous for the quality of his instruments.

In addition to an array of political opinions, Germans brought with them a variety of religious preferences. Most were Protestant (usually Lutheran), one-third were Roman Catholic, and a significant number were Jewish.

Germans settled more often in rural areas. Many were independent farmers, skilled workers, and shopkeepers. More so than the Irish, they migrated in families and groups. This communal quality helped them better sustain elements of their language and culture.

Nativism

The flood of immigrants created a backlash among a growing number of "nativists," people born in the United States who resented the newcomers. The flood of Irish and German Catholics especially aroused hostility among Protestant nativists.

nativists Native-born Americans who viewed immigrants as a threat to their job opportunities and way of life.

Know-Nothings Nativist, anti-Catholic third party organized in 1854 in reaction to large-scale German and Irish immigration.

Roving gangs of **nativists** terrorized and even murdered Catholic immigrants to keep them from voting. The Order of the Star-Spangled Banner, founded in New York City in 1849, grew into a powerful political group known officially as the American Party. Members pledged never to vote for foreign-born or Catholic candidates. When asked about the secretive organization, they were told to say, "I know nothing," a phrase that gave rise to the informal name for the party: the **Know-Nothings**.

The Know-Nothings demanded that immigrants and Roman Catholics be excluded from public office and that the waiting period for naturalization (earning citizenship) be increased from five years to twenty-one. Their battle cry was "America for Americans," and many of them engaged in riotous violence, assaulting Catholic neighborhoods and burning churches, convents, and homes.

Nativists generated intense opposition. Abraham Lincoln expressed his revulsion at the anti-immigrant party in a letter to a friend in 1855:

> I am not a Know-Nothing—that is certain. How could I be? How can anyone who abhors the oppression of negroes, be in favor of degrading classes of white people just because of their religion or their place of origin? As a nation, we began by declaring that "all men are created equal." We now practically read it "all men are created equal, except negroes." When the Know-Nothings get control, it will read "all men are created equals, except negroes and foreigners and Catholics."

For a while, the Know-Nothings threatened to control New England, New York, and Maryland, but the anti-Catholic movement subsided when slavery became the focal issue of the 1850s; and after 1856, members opted for either the Republican or the Democratic Party. By 1860, the nativist American Party was dead.

The United States attracted the poor and dispossessed from many lands. Like the Irish and Germans who were the majority of new arrivals in the first half of the nineteenth century, most immigrants were fleeing either economic hardship or political persecution. Yet the influx of foreigners also stoked anti-immigrant sentiment in the United States—a recurring theme in American history—as well as racial and religious tensions. The nativist strain in politics subsided by 1860 but would reemerge at the end of the century.

KNOW-NOTHINGS This political cartoon (ca. 1850) visualizes the Know-Nothings' common complaints: that in contrast to hardworking Americans, the Irish and German immigrants were drunkards who were stealing American elections and disrupting the political status quo.

Organized Labor and New Professions

While most Americans continued to work as farmers during the nineteenth century, a growing number found employment in new or expanding enterprises: textile mills, shoe factories, banks, railroads, publishing, retail stores, teaching, preaching, medicine, law, construction, and engineering. Technological innovations (steam power, power tools, and new modes of

> **CORE OBJECTIVE**
> **4.** Evaluate the impact of the expanding capitalist "market economy" on workers, professionals, and women.

THE SHOE FACTORY When Philadelphia shoemakers went on strike in 1806, a court found them guilty of a "conspiracy to raise wages." Here, shoemakers work in the bottoming room at a Massachusetts shoe factory.

transportation) and their social applications (mass communication, turnpikes, the postal service, banks, and corporations) transformed the nature of work for many Americans, both men and women.

Early Unions

Proud artisans, mechanics, and master craftspeople, who controlled their labor and invested their work with an emphasis on quality rather than quantity, resented the spread of mills and factories in the early nineteenth century. These artisans and the shoes, jewelry, furniture and other items they produced found themselves struggling to compete with the low prices made possible by the new factories and mass-production workshops.

A growing fear that they were losing status led artisans in the major cities to become involved in politics and unions. At first, they organized themselves into interest groups representing their individual skills or trades. Such "trade associations" were the first type of labor unions. They pressured politicians for tariffs to protect their industries from foreign imports, provided insurance benefits, and drafted regulations to improve working conditions.

> Trade associations of skilled craftspeople

Early labor unions were prosecuted as unlawful conspiracies. In 1806, for instance, Philadelphia shoemakers were found guilty of conspiring "to raise their wages." The court's decision broke the union. In 1842, though, the Massachusetts Supreme Court issued a landmark ruling in *Commonwealth v. Hunt* declaring that forming a trade union was not in itself illegal, nor was a demand that employers hire only members of the union. The court also said that union workers could strike if an employer hired laborers who refused to join the union.

By the 1830s, however, organization on a larger scale began to take hold. In 1834, the **National Trades' Union** was formed to organize the citywide

National Trades' Union Organization formed in 1834 to organize all local trade unions into a stronger national association; dissolved amid the economic depression in the late 1830s.

trade unions into a stronger national association. At the same time, shoemakers, printers, carpenters, and weavers established national craft unions.

Women also formed trade unions. Sarah Monroe, who helped organize the New York Tailoresses' Society, explained that it was intended to defend "our rights." If it was "unfashionable for men to bear [workplace] oppression in silence," she wondered, "why should it not also become unfashionable with the women?"

Strikes led by women followed in industrial cities such as New York (1825), Baltimore (1833), and Lowell (1834). But women, as Louise Mitchell of the New York Tailoresses' Society explained, faced unique obstacles to improving their working conditions. "When we complain to our employers and others, of the inequality of our wages with that of the men's," she said, "the excuse is, they [men] have families to support, from which females are exempt." Mitchell called that a "sad mistake."

The Rise of the Professions

The dramatic social changes of the first half of the nineteenth century opened up an array of new **professions**. Bustling new towns required new services—retail stores, printing shops, post offices, newspapers, schools, banks, law firms, medical practices, and others—that created more high-status professions than had existed before.

professions Occupations requiring specialized knowledge of a particular field; the Industrial Revolution and its new organization of labor created an array of professions in the nineteenth century.

Teaching Teaching became one of the fastest-growing professions. Horace Mann of Massachusetts was instrumental in demanding free public education for all children as the best way to transform youths into citizens. Many states, especially in the North, agreed, and the number of schools exploded during the second quarter of the nineteenth century.

Mann also helped create "normal schools" to train teachers. Public schools initially preferred men as teachers, usually hiring them at age seventeen or eighteen. The pay was so low that few stayed in the profession their entire career, and eventually women replaced male teachers. But initially, for many educated young men, teaching offered independence and social status, as well as an alternative to the rural isolation of farming.

Law, Medicine, and Engineering Teaching was a common stepping-stone for men who became lawyers. In the decades after the American Revolution, young men would teach for a year or two before joining an experienced attorney as an apprentice (what today would be called an *intern*). They would learn the practice of law in exchange for their labors.

New professions for men

Like attorneys, physicians in the early nineteenth century often had little formal academic training. Healers of every stripe assumed the title of *doctor* and established medical practices without regulation. Most were self-taught or had assisted a physician for several years, occasionally supplementing their internships with a few classes at the handful of medical schools. By 1860, there were 60,000 self-styled physicians, many of whom were "quacks," or frauds.

THE COUNTRY SCHOOL A one-room schoolhouse in rural New England, as depicted by Winslow Homer in 1871. The young teacher presides over her class, which, as was customary, is arranged with boys mostly on one side of the room and girls on the other. **What changes in American education took place in the mid-eighteenth century?**

Industrial expansion also spurred the profession of engineering, a field that, by the outbreak of the Civil War, would become the largest professional occupation for men. Specialized expertise was required for the design and construction of canals and railroads; the development of machine tools and steam engines; and the building of roads, bridges, and factories.

Women in the Professional Workforce

New professions for women

During the first half of the nineteenth century, the only professions considered acceptable for women were nursing (often midwifery, the delivery of babies) and teaching. Women also found outlets in the creative arts as writers, artists, and actors.

A few women, however, pursued careers in male-dominated professions. Elizabeth Blackwell of Ohio gained admission to Geneva Medical College (now Hobart and William Smith College) in western New York despite the disapproval of the faculty. When she arrived at her first class, a hush fell upon the students "as if each member had been struck with paralysis."

Blackwell, however, had the last laugh when she finished first in her class in 1849, but thereafter the medical school refused to admit any more women. The first woman to earn a medical degree, Blackwell went on to create the New York Infirmary for Women and Children and later was a professor of gynecology at the London School of Medicine for Women.

Equal Opportunities

The dynamic market economy helped spread the idea that individuals should have an equal opportunity to better themselves through their abilities and hard work. In America, observed a journalist in 1844, "one has as good a chance as another according to his talents, prudence, and personal exertions."

More and more Americans held on to that promise. As the combined forces of industrialization and urbanization gave rise to a wide range of jobs and professions—from schoolteaching and banking to medicine and engineering—workers became more demanding about the conditions under which they were willing to labor, and they organized trade associations and labor unions to press for equal treatment in the workplace.

That same desire to rise economically, which prompted so many White immigrants to risk everything to come to the United States, was also shared by people who had never enjoyed equal opportunities to pursue their American dream: namely, African Americans and women. By the 1830s, they, too, began to organize and more forcefully demand their right to "life, liberty, and the pursuit of happiness."

The desire of "common people" to pursue economic opportunities would quickly spill over into the political arena. The great theme of political life in the first half of the nineteenth century would be the continuing democratization of opportunities for White men, regardless of income or background, to vote and hold office—and the continuing exclusion of everyone else.

FIRST FEMALE DOCTOR The first American woman to earn a medical degree, Elizabeth Blackwell went on to establish the New York Infirmary for Women and Children and later was professor of gynecology at the London School of Medicine for Women.

Reviewing the
CORE OBJECTIVES

- **The Market Revolution**
Canals and other improvements in transportation—such as *steamboats*, which could be used on the nation's rivers and lakes—allowed goods to reach markets more quickly and cheaply, helping to create a national *market economy* in which people bought and sold goods at longer distances. *Clipper ships* shortened the amount of time to transport goods across the oceans. The *railroads* (which expanded rapidly during the 1850s) and the *telegraph system* diminished the isolation of the West and united the country economically and socially. The *Erie Canal* (1825) contributed to New York City's emerging status as the nation's economic center even as it spurred the growth of Chicago and other midwestern cities. Improvements in transportation and communication linked rural communities to a worldwide marketplace.

- **Industrial Development**
Inventions in machine tools and technology spurred an *Industrial Revolution* during the nineteenth century. The *cotton gin* dramatically increased cotton production, and a rapidly spreading culture of *cotton* capitalism boomed in the United States, with a resultant increase in slavery. Other inventions, such as John Deere's steel plows and the mechanized *McCormick reapers*, helped Americans—especially westerners—farm their land more efficiently and more profitably. In the North, mills and factories, at first water-powered and eventually powered by coal-fired steam engines, spread rapidly. They initially produced textiles for clothing and bedding from southern cotton, as well as iron, shoes, and other products. The federal government's tariff policy encouraged the growth of domestic manufacturing, especially cotton textiles, by reducing imports of British cloth. Between 1820 and 1840, the number of Americans engaged in manufacturing increased 800 percent. Many mill workers, such as the women employed in the *Lowell system* of New England textile factory communities, worked long hours for low wages in unhealthy conditions. Industrialization, along with increased commerce, helped spur the growth of cities.

- **Immigration** The promise of cheap land and good wages drew millions of immigrants to America. By 1844, about 14.5 percent of the population was foreign-born. Many of those who arrived in the 1840s came from places outside the Protestant regions of northern Europe that had supplied most of America's previous immigrants. The devastating potato famine led to an influx of poor Irish Catholic families. By the 1850s, they represented a significant portion of the urban population in the United States, constituting a majority in New York and Boston. German migrants, many of them Catholics and Jews, came to the country at the same time. Not all native-born Americans welcomed the immigrants. *Nativists* became a powerful political force in the

1850s, with the *Know-Nothings* nearly achieving major-party status with their message of excluding immigrants and Catholics from the nation's political community.

■ **Organized Labor and New Professions**
Skilled workers (artisans) in American cities had long formed trade associations to protect their members and to lobby for their interests. As the Industrial Revolution spread, some workers expanded these organizations nationally, forming the *National Trades' Union*. The growth of the *market economy* also expanded opportunities for those with formal education to serve in new or expanding *professions*. The number of physicians, teachers, engineers, and lawyers grew rapidly. By the mid-nineteenth century, women, African Americans, and immigrants began to agitate for equal social, economic, and political opportunities.

KEY TERMS

market economy p. 334
steamboats p. 336
Erie Canal (1825) p. 337
railroads p. 338
clipper ships p. 339
telegraph system p. 341
Industrial Revolution p. 342
cotton gin p. 344
cotton p. 344
McCormick reapers p. 349
Lowell system p. 350
nativists p. 358
Know-Nothings p. 358
National Trades' Union p. 360
professions p. 361

CHRONOLOGY

1793 Eli Whitney invents the cotton gin
1807 Robert Fulton and Robert Livingston launch steamship transportation on the Hudson River in New York
1825 Erie Canal opens in upstate New York
1831 Cyrus McCormick invents a mechanical reaper
1834 National Trades' Union is organized
Lowell factory women launch their strike
1837 John Deere invents the steel plow
1842 Massachusetts Supreme Judicial Court issues *Commonwealth v. Hunt* decision
1845 The *Rainbow*, the first clipper ship, is launched
Irish potato famine
1846 Elias Howe invents the sewing machine
1848 California gold rush begins
1854 Know-Nothings party (the American Party) is formed

InQuizitive

Go to InQuizitive to see what you've learned—and learn what you've missed—with personalized feedback along the way.

PARADE OF THE VICTUALLERS (1821) On a beautiful day in March 1821, Philadelphia butcher William White organized a parade celebrating America's high-quality meats. This colored aquatint by Joseph Yeager, originally drawn by John Lewis Krimmel, captures the new, vibrant nationalism that emerged in America after the War of 1812.

Nationalism and Sectionalism

1815–1828

After the War of 1812, the British stopped interfering with American shipping. The United States could now develop new industries and exploit new markets around the globe. The result was a surge of economic development. By 1828, the young agrarian republic was poised to become a sprawling commercial nation connected by networks of roads and canals as well as regional economic relationships—all energized by a spirit of enterprise and experimentation.

Yet for all the optimism exhibited by Americans after the war, the fundamental tension between *nationalism* and *sectionalism* remained: how to balance the different needs of the nation's three diverse regions—North, South, and West—with the national interest.

Some sectionalists focused on promoting their region's priorities: shipping and manufacturing in the North, canals and roads in the Midwest, slavery-based agriculture in the South. Nationalists, on the other hand, promoted the interests of the nation as a whole. This required each region to recognize that no single section could get all it wanted without threatening the survival of the nation. Among the issues dividing the young republic, the passions aroused by the expansion of slavery proved to be the most difficult to resolve.

CORE OBJECTIVES

1. Analyze how the spirit of nationalism that emerged after the War of 1812 affected economic policies and judicial decisions.

2. Explain how Henry Clay's American System fueled the rise of sectional conflict during this era.

3. Identify the social and economic factors that led to the demise of the "Era of Good Feelings."

4. Explain how the federal government's diplomatic accomplishments during James Monroe's presidency reflected the policies expressed in the Monroe Doctrine.

5. Evaluate the social and political factors that contributed to Andrew Jackson's success in the 1828 election.

> **CORE OBJECTIVE**
>
> **1.** Analyze how the spirit of nationalism that emerged after the War of 1812 affected economic policies and judicial decisions.

A New Nationalism

After the War of 1812, Americans experienced a wave of patriotic excitement. They had won their independence from Britain for a second time, and postwar prosperity fed a widespread sense of optimism. In a message to Congress in 1815, President James Madison revealed how the challenges of the war, especially the weaknesses of the armed forces and federal finances, had changed his attitudes toward the role of the federal government.

Economic Nationalism

Now, Madison and other leading southern Republicans, such as South Carolina's John C. Calhoun, acted like nationalists rather than states' rights sectionalists. They abandoned many of Thomas Jefferson's presidential policies (reducing the armed forces and opposing a national bank, for example) in favor of the *economic nationalism* promoted earlier by Federalists Alexander Hamilton and George Washington.

Madison now supported a larger army and navy, a new national bank, and tariffs to protect American manufacturers from foreign competitors. "The Republicans have out-Federalized Federalism," one New Englander commented.

> Economic nationalism: New national bank and currency

The Bank of the United States

After President Madison and congressional Republicans allowed the charter for the First Bank of the United States to expire, in 1811, the nation's finances had fallen into a muddle. States began chartering local banks with little or no regulation, and their banknotes (paper money) flooded the economy with different currencies of uncertain value. Imagine trying to do business on a national basis when each state-chartered bank had its own currency, which often was not accepted by other banks or in other states.

In response, President Madison in 1816 convinced Congress to establish the **Second Bank of the United States** (B.U.S.). The new B.U.S.—which, like its predecessor, was based in Philadelphia and was chartered for twenty years—was intended primarily to support a stable *national* currency that would promote economic growth.

In return for issuing national currency and opening branches in every state, the new B.U.S. had to handle all federal government funds, lend the government up to $5 million upon demand, and pay it $1.5 million annually.

Second Bank of the United States Established in 1816 after the first national bank's charter expired; it stabilized the economy by creating a sound national currency; by making loans to farmers, small manufacturers, and entrepreneurs; and by regulating the ability of state banks to issue their own paper currency.

A Protective Tariff

The long controversy with Great Britain over shipping rights convinced most Americans of the need to end their dependence on imported British goods. Efforts to develop iron and textile industries, begun in New York and New England during the embargo of 1807, had accelerated during the War of 1812, when America lost access to European goods.

After the war ended, however, British companies flooded U.S. markets with their less-expensive products. In response, northern manufacturers lobbied Congress for tariffs to protect their new industries from "unfair" British competition. Congress responded by passing the **Tariff of 1816**, which placed a 20–25 percent tax on a long list of imported goods.

Debates over federal tariffs followed, partly because they benefited manufacturers rather than consumers or farmers. This also meant that tariffs benefited some regions (the Northeast) more than others (the South), thus aggravating sectional tensions.

Internal Improvements

The final major element of economic nationalism in the first half of the nineteenth century involved federal financing of **internal improvements** (what today is called infrastructure), specifically the construction of roads, bridges, canals, and harbors. Most American rivers flowed from north to south, so the nation needed a network of roads running east to west.

Following the successful creation of the first stretches of the Cumberland Pike, later called the National Road, a movement for paved roads in the northeastern states gathered momentum. The first section, the Philadelphia-Lancaster Turnpike, opened in 1794. (The term *turnpike* derived from a pole, or pike, at the tollgate, which was turned by the turnpike owner to admit traffic in exchange for a small fee, or toll.) By 1821, some 4,000 miles of turnpikes had been built, and stagecoach and freight companies emerged to move more people and cargo at lower rates.

The use of federal money to finance internal improvements remained controversial, however. Some critics resisted when it seemed like a new road or canal would spur development in only one region of the country at the expense of the whole. Others argued that the U.S. Constitution did not allow for such activities; only the local and state governments, or private investors, they claimed, should fund road, canal, and harbor projects.

Judicial Nationalism and the Supreme Court

The postwar emphasis on economic nationalism also flourished in the Supreme Court, where Chief Justice John Marshall strengthened the constitutional powers of the federal government at the expense of states' rights. Marshall was a consistent nationalist who viewed his cousin Thomas Jefferson as a danger for promoting states' rights over federal authority.

Marshall's judicial nationalism affirmed that the Supreme Court had the authority (and responsibility) to judge the constitutionality of state and federal legislative actions (this oversight was called *judicial review*). In the pathbreaking case of *Marbury v. Madison* (1803), the Court had, for the first time, declared a federal law unconstitutional. In other cases, the Court ruled that the Constitution, as well as the nation's laws and treaties, could remain the supreme law of the land only if the U.S. Supreme Court could review and at times overturn the decisions of state courts.

Economic nationalism: Tariff of 1816 and federal financing for "internal improvements"

Tariff of 1816 Taxes on various imported items to protect America's emerging iron and textile industries from British competition.

internal improvements Construction of roads, canals, and other infrastructure projects intended to facilitate the flow of goods and people.

JOHN MARSHALL A pillar of judicial nationalism, Marshall became chief justice of the U.S. Supreme Court at the young age of forty-six, ruling on *Marbury v. Madison* just two years later.

Protecting Contract Rights

The Supreme Court made two major decisions in 1819 that strengthened the power of the federal government at the expense of the states. One, **Dartmouth College v. Woodward** (1819), stopped an effort by the New Hampshire legislature to alter the charter of Dartmouth College and to change the way it created its board of trustees. The college's original charter, wrote John Marshall in drafting the Court's majority opinion, was a valid contract that the state legislature had violated, an act forbidden by the U.S. Constitution.

This decision implied an enlarged definition of *contract* that seemed to put corporations (in this case, Dartmouth) beyond the reach of the states that had chartered them. Thereafter, the state-written charters that incorporated organizations and businesses commonly included provisions that made the charters subject to modification. Such provisions were then part of the "contract."

Protecting a National Currency

The second major Supreme Court case of 1819 was Chief Justice Marshall's most significant interpretation of the constitutional system: **McCulloch v. Maryland** (1819). James McCulloch, a B.U.S. clerk in Baltimore, had refused to pay the state taxes on B.U.S. currency that were required by a Maryland law. The state indicted McCulloch. Acting on behalf of the national bank, he appealed to the Supreme Court, which ruled unanimously that Congress had the authority to charter the B.U.S. and that states had no right to ban or to tax the national bank.

Speaking for the Court, Chief Justice Marshall ruled that Congress had the right (that is, one of its "implied powers") to take any action not forbidden by the Constitution as long as the purpose of such laws was within the "scope of the Constitution." One great principle that "entirely pervades the Constitution," Marshall wrote, is "that the Constitution and the laws made in pursuance thereof are supreme: . . . They control the Constitution and laws of the respective states, and cannot be controlled by them." The effort by a state to tax a federal bank was therefore unconstitutional, for the "power to tax involves the power to destroy."

Interstate Commerce

John Marshall's last great decision, **Gibbons v. Ogden** (1824), affirmed the federal government's supremacy in regulating interstate commerce. In 1808, the New York legislature granted Robert Fulton and Robert R. Livingston the exclusive right to operate steamboats on the state's rivers and lakes. Fulton and Livingston then gave Aaron Ogden, a former New Jersey governor, the exclusive right to ferry people and goods up the Hudson River between New York and New Jersey. Georgia planter Thomas Gibbons, however, operated ships under a federal license that competed with Ogden.

On behalf of a unanimous Court, Marshall ruled in *Gibbons v. Ogden* that the monopoly granted by the state to Ogden conflicted with the federal

---

Judicial nationalism: Dartmouth College v. Woodward (1819)

Judicial nationalism: McCulloch v. Maryland (1819)

Dartmouth College v. Woodward (1819) Supreme Court ruling that enlarged the definition of contract to put corporations beyond the reach of the states that chartered them.

McCulloch v. Maryland (1819) Supreme Court ruling that prohibited states from taxing the Bank of the United States.

Gibbons v. Ogden (1824) Supreme Court case that gave the federal government the power to regulate interstate commerce.

STEAMBOAT TRAVEL ON THE HUDSON RIVER (1811) This watercolor of an early steamboat was painted by a Russian diplomat, Pavel Petrovich Svinin, who was fascinated by early technological innovations and the unique entrepreneurial culture of America.

license issued to Gibbons. Marshall added that Congress could regulate not only commerce between states but also activities within a state that were "connected with" interstate commerce.

> Judicial nationalism: *Gibbons v. Ogden* (1824)

Thomas Jefferson detested Marshall's judicial nationalism. To Jefferson, the Court's ruling in the *Gibbons* case revealed how "the Federal branch of our Government is advancing towards the usurpation of all the rights reserved to the States, and the consolidation in itself of all powers, foreign and domestic."

Jefferson's words foreshadowed a conflict over state and federal power that would persist for decades to come. But for now, in the aftermath of the War of 1812, political leaders felt an urgent need to institute a set of policies that would bind the states more closely together, both economically and politically, in order to promote national prosperity. Internal improvement projects such as the National Road boosted the country's economic development by forging more connections among the states and regions. At the same time, a series of landmark Supreme Court decisions enhanced the power of the federal government to oversee and promote the national economy.

CHAPTER 9 Nationalism and Sectionalism

> **CORE OBJECTIVE**
>
> **2.** Explain how Henry Clay's American System fueled the rise of sectional conflict during this era.

Debates over the American System

The major economic initiatives debated by Congress after the War of 1812—the national bank; federal tariffs; and federally financed roads, bridges, and canals—were interrelated pieces of a comprehensive economic plan called the **American System**. The term was coined by Henry Clay, the powerful Kentucky congressman, to refer to economic nationalism. Clay wanted to free America's economy from its dependence on Great Britain while tying together the diverse regions of the nation politically. "I know of no South, no North, no East, no West to which I owe my allegiance," he asserted. "The Union is my country."

In promoting the American System, Clay sought to promote each region's top economic priority. He argued that high tariffs on imports were needed to block the sale of British products in the United States in order to protect new industries in New York and New England. To convince western states to support those tariffs, Clay first called for the federal government to use tariff revenues to build much-needed infrastructure—roads, bridges, canals, and other internal improvements—in the frontier West. Second, Clay's American System would raise prices for the purchase of federal lands and "distribute" the additional revenue to the states to help finance more roads, bridges, and canals. Third, Clay endorsed a strong national bank to create a single national currency and to regulate the unstable state and local banks.

Sectional Conflicts

Clay's program depended on the willingness of each region to compromise. For a while, it worked. But debates soon arose that helped set the pattern of deepening sectional disputes over economic issues.

Critics argued that higher prices for federal lands would discourage western migration and that tariffs benefited the northern manufacturing sector at the expense of southern and western farmers and the "common" people, who had to pay higher prices for the goods produced by tariff-protected industries.

Many westerners and southerners also feared that the Philadelphia-based Second B.U.S. would become so powerful and corrupt that it could dictate the nation's economic future at the expense of particular regions. Missouri senator Thomas Hart Benton feared that the West would be "devoured" by the East. Westerners, Benton worried, "are in the jaws of the monster! A lump of butter in the mouth of a dog! One gulp, one swallow, and all is gone!"

Support for federal spending on internal improvements came largely from the West, while many New Englanders and southerners argued that the states should fund such projects.

On his last day in office, in 1817, even President Madison, a supporter of internal improvements himself, vetoed a bill funding more construction because he grew concerned that such federal expenditures were

HENRY CLAY A committed nationalist, Clay was the chief architect of the American System. Here he is pictured on a $50 bill issued in the 1860s, long after his death.

American System Economic plan championed by Henry Clay of Kentucky that called for federal tariffs on imports, a strong national bank, and federally financed internal improvements—roads, bridges, canals—all intended to strengthen the national economy and end American economic dependence on Great Britain.

not authorized by the Constitution. As a result, internal improvements remained, with few exceptions, largely the responsibility of the states for another 100 years.

The Future of Slavery

In championing his American System, Henry Clay was forced to resolve explosive sectional conflicts over slavery in the western territories and states. Many Americans heading westward across the Appalachian Mountains were southerners committed to cotton production and the slavery system that supported it. The possibility of new western states becoming "slave states" created the greatest political conflict of the nineteenth century. Thomas Jefferson said the conflict "filled me with terror. I considered it at once as the [death] knell of the Union."

Like Jefferson, Clay lived with the contradiction of being a slave owner who denounced the evils of slavery and understood its potential to tear the nation apart. "I consider slavery as a curse—a curse to the master, a wrong, a grievous wrong to the slave," he explained. Nonetheless, he insisted that slavery had become essential to the southern way of life.

Clay grappled with the tension between sectionalism and nationalism that had been a defining feature of American political culture since the nation's founding. His American System asserted the authority of the federal government over that of the states and territories. Although the entire United States stood to benefit from its economic development, some Americans still feared that the tariff or the B.U.S. favored one section over the rest. And the South's attachment to slavery threatened to derail the nationalist project altogether.

> Conflict over extending slavery into the western states

"An Era of Good Feelings"

In the 1816 presidential election, Republican presidential candidate James Monroe, another Virginian, overwhelmed his Federalist opponent, Rufus King of New York, by a 183–34 margin in the Electoral College. The nation that Monroe would preside over was remarkably changed from the new republic led by George Washington. By 1817, the Union had nineteen states; five more would be added under Monroe.

> **CORE OBJECTIVE**
> **3.** Identify the social and economic factors that led to the demise of the "Era of Good Feelings."

James Monroe

James Monroe was eminently qualified to be president. He had served as a representative in the Virginia Assembly; as governor of the state; as a representative in the Confederation Congress; as a U.S. senator; and as U.S. minister (ambassador) to Paris, London, and Madrid. Under President Madison, he had served as secretary of state and doubled as secretary of war.

Monroe's administration began with the nation at peace and its economy flourishing. A Boston newspaper said the new president was

INDEPENDENCE DAY CELEBRATION (1819) James Monroe's election and his presidential tour that followed became associated with an "Era of Good Feelings," here envisioned in watercolor by John Lewis Krimmel. In reality, Monroe's presidency was tainted by the Panic of 1819 and the controversial Missouri Compromise.

determined to usher in an "Era of Good Feelings," and the label became a popular catchphrase for the strong economy and political goodwill during Monroe's administration.

The nationalist priorities during the so-called Era of Good Feelings did not last long, however, for sectional loyalties continued to clash with national perspectives. Two crucial events warned of stormy times ahead: the financial Panic of 1819 and the political conflict over statehood for the Missouri Territory.

The Panic of 1819

Collapse of cotton prices

The **Panic of 1819** resulted from the sudden collapse of cotton prices after British textile mills quit buying high-priced American cotton—the nation's leading export—in favor of cheaper cotton from other parts of the world, especially the British colonies of Egypt and India. As the price of cotton fell and the flow of commerce slowed, banks failed, businesses went bankrupt, and unemployment soared. New factory owners struggled to find markets for their goods and to fend off more-powerful foreign competitors.

Other factors caused the financial panic to become a depression. Business owners, farmers, and land speculators had recklessly borrowed money to expand their business ventures or purchase more land. With the collapse of crop prices and the decline of land values during and after 1819, both land speculators and settlers saw their income plummet.

Unregulated banks exacerbate the financial crisis

The reckless lending practices of the unregulated new state banks compounded the economic confusion. Between 1815 and 1818, the number of banks grew by some 30 percent. To generate more loans, the wobbly new banks issued more paper money. Even the B.U.S., which was supposed to provide financial stability, succumbed to the easy-credit mania and extended too many loans.

Panic of 1819 A financial panic that began a three-year economic crisis triggered by reduced demand in Europe for American cotton, declining land values, and reckless practices by local and state banks.

The economic depression lasted about three years, and people blamed the B.U.S. After the panic subsided, many Americans—especially in the South and the West—remained critical of the national bank.

Slave versus Free States

As the financial panic deepened, another cloud appeared on the horizon: the onset of a fierce sectional controversy between North and South over extending slavery into the new western territories.

By 1819, the United States had an equal number of slave and free states—eleven of each. The Northwest Ordinance (1787) had *banned* slavery north of the Ohio River, and the Southwest Ordinance (1790) had *authorized* slavery south of the Ohio. In the vast region west of the Mississippi River, however, no move had been made to extend the dividing line across the vast Louisiana Territory, where slavery had existed since France and Spain first colonized the area. At the time, the Missouri Territory encompassed all of the Louisiana Purchase except the state of Louisiana and the Arkansas Territory.

In 1819, the year that Spain agreed to transfer Florida to the United States, residents of the Missouri Territory approached the U.S. Congress about applying for statehood. It would be the first state west of the Mississippi River, and a majority of its residents wanted to allow slavery.

At that point, Representative James Tallmadge Jr., an obscure New York Republican, stunned Congress by proposing to ban the transport of enslaved people into Missouri.

Tallmadge's amendment infuriated southern slave owners, many of whom had developed a profitable trade selling enslaved people to be taken into the western territories. In addition, southerners worried that the addition of Missouri as a free state would tip the balance of power in the Senate against the slave states. Their fears were heightened when Congressman Timothy Fuller, an anti-slavery Democratic Republican from Massachusetts, declared that it was both "the right and duty of Congress" to stop the spread "of the intolerable evil and the crying enormity of slavery." After fiery debates, the House, with its northern majority, passed the Tallmadge Amendment by a vote that was almost strictly sectional. The Senate, however, rejected it—also along sectional lines.

> The Tallmadge Amendment

The Missouri Compromise

At about the same time, Maine, which had been part of Massachusetts, applied for statehood. The Senate decided to link Maine's request for statehood with Missouri's, voting to admit Maine as a free state and Missouri as a slave state, thus maintaining the political balance between free and slave states.

Illinois senator Jesse Thomas revised the so-called **Missouri Compromise** by introducing an amendment to exclude slavery in the rest of the Louisiana Purchase territory north of latitude 36°30′, Missouri's southern border. Slavery thus would continue in the Arkansas Territory and in Missouri but

Missouri Compromise (1820) Legislative decision to admit Missouri as a slave state while prohibiting slavery in the area west of the Mississippi River and north of the parallel 36°30′.

Comparing PERSPECTIVES

SLAVERY AND FREEDOM ACROSS BORDERS

From: "Emancipation of Slaves in Texas," *Georgia Messenger*, **December 12, 1826.**

This news article from a Georgian newspaper addresses the ending of slavery in Mexico. In response, slaveholders in the Province of Texas moved their enslaved people, whom they regarded as property, to other regions.

ARKANSAS, Oct. 10.

Emancipation of Slaves in Texas.
We learn by a gentleman of this place, who arrived a few days since from Miller county, that a citizen of that county had returned just before he started, from the Province of Texas, bringing information that great excitement prevailed throughout the several Colonies in that country, when he left there, in consequence of the recent passage of a law by the Mexican Government, for the Emancipation of all the Slaves in the Province of Texas, and that orders had been received for carrying it into immediate effect. As may well be supposed, this information produced the greatest consternation among the slave holders, all of whom had emigrated to that country under an assurance, as we are informed, from the local authorities of Texas, that they could hold their slaves; though we are under the impression that slavery is prohibited throughout the Republic, by the Constitution of Mexico.

    The large slave-holders were hurrying off their slaves in great numbers, into Louisiana and Arkansas; and we have heard of several persons who emigratad [sic] from this Territory, who have recently crossed the line into Louisiana, with their slaves. Those persons who have but few slaves, have held meetings, at which it was resolved, that they would stand by each other in resisting the execution of the law, until they can gather this year's crop, after which they have determined to leave the country.

From: C. A. Wickliffe, "Fugitive Slaves," *Niles' Register*, June 24, 1826.

These two letters are from the correspondence between Mr. Wickliffe and Secretary of State Henry Clay regarding the status of freedom-seeking enslaved people who now lived in Canada.

FUGITIVE SLAVES. The following correspondence between Mr. Wickliffe and the secretary of state, has been recently published—

WASHINGTON, April 12.

Hon. H. Clay, secretary of state,

Sir.—You will recollect that, during the last congress, the attention of the representatives from Kentucky was called, by resolution of the legislature, to the growing evil under which many of the citizens of that state labor, from the countenance and protection which their fugitive slaves receive from the authorities of the government of Upper Canada.

If my recollection serves me correctly, to you was assigned, by your colleagues, the duty of presenting this subject to the attention of the executive of the United States. The evil is increasing, and the citizens of Kentucky have no information, what efforts, if any, have been made by the executive of the United States with the British nation, to check it. It was desirable, that it should be made the subject of negotiation between the two governments. If the attention of the president of the United States, with that view, has been called to the subject, if not inconsistent with your views of propriety, I will thank you for any information upon the subject, which your relation with the government of the United States may enable you to give.

Accept on this occasion, my renewed assurances of respect and esteem, C. A. WICKLIFFE.

Questions

1. In 1826, Texas was a province of New Spain. According to this news report, how were American slaveholders living in Texas affected by the emancipation of enslaved people in Mexico?

2. How does C. A. Wickliffe suggest that the United States and Canada address the "growing evil" of fugitive slaves seeking their freedom?

3. What do these documents teach us about slavery and freedom in the United States and its neighbors in the early nineteenth century?

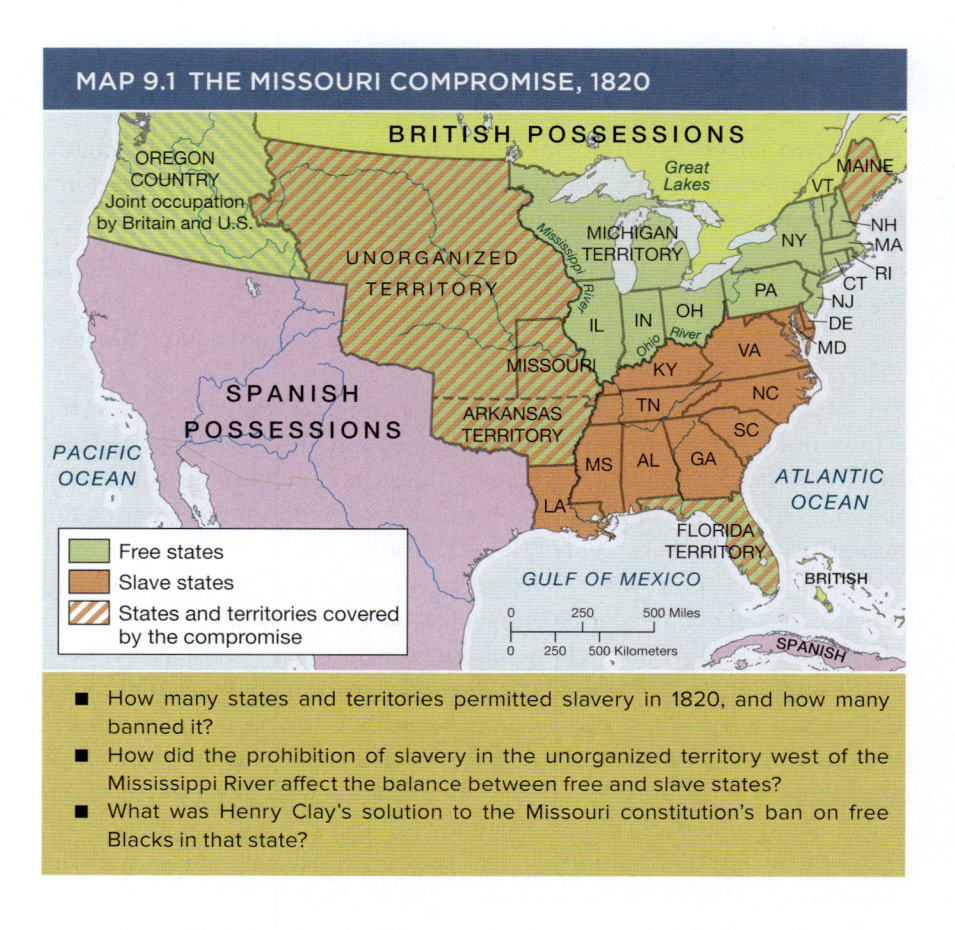

MAP 9.1 THE MISSOURI COMPROMISE, 1820

- How many states and territories permitted slavery in 1820, and how many banned it?
- How did the prohibition of slavery in the unorganized territory west of the Mississippi River affect the balance between free and slave states?
- What was Henry Clay's solution to the Missouri constitution's ban on free Blacks in that state?

would be excluded from the remainder of the area west of the Mississippi River. By a narrow margin, the Thomas Amendment passed on March 2, 1820.

Then another issue arose. The pro-slavery faction in Missouri's constitutional convention inserted into the proposed state constitution a provision banning free Blacks and mixed-race people.

The resulting dispute threatened to unravel the deal to admit Missouri as a state until Speaker of the House Henry Clay fashioned a "second" Missouri Compromise whereby Missouri would be admitted as a state only if its legislature pledged never to deny free Blacks their constitutional rights. He then set about convincing others to support his proposal. A New Hampshire congressman observed that Clay "uses no threats or abuse—but is mild, humble, and persuasive—he begs, he instructs, adjures, and beseeches us to have mercy on the people of Missouri." Clay's aggressive action worked. On August 10, 1821, Missouri became the twenty-fourth state (see Map 9.1).

The Missouri Compromise and the debate surrounding it revealed a widening sectional divide: the Northeast dominating in shipping, commerce, and manufacturing; the Midwest centering on small farms; and the South becoming more and more dependent on cotton and slavery. The Era of Good Feelings had also given way to the Panic of 1819, which further inflamed sectionalist sentiment in all three regions. Although Henry Clay's compromise plan temporarily preserved the fragile balance between slave and free states, the country's relentless westward expansion ensured that the unresolved issue would not go away.

Nationalist Diplomacy

Henry Clay's *economic* nationalism and John Marshall's *judicial* nationalism were reinforced by efforts to practice *diplomatic* nationalism. Secretary of State John Quincy Adams aggressively exercised America's growing power to clarify and expand the nation's boundaries. He also wanted Europeans to recognize America's dominance in the Western Hemisphere.

> **CORE OBJECTIVE**
> **4.** Explain how the federal government's diplomatic accomplishments during James Monroe's presidency reflected the policies expressed in the Monroe Doctrine.

Relations with Britain

The Treaty of Ghent (1814) had ended the War of 1812, but it left unsettled several disputes between the United States and Great Britain.

During James Monroe's presidency, John Quincy Adams oversaw the negotiations of two important treaties that eased tensions with Great Britain. First, the Rush-Bagot Agreement of 1817 (named after the diplomats who arranged it) limited the number of warships on the Great Lakes. Second, the Convention of 1818 settled the disputed northern boundary of the Louisiana Purchase by extending it along the 49th parallel westward from what would become Minnesota to the Rocky Mountains. West of the Rockies, the Oregon Country would be jointly occupied by the British and the Americans.

> The Rush-Bagot Agreement of 1817 and the Convention of 1818

Florida

Still another disputed boundary involved western Florida. Spanish control over Florida during the early nineteenth century was more a technicality than an actuality. Spain was now a declining power, unable to enforce its obligations under Pinckney's Treaty of 1795 to keep Indigenous Americans in the region from launching raids into southern Georgia.

In 1816, U.S. soldiers clashed with Black freedom seekers who had taken refuge in a British fort in West Florida, in the present-day Florida Panhandle. At the same time, Seminole warriors fought White settlers in the area. In 1817, White Americans burned a Seminole village on the border, killing five Indigenous people.

At that point, Secretary of War John C. Calhoun ordered General Andrew Jackson to lead an army from Tennessee into Florida, igniting what became known as the First Seminole War. Jackson was told to pursue Indigenous people into Spanish Florida but not to attack any Spanish forts.

> The first Seminole War

When it came to Spaniards or Indigenous Americans, few White Tennesseans—and certainly not Andrew Jackson, the hero of the Battle of New Orleans—bothered with legal technicalities. In early 1818, without presidential approval, General Jackson's force of 2,000 federal soldiers,

MASSACRE OF THE WHITES BY INDIANS AND BLACKS IN FLORIDA (1836) Published in a White southerner's account of the Seminole War, this is one of the earliest known depictions of African Americans and Indigenous Americans fighting as allies. **What motivated Americans to attack Indigenous Americans to the west?**

volunteer Tennessee militiamen, and Indigenous allies crossed into Spanish Florida from southern Georgia.

The Americans assaulted a Spanish fort at St. Marks and destroyed several Seminole villages along the Suwannee River. They also captured and court-martialed British traders accused of provoking attacks by Indigenous people. When told that a military trial of the British citizens was illegal, Jackson gruffly replied that the laws of war did not "apply to conflicts with savages." Jackson ordered the immediate execution of the British troublemakers, an illegal action that angered the British government and alarmed President Monroe's cabinet. But the impulsive general kept moving. In May, he captured Pensacola, the Spanish capital of West Florida, and established a provisional American government.

While Jackson's military exploits excited American expansionists, they aroused resentment in Spain and concern in Washington, D.C. Spain demanded that its territory be returned and that the American general be punished for violating international law. Monroe's cabinet was at first prepared to disavow Jackson's illegal acts. Privately, Calhoun criticized Jackson for disobeying orders—a stand that would later cause bad blood between them.

A Transcontinental Nation

With the fate of Florida a foregone conclusion, John Quincy Adams turned his eye to a larger goal: extending the contested western boundary of the Louisiana Purchase to the Pacific coast. In lengthy negotiations with Spain, Adams gradually gave ground on American claims to Texas, then a province of New Spain, but stuck to his demand for the Louisiana Purchase boundary.

In 1819, Adams convinced the Spanish to sign the **Transcontinental Treaty** (also called the Adams-Onís Treaty), which gave all of Florida to the

Transcontinental Treaty (1819) Treaty between Spain and the United States that clarified the boundaries of the Louisiana Purchase and arranged for the transfer of Florida to the United States in exchange for cash.

MAP 9.2 BOUNDARY TREATIES, 1818–1819

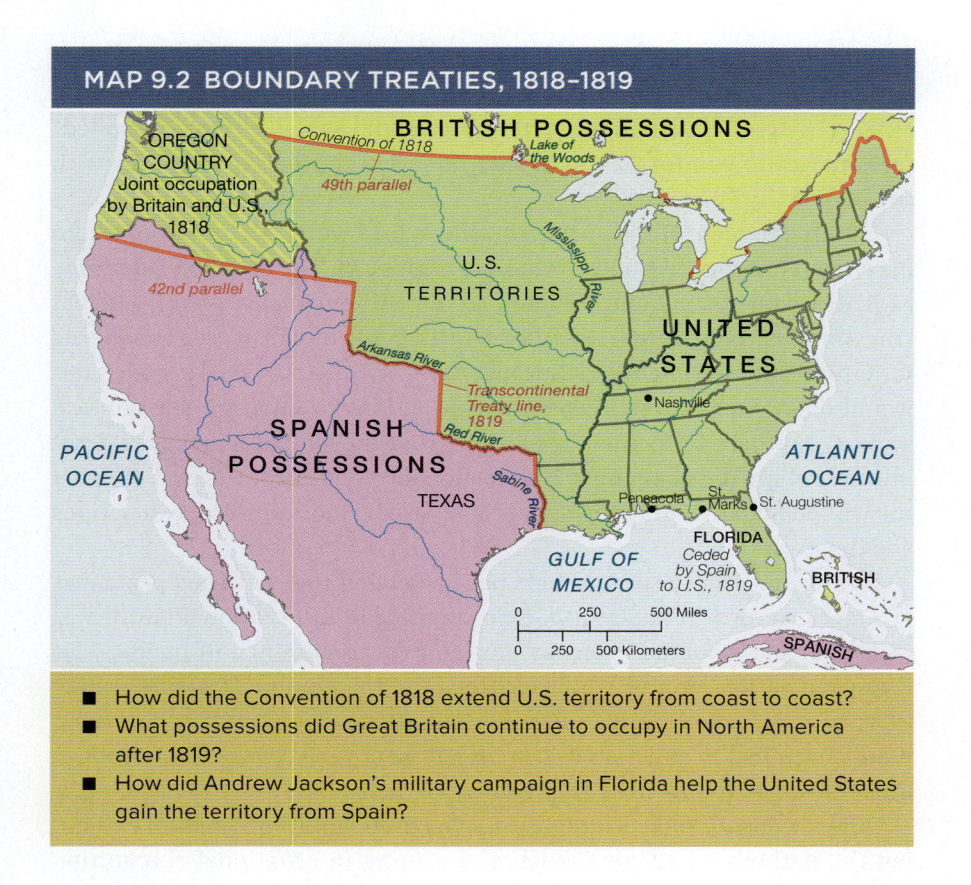

- How did the Convention of 1818 extend U.S. territory from coast to coast?
- What possessions did Great Britain continue to occupy in North America after 1819?
- How did Andrew Jackson's military campaign in Florida help the United States gain the territory from Spain?

United States in exchange for $5 million. Florida thus became a U.S. territory; in 1845, it would become a state. The treaty also addressed the western boundary separating the Louisiana Territory from New Spain, establishing that it would run from the Gulf of Mexico north to the 42nd parallel and then west to the Pacific coast. The United States now spanned the continent (see Map 9.2).

The Monroe Doctrine

The most important diplomatic policy crafted by President Monroe and Secretary of State Adams was designed to prevent future European colonialism in the Western Hemisphere. One consequence of the Napoleonic Wars raging across Europe and the French occupation of Spain and Portugal was a series of independence movements among the Spanish colonies. Between 1809 and 1830, Spain lost almost its entire empire in the Americas: La Plata (later Argentina), Bolivia, Chile, Ecuador, Peru, Colombia, Mexico, Paraguay, Uruguay, and Venezuela had all proclaimed their independence, as had Portuguese Brazil, and the United States was the first nation to recognize them. The only areas still under Spanish control were the islands of Cuba and Puerto Rico and the colony of Santo Domingo on the island of Hispaniola.

In 1823, rumors reached America that the monarchs of Europe were planning to help Spain recover its lost Latin American colonies. After an

> Transcontinental Treaty makes Florida a U.S. territory

Monroe Doctrine (1823)
U.S. foreign policy that barred further colonization in the Western Hemisphere by European powers and pledged that there would be no American interference with any existing European colonies.

Monroe declares opposition to recolonization of the Americas

attempt to enlist British support in opposing new incursions by European nations failed, Secretary of State Adams urged President Monroe to go it alone. He stressed that "it would be more candid as well as more dignified" for America to ban further European intervention than to tag along with the British.

Monroe agreed. He incorporated the substance of Adams's views into his annual message to Congress in December 1823. The **Monroe Doctrine**, as it was named a generation later, contained four major points: (1) that "the American continents . . . are henceforth not to be considered as subjects for future colonization by any European powers"; (2) that the United States would oppose any attempt by European nations to impose their political system anywhere in the hemisphere; (3) that the United States would not interfere with the remaining European-controlled colonies; and (4) that the United States would keep out of the internal affairs of European nations and their wars.

Although the Monroe Doctrine became one of the cherished principles of American foreign policy, it had no standing in international law; it was merely a bold statement sent by an American president to Congress. No European nation recognized the legitimacy of the Monroe Doctrine. And to this day, it has no official standing in international law. Over time, however, it has continued to guide American foreign policy in the event of European intervention in the Western Hemisphere.

American nationalists largely achieved their ambitious goals of extending the nation's geographic reach and gaining international recognition for the United States. A series of treaties and agreements defused simmering conflicts with Great Britain and Spain, the two remaining colonial powers in North America, and clarified the nation's boundaries as it expanded westward from the Atlantic to the Pacific Oceans. At the same time, the military campaign in Spanish Florida led by future president Andrew Jackson demonstrated that America was also determined to back diplomacy with force.

The Rise of Andrew Jackson

CORE OBJECTIVE

5. Evaluate the social and political factors that contributed to Andrew Jackson's success in the 1828 election.

America had become a one-party political system after the War of 1812. The refusal of the Federalists to support the conflict against Great Britain had virtually killed the party. In 1820, President Monroe was reelected without opposition.

While the Democratic-Republican Party was dominant for the moment, however, it was about to follow the Federalists into oblivion. If Monroe's first term was the Era of Good Feelings, his second term became the Era of Bad Feelings, as sectional controversies erupted into disputes so violent that they gave birth to a new political party: the Democrats, led by Andrew Jackson of Tennessee.

A Self-Made Man

Born in 1767 along the border between the Carolinas, Jackson grew up in a struggling single-parent household. His father was killed in a farm accident three weeks before Andrew was born, forcing his widowed mother, Elizabeth, to scratch out a living as a housekeeper while raising three sons.

During the Revolutionary War, the Jackson boys fought against the British. One of them, sixteen-year-old Hugh, died during a battle; another, Robert, died while trudging home from a prisoner-of-war camp in Camden, South Carolina. In 1781, fourteen-year-old Andrew Jackson was captured. When a British officer demanded that the boy shine his boots, Andrew refused, explaining that he was a prisoner of war and expected "to be treated as such." The angry officer slashed him with his sword, leaving ugly scars on Jackson's head and hand. Soon after young Andrew was released, his mother died of cholera.

After the Revolution, the orphaned Jackson went to Charleston, South Carolina, where he learned to love racehorses, card games, gambling, carousing, and fine clothes. He returned home and tried saddle-making and teaching before moving to Salisbury, North Carolina, where he earned a license to practice law. He also enjoyed life. A friend recalled that Jackson was "the most roaring, rollicking, game-cocking, card-playing, mischievous fellow that ever lived in Salisbury."

In 1788, at age twenty-one, Jackson moved to Nashville, Tennessee, and became an attorney. Eight years later, when Tennessee became a state, voters elected him to the U.S. House (he would later be elected to the Senate), but he served only a year before returning home and becoming a judge. Jackson also made a lot of money, first as an attorney, then as a buyer and seller of horses, land—and enslaved people, as many as 160 of whom labored on his cotton plantation, called the Hermitage, some twelve miles outside Nashville.

Many American political leaders cringed at the thought of the combative, short-tempered Jackson, who had run roughshod over international law when fighting the British and Seminoles in Florida, presiding over the nation. John Quincy Adams scorned Jackson "as a barbarian and savage who could scarcely spell his name."

ANDREW JACKSON The controversial general was painted by Anna Claypoole Peale in 1819, the year of his military exploits in Florida.

One-Party Politics

No sooner had James Monroe started his second presidential term, in 1821, than leading Republicans began seeking nominations to be the next president, including two members of the cabinet: Secretary of the Treasury William H. Crawford and Secretary of State John Quincy Adams. The powerful Speaker of the House, Henry Clay, also hungered for the presidency. And then there was Andrew Jackson, who was elected to the Senate in 1823. The emergence of so many strong candidates revealed how fractured the Republican Party had become.

Crawford's friends emphasized his devotion to states' rights and strict construction (interpretation) of the Constitution. For his part, Clay continued to champion his American System. Adams shared Clay's belief that the national government should finance internal improvements to stimulate economic development, but he was less strongly committed to tariffs.

Candidate Jackson

Jackson's appeal as "the common man"

As a self-made military hero, Andrew Jackson was an attractive candidate, especially to voters of Irish and Scots-Irish backgrounds. In Jackson, the Irish immigrants found a hero who had defeated the hated English in the Battle of New Orleans. In addition, the Irish immigrants' distaste for aristocracy, which they associated with centuries of English rule, attracted them to a politician who was proud of his rise from poverty.

The Election of 1824

A deadlocked election

The initial results of the 1824 election were inconclusive. In the Electoral College, Jackson received 99 votes; Adams, 84; Crawford, 41; and Clay, 37. Jackson, however, did not have the necessary majority of the votes. In such a circumstance, as in the 1800 election, the Constitution specified that the House of Representatives would make the final selection from among the top three candidates. By the time the House could convene, however, Crawford had suffered a stroke and dropped out.

The election was humiliating for Henry Clay and his American System; voters in New England and New York opposed his call for federal funding of internal improvements, and the South rejected his promotion of the protective tariff.

Whatever else might have been said about the outcome, one thing seemed apparent—the election revealed how deeply divided the nation had become. Sectionalism had defeated nationalism as the Republicans split into warring regional factions.

The "Corrupt Bargain"

Once the deadlocked election had been thrown into the House of Representatives, however, Clay's influence as Speaker of the House would prove decisive. While Adams and Jackson courted Clay's support, he claimed they provided only a "choice of evils." But he regarded Jackson as a "military chieftain" unfit for the presidency and predicted that his election would "be the greatest misfortune that could befall the country."

Although Clay and Adams disliked each other, the nationalist Adams supported most of what Clay wanted policy-wise, particularly high tariffs, transportation improvements, and a strong national bank. Clay also expected Adams to name him secretary of state, the office that usually led to the White House. A deal between Clay and Adams broke the deadlock. Clay endorsed Adams, and the House of Representatives elected Adams with 13 state-delegation votes to Jackson's 7 and Crawford's 4.

The controversial victory proved costly for Adams, however, as it united his foes and crippled his administration before it began. Jackson

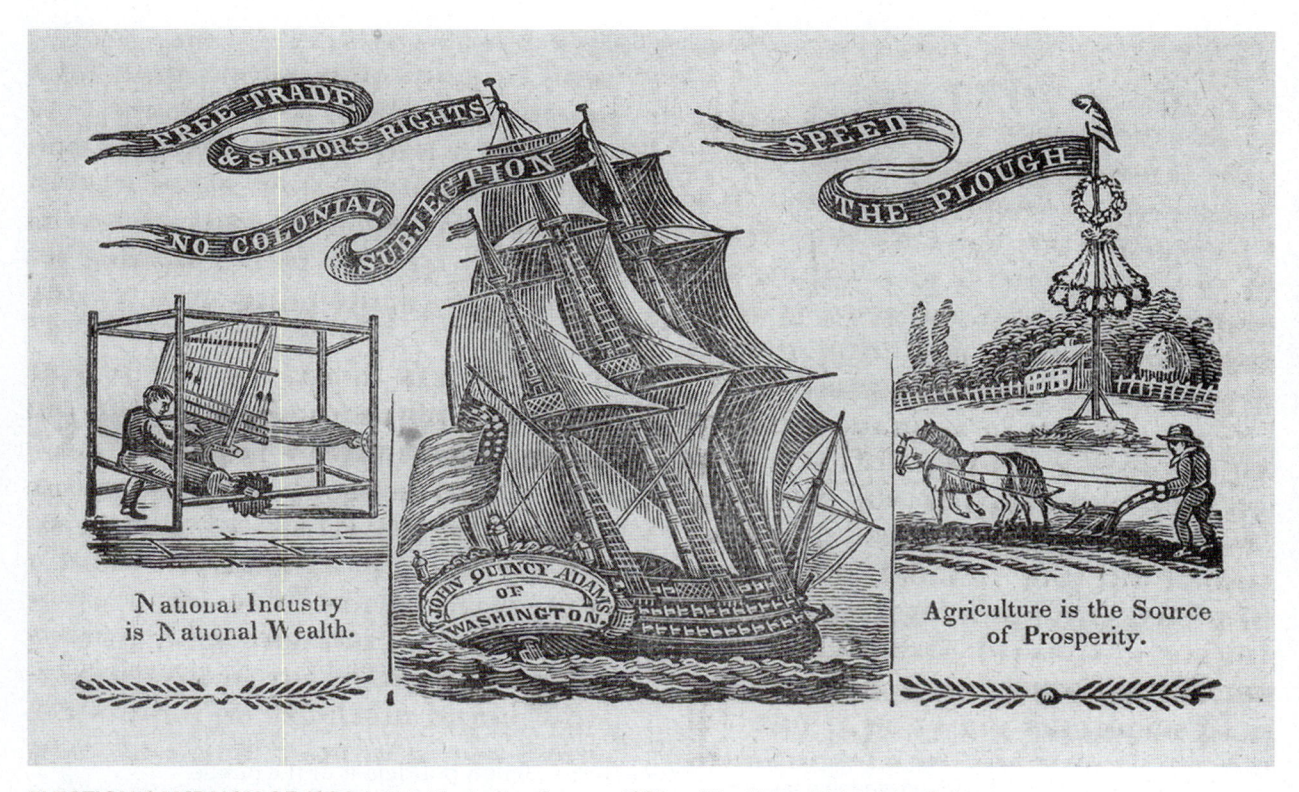

ELECTION CAMPAIGN OF 1824 In this illustration from an 1824 political broadside, John Quincy Adams advertises his allegiance to Henry Clay's American System. His presidential platform is portrayed as a ship sailing under the banners of "No Colonial Subjugation" and "Free Trade." **How did Adams's platform differ from Andrew Jackson's?**

dismissed Clay as a "scoundrel," the "Judas of the West," who had entered into a self-serving **"corrupt bargain"** with Adams. Their "corruptions and intrigues," he charged, had "defeated the will of the People."

Almost immediately, in 1828, Jackson's supporters launched a campaign to undermine the Adams administration and elect their hero president. Crawford's supporters soon moved into the Jackson camp, as did the new vice president, John C. Calhoun of South Carolina, who quickly found himself at odds with the president.

John Quincy Adams

Adams had been groomed for greatness by his parents, John and Abigail, the nation's second president and his accomplished wife. He began keeping a diary at age twelve and made daily entries until his death, eventually filling some 14,000 pages of text. In his diary, Adams often reflected on the stain of slavery. The Constitution that his father had helped enact was, he decided, "morally and politically vicious" for its tolerance of slavery, and therefore "inconsistent with the principles upon which alone our Revolution can be justified."

Adams's political experience was unmatched. He had been ambassador to four European nations, during which time he became fluent in three

"corrupt bargain" Scandal in which presidential candidate and Speaker of the House Henry Clay secured John Quincy Adams's victory over Andrew Jackson in the 1824 election, supposedly in exchange for naming Clay secretary of state.

languages: German, Dutch, and French. After graduating from Harvard, he served as a U.S. senator, a Harvard professor, and as secretary of state. He had helped negotiate the treaty ending the War of 1812 and had drafted the Monroe Doctrine (1823). And he promoted American isolation from global wars and causes.

Yet for all his accomplishments, John Quincy Adams proved to be an ineffective president, undercut from the start by the controversy surrounding his deal with Henry Clay. In his inaugural address, Adams promised to govern with "talents and virtue" but admitted to voters that he was "less possessed of your confidence . . . than any of my predecessors."

Adams lacked the common touch and the politician's gift for compromise. "I am," he confessed, "a man of reserved, cold, austere, and forbidding manners." The stiff and stern Adams was unable to "reform" himself. His sour personality was shaped in part by family tragedies: he saw two brothers and two sons die from alcoholism. Adams himself suffered from chronic bouts of depression that reinforced his grim outlook and tendency toward self-pity, qualities that did not endear him to fellow politicians or the public.

Adams also detested the democratic politicking that Andrew Jackson represented. He worried, as his father had, that republicanism was degenerating into government *by* the people, many of whom, in his view, were uneducated and incompetent. He wanted politics to be a "sacred" arena for the "best men," a profession limited to the "most able and worthy" leaders motivated by a sense of civic duty rather than a selfish quest for power and stature.

JOHN QUINCY ADAMS Considered a brilliant man but an ineffective leader, Adams appears here in his study in 1843. He was the first U.S. president to be photographed.

An Activist Government

Public opposition to Adams's activist government

John Quincy Adams was determined to create an activist federal government with expansive goals. His first State of the Union message, in December 1825, included a grand blueprint for national development, but it was set forth so bluntly that it became a political disaster.

The federal government, Adams stressed, should finance vast internal improvements (new roads, canals, harbors, and bridges), create a national university, support scientific explorations of the Far West, build astronomical observatories, and establish a department of the interior to manage government-owned lands. He challenged Congress to approve his proposals and not be paralyzed "by the will of our constituents."

The reaction was overwhelmingly negative. Newspapers charged that Adams was behaving like an aristocratic tyrant, and Congress rejected all of his proposals. The disastrous start shattered Adams's confidence. He wrote in his diary that he was in a "protracted agony of character and reputation."

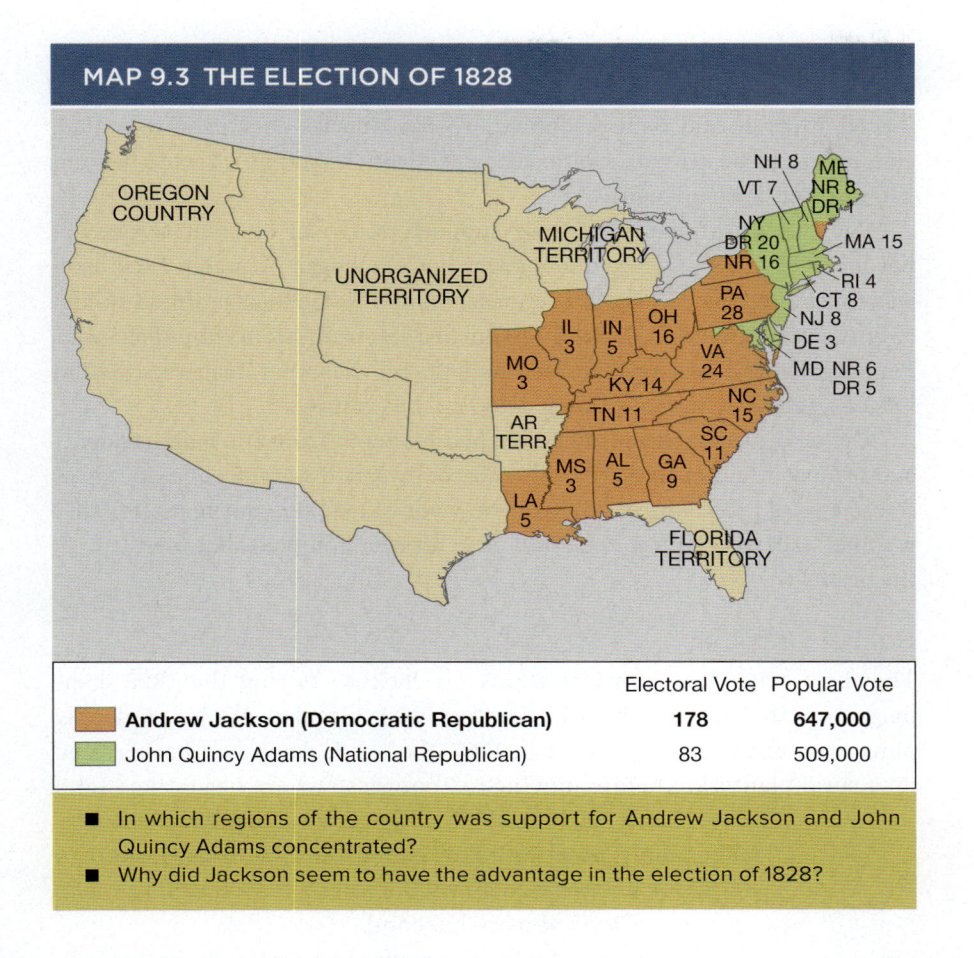

MAP 9.3 THE ELECTION OF 1828

	Electoral Vote	Popular Vote
■ Andrew Jackson (Democratic Republican)	178	647,000
■ John Quincy Adams (National Republican)	83	509,000

- In which regions of the country was support for Andrew Jackson and John Quincy Adams concentrated?
- Why did Jackson seem to have the advantage in the election of 1828?

Adams's effort to expand the powers of the federal government divided the Democratic-Republican Party. Those who agreed with the economic nationalism of Adams and Clay began calling themselves National Republicans. Those Democratic Republicans supporting Andrew Jackson and states' rights would eventually drop the name Republican and become simply Democrats.

> A partisan split between the Democrats and Republicans

President Adams proved to be a stubborn visionary unable to excite voters with his ideas. The nation was not ready for a dominant federal government—but it was ready for a charismatic and domineering president.

The Election of 1828

The defiant congressional opposition to the Adams presidency launched the **campaign of 1828** between the National Republicans and the Jacksonian Democrats (see Map 9.3). Both sides engaged in vicious personal attacks.

"The floodgates of falsehood, slander, and abuse have been hoisted" by the Adams campaign, a Jackson supporter observed, "and the most nauseating filth is [being] poured" on Jackson's head. Adams's supporters denounced Jackson as a hot-tempered, ignorant barbarian and slave trader who had participated in numerous frontier brawls, a man whose fame rested upon his reputation as a killer.

campaign of 1828 Bitter presidential contest between Democrat Andrew Jackson and National Republican John Quincy Adams (running for reelection), resulting in Jackson's victory.

Such charges were not inaccurate. The iron-willed Jackson had always displayed an explosive temper. He loved a good fight. In 1806, he challenged attorney and rival racehorse breeder Charles Dickinson to a duel, claiming that the arrogant young attorney had not paid off a racing bet and had insulted Jackson's wife.

The two proud men and their supporters agreed to meet across the border in Kentucky, where dueling was not yet illegal. Although Dickinson was considered the best shot in Tennessee and was said to have already killed twenty-six men in duels, Jackson let him fire first from twenty-four feet away. For his gallantry, Jackson received a bullet in his chest that fractured ribs and lodged so close to his heart that it could not be removed.

The wounded Jackson then clenched his teeth from the pain, straightened himself, patiently took aim, and coolly killed his foe. The doctor at the scene told Jackson, "I don't see how you stayed on your feet after that wound." Jackson replied, "I should have hit him if he had shot me through the brain."

Rachel Jackson

Defamatory attacks on Rachel Jackson

The most scurrilous political attack on Jackson during the 1828 campaign was that he had lived in adultery with his wife, Rachel, a deeply pious woman. Born in Virginia in 1767, Rachel Jackson had been raised on a rural plantation before moving to Tennessee where her father, John Donelson, led the establishing of what became Nashville. The family later moved to Harrodsburg, Kentucky, where in 1785 Rachel married Lewis Robards, a land speculator who proved to be an abusive husband.

During one of several periods of separation from Robards, Rachel returned to Nashville. Her mother was living there again after the death of Rachel's father and, it turned out, was renting a room to Andrew Jackson, then a young attorney recently arrived from South Carolina. Rachel was known as a charming, vivacious woman with special talents as a dancer and horsewoman. Upon meeting Rachel, Jackson was smitten with her.

In 1790 Lewis Robards gained legal permission to seek a divorce. Rachel, along with Andrew Jackson, mistakenly assumed a divorce had already been granted, and in August 1791 they were married. Two years later, when they learned that Robards had not instituted formal divorce proceedings until September 1793, they underwent a second marriage ceremony on January 17, 1794.

Over thirty-five years later, when Jackson became a presidential candidate, ugly rumors began to circulate about the "irregularities" of his marriage. Adams's supporters insisted that an "adulteress" had no business being the nation's First Lady. A furious Jackson blamed Henry Clay

RACHEL JACKSON The wife of President-elect Andrew Jackson was subjected to a brutal political attack on her character during the 1828 election. She would die just a few weeks before Jackson was inaugurated.

for the slurs against his wife, calling the Kentuckian "the basest, meanest scoundrel that ever disgraced the image of his god." Thereafter, the two proud men developed a consuming hatred for each other and a bitter political rivalry.

Candidate Jackson benefited from a growing spirit of democracy in which many voters viewed John Quincy Adams as an elitist. When Adams's supporters began referring to the rough-hewn Jackson as a "jackass," the Tennessean embraced the name, using the animal as a symbol for his "tough" campaign. The jackass eventually became the enduring symbol of the Democratic Party.

Jackson prevailed and easily defeated Adams in the 1828 election. But he never forgot or forgave the attacks on his wife.

Rachel Jackson did not follow her husband to the White House. On December 22, just a few weeks before Jackson's inauguration, she succumbed to a heart attack. She was buried in her inauguration gown and slippers. Jackson had the following inscription etched into her tombstone: "A being so gentle and so virtuous, slander might wound, but could not dishonor."

The "Common Man" in Politics

Jackson's 1828 campaign explicitly appealed to the "common" voters, many of whom were able to vote in a presidential election for the first time. After the Revolution, and especially after 1800, more and more White men had gained the right to vote. Only Virginia and the Carolinas, still dominated by the planter elite, continued to resist the democratizing trend.

> Democratization of voting

The extension of voting rights to people with little or no wealth led to the election of politicians who arose from the people rather than from the social elite. Jackson, a frontiersman of humble origin who had made a fortune and scrambled up the political ladder by will and tenacity, fit this more democratic ideal. "Adams can write," went one of the campaign slogans, "but Jackson can fight."

The "democratization" of politics also led many free Black men in northern states to vote for the first time. But that did not last long. States such as New York, in its 1821 constitution, instituted new voting restrictions on Black voting at the same time that it extended the right to vote to all White men. Pennsylvania (in 1838) and New Jersey (in 1807) likewise outlawed Black voting during this period of "democratization."

Freedom's Journal

African Americans protested these restrictions on their rights and in 1827 launched *Freedom's Journal*, the first weekly newspaper published by and for Black people. Based in New York City, the editors Samuel Cornish and John Russwurm stressed that their newspaper would meet a pressing need for African Americans to resist discriminatory "schemes" affecting "our brethren."

> First African American Newspaper

Cornish was the pastor of the First Colored Presbyterian Church in New York City, and Russwurm was the first African American to graduate from

FREEDOM'S JOURNAL The first weekly newspaper published by and for African Americans was launched in New York City. The editors, Samuel Cornish and John Russwurm, both freeborn, stressed that their newspaper would meet a pressing need for African Americans to publicly debate and protest slavery and other inequalities facing Black people.

an American college (Bowdoin College in Maine). The two young editors were eager to fill their newspaper with "whatever concerns us as a people" and enable readers and contributors to "plead our own cause. Too long have others spoken for us."

The editors pledged to inform their readers about the daily injustices experienced by African Americans in the hope of ending the practice of slavery forever. Within a few years, thanks to the example of *Freedom's Journal*, there were more than a dozen newspapers owned by Black editors and focused on slavery and racial equality. The growth of the Black press would help fuel the rise of the abolitionist movement in the decades to come and ensure that slavery would remain the major sectionalist issue in American politics.

President Jackson

In winning the 1828 election, Andrew Jackson had captured every state west and south of Pennsylvania. His 178 Electoral College votes trounced Adams' 83. Equally important was the surge in voter turnout that brought more than twice as many men to the polls as in the 1824 election (see again Map 9.3).

John Quincy Adams was stunned by his defeat. He was only the second president to be denied a second term (his father had been the first). But the younger Adams was elated to leave the White House. "The four most miserable years of my life," he later noted, "were my four years in the presidency."

Although Adams's nationalist agenda had been largely thwarted by a Congress dominated by slave-state representatives, Jackson would prove more adept at wielding the power of the executive branch to serve the interests of particular states. The trajectory of Andrew Jackson's career—from hardscrabble backwoodsman to military hero to slave owner and combative politician—mirrored the aspirations of many White Americans in the nation's maturing democracy. And although he was hated by some of his fellow Republicans, including Adams and James Monroe, Jackson appealed to the expanding electorate through his common-man image and disdain of convention. His populist style would come to define what became a new era of democracy in the United States.

> Dramatic expansion of democracy revealed in 1828 presidential election

Reviewing the
CORE OBJECTIVES

- **A New Nationalism** After the War of 1812, the federal government pursued many policies to strengthen the national economy. The *Tariff of 1816* protected American manufacturers from foreign competition, and the *Second Bank of the United States* provided a stronger national currency. Madison, Monroe, and Adams all encouraged an active role for the federal government in promoting economic growth. Led by John Marshall, the Supreme Court limited the powers of states and strengthened the power of the federal government in *Dartmouth College v. Woodward* (1819) and *McCulloch v. Maryland* (1819). The Marshall court interpreted the Constitution as giving Congress the right to take any action not forbidden by the Constitution as long as the purpose of such laws was within the "scope of the Constitution." In *Gibbons v. Ogden* (1824), the Marshall court established the federal government's authority over interstate commerce.

- **Debates over the American System** Henry Clay's *American System* supported economic nationalism by endorsing a national bank, a protective tariff, and federally funded *internal improvements* such as roads and canals. Many Americans, however, remained more tied to the needs of their sections of the country. People in the different regions—Northeast, South, and Midwest—disagreed about which economic policies best served their interests. As settlers streamed west, the extension of slavery into the new territories became the predominant political concern, eventually requiring both sides to compromise repeatedly to avoid civil war.

- **"An Era of Good Feelings"** James Monroe's term in office was initially labeled the Era of Good Feelings because it began with peace and prosperity. Two major events spelled the end of the Era of Good Feelings: the financial *Panic of 1819* and the controversial *Missouri Compromise* (1820). The explosive growth of the cotton culture transformed life in the South, partly by encouraging the expansion of slavery, which moved west with migrating southern planters. In 1819, however, the sudden collapse of world cotton prices devastated the southern economy. The Missouri Compromise, a short-term solution to the issue of allowing slavery in the western territories, exposed the emotions and turmoil that the tragic system generated.

- **Nationalist Diplomacy** The main diplomatic achievements of the period after the War of 1812 defined America's contested boundaries and eased tensions with Great Britain. To the north, U.S. diplomats established northern borders with Canada. To the south, the *Transcontinental Treaty* (1819) with Spain extended the boundaries of the United States. The *Monroe Doctrine* (1823) declared that the Americas were no longer open to European colonization.

- **The Rise of Andrew Jackson** The demise of the Federalists ended the first party system in America, leaving the Republicans as the only national party. The seeming unity of the Republicans was shattered by the election of 1824, which Andrew Jackson lost as a result of what he believed was a *"corrupt bargain"* between John Quincy Adams and Henry Clay. Jackson won the presidency in the *campaign of 1828* by rallying southern and western voters with his promise to serve the interests of common people. His election opened a new era in national politics that reflected the democratization of voting in most states (at least for White men).

KEY TERMS

Second Bank of the United States *p. 368*
Tariff of 1816 *p. 369*
internal improvements *p. 369*
Dartmouth College v. Woodward (1819) *p. 370*
McCulloch v. Maryland (1819) *p. 370*
Gibbons v. Ogden (1824) *p. 370*
American System *p. 372*
Panic of 1819 *p. 374*
Missouri Compromise (1820) *p. 375*
Transcontinental Treaty (1819) *p. 380*
Monroe Doctrine (1823) *p. 382*
"corrupt bargain" *p. 385*
campaign of 1828 *p. 387*

CHRONOLOGY

1811 Construction of the National Road begins
1816 Second Bank of the United States is established
First protective tariff goes into effect
1817 Rush-Bagot Agreement between the United States and Great Britain
1818 The Convention of 1818 establishes the northern border of the Louisiana Purchase; Britain and the United States agree to their joint occupation of Oregon
1819 Supreme Court issues *McCulloch v. Maryland* decision
The United States and Spain agree to the Transcontinental Treaty
The Tallmadge Amendment is passed
1820 Congress accepts the Missouri Compromise
1823 President Monroe enunciates the principles of the Monroe Doctrine
1824 Supreme Court issues *Gibbons v. Ogden* decision
John Quincy Adams wins the presidential election by what some critics claim is a "corrupt bargain" with Henry Clay
1828 Andrew Jackson wins the presidential contest

InQuizitive

Go to InQuizitive to see what you've learned—and learn what you've missed—with personalized feedback along the way.

HARD TIMES IN THE JACKSONIAN ERA Although it is said that Andrew Jackson championed the "poor and humble," his economic policies contributed to the Panic of 1837, a financial crisis that hit the working class the hardest. This cartoon illustrates New York City during the seven-year economic depression: a frantic mob storms a bank, while in the *foreground* a widow begs on the street with her child, surrounded by a banker or landlord and a barefoot sailor. At *left* are a drunken member of the Bowery Toughs gang and a down-on-his-luck militiaman. The cartoonist places the blame on Jackson, whose hat, glasses, and pipe overlook the scene. The banner about "specie," or payments in gold rather than paper money, illustrates the controversy over banks and bankers during the Jacksonian era.

CHAPTER 10

A New Democratic Era

1828–1840

As the United States entered a new era, the nation began to solidify ideals of democracy. More Americans participated in national politics and exercised their right to vote. Previous property restrictions were lifted, allowing more people the opportunity to run for office. American citizens chose political parties and rallied behind their parties' principles. Even with these changes, however, groups of people remained marginalized, and it was in this context that Andrew Jackson became the seventh president of the United States.

President Andrew Jackson was a unique character and, to some, a transformational leader. To others, he was a disruptor of the lives of Indigenous and enslaved people. He was the first president from a western state (Tennessee), the first to have been born in a log cabin, the first *not* to come from a prominent colonial family, the first to be censured by the Senate, the first to enact Indigenous removal, the first to experience an attempted assassination, and the first to carry two bullets in his body from a duel and a barroom brawl. Most important, Jackson was the polarizing figure of a new democratic era.

Jackson had a gaunt, chiseled face topped by a shock of unruly white hair. A self-made man, he believed in simple pleasures; he read three chapters of the Bible each day. He smoked a corncob pipe and chewed tobacco. (As president, he had a servant place twenty gold spittoons throughout the White House.) Jackson was dubbed "Old Hickory" because of his grit and toughness; yet despite appearances, he was not in good health when he assumed the presidency. He suffered from blinding headaches, a constant

CORE OBJECTIVES

1. Describe how Democracy expanded and contracted during this period.
2. Evaluate Jackson's response to the nullification crisis.
3. Analyze Jackson's legacy regarding the status of Indigenous people in American society.
4. Explain the causes of the economic depression of the late 1830s and the emergence of the Whig Party.
5. Assess the strengths and weaknesses of Jackson's presidency.

cough, and other ailments that led his rival Henry Clay to describe him as "feeble in body and mind."

Despite his physical challenges, Jackson relished the rough-and-tumble combat of the raucous new democratic political culture. "I was born for a storm," he once boasted.

Jackson certainly took the nation by storm. No political figure was more widely loved or more deeply despised than he. As a soldier, lawyer, slave-owning planter, and politician, he helped create and shape the Democratic Party, and he ushered new elements of presidential campaigning into the electoral process. Jackson championed the emergence of the "common man" in politics (by which he meant White men only) and resolved to *"preserve the union of these states, although it may cost me my life."*

Jackson led the nation into a new era in which more people became involved with the political process. Yet even in this expansive period, Jackson's leadership excluded and literally removed some people from the franchise. Women, the enslaved, and Indigenous people were not able to participate in the political process in the same way as White men. Such inequalities led to conflicts that would divide the nation in the years to come.

> CORE **OBJECTIVE**
> **1.** Describe how Democracy expanded and contracted during this period.
>
> Promoting the "common man"

Democratization and the Role of the Federal Government

Andrew Jackson's election marked the culmination of thirty years of democratic innovations in politics. During the 1820s and 1830s, political life was transformed as more and more landless White men were allowed to vote and to hold office. "The principle of universal suffrage," announced the *U.S. Magazine and Democratic Review*, "meant that white males of age constituted the political nation." Jackson's populist goal was to elevate the "laboring classes" of White men who "love liberty and desire nothing but equal rights and equal laws." No longer was politics the arena for only the most prominent and wealthiest Americans.

Political Democracy

Campaigning was also democratized. Politics became the most popular form of mass entertainment, as people from all walks of life passionately engaged in political campaigns. Even the disenfranchised (especially women and enslaved and free Blacks) understood the importance of participation in political activities. Politics was "the only pleasure an American knows," observed visiting Frenchman Alexis de Tocqueville. "Even the women frequently attend public meetings and listen to political harangues as a recreation from their household labors."

Indeed, during this period women participated in religious and charitable organizations that focused on issues of concern to them. They lobbied for social services and a share of public money to support widows, orphans, pregnant women, and the aged. Women also spoke out about the welfare system; and challenged their exclusion from politics, using political language to fight for their rights.

Aside from the disenfranchised, Jackson benefited from a powerful Democratic Party "machine" run by his trusted secretary of state (later his vice president) Martin Van Buren, a New York lawyer with a keen political sense. Unlike the founders who had drafted the Constitution, Van Buren did not worry over the rise of political parties. He saw them as necessary elements of a republic. And he played a significant role in nurturing Jackson's Democratic Party.

> An openly partisan president

Democracy, of course, is a slippery and elastic concept, and Jacksonians rarely defined what they meant by the "rule of the people." Noah Webster, the Connecticut Federalist who produced the nation's first dictionary of homegrown American English, complained that "the men who have preached these doctrines [of democracy] have never defined what they mean by the *people*, or what they mean by *democracy*, nor how the *people* are to govern themselves."

Anti-Democratic Impulses

Jacksonian Democrats also showed little concern for the *undemocratic* constraints on African Americans, Indigenous Americans, and women, all of whom were denied political and civil rights.

Many southern slaveowners worried that the surge of democratic activism would eventually threaten the slave system. Virginian Muscoe Garnett, a planter and attorney, declared that "democracy is indeed incompatible with slavery, and the whole system of Southern society."

As the first president to view himself as a representative of "the people," Jackson resolved to exercise expanded executive powers at the expense of the legislative and judicial branches. The ruling political and economic elite must be removed, he said, for "the people" are "the government, the sovereign power" in the United States, and they had elected him president.

> Expanded presidential authority

Democracy Unleashed

Jackson's inauguration ceremony set the tone for his controversial presidency. The self-described people's president stepped out of the U.S. Capitol at noon on March 4, 1829. Waiting for him in the cold were 15,000 people who collectively roared and waved their hats when they saw Jackson emerge. "I've never seen anything like it before," marveled Daniel Webster, the renowned senator from Massachusetts.

ALL CREATION GOING TO THE WHITE HOUSE (1840) In this depiction of Jackson's inauguration party, satirist Robert Cruikshank draws a visual parallel to Noah's Ark, suggesting that people of all walks of life were now welcome to what would be called the White House.

Concerns about Jackson's fitness for the presidency were heightened by riotous scenes at the White House immediately after his inauguration ceremony. In a symbolic effort to reach out to the "common" people, Jackson announced that he was opening the party to anyone. To his surprise, the huge crowd of jubilant supporters turned into a drunken, raucous mob, smashing dishes and glasses and breaking furniture inside the White House.

Upon taking office, the nation's seventh president wanted to reduce federal spending, pay off the federal debt (a "national curse"), destroy the Second Bank of the United States (B.U.S.), and relocate the "ill-fated race" of Indigenous Americans from the East to the West so that Whites could exploit the native peoples' ancestral lands. In pursuing these ambitious goals, he exercised presidential authority more boldly than any of his predecessors.

The Spoils System and Presidential Conventions

Spoils system

To dislodge the eastern political elite, Jackson launched a policy he called "rotation in office," whereby he replaced many federal officials with his supporters. He argued that government jobs belonged to the people, not to career bureaucrats. During Jackson's two presidential terms, he replaced about one-fifth of the federal officeholders with his friends and supporters, not all of whom were qualified for their new positions. Such partisan behavior came to be called "the spoils system," since, as a prominent Democrat declared, "to the victor goes the spoils."

Birth of presidential nominating conventions

Jackson also sought to "democratize" the way that presidential candidates were selected. Ever since the presidency of George Washington, most nominees had been chosen by party caucuses of prominent congressmen and senators. Jackson hated the idea of legislators nominating presidents. In 1831, he convinced the Democrats to stage their first presidential nominating convention as a means of involving more people in the process of selecting a candidate. The innovation of presidential nominating conventions reinforced Jackson's image as a man of the people fighting against entrenched party leaders.

Divided Cabinet

Yet Jackson soon found himself preoccupied with squabbles within his own cabinet. From the outset, his administration was divided between supporters of Secretary of State Martin Van Buren, a New Yorker, and the allies of Vice President John C. Calhoun of South Carolina. Both men wanted to succeed Jackson as president.

Jackson turned mostly to Van Buren for advice because he did not trust Calhoun, a Yale graduate of towering intellect and fiery self-interest. Calhoun was focused on defending southern interests, especially the preservation of slavery, which had made him a wealthy planter. Van Buren accompanied Jackson on horseback rides around the capital and found ways to displace Vice President Calhoun as the nation's second most powerful political figure; several years later, in 1837, Van Buren became president himself.

Internal Improvements

Jackson used his executive authority to limit the role of the federal government—while at the same time delivering additional blows to John C. Calhoun and to Henry Clay, the man Jackson blamed for having "stolen" the 1824 election from him.

In 1830, Congress passed a bill pushed by Calhoun and Clay that authorized the use of federal funds to build a sixty-mile-long road across the state of Kentucky from Maysville to Lexington, Clay's hometown. Urged on by New Yorker Martin Van Buren, who wanted to preserve the Erie Canal's monopoly over western trade, Jackson vetoed the bill. The president claimed that the proposed Maysville Road was a "purely local matter," because it would run solely through Kentucky. Therefore, that single-state boundary placed the project outside the domain of Congress, which had authority only over *interstate* commerce. The veto left Clay stunned. "We are all shocked and mortified by the rejection of the Maysville Road," he wrote to a friend.

> Jackson vetoes the Maysville Road Bill

The Bank War

Andrew Jackson showed the same principled resolve in dealing with the national bank. The charter for the First Bank of the United States (B.U.S.) had expired in 1811 but was renewed in 1816 as the Second Bank of the United States, and it soon became the largest corporation in the nation. The Second B.U.S. held all federal funds—mostly the proceeds from land sales and tariff revenues. It also issued paper money (backed by gold and silver) as the national currency. Headquartered in Philadelphia and supported by twenty-nine branches around the nation, the B.U.S. had helped accelerate business expansion by making loans to individuals, businesses, and state banks. It had also supplied a stable currency by requiring the 464 state banks to keep enough gold coins in their vaults to back their own paper currency. With federal revenues soaring from land sales during the early 1830s, the B.U.S., led by Nicholas Biddle, had accumulated massive amounts of money—and economic power.

Even though the B.U.S. benefited the national economy, it had been controversial from the start. Local banks and state governments, especially those in the South and West, feared its growing "monopolistic" power. Southerners and westerners claimed that Biddle and the massive B.U.S. were restricting lending by state banks and impeding businesses from borrowing.

Throughout his life Andrew Jackson, like many westerners, had hated banks and bankers, whom he called "vipers and thieves." He admitted that he had "always been afraid of banks"—especially the national bank—because they exercised too much power. He distrusted paper money because in his opinion banks printed too much of it, causing prices to rise (inflation). "I

KING ANDREW THE FIRST (1833) Opponents considered Jackson's veto of the Maysville Road Bill an abuse of power. This cartoon shows "King Andrew" trampling on the Constitution, internal improvements, and the Bank of the United States.

RECHARTERING THE BANK
Jackson's effort to defeat the recharter of the B.U.S. is likened to fighting a hydra, a many-headed serpent from Greek mythology. Just as the mythical hydra sprouted two heads when one was severed, for every B.U.S. supporter that Jackson subdues, even more B.U.S. supporters emerge to take his place.

think it right to be perfectly frank with you," Jackson told Biddle in 1829. "I do not dislike your Bank any more than [I dislike] all banks."

Early on, the president resolved to destroy the B.U.S., pledging "to put his foot upon the head of the monster and crush him to the dust." The national bank may have become too powerful, but the **Bank War** between Jackson and Biddle revealed, as some historians argue, that the president never understood the bank's role or policies. The national bank had in fact provided a stable currency for the expanding economy, as well as a mechanism for controlling the pace of economic growth by regulating the ability of branch banks and state banks to issue paper currency.

The Recharter Effort

Nicholas Biddle was confident about the Second Bank's future. Leaders of the newly named National Republican Party, especially Henry Clay and Daniel Webster (who was legal counsel to the B.U.S. as well as a senator), had assured him that Congress would renew the charter before the 1832 presidential election. "This worthy President," he claimed, "thinks because he has scalped Indians . . . he is to have his way with the Bank." Biddle was certain that the B.U.S. "will destroy" Jackson instead.

Biddle and his political allies, however, failed to grasp both Jackson's tenacity and the depth of public resentment toward the national bank. In the end, Biddle, Clay, and the National Republican Party (also called the Anti-Jackson Party) unintentionally handed Jackson a powerful issue on the eve of the 1832 election.

Bank War The political struggle in the early 1830s between President Jackson and financier Nicholas Biddle over the renewing of the Second Bank's charter.

Early in the summer of 1832, both houses of Congress passed the Bank Recharter Bill. A month later, however, Jackson vetoed the bill. The president claimed that the B.U.S. was both unconstitutional (although the Supreme Court disagreed) and "dangerous to our liberties." The B.U.S. made "the rich richer and the potent more powerful," he charged, while discriminating against "the humble members of society—the farmers, mechanics, and laborers."

Daniel Webster accused Jackson of using the bank issue "to stir up the poor against the rich." To Henry Clay, Jackson's veto represented another example of the president's desire to concentrate "all power in the hands of one man." In the end, Clay and Webster could not convince the Senate to override the veto, thus setting the stage for a nationwide debate and a dramatic presidential campaign.

By now, Jackson had clearly articulated his beliefs about democracy, the presidency, and the role of government in the nation's economy. He wanted to make the democratic process and economic opportunity accessible to the "common man," and while this expansion of the democratic process did not include women, Black people, or Indigenous people, each of these groups began to participate more in political activities. Jackson, however, wanted to expand the role of the president—especially in economic matters. He sought to reduce federal spending and do away with the powerful Second B.U.S.—moves that angered his opponents. Soon, he would face a new controversy stirred up by his fellow southerners.

> Jackson vetoes renewal of B.U.S. charter

Nullification

Critics claimed that Jackson's behavior in vetoing the Maysville Road Bill and the B.U.S. recharter was "monarchical" in its defiance of the will of Congress. Jackson, however, remained determined to strengthen the executive branch in order to strengthen the Union. His commitment to nationalism over sectionalism was especially evident in his handling of the nullification crisis in South Carolina.

Calhoun and the Tariff

Vice President John C. Calhoun became President Jackson's fiercest critic because of changing conditions in his home state of South Carolina. The financial Panic of 1819 had sparked a nationwide economic depression; and throughout the 1820s, South Carolina had suffered from falling cotton prices.

Most South Carolinians blamed their economic woes on the Tariff of 1828, which was labeled the **Tariff of Abominations**. By taxing British textiles coming into U.S. markets, the 1828 tariff hurt southern cotton growers by reducing British demand for raw cotton from America. It also hurt southerners by raising prices for imported products.

> **CORE OBJECTIVE**
> **2.** Evaluate Jackson's response to the nullification crisis.

Tariff of Abominations (1828)
A tax on imported goods, including British cloth and clothing, that strengthened New England textile companies but hurt southern consumers, who experienced a decrease in British demand for raw cotton grown in the South.

NULLIFICATION The enormous "Union Pie" symbolizes the United States being devoured by different states and nations. South Carolina appears as a gluttonous colonist indulging in its own self-interests while threatening to divide the Union.

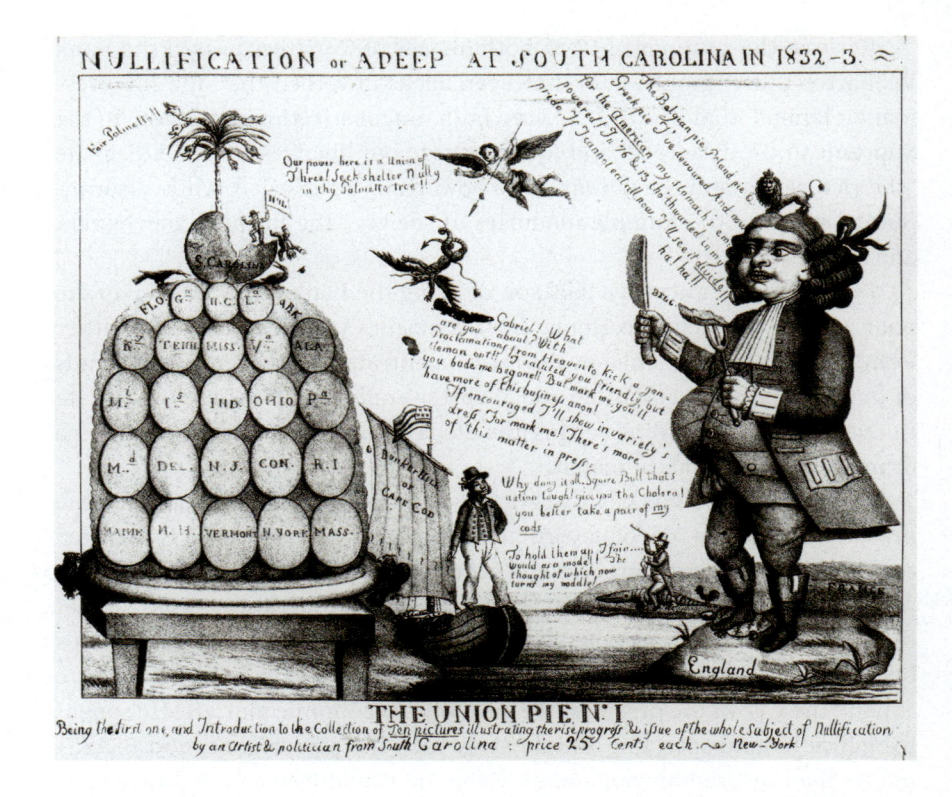

But the tariff was not the only factor explaining South Carolina's problems. Thousands of acres of farmland across the state were nutritionally exhausted from constant overplanting. In addition, South Carolina cotton planters now faced competition from the new cotton-growing states in the Old Southwest: Alabama, Mississippi, Louisiana, and Arkansas.

In a pamphlet he wrote in secret called the *South Carolina Exposition and Protest* (1828), Calhoun claimed that the Tariff of 1828 favored the interests of New England textile manufacturing over southern agriculture. Under such circumstances, he argued, a state could "nullify," or veto, a federal law it deemed unconstitutional.

Nullification was the ultimate weapon for those determined to protect states' rights against federal authority. As President Jackson and others pointed out, however, allowing states to pick and choose which federal laws they wanted to follow would create chaos.

The Webster-Hayne Debate

> Webster-Hayne debate: States' rights vs. national unity

The controversy over the Tariff of 1828 simmered until 1830. In a fiery speech that year, Senator Robert Y. Hayne of South Carolina argued that antislavery Yankees were invading the South, "making war upon her citizens, and endeavoring to overthrow her principles and institutions." In Hayne's view, the Union was created by the states, and the states therefore had the right to nullify—or ignore—federal laws they did not like.

nullification The right claimed by some states to veto a federal law they deemed unconstitutional.

Massachusetts senator Daniel Webster challenged Hayne's arguments. Blessed with a thunderous voice and a theatrical flair, Webster was an unapologetic Unionist determined "to strengthen the ties that hold us together." If states were allowed to nullify a federal law, he argued, the Union would be nothing but a "rope of sand." South Carolina's defiance of federal authority, Webster charged, "is nothing more than resistance by *force*—it is disunion by *force*—it is secession by *force*—it is civil war." (Secession is the formal withdrawal of a state from the Union.)

Webster's powerful closing statement appeared in virtually every newspaper in the nation: "Liberty and Union, now and forever, one and inseparable." Even Hayne was awestruck. He told Webster that "a man who can make such speeches as that ought never to die."

In the end, Webster had the better argument. Most political leaders agreed that the states could not act separately from the national government. The president was pleased. As Jackson said, the Constitution and its laws remained "supreme."

Jackson versus Calhoun

The fact that Andrew Jackson, like John C. Calhoun, was a cotton-planting owner of enslaved people led many southerners to assume that the president would support their resistance to the federal tariff. Jackson was indeed sympathetic—until Calhoun and others in South Carolina threatened to "nullify" federal laws. Jackson then turned on them.

In April 1830, the Democratic Party hosted members of Congress at the first annual Jefferson Day dinner to honor the birthday of the former president. When it was Jackson's turn to propose a toast to Jefferson's memory, he rose to his feet, raised his glass, glared at Calhoun, and announced: "Our Union—it must be preserved!"

People gasped, knowing that the vice president must reply. Calhoun, trembling with emotion, countered with a defiant toast to "the Union, next to our liberty the most dear!" In that dramatic exchange, Jackson and Calhoun laid bare the fundamental tension between federal authority and states' rights that has remained to this day an animating theme of the American republic.

A New Cabinet

The animosity between Jackson and Calhoun deepened, and soon the president took a dramatic step suggested by Secretary of State Martin Van Buren. During one of Jackson and Van Buren's frequent horseback rides together,

WEBSTER'S REPLY TO SENATOR HAYNE Shortly before his death, a sculpture was made of the eloquent Massachusetts senator Daniel Webster by Thomas Ball, commemorating Webster's denunciation of nullification in the Webster-Hayne debate. A cast of this statue was placed in New York's Central Park in 1876, with a pedestal quoting Webster's final line: "Liberty and Union, now and forever, one and inseparable."

JACKSON'S KITCHEN CABINET
Faced with a cabinet deeply divided, as pictured, Jackson and his closest adviser, Martin Van Buren, emptied the cabinet of Calhoun supporters and filled it instead with Jackson loyalists.

Van Buren offered himself up as a political sacrifice as a way to remove all Calhoun supporters from the cabinet.

As the first step in the cabinet coup, Van Buren convinced Secretary of War John Eaton to resign on April 4, 1831. Four days later, Van Buren resigned as secretary of state. "The long agony is over," crowed Samuel Ingham, the secretary of the Treasury, in a letter to Attorney General John Berrien. "Mr. V. B. and Major Eaton have resigned." What Ingham and Berrien did not realize was that a few days later, Jackson would force them—both Calhoun supporters—to resign as well. Jackson now had a clean slate on which to create another cabinet.

Critics saw through the secretary of state's scheme: "Mr. Van Buren may be called the 'Great Magician,'" wrote the *New York Courier*, "for he *raises his wand, and the whole Cabinet disappears*." Others claimed that the cabinet purge showed that Jackson did not have the political skill to lead the nation. One newspaper announced that the ship of state "is sinking . . . and the hero of two wars and a half has not the skill to keep it afloat."

Jackson's "Kitchen Cabinet"

By the end of August 1831, President Jackson had appointed a new cabinet. At the same time, he increasingly relied upon the advice of Martin Van Buren and others making up his so-called "Kitchen Cabinet"—an informal group of close friends and supporters, many of them Democratic newspaper editors.

The Kitchen Cabinet soon convinced Jackson to drop an earlier pledge to serve only one term. They explained that it would be hard for Van Buren, the president's chosen successor, to win the 1832 Democratic nomination because Calhoun would do everything in his power to stop him—and might win the nomination himself.

The South Carolina Nullification Ordinance

In the fall of 1831, President Jackson tried to defuse the conflict with South Carolina by calling on Congress to reduce the tariff. Congress responded with the Tariff of 1832, which lowered taxes on many imported items.

The new tariff, however, was not enough to satisfy Calhoun and others in his home state. South Carolina seethed with resentment toward Jackson and the federal government. Living in the only state where enslaved Africans were a majority of the population, White South Carolinians feared that if the northern representatives in Congress were powerful enough to create such discriminatory tariffs, they might eventually vote to end slavery.

In November 1832, just weeks after Andrew Jackson was elected for a second term, a South Carolina state convention overwhelmingly adopted a nullification ordinance that repudiated the "unconstitutional" federal tariff acts of 1828 and 1832 (declaring them "null, void, and no law"). If federal authorities tried to use force to collect the tariffs, South Carolina would secede from the Union, the ordinance vowed. The state legislature then chose Senator Robert Hayne as governor and elected Calhoun to succeed him as U.S. senator. Calhoun resigned as Jackson's vice president so that he could defend the nullification policy in the Senate and protect his state's investments in slavery.

> South Carolina threatens to secede from the Union

Jackson's Firm Response

In the nullification crisis, South Carolina, "feisty as a gamecock," found itself standing alone. Other southern states expressed sympathy, but none endorsed nullification. President Jackson's public response was measured yet forthright. He promised to use "firmness and forbearance" with South Carolina but stressed that nullification "means insurrection and war; and the other states have a right to put it down."

In private, however, Jackson was furious. He threatened to hang Calhoun, Hayne, and other "nullifiers" if any bloodshed occurred. "Surely the president is exaggerating," Governor Hayne of South Carolina remarked to Senator Thomas Hart Benton of Missouri. Benton, who years before had been in a fistfight with Jackson, replied: "I have known General Jackson a great many years, and when he speaks of hanging [people] it is time to look for a rope."

In his annual message to the nation, delivered December 4, 1832, Jackson appealed to the people of South Carolina not to follow leaders such as Calhoun: "The laws of the United States must be executed. . . . Those who told you that you might peaceably prevent their execution, deceived you. . . . Their object is disunion. . . . Disunion by armed force is treason."

Clay's Compromise

President Jackson then sent federal soldiers and a warship to Charleston, the South Carolina port city. Governor Hayne responded by mobilizing the state militia, and the two sides verged on civil war. In early 1833, the president

> Jackson asks Congress to issue a Force Bill

Force Bill (1833) Legislation, sparked by the nullification crisis in South Carolina, that authorized the president's use of the army to compel states to comply with federal law.

requested from Congress a **Force Bill** authorizing him to use the U.S. Army to "force" compliance with federal law in South Carolina. At this, Calhoun exploded on the Senate floor, exclaiming that he and others defending his state's constitutional rights were being threatened "to have our throats cut, and those of our wives and children."

Calhoun and the nullifiers, however, soon backed down. And the South Carolina legislature postponed implementation of the nullification ordinances in hopes that Congress would pass a more palatable tariff bill. Passage of a compromise bill, however, depended upon the support of Senator Henry Clay, himself a planter who owned about 120 enslaved people.

In February 1833, Clay circulated a plan to reduce the federal tariff gradually. It was less than South Carolina preferred, but it got the nullifiers out of the dilemma they had created. On March 1, Congress passed both the compromise tariff and the Force Bill.

Calhoun supported the compromise: "He who loves the Union must desire to see this agitating question [the tariff] brought to a termination." He rushed home to convince the South Carolina convention to rescind its nullification of the tariff acts. In a face-saving gesture, the delegates also nullified the Force Bill, which Jackson no longer needed.

Both sides claimed victory. Jackson had upheld the supremacy of the Union, and South Carolina had secured a reduction of the federal tariff. But there remained the fundamental issue of southern slaveholders feeling increasingly threatened by growing anti-slavery sentiment in the North. "The struggle, so far from being over," a defiant Calhoun wrote, "is not more than fairly commenced."

In retrospect, how had Jackson responded to the nullification crisis? The events had raised the thorny issue of states' rights versus the supremacy of the Union. When the South Carolina convention nullified two tariffs, Jackson had determinedly pushed through legislation that permitted the army to force the state to comply with the tariffs (the Force Bill). Congress passed both the Force Bill and a compromise tariff that satisfied both sides. In the end, Jackson could still maintain that using the executive branch to support nationalism over sectionalism had succeeded.

CORE **OBJECTIVE**
3. Analyze Jackson's legacy regarding the status of Indigenous people in American society.

Jackson's Policy on Indigenous Americans

If President Jackson's firm stance against nullification constituted one of his finest hours, his forcible removal of Indigenous people from their ancestral lands showed another side of him. Like most White frontiersmen, Jackson believed that Indigenous people and land-hungry settlers could never live in harmony. His solution was to relocate the former.

After Jackson's election in 1828, he ordered that the remaining eastern tribes (those east of the Mississippi River) be moved west of the Mississippi,

HISTORICAL CARICATURE OF THE CHEROKEE NATION (1886) This image captures the competing pressures to partition Indigenous nations: U.S. courts, missionaries, railroads, individual states, and the federal government all want a piece of Indigenous lands.

to parts of Arkansas and later Oklahoma. State laws in Alabama, Georgia, and Mississippi had already abolished tribal units and stripped them of their powers, rejected ancestral Indigenous land claims, and denied them the right to vote or testify in court. Jackson claimed that relocating the eastern Indigenous people was an act of mercy, a "wise and humane policy" that would save them from "utter annihilation." However, this was not the perspective of the Indigenous peoples. This was their land, they maintained, and it had been for centuries prior to European settlement.

Removal of Indigenous Americans

In response to a request from Jackson, and despite Indigenous groups' arguments against it, Congress debated the **Indian Removal Act** in 1830. This legislation authorized Jackson to ignore previous treaty commitments and force the nearly 100,000 Indigenous people remaining in the East and South to move to federal lands west of the Mississippi River (see Map 10.1).

Indigenous groups—particularly members of the Five Nations, the Cherokee, Creek, Chickasaw, Seminole, and Choctaw—advocated for their protection and rejected removal. Their leaders were offended by the broken treaties. The U.S. government had made eighty-six treaties with twenty-six different Indigenous nations during Jackson's administration. Now, as a federal agent reported: "They see that our professions are insincere, that our promises are broken, that the happiness of the Indian is a cheap sacrifice to the acquisition of new lands."

In late May 1830, the Senate passed the Indian Removal Act by a slim margin. The Cherokee responded by announcing that "we see nothing but ruin before us."

Indian Removal Act (1830) A law permitting the forced relocation of Indigenous peoples to federal lands west of the Mississippi River in exchange for the land they occupied in the East and South.

Indigenous People Resist Resettlement

By 1836, some 46,000 Indigenous Americans, including most who resided in northern areas of the Midwest, had been relocated across the Mississippi River. In Illinois and the Wisconsin Territory, however, Sauk and Fox people fought to regain their ancestral lands.

The Black Hawk War erupted in 1832, when Chief Black Hawk led 1,000 Sauks—men, women, and children who had been relocated to the Iowa Territory—back across the Mississippi River to their homeland in Illinois, land shared with the Fox Nation (see again Map 10.1). After several skirmishes, Indiana and Illinois militia chased the Sauk and Fox into the Wisconsin Territory and caught them on the eastern bank of the Mississippi, a few miles downstream from the mouth of the Bad Axe River. In what became known as the Bad Axe Massacre, the militiamen murdered hundreds of women and children as they tried to escape. Six weeks later, Black Hawk was captured and imprisoned.

In Florida, the Seminole Nation, which consisted of communities of Indigenous people and Black Indigenous (freedom-seeking enslaved people who lived in separate communities in Seminole lands), forcefully resisted the federal removal policy. For eight years, the Seminole would fight a guerrilla war in the swamps of the Everglades—the longest, most costly, and deadliest war ever fought by Indigenous Americans. Some 1,500 fighters were killed on both sides.

BATTLE ICON FOR SEMINOLE WAR IN FLORIDA Seminole leader Osceola was an American Indigenous leader during the Second Seminole War. He led the young Native Americans who opposed the Treaty of Payne's Landing (1832) to withdraw into the Everglades and fight back, employing guerrilla tactics. Osceola was seized under a flag of truce in 1837 and died in prison.

HIDING IN A MANGROVE SWAMP During the Second Seminole War (1835–1842), an armed group of Seminoles crouch under the roots of a mangrove in the Florida Everglades, unseen by the U.S. Marine boat passing by. Seminole resistance to relocation waned after 1837, and by 1842 only a few hundred Seminoles remained in Florida. While the war was officially declared over, no peace treaty was ever signed.

The Cherokee

Members of the Cherokee Nation also defied the federal removal policy, but their leaders chose to use the courts as their battleground. Cherokee people had long occupied northwest Georgia and the mountainous areas of northern Alabama, northwest South Carolina, eastern Tennessee, and western North Carolina. In 1827, relying upon their established treaty rights, they adopted a constitution as an independent nation in which they declared that they were not subject to the laws or control of any state or federal government. Georgia officials had other ideas.

Cherokee Nation v. Georgia (1831)

In 1828, shortly after Andrew Jackson's election, the Georgia government announced that after June 1, 1830, the authority of state law would extend to the Cherokee. The "barbarous and savage tribes" must give way to the march of White civilization, stated Governor George Gilmer. Under the new state laws, members of the Cherokee Nation would not be allowed to vote, own property, or testify against Whites in court. The continuing profitability of cotton and the discovery of gold in north Georgia in 1829 had increased Whites' lust for Cherokee land and led to the new law, which prohibited the Cherokee from digging for gold on their own lands. In response, Cherokee leaders sought relief in the U.S. Supreme Court, arguing, "We wish to remain on the land of our fathers. We have a perfect and original right to remain without interruption or molestation."

Challenges in the Courts In *Cherokee Nation v. Georgia* (1831), Chief Justice John Marshall ruled that the Cherokee had "an unquestionable right" to maintain control of their ancestral lands, but that the Court could not render a verdict because of a technicality: the Cherokee had filed suit as a "foreign nation," but in Marshall's view Indigenous groups were "domestic dependent nations." If it was true that "wrongs have been inflicted," Marshall explained, "this is not the tribunal which can redress the past or prevent the future."

The following year, the Supreme Court *did* rule in favor of the Cherokee in *Worcester v. Georgia* (1832). The case arose when Georgia officials arrested a group of White Christian missionaries who were living among Cherokee people in violation of a state law forbidding such interaction. Two of the missionaries, Samuel Worcester and Elihu Butler, were sentenced to four years at hard labor. They appealed to the Supreme Court.

In the *Worcester* case, Marshall said the missionaries must be released. The anti-Cherokee laws passed by the Georgia legislature, he declared, had violated "the Constitution, laws, and treaties of the United States." He added that the Cherokee Nation was "a distinct political community" within which Georgia law had no force.

Jackson, however, forced the Cherokee and other Indigenous nations to either abide by discriminatory new state laws or relocate to federal lands

CHEROKEE DIVIDED While many other members of the Cherokee elite fought against Jackson's policies, Elias Boudinot, editor of the first Native American newspaper, *Cherokee Phoenix*, signed the Treaty of New Echota in 1835. As a result of his support of the treaty, which ceded all Cherokee territory east of the Mississippi River to the U.S. government in exchange for new homelands in Indian Territory, Boudinot was subsequently murdered by a rival faction of Cherokee.

west of the Mississippi River. Jackson told leaders of the Creek Nation that they and his "white children" could not live "in harmony and peace" if the Creek people remained on their ancestral lands.

Despite efforts to remain on their lands, and after a series of fraught negotiations, Indigenous Americans were expelled into lands designated by the U.S. government that appear on maps as "Indian Lands" or "Indian Territory." The Choctaw people were the first to be forcibly removed in 1831–1833, followed by the Creek in 1836–1837, the Chickasaw in 1837, and then the Cherokee in 1838–1839 (Map 10.1).

Indigenous Peoples and White Customs The irony of the new Georgia policy was that the Cherokee had in fact adopted many customs of White America. They had abandoned traditional hunting practices to develop farms; built roads, schools, and churches; and established trading posts and newspapers. Some had married Whites, adopted their clothing and food, and converted to Christianity.

The Cherokee also had their own constitution modeled after the U.S. Constitution. They elected as their first president John Ross, a wealthy, mixed-race Christian who had served with General Andrew Jackson's forces against the Creek. The Cherokee, Ross told the U.S. Senate, were "like the white man in manners, morals, and religion."

In fact, members of all of the Five Nations owned enslaved people. For example, Rebecca McIntosh Hawkins Hagerty, a member of the Creek Nation in Georgia, moved to Texas prior to removal and set up a plantation. Married twice, she inherited land and enslaved people through both of her husbands. By 1860, she had become one of the largest female slaveholders in Texas. Her story indicates that Indigenous people responded differently to the challenges of the Jacksonian era; and that for some, slaveholding was an option. In yet another irony, captive Indigenous people brought enslaved people to serve them in their new lives in Indian Territory.

REBECCA MCINTOSH HAWKINS HAGERTY Daughter of the Creek chief William McIntosh. Through two marriages, one to a mixed-blood Creek, she became one of the richest planters in Texas, where she enslaved more than 100 people.

Worcester v. Georgia (1832)

The Trail of Tears

The federal officials responsible for implementing the Indian Removal Act developed a strategy of divide-and-conquer with the Cherokee. In 1835, for example, a minority faction among the Cherokee led by Major Ridge ("He Who Walks on Mountaintops") signed the fraudulent Treaty of New Echota, which called for the relocation of the Cherokee Nation to Oklahoma. New Echota was the capital of the Cherokee Nation (currently Gordon County, Georgia), and the signing of this treaty led to the dismantling of a community who had lived in the area for generations. Cherokee president John Ross was outraged. Ever since the Europeans arrived, he asserted, "we have been made to drink the bitter cup of humiliation . . . our country and the graves of our fathers torn from us." Ridge, however, urged submission to

President Jackson's orders: "They are strong, and we are weak. We are few, they are many."

Although 90 percent of the Cherokee people rejected the New Echota Treaty, the U.S. Senate readily accepted it and the U.S. Army set about enforcing its provisions. Major Ridge knew that his decision to abide by the federal decree outraged most Cherokee. "I have signed my death warrant," he muttered. Indeed, he had. In 1839, rival Cherokee executed Ridge and his son, John.

By 1838, when Martin Van Buren was president, 17,000 Cherokee were evicted and forcibly moved west under military guard on the **Trail of Tears,** an 800-mile forced removal to ceded territory in present-day Oklahoma which was, according to a White Georgian, "the cruelest work I ever knew." Thousands of Indigenous people, including John Ross's wife, died along the way from exposure, disease, or starvation.

Elder Cherokee women such as Nanyehi had rejected the forced removal; she worked with twelve other women on the Women's Council to plead with

JOHN ROSS John Ross was Principal Chief of the Cherokee Nation for nearly four decades, and led the fight to stop the Cherokee's removal from their eastern homelands. However, Ross and his people were eventually relocated to Indian Territory (Oklahoma) through the Trail of Tears.

Trail of Tears (1838–1839)
The forced, 800-mile journey of Indigenous people from the southern Appalachians to Indian Territory.

CONTEMPORARY VIZUALIZATION OF NANYEHI Nanyehi was born into the Cherokee Nation in 1738 in Chota, Tennessee. For her heroics in the Battle of Taliwa (1755), the Cherokee Nation awarded her the title Gighau, "Beloved Woman," making her the only female voting member of the Cherokee General Council. She also became the leader of the Women's Clan Council, and she was authorized to serve on behalf of and negotiate for her people, which she would do throughout the Cherokee-American War years. One of her final acts in 1817 was to write a letter to the Cherokee General Council to protest the continued removal of Cherokee from the native lands and the sale of those lands.

the men in their community: "Your mothers, your sisters, ask and beg of you not to part with any more of our land." Despite such pleas, even young Cherokee girls such as Eliza Whitmire had no choice but to succumb to the Trail of Tears, enduring the horror and suffering of their people. "The trip was made in the dead of winter and many died for exposure from sleet and snow," Eliza shared years later in her narrative, citing her "bitter" memories of this experience as a young child.

Yet Van Buren told Congress in December 1838 that he took "sincere pleasure" in reporting that the Cherokee people had been relocated. "You can expel us by force, we grant," Chief John Ross wrote to Van Buren in

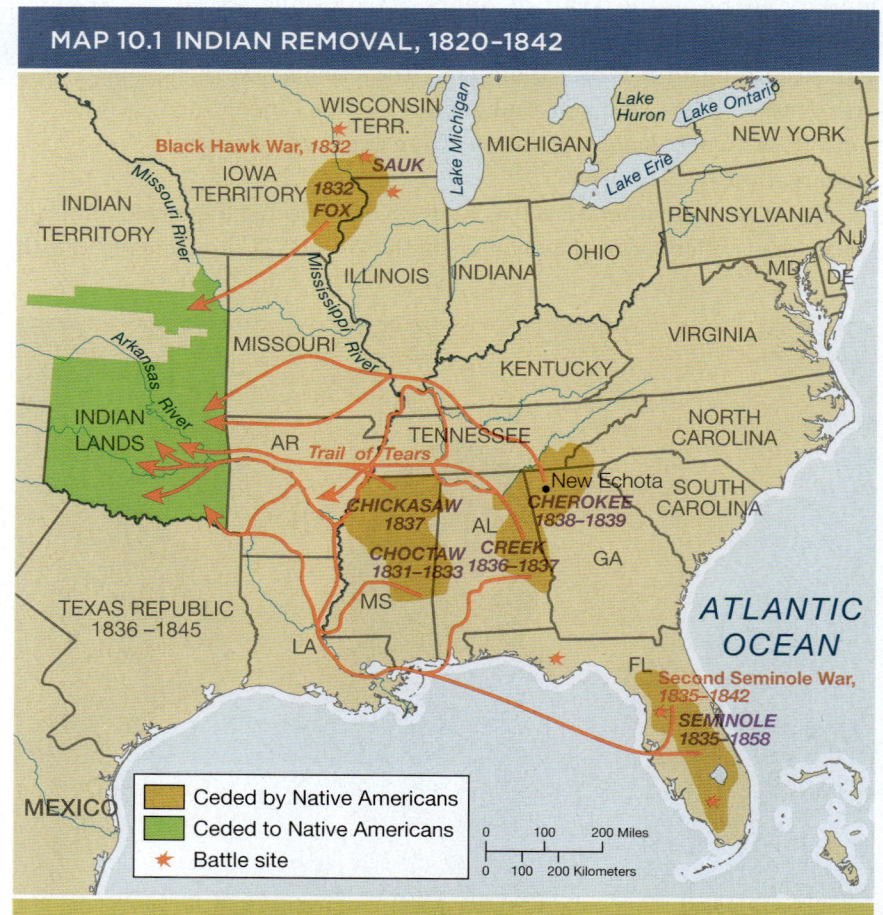

MAP 10.1 INDIAN REMOVAL, 1820–1842

- Identify each Indigenous group, and follow the arrows showing their routes to the "Indian Lands" ceded to them. Using the map as well as the map key, estimate how far each group had to travel, the kinds of terrain they traversed, and the difficult conditions they faced along the way.
- Using the map key, identify the lands ceded to the U.S. government by the Choctaw, Chickasaw, Creek, Seminole, and Cherokee peoples. Why do you suppose the U.S. government wanted lands in those locations?
- According to your understanding of the chapter text, why were Indigenous groups not forced to move before the 1800s?

TRAIL OF TEARS Thousands of Cherokee died on a nightmarish 800-mile forced march from Georgia to Oklahoma after being evicted from their native lands.

1838, "but you cannot make us call it fairness." A few Cherokee held out in the mountains of North Carolina; they became known as the Eastern Band of Cherokee.

President Van Buren predicted that the controversies dogging his administration would disappear over time, but that the forced removal of the Indigenous people would "endure . . . as long as the government itself." Over 150 years later, in 2009, Congress passed and President Barack Obama signed an official document apologizing for the Trail of Tears.

Jackson's legacy regarding Indigenous people in U.S. society reflected his firm personal belief that White settlers and Indigenous people could never live in harmony. Despite fierce controversy, the Indian Removal Act that he proposed—and obtained—had the effect of forcing many thousands of Indigenous people to unwillingly leave their homelands and relocate to territory west of the Mississippi. Women and men alike rejected removal and sought to encourage the leaders of their communities not to comply. Many perished on the brutally long and difficult trek.

Ultimately, only a few Cherokee and Seminole remained in the Southeast—and the U.S. government was able to claim (and sell) fertile agricultural land that it had forced the Indigenous people to cede.

Comparing PERSPECTIVES

THE POSSESSION AND DISPOSSESSION OF NATIVE LANDS

From: Letter from John Ross to Andrew Jackson, January 23, 1835.

In this letter, John Ross, chief of the Cherokee, requests that President Andrew Jackson allow the Cherokee to remain on their native land. Ross rejects the removal to land west of Arkansas and asks for relief from the Cherokee people's "sufferings" so that they might discuss terms for peace "on the land of their nativity."

It is Known to your Excellency, that the history of the Cherokee Nation since the year 1829, up to the present, has been on its part, One of repeated, Continued unavailing struggle against the Cruel policy of Georgia; On the part of that State, it has been One, of unparalleled aggravated Acts of Oppression upon the Nation. Actuated by an unextinguishable love of Country, Confiding implicitly in the good faith of the American Govt. and believing that the Govt. priding itself, as it does, upon its justice and humanity would, not only not disregard its own plighted faith, but would eventually interpose to prevent it from being disregarded, and trampled into dust by the State of Georgia, Being fully convinced in their Own judgement that they could not prosper as well any where else as upon their Native land, The Cherokees have successively appealed to the Executive, Legislative and Judiciary Departments of this Govt. for redress of Wrongs Committed and security against injuries apprehended, but as yet those appeals have been unavailing....

The Crisis of the fate of the Cherokee people, seems to be rapidly approaching, And the time has come, when they must be relieved of their sufferings. They having fully determined against a removal to Arkansas. The Undersigned Delegation would therefore most respectfully and earnestly ask to be informed, Upon what terms will the President negotiate for a final termination of those sufferings, that their people may repose in peace and comfort on the land of their nativity, under the enjoyment of such rights and privileges as belongs to freemen.

From: Andrew Jackson, "To the Cherokee Tribe of Indians East of Mississippi River," March 16, 1835.

Andrew Jackson addresses the Cherokee Nation directly, urging them to give up the fight for their homeland. Jackson argues that they will be much better off if they remove to land west of the Mississippi, and he hopes they will accept this advice he gives them as a friend.

I have no motive, my friends, to deceive you. I am sincerely desirous to promote your welfare. Listen to me, therefore, while I tell you that you cannot remain where you now are. Circumstances that cannot be controlled, and which are beyond the reach of human laws, render it impossible that you can flourish in the midst of a civilized community. You have but one remedy within your reach. And that is, to remove to the West and join your countrymen, who are already established there. And the sooner you do this, the sooner you will commence your career of improvement and prosperity. . . .

. . .

. . . As certain as the sun shines to guide you in your path, so certain is it that you cannot drive back the laws of Georgia from among you. Every year will increase your difficulties. Look at the condition of the Creeks. See the collisions which are taking place with them. See how their young men are committing depredations upon the property of our citizens, and are shedding their blood. This cannot and will not be allowed. Punishment will follow, and all who are engaged in these offences must suffer.

Questions

1. What arguments does John Ross use to appeal to Andrew Jackson for the Cherokee people to remain on their native land?

2. What is the tone of Jackson's address to the Cherokee, and in what manner does he convey his thoughts?

3. Given the two perspectives, what could have been the motivation for each side? How did this issue and its outcome contribute to Indigenous peoples' relations with the federal government?

> **CORE OBJECTIVE**
>
> **4.** Explain the causes of the economic depression of the late 1830s and the emergence of the Whig Party.

Political Battles

Andrew Jackson's controversial policies regarding the Indigenous people, nullification, and the B.U.S. aroused intense opposition. Some congressional opponents talked of impeaching him; while other, unidentified people sent him death threats.

In January 1835, the threat became real. After attending the funeral service for a member of Congress, Jackson was leaving the Capitol when an unemployed English-born housepainter named Richard Lawrence emerged from the shadows and pointed a pistol at the president's heart. When he pulled the trigger, however, the gun misfired. Jackson lifted his walking stick and charged at Lawrence, who pulled out another pistol—but it, too, miraculously misfired. Jackson claimed that his political foes, including John C. Calhoun, had planned the attack. A jury, however, decided that Lawrence, the first person to try to kill a U.S. president, was insane and ordered him confined in an asylum.

A Third Party

> The Anti-Masonic Party

In 1832, for the first time in a presidential election, a third party entered the field. The grassroots movement known as the Anti-Masonic Party grew out of popular hostility toward the Masonic fraternal order, a large, all-male social organization that originated in Great Britain early in the eighteenth century. By 1830, there were some 2,000 Masonic "lodges" scattered across the United States with about 100,000 members, including Andrew Jackson and Henry Clay.

Suspicions of the Masonic order as a secret elite organization intent on undermining democracy was an unlikely foundation upon which to build a lasting political party. The Anti-Masonic Party, however, had three important firsts to its credit: in addition to being the first third party, it was the first party to hold a national convention to nominate a presidential candidate and the first to announce a "platform" of specific policy goals.

The 1832 Election

In preparing for the 1832 election, the Democrats and the National Republicans followed the example of the Anti-Masonic Party by holding presidential nominating conventions of their own for the first time. In December 1831, the National Republicans gathered to nominate Henry Clay.

Eager to demonstrate popular support for his own party's candidates, Jackson endorsed the idea of a nominating convention for the Democratic Party as well. Subsequently the Democratic convention named New Yorker Martin Van Buren as Jackson's running mate. However, unlike the other two parties, the Democrats adopted no formal platform and relied upon the popularity of the president to carry their cause.

The outcome was an overwhelming endorsement of Jackson, who received 219 Electoral College votes—versus 49 for Clay, 11 for the Independent Governor John Floyd of Virginia, and 7 for the Anti-Masonic candidate William Wirt—and a solid popular-vote victory, 688,000 to 530,000. Dazzled by the president's strong showing, Wirt observed that Jackson could "be President for life if he chooses."

> Jackson and Van Buren win the 1832 election

The Removal of Government Deposits

Andrew Jackson interpreted his lopsided reelection as a "decision of the people against the bank." Having vetoed the charter renewal of the B.U.S., he ordered the Treasury Department to transfer federal monies from the national bank to twenty-three state banks—called "pet banks" by Jackson's critics because many were run by Jackson's friends and allies. When the Treasury secretary balked, a furious Jackson fired him.

Transferring the government's deposits from the B.U.S. to the pet banks was likely illegal but went unchallenged. However, the Senate, led by Henry Clay, voted in March 1834 to *censure* (issue a formal statement of disapproval) Jackson for it—the first time an American president was reprimanded instead of being impeached. Jackson was so angry after being censured that he wanted to challenge Clay to a duel.

Biddle's Response

Nicholas Biddle responded to Jackson's actions by ordering the B.U.S. to quit making loans, and demanded that state banks exchange their paper currency for gold or silver coins as quickly as possible. Through such deflationary policies that reduced the amount of money circulating in the economy, the desperate Biddle was trying to create an economic depression to reveal the importance of maintaining the national bank. An enraged Jackson said the B.U.S. under Biddle was "trying to kill me, but I will kill it!"

Jackson prevailed in the Bank War; the B.U.S. would shut down by 1841. With the restraining effects of Biddle's national bank removed, hundreds of new state banks sprouted like mushrooms, each printing its own paper currency to lend to land speculators and new businesses.

> Jackson's "pet banks" create financial chaos

Jackson's war on the national bank ended up sparking the sort of actions on the part of small state banks that he most feared. As Senator Thomas Hart Benton, one of Jackson's most loyal supporters, said in 1837, those who helped kill the B.U.S. did not intend to create a "wilderness of local banks."

But that is what happened. During what was called the "free banking era" after 1837, anyone who could raise a certain minimum amount of money (capital) could open a bank. And many speculators did. With no central bank to regulate and oversee the operations of "wildcat" banks, many of them went bankrupt after only a few months or years.

Distribution Act (1836) A law requiring distribution of the federal budget surplus to the states, creating chaos among unregulated state banks dependent on such federal funds.

The Money Question

During the 1830s, the federal government acquired huge amounts of money from the sale of government-owned lands. Initially, the Treasury department used the annual surpluses from land sales to pay down the accumulated federal debt, which it eliminated in 1835, the first time that any nation had done so. By 1836, the federal budget was generating an annual budget surplus, which led to intense discussions about what to do with the increasingly worthless paper money flowing into the Treasury's vaults.

The surge of unstable paper money issued by state banks peaked in 1836, when events combined suddenly to destroy the value of the bank notes. Two key developments, the passage of the **Distribution Act** and the Specie Circular, together played havoc with the economy and devastated the nation's financial system.

The Distribution Act (1836)

In June 1836, Congress approved the Distribution Act that required the federal government to "distribute" surplus revenue from land sales to the states by "depositing" the funds into eighty-one state banks in proportion to each state's representation in Congress. The state governments would then draw upon those deposits to fund roads, bridges, and other internal improvements, including the construction of new public schools.

Specie Circular (1836)

A month later, President Jackson issued the Specie Circular (1836), which announced that the federal government would accept only specie (gold or silver coins) in payment for land purchased by speculators (farmers could still pay with paper money). Westerners opposed the Specie Circular because most of the government land sales were occurring in the western states. They helped convince Congress to pass an act overturning Jackson's policy. The president, however, vetoed it.

THE DOCTORS PUZZLED, OR THE DESPERATE CASE OF MOTHER U.S. BANK (1833) In this satire of Andrew Jackson's Distribution Act and Specie Circular, the B.U.S. is portrayed as an oversized patient vomiting gold and silver coins into pans representing local banks. Henry Clay, Daniel Webster, and John C. Calhoun discuss various prescriptions while Jackson leans on the windowsill, insisting he knows the best cure.

Once enacted, the Distribution Act and the Specie Circular put added strains on the nation's already-tight supplies of gold and silver. Eastern banks had to transfer much of their gold and silver reserves to western banks. As banks reduced their reserves of gold and silver coins, they had to reduce their lending. Soon, the once-bustling economy began to slow into a recession as the money supply contracted. Nervous depositors rushed to their local banks to get their money out.

Censoring the Mail

While concerns about the strength of the economy grew, slavery again emerged as a national issue. In 1835, northern abolitionist organizations began mailing anti-slavery pamphlets and newspapers to prominent White southerners, hoping to convince them to end the "peculiar institution."

Francis Pickens of South Carolina urged southerners to stop abolitionists from spreading their "lies." Angry pro-slavery South Carolinians in Charleston broke into the federal post office, stole bags of abolitionist mailings, and ceremoniously burned them. Southern state legislatures passed laws banning such "dangerous" publications. Jackson asked Congress to pass a federal censorship law that would prohibit "incendiary" materials intended to incite "the slaves to insurrection."

Congress took action in 1836; but instead of banning abolitionist materials, a bipartisan group reaffirmed the sanctity of the federal mail. Southern post offices began censoring the mail anyway, arguing that federal authority ended when the mail arrived at the post office door. Jackson decided not to enforce the congressional action, creating what would become a growing split in the Democratic Party over the future of slavery.

> Controversy over the censorship of abolitionist literature

The controversy over the mails proved to be a victory for the growing abolitionist movement. One anti-slavery publisher said that instead of stifling their efforts, Jackson and the southern radicals "put us and our principles up before the world—just where we wanted to be." Abolitionist groups now started mailing their pamphlets and petitions to members of Congress. At this, James Hammond, a pro-slavery South Carolinian, called for Congress to ban such anti-slavery petitions. When that failed, Congress in 1836 adopted an informal solution suggested by Martin Van Buren: whenever a petition calling for the end of slavery appeared, someone would immediately move that it be tabled rather than discussed. This "gag rule," Van Buren claimed, would preserve the "harmony of our happy Union."

> Van Buren's "gag rule" stifles abolitionists

The Whig Coalition

President Jackson's war on the B.U.S. led his opponents to create a new anti-Jackson political party. They claimed that he was ruling like a monarch, sarcastically dubbed him "King Andrew I," and called his Democratic supporters *Tories* (a reference to those who had supported the British monarchy during the American Revolution). The new anti-Jackson coalition called itself the **Whig Party**, a name that had been used by the Patriots of the American Revolution (as well as by the parliamentary opponents of the Tories in Britain).

> Whigs vs. "King Andrew I"

Whig Party A political party founded in 1834 in opposition to the Jacksonian Democrats; supported federal funding for internal improvements, a national bank, and high tariffs on imports.

two-party system The domination of national politics by two major political parties, such as the Whigs and the Democrats during the 1830s and 1840s.

The Whig Party grew directly out of a coalition of National Republicans led by John Quincy Adams, Henry Clay, and Daniel Webster. The Whigs also found support among Anti-Masons and even some Democrats who resented President Jackson's war on the national bank. For the next twenty years, the Whigs and the Democrats would be the two major political parties, and for a second time a **two-party system** emerged.

The Whigs supported Henry Clay and his American System of economic nationalism. They favored federal support for internal improvements to foster economic growth. They also supported a national bank and high tariffs. In the South, the Whigs tended to be bankers and merchants. In the West, they were mostly farmers who valued government-funded infrastructure improvements: more roads, canals, and railroads. Unlike the Democrats, who attracted Catholic voters among German and Irish immigrants, northern Whigs tended to be native-born Protestants—Congregationalists, Presbyterians, Methodists, and Baptists—who advocated the abolition of slavery and efforts to restrict alcoholic beverages.

The Election of 1836

In 1835, eighteen months before the presidential election, the Democrats nominated Jackson's handpicked successor, Vice President Martin Van Buren. The Whig coalition, united chiefly in its opposition to Jackson, adopted a strategy of nominating multiple candidates, hoping to throw the election into the House of Representatives.

> Martin Van Buren wins the election of 1836

The Whigs put up three regional candidates: New Englander Daniel Webster, Hugh Lawson White of Tennessee, and William Henry Harrison of Indiana. But the multi-candidate strategy failed. In the popular vote of 1836, Van Buren defeated the entire Whig field, winning 170 electoral votes while the others collected only 113 combined.

The Eighth President

Born into a family of Dutch-speaking New York farmers, Martin Van Buren remains the only president for whom English was a second language. Like Andrew Jackson, Van Buren was an outsider and took great pride in his successful efforts to strip the political "old guard" of their powers. Van Buren was largely responsible for the formation of the Democratic Party. Elected governor of New York in 1828, he had resigned to become Andrew Jackson's secretary of state, then became vice president in 1833.

Martin Van Buren had been Jackson's closest political adviser and ally, but many in government thought he was too self-centered. John Quincy Adams wrote in his diary that Van Buren was "by far the ablest" of the Jacksonians, but he had wasted "most of his ability upon mere personal intrigues. His principles are all subordinate to his ambition."

At his inauguration, Van Buren promised to follow "in the footsteps of President Jackson." Before he could do so, however, the nation's financial sector began to collapse. On May 10, 1837, several large state banks in New York, running out of gold and silver, suddenly refused to convert customers'

MARTIN VAN BUREN Van Buren earned the nickname of "Little Magician" not only for his short stature but also for his "magical" ability to exploit his political and social connections.

paper money into coins. Other banks across the nation quickly did the same. This financial crisis, the worst yet faced by the young nation, would become known as the **Panic of 1837**. It would soon mushroom into the republic's worst depression, lasting seven years.

The Panic of 1837

The financial crisis had started in Europe. During the mid-1830s, Great Britain, America's largest trading partner, experienced an acute financial crisis when the Bank of England, worried about a run on the gold and silver in its vaults, curtailed its loans. This forced most British companies to reduce their trade with America. As British demand for American cotton plummeted, so did the price they were willing to pay for cotton.

As creditors hastened to foreclose on struggling businesses and farms unable to make their debt payments, U.S. government spending plunged. Many canals under construction were shut down, and many state governments could not repay their debts. By early fall, 90 percent of the nation's factories had closed. Workers who still had jobs saw their wages plummet, sometimes in half. Hundreds of thousands of people across the nation were not only jobless but homeless as well.

Not surprisingly, the economic crisis frightened people. As a newspaper editorial complained, the economy "has been put into confusion and dismay by a well-meant, but *extremely mistaken*" pair of decisions by Congress and President Jackson: the Specie Circular and the elimination of the B.U.S.

The first "mistake" was the Specie Circular. Its requirement that all federal land purchases be transacted in gold or silver coins greatly reduced government land sales, thus pinching the federal budget. Struggling American banks had to borrow gold from European banks, but they could not get enough to prevent a financial panic and a deepening depression.

Jackson's second mistake was his decision to eliminate rather than reform the B.U.S. It could have acted as a stabilizing force amid the financial panic. Instead, unregulated state banks around the country flooded the economy with paper money that was basically worthless because it lacked adequate backing in gold or silver.

In April 1836, *Niles' Weekly Register*, the nation's leading business journal, reported that the economy was "approaching a momentous crisis." State governments canceled plans to build roads, bridges, railroads, canals, and ports. Forty percent of the state banks shut their doors. Even the federal government itself, having put most of its gold and

Panic of 1837 A financial calamity in the United States brought on by a dramatic slowdown in the British economy and falling cotton prices, failed crops, high inflation, and reckless state banks.

> Reasons for the Panic: European economy

> Reasons for the Panic: Jackson's policies

JACKSONIAN TREASURY NOTE A parody of the often-worthless fractional notes issued by local banks and businesses in lieu of coins. These notes proliferated during the Panic of 1837, with the emergency suspension of gold and silver payments. In the main scene, Martin Van Buren, depicted as a monster on a wagon driven by John C. Calhoun, is about to pass through an arch labeled "Wall Street" and "Safety Fund Banks."

silver in state banks, was verging on bankruptcy. The *National Intelligencer* newspaper reported in May that the federal treasury "has not a dollar of gold or silver in the world!"

Poor people, enslaved Blacks, and Indigenous Americans, as always, were particularly hard hit. By the fall of 1837, one-third of workers were jobless, and those still fortunate enough to have jobs had their wages slashed. At the same time, prices for food and clothing soared. As the winter of 1837 approached, a New York City journalist reported that the nation had a "poverty-struck feeling."

Politics amid Depression

The unprecedented economic calamity sent shock waves through the political system. Critics called the president "Martin Van Ruin" because he did not believe that the government had any responsibility to rescue hard-pressed farmers, bankers, or businessmen or to provide relief for the jobless and homeless.

How best to deal with the economic depression clearly divided Democrats from Whigs. Unlike Van Buren, the Whig Henry Clay insisted that suffering people were "entitled to the protecting care of a parental Government." To him, an enlarged role for the federal government was the price of a maturing, expanding republic in which elected officials had an obligation to promote public "safety, convenience, and prosperity." In contrast, Van Buren and the Democrats believed that the government had no such obligations. Henry Clay, among others, savaged the president for his "cold and heartless" attitude.

An Independent Treasury

Martin Van Buren believed that the federal government should stop risking its cash deposits in insecure pet banks. Instead, he wanted to establish an independent Treasury system whereby the government would keep its funds in its own bank vaults and do business entirely in gold or silver, not in paper currency. Van Buren wanted the federal government to regulate the nation's supply of gold and silver and let the marketplace regulate the supply of paper currency.

It took Van Buren more than three years to convince Congress to pass the **Independent Treasury Act** on July 4, 1840. Although it lasted little more than a year (the Whigs repealed it in 1841), it would be restored in 1846. Not surprisingly, the state banks that lost control of the federal funds howled in protest.

The "Log Cabin and Hard Cider" Campaign

By 1840, an election year, the Van Buren administration and the Democrats were in deep trouble. The depression continued to worsen and the suffering spread, leading the Whigs to grow confident they could win the presidency. At their nominating convention, they passed over Henry Clay, the Kentucky legislator who had been Jackson's consistent foe, in favor of William

Independent Treasury Act (1840)

Independent Treasury Act (1840) A system created by President Martin Van Buren that moved federal funds from favored state banks to the U.S. Treasury, whose financial transactions could only be in gold or silver.

Henry Harrison, whose credentials were impressive: victor at the Battle of Tippecanoe against Tecumseh's Shawnee warriors in 1811, former governor of the Indiana Territory, and former congressman and senator from Ohio. To balance the ticket geographically, the Whigs nominated John Tyler of Virginia as their vice president.

The Whigs refused to take a stand on major issues. They did, however, seize upon a catchy campaign slogan: "Tippecanoe and Tyler Too." When a Democratic newspaper declared that General Harrison was the kind of man who would spend his retirement "in a log cabin [sipping hard apple cider] on the banks of the Ohio [River]," the Whigs chose the cider and log cabin symbols to depict Harrison as a simple man sprung from the people, in contrast to Van Buren's wealthy, aristocratic lifestyle. (Harrison actually was born into one of Virginia's wealthiest families.)

Harrison defeated Van Buren easily, winning 234 electoral votes to his opponent's 60. The Whigs had promised a return to prosperity without explaining how it would happen. It was simply time for a change. The most remarkable aspect of the election of 1840 was the turnout. More than 80 percent of White American men voted, many for the first time—the highest turnout before or since.

> Harrison wins the 1840 election with record-breaking voter turnout

Overall, Andrew Jackson's use of the presidential veto, combined with his bank policies, triggered opposition that led to the election of William Henry Harrison, a Whig. The Whig Party had formed in direct response

UNCLE SAM'S PET PUPS! (1840) A woodcut showing William Henry Harrison luring "Mother Bank," Andrew Jackson, and Martin Van Buren into a barrel of hard (alcoholic) cider. While Jackson and Van Buren sought to destroy the Bank of the United States, Harrison promised to re-establish it—which is why he provides "Mother Bank" a refuge in this scene.

to Jackson's authoritarian moves as president. Moreover, in response to reduced British trade with America in the mid-1830s, which caused the U.S. economy to falter, Jackson had sought legislation that further destabilized the economy—the Distribution Act and the Specie Circular. Although a more severe economic depression and the financial Panic of 1837 occurred under President Van Buren, these prior moves by Jackson had set the process in motion and generated support for the Whigs. Now entering a new era, the next president would lead the nation in a slightly different direction.

> **CORE OBJECTIVE**
> **5.** Assess the strengths and weaknesses of Jackson's presidency.

Beyond Jackson's Legacy: A New Era

The nation that new president William Henry Harrison governed was vastly different from the one led by George Washington and Thomas Jefferson. Much of that difference had developed during the years of Andrew Jackson's presidency. In 1828, when Jackson took office, the United States boasted twenty-four states and nearly 13 million people, many of them recent arrivals from Germany and Ireland. The national population was growing at a phenomenal rate, doubling every twenty-three years.

During the so-called Jacksonian era, the nation also witnessed continuing industrialization; rapidly growing cities; rising tensions between the North and South over slavery; accelerating westward expansion; and the emergence of the second two-party system, featuring Democrats and Whigs.

A surge in foreign demand for southern cotton and other American goods, along with substantial British investment in an array of new American enterprises, helped generate an economic boom and a transportation revolution. The fact that president-elect Jackson rode to his inauguration in a horse-drawn carriage and left Washington, D.C., eight years later on a train symbolized the dramatic changes occurring in American life.

A New Political Landscape

A transformational figure in a transformational era, Andrew Jackson helped reshape the political landscape. Even his ferocious opponent Henry Clay acknowledged that Jackson had "swept over the Government . . . like a tropical tornado."

Yet Jackson was a controversial figure, too. He left a messy, even contradictory, legacy. He championed opportunities for the "common man" to play a greater role in the political arena. He helped establish the modern Democratic Party and attracted to it the working poor and immigrants from eastern cities, as well as farmers from the South and East. He also saved the Union by suppressing the nullification crisis.

In his 1837 farewell address, Jackson stressed his crusade on behalf of "the farmer, the mechanic, and the laboring classes of society—the bone and sinew of the country—men who love liberty and desire nothing but equal rights and equal laws."

And, with great fanfare on January 1, 1835, Jackson announced that the government had paid off the national debt accumulated since the Revolutionary War, a debt that he called a "national curse."

Jackson's concept of "the people," however, was limited to a democracy of White men—as it had been for all previous presidents. The phenomenon of Andrew Jackson that some see as the heroic symbol of the common man and the democratic ideal continues to spark historical debate, as it did during his lifetime.

Jackson was so convinced of the rightness of his ideals that he was willing to defy constitutional limits on his authority. He did not embrace the rule of law unless he was the one making the laws. In this sense, he was both the instrument of democracy and its enemy, protecting "the humble people" and the Union by expanding presidential authority in ways that the founders had never envisioned—including removing federal money from the national bank, replacing government officials with party loyalists, censoring the mails, and ending nullification in South Carolina. In doing so, he both symbolized and aggravated the perennial tension in the American republic between a commitment to democratic ideals and the exercise of presidential power, states' rights, and federal actions.

Reviewing the
CORE OBJECTIVES

- **Jackson's Views and Policies** The Jacksonians sought to democratize the political process and expand economic opportunity for the "common man" (that is, "poor and humble" White men). As the representative of "the people," he expanded the role of the president in economic matters, reducing federal government spending and eliminating the powerful Second Bank of the United States. However, his policies excluded women, the enslaved, and Indigenous people. Jackson's view of democracy was limited, and marginalized groups sought ways to exercise their rights. His *Bank War* was hugely popular, but Jackson did not foresee its long-term economic consequences. In addition, his views on limited government were not always reflected in his policies. He left in place the high taxes on imports from the *Tariff of Abominations* (1828) until opposition in the South created a national crisis.

- **Nullification Controversy** The concept of *nullification*, developed by South Carolina's John C. Calhoun, allowed a state to reject a federal law. When a South Carolina convention nullified the Tariffs of 1828 and 1832, Jackson requested that Congress pass a *Force Bill* (1833) authorizing the U.S. Army to compel compliance with the tariffs. After South Carolina, under the threat of federal military force, accepted a compromise tariff put forth by Henry Clay, the crisis was over—and both sides claimed victory.

- **Indian Removal Act of 1830** The *Indian Removal Act* authorized the relocation of Indigenous peoples living in the East to federal lands west of the Mississippi River. Cherokee leaders used the federal court system in *Cherokee Nation v. Georgia* and *Worcester v. Georgia* to try to block this relocation. Despite the Supreme Court's decisions in their favor, President Jackson forced them to move; the event itself and the brutally difficult route they took came to be called the *Trail of Tears* (1838–1839). Other nations such as the Chickasaw and Creek negotiated their removal; and by 1840, only a few Seminole and Cherokee holdouts remained in remote areas of the Southeast.

- **Democrats and Whigs** Jackson's behavior, especially his use of the veto, led many to jokingly regard him as "King Andrew the First." Groups who opposed him organized a new political party known as the *Whig Party*, thus producing the country's second *two-party system*. Two acts—the *Distribution Act* (1836) and the Specie Circular—ultimately destabilized the nation's economy. Andrew Jackson's ally and vice president, Martin Van Buren, succeeded Jackson as president; but Jacksonian bank policies led to the financial *Panic of 1837* and an economic depression. Van Buren responded by persuading Congress to pass the *Independent Treasury Act* (1840) to safeguard the nation's economy, but offered no help for individuals in distress. The economic calamity ensured a Whig victory in the election of 1840.

■ **The Jackson Years** Andrew Jackson's America was very different from the America of 1776. Most White men had gained the vote when states removed property qualifications for voting, but political equality did not mean economic equality. Democrats wanted every American to have an equal chance to compete in the marketplace and in the political arena, but they never promoted equality of results.

KEY TERMS

Bank War *p. 400*

Tariff of Abominations (1828) *p. 401*

nullification *p. 402*

Force Bill (1833) *p. 406*

Indian Removal Act (1830) *p. 407*

Trail of Tears (1838–1839) *p. 411*

Distribution Act (1836) *p. 418*

Whig Party *p. 419*

two-party system *p. 420*

Panic of 1837 *p. 421*

Independent Treasury Act (1840) *p. 422*

CHRONOLOGY

1828	Andrew Jackson wins presidential election
	Tariff of Abominations goes into effect
1830	Congress passes the Indian Removal Act
1831	Supreme Court issues *Cherokee Nation v. Georgia* decision
1831–1833	Choctaw removal
1832	Supreme Court issues *Worcester v. Georgia* decision
	Andrew Jackson vetoes the Bank Recharter Bill
	South Carolina passes the Nullification Ordinance
1833	Congress passes the Force Bill, authorizing military force in South Carolina
	Congress passes Henry Clay's compromise tariff, with Jackson's support
1835	Treaty of Echota between the U.S. government and the Cherokee Nation signed, which leads to the Trail of Tears
1836	Democratic candidate Martin Van Buren is elected president
1836–1837	Creek removal
1837	Chickasaw removal
	Financial panic deflates the economy
1838–1839	Cherokee Trail of Tears
1840	Independent Treasury Act is established
1840	Whig candidate William Henry Harrison is elected president

InQuizitive

Go to InQuizitive to see what you've learned—and learn what you've missed—with personalized feedback along the way.

THE SOUTH A region known for its rich agricultural resources and distinct communities, the South represented the southern United States during the four decades before the Civil War, 1820–1860. The region operated under an agrarian economy based predominantly on enslaved labor on plantations and farms of various sizes. Here, enslaved people labored against their will cultivating rice, cotton, sugar, and tobacco. They generated wealth for the White planter elite, a group of enslavers who also served as the ruling class.

CHAPTER 11

The South and Slavery

1800–1860

Early in the nineteenth century, before the Civil War, the southern states consolidated an identity distinct from other regions of the nation. Unique climatic and soil conditions supported an agrarian way of life featuring fertile plantations and small farms, which yielded an economy and a way of life based solely on agriculture—and on the labor of enslaved Africans.

The South also had a higher proportion of native-born Americans (including the children of enslaved Africans). The region attracted few European immigrants. The main shipping routes from Britain and Europe took immigrants to northern port cities such as Boston, New York, and Philadelphia, and most immigrants could not afford to travel from there to the South. Moreover, European immigrants, most of whom were manual laborers, could not compete with the widespread system of enslaved labor in the South.

The southern states remained largely rural and agricultural long after the rest of the nation had embraced cities, hired immigrants, and built factories, but the South was also instrumental in enabling the nation's industrial development. After the War of 1812, southern-grown cotton fed the bustling textile mills of Great Britain and New England. The price of raw cotton doubled in the first year after the war, and the fibrous "white gold" quickly displaced sugar as the most profitable crop produced by enslaved labor. Its stunning profitability

CORE OBJECTIVES

1. Explain how racial capitalism contributed to inequalities in the South.
2. Discuss the role that cotton production and slavery played in the South's economic and social development.
3. Explain why most White Southerners—enslavers as well as those who did not have the means to own enslaved people—supported the expansion of slavery.
4. Describe the impact of slavery on African Americans, both free and enslaved, throughout the South.
5. Analyze how enslaved people resisted the conditions they were forced to endure.

soon entwined the economies of the North and South with those of much of the world (see Chapter 8). As a result, during this period the South became the nation's "cotton kingdom."

Racial Capitalism

> **CORE OBJECTIVE**
> 1. Explain how racial capitalism contributed to inequalities in the South.

In the South, a cotton empire developed where Northern financiers, shippers, and merchants provided an industrial and financial infrastructure in which large-scale cotton production could thrive. It was in the South that a new form of capitalism found its roots: racial capitalism.

Slavery was a profit-making system built upon forced labor; and it was a form of racial capitalism that created vast inequalities in income, wealth, power, and status. These disparities were so great that the monetary value of enslaved people exceeded the total wealth that the entire nation generated from railroads and factories.

Enslaved people knew they were valuable and that their labor in the fields, factories, universities, and other settings kept the United States strong during the nineteenth century. It was such common knowledge that a group of enslaved people in Virginia asked, "Didn't we clear the land, and raise the crops of corn, of tobacco, rice, of sugar, of everything? And then didn't the large cities in the North grow up on the cotton and the sugars and the rice that we made?"

> Racial hierarchies in the South

Yet most White Southerners viewed those held in bondage not as human beings but rather as property. A South Carolina planter asserted that the enslaved "are yet the best stock a man can own.... The truth is there is no investment so safe & so profitable as land & negroes." Indeed, the profitability and convenience of owning laborers created a sense of social unity among Whites that bridged class differences. Poor Whites who owned no enslaved people, and resented those who did, could still claim racial superiority over Black people. These attitudes ensured that racial capitalism would thrive throughout the South.

The Cotton Kingdom

> **CORE OBJECTIVE**
> 2. Discuss the role that cotton production and slavery played in the South's economic and social development.

Within the South's cotton kingdom were three distinct patterns of economic development and diverging degrees of commitment to slavery.

Throughout the first half of the nineteenth century, the seven states of the Lower South (South Carolina, Georgia, Florida, Alabama, Mississippi, Louisiana, and parts of Texas) grew increasingly reliant on cotton production, which was highly dependent upon slave labor. By 1860, enslaved people represented nearly half the population of the Lower South.

The states of the Upper South (Virginia, North Carolina, Tennessee, and Arkansas) had more varied agricultural economies—a mixture of large commercial plantations and small family farms, where crops were grown mostly for household use. Many states also had large areas without slavery, especially in the mountains of Virginia, the western Carolinas, eastern Tennessee, and northern Georgia, where the soil and climate were not suited to growing cotton or tobacco.

In the Border South (Delaware, Maryland, Kentucky, and Missouri), slavery was slowly disappearing because cotton could not thrive there. By 1860, fully 90 percent of Delaware's Black population and half of Maryland's were already free.

Tobacco, Rice, Sugar, and Livestock

After the Revolution, as the tobacco fields in Virginia and Maryland lost their fertility, tobacco farming spread into Kentucky and as far west as Missouri. Rice continued to be grown in the coastal areas (low country) of the Carolinas and Georgia, where fields could easily be flooded and drained by tidal rivers flowing into the ocean. Sugarcane, like rice, was also expensive to produce, requiring machinery to grind the cane to release the sugar syrup. During the early nineteenth century, only southern Louisiana focused on sugar production; but as slavery expanded into Texas after that area gained independence from Mexico in 1836, so too did sugar production.

In addition to such cash crops, the South led the nation in the production of livestock: hogs, horses, mules, and cattle. Enslaved cowboys worked in the livestock industry and served as tanners, cattlemen, horse-breakers, and drivers, and in many other roles. Some drove cattle to markets across county and state lines. Other enslaved workers labored in iron, coal, and brick-making factories in industrial settings. In the Chesapeake region of Virginia and Maryland, there were about sixty-five ironworks factories with 4,500 enslaved workers. Yet no industry or crop dominated more than cotton.

> Diverse industries all reliant on enslaved labor

"King Cotton"

During the first half of the nineteenth century, cotton surpassed rice as the most profitable cash crop in the South. Southern cotton drove much of the nation's economy and played a key role in the Industrial Revolution, feeding the textile mills in New England and Great Britain.

Cotton became one of the transforming forces in nineteenth-century history. It shaped the lives of the enslaved workers who cultivated it, the planters who grew rich from it by using enslaved labor, the predominantly Northern shipowners who transported it, the mill girls who turned it into fabric and thread, the merchants who sold it, the people who wore it, and the politicians who warred over it. "Cotton is King," exclaimed the *Southern Cultivator* journal in 1859, "and wields an astonishing influence over the world's commerce."

The cotton kingdom was made possible by two technological developments. Until the late eighteenth century, cotton fabric had been a rarity that was produced by women in India using handlooms. Then British inventors developed machinery, including the power loom, to convert raw cotton into thread and cloth. At the same time, Eli Whitney's invention of the cotton gin

> Technological innovations: British textile mills and the cotton gin

ATOP THE COTTON KINGDOM
This photograph offers a glimpse of the staggering rates of cotton production. Cotton bales fill this Mississippi River steamboat to capacity and are so densely packed and plentiful that men can walk on top of them.

in the United States sped up the work of removing the plant's sticky seeds and preparing the fiber for processing (see Chapter 8).

Together, these two mechanical breakthroughs helped create the world's largest industry—and transformed the South. By 1815, just months after General Andrew Jackson's victory over British troops at New Orleans, some thirty British ships docked at the city's wharves because, as an American merchant reported, "Europe must, and will have, cotton for her manufacturers." During that year alone, more than 65,000 bales of cotton were shipped down the Mississippi River to the port of New Orleans. By 1860, southern states were providing 77 percent of the cotton used in Britain's textile mills and 90 percent of the fiber used in France's mills.

The Lower South (the Old Southwest)

> Massive migration to Lower South / Old Southwest

Because of its warm climate and plentiful rainfall, much of the Lower South became the global leader in cotton production. The region's cheap, fertile land, combined with the profits provided by cotton and the sale of enslaved people, generated a frenzied mobility as people eager to better themselves searched for more opportunities and better land. Henry Watson, a New Englander who moved to Alabama, complained in 1836 that "nobody seems to consider himself settled [here]; they remain one, two, three or four years & must move on to some other spot."

A Fertile Cotton Kingdom The so-called cotton kingdom moved south and west during the first half of the nineteenth century. As Virginia and the Carolinas experienced soil exhaustion from the overplanting of tobacco and cotton, restless farmers and many sons of enslavers moved to the **Old Southwest**—western Georgia, Alabama, Mississippi, Louisiana, Arkansas,

Old Southwest The region covering western Georgia, Alabama, Mississippi, Louisiana, Arkansas, and Texas, where low land prices and fertile soil attracted droves of settlers after the American Revolution.

MAP 11.1 COTTON PRODUCTION, 1821

Each dot represents 1,000 bales of cotton.

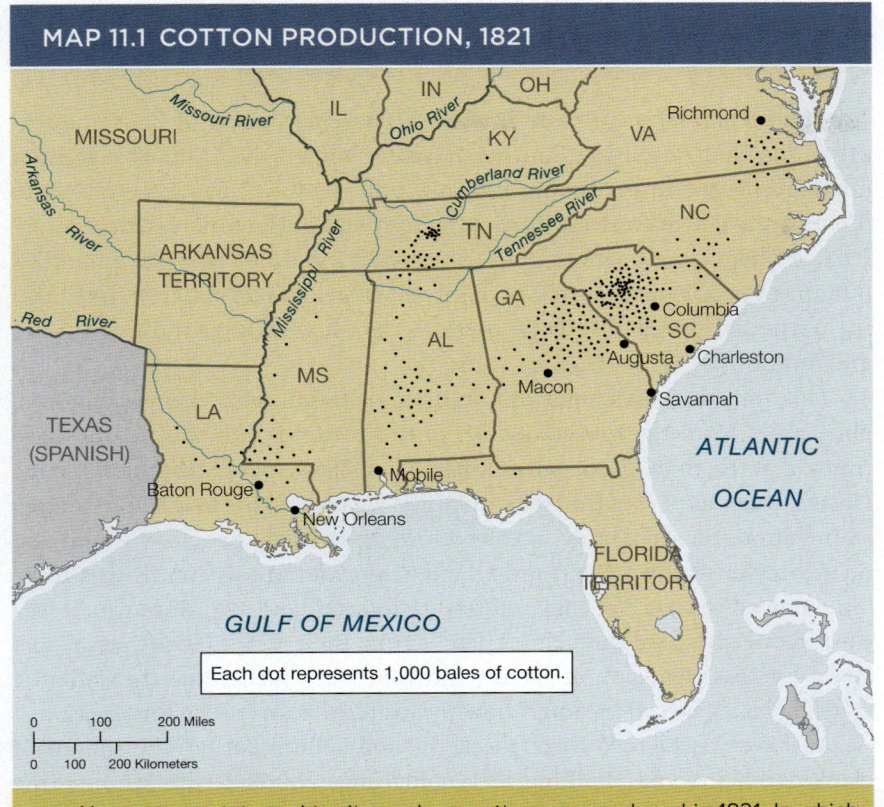

- Name every state and territory where cotton was produced in 1821. In which two states was cotton production the densest?
- Name the rivers that flow through the areas of cotton production in 1821. Which rivers allowed transport of baled cotton to the port at New Orleans?
- According to the chapter text, why was cotton so profitable? What were its main destinations?

and, eventually, Texas. There they found cheap land and fertile soil—a promised land made possible by the worldwide demand for cotton clothing.

Many Southern White women were not happy about leaving the coastal states for the southwestern frontier. As Mary Ann Taylor prepared to leave South Carolina for Alabama, she confessed to a friend, "You *cannot* imagine the state of despair I am in." Her despair deepened when she reached Alabama in 1834. There she was "surrounded by strangers with whom I have not a single congenial feeling."

In 1820, Virginia, the Carolinas, and Georgia had produced two-thirds of the nation's cotton (see Map 11.1). By 1830, the states in the Old Southwest had overtaken them as the leading cotton-growing region. An acre of land in South Carolina produced about 300 pounds of cotton; while an acre in Alabama or in the Mississippi delta, a 200-mile-wide strip of fertile soil between the Yazoo and Mississippi Rivers, could generate 800 pounds. It was the most profitable farmland in the world. As a British visitor noted, people in the Old Southwest "buy cotton, sell cotton, think cotton, eat cotton, drink cotton, and dream cotton. They marry cotton wives, and unto them are born cotton children.... It is the great staple—the sum and substance of Alabama."

> Domestic slave trade forces a million enslaved people into the cotton South

The Domestic Slave Trade Enslaved Blacks had many of the same reservations that migrating Southern White women did. Almost a million enslaved people in Maryland, Virginia, and the Carolinas were forced to move to the Old Southwest during the first half of the nineteenth century. Packed onto steamboats or coerced to walk hundreds of miles in coffles (chains of people handcuffed in pairs and wearing iron collars), they lived in "perpetual dread" of the Gulf states' harsh working conditions, heat, and humidity.

This forced resettlement of a million enslaved men, women, children, and babies from the tobacco South to the cotton South was nearly three times greater than the total number of enslaved people brought to the United States as part of the transatlantic slave trade. This new traffic, known as the domestic slave trade, involved forcing enslaved people—by land and on steamships—down the Cumberland, Ohio, and Mississippi Rivers to be "sold down the river," as they referred to it (see Map 11.2). Moreover, it was the forced removal of Indigenous people from their native lands that opened space for the expansion of slavery into the West, just as the transatlantic trade had once forced the migration of captive Africans to the Americas.

As slavery expanded throughout the antebellum period, the sounds of clanking chains and shuffling feet, sometimes coupled with whimpering cries and simmering anger, were quite common. Virginia congressman John Randolph complained that the roads near his home were "thronged with droves of these wretches & the human carcass-butchers, who drive them on the hoof to market." Enslaved people such as W. L. Boost witnessed the coffles of people passing by: "I could hear them mournin' and prayin'."

SLAVE COFFLE This drawing, which appeared in the abolitionist newspaper *The Genius of Universal Emancipation* in 1821, shows enslaved people in coffles (people fastened together in shackles and handcuffs) as they are forcibly moved to deeper regions of the South.

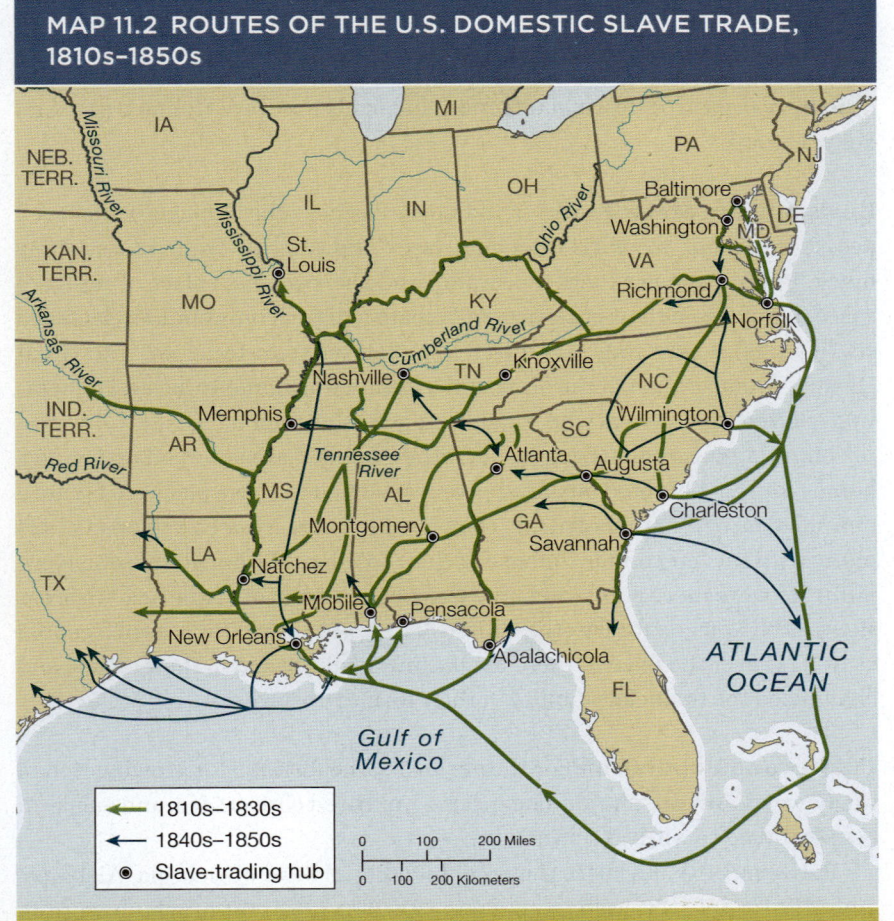

MAP 11.2 ROUTES OF THE U.S. DOMESTIC SLAVE TRADE, 1810s–1850s

- 1810s–1830s
- 1840s–1850s
- Slave-trading hub

- Trace and name the rivers that carried enslaved laborers south and west during the domestic slave trade. On what other bodies of water did they travel as well?
- How many slave-trading hubs appear on this map? In what states are they located? How many hubs are located on rivers?
- Compare the pattern of movement shown on this map with the patterns of population growth and cotton production on Map 11.3. What similarities do you see? According to the chapter text, how are the three factors—slave trade, population growth, cotton production—interrelated?

The enslaved people who were sent "downriver" struggled with being torn from their families and friends. One song expressed their anguish: "Massa sell poor negro, ho, heave, O! / Leave poor wife and children, ho, heave, O!" Some tried to run away. Others maimed themselves to avoid being "sent south." One woman killed herself because "they have carried my children off with 'em."

The steady stream of enslaved Black people arriving in the Cotton South performed backbreaking labor in an environment of danger, disease, and deprivation. They worked from sunup to sundown in the fields, repeatedly bending and standing to pull the cotton fiber out of the boll. Some suffered with cuts on their hands and other injuries related to repetitive motion. Deprived of healthy, well-balanced meals, enslaved people were often malnourished and susceptible to diseases such as smallpox, yellow fever, and dysentery (a gastrointestinal infection that leads to severe stomach pain and dehydration).

Resisting the Slave Trade In marshy areas near the Gulf coast, enslaved people were put to work removing trees and stumps from the swampy muck. But for some of them the swampland also became a place of refuge, a space to hide from their enslavers and create maroon communities (secluded settlements) where they could live in a state of semi-freedom. The Great Dismal Swamp of North Carolina and Virginia was home to several generations of freedom seekers who sought refuge in this region.

> *Escaping from the slave trade*

Mountainous regions, caves, and other wooded areas served as the new homes for self-liberated enslaved people who fled to these places to create a new life free of external control. They lived in these isolated regions in harmony with the land and in defense of their freedom. Although maroon communities were more common in the Caribbean and South America—in areas such as the Amazon forest—the United States offered such spaces of freedom as well. Those who lived in these communities succeeded in their escape and challenged the financial stability of their former enslavers.

> *Population growth and cotton production*

Profits and Population For the enslavers, the formula for growing rich in the Lower South was simple: cheap land, improved cotton seed, and enslaved people forced to work at a swift pace.

Between 1810 and 1840, the combined population of Georgia, Alabama, and Mississippi increased from about 300,000 (252,000 of whom were in Georgia) to 1,657,799. As Virginian Richard Ambler made his way to Alabama, he marveled that "the number of emigrants surpasses all calculations. . . . For six or eight miles at a time you see an uninterrupted line of walkers, wagons, and carriages." By 1860, annual cotton production in the United States had grown to 4 *million* bales (bundles of cotton weighing between 400 and 500 pounds each).

The Spreading Cotton Kingdom

> *Mississippi River becomes a cotton highway*

By 1860, the center of the **cotton kingdom** stretched from eastern North Carolina, South Carolina, and Georgia through the Alabama–Mississippi "black belt" (so called for the color of the fertile soil), through Louisiana, on to Texas, and up the Mississippi Valley as far as southern Illinois (see Map 11.3).

With the emergence of steamboats, the Mississippi River became the cotton highway, transporting millions of bales downriver from Kentucky, Tennessee, Arkansas, Mississippi, and Louisiana to New Orleans. From there, ships took the cotton to New York City, New England, Great Britain, and France. By 1860, King Cotton accounted for more than half of all U.S. exports.

cotton kingdom The cotton-producing region, relying predominantly on slave labor, that extended from North Carolina west to Louisiana and reached as far north as southern Illinois.

MAP 11.3 POPULATION GROWTH AND COTTON PRODUCTION, 1821–1859

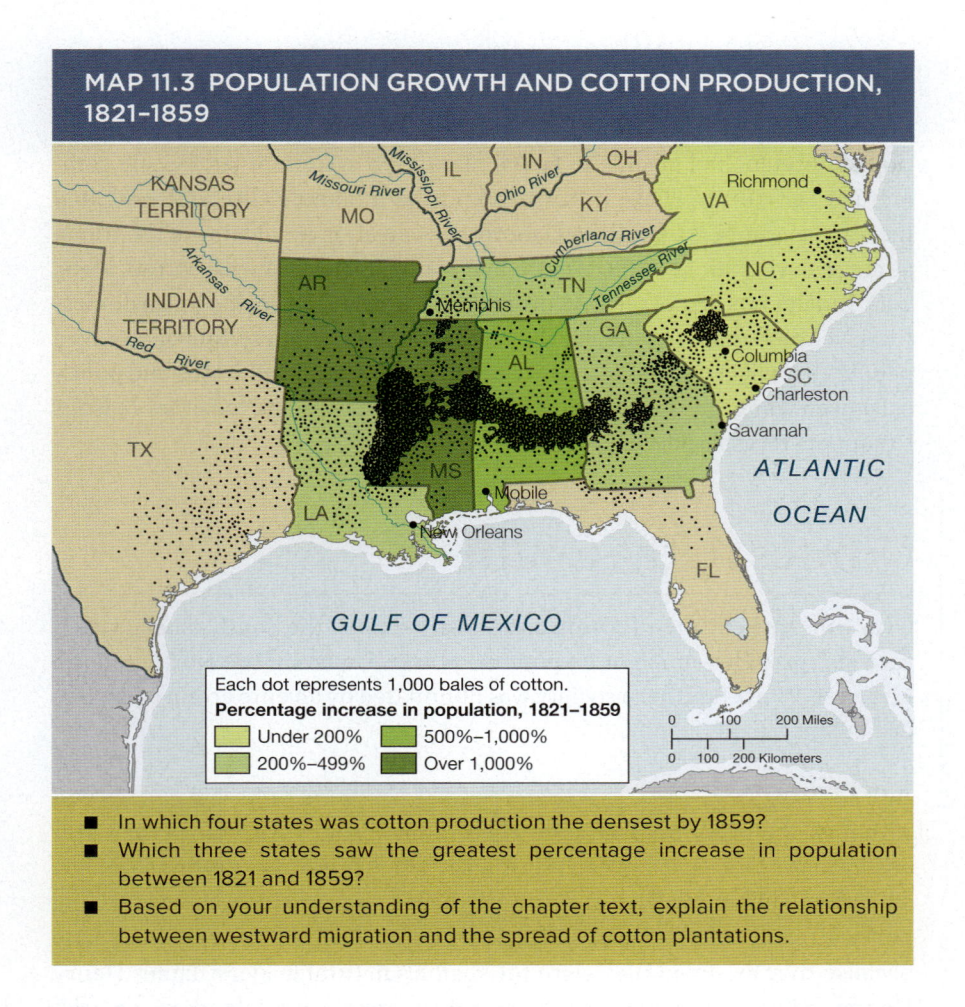

Each dot represents 1,000 bales of cotton.

Percentage increase in population, 1821–1859
- Under 200%
- 200%–499%
- 500%–1,000%
- Over 1,000%

- In which four states was cotton production the densest by 1859?
- Which three states saw the greatest percentage increase in population between 1821 and 1859?
- Based on your understanding of the chapter text, explain the relationship between westward migration and the spread of cotton plantations.

That same year, two-thirds of the richest Americans lived in the South. Cotton-growing was the most visible sign of economic success—and enterprising young White men judged their wealth and status by the number of human beings they owned.

The soaring profitability of cotton fostered a false sense of security. In a speech to the U.S. Senate in 1858, South Carolina's former governor James Henry Hammond, who owned a huge cotton plantation worked by more than 300 enslaved laborers, warned critics: "You dare not make war on cotton. No power on earth dares make war upon it. Cotton is King."

What Hammond failed to acknowledge was that the Southern economy had grown dangerously dependent on European demand for raw cotton. By 1860, Great Britain was importing more than 80 percent of its cotton from the South. Southern leaders did not anticipate what they could least afford: a collapse in world demand for Southern cotton. Yet in 1860, the expansion of the British textile industry peaked and the selling price of Southern cotton began a steady decline. By then, however, it was too late to change; the Lower South was committed to large-scale cotton production for generations to come.

> Unsustainable Southern dependence on British demand for cotton

Indeed, by now the South had become fully committed to both a cotton economy and a social structure built around the forced labor of enslaved Africans. Successful cotton production and eager markets, both domestic and foreign, had given rise to the plantation system of large-scale commercial agriculture. This, in turn, supported a planter elite and exploited increasing numbers of enslaved laborers—even after the closing of the transatlantic slave trade in 1808. Wealth and status associated with cotton, along with Indigenous dispossession, propelled westward expansion and a domestic slave trade that encouraged the buying, breeding, and selling of enslaved people. A small class of planter elite came to enjoy outsized status and political power, while Southern Whites of the lower class discovered other reasons to support race-based slavery.

Whites in the South

Over time, the culture of cotton and slavery shaped the South's social structure and provided much of its political power. Unlike in the North and the Midwest, White Southern society was dominated by an elite group of enslavers and merchants.

Enslavers

Although the percentage of large plantations (estates with more than fifty enslaved people) varied in each southern state, their owners exercised overwhelming influence. The enslavers behaved like aristocrats—controlling political, economic, and social life, partly because of self-interest and partly because they assumed they were the region's natural leaders. James Henry Hammond argued that slavery "does indeed create an aristocracy—an aristocracy of talents, of virtue, of generosity, and courage."

What distinguished a plantation from a farm—in addition to the plantation's sheer size—was the use of a large number of enslaved workers supervised by drivers and overseers. If, as historians have agreed, one had to own at least twenty laborers to be called a **planter**, only 1 out of 30 Whites in 1860 qualified. Eleven planters, among the wealthiest people in the nation, owned 500 enslaved people each—and one planter, a South Carolina rice grower, owned 1,000. The total number of slaveholders added up to a minority of White Southerners—383,637 out of 8 million.

Over time, enslavers and their wives (sometimes called mistresses) grew accustomed to being waited on by enslaved people, day and night. A Virginia planter told a British visitor that a Black girl slept in the master bedroom. When his British guest asked why, he replied: "Good heaven! If I wanted a glass of water during the night, what would become of me?" When not working, enslavers enjoyed hunting, horse racing, and playing card games.

Most Southern White men, but especially the enslavers and political elite, embraced an unwritten social code centered on personal honor in which they felt compelled to defend their reputation—with words, fists, or

---

CORE OBJECTIVE
3. Explain why most White Southerners—enslavers as well as those who did not have the means to own enslaved people—supported the expansion of slavery.

The planter elite

planters Owners of large farms in the South that were worked by twenty or more enslaved people and supervised by overseers.

A SOUTHERN PLANTATION
In this 1859 engraving of a rice planter's mansion, a set of humble cabins that house the plantation's enslaved workers is visible behind the mansion.

guns. Duels to the death (called affairs of honor) were the ultimate expressions of manly virtue.

Honor and violence: Dueling

Although not confined to the South, dueling was much more common there than in the rest of the nation. Many prominent Southern leaders—congressmen, senators, governors, editors, and planters—engaged in duels, although dueling was technically illegal in many states.

The Plantation Mistress

The South, like the North, was a male-dominated society, only more so because of the slavery system. South Carolinian Christopher Memminger explained that slavery heightened the need for a hierarchical social and family structure. White wives and children, he stressed, needed to be as subservient and compliant as enslaved Blacks were required to be. "Each planter," he declared, "is in fact a Patriarch" who requires "obedience and subordination."

White women on the plantation

Conflicting Realities The **plantation mistress** may have been expected to be meekly submissive, but few were the frail, helpless creatures that many husbands demanded. In fact, many of these women were the female counterparts of their husbands. Some brought riches and enslaved people to their marriages through generations of wealth passed down from their fathers.

These women were active participants in the system of slavery. Many mistresses doled out work assignments and punishments; many organized private and public slave auctions. Often, they treated their enslaved workers harshly, and enslaved people noted that some of these women were more sadistic than their husbands. Some wives, however, were not so harsh. One enslaved worker said that her mistress "was with all the slave women every

plantation mistress The matriarch of a planter's household, responsible for supervising the domestic aspects of the estate.

MARY BOYKIN CHESNUT
Chesnut's diary describing Southern life and the Civil War, published posthumously, was awarded the Pulitzer Prize in 1981.

time a baby was born. Or, when a plague of misery hit the folks, she knew what to do and what kind of medicine to chase off the aches and pains."

Some White women complained that they also were, in a way, enslaved. Mary Boykin Chesnut, a plantation mistress in South Carolina, believed that "there is no slave, after all, like a wife." She admitted that she had few rights, since her husband was the "master of the house." George Fitzhugh, a Virginia attorney and writer, spoke for most White Southern men when he said that a "man loves his children because they are weak, helpless, and dependent. He loves his wife for similar reasons."

Despite some mistresses' complaints about their own situation, enslaved women did not see themselves in alignment with their mistresses and often spent time begging them for fair treatment—to no avail. For example, Fanny Kemble of Philadelphia, who married into a family with large plantations in Georgia, rejected enslaved women's attempts to relate to her. In her mind, "their dirt and bad smells about their houses were most revolting to all senses."

Sexual Behavior White women living in a slaveholding culture confronted a double standard in terms of moral and sexual behavior. They were expected to be exemplars of Christian morality and sexual purity and to obey their fathers and husbands, even as the men engaged in gambling, drinking, carousing, and sexually assaulting enslaved women. "The enjoyment of a Negro or Mulatto [person of mixed race] woman is spoken of as quite a common thing," a guest of Southern enslavers noted in 1764. "No reluctance, delicacy, or shame is made about the matter." The practice of White owners assaulting enslaved men, women, and children was common because the crime of rape did not apply; an enslaver could treat his human property as he wished.

"God forgive us," Mary Chesnut wrote, "but ours is a monstrous system. Like the patriarchs of old, our men live all in one house with their wives and their [enslaved] concubines [lovers]. . . . Any lady is ready to tell you who is the father of all the mulatto children in everybody's household but her own. Those, she seems to think, drop from the clouds."

Overseers and Drivers

White plantation overseers ▶ The Whites who worked on large plantations were usually overseers, who managed the enslaved people and were also responsible for maintaining the buildings, fences, and grounds. Usually, they were farmers or skilled workers, or sons of enslavers, or simply poor Whites eager to rise in stature. Some were themselves slaveholders.

The overseers relocated often in search of better wages and cheaper land. A Mississippi planter described White overseers as "a worthless set of vagabonds." Frederick Douglass, who escaped from slavery in Maryland, said his overseer was "a miserable drunkard, a profane swearer, and a savage monster" armed with a blood-stained bullwhip and a club that he used so cruelly that he even "enraged" the plantation owner.

OVERSEEING ENSLAVED WORKERS A well-dressed overseer supervises a line of enslaved people, including children, harvesting sugarcane.

Usually, the highest managerial position an enslaved person could hope for was that of driver, a favored man whose job was to oversee a small group ("gang") of enslaved people, getting them up and organized each morning by sunrise, and then directing their work (and punishing them) until dark. There were many examples of enslaved people murdering drivers because of their cruel treatment.

"Plain White Folk"

The most numerous White Southerners were small farmers—the so-called **plain White folk**, usually uneducated and often illiterate, eking out hardscrabble lives of bare self-sufficiency. These small farmers ("yeomen") lived with their families in two-room cabins, raised a few hogs and chickens, grew some corn and cotton, and traded with neighbors more than they bought from stores. Women on these farms worked in the fields during harvest time but spent most of their days doing household chores while raising lots of children.

Southern yeomen farmers tended to be fiercely independent and suspicious of government authority, and they overwhelmingly identified with the Democratic Party of Andrew Jackson and the spiritual energies of the evangelical Protestant denominations such as Baptists and Methodists.

Although only a minority of the small-farm owners held enslaved people, most supported slavery for economic and racial reasons. They feared that the enslaved people, if freed, would compete with them for land and jobs, and they enjoyed the privileged status that race-based slavery afforded them. As a White farmer told a Northern traveler, "Now suppose they [enslaved people] was free. You see they'd all think themselves as good as we."

plain White folk Yeoman farmers in the South who lived and worked on their own small farms, growing food and cash crops to trade for necessities.

"Poor Whites"

Poor White Southerners living on the fringes

Visitors to the South often had trouble telling yeoman farmers apart from the "poor Whites," the desperately poor people who were relegated to the least desirable land and lived on the fringes of polite society. The poor Whites, often derided as "crackers," "hillbillies," or "trash," were usually day laborers or squatters who owned neither land nor enslaved people. Some 40 percent of White Southerners worked as tenants, renting land; or as farm laborers, toiling for others. They were often forced to take refuge in the pine barrens, the mountain hollows, and the swamps after having been pushed aside by the more enterprising and the more successful members of Southern society. They usually lived in log cabins, barely managing to keep their families clothed, warm, dry, and fed.

Overall, despite the sharp class differences that slavery created, most White Southerners were fiercely loyal to the institution. The planter elite and their sons, of course, wanted to expand slavery so they could establish even bigger plantations on cheap, fertile land in the Old Southwest. Lower-class Whites, too, supported the institution because they feared competition if enslaved people were to be freed—and it boosted their self-esteem to look down on an even lower class of enslaved laborers. These attitudes served to reinforce inequality throughout the South.

Enslaved People in the South

CORE OBJECTIVE
4. Describe the impact of slavery on African Americans, both free and enslaved, throughout the South.

However immoral and degrading, slavery was the fastest-growing element of Southern life during the first half of the nineteenth century. In 1790, the United States had fewer than 700,000 Black enslaved people. By 1830, they numbered more than 2 million—and by 1860, 4 million (see Maps 11.4 and 11.5). As the enslaved population grew, slave owners felt the need to develop a complex system of rules, regulations, and restrictions.

White Supremacy and Slave Codes

Most Southern enslavers justified owning other human beings by touting White supremacy. "We believe the negro to belong to an inferior race," one planter asserted. Thomas R. R. Cobb, a Georgia lawyer, proclaimed that African Americans were better off "in a state of bondage."

Slave codes controlling Black people

Black babies became enslaved at birth; enslaved people could be moved, sold, rented out, whipped, or raped, as their enslaver saw fit. Formal slave codes (restrictive legislation that sought to control Black people) were quite common. Each state governed the treatment of enslaved people: they could not leave their enslaver's land or household without permission in the form of a pass, they had nightly curfews, and some enslavers incorporated "bed checks" to make sure the enslaved people were in their cabins by 9:00 P.M.

Some codes made it a crime for enslaved people to learn to read and write, for fear that they might use notes to plan a revolt. One formerly enslaved man from Kentucky, John W. Fields, remembered that the White slaveholders "were very harsh if we were caught trying to learn or write. . . . Our ignorance was the greatest hold the South had on us." Enslaved people in most states could not testify in court; legally marry; own firearms; or hit a White man, even in self-defense.

Whites believed that effective management required teaching enslaved people to understand that they were *supposed to be* treated like animals. As Henry Garner, a freedom seeker, explained, the aim of slaveholders was "to make you as much like brutes as possible." Other Whites justified slavery as a form of benevolent paternalism. George Fitzhugh believed that the enslaved Black person was "but a grown-up child and must be governed as a child."

Profits and Exploitation

Such self-serving paternalism had one purpose: profits. Enslavers, explained a White Southerner, "care for nothing but to buy Negroes to raise cotton & raise cotton to buy Negroes." Many viewed enslaved people as a form of human capital—merely commodities to be bought and sold.

> Exploitation of enslaved families

Those in the business of buying and selling enslaved people grew wealthy. One such businessman reported in the 1850s that "a [colored person] that wouldn't bring over $300, seven years ago, will fetch $1000, cash, quick, this year." Thomas Clemson of South Carolina candidly explained, "My object is to get the most I can for the property [enslaved people]. . . . I care but little to whom and how they are sold, whether together [as families] or separated."

Few slave owners balked at splitting up enslaved families. Charles Ball was about four years old in Maryland when his owner died. To settle the owner's debts, the owner's family sold Ball, his mother, and his siblings to different buyers. Decades later, Ball recalled the trauma when his weeping mother "saw me leaving her for the last time" and grabbed him down from the buyer's horse. "My master . . . endeavored to soothe her distress by telling her that he would be a good master to me." Still, his mother would not let go. She begged the slave owner to buy her and the rest of her children.

At that point, the man who had bought Ball's mother "came running in pursuit of her with a raw hide [whip] in his hand. When he overtook us, he told her . . . to give that little Negro to its owner and come back with him. My mother . . . cried, 'Oh, master, do not take me from my child!' Without making any reply, he gave her two or three heavy blows on the shoulders with his raw hide, snatched me from her arms, handed me to my [new] master, and seizing her by one arm, dragged her back towards the place of sale."

Four-year-old Ball was then locked in chains, dragged across the Patuxent River, and marched some 500 miles across Virginia and North Carolina before finally reaching his new home on the South Carolina coast. Years later, after he had escaped to freedom, the memory of his family being sold and separated remained an open wound: "Young as I was, the horrors of that day sank deeply into my heart, and even at this time, though half a century has elapsed, the terrors of the scene return with painful vividness upon my memory."

MAP 11.4 THE ENSLAVED POPULATION, 1820

Each dot represents 200 enslaved people.

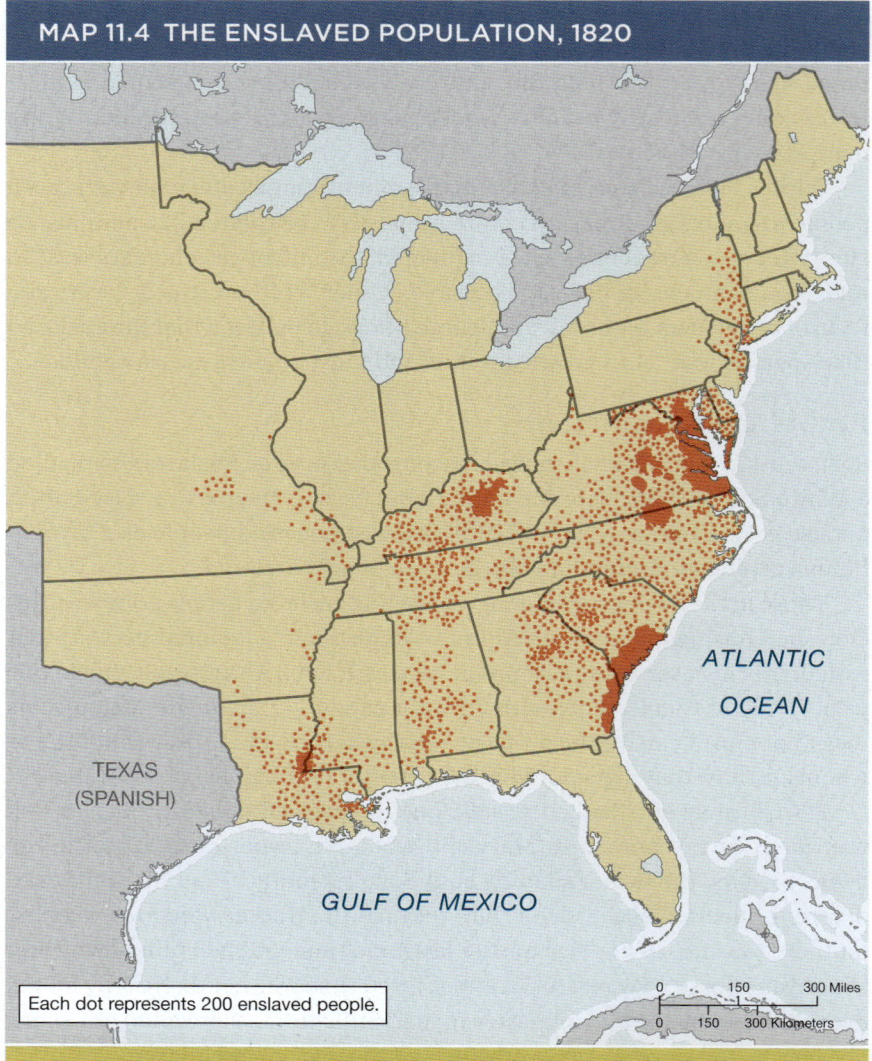

- Consider where the largest populations of enslaved people were clustered in 1820. According to the chapter text, why were most enslaved people in these regions and not in others?
- In how many states do the dots representing 200 enslaved people in 1820 cluster so closely that they merge together? Now look at Map 11.5 and do the same count. How have the numbers changed?
- Comparing Maps 11.4 and 11.5, how many states that had enslaved populations in 1820 no longer had any in 1860? How do you explain this?

"Free Persons of Color"

African Americans who were not enslaved were called "free persons of color." In fact, however, they were anything but free; they occupied an uncertain social status between slavery and freedom. In South Carolina, for example, free Blacks had to pay an annual tax and were not allowed to leave the state. After 1823, they were required to have a White "guardian" and an identity card.

MAP 11.5 THE ENSLAVED POPULATION, 1860

Each dot represents 200 enslaved people.

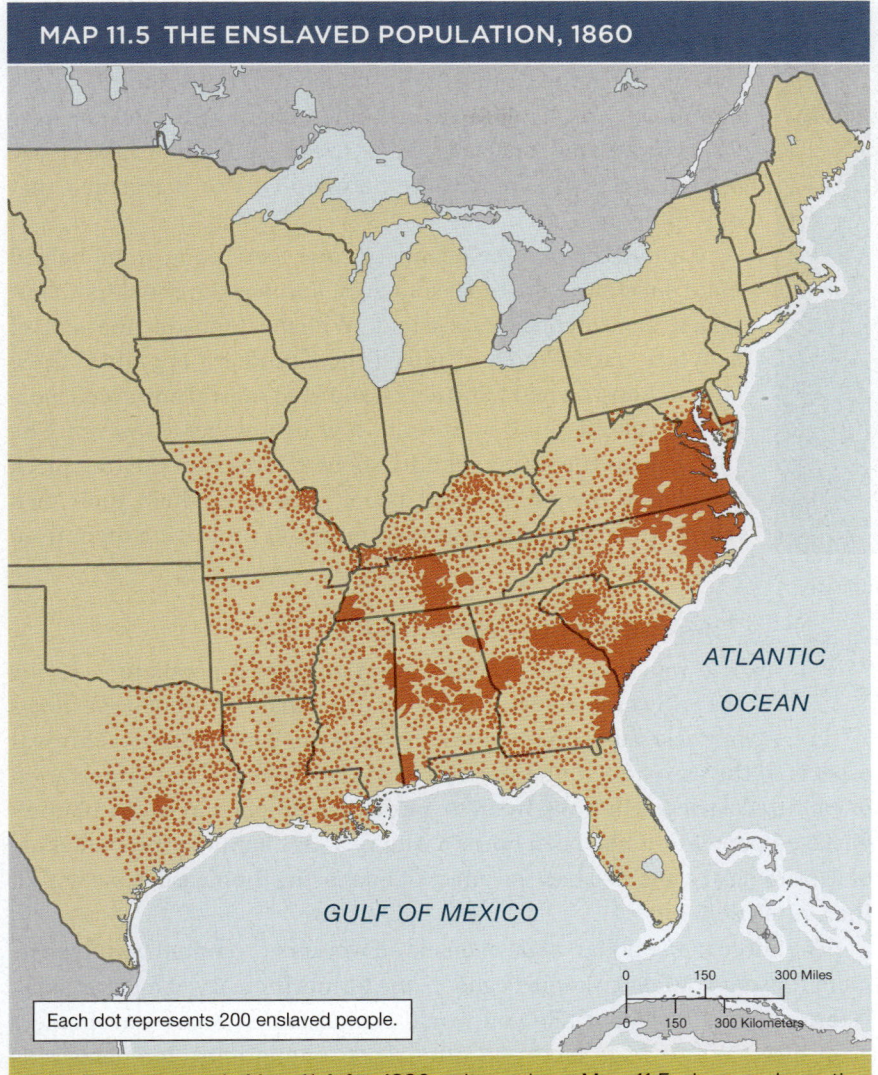

- Compared with Map 11.4 for 1820, where does Map 11.5 show a dramatic westward increase in the enslaved population by 1860? What change in the map for 1860 shows how the nation's growth enabled this westward surge?
- According to the chapter text, why did slavery spread west? Why did many enslaved people resist migrating west?
- Compare Maps 11.4 and 11.5 with Maps 11.1 and 11.3 showing cotton production. What patterns do you see?

Individual Black people came to be "free" in a number of ways. Some enslaved people were able to purchase their freedom, and others were freed (manumitted) by their owners. By 1860, approximately 250,000 free people of color lived in the slave states, most of them in coastal cities such as Baltimore, Charleston, Mobile, and New Orleans. Some were tailors or shoemakers or carpenters; others were painters, bricklayers, butchers, blacksmiths, or barbers. Still others worked on the docks or on ships. Free Black women usually worked as seamstresses, laundresses, or house servants.

YARROW MAMOUT As an enslaved African Muslim, Mamout purchased his freedom, acquired property, and settled in present-day Washington, D.C. Charles Willson Peale executed this portrait in 1819, when Mamout was over 100 years old.

Among the free Black population were "Mulattoes," or people of mixed ancestry. The 1860 census reported 412,000 mixed-race people in the United States, or about 10 percent of the Black population—probably a drastic undercount. In cities such as Charleston, and especially New Orleans, people of mixed race occupied a status somewhere between that of Blacks and that of Whites.

Although most free people of color were poor, some helped build substantial fortunes and even became slaveholders themselves. In Natchez, Mississippi, William Johnson, the son of a White father and a mixed-race mother, operated three barbershops, owned 1,500 acres, and held several enslaved laborers. Slaveholders of color were few in number, however. The 1830 census reported that only about 2 percent of the free Black population owned enslaved people—many of them their own family members, purchased as a means of protecting them from White enslavers.

The World of the Slave Trade

The rapid increase in the nation's enslaved population during the early nineteenth century occurred mainly through the births of enslaved people already living in the United States. This was especially the case after Congress outlawed the purchase and importation of captured Africans in 1808. By 1820, more than 80 percent of the nation's enslaved population had been born in America. But banning the trafficking of captured Africans also had the effect of increasing their cash value within the United States.

> Slave market multiplies

The surge in the dollar value of enslaved workers prompted better treatment for some. "Massa was purty good," one formerly enslaved man recalled. "He treated us jus' 'bout like you would a good mule." Some slaveholders even hired White wage laborers—often Irish immigrants—for dangerous work rather than risk the lives of the more valuable enslaved workers.

An Expanding Slave Market Between 1800 and 1860, the average price of enslaved people *quadrupled*, and breeding and selling enslaved people became a big business. Over a twenty-year period, a Virginia plantation owned by John Tayloe III recorded 252 enslaved births and 142 deaths of enslaved people, thus providing him with 110 extra enslaved individuals to be deployed on the plantation, given to his sons, or sold to traders.

Markets and auction houses sprang up in every southern city. New Orleans alone had twenty slave-trading businesses. Each year, thousands of enslaved people circulated through the city's "slave pens," forced to become products with prices. They were bathed and groomed; "fattened up" like cattle, with bacon, milk, and butter; assigned categories such as Prime, No. 1, No. 2, and Second Rate; and packaged for sale in identical blue suits or dresses. On auction day, they were paraded into the sale room.

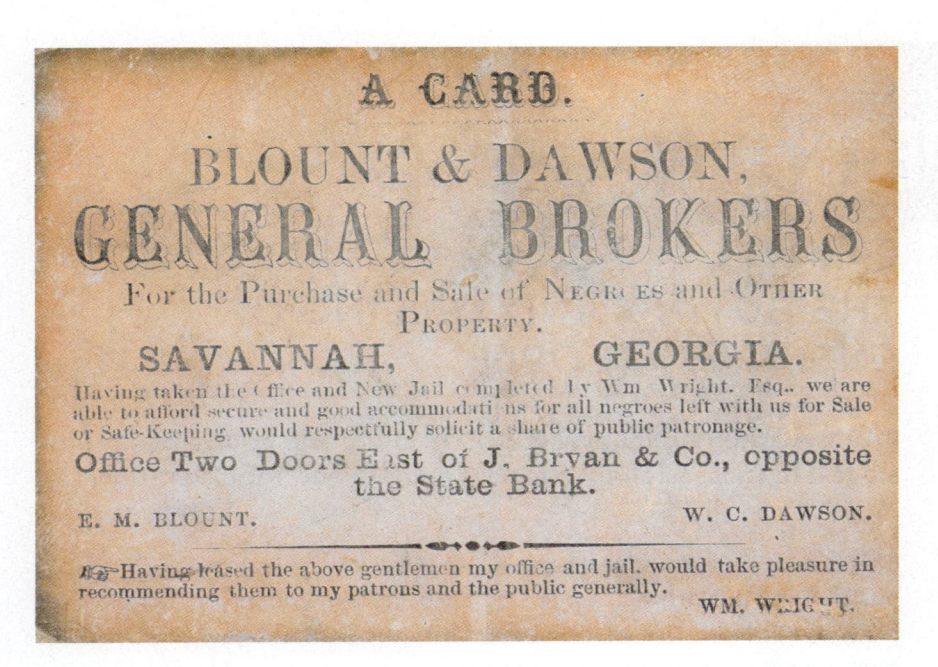

THE BUSINESS OF SLAVERY
This advertisement for Blount & Dawson, "General Brokers for the Purchase and Sale of Negroes and Other Property," guarantees its clients "secure and good accommodations for all negroes left with us for Sale or Safe-Keeping" in its newly acquired jail, opposite the state bank.

Buyers physically inspected each enslaved person on the auction block. They forced the enslaved people to undress; then inspected their naked bodies, poking, squeezing, and searching for signs of disease or deformities. As formerly enslaved Solomon Northup noted, "scars on a slave's back were considered evidence of a rebellious or unruly spirit and hurt [the enslaved person's chances for] sale." Once the inspections ended, buyers bid on the enslaved people, purchased them, and transported them to their new workplaces.

The Market in Enslaved Women and Children Almost a million people were "sold South" or "sold downriver" and taken to the Old Southwest during the first half of the nineteenth century (see again Map 11.2).

The separation of children from parents and husbands from wives remained the worst aspect of the slave trade. In Missouri, one enslaved woman saw six of her seven children, ages one to eleven years, sold to six different owners. Only Louisiana and Alabama prohibited separating a child younger than age ten from his or her mother, and no state prevented the separation of an enslaved husband from his wife.

Slave markets in New Orleans engaged in what was called the "fancy trade," which meant selling women as forced sexual partners. "I sold your fancy girl Alice for $800," a New Orleans slave trader wrote to a partner in Richmond. "There is great demand for fancy maids."

A reporter watching a slave sale in New Orleans spied on the auction block "one of the most beautiful women [he] had ever saw. She was about sixteen, dressed in a cheap striped woolen gown, and bareheaded." Her name was Hermina, and she was "sold for $1250 [$35,000 today] to one of the most lecherous brutes I ever set eyes on."

Comparing PERSPECTIVES

THE BUYING AND SELLING OF ENSLAVED PEOPLE

From: Auction Announcement, "178 sugar and cotton plantation slaves! In succession of Wm. M. Lambeth and for a partition," March 13–14, 1855.

This slave auction advertisement showcases the sale of 178 people enslaved by the late William M. Lambeth, in New Orleans, to be held over two days in 1855. The advertisement lists the names, ages, and trades of each individual being sold at auction.

Will be Sold at Auction, . . . in the city of New Orleans, . . . Slaves comprising the gangs of the WAVERLY and MEREDITH PLANTATIONS, belonging to the succession of William M. Lambeth, deceased.

TERMS.

One-third cash, and the remainder at 12 months' credit. . . . All sales to be completed within ten days from adjudication, or the Slaves will be re-sold for account and risk of the former purchaser after ten days' advertisement in one city paper, and without further notice or other putting in default.

. . . The slaves will be sold singly, and when in families, together. They can be seen three days previous to sale, on application at the office of the Auctioneers, No. 8 Banks' Arcade.

. . .

ONE FAMILY.

1. Frank Bond, 45 years, good teamster and field hand.
2. Eliza, 35 years, choice field hand.
3. Sarah, Infant.
4. Louisa, 4 years.
5. Harriet, 6 years.
6. Mary Jane, 9 years.
7. Washington, 11 years, likely boy.

---

8. Caroline, 14 years, likely intelligent girl.
9. Margaret, 16 years, choice field hand.

. . .

ONE FAMILY—(Choice.)

18. Anthony Moore, about 30 years, fine engineer and field hand.
19. Sarah Moore, 32 years, good field hand; tonsils occasionally inflamed.
20. Infant, 2 months.
21. Anthony, 3 years.
22. Stephen, 5 years.
23. Nace, 9 years.
24. Sophy, 12 years, likely.

. . .

ONE FAMILY.

41. Solomon White, 40 years, a No. 1 field hand and fine filterer.
42. Cloe, 42 yrs., good servant and nurse—manager of trash gang.
43. Joe B., 24 yrs., fine field hand and axeman, slightly lame from cut on instep.

From: Receipt of Sale of 58 slaves [Sale by Josiah Brown to A. C. Horton, who was taking them to Texas], July 25, 1860.

This receipt was received from Albert C. Horton of Matagorda, Texas, on account of his purchase of fifty-eight enslaved individuals. It shows that the amount paid in cash was $13,700, of a total balance of $32,700. This receipt also lists a number of enslaved individuals considered "defective."

(Copy of Receipt given to Gov. Albert C. Horton)

Charleston S°Cª 25th July 1860

Received from Albert C. Horton of Matagorda Texas, on account of Purchase money of Fifty eight (58) negro Slaves, Thirteen thousand seven hundred Dollars in Cash, the Balance, namely Thirty two thousand Seven hundred ($32,700) Dollars with Interest from date being secured by two Bonds each in the amount of Sixteen thousand three hundred and Fifty ($16,350) Dollars, upon one of which Ziba B. Oakes is Co-Obligor, with further collateral Security, namely Drafts on Nelson Clements of New York in favor of said A C Horton & others, proceeds of said Drafts to be applied to payment of said Bonds, and as additional security a Mortgage of the said Negro Slaves and a Mortgage of good & sufficient Real Estate, the property of the said A C Horton, near Matagorda Texas, the negroes below being defective as follows — Peter lost one finger, Patty & Clarissa umbilical hernia, Lucy simple minded, Sarah Hefty & Betty prolapsus, Anthony slight rupture.

In my presence signed Josiah L. Brown Signed
signed Josiah L. Brown Signed

Questions

1. How are enslaved families described in this auction advertisement? What do documents such as these reveal about their family lives?

2. Judging from the receipt excerpted here, what were the terms of sale of enslaved people—from the enslavers' perspective?

3. What type of personal information is revealed through transactions that commodified enslaved people?

ESTATE SALE AND AUCTION OF ENSLAVED PEOPLE This engraving from 1842 depicts an estate sale in New Orleans where enslaved people are auctioned off alongside art and other valuable items. An enslaved man, woman, and child stand on the auction block. **How were enslaved people treated and evaluated in auctions such as this one?**

The same reporter noted that "a noble-looking woman with a bright-eyed seven-year-old" son were offered for sale as a pair. When no one bid on them, the auctioneer offered them separately. A man from Mississippi bought the boy, while the mother went to a Texan. As her son was dragged away, the woman "burst forth into the most frantic wails that ever despair gave utterance to."

Slavery as a Way of Life

Plantation field hands

The lives of enslaved people differed greatly from place to place, depending in part on the owners themselves; partly on whether the owners were focused on growing rice, sugar, tobacco, or cotton; and partly on the owners' location, whether on a farm or in a city. Although many enslaved people were artisans or craftsmen (carpenters, blacksmiths, furniture-makers, butchers, ship pilots, house servants, cooks, nurses, maids, weavers, basketmakers, and so on), the vast majority were **field hands** who were often organized into work gangs supervised by a Black driver or a White overseer. Some enslaved people were "hired out" to other enslavers or to merchants, churches, or businesses. Others worked on Sundays or holidays to earn cash of their own.

field hands Enslaved people who toiled in the cotton or cane fields in organized work gangs.

Enslaved plantation workers were usually housed in one- or two-room cabins with dirt floors. The wealthiest enslavers built workers' cabins out of brick. Beds were a luxury, even though they were little more than boards covered with straw. Most enslaved people slept on the floor, with only a coarse blanket for warmth. They received a set of cheap linen or cotton clothing twice a year, but shoes were generally provided only in winter; enslaved people went barefoot most of the year. About half of their babies died in their first year, a death rate more than twice that of Whites. The food given to enslaved people was cheap and monotonous: cornmeal, pork, molasses, and chicken.

Field hands worked from sunrise to sunset, six days a week. Solomon Northup remembered picking cotton until it was "too dark to see, and when the moon is full, they oftentimes labor till the middle of the night." Each evening, the overseer or planter weighed the baskets and recorded that weight next to each picker's name on a slate board. Those who fell short of the daily goal were whipped.

At times, plantation laborers continued to work at night ginning cotton, milling sugarcane, grinding corn, or doing other indoor tasks. Women, remembered one enslaved person, "had to work all day in de fields an' den come home an' do the housework at night." Sundays were precious days off on many estates and small farms. Enslaved people used this time to hunt, fish, dance to banjo and fiddle music, tell stories, or tend their own small gardens. They also could use it to attend religious gatherings.

The Violence of Slavery

Although some owners and enslaved people developed close and even affectionate relationships, slavery remained a system rooted in brutal force. The difference between a good owner and a bad one, according to one enslaved man, was the difference between one "who did not whip you too much" and one who "whipped you till he'd bloodied you and blistered you."

> Brutal violence against the rural enslaved population

Allen Sidney, formerly an enslaved person, recalled an incident on a Mississippi plantation. An enslaved worker who fell behind while picking cotton resisted when a Black driver started to "whip him up." Upon seeing the fracas, the White overseer, mounted on horseback, galloped over and shot the resisting worker, killing him. "None of the other slaves," Sidney noted, "said a word or turned their heads." They were so fearful of being shot themselves that they "kept on hoeing as if nothing had happened." At times, Whites turned the punishment of enslaved people into public spectacles that struck fear into anyone else considering rebellion or escape.

Urban Slavery

Enslaved people living in southern cities such as Richmond, Memphis, Atlanta, New Orleans, or Charleston had a much different experience from those on isolated farms and plantations. "A city slave is almost a freeman," claimed an enslaved person living in Maryland.

> Greater mobility for enslaved people in the cities

Those who worked in urban households tended to be better fed and clothed. They interacted not only with their White owners but also with the community around them—shopkeepers and police, neighbors and strangers. Some were hired out to others and allowed to keep a portion of their wages. In general, enslaved people in cities enjoyed greater mobility than their counterparts in rural areas and were able to experience something closer to freedom.

Enslaved Women

Although enslaved men and women often performed similar chores, they did not experience slavery in the same way. "Slavery is terrible for men," the formerly enslaved North Carolinian Harriet Jacobs stressed in her autobiography, *Incidents in the Life of a Slave Girl*, "but it is far more terrible for women."

> Enslaved women and reproduction

Once slaveholders realized how profitable a fertile enslaved woman would be by giving birth to babies that could later be sold, they coerced enslaved women into having as many children as possible. Some owners rewarded pregnant enslaved women by giving them less work and more food and by gifting new mothers with dresses and silver dollars.

But if motherhood provided these women with benefits, it also was exhausting. Within days after childbirth, the mothers were put to work spinning, weaving, or sewing. A few weeks thereafter, they were sent back to the fields; breastfeeding mothers were often forced to take their babies with them, strapped to their backs. Enslaved women were expected to do "man's work": cut trees, haul logs, spread fertilizer, plow fields, dig ditches, slaughter animals, hoe corn, and pick cotton—whether or not they were toting a new child.

> Enslaved women and sexual abuse

Enslaved girls, women, and some men were often sexually abused by their owners, both men and women. Hundreds of thousands of mixed-race children provided physical proof of interracial sexual assault.

James Henry Hammond, a prominent South Carolina planter and politician, confessed that he sexually assaulted one of his enslaved women, Sally Johnson, who bore several of his children—all of whom he kept in slavery as "their happiest earthly condition." He also abused one of Sally's daughters, twelve-year-old Louisa.

The women responded in different ways. Some fiercely resisted the advances—and were usually whipped or even killed for their disobedience. Others aborted or killed their babies rather than see them grow up in slavery.

Celia

Often, enslaved people could improve their circumstances only by making horrible choices that offered no guarantee of success. The tragic story of a girl named Celia reveals the moral complexity of slavery for African American women and the limited legal options available to them.

In 1850, fourteen-year-old Celia was purchased by Robert Newsom, a prosperous Missouri farmer who told his daughters that he had bought the girl to be their servant. In fact, however, the recently widowed Newsom wanted a sex slave. After purchasing Celia, he raped her; and for the next five years he continued to do so, even building her a brick cabin fifty yards from his house. During that time, she gave birth to two of his children.

Eventually, Celia reached her breaking point. She warned Newsom that the rapes must stop. He paid no attention. On June 23, 1855, the sixty-five-year-old Newsom entered Celia's cabin, ignored her frantic appeals, and kept assaulting her until she struck and killed him with a large stick and then burned his body in the fireplace.

Celia was not allowed to testify at her murder trial because she was an enslaved person. The judge and jury, all White men, pronounced her guilty, and on December 21, 1855, she was taken to the Calloway Courthouse in Fulton, Missouri, and "hanged until she died."

Celia's grim story illustrates the lopsided power structure in Southern society at the time. She bore a double burden, being both an enslaved person and a woman living in a male-dominated society that was rife with racism and sexism.

The impact of slavery on all African Americans, whether enslaved or free, was all-encompassing and extreme. Free Blacks had more rights and acquired wealth but still were treated similarly to those in bondage. Slave codes legally restricted the rights and actions of enslaved persons, including limiting their movement and denying them the opportunity to learn to read and write. But nothing proved more threatening than the ever-expanding slave trade, which left enslaved men, women, and children in constant fear of being sold away from their families. Some of them were sold to enslavers in cities or on smaller farms, but the vast majority were sent to work on large plantations as field hands, laboring under the watch of often-violent overseers. Women faced the added threat of sexual abuse, though some of them, like Celia, found that fighting back was the only way to protect themselves and their families.

Forging an Enslaved Community

Enslaved African Americans were victims of terrible injustice and abuse, but such an obvious truth neglects important evidence of their endurance, resilience, and achievement. The captured Africans who were brought to America represented a variety of ethnic, linguistic, and tribal origins. Wherever they could, they forged their own sense of community, asserted their individuality, and devised many ways of resisting their confinement. Many **spirituals** (sacred folk songs) expressed the longing to be free. Although most enslaved people were prohibited from marrying, the law did not prevent them from choosing partners and forging a family life within the rigid constraints of slavery.

> CORE **OBJECTIVE**
> **5.** Analyze how enslaved people resisted the conditions they were forced to endure.

spirituals Songs with religious messages sung by enslaved people to help ease the strain of field labor and to voice their suffering at the hands of their masters and overseers.

ENSLAVED FAMILY IN A GEORGIA COTTON FIELD
An enslaved family toils in a cotton field together, the young children working alongside the men and women. **What factors extended enslaved African Americans' concept of family?**

The Enslaved Family

Marriages between enslaved people had no legal status, but many slaveholders accepted unofficial marriages as a stabilizing influence; a Black man who supported a family, they assumed, would be more reliable and obedient. Even when enslavers did not sanction a marriage, enslaved people went ahead and secretly married, forming nuclear families with the father as the head of the household.

Childhood was short-lived for those born to enslaved parents. At five or six years of age, children were put to work; they collected trash and firewood, picked cotton, scared away crows from planted fields, weeded gardens and fields, and ran errands. By age ten they were full-time field hands.

Because the slave trade often separated enslaved families, enslaved African Americans also extended the fellowship of family to those who worked together, with older enslaved women being addressed as "granny" and coworkers as "sis" or "brother."

African American Religion

Among the most important elements of African American culture was its dynamic religion. This was a unique mixture of African, Caribbean, and Christian elements, often practiced in secret and at night because many slaveholders feared that enslaved workers might use group religious services to organize rebellions.

In religion, enslaved people found both relief for the soul and release for their emotions. "We used to slip off into the woods," a formerly enslaved person recalled, "... to sing and pray to our own liking. We prayed for freedom."

PLANTATION BURIAL (1860) The enslaved people owned by Mississippi governor Tilghman Tucker gather in the woods to bury and mourn for one of their own. The painter of this scene, Englishman John Antrobus, would serve in the Confederate army during the Civil War.

> African American religion and spirituals

Most Africans brought with them to the Americas a belief in a Creator, or Supreme God, whom they could recognize in the Christian God and whom they might identify with Christ, the Holy Ghost, and the saints. But they also maintained African religious beliefs in magic and conjuring (connecting with spirits for the purpose of healing and protection). By 1860, about 20 percent of enslaved adults had joined Christian denominations. Many others blended aspects of the Christian faith into their own forms of worship.

Enslaved people found the Bible inspiring in its support for the poor and oppressed, and they embraced its promise of salvation through the sacrifice of Jesus. Likewise, the spirituals' lyrics offered the promise of deliverance from worldly woes. One popular spiritual, "Go Down, Moses," derived from the plight of the ancient Israelites held captive in Egypt, says: "We need not always weep and moan, / Let my people go. / And wear these slavery chains forlorn, / Let my people go." Nevertheless, despite the soothing promises of salvation, anger and resentment were often present among the enslaved population.

Slave Rebellions

Southern Whites feared slave uprisings more than anything. As a prominent Virginian explained, a slave revolt would "deluge the southern country with blood." Any sign of resistance or rebellion, therefore, risked a brutal response. Despite those responses, the nineteenth-century South witnessed four major slave insurrections.

> Gabriel's foiled rebellion

Gabriel's Rebellion In August 1800, a twenty-four-year-old enslaved man named Gabriel, who worked as a blacksmith near Richmond, Virginia, decided to launch a revolt. His plan was to kill his owner and then gather perhaps a thousand other enslaved people, free Blacks, working-class Whites, abolitionists, and Quakers. His rebel army would then seize key points in the city, capture the governor (future president James Monroe), and terrorize the White elite.

The rebellion never occurred, though, because two enslaved workers on a neighboring plantation alerted Whites to the scheme. Gabriel, his two older brothers, and twenty-four of his fellow "soldiers" were captured, tried, and hanged. Before his execution, Gabriel explained that he had only been imitating George Washington: "I have ventured my life in endeavoring to obtain the liberty of my countrymen."

German Coast Uprising In early 1811, the largest slave revolt in American history occurred just upriver from New Orleans, on a ribbon of land known as the German Coast. There, wealthy sugarcane planters had acquired one of the largest populations of enslaved people in North America, and many of those enslaved people were ripe for revolt. Sugarcane was known as a "killer crop" because the working conditions were so harsh.

> Deslondes's rebellion

Late on January 8, a group of enslaved people broke into their owner's plantation house along the Mississippi River. The planter escaped, but his son was hacked to death. The leader of the assault was Charles Deslondes, a trusted overseer who was the light-skinned son of a planter. Deslondes and his fellow rebels seized weapons, horses, and militia uniforms from the plantation. Reinforced by more enslaved people and emboldened by liquor, they headed toward New Orleans, burning houses and killing Whites along the way. Over the next two days, the ranks of the rebels swelled to over 200.

Their success, however, was short-lived. Angry Whites—as well as several free Blacks who were later praised for their "tireless zeal and dauntless courage"—suppressed the insurrection. U.S. Army units and local militiamen joined the effort.

Deslondes and as many as 100 enslaved people were tortured, killed, and beheaded. Their heads were placed on poles along the Mississippi River to strike fear into other enslaved workers. A month after the rebellion was put down, a White resident noted that "all the negro difficulties have subsided and gentle peace prevails."

> The Vesey plot

Denmark Vesey Revolt The Denmark Vesey plot in Charleston, South Carolina, discovered in 1822, involved a similar effort to assault the White population. Vesey, born in 1767 on the Caribbean island of St. Thomas, was bought by a slave trader based in Charleston. In 1799, Vesey purchased a lottery ticket and won $1,500, which he used to buy his freedom. He then opened a carpentry shop and organized a Bible study class in the African Methodist Episcopal Church. His family, however, remained enslaved, and he could visit them only with the permission of their masters.

In 1822, Vesey and several others plotted a massive slave revolt. They would first capture the city's arsenal and distribute its hundreds of rifles to free and enslaved Blacks, who outnumbered Whites in the city. All the Whites would be killed, along with any Blacks who refused to join the rebellion. Vesey's plan then would have them burn the city, seize ships in the harbor, and head for the independent Black nation known as the Republic of Haiti, where enslaved people in the former French sugar colony (then called Saint-Domingue) had staged a successful revolt in 1791–1804.

Vesey's plot, however, never got off the ground. As Vesey and others secretly tried to recruit enslaved people, one of the potential recruits told his master what was going on. Soon Vesey and a hundred other supposed rebels were captured and tried. The court found Vesey guilty of plotting a slave uprising intended to "trample on all laws, human and divine; to riot in blood, outrage, rapine . . . and conflagration, and to introduce anarchy and confusion in their most horrid forms." Vesey and thirty-four others were executed; three dozen more were transported to Spanish Cuba and sold.

Denmark Vesey's planned rebellion led officials in South Carolina to place even more restrictions on the mobility of free Blacks and Black religious gatherings.

Nat Turner's Rebellion The Nat Turner rebellion of August 1831, in Southampton County, Virginia, again panicked Whites throughout the South. Turner, a trusted Black overseer, was also a preacher who believed God had instructed him to lead a slave rebellion. The revolt began when a small group of enslaved people joined Turner in killing his owner's family. Arming themselves with axes and swords, farm tools and muskets, they then repeated the process at other farmhouses, where other enslaved people joined in. Before the revolt ended, fifty-seven Whites had been killed, most of them women and children.

A crowd of federal troops, Virginia militiamen, and volunteers responded by killing nearly 200 enslaved people. Seventeen were hanged; several were decapitated, and their heads were placed on poles along the highway. Turner, called the "blood-stained monster," avoided capture for six weeks but was finally caught, tried, and found guilty. While waiting to be hanged, he was asked if the revolt was worth it. "Was not Christ crucified?" he replied.

More than any other slave uprising, **Nat Turner's Rebellion** terrified Whites across the South. The Virginia legislature debated whether slavery should be abolished. That proposal was defeated, and instead the delegates restricted the ability of enslaved people to learn to read and write and gather for religious meetings. "We were no more than dogs," an enslaved woman recalled. "If they caught us with a piece of paper in

Nat Turner's Rebellion (1831)
An insurrection in rural Virginia led by Black overseer Nat Turner, who killed slave owners and their families; in turn, federal troops indiscriminately killed hundreds of enslaved people in the process of putting down Turner and his rebels.

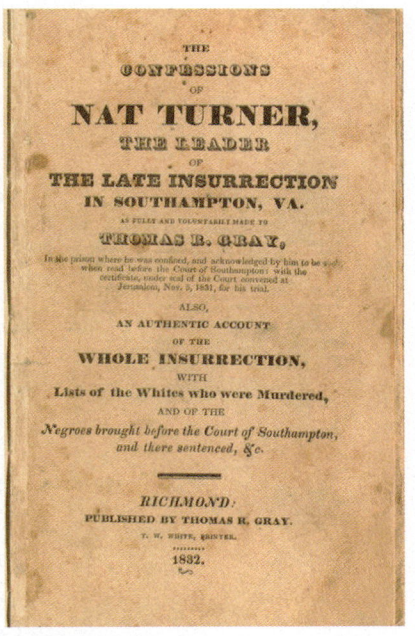

THE CONFESSIONS OF NAT TURNER
Following Nat Turner's trial and conviction, his lawyer, Thomas R. Gray, published an account of Turner's life and rebellion in which Gray explained that Turner believed that God had called upon him to murder slave owners. **What sentiments did Turner's rebellion, and accounts such as this, provoke among White Southerners?**

our pockets, they'd whip us. They was afraid we'd learn to read and write, but I never got the chance."

After Nat Turner's Rebellion, southern states created vigilante groups of Whites to patrol their communities looking for freedom seekers. One formerly enslaved person highlighted the "thousand obstacles thrown in the way of the flying slave. Every White man's hand is raised against him—the patrollers are watching for him—the hounds are ready to follow on his track."

> Whites' indiscriminate murder of enslaved people in response to rebellion

The Dream of Freedom

Yet thousands of enslaved people kept running away each year—a powerful example of the enduring dream of freedom and the courage of those who yearn for it. Frederick Douglass decided that risking death was better than staying in bondage: "I had as well be killed running as die standing." In 1834, Douglass and two other enslaved people on the Maryland coast stole a canoe and paddled toward the Chesapeake Bay and freedom. They were caught, however, and jailed. His owner threatened to sell him to a friend in Alabama; but in the end, Douglass was kept and taught a skill: caulking the seams in ships. He escaped again, successfully, four years later.

> Running away and everyday forms of resistance

As Douglass experienced initially, the odds were stacked against escape, partly because most enslaved people could not read; had no maps; and could not use public transportation such as stagecoaches, steamboats, and railroads. Blacks, whether free or enslaved, had to have a pass or official emancipation papers to go anywhere on their own. Most freedom seekers were tracked down by bloodhounds or bounty hunters. Even in the 1850s, the height of efforts by many Northerners to help freedom seekers through the Underground Railroad, only 1,000 to 1,500 enslaved people each year made it to safety.

Those who did not escape resisted in other ways on their plantations. They often faked illness, engaged in sabotage, stole or broke tools, or destroyed crops or livestock.

The South: A Region Apart

The recurring theme of Southern politics and culture from the 1830s to the outbreak of the Civil War in 1861 was the region's determination to remain a society dominated by Whites who debased people of color. Slavery increasingly became the paramount issue that controlled all else. A South Carolinian explained that "slavery with us is no abstraction—but a great and vital fact. Without it, our every comfort would be taken from us."

Protecting their right to own, transport, and sell enslaved people in the new western territories became the overriding focus of White Southern political leaders. Throughout the 1830s, southern state legislatures were, as one historian noted, "one and indivisible" in their efforts to preserve and expand slavery. Virginia's General Assembly, for example, declared that only the southern states had the right to control slavery, and that such control must be "maintained at all hazards." The Georgia legislature agreed, announcing that "upon this point there can be no discussion—no compromise—no doubt."

The increasingly militant efforts of Northerners to restrict or abolish slavery only reinforced the sense of Southern unity while provoking an emotional defensiveness that would ultimately result in secession and war—and the unexpected end of slavery. In the meantime, enslaved people continued to resist through passive or overt acts of rebellion; reliance on their own communities, family ties, and culture; and religious faith that offered hope for their eventual deliverance.

Reviewing the
CORE OBJECTIVES

- **Racial Capitalism** As a profit-making system based on forced labor and large-scale agricultural production financed by Northern manufacturing interests, racial capitalism in the South created extreme inequalities in income, power, and prestige.

- **A Cotton Economy** Throughout the pre–Civil War era, the South became increasingly committed to a cotton economy dependent upon slave labor. Despite efforts to diversify the economy, the wealth and status associated with cotton—as well as soil exhaustion and falling prices from Virginia to Georgia—prompted the westward expansion of the plantation culture to the *Old Southwest*. Moreover, sons of Southern enslavers wanted to take advantage of cheap land on the western frontier in order to make their own fortunes. By 1860, the *cotton kingdom* stretched from the Carolinas and Georgia through eastern Texas and up the Mississippi River to Illinois. More than half of all enslaved people worked on cotton plantations.

- **Southern White Culture** White society was divided between the planter elite, or those who owned at least twenty enslaved people, and all the rest. *Planters* made up around 4 percent of the White population and exercised a disproportionately powerful political and social influence. Other Whites owned a few enslaved people, but most Whites owned none. A majority of Whites were *plain White folk*—simple farmers who raised corn, cotton, hogs, and chickens. Southern White women spent most of their time on household chores. The *plantation mistress* supervised her enslaved people in the home and household. Most Whites were fiercely loyal to the institution of slavery. Even those who owned no enslaved people feared the competition they believed they would face if enslaved people were freed, and they enjoyed the privileged status that race-based slavery gave them.

- **Southern Black Culture** As the Southern economy became more dependent on slave labor, the enslaved population faced more regulations and restrictions on their behavior (slave codes). The vast majority of southern Blacks were enslaved people who served as *field hands*. They had few rights; and could be bought, sold, and moved at any time. Their own movements were severely limited, and they had little ability to defend themselves. Any violation of these restrictions could result in severe punishments, though enslaved women found that fighting back was necessary to protect themselves from sexual abuse. A small percentage of Southern Blacks were free. Many of the free Blacks had mixed-race parentage. Free Blacks often worked for wages in towns and cities.

- **African American Resistance and Resilience** The enslaved population responded to their oppression in a variety of ways. Although many enslaved people attempted to run away, only a few rebelled openly because the consequences were so harsh. Organized revolts such as *Nat Turner's Rebellion* (1831) in Virginia were rare. Most enslaved people survived their hardships by relying on their own communities, family ties, and Christian faith; and by developing their own culture, such as the singing of *spirituals* to express frustration, sorrow, and hope for their eventual deliverance.

KEY TERMS

Old Southwest *p. 432*
cotton kingdom *p. 436*
planters *p. 438*
plantation mistress *p. 439*
plain White folk *p. 441*
field hands *p. 451*
spirituals *p. 453*
Nat Turner's Rebellion (1831) *p. 457*

CHRONOLOGY

1790	Enslaved population of the United States reaches nearly 700,000
1800	Gabriel's Rebellion in Richmond, Virginia
1808	U.S. participation in the international slave trade is outlawed
1811	Charles Deslondes organizes revolt in Louisiana
1815	Annual cotton production in the United States is 150,000 bales
1822	The Denmark Vesey plot is discovered in Charleston, South Carolina
1830	Enslaved population exceeds 2 million in the United States
1831	Nat Turner leads slave insurrection in Virginia
1840	Population in the Old Southwest tops 1.5 million
1860	Annual cotton production in the United States reaches 4 million bales
	Enslaved population in the United States reaches 4 million

InQuizitive

Go to InQuizitive to see what you've learned—and learn what you've missed—with personalized feedback along the way.

461

KAATERSKILL CLOVE (1858) In the wake of the Enlightenment, the Romantic ideals of personal spirituality and reverence for the uncorrupted natural world swept America. This painting, by the artist Harriet Cany Peale, depicts a cleft in New York's Catskill Mountains visited regularly by transcendentalist landscape painters. A love of nature shared by women and men alike emerged as an influential cultural force in the first half of the nineteenth century.

Religion, Romanticism, and Reform

1800–1860

CHAPTER 12

During the first half of the nineteenth century, the United States was overflowing with restless energy and confidence in the future. "America is the country of the Future," the Massachusetts philosopher-poet Ralph Waldo Emerson observed. "It is a country of beginnings, of projects, of designs, and expectations."

However, the dynamic young republic was also experiencing growing pains as the market economy widened the gap between rich and poor. At the same time, sectional tensions over economic policies and increasingly heated debates over the future of slavery created a combative political environment whose conflicts overflowed into social and cultural life.

During these decades, Americans became as interested in religious salvation as they were in exercising political rights. A theological revolution led most Christians to reject the Calvinist belief in predestination (that God had chosen only a select few for salvation). Salvation, they argued, was open to everyone, not just the "elect." By this logic, sin was voluntary rather than innate. People were not helplessly depraved; they could choose salvation and improve themselves and society. Such notions democratized Christianity by giving everyone the path to salvation.

Growing numbers of evangelical Christians believed that America had a God-given mission to provide a shining example of representative

CORE OBJECTIVES

1. Describe the major changes in religious life in the early nineteenth century and assess their influence on American society.

2. Examine the emergence of transcendentalism in American culture in the early nineteenth century.

3. Explain why major social reform movements emerged in the early nineteenth century and analyze their influence on American society and politics.

4. Evaluate the evolution of the antislavery movement in the first half of the nineteenth century and describe how it affected the cause of women's rights.

democracy, much as Puritan New England had once stood as an example of an ideal Christian community. The concept of a godly mission to create an ideal society (often called manifest destiny) remained compelling throughout the nineteenth century.

America's God-given mission also contained an aspiration toward perfectionism: the blessed nation could become more perfect by improving morals and by combating social problems. Throughout the first half of the nineteenth century, reform-minded Americans fanned out across the United States to act on their faith and root out injustice and suffering. They shared a faith in progress that inspired significant transformations in social and cultural life. Painters and writers produced what would become classic works in American arts and literature, and ministers and activists secured major advances in human rights.

That faith in progress was also tested, triggering cynicism and disillusionment at times. But these decades showed that outside the realm of formal politics, Americans all across the nation were engaged in a vibrant cultural debate about what values and ideals should guide the nation into the future.

> CORE **OBJECTIVE**
> **1.** Describe the major changes in religious life in the early nineteenth century and assess their influence on American society.

A More Democratic Religion

The energies of the rational Enlightenment and the spiritual Great Awakening flowed from the colonial period into the nineteenth century. In different ways, these two powerful modes of thought—one promoting logic and science; the other emphasizing personal redemption and religious fervor—led many Christians to embrace a more democratic spiritual outlook that offered salvation to everyone. A growing number of Protestant churches stressed that everyone is capable of perfection through the guiding light of Christ and their own activism.

Rational Religion

> The rise of *Deism*

Interest in Enlightenment ideas such as Deism increased after the American Revolution. Deists, including such prominent leaders as Thomas Jefferson and Benjamin Franklin, prized science and reason over unquestioning faith. They believed in a rational God—the creator of the rational universe—and that all people were equal in the eyes of God (though most Deists refused to accept that enslaved Africans were equal too). They also defended free speech and opposed governments' efforts to force a particular religious faith on the people.

Unitarianism and Universalism

The ideals of Enlightenment rationalism that excited Deists made inroads into Protestantism. By the end of the eighteenth century, well-educated New Englanders, most of them Congregationalists, were embracing Unitarianism. This was a "liberal" faith that emphasized the compassion of a loving God, the superiority of reason over emotional forms of worship, the rejection of the Calvinist belief in predestination, and a general rather than literal reading of the Bible.

Unitarians abandoned the concept of the Trinity (God as the Father, the Son, and the Holy Ghost) that had long been central to the Christian faith, believing instead that God and Jesus were separate. Jesus was a saintly man (but not divine) who set a shining example. Unitarians also stressed that people were not inherently sinful. By following the teachings of Jesus and trusting their own consciences, *all* people were eligible for salvation. Churches that adopted the *Unitarian* outlook were especially popular with the educated elite in major cities such as Boston.

A parallel anti-Calvinist movement, Universalism, attracted a different—and much larger—social group: the working poor. In 1779, John Murray, a British clergyman, founded the first Universalist church, in Gloucester, Massachusetts. Like the Unitarians, **Universalists** proclaimed the dignity and worth of all people. They stressed that believers must liberate themselves from the governance of priests and ministers and use their own God-given reasoning to explain the mysteries of existence.

To Universalists and Unitarians alike, hell was a myth; it did not exist. Salvation was "universal," available to everyone through the sacrifice of Jesus. In essence, Universalists thought God was too caring to damn people, while Unitarians thought people were too good to be damned.

The Second Great Awakening

The rise of Universalism and Unitarianism did not mean that traditional religious beliefs were disappearing. In fact, conservative evangelism remained widespread. During the first Great Awakening in the early 1700s, traveling revivalists had promoted an intense and personal relationship with God. In addition, Anglicanism suffered from being aligned with the Church of England; it lost its status as the official religion in most states after the American Revolution. To help erase their pro-British image, Virginia Anglicans renamed themselves *Episcopalians*.

Around 1800, the United States experienced a massive wave of religious revivals called the **Second Great Awakening**, or the Great Revival. This second wave rejected Enlightenment rationalism. It also appealed to people who were feeling unsettled by the secularism (indifference to religion) that seemed to thrive amid the rapid growth of industries and cities and the increasingly divisive politics of the era. While all denominations grew, new evangelical sects—Baptists, Methodists, and Presbyterians—experienced explosive popularity. In 1780, the nation had only 50 Methodist churches; by 1860, there were 20,000, far more than any other denomination.

The Second Great Awakening involved two centers of activity. One developed among New England colleges that were founded as religious centers of learning, then spread across western New York into Pennsylvania and

Unitarians Members of the liberal New England Congregationalist offshoot, often well educated and wealthy, who profess the oneness of God and the goodness of rational worshippers.

Universalists Generally working-class members of a New England religious movement who believed in a merciful God and universal salvation.

Second Great Awakening A religious revival movement that arose in reaction to the growth of secularism and rationalist religion; it spurred the growth of the Baptist and Methodist denominations.

Ohio, Indiana, and Illinois. The other emerged in the backwoods of Tennessee and Kentucky and spread across rural America. Both shared a simple message: Salvation is available to *anyone* who repents and embraces the teachings of Christ.

Frontier Revivals

In its frontier phase, the Second Great Awakening generated tremendous excitement and emotional excesses. It gave birth to two religious phenomena—the traveling evangelist and the camp meeting.

Many Americans readily believed in magic, dreams, visions, miraculous healings, and speaking in tongues (a spontaneous babbling brought on by the workings of the Holy Spirit). Evangelists and "exhorters" (spiritual speakers who were not formal ministers) with colorful nicknames such as Jumpin' Jesus and Mad Isaac found ready audiences among isolated frontier folk hungry for spiritual intensity and community.

Mass revivals along the western frontier were family-oriented, community-building events that bridged social, economic, political, and even racial

> New religious phenomenon: camp meetings

RELIGIOUS REVIVALISM Frontier revivals and prayer meetings ignited religious fervor within both minister and participant. In this 1830s camp meeting, the women are so intensely moved by the sermon that they shed their bonnets and fall to their knees.

divisions. Women, especially, flocked to the revivals and served as the backbone of religious life on the frontier.

The first such revival occurred in 1801 on a Kentucky hillside called Cane Ridge. A Scots-Irish Presbyterian minister named James McGready invited Protestants to attend, and as many as 20,000 camped in tents for nine days. McGready helped his parishioners choose Christ by vividly portraying heaven's "glories" while reminding them of "hell and its horrors." His theatrical sermons left his listeners "powerless, groaning, praying, and crying for mercy."

The frontier revivals generated powerful emotions and unusual behavior. Some people went into trances; others contracted the "jerks," a spasmodic twitching.

As news of the unscrubbed energy of the Cane Ridge gathering spread, evangelists, especially Methodists, organized similar revivals. "Hell is trembling, and Satan's kingdom falling," reported a South Carolinian in 1802. "The sacred flame" of religious revival is "extending far and wide." In 1776, about one in six Americans belonged to a church; by 1850, it was one in three.

Denominational Growth

Though Baptists and Methodists predominated, **frontier revivals** also included Presbyterians, whose faith was especially appealing to those with Scots-Irish backgrounds. The Presbyterians agreed with the Congregationalists on theology, leading them to merge and form united congregations. The result through much of the Old Northwest (Ohio, Michigan, Indiana, and Illinois) was that New Englanders became Presbyterians by way of the "Presbygational" churches.

PETER CARTWRIGHT AND HIS WIFE FRANCINE GAINES Cartwright experienced a religious epiphany at a frontier revival meeting, and henceforth became a traveling evangelist, the first to integrate evangelical preaching into politics.

frontier revivals A religious revival movement within the Second Great Awakening that took place in frontier churches in western territories and states in the early nineteenth century.

BLACK METHODISTS HOLDING A PRAYER MEETING (1811) This caricature of an African American Methodist meeting in Philadelphia shows a preacher in the church doorway, while his congregation engages in exuberant worship. **How does this illustration compare with the frontier prayer meeting depicted on page 466?**

The Baptist theology was grounded in biblical fundamentalism—a certainty that every word in the Bible was divinely inspired and literally true. Baptists believed that *everyone* could gain salvation by choosing (via *free will*) to receive God's grace and being baptized as adults rather than as infants. Baptists also stressed the social equality of everyone in God's view.

> Mechanisms of religious dissemination: circuit riders

Methodists, who also believed in free will, developed the most effective evangelical method: the "circuit rider," an evangelist ("itinerant") on horseback who sought converts in remote frontier settlements.

Revivalism and African Americans

Free African Americans were especially attracted to the emotional energies of the Methodist and Baptist churches, in part because some White circuit riders opposed slavery. Richard Allen, a formerly enslaved person in Philadelphia, claimed in 1787 that "there was no religious sect or denomination that would suit the capacity of the colored people as well as the Methodist." He decided that the "plain and simple gospel suits best for any people; for the unlearned can understand [it]." Even more important, the Methodists actively recruited Black people.

> The rise of the African Methodist Episcopal Church

Yet racial tensions increased as the mostly White Methodist churches required Black congregants to sit in designated pews. Such discrimination led Allen and others to organize the Bethel African Methodist Episcopal Church in 1793. In 1816, as racial discrimination continued, Allen established a new denomination: the African Methodist Episcopal (AME) Church.

Starting with only five churches and eight clergymen, the AME denomination grew quickly and moved far beyond its origins in Philadelphia. By 1846 it boasted 296 churches, most located across the northern states, along with 200 ministers. During the nineteenth century, the AME Church fought against racist laws and promoted economic and educational opportunities for people of color.

Women's Leadership

The camp meetings offered a needed social outlet to isolated rural folk, especially women. Evangelical ministers repeatedly applauded the spiritual energies of women and affirmed their right to give public witness to their faith and to play a leading role in efforts at social reform.

At a time when women were banned from preaching, Jarena Lee, a free Black woman who lived near Philadelphia, was the first African American woman to become a minister in the AME. As she wrote, "If the man may preach, because the Saviour died for him, why not the woman? Seeing [as] he died for her also." Lee became a tireless revivalist; according to her records, she "traveled 2,325 miles and preached 178 sermons."

Revivals offered women ample opportunities to assume leadership roles as traveling evangelists. Phoebe Worrall Palmer, a camp-meeting exhorter,

JARENA LEE A pathbreaking revivalist, Lee traveled thousands of miles on foot to preach to diverse crowds across America. Lee also published a detailed autobiography about her religious experiences, spreading her message through print, as well.

claimed her right to preach by citing the biblical emphasis on obeying God rather than man. "It is always right to obey the Holy Spirit's command," she stressed, "and if that is laid upon a woman to preach the Gospel, then it is right for her to do so; it is a duty she cannot neglect without falling into condemnation."

> Religioius leadership for women

Religion and Reform

During this period, regions roiled by revival fever were compared to forests devastated by fire. Western New York experienced so much intense evangelical activity that people labeled it the *burned-over district*.

Charles G. Finney

The most successful evangelist in the burned-over district was a Presbyterian minister named Charles Grandison Finney. In the winter of 1830–1831, he preached for six months in Rochester, an Erie Canal boomtown in upstate New York, and became the nation's most celebrated minister.

While rural camp-meeting revivals attracted farm families and other working-class groups, Finney's audiences were more-prosperous city dwellers in places like New York City. "The Lord," Finney declared, "was aiming at the conversion of the highest classes of society."

> Finney and the religious revival in New York

Finney focused on one question: What role can the individual play in earning salvation? He and other free-will evangelists insisted that everyone, rich or poor, male or female, Black or White, could *choose* to be saved. Finney also emphasized that Christians must first perfect themselves before "reforming the world."

The invigorating revivals led by Finney and others provided much of the energy behind the widespread reform impulse that swept across America during the first half of the nineteenth century.

The Mormons

The Second Great Awakening also spawned new religious groups. The burned-over district in New York gave rise to several significant movements; among them was Mormonism. Its founder, Joseph Smith Jr., the child of an intensely religious Vermont farm couple who settled in the western New York village of Palmyra, was raised amid the excitement of nearly constant revivalism.

In 1823, eighteen-year-old Smith reported that an angel named Moroni had appeared by his bedside to report that God needed his help. The angel then led him to a hillside near his father's farm, where he had unearthed a box containing golden tablets on which was etched, in an ancient language, a lost "gospel" explaining the history of ancient America. It described a group of Israelites ("Nephites") who crossed the Atlantic and settled America 2,100 years before Columbus. After his death and resurrection, Jesus Christ appeared before the "Nephites" in the New World.

> Joseph Smith founds Mormonism

Smith set about laboriously translating the inscriptions on the plates. In 1830, either he or a friend paid for the publication of the first 5,000 copies of

NAUVOO The magnificent scale and stately architecture of Joseph Smith's original temple in Nauvoo is captured in this 1890 print. **How did Joseph Smith organize the new community of Nauvoo?**

Mormon Church The Church of Jesus Christ of Latter-day Saints, founded by Joseph Smith, emphasizing universal salvation and a modest lifestyle; often persecuted for its separateness and the practice of polygamy.

the 500-page text he called *The Book of Mormon: An Account Written by the Hand of Mormon upon Plates Taken from the Plates of Nephi*.

With this book as his gospel, young Smith became Jesus's prophet. He began telling others the story of his "marvilous [sic] experience" and gathering thousands of converts (whom he referred to as saints) who shared his desire to live together in accordance with the teachings of Jesus. Eventually, Smith formed what came to be called the Church of Jesus Christ of Latter-day Saints, informally known as the **Mormon Church**. In keeping with the teaching of Jesus and the democratic spirit of the times, Smith maintained that God, angels, and people were all members of the same flesh-and-blood species. "God is a man like one of you," Smith told his followers.

In his role as prophet and conveyor of the gospel, Smith dismissed as frauds all Christian denominations (Protestant and Catholic); criticized the sins of the rich; preached universal salvation; denied that there was a hell; urged his followers to avoid liquor, tobacco, and caffeine; and claimed that the Second Coming of Christ was near. Smith promised to create not just a new religious denomination but "a new a nation, a new Israel, a people bound as much by heritage and identity as by belief." Within a few years, he had gathered thousands of converts ("saints"), most of them poor farmers who were drawn to Smith's message as a welcome refuge from what they believed was an increasingly chaotic and dangerous world.

Years of Persecution From the beginning, Mormon "saints" tested the nation's social and democratic boundaries with their secret rituals and their chosen separateness. In their search for a "promised land" free from persecution, the Mormons moved from western New York to Ohio, and then to Missouri (see Map 12.1).

Forced out of Missouri in 1839, Smith and the Mormons moved to the half-built town of Commerce, Illinois, along the Mississippi River. They renamed the town Nauvoo, a rough translation of a Hebrew word meaning "beautiful land."

Within five years, Nauvoo had become the second largest city in the state, and Joseph Smith—the Prophet—and his saints referred to it as the Kingdom of God. The community established a new form of theocratic government with its own constitution. As "the Prophet," Smith had substantial control over the community. He owned the hotel and general store; published the newspaper; and served as mayor, chief justice, and commander of the city's army. With his strong belief in priestly authority, Smith began excommunicating dissidents.

A More Democratic Religion

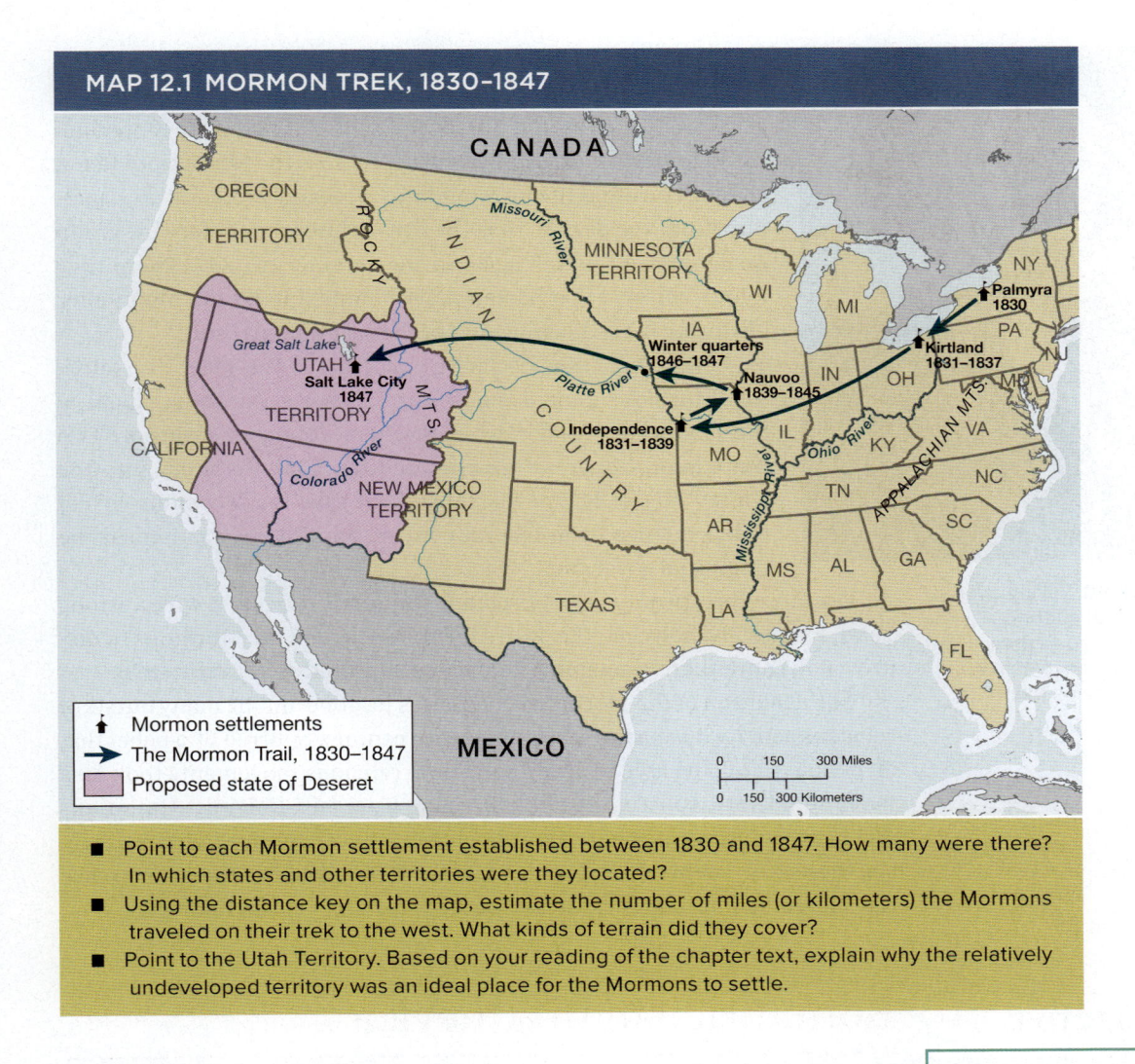

MAP 12.1 MORMON TREK, 1830–1847

- Mormon settlements
- The Mormon Trail, 1830–1847
- Proposed state of Deseret

- Point to each Mormon settlement established between 1830 and 1847. How many were there? In which states and other territories were they located?
- Using the distance key on the map, estimate the number of miles (or kilometers) the Mormons traveled on their trek to the west. What kinds of terrain did they cover?
- Point to the Utah Territory. Based on your reading of the chapter text, explain why the relatively undeveloped territory was an ideal place for the Mormons to settle.

Smith pushed conventional marital boundaries, too, when he announced that God wanted men to have multiple wives—"plural marriage" (polygamy). Smith himself led by example, claiming more than two dozen wives. In 1844, Mormon dissenters, including Smith's first wife, Emma, denounced his polygamy. The result was not only a split in the church but also an attack on Nauvoo by non-Mormons.

>Dissent over the issue of polygamy

When an opposition newspaper was destroyed, Smith and his brother Hyrum were arrested and charged with organizing the incident and the riot that followed. While the two Mormon leaders awaited trial, a mob from surrounding communities stormed the jail and killed them.

Brigham Young The Mormons quickly found a new leader in Brigham Young, who had been Smith's most trusted adviser. Young led the Mormons through a period of transition and upheaval. Because Mormons continued to be the targets of criticism in Illinois, Young looked for another home for the controversial sect. That home turned out to be 1,300 miles away, near

BRIGHAM YOUNG Taking over from Joseph Smith after his death, Young served as president of the Mormons for thirty years and led them on their exodus to Utah.

the Great Salt Lake in the Utah Territory—a vast, sparsely populated area that was then part of Mexico (see again Map 12.1). To get there, Young set out during the winter of 1846 with more than 2,000 followers, in a harrowing trek across the Mississippi River, Great Plains, and Rocky Mountains. Freezing temperatures, malnutrition, and disease took the lives of hundreds before the group finally arrived in Salt Lake in the summer of 1847. There they found "a broad and barren plain hemmed in by the mountains, blistering in the burning rays of the mid-summer sun."

Young, however, declared that "this is the place" to settle. The Mormons named their "state" Deseret (meaning "Land of the Honeybee") and elected Brigham Young as governor. Two years later, Congress incorporated the Utah Territory into the United States. The new arrangement gave the Mormons virtual independence from federal control, and Young was named the territorial governor.

For more than twenty years, Brigham Young ruled Deseret with a strong hand. Eventually, however, the desire for statehood led the Mormons to disavow polygamy, thereby enabling Utah to be admitted as a state in 1896.

The evolution of the Mormon Church was just one among many bursts of religious activity during the early nineteenth century. Spurred by a belief that all people should be able to attain salvation, religious movements took on a more democratic spiritual outlook. Ranging from anti-Calvinist Unitarians and Universalists, to various evangelical sects, to community-building revivals, these movements drew people together from all across the nation, gave rise to new denominations, and set the stage for other social reforms.

CORE OBJECTIVE

2. Examine the emergence of transcendentalism in American culture in the early nineteenth century.

Romanticism in America

The revival of religious life during the early 1800s was one of many efforts to unleash spiritual energies throughout the United States and Europe. Another great cultural shift was the Romantic movement in thought, literature, and the arts. Romanticism began in Europe as a rebellion against the well-ordered rational world promoted by scientific objectivity. After all, some people began to ask, weren't there more things in the world than science and logic could categorize and explain—such as spontaneous moods and feelings, or mysterious and half-seen things?

When science could neither prove nor disprove concepts, the Romantics insisted that people were justified in believing what they felt. They preferred the stirrings of the heart over the calculations of the head, and the mystical over the rational. Many well-educated young Americans embraced this emphasis on individual creativity, emotional fervor, and the virtues of common people and civic democracy. The engine of social progress, they argued, should be an individual's faith and belief rather than the rational world of political and religious decrees.

THE OXBOW This 1836 landscape by the American artist Thomas Cole is an iconic work of Romanticism, capturing the view from Mount Holyoke, Massachusetts, after a thunderstorm. **What might Cole be symbolizing by his juxtaposition of untamed wilderness to the left and domesticated farmland to the right?**

Transcendentalism

The most intense American advocates of Romantic ideals were the transcendentalists of New England. Transcendentalism was a vibrant philosophical and literary movement that promoted a radical individualism and personal spirituality liberated from the strict requirements of organized religion and societal institutions.

The word **transcendentalism** derived from an emphasis on thoughts and actions that transcend (or rise above) the constraints of logic and tradition in the physical world. Transcendentalism, said the poet and philosopher Ralph Waldo Emerson, meant an interest in areas "a little beyond" the scope of reason. To Emerson, Henry David Thoreau, Margaret Fuller, and other transcendentalists, a life centered on intense contemplation and radical individualism took priority over what they saw as the stifling dogmas of organized religion. In their view, individuals could access spiritual truths through their own intuition rather than being told what to think by ministers.

> The rise of transcendentalism in New England

transcendentalism The philosophy of New England writers and thinkers of the nineteenth century who advocated personal spirituality, self-reliance, social reform, and harmony with nature.

Transcendentalists were passionate rebels who revolted against traditional assumptions and boundaries. Thoreau, for example, yearned to speak and write "without bounds." The transcendentalists celebrated "self-reliance" over conformity and embraced a pure form of personal spirituality uncorrupted by theological dogma and denominational creeds.

In short, transcendentalists wanted everyone to be courageous enough to think their own thoughts and develop their own beliefs. To them, self-discovery was the essential goal in life. "Trust thyself," Emerson insisted, "To be yourself in a world that is constantly trying to make you something else is the greatest accomplishment."

At times, however, the efforts of Emerson and others to unleash the self from society led to self-absorbed elitism. Transcendentalism, warned writer Nathaniel Hawthorne, often careened "into anarchism." Yet the intense rebelliousness struck a responsive chord with many like-minded Americans. By the 1830s, New England transcendentalism had become one of the most influential forces in American culture.

Ralph Waldo Emerson

Ralph Waldo Emerson embodied the transcendentalist gospel. To Emerson, self-knowledge opened the doors to self-improvement and self-realization. During the 1840s, he became the nation's most popular public speaker, crisscrossing the country encouraging self-reliance. He challenged the young republic to create its own distinctive cultural outlook in literature, art, and thought. "We have listened too long to the courtly muses of Europe," he said. "We will walk on our own feet; we will work with our own hands; we will speak with our own minds."

The descendant of eight generations of clergymen, Emerson graduated from Harvard College in 1821 and became a Unitarian minister in 1829. But three years later, following the death of his wife, he turned away from organized religions. He sought instead to cultivate a personal spirituality in communion with nature. As he explained, "I like the silent church before the service begins, better than any preaching."

After traveling in Europe, Emerson settled in Concord, Massachusetts, and became an essayist, poet, and lecturer (as he put it, a "preacher to the world"). He celebrated the individual's unlimited potential—if people would only learn to think for themselves and defy traditional assumptions and beliefs.

In 1836, Emerson published the pathbreaking book *Nature*, which helped launch the transcendental movement. In it, he stressed that people could "transcend" the limitations of their everyday world and discover the "spirit" animating the universe.

Emerson included women in that belief but also viewed them differently. They possessed unique "tastes and genius," he wrote. Men may have been defined by "intellect," but women could boast of "affection," the ability to

RALPH WALDO EMERSON Emerson is most remembered for leading the transcendentalist movement, and his message of self-reliance affirmed the integrity of the individual and inspired generations of thinkers.

empathize with the condition of others. For that reason, Emerson explained, "[t]he man goes abroad, and works in the world. The woman stays at home and draws him to his place."

Emerson's early beliefs echoed the gender stereotypes of his time, but he conceded, in his 1844 essay "The Poet," that both men and women could tap the divine source of inspiration and creativity. "The soul," he wrote, "has no sex." Likewise, women had an equal capacity for "genius" as men and therefore should be given access to the best educational opportunities. Women of keen intelligence liked what Emerson said, and many embraced transcendentalism.

The Transcendental Club

In 1836, a diverse, informal discussion group that came to be called the Transcendental Club began to meet in Boston and nearby Concord to discuss philosophy, literature, and religion. In describing life in Concord, writer Nathaniel Hawthorne said there "never was a poor, little country village infested with such a variety of queer, strangely dressed, oddly behaved mortals." Those "oddly behaved mortals" were mostly thinkers rather than doers, who promoted a rebellion against the social and cultural status quo.

Margaret Fuller One founding member of this group, Margaret Fuller, was an illustrious American journalist, editor, and critic. She was also a dazzling conversationalist who helped organize the club's wide-ranging "Conversations" that took up questions related to social reform. In 1839 she began a conversation group among Boston's women that led to the classic treatise *Woman in the Nineteenth Century*.

Fuller sought to embolden the women in the Transcendental Club to think and act for themselves. As part of this effort, she helped launch and edit *Dial* (1840–1844), an experimental transcendentalist magazine. "A much greater range of occupations," Fuller asserted, must be made available to women to enable them to express their full potential. Fuller herself, though, never had a chance to reach her own full potential. She drowned in a shipwreck at age forty.

MARGARET FULLER Margaret Fuller (May 23, 1810–July 19, 1850) was an illustrious American journalist, editor, and critic. In 1839 she began a conversation group among Boston's women that led to the classic treatise *Woman in the Nineteenth Century*. Drowned in a shipwreck with her husband and baby boy, Margaret Fuller is the tragic heroine of the transcendentalist movement.

> Women and transdendentalism

Henry David Thoreau

Ralph Waldo Emerson's younger friend Henry David Thoreau practiced the thoughtful self-reliance and pursuit of perfection that Emerson preached. "I like people who can do things," Emerson said, and Thoreau could do many things: carpentry, masonry, painting, surveying, sailing, gardening, lecturing.

Born in Concord in 1817, Thoreau graduated from Harvard, worked as a teacher, and helped his father, a pencil-maker. Like Emerson, however, Thoreau frequently escaped to the woods. He viewed "the indescribable innocence" of nature as a living Bible, a reflection of the divine; the earth and its creatures were to him a form of sacred poetry, full of hidden meanings. At

HENRY DAVID THOREAU A model transcendentalist, Thoreau celebrated the right and willingness of individuals to think and act for themselves, influencing activists throughout the twentieth century and since.

the same time, he believed that Christian churches had become dying institutions. His priorities were inward.

Thoreau showed little interest in social life and no interest in wealth. "The mass of men," he wrote, "lead lives of quiet desperation" because they are preoccupied with making money and exploiting nature at the expense of self-discovery. Thoreau committed himself to what Emerson called a simple life centered on "plain living and high thinking."

In 1844, when Emerson bought fourteen acres along Walden Pond, Thoreau decided to embark upon an unusual experiment in self-reliance. On July 4, 1845, just shy of his twenty-eighth birthday, he took to the woods to live in a tiny, one-room cabin he had built at Walden Pond, a mile outside of Concord. His hut featured three chairs: "one for solitude, two for friendship, and three for society."

Living alone at Walden Pond was Thoreau's personal declaration of independence. His goal was to discover what nature "had to teach" about those things that money can't buy. "I went to the woods because I wished to live deliberately," he wrote in *Walden, or Life in the Woods* (1854), "... and not, when I came to die, discover that I had not lived." Thoreau ate only one meal a day and disdained coffee, alcohol, jam, tobacco, and salt. He regarded sex with disgust and suspicion. His minimalist ethic led Emerson to observe that he "was never affectionate, but superior, didactic," forever scorning his neighbors and claiming that he was "more favored by the gods."

To Thoreau, there was something sacred and liberating about nature's beauty and sensuality. His ecstatic descriptions of the natural world have made him the patron saint of the environmental movement. "In wildness is the preservation of the world," he wrote, and his scriptural statement later became the motto of the Sierra Club.

During Thoreau's two years, two months, and two days at Walden Pond, his conscience was pricked by the abolitionist movement. He gave shelter to an enslaved man seeking freedom and considered President James K. Polk's declaration of war against Mexico an unjust action pushed by southern cotton planters eager to add more slave territory (see Chapter 13). His disgust for the war led him to refuse to pay taxes, for which he was put in jail (for only one night; an aunt paid his overdue tax bill).

This incident inspired Thoreau to write his classic essay "Civil Disobedience" (1849), which would influence Martin Luther King Jr. in shaping the peaceful protest movement 100 years later. "If the law is of such a nature that it requires you to be an agent of injustice to another," Thoreau wrote, "then, I say, break the law."

An American Literature

> Impact of transcendentalism on American literature

The poet Edgar Allan Poe scorned transcendentalism as "an idealistic scheme concocted by unstable minds for the discovery of non-existent truths." Yet the transcendentalists did help inspire a generation of writers eager to create distinctively American forms of literature.

In fact, the 1840s and 1850s brought an outpouring of writing. Among the works produced were *Representative Men* by Emerson; *Walden, or Life in the Woods* by Thoreau; *The Scarlet Letter* and *The House of the Seven Gables* by Nathaniel Hawthorne; *Forest Leaves* by Frances Ellen Watkins Harper; *Leaves of Grass* by Walt Whitman; *Woman in the Nineteenth Century* by Margaret Fuller; and hundreds of unpublished poems by Emily Dickinson.

The poems, short stories, and novels published in these decades were as extraordinary in literary style as they were penetrating in their exploration of basic human struggles. Little about life and death, suffering and injustice, escaped these writers' notice. Their works harnessed the power of words to unsettle Americans' conventional ways of viewing the society around them—and helped inspire movements for social change.

Nathaniel Hawthorne

Nathaniel Hawthorne, the supreme writer of the New England group, never shared the sunny optimism of his neighbors or their perfectionist belief in social reform. A native of Salem, Massachusetts, he was haunted by the knowledge of evil bequeathed to him by his Puritan forebears. One (John Hathorne) had been a judge at the Salem witchcraft trials. After college, Hawthorne worked in obscurity in Salem before earning a degree of fame with *Twice-Told Tales* (1837). The central theme of his stories and novels was sin and its consequences: pride and selfishness, secret guilt, and the impossibility of rooting sin out of the human soul.

Emily Dickinson

Emily Dickinson, the most strikingly original of the New England poets, lived with her parents and sister in Amherst, Massachusetts. There, in a simply furnished corner bedroom on the second floor of the family house, Dickinson found independence and self-expression in poetry, ever grateful that "one is one's self & not somebody else." Only 10 or so of her almost 1,800 poems appeared in print (anonymously) before her death in 1886 at age fifty-five. As she once prophetically wrote, "Success is counted sweetest/By those who ne'er succeed."

Once, when her niece Matty visited, Dickinson locked the bedroom door and excitedly announced, "Matty: here's freedom," for in her room her soul had "moments of Escape." Dickinson lived what her niece called a life of "exquisite self-containment," in part because her patriarchal and often tyrannical father prohibited her from exploring the world of ideas outside the home. Enlivened by "the light of insight and the fire of emotion," Dickinson wrote verse remarkable for its simplicity, brevity, and depth.

Dickinson's isolation and lifelong religious doubts led her to explore the "white heat" of heartbreak and disappointment in ways unusual for the time. Her themes were often elemental: life, death, fear, loneliness, nature,

EMILY DICKINSON Although her works were rarely published during her lifetime, Dickinson offered the literary world of New England a fresh female voice.

and above all, the withdrawal of God, "a distant, stately lover" who no longer could be found.

Edgar Allan Poe

Edgar Allan Poe was fascinated by the menace of death. Born in Boston in 1809 and orphaned as a child, he was raised by foster parents in Richmond, Virginia. In 1837 he moved to Philadelphia, where he edited magazines and wrote scathing reviews and terrifying mystery stories. Poe is considered to be the creator of the detective story.

The poem "The Raven," about a man who lost his lover, made Poe a household name. In 1847, however, his young wife died of tuberculosis. Thereafter, he was seduced as much by alcohol and drugs as by writing. He died at age forty of mysterious causes, leaving behind an extraordinary collection of "unworldly" tales and haunting poems. He used horror to explore the darkest corners of human psychology. To him, fear was the most powerful emotion, so he focused on making the grotesque and supernatural seem disturbingly real. His short stories "The Tell-Tale Heart" and "The Pit and the Pendulum" especially accomplished this goal.

Frances Ellen Watkins Harper

In poetry and fiction, Frances Ellen Watkins Harper discovered an outlet for confronting the pain and suffering of racial injustice. Born in 1825 to a free Black family in Baltimore, Maryland, Harper attended her uncle's school until the age of thirteen, when economic need required her to begin working. She continued educating herself for the rest of her life by reading books.

Harper later moved to Philadelphia, where she encountered the indignities of racial segregation in her daily life. In 1858, she refused to give up her seat in a segregated railroad car, which so angered the conductor that he refused her money when she tried to pay for her ticket. So "I threw it down on the car floor," she recalled, and walked off. Harper's act of civil disobedience was part of a larger series of boycotts and lawsuits by Black people in the northern states against racial inequality—known as the *first civil rights movement*.

Harper's first two books, *Forest Leaves* (1845) and *Poems on Miscellaneous Subjects* (1854), were collections of protest poetry that together sold 50,000 copies—an extraordinary number for the time. In these works she condemned slavery and described the trauma it inflicted on enslaved families. Harper's poem "The Slave Auction" revealed the anguish of mothers whose children were sold away: "And mothers stood with streaming eyes / And saw their dearest children sold; / Unheeded rose their bitter cries, / While tyrants bartered them for gold."

Harper crisscrossed the northern states delivering searing critiques of slavery. "It may be that God Himself has written upon both my heart and brain," she reflected, "a commissary to use time, talent, and energy in the cause of freedom."

FRANCES ELLEN WATKINS HARPER An accomplished poet and novelist, in 1859 Harper became the first African American woman to publish a short story. While fighting for racial justice in her writing and in her speeches, she also took up the cause of women's rights and in 1896 co-founded the National Association of Colored Women's Clubs.

Walt Whitman

The most controversial writer during the nineteenth century was Walt Whitman, a New York journalist and poet. Born in 1819, he was a self-promoting, robust personality. Whitman wrote about industrial development, urban life, working men, sailors, and "simple humanity."

By the time he met Ralph Waldo Emerson, Whitman had been "simmering, simmering." Emerson "brought him to a boil" with his emphasis on defying tradition and celebrating the everyday aspects of life, including sexuality and the body. These themes found their way into Whitman's controversial first book of unconventional, free-verse poems, *Leaves of Grass* (1855). In its first year, it sold ten copies. One reviewer called it "an intensely vulgar, nay, absolutely *beastly* book." *Leaves of Grass*, however, became more influential with each passing year.

Whitman's poems were seasoned with frank sexuality and homoerotic overtones. Although *Leaves of Grass* was banned in Boston because of its explicit sexuality, Emerson found it "the most extraordinary piece of wit and wisdom that America has yet contributed." More conventional literary critics, however, shuddered at the shocking "grossness" of Whitman's homosexual references ("manly love"; "the love of comrades"; "for the friend I love lay sleeping by my side"). Yet Whitman could never be truly honest about his own sexuality (he identified as gay or bisexual in today's terms), for even discussing such topics was a crime in the nineteenth century.

Whitman's verse evoked the everyday struggle to live openly in same-sex relationships—one that a young woman named Charity Bryant knew well. After being kicked out of her father's house in Massachusetts and ostracized for her love of women, the thirty-year-old Bryant moved to Weybridge, Vermont, in 1807. There she met Sylvia Drake, and their attraction was immediate. Bryant and Drake moved in together a few months later and started building a new life as a "fond wife" and "husband," as Bryant's nephew, the poet William Cullen Bryant, called them. The two women could not legally marry—but they were later buried together under a single headstone.

Newspapers

The flowering of American literature coincided with a massive expansion in newspaper readership sparked by rapid improvements in printing technology. The availability of newspapers costing only a penny transformed daily reading into a form of popular entertainment.

By 1850, newspapers had forged a network of essential communications across the United States. As readership soared, the content of the papers expanded beyond political news and commentary to include society gossip, sports, and reports of sensational crimes and accidents. "We do not care for the Bible," Henry David Thoreau declared, "but we do care for the

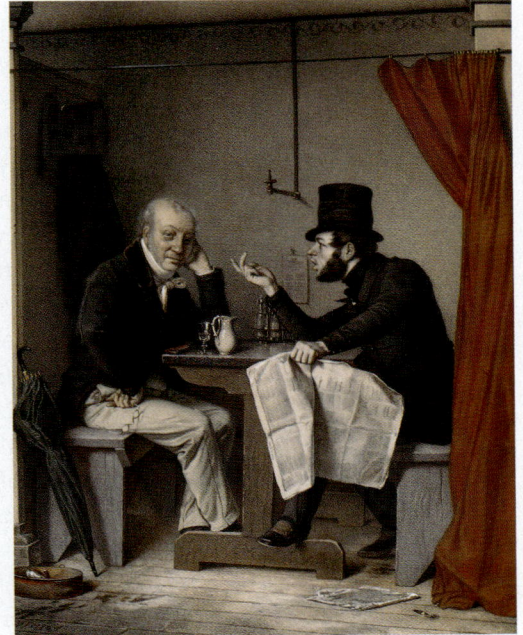

POLITICS IN AN OYSTER HOUSE (1848) Commissioned by social activist John H. B. Latrobe, this painting captures the public conversations that were fueled by newspapers and other print periodicals. **What issues were being tackled by activists in the mid-1800s?**

newspaper," for it served as "a Bible which we read every morning and every afternoon, standing and sitting, riding and walking."

Thoreau's words underscore that by this time many Americans were viewing themselves, and their world, in new ways. Rebelling against the rational outlook promoted by scientific objectivity, Romantics and transcendentalists cultivated a more personal spiritual idealism through individual reflection and an emphasis on faith and intuition over reason. Men and women, White and Black, expressed these impulses in an outpouring of fiction and poetry. The works of Ralph Waldo Emerson, Emily Dickinson, Frances Ellen Watkins Harper, and Walt Whitman, for example, all explored fundamental themes of human life, death, and suffering, and in some cases called for social change.

The Reform Impulse

> **CORE OBJECTIVE**
> **3.** Explain why major social reform movements emerged in the early nineteenth century and analyze their influence on American society and politics.

By the 1840s, the United States was awash in social reform movements led by dreamers and activists, mostly women, who fought against social injustice and perceived immorality. Lyman Beecher, a prominent preacher and champion of evangelical Christian revivalism (and the father of writer Harriet Beecher Stowe), stressed that the Second Great Awakening was not focused simply on promoting individual conversions; it was also intended to "reform human society."

Certain social and economic changes—including the Panic of 1837 and the ensuing economic depression—motivated many reformers too. The rise of an urban middle class enabled growing numbers of women to hire cooks and maids, thus freeing them to devote more time to societal concerns. Many joined churches and charitable organizations, most of which were led by men.

Both women and men belonging to evangelical societies fanned out across America to organize Sunday schools, spread the gospel, and distribute Bibles to the children of the working poor. Other reformers tackled issues such as prison and workplace conditions, care of the disabled, temperance (reducing the consumption of alcoholic beverages), women's rights, and the abolition of slavery. These efforts sought to improve the lives of the poor, the disenfranchised, and the enslaved.

Temperance

The **temperance** crusade was among the most widespread of the reform movements. Many people argued that most social problems of the time were rooted in alcohol abuse. William Cobbett, an English reformer who traveled in the United States, noted in 1819 that virtually every time he visited an American home his hosts asked him "to drink wine or spirits, even *in the morning.*"

In 1826, a group of ministers in Boston organized the American Society for the Promotion of Temperance, which sponsored lectures, press campaigns, and the formation of local and state societies. A favorite tactic was to ask everyone

temperance A widespread reform movement led by militant Christians that focused on reducing the use of alcoholic beverages.

THE DRUNKARD'S PROGRESS This 1846 pro-temperance print outlines a nine-step process of alcoholism, beginning with "a glass with a friend" and ending with "death by suicide." Below the arc are a weeping wife and her child.

who pledged to quit drinking to put by their signature a letter *T* for "total abstinence." With that, a new word entered the English language: *teetotaler*.

Like nearly every reform movement of the day, the temperance movement had a wing of absolutists. In this case, such motivated individuals formed the American Temperance Union in 1833 and later called for abstinence from *all* alcoholic beverages—which caused moderates to abstain from the temperance movement.

Social reform can be a conservative force. Those who feared the Jacksonian appeal to the working class and worried about the surge of poor immigrants from Ireland and Germany, or who dreaded change itself, promoted reform as a means of restoring social control. They were afraid of anything that upset the social status quo.

> Reform as social control

For example, fears that Americans were turning away from the Protestant faith led Lyman Beecher and other evangelicals to found societies such as the American Bible Society, the American Sunday School Union, and the American Tract Society—all designed to shore up the centrality of religion and churches in community life. Evangelical reformers sought to restrict freedom: no more Sunday mail service or Sunday recreation, no more families without Bibles, no communities without ministers, no more liquor.

Prisons and Asylums

The Romantic belief that people are innately good brought about major changes in the treatment of prisoners, the disabled, and orphans. Public institutions (often called asylums) emerged for the treatment of social ills. If removed from society, the theory went, the needy and deviant could be made whole again. However, the underfunded and understaffed asylums often became breeding grounds for brutality and neglect.

Romanticism and rehabilitative justice

The idea of the penitentiary—a place where the guilty paid for their crimes but also underwent rehabilitation—developed as a new approach to reforming criminals. An early model of the system was Auburn Penitentiary, which opened in New York in 1816.

The prisoners at Auburn had separate cells and gathered only for meals and group labor. Discipline was severe. The men marched in lockstep and were never put face-to-face or allowed to talk. The system, its advocates argued, had a beneficial effect on the prisoners and saved money, since the facility's workshops supplied prison needs and produced goods for sale at a profit. By 1840, the nation had twelve Auburn-type penitentiaries.

The reform impulse also found an outlet in the care of the mentally ill. Before 1800, those judged to be "insane" were usually confined at home, with hired keepers, or in jails or almshouses. After 1815, however, asylums devoted specifically to mentally ill people began to appear.

Dorothea Dix's activism for the mentally ill

The most important figure in boosting awareness of mental illness was Dorothea Lynde Dix. A pious Boston schoolteacher, she was asked to instruct a Sunday-school class at a prison in 1841. There she found a roomful of people whose mental health had been completely neglected. The scene so disturbed her that she began a two-year investigation of jails and almshouses throughout Massachusetts. Subsequently, in a report to the state legislature in 1843, Dix revealed that people were confined "in *cages, closets, cellars, stalls, pens! Chained, naked, beaten with rods,* and *lashed* into obedience." Her crusading efforts spread throughout the country and abroad. In the process, she helped to transform social attitudes toward mental illness.

Early Public Schools

America at this time, like most rural societies, offered few educational opportunities. That changed in the first half of the nineteenth century as reformers lobbied for **public schools** to serve all children. The working poor wanted free schools to give their children an equal chance to pursue the American dream. Education, reformers argued, would improve manners while reducing crime and poverty.

A well-informed, well-trained citizenry was considered one of the basic premises of a republic. Because political power resided with the people, as the Constitution asserted, the citizenry needed to be well educated. By 1830, however, no state had a public school system.

Horace Mann of Massachusetts, a state legislator and attorney, led the early drive for statewide, tax-supported public schools. He proposed that the

public schools Established during the 1800s, elementary and secondary schools funded by the state and free of tuition—and open to all children.

THE GEORGE BARRELL EMERSON SCHOOL, BOSTON (CA. 1850) Although higher education for women initially met with some resistance, seminaries such as this one started in the 1820s and 1830s and taught women mathematics, physics, and history as well as music, art, and social graces.

schools be free to all children regardless of gender, class, race, or ethnicity—including immigrant children. Universal access to education, Mann argued, would be "the great equalizer of the conditions of men—the balance-wheel of the social machinery."

Mann saw public schools as the only way to ensure that everyone had a basic level of knowledge and skills. Schooling would also reinforce values such as hard work and clean living. "If we do not prepare children to become good citizens, if we do not enrich their minds with knowledge," Mann warned, "then our republic must go down to destruction."

By the 1840s, most states in the North and Midwest had joined the public school movement. Still, funds for buildings, books, and equipment were limited; teachers were poorly paid and often poorly prepared. Most students going beyond the elementary grades attended private academies, often organized by churches. In 1821, Boston English High School opened as the nation's first free public *secondary* school. Beginning in 1827, Massachusetts required every town of 500 or more residents to have a high school. Most of these schools were segregated by race, however, leading Black families in Boston to launch a movement for desegregation in Massachusetts.

In 1847, an African American parent, Benjamin Roberts, argued in a lawsuit that his five-year-old daughter Sarah had the right to attend the same schools as White students. However, in 1849 the Massachusetts Supreme Court denied Roberts's appeal, ruling that all-White schools were allowed as long as schools for Black children were equal in quality. Although this ruling was a setback to proponents of integration, the *Roberts* case triggered a wave of protests that led to the state legislature passing the Anti-Segregation Act of 1855, which prohibited racially segregated public schools. Massachusetts was the first state to do so. This turn of events marked an important victory for the nation's first civil rights movement.

> Regional inequalities in access to education

With only a few exceptions, southern states did not establish public schools until after the Civil War. In most states, enslaved children were prohibited from learning to read and write or to attend school at all. One of the exceptions, North Carolina led the way in state-supported education, enrolling more than two-thirds of its White school-age population by 1860. But the school year was only four months long because of the need for children to help with farm work.

The disparities between North and South in educational opportunities contributed to the growing economic and cultural differences between the two regions.

Utopian Communities

Amid the climate of reform, the quest for everyday utopias—ideal communities with innovative social and economic relationships—flourished. Plans for creating heaven on earth had long been an American passion, at least since the Puritans set out to build a holy colony in New England.

During the nineteenth century, more than 100 **utopian communities** were created. Religious motives animated many of them, while others reflected faith in the Enlightenment ideal that every social problem had a solution discoverable by scientific study.

Some utopias were *communitarian* experiments emphasizing the welfare of the entire community rather than individual freedom and private profits. Others experimented with "free love," socialism, and special diets. What they shared was a conviction that mainstream society was fundamentally flawed and irredeemable.

The Shakers Communities founded by the Shakers (the United Society of Believers in Christ's Second Appearing) proved to be long-lasting. Ann Lee (whom the Shakers would call Mother Ann) was born in England in 1736 and grew up as the illiterate daughter of a blacksmith, with seven siblings. Early on she came to believe in the "depravity of human nature and the odiousness of sin." No sooner did she marry than she was constantly pregnant, bearing four children, none of whom lived beyond six years of age. The trauma of childbirth and the loss of her children convinced Ann Lee that sexual activity was "indecent" and sinful. She eventually took shelter among a group of renegade Shaking Quakers who nurtured in her the dream of a celibate, spotlessly clean utopia devoted to the Second Coming of Christ in which she would play the role of Jesus's female counterpart. She also believed that God and Jesus spoke directly to her (a phenomenon known as direct revelation).

As Ann Lee recounted her visions of Christ, listeners decided that "the candle of the Lord was in her hand." She was both a prophet and a seer who equated cleanliness, hard work, and chastity with saintliness. Under her leadership, the Shakers publicly attacked the Anglican Church, adopted lives of strict celibacy, and developed unique forms of worship featuring loud singing, "inspired" dancing, speaking in unknown tongues, and "shaking," which accounts for their name.

utopian communities During the nineteenth century, ideal communities that offered innovative social and economic relationships to those who were interested in achieving salvation—now.

After immigrating to America in 1874, Ann Lee and her followers settled on 200 acres in New York that they named New Lebanon. They built a log cabin that housed men on the first floor and women on the second. Then they set about pursuing their goal of Christian perfection.

Mother Ann died in 1784, but new leaders spread the Shaker movement from New York into New England, Ohio, and Kentucky. By 1830, an estimated 4,000 Shakers lived in about twenty settlements. In these communities, there were no pets, no rugs (favorite hiding places of the devil, they believed), no more than one rocking chair in a room. All property was held in common, and men and women were seen as equal. People of color were welcome. Shaker farms became leading sources of garden seed and medicinal herbs, and many Shaker products, especially handcrafted furniture, came to be prized for their simple beauty.

The Shakers took great pride in their ability to create stable colonies outside the mainstream of American life. As Mother Ann observed, "We are the people who turned the world upside down" by displaying their utopian faith in the perfectibility of life on earth.

> Ann Lee founds New Lebanon Shaker Society

Oneida John Humphrey Noyes, founder of the Oneida Community in upstate New York, developed a much different vision of the ideal community. The son of a Vermont congressman, Noyes attended Dartmouth College and Yale Divinity School. But in 1834 he was expelled from Yale and his license to preach was revoked after he announced that he was a "perfect" person, free of all sin, and that God had singled him out to lead others to perfection. In 1836, Noyes gathered a group of "Perfectionists" in Putney, Vermont. Like the Shakers, this community banned private property, and everyone labored for the common good.

> John Humphrey Noyes founds the Oneida Community

Ten years later, Noyes announced a new doctrine, "complex marriage," which meant that every man in the community was married to every woman, and vice versa. "In a holy community," he claimed, "there is no more reason why sexual intercourse should be restrained by law than why eating and drinking should be." Local authorities disagreed, and they charged Noyes with adultery for practicing his theology of "free love."

Noyes fled to New York and in 1848 established the Oneida Community, which became famous for producing fine silverware. Oneida would survive by promoting free sex. Adults had multiple sexual partners and access to surprisingly effective birth control methods. Noyes separated couples that grew too fond of each other (he termed their attachment "sticky love"). He also conducted experiments

ONEIDA COMMUNITY Known for its practice of "complex marriage," Oneida was a utopian community that disavowed private property and emphasized "free love." In this photo from 1870, members of the Oneida Community relax on the front lawn of the Oneida Mansion.

"A DOWNRIGHT GABBLER" (1829) Frances Wright became the target of angry backlash for daring to speak publicly as a woman. This cartoon depicts her as an unattractive "gabbler" forcing a man into the subservient role of holding her bonnet.

in scientific breeding, during which he paired couples based on their positive genetic attributes. Over ten years, Oneida produced sixty-two children from these pairings, ten of whom were fathered by Noyes. It was Noyes that Ralph Waldo Emerson had in mind when he wrote that many reformers "have their high origin in an ideal justice, but they do not retain the purity of an idea."

Nashoba Indeed, utopian communities struggled to live up to the visions that founded them. In Nashoba, Tennessee, near Memphis, Frances Wright dreamed of building a model interracial community to replace slavery. Born in Scotland and orphaned at an early age, Wright had moved to the United States as a young woman and published her observations about American culture in *Views of Society and Manners in America*. An advocate for the rights of women and enslaved people, Wright became one of the first women to speak to a mixed-gender audience. (It was socially unacceptable at the time for women to lecture to men in public.) Never one to mince words, she declared that slavery was "revolting" and "evil."

Wright retreated to Nashoba in 1825 to create an experimental community, but her commitment to social justice proved inconsistent. The land she purchased had earlier been confiscated from the Chickasaw people by the U.S. government (though she retained its Chickasaw name, Nashoba, meaning "wolf"). Then she purchased, but did not liberate, eleven enslaved adults and children living on the property. Wright refused to believe that enslaved people should be given their freedom outright, and required them instead to earn it by working for wages and purchasing their own freedom.

> Frances Wright experiments with interracial community

Wright felt that her Nashoba experiment would provide the best example for ending slavery gradually throughout the South because it compensated slave owners for their financial losses. The Nashoba community, however, was short-lived. After just three years, it disbanded because of financial constraints and persistent opposition from neighboring White farmers. Wright eventually freed her enslaved workers, but took them to Haiti to spend the rest of their lives there so they would not compete against White laborers in the United States.

New Harmony After Nashoba collapsed, Frances Wright moved to another utopian experiment under way in New Harmony, Indiana. There she encountered Robert Owen, a self-made British textile industry magnate who had packed his bags and left everything behind in Scotland in 1825. Owen was already known in Great Britain for providing fair working conditions to his laborers, such as an eight-hour workday and free medical care. But it was in the United States, a place he believed was less corrupted by tradition and custom, where Owen thought he could bring an entirely new moral order into existence.

After purchasing 20,000 acres of land, Owen set to work. New Harmony's constitution explained that it would offer a "community of equality and independence," one in which property was communally owned, houses were nearly identical, children were reared by the whole community, and residents enjoyed an "equality of rights, uninfluenced by sex or condition."

Women like Frances Wright participated equally in governing the New Harmony community, and Wright herself edited its newspaper. But its constitution excluded "persons of color," and within a couple of years numerous internal factions splintered New Harmony and spelled the doom of the entire experiment.

The demise of New Harmony reflected the fundamental tension inherent in all perfectionist schemes: how to maintain solidarity when residents with different personalities and convictions display conflicting notions of paradise. Ultimately, only a few utopian communities survived.

Utopianism joined the temperance, prison reform, and public school movements in a larger push for social and political change that promised to improve everyday life in the rapidly changing world of the early nineteenth century. All of these reform efforts were encouraged by the shifts in faith and belief that had been brought about by religious movements and by the rise of Romanticism. And the push for change did not end there: the same impulses also set the stage for the rise of the anti-slavery movement and the crusade for women's rights.

Anti-Slavery and Women's Rights Movements

Many people who participated in communitarian experiments and other reform movements also played key roles in the abolitionist movement. But the roots of the anti-slavery movement ran deepest in Black communities. The determined resistance of enslaved people made slavery's future an unavoidable issue, and by the 1830s the courage of Black abolitionists attracted increasing numbers of Whites into the organized fight for abolition.

The cause of human freedom taken up by the abolitionists also led many of them to organize on behalf of women as well. A women's rights movement thus emerged by the 1840s and would advocate for political rights and equality well into the next century.

> **CORE OBJECTIVE**
> **4.** Evaluate the evolution of the anti-slavery movement in the first half of the nineteenth century and describe how it affected the cause of women's rights.

The Underground Railroad

Between 1810 and 1850, tens of thousands of enslaved people in the South fled north. Freedom seekers would make their way, usually at night, from one "station," or safe house, to the next. The systems of safe houses and shelters in the border states such as Maryland and Kentucky (and farther north)

> The Underground Railroad leads tens of thousands to freedom

were referred to as the **Underground Railroad**. The "conductors" helping the freedom seekers included freeborn Blacks, White abolitionists, formerly enslaved people, and Indigenous people.

In Philadelphia, William Still, a free Black man who was a clerk at the Pennsylvania Society for the Abolition of Slavery, helped almost 800 freedom-seekers make their way to Canada during his fourteen years as a conductor on the Underground Railroad. "It was my good fortune to lend a helping hand to the weary travelers flying from the land of bondage," he later recounted.

Some courageous fugitive slaves returned to the South to organize even more escapes. Harriet Tubman, the most celebrated member of the Underground Railroad, was born an enslaved person on Maryland's Eastern Shore in 1820 but escaped to Philadelphia in 1849, traveling some 90 miles on foot across Delaware. "I was free," she recalled, "but there was no one to welcome me to the land of freedom. I was a stranger in a strange land." Dressed like a man, she would return to the South nineteen times to help 300 freedom seekers, including her parents and brothers, and "never lost a passenger." She always carried a pistol, and if a freedom-seeking person panicked about escaping, she would pull out her gun, point it at the ambivalent runaway, and say, "You'll be free or die a slave."

David Walker

Another powerful voice urging enslaved people to fight was that of David Walker, a free Black man who owned a used clothing store in Boston serving mostly seamen. In 1829, he published *Appeal to the Colored Citizens of the World*, a pamphlet that denounced the hypocrisy of White Christians in the South for defending slavery. He urged enslaved people to revolt. "The whites want slaves, and want us for their slaves," Walker warned, "but some of them will curse the day they ever saw us." He challenged African Americans, enslaved and free, to use the "crushing arm of power" to gain their freedom. "Woe, woe will be to you," he threatened Whites, "if we have to obtain our freedom by fighting."

Copies of Walker's *Appeal* were secretly carried to the South by Black sailors who had frequented his shop, but Whites in major cities seized the "vile" pamphlet. In 1830, the state of Mississippi outlawed efforts to "print, write, circulate, or put forth . . . any book, paper, magazine, pamphlet, handbill or circular" intended to arouse the "colored population" by "exciting riots and rebellion." By then, however, David Walker had been discovered dead near the doorway of his shop. Though some people feared he was murdered, it is now believed that Walker succumbed to tuberculosis.

Colonization

It took longer for White Americans to follow Walker's radical lead. Many of those with misgivings about slavery, like Frances Wright, initially preferred a gradual form of abolition. Such gradualism was evident in the formation of the **American Colonization Society (ACS)** in Washington, D.C., in 1816.

Walker's Appeal *leads Mississippi to censor incendiary texts*

Underground Railroad A secret system of routes, safe houses, and abolitionists that helped freedom seekers reach freedom in the North.

American Colonization Society (ACS) Established in 1816, an organization whose mission was to send freed, formerly enslaved people to Africa.

Its mission was to raise funds to "repatriate" free Blacks back to Africa. Its supporters included James Madison, Andrew Jackson, and Daniel Webster.

Some White Americans embraced the colonization movement because they opposed slavery; others saw it as a way to get rid of free Black people. "We must save the Negro," one missionary explained, "or the Negro will ruin us." White supremacy remained a powerful assumption.

Most leaders of the free Black community denounced the colonization idea. The United States, they stressed, was their native land, and they had as valid a claim on U.S. citizenship as anyone else. "America is more our country than it is the whites'," argued David Walker. "We have enriched it with our blood and tears."

Nevertheless, the ACS acquired land on the Ivory Coast of West Africa, and on February 6, 1820, the *Elizabeth* sailed from New York with 88 emigrants who formed the nucleus of a new nation—the Republic of Liberia. Thereafter, however, the African colonization movement waned. During the 1830s, only 2,638 African Americans migrated to Liberia. In all, only about 15,000 resettled in Africa—a very small fraction of the American Black population.

> American Colonization Society sends free Black people to West Africa

From Gradualism to Abolitionism

The 1830s marked a turning point. As more and more Americans began to realize that *gradual* approaches to ending slavery were insufficient, they started advocating for *immediate* **abolitionism** everywhere.

Some were inspired by the anti-slavery movement in Great Britain, which led to the emancipation of 800,000 enslaved people across its empire beginning in 1834. Most of those emancipated were in Britain's Caribbean colonies, including Barbados and Jamaica, and British abolitionists helped convince American anti-slavery leaders to adopt an aggressive new strategy. Equally important was the realization that slavery in the cotton states of the South was not dying out; in fact, it was growing rapidly.

To the new generation of reformers who came of age amid the Second Great Awakening, slavery was a sin and Christians had an obligation to purge all sins, personal and societal. In the idea of immediate emancipation, the abolitionists found a perfectionist formula for casting off the guilt of slavery. Theirs would be a moral crusade rather than a political movement. As the American Anti-Slavery Society promised, "We shall send forth agents to lift up the voice of remonstrance, of warning, of entreaty, and of rebuke" against slaveholders everywhere.

> Religious revivalism strengthens the abolitionist movement

William Lloyd Garrison

A zealous White activist named William Lloyd Garrison became an influential leader in the emerging abolitionist movement. Born in 1805 in Newburyport, Massachusetts, Garrison learned the printing trade before moving to Boston. There he embraced the reform spirit of the era, writing anonymous letters and essays denouncing alcohol abuse, Sabbath-breaking, and war.

It was slavery, however, that most excited Garrison's indignation. In 1831, free Black northerners helped convince Garrison to launch an anti-slavery

abolitionism A movement that called for an immediate end to slavery throughout the United States.

MASTHEAD OF *THE LIBERATOR* Masthead of the abolitionist newspaper *The Liberator*, dated Friday, April 21, 1861. William Lloyd Garrison's weekly newspaper appealed to the morality of its readers to abolish African American slavery. In the center is an image of Jesus Christ and the text, "I come to break the bonds of the oppressor."

newspaper, *The Liberator*. Of the first 500 subscribers, 450 were free Black people, leading Garrison to acknowledge that people of color kept *The Liberator* afloat—"It is their organ."

In the first issue, Garrison condemned "the popular but pernicious doctrine of gradual emancipation." He dreamed of immediate equality in all spheres of American life. In pursuing that dream, he vowed, "I am in earnest—I will not equivocate—I will not excuse—I will not retreat a single inch—and I WILL BE HEARD."

Garrison's courage in denouncing slavery as "the one great, distinctive, all-conquering sin in America" outraged slaveholders in the South, as well as some Whites in the North. In 1835, a mob of angry Whites dragged him through the streets of Boston. The South Carolina and Georgia legislatures promised a $5,000 reward to anyone who kidnapped Garrison and brought him south for trial.

> Founding of the American Anti-Slavery Society

But Garrison's unflagging efforts made the impossible—abolition—seem possible. Soon two wealthy New York City silk merchants, Arthur and Lewis Tappan, were providing financial support. In 1833 they joined with Garrison and a group of Quaker reformers, free Black activists, and evangelicals to organize the American Anti-Slavery Society (AASS).

In 1835, the AASS began flooding the South with anti-slavery pamphlets and newspapers. The materials so enraged southern slaveholders that a Louisiana community offered a $50,000 reward for the capture of the "notorious abolitionist, Arthur Tappan, of New York." Post offices throughout the South began destroying "anti-slavery propaganda."

By 1840, some 160,000 people in more than 200 local branches belonged to the American Anti-Slavery Society, which stressed that "slaveholding is a heinous crime in the sight of God, and that the duty, safety, and best interests of all concerned, require its immediate abandonment." The AASS argued that Black people should have full social and civil rights.

Black Leadership

Although many Whites joined the fight to end slavery, most of them, unlike William Lloyd Garrison, still insisted that Black people were socially inferior. Many of these Whites expected free Black people to take a back seat in the movement.

Yet free African Americans were crucial in transforming the struggle against slavery into a more ambitious fight against racial discrimination, which remained widespread in most states. Black people were barred from public places in the North—churches, schools, hotels, railroad stations, and cemeteries. As Garrison reported from Boston, "Hardly any doors but those of our state prisons were open to our colored brethren."

William Wells Brown Much of the energy and effectiveness of the abolitionist movement derived from the compelling testimonies provided by formerly enslaved people. These included the voices of William Wells Brown, a freedom seeker from Kentucky; Frederick Douglass, who had escaped from Maryland; and Sojourner Truth, a freedom seeker from New York.

Brown was just twenty years old when he escaped from his owner, a steamboat pilot on the Ohio River. An Ohio Quaker named Wells Brown provided shelter to the freedom seeker, and Brown adopted the man's name while forging a new identity as a free man. He settled in Cleveland, Ohio, where he became a dockworker. He married, had three children, and helped freedom seekers cross the border into Canada. By 1842, he had learned to read and write, had begun to publish columns in abolitionist newspapers, and was in great demand as a speaker at anti-slavery meetings. In 1847 he moved to Boston, where the Massachusetts Anti-Slavery Society hired him as a traveling lecturer.

That same year, the organization published Brown's autobiography, *Narrative of William W. Brown, A Fugitive Slave, Written by Himself*, which became a best seller. Brown gave thousands of speeches calling for an end to slavery and for equality for both Blacks and women. He stressed that African Americans were "endowed with those intellectual and amiable qualities which adorn and dignify human nature."

Narrative of William W. Brown (1847)

Frederick Douglass Frederick Douglass was an even more effective spokesman for abolitionism. Born enslaved in Maryland to a mother he rarely saw, Douglass suspected that his White owner was also his father. At age eight he was sent to Baltimore as an enslaved house servant. There he taught himself to read. When Douglass was about fifteen years old, his owner sent him to a plantation to strip him of his "rebelliousness," but the experience only hardened his resolve to escape.

Back in Baltimore, Douglass was rented out to a shipyard. There, in 1838, he plotted his escape from slavery. After disguising himself as a sailor and forging documents certifying that he was free, he escaped from Maryland and made his way to New Bedford, Massachusetts, where he heard William Garrison speak and felt "my heart bounding at every true utterance against the slave system." Two years later, while attending another rally at which Garrison spoke, Douglass rose spontaneously to endorse Garrison's pleas. There "opened upon me a new life—a life for which I had had no preparation."

The Massachusetts Anti-Slavery Society recruited Douglass as a traveling speaker, sending him across New England and west to Ohio and Indiana. At numerous abolitionist gatherings, he recounted his painful encounters with "the whip, the chain . . . and all the other bloody paraphernalia of the slave system." Through his writings and presentations, Douglass became the best-known man of color in America and the courageous voice of the abolitionist movement. "I appear before the immense assembly this evening as a thief and a robber," he told a Massachusetts group in 1842. "I stole this head, these limbs, this body from my master, and ran off with them."

> *Narrative of the Life of Frederick Douglass* (1845)

After publishing his *Narrative of the Life of Frederick Douglass, An American Slave* (1845), Douglass, fearing that his prominence would make him accessible to fugitive slave catchers, left for an extended lecture tour of

FREDERICK DOUGLASS AND SOJOURNER TRUTH Douglass *(left)* escaped slavery and came to Massachusetts, where he began his career as a traveling speaker and advocate for abolitionism, eventually earning enough money to purchase his freedom and founding the *North Star,* an abolitionist newspaper. Sojourner Truth *(right)*, freed from slavery, was a captivating speaker who toured the North advocating for abolitionism and women's rights.

the British Isles. He returned two years later with enough money to purchase his freedom. He then started an abolitionist newspaper, the *North Star*, in Rochester, New York. He named the newspaper after the star that freedom seekers used to guide themselves toward freedom.

Sojourner Truth African American women also were enormously influential in the abolitionist movement. Sojourner Truth was born to enslaved parents in upstate New York in 1797. She was given the name Isabella but renamed herself in 1843 after experiencing a conversation with God, who told her "to travel up and down the land" preaching "the truth" against slavery.

An enslaved person until she was freed in 1827, Truth spoke with conviction about the evils of slavery and the ways it denied Black women the respect and rights that they deserved. She traveled throughout the North during the 1840s and 1850s, citing her own experiences as justification for equal recognition. As she told the Ohio Women's Rights Convention in 1851, "I have plowed, and planted, and gathered into barns, and no man could head [surpass] me—and ar'n't I a woman? I have borne thirteen children, and seen 'em mos' all sold off into slavery, and when I cried out with a mother's grief, none but Jesus heard—and ar'n't I a woman?"

Through such compelling testimony, Sojourner Truth tapped the distinctive energies that women brought to reformist causes. "If the first woman God ever made was strong enough to turn the world upside down all alone," she concluded in her address to the Ohio gathering, "these women together ought to be able to turn it back and get it right side up again!"

Women's Rights

As abolition gained momentum, the issue of equal rights for women became more widely debated. Some anti-slavery activists joined Sojourner Truth in asserting that the fight for freedom from slavery required a more universal fight for the liberation of all people—including women. After all, shouldn't a nation built on the principles of liberty and equality extend the same rights to women as it did to men? Growing numbers of women in the 1840s answered yes to this question, though they were not all of one mind about how best to proceed.

Catharine Beecher

Some argued that women should focus on enhancing home life. One supporter of this view was Catharine Beecher, the daughter of White religious leader Lyman Beecher. She was also the sister of writer Harriet Beecher Stowe and of clergymen Henry Ward Beecher and Charles Beecher.

In 1842, Catharine Beecher published *A Treatise on Domestic Economy*, which promoted the **cult of domesticity**. This powerful idea called upon women to accept and celebrate their role as manager of the household and nurturer of the children, separate from the man's sphere of work outside the home (also known as "separate spheres"). Beecher argued that young women

cult of domesticity A pervasive nineteenth-century ideology urging women to celebrate their role as manager of the household and nurturer of the children.

Seneca Falls Convention (1848) The convention organized by feminists Lucretia Mott and Elizabeth Cady Stanton to promote women's rights and issue the pathbreaking Declaration of Rights and Sentiments.

Declaration of Rights and Sentiments (1848) A document based on the Declaration of Independence that called for gender equality, written primarily by Elizabeth Cady Stanton and signed by Seneca Falls Convention delegates.

should be trained not for careers outside the home but for a life centered in the household. Reflecting this perspective, women were barred from the ministry and most other professions. They could not vote or serve on juries. College was rarely an option. A wife often had no control over her property or her children. She could not make a will, sign a contract, or bring suit in court without her husband's permission. At this point, the cult of domesticity seemed to be holding women in place.

Seneca Falls

Gradually, other women began to protest their subordinate status, and some men began to listen. In 1848, Lucretia Mott, a Philadelphia Quaker, and Elizabeth Cady Stanton of New York called a convention to gather in Stanton's hometown of Seneca Falls, in western New York, to discuss "the social, civil, and religious condition and rights of women."

Already leaders in the abolitionist movement—Mott had founded the Female Antislavery Society of Philadelphia in 1833—the two White women met at the 1840 World Anti-Slavery Convention in London. Stanton was there on her honeymoon, having just married a fellow abolitionist in a ceremony where she refused to use the word *obey* in her vows. Stanton and Mott soon discovered that, as women, they were not allowed to participate in the convention proceedings and could only attend meetings while sitting behind a curtain. Outraged by this unequal treatment from those who claimed to care deeply about human freedom, Stanton and Mott went back to the United States more determined than ever to organize for women's rights.

By July 19, 1848, when the **Seneca Falls Convention** convened, revolution was in the air. In Europe, militant nationalists—including many women—were rebelling against monarchies and promoting unification. In France, the Society for the Emancipation of Women was demanding that women receive equal political rights. Earlier, in April, the French government had abolished slavery in its Caribbean colonies; in June, European reformers had called for "the complete, radical abolition of all the privileges of sex, of birth, of race, of rank, and of fortune."

The activists at Seneca Falls did not go that far, but they did issue a clever revision of the Declaration of Independence. Their **Declaration of Rights and Sentiments** proclaimed that "all men and women are created equal." All laws that placed women "in a position inferior to that of men, are contrary to the great precept of nature, and therefore of no force or authority." The Declaration's most controversial demand was the right to vote.

ELIZABETH CADY STANTON Stanton, in 1856, was a young mother who organized the Seneca Falls Convention. She devoted the rest of her life to the organized fight for women's rights.

Such ambitious goals and strong language were too radical for many of the 300 delegates—and for most Americans. The editors of the *Philadelphia Public Ledger* asked why women would want to climb down from their domestic pedestal and get involved with politics: "A woman is nothing. A wife is everything. A pretty girl is equal to ten thousand men, and a mother is, next to God, all powerful." Despite such opposition, the Seneca Falls gathering represented an important first step in the campaign for women's rights. Thirty-two men joined the women in signing the Declaration of Rights and Sentiments—including Frederick Douglass, who would become a forceful supporter of women's rights.

> Declaration of Rights and Sentiments calls for women's right to vote

Thereafter, from 1850 until the outbreak of the Civil War in 1861, women's rights advocates held conventions, delivered lectures, and circulated petitions. Women nationwide did not gain the vote in the nineteenth century, but they did make legal gains. In 1839, Mississippi became the first state to grant married women control over their property; by the 1860s, eleven more states had done so.

Black Women's Rights

No Black women attended the Seneca Falls Convention. As the poet and writer Frances Ellen Watkins Harper later explained, "You white women speak here of rights. I speak of wrongs." Black women confronted racist indignities in their everyday lives that led them to push for equality in ways that went beyond the right to vote.

Black women mobilized within African American communities, especially in churches, and followed the revivalist Jarena Lee's pioneering footsteps by pushing for all women to be allowed to preach in churches. In 1848, Black women attended the National Convention of Colored Citizens in Cleveland, Ohio, where they helped pass a resolution proclaiming "the equality of the sexes."

> Black Convention advocates for women's equality

Maria Miller Stewart, a public speaker and writer based in Boston, declared that Black women like her could not separate the pursuit of women's rights from the fight against racism and slavery. The two were intertwined. "Oh, ye daughters of Africa, awake! Awake! Arise!" she argued, "No longer sleep nor slumber, but distinguish yourselves." As mothers, she explained, "We have done the duties of women, and we have done them well. But we have not been esteemed for it, and now we are coming out demanding our rights."

Meanwhile, amid these growing calls for rights from Black and White women alike, the struggle to abolish slavery was becoming more complex.

Splits Within the Abolitionist Movement

As the movement for abolition spread, debates over tactics intensified. The Garrisonians, who felt that slavery had corrupted all aspects of American life, embraced every important reform movement of the day: abolition, temperance, pacifism, vegetarianism, and women's rights. William Lloyd Garrison's unconventional religious ideas and social ideals led him to break with the

Comparing PERSPECTIVES

RIGHTS FOR WOMEN AND ENSLAVED PEOPLE

From: "Declaration of Sentiments," *Report of the Women's Rights Convention Held at Seneca Falls, NY,* July 19–20, 1848.

The 1848 Seneca Falls Convention, organized by Elizabeth Cady Stanton and Lucretia Mott, advocated for women's rights, including the right to vote. Attendees signed the Declaration of Rights and Sentiments, modeled on the Declaration of Independence, to explain why the cause of women's rights had become urgent.

We hold these truths to be self-evident: that all men and women are created equal; that they are endowed by their Creator with certain inalienable rights; that among these are life, liberty, and the pursuit of happiness.

The history of mankind is a history of repeated injuries and usurpations on the part of man toward woman, having in direct object the establishment of an absolute tyranny over her. To prove this, let facts be submitted.

He has never permitted her to exercise her inalienable right to the elective franchise.

He has compelled her to submit to laws, in the formation of which she had no voice.

He has withheld from her rights which are given to the most ignorant and degraded men—both natives and foreigners.

Having deprived her of this first right of a citizen, the elective franchise, thereby leaving her without representation in the halls of legislation, he has oppressed her on all sides.

He has taken from her all rights in property, even to the wages she earns.

Now, in view of this entire disfranchisement of one-half the people of this country, their social and religious degradation,—in view of the unjust laws above mentioned, and because women do feel themselves aggrieved, oppressed, and fraudulently deprived of their most sacred rights, we insist that they have immediate admission to all the rights and privileges which belong to them as citizens of these United States.

From: Frederick Douglass, "What to the Slave Is the Fourth of July?" July 5, 1852.

Frederick Douglass escaped slavery in 1838 and became a widely celebrated orator for the abolitionist movement. On July 5, 1852, one day after the nation's celebration of independence, he stood before an audience in Rochester, New York, to explain what this annual holiday meant to people who were enslaved.

This, for the purpose of this celebration, is the 4th of July. It is the birthday of your National Independence, and of your political freedom.

I have said that the Declaration of Independence is the ringbolt to the chain of your nation's destiny; so, indeed, I regard it. The principles contained in that instrument are saving principles. Stand by those principles, be true to them on all occasions, in all places, against all foes, and at whatever cost.

Fellow-citizens, pardon me, allow me to ask, why am I called upon to speak here to-day? What have I, or those I represent, to do with your national independence? Are the great principles of political freedom and of natural justice, embodied in that Declaration of Independence, extended to us?

What, to the American slave, is your 4th of July? I answer; a day that reveals to him, more than all other days in the year, the gross injustice and cruelty to which he is the constant victim. To him, your celebration is a sham; your boasted liberty, an unholy license; your national greatness, swelling vanity; your sounds of rejoicing are empty and heartless; your shouts of liberty and equality, hollow mockery; your prayers and hymns, your sermons and thanksgivings, with all your religious parade, and solemnity, are, to him, mere bombast, fraud, deception, impiety, and hypocrisy.

I do not despair of this country. There are forces in operation, which must inevitably, work the downfall of slavery. *"The arm of the Lord is not shortened,"* and the doom of slavery is certain. I, therefore, leave off where I began, with *hope*. While drawing encouragement from "the Declaration of Independence," the great principles it contains, and the genius of American Institutions, my spirit is also cheered by the obvious tendencies of the age.

Questions

1. According to the Declaration of Sentiments, in what ways do American women experience "absolute tyranny" in their everyday lives?

2. According to Frederick Douglass, what do enslaved people see when they look out on the nation's celebrations of July 4?

3. Compare how Frederick Douglass and the signers of the Declaration of Sentiments refer, directly or indirectly, to the Declaration of Independence. How do each draw inspiration from the nation's founding document to support their arguments for equal rights?

established Protestant churches, which, to his mind, were in league with slavery, as was the federal government. The U.S. Constitution, he charged, was "a covenant with death and an agreement with hell."

Other reformers saw American society as fundamentally sound, and concentrated on purging it of slavery. Garrison struck them as an unrealistic fanatic whose radicalism hurt the cause. That is what led Arthur and Lewis Tappan to break with Garrison and form a new abolitionist organization, the American and Foreign Antislavery Society.

Outspoken Women

The Tappans and their followers also believed that women should remain subordinate members of the abolitionist movement, so they fought against their assumption of leadership roles. But women remained undeterred, becoming the majority of the movement's foot soldiers while linking the causes of anti-slavery and women's rights.

The Grimké Sisters The scandalous activities of the Grimké sisters kept women's rights center stage in the abolitionist movement. Sarah and Angelina Grimké, born to a wealthy South Carolina family, grew up on a rice plantation worked by enslaved people. In 1821, soon after her father's death, Sarah moved to Philadelphia, joined the Society of Friends (Quakers), and renounced slavery. Angelina followed her eight years later, and in 1835 the sisters joined the abolitionist movement, speaking to northern women's groups. Angelina often declared that if southern White women would stand up against slavery they could "overthrow this horrible system of oppression and cruelty." Upon reading this, the mayor of Charleston told Angelina's mother that her daughters would be jailed if they returned home.

THE GRIMKÉ SISTERS After moving away from their slave-holding family, Sarah *(left)* and Angelina *(right)* Grimké devoted themselves to abolitionism and feminism.

The Grimké sisters traveled widely and soon began speaking to audiences of both women and men. Their unconventional behavior in addressing mixed-gender audiences prompted sharp criticism from ministers. Catharine Beecher also reminded the sisters that women occupied "a subordinate relation in society to the other sex" and that they should limit their activities to the "domestic and social circle."

Angelina Grimké firmly rejected such arguments: "The investigation of the rights of the slave has led me to a better understanding of my own [rights]." For centuries, she noted, women had been raised to view themselves as "inferior creatures." Now, she insisted, "It is a woman's right to have a voice in all laws and regulations by which she is to be governed, whether in church or in state." Soon, she and her sister began linking their efforts to free enslaved people with their desire to free women from male domination. "Men and women are CREATED EQUAL!" Sarah Grimké asserted. "Whatever is right for man to do is right for woman."

> White women unite abolition of slavery and women's rights

Abigail Kelley The powerful appeal of abolitionism and women's rights is illustrated in the colorful life of Abigail "Abby" Kelley. A teacher, born in Pelham, Massachusetts, in 1811, she embraced abolitionism after attending a lecture by William Lloyd Garrison and joined the Female Anti-Slavery Society.

By 1840, Kelley became the first woman elected as an officer in the American Anti-Slavery Society. Many male abolitionists were furious. One of them described Kelley as one of those "women of masculine minds and aggressive tendencies... who cannot be satisfied in domestic life." The prejudice she experienced from the Society's male officers revealed to her that she and other women "were manacled [chained] *ourselves*."

> Abigail Kelley becomes an officer in the American Anti-Slavery Society

During the 1850s, Kelley also began to champion women's rights and temperance. She spoke at the fourth National Woman's Rights Convention in Cleveland. Lucy Stone, one of the women's rights leaders, called Kelley a heroine who "stood in the thick of the fight for the slaves, and at the same time, she hewed out that path over which women are now walking toward their equal political rights."

The Liberty Party

Another faction of the American Anti-Slavery Society had grown skeptical that the nonviolent "moral suasion" promoted by William Lloyd Garrison would ever lead to abolition. They decided that political action would be the most effective way to pursue their goal. In 1840, activists formed the Liberty Party to elect an American president who would restrict the spread of slavery. The Liberty Party's presidential nominee, James Gillespie Birney, was a former Alabama slaveholder turned anti-slavery activist. His slogan was "vote as you pray, and pray as you vote." The platform called not for immediate abolition but for banning slavery in the western territories and the District of Columbia.

> Formation of the Liberty Party (1840)

Yet the Liberty Party found few supporters. In the 1840 election, Birney polled only 7,000 votes. In 1844, however, he would win 60,000. Thereafter, an anti-slavery party contested every national election until the Thirteenth Amendment officially ended slavery in 1865.

Reactions to Abolitionism

Despite the growing efforts of anti-slavery organizations, racism remained widespread in the North, especially among the working poor. Abolitionist speakers confronted hostile White crowds who disliked Black people or found that anti-slavery agitation was bad for business, and sometimes these confrontations led to violence. Meanwhile, in the cotton-producing South, prominent leaders raised their voices in loud defense of slavery.

Elijah P. Lovejoy

In 1837, a mob in Illinois killed Elijah P. Lovejoy, a White editor of an anti-slavery newspaper. This violent act gave the movement a martyr to the causes of both abolition and freedom of the press.

Lovejoy had begun his career as a Presbyterian minister in New England. After receiving a "sign by God" to focus his life on the "destruction of slavery," he moved to St. Louis, in slaveholding Missouri, where his newspaper denounced alcohol, Catholicism, and slavery. When a pro-slavery mob destroyed his printing office, he moved across the Mississippi River to a warehouse in Alton, Illinois, where he tried to start an anti-slavery society. White mobs, however, twice again destroyed his printing press. When a new press arrived, Lovejoy and several supporters armed themselves and took up defensive positions.

> **Mob violence against abolitionists**

On November 7, 1837, ruffians began throwing stones and firing shots into the building. One of Lovejoy's allies fired back, killing a rioter. The mob then set fire to the warehouse. A shotgun blast killed Lovejoy, and his murder aroused a frenzy of indignation. John Quincy Adams said the murder "sent a shock as of any earthquake throughout this continent."

In Illinois, young Abraham Lincoln felt those shockwaves. Lovejoy's murder, he noted, was an "ill omen," for the "mob violence" threatened America's core values: "liberty and equal rights."

At one of the hundreds of memorial services for Lovejoy across the North, a grizzled abolitionist named John Brown rose, raised his right hand, and declared, "Here, before God, in the presence of these witnesses, from this time, I consecrate my life to the destruction of slavery!" Only violence, Brown and other militants decided, could dislodge the sin of slavery. Brown forced his family members to pledge with him that they would wage "war on slavery." Their war would shake the nation over the next two decades.

The Defense of Slavery

> **Attempts to justify slavery with the Bible**

The growing strength and visibility of the abolitionist movement, coupled with the profitability of cotton, prompted southerners to launch an aggressive defense of slavery. During the 1830s and after, pro-slavery leaders worked out an elaborate rationale for what they considered the benefits of slavery. The Bible was their favorite weapon. Had not the patriarchs of the Hebrew Bible held people in bondage? Had not Saint Paul advised servants to obey their masters, and told a runaway servant to return to his master? And had not Jesus remained silent on slavery?

Soon, bolder arguments emerged. In February 1837, South Carolina's John C. Calhoun told the Senate that slavery was "good—a great good," rooted in the Bible. He asserted that Africans who had been brought to America "had never existed in so comfortable, so respectable, or so civilized a condition, as that which is now enjoyed in the Southern states." If slavery were abolished, Calhoun warned, White racial supremacy would be compromised.

One of Calhoun's friends, James Henry Hammond, was the South's loudest defender of slavery. A South Carolina planter, like Calhoun, he proclaimed that the people he enslaved were "happy, content . . . and utterly incapable, from intellectual weakness, ever to give us any trouble by their aspirations." He rejected the "ridiculously absurd . . . dogma of Mr. Jefferson, that 'all men are born equal.'"

Hammond, Calhoun, and others also claimed that if freed, Black people would be a danger to themselves and to others. White workers, in their view, feared the competition for jobs if enslaved people were to be freed.

In 1859, the writer Frances Ellen Watkins Harper predicted that the reign of the "wicked" who championed slavery would soon end. "God will do right by us," she wrote, and an improved nation would emerge. Harper shared the optimism about individual and national progress that had inspired so many of the reformers in the first half of the nineteenth century. Her faith in moral progress was grounded in the assumption that human freedom must triumph over slavery.

By midcentury, a rapidly growing number of Americans agreed with Harper that southern slavery was an abomination that should not spread its evils into the western territories—and should be abolished altogether. That changing attitude represented a success for the anti-slavery movement, which had been gaining momentum since the 1830s thanks to the initiative taken by Black people and the increasing numbers of White participants who joined them. Women, both Black and White, were crucial to abolitionist organizing. But even as they grew more influential, their own unequal treatment within the movement helped launch the organized push for women's rights. Having triggered a polarizing debate surrounding both women's rights and anti-slavery, the abolitionist crusade would reach a fiery climax in the Civil War.

Reviewing the
CORE OBJECTIVES

- **Religious Developments** *Unitarians* and *Universalists* in New England challenged the notion of predestination by arguing that all people could receive salvation, not just a select few. The evangelical preachers of the *Second Great Awakening* generated fiery *frontier revivals*. The more democratic sects, such as Baptists and Methodists, which promoted the idea of free-will salvation, gained huge numbers of converts, including women and African Americans. Religion inspired reform movements in western New York, which was also the birthplace of several religious movements, including the Church of Jesus Christ of Latter-day Saints (often called the *Mormon Church*).

- **Transcendentalists** Transcendentalists were poets, writers, artists, ministers, and philosophers who embraced a moral and spiritual idealism (Romanticism) in reaction to scientific rationalism and Christian orthodoxy. They sought to "transcend" reason and the material world and encourage independent reflection. At the same time, *transcendentalism* influenced the works of novelists, essayists, and poets, who created a uniquely American literature. This outpouring of new writing inspired readers to see, think about, and improve themselves and the world around them—and at times lent direct support to emerging social movements.

- **Social Reform Movements** The shifting cultural foundation in religion, arts, and literature helped inspire an unprecedented wave of social reform movements during a time of rapid economic, political, and social upheaval. The most widespread movement was for *temperance*, the elimination of excessive drinking. Women were among the most energetic participants in the temperance movement and in other social reform movements, calling for the improvement of prisons and asylums, and for greater access to education through *public schools*. Amid the pervasive climate of reform during the early nineteenth century, more than 100 *utopian communities* were established, including the Shakers and the Oneida Community.

- **Anti-Slavery Movement and Women's Rights** The determined resistance of enslaved people drew more and more Americans into the anti-slavery movement. African Americans in the North joined with White allies to create an *Underground Railroad*—a network of safe havens and abolitionists, both White and Black, which helped freedom seekers escape their bondage in the South. Though other opponents of slavery had promoted less radical solutions, including the *American Colonization Society's* call for gradual emancipation and the resettlement of free African Americans to colonies in Africa, *abolitionism* emerged in the 1830s to demand an immediate and complete end of slavery. Some abolitionists went even further, calling for full social and political equality, although they disagreed over tactics. At the center of their disagreements was a conflict over the role of women.

Women may have been the majority of abolitionists, but their unequal treatment by fellow anti-slavery activists helped launch the women's rights movement. At the *Seneca Falls Convention* (1848), White women drafted the *Declaration of Rights and Sentiments* (1848), while Black women gathered in their own churches and conventions to address the unique inequalities facing women of their race.

KEY TERMS

Unitarians *p. 465*

Universalists *p. 465*

Second Great Awakening *p. 465*

frontier revivals *p. 467*

Mormon Church *p. 470*

transcendentalism *p. 473*

temperance *p. 480*

public schools *p. 482*

utopian communities *p. 484*

Underground Railroad *p. 488*

American Colonization Society (ACS) *p. 488*

abolitionism *p. 489*

cult of domesticity *p. 493*

Seneca Falls Convention (1848) *p. 494*

Declaration of Rights and Sentiments (1848) *p. 494*

CHRONOLOGY

1825 Frances Wright establishes utopian community in Nashoba, Tennessee

1826 American Society for the Promotion of Temperance organized

1830 Percentage of American churchgoers has doubled since 1800

Joseph Smith reveals *The Book of Mormon*

1830–1831 Charles G. Finney leads revivals in upstate New York

1831 William Lloyd Garrison begins publishing *The Liberator*

1833 American Anti-Slavery Society is founded

1836 Transcendental Club holds its first meeting

1837 Abolitionist editor Elijah P. Lovejoy is murdered

1840 Abolitionists form the Liberty Party

1845 *Narrative of the Life of Frederick Douglass* is published

1846 Mormons, led by Brigham Young, make the difficult trek to Utah

1848 At the Seneca Falls Convention, White feminists issue the Declaration of Rights and Sentiments

National Convention of Colored Citizens in Cleveland, Ohio, passes resolution affirming the equality of women

1851 Sojourner Truth delivers her famous speech "Ar'n't I a Woman?"

1854 Henry David Thoreau's *Walden, or Life in the Woods* is published

InQuizitive

Go to InQuizitive to see what you've learned—and learn what you've missed—with personalized feedback along the way.

THINKING LIKE A HISTORIAN

DEBATING Separate Spheres

Politics and present-day events often influence *historiography*, the study of how historians develop contrasting interpretations over time. In the 1960s, *social* history gained popularity as scholars sought to tell the story of previously unrepresented groups—the poor, women, racial and ethnic minorities. Three concepts of great importance to social historians are *race, class,* and *gender*. Part 3, *"An Expansive Nation,"* shows how historians use these concepts to debate the importance of the "separate spheres" ideology. In the first half of the nineteenth century, before the Civil War, the separate spheres ideology promoted separate and distinct roles for women and men. The female sphere was "domestic," within the home, while the male sphere was centered on economic and political life.

This exercise has two tasks:

PART 1: Compare the two secondary sources on women and separate spheres.
PART 2: Using primary sources, evaluate the arguments of the two secondary sources.

PART I Comparing Secondary Sources

Below are secondary sources from two social historians. The first is from Catherine Clinton of the University of Texas at San Antonio; the second, from Nancy Hewitt of Rutgers, the State University of New Jersey. Both Clinton and Hewitt use race, class, and gender analysis to assess how the dominant tradition of separate spheres impacted women and how women responded.

In comparing the views of these two scholars, answer the following questions. Use specific examples in the selections to support your answers.

- What is the subject of each article?
- What classes of women does each author highlight?
- According to each author, how did the ideology of separate spheres impact women?
- In what ways does each author use race, class, and gender to construct her argument?

Secondary Source 1

Catherine Clinton, "The Ties That Bind," 1984

The nineteenth century ushered in a social as well as an economic revolution for American women. The refinement of middle-class ideology profoundly affected females during the antebellum [pre–Civil War] era. . . . The creation of the cult of domesticity, the redefinition of the home as women's domain, was a delicate process designed to channel women's contributions into a proper course. . . .

[I]nstead of liberty and equality, subordination and restriction were drummed into women, a refrain inherited from the colonial era. Women's only reward was lavish exaltation of their vital and unmatchable contributions to the civic state as mothers. This rejuvenated ethic was accompanied by a confinement to the domestic sphere.

Once segregated from men by the confines of a new ideological order, women set about turning their liabilities into assets. Forbidden traditional pathways to success, post-Revolutionary women pursued other means of achieving esteem and influence within their society. These alternatives were pioneered by women who were in search of new influence but who refrained from invading the male domain—not for the sake of modesty, but rather as a strategy. . . .

Woman's domain was, despite confinement, expansive. She was charged with the moral, spiritual, and physical well-being of her entire family. . . . She was supervisor of the education of her children, tender of the hearth, and the symbol of the home. These indispensable functions, although primarily carried out within the home, were not restricted to it. Women perceived that they might extend female jurisdiction into the public and hitherto exclusively male realm by using their "domestic" role as a lever—wedging themselves into positions of power, however limited, through exploitation of their domesticity. In the early decades of the century, creative women took their rather circumscribed nooks and crannies, within the culture, and turned them into springboards. Women's talents and contributions were soon apparent within the larger social arena.

Source: Clinton, Catherine. "The Ties That Bind." Chap. 3 in *The Other Civil War: American Women in the Nineteenth Century*. New York: Hill & Wang, 1984. 40–42.

Secondary Source 2

Nancy A. Hewitt, "Beyond the Search for Sisterhood: American Women's History in the 1980s," 1985

The bonds that encircled past generations of women were initially perceived as restrictive, arising from female victimization at the hands of patriarchs in such institutions as medicine, education, the church, the state, and the family. Historians soon concluded, however, that oppression was a double-edged sword; the counterpart of subordination in or exclusion from male-dominated domains was inclusion in an all-female enclave. The concept of womanhood, it soon appeared, "bound women together even as it bound them down."

The formative works in American women's history have focused on the formation of these separate sexual spheres, particularly among the emerging urban bourgeoisie in the first half of the nineteenth century. Reified [reinforced] in prescriptive literature, realized in daily life, and ritualized in female collectivities, this 'woman's sphere' came to be seen as the foundation of women's culture and community in antebellum [pre–Civil War] America. . . . The community that has become the cornerstone of North American women's history was discovered within the Victorian middle class. . . . Yet evidence from the lives of slaves, mill operatives, miners' wives, immigrants, and southern industrial workers as well as from "true women" indicates that there was no single woman's culture or sphere. There was a culturally dominant definition of sexual spheres promulgated by an economically, politically, and socially dominant group.

That definition was firmly grounded in the sexual division of labor appropriate to that class, just as other definitions developed based on the sexual division of labor in other class and racial groups. All these divisions were characterized by sufficient sex-stereotyping to assure the formation of distinct female circles of labor and distinct rituals and values rooted in that laboring experience.

To date historians have focused on the parallels in the establishment of women's spheres across classes, races, and ethnic groups and have asserted certain commonalities among them, assuming their common origin in the modernization of society during the nineteenth century.

A closer examination now reveals that no such universal sisterhood existed, and in fact that the development of a sense of community among various classes of women served as a barrier to an all-embracing bond of womanhood. Finally, it is now clear that privileged women were willing to wield their sex-specific influence in ways that, intentionally or unintentionally, exploited other women in the name of "true-womanhood."

Source: Hewitt, Nancy A. "Beyond the Search for Sisterhood: American Women's History in the 1980s." *Social History* 10 (1985): 299–321.

PART II Using Primary Sources to Evaluate Secondary Sources

When historians are faced with conflicting interpretations of the past, they often look at primary source material as part of the process of evaluating the different arguments. Below are three excerpts from political statements by three remarkable but very different women. The first is from Lucretia Mott, a White, middle-class, and highly educated woman who became a prominent Quaker speaker, leading abolitionist, and co-organizer of the first women's rights convention, the Seneca Falls Convention. The second excerpt is from Sojourner Truth, a formerly enslaved woman who became a leading abolitionist and activist for women's rights. The final excerpt is from Harriett Robinson, who grew up in a White working-class family headed by a widowed mother and began working in the textile mills of Lowell, Massachusetts, at the age of ten.

While not all these documents directly address the term *separate spheres*, each addresses women's place in American society.

Carefully read each of the primary sources and answer the following questions. Decide which of the primary source documents support or refute Clinton's and Hewitt's arguments about women's separate sphere. Be sure to identify which specific components of each historian's argument the documents support or refute.

- How did the ideology of separate spheres impact the lives of these three women?
- Which of the primary sources do you think Clinton and Hewitt would find most useful, and how might the authors use them to support their arguments?
- Which of the secondary sources do you think is best supported by the primary source evidence?
- What have these primary sources taught you about using race, class, and gender in historical analysis?

Primary Source 1

Lucretia Mott, *Discourse on Women*, 1849

This age is notable for its works of mercy and benevolence—for the efforts that are made to reform the inebriate and the degraded, to relieve the oppressed and the suffering. Women as well as men are interested in these works of justice and mercy. They are efficient co-workers, their talents are called into profitable exercise, their labors are effective in each department of reform. The blessing to the merciful, to the peacemaker is equal to man and to woman. It is greatly to be deplored, now that she is increasingly qualified for usefulness, that any view should be presented, calculated to retard her labors of love.

Why should not woman seek to be a reformer? . . . [I]f she is to fear to exercise her reason, and her noblest powers, lest she should be thought to "attempt to act the man," and not "acknowledge his supremacy"; if she is to be satisfied with the narrow sphere assigned her by man, nor aspire to a higher, lest she should transcend the bounds of female delicacy; truly it is a mournful prospect for woman. We would admit all the difference, that our great and beneficent Creator has made, in the relation of man and woman, nor would we seek to disturb this relation; but we deny that the present position of woman is her true sphere of usefulness: nor will she attain to this sphere, until the disabilities and disadvantages, religious, civil, and social, which impede her progress, are removed out of her way. These restrictions have enervated her mind and paralyzed her powers. . . .

So far from her "ambition leading her to attempt to act the man," she needs all the encouragement she can receive, by the removal of obstacles from her path, in order that she may become a "true woman." As it is desirable that man should act a manly and generous part, not "mannish," so let woman be urged to exercise a dignified and womanly bearing, not womanish. Let her cultivate all the graces and proper accomplishments of her sex, but let not these degenerate into a kind of effeminacy, in which she is satisfied to be the mere plaything or toy of society, content with her outward adornings, and with the tone of flattery and fulsome adulation too often addressed to her. True, nature has made a difference in her configuration, her physical strength, her voice, etc.—and we ask no change, we are satisfied with nature. But how has neglect and mismanagement increased this difference! It is our duty to develop these natural powers, by suitable exercise, so that they may be strengthened "by reason of use."

Source: Mott, Lucretia. *Discourse on Women*. Philadelphia, Penn.: T. B. Peterson, 1850.

Primary Source 2

Sojourner Truth, "And Ar'n't I a Woman?" 1851

And ar'n't I a woman? Look at me! Look at my arm! (*And she bared her right arm to the shoulder, showing her tremendous muscular power.*) I have plowed, and planted, and gathered into barns, and no man could head [surpass] me—and ar'n't I a woman? I could work as much and eat as much as a man when I could get it and bear de lash as well—and ar'n't I a woman? I have borne thirteen children, and seen 'em mos' all sold off to slavery, and when I cried out with my mother's grief, none but Jesus heard me—and ar'n't I a woman? . . . If my cup won't hold but a pint, and your'n holds a quart, wouldn't ye be mean not to let me have my little half-measure full? . . . He say women can't have as much rights as men, 'cause Christ wan't a woman! Whar did your Christ come from? . . . From God and a woman! Man had nothin' to do with Him.

Source: Truth, Sojourner. "And Ar'n't I a Woman?" (Speech at the Ohio Women's Rights Convention, 1851, Akron, Ohio). *History of Woman Suffrage.* Vol. 1, *1848–1861.* Edited by Elizabeth Cady Stanton, Susan B. Anthony, and Matilda Joslyn Gage. Rochester, NY: Susan B. Anthony, 1887.

Primary Source 3

Harriet H. Robinson, *Loom and Spindle, or Life among the Early Mill Girls*, 1898

One of the first strikes of cotton-factory operatives that ever took place in this country was that in Lowell, in October, 1836. When it was announced that the wages were to be cut down, great indignation was felt, and it was decided to strike, en masse. This was done. The mills were shut down, and the girls went in procession from their several corporations to the "grove" on Chapel Hill, and listened to "incendiary" speeches from early labor reformers. One of the girls stood on a pump, and gave vent to the feelings of her companions in a neat speech, declaring that it was their duty to resist all attempts at cutting down the wages. This was the first time a woman had spoken in public in Lowell, and the event caused surprise and consternation among her audience.... It was estimated that as many as twelve or fifteen hundred girls turned out, and walked in procession through the streets. They had neither flags nor music, but sang songs, a favorite (but rather inappropriate) one being a parody on "I won't be a nun."

Oh! isn't it a pity, such a pretty girl as I—

Should be sent to the factory to pine away and die?

Oh! I cannot be a slave,

I will not be a slave,

For I'm so fond of liberty

That I cannot be a slave.

Source: Robinson, Harriet H. *Loom and Spindle, or Life among the Early Mill Girls*. New York: Thomas Y. Crowell & Company, 1898.

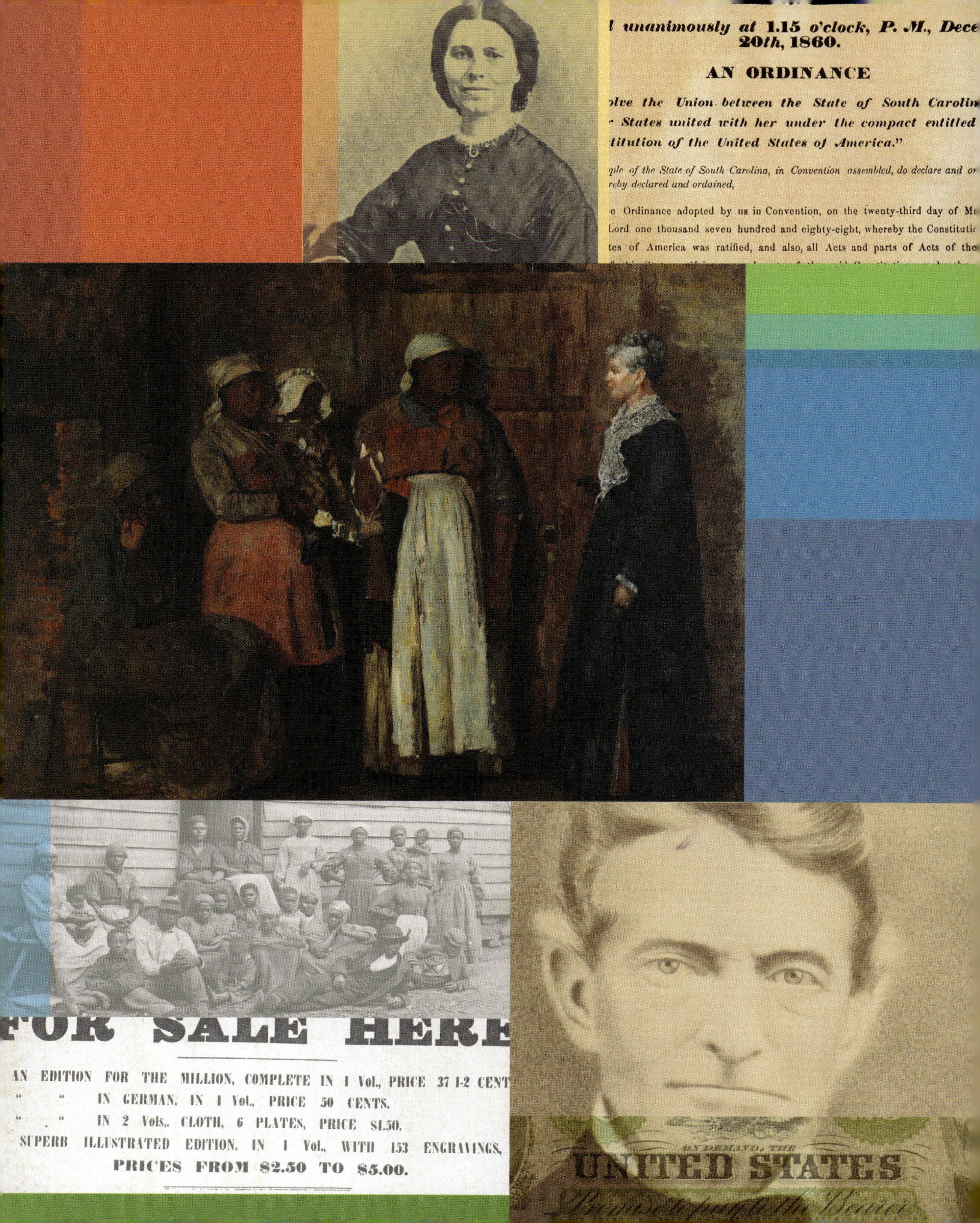
unanimously at 1.15 o'clock, P. M., Dece
20th, 1860.
AN ORDINANCE
olve the Union between the State of South Carolin
States united with her under the compact entitled
titution of the United States of America."
ple of the State of South Carolina, in Convention assembled, do declare and or
reby declared and ordained,
e Ordinance adopted by us in Convention, on the twenty-third day of M
Lord one thousand seven hundred and eighty-eight, whereby the Constituti
tes of America was ratified, and also, all Acts and parts of Acts of the
FOR SALE HERE
AN EDITION FOR THE MILLION, COMPLETE IN 1 Vol., PRICE 37 1-2 CENT
" " IN GERMAN, IN 1 Vol., PRICE 50 CENTS.
" " IN 2 Vols., CLOTH, 6 PLATES, PRICE $1.50.
SUPERB ILLUSTRATED EDITION, IN 1 Vol., WITH 153 ENGRAVINGS,
PRICES FROM $2.50 TO $5.00.
ON DEMAND, THE
UNITED STATES

A House Divided and Rebuilt

PART 4

By the end of the 1840s, the United States had expanded its territory to include Texas, California, and the Pacific Northwest. Years of warfare and lopsided government treaties had made that possible. The far western regions of the continent were controlled by Mexico and by Indigenous nations and empires that resisted White American expansion and vied for supremacy in the West. Only by conquering and displacing these other continental powers could the United States amass an empire of its own extending from the Atlantic to the Pacific.

Managing the newly acquired western territories became the nation's flashpoint issue. The economic and political differences among the nation's three distinctive regions—North, South, and West—grew even more explosive.

During the first half of the nineteenth century, a series of political compromises had left the fundamental issue of slavery and its future unsettled, but growing numbers of anti-slavery activists opposed efforts to extend slavery into the western territories that had been acquired from Mexico and Indigenous nations. Moreover, the 1850s witnessed the emergence of a new generation of national politicians who were less willing to compromise over the expansion of slavery.

The election of Abraham Lincoln in 1860 initially prompted eleven southern states to rebel against the United States. They believed that the basis of the southern economy, the "peculiar institution" of slavery, had to be protected at all costs. When Confederate cannons fired on Fort Sumter in Charleston Harbor and forced its surrender in April 1861, northerners, led by President Lincoln, mobilized for a civil war to restore the Union. The war would take the lives of more than 700,000 people in four years of fighting and would transform the nation in the process.

The United States' victory in 1865 ended slavery and preserved American democracy, but what kind of democracy would it be? The rights and status of the liberated African Americans remained uncertain. Although they were legally free, formerly enslaved people faced enormous challenges in their efforts to acquire money, property, homes, or education. While the Fourteenth Amendment (1868) guaranteed equal citizenship rights and the Fifteenth Amendment (1870) protected Black men's rights to vote, White southerners often violated the new federal laws. African Americans had to build newly free lives while confronting waves of discrimination and violence inflicted by those determined to protect the supremacy of White people.

The victorious American government also continued to extend its control over the West, dispatching U.S. soldiers from Civil War battlefields to the Great Plains to force Indigenous peoples off their ancestral lands and onto reservations. A new round of so-called "Indian wars" followed as Indigenous nations resisted being assimilated into American society. The Civil War may have ended, but the era of Reconstruction that followed witnessed violent conflicts over who was an American citizen—and what rights and protections that entailed.

EMIGRANTS CROSSING THE PLAINS, OR THE OREGON TRAIL (1869) German American painter Albert Bierstadt captures the majestic sights of the frontier, though the transcontinental trek was also grueling and bleak for many settlers.

Western Expansion and Southern Secession

1830–1861

CHAPTER 13

During the 1840s and after, Americans increasingly pushed beyond the nation's borders in search of more land, wealth, and power. Some looked south to Cuba and Central America. One such American, William Walker, a pistol-wielding lawyer and journalist, was eager to expand slavery into Central America. After sailing from San Francisco in 1855 on an unauthorized military expedition into Nicaragua, he and his men seized the city of Granada. Walker named himself the nation's president, only to be ousted two years later. Other similar expeditions targeted Cuba, Mexico, and Honduras.

Most Americans, however, invested their energy and firepower in expanding the United States' geographic reach westward to the Pacific. By 1860, some 4.3 million people had crossed the mile-wide Mississippi River and spread out across the Great Plains, over the Rocky Mountains, and along the Pacific coast.

People migrated westward mainly for economic reasons, usually fueled by gold fever or land lust. Trappers, farmers, miners, ministers, merchants, hunters, ranchers, teachers, servants, and prostitutes, among others, headed west. Others—such as Mormons and

CORE OBJECTIVES

1. Explain how, why, and where Americans moved west of the Mississippi River during the 1830s and 1840s.
2. Examine the causes of the Mexican-American War and its impact on national politics.
3. Describe how the federal government tried to resolve the issue of slavery in the western territories during the 1850s.
4. Analyze the appeal of the Republican Party to northern voters and how it led to Abraham Lincoln's victory in the 1860 presidential contest.
5. Explain why seven southern states seceded from the Union shortly after Lincoln's election in 1860.

Christian missionaries—sought religious freedom and the chance to win converts to their faith. Indigenous and Hispanic peoples who had long inhabited the region now faced an onslaught of American settlers.

Westward expansion was especially crucial to White southerners. To them, the West offered access to new lands on which enslaved people could grow cotton. They also wanted access to the Pacific coast trade routes for expanding the cotton trade into Asian markets. The West promised more political power, too, as the creation of new western states could boost pro-southern representation in Congress. These goals led southern politicians to become the nation's most aggressive expansionists. They imagined a future in which the North American continent would become one great slave-owning empire.

Standing in their way, however, were northerners who possessed a different vision for settling the continent that did not include the expansion of slavery. Early compromises on this issue soon gave way to bitter, irreconcilable division. Southern leaders eventually concluded that seceding from the United States, and sending the nation spiraling into civil war, was the only way to protect their interests and their vision for the continent.

> CORE **OBJECTIVE**
>
> **1.** Explain how, why, and where Americans moved west of the Mississippi River during the 1830s and 1840s.

Moving West

An anonymous journalist writing in 1845 gave a catchy name to America's aggressive spirit of westward expansion. "Our manifest destiny," the author wrote, "is to overspread the continent allotted by Providence for the free development of our yearly multiplying millions . . . [and for the] great experiment of liberty."

The idea of a "**manifest destiny**" implied that the United States had a God-given mission to extend its Christian republic and capitalist civilization from the Atlantic to the Pacific—and beyond. It offered a powerful, if self-serving, religious justification for expansion at the expense of Indigenous and Hispanic people, as well as the Spaniards and the British, all of whom resided in the western territories that Americans coveted.

The Western Frontier

> Western migration

Most of the new western settlers were American-born Whites from the Upper South and the Midwest. Very few free Black people joined in the migration. What spurred the migration westward was the nation's continuing population explosion and the widespread desire for *land*. Indeed, Americans viewed owning land as the essential condition of liberty. Voting rights initially were tied to land ownership, and farming or ranching provided the best opportunity for self-sufficiency.

Although some people traveled 13,000 miles by sea from New York City or Boston to California, most took the overland route across the Mississippi

manifest destiny The widespread belief that America was "destined" by God to expand westward across the continent into lands claimed by Native Americans as well as European empires.

MAP 13.1 OVERLAND TRAILS

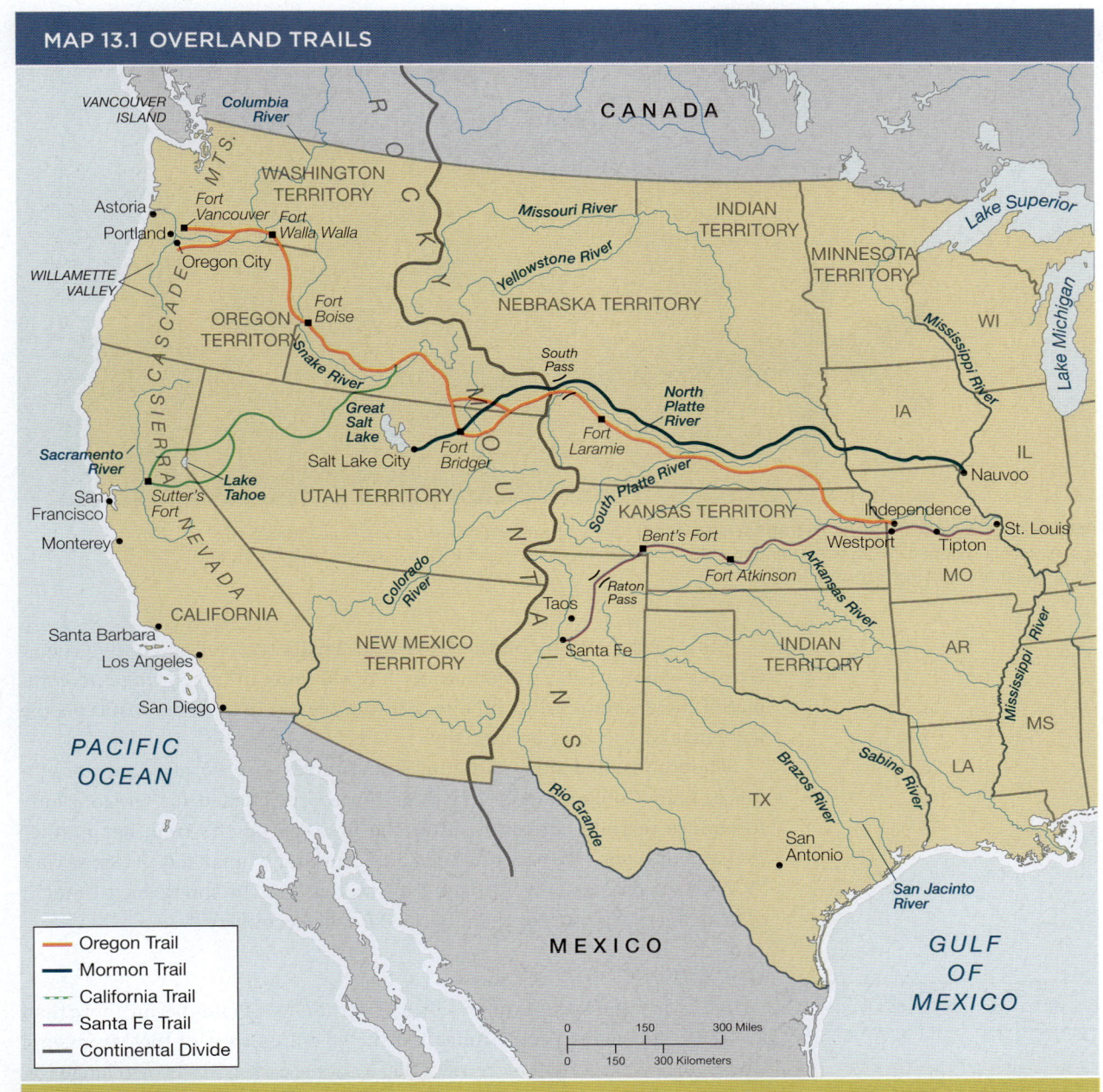

Legend:
- Oregon Trail
- Mormon Trail
- California Trail
- Santa Fe Trail
- Continental Divide

- Using the distance key at the bottom of the map, estimate the number of miles or kilometers each trail covered.
- For each trail, name the rivers and mountains that migrants on that route had to cross.
- Judging from your chapter reading as well as the map features, what were the perils of the Overland Trails? Which of these hardships are not shown on the map?

River, the Great Plains, and the Rocky Mountains (see Map 13.1). Between 1841 and 1867, 400,000 men, women, and children made the trek to California or Oregon. As many as 70,000 Mormons also emigrated to the Far West, making them one of the leading groups engaged in western settlement.

FUR TRADERS DESCENDING THE MISSOURI (1845) Originally titled *French-Trader, Half-Breed Son*, this oil painting depicts a White settler paddling down the river with his half–Native American son—not an uncommon sight in early America.

Most of the settlers on the **Overland Trails** traveled in family groups. Oregon-bound wagon trains usually left Missouri in late spring and completed the grueling 2,000-mile trek by winter. By 1845, some 5,000 people were making the journey annually.

Thousands died along the trails from hunger, disease, accidents, or violence. Lucy Cooke's family left their Iowa farm headed for Oregon, only to endure terrible hardships. After the first day on the trail, her mother exclaimed, "I wish we never had started." Another woman felt the same way. "What had possessed my husband," she wailed, "that he should have thought of bringing us way out through this God forsaken country?"

Indigenous Plains Peoples

> Conflicts over Indigenous lands

In 1840, when the massive migration across the Great Plains began, more than 325,000 Indigenous people inhabited the vast area west of the Mississippi River. They represented more than 200 nations, each with its own language, religion, cultural practices, and system of governance. Some were farmers, like the Lipan Apache and Pueblo; others were nomadic hunters, such as the Lakota and Comanche, following bison herds. They were joined by other Indigenous societies that had been forcibly removed from the eastern United States.

The **Comanche** had become the dominant people of the Southwest over the previous century. Commanding an empire (*Comanchería*) that stretched across the Great Plains and into New Mexico and Texas (see Map 13.2), the Comanche were a nomadic people who ruled on horseback. Their aim was not to control the land itself but the most valuable resources on it—especially bison and horses. Using a mix of diplomacy and often brutal violence, the

Overland Trails Trail routes followed by wagon trains bearing settlers and trade goods from Missouri to the Oregon Country, California, and New Mexico, beginning in the 1840s.

Comanche A Native American nomadic tribe from the southern Plains of North America. Comanche people today belong to the federally recognized Comanche Nation.

MAP 13.2 COMANCHE EMPIRE

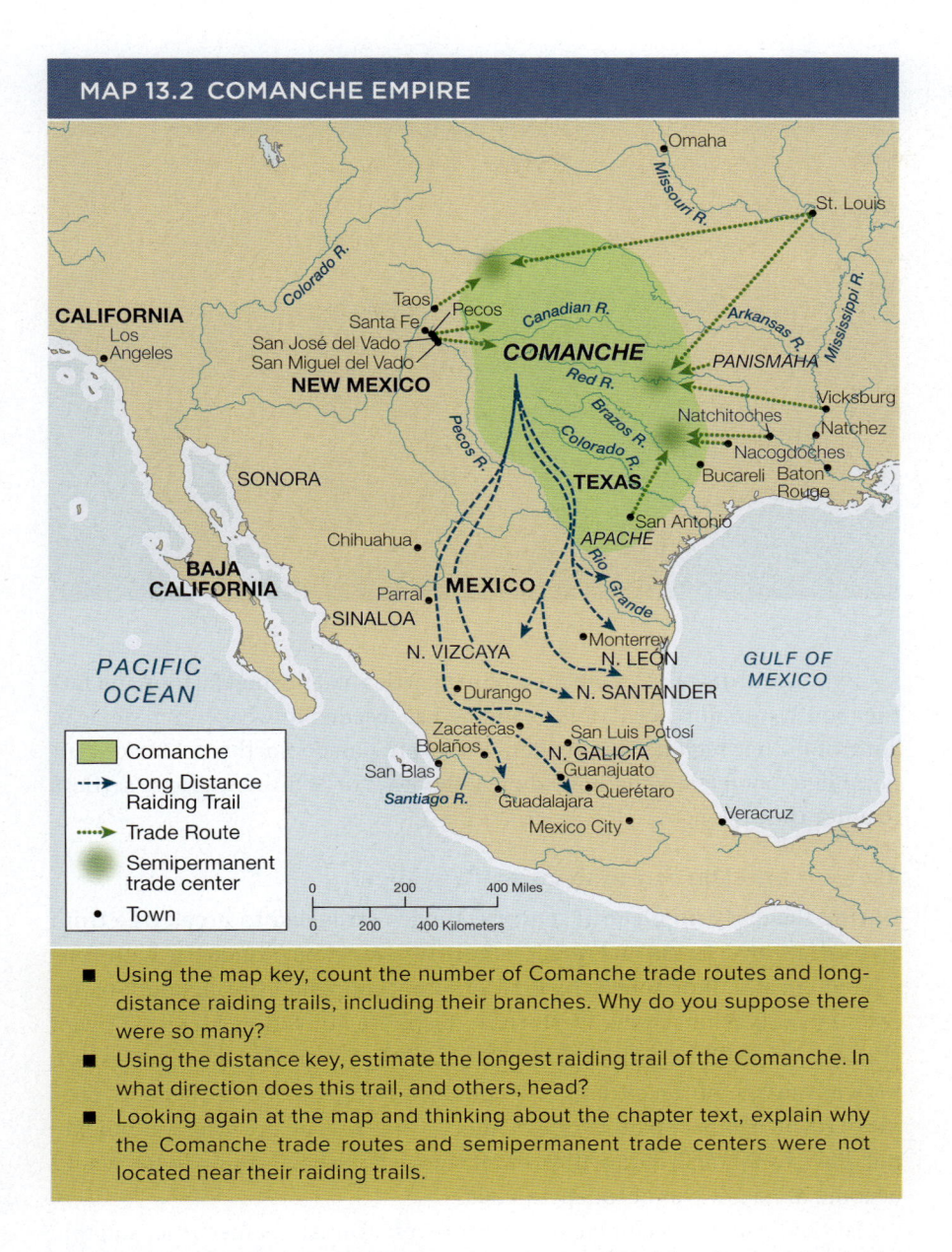

- Using the map key, count the number of Comanche trade routes and long-distance raiding trails, including their branches. Why do you suppose there were so many?
- Using the distance key, estimate the longest raiding trail of the Comanche. In what direction does this trail, and others, head?
- Looking again at the map and thinking about the chapter text, explain why the Comanche trade routes and semipermanent trade centers were not located near their raiding trails.

Comanche traveled long distances, seizing livestock by the thousands. By the early 1800s, the empire monopolized the region's horse trade and had established themselves as an economic powerhouse.

Comanche men who acquired horses gained status and wealth—as well as wives. They needed women to process the bison they hunted and to care for the horses they captured. One wife was not enough to perform all that labor herself, however, so Comanche men took up to ten wives and embraced polygyny (having multiple wives). Many of the wives were captives who had been seized during raiding missions and then sold as enslaved people. Their new owners married them and then incorporated them into their families, giving each woman the title of "chore wife."

> Comanche society and culture

COMANCHE VILLAGE, WOMEN DRESSING ROBES AND DRYING MEAT (1834–1835) Comanche women's work to process bison into leather and meat is depicted by the artist George Catlin, who traveled the West in the 1830s.

By the mid-1800s, Comanche raiding parties had pushed farther and farther south into northern Mexico and had succeeded in weakening Mexican control in that region. This sequence of events made northern Mexico vulnerable to conquest—and helped pave the way for White American settlers to enter the region.

Mexico and the Spanish-Speaking West

During the early nineteenth century, Mexico struggled to break free from Spanish control. In 1807, a French army led by Napoléon Bonaparte had occupied Spain and imprisoned the king, creating confusion throughout Spain's colonial possessions in the Western Hemisphere—including Mexico. Miguel Hidalgo y Costilla, a Creole priest (born in Mexico of European ancestry), took advantage of the situation to convince Indigenous and Hispanic people to revolt against Spanish rule in Mexico in 1810. The uprising was quickly put down by Spanish authorities, but it signaled the beginning of what would become Mexico's War of Independence.

In 1820, Mexicans launched another revolt against Spanish rule, and this time they succeeded. The last Spanish officials withdrew in 1821, enabling Mexico to become an independent republic. However, it struggled to develop a stable government and an effective economy, given that its wide-ranging territory was divided into nineteen different states, some of which were sparsely populated.

Amid the political upheaval in Mexico, Americans rushed to settle in Texas, which was part of Coahuila y Tejas, the northernmost Mexican state. Though permitted by the Mexican government to enter the region, the influx of Americans worried one Mexican official, who called for restrictions on American immigration: "Where others send invading armies," he explained, Americans "send their colonists."

THE JOURNEY WEST A photo from the nineteenth century shows a westward-bound man and woman beside their covered wagon. Life on the Overland Trails was rough and tiring, and even in these moments of apparent rest the pioneers had to cook their meals, tend to their horses or oxen, and maintain their wagon. **What challenges did the westward-bound face on their journey?**

During the 1830s and 1840s, thousands of White settlers also traversed the Santa Fe Trail from Missouri to New Mexico (see again Map 13.1). The trek was not for the fainthearted. In 1847 alone, Comanche warriors, joined by Kiowas and Pawnees, killed 47 Americans, destroyed 330 wagons, and stole 6,500 horses, cattle, and oxen along the trail.

At the same time, the inability of the Mexican government to subdue the Comanche in northern Mexico led some White Americans to conclude that the Mexican people were too weak to govern their sprawling nation. This attitude deepened longstanding prejudices toward Spanish-speaking peoples and heightened American interest in acquiring Mexican territory. Senator Lewis Cass from Michigan expressed the expansionist view when he declared: "We do not want the people of Mexico, either as citizens or as subjects. All we want is their . . . territory."

> The Santa Fe Trail to New Mexico

Mountains and Oregon Country

Other western areas were far different from Texas and New Mexico. The Oregon Country, as it was originally called, included what became the states of Oregon, Idaho, and Washington; parts of Montana and Wyoming; and the Canadian province of British Columbia. It was an unsettled region claimed by both Great Britain and the United States. By the Convention of 1818 (see Chapter 9), the two nations had agreed to "joint occupation" of the Oregon Country, each drawn there initially by the profitable trade in fur pelts.

The Great Migration Word of Oregon's fertile soil and mild climate spread eastward. By the late 1830s, farmers, missionaries, fur traders, and shopkeepers were traveling along the Oregon Trail, a 2,100-mile pathway that became the most strategic land route in North America. It spanned half

> The Oregon Trail to British-American Oregon Country

Oregon Fever The lure of fertile land and economic opportunities in the Oregon Country that drew hundreds of thousands of settlers westward, beginning in the late 1830s.

the continent from Missouri to Oregon, passing over flood-swollen rivers, scorching deserts, and treacherous mountain passes to the Pacific coast.

Soon, **Oregon Fever** swept the nation, "raging like any other contagion," as a journalist wrote in 1843. In 1841 and 1842, the first sizable wagon trains made the trip, and in 1843 the movement to the Oregon Country became one of the largest voluntary overland migrations in history.

For many, the migration across the punishing terrain came to symbolize the mythic American Dream, whereby a determined people risked everything to gain their own land and enjoy prosperity and independence. "Eastward I go only by force," said poet Henry David Thoreau. "But westward I go free."

Most of the people migrating to Oregon walked the 2,000-plus miles. All their food and worldly goods were packed in wagons called "prairie schooners" or Conestogas, named for the valley in Pennsylvania where they were first built. They were pulled by teams of four mules or oxen. One settler remembered that the wagon trains were like mobile communities: "Everybody was supposed to rise at daylight, and while the women were preparing breakfast, the men rounded up the cattle, took down the tents, yoked the oxen to the wagons, and made everything ready to start" once breakfast was over.

The wagon trains followed the Oregon Trail westward from Independence, Missouri, along the winding North Platte River into what is now Wyoming; through South Pass to Fort Bridger; then down the Snake River through what is now Idaho to the salmon-filled Columbia River. From there, they moved through the Cascade Mountains to their goal: Oregon's fertile Willamette Valley (Map 13.1). By 1845, about 5,000 people had settled there.

The arduous westward journey, usually five to six months long, was full of hardship amid climatic extremes: broiling summers, fierce thunderstorms and tornadoes, and bitterly cold winters. Wagons broke down, mules and oxen died, and diseases took their toll.

Cholera

Cholera claimed many lives. Tainted water and contaminated food spread the poisonous bacteria, which multiplied rapidly in the small intestine. Infected people experienced acute diarrhea followed by convulsions and vomiting; most died within hours of contracting the disease. Illinois emigrant John Nevin King found it awful to see "an acquaintance at noon well and in the enjoyment of health and learn in the evening that he is a corpse." On average, one grave appeared every eighty yards along the overland trails.

Despite the hardships and gruesome deaths, the growing numbers of migrants along the Oregon Trail tore through Native American lands and culture. Bison disappeared, and nations such as the Cheyenne and the Arapaho were forced to split into northern and southern branches. The Cayuse nation grew so frustrated with the large numbers and unfair trading practices of the Americans that in 1847, when they suspected two American missionaries of poisoning them, they attacked and killed fourteen people. The Americans retaliated with a series of massacres that left thousands of Native Americans dead.

The Settlement of California

California was also a powerful magnet for settlers. By the nineteenth century, Spanish Catholic missionaries, aided by Spanish soldiers, controlled most of the Native people living along the California coast. The friars enticed the Indigenous people into coastal "missions" by offering them gifts or impressing them with seemingly magical religious rituals. Once inside the missions, they were baptized as Catholics, taught Spanish, and stripped of their cultural heritage.

Catholic Missions The California Catholic missions served as churches, fortresses, homes, schools, and outposts of Spanish rule. They quickly became agricultural enterprises, producing crops, livestock, clothing, and household goods—both for profit and to supply the neighboring presidios (military garrisons). Indigenous people performed most of the labor. Instead of wages, they received clothing, food, housing, and religious instruction.

Native people who resisted were whipped or imprisoned, and those attached to the missions died at an alarming rate. Infectious disease was the primary threat, but the grueling labor regimen took a high toll as well. The Indigenous population along the California coast declined from 72,000 in 1769 to 18,000 by 1821.

> Spanish impact on Indigenous peoples in California

With Mexican independence in 1821, the Spanish missions slowly fell into disuse. By the time the first American settlers began to trickle into California, they found a vast, beautiful province with a small, scattered population of 6,000 Mexicans ruled by a few dominant *caballeros* or *rancheros*. These "gentlemen" owned the largest ranches in the province and hungered for more land.

In 1833–1834, the *rancheros* persuaded the Mexican government to pass the "secularization act," which had a disastrous effect on the Indigenous people. It allowed the government to take the missions, release the people from

> *Rancheros* dominate Mexican-owned California

SPANISH MISSIONS The Spanish mission Santa Clara de Asis, California, in 1777 was one of a series of religious outposts founded by Spanish Catholics to spread the Christian doctrine to the Native Americans. Once part of the missions, Native Americans were stripped of their cultural traditions and forced to work on mission lands.

SUTTER'S FORT Marking the end of the California Trail, Sutter's Fort was a prominent trading hub that depended on the labor and craftsmanship of the Native Americans who worked for Sutter. **How were the Native Americans at Sutter's Fort treated?**

church control, and transfer the missions' farmlands to *rancheros*. Within a few years, the government issued 700 new *rancho* grants of 4,500 to 50,000 acres along the California coast. These sprawling ranches resembled southern cotton plantations.

> Sutter's Fort and the development of the Sacramento Valley

John Sutter Among the newly arrived White Americans in California was forty-four-year-old John Augustus Sutter, a German-Swiss entrepreneur who had left behind his wife, four children, crushing debts, and a warrant for his arrest to make his fortune. At the junction of the Sacramento and American Rivers (later the site of the city of Sacramento), Sutter put local Indigenous and White laborers to work building a fort with walls eighteen feet tall. The fort, completed in 1843, was built on 230 acres of land granted to Sutter by the Mexican government. It would protect the settlers while also serving as a fur-trading post.

The people working for Sutter made wool blankets and hats; cultivated vast acres of wheat and corn; and raised herds of cattle, sheep, hogs, and horses. Sutter paid some of his workers, but enslaved others—particularly Native people, whom he whipped, jailed, and even executed when they disobeyed his orders. In the process, Sutter helped spur the American settlement of Hispanic California.

By 1845, there were perhaps 800 White American settlers in California, along with approximately 10,000 *Californios* (Hispanic Californians) and 150,000 Indigenous people. California's Mexican governor warned, "We find ourselves threatened by hordes of Yankee emigrants, who have already begun to flock into our country, and whose progress we cannot arrest."

> The Donner Party and cannibalism

The Donner Party The most tragic story of settlers traveling to California involved the group headed by George Donner, a sixty-two-year-old farmer from Illinois. In mid-April 1846, Donner led his family and seventy-four others from Springfield, Illinois, to the Oregon Trail.

The group started too late in the spring and took a shortcut that turned into a disaster. They had brought too little food, water, and clothing, and their inexperience proved to be fatal. In the Utah Territory's Wasatch Mountains, the party got lost, wasting three precious weeks. Then, crossing the desert before the Great Salt Lake, they suffered in the heat. Over 100 oxen were lost, forcing them to abandon several wagons with precious supplies.

Reaching Truckee Pass in eastern California, the Donner Party confronted a two-week blizzard. By December, the settlers—half of them children—were marooned by twenty feet of snow, with only enough food to last through the end of the month. Seventeen of the strongest members, calling themselves the "Forlorn Hope," decided to cross the pass on their own but became trapped by more snow. Two turned back; eight more died of exposure and starvation. Only seven of the "Forlorn Hope" group reached the Sacramento Valley.

By the time a rescue party reached the main camp two months later, thirteen people had died, and cannibalism had become common. The rescuers were horrified to find around the fire the bones, skulls, and half-eaten limbs of those who had died. As the survivors were led over the pass, George Donner and his wife, Tamsen, too weak and distressed to walk, stayed behind to die.

American Settlements in Texas

The northern Mexican province of Texas was a vast region sweeping westward from Louisiana to the Rocky Mountains in the north and the Rio Grande in the south (in Spanish, *Rio Grande* means "Big River"). During the 1820s, the United States had twice offered to buy Texas, but the Mexican government refused to sell. Meanwhile the Comanche, along with the Kiowa and Lipan Apache, continued to challenge Mexico for supremacy over the region.

By 1823, 3,000 Americans (or *Texians*, also called *Anglos* because they spoke English) were living in Texas. Most had migrated from southern states and snapped up inexpensive lands in east Texas that boasted the same rich soils as the cotton-growing South. They dreamed of great cotton wealth to be made in Texas—and they forced enslaved people to move with them.

> "Texians" settle lands in northern Mexico

The leading promoter of American settlement in Mexican-controlled Texas was Stephen Fuller Austin, a land developer (*empresario*). His father, Moses Austin, had convinced the Mexican government that American settlers could provide a buffer zone between Comanches to the north and Mexicans in the south.

Moses Austin died before he could enact his plan, but his son Stephen set it in motion in 1822. Thousands of hardy souls settled in Austin's Anglo-Texas "colony," on the lower Brazos and Colorado Rivers. Stephen Austin intended his colony to be a thriving community of cooperating families that would "redeem Texas from the wilderness."

Americans who rushed to settle in Austin's colony received 177 free acres and had access to thousands of acres of common pasture for ranching (Austin himself received 65,000 acres from the Mexican government). They settled close to the Gulf of Mexico coast, where they gained access to the port of

New Orleans for exporting cotton to the rest of the world. By 1827, they were exporting 400,000 pounds of cotton per year.

Soon, Mexican leaders grew worried that the Austin colony was maintaining close ties to the United States. In 1828, a Mexican military official visited Austin's settlement. Afterward, he reported that the effort by Americans to seize Texas from Mexico "will start from this colony" because the Mexican government was not taking "vigorous measures to prevent it." For their part, the settlers displayed a contempt for the brown-skinned Mexican people and became increasingly convinced that Mexico's unstable government was a threat to their interests.

Mexican officials became so concerned about the Americans living in Texas that in 1830 they outlawed immigration from the United States and built forts housing Mexican soldiers to enforce the new law.

Americans kept coming anyway—some of them as illegal immigrants. By 1835, the Texians and the people they enslaved outnumbered the Tejanos 10 to 1. In a letter to his cousin in 1835, Stephen Austin left no doubt about his plans: "It is very evident that Texas should be effectually, and fully, *Americanized*. . . . *Texas must be a slave country. It is no longer a matter of doubt*."

A Southbound Underground Railroad

> Enslaved people flee to Mexico

Austin understood that Mexico was becoming a country opposed to slavery. Its government had banned the importation of enslaved people in 1824; and then its new 1827 constitution began gradually freeing enslaved people across Mexico, before abolishing slavery outright ten years later. The Mexican government exempted Texians from some of its abolition policies but still angered the slaveowners in 1849 by declaring that "the slaves of other countries" who reached Mexico would be "free by the act of stepping on the national territory."

Enslaved people in Texas and the United States then seized the opportunity created by this policy and began fleeing deeper into Mexico to secure their freedom. They effectively created a new southbound Underground Railroad. By the 1860s, an estimated 3,000 to 5,000 individuals enslaved by Americans had successfully fled to Mexico. They included Mathilde Hennes, a woman enslaved in a part of Louisiana where nine enslaved people had been hanged in 1837 for daring to consider fleeing to Mexico. Undaunted, Hennes took off for Tamaulipas and went to work for wages as a house servant. Her former owner followed hotly on her footsteps but was arrested by Mexican police for attempted kidnapping. Hennes continued to live in Mexico with her freedom protected.

The Texas War for Independence

Political turmoil in Mexico aggravated the growing tensions with slave-owning American colonists. The Mexican government was "a plundering, robbing, autocratical, aristocratical jumbled up govt which is in fact no govt at all," fumed one of the Texians. "There is no security for life, liberty, or property." Mexican governance was indeed chaotic. The presidency changed hands constantly—General Antonio López de Santa Anna served in the position eleven times between 1833 and 1854.

Santa Anna himself was eccentric—he later gave his amputated leg a funeral—and he ruled like a dictator. Determined to tighten his grip on the growing American presence in Texas, he imprisoned Stephen Austin for treason in 1834 and sent troops into Texas. He also talked openly about enforcing anti-slavery laws there. Texians feared that the Mexican president planned to free "our slaves and to make slaves of us" by encouraging a rebellion. When enslaved people in Brazoria were caught planning such a revolt, the Texians whipped and hanged more than 100 of them.

By the fall of 1835, Texians resolved to be free of Mexican interference. They rebelled against the "despotism" of Santa Anna's government. In response, a furious Santa Anna ordered all Americans expelled from Texas and all rebels arrested and executed. As sporadic fighting erupted, hundreds of armed volunteers from southern states rushed to assist the 30,000 Texians in the **Texas Revolution** against a Mexican nation of 7 million people. "The sword is drawn!" Stephen Austin proclaimed, promising 800 acres of land to anyone who joined the rebellion.

The Alamo At San Antonio, in southern Texas, Santa Anna's 1,800-man army assaulted a small group of fewer than 200 Texians, Tejanos, and recently arrived American volunteers holed up in an abandoned Catholic mission called the Alamo. Leading the outmanned rebels was William B. Travis, a hot-tempered, pro-slavery, twenty-six-year-old Alabama lawyer and teacher. He ignored orders to retreat, insisting that "death was preferable to disgrace."

Among the Americans at the Alamo, the most celebrated was David Crockett, a Tennessee frontiersman, bear hunter, and sharpshooter who had fought the Creek Indians under Andrew Jackson and served as an anti-Jackson Whig congressman. Having lost his reelection bid, he encouraged those Tennesseans who voted against him to "go to hell, and I will go to Texas." Upon his arrival in San Antonio, Crockett told the Alamo defenders that he had come "to aid you all that I can in your noble cause."

Also among those at the Alamo was Juan Seguín, the son of a prominent Tejano family in San Antonio. At age eighteen, he had become the mayor (*alcalde*) of San Antonio. Like many other Mexicans living in Texas, he resented Santa Anna's tyranny so much that he joined the Texas independence movement and was made a captain in the Texian army.

In February 1836, Santa Anna demanded that the Americans in the Alamo surrender. Travis answered with cannon fire and a letter, promising that he was determined to "die like a soldier. *I shall never surrender or retreat. . . . VICTORY OR DEATH!*" Santa Anna's forces then launched a series of assaults. During the fighting, Travis sent Seguín to gather reinforcements and to deliver a message to Sam Houston, the commander of the Texian army: the Texans at the Alamo would "never surrender or retreat."

Texas Revolution (1835–1836)
A conflict between Texas colonists and the Mexican government that resulted in the creation of the separate Republic of Texas in 1836.

Texas Revolution against Santa Anna (1835–1836)

Battle of the Alamo (1836)

THE ALAMO David Crockett, pictured fighting with his rifle over his head after running out of bullets, joined the legendary battle to defend the Alamo against the Mexican army. **What were the consequences of the Battle of the Alamo?**

For eleven days, the Mexicans suffered heavy losses. Then, before dawn on March 6, the Alamo defenders awakened to the sound of Mexican bugles playing the dreaded "Degüello" ("Take No Prisoners"). Wave after wave of Santa Anna's men attacked. They were twice forced back, but on the third try, they broke through the battered north wall. As Travis was directing his men, a bullet smashed into his forehead, killing him instantly. The rebels ran out of bullets but fought on with tomahawks, knives, and rifle butts. In the end, however, virtually all were killed. A few days later, Juan Seguín returned with more troops, only to discover that they were too late.

Victory at the Alamo was costly for the Mexicans, however, as they lost more than 600 soldiers and also alienated many Texians. While Santa Anna proclaimed a "glorious victory," his aide wrote in his diary, "One more such 'glorious victory' and we are finished."

The furious fighting at the Alamo turned the rebellion into a war for Texas independence. On March 2, 1836, delegates from all fifty-nine Texas towns met at Washington-on-the-Brazos, 150 miles northeast of San Antonio. There they signed a declaration of independence from Mexican control. Over the next seventeen days, they drafted a constitution establishing the Republic of Texas.

Two weeks later, at the Battle of Coleto, a Mexican force again defeated a smaller Texian army. The Mexicans marched 465 captured Texians to a fort in the nearby town of Goliad. Despite pleas from his men to show mercy, Santa Anna ordered the captives killed as "pirates and outlaws." On Palm Sunday, March 27, 303 Texians were marched out of Goliad and shot. The massacres at the Alamo and Goliad fueled a burning desire for revenge among the Texians.

Sam Houston The commander-in-chief of the still-forming Texian army was Sam Houston, a hard-drinking frontiersman born in Virginia and raised in eastern Tennessee. As a young teen, he had left his widowed mother and eight siblings and lived among the Cherokee for a time, learning their language and customs.

Like David Crockett, Sam Houston had served under General Andrew Jackson during the War of 1812. At the Battle of Horseshoe Bend in Alabama in 1814, he was seriously wounded but insisted on rejoining his unit, only to be shot twice in the right arm and shoulder.

After the war, Sam Houston became an attorney, a U.S. congressman, and, in 1827, governor of Tennessee. In 1829, despondent and often drunk, he resigned the governorship and went "home" to the Cherokee in the Arkansas Territory. There he married a Cherokee woman and was formally "adopted" by the Cherokee Nation. A few years later he moved to Texas, became a Mexican citizen, and started a law practice.

When the Americans in Texas declared their independence from Mexico on March 4, 1836, Houston became "Commander-in-Chief of the Armies of the Republic of Texas." Houston was a risk taker—a quality the Texians sorely needed against the much larger Mexican army.

The Battle of San Jacinto After learning of the massacre at the Alamo, Houston's troops retreated, hoping that Santa Anna's pursuing army would make a mistake. On April 21, 1836, the overconfident Mexican general let his guard down setting up their encampment in a vulnerable location. Houston's army of 900 determined fighters engaged Santa Anna's 1,600 troops on that site near the San Jacinto River, about twenty-five miles southeast of what is now the city of Houston. At 4:30 in the afternoon, the Texians charged the Mexican lines screaming "Remember the Alamo! Remember Goliad!" The Texians and Tejanos overwhelmed the Mexicans.

The battle lasted only eighteen minutes, but Houston's troops spent the next two hours slaughtering fleeing Mexican soldiers. It was, said a Texian, a "frightful sight to behold." Some 650 Mexicans were killed and 300 captured. The Texians lost only 11 men.

General Santa Anna escaped, only to be captured the next day. Brought before Sam Houston, the Mexican leader begged the Texian commander to be "generous to the vanquished." Houston replied, "You should have remembered that at the Alamo." In the end, Santa Anna bought his freedom by signing a treaty recognizing the independence of the Republic of Texas.

SAM HOUSTON Having led the Texans to a sweeping victory over the Mexicans in the Battle of San Jacinto, Houston went on to serve as the first president of the Republic of Texas.

Santa Anna is defeated

The Lone Star Republic

In 1836, the Lone Star Republic, as Texians called their new nation, legalized slavery and banned free Black people. Voters elected Sam Houston the Republic's first president. But they still faced another adversary in the region—the Comanche, who alarmed the Texians by continuing to extend their trading empire throughout Texas (see again Map 13.2). The need for protection encouraged the Texians to vote overwhelmingly for annexation to the United States. But the issue of statehood for Texas soon became entwined within the growing sectional dispute over slavery.

> *Delayed recognition of the Republic of Texas*

President Andrew Jackson wanted Texas to join the United States. He knew, however, that adding Texas as a slave state would ignite a quarrel between North and South that would fracture the Democratic Party and endanger the election of New Yorker Martin Van Buren, his handpicked successor. Worse, any effort to add Texas to the Union would likely mean a war with Mexico, which refused to recognize Santa Anna's granting of Texian independence. So Jackson delayed official recognition of the Republic of Texas until his last day in office, early in 1837. Van Buren then did as predicted: he avoided all talk of Texas annexation during his single term as president.

The Tyler Presidency and Texas

When William Henry Harrison became president in 1841, he was the oldest man (sixty-eight) and the first Whig to win the office. The Whigs had emerged in opposition to Andrew Jackson, promoting federal government support for internal improvements and economic growth through high tariffs. Harrison, however, was elected primarily on the strength of his military record—a singular victory at the Battle of Tippecanoe thirty years before. In the end, it mattered little, for Harrison served the shortest term of any president.

> *Death of William Henry Harrison*

Exactly one month after his inauguration, Harrison died of pneumonia, the first president to die in office. Vice President John Tyler of Virginia assumed the presidency. At fifty-one, the tall, thin, slave-owning Virginian was the youngest president to date; but he had lots of political experience, having served as a state legislator, governor, congressman, and senator.

Now, as president, Tyler began working to make Texas the twenty-eighth state. At the same time, however, he opposed fellow Whig Henry Clay's so-called American System—a program that called for the federal government to promote industrial development.

> *Conflicts between Clay and Tyler*

When Congress met in a special session in 1841, Clay introduced a series of controversial resolutions. He demanded that a new Bank of the United States be created. He also pledged to revive the "distribution" program whereby the money raised from federal land sales went to the states, and he urged that tariffs be raised on imported goods.

Clay then used threats and intimidation to push his program through Congress. Legislators began calling him "the Dictator." With more tact, Clay might have avoided a series of nasty disputes with Tyler over financial issues. Driven by his lust to be president, however Clay abandoned any instinct to compromise and bullied legislators to follow his lead.

Although Tyler agreed to sign a higher tariff bill, he vetoed Clay's pet project of a new national bank. Clay responded by calling the president a traitor to his party. He then convinced Tyler's entire cabinet to resign, except for Secretary of State Daniel Webster. Tyler replaced the defectors with anti-Jackson Democrats who, like him, had become Whigs.

Tyler vetoes national bank bill

The Whigs then took the unprecedented step of expelling Tyler from the party, dismissing him as "His Accidency" and the "Executive Ass." By 1842, Tyler had become a president without a party, shunned by both Whigs and Democrats but loved by those promoting territorial expansion. A festering economic depression coincided with the political turmoil, but Tyler remained determined to annex Texas.

Efforts to Annex Texas

In April 1843, South Carolinian John C. Calhoun, then secretary of state, sent to the Senate for ratification a treaty annexing Texas. There it died by a vote of 35–16. Northern senators, many of whom were abolitionists, refused to add another slave state. Others feared that annexing Texas would trigger a war with Mexico.

Texas annexation treaty defeated

By now, Texan leaders were frustrated that independence had not led to annexation. Sam Houston threatened to expand the Republic of Texas to the Pacific. But with little money in the treasury, rising government debt, and continuing tensions with the Comanche and with Mexico, the new republic was in no position to spread its borders.

The Lone Star Republic had no infrastructure—no banks, no schools, and no industries. It remained a frontier community of scattered log cabins and few cities. Houston decided that Texas had two choices: annexation to the United States or closer economic ties to Great Britain, which had begun to buy cotton from Texas planters. Meanwhile, thousands more Americans poured into Texas. The population more than tripled between 1836 and 1845, from 40,000 to 150,000, and the enslaved Black population grew even faster than the White population.

The Election of 1844

Both political parties initially hoped to keep the divisive Texas issue out of the 1844 presidential campaign.

At the Democratic Convention, however, annexationists, including Andrew Jackson, nominated James Knox Polk, former Speaker of the House and former governor of Tennessee. Like Tyler, Polk was an aggressive expansionist. On the ninth ballot, he became the first "dark horse" (unexpected) candidate to win a major-party nomination. At Polk's insistence, the Democrats' platform called for the annexation of both the Oregon Country and Texas.

ELECTION OF 1844 A political cartoon depicts the decline of the Whig Party—represented by a raccoon—from 1810 to 1844. What used to be a plump, well-fed raccoon was now an emaciated animal with a fraction of the strength. **Based on the 1844 election, how accurate was this illustration's representation of the Whigs?**

By promoting southern and western expansionism, the Democrats forced the Whigs' candidate Henry Clay to alter his position at the last minute. Once opposed to adding Texas to the United States, Clay dropped his "objection to the annexation" if it could be achieved "without dishonor, without war, with the common consent of the Union, and upon just and fair terms."

> James K. Polk elected president (1844)

Clay's change of heart shifted more anti-slavery votes to the new Liberty Party (the anti-slavery party that formed in 1840), which increased its count in the presidential election from about 7,000 in 1840 to more than 62,000 in 1844. In the western counties of New York, the Liberty Party drew just enough votes from Clay and the Whigs to give the state to Polk and the Democrats.

James K. Polk

Born near Charlotte, North Carolina, Polk had graduated first in his class at the University of North Carolina, then moved to Tennessee, where he became a successful lawyer, planter, and political figure. He served fourteen years in Congress (four as Speaker of the House) and two years as governor.

At age forty-nine, Polk was the youngest president up to that time. Polk owed his election to two people: Andrew Jackson, his hero and mentor; and Sarah Childress Polk, his politically savvy wife who served as his unofficial chief of staff. She managed his correspondence and used her considerable social skills to practice what was called "parlor politics," hosting numerous dinner gatherings with political figures where she smoothed over her husband's prickly personality.

The Polks never had children, and they depended on enslaved men and women to run their household, including at the White House. This gave Sarah freedom to involve herself in political affairs. "Why should you stay at home?" James once asked, "To take care of the house?" Sarah never went so far as to advocate for women's rights, but her formidable skills as a politician nevertheless helped thrust her husband into the presidency and into the firestorm over western expansion.

JAMES AND SARAH POLK Like other political couples of their time, James and Sarah Polk formed a partnership when they married in 1824 that enabled Sarah to influence American politics long before women could vote.

The State of Texas

Texas joined the United States just *before* James K. Polk became president. In John Tyler's final months as president, he had convinced Congress to annex Texas. On March 1, 1845, Tyler signed the resolution admitting Texas to the Union as the fifteenth slave state.

Meanwhile, after gaining their independence from Mexico, White Texans had turned on the Tejanos (Mexican-born Texans) who had supported the revolution. "White folks and Mexicans were never made to live together," an American woman explained to a visiting journalist. "The Mexicans had no business [living] here." By then, Tejanos were being uprooted and expelled.

In 1857, White Texan wagon drivers (teamsters) killed seventy-five Mexican-born competitors in what was called the Cart War. Juan Seguín, who had led a cavalry unit against Mexican forces at San Jacinto and had served as mayor of San Antonio, lamented that he "had become a foreigner in my native land."

Expulsion of the Tejanos

Polk's Goals

Perhaps because he pledged to serve only one term, Polk was a president in a hurry. His top priority was territorial expansion. He wanted to add Oregon, California, and New Mexico to the Union. In keeping with long-standing Democratic beliefs, Polk wanted lower tariffs to allow more foreign goods to compete in the American marketplace and thereby help drive consumer prices down. Congress agreed by approving a new tariff law in 1846.

Polk's goals: territorial expansion, reducing import tariffs

Polk also twice vetoed Whig-passed bills for federally funded infrastructure projects. His efforts to reverse Whig economic policies satisfied the slave-owning South but angered northerners and westerners. The northerners wanted higher tariffs to protect their industries from British competition, and the westerners wanted federally financed roads and harbors.

Oregon

Meanwhile, the dispute with Great Britain over the Oregon Country boundary heated up as expansionists insisted that Polk take the whole region rather than split it with the British. Polk was willing to go to the brink of war to do so. "If we do have war," the president blustered, "it will not be our fault."

Fortunately, the British were not willing to risk war. On June 15, 1846, James Buchanan, Polk's secretary of state, signed the Buchanan-Pakenham Treaty. This agreement extended the border between the United States and British possessions in Canada westward to the Pacific coast along the 49th parallel (see Map 13.3). The region south of that line became part of the United States and would be known as the Oregon Territory.

Buchanan-Pakenham Treaty (1846): Oregon becomes American territory

It took a combination of treaties and violence for White Americans to gain control over lands in the West. Those who had migrated west during the 1830s and 1840s were driven by a desire for land and a firm belief in their "manifest destiny." But they soon discovered that their expansionist goals collided with those of European, Mexican, and Indigenous nations, all of which claimed western lands as their own. To gain this vast territory, the Americans therefore had to negotiate or fight—or sometimes a mix of both. They fought deadly battles against Indigenous societies, resisted Mexican control over Texas, and negotiated with the British Empire to extend a crucial border westward to the Pacific coast. These gains did not end the United States' desire for expansion, however. Indeed, a war with Mexico was already brewing.

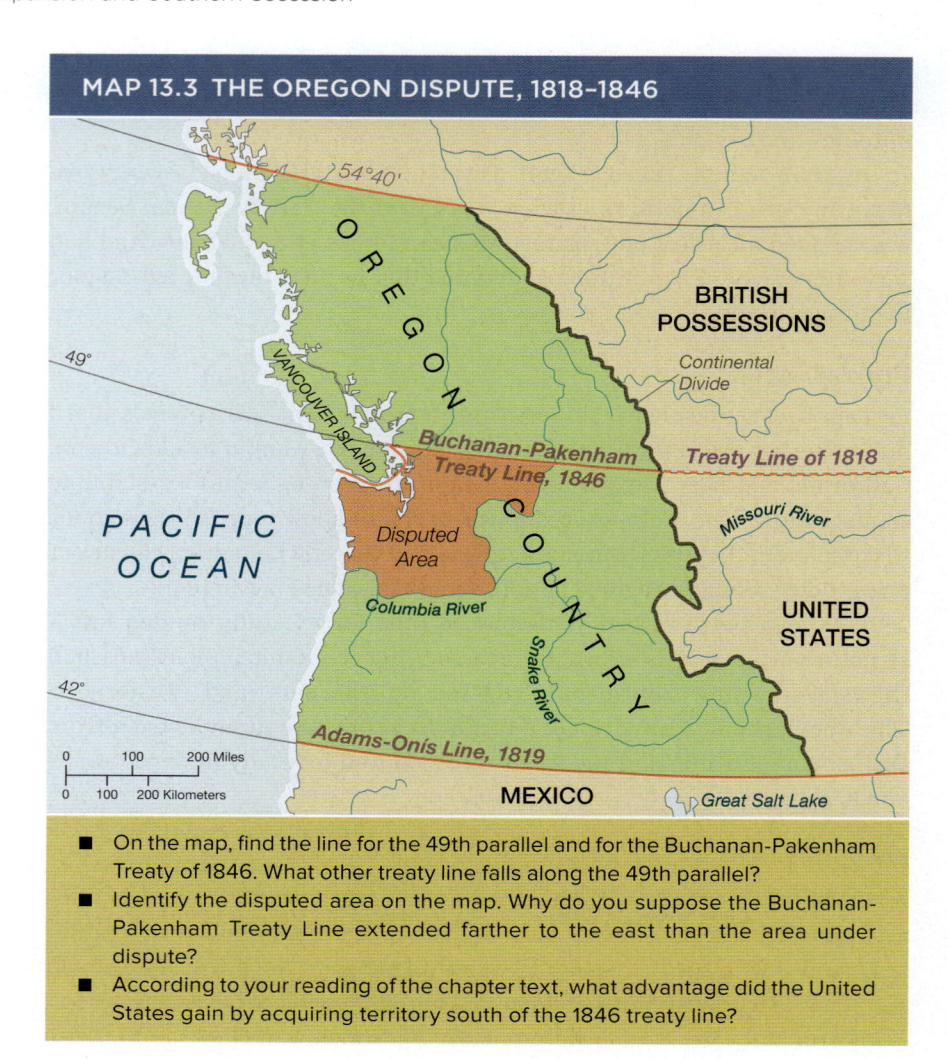

MAP 13.3 THE OREGON DISPUTE, 1818–1846

- On the map, find the line for the 49th parallel and for the Buchanan-Pakenham Treaty of 1846. What other treaty line falls along the 49th parallel?
- Identify the disputed area on the map. Why do you suppose the Buchanan-Pakenham Treaty Line extended farther to the east than the area under dispute?
- According to your reading of the chapter text, what advantage did the United States gain by acquiring territory south of the 1846 treaty line?

CORE OBJECTIVE
2. Examine the causes of the Mexican-American War and its impact on national politics.

Polk and Congress declare war

The Mexican-American War

On March 6, 1845, two days after James K. Polk became president, the Mexican government broke off relations with the United States to protest the annexation of Texas. Polk wanted a war with Mexico, which would likely end with the U.S. acquisition of California and New Mexico—but he did not want Americans to fire the first shot. So he sent several thousand troops, under General Zachary Taylor, to the Rio Grande. That was some 150 miles south of the Nueces River, which both sides had publicly recognized as the southern border (see Map 13.4). The Mexican government resisted Polk's attempt to extend the southern border to the Rio Grande.

On the evening of May 9, President Polk learned that Mexican troops had attacked U.S. soldiers along the Rio Grande. Eleven Americans were killed. The president now had the pretext for war that he had been seeking. Polk asked Congress for a declaration of war, only to have a Delaware senator insist that sending troops to the Rio Grande had been "as much an act of aggression on our part as is a man pointing a pistol at another's heart."

Despite such concerns, Congress complied with Polk's request and authorized the recruitment of 50,000 soldiers. In the South, where expansion fever ran high, the war was immensely popular. So many men rushed to volunteer that thousands had to be turned back. Eventually, 112,000 Whites served in the war (Black people were banned from military service).

On balance, the United States had formidable advantages in the war. America's population was 20 million compared with Mexico's 7 million. The Mexican economy was essentially bankrupt, while America's prospered. The U.S. forces had better weapons, training, resources, and leadership. The Mexicans' main advantage was that they were fighting on their own territory.

Opposition to the War

In New England and among northern abolitionists, however, there was much less enthusiasm for "Mr. Polk's War." Congressman John Quincy Adams, the former president, called it "a most unrighteous war." The fiery Boston abolitionist William Lloyd Garrison charged that the war was one of American "aggression, of invasion, of conquest."

Most Whigs across the North, including a young Illinois congressman named Abraham Lincoln, also opposed the war, stressing that President Polk had maneuvered the Mexicans into attacking. The United States, many insisted, had no reason for placing its army in the disputed border region between Texas and Mexico.

Heading into Battle

Many of the U.S. soldiers fighting in Mexico were frontier toughs who lacked uniforms, equipment, and discipline.

They abused and slaughtered Mexicans wherever they found them—men, women, and children. George Gordon Meade, who would become a celebrated Union general during the Civil War, noted that the undisciplined Americans murdered Mexicans simply "for their amusement."

The Mexican-American War, from March 1846 to April 1848, was fought on four fronts: southern Texas, central Mexico, New Mexico, and California. Early on, in 1846, the U.S. Army scored victories north of the Rio Grande, at Palo Alto (May 8) and Resaca de la Palma (May 9). On May 18, General Zachary Taylor's army crossed the Rio Grande and occupied Matamoros (see again Map 13.4). Those quick victories brought instant popularity to Taylor, a slave-owning Louisiana Whig. Polk agreed to public demand that Taylor be made overall commander.

Zachary Taylor becomes commander

The Annexation of California

Of all the Mexican territories President Polk coveted, California was the grand prize, for he saw it as the commercial gateway to the riches of Asia. Accordingly, he fashioned an elaborate scheme to seize Mexico's westernmost province.

MAP 13.4 THE MEXICAN-AMERICAN WAR, 1846–1848

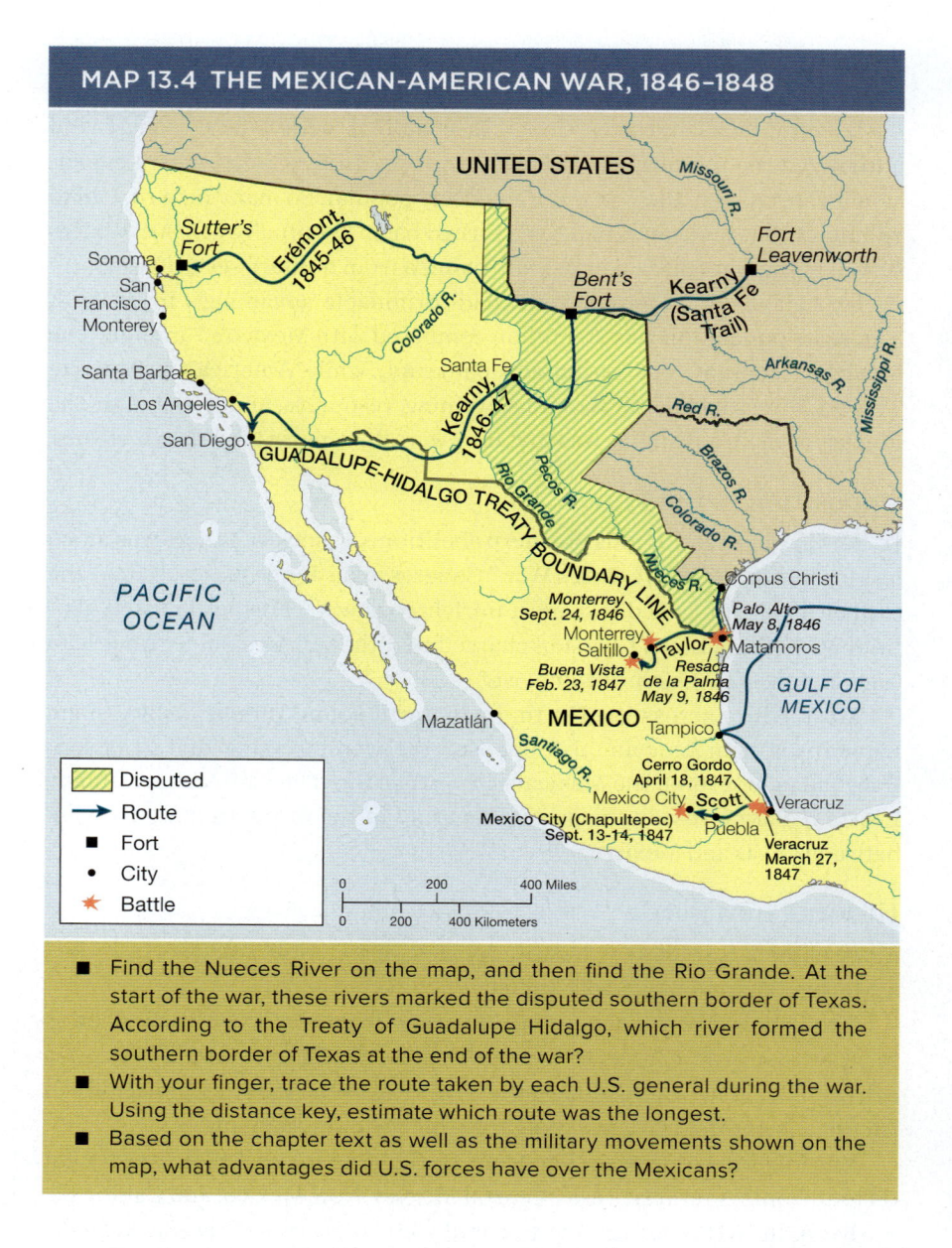

- Find the Nueces River on the map, and then find the Rio Grande. At the start of the war, these rivers marked the disputed southern border of Texas. According to the Treaty of Guadalupe Hidalgo, which river formed the southern border of Texas at the end of the war?
- With your finger, trace the route taken by each U.S. general during the war. Using the distance key, estimate which route was the longest.
- Based on the chapter text as well as the military movements shown on the map, what advantages did U.S. forces have over the Mexicans?

Polk's plan centered on using John C. Frémont, an ambitious junior army officer famous for having helped map the Oregon Trail. Near the end of 1845, Frémont recruited sixty-two frontiersmen, scientists, soldiers, marksmen, and hunters for a secret mission and led them into California's Sacramento Valley (Map 13.4). His official purpose was to find the best route for immigrants; his actual goal was to conquer Mexican California.

Frémont was a free-spirited adventurer who disobeyed orders, violated promises, and rarely acknowledged mistakes. Once in California, he and his troops abandoned their exploration and research mission and focused instead on organizing a rebellion against the Mexican officials. The Mexican governor quickly ordered Frémont and his "band of robbers" to leave.

CALIFORNIA BEAR FLAG REVOLT OF 1846 John C. Frémont's soldiers joined other Americans in proclaiming the Republic of California on June 14, 1846. They hoisted a flag that reflected their aspirations: The bear conveyed strength; while the star, a symbol of sovereignty, represented their desire to govern themselves as an independent republic.

They grudgingly did so, traveling north to Oregon, only to return after receiving secret messages from President Polk. The messages revealed that the United States would soon be at war with Mexico and that Frémont should seize control of California. Frémont's men then joined other Americans in capturing Sonoma, the largest settlement in northern California, in June 1846. They proclaimed the Republic of California and hoisted a flag featuring a grizzly bear and star, a version of which would later become the state flag.

What became known as the Bear Flag Republic lasted only a month, however. In July, the commander of the U.S. Pacific Fleet, having heard of the outbreak of hostilities with Mexico, sent troops ashore at Monterrey to raise the American flag and claim California as part of the United States.

Before the end of July, another navy officer, Robert F. Stockton, led the American occupation of Santa Barbara and Los Angeles, on the southern California coast. By mid-August 1846, Mexican resistance in California had evaporated. Stockton then declared himself governor, with Frémont as military governor in the north.

At the same time, another U.S. military expedition headed for New Mexico. On August 18, General Stephen Kearny and a small army entered Santa Fe. Kearny then led 300 men westward toward southern California, where they joined Stockton's forces at San Diego (Map 13.4). They took control of Los Angeles on January 10, 1847, and the remaining Mexican forces surrendered.

> California becomes an American territory (1846)

> U.S. Army takes New Mexico (1846)

War in Northern Mexico

Both California and New Mexico had been taken from Mexican control before General Zachary Taylor fought his first major battle in northern Mexico. In September 1846, Taylor's army assaulted the fortified city of Monterrey (Map 13.4), which surrendered after a five-day siege. The dictator General Antonio López de Santa Anna, who had been forced out of power in 1845, had previously sent word to Polk from his exile in Cuba that he would secure an end to the war if allowed to return to Mexico.

> Santa Anna returns to Mexico

In August 1846, on Polk's orders, Santa Anna was permitted to return to Mexico on the condition that he stay out of politics and the military. The Mexican leader had lied, however. Soon he was again president of Mexico and in command of the Mexican army. In October 1846, he prepared to attack. When the Mexican general invited the outnumbered Americans to surrender, Zachary Taylor responded, "Tell him to go to hell."

> The Battle of Buena Vista (1847)

That launched the hard-fought Battle of Buena Vista (February 22–23, 1847). Both sides claimed victory, but the Mexicans suffered five times as many casualties as the Americans. One of the U.S. soldiers killed was Henry Clay, Jr., whose famous father had lost to Polk in the 1844 presidential campaign. The elder Clay, devastated by his son's death, condemned Polk's "unnecessary" war of "offensive aggression" and opposed any effort to use the war as a means of acquiring Mexican territory "for the purpose of introducing slavery into it."

In August, General Winfield Scott's outnumbered invasion force marched from Veracruz on the eastern coast toward heavily defended Mexico City, the national capital some 200 miles away. After four battles in which they overwhelmed the Mexican defenders and killed hundreds of civilians, U.S. forces arrived at the gates of Mexico City in early September 1847 (Map 13.4).

The Saint Patrick's Battalion

General Winfield Scott's triumphant assault on Mexico City was not without problems. Since the start of the war, some 7,000 American soldiers had deserted. Several hundred of them, mostly poor Catholic Irish and German immigrants who resented the abuse inflicted on them by Protestant officers, changed sides and formed the Saint Patrick's Battalion in the Mexican army.

During one of the battles for Mexico City, the Americans captured seventy-two of the Catholic defectors, most of whom were sentenced to death.

At dawn on September 13, 1847, the *San Patricios* (as these fighters were called), their hands and feet bound, were made to stand in the hot sun in sight of Chapultepec, the last Mexican fortress protecting Mexico City. There they were forced to watch the battle unfold. When the American troops scaled the walls of the fortress and raised the U.S. flag, the *San Patricios* were all hanged simultaneously.

The Treaty of Guadalupe Hidalgo (1848)

After the fall of Mexico City, the Mexican leader Santa Anna resigned and fled the country. Peace talks began early the next year. News of the victory thrilled American expansionists. The editor John O'Sullivan, who had popularized the phrase "manifest destiny," shouted, "More, More, More! Why not take all of Mexico?"

By the **Treaty of Guadalupe Hidalgo**, signed in February 1848, a humiliated Mexico gave up half its entire territory: all of Texas north of the Rio Grande; the territories that would become the states of California, Arizona, New Mexico; and significant parts of Colorado, Utah, Wyoming, and Nevada (Map 13.4).

Treaty of Guadalupe Hidalgo (1848) The treaty between the United States and Mexico that ended the Mexican-American War.

The treaty guaranteed the 150,000 Indigenous people and the 80,000 Mexicans living in the ceded territories that they could keep their property, receive U.S. citizenship, and retain their Catholic religion. About 90 percent of them chose to stay in the new American territories.

Over time, however, as Americans streamed in, the ruthless among them cheated and killed Mexican-born residents and Native people. Mexican Americans were forced to accept the lowest-paying jobs under the worst working conditions. Most of them were manual laborers, *vaqueros* (cowboys), miners, railroad workers, or cartmen, transporting food and supplies. Others had their lands confiscated by the Americans.

> Americans' treatment of the Mexicans and Native Americans

Except for a small addition made by the Gadsden Purchase of 1853, the annexations of Mexican territory rounded out the continental United States and nearly doubled its size. In return for what President Polk called "an immense empire," the United States paid Mexico $15 million. The disgraced Mexican leader Santa Anna spoke for most Mexicans when he said the treaty would always be a source of "eternal shame and bitter regret for every Mexican."

The War's Legacies

The Mexican-American War marked the first time that U.S. military forces had defeated and occupied another country. More than 13,000 Americans died in the conflict, 11,550 of them from disease. The war remains one of the deadliest in American history in terms of the percentage of soldiers killed. Of every 1,000 U.S. soldiers in Mexico, some 110 died.

The U.S. victory helped end the prolonged economic depression. As the years passed, however, critics charged that the conflict was a shameful war of conquest directed by a president bent on acquiring new territory for the likely expansion of slavery. Ulysses S. Grant, who fought in the war, later called it "one of the most unjust wars ever waged by a stronger against a weaker nation."

The acquisition of the northern Mexican provinces made the United States a transcontinental nation and led to a dramatic expansion of the federal government. In 1849, Congress created the Department of the Interior to supervise the distribution of land, the creation of new territories and states, and the "protection" of Indigenous people and their reservations. Americans now had their long-coveted western empire, although it was built upon the conquest and exploitation of Mexican and Native peoples.

The Mexican-American War had resulted from a chain of events beginning with the U.S. annexation of Texas in 1845. Subsequent U.S. efforts to formally acquire Texas, California, and New Mexico met resistance from the Mexican government. President Polk, eager for war, dispatched U.S. troops to the Rio Grande; and when Mexican troops crossed the river to fire on the American soldiers, the U.S. Congress authorized a declaration of war. The conflict soon radiated far beyond Texas and provoked a contentious political debate in American politics. Tensions between northern and southern leaders intensified as they battled over whether to support the war, and whether slavery should be extended to any of the new territories acquired from Mexico.

Slavery in the Territories

> **CORE OBJECTIVE**
> **3.** Describe how the federal government tried to resolve the issue of slavery in the western territories during the 1850s.

As tensions surrounding the Mexican War revealed, by midcentury the political storm clouds were forming over the fate of slavery. The United States had developed two different societies, one in the North and the other in the South, and now the addition of the West put them at odds over the nation's future. In 1833, Andrew Jackson had predicted that pro-slavery firebrands like John C. Calhoun "would do any act to destroy this union and form a southern confederacy bounded, north, by the Potomac River." By 1848, Jackson's prediction seemed close to reality.

The Wilmot Proviso

President Polk had assumed that the expansion of American territory to the Pacific would strengthen "the bonds of Union." Instead, the fate of slavery in the new western territories ignited a violent political debate.

On August 8, 1846, only three months into the Mexican-American War, an obscure Democratic congressman from Pennsylvania, David Wilmot, delivered a speech to the House of Representatives in which he proposed that if any Mexican territory should be acquired, slavery would be banned there.

The **Wilmot Proviso** reignited the debate over the westward expansion of slavery that had been lurking since the Missouri controversy of 1819–1821

Wilmot Proviso (1846) A proposal by Congressman David Wilmot, a Pennsylvania Democrat, to prohibit slavery in any lands acquired in the Mexican-American War.

THE WILMOT PROVISO Zachary Taylor promised during his presidential campaign in 1848 that he would not veto the proviso after being elected, even though he was a slaveowner. This political cartoon, "Old Zack at Home," points out his seeming hypocrisy.

(see Chapter 9). The Missouri Compromise had provided a temporary solution by protecting slavery in states where it already existed but not allowing it in newly acquired territories north of the 36°30′ latitude. Now, with the territories taken from Mexico, the political dispute over slavery would explode.

The House of Representatives approved the Wilmot Proviso, but the Senate balked. President Polk dismissed the proviso as "mischievous and foolish" but privately worried that "the slavery question is assuming a fearful... aspect" that might "ultimately threaten the Union itself." If slavery were banned from the western territories, all new states would be free states, thus putting at risk the future of slavery everywhere and shifting the political balance in Congress against the slave states.

> Congressional controversy over the Wilmot Proviso

Polk convinced Wilmot to withhold his amendment from any bill dealing with the annexation of Mexican territory. By then, however, others were ready to take up the cause. In one form or another, Wilmot's proposal would frame the furious debate in Congress over the expansion of slavery. Abraham Lincoln recalled that during his one term as a congressman, in 1847–1849, he voted for restricting slavery in the new territories forty times.

Senator John C. Calhoun, meanwhile, countered Wilmot's proviso with a pro-slavery plan, which he introduced in early 1847. Calhoun insisted that Wilmot's effort to exclude enslaved people from territories would violate the Fifth Amendment, which forbids Congress from depriving any person of life, liberty, or property without due process of law. Enslaved people, he argued, were *property*.

By this logic, Calhoun turned the Bill of Rights into a protector of slavery. Senator Thomas Hart Benton of Missouri, a slaveowner but also a nationalist eager to calm sectional tensions, found in Calhoun's stance a set of dangerous abstractions "leading to no result." Wilmot and Calhoun together, he said, had fashioned a pair of scissors. Neither blade alone would cut very well, but joined together they could sever the nation in two.

Popular Sovereignty

Thomas Hart Benton and others tried to deflect the brewing conflict over slavery by suggesting that Congress simply extend the Missouri Compromise line, dividing free and slave territory at the latitude of 36°30′, all the way to the Pacific Ocean. Senator Lewis Cass of Michigan suggested a different solution: that the citizens of each territory "regulate their own internal concerns in their own way" and decide for themselves whether slavery would be legal. This would take the issue out of Congress and put it in the hands of those directly affected. **Popular sovereignty**, as Cass called his idea, appealed to many who were eager to protect states' rights.

President Polk had promised to serve only one term, and, having accomplished his goals, he refused to run again in 1848. Cass won the Democratic presidential nomination for president, but the party refused to endorse his

popular sovereignty The legal concept by which the White male settlers in a U.S. territory would vote to decide whether to permit slavery.

Free-Soil Party A political coalition created in 1848 that opposed the expansion of slavery into the new western territories.

popular sovereignty plan, since it angered anti-slavery members as well as the pro-slavery Democrats who believed the federal government should protect slavery across the nation.

The Whigs again passed over their party leader, Henry Clay, and nominated General Zachary Taylor, the hero of the Mexican-American War. Taylor owned a Louisiana plantation with 145 enslaved people. Yet he opposed the extension of slavery into new western territories.

The Free-Soil Movement

The anti-slavery crusade was not easily silenced. Many Americans who cared little about the welfare of enslaved people supported banning slavery in the western territories acquired from Mexico. Some, like Senator Henry Clay, recognized that the Mexican government had already outlawed slavery in the region: "I cannot vote to convert a territory already free into a slave territory." Other opponents of slavery's expansion did not want to see new slave states gaining political power in Congress, or enslaved people competing with free workers in the West. As a result, keeping slavery out of the territories became the rallying cry for the Free-Soil Party, a new political organization that focused solely on stopping the spread of slavery.

The **Free-Soil Party** attracted northern Democrats and Whigs opposed to slavery, and members of the abolitionist Liberty Party. In 1848, Free-Soilers nominated former president Martin Van Buren as their presidential candidate. The party's platform stressed that slavery would not be allowed in the western territories.

In the 1848 election, the Free-Soilers split the Democratic vote enough to throw New York to Zachary Taylor; they split the Whig vote enough to give Ohio to the Democrat, Lewis Cass. Nationwide, however, Van Buren's approximately 291,000 third-party votes lagged well behind the totals of 1,361,000 for Taylor and 1,222,000 for Cass.

The California Gold Rush

Meanwhile, a new issue had emerged to complicate the growing debate over territorial expansion and slavery. On January 24, 1848, a group of Mormon and Indigenous laborers building a sawmill in eastern California discovered gold nuggets on the 50,000-acre property of John A. Sutter, along the south fork of the American River. Nine days later, California would be labeled the "great prize" transferred to the United States through the treaty ending the Mexican-American War.

Word of the gold strike raced across the country and then much of the world. In 1849, nearly 100,000 Americans, mostly young men infected with "gold fever," quit jobs, left farms, deserted from the army, abandoned wives and children, and sold businesses to set off for the California Territory. Within a matter of weeks, gold seekers vastly outnumbered the disinherited Mexican population. Thousands more came from across the world—Mexico, Central and South America, Canada, Australia, New Zealand, Asia, and Europe.

A U.S. Army officer reported that the "vast deposits of gold" had "entirely changed the character of Upper California." Within two years, San Francisco was transformed from a sleepy coastal village of 800 residents to a bustling city of 20,000.

"We are on the brink of an Age of Gold," gushed Horace Greeley, editor of the *New York Tribune*. "Go west, young man, go west!" So many men left New England for California that it would take years to restore the region's gender balance, leading some women to form ambiguous same-sex partnerships in what novelist Henry James later called "Boston marriages."

Gold seekers, called "forty-niners," found the long trip to California grueling beyond description. The favored route was by sea around the southern tip of South America and then up the Pacific coast to San Francisco. The 13,000-mile journey took an average of six months, twice as long as the trek overland.

For all its hardships, however, the **California gold rush** became one of the greatest mass migrations in American history. Between 1851 and 1855, the "diggings" throughout California produced almost half the world's output of gold, and the nation's supply of gold coinage increased twentyfold.

Conquering Indigenous Americans and Mexican Americans

For Indigenous people in California, however, the gold rush was a disaster. In 1848, there were 150,000 in the territory, ten times more than Whites; by 1870, there were only 30,000 (an 80 percent decrease). Starvation, disease, and a declining birth rate took a heavy toll. But many, perhaps 40 percent, were murdered by gold miners, soldiers, and others.

In 1850, the California legislature allowed Whites to force "unemployed Indians" to work for them in exchange for food and clothing. Some miners went further, forcing them out of the diggings and killing those who resisted. The next year, California's territorial governor pledged to continue "a war of extermination . . . between the two races until the Indian race becomes extinct." His commitment to exterminating Indigenous people contradicted the Treaty of Guadalupe Hidalgo, which granted U.S. citizenship to the Indigenous peoples in California.

With the governor's approval and the added enticement of bounties paid for Indigenous scalps or ears, bands of White "Indian-killers" roamed the state, massacring Indigenous people. Sally Bell, a Sinkyone survivor of one of the raids, reported that "some white men came. They killed my grandfather and my mother and my father. . . . Then they killed my baby sister and cut her heart out and threw it in the brush where I ran and hid."

GOLD MINERS Chinese immigrants and White settlers mine for gold in the Auburn Ravine of California in 1856. **What were living and working conditions like in the mining camps?**

Mass migration to California

California gold rush (1849) A massive migration of gold hunters, mostly young men, who transformed the national economy after extensive amounts of gold were discovered in northern California.

SAN FRANCISCO A view of San Francisco during 1849 shows the city in the midst of rapid growth. The Bay is crowded with ships, and a blend of tents and newly constructed buildings dot the coastline.

Actions against Mexican Californios

The influx of miners into California proved deadly for Mexican *Californios*. "Mexicans have no business in this country," a miner wrote in a letter to the *Stockton Times*. "I don't believe in them. The men were made to be shot at, and the women were made for *our* purposes. I'm a white man—I am. A Mexican is pretty near black. I hate all Mexicans." In 1850, White miners convinced the new state legislature to pass a Foreign Miners' Tax that drove most Mexicans from the diggings.

Mining Life

Sacramento became the staging area for the northern gold rush. New business enterprises—saloons, taverns, gambling halls, restaurants, laundries, general stores—emerged to serve the miners. One of the new businesses made sturdy denim work pants, their pockets reinforced by copper rivets. Developed in San Francisco by the German-Jewish immigrant Levi Strauss, the blue jeans—originally called "those pants of Levi's"—today are known as just Levi's.

The flannel-shirted forty-niners included people from every social class and every state and territory, as well as local Indigenous and enslaved people. Louis Manigault, the son of a South Carolina rice planter, reported that California was "filled with castoffs and exiles from almost every nation, the true and perfect scum of the Earth."

Chinese immigrants in California

The miners were mostly unmarried men of varied ethnic and cultural backgrounds, including some 20,000 Chinese immigrants. In fact, a Chinese shipowner recruited immigrants by portraying California as utopia: "Americans are very rich people. They want the Chinese to come and will make him welcome. There will be big pay, large houses, and food and clothing of the finest description. . . . Never fear, and you will be lucky." Few Chinese immigrants were interested in staying in California; they wanted to strike it rich and return home.

Mining camps sprang up like mushrooms and disappeared almost as rapidly. As soon as rumors of a new strike circulated, prospectors abandoned one site for another; when no more gold could be found, they picked up and moved on again.

The mining camps and shantytowns may have had colorful names—Grizzly Flats, Lousy Ravine, Petticoat Slide, Piety Hill—but they were raw, dirty, lawless, disease-ridden, and dangerous places. "In the short space of twenty-four days," one miner reported, "we have had murders, fearful accidents, bloody deaths, a mob, whippings, a hanging, an attempt at suicide, and a fatal duel."

Women were as rare in the mining camps as liquor and guns were abundant. In 1850, less than 3 percent of the population of the Southern California mines was female, though that number rose to 20 percent over the next decade as more women headed west. The women who dared to live in the camps could demand a premium for their work as cooks, laundresses, entertainers, and prostitutes.

> Women in California

It took four years for Mary Harrison Newell to join her husband, William, in California. After his departure in 1849 and the death of their infant son six months later, a distraught Mary had pleaded with William to return home to Delaware. He refused. "How can I now leave all and go home to be dependent on others," William demanded, believing that a man like him needed to strike it rich before heading back east. Mary eventually gave in and boarded a ship to California, but their reunion was short-lived—William died the next year.

For most forty-niners, the gold rush brought more frustration and failure than wealth. Within six months of arriving in California in 1849, one gold seeker in every five was dead. The gold fields and mining towns were so dangerous that insurance companies refused to provide coverage. Suicides were common, and disease and drunkenness were rampant.

California Statehood

New president Zachary Taylor decided in 1849 to use California's request for statehood to end the congressional stalemate over slavery. Why not make California and New Mexico free states immediately, he argued, and thereby bypass the volatile issue of slavery?

Californians, however, were ahead of him. By December 1849, without consulting Congress, they had put a free-state (no-slavery) government into operation. New Mexico responded more slowly, but by 1850 it had also adopted a free-state constitution.

> California and New Mexico establish free-state governments

Yet while banning African American slavery, the new western states preserved *peonage* (involuntary servitude) of Native Americans. In California, the Indian Act (1850) allowed 25,000 "unemployed" Indigenous people, including thousands of children, to be auctioned off to White settlers as forced laborers. Five years later, the state legislature passed the Anti-Vagrancy Act. It was directed at those of "Spanish and Indian blood" and allowed police to arrest any person suspected of not working and force them to labor, usually on ranches or in mines.

The Compromise of 1850

In his annual message in late 1849, President Zachary Taylor endorsed immediate statehood for California and urged Congress to avoid injecting slavery into the issue. The new Congress, however, was in no mood for simple solutions.

CLAY'S COMPROMISE (1850)
Warning against an impending sectional conflict, Henry Clay takes the Senate floor to outline his plan for "compromise and harmony."

Angry southerners threatened to leave the United States if Taylor brought in California and New Mexico as free states. Doing so, they feared, would upset the political balance of fifteen slave states and fifteen free states.

The spotlight then fell on the Senate, where an all-star cast—Henry Clay, John C. Calhoun, and Daniel Webster (all of whom would die within two years), with William H. Seward, Stephen A. Douglas, and Jefferson Davis in supporting roles—staged one of the great dramas of American politics: the **Compromise of 1850** (see Map 13.5).

Saving the Union

With southern extremists threatening secession, congressional leaders again turned to an aging Henry Clay. As Abraham Lincoln acknowledged, Clay was "regarded by all, as *the* man for the crisis."

On January 29, 1850, having gained Daniel Webster's support, Henry Clay presented to Congress several resolutions meant to settle the controversy. The resolutions ranged from admitting California as a free state to getting the federal government involved in the business of capturing fugitive slaves, also called freedom seekers.

Clay's cluster of proposals became in substance the Compromise of 1850, but only after months of negotiations punctuated by the most contentious debates in congressional history. On March 4, a grim John C. Calhoun, the unbending defender of slavery, left his sickbed, draped himself in a black cloak, and sat in the Senate chamber, where he listened to a colleague read his defiant rejection of Clay's proposal.

Compromise of 1850 A package of five bills presented to Congress by Henry Clay intended to avoid secession or civil war by reducing tensions between North and South over the status of slavery.

MAP 13.5 THE COMPROMISE OF 1850

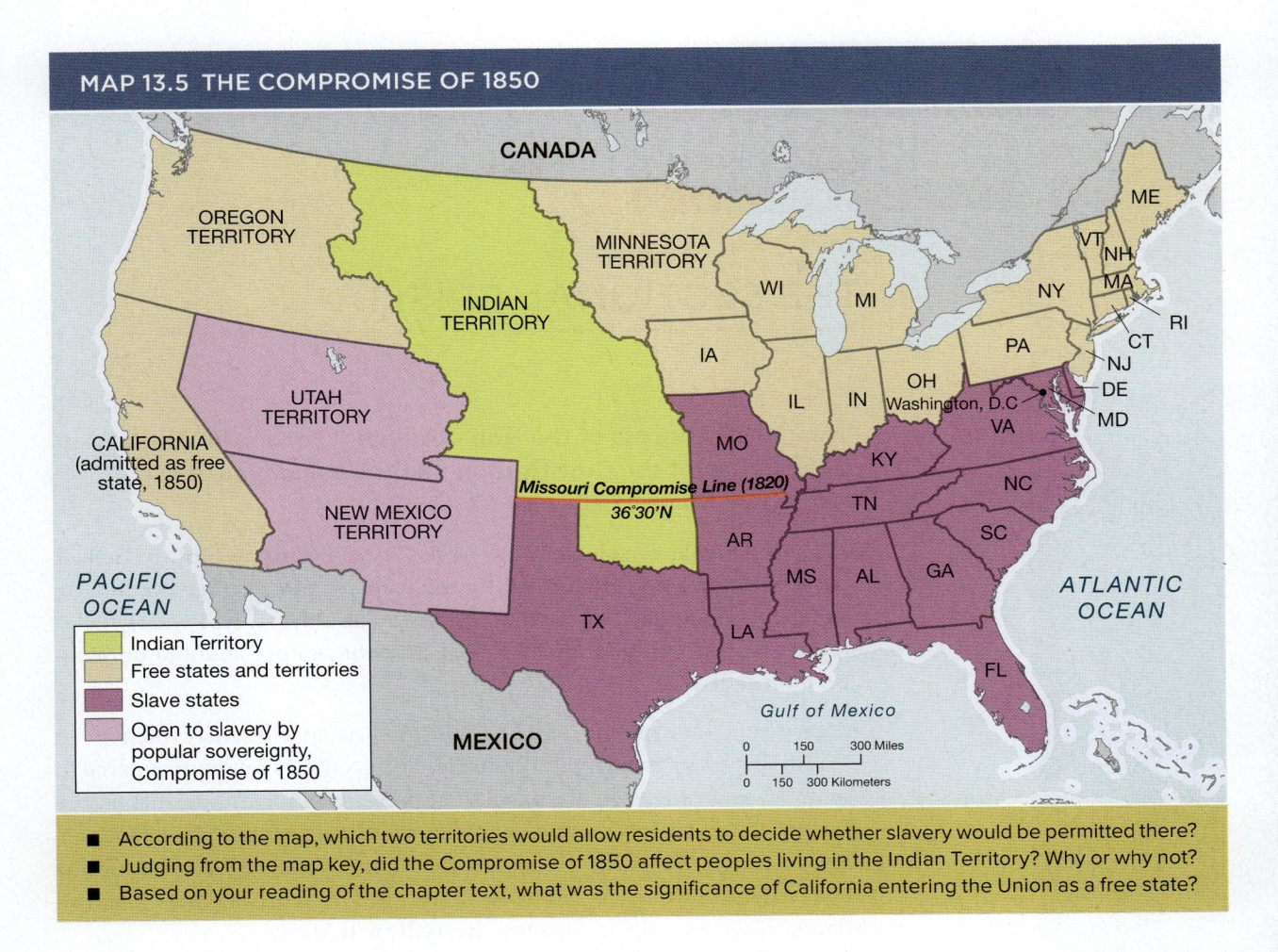

- According to the map, which two territories would allow residents to decide whether slavery would be permitted there?
- Judging from the map key, did the Compromise of 1850 affect peoples living in the Indian Territory? Why or why not?
- Based on your reading of the chapter text, what was the significance of California entering the Union as a free state?

Three days later, Calhoun, who would die in just three weeks, returned to the Senate to hear the "golden-throated" Daniel Webster. "I wish to speak today," Webster began, "not as a Massachusetts man, not as a Northern man, but as an American. . . . I speak today for the preservation of the Union." He criticized extremists on both sides for their "violent" actions and suggested that some new territories should become slave states and others free states.

Webster's evenhanded speech angered extremists on both sides—in part because it was four hours long. On March 11, William Seward, the hook-nosed and shaggy-browed Whig senator from New York who had long been a fearless critic of slavery, declared that *any* compromise with slavery was "radically wrong and essentially vicious." There was, he said, "a *higher law* than the Constitution," and it demanded the abolition of slavery. A Georgia newspaper said that Seward should be dressed in a straitjacket and taken to a lunatic asylum.

Compromise Efforts

On July 4, 1850, Congress celebrated Independence Day by gathering at the base of the unfinished Washington Monument. While listening to the

> Death of President Zachary Taylor

Comparing PERSPECTIVES

THE SECTIONAL CRISIS

From: "The Address of the Hon. Abraham Lincoln, in Vindication of the Policy of the Constitution and the Principles of the Republican Party," February 27, 1860.

Abraham Lincoln traveled to New York City in February 1860 to deliver a speech before a gathering of Republicans at the Cooper Union. The speech, in which Lincoln outlined his views on slavery, was widely celebrated and helped earn him the 1860 Republican presidential nomination later that year.

Judging by all they say and do, let us determine, what will satisfy them.

Will they be satisfied if the Territories be unconditionally surrendered to them? We know they will not. In all their present complaints against us, the Territories are scarcely mentioned. What will convince them? This, and this only: cease to call slavery *wrong*, and join them in calling it *right*. And this must be done thoroughly—done in *acts* as well as in *words*. Silence will not be tolerated—we must place ourselves avowedly with them.

If slavery is right, all words, acts, laws, and constitutions against it, are themselves wrong. If it is right, we cannot justly object to its nationality—its universality; if it is wrong, they cannot justly insist upon its extension—its enlargement. All they ask, we could readily grant, if we thought slavery right: all we ask, they could as readily grant, if they thought it wrong. Their thinking it right, and our thinking it wrong, is the precise fact upon which depends the whole controversy. Thinking it right, as they do, they are not to blame for desiring its full recognition, as being right; but, thinking it wrong, as we do; can we yield to them? Can we cast our votes with their view, and against our own? In view of our moral, social, and political responsibilities, can we do this?

Wrong as we think slavery is, we can yet afford to let it alone where it is, but can we, while our votes will prevent it, allow it to spread into the National Territories, and to overrun us here in these Free States?

From: "An Address Setting Forth the Declaration of the Immediate Causes Which Induce and Justify the Secession of Mississippi from the Federal Union and the Ordinance of Secession," 1861.

Following Lincoln's election to the presidency, Mississippi political leaders held a convention to decide whether to secede from the United States. On January 9, 1861, they voted yes, making their state the second to leave the Union behind South Carolina. Mississippi leaders then published a declaration outlining their reasons for seceding.

In the momentous step which our State has taken of dissolving its connection with the government of which we so long formed a part, it is but just that we should declare the prominent reasons which have induced our course.

Our position is thoroughly identified with the institution of slavery—the greatest material interest of the world. Its labor supplies the product which constitutes by far the largest and most important portions of the commerce of the earth. These products are peculiar to the climate verging on the tropical regions, and by an imperious law of nature, none but the black race can bear exposure to the tropical sun. These products have become necessities of the world, and a blow at slavery is a blow at commerce and civilization. That blow has been long aimed at the institution, and was at the point of reaching its consummation. There was no choice left us but submission to the mandates of abolition, or a dissolution of the Union, whose principles had been subverted to work out our ruin.

It [abolition] refuses the admission of new slave States into the Union.

It tramples the original equality of the South under foot.

It has nullified the Fugitive Slave Law in almost every free State.

It advocates negro equality, socially and politically, and promotes insurrection and incendiarism in our midst.

It has enlisted its press, its pulpit and its schools against us, until the whole popular mind of the North is excited and inflamed with prejudice.

Utter subjugation awaits us in the Union, if we should consent longer to remain in it. It is not a matter of choice, but of necessity. We must either submit to degradation, and to the loss of property worth four billions of money, or we must secede from the Union framed by our fathers.

Questions

1. Describe Abraham Lincoln's position on the future of slavery. What was he willing to do to "satisfy" proslavery interests—and what was he unwilling to do?

2. Describe the position of Mississippi political leaders. What did they think would happen if they remained in the Union?

3. Comparing positions on these issues, why did speeches like Abraham Lincoln's fail to satisfy Mississippi leaders and prevent them from seceding?

patriotic speeches, President Zachary Taylor collapsed in the heat and humidity. Five days later, he died of a violent stomach disorder, likely caused by tainted food or water.

Taylor's shocking death bolstered the chances of a compromise in Congress, for his successor, Vice President Millard Fillmore, supported Clay's proposals. It was a striking reversal: Taylor, the Louisiana slaveowner, had been ready to make war on his native South; Fillmore, who southerners thought opposed slavery, was ready to make peace.

The new president benefited from the support of Stephen A. Douglas of Illinois, a rising star in the Democratic Party, the youngest man in the Senate, and a friend of the South. Douglas suggested that the best way to approve Clay's "comprehensive scheme" was to separate the proposals and vote on each of them, one at a time. The plan worked. By September 20, President Fillmore had signed the last of the measures into law.

The Compromise of 1850 passes

In its final version, the Compromise of 1850 (see again Map 13.5) included five key elements:

(1) California entered the Union as a free state, ending forever the balance of free and slave states.
(2) The Texas–New Mexico Act made New Mexico a separate territory and set the Texas state boundary at its present location. In return for giving up its claims to much of New Mexico, Texas received $10 million to erase the state's debt.
(3) The Utah Act set up the Utah Territory and gave the territorial legislature authority over "all rightful subjects of legislation," including slavery.
(4) A Fugitive Slave Act required the federal government and the northern states to help capture and return freedom seekers to the South.
(5) As a gesture to anti-slavery groups, the slave trade, but not slavery itself, was abolished in the District of Columbia.

The Fugitive Slave Act

The **Fugitive Slave Act** was the most controversial element of the Compromise of 1850. It did more than strengthen the hand of slave-catchers; it sought to recover freedom seekers who had already escaped. The law even enabled slave-traders to kidnap free Blacks in northern "free" states, claiming that they were fugitive slaves; and it required citizens to help locate and capture any freedom seekers who had successfully escaped. In addition, the act dispatched federal commissioners to hear disputes between freedom seekers and slave-catchers in a corrupt set of legal proceedings designed to favor the catchers. There was no jury, no testimony was allowed from the fugitives, and the commissioners themselves were paid $10 for returning runaways to slavery—but only $5 to free them.

Abolitionists fumed. Ralph Waldo Emerson urged people to break the new law. In New York, Reverend Jermain Loguen, himself a freedom seeker, shouted: "I don't respect this law—I don't fear it—I won't obey it! It outlaws me, and I outlaw it."

Fugitive Slave Act (1850)
A part of the Compromise of 1850 that authorized federal officials to help capture and then return freedom seekers to their owners without trials.

In late October 1850, two slave-catchers from Georgia arrived in Boston, determined to use the Fugitive Slave Act to recapture William and Ellen Craft. The Crafts had escaped to the North by dressing light-skinned Ellen as a male slaveowner, with her husband, William, posing as her personal servant. Abolitionists mobilized to prevent the Crafts from being seized by the southern "man stealers." After five days, the slave-catchers gave up and returned to Georgia.

Anthony Burns had a much different experience, however. In 1853, he had escaped from slavery in Virginia and settled in Boston. The following year, his former owner captured him on his way home from work. Although Burns, as a freedom seeker, had no legal rights, his anti-slavery attorneys found ingenious ways to postpone the court date when he would be released to his former owner.

Then something extraordinary occurred. Some 7,000 abolitionists, Black as well as White, stormed the courthouse in an effort to free Burns. During the commotion, a U.S. marshal was killed and a dozen more people were wounded. Some 1,500 federal troops were sent to restore order and ensure that Burns's hearing proceeded on schedule. The judge ruled that Burns must be returned to Virginia and his enslaved existence there.

Amos Lawrence, one of the wealthiest men in Boston, was transformed by the government's effort to return Burns to a life of forced servitude. He wrote to his uncle that "we went to bed one night old-fashioned, conservative, Compromise Union Whigs and waked up stark mad Abolitionists." Lawrence and other abolitionists began to endorse the use of violence to end slavery altogether.

Soon, several northern states countered the Fugitive Slave Act by passing what were called personal liberty laws. Some of these state laws allowed jury trials for freedom seekers who had been captured and others prohibited state authorities from cooperating with slave catchers. Still others imposed stiff penalties on anyone who falsely accused African Americans of being freedom seekers.

ELLEN CRAFT Ellen Craft wore the disguise of a young male slaveowner when she and her husband, William, successfully fled slavery to freedom. The Crafts later moved to England, which they believed was safer than the United States, and published *Running a Thousand Miles to Freedom*, a firsthand account of their escape from slavery.

Slavery: A Fate Worse than Death

The Fugitive Slave Act polarized the debate over the future of slavery. It also generated tragic consequences, the most poignant of which occurred along the Kentucky-Ohio border. In early 1856, a twenty-two-year-old enslaved woman named Margaret "Peggy" Garner escaped from Maplewood, a northern Kentucky plantation. With her were her husband, Robert; four children; and several other enslaved families. They stole horses and a sleigh and made their way sixteen miles to the frozen Ohio River. At dawn, the seventeen escapees walked across the iced-over waterway and made their way to Cincinnati, where they split up. At long last, they were free—or so they thought.

Within hours, slave-catchers, federal marshals, and Archibald Gaines, the owner of Maplewood, found Garner and others barricaded in what they

Trial of Peggy Garner

MARGARET "PEGGY" GARNER This image depicts Margaret Garner, the determined freedom seeker who escaped from Kentucky to Ohio with four of her children, one of whom she killed when discovered by slave-catchers. She said she did not want her children raised in slavery.

thought was a safe house. The posse stormed the house. Frantic with fright, Margaret killed her two-year-old daughter Mary with a butcher knife rather than see her returned to slavery. She was about to kill her other children and then herself when marshals arrested her.

Accounts of the incident spread quickly across the nation and the world. On her trial's final day, Garner called slavery a fate "more cruel than death," especially for young women subject to daily sexual assaults. It was better, she said, for her children "to go home to God than back to slavery."

In the end, the Ohio judge ruled that Garner was "property" to be returned to slave-state Kentucky. Yet no sooner was she back in Kentucky than abolitionists in Ohio got the state to issue warrants to have her returned to be tried for murder. (They assumed the governor would pardon her if convicted.) These efforts prompted Archibald Gaines to sell Margaret and her children to his brother in Arkansas. She died of typhoid fever two years later.

Uncle Tom's Cabin

During the 1850s, anti-slavery advocates gained a powerful new weapon in the form of Harriet Beecher Stowe's best-selling novel *Uncle Tom's Cabin; or Life among the Lowly* (1852). Stowe reflected the powerful moral and religious underpinnings of the abolitionist movement. The sister and daughter of prominent ministers, and the wife of a theology professor, she had absorbed the deep religiosity and moral activism of her family. While raising six children in Cincinnati, Ohio, during the 1830s and 1840s, she encountered freedom seekers who had crossed the Ohio River from Kentucky.

Stowe detested the Fugitive Slave Act. In the spring of 1850, having moved to Maine, she began writing *Uncle Tom's Cabin*. "The time has come," she wrote, "when even a woman or a child who can speak a word for freedom and humanity is bound to speak." The novel ended with Stowe predicting that Almighty God's wrath would destroy America if slavery were not abolished.

Uncle Tom's Cabin was a smashing success. By the end of its first year, it had sold 300,000 copies in the United States and more than a million in Great Britain. By 1855, it was "the most popular novel of our day."

Abolitionist leader Frederick Douglass, who had escaped slavery himself, said that *Uncle Tom's Cabin* was like "a flash" that lit "a million campfires in front of the embattled host of slavery." The book incensed the South's enslavers, one of whom called Stowe "that wretch in petticoats."

Uncle Tom's Cabin is a bestseller

The Election of 1852

In 1852, the Democrats chose Franklin Pierce of New Hampshire as their presidential candidate; their platform endorsed the Compromise of 1850. For their part, the Whigs repudiated Millard Fillmore, who had faithfully supported the Compromise of 1850, and chose General Winfield Scott, another hero of the Mexican-American War.

Scott, an inept campaigner, carried only Tennessee, Kentucky, Massachusetts, and Vermont. Pierce overwhelmed him in the Electoral College, 254 to 42, although the popular vote was close: 1.6 million to 1.4 million. The third-party Free-Soilers mustered only 156,000 votes for John P. Hale.

The forty-eight-year-old Pierce promoted western expansion, even if it meant adding more slave states to the Union. Yet he also acknowledged that the nation had recently survived a "perilous crisis," and he urged both North and South to avoid aggravating the other.

Franklin Pierce elected president (1852)

By the end of his first year in office, Democratic leaders had decided he was a failure. By trying to be all things to all people, Pierce was labeled a "doughface": a "Northern man with Southern principles."

The Kansas-Nebraska Crisis

During the mid–nineteenth century, as tensions over slavery were simmering between North and South, American merchants discovered the vast markets of Asia. As commerce with China and Japan grew, so did demand for a transcontinental railroad line connecting the eastern seaboard with the Pacific coast to facilitate trade with Asia. The issue reignited the debate over the westward extension of slavery.

In 1852 and 1853, Congress debated several proposals for a transcontinental rail line. Secretary of War Jefferson Davis of Mississippi favored a southern route across the territories acquired from Mexico. Senator Stephen Douglas of Illinois insisted that Chicago be the transcontinental railroad's Midwest hub. Both proposed routes extended through lands controlled by eighteen Indigenous nations—something another senator, William Seward of New York, could not ignore. "Where will they go?" he asked. "Back across the Mississippi? . . . To the Himalayas?"

Democrats pass Kansas-Nebraska Act

The Cherokee were aghast at the Americans. "No matter how little is left the red man," warned an editorial in the *Cherokee Advocate*, the federal government would not "rest until the Indians are made landless and homeless."

Kansas-Nebraska Act (1854)
Controversial legislation that created two new territories taken from Native Americans, Kansas and Nebraska, where resident males would decide whether slavery would be allowed (popular sovereignty).

Unconcerned about the fate of Indigenous people, Douglas plowed ahead and urged Congress to pass the **Kansas-Nebraska Act** so that the vast northern territory west of Missouri and Iowa could be settled by Whites. To win the support of southern legislators, Douglas championed the principle of popular sovereignty, under which the voters themselves in each new western territory would decide whether to allow slavery. The legislation offered a way of getting around the 1820 Missouri Compromise, which excluded slavery north of the 36th parallel, where Kansas and Nebraska were located.

Southerners demanded more, however, and Douglas complied. He supported the formal repeal of the Missouri Compromise and the creation of *two* new territorial governments: Kansas, west of Missouri; and Nebraska, which then included the Dakotas (see Map 13.6). In 1854, Douglas and the Democrats pushed through the Kansas-Nebraska Act by a vote of 37–14 in the Senate and 113–100 in the House. The anti-slavery faction in Congress—mostly Whigs—had been crushed, and the national Whig Party died with them.

The political chaos had been building since the end of the Mexican-American War, when the United States' acquisition of new western territories stirred up debate about the future of slavery. Pro-slavery and anti-slavery leaders kept making attempts at compromise—including the Compromise of 1850, which established California as a free state and included the Fugitive Slave Act of 1850, which authorized federal officials to help capture people who escaped slavery and return them to their owners. The Kansas-Nebraska Act of 1854, with its call for "popular sovereignty" in those territories, reopened the possibility of extending slavery into a region where it had been banned since 1820. Increasingly, these compromises satisfied no one. This put a strain on the Whigs and the Democrats that had already given rise to the Free-Soil Party—and would now lead to more new parties.

CORE OBJECTIVE
4. Analyze the appeal of the Republican Party to northern voters and how it led to Abraham Lincoln's victory in the 1860 presidential contest.

The Emergence of the Republican Party

The dispute over the Kansas-Nebraska Act led northern Whigs to align with one of two new national political parties. One was the American ("Know-Nothing") Party, which had emerged in opposition to the surge of mostly Catholic immigrants from Ireland and Germany during the 1840s. The Know-Nothings proposed that newcomers be denied citizenship and the right to run for public offices. In the early 1850s, Know-Nothings won several local elections in Massachusetts and New York.

The other new party, the Republican Party, attracted even more northern Whigs. The party coalesced in 1854 when the anti-slavery "conscience Whigs" split from the southern pro-slavery "cotton Whigs." They then joined with independent Democrats and Free-Soilers to form a Republican Party dedicated to excluding slavery from the western territories.

MAP 13.6 THE KANSAS-NEBRASKA ACT, 1854

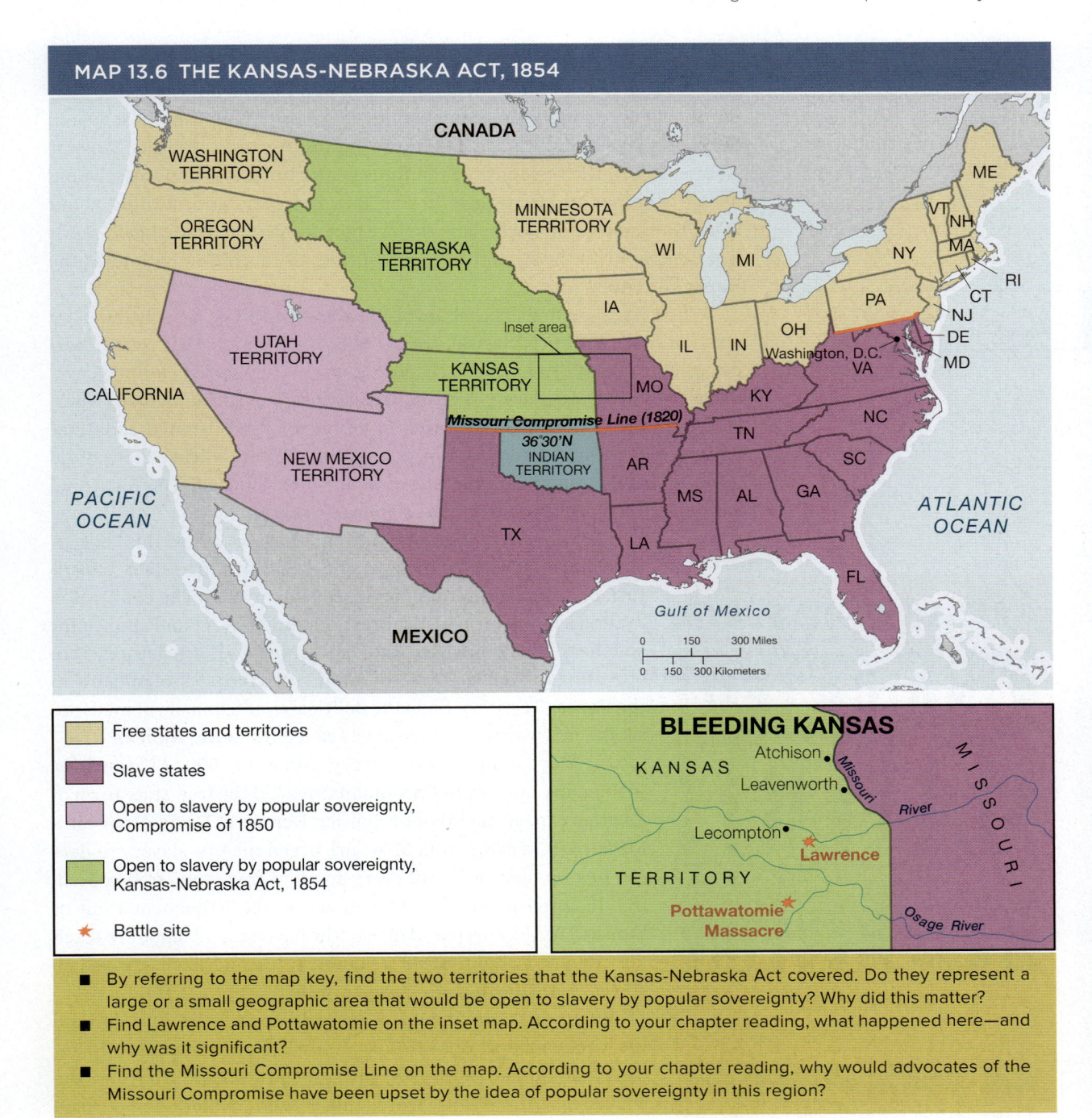

Legend:
- Free states and territories
- Slave states
- Open to slavery by popular sovereignty, Compromise of 1850
- Open to slavery by popular sovereignty, Kansas-Nebraska Act, 1854
- ★ Battle site

BLEEDING KANSAS (inset): Atchison, Leavenworth, Lecompton, Lawrence, Pottawatomie Massacre

- By referring to the map key, find the two territories that the Kansas-Nebraska Act covered. Do they represent a large or a small geographic area that would be open to slavery by popular sovereignty? Why did this matter?
- Find Lawrence and Pottawatomie on the inset map. According to your chapter reading, what happened here—and why was it significant?
- Find the Missouri Compromise Line on the map. According to your chapter reading, why would advocates of the Missouri Compromise have been upset by the idea of popular sovereignty in this region?

Abraham Lincoln made the transition from Whig to Republican. He said that the passage of Douglas's Kansas-Nebraska Act angered him "as he had never been before." Unless the North mobilized to stop the efforts of proslavery southerners, Lincoln believed, the future of the Union was endangered. From that moment on, he focused his career on reversing the Kansas-Nebraska Act and preventing the extension of slavery into any new territories.

Bleeding Kansas (1856) Journalists' name for a series of violent conflicts in the Kansas Territory between anti-slavery and pro-slavery factions over the status of slavery.

> Anti-abolitionist voting fraud in Kansas

Bleeding Kansas

The passage of the Kansas-Nebraska Act soon placed Kansas at the center of the increasingly violent debate over slavery. While Nebraska would become a free state, Kansas was up for grabs. According to the Kansas-Nebraska Act, the residents of the Kansas Territory, not Congress, would decide whether to allow slavery. The law, however, said nothing about *when* Kansans would decide about slavery, so each side tried to gain political control of the vast territory and worked to recruit emigrants to the Kansas territory.

When Kansas's first federal governor arrived in 1854, he scheduled an election for a territorial legislature in 1855. On Election Day, 5,000 "border ruffians" from Missouri crossed into Kansas. They seized polling places, illegally elected pro-slavery legislators (casting four times as many votes as there were residents), and vowed to kill every "God-damned abolitionist in the Territory." The governor denounced the fraudulent vote but did nothing to alter the results for fear of being killed himself. The territorial legislature then declared the territory open to slavery.

Outraged free-state advocates in Kansas spurned this "bogus" legislature and elected their own delegates to a "free state" constitutional convention that met in Topeka in 1855. The convention drafted a new state constitution excluding slavery and applied for statehood. By 1856, a free-state "governor" and "legislature" were operating in Topeka; thus, there were two illegal governments in the Kansas Territory. Soon the political conflict mushroomed into a local civil war, which journalists called **Bleeding Kansas**.

In May 1856, a pro-slavery force of 500 Missourians, Alabamans, and South Carolinians invaded the free-state town of Lawrence, near the Missouri border. Democrat David Atchison, a former U.S. senator from Missouri, urged the pro-slavery raiders not to stop fighting "until every spark of free-state, free-speech, free-[colored people], or free in any shape is quenched out of Kansas." As they prepared to use "the bayonet and blood" to teach the "damned abolitionists a southern lesson," Atchison yelled: "Boys, this is the happiest day of my life!"

What became known as the Sack of Lawrence ignited the vengeance of abolitionist John Brown. He believed that Christians must "break the jaws of the wicked," and that the wickedest Americans were those who owned and traded enslaved people. Upon meeting Brown, many declared him crazy; those who supported his efforts thought he was a saint. He was some of both.

By the mid-1850s, the fifty-five-year-old Brown, the father of twenty children, had left his home in Springfield, Massachusetts, to become a merciless holy warrior against slavery. In his view, Black people deserved both liberty and full social equality.

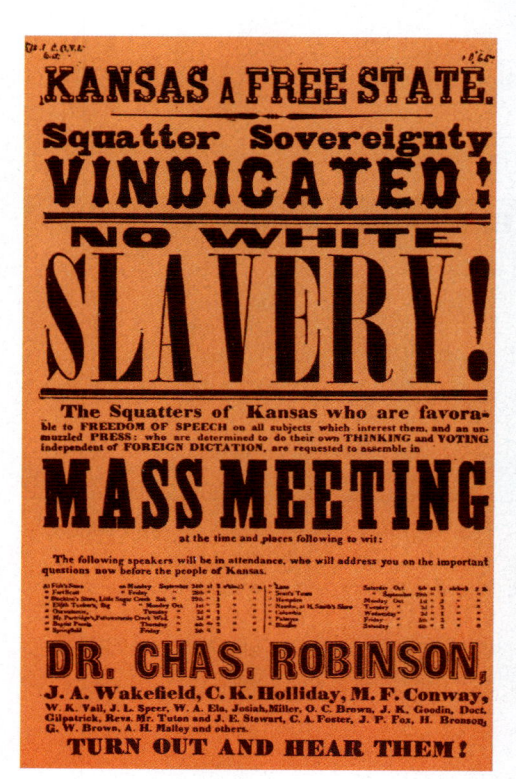

KANSAS A FREE STATE This broadside advertises a series of mass meetings in Kansas in support of the free-state cause, based on the principle of "squatter" or popular sovereignty.

Two days after the attack on Lawrence, Brown led four of his sons to Pottawatomie, Kansas, a pro-slavery settlement near the Missouri border. There they dragged five men from their houses and hacked them to death with swords. "God is my judge," Brown told one of his sons afterward. "We were justified under the circumstances."

> The Pottawatomie Massacre

The Pottawatomie Massacre (May 24–25, 1856) ignited a guerrilla war in the Kansas Territory. Later that summer, pro-slavery Missourians raided a free-state settlement at Osawatomie, Kansas. They looted and burned houses and shot Frederick Brown, John's son, through the heart, killing him. By the end of 1856, about 200 settlers had been killed in Bleeding Kansas.

Violence in the Senate

Just two days before the Pottawatomie Massacre, an ugly incident in the U.S. Senate had shocked the nation. Republican senator Charles Sumner of Massachusetts had delivered a fiery speech that insulted slaveowners, including Andrew Pickens Butler, an elderly senator from South Carolina.

Sumner's speech enraged Butler's young cousin, Preston S. Brooks, a hot-headed South Carolina congressman. Resolving on the spot to defend the honor of his family, state, and region, he strode into the Senate, confronted Sumner, and began beating him about the head and shoulders with a gold-knobbed cane. Sumner nearly died; he would not return to the Senate for almost four years.

Southerners celebrated Brooks as a hero; dozens of supporters sent him new canes, one of which carried the inscription: "Hit Him Again." In satisfying his rage, though, Brooks had created a martyr—"Bleeding Sumner"—for the anti-slavery cause. A New Hampshire newspaper said the brutal beating had aroused "hostility against the Slave Power more intense than ever." Brooks's assault on Sumner thus had an unintended political effect: it drove more northerners into the new Republican Party.

> "Bleeding Sumner": A Republican martyr

Sectional Squabbles

The violence during the spring of 1856 spilled over into the presidential election—one in which the major parties could no longer evade the slavery dilemma. At its first national convention, the Republican Party fastened on John C. Frémont, the dashing western explorer nicknamed "the Pathfinder" who had led the conquest of Mexican-controlled California. The Republican platform borrowed heavily from the former Whigs. It endorsed federal funding for a transcontinental railroad and other transportation improvements, and it denounced the repeal of the Missouri Compromise and the "barbarism" of slavery. For the first time, a major-party platform had taken a stand against the expansion of slavery.

In picking a candidate, the Democrats dumped the unpopular Franklin Pierce. He remains the only elected president to be denied re-nomination by his own party. Instead, they nominated James Buchanan of Pennsylvania, a former senator and secretary of state who had long sought the nomination. The Democratic platform endorsed the Kansas-Nebraska Act, called for vigorous enforcement of the fugitive slave law, and stressed that Congress should not interfere with slavery in states or territories.

In the 1856 campaign, the Republicans had few southern supporters and only a handful in the border slave states of Delaware, Maryland, Kentucky, and Missouri. Buchanan, the Democrat, thus went into the campaign as the candidate of the only party with a national reach. Millard Fillmore ran as the candidate of the American Party, focusing on opposing Catholic immigrants from Germany and Ireland. Frémont swept the northernmost states with 114 electoral votes, but Buchanan added five free states—Pennsylvania, New Jersey, Illinois, Indiana, and California—to his southern majority for a total of 174. Fillmore garnered almost 22 percent of the votes but won only Maryland's eight electoral votes.

President James Buchanan

James Buchanan had built his career on his commitment to states' rights and his aggressive promotion of territorial expansion. Saving the Union, he believed, depended upon making concessions to the South. Republicans charged that he lacked the backbone to stand up to the South's enslavers who dominated the Democratic majorities in Congress.

The sixty-five-year-old Buchanan was—and remains—America's only president who was a lifelong bachelor. (His niece, Harriet Lane, handled the duties of First Lady during his term in office.) He was also rumored to be the first gay president.

To be gay, lesbian, or bisexual in the mid-nineteenth century was to risk arrest or social censure—or both. Most states enforced "anti-sodomy" laws prohibiting "unnatural acts," forcing same-sex relationships underground. For that reason, historians struggle to know with certainty the sexual orientation of people who were determined to keep it concealed.

That is the case with James Buchanan. Before becoming president, he had lived for sixteen years with Democrat William Rufus King, a former U.S. senator from Alabama who had also served as ambassador to France. King and Buchanan attended many official functions and social events together. And they shared a bed. To be sure, it was not uncommon in the nineteenth century for single men to room together or even sleep together. In the case of Buchanan and King, however, there seemed to be more at stake than simple expediency. Friends referred to King as Buchanan's "better half," and one congressman nicknamed him "Mrs. B." When King left for Paris, Buchanan confessed that he was "now 'solitary and alone,' having no companion in the house with me. I have gone a wooing to several gentlemen but have not succeeded with any one of them."

By the time of the 1856 presidential campaign, Democratic newspaper editors scrambled to spin Buchanan's unmarried status into a virtue. One claimed that Buchanan "married his Country over forty years ago and has taken good care of her." A single man like Buchanan would be a loyal and restrained president, his supporters argued, unlike his reckless opponent, John C. Frémont, who had eloped with his wife, Jessie. That, they charged,

> James Buchanan elected president (1856)

was an act of unrestrained passion that revealed Frémont to be lacking in morals and character.

Regardless of the way Buchanan conducted his private life, there is no doubt that he was a "doughface," a northerner with southern sympathies. No sooner was he elected president than he chose mostly slave-state men for his cabinet.

Although Buchanan had vast political experience, he had limited leadership ability—and bad luck. During his first six months in office in 1857, several events would bring about his undoing, beginning with a sharp downturn in the economy.

The Panic of 1857

By the summer of 1857, the economy was growing too fast. Too many railroads and factories were being built, and European demand for American corn and wheat was slackening. The result was a financial panic triggered by the failure of the Ohio Life Insurance and Trust Company. If such a prestigious company could fail, people worried, the entire economy might collapse.

Upon hearing the news, fearful customers began withdrawing their money from banks. This forced banks to call in loans, causing many businesses to go bankrupt. By the fall, tens of thousands had lost their jobs, and virtually every bank in New York City had closed its doors.

Amid the growing hysteria over the economic collapse, President Buchanan refused to intervene in what came to be called the Panic of 1857. In December of that year, preferring to make changes to the financial system rather than helping those affected—"reform not relief"—Buchanan pledged the federal government would do nothing to address the suffering caused by the financial panic.

> Buchanan's nonintervention in financial panic

The *Dred Scott* Case

A few months earlier, in his inaugural address, President Buchanan had asserted that the Supreme Court should decide the issue of slavery in the western territories. Two days later, on March 6, 1857, the Court delivered a momentous decision in the long-awaited case of **Dred Scott v. Sandford**, which had taken eleven years to work its way through the state and federal courts. The *New York Times* declared it "the most important decision ever made by the Supreme Court."

> The *Dred Scott* decision (1857)

Scott, enslaved from birth in Virginia, had been taken to St. Louis in 1830, where slavery was legal. There he was sold to an army surgeon, who took him to Illinois, then to the Wisconsin Territory (later Minnesota), and finally back to St. Louis in 1842. While in the Wisconsin Territory, Scott married Harriet Robinson, a woman also enslaved in Virginia who had lived in Pennsylvania before being forced to the western territory by her owner, a government agent negotiating with the Dakota and Obijwe peoples. Dred and Harriet Scott had two daughters, Eliza and Lizzie.

In 1846, the Scotts, with the aid of abolitionist attorneys, each filed lawsuits in Missouri, claiming that their residence in the free regions of Illinois,

Dred Scott v. Sandford (1857)
The U.S. Supreme Court ruling that enslaved people were not U.S. citizens and that Congress could not prohibit slavery in territories.

DRED AND HARRIET SCOTT
Dred and Harriet Scott agreed to sit for these portraits for the New York-based *Frank Leslie's Illustrated Newspaper* just after the Supreme Court issued its monumental decision rejecting their arguments for freedom.

Pennsylvania, and the Wisconsin Territory had made them "free" because slavery was outlawed in those areas. Harriet's lawyers eventually dropped her lawsuit, believing that the outcome of her husband's case would also decide her fate and that of their daughters. Her name then disappeared from the legal proceedings.

A Missouri jury decided in Dred Scott's favor, but the state supreme court ruled against him. When the case finally arose on appeal to the U.S. Supreme Court, the nation anxiously awaited its ruling.

Seven of the nine justices were Democrats, and five of the seven were southern slaveowners. Buchanan violated the separation of powers between the judicial and executive branches by browbeating a justice to go along with the southerners. The final vote was 7–2 against Scott.

Chief Justice Roger B. Taney of Maryland, a devoted supporter of the South and of slavery, wrote the majority opinion. He ruled that Scott lacked legal standing because, like all enslaved people, he was *property*, not a human being. He was not a U.S. citizen and could never become one, nor was he eligible to file suit in a court. When the Constitution was drafted in 1787, Taney claimed, all African Americans, even those who were legally free, were deemed "an inferior and subject race" that the Constitution had implicitly excluded from citizenship.

The *Dred Scott* case directly challenged the concept of popular sovereignty. If Congress could not exclude slavery from a territory, as Taney argued, then neither could a territorial government created by an act of Congress. Suddenly, all the West—and the North—was open to slavery.

Pro-slavery advocates celebrated the Court's decision, as did President Buchanan. A Georgia newspaper said the decision "covers every question regarding slavery and settles it in favor of the South." Republicans and abolitionists, by contrast, protested the *Dred Scott* decision because it nullified the very basis of the anti-slavery movement—the argument that the enslaved were people, not property.

The Scotts managed to gain their freedom anyway when abolitionists purchased and liberated them later that year. Dred went to work as a hotel porter in St. Louis until he became ill and died in 1858, while Harriet worked as a laundress and lived long enough to witness the liberation of all enslaved people in the United States.

The Lecompton Constitution (1857)

> Kansans twice reject the Lecompton Constitution

Meanwhile, in the Kansas Territory, the fight over slavery intensified. Just before James Buchanan's inauguration, in early 1857, the pro-slavery territorial legislature scheduled a constitutional convention. The governor vetoed the measure, but the legislature overrode his veto. The governor resigned in protest, and Buchanan replaced him with Robert J. Walker, a Pennsylvania native who had gone to Mississippi three decades before and become a slaveowner.

With Buchanan's approval, Governor Walker pledged to free-state Kansans (the overwhelming majority of residents) that the new constitution would receive a fair vote. But the delegates at Lecompton did not represent the majority, and they drafted a constitution, known as the Lecompton Constitution, that allowed slavery to be continued in Kansas. Opponents reacted by boycotting the referendum, thus allowing it to be approved and sent to Congress for endorsement. A new wave of outrage swept across the northern states. Governor Walker, having promised a fair election, resigned his post in protest of the Lecompton Constitution.

Before long, the new acting governor convened the anti-slavery legislature. It called for another election to vote the Lecompton Constitution up or down. Most pro-slavery settlers boycotted this election. The result was decisive: 10,226 voted against the constitution, while only 138 voted for it. In April 1858, the U.S. Congress ordered that Kansans vote again. They did so, rejecting the Lecompton Constitution, 11,300–1,788. With that vote, Kansas cleared the way for its eventual admission as a *free* state.

Douglas versus Lincoln (1858)

The controversy over slavery in Kansas fractured the Democratic Party. Stephen A. Douglas, one of the few remaining Democrats with support in both the North and the South, struggled to keep the party from fragmenting. First, however, he had to secure his home base in Illinois, where in 1858 he faced a demanding Senate reelection campaign.

To challenge Douglas, Illinois Republicans selected a respected lawyer from Springfield, Abraham Lincoln. Lincoln was the son of a frontier farmer/carpenter so poor that he rented out his hardworking son to neighbors.

LINCOLN AND DOUGLAS A tall, rawboned, small-town lawyer, Abraham Lincoln *(left)* was motivated by the Kansas-Nebraska Act to vie for an Illinois Senate seat, running against the current Democratic senator and author of the act, Stephen Douglas *(right)*.

When Abraham was seven years old, the family moved from Kentucky across the Ohio River to Indiana. Two years later, Lincoln's "angel mother" (as he called her) died, and his father remarried. In 1830, the Lincolns moved to Illinois, where young Lincoln worked in Springfield as a farmer, rail-splitter, and surveyor. He later became an attorney and married Mary Todd, an independent-minded woman who had been raised in a wealthy, slave-owning family in Kentucky.

In 1834, Lincoln was elected to the Illinois legislature, where he served four successive terms as a Whig. He was a true believer in Henry Clay's leadership and Clay's promotion of the American System. "My politics are short and sweet," Lincoln said. "I am in favor of a national bank. I am in favor of the internal improvement system and a high protective tariff." And he was opposed to the expansion of slavery into the western territories.

In 1846, Lincoln won a seat in the U.S. Congress while pledging to serve only one term. After his single unremarkable term, he returned to lawyering in Springfield. In 1854, however, his disgust at Douglas's Kansas-Nebraska Act drew him back into the political arena.

Lincoln hated slavery but was not yet an abolitionist. He did not believe that the nation should force the South to end "the monstrous injustice" of slavery, but he did insist that slavery be banned in the new western territories.

Lincoln joined the Republican Party in 1856, and two years later he emerged as the obvious choice to oppose Douglas in the Illinois senatorial race. At that point, Lincoln sought to raise his profile by challenging Douglas to a series of debates. The seven **Lincoln-Douglas debates** took place between August 21 and October 15, 1858. They attracted thousands of spectators and transformed the statewide race into a battle for the future of the entire republic.

The two men differed as much physically as they did politically. The brash and brilliant Douglas was short and stocky, barely five feet tall, but he had an enormous head that inspired the nickname "the Little Giant." He wore custom-tailored suits and traveled to the debates in a private railroad car.

By contrast, Lincoln was homely—tall (six feet four inches) and thin, with a long neck, big ears, and deep-set, brooding eyes. Poet Walt Whitman said that Lincoln's face was "so awful ugly it becomes beautiful." His coarse black hair never looked the same from day to day, and his ill-fitting suits made him so unkempt a Bostonian considered Lincoln "the ugliest man" he had ever seen.

Lincoln, however, dazzled people with the rawboned genius of his speeches, which were highlighted by folksy humor and biblical eloquence. His opponent, Stephen Douglas, acknowledged that Lincoln was "the strong man of the [Republican] party—full of wit, facts, dates, and the best stump speaker . . . in the West."

The basic dispute between the two candidates, Lincoln insisted, lay in Douglas's indifference to the immorality of slavery. Douglas, he said, did not care whether slavery in the territories was "voted up, or voted down."

Lincoln-Douglas debates over the issue of slavery in the West

Lincoln-Douglas debates (1858) In the Illinois race between Republican Abraham Lincoln and Democrat Stephen A. Douglas for a seat in the U.S. Senate, a series of seven dramatic debates focusing on the issue of slavery in the territories.

Instead, he was preoccupied only with process (Douglas continued to tout popular sovereignty); Lincoln claimed to be focused on principle. "I have always hated slavery as much as any abolitionist," he stressed. The American government, he predicted, could not "endure, permanently half *slave* and half *free*.... It will become *all* one thing or *all* the other."

Douglas responded that the United States was founded on the principle of White supremacy. "It was made by the white man, for the benefit of the white man, to be administered by the white man." Blacks and "Indians," he added, were members of an "inferior race."

Although Lincoln won the popular vote, Douglas won the Senate seat because he had the support of the Democratic-controlled state legislature, which chose the winner. Lincoln's energetic campaign, however, had made him a national figure.

An Insecure South

In May 1858, the free state of Minnesota entered the Union; in February 1859, another nonslave territory, Oregon, gained statehood. The slave states were quickly becoming a besieged minority, and their political insecurity deepened.

> Continued violence in Congress

As tensions over the future of slavery rose, decorum in Congress plummeted. Legislators threatened one another with clenched fists. A few of them killed opponents in duels. In 1858, members of Congress engaged in the largest brawl ever staged on the floor of the House of Representatives.

Harsh words about slavery incited the free-for-all. According to a reporter, the House floor "was a sea of writhing bodies, a dozen Southerners pummeling—or being pummeled by—a dozen Northerners. The Speaker shouted and rapped for order, and the sergeant at arms, thinking he could make a difference, rushed among the combatants showing the House mace (a heavy club). One representative picked up a heavy stoneware spittoon and rushed into the fray. Several Quakers urged calm and peace.

Like the fighting members of Congress, more and more Americans decided that compromise over the extension of slavery was impossible. The editor of a pro-slavery Kansas newspaper confessed he wanted to kill abolitionists: "If I can't kill a man, I'll kill a woman; and if I can't kill a woman, I'll kill a child."

Some southerners were already talking of secession again. Former Alabama congressman William L. Yancey, the leader of the most radical advocates of secession (known as "fire-eaters"), boasted that it would be easy "to precipitate the Cotton States into a revolution."

John Brown's Raid (1859)

Such violent threats drove John Brown to desperation. On the cool, rainy night of October 16, 1859, Brown crossed the Potomac River from Maryland with about twenty young men, including three of his sons and five African Americans. They walked five miles to the federal rifle arsenal in Harpers

> Raid on Harpers Ferry (1859)

JOHN BROWN On his way to the gallows, Brown predicted that slavery would end only "after much bloodshed."

Ferry, Virginia (now West Virginia). There they took the sleeping residents by surprise, cut the telegraph lines, and occupied the arsenal with its 100,000 rifles.

Brown then sent several men to kidnap prominent slaveowners and arm thousands of enslaved people in the area, in the hope of triggering mass uprisings. "I want to free all the negroes in this state," Brown said. "If the citizens interfere with me, I must burn the town and have blood."

Only a few enslaved people heeded the call, however, and by dawn, enraged townsmen had surrounded the raiders. Brown and a dozen of his men, along with eleven White hostages and two of their enslaved workers, holed up in the firehouse.

In response, hundreds of armed men poured into Harpers Ferry. Among them was Lieutenant Colonel Robert E. Lee, who arrived with a force of U.S. Marines. On the morning of October 18, the marines broke down the firehouse's barricaded doors and rushed in. The siege was over. Brown's men had killed four townspeople and wounded another dozen. Of their own group, ten were killed (including two of Brown's sons), and five were captured; another five escaped.

A jury quickly convicted John Brown and his accomplices of treason, murder, and "conspiring with Negroes to produce insurrection." A wounded Brown delivered a stirring speech: "Now, if it is deemed necessary that I should forfeit my life for the furtherance of the ends of justice, and mingle my blood further with the blood of my children and with the blood of millions in this slave country whose rights are disregarded by wicked, cruel, and unjust enactments, I say, let it be done."

On December 2, 1859, Brown, wearing a black coat and black pants stained with blood, climbed into a wagon, sat on his empty black walnut coffin, and rode to the gallows, which was surrounded by 1,500 soldiers. (Among the onlookers was a popular actor named John Wilkes Booth, who would later assassinate Abraham Lincoln.)

If Brown had failed to ignite a massive slave rebellion, he had become a martyr for the anti-slavery cause. In the North, church bells tolled in his honor, and cannons fired salutes. In the South, he had stirred the region's worst nightmare: that armed enslaved people would revolt. John Brown, wrote the African American abolitionist Frederick Douglass, "began the war that ended American slavery."

Throughout the fall and winter of 1859–1860, rumors of abolitionist conspiracies and slave insurrections swept through the southern states. Some 300 abolitionists were murdered or forced out of the region.

> Brown's raid ignites Southern fears of abolitionists

The Democrats Divide (1860)

Amid such hysteria, the nation mobilized for another presidential election, destined to be the most fateful in its history. In April 1860, Democrats gathered for what would become a disastrous nominating convention in Charleston, South Carolina.

President Buchanan had decided not to seek a second term, leaving Stephen A. Douglas as the front-runner. Douglas's northern supporters tried to straddle the issue of slavery by promising to defend the institution in the South while assuring northerners that it would not spread to new states. Southern militants, however, used the *Dred Scott* ruling to demand federal protection for slavery in the territories as well as the states.

When the pro-slavery advocates lost, delegates from eight southern states walked out and the convention disintegrated. Before departing, a plantation-owning delegate left no doubt about the reason for the split: "Slavery is our King; Slavery is our truth; Slavery is our divine right." Douglas's supporters reassembled in Baltimore on June 18 and nominated him for president.

> Southern and Northern Democrats split over slavery in 1860 election

Southern Democrats met first in Richmond and then in Baltimore, where they adopted the pro-slavery platform that had been defeated in Charleston. They named John C. Breckinridge, vice president under Buchanan, as their candidate because he promised to protect the right of emigrants to take their enslaved people to the western territories. Thus another cord binding the nation together had snapped: the fracturing of the Democratic Party made a Republican victory in 1860 almost certain.

Lincoln's Election (1860)

The Republicans gathered in Chicago, where everything came together for Abraham Lincoln. Inside the convention building, the "wildest excitement and enthusiasm" swelled to a "perfect roar" as Lincoln was nominated. The convention reaffirmed the party's opposition to the extension of slavery and endorsed a series of traditional Whig policies promoting a higher protective tariff, free farms (homesteads) on federal lands in the West, and federally financed internal improvements, including a transcontinental railroad.

In the border states of Maryland, Delaware, Kentucky, and Missouri, former Whigs made one more try at sectional reconciliation. Meeting in Baltimore a week before the Republicans met in Chicago, they reorganized as the Constitutional Union Party and nominated John Bell of Tennessee for president. Their platform promoted "the Constitution of the Country, the Union of the States, and the Enforcement of the Laws."

The bitterly contested presidential campaign became a choice between Abraham Lincoln and Steven A. Douglas in the North (Lincoln was not even on the ballot in the South), and between Breckinridge and Bell in the South. Douglas, the only candidate to mount a nationwide campaign, promised that he would "make war boldly against" extremists in both regions. His heroic effort, however, did little good.

At midnight on November 6, Lincoln won with 39 percent of the popular vote, the smallest plurality ever, but he captured a clear majority (180 votes) in the Electoral College (see Map 13.7). He carried *all* eighteen free states but *none* of the slave states. Douglas came in second and had worn himself out in doing so. He would die just seven months later at age forty-eight.

> Abraham Lincoln elected president (1860)

MAP 13.7 THE ELECTION OF 1860

		Electoral Vote	Popular Vote
■	**Abraham Lincoln (Republican)**	180	1,866,000
■	Stephen A. Douglas (Democrat—northern)	12	1,383,000
■	John C. Breckinridge (Democrat—southern)	72	848,000
■	John Bell (Constitutional Union)	39	593,000

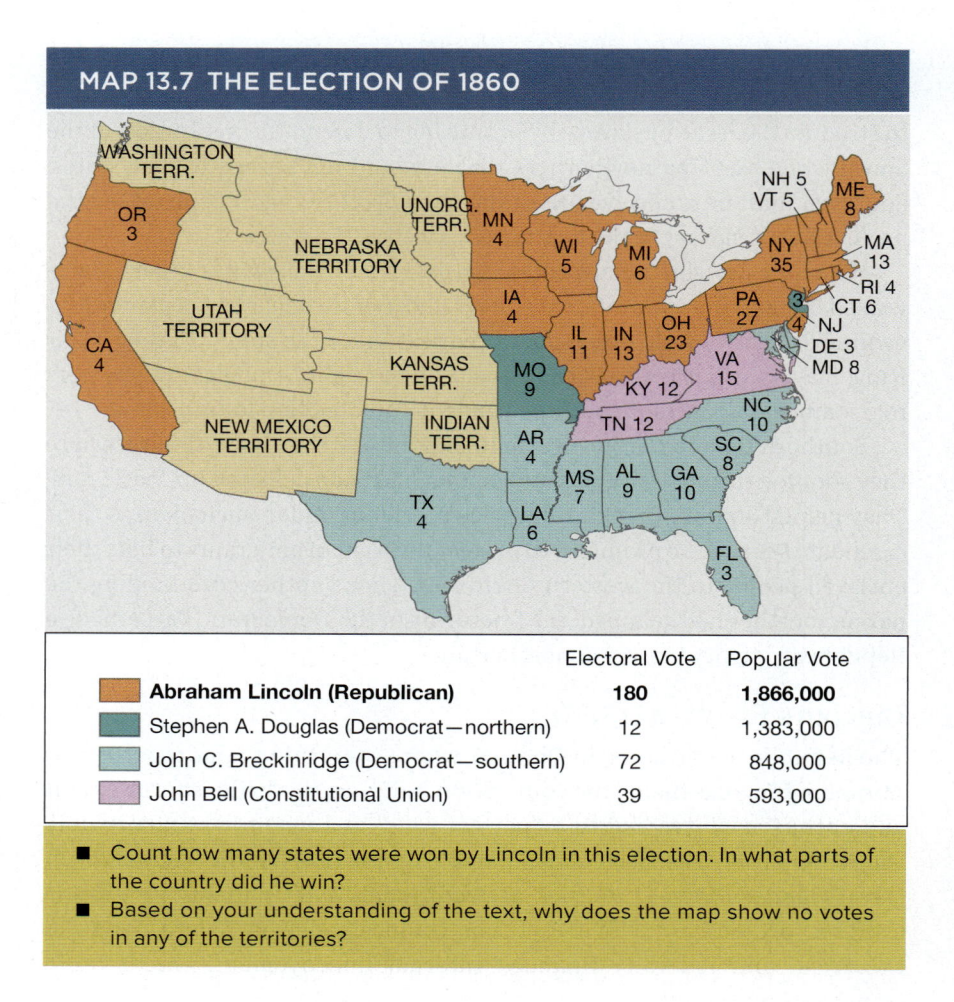

- Count how many states were won by Lincoln in this election. In what parts of the country did he win?
- Based on your understanding of the text, why does the map show no votes in any of the territories?

Lincoln's political experience was meager, his learning limited, and his popular support shallow. Yet ultimately the unassuming lawyer from Springfield, Illinois, would become, as Walt Whitman wrote, "the grandest figure yet, on all the crowded canvas of the Nineteenth Century."

All eyes would turn to Lincoln in the weeks and months ahead. His controversial election had thrust the future of slavery to the center of American politics and had ended the many years of political evasion and compromise. The time had finally come to decide what kind of nation would continue extending its reach across the North American continent—slave or free? Against the backdrop of violent pro-slavery and anti-slavery events in Kansas, the Supreme Court's pro-slavery *Dred Scott* decision, and the Lincoln-Douglas debates, the Republican Party's anti-slavery platform had appealed to northern voters. Their states' Electoral College votes delivered victory to Lincoln in the 1860 election. But victory did not settle the sectional conflict—far from it. While many northerners worried whether their new president could hold the fractured nation together, outraged White southerners defiantly pushed the nation to a breaking point.

The Southern Response

> **CORE OBJECTIVE**
> **5.** Explain why seven southern states seceded from the Union shortly after Lincoln's election in 1860.

Between November 8, 1860, when Abraham Lincoln was elected, and March 4, 1861, when he was inaugurated, the United States of America disintegrated. Lincoln's election panicked southerners, who believed that the Republican Party, as a Richmond newspaper asserted, was founded for one reason: "hatred of African slavery."

After Lincoln's victory, South Carolina's entire congressional delegation resigned. The state's legislature then appointed a convention to decide whether it should secede from the Union. Nearly all the delegates owned enslaved people. Delegate Thomas Jefferson Withers declared that the "true question for us all is how shall we sustain African slavery in South Carolina from a series of annoying attacks?"

> South Carolina secedes

Meeting in Charleston on December 20, 1860, the special convention unanimously approved an Ordinance of Secession separating South Carolina from the United States. James L. Petigru, one of the few Unionists in Charleston, quipped that his newly independent home state "is too small to be a Republic and too large to be an insane asylum."

As the news spread across the state, church bells rang and shops closed. "THE UNION IS DISSOLVED!" screamed the headline of the *Charleston Mercury*.

President Buchanan's Waiting Game

Other southern states, especially those where the cotton economy reigned supreme, soon followed South Carolina's lead in descending into disunion. The imploding nation desperately needed a bold, decisive president to intervene. Instead it suffered under the final weeks in office of James Buchanan, who blamed the crisis on fanatical abolitionists. He declared secession illegal, then claimed that he lacked the constitutional authority to stop it. "I can do nothing," he sighed. In the face of the president's clueless inaction, armed southern firebrands surrounded federal forts in the seceded states.

Among the federal facilities under siege was Fort Sumter, nestled on a tiny island at the mouth of Charleston Harbor. When South Carolina secessionists demanded that U.S. Army Major Robert Anderson surrender the fort, he refused.

On January 5, 1861, President Buchanan sent an unarmed commercial steamship, the *Star of the West*, to resupply Fort Sumter. As the ship approached Charleston Harbor after midnight four days later, cannons operated by cadets from The Citadel, the state's military college, opened fire and drove it away. It was an act of war, but Buchanan chose to ignore the attack, hoping that a compromise might avert civil war. Southern leaders, however, were not in a compromising

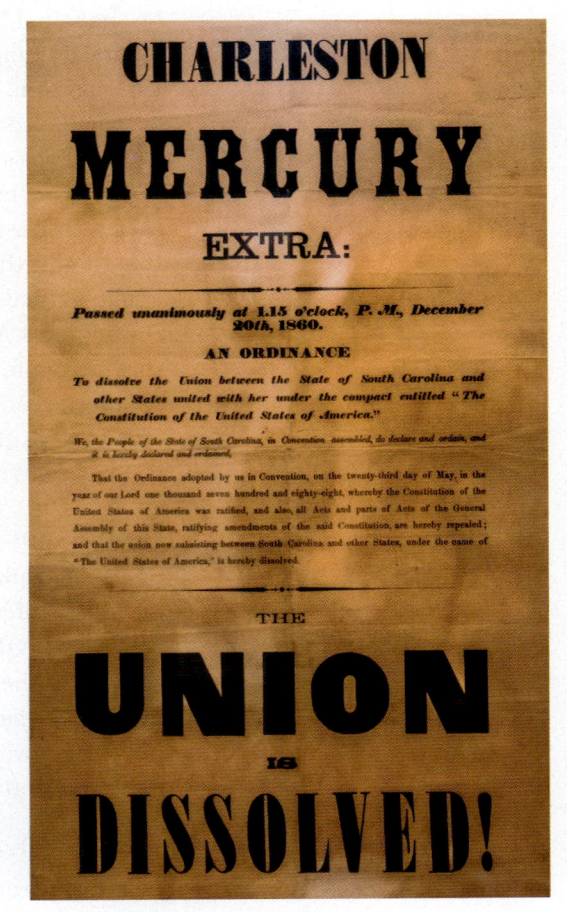

"THE UNION IS DISSOLVED!" A newspaper headline announcing South Carolina's secession from the Union.

mood. "We spit on every plan to compromise," sneered a secessionist. That same day, Mississippi left the Union, followed by Alabama three days later.

Secession of the Lower South (1861)

By February 1, 1861, the other states of the Lower South—Florida, Georgia, Louisiana, and Texas—had also seceded. Although their secession ordinances mentioned various grievances against the federal government, they made clear that the primary reason for leaving the Union was their determination to preserve slavery.

On February 4, 1861, fifty representatives of the seceding states—all but one of whom were slaveowners—met in Montgomery, Alabama, where they adopted a constitution for the Confederate States of America (CSA). The document was modeled closely after the federal constitution, but with some key revisions. Unlike the 1787 constitution, the Confederacy's founders mandated that "the institution of negro slavery, as it now exists in the Confederate States, shall be recognized and protected" by the new government, and an individual's right to own enslaved "property" and transport it to other states could not be "impaired." In addition, the Confederate constitution outlawed tariffs and federal funding for internal improvements, and it gave the president only one six-year term. The CSA was to have only an agricultural economy.

> The formation of the Confederacy

The delegates unanimously elected Mississippi's Jefferson Davis as the Confederacy's president. A West Point graduate who had been a highly decorated officer in the Mexican-American War, Davis became a U.S. senator and then served as secretary of war under President Franklin Pierce. Davis claimed that "if only the North would recognize our independence, all would be well." Yet he warned southerners to prepare for "a long and bloody conflict."

> Jefferson Davis elected Confederate president

Georgia's Alexander H. Stephens, Davis's vice president, told supporters that the Confederacy was founded to sustain the slave system upon which the southern economy depended. The new southern republic, he said, embodied "the great truth that the negro is not equal to the white man; that slavery, subordination to the superior [White] race, is his natural and normal condition."

Compromise Efforts Fail

Earlier, as talk of civil war had been growing, several members of Congress had desperately sought a compromise. John J. Crittenden of Kentucky, an enslaver and the oldest member of the Senate, had suggested that slavery be allowed in the western territories *south* of the 1820 Missouri Compromise line (36°30′ parallel) and be guaranteed to continue where it already existed. Lincoln, however, opposed any plan that would expand slavery westward, and at his urging, the Senate defeated the Crittenden Compromise, 25–23.

Lincoln's Inauguration

In mid-February 1861, Abraham Lincoln boarded a train in Springfield, Illinois, headed to Washington, D.C., for his inauguration.

In his inaugural address on March 4, the most highly anticipated speech in U.S. history, Lincoln repeated his pledge not "to interfere with the institution of slavery in the states where it exists" because he did not believe he had constitutional authority to do so. Yet the immediate question had shifted to secession. Lincoln insisted that "the Union of these States is perpetual," and therefore the notion of a Confederate nation was a fiction. No state, he stressed, "can lawfully get out of the Union." He pledged to defend "federal forts in the South," such as Fort Sumter in Charleston, but beyond that "there [would] be no invasion, no using of force against or among the people anywhere."

In closing, Lincoln appealed for regional harmony:

> We are not enemies, but friends. We must not be enemies. Though passion may have strained, it must not break our bonds of affection. The mystic chords of memory, stretching from every battlefield and patriot grave to every living heart and hearthstone all over this broad land, will yet swell the chorus of the Union, when again touched, as surely they will be, by the better angels of our nature.

Most White southerners were not impressed. A North Carolina newspaper warned that Lincoln's speech made civil war "inevitable."

The End of the Waiting Game

On March 5, 1861, his first day in office, President Lincoln found a letter on his desk from Major Robert Anderson, the army commander at Fort Sumter. Anderson reported that his men had enough food for only a few weeks and that the Confederates were encircling the fort with a "ring of fire."

On April 4, Lincoln ordered unarmed ships to resupply the sixty-nine soldiers at Fort Sumter. On April 11, Confederate General Pierre G. T. Beauregard, who had studied under Major Anderson at West Point, demanded that his former professor surrender Fort Sumter. Anderson refused. At four-thirty in the morning of April 12, Confederate cannons began firing on Fort Sumter. After some thirty-four hours, his ammunition exhausted, Anderson lowered the "Stars and Stripes."

Civil War begins (April 12, 1861)

The Confederate attack on Fort Sumter changed everything. It "has made the North a unit," New York Democratic congressman Daniel Sickles wrote. "We are at war with a foreign power." The abolitionist Frederick Douglass observed that "war begins where reason ends," and the South's consuming concern about the future of slavery confirmed the logic of his statement.

By this point, the northern and southern states were not just ideological and political adversaries; the secession of seven states and the Confederate attack on Fort Sumter had turned them into military foes as well. The states had seceded because they feared that Lincoln would abolish slavery everywhere, even though Lincoln himself had promised repeatedly that he would not interfere with slavery in the South—he only wanted to stop its expansion to the West. Once South Carolina seceded, however, six other states followed and together formed the Confederate States of America. After the Confederate attack on Fort Sumter in Charleston Harbor, six more southern states seceded, sending the North and South down a deadly road to civil war.

Reviewing the
CORE OBJECTIVES

- **Westward Migration** In the 1830s, White Americans came to believe in *manifest destiny*—the theory that the U.S. expansion to the Pacific coast was divinely ordained. This overlooked the reality that the West was already controlled by powerful European and Indigenous empires, such as that of the *Comanche*, who were ready to fight the United States for dominance over the continent. Large numbers of Americans set out anyway on the *Overland Trails* to settle in Oregon (*Oregon Fever*) and California, and many southerners (*Texians*) moved to the Mexican province of Texas with their enslaved people. The Mexican government gradually outlawed slavery, however, and in 1830 forbade further immigration. Texians rebelled, winning their independence from Mexico in the *Texas Revolution* (1835–1836). Texas, however, would not become a state for another decade because the U.S. government was determined to avoid both war with Mexico and the divisive issue of adding another slave state to the nation.

- **Mexican-American War** As the Comanche continued to push deeper into the Republic of Texas, and Texian calls for American protection escalated, the United States finally annexed Texas in 1845. But the Mexican government refused to recognize the loss of its northern province. Meanwhile, President Polk sought to acquire California, New Mexico, and Texas from Mexico, but negotiations failed. When Mexican troops crossed the Rio Grande and fired on U.S. soldiers, Polk urged Congress to declare war, which U.S. forces won. By the terms of the *Treaty of Guadalupe Hidalgo* (1848), Mexico ceded California and New Mexico to the United States and gave up claims to disputed land north of the Rio Grande.

- **Slavery in the Territories** The *Wilmot Proviso* (1846) never became law; but by seeking to ban slavery in the newly acquired Mexican territories, it outraged pro-slavery legislators. The controversy helped create a new *Free-Soil Party* that demanded the banning of slavery in the new territories. In 1849, the *California gold rush* further escalated sectional tensions. Most Californians wanted their territory to become a free state. Southerners feared losing federal protection of slavery if free states outnumbered slave states. Some political leaders urged the voters in each territory to decide the issue themselves (*popular sovereignty*). The *Compromise of 1850* allowed California to enter the Union as a free state; established the territories of Texas, New Mexico, and Utah without direct reference to slavery; banned the slave trade in Washington, D.C.; and strengthened the *Fugitive Slave Act* (1850). Tensions turned violent with passage of the *Kansas-Nebraska Act* (1854), which overturned the Missouri Compromise by allowing slavery in the territories where it had been banned in 1820.

- **The Republican Party's Appeal** Northerners were outraged by violent pro-slavery mobs as the territory of Kansas prepared to enter the Union. Yet anti-slavery radicals could also be violent, such as John Brown in *Bleeding Kansas* (1856). The Supreme

Court's pro-slavery *Dred Scott v. Sandford* (1857) decision further fueled sectional conflict. The *Lincoln-Douglas debates* (1858) in Illinois centered on the controversy over extending slavery into the territories. Northern voters increasingly gravitated toward the anti-slavery Republican Party. Republicans also advocated for protective tariffs and the development of national infrastructure, which appealed to northern manufacturers and commercial farmers. In the 1860 presidential election, Abraham Lincoln carried every free state and won a clear Electoral College victory.

■ **The Secession of the Lower South** South Carolina seceded from the Union a month after Lincoln's presidential victory. Before Lincoln was inaugurated, six other states joined South Carolina to form the Confederate States of America (CSA). South Carolinians bombarded Fort Sumter in Charleston Harbor, and so the Civil War began.

KEY TERMS

manifest destiny *p. 514*
Overland Trails *p. 516*
Comanche *p. 516*
Oregon Fever *p. 520*
Texas Revolution (1835–1836) *p. 525*
Treaty of Guadalupe Hidalgo (1848) *p. 536*
Wilmot Proviso (1846) *p. 538*
popular sovereignty *p. 539*
Free-Soil Party *p. 540*
California gold rush (1849) *p. 541*
Compromise of 1850 *p. 544*
Fugitive Slave Act (1850) *p. 548*
Kansas-Nebraska Act (1854) *p. 552*
Bleeding Kansas (1856) *p. 554*
Dred Scott v. Sandford (1857) *p. 557*
Lincoln-Douglas debates (1858) *p. 560*

CHRONOLOGY

1750–1850	Comanche Empire
1821	Mexico gains independence from Spain and begins abolishing slavery
1836	American "Texians" are defeated at the Alamo
1845	United States annexes Texas
1846	Mexican-American War begins
1848	Treaty of Guadalupe Hidalgo ends Mexican-American War
1849	California gold rush begins
1854	Congress passes Kansas-Nebraska Act
	Republican Party is founded
1856	Bleeding Kansas
1857	*Dred Scott v. Sandford* and Lecompton Constitution
1858	Lincoln-Douglas debates
1859	John Brown's raid at Harpers Ferry, Virginia
1860–1861	Seven southern states secede from the Union
March 4, 1861	Abraham Lincoln is inaugurated president
April 1861	Fort Sumter falls to Confederate forces

InQuizitive

Go to InQuizitive to see what you've learned—and learn what you've missed—with personalized feedback along the way.

LINCOLN'S DRIVE THROUGH RICHMOND (1866) Shortly after the Confederate capital of Richmond, Virginia, fell to Union forces in April 1865, President Abraham Lincoln visited the war-torn city. Formerly enslaved people and White Unionists enthusiastically approached his carriage.

CHAPTER 14

The War of the Union

1861–1865

The fall of Fort Sumter started the Civil War and triggered a wave of patriotic bluster on both sides. A White Southern woman prayed that God would "give us strength to conquer the Yankees, to exterminate *them*, to lay waste every Northern city, town and village, to destroy them utterly." Northern sentiment was similarly bloodthirsty. Writer Nathaniel Hawthorne reported from Massachusetts that his transcendentalist friend Ralph Waldo Emerson was "breathing slaughter" as the Union army prepared for its first battle. Emerson, a pacifist, now said that "sometimes gunpowder smells good."

Southerners claimed their constitutional *right* to secede from the United States. Confederate president Jefferson Davis argued that secession was necessary to defend themselves against a "tyrannical majority"—meaning those Northerners who had elected President Abraham Lincoln, the anti-slavery Republican.

Davis and his fellow Confederate leaders emphasized that protecting slavery from attacks by Republicans justified secession. The South Carolina Declaration on the Immediate Causes of Secession, for example, explained that the state left the Union because of the "increasing hostility on the part of the non-slaveholding states to the institution of slavery." Georgian Alexander Stephens, vice president of the Confederate States of America, said that slavery was the "immediate cause" of secession and war and that the supremacy of White people must remain

CORE OBJECTIVES

1. Identify the respective advantages of the North and South as the Civil War began, and explain how they affected the military strategies of the Union and the Confederacy.

2. Evaluate Abraham Lincoln's decision to issue the Emancipation Proclamation and its impact on the war.

3. Analyze how the war affected social and economic life in the North and South.

4. Describe the military turning points in 1863 and 1864 that ultimately led to the Confederacy's defeat.

5. Explain how the Civil War changed the nation.

JEFFERSON DAVIS President of the Confederacy.

the "cornerstone" of the Confederacy. The "great truth" on which the Confederate government was founded, he stressed, is "that the negro is not equal to the White man; that slavery—subordination to the superior race—is his natural and normal condition."

President Lincoln resolved to pull the South back into the Union. To do so, he reassured Southerners that the "paramount object in this struggle *is* to save the Union and is *not* either to save or to destroy slavery. If I could save the Union without freeing *any* slave I would do it, and if I could save it by freeing *all* the slaves I would do it; and if I could save it by freeing some and leaving others alone I would also do that." While remaining opposed to any westward expansion of the slave system, he promised Southerners that they could retain their enslaved people.

None of the Confederate states took Lincoln at his word. White Southerners believed the "Black Republican," as they called the president, was determined to end slavery everywhere. Given this contentious atmosphere, the next four years would put the United States to its greatest test—and would determine whether its young democracy could endure four years of devastating warfare.

CORE OBJECTIVE

1. Identify the respective advantages of the North and South as the Civil War began, and explain how they affected the military strategies of the Union and the Confederacy.

Mobilizing Forces in the North and South

On April 15, 1861, three days after the Confederate attack on Fort Sumter, Lincoln directed the "loyal" states to supply 75,000 militiamen for ninety days to suppress the rebellion. The Civil War would force everyone—men and women, White and Black, immigrants, Hispanic-Americans, and Native Americans, free and enslaved—to choose sides.

Choosing Sides

The first seven states that seceded—South Carolina, Mississippi, Florida, Alabama, Georgia, Louisiana, and Texas—were all from the Lower South, where the cotton economy was strongest and where most enslaved people lived. All the states in the Upper South, especially Tennessee and Virginia, had areas (mainly in the mountains) where White people were poor, enslaved people were scarce, and Union support remained strong. Nevertheless, the outbreak of fighting led four more Southern slave states to join the Confederacy: Virginia, Arkansas, Tennessee, and North Carolina (see Map 14.1).

Of the slaveholding states along the border between North and South, Delaware remained in the Union; but Maryland, Kentucky, and Missouri went through bitter struggles to decide which side to support. "I think to lose Kentucky is nearly the same as to lose the whole game," Lincoln told a friend. If Kentucky were to join the Confederacy, "we cannot hold Missouri, nor, as I think, Maryland." Lincoln was so determined to keep slaveholding Kentucky on the Union side that he muffled all talk of abolition.

MAP 14.1 SECESSION, 1860–1861

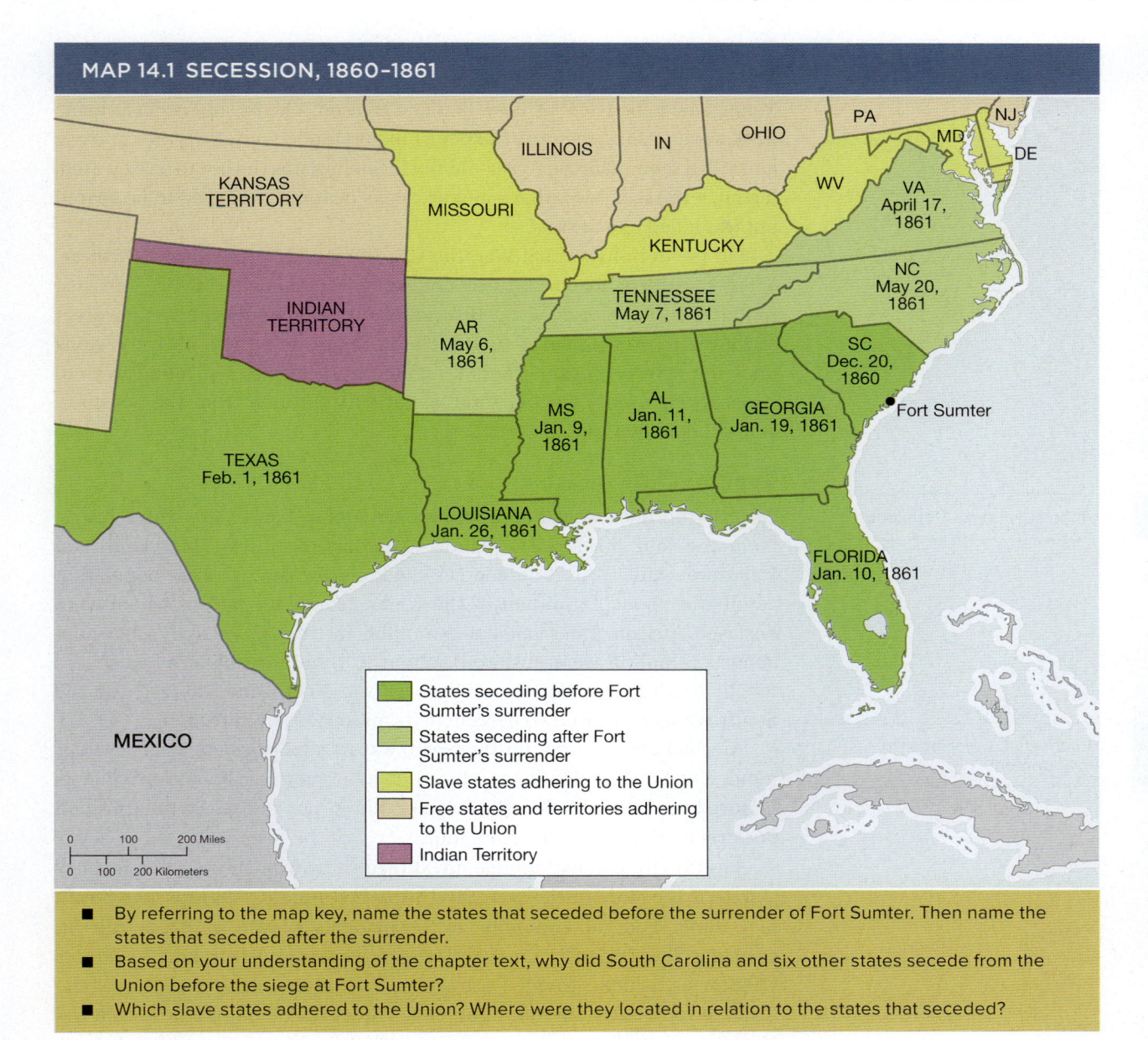

Legend:
- States seceding before Fort Sumter's surrender
- States seceding after Fort Sumter's surrender
- Slave states adhering to the Union
- Free states and territories adhering to the Union
- Indian Territory

States and secession dates shown on map:
- SC: Dec. 20, 1860
- MS: Jan. 9, 1861
- FLORIDA: Jan. 10, 1861
- AL: Jan. 11, 1861
- GEORGIA: Jan. 19, 1861
- LOUISIANA: Jan. 26, 1861
- TEXAS: Feb. 1, 1861
- AR: May 6, 1861
- TENNESSEE: May 7, 1861
- VA: April 17, 1861
- NC: May 20, 1861

- By referring to the map key, name the states that seceded before the surrender of Fort Sumter. Then name the states that seceded after the surrender.
- Based on your understanding of the chapter text, why did South Carolina and six other states secede from the Union before the siege at Fort Sumter?
- Which slave states adhered to the Union? Where were they located in relation to the states that seceded?

If Maryland had seceded, Confederates would have surrounded Washington, D.C. To keep Maryland in the Union, Lincoln had pro-Confederate leaders there arrested. The fragile neutrality of Kentucky lasted until September 3, when Confederate and Union armies moved into the divided state. Kentucky voters elected a Southern-sympathizing governor and a Unionist majority in the state legislature—as did Missouri, a state with many European immigrants, most of whom were German and overwhelmingly sided with the Union.

In areas of the South where Union sentiment remained strong, such as eastern Tennessee and Western Virginia, the Civil War was brutally uncivil.

In January 1863, Confederate soldiers in Madison County, North Carolina, captured thirteen men and boys and began marching them to Knoxville, Tennessee, to be tried for desertion and treason. The prisoners never made it, however. Along the way, the detachment stopped, lined up the captives, and killed them. Thirteen-year-old David Shelton was the last to be executed, having witnessed his father's and brother's deaths. He begged to be spared but was killed like the rest.

On the eve of the Civil War, the U.S. Army had 1,000 officers. Of these, about 25 percent, like the future Confederate general Robert E. Lee, resigned to join the Confederate army. But similarly, many Southerners made great sacrifices to remain loyal to the Union. Some left their native regions once the fighting began; others remained in the South but found ways to support the Union. Of that total, about 100,000 men from the Southern states fought *against* the Confederacy.

Regional Advantages

Union advantage: Population

Once battle lines were finally drawn, the Union had twenty-three states, including four border slave states—Missouri, Kentucky, Maryland, and Delaware—while the Confederacy had eleven states. The population count was about 22 million in the Union (some 400,000 of whom were enslaved African Americans) to 9 million in the Confederacy (of whom about 3.5 million were enslaved). About 2.75 million soldiers and sailors fought in the Civil War—2 million for the North and 750,000 for the South, which mobilized 80 percent of its military-age White men.

Union advantage: Industrial development

An even greater asset for the North was its superior industrial development. The Southern states produced just 7 percent of the nation's manufactured goods. The Union states generated 97 percent of the firearms and 96 percent of the railroad equipment.

The North also had a huge advantage in transportation, particularly ships. At the start of the war, the Union had ninety warships; the South had none. Federal gunboats and transports played a direct role in securing the Union's control of the Mississippi River and its larger tributaries, which provided easy invasion routes into the center of the Confederacy. Early on, the Union navy's blockade of major Southern ports sharply reduced the amount of cotton that could be exported to Britain and France as well as the flow of goods (including military weapons) imported from Europe.

Confederate advantage: Defending its own territory

The Confederates, however, had major geographic and emotional advantages: they could fight on their own territory in defense of their homeland. In warfare, it is usually easier to defend than to attack, since defending troops have the opportunity to dig protective trenches and fortifications. In the Civil War, armies that assaulted well-defended positions were mauled 90 percent of the time. Many Confederate leaders thought that if they could hold out long enough, disgruntled Northern voters might convince Lincoln and Congress to end the war.

A Conflict of Goals

The Confederacy's top priority was to convince the Union and the world to recognize its newly declared independence. The United States, by contrast, fought to restore the Union, as Abraham Lincoln repeatedly said.

After the fall of Fort Sumter, newspaper editors and politicians on both sides pressured the generals to strike quickly. "Forward to Richmond!" screamed a New York newspaper headline. Most people thought the war would be, in President Lincoln's words, "a short and decisive one." They were sorely wrong.

In the summer of 1861, Jefferson Davis told General Pierre G. T. Beauregard to rush the main Confederate army to Manassas Junction, a railroad crossing in northern Virginia, about twenty-five miles west of Washington. Lincoln hoped that the Union army (often called *Federals*) would overrun the outnumbered Confederates and quickly push on to Richmond, only 107 miles to the south.

> Early expectations for the war

First Bull Run

When word reached Washington, D.C., that the armies were converging for battle, hundreds of civilians packed picnic lunches and rode out to watch, assuming that the first clash of arms would be short, glorious, and bloodless.

It was a hot, dry day on July 21, 1861, when 37,000 untested Union recruits marched to battle, some of them breaking ranks to eat blackberries or drink water from streams along the way. Many of them died with the berry juice still on their lips as they engaged the Confederates, who were dug in behind a tree-choked branch of the Potomac River called Bull Run.

For most soldiers, the battle provided their first taste of the chaos and confusion of combat. Many were disoriented by the smoke from

BULL RUN Moments before battle, a spectator in a top hat chats with Union soldiers *(bottom right)*, while an artist sketches the passing troops heading to combat *(at left)*.

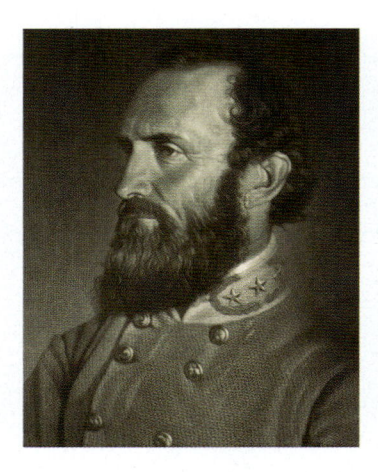

THOMAS "STONEWALL" JACKSON
The aggressive commander of a Confederate brigade at Bull Run, Jackson would later die of friendly fire in the Battle of Chancellorsville.

Confederate advantage: Victory at First Battle of Bull Run (1861)

Union strategy: Naval blockade and control of rivers

gunpowder and the screaming of fallen comrades. Because neither side yet wore standard-colored uniforms, the soldiers had trouble identifying friend from foe.

The Union troops almost won the battle early in the afternoon. "We fired a volley," wrote a Massachusetts private, "and saw the Rebels running. . . . The boys were saying constantly, in great glee, 'We've whipped them.' 'We'll hang Jeff Davis from a sour apple tree.' 'They're running.' 'The war is over.'"

But Confederate reinforcements poured in. So did crucial information about the location and size of U.S. forces, courtesy of Rose O'Neal Greenhow, a Southern-sympathizing resident of Washington, D.C., who used her friendships with prominent U.S. politicians to learn about Union battle preparations. She then passed that information on to the Confederates—and was arrested by U.S. officials on the charge of espionage.

A South Carolina officer rallied his troops by pointing to the example of Thomas Jackson: "Look! There is General Jackson with his Virginians, standing like a stone wall!" Jackson, a professor at Virginia Military Institute who had graduated from West Point, ordered his men to charge, urging them to "yell like furies!" From that day forward, "Stonewall" became Jackson's nickname and he would become the most celebrated—and feared—Confederate field commander.

The Union army panicked, and fleeing soldiers and terrified civilians clogged the road to Washington, D.C. The victorious Confederates, however, were so disorganized and exhausted that they failed to give chase.

The news of the Confederate victory at Bull Run shocked Northerners. Senator Benjamin Wade, an Ohio Republican, reported from Washington, D.C., that "all is gloomy & despairing here." The surprising Yankee defeat triggered sharp criticism of President Lincoln. Another Republican denounced Lincoln as "an admitted failure" who "has no will, no courage, no executive capacity."

The hallmark of Lincoln's presidency, however, was his ability to acknowledge mistakes, to learn from them, and to move forward. The self-educated president with limited political and executive experience surrounded himself with capable cabinet members and advisers, both Republicans and Democrats, conservatives and radicals. All were independent thinkers with their own agendas, yet Lincoln found a way to forge them into an effective team. With each passing year, Lincoln would become more sure of himself. He grew into greatness as the war grew in scope and unspeakable horrors.

The Union's "Anaconda" Plan

The Battle of Bull Run demonstrated that the war would not be decided with one sudden stroke, as many had assumed. General Winfield Scott, the seventy-five-year-old commander of the Union effort, devised a three-pronged strategy. First, the Army of the Potomac, the main Union army, would defend Washington, D.C., and exert constant pressure on the Confederate capital at Richmond.

Second, the Federal navy's blockade of Southern ports would cut off the Confederacy's access to foreign goods and weapons. The third component called for other Union armies to divide the Confederacy by pushing south along the crucial inland water routes: the Mississippi, Tennessee, and Cumberland Rivers. This so-called **Anaconda Plan** was intended to slowly trap and crush the Southern resistance, like an anaconda snake strangling its prey.

Anaconda Plan During the Civil War, the Union's primary strategy calling for a naval blockade of major Southern seaports and then dividing the Confederacy by gaining control of the Tennessee, Cumberland, and Mississippi Rivers.

Confederate Strategy

The Confederate plan was simpler. If the Union forces could be stalemated and the war prolonged, as Jefferson Davis and others hoped, then the British or French, desperate for cotton from the South, might be persuaded to join the cause. Or perhaps a long war would change public sentiment in the North and force President Lincoln to seek a negotiated settlement. So, while armies were forming in the South, Confederate diplomats were seeking military and financial assistance in London and Paris. They won a promise from France to recognize the Confederacy as a new nation *if* Great Britain would do the same. But the British refused, partly in response to pressure from Lincoln and partly out of their desire to maintain trade with the United States.

Confederate strategies: Prolonged war to erode Northern support and cotton diplomacy in Europe

Forming Armies

Once fighting began, President Lincoln called for 500,000 more men, a staggering number that the Confederacy struggled to match. Although the average age of soldiers in the Civil War was twenty-six, the Union army included more than 100,000 soldiers younger than fifteen. Almost a fifth of Union soldiers and sailors were immigrants—French, German, Polish, Italian, other Europeans; and Caribbean, Central, and South Americans—and many could not speak English. The Union army also included 50,000 Canadians and an equal number of Englishmen. Some 210,000 Irish-born men served in the war, 170,000 of them on the Union side. At the outset of the war, Mexican Americans, Puerto Ricans, and Cubans living throughout the United States joined both armies, with their total number rising to 10,000 by the end of the war.

Diverse Union army

Immigrants fought for many reasons: strong political beliefs, cash bonuses, extra food, the need for a steady job. Regardless of the reason, the higher proportion of immigrants in the Union army gave it an ethnic diversity that was largely absent in the Confederate ranks.

UNION SOLDIERS Smoking their pipes, these soldiers share a moment of rest and a bottle of whiskey.

The Confederacy's smaller male population forced Jefferson Davis to enact a conscription law (mandatory military draft). On April 16, 1862, all White males between the ages of eighteen and thirty-five were required to serve in the army for three years. "From this time until the end of the war," a Tennessee soldier wrote, "a soldier was simply a machine, a conscript.... All our pride and valor had gone."

> Confederate army draft, with loopholes

The conscription law included controversial loopholes. A draftee might avoid service either by paying a "substitute" who was not of draft age or by paying $500 to the government. Elected officials and key civilian workers, as well as planters with twenty or more enslaved persons, were exempted from military service.

The Union waited nearly a year before forcing men into service. Then in 1863, with the war going badly, the U.S. government began to draft men. As in the South, Northerners found ways to avoid military service. A draftee might pay $300 to avoid service, and exemptions were granted to selected federal and state officeholders and to others on medical or compassionate grounds. Such exemptions led to bitter complaints on both sides about the conflict being "a rich man's war and a poor man's fight."

Why They Fought

Most of those who fought were volunteers. Why did they risk their lives? The reasons varied, but many stressed that they felt compelled by masculine duty, honor, and patriotism. One Union volunteer enlisted because he felt a powerful "sense of duty to my country and myself . . . to give up *life* if need be . . . in the battle for freedom & right, opposed to slavery & wrong." Similarly, a Texas private insisted that he and other Confederates were "fighting for matters real and tangible . . . our property [enslaved laborers] and our homes."

A New York Private Nineteen-year-old Lyons Wakeman, the eldest of nine children in an upstate New York farm family, enlisted in the Union army in 1862. In exchange for a $152 cash bonus, the five-foot-tall, blue-eyed Wakeman signed up for three years. The pay was $13 a month. Initially, at least, army life was tolerable, and the prospect of death did not faze Wakeman: "I don't fear the rebel bullets, nor do I fear the cannon. If it is God's will for me to be killed here, it is my will to die." In letters home, first from Virginia and later from Louisiana, Private Wakeman asked about the family farm, how many hogs were slaughtered, what the new barn looked like, and how much it might cost to buy a farm on the Wisconsin prairie.

Yet Wakeman never became a farmer. In a fierce battle, the New Yorker faced "enemy bullets with my regiment. I was under fire about four hours and lay on the field of battle all night." Wakeman did not die from wounds

LYONS WAKEMAN Private Lyons Wakeman, born Sarah Rosetta Wakeman, served in the Union army.

but did succumb a few weeks later to dysentery (chronic diarrhea) after drinking from a stream contaminated with the carcasses of dead horses. Wakeman was buried in a New Orleans cemetery, under a headstone that simply read: "Lyons Wakeman—N.Y."

What might have been added was that Lyons Wakeman, it turned out, was born a woman. Given the name Sarah Rosetta Wakeman, she, like hundreds of women on both sides, had disguised her gender to serve in the war. Why? Was it simply patriotism? Or did it also involve seizing the opportunity afforded by the war to explore an alternative gender role?

What Was at Stake Many Confederates were convinced that defeat would enslave Whites in the South. "If we was to lose," a Mississippi private wrote his wife in 1862, "we would be slaves to the Yanks and our children would have a yoke of bondage thrown around their necks."

Most Confederates could not imagine life without enslaving Black people. "This country without slave labor would be completely worthless," wrote a Mississippi lieutenant. "We can only live & exist by that species of labor: hence I am willing to fight to the last."

Many Union soldiers were fighting to preserve the Union rather than to free men, women, and children in bondage, but a substantial number of Yankee soldiers insisted that winning the war meant ending slavery. "Any country that allows the curse of Slavery... should be cursed," an Illinois soldier wrote home, "and I believe in my soul that God allowed this war for the very purpose of clearing out the evil and punishing us as a nation for allowing it."

Despite the patriotic fervor of 1861, people remained ambivalent about their loyalties. In Virginia, for example, Confederate Joseph Waddell admitted in his diary that he actually regretted secession. "I never ceased to deplore the disruption [of the Union], and never could have loved my country and government as I loved the old United States."

> Soldiers and the question of slavery

Divided Families The Civil War divided families. President Lincoln's wife, Mary Todd of Kentucky, for example, saw her youngest brother join the Confederate army, as did three of her half-brothers and three brothers-in-law.

Kinfolk also fought against each other. In June 1862, brothers Alexander and James Campbell fought against each other during a battle on James Island, South Carolina. Alexander joined the Union forces in assaulting a Confederate fort, where his brother served. Afterward, James wrote to his brother, expressing astonishment that Alexander had been among the Union attackers. "I was... doing my best to Beat you, but I hope that you and I will never again meet face to face." But if they should meet again in battle, he urged his brother to "do your duty to your cause, for I can assure you I will strive to discharge my duty to my country & my cause."

The Life of a Soldier

Because most of the fighting occurred in the spring and summer, soldiers spent far more time preparing for war than fighting. A Pennsylvania private wrote home that "the first thing in the morning is drill. Then drill, then drill again. Then drill, drill, a little more drill, then drill, lastly drill."

When not training, soldiers relaxed outdoors in makeshift shelters or small tents—talking; reading; playing cards or checkers; singing songs; smoking pipes; washing and mending clothes; and fighting lice, ticks, chiggers, and mosquitoes. Their diet was dull: baked bread crackers (called hardtack), salted meat (pork or beef), and coffee.

Some soldiers on both sides were so overwhelmed by the rigors of combat and camp life or so concerned about their families and farms that they deserted, even though they risked execution if caught. Desertions soared with each passing year, as did incidents of drunkenness, thievery, and insubordination. Punishments varied. Some deserters were shot or hanged. Others were tied to a ball and chain, forced to bury dead horses or tend to animals, or drummed out of the service.

Prisoner-of-war camps

More than 400,000 soldiers on both sides were sent to prisoner-of-war camps, where conditions were so miserable that some 30,000 Union prisoners and nearly 26,000 Confederates died in captivity. The worst of the prisons was Camp Sumter, in southwest Georgia near Andersonville. Built to house 10,000 prisoners, it overflowed with 45,000 Union soldiers. Nearly a third of them died in captivity.

Becoming Warriors

Few of those who fought in the Civil War had any combat experience. Sullivan Ballou, a thirty-two-year-old Rhode Island lawyer and legislator who enlisted in the Union army, wrote to his wife in July 1861 that he would have loved nothing more than to have stayed home and seen their

DAILY LIFE These souvenir cards show various aspects of life in Civil War camps, from enduring illnesses and a bland diet of hardtack to getting stuck in the mud and hiding from enemy fire.

SURGEONS CALL.

STUCK IN THE MUD.

HARD TACK.

A SHELL IS COMING.

sons grow to "honorable manhood," but his ultimate priority was serving his country. A week later, Ballou was killed in the first Battle of Bull Run. In his last letter to his wife, he had expressed a premonition of death: "Do not mourn me dead. . . . Wait for me, for we shall meet again."

Black People Mobilize

Among the Americans most determined to join the fight were people in bondage. As had happened during the Revolutionary War and the War of 1812, enslaved African Americans took advantage of the confusion created by the war to liberate themselves. They began fleeing to U.S. military posts, where they offered to work for, and even enlist in, the U.S. Army. Initially, military commanders did not know what to do with them—or what to call them. Were they "freedmen" or "vagrants" or something else?

President Lincoln struggled to answer those questions. When fighting began in 1861, the need to keep the border slave states (Delaware, Kentucky, Maryland, and Missouri) in the Union dictated caution on the volatile issue of emancipation. In August 1862, for example, Lincoln worried that "to arm the negroes would turn 50,000 bayonets from the loyal Border states *against* us that were *for* us." Lincoln also harbored doubts about his constitutional authority to end slavery.

Enslaved people continued to flee to Union camps anyway. By late May 1861, after listening to three men named James Baker, Shepard Mallory, and William Townsend claim that allowing them inside Union lines would draw labor away from the Confederates and hamper their war effort, U.S. General Benjamin Butler agreed. He designated them as "contraband of war"—a military phrase referring to captured enemy property—and permitted them to stay. They were not yet legally free, but the promise

> Enslaved people support the Union

> "Contrabands of war"

FREEDOM SEEKERS This August 1861 illustration that appeared in a Northern newspaper depicts men, women, and children fleeing slavery and seeking refuge with the U.S. Army at Fort Monroe, Virginia.

ROBERT SMALLS Robert Smalls, a twenty-three-year-old enslaved man who was a harbor pilot, stole the Confederate gunboat C.S.S. *Planter*, steered it to the Union side, and was lauded as a hero in the North.

contrabands During the Civil War, freedom seekers who sought refuge in Union military camps or who lived in areas of the Confederacy under Union control.

of a new life in Union army camps eventually led a half million more enslaved people to seek protection among Union armies during the war. They were known as **contrabands**, but the more accurate term for them was *refugees*. Butler's policy marked an important step in the path toward emancipation by the end of the war.

Perhaps the most dramatic instance of enslaved people's rebelliousness occurred in Charleston Harbor. On May 13, 1862, twenty-three-year-old Robert Smalls, an enslaved harbor pilot aboard the Confederate gunboat *Planter*, stole the ship and headed out to sea in a desperate quest for freedom. Sneaking past Confederate forts and cannons, he guided the *Planter* up the Cooper River and docked at a wharf where his wife, his child, and the families of his crew were waiting.

Once the seventeen Black passengers were aboard, the gunboat crept out of the harbor. As the sun rose, Smalls had a crew member hoist a white bedsheet to signal their intention to surrender as he steered toward the Union fleet then blockading Charleston Harbor. A warship summoned Smalls onboard, whereupon he announced: "I am delivering this war material, including these cannons, and I think Uncle Abraham Lincoln can put them to good use."

Smalls was hailed as a hero in the North. He met with President Lincoln at the White House, toured Northern cities urging that Black men be allowed to serve in the Union army and navy, and became a ship pilot for the Union navy. After the war, he became a South Carolina legislator and U.S. congressman.

Fighting in the West

Civil War combat spilled across the Mississippi River into the Great Plains and all the way to California. In 1862, a small Confederate army tried to conquer the New Mexico Territory to gain control of the western region, including the gold fields of Colorado and the ports of California. But the attack was repelled by Union forces led by the New Mexico Volunteer Infantry, which boasted 157 Hispanic officers.

Amid sporadic fighting, western settlement slowed but did not stop. New discoveries of gold and silver in eastern California and in Montana and Colorado lured more prospectors. Dakota, Colorado, and Nevada gained territorial status in 1861; Idaho and Arizona in 1863. Both Montana and silver-rich Nevada gained statehood in 1864.

Kansas and Indigenous Nations

Native Americans pick sides

The most intense fighting west of the Mississippi occurred along the Kansas–Missouri border, where the disputes that had developed between pro-slavery and anti-slavery settlers in the 1850s turned into brutal guerrilla warfare.

The most prominent pro-Confederate leader in the western region was William Quantrill. In destroying the anti-slavery stronghold of Lawrence, Kansas, in 1863, Quantrill ordered his followers—who were mostly teenagers—to "kill every male and burn every house." By the end of the day, they had massacred 182 men and boys. Their opponents, the Jayhawkers (originally a slang term meaning "thieves"), responded by torturing and hanging pro-Confederate prisoners, burning houses, and destroying livestock.

Many Indigenous nations were caught up in the war. Some 20,000 Native Americans allied with one side or the other, and in Oklahoma they fought against each other. Some Native Americans among the "Five Civilized Tribes" (Cherokee, Chickasaw, Choctaw, Creek, and Seminole) enslaved African American people and felt a bond with Southern Whites. Stand Watie, an Oklahoma Cherokee leader, chose the Confederacy in 1861, then raised a volunteer regiment called the Cherokee Mounted Rifles. By the end of the war, he had been promoted to brigadier general and was the principal chief of the Confederate Cherokee.

Oklahoma's proximity to Texas also influenced the Choctaw and Chickasaw to support the Confederacy. The Cherokee, Creek, and Seminole were more divided in their loyalties. Caught in the crossfire of battle, one-third of Cherokee women ended up as widows by the end of the war.

STAND WATIE Stand Watie commanded the Confederate Indian cavalry of the Army of the Trans-Mississippi after the Cherokee Nation allied with the Confederacy.

Texans in the War

Although Texas would never be a primary battleground, it did have an outsized influence on the Civil War, sending vast numbers of soldiers to the East. No sooner was war declared than 25,000 Texans volunteered. Eventually more than half of the military-aged men in Texas fought in the war. One of them explained that he was willing to go to war because "we want more slaves—we need them."

Several Texans emerged as prominent Confederate generals, and Texas units were ethnically diverse. The 4,400-strong Texas Brigade led by John Bell Hood included Mexicans, Native Americans, and Europeans—English, Welsh, Irish, Scots, Germans, and French. They became one of the most celebrated units in the war, in part because they absorbed the highest rate of casualties. Only 600 were still serving at the war's end.

Texan and Tejano cowboys also drove vast herds of longhorn steers hundreds of miles east across Louisiana and the Mississippi River to feed Confederate armies.

Not all Texans chose the Confederate cause, however. Among the Union soldiers from Texas were many Tejanos and Mexican nationals. Their motives were varied, but many sought revenge against White Texans who had taken their lands. Others were attracted by the enlistment bonuses and military pay. If captured by Confederates, Texas Unionists often paid with their lives. Several dozen were executed as traitors.

Kentucky and Tennessee

> Union victories at Fort Henry, Fort Donelson, and Nashville

Early in 1862, General Ulysses S. Grant made the first Union thrust against the Confederate army that was defending Tennessee. Moving on boats out of Illinois and Kentucky, the Union army captured two hastily built Confederate strongholds: Fort Henry, on the east bank of the Tennessee River, on February 6, 1862; and nearby Fort Donelson, perched on a hill overlooking the Cumberland River, where, on February 16, some 12,000 Confederates met the demands of General Grant and surrendered immediately and unconditionally. Eight days later, Union forces took control of Nashville, Tennessee's capital (see Map 14.2).

> Early victories ensure Kentucky's loyalty to the Union

These first major Union victories ignited wild celebrations throughout the North. They helped ensure that Kentucky would stay within the Union and gave the North access to two key rivers, the Cumberland and the Tennessee. At the same time, the victory at Fort Donelson gave the shy and unassuming Grant a catchy nickname matching his initials: "Unconditional Surrender" Grant. The *New York Times* reported that Grant's "prestige is second now to that of no general in the army." Admirers rushed him 10,000 cigars, and he soon began smoking 20 a day. (He would die in 1885 of throat cancer.)

President Lincoln's delight with Grant's victories, however, was tempered by the death of Lincoln's eleven-year-old son, Willie, of typhoid fever. The tragedy "overwhelmed" the president. A White House staff member said she had never seen "a man so bowed down in grief." Mary Todd Lincoln was so distraught that she was unable to attend Willie's funeral.

Shiloh

After the defeats in Tennessee, the Confederate forces fled southward before regrouping under General Albert Sydney Johnston at Corinth, in northern Mississippi, near the Tennessee border (see again Map 14.2). Their goal was to protect the Memphis and Charleston Railroad that linked the lower Mississippi Valley and the Atlantic coast. At dawn on Sunday, April 6, General Johnston launched a surprise attack.

The Confederates, screaming their blood-curdling "Rebel yell," struck the unsuspecting Union lines near Shiloh, a tiny Methodist church in the center of the Union camp in southwestern Tennessee. Many of Grant's 42,000 troops, half of whom had yet to see combat, were still sleeping or eating breakfast; some died in their tents. Panic-stricken soldiers dropped their weapons and ran for the river.

After a day of confused fighting and terrible losses on both sides—including the Confederate commander, General Johnston—the fleeing Union soldiers were pinned against the river as heavy rain began to fall. Union general William Tecumseh Sherman found Grant and said, "We've had the devil's own day, haven't we?" Grant puffed on his cigar and replied, "Yes, but we will lick 'em tomorrow though."

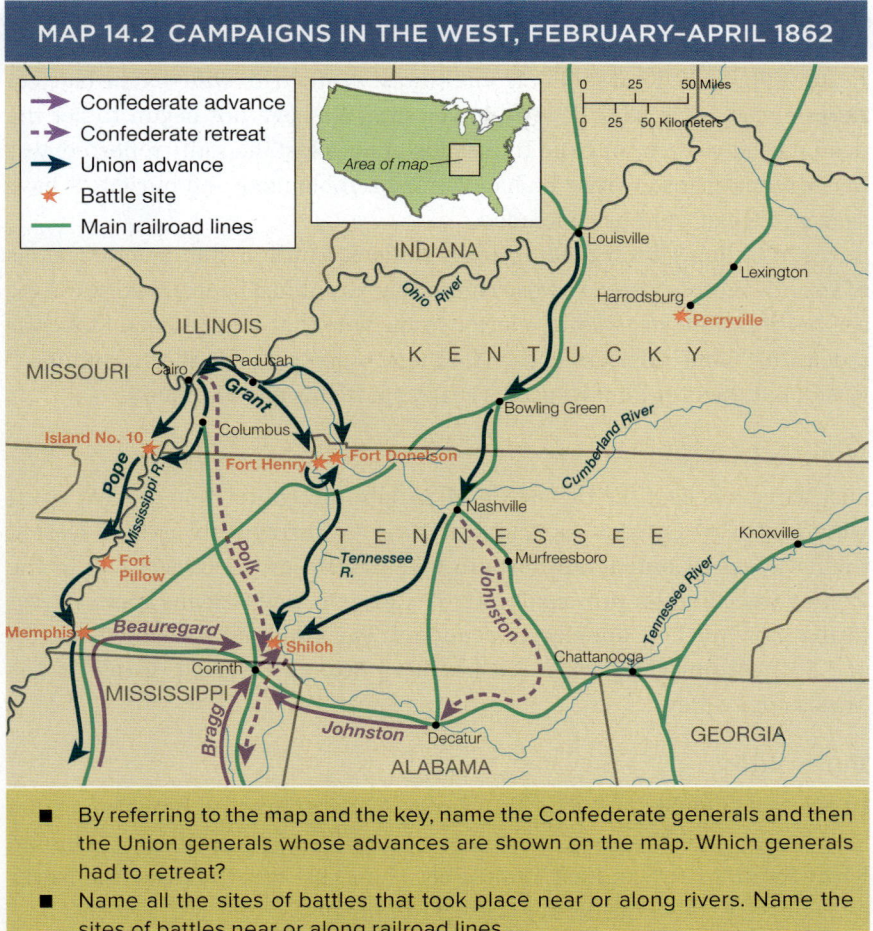

MAP 14.2 CAMPAIGNS IN THE WEST, FEBRUARY–APRIL 1862

- By referring to the map and the key, name the Confederate generals and then the Union generals whose advances are shown on the map. Which generals had to retreat?
- Name all the sites of battles that took place near or along rivers. Name the sites of battles near or along railroad lines.
- Find the site of the Battle of Shiloh. According to the chapter text, how did this battle play out, and what were the costs to the Union as a result?

The new Confederate commander, Pierre G. T. Beauregard, telegraphed President Jefferson Davis that his army had scored "a complete victory, driving the enemy from every position." His celebration, however, was premature.

Reinforced by 25,000 fresh Union troops, Grant's army took the offensive at dawn the next day, and the Confederates glumly withdrew twenty miles to Corinth (Map 14.2). The Union troops were too battered and weary to pursue. Confederate private Sam Watkins observed that "those Yankees were whipped, fairly whipped, and according to all the rules of war they ought to have retreated. But they didn't."

Shiloh, a Hebrew word meaning "Place of Peace," had become a place of anguish. The battle's first day was the bloodiest in American history to that point. Viewing the scene afterward, said General Sherman, "would have cured anybody of war."

> **Devastating casualties at the Battle of Shiloh**

Of the 100,000 men who participated in the fighting, a quarter were killed or wounded—seven times the casualties at the Battle of Bull Run. Lester Filley, a Federal soldier from Illinois, wrote to his wife that he had just experienced "4 as hard days as I ever saw. We have not begun to get the dead buried yet." Among the thousands of lives lost, he sadly reported, was her brother, whose corpse he had wrapped in blankets and buried. "I have seen enough of war," he concluded.

After Shiloh, Union general Henry Halleck, a military bureaucrat jealous of Grant's success, spread a false rumor that Grant had been drinking during the battle. Grant insisted in a letter to his wife that he had been "sober as a deacon." Some advisers urged Abraham Lincoln to fire the "unmilitary" Grant, but the president refused: "I can't spare this man; he fights."

New Orleans

> **Union seizes New Orleans**

Just three weeks after the Battle of Shiloh, the Union won a great naval victory at New Orleans, as Admiral David G. Farragut's warships blasted their way past Confederate forts to take control of the largest city in the Confederacy and its principal port. The loss of New Orleans was a devastating blow to the Confederate economy. The Union army gained control of 1,500 cotton plantations and liberated 50,000 enslaved people in the Mississippi Valley.

Perryville

In the late summer of 1862, Confederate General Braxton Bragg's Army of Mississippi, 30,000 strong, used railroads to link up with General Edmund Kirby Smith's Army of East Tennessee. Their goal was to invade the North by taking control of the border state of Kentucky.

The Confederates met the Union Army of Ohio, led by General Don Carlos Buell, at the central Kentucky village of Perryville in October 1862. The outnumbered Confederates attacked the Union lines, pushing them back more than a mile. When Bragg learned that Union reinforcements were approaching, however, he ordered his army to withdraw south toward Tennessee. The Union retained control of Kentucky for the rest of the war.

Fighting in the East

> **George B. McClellan heads the Army of the Potomac**

The fighting in the East remained sporadic for nine months after the first battle at Bull Run. In the wake of the Union defeat there, Lincoln had appointed General George B. McClellan as head of the Army of the Potomac. The thirty-four-year-old McClellan, who encouraged journalists to call him "Little Napoleon," set about building the Union's most powerful, best-trained army.

Yet for all his boundless self-confidence and organizational ability, McClellan was hesitant to attack. Months passed while he trained his massive army to meet the superior numbers of Confederates he mistakenly believed were facing him. Lincoln finally lost his patience as commander-in-chief and ordered McClellan to attack.

McClellan's Peninsular Campaign

In mid-March 1862, McClellan moved his army of 122,000 men on 400 ships and barges down the Potomac River and through the Chesapeake Bay to the mouth of the James River at the tip of the Yorktown peninsula (see Map 14.3). The troops were within sixty miles of the Confederate capital of Richmond, Virginia. Thousands of residents fled the city in panic, but McClellan waited too long to strike. A frustrated Lincoln told McClellan that the war could be won only by *engaging* the Rebel army. "Once more" Lincoln telegraphed, "it is indispensable that you strike a blow."

On May 31, 1862, Confederate General Joseph E. Johnston struck McClellan's army along the Chickahominy River, six miles east of Richmond. In the Battle of Seven Pines (Fair Oaks), only the arrival of Federal reinforcements prevented a disastrous Union defeat. Both sides took heavy casualties, and Johnston was severely wounded.

At this point, Robert E. Lee assumed command of the main Confederate army, the Army of Northern Virginia, a development that changed the course of the war. Lee, a slave-owning planter, had graduated second in his class at West Point. During the Mexican-American War, he had impressed General Winfield Scott as the "very best soldier I ever saw in the field." Lee would prove to be a daring strategist who was as aggressive as McClellan was timid.

On July 9, when Lincoln visited McClellan's headquarters on the coast of Virginia, the general complained that the administration had failed to support him and lectured the president on military strategy. Such insubordination was ample reason to relieve McClellan of his overall command. After returning to Washington, Lincoln named Henry Halleck general-in-chief of all Union forces.

ROBERT E. LEE The Confederacy's leading general, Lee served as military adviser to President Jefferson Davis and as commander of the Army of Northern Virginia.

> Robert E. Lee heads the Army of Northern Virginia

The Second Battle of Bull Run

General McClellan was ordered to move his Army of the Potomac back to Washington, D.C., and join General John Pope, commander of the Union Army of Virginia, in a new assault on Richmond. Robert E. Lee realized that his only chance was to drive a wedge between the two larger Union armies so that he could deal with them one at a time. He moved northward to strike Pope's army before McClellan's troops could arrive. On August 30, 1862, at the Second Battle of Bull Run (or Manassas)—fought on almost the same site as the earlier battle—Lee boldly divided his forces, sending Stonewall Jackson's troops around the flank to attack from the rear (see Map 14.4). A confused Pope assumed that he faced only Jackson, but Lee's main army by that time had joined in.

MAP 14.3 THE PENINSULAR CAMPAIGN, 1862

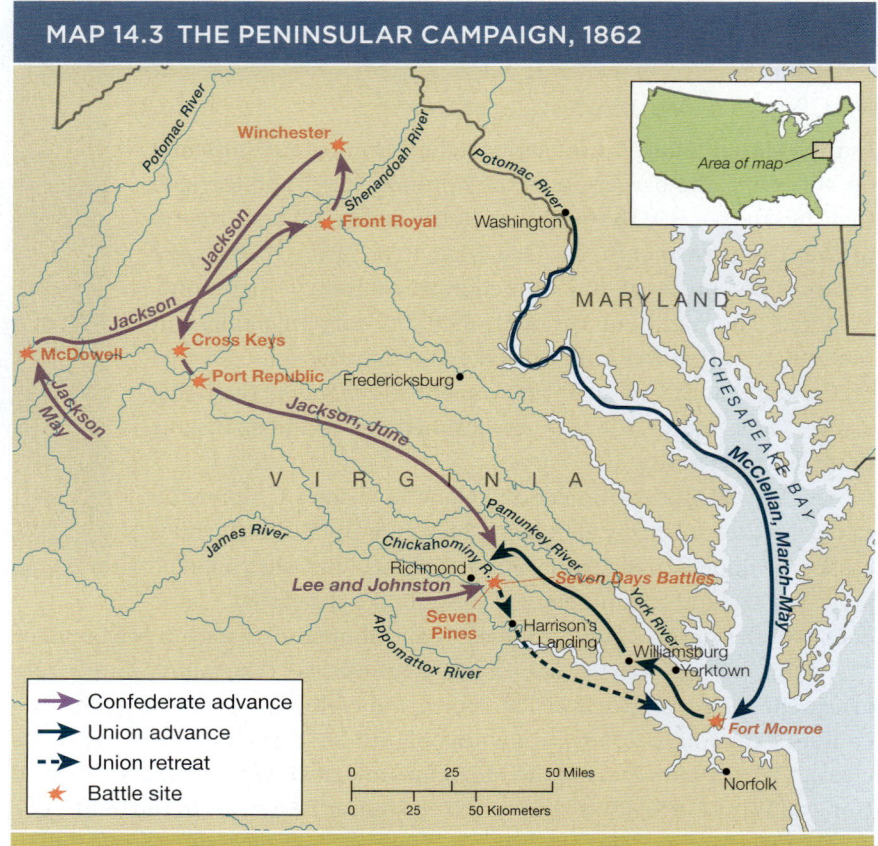

- Using your finger, trace General George B. McClellan's initial advance from Washington, D.C., to the tip of the Yorktown peninsula. Did any of that advance take place on land?
- Using the map and the key for reference, name the battle sites attacked by General Thomas "Stonewall" Jackson and his troops.
- Find Richmond on the map. Based on your understanding of the chapter text, what was General McClellan's strategy for attacking this city? Was it a decisive success? Why or why not?

Confederate victory at the Second Battle of Bull Run (1862)

The crushing Confederate attack drove the larger Union army from the field, giving the Confederates a sensational victory. The news of another defeat left Lincoln depressed, and he relieved Pope of command on September 12. A Rebel soldier wrote home that "General Lee stands now above all generals in modern history. Our men will follow him to the end."

Despite this Confederate victory, the North had entered the war with a decided advantage over the South. The Union had a larger population (thus more replacement soldiers and sailors) and the capability to produce weapons, ships, and railroad equipment. These advantages in resources enabled Union generals to pursue an offensive strategy. They sought to capture the Confederate capital of Richmond, impose a naval blockade on Southern ports, take control of the Mississippi River, and break the Confederates' morale. Confederate generals, meanwhile, determined to hold their homeland, pursued a defensive strategy that sought to blunt Union strength and numbers and protect Richmond. Over a year into the war, however, the outcome was still uncertain.

Emancipation

The Confederate victories in 1862 devastated morale in the North and convinced Lincoln that he had to take bolder steps to win the war, including the abolition of slavery.

As the Union army expanded its reach across the Confederacy in 1862, enslaved people had continued to pressure the U.S. government to liberate them. They fled wherever the army appeared, and thousands of men, women, and children took up residence in refugee camps. Their large numbers astonished Union officials. Enslaved people "have long had their ears open and their minds active," one explained, "watching for their moment of deliverance." They believed this was their moment.

As time passed and the number of refugees soared, Union armies established some 500 camps to house them in cast-off tents or slapdash cabins. The camps were intended to protect freedom-seeking people from returning to slavery, but they were often disease-ridden and dangerous places that were targeted by Confederates for destruction. "There is scarcely one of them all which has escaped guerrilla atrocities," lamented one Union official. Still, the former-enslaved-turned-refugees preferred to live in Union army camps rather than with their former Southern overlords.

> **CORE OBJECTIVE**
> **2.** Evaluate Abraham Lincoln's decision to issue the Emancipation Proclamation and its impact on the war.

"CONTRABANDS" Formerly enslaved people freed during the war's chaos are photographed on a farm in Cumberland Landing, Virginia, in 1862.

FREEDMAN'S VILLAGE A photograph of students with their books at Freedman's Village in Virginia. Long denied an education while enslaved, children and adults alike seized the opportunity to attend schools such as this one in refugee camps across the South.

Some of the camps even began to look more like permanent towns. One in Arlington, Virginia, known as "Freedman's Village," boasted schools, churches, and parks named after sympathetic U.S. officials, such as Lincoln Park. Residents did not name anything after the man who owned the land before the U.S. Army seized it—Confederate general Robert E. Lee. His Arlington plantation would also become the site of the United States' largest national cemetery.

"What Shall We Do with the Negro?"

However much Lincoln—and others—asserted that the conflict was about saving the Union rather than ending slavery, the prolonged war changed his outlook. In 1862, the editors of the *New York Times* asked, "What Shall We Do with the Negro?" Lincoln's answer was to edge toward ending slavery as a way to win the war.

In March 1862, he urged representatives of the four border slave states to begin the gradual emancipation of their enslaved people. On April 16, he signed an act that abolished slavery in the District of Columbia. By June 19, he had signed another bill that excluded slavery from the western territories; in July, the Republican-controlled Congress passed the Second Confiscation Act, which declared that contrabands—that is, refugees—who had made it to Union army camps were "forever free."

> Emancipation as a military necessity

Lincoln had learned something from the tens of thousands of enslaved people who had already fled into Union army camps. They had weakened the Confederate war effort by fleeing—and helped the United States by working as laborers for the army. Lincoln realized that as commander-in-chief he could go further and eliminate slavery in all the Confederate states as a necessary step to win the war and save the Union. In July 1862, he confided to his cabinet that emancipation had become "a military necessity, absolutely necessary to the preservation of the Union. We must free the slaves or be ourselves subdued." Secretary of State William H. Seward agreed but advised Lincoln to delay the announcement until after a Union battlefield victory, to avoid being viewed as desperate.

Antietam: A Turning Point

Robert E. Lee made his own momentous decision in the summer of 1862: he would lead his troops north into Pennsylvania and force the "much weakened and demoralized" Army of the Potomac and its "timid" commander George McClellan to leave northern Virginia, thereby relieving the pressure on Richmond, the Confederate capital. "The idea of waiting for blows, instead of inflicting them, is altogether unsuited to the genius of our people," explained the *Richmond Examiner*.

Lee hoped to gain British and French recognition of the Confederacy, which would bring his troops desperately needed supplies. In addition, Lee and Jefferson Davis planned to capture Maryland (with its many Confederate supporters); separate it from the Union; and gain control of its farms, crops, and livestock.

In September 1862, Lee and his 40,000 troops pushed north across the Potomac River into western Maryland amid sweltering heat and humidity. "I have never seen such a mass of filthy, strong-smelling men," said a Marylander. "They are the roughest looking set of creatures I ever saw, their features, hair, and clothing matted with dirt and filth."

On September 17, Union and Confederate armies clashed in the furious **Battle of Antietam** (Sharpsburg; see again Map 14.4). Had Union soldiers not discovered Lee's battle plans wrapped around three cigars that a Rebel courier had carelessly dropped on the ground, the Confederates might have won.

And had McClellan moved his 10,000 men more quickly, he could have destroyed Lee's Army of Northern Virginia while it was scattered and still on the march, since McClellan's army was twice as large as Lee's. As always, however, McClellan mobilized slowly, enabling Lee and his troops to regroup at Sharpsburg, Maryland, between Antietam Creek and the Potomac River.

There, over the course of fourteen hours, the Union army launched repeated attacks. The fighting was savage; an officer counted "hundreds of dead bodies lying in rows and in piles." The scene was "sickening, harrowing, horrible. O what a terrible sight!" With nearly 23,000 killed and wounded on both sides, it was the bloodiest single day of the war and the bloodiest day in American history.

The next day, Lee braced for another Federal attack that never came. That night, cloaked by fog and drizzling rain, the battered Confederates slipped back across the Potomac River to the safety of Virginia.

Although the battle was technically a draw, Lee's invasion northward had failed. McClellan, never known for his modesty, told his wife that he

Battle of Antietam (1862)
A turning-point battle near Sharpsburg, Maryland, leaving almost 25,000 soldiers dead or wounded, in which Union forces halted a Confederate invasion of the North.

The Battle of Antietam (1862)

CASUALTIES AT THE BATTLE OF ANTIETAM A photograph taken on September 19, 1862, captures a wagon road known as "Bloody Lane." Used as a rifle pit by Confederate troops, it served as their gravesite after the deadliest day in American history.

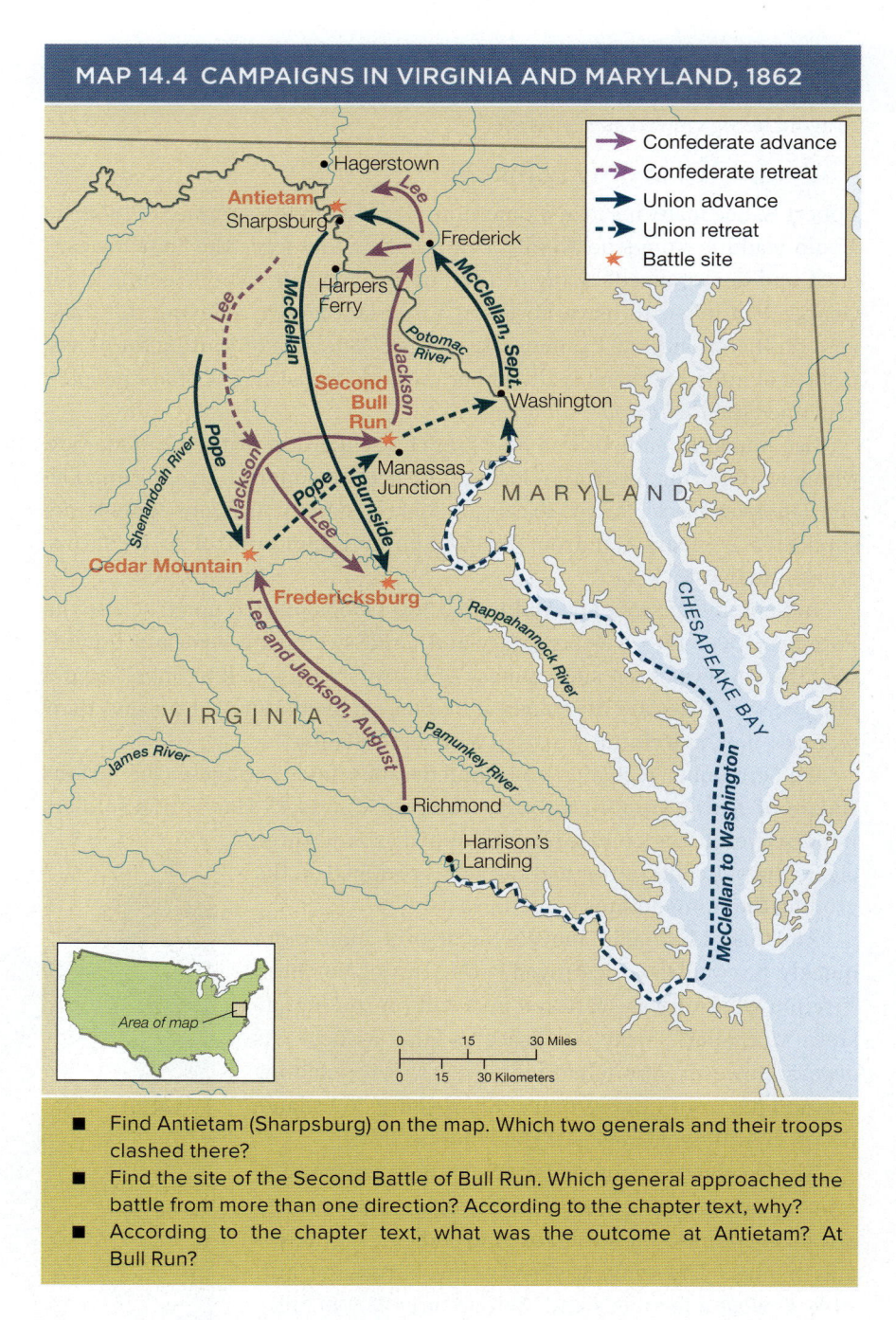

MAP 14.4 CAMPAIGNS IN VIRGINIA AND MARYLAND, 1862

- Find Antietam (Sharpsburg) on the map. Which two generals and their troops clashed there?
- Find the site of the Second Battle of Bull Run. Which general approached the battle from more than one direction? According to the chapter text, why?
- According to the chapter text, what was the outcome at Antietam? At Bull Run?

"had fought the battle splendidly" against great odds. To him, the Battle of Antietam was "the most terrible battle of the age." Some 6,400 soldiers on both sides were killed—twice as many as at Shiloh—and another 17,000 were wounded or listed as missing.

President Lincoln was pleased that Lee's army had been forced to retreat, but he was disgusted by McClellan's failure to pursue the Confederates and win the war. The president sent a sarcastic message to the general:

"I have just read your dispatch about sore-tongued and fatigued horses. Will you pardon me for asking what the horses of your army have done . . . that fatigues anything?" Failing to receive a satisfactory answer, Lincoln sacked McClellan as commander of the Army of the Potomac. Never again would McClellan command troops, but he would challenge Lincoln for the presidency in 1864.

The Battle of Antietam revived sagging Northern morale and dashed the Confederacy's hopes of forging military alliances with Great Britain and France. It also convinced Lincoln to transform the war from an effort to restore the Union to a crusade to end slavery.

Emancipation Proclamation

On September 22, 1862, five days after the Battle of Antietam, President Lincoln issued the preliminary **Emancipation Proclamation**, which changed the course of history. It warned Confederate leaders that if they did not stop fighting and return to the Union, all enslaved people still under their control would be made "forever free" in exactly 100 days, on January 1, 1863.

The Emancipation Proclamation was not based on ideas of racial equality or abstract ideals of human dignity. It was, according to Lincoln, a "military necessity" and therefore a legitimate use of presidential "war powers."

Lincoln's concept of military-necessitated emancipation was limited, however; it would free only those enslaved people in areas of the Confederacy still in rebellion against the United States. It had no bearing on enslaved people in the four border states that remained in the Union, or in Tennessee and southern Louisiana, which had been reoccupied by Federal forces. Lincoln did not believe he had constitutional authority

Emancipation Proclamation (1863) The military order issued by President Abraham Lincoln that freed enslaved people in areas still controlled by the Confederacy.

> Civil War becomes a war to end slavery

UNION VIEW OF THE EMANCIPATION PROCLAMATION In this 1863 painting, a thoughtful Lincoln composes the proclamation with the Constitution and the Holy Bible in his lap. The Scales of Justice hang on the wall behind him.

as president to abolish slavery in these "loyal" areas. But he could act as commander-in-chief of the armed forces and end slavery wherever military necessity demanded it.

When Lincoln signed the actual Emancipation Proclamation in January, however, he amended his original message, adding that the proclamation was "an act of justice" as well as a military necessity. "I never, in my life, felt more certain that I was doing the right thing than I do in signing this paper," he reflected. Simply restoring the Union was no longer the purpose of the war; the transformation of the South and the slave system was now the goal.

Reactions to Emancipation

African Americans across the warring nation gathered in churches and held services on New Year's Eve, waiting expectantly for the news that the president had at last signed the Emancipation Proclamation. "The occasion, wherefore, was one of hope and fear," Frederick Douglass recalled. "We were waiting and listening as for a bolt from the sky, which should rend [tear away] the fetters [chains] of four million slaves."

The news triggered celebrations highlighted by singing, dancing, and parades. At Camp Saxton, a former plantation on the coast of South Carolina, the First South Carolina Volunteers, a Union regiment made up of formerly enslaved men, gathered on January 1. After the Emancipation Proclamation was read aloud, it was "cheered to the skies." As Colonel Thomas W. Higginson, the unit's commander, unfurled an American flag, the Black troops spontaneously began singing "My country 'tis of thee / Sweet land of liberty / Of thee I sing!" "I never saw anything so electric," Higginson reported.

EMANCIPATION DAY The January 1 celebrations like this one in South Carolina became an annual holiday in Black communities. These observances were originally known as Emancipation Day. Today the holiday is celebrated nationally on June 19, or Juneteenth.

Northerners had more mixed reactions to Lincoln's proclamation. The *New York Times* proclaimed that "there has been no more far reaching document ever issued since the founding of this government." Democrats, however, called his decision dictatorial, unconstitutional, and catastrophic. In the months following the proclamation, thousands of White Union troops deserted, explaining that they did not enlist to free the enslaved, much less to provide racial equality. In the November elections, Democrats took twenty-eight Republican seats in Congress.

Yet Lincoln forcefully responded to his critics. "You say you will not fight to free negroes," he wrote. "Some of them seem willing to fight for you; but, no matter. Fight you, then, exclusively to save the Union. I issued the [emancipation] proclamation on purpose to aid you in saving the Union."

Of course, the proclamation incensed Confederate leaders and slave owners, who predicted it would ignite a race war. They redoubled their efforts to stop enslaved people from escaping to U.S. Army camps.

Still, the enslaved kept risking their lives to gain freedom. Clarissa Burdett was one of them. Like thousands of women and children in the border state of Kentucky, she was not freed by the Emancipation Proclamation—but it inspired her to flee anyway. Her husband, Elijah, had already escaped and joined the Twelfth U.S. Colored Artillery unit at Camp Nelson. But "[w]hen my husband enlisted," she later recalled, "my master beat me over the head with an axe handle saying as he did so that he beat me for letting Ely Burdett go off."

Eventually, in 1865, Clarissa ran for her life, so desperate to avoid her owner's violent abuse that she left behind her four children, who were too young to escape quickly. U.S. Army troops were so horrified by her injuries

CONFEDERATE VIEW OF THE EMANCIPATION PROCLAMATION In this political cartoon, Lincoln pens the proclamation with his foot trampling on a bound copy of the Constitution. The devil holds the inkwell before him, and demonic faces are hidden in his furnishings.

that they stormed her plantation and arrested its owner, charging him with "inhumanly beating Clarissa Burdett." They also rescued her children.

Union armies continued to be forces of liberation as they advanced deeper into the Confederate states, freeing enslaved people and circulating thousands of copies of the Emancipation Proclamation. A Union general said that the news of emancipation "was like an earthquake. It shook and shattered the whole previously existing social system."

> **Union effort boosted by freed African Americans and European sympathy**

As Lincoln had hoped, the Emancipation Proclamation boosted the Union war effort. It enabled African Americans to enlist in the Union army, and it undermined support for the Confederacy in Europe. The conversion of the Civil War from a conflict to restore the Union into a crusade to end slavery gave the Federal war effort moral legitimacy in the eyes of Europeans.

Fredericksburg

> **Ambrose E. Burnside made general**

In his search for an effective commanding general, Lincoln turned in the fall of 1862 to Ambrose E. Burnside, whose greatest attribute was that he looked like a general: tall and imposing, with massive facial hair that gave rise to the term *sideburns*. Twice before, Burnside had turned down the job, saying he was unfit for such responsibility. Now he accepted, although he remained wracked by self-doubts.

Burnside decided to try again to capture Richmond, the Confederate capital. In mid-November 1862, he positioned most of the 122,000 men in the Army of the Potomac east of the icy Rappahannock River overlooking the town of Fredericksburg, Virginia (Map 14.4). Robert E. Lee rushed his Army of Northern Virginia to defend the town.

As the days passed, Lee's outnumbered forces established impregnable positions along a line of ridges and behind a stone wall at the base of Marye's Heights, west of Fredericksburg. The Confederates positioned so many cannons atop the ridge that a Union soldier predicted what would happen next: "It looks to me as if we are going over there to get murdered."

On December 13, the Union soldiers began to assault Lee's entrenched positions. Confederate cannons and muskets chewed up the Federals as they advanced uphill across a half mile of open land. The series of six futile assaults was, a Union general regretted, "a great slaughter-pen." The awful scene of dead and dying Federals, some stacked three deep on the battlefield, led General Lee to remark: "It is well that war is so terrible—we should grow too fond of it."

> **Union defeated at Battle of Fredericksburg (1862)**

After 12,600 Federals were killed or wounded, compared with fewer than 5,300 Confederates, a weeping General Burnside told his shattered army to withdraw across the river as darkness fell. When Burnside rode past his retreating men, his aide called for three cheers for their commander. All he got was sullen silence. It was the worst Union defeat of the war.

The year 1862 ended with a stalemate in the East and a mired-down Union thrust in the West. Northern morale plummeted. Many Democrats were calling for a negotiated peace, and Republicans—even Lincoln's own cabinet members—grew increasingly critical of the president's leadership. "If there is a worse place than hell," Lincoln sighed, "I am in it."

New York City Draft Riots

Lincoln's proclamation freeing enslaved people in the Confederacy created anxiety and anger among many Northern laborers, who feared that formerly enslaved people would migrate north and take their jobs. In New York City, such fears erupted into violence. In July 1863, a group of 500 White laborers, led by volunteer firemen, assaulted the army draft office, shattered its windows, and burned it down.

Swollen by thousands of working-class Whites, mostly Irish, the rioters then ruthlessly began taking out their frustrations on Black people. For four days and nights, mobs rampaged through the streets of Manhattan, tearing up rail lines, cutting telegraph wires, toppling streetcars, and randomly attacking African Americans. The protesters also burned down more than fifty buildings, including the mayor's home, police stations, two Protestant churches—and the Colored Orphan Asylum, forcing 233 children to flee.

The violence killed 120 people and injured thousands. Only the arrival of Union soldiers ended it.

Black Soldiers and Sailors

In July 1862, in an effort to strengthen the Union war effort, the U.S. Congress had passed the **Militia Act**, which authorized the army to use formerly enslaved people as laborers or soldiers. (Black men were already eligible to serve in the navy.) But only after the formal signing of the Emancipation Proclamation in January 1863 did the Union army recruit Black men in large numbers. Doing so represented the most revolutionary episode of the war.

On May 22, 1863, the U.S. War Department created the Bureau of Colored Troops to recruit free Blacks and formerly enslaved people. James Henry Gooding, a twenty-six-year-old Black enlistee from New Bedford, Massachusetts, declared that "if they [African Americans] are ever to attain . . . any position in the civilized world, they must forgo comfort . . . and fight for it."

More than 180,000 Black men enlisted in the army, most of them formerly enslaved and 80 percent from Southern states. In the navy, African Americans accounted for about a fourth of all enlistments.

Initially, Black soldiers were not allowed in combat, but the need to win the war changed that. A White Union army private reported in the late spring of 1863 that the Black troops "fight like the Devil." Their tenacity in part reflected their determination to liberate their people. "I do really think

Militia Act (1862) A congressional measure that permitted formerly enslaved people to serve as laborers or soldiers in the U.S. Army.

Northern resistance to fighting a war for emancipation

BLACK UNION ARMY SERGEANT Wearing the uniform and sword of the North, this Black Union sergeant poses with a copy of J. T. Headley's *The Great Rebellion* in his hand.

Comparing PERSPECTIVES

THE END OF SLAVERY

From: *The Secret Eye: The Journal of Ella Gertrude Clanton Thomas,* **May 29 and June 12, 1865.**

Ella Gertrude Clanton Thomas, a wealthy, slave-owning woman in Georgia, kept a journal in which she described the departure of each enslaved person who left her plantation to seek freedom.

Monday, May 29, 1865 Out of all our old house servants not one remains except Patsey and a little boy Frank. We have one of our servants Uncle Jim to take Daniel's place as driver and butler and a much more efficient person he proves to be. Nancy has been cooking since Tamah left. On last Wednesday I hired a woman to do the washing. Thursday I expected Nancy to iron but she was sick. In the same way she was sick the week before when there was ironing to do. I said nothing but told Patsey to get breakfast. After it was over I assisted her in wiping the breakfast dishes, a thing I never remember to have done more than once or twice in my life. I then thoroughly cleaned up the sitting room and parlour....

Immediately after breakfast as I was writing by the window Turner directed my attention to Nancy with her two children, Hannah and Jessy, going out of the gate. I told him to enquire "Where she was going." She had expected to leave with flying colours but was compelled to tell a falsehood for she replied "I will be back directly." I knew at once that she was taking "french leave" and was not surprised when I went into her room sometime afterwards to find that all her things had been removed. I was again engaged in housework most of the morning....

Yesterday numbers of the negro women some of them quite black were promenading up the streets with black lace veil shading them from the embrowning rays of a sun under whose influence they had worked all their life.... On Thursday Rev Dr Finch of the Federal Army addressed the citizens on the subject of their late slaves and Saturday addressed the Negroes at the parade ground on *their* duty. I think now they have the Negroes free they don't know what to do with them.

Belmont, Monday, June 12, 1865 I must confess to you my journal that I do most heartily dispise Yankees, Negroes and everything connected with them.

From: "Letter from a Freedman to His Old Master," *Cleveland Daily Leader*, **August 28, 1865.**

Jourdon Anderson fled the Tennessee plantation where he was enslaved and moved to Ohio with his wife, Mandy. When their former owner demanded their return, Anderson responded in a letter that was published in a Northern newspaper.

Letter from a Freedman to his Old Master.

DAYTON, OHIO, August 7.

To my old Master, Col. P. H. Anderson, Big Spring, Tennessee:

SIR; I got your letter and was glad to find that you had not forgotten Jourdon and that you wanted me to come back and live with you again, promising to do better for me than any body else can. I have often felt uneasy about you.... Although you shot at me twice before I left you, I did not want to hear of your being hurt, and am glad you are still living....

As to my freedom, which you say I can have, there is nothing to be gained on that score, as I got my free papers in 1864, from the Provost Marshal General of the Department at Nashville.

Mandy says she would be afraid to go back without some proof that you are sincerely disposed to treat us kindly and justly—and we have concluded to test your sincerity by asking you to send us our wages for the time we served you. This will make us forget and forgive old scores, and rely on your justice and friendship in the future. I served you faithfully for 32 years, and Mandy 20 years, at $25 per month for me, and $2 per week for Mandy. Our earning would amount to $11,680—Add to this the interest for the time our wages has been kept back and deduct what you paid for our clothing, and three doctor's visits to me, and pulling a tooth for Mandy, and the balance will show what we are in justice entitled to....

We trust the good Maker has opened your eyes to the wrongs which you and your fathers have done to me and my fathers, in making us toil for you for generations without recompense.

From your old servant,
JOURDON ANDERSON

P. S.—Say howdy to George Carter, and thank him for taking the pistol from you when you were shooting at me.

Questions

1. Describe Ella Gertrude Clanton Thomas's reaction to the departures of enslaved people from her plantation. What seems to concern her the most?

2. Describe Jourdon Anderson's reaction to his former owner's request that he return to the plantation. What does he want his former owner to understand?

3. Compare Thomas's and Anderson's experiences with the end of slavery. How easily did each of them adjust to the reality of freedom?

that it's God's will that this war Shall not end till the Colored people get their rights," Union soldier Jacob Christy, a free Black man from Pennsylvania, wrote home in 1864, and "I shall die a trying for our rights so that others that are born hereafter may live and enjoy a happy life."

> **Inequalities in the Union army**

To be sure, racism influenced the status of African Americans in the military. Black soldiers and sailors served in all-Black units led by White officers. Initially, they were paid less than Whites ($7 per month versus $16 for White recruits) and were ineligible for the enlistment bonus paid to Whites. Still, as Frederick Douglass declared, "this is no time for hesitation. . . . This is our chance, and woe betide us if we fail to embrace it."

Commenting on Union victories at Port Hudson and Milliken's Bend, Louisiana, President Lincoln reported that "some of our commanders . . . believe that . . . the use of colored troops constitutes the heaviest blow yet dealt to the rebels." One African American soldier who recognized his former owner among a group of Confederate prisoners called out: "Hello, master. Bottom rail on top this time!"

Why had Lincoln issued the Emancipation Proclamation, freeing people enslaved in the Confederate states? He realized that winning the war required abolishing slavery there: doing so would deprive the South of its valuable captive labor force. The immediate effect of the Proclamation was a striking increase in the already-large numbers of enslaved people fleeing to Union army camps. Thanks to Congress's passage of the Militia Act allowing Black men to enlist in the Union army, the surge in numbers gave the Union a marked advantage over the Confederacy.

> **CORE OBJECTIVE**
> **3.** Analyze how the war affected social and economic life in the North and South.

The War behind the Lines

Feeding, clothing, supplying, and nursing the vast armies required tremendous sacrifices. Farms and villages were transformed into battlefields, churches became makeshift hospitals, civilian life was disrupted, and families grieved for those who would not be coming home.

Civil War Medicine

Medical knowledge lagged behind the development of military weapons during the war. Doctors did not yet understand how germs created infections, leading them to perform surgeries without disinfecting instruments or washing their hands. Antibiotics had not been developed, which meant that soldiers quickly succumbed to deadly infections. Amputation, the most common treatment for gunshot wounds to the arm or leg, saved many lives; but stomach wounds were usually fatal because the resulting infection (peritonitis) could not be prevented. Pain-killing medicines were also in short supply—and the opium shared with some wounded soldiers led to addictions.

But the war's medical emergency also gave doctors a laboratory for acquiring new knowledge about surgical techniques and the spread of infectious diseases. Many innovations resulted that transformed American medicine, from the development of the triage system of evaluating the seriousness of wounds, to the rise of the prosthetic industry. The U.S. Army also created the first ambulance system to make sure wounded men got to hospitals as quickly as possible. It saved countless men's lives and helps explain why the war's death toll was not higher.

Women and the War

"No conflict in history," a journalist wrote, "was such a woman's war as the Civil War." Women played prominent roles in both the North and South, as the war loosened traditional restraints on female activity and mobilized women to support the warring armies.

In Greenville, South Carolina, when T. G. Gower went off to fight, his wife, Elizabeth, took over the family business, converting production in their carriage factory to military wagons and ambulances. Three thousand Northern women worked as nurses with the U.S. Sanitary Commission, which provided medical relief and other services for soldiers. Many Northern women, Black and White, supported the "freedmen's aid" movement that sent food, clothing, and money to the South to help those who had escaped slavery.

In the North, thousands of women served as untrained nurses and health-related volunteers. Dorothea Lynde Dix, who was appointed

WOMEN IN THE WAR EFFORT Claiming that her place was "anywhere between the bullet and the battlefield," Clara Barton *(left)* oversaw the distribution of medicines to Union troops and later helped found the American Red Cross. Susie King Taylor *(right)* served as a nurse in Union-occupied Georgia and later operated a school for freed people.

superintendent of Union nurses in 1861, recruited "plain looking" women between the ages of thirty-five and fifty who wore no jewelry and could "bear the presence of suffering and exercise entire self-control" as military nurses.

Clara Barton, who later founded the American Red Cross, decided to go to the battlefields on her own, delivering medical supplies and food. At Fredericksburg, she nursed some 1,200 wounded in a single building. "I wrung the blood from the bottom of my clothing before I could step," she reported, "for the weight about my feet" kept her from moving.

In many Southern towns and counties, the home front was depleted of men and became a world of White women and children and enslaved African Americans. A resident of Lexington, Virginia, reported that there were "no men left" in town by mid-1862. White women suddenly found themselves working as full-time farmers or plantation managers, clerks, and schoolteachers. Enslaved women took advantage of the moment to flee to freedom behind U.S. lines.

Other women traveled with the armies, cooking meals, writing letters, and assisting with amputations. Phoebe Pember, a prominent Jewish widow from Charleston, helped manage Richmond's huge Chimborazo Hospital. She proudly observed that the White women of the Confederacy "incited the men to struggle for their liberties" and shared an intense hatred of Yankees: "They were the first to rebel, the last to succumb."

Women Who Fought

Both armies' combat operations included hundreds of women. Some disguised themselves as men and served as soldiers, including Loretta Jean Velazquez, a Cuban immigrant from New Orleans. She claimed to have enlisted twice as a soldier (using the name Harry T. Buford) and fought at Bull Run and Shiloh before her identity was discovered by an army doctor. Others mobilized at home, like the White women of New Orleans, who resisted the presence of U.S. troops in their city by spitting in their faces and dumping chamber pots on their heads. Still others fed guerrilla fighters or harbored deserters and spies.

HARRIET TUBMAN, CIVIL WAR SPY The open, freedom seeker turned spy Harriet Tubman is depicted in a Civil War encampment, leaning against an army rifle, with soldiers' tents visible in the background. Thirty years later, Tubman appealed to the U.S. government for compensation for her service to the U.S. military—a soldier's pension—but her request was denied.

Several dozen women served as spies—the most daring of whom was Harriet Tubman. She had already risked death many times to liberate seventy enslaved people from Maryland who escaped on the Underground Railroad in the decades before the war. On June 2, 1863, Tubman took command of her own military expedition in coastal South Carolina. Guided by secret intelligence she gathered from a local network of enslaved people, Tubman led three ships carrying Black U.S. soldiers up the Combahee River. Along the way, she guided the boats to avoid Confederate torpedoes submerged in the water.

As the ships moved upriver in the dark of night, they stopped several times to pick up freedom-seeking enslaved people who had gathered at the river's edge. "I never saw such a sight," Tubman recalled. "Sometimes the women would come with twins hanging around their necks . . . bags on their shoulders, baskets on their heads, and young ones tagging along behind." By dawn the boats had managed to outrun Confederate forces that were pursuing them, while destroying plantations and rice fields along the way. All told, Tubman's daring raid safely delivered 750 people to freedom.

New Yorker Mary Edwards Walker, a Union battlefield surgeon, was captured and imprisoned by Confederates for spying, but later was released in a prisoner exchange. She was the only woman in the war (and since) to be awarded the Congressional Medal of Honor—the nation's highest military award.

Wartime Government

As the war continued to rage on the nation's battlefields, a political revolution in Washington, D.C., resulted from the shift in congressional power from the South to the North after secession.

In 1862, the Republican-dominated Congress sought to promote the "prosperity and happiness of the whole people" by passing a more comprehensive tariff bill (called the Morrill Tariff in honor of its sponsor, Vermont Republican congressman Justin Smith Morrill) to raise government revenue and "protect" America's manufacturing, agricultural, mining, and fishing industries from foreign competition.

Republicans in Congress, with Lincoln's support, enacted legislation reflecting their belief that the federal government should actively promote economic development. To that end, Congress approved the **Pacific Railway Act (1862)**, which provided funding and grants of land for construction of a 1,900-mile-long transcontinental railroad line from Omaha, Nebraska, to Sacramento, California. In addition, a **Homestead Act (1862)** granted 160 acres of public land to each settler who agreed to work the land for five years. To help farmers become more productive, Congress created a new federal agency, the Department of Agriculture.

Two other key pieces of legislation were the **Morrill Land-Grant College Act (1862)**, which provided states with 30,000 acres of federal land to finance the establishment of public universities that would teach "agriculture and mechanic arts"; and the **National Banking Act (1863)**, which created national banks that could issue paper money that would be accepted across the country. These wartime measures had long-term significance for the growth of the national economy—and the expansion of the federal government.

Union Finances

Back in December 1860, the federal Treasury had been virtually empty. Once the war started in April 1861, Congress needed money fast—and lots of it. It focused on three options: raising taxes, printing paper money, and

> Republicans expand national economy and federal government

Pacific Railway Act (1862) Legislation under which Congress provided funding for a transcontinental railroad from Nebraska west to California.

Homestead Act (1862) Legislation granting 160 acres of government-owned land to settlers who agreed to work the land for at least five years.

Morrill Land-Grant College Act (1862) A federal statute that granted federal lands to states to help fund the creation of land-grant colleges and universities, which were founded to provide technical education in agriculture, mining, and industry.

National Banking Act (1863) Legislation through which the U.S. Congress created a national banking system to finance the enormous expense of the Civil War. It enabled loans to the government and established a single national currency, including the issuance of paper money ("greenbacks").

selling government bonds to investors. The taxes came chiefly in the form of the Morrill Tariff on imports and a 3 percent tax on manufactures and most professions.

In 1862, Congress created what would become the Internal Revenue Service to collect the first income tax on citizens and corporations. Yet only 250,000 people out of a population of 39 million had income high enough to pay taxes.

In the end, the tax revenues met only 21 percent of wartime expenditures. To fill the gap, Congress approved the printing of paper money to help finance the war. With the Legal Tender Act of 1862, the Treasury issued $450 million in new paper currency, called *greenbacks* because of the green ink used to print the bills. The federal government also relied upon the sale of bonds.

Confederate Finances

Compared to the Union's, Confederate efforts to finance the war were a disaster. Jefferson Davis had to create a Treasury department and a revenue-collecting system from scratch. Moreover, the South's agrarian economy was land-rich but cash-poor. While the Confederacy owned 30 percent of America's assets (businesses, land, enslaved people) in 1861, its currency in circulation was only 12 percent of that in the North.

In its first year, the Confederacy created a property tax. By 1863, the desperate Confederate Congress began taxing nearly everything, but enforcement was poor and evasion easy. Altogether, taxes covered no more than 5 percent of Confederate war costs, and bond issues accounted for less than 33 percent. Treasury notes (paper money) accounted for more than 60 percent.

During the war, the Confederacy issued more than $1 billion in paper money, which, along with a shortage of consumer goods, caused inflation.

STATE CURRENCY Both the Union and the Confederacy issued paper money to stimulate the economy. The patriotic art on the notes honored soldiers and other important figures. Generally, the better the art on the note, the more it was trusted.

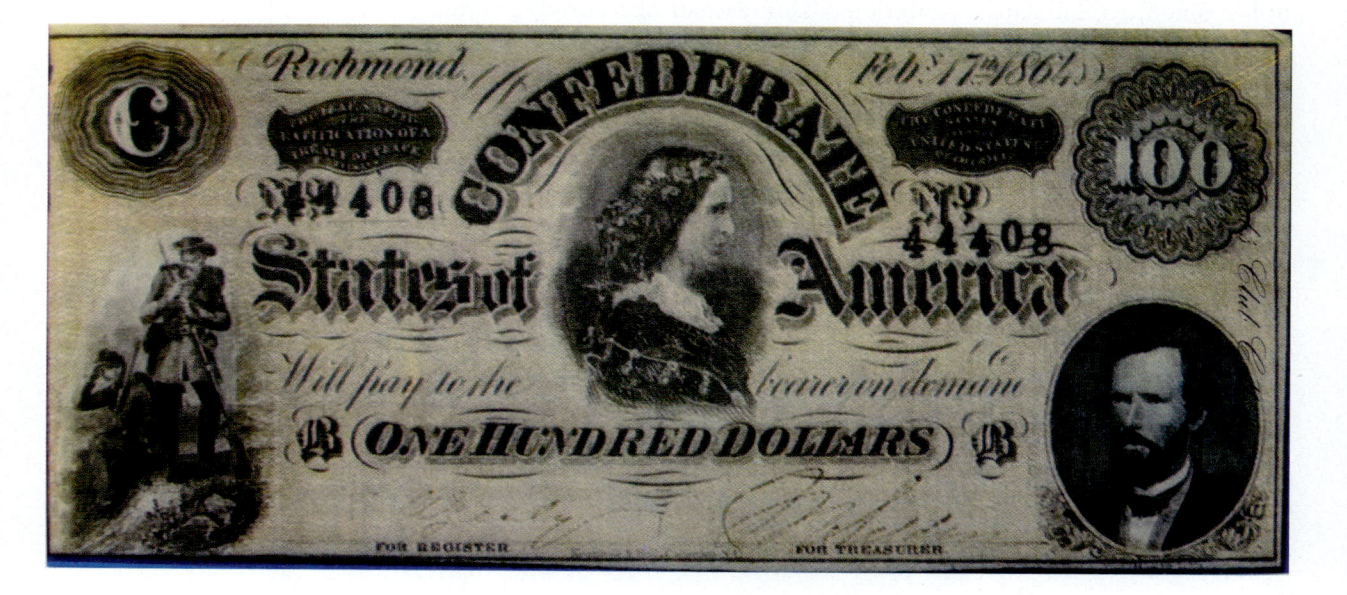

By 1864, a turkey sold in the Richmond market for $100 and bacon was $10 a pound. Such steep price increases caused great distress; and frustrations over the burdens of war erupted into rioting, looting, and mass protests.

By 1865, some 100,000 Confederate soldiers, hungry, weary, and frustrated by delayed pay, were deserting and heading home. As one said, he and his comrades were "tired of fighting for this negro-owning aristockracy [*sic*]."

Union Politics

The North also had its share of dissension and factionalism, but President Lincoln proved to be a remarkable conflict manager. He loved the jockeying of backroom politics, and he excelled at fending off uprisings and attempts to subvert his leadership.

Led by Thaddeus Stevens in the House and Charles Sumner in the Senate, the so-called Radical Republicans wanted more than the Confederacy's defeat; they wanted to "reconstruct" the rebellious region by having Union armies seize Southern plantations and give the land to the formerly enslaved workers. Most Republicans, however, continued to back Lincoln's more cautious approach.

The Democratic Party was devastated by the loss of its long-dominant Southern wing and the death of its nationalist spokesman, Stephen A. Douglas. Peace Democrats favored restoring the Union "as it was [before 1860] and the Constitution as it is." They reluctantly supported Lincoln's war policies but opposed Republican economic legislation. Those referred to as the War Democrats, such as Tennessee senator Andrew Johnson and Secretary of War Edwin M. Stanton, backed Lincoln.

Civil Liberties

Growing support for the enemy in the North led President Lincoln to crack down hard. His challenge was to balance the urgent needs of winning a war with the protection of civil liberties. Using his authority as commander-in-chief, Lincoln exercised emergency powers, including suspending the writ of habeas corpus, which guarantees arrested citizens a speedy hearing before a judge. The Constitution states that the government may suspend habeas corpus only in cases of foreign invasion, but Supreme Court justice Roger Taney and several congressional leaders argued that Congress alone had the authority to take such action.

> Lincoln suspends *habeas corpus*

By the Habeas Corpus Act of 1863, Congress allowed the president to have people arrested on the "suspicion" of treason. Thereafter, Union soldiers and local sheriffs arrested thousands of Confederate sympathizers in the Northern states without using a writ of habeas corpus. Union general Henry Halleck jailed a Missourian for saying, "[I] wouldn't wipe my ass with the stars and stripes."

Confederate Politics and States' Rights

As the war dragged on, discontented Confederates directed much of their frustration toward their leaders. A Richmond newspaper reported in 1862 that the Confederacy had "reached a very dark hour" because of Jefferson Davis's faulty leadership. It described the Rebel leader as "cold, haughty, peevish, narrow-minded, pig-headed, [and] malignant."

Poor White Southerners resented the planter elite while food grew scarce and prices skyrocketed. In August 1862, planter/politician J. F. H. Claiborne wrote a letter to the Mississippi governor in which he acknowledged, "We are proving our loyalty by starvation." The military's demands for food and supplies pitted the needs of civilians against those of the army. Women struggling to feed their families pleaded with Confederate leaders to send their husbands and sons home. "My record of misfortune has been unparalleled," wrote Elizabeth Patterson of Virginia, after losing three sons and her husband to the war. "In every conceivable way my family have striven to benefit the Confederacy," but now she wanted her only remaining son discharged from military service and sent home. She got no response.

Women lead riots in the South

In spring 1863, the desperate situation led women across the South to riot. In cities such as Atlanta, Mobile, and Richmond, they gathered by the hundreds to demand that something be done. In Richmond, on April 2, 1863, Mary Jackson and Minerva Meredith led hundreds of women (and some men) on a march to the governor's mansion to demand that bread in Confederate warehouses be shared with civilians. "We are starving!" they shouted. When the governor announced that nothing could be done, the protesters, many of them armed with guns and knives, cried, "Bread or blood!"—words chanted in other cities too. The protesters broke into markets and stores, taking shoes and clothing as well as food. The bread riot ended only when President Davis arrived and threatened to shoot the demonstrators. Over several days, police arrested forty-four women and twenty-nine men.

President Davis's greatest challenge came from Southern politicians who criticized the "tyrannical" powers of the Confederate government. Critics asserted states' rights against the Confederate government. Georgia governor Joseph Brown explained that he had joined the Confederacy to "sustain the rights of the states and prevent the consolidation of the Government, and I am still a *rebel*... *no* matter who may be in power."

While Abraham Lincoln was a shrewd pragmatist, Jefferson Davis was a brittle ideologue. Once he made a decision, nothing could change his mind, and he could never admit his mistake. South Carolina's James Henry Hammond charged that Davis displayed "the most perverse & mulish obstinacy, spleen, spite & illimitable conceit & vanity."

Such a dogmatic personality was ill suited to be the chief executive of a new—and quarrelsome—nation. Confederate cabinet members resigned almost as soon as they were appointed. During its four years, the Confederacy had three secretaries of state and six secretaries of war.

The war was taking its toll on many aspects of social and economic life across the warring nation. The pressures of supplying and nursing the huge armies required enormous sacrifices and prompted many women to get involved in the war effort. All facets of civilian life were disrupted. Farms and villages became battlefields, while churches became makeshift hospitals and morgues. Death and grief were inescapable. Economically, the North worked to absorb the war's staggering costs through taxes, tariffs, government bonds, and the issuing of paper money. In the cash-poor South, however, the government printed so much paper money that it caused severe inflation of consumer prices, which led to even more personal trauma and civil unrest.

The Faltering Confederacy

Amid the political infighting, the war ground on. The Confederate strategy of fighting mostly a defensive war was working well, and President Lincoln was still searching for a general-in-chief comparable to Robert E. Lee.

> **CORE OBJECTIVE**
> **4.** Describe the military turning points in 1863 and 1864 that ultimately led to the Confederacy's defeat.

Chancellorsville

After the Union disaster at the Battle of Fredericksburg at the end of 1862, President Lincoln fired Ambrose Burnside and appointed General Joseph "Fighting Joe" Hooker to lead the Army of the Potomac. With a force of 130,000 men, the largest Union army yet gathered, an overconfident Hooker attacked the Confederates at Chancellorsville, in eastern Virginia, during the first week of May 1863 (see Map 14.5). "My plans are perfect," Hooker boasted. "May God have mercy on General Lee, for I will have none."

Hooker spoke too soon. Lee, with perhaps half as many troops, divided his army and enabled Stonewall Jackson's 28,000 Confederates to surprise the Union army by smashing into its exposed right flank. Jackson's stunning attack resulted in a devastating defeat for the Union. "My God, my God," moaned Lincoln when he heard the news. "What will the country say?"

The Confederate triumph was costly for the victors, however. As night fell during the second day of battle, General Jackson and several aides rode out beyond the Rebel lines to locate Union forces. Shooting erupted in the darkness, and nervous Confederates mistakenly opened fire on Jackson's group. Three bullets struck the celebrated commander, shattering his left arm and right hand. The next day, a surgeon amputated his arm. The indispensable Jackson seemed to be recovering, but he then contracted pneumonia and died. "I have lost my right arm," Lee lamented, and "I do not know how to replace him."

ULYSSES S. GRANT In Grant, President Lincoln finally found a general to rival Robert E. Lee. Grant is pictured here at his headquarters in City Point (now Hopewell), Virginia.

Vicksburg

While General Robert E. Lee frustrated the Federals in the East, General Ulysses S. Grant had been inching his army down the Mississippi River toward the Confederate stronghold of Vicksburg, Mississippi, a busy commercial town situated on high bluffs overlooking a bend in the river (see again Map 14.5). Capturing the most important Rebel outpost in the western theater, Grant stressed, "was of the first importance," because Vicksburg was the only rail and river junction between Memphis, Tennessee, and New Orleans. By gaining control of the lower Mississippi River, the Union could cut off and isolate Texas, Arkansas, and most of Louisiana from the rest of the Confederacy.

While Union warships sneaked past the Confederate cannons overlooking the river, Grant moved his army eastward across Mississippi, living off the land on a campaign that President Lincoln later called "one of the most brilliant in the world." In three weeks, Grant's men marched 180 miles, won five battles, and captured some 6,000 prisoners before pinning the main Rebel army inside Vicksburg so tightly that "not a cat could have crept out ... without being discovered."

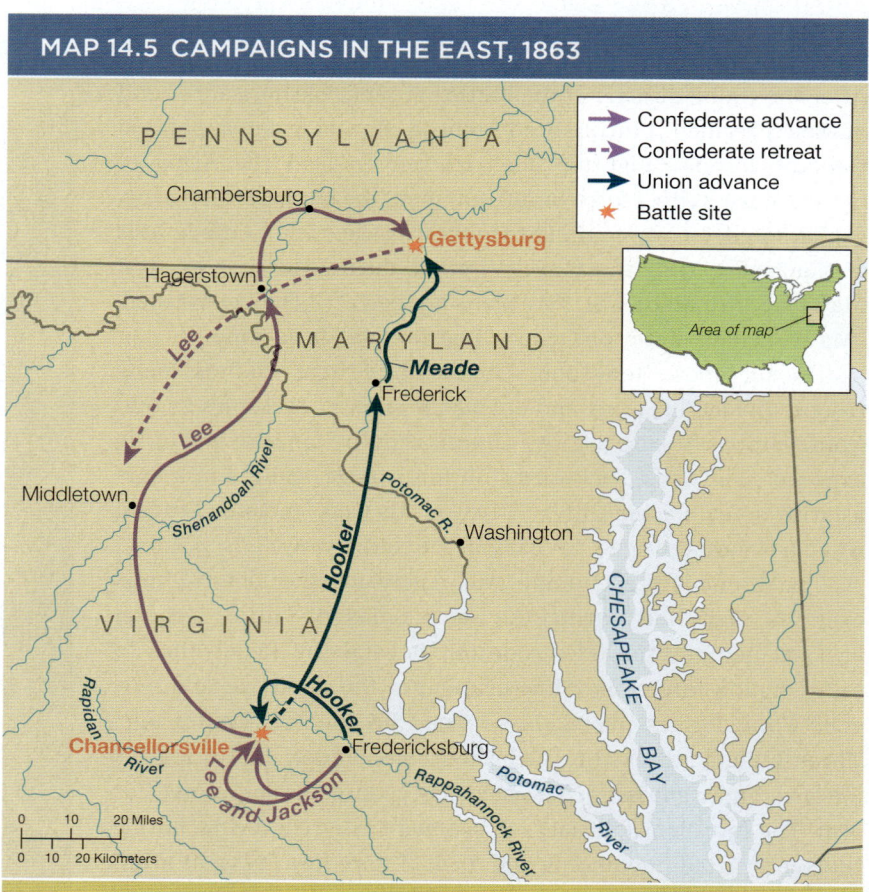

MAP 14.5 CAMPAIGNS IN THE EAST, 1863

- Locate Chancellorsville on the map. Judging from the arrows showing Union and Confederate advances there, who had the advantage—and why?
- Find Gettysburg on the map, and then trace General Robert E. Lee's northward advance from Chancellorsville to Gettysburg. What states did his troops pass through?
- Based on your understanding of the chapter text, explain why Gettysburg was a major turning point in the Civil War.

In late May and early June 1863, Federal troops dug twelve miles of interconnected trenches around the besieged city and positioned 220 cannons to make life miserable for the Vicksburg defenders and civilians. Yet taking the river city would not be easy. One of Grant's generals declared that "no place on earth is favored by nature with natural defense such as Vicksburg."

In the **Battle of Vicksburg**, Grant decided to use constant bombardment from gunboats and cannons to starve and gradually wear down the trapped Confederate soldiers, 10 percent of whom would be killed or wounded. Many civilian residents were forced to live in cellars or caves dug as protection from the unending shelling. A woman trapped by the siege stressed that "we are utterly cutoff from the world, surrounded by a circle of fire. The fiery shower of [Union] shells goes on day and night."

The Confederate soldiers and the city's residents could neither escape, nor be reinforced, nor be resupplied with food and ammunition. Living conditions for both military personnel and civilians deteriorated rapidly.

General John C. Pemberton, the Confederate commander at Vicksburg, wrote Jefferson Davis that the situation was "hopeless." A group of ragged soldiers pleaded with their commander: "If you can't feed us, you had better surrender us, horrible as that idea is." Yet Pemberton, a Pennsylvanian whose Virginia-born wife convinced him to fight for the Confederacy, was determined to outlast Grant's troops.

Gettysburg

Vicksburg's dilemma led Jefferson Davis to ask General Lee to send troops from Virginia to Mississippi to break the Union siege. Lee, however, thought he had a better plan. He would make another daring strike into the North in hopes of forcing the Union army surrounding Vicksburg to rush home to defend the Northern heartland. He also wagered that a bold offensive to the north would persuade peace-seeking Democrats to try again to end the war on terms favorable to the Confederacy. The stakes were high.

Targeting the North in Pennsylvania In June 1863, the fabled Army of Northern Virginia, which Lee said was made up of "invincible troops" who would "go anywhere and do anything if properly led," moved northward, taking thousands of animals and wagons as well as throngs of enslaved people for support.

Once the Union commander General George Meade realized that the Confederates were again marching north, he gave chase, knowing that the next battle would "decide the fate of our country and our cause." As Lee's army moved into Pennsylvania, the Confederate general lost track of the Federals following him because of the unexplained absence of General J. E. B. Stuart's 5,000 horse soldiers, who were Lee's "eyes and ears."

Neither side expected Gettysburg, a hilly farming town in southeastern Pennsylvania, to be the site of the largest battle ever fought in North America

Battle of Vicksburg (1863)
A protracted battle in northern Mississippi in which Union forces under Ulysses S. Grant besieged the last major Confederate fortress on the Mississippi River, forcing the inhabitants into starvation and then submission on July 4, 1863.

Ulysses S. Grant holds Vicksburg under siege

General Lee leads Confederate troops north

Battle of Gettysburg (1863)

PICKETT'S CHARGE In a courageous and doomed effort, the Confederate soldiers *(in the foreground)* led by General George Pickett prepare to advance on a line of well-armed Union troops.

(Map 14.5). Unsuspecting Confederate troops entered the town at dawn on June 30 and collided with Union cavalry units that had been tracking their movements.

The main forces of both sides—65,000 Confederates and 85,000 Federals—then raced to the scene, and on July 1, the armies clashed in what came to be called the **Battle of Gettysburg**, the most dramatic contest of the war.

On July 2, wave after wave of screaming Confederates assaulted Meade's army, pushing the Federals back but never breaking through. A wounded Confederate officer scrawled a note before he died: "Tell my father I died with my face to the enemy." Some 16,000 men were killed or wounded on both sides during the second day. Worse was to come.

The next day, against the objections of his senior general, Georgian James Longstreet, Robert E. Lee risked all on a gallant but doomed assault against the well-defended Union lines arrayed along Cemetery Ridge. For two hours, both sides bombarded the other, leading a Union soldier to write that it felt "as if the heavens and earth were crashing together."

Pickett's "grand charge"

Pickett's Charge Then, at two o'clock on the broiling summer afternoon, the cannons stopped. Three Confederate infantry divisions—about 12,500 men—rose together and emerged from the woods into the brilliant sunlight. General George Pickett, commander of the lead division, told his men, "Charge the enemy and remember Old Virginia!"

A gray wave of sweating Rebels began a mile-long dash up a grassy slope of newly mown hay crisscrossed with split-rail fences. Awaiting them behind a low stone wall at the top of Cemetery Ridge were 120 Union cannons and thousands of riflemen.

When the Federals opened fire, the attacking Rebels were "enveloped in a dense cloud of dust. Arms, heads, blankets, guns, and knapsacks were

Battle of Gettysburg (1863)
A monumental three-day battle in southern Pennsylvania, widely considered a turning point in the Civil War, in which Union forces defeated Lee's Confederate army and forced it back into Virginia.

tossed into the clear air." Half of the Confederates were killed or wounded. Only a few made it to the Union lines, where they grappled with Federals in hand-to-hand combat. The Union line held, and the Confederates fell back.

With stunning suddenness, the carnage was over. The surviving Confederates retreated to the sheltering woods, and the once-roaring battlefield was left covered with the corpses of men and horses, a scene made ghastlier by the "moanings and groanings" of thousands of wounded.

A HARVEST OF DEATH Timothy H. O'Sullivan's grim photograph shows some of the dead at Gettysburg.

"This horrid war" Each corpse told a poignant story. Scattered beside a dead Federal officer were papers granting him leave to go home and be married, and a letter from his soon-to-be bride expressing her "happiness at the approaching event."

What General Lee had called the "grand charge" was a grand failure. As he watched the survivors struggle back, he muttered, "All this has been my fault. It is I who have lost this fight." He ordered General Pickett to prepare his battered division for another attack, only to have Pickett reply: "General Lee, I have no division now." Half his men lay dead or wounded.

Lee sought to console Pickett by assuring him that he and his troops "have covered yourselves with glory." Pickett would have none of it. "Not all the glory in the world, General Lee, can atone for the widows and orphans this day has made."

Some 42,000 on both sides were dead, wounded, or missing after three days at Gettysburg. Hundreds of horses were also killed and left to rot. A Union soldier wrote home: "Great God! When will this horrid war stop?"

Lee's Retreat

Again, as after the Battle of Antietam, Robert E. Lee's mangled army retreated to Virginia (Map 14.5)—and again, the Federals were slow to give chase. Had General Meade quickly pursued Lee's battered army, he might have ended the war. President Lincoln was outraged: "We had them within our grasp! Your golden opportunity is gone, and I am distressed immeasurably because of it."

The war would grind on for another twenty-one months. Still, Confederate morale plummeted. A Georgia soldier wrote his mother that "the Army is broken hearted" and "don't care which way the war closes, for we have suffered very much."

Lee's desperate gamble had failed in every way, not the least being its inability to relieve the pressure on the Confederate army trapped in Vicksburg, Mississippi. On July 4, General John Pemberton, the Confederate commander at Vicksburg, surrendered, ending the forty-seven-day siege. Union vessels now controlled the Mississippi River, and the Confederacy was effectively split in two.

The Gettysburg Address

After the Battle of Gettysburg, a group of Northern states funded a military cemetery in commemoration of the thousands killed in the battle. On November 19, 1863, President Lincoln spoke to 15,000 people gathered to dedicate the new national cemetery. In his brief remarks (only nine sentences), known now as the Gettysburg Address, he expressed the pain and sorrow of the uncivil war. The prolonged conflict, he stressed, was testing whether a nation "dedicated to the proposition that all men are created equal . . . can long endure." In stirring words, Lincoln predicted that "this nation, under God, shall have a new birth of freedom—and that government of the people, by the people, and for the people, shall not perish from the earth."

Chattanooga

The third Union triumph of 1863 occurred in southern Tennessee around Chattanooga, the river port that served as a gateway to northern Georgia. A Union army led by General William Rosecrans took Chattanooga on September 9 and then chased General Braxton Bragg's Confederate forces into the north Georgia mountains, where they clashed at Chickamauga (a Cherokee word meaning "river of death").

The result was horrific. Some 35,000 soldiers on both sides were killed or wounded. On the second day, Rosecrans nearly lost the battle when he rushed troops to close a gap in the Union line—a gap that did not exist. His mistake did open a gap in his own lines, however, and Confederate troops stormed through, sending Rosecrans and most of his army reeling back to Chattanooga.

The Union command rushed in reinforcements; and on November 24 and 25, the Federal troops dislodged the Confederates from Lookout Mountain and Missionary Ridge, thereby gaining effective control of Tennessee. The South had lost the war in the West.

The Battle of Chattanooga secures Union victory in the West

The North Prevails

The dramatic Union victories at Vicksburg, Gettysburg, and Chattanooga seemed to turn the tide against the Confederacy. During the summer and fall of 1863, however, Union generals in the East lost the momentum Gettysburg had provided.

By 1864, Robert E. Lee, whose offer to resign after Gettysburg was refused by Jefferson Davis, was ready to renew the war. His men were "in fine spirits and anxious for a fight." Still, the tone had changed. Confederate leaders had long assumed they could win the war. Now, they began to worry about defeat.

A Wartime Election

War or no war, 1864 was a presidential election year in the United States, and by autumn the contest would become a referendum on the war itself. Abraham Lincoln became convinced that he would lose without a dramatic change in the course of the war. "This war is eating my life out," Lincoln confessed to an Illinois friend in 1864. "I have a strong impression I shall not live to see the end."

Radical Republicans, frustrated that the war had not been won, tried to prevent Lincoln's nomination for a second term, but he consistently outmaneuvered them. Once Lincoln was assured of the nomination, he selected Andrew Johnson, a War Democrat from Tennessee, as his running mate on the "National Union" ticket. Johnson was the only U.S. senator from the Southern states to remain in Congress and not join the Confederacy in 1861. By choosing Johnson as his running mate, Lincoln sought to make a bipartisan appeal to Union voters, both Republicans and Democrats.

The Democratic Party nominated General George B. McClellan, the former Union commander who had clashed with Lincoln. McClellan pledged to end the war and, if the Rebels refused to return to the Union, to allow the Confederacy to "go in peace."

To save the Union—and his presidency—Lincoln had brought General Grant, his best commander, to Washington, D.C., in March 1864; promoted him to general-in-chief; and given him overall command of the war effort, promising all the troops and supplies he needed.

A New York newspaper reported that Lincoln's presidency was now "in the hands of General Grant, and the failure of the General will be the overthrow of the president." When a delegation visited the White House to complain about Grant's reputation as a heavy drinker, Lincoln told the visitors that if he could find the brand of whiskey Grant used, he would distribute it to the rest of his generals.

Grant's Strategy

General Grant was a hard-nosed warrior with unflagging energy and persistence. One soldier said that Grant always looked like he was "determined to drive his head through a brick wall and was about to do it." Yet the Union commander hated war. "I never went into battle willingly or with enthusiasm," he admitted. Nevertheless, he was a brilliant military strategist driven by a simple concept: "Find out where your enemy is, get to him as soon as you can, and strike him as hard as you can, and keep moving on."

Grant's predecessors had focused on trying to capture Richmond; his priority was to defeat Confederate armies. He would wage a relentless war of attrition, one in which victory would favor the side that could absorb the most punishment and keep fighting. Grant, as Abraham Lincoln noted, understood that winning the war was a matter of "awful arithmetic." The Union had the greater numbers of soldiers and weaponry, so victory was "only a matter of time."

> Grant's strategy of hard war

FORT PILLOW MASSACRE Confederate General Nathan Bedford Forrest oversaw the brutal execution of roughly 300 surrendered Union soldiers, most of them Black, at Fort Pillow in 1864.

To that end, Grant ordered the three largest Union armies, one in Virginia, one in Tennessee, and one in Louisiana, to launch offensives in the spring of 1864. No more short battles followed by long pauses. They were to force the outnumbered Confederates to keep fighting, day after day, week after week, until they were worn out.

Grant assigned his trusted friend General William Tecumseh Sherman, a rail-thin, red-haired Ohioan, to lead the Union army in Tennessee southward and apply a strategy of "complete conquest." Sherman and Grant would now wage total war, or what was called "hard war" at the time, which meant destroying any property that might have military value. It was a ruthless and costly plan, but in the end, it would prove effective in shortening the war.

Fort Pillow Massacre

As the war ground on, the fighting grew more brutal. The worst war crime occurred at Fort Pillow on the western edge of Tennessee. Built in 1861 by Confederates, Fort Pillow was perched on a bluff overlooking a bend in the Mississippi River some forty miles north of Memphis, Tennessee. In 1862, as Union forces took control of the Mississippi, Confederates abandoned the fort and Union troops had moved in.

On April 12, 1864, Confederates under General Nathan Bedford Forrest, a former slave trader and planter, assaulted Fort Pillow and murdered some 300 surrendering Union soldiers. Most of them were African Americans. A Confederate sergeant reported that "the slaughter was awful. Words cannot describe the scene."

As word of the Fort Pillow Massacre spread among soldiers, violence begat violence. A few weeks later, a Union soldier from Wisconsin fighting in north Georgia wrote to his future wife about a recent battle: "Twenty-three of the Rebs surrendered but our boys asked if they remembered Fort Pillow and killed all of them. Where there is no officer with us, we take no prisoners.... We want revenge for our brother soldiers and will have it."

Chasing Lee

> Battle of the Wilderness (1864)

In May 1864, General Grant's massive Army of the Potomac, numbering about 115,000 (nearly twice the size of General Lee's Army of Northern Virginia), moved south across the Rappahannock and Rapidan Rivers in eastern Virginia (see Map 14.6). In the nightmarish Battle of the Wilderness (May 5–6), halfway between Washington, D.C., and Richmond, the armies clashed in an impenetrable tangle of scrub oaks, stunted pines, and thorny thickets interspersed with ravines, streams, and swamps.

Exploding shells set off brushfires that burned many wounded soldiers to death.

At one point, the Union forces threatened to overrun Lee's headquarters. Lee himself helped organize a counterattack, lining up soldiers from Texas to lead the effort. His mood brightened as the Confederates swept the Federals from the field.

Grant's men suffered more casualties than the Confederates, but the Rebels struggled to find replacements. Always before, when bloodied by Lee's troops, Union armies had quit fighting to rest and nurse their wounds, but now Grant refused to halt. His army continued to push southward, forcing the Confederates to keep fighting.

When General John B. Gordon boasted after the Battle of the Wilderness that Grant was retreating, Lee corrected him: "You are mistaken, quite mistaken. Grant is not retreating; he is not a *retreating* man."

Pushing Southward Lee predicted that Grant's army would head for Spotsylvania, which it did. There, it engaged Lee's men near Spotsylvania Court House, eleven miles southwest of Fredericksburg, on the road to Richmond (see again Map 14.6). For twelve brutally hot days in May, the opposing armies were locked in some of the fiercest combat of the war. The result was inconclusive, with both sides declaring victory.

In the first days of June 1864, Grant ordered a poorly coordinated frontal assault on Lee's entrenched Rebels ten miles east of Richmond, at Cold Harbor (the name derived from a tavern that offered overnight rooms but no hot meals).

> Grant suffers terrible defeat at Cold Harbor

In twenty minutes, amid pitiless heat and choking dust, almost 4,000 Federals, caught in a blistering crossfire, were killed or wounded; the Rebel casualty count was only 1,500. It was, according to a Union general, "one of the most disastrous days the Army of the Potomac has ever seen." A Confederate commander reported that "it was not war; it was murder."

The frightful losses nearly unhinged Grant, who later admitted that the botched attack was his greatest mistake as a commander. Critics called Grant "a butcher" who was indifferent to the lives of his soldiers. In just two months, Grant's massive offensive across Virginia, labeled the Overland Campaign, had cost some 65,000 killed, wounded, or missing Union soldiers while the Confederate losses were only half that number.

> Outcry against Grant

Yet Grant, for all his mistakes, knew that his army could replace its dead and wounded; the Confederates could not. A Union victory, he insisted, "was only a question of time." And, Grant reminded Lincoln, he was slowly pushing Lee's army toward Richmond, backing the Confederates into a corner from which they could not escape.

After Cold Harbor, Grant brilliantly maneuvered his battered forces around Lee's army, crossed the James River, and headed for Petersburg, a major supply center and railroad hub just twenty-five miles south of Richmond. As the opposing armies dug in above and below Petersburg, Grant began a long siege of the trapped Confederate army, tightening the noose as he had done at Vicksburg.

MAP 14.6 GRANT IN VIRGINIA, 1864–1865

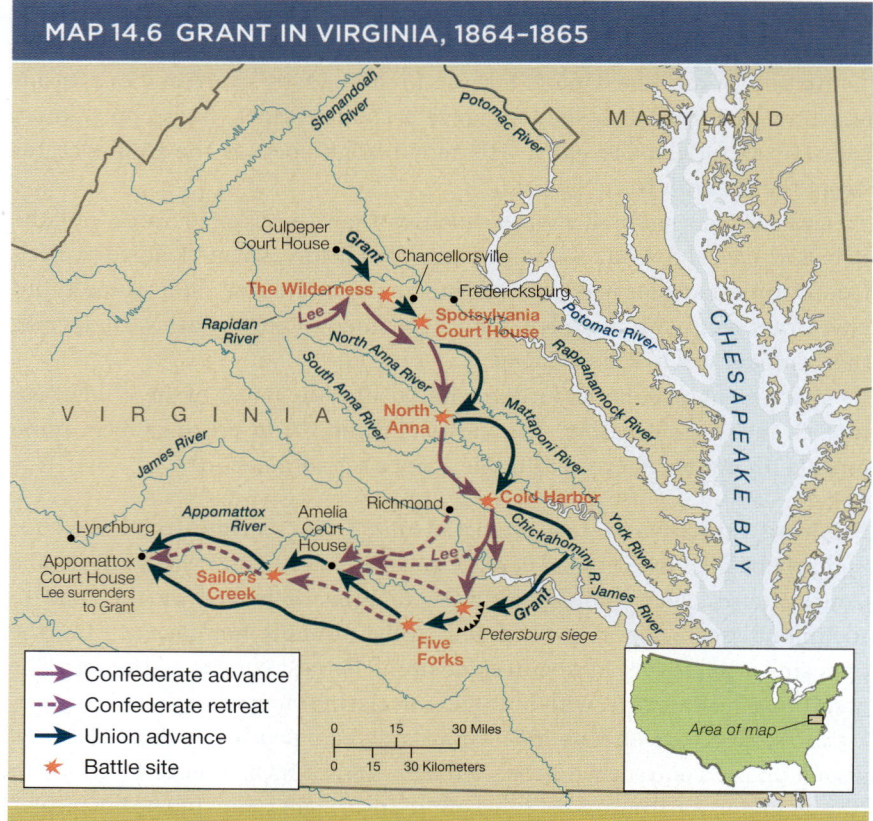

- Find the arrows showing General Ulysses S. Grant's southward advance toward the Battle of the Wilderness, and his troops' movements after that. What do the progressing solid arrows tell you about his success?
- Locate the site of the siege of Petersburg. Using the mileage key as a guide, estimate how far from Virginia's capital of Richmond the siege took place. Why did the Confederate forces want to keep Grant from heading north from Petersburg?
- Based on your reading of the chapter text, why did Grant have the advantage at Petersburg? How long did the siege last?

At the end of August, Robert E. Lee reported to Jefferson Davis that Grant was "reducing us by starvation." For eight more months, the opposing armies held each other in check around Petersburg. Grant's troops were generously supplied by Union vessels moving up the James River, while the besieged Confederates wasted away.

Petersburg had become Lee's prison, while disasters piled up for the Confederacy elsewhere. He admitted that it was "a mere question of time" before he would have to retreat or surrender.

Sherman Pushes South

Meanwhile, General Grant ordered William Tecumseh Sherman to drive through the heart of Dixie and inflict "all the damage you can." As Sherman moved his army south from Chattanooga toward the crucial railroad hub in Atlanta, he sent a warning to the city's residents: "Prepare for my coming."

By the middle of July, Sherman's troops had reached the outskirts of heavily fortified Atlanta, trapping 40,000 Confederate soldiers there led by General John Bell Hood, the Confederate commander from Texas (see Map 14.7). General Grant viewed Hood as "a gallant brave fellow" but believed he would likely "dash out and fight every time you raised a [Union] flag before him." And that is just what Grant and Sherman wanted him to do.

Hood's arm had been shattered at Gettysburg, and he had lost a leg in Tennessee. Strapped to his saddle, he refused simply to "defend" Atlanta; instead, he attacked. Three times in eight days, the Confederates lashed out at the Union lines encircling the city. Each time, they were repulsed, suffering *seven* times as many casualties as the Federals.

Finally, on September 1, the Confederates evacuated the city. Sherman then moved in, gleefully telegraphing Lincoln in September 1864, "Atlanta is ours and fairly won." Confederates were crestfallen at the news. A distraught Mary Chesnut decided "the end has come. . . . We are going to be wiped off the face of the earth. . . . No hope."

Sherman's soldiers stayed in Atlanta until November, resting and resupplying themselves. The 20,000 residents were told to leave before he destroyed much of the city. When they protested, the Union commander replied: "War is cruelty." His men then set fire to the city's railroad station, shops, mills, hotels, and businesses. After Grant congratulated Sherman, he ordered him to commence another campaign, for "we want to keep the enemy constantly pressed to the end of the war."

> Sherman seizes and burns Atlanta

DESTROYING SOUTHERN RAILROADS General William Tecumseh Sherman's troops cut a swath of destruction across Georgia in their "March to the Sea." Here, Union troops rip up railroad tracks in Atlanta.

election of 1864 Abraham Lincoln's successful reelection campaign capitalizing on Union military successes in Georgia to defeat his Democratic opponent, former general George B. McClellan, who ran on a peace platform.

Lincoln Reelected

William Tecumseh Sherman's conquest of Atlanta enabled Abraham Lincoln to win a second term in the **election of 1864**. Up to that point, President Lincoln was convinced that he would lose his reelection bid. "I am a beaten man, unless we have some great victory," he predicted at the end of August. Now, with Sherman's victories, the tide had turned in Lincoln's favor. As a Republican senator said, the Union army's success in Georgia "created the most extraordinary change in public opinion here [in the North] that ever was known." A Union newspaper editor reported that the fall of Atlanta "has secured a sudden unanimity for Mr. Lincoln."

In the 1864 election, the Democratic candidate, George McClellan, carried only New Jersey, Delaware, and Kentucky, winning just 21 Electoral College votes to Lincoln's 212 and 1.8 million popular votes (45 percent) to Lincoln's 2.2 million (55 percent). Union soldiers and sailors voted in large numbers, and almost 80 percent voted for Lincoln. The president's victory ensured that Union armies would keep the pressure on the Confederates. There would be no negotiated peace.

Sherman's "March to the Sea"

In November 1864, General Sherman led 60,000 soldiers out of Atlanta on their fabled 300-mile "March to the Sea" southeastward to the coastal city of Savannah (see again Map 14.7). Sherman planned to wage a modern war against all Confederates—soldiers and civilians—and their economy. He intended to "whip the rebels, to humble their pride, to follow them into their inmost recesses, and make them fear and dread us." Showing Rebel sympathizers the "hard hand of war," he believed, would shatter civilian morale and trigger a wave of military desertions. It would also "ruin Georgia" as a source of Confederate supplies.

General John Bell Hood's Confederate Army of Tennessee, meanwhile, tried a desperate gamble by heading in the opposite direction, pushing northward into Alabama and then Tennessee (Map 14.7). Hood hoped to trick Sherman into chasing him, but Sherman refused to take the bait. He was determined to keep his main army moving southward to the Georgia coast and then into South Carolina, the seedbed of secession.

Sherman, however, did send General George Thomas and 30,000 soldiers to shadow Hood's Confederates. The two forces clashed in the Battle of Franklin (November 30, 1864), near Nashville, where Hood's 18,000 soldiers launched a suicidal frontal assault against entrenched Union troops backed by cannons.

> Hood's Confederate Army of Tennessee defeated

In just five hours, Hood lost six generals and saw 6,252 of his men killed or wounded, a casualty figure higher than Pickett's charge at Gettysburg and three times that of the Union troops at Franklin. The following morning, a Tennessee private noted that the battlefield resembled "a grand holocaust of death.... The dead were piled the one on the other all over the ground."

Two weeks later, in the Battle of Nashville, the Federals scattered what was left of Hood's bloodied army.

Sherman's "March to the Sea" became infamous among Southerners as a supposed example of Union ruthlessness. After the war, however, a Confederate officer acknowledged that the campaign had been well conceived and well managed. "I don't think there was ever an army in the world that would have behaved better, in a similar expedition, in an enemy country. Our army certainly wouldn't have."

On December 24, 1864, General Sherman sent a whimsical telegram to President Lincoln offering him the coastal city of Savannah, Georgia, as a Christmas present. By the time Union troops arrived in Savannah, they had freed more than 40,000 enslaved people, burned scores of plantation buildings, and destroyed the railroads. "God bless you, Yanks!" shouted a formerly enslaved man. "Come at last! God knows how long I been waitin'."

> **Sherman's "March to the Sea" (1864)** The Union army's devastating march through Georgia from Atlanta to Savannah led by General William T. Sherman, intended to demoralize civilians and destroy the resources the Confederate army needed to fight.

South Carolina

On February 1, 1865, Sherman's army headed north across the Savannah River into South Carolina, the "hell-hole of secession." Sherman reported that his "whole army is burning with an insatiable desire to wreak vengeance upon South Carolina. I almost tremble at her fate, but feel she deserves all that seems in store for her."

South Carolina paid a high price for having led the Southern states out of the Union. Sherman's men burned more than a dozen towns, including Barnwell, which they called "Burnwell." On February 17, 1865, they captured the state capital of Columbia (Map 14.7). Soon thereafter, Charleston surrendered.

It was no accident that Sherman ordered two all-Black regiments to lead the Union troops into the city. On April 14, the Union commander gave Major Robert Anderson, now retired from active service, the honor of raising the U.S. flag once again over the fort.

A Losing Cause

During late 1864 and early 1865, the Confederacy found itself besieged on all sides. Some Rebel leaders wanted to negotiate a peace settlement, but Jefferson Davis stubbornly rejected any talk of surrender. If his armies should be defeated, he wanted soldiers to scatter and fight an unending guerrilla war. "The war came and now it must go on," he insisted, "till the last man of this generation falls in his tracks, and his children seize his musket and fight our battle."

> Jefferson Davis refuses to surrender

A Second Term

While Confederate forces made their last stands, Abraham Lincoln prepared for his second term as president. The weary commander-in-chief had weathered constant criticism during his first term, but he now garnered praise. The

MAP 14.7 SHERMAN'S CAMPAIGNS, 1864–1865

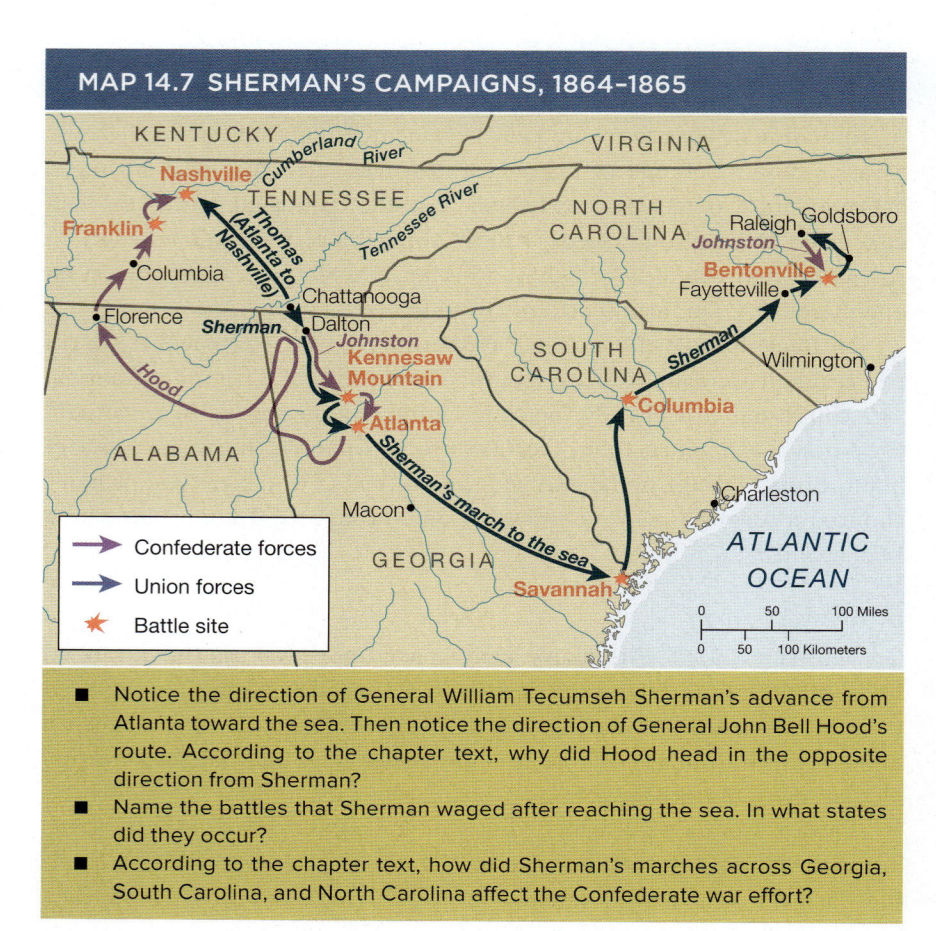

- Notice the direction of General William Tecumseh Sherman's advance from Atlanta toward the sea. Then notice the direction of General John Bell Hood's route. According to the chapter text, why did Hood head in the opposite direction from Sherman?
- Name the battles that Sherman waged after reaching the sea. In what states did they occur?
- According to the chapter text, how did Sherman's marches across Georgia, South Carolina, and North Carolina affect the Confederate war effort?

Chicago Tribune observed that Lincoln "has slowly and steadily risen in the respect, confidence, and admiration of the people."

On March 4, 1865, amid rumors of a Confederate attempt to abduct or assassinate the president, some 30,000 people, half of them African Americans, defied frigid weather to attend Lincoln's second inauguration in Washington, D.C. Dressed in a black suit and stovepipe hat, Lincoln delivered his address in the open air on the east portico of the Capitol. Sharpshooters lined the roofs to protect the president—and with good reason. Looking down from the Capitol porch, not 100 feet away, was twenty-six-year-old stage actor John Wilkes Booth, who five weeks later would kill the president in a desperate attempt to do something "heroic" for his beloved South.

Lincoln's five-minute second inaugural address (703 words) was more a powerful sermon than a typical political speech. He chose not to celebrate Union victories, nor did he denounce Confederates. Instead, Lincoln revealed what he had learned during four years of killing and suffering and untold stories of heartbreak and mourning in homes across both nations. He insisted that everyone bore some guilt for the shame of racial injustice and the tragic but just war to end it.

> Lincoln's second inaugural address (1865)

Lincoln longed for peace. "Fondly do we hope—fervently do we pray—that this mighty scourge of war may speedily pass away." As Lincoln looked ahead to a "just and lasting peace," he stressed that the understandable urge for vengeance against the Rebels must be stifled by humility and forgiveness. Reconciliation must be pursued "with malice toward none; with charity for all." Those eight words captured his hopes for a restored Union.

Appomattox

During the spring of 1865, General Grant's army kept pounding the encircled Rebels defending Petersburg, Virginia. Robert E. Lee had no way to replace the men he was losing, and his dwindling army couldn't kill enough Yankees to make Grant quit. On April 2, 1865, after General Philip Sheridan's cavalry cut off the last railroad serving the Confederate army in Petersburg, a desperate Lee made a desperate decision: the badly outnumbered Confederates abandoned Petersburg and headed west, with the Union army in hot pursuit (Map 14.6).

At the same time, the Confederate government fled Richmond—but not before burning anything of value. While the fires raged, Union troops, led by the all-Black Fifth Massachusetts Cavalry, entered the capital of the dying Confederacy. African Americans lined the streets to welcome the soldiers. They shouted, danced, prayed, and sang songs of liberation. The next day, April 4, Abraham Lincoln toured the fallen capital. "The colored population," wrote a Black reporter for a Philadelphia newspaper, "went wild with excitement."

On April 7, General Grant sent a note urging General Lee to surrender. With the remnants of his army virtually surrounded, Lee recognized that "there is nothing left for me to do but go and see General Grant, and I would rather die a thousand deaths."

Two days later, four years to the day since the Confederate attack on Fort Sumter, the tall, formal Lee, in his dress uniform, ceremonial sword, and shined boots, met the short, mud-spattered Grant in a small brick house in the village of **Appomattox Court House**. Grant apologized for his "rough" appearance, explaining that he had left behind his dress uniform. Lee, in turn, stressed that he was in a new uniform because it was the only one he had left, and he fully expected to be arrested after surrendering.

After some awkward exchanges about their service as junior officers in the Mexican-American War, Lee asked Grant about the terms of surrender. In keeping with Lincoln's desire for a gracious peace with "malice toward none," Grant let the Confederates keep their pistols, horses, and mules, and he promised that none of them would be tried for treason. Lee replied that "this would have a most happy effect" upon his men and accepted the terms as "more than he expected." He then confessed that his men were starving, and Grant ordered that they be provided food.

Appomattox Court House
The Virginia village where Confederate general Robert E. Lee surrendered to Union general Ulysses S. Grant on April 9, 1865.

Lee prepares to surrender at Appomattox Court House

THE END OF THE WAR
Confederate General Robert E. Lee (*right*) surrenders to Union General Ulysses S. Grant (*left*) at Appomattox Court House on April 9, 1865.

After signing the surrender documents, Lee mounted his horse. Grant and his men saluted him, raising their hats, and Lee responded in kind before returning to his defeated army. Grant ordered that there be no cheering or gloating from his soldiers. "The war is over," he said, adding that "the rebels are our countrymen again."

The next day, as the gaunt Confederates formed ranks for the last time, Joshua Chamberlain, the Union general in charge of the surrender ceremony, told his men to salute the Rebel soldiers as they paraded past to give up their muskets. His Confederate counterpart signaled his men to do likewise. Chamberlain remembered that there was not a sound, simply an "awed stillness . . . as if it were the passing of the dead."

The remaining Confederate forces in Texas and North Carolina surrendered in May. Jefferson Davis, who had fled Richmond ahead of the advancing Federal troops, was captured in Georgia on May 10. He was eventually imprisoned in Virginia for two years.

Some Confederates never surrendered. They fled to Caribbean islands or to Central or South America or to Europe. In June 1865, General Joseph Shelby of Missouri and almost a thousand Rebel troops crossed the Rio Grande and entered Mexico. Once they reached Mexico City, the government gave them land to form a refugee colony, but most of the expatriates returned to the United States within a few years.

Other unrepentant Confederates vowed revenge. Actor John Wilkes Booth wrote in his diary that "something *decisive* and great must be done." He began plotting with others to kill President Lincoln and members of his cabinet.

How had the nation gotten to this point? The Confederacy's defeat was largely the result of the Battles of Vicksburg and Gettysburg in 1863, as well as—in 1864—the relentless attacks on Southern troops by Union General Ulysses Grant and the conquest of Georgia and South Carolina by General Sherman. These battles cost the South a major loss in troops and morale; and after Lincoln's reelection in 1864, the Southern resistance weakened further and eventually collapsed. By the time of the Confederacy's surrender, the nation had been irrevocably transformed.

> CORE **OBJECTIVE**
> **5.** Explain how the Civil War changed the nation.

A Transformational War

The Civil War was the most traumatic event in American history. "We have shared the incommunicable experience of war," reflected Oliver Wendell Holmes, Jr., a twice-wounded Union officer who would become chief justice of the Supreme Court. "We have felt, we still feel, the passion of life to its top."

Throughout the South, however, a vengeful gloom took hold of the former Confederates. In Virginia, Edmund Ruffin, the fervent secessionist who had fired the first shot at Fort Sumter in 1861, was devastated by the Confederate surrender. In the final entry to his diary, he wrote: "I hereby declare my unmitigated hatred to Yankee rule—to all political, social and business connections with the Yankees and to the Yankee race." He then put a shotgun barrel in his mouth and blew off the top of his head.

The war had transformed the nation. A *New York Times* editorial reflected that the war had left "nothing as it found it.... It leaves us a different people in everything."

The Union Preserved

Northern victory restored the Union—and transformed it. What Lincoln called the "monstrous injustice" of slavery had been abolished, and a key issue had been resolved: no state had the right to divorce itself from the Union. The political balance of power in Congress, the U.S. Supreme Court, and the presidency had shifted from South to North. And the war had strengthened the Republican Party and boosted the Northern economy's industrial development, commercial agriculture, and western settlement.

The Homestead Act (1862) made more than a billion acres in the West available to new settlers who could extend U.S. influence and power over the ancestral lands of Indigenous nations. The power and scope of the federal government were expanded at the expense of states' rights. In 1860, the annual federal budget was $63 million; by 1865, it was more than $1 billion.

> Impacts of war: Expansion of federal government

By the end of the war, the Union was spending $2.5 million per day on the military effort, and new industries had been established to meet its needs for weapons, uniforms, food, equipment, and supplies. The massive amounts of preserved food required by the Union armies, for example, helped create the canning industry and transformed Chicago into the meatpacking capital of the world.

> Impacts of war: New industries

Federal contracts also provided money that was needed to accelerate the growth of new industries, such as the production of iron, steel, and petroleum, thus laying the groundwork for a postwar economic boom. Ohio senator John Sherman, in a letter to his brother, General William Tecumseh Sherman, said the war had dramatically expanded the vision "of leading capitalists" who now talked of earning "millions as confidently as formerly of thousands."

The war also influenced world events. Southern-grown cotton had fed national prosperity during the first half of the nineteenth century, but the onset of war in 1861 changed that. In 1860, the South had sent nearly 4 million bales of cotton to Europe. By 1862, hardly any arrived in Europe. By cutting off this supply of cotton to Great Britain and Europe, the war fueled global colonialism, as European nations looked for other sources of cotton in India, Egypt, and West Africa.

> Impacts of war: New competition for cotton exporters

The First "Modern" War

In many respects, the Civil War was one of the first modern wars. Its scope and scale were unprecedented, as it was fought across an entire continent. For the first time, armies used railroads and steamboats to move around and photographers used cameras to record the carnage.

New forms of weaponry

Unlike previous conflicts, much of the fighting had been distant and impersonal, in part because of improvements in the effectiveness of muskets, rifles, and cannons. Men were killed at long distance, without knowing who had fired the shots that felled them. Among the array of new weapons and instruments were cannons with "rifled," or grooved, barrels for greater accuracy; repeating rifles; ironclad ships; railroad artillery; the first military telegraph; observation balloons; and wire entanglements. Civilians could also follow the war by reading the newspapers that sent reporters to the front lines, or by visiting exhibitions of photographs taken at the battlefields and camps.

Devastating human losses

Powerful new weapons escalated the war's death toll. More than 750,000 soldiers and sailors (38,000 of whom were Black men fighting for the Union) died—a number that exceeds the total deaths in all other American wars combined. Of the surviving combatants, 50,000 returned home with one or more limbs amputated. Disease, however, was the greatest threat to soldiers, killing twice as many as were lost in battle. Some 50,000 civilians died as well, and virtually every community had uncounted widows and orphans.

The modern funeral industry emerged as a result, with new innovations such as the embalming that allowed those killed in battle to be transported home for burial. The National Cemetery system was also established during the war to make sure that all U.S. soldiers, no matter their rank, would receive a proper burial.

Freedom for All

The Emancipation Proclamation had not freed all enslaved people in the South, only those in areas under Confederate control. Its limitations—and the question of whether the proclamation itself could withstand a legal challenge—led to calls for a new constitutional amendment abolishing slavery.

Women's rights leaders were especially vocal in demanding a complete end to slavery. After putting their movement on hold and organizing no conventions during the war, they turned instead to the fight against slavery. Susan B. Anthony and Elizabeth Cady Stanton were among the founders of a new organization, the **Women's Loyal National League**, that launched a massive petition drive in 1864 calling on Congress to pass a constitutional amendment abolishing slavery everywhere in the United States. "Women, you cannot vote or fight for your country," Stanton pleaded. "Your only way to be a power in the Government is through the exercise of this, one, sacred, *Constitutional* 'right of petition.'"

Signatures poured in. The League sent the petitions to the abolitionist senator Charles Sumner of Massachusetts, who later credited the petition drive with energizing the passage of the Thirteenth Amendment.

Thirteenth Amendment

It was not until the war entered its final months, however, that the amendment became a legal reality. President Lincoln himself had shifted from

Women's Loyal National League (1863) An organization that was formed to campaign for an amendment to the U.S. Constitution that would abolish slavery. Petitions with almost 400,000 signatures presented to Congress contributed to passage of the Thirteenth Amendment.

viewing emancipation as a military weapon to seeing it as the mainspring of the conflict itself. At last, he had become an abolitionist.

Three major steps toward universal abolition occurred by the end of February 1865, three months before the war ended. Missouri and then Tennessee abolished slavery; and at Lincoln's insistence, the U.S. House of Representatives passed the proposed amendment to the Constitution that banned slavery everywhere (the Senate had passed it the previous April). Every Republican voted in favor. As the final tally was announced, the House erupted in "an outburst of enthusiasm." Men threw their hats, and some "wept like children."

Upon ratification by three-fourths of the reunited states, the **Thirteenth Amendment** became law eight months after the war ended, on December 18, 1865. That date, said the *New York Times*, "will be forever memorable in the annals of the republic." The amendment removed any lingering doubts about the legality of emancipation. And it guaranteed that the most important result of the Civil War would be the liberation of nearly 4 million enslaved men, women, and children.

The "Vast Future"

In his first message to Congress in December 1861, Lincoln had recognized what was at stake: "The struggle of today is not altogether for today; it is for a vast future also." At the center of that future was the nation's democratic institutions and ideals. Two years later, in his 1863 Gettysburg Address, Lincoln had urged Americans to not let so many soldiers die in vain and to make sure that "government of the people, by the people, for the people, shall not perish from the earth."

Now, in April 1865, the American republic had not perished—it had been saved. But it had been irrevocably changed—through the abolition of slavery and the adoption of the Thirteenth Amendment, through increased power for the federal government, and through a shifting of political and economic power from the South to the North. In this atmosphere, abolishing slavery and defeating secession turned out only to be the beginning of a long debate about what a government "by the people" should look like. What sort of nation, "conceived in liberty" and rededicated to the founding ideal that "all men are created equal," could be rebuilt out of the ashes of war? Addressing that fundamental issue would begin the challenging work of Reconstruction.

Thirteenth Amendment (1865)
The amendment to the U.S. Constitution that ended slavery and freed all enslaved people in the United States.

Thirteenth Amendment: Abolition of slavery

An indissoluble Union

Reviewing the
CORE OBJECTIVES

- **Civil War Strategies** The Confederacy had a geographic advantage of fighting a defensive war on its own territory. The Union, however, had a larger population and greater industrial capability, particularly in the production of weapons, ships, and railroad equipment. Initial hopes for a rapid Union victory died at the First Battle of Bull Run. The Union then adopted the *Anaconda Plan*, which involved imposing a naval blockade on Southern ports and slowly crushing resistance on all fronts.

- **Emancipation** Enslaved people, by fleeing plantations in the South and entering Union army lines, had exerted pressure on the U.S. government to liberate them—and President Lincoln came to see that winning the war required ending slavery. He justified the *Emancipation Proclamation* (1863) as a military necessity because it would deprive the South of its captive labor force. After the *Battle of Antietam* in September 1862, he announced his plans to free the enslaved people living in areas under Confederate control. Large numbers of enslaved people freed themselves by escaping to Union camps and working for the army. In July 1862, with the *Militia Act*, Congress had declared that formerly enslaved people (*contrabands*) could enlist in the Union army too.

- **Social and Economic Life during Wartime** The Union government proved much more capable with finances than did its Confederate counterparts, and was better able to absorb the war's soaring costs. The U.S. government also promoted economic development through the *Homestead Act* (1862), *Pacific Railway Act* (1862), *National Banking Act* (1863), and *Morrill Land-Grant College Act* (1862). The Confederacy, in contrast with the Union, suffered when its Treasury Department printed too much money and created spiraling inflation. These conditions led Southern White women to protest and riot. Women throughout the nation also joined the war effort as spies and soldiers (the latter in disguise as men), and as nurses in military hospitals. Civil War medicine struggled to meet the war's emergencies. But new innovations such as the triage and ambulance systems helped keep the death toll from soaring even higher.

- **The Winning Union Strategy** The Union victories at the *Battle of Vicksburg* and the *Battle of Gettysburg* in July 1863 were a major turning point of the war. With the capture of Vicksburg, Union forces cut the Confederacy in two, depriving armies in the eastern Confederacy of western supplies and manpower. General Robert E. Lee and the Army of Northern Virginia lost a third of its troops after the defeat at Gettysburg. In 1864, Lincoln placed General Ulysses S. Grant in charge of the Union's war efforts; thereafter, Grant's forces constantly attacked Lee's in Virginia while, farther south, General William Tecumseh *Sherman's "March to the Sea"* (1864) resulted in the Union's conquest of Georgia and South Carolina. Sherman's successes helped propel Lincoln to victory in the *election* *of 1864*. After that, Southern resistance wilted, forcing Lee to surrender his army to General Grant at *Appomattox Court House* in April 1865.

■ **The Significance of the Civil War** The Civil War involved the largest number of casualties of any American war, and the Union's victory changed the course of the nation's development. Most important, the war ended slavery, embodied in the adoption of the *Thirteenth Amendment* to the U.S. Constitution in late 1865 (which had been boosted by the *Women's Loyal National League*'s petition drive). Not only did the power of the federal government increase, but the center of political and economic power shifted away from the South and the planter class.

KEY TERMS

Anaconda Plan *p. 577*

contrabands *p. 582*

Battle of Antietam (1862) *p. 591*

Emancipation Proclamation (1863) *p. 593*

Militia Act (1862) *p. 597*

Pacific Railway Act (1862) *p. 603*

Homestead Act (1862) *p. 603*

Morrill Land-Grant College Act (1862) *p. 603*

National Banking Act (1863) *p. 603*

Battle of Vicksburg (1863) *p. 609*

Battle of Gettysburg (1863) *p. 610*

election of 1864 *p. 618*

Sherman's "March to the Sea" (1864) *p. 619*

Appomattox Court House *p. 621*

Women's Loyal National League (1863) *p. 624*

Thirteenth Amendment (1865) *p. 625*

CHRONOLOGY

April 1861	Virginia, North Carolina, Tennessee, and Arkansas join the Confederacy
	West Virginia splits from Virginia to stay with the Union
May 1861	Enslaved people are allowed to remain in U.S. Army camps as "contraband of war"
July 1861	First Battle of Bull Run (Manassas)
April–August 1862	Battles of Shiloh, Second Bull Run, and Antietam
July 1862	Congress passes the Militia Act
January 1863	Emancipation Proclamation goes into effect
May–July 1863	New York City draft riots
	Battles of Vicksburg and Gettysburg
January 1864	Women's Loyal National League seeks constitutional amendment to ban slavery in all states
March 1864	General Grant takes charge of Union military operations
September 1864	General Sherman seizes and burns Atlanta
November 1864	Lincoln is reelected
	Sherman's "March to the Sea"
April 9, 1865	General Lee surrenders at Appomattox Court House
1865	Thirteenth Amendment is ratified

THOMAS NAST'S *EMANCIPATION* (1865) Thomas Nast's *Emancipation* represents his vision of an optimistic future for Black people in the United States after emancipation. The central scene of a joyous family contrasts with the background depicting enslavement prior to emancipation.

CHAPTER 15

The Era of Reconstruction

1865–1877

In the spring of 1865, the terrible conflict finally ended. The United States was a "new nation," said an Illinois congressman, because it was now "wholly free." At a cost of some 750,000 lives and the destruction of the Southern economy, the Union had won the war and almost 4 million enslaved African Americans had seized their freedom.

Most civil wars, however, never end completely. Peace did not bring everyday equality or civil rights to people of color, nor did it end racism—in the South or in the North. Many White Southerners opposed the decision of Confederate generals to surrender their armies, and many more Southerners bitterly resented the freeing of the enslaved population. Racism persisted in the North, too. The *New York Times* declared that African Americans, even if freed from slavery, had no more business voting than did women or Native Americans, and that it was "little short of insane" to think otherwise.

The defeated Confederates had seen their world turned upside down. The abolition of slavery, the disruptions to the South's economy, and the horrifying human losses and physical devastation had shattered the plantation system and upended racial relations in the South. "Change, change, indelibly stamped upon everything I meet, even upon the faces of the people!" sighed Alexander Stephens, vice president of the former Confederacy. His native region now had to adjust to a new order as the U.S. government set about reconstructing the South and using federal troops to police defiant former Confederates.

CORE OBJECTIVES

1. Identify the federal government's major challenges in reconstructing the South after the Civil War.
2. Describe how and why the federal government's Reconstruction policies changed over time.
3. Assess the attitudes of White and Black Southerners toward various Reconstruction programs and requirements.
4. Analyze the political and economic factors that helped end Reconstruction in 1877.
5. Explain the significance of Reconstruction to the nation's future.

> DEAR EDITOR—I desire to find my parents. Grandmother was Charity Thompson, mother, Edna Thompson. At the death of first owner, Swan Thompson, property was divided and Sylvester Williams took charge of mother. I had a brother Orange. All were in Carroll county, Mississippi. Aunt Lydia belonged to Bill Thompson; another aunt was Janey Newman. Father, John Moore, was born in South Carolina. My mother said, the morning she was going to leave, "My son you must be a good child." I was standing in my father's house by a little table near the door, he said to me, "My son you are five years old to-day." It was in 1834. Miss Lureasy Cuff was standing in the house and talking to my mother, and saying, "I think pa should give Si to me, because I raised him to what he is." Uncle Thomas drove the wagon when mother left. She had two children then, Si and Orange. Address me at Midway, Texas.
> SI. JOHNSON.

"INFORMATION WANTED" Newly freed people desperate for information about the whereabouts of their kin often posted newspaper advertisements like this one. Such notices were widely circulated and read aloud in Black churches.

Formerly enslaved people felt just the opposite. The Yankees had fought for their liberation. No longer would enslaved workers be sold and separated from their families, or prevented from learning to read and write or from attending church without White supervision. "I felt like a bird out of a cage," said formerly enslaved Houston Holloway of Georgia, who had been sold to three different owners before he was twenty years old. "Amen. Amen. Amen. I could hardly ask to feel any better than I did that day."

Many previously enslaved people rushed to reunite with long-lost family members. Not always knowing where their husbands, wives, and children had been taken by the slave trade, they hit the road, traveling hundreds of miles to former plantations or into cities where someone might know something about their relatives' whereabouts. Spottswood Rice, a Black soldier from Missouri, knew exactly where his daughter was but still had to confront his former enslaver to get her freed. "[N]ow I want you to understand that mary is my Child," he demanded in a letter while lying in a hospital bed recovering from war injuries, and "the longor you keep my Child from me the longor you will have to burn in hell."

All across the South, however, violence rained down on formerly enslaved people who dared to seize their freedom. The simple acts of going to church or sending a child to school could subject a person to beatings and murder. A "perfect reign of terror" was how a Black minister in Kentucky described the world into which he had been liberated.

Such brutality testified to the extraordinary challenges the nation faced in reconstructing a ravaged and resentful South while helping to transform formerly enslaved people into free workers and citizens. It would not be easy. The Rebels had been conquered, but they were far from being loyal Unionists, and few of them supported the federal effort to create a multiracial democracy in the newly reunited nation.

The Reconstruction era, from 1865 to 1877, witnessed a complex debate about the role of the federal government in punishing the South and protecting civil rights. Some Northerners wanted the former Confederate states returned to the Union with few or no changes. Others wanted Confederate leaders imprisoned or executed and the South rebuilt in the image of the rest of the nation. Still others cared little about reconstructing the South; they wanted the federal government to focus on promoting economic growth in the North and expanding westward.

Although the Reconstruction era lasted only twelve years, it was one of the most challenging and significant periods in U.S. history. At the center of the debate over how to rebuild the nation were profound questions: Who is deserving of citizenship, and what rights does it entail? What role should the federal government play in ensuring freedom and equality? Those questions are still shaping American life 160 years later.

The War's Aftermath in the South

In the spring of 1865, White Southerners were exhausted. Fully one-fifth of Southern White males had died in the war; many others had been maimed for life. The economy was also ravaged. Property values had collapsed. In the year after the war ended, eighty-one Mississippi plantations were sold for one-tenth of what they had been worth in 1860. Confederate money was worthless, tens of thousands of horses and mules had been killed, and countless farm buildings and pieces of agricultural equipment had been destroyed.

Many of the South's largest cities—Richmond, Atlanta, Columbia—were devastated. Most railroads and many bridges were damaged or destroyed; and Southerners, White and Black, were homeless and hungry. Charleston, the birthplace of secession, had become a place of "vacant houses, of widowed women, of rotting wharves, of deserted warehouses, of weed-wild gardens, of miles of grass-grown streets, of acres of pitiful and voiceless barrenness."

> **CORE OBJECTIVE**
> **1.** Identify the federal government's major challenges in reconstructing the South after the Civil War.

RICHMOND AFTER THE CIVIL WAR Before evacuating the capital of the Confederacy, Richmond, Virginia, residents set fire to warehouses and factories to prevent their falling into Union hands. Pictured here is one of Richmond's burnt districts in April 1865. Women in mourning attire walk among the ruins.

> Economic disparities between the North and South

Between 1860 and 1870, wealth in the North grew by 50 percent while wealth in the South dropped by 60 percent. Emancipation wiped out almost $3 billion invested in the slave labor system, which had enabled the explosive growth of the cotton culture. Not until 1879 would the cotton crop again equal the record harvest of 1860. Tobacco production did not regain its prewar level until 1880, the sugar crop of Louisiana did not recover until 1893, and the rice economy along the coasts of South Carolina and Georgia never regained its prewar levels of production.

In 1860, just before the Civil War, the South had generated 30 percent of the nation's wealth; in 1870, it produced but 12 percent. Amanda Worthington, a planter's wife from Mississippi, could not believe "that we are no longer wealthy—yet thanks to the Yankees, the cause of all unhappiness, such is the case."

The anger and resentment of White people made it even more difficult for newly freed people to build new lives in the South. What they wanted most was to live the opposite of what they had experienced while enslaved—to be paid for their labor, to reunite with their family members, to gain education for their children, and to enjoy full participation in political life. They were determined to become owners of land on which they could build their own houses, churches, schools, and wealth. Most Southern Whites were just as determined to prevent that from happening.

> Legal and social controversies over Reconstruction

Any process of "reconstructing" the former Confederacy was going to be complicated and controversial and would have to address the most difficult issue: what would the political, social, and economic status of the freedpeople be? They were free, but were they citizens? Would they be entitled to equality? If not, what was their status? Likewise, what was the status of the former Confederate states, and how would they be reintegrated into the nation's political life? As work on these complex challenges got under way, differing priorities meant that everyone involved would clash over the best way to accomplish Reconstruction.

> **CORE OBJECTIVE**
> **2.** Describe how and why the federal government's Reconstruction policies changed over time.

Battles over Political Reconstruction

Reconstruction of the former Confederate states began during the war and went through several phases, the first of which was called Presidential Reconstruction. In 1862, President Abraham Lincoln had named army generals to serve as temporary military governors for conquered Confederate areas. By the end of 1863, he had formulated a plan to reestablish governments in the former Confederate states.

Lincoln's Wartime Reconstruction Plan

> Presidential Reconstruction: Lincoln's Plan

In late 1863, President Lincoln issued a Proclamation of Amnesty and Reconstruction, under which a former Confederate state could rejoin the

Union and re-create its state government once 10 percent of those who had voted in 1860 swore allegiance to the Constitution. All ex-Confederates, except for high-ranking Confederate military and civilian leaders, also received a presidential pardon acquitting them of treason.

Congressional Wartime Reconstruction Plans

A few conservative and most moderate Republicans supported President Lincoln's "10 percent" program that immediately restored Southern state governments in Tennessee, Arkansas, and Louisiana. **Radical Republicans**, however, favored a more drastic transformation of Southern society that would grant freedpeople full citizenship. Many Radicals were abolitionists who believed that all people, regardless of race, were equal in God's eyes. They wanted no compromise with the "sin" of racism. They also hoped to replace the White, Democratic planter elite with a new generation of small farmers. "The middling classes who own the soil, and work it with their own hands," explained Radical leader Thaddeus Stevens, "are the main support of every free government."

In 1864, with war still raging, the Radicals in Congress tried to take charge of Reconstruction by passing the Wade-Davis Bill, named for two leading Republicans. In contrast to Lincoln's 10 percent Reconstruction plan, the Wade-Davis Bill required that a *majority* of White male citizens declare their allegiance to the Union before a formerly Confederate state could be readmitted.

The bill never became law, however, because Lincoln vetoed it. In retaliation, Radicals issued the Wade-Davis Manifesto, which accused Lincoln of exceeding his constitutional authority. Unfazed by the criticism, Lincoln continued his efforts to restore the Confederate states to the Union while assisting freedpeople in the South.

> Lincoln vetoes Wade-Davis bill

The Freedmen's Bureau

In early 1865, Congress approved the Thirteenth Amendment to the Constitution, officially abolishing slavery in the United States. It became law in December. Yet what did freedom mean for the formerly enslaved, most of whom had no land, no home, no food, no paying job, and no education? "Liberty has been won," Senator Charles Sumner noted. "The battle for Equality is still pending."

To address the complex issues raised by emancipation, Congress on March 3, 1865, created within the War Department the Bureau of Refugees, Freedmen, and Abandoned Lands (known as the **Freedmen's Bureau**) to assist "freedmen and their wives and children." Its task was daunting. When General William Tecumseh Sherman learned that his friend, General Oliver O. Howard, had been appointed to lead the Freedmen's Bureau, he warned: "It is not . . . in your power to fulfill one-tenth of the expectations of those who framed the Bureau."

Undeterred by such concerns, Howard declared that emancipated people "must be free to choose their own employers and be paid for their labor." He

> Establishment of the Freedmen's Bureau (1865)

Radical Republicans Congressmen who identified with the abolitionist cause and sought swift emancipation of the enslaved, punishment of the Rebels, and tight controls over former Confederate states.

Freedmen's Bureau A federal Reconstruction agency established to protect the legal rights of formerly enslaved people and to assist with their education, jobs, health care, and land ownership.

FREEDMEN'S SCHOOL IN NORTH CAROLINA Students and their teachers gather outside one of the thousands of new freedmen's schools established after the war, often with the help of the Freedmen's Bureau.

assigned army officers to negotiate labor contracts between freedpeople and White landowners, many of whom resisted. The Bureau also provided the now-free African Americans with medical care, clothing, shelter, and food. By 1868, the Bureau had distributed more than 20 million meals. In addition, it assisted formerly enslaved people in seeking justice in courts, managed abandoned lands, and helped formalize marriages and find relatives.

> Establishing schools for freedpeople

The Bureau also supported freedpeoples' efforts to establish schools and colleges. A Mississippi freedman explained that education was his essential priority, for it "was the next best thing to liberty." That belief led freedpeople to establish an estimated 500 schools on their own even before the Freedmen's Bureau arrived in the South. By 1870, the Bureau supervised more than 4,000 schools serving almost 250,000 students in the former Confederate states. Bureau-supported schools provided a crucial transition to conventional public schools that Southern states eventually created. To staff them, the Bureau recruited thousands of teachers from both the North and the South. Most were women, and one-third of them were Black.

Among these was Ruth A. Grimes, who established a school in Union Point, Georgia, very quickly after her liberation from slavery. She acknowledged that "my Education is feeble compared to the people North but . . . the little I know I am willing to impart with my fellow people." Charlotte Forten, one of the African American teachers from the North, had been formally educated at Salem Normal School (now Salem State University) before venturing south after the war. She marveled at the passion for learning displayed by her students: "I never before saw children so eager to learn."

Yet the Freedmen's Bureau had significant limitations. It never had more than 900 agents across thirteen states to support 3.5 million formerly enslaved people spread across a million square miles—not nearly enough to implement the Bureau's broad goals. The number of federal troops supporting the Freedmen's Bureau was also inadequate. As a Texas officer stressed, the Bureau agents were helpless "unless in the vicinity of our troops."

Empowering Freedpeople

In July 1865, hundreds of African Americans gathered on St. Helena Island off the South Carolina coast. There, Martin Delany, the highest-ranking Black officer in the U.S. Colored Troops, addressed them. Before the Civil War, he had been a prominent African American abolitionist in the North. Now, Major Delany assured the gathering that slavery had indeed been "absolutely abolished." But abolition, he stressed, was less the result of Abraham Lincoln's leadership than it was the outcome of formerly enslaved people and free Blacks like himself arming themselves and fighting the Confederacy. Slavery was dead, and freedom was now in their hands. "Yes, yes, yes!" his listeners shouted.

MAJOR MARTIN DELANY African American abolitionist, journalist, physician, soldier, and writer, and arguably the first proponent of Black nationalism, Delany is credited with the Pan-African slogan of "Africa for Africans."

Delany then urged his audience to continue relying on themselves. Do not accept the labor terms offered by your former owners, he advised. After all, how can one trust a man who "never earned a single Dollar in his life"? "You men and women, every one of you around me, made thousands and thousands of dollars," he reminded them; "you always have been the means of riches." He then told the freedpeople that their best hope was to acquire land and become independent farmers: "Get a community and get all the lands you can." Rely on one another, and be skeptical of advice from White people who "never tell you the truth."

Several White planters attended Delany's talk, and an army officer at the scene reported that they "listened with horror depicted in their faces." The planters feared that such speeches would incite "open rebellion" among Southern Black people.

The Freedman's Bank

Long before emancipation, enslaved people had been able to earn additional money by doing extra work on their owner's plantation or neighboring ones. The creation of the Freedman's Bank by Congress immediately after the Civil War finally provided the opportunity for all Black people to safely invest the money they had saved and now were earning as freedpeople. African Americans also fundamentally understood that in order to get ahead in life they would need to buy property, whether farmland or buildings. Ultimately, more than 100,000 freedpeople would place their money in the new bank, working toward their dreams with deposits totaling over $50,000,000.

Within ten years of its founding, however, the bank's directors (mostly prominent White financiers) were taking advantage of changes made by Congress to the bank's bylaws that enabled them to gut the bank for their

FREEDMAN'S SAVINGS AND TRUST COMPANY A photograph of the Freedman's Bank headquarters in Washington, D.C. At its height, the bank had branches in seventeen states across the nation.

own personal uses. As a result, the Black investors lost more than 80 percent of their investments. Freed Black people for some time thereafter returned to hiding their money in their house or yard, afraid to trust banks run by White people. This tragic turn of events in part set back the development of a Black middle class by decades.

The Assassination of Lincoln

The president who had yearned for a peace "with malice toward none, with charity for all" offered his last view of Reconstruction in the final speech of his life. On April 11, 1865, Lincoln rejected calls for a vengeful peace. He wanted "no persecution, no bloody work," no hangings of Confederate leaders, and no extreme efforts to restructure social and economic life in the South.

Three days later, on April 14, Lincoln and his wife attended a play at Ford's Theatre in Washington, D.C. With his trusted bodyguard having been called away to Richmond, Lincoln was defenseless as twenty-six-year-old John Wilkes Booth, a celebrated actor and an ardent Confederate, slipped into the presidential box and shot the president behind the left ear. As Lincoln slumped forward, Booth pulled out a knife, stabbed the president's military aide, and jumped from the box to the stage, breaking his leg in the process. He then mounted a waiting horse and fled the city. Lincoln died nine hours later, the first president to be killed in office.

LINCOLN'S FUNERAL PROCESSION After President Abraham Lincoln's assassination, his body was taken on a two-week-long funeral procession through five different states, allowing millions of people the chance to see his casket. This photograph was taken on April 25, 1865, when the procession passed through New York City. A young Theodore Roosevelt watched the parade from the window of his family's mansion, pictured on the left.

The government was suddenly leaderless, and the nation was overwhelmed with shock, horror, and anguish. Frederick Douglass described Lincoln's murder as "an unspeakable calamity." In his view, Lincoln was "the black man's President: the first to show any respect for their rights as men" by rising "above the prejudice of his times." Confederates had a different view. A seventeen-year-old South Carolina girl celebrated the news of Lincoln's murder. As she wrote in her diary, "Old Abe Lincoln has been assassinated!"

> Lincoln assassinated (April 14, 1865)

Vice President Andrew Johnson became the new president shortly after Lincoln was declared dead. Eleven days later, U.S. troops found John Wilkes Booth hiding in a Virginia tobacco barn. The soldiers set fire to the barn; a few minutes later, one of them shot and killed Booth. As he lay dying, the assassin whispered, "Tell my mother I died for my country."

Three of Booth's collaborators were convicted by a military court and hanged, as was Mary Surratt, a middle-aged widow who owned the Washington boardinghouse where the assassination had been planned. Surratt and her extended family were ardent supporters of the Confederacy.

The outpouring of grief after Lincoln's death transformed the fallen president into a sacred symbol. Lincoln's body lay in state for several days in Washington, D.C., before being transported 1,600 miles by train for burial in Springfield, Illinois. In Philadelphia, 300,000 mourners paid their last respects; in New York City, 500,000 people viewed the president's body. On May 4, Lincoln was laid to rest.

Johnson's Reconstruction Plan

The new president, Andrew Johnson of Tennessee, was a pro-Union Democrat who had been added to Lincoln's National Union ticket in 1864 to help the president win reelection. Combative and self-righteous, Johnson hated both the White Southern elite and the idea of racial equality.

Like Lincoln, Johnson was a self-made man, but he displayed none of Lincoln's eloquence. Born in 1808 in a log cabin near Raleigh, North Carolina, he lost his father when he was three years old and never attended school. His illiterate mother apprenticed him to a tailor to learn a trade. He ran away from home at age thirteen and eventually landed in Greeneville, in the mountains of East Tennessee. There he taught himself to read, and his sixteen-year-old wife showed him how to write and do basic arithmetic.

Over time, Johnson prospered and acquired at least five enslaved people. A natural leader, he served as mayor, state legislator, governor, congressional representative, and U.S. senator. A friend described the trajectory of Johnson's life as "one intense, unceasing, desperate upward struggle" during which he identified with poor farmers and came to hate the "pampered, bloated, corrupted aristocracy" of wealthy planters.

During the Civil War, Johnson supported "putting down the [Confederate] rebellion, because it is a war [of wealthy plantation owners] against democracy." Yet Johnson also shared the racist attitudes of most Southern Whites. "Damn the negroes," he exclaimed during the war. "This is a country for

ANDREW JOHNSON
A Jacksonian Democrat from Tennessee, Johnson stepped into the role of president after Abraham Lincoln's assassination. Johnson introduced a Reconstruction plan that required Southern states to ratify the Thirteenth Amendment and limited the political power of rich former Confederates.

> Johnson revises Lincoln's plan for reconstruction

white men," he exclaimed, "and by God, as long as I am president, it shall be a government for white men."

Early in his presidency, Johnson stressed that he would continue Lincoln's policies in restoring the former Confederate states to the Union—however, Johnson's **Presidential Reconstruction Plan** included a few twists. In May 1865, he issued a new Proclamation of Amnesty that excluded not only those high-ranking Confederate leaders whom Lincoln had barred from a presidential pardon but also anyone with property worth more than $20,000. Johnson was determined to keep the wealthiest Southerners from regaining political power.

Surprisingly, however, by 1866 President Johnson had pardoned some 7,000 former Confederates, and he eventually pardoned most of the White "aristocrats" he claimed to despise. What brought about this change of heart? Johnson had decided that he could buy the political support of prominent Southerners by pardoning them, improving his chances of reelection.

Johnson appointed a Unionist as provisional governor in each state in the South. Each governor called a convention of men elected by "loyal" (not Confederate) voters. Johnson's plan required that each state convention ratify the Thirteenth Amendment. Except for Mississippi, each former Confederate state held a convention that met Johnson's requirement.

Freedmen's Conventions

Freedpeople were eager to counter the Whites-only state conventions organized under President Johnson's Reconstruction plan. They began meeting and marching, demanding not just freedom but citizenship and full civil rights, land of their own, and voting rights. Especially in large cities such as New Orleans, Mobile, Nashville, Memphis, and Charleston, they organized regular meetings, chose leaders, protested mistreatment, learned the workings of the federal bureaucracy, and sought economic opportunities.

> African Americans mobilize at freedmen's conventions

During the summer and fall of 1865, emancipated Southerners and free Black people from the North and South organized freedmen's conventions (sometimes called Colored Conventions). The conventions met in state capitals "to impress upon the white men," as the Reverend James D. Lynch told the Tennessee freedmen's convention, "that we are part and parcel of the American republic." Men assumed leadership of the conventions, but women also attended and supported the proceedings by editing convention documents and hosting attendees at nearby boardinghouses.

The North Carolina freedmen's convention elected as its president James Walker Hood, a free Black man from Connecticut. In his acceptance speech, he said: "We and the white people have to live here together. Some people talk of emigration for the Black race, some of expatriation, and some of colonization. I regard this as all nonsense. We have been living together for a hundred years and more, and we have got to live together still." Hood then demanded three constitutional rights for African Americans: the right to testify in courts, the right to serve on juries, and "the right to carry [a] ballot to the ballot box."

Presidential Reconstruction Plan President Andrew Johnson's plan to require Southern states to ratify the Thirteenth Amendment, disqualify wealthy former Confederates from voting, and appoint a Unionist governor.

FREEDMEN'S CONVENTION In this 1868 woodcut, a group of freedpeople in the South meet to discuss their political and social resolutions.

The freedmen's conventions demanded that their voices be heard. As the Virginia convention asserted, "Any attempt to reconstruct the states . . . without giving to American citizens of African descent all the rights and immunities accorded to white citizens . . . is an act of gross injustice."

The conventions laid a foundation for Black political organizing and influence that would, in the years ahead, propel some of the convention delegates into elected office. The events also succeeded in gaining the attention of Radical Republicans in Washington, D.C., who were listening and were ready to take up the cause of full citizenship rights for African American people.

The Radical Republicans

President Johnson's initial assault on the Southern planter elite pleased Radical Republicans, but not for long. The most devout Radicals, led by Thaddeus Stevens of Pennsylvania and Charles Sumner of Massachusetts,

Comparing PERSPECTIVES

RECONSTRUCTING DEMOCRACY

From: *Proceedings of the State Convention of Colored Men Held at Lexington, KY,* **November 26–28, 1867.**

Immediately after the Civil War, Black Americans across the nation drew on a long tradition of organizing conventions to make claims for equality and citizenship rights. The convention held in Lexington, Kentucky, in 1867.

To the Honorable House of Representatives and Senate of the United States:

The colored people of the Commonwealth of Kentucky, through their delegates in convention assembled, most respectfully petition your Honorable Bodies to grant us the right of suffrage. Your petitioners would further represent that they are now, and ever have been, loyal to the Government of the United States, more than thirty thousand of their brothers and sons having enlisted in the army of the Union during the late war; that they are peaceable, law-abiding citizens, who pay taxes as other people, and, inasmuch as the color of our skins did not, in time of war, prevent the government from claiming our allegiance, and causing us to bear arms in its defence, and it is a well-established principle of just government, that allegiance and protection go together, the one being the consideration of the other, and, inasmuch as the Declaration of Independence promises the equality of the people, and it is the expressly declared duty of Congress under the Constitution to guarantee to every State in the Union a republican form of government; and, inasmuch as many white persons of no greater degree of intelligence than ourselves are allowed to go to the polls and vote in this Commonwealth, and thousands of men who fought against the Government in the late war also vote, now, therefore, we earnestly pray your Honorable Bodies, in such way and manner as it may properly and legally be done, to enact such laws or amend the Constitution of the United States, so as to secure to every citizen in this Commonwealth who may have been a slave, or is the descendant of a slave, or by reason of race or color is deprived of equal rights, to vote at all elections.

From: "A Southern Speech: General Wade Hampton on the Crisis," *New York Times*, October 17, 1866.

Wade Hampton III came from one of South Carolina's wealthiest slave-owning families. After serving as a high-ranking general in the Confederate army, he returned to his burned-out plantation to find that the Union army had burned it and the enslaved people had fled. Hampton became a vocal critic of Congressional Reconstruction.

A SOUTHERN SPEECH.

GEN. WADE HAMPTON ON THE CRISIS.

For four years the South was the victim of a cruel and unnecessary war—a war marked on the part of her opponents by a barbarity never surpassed, if equaled, in the annals of civilised warfare.

But, fellow-citizens, was the South ever disloyal to the Constitution of the United States? I deny that she ever was, and I challenge her most bitter enemy to adduce one single instance in which she has been. From the adoption of that Constitution, up to the time when she framed one of her own governance no one can lay to her charge a single violation of any clause of that instrument. Did she ever propose to change it? Did she ever evade any of its provisions? Did she ever denounce it as a "league with hell and a covenant with the devil"? Nay more, when she framed a Constitution for herself did she not adopt the old and honored one almost word for word? Had the North been but half as loyal as the South has ever been, no war would have desolated our country.

For four years the North waged war upon us, only, as she solemnly declared, to bring us back into the Union. More than a year ago the South expressed her willingness to return, and yet she is now as effectually out of the Union as if she had never formed a part of it. The North professed to fight for the Constitution. As soon as she had the power to do so, she changed that Constitution, and she violated its sacred provisions.

Of all the inconsistencies of which the North has been guilty—and their name is legion—none is greater than that by which she forced the Southern States while rigidly excluding them from the Union, to rectify the Constitutional Amendment abolishing slavery, which they could do legally only as States of that Union. But the deed has been done.

Questions

1. Summarize the main points of the petition written by the delegates at the Lexington convention. What do they urge Congress to do?

2. Summarize the main points of Wade Hampton's speech. How does he feel about Congress's treatment of the South during Reconstruction?

3. Compare these two discussions of the Constitution. How do the convention delegates and Wade Hampton feel about amending the Constitution—and how does each statement invoke "loyalty" to American principles in order to justify its position?

wanted Reconstruction to provide social and political equality for Black people.

Johnson, however, balked at such an expansion of federal authority. He was committed to the states' rights to control their affairs. When the U.S. Congress met in December 1865 for the first time since the end of the war, the new state governments in the South looked remarkably like the former Confederate governments. Controlled by White Southerners, the states had refused to extend voting rights to the newly freed African Americans.

> Little change among southern representatives

White voters in Southern states elected former Confederate leaders as their new U.S. senators and congressmen. Across the South, four Confederate generals, eight colonels, six Confederate cabinet members, and several Confederate legislators were elected as new U.S. senators and congressmen. Outraged Republicans denied seats to all such "Rebel" officials and appointed a Joint Committee on Reconstruction to develop a new plan to bring the former Confederate states back into the Union.

The Joint Committee discovered that White violence against Black people in the South was widespread and unrelenting. A freedman from Shreveport, Louisiana, testified that Whites still bullwhipped Blacks as if they were enslaved. He estimated that 2,000 freedpeople had been killed in Shreveport in 1865.

> Race massacres

In 1866, White mobs angered by signs of Black progress murdered African Americans in Memphis and New Orleans. In Memphis, a clash between city police and African American military veterans triggered a race massacre in which rampaging Whites raped and murdered Blacks before setting fire to their neighborhoods. Over two days, Black schools and churches were destroyed. Forty-six African Americans and two Whites were killed. Only the arrival of federal troops quelled the violence.

The racial violence, Radical Republicans argued, resulted from Andrew Johnson's lenient policy toward White supremacists. Senator Charles

RACE MASSACRE IN MEMPHIS, TENNESSEE In 1866, African Americans were murdered by White mobs in Memphis, Tennessee. Black neighborhoods, schools, and churches were destroyed. Forty-six African Americans were killed.

Sumner asked, "Who can doubt that the President is the author of these tragedies?" Ultimately, the race riots helped spur the Republican-controlled Congress to pass the Fourteenth Amendment (1866), extending federal civil rights protections to African Americans.

Black Codes

The all-White Southern state legislatures had also passed laws discriminating against formerly enslaved people. These **Black codes**, as a White Southerner explained, would ensure "the ex-slave was not a free man; he was a free Negro."

Black codes varied from state to state. In South Carolina, African Americans were required to remain on their former plantations, forced to labor from dawn to dusk. Mississippi prohibited Black people from hunting or fishing to feed their families, making them even more dependent on their White employers.

Some Black codes recognized Black marriages but prohibited interracial marriage. Mississippi stipulated that "no white person could intermarry with a freedman, free negro, or mulatto." Violators faced life in prison.

The codes also barred African Americans from voting, serving on juries, or testifying against Whites. In Mississippi, every Black male over eighteen had to be apprenticed to a White, preferably a former slave owner. Any Black people not apprenticed or employed by January 1866 would be jailed as "vagrants." If they could not pay the vagrancy fine—and most could not—they were jailed and forced to work for Whites as convict laborers in chain gangs.

Convict Leasing

The system of leasing convicts to White employers, known as convict leasing, was one of the most exploitative labor systems in history. People convicted of crimes (often African American men and women who were falsely accused) were hired out by county and state governments to work for individuals and businesses—coal mines, lumber camps, brickyards, railroads, quarries, mills, and plantations. They received no pay for their labor and often worked in inhumane and brutal conditions. More than 10 percent died on the job.

Convict leasing, in other words, was a thinly disguised form of slavery. It was also considered legal. The Thirteenth Amendment had abolished slavery "except as punishment for a crime"—a crucial phrase that would allow the system of convict leasing to flourish. A Virginia Supreme Court justice also justified the system by arguing in *Ruffin v. Commonwealth* (1871) that an incarcerated person "not only forfeited his liberty, but all his personal rights. . . . He is for the time being the slave of the State."

States viewed the "convict lease" system as a means of controlling Black labor while cutting the expense of housing prisoners. Many prisons in the South had been destroyed during the war, and states lacked the funds to rebuild them. Convict leasing increased government revenue in these struggling states, until the system was gradually abolished by 1928.

Black codes Laws passed in southern states to restrict the rights of formerly enslaved people.

> Southern states issue Black codes

> Exploitative labor practices under "convict leasing"

"SLAVERY IS DEAD (?)" Thomas Nast's 1867 cartoon argues that Black people were still being treated as if they were enslaved despite the passage of the Fourteenth Amendment. This detail illustrates a case in Raleigh, North Carolina: a Black man was whipped for a crime despite federal orders prohibiting such forms of punishment.

> Congress passes the Civil Rights Act

> Republicans pass the Fourteenth Amendment (1866)

Fourteenth Amendment (1866)
An amendment to the U.S. Constitution guaranteeing equal protection under the law to all U.S. citizens, including formerly enslaved people.

Systems such as convict leasing, and the Black codes in general, were "returning us to slavery again," as a formerly enslaved man protested to President Johnson. Republicans were infuriated. "We [Republicans] must see to it," Senator William Stewart of Nevada resolved, "that the man made free by the Constitution of the United States is a freeman indeed."

Johnson's Battle with Congress

Early in 1866, the Radical Republicans openly challenged Andrew Johnson over Reconstruction policies after he vetoed a bill renewing funding for the Freedmen's Bureau.

By mid-March, the Radical-led Congress passed the pathbreaking Civil Rights Act, the first federal law to define citizenship. It declared that "all persons born in the United States," including the children of immigrants, but excluding Native Americans, were citizens entitled to "full and equal benefit of all laws."

The Civil Rights Act infuriated President Johnson. Congress, he fumed, did not have constitutional authority to grant citizenship to Black people. Claiming that the proposed legislation trespassed on states' rights, and that it also discriminated against White people, Johnson vetoed it. The Republicans overrode the veto. The government, said Senator Richard Yates of Illinois, never intended "to set 4 million slaves free . . . and at the same time leave them without the civil and political rights which attach to a free citizen." It was the first time that Congress had overturned a presidential veto of a major bill. From that point on, Johnson steadily lost both public and political support.

Fourteenth Amendment

To remove all doubt about the legality of the new Civil Rights Act, Congress passed the **Fourteenth Amendment** to the Constitution in 1866. (It gained ratification in 1868.) The Amendment guaranteed citizenship to anyone born in the United States (known as birthright citizenship), including formerly enslaved people and immigrant children.

The Fourteenth Amendment overturned the Black codes by prohibiting any efforts to violate the civil rights of any "citizens"; to deprive any person "of life, liberty, or property, without due process of law"; or to "deny any person . . . the equal protection of the laws." The Fourteenth Amendment gave the federal government responsibility for protecting (and enforcing) civil rights.

President Johnson urged the Southern states to refuse to ratify the amendment. He also predicted that the Democrats could win the congressional elections in November and then nix the amendment.

Johnson versus the Radical Republicans

To win votes for Democratic candidates in the 1866 congressional elections, Andrew Johnson went on a nineteen-day speaking tour during which he gave more than 100 speeches promoting his plan for reconstructing the South. He drew large crowds in Baltimore, Philadelphia, and New York City, during which he denounced Radical Republicans as traitors who should be hanged. His partisan speeches, however, backfired.

In Cleveland, Ohio, Johnson savaged Radical Republicans as "factious, domineering, tyrannical" men. When a heckler shouted that Johnson should hang Jefferson Davis as a war criminal, the thin-skinned president retorted, "Why not hang Thad Stevens?" Then a crowd member yelled, "Is this dignified?" Johnson shouted back: "I care not for dignity."

The backlash was intense. One newspaper denounced Johnson's remarks as "the most disgraceful speech ever delivered" by a president. Even the pro-Johnson *New York Times* concluded that the president's behavior was "compromising his official character."

Voters agreed. The 1866 congressional elections brought a devastating defeat for Johnson and the Democrats; in each house, Radical Republican candidates won more than a two-thirds majority, the margin required to override presidential vetoes. Congressional Republicans would now take over the process of reconstructing the former Confederacy.

> Republicans win two-thirds majority in Congress

Congress Takes Charge of Reconstruction

In March 1867, Congress passed, over President Johnson's vetoes, laws that laid out the requirements for the former Confederate states to be readmitted to the Union under its new Reconstruction plan.

At the center of the plan was the Military Reconstruction Act. It abolished the governments "in the Rebel States" that had been established under Johnson's lenient Reconstruction policies. In their place, Congress established military control over ten of the eleven former Confederate states. (Tennessee was exempted because it had already ratified the Fourteenth Amendment.) The ten states were divided into five "military districts," each commanded by an army general (see Map 15.1).

> Military Reconstruction Act (1867)

The Military Reconstruction Act required each former Confederate state to write a new constitution that guaranteed all adult males the right to vote—Black or White, rich or poor, landless or property-owning. Women, Black or White, were still not included as voters.

The act also stipulated that the new state constitutions were to be drafted by conventions elected by male citizens "of whatever race, color, or previous condition." Once a majority of voters ratified the new constitutions, the state legislatures had to ratify the Fourteenth Amendment; once the amendment became part of a new state constitution, the former Confederate states would be entitled to send representatives to Congress. Several hundred African American delegates participated in the constitutional conventions.

MAP 15.1 RECONSTRUCTION, 1865–1877

- States with Reconstruction governments
- ____ Border around the five military districts of the Reconstruction Act of 1867
- 1868 Date of readmission to the Union
- 1870 Date of reestablishment of conservative Democratic rule
- 2 Military districts set up by the Reconstruction Act of 1867

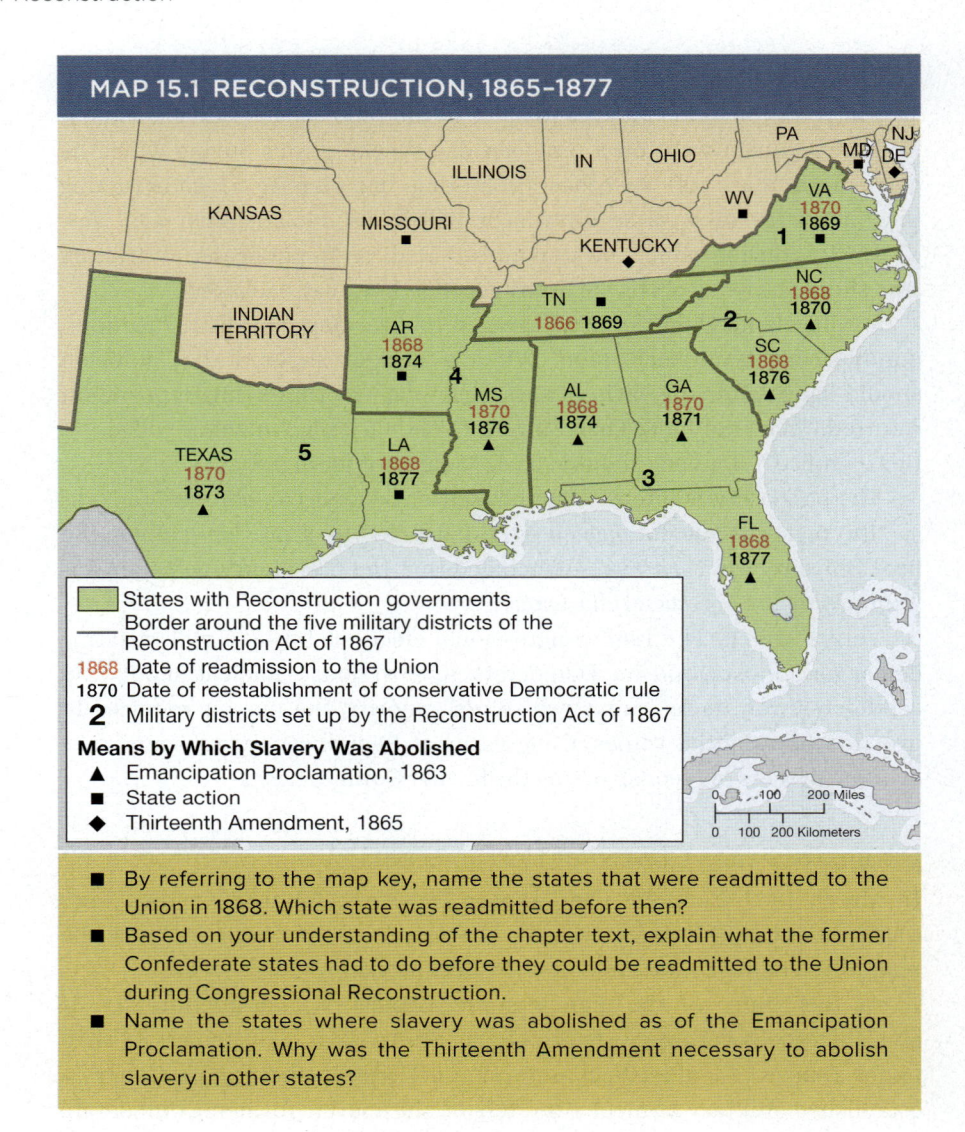

Means by Which Slavery Was Abolished
- ▲ Emancipation Proclamation, 1863
- ■ State action
- ♦ Thirteenth Amendment, 1865

- By referring to the map key, name the states that were readmitted to the Union in 1868. Which state was readmitted before then?
- Based on your understanding of the chapter text, explain what the former Confederate states had to do before they could be readmitted to the Union during Congressional Reconstruction.
- Name the states where slavery was abolished as of the Emancipation Proclamation. Why was the Thirteenth Amendment necessary to abolish slavery in other states?

Taken together, these procedures represented what came to be called **Congressional Reconstruction** (also known as Radical Reconstruction). It embodied the most sweeping peacetime legislation in American history to that point. It sought to ensure that freedpeople could participate in the creation of new state governments in the former Confederacy. As Thaddeus Stevens explained, the Congressional Reconstruction plan would create a "perfect republic" based on the principle of *equal rights* for all citizens.

Impeaching the President

The first two years of Congressional Reconstruction produced dramatic changes in the South, as new state legislatures rewrote their constitutions and ratified the Fourteenth Amendment. Radical Republicans were in control of Reconstruction, but one person still stood in their way—Andrew Johnson.

Congressional Reconstruction
A phase of Reconstruction directed by Radical Republicans in Congress and based on the Military Reconstruction Act; primary goal was to protect citizenship rights of freed people.

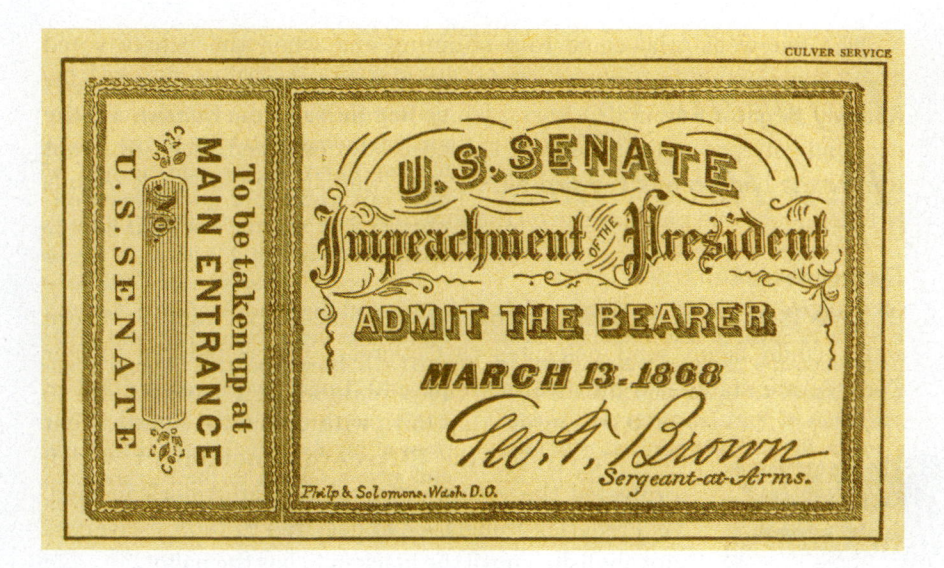

TICKET TO THE U.S. SENATE IMPEACHMENT TRIAL OF ANDREW JOHNSON President Andrew Johnson's impeachment trial was the first in American history. To follow the trial's progress, spectators needed a ticket to gain admission into the U.S. Senate chambers.

During 1867 and early 1868, more and more Radicals decided that the president must be removed from office.

Johnson himself opened the door to impeachment (the formal process by which Congress charges the president with "high crimes and misdemeanors") when he suspended Secretary of War Edwin Stanton, who had refused to resign despite his harsh criticism of the president's Reconstruction policy. Johnson soon decided that suspending Stanton was not enough, and in February 1868 he fired the secretary of war and replaced him with Ulysses S. Grant. Stanton, however, refused to leave his office, claiming that his appointment was protected by the Tenure of Office Act. The act stipulated that the Senate must approve any presidential effort to remove federal officials whose appointments the Senate had confirmed. It had been passed the year before to prevent Johnson from firing his most outspoken critics.

Stanton locked himself in the War Department until the Senate voted to override President Johnson's firing of him. The Radicals now saw their chance. By removing Stanton without congressional approval, Johnson had violated the law.

On February 24, 1868, the Republican-dominated House passed eleven articles of impeachment (that is, specific charges against the president), most of which dealt with Stanton's firing. In reality, the essential grievance against the president was that he had opposed the policies of the Radical Republicans and in doing so had brought "disgrace, ridicule, hatred, contempt, and reproach" onto the Congress. According to Secretary of the Navy Gideon Welles, Radicals were so angry at Johnson that they "would have tried to remove him had he been accused of stepping on a dog's tail."

The first Senate trial of a sitting president began on March 5, 1868. The Republicans held a majority, but not the two-thirds required to convict. It was a dramatic spectacle before a packed gallery of journalists, foreign dignitaries, and political officials.

> Impeachment of President Johnson

Fifteenth Amendment (1870)
An amendment to the U.S. Constitution forbidding states to deny any male citizen the right to vote on grounds of "race, color or previous condition of servitude."

The five-week trial came to a stunning end when the Senate voted 35–19 for conviction, only *one* vote short of the two-thirds needed for removal. Senator Edmund G. Ross, a young Republican from Kansas, cast the deciding vote preventing removal. Evidence later emerged suggesting that Ross's vote had been purchased by Johnson, who appointed Ross's friends to federal jobs and may have given the senator a $150,000 cash payment.

Expanding Voting Rights

In June 1868, congressional Republicans announced that eight Southern states could again send delegates to Congress. The remaining former Confederate states—Virginia, Mississippi, and Texas—were readmitted in 1870 (see again Map 15.1), with the added requirement that they ratify the **Fifteenth Amendment**, which protected the voting rights of African American men. As Frederick Douglass had declared in 1865, "slavery is not abolished until the black man has the ballot."

The Fifteenth Amendment prohibited states from denying a citizen's right to vote on grounds of "race, color, or previous condition of servitude." Prior to its ratification, the individual states determined voting eligibility.

The Fifteenth Amendment did not prohibit states from denying the right to vote to women. Radical Republicans tried to deflect the issue by declaring that it was the "Negro's hour." Anyway, argued Senator Richard Yates, allowing a woman to vote would be "destructive of her womanly qualities." Women, both Black and White, would have to wait.

Prejudice against Chinese Americans

Chinese Americans were also ignored by the Fifteenth Amendment. Since the gold rush of the 1840s, Chinese laborers had migrated to western states to work as miners and to help construct the transcontinental railroad (see Chapter 13). Men arrived first; then increasing numbers of women and children followed. By 1870, over 60,000 Chinese Americans were living in the United States, many of them in newly established communities in cities such as San Francisco.

But in California, Nevada, and Oregon, state laws still prevented them from voting. In *People v. Hall*, an 1857 California Supreme Court case, the justices had described the Chinese as "a race of people whom nature has marked as inferior, and who are incapable of progress."

During Reconstruction, elected officials from the western states insisted that citizenship and voting rights were appropriate for Black people but not Asians. The Chinese, asserted a senator from Oregon, were "a different race

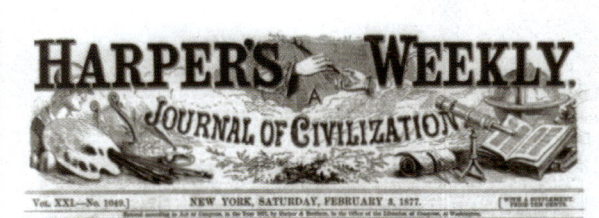

CONTINUED ANTI-CHINESE SENTIMENT Arriving in San Francisco as new laborers, Chinese immigrants had their belongings closely inspected by customs officers. Deemed racially inferior by White Americans, the Chinese were not granted voting rights despite the Fifteenth Amendment.

entirely" and should not be allowed to vote. Some of his colleagues suspected that Chinese immigrants remained too controlled by China and could never become loyal American citizens. A Nevada congressman added that there were not "ten American citizens" in the Far West "who favor Chinese suffrage."

In the end, California and Oregon refused to ratify the Fifteenth Amendment because of the Chinese issue. Federal policies continued to bar Chinese Americans from exercising citizenship rights until 1952, when Asian Americans were made eligible for citizenship and voting. Indigenous people were likewise precluded from citizenship until 1924.

> Chinese Americans barred from voting

Federal Reconstruction policies had changed several times throughout the postwar period. Abraham Lincoln and Andrew Johnson initially sought a quick reinstatement of Southern governments; this resulted, however, in the enactment of Black codes that restricted the rights of newly freed people. Radical Republicans, in response, opted for a more radical approach that would end the plantation elite's control of the South's state governments. Ultimately, under their Congressional Reconstruction plan, former Confederate states were required to ratify the Fourteenth and Fifteenth Amendments expanding African Americans' rights before being readmitted to the Union.

Black Society under Reconstruction

> **CORE OBJECTIVE**
> **3.** Assess the attitudes of White and Black Southerners toward various Reconstruction programs and requirements.

When a federal official asked Garrison Frazier, a freedman from Georgia, if he and others wanted to live among White people, Frazier said that they preferred "to live by ourselves, for there is a prejudice against us in the South that will take years to get over." In forging new lives, Frazier and many other formerly enslaved people set about creating their own social institutions.

U.S. soldiers and observers in the North often expressed surprise that formerly enslaved people did not leave the South. As a group of African Americans explained, they did not want to abandon "land they had laid their fathers' bones upon." A Union officer noted that Black people in the South seemed "more attached to familiar places" than any other group in the nation.

Black Churches and Schools

Part of the attraction of remaining in the South involved freedpeople's attachment to their churches. Religious life in the South had been transformed during and after the war. Many formerly enslaved people identified with the biblical Hebrews, who were led out of slavery into the "promised land." Emancipation thus demonstrated that God was on *their* side. Before the war, enslaved people who attended White churches were forced to sit in the back and listen to pro-slavery preaching. After the war, freedpeople

THE FIRST AFRICAN CHURCH, RICHMOND, VIRGINIA In June 1874, *Harper's Weekly* featured this illustration of the First African Baptist Church of Richmond, Virginia.

established their own churches that became the crossroads for Black community life.

> African American churches

Ministers emerged as social and political leaders. Many African Americans became Baptists or Methodists, partly because these were already the largest denominations in the South and partly because they reached out to the working poor. In 1866 alone, the African Methodist Episcopal (AME) Church gained 50,000 members. By 1890, more than 1.3 million African Americans in the South had become Baptists, nearly three times as many as had joined any other denomination.

> African American schools

African American communities also worked to establish schools. Starting schools, said a formerly enslaved person, was the "first proof" of freedom. White elites, however, feared that learning might distract poor Whites and Black people from their work in the fields, or encourage them to leave the South in search of better social and economic opportunities. Or it might empower them to organize and push for political change in the South.

The opposition of Southern Whites to Black education made public schools all the more important to African Americans. Republican-led governments in Southern states established new public school systems throughout the region, with 1,500 schools in Texas alone by 1872. New colleges and universities were established to help train teachers to work in these schools. By 1900, over 90 Black colleges and universities had been established, such as Hampton Institute in Virginia and Howard University in Washington, D.C.

South Carolina's Mary McLeod Bethune rejoiced in the new opportunities: "The whole world opened to me when I learned to read." She walked five miles to school every day as a child, earned a scholarship to college, and by

1904 became the first Black woman to found a school that became a four-year college: Bethune-Cookman University, in Daytona Beach, Florida.

The Union League

The Fifteenth Amendment had enormous political consequences. No sooner was it ratified than Republicans from the North, Black and White, sought to convince freedmen to join the party of Lincoln. To do so, they organized Union Leagues throughout the former Confederacy. Republicans had founded the Union League (also called the Loyal League) in 1862 to rally voters behind Lincoln, the war, and the party. By late 1863, the league claimed over 700,000 members in 4,554 councils across the nation.

In the postwar South, these Union League chapters were organized like fraternities, with formal initiations and rituals and secret meetings to protect the freedpeople from being persecuted by angry White Democrats. The leagues met in churches, schools, homes, and fields, often listening to speakers from the North who traveled the South extolling the Republican Party and encouraging Blacks to register and vote.

> Union Leagues mobilize Black voters

With the help of the Union Leagues, some 90 percent of freedmen in the South registered to vote—almost all of them as Republicans—and they voted in record numbers (often 80–90 percent). Their doing so often required great courage. Throughout the postwar South, angry Whites persecuted, evicted, or fired African American workers who "exercised their political rights," as a Union officer reported from Virginia. Those who made it to the polling place had to contend with Democrats brandishing weapons and cursing at them to stop them from voting.

> Risks of voting

Yet the net result of the Union Leagues was a remarkable mobilization of Black people whose votes enabled men of color to gain elected offices for the first time in the former Confederate states. Francis Cardozo, a Black minister who served as president of the South Carolina Council of Union Leagues, declared in 1870 that South Carolina had "prospered in every respect" as a result of the enfranchisement of Black voters enabled by the Union Leagues.

African American Political Leadership

Black military veterans formed the core of the first generation of African American political leaders in the postwar South. Military service had given many formerly enslaved people their first opportunities to learn to read and write and had alerted them to new possibilities for economic advancement and leadership. In addition, fighting for the Union cause had instilled a fervent sense of nationalism. A Virginia freedman explained that the United States was "now *our* country—made emphatically so by the blood of our brethren."

New African American voters helped elect nearly 800 Black men—most of them formerly enslaved—as state legislators. In Louisiana, Pinckney Pinchback, a Northern free Black man and former Union soldier, was elected lieutenant governor. Other African Americans were elected to federal offices. There were two Black senators in Congress, Hiram Revels and Blanche

> African American men elected to office

AFRICAN AMERICAN POLITICAL FIGURES OF RECONSTRUCTION As Black people gained the right to vote, formerly enslaved men were elected to positions in government. Among these, Blanche K. Bruce *(left)* and Hiram Revels *(right)* served in the U.S. Senate. Between them is Frederick Douglass, a major figure in the abolitionist movement who was later appointed U.S. ambassador to the Republic of Haiti.

K. Bruce, while fourteen Black congressmen served in the U.S. House of Representatives.

One was Robert Smalls of South Carolina, the war hero who had seized the Confederate steamer *Planter* and piloted it into Union lines in 1863 (see Chapter 14). Awarded prize money by Congress for that daring act, Smalls purchased the land of his former enslaver, established a store and a newspaper, and hired a teacher to help him learn to read and write. He then moved quickly into politics. "My race needs no special defense," he argued after being elected to the South Carolina legislature in 1868, "for the past history of them in this country proves them to be the equal of any people anywhere. All they need is an equal chance in the battle of life."

In Congress, where he served for five terms, Robert Smalls advocated for U.S. troops to remain in the Reconstruction South, knowing full well that White South Carolinians were waiting for a chance to stop his climb into political leadership.

Southern Whites complained that emancipated Blacks were illiterate and had no civic experience. In this regard, however, Blacks were no different from millions of poor or immigrant White males who had been voting and serving in office for years. Beverly Nash, an African American delegate to the South Carolina convention of 1868, told his colleagues, "We are not prepared for this suffrage [the vote]. But we can learn. Give a man tools and let him commence to use them, and in time he will learn a trade. So it is with voting."

The Quest for Land

> Land grants to freedpeople revoked by President Johnson

Many freedpeople argued that what they needed most was land. In several Southern states, Black people had been allowed to rent or purchase land seized by Union armies in Confederate areas during the war. But Andrew Johnson reversed such transfers of property to formerly enslaved people.

In South Carolina, the Union general responsible for evicting freedpeople urged them to "lay aside their bitter feelings, and become reconciled to their old masters." The assembled freedmen instead shouted, "No, never!" and "Can't do it!"

They knew that ownership of land was the foundation of their freedom. They may have had no deeds or titles for the land they now worked, but it had been "earned by the sweat of *our* brows," said a group of Alabama freedmen. "Didn't we clear the land and raise de crops?" a Virginia freedman argued, "We have a right to [that] land."

Thousands of evicted people were forced to return their farms to White owners. In addition, it was virtually impossible for Black people to take out loans to buy farmland because few banks were willing to lend to them, and few White landowners were willing to sell to Black buyers. A formerly enslaved man in Mississippi said that he and others were left with nothing: "no *land*, no *house*, not so much as a place to lay our head."

Sojourner Truth, the women's rights leader and abolitionist, had an idea for getting land into the hands of formerly enslaved people: she launched a petition drive urging the federal government to set aside western lands for freedpeople. Truth lobbied Congress and went on a speaking tour in 1870–1871, telling anyone who would listen that her plan would pay "a little of that great debt we owe to this long oppressed people." Not enough political leaders listened, however, and the plan went nowhere.

Sharecropping

Many Black people in the South realized that their only chance to make a living was by working for pay for their former owners. In fact, the Freedmen's

SHARECROPPERS This 1899 photograph by Frances Benjamin Johnston, one of the earliest female photojournalists, shows a sharecropping family outside their Virginia cabin.

sharecropping A farming system developed after the Civil War by which landless workers farmed land in exchange with the landowner for farm supplies and a share of the crop.

Sharecropping replaces slavery

Bureau and federal soldiers urged and even ordered them to sign labor contracts with local Whites that would pay them to do the same work on the same land that they had tilled while enslaved. Many planters, however, conspired to limit the amount of wages paid to freedmen. "It seems humiliating to be compelled to bargain and haggle with our own servants about wages," complained a White planter's daughter.

Other freedpeople participated in a new labor system: **sharecropping**. It worked like this: Black laborers would rent a portion of land on which to raise crops and then pay the rent by giving the landowner a *share* of the crop. White landowners might provide seed and tools, or sometimes local merchants loaned the supplies but required repayment in the future, at high interest rates. This essentially re-enslaved the workers because, as a federal army officer said, no matter "how much they are abused, they cannot leave without permission of the owner." If they left, they would forfeit their portion of the crop; if they stayed, it became nearly impossible to repay their debts. Workers who violated the terms of the contract could be evicted, leaving them jobless and homeless—and subject to arrest as vagrants.

The rapid growth of sharecropping revealed that most White plantation owners and small farmers were determined to control African Americans as if they were still enslaved. And if bad weather or insects or disease stunted the harvest, it pushed the sharecropper deeper in debt.

Many freed Blacks initially preferred sharecropping over working for wages, since it freed them from day-to-day supervision by White landowners. Over time, however, most sharecroppers, Black and White, found themselves deeply in debt, with little choice but to remain tied to the same discouraging system of dependence that felt much like slavery. As one freedman acknowledged, "freedom could make folks proud, but it didn't make 'em rich."

"Carpetbaggers" and "Scalawags"

White Southerners who resisted Reconstruction called Whites who served in the South's new Republican state governments "carpetbaggers" or "scalawags." Carpetbaggers, critics argued, were the 30,000 scheming Northerners who rushed south with their belongings in cheap suitcases made of carpeting ("carpetbags") to grab political power or buy plantations.

Northerners who moved south

Some Northerners who migrated south were indeed corrupt opportunists. However, most were Union military veterans drawn to the South by the desire to rebuild the region's wrecked economy. Many other so-called carpetbaggers were teachers, social workers, attorneys, physicians, editors, and ministers motivated by a genuine desire to help free Blacks and poor Whites.

For example, Union General Adelbert Ames, who won the Congressional Medal of Honor, stayed in the South after the war because he felt a "sense of Mission with a large M" to help formerly enslaved people develop healthy communities. He served as the military governor of Mississippi before being elected a Republican U.S. senator in 1870.

Southern Democrats especially hated the scalawags, or southern White Republicans, calling them traitors to their region. A Nashville newspaper editor described them as the "merest trash." They were prominent in the mountain counties of Georgia, Tennessee, and Alabama. Among the scalawags were several distinguished figures, including former Confederate General James Longstreet, who decided that the Old South must change its ways. He became a successful cotton broker in New Orleans, joined the Republican Party, and supported Radical Reconstruction.

Southern Violence

With each passing year during Reconstruction, African Americans suffered increasing exploitation and abuse. The Black codes created by White state governments in 1865 and 1866 were only the first of many efforts to deny equality. Whites continued to use terror, intimidation, and violence to disrupt Black Republican meetings, target Black and White Republican leaders for beatings or killings, and prevent Black people from exercising their political rights.

In Texas, a White farmer, D. B. Whitesides, told a former enslaved man named Charles Brown that his newfound freedom would do him "damned little good . . . as I intend to shoot you"—which he did, shooting Brown in the chest as he tried to flee. Whitesides then rode his horse beside Brown and asked, "I got you, did I Brown?" "Yes," a bleeding Brown replied. "You got me good." Whitesides yelled that the wound would teach "[Blacks like you] to put on airs because you are free."

Such violent incidents revealed a harsh truth: the death of slavery did not mean the birth of true freedom for African Americans. Secretive terrorist groups—including the Ku Klux Klan, the Knights of the White Camelia, the White Line, and the White League—emerged to resist Radical Reconstruction and to harass, intimidate, torture, and even kill African Americans.

> Rise of White supremacy groups

VISIT OF THE KU-KLUX African Americans in the South lived in constant fear of racial violence, as this 1872 engraving from *Harper's Weekly*, published to elicit Northerners' sympathy, illustrates.

Ku Klux Klan A secret terrorist organization founded in Pulaski, Tennessee, in 1866 targeting formerly enslaved people who voted and held political offices, as well as people the KKK labeled as carpetbaggers and scalawags.

The **Ku Klux Klan** (KKK) was formed in 1866 in Pulaski, Tennessee. The name *Ku Klux* derived from the Greek word *kuklos*, meaning "circle" or "band"; *Klan* came from the English word *clan*, meaning "family." The Klan, and other groups like it, began as a social club, with intimidating costumes and secret rituals. But its members, most of them former Confederate soldiers, soon began harassing Black and White Republicans.

General Philip Sheridan, who supervised the military district that included Louisiana and Texas, reported that Klansmen were terrorists intent on suppressing Black political participation. Klansmen marauded at night on horseback, spreading rumors, issuing threats, and burning schools and churches. "We are going to kill all the Negroes," a White supremacist declared during one massacre.

The Legacy of Congressional Reconstruction

The widespread terror of racial violence eventually undermined the Republican state governments. Yet they still left behind an important accomplishment: the new constitutions they created remained in effect for years, and later constitutions incorporated many of their most progressive features.

Radical Republican achievements

Some of the significant innovations instituted by the Republican state governments protected Black voting rights and shifted state offices from appointed to elected positions in order to weaken the "good old boy" tradition of rewarding political supporters with state government jobs. As well, these governments provided free public schools for the first time in most counties in the South, allowed women to keep their private property rather than transfer it to their husbands, and rebuilt an extensive railroad network destroyed during the war.

Southern Republicans also gave more attention to the poor and to orphanages, asylums, and institutions for the deaf and blind of both races. Sorely needed infrastructure—roads, bridges, and buildings—was repaired or rebuilt. African Americans achieved rights and opportunities that would repeatedly be violated but would never completely be taken away, at least in principle, such as equality before the law and the rights to own property, attend schools, learn to read and write, enter professions, and carry on business.

Yet government officials also engaged in corrupt practices that were common to politics in the nineteenth century. Bribes and kickbacks, by which companies received government contracts in return for giving government officials cash or stock, were widespread. In Louisiana, twenty-six-year-old Henry Clay Warmoth somehow turned an annual salary of $8,000 into a million-dollar fortune during his four years as governor. "I don't pretend to be honest," he admitted. "I only pretend to be as honest as anybody in politics." Warmoth would eventually be impeached and removed from office.

As was true in the North and the Midwest, state governments in the South awarded money to corporations, notably railroads, under conditions that invited shady dealings and outright corruption. Some railroad corporations received state funds but never built railroads, and bribery was rampant.

But the Radical Republican regimes did not invent such corruption, nor did it die with them. Warmoth recognized as much: "Corruption is the fashion" in Louisiana, he explained.

By now, Reconstruction had drawn different responses from White and Black Southerners. Most freedpeople chose to remain in familiar surroundings in the South, establishing independent churches and schools in their communities and participating in politics. Yet land ownership had gone back into the hands of the White elite, so Black farmers had no choice but to become sharecroppers with little hope of rising out of poverty. Apart from the elite, many White Southerners blamed their own poverty on the formerly enslaved, leading them to participate in violent intimidation of Black people and their allies who supported Reconstruction efforts.

The Grant Administration

Andrew Johnson's crippled presidency created an opportunity for Republicans to elect one of their own in 1868. Both parties wooed Ulysses S. Grant, the "Lion of Vicksburg" credited by most with the Union victory in the Civil War. His differences with Johnson, however, had pushed him toward the Republicans, who unanimously nominated him as their presidential candidate.

> **CORE OBJECTIVE**
> **4.** Analyze the political and economic factors that helped end Reconstruction in 1877.

The Election of 1868

The Republican Party platform endorsed Congressional Reconstruction. More important, however, were the public expectations driving the candidacy of Ulysses S. Grant, whose campaign slogan was "Let us have peace." Grant promised that if elected, he would enforce the laws and promote prosperity for all.

Democrats shouted defiance, however. "This is a White man's country," they claimed, so "let White men rule." The Radical Republicans, Democrats charged, were subjecting the South "to military despotism and Negro supremacy."

Democratic delegates nominated Horatio Seymour, the wartime governor of New York and a passionate critic of Congressional Reconstruction, who dismissed the Emancipation Proclamation as "a proposal for the butchery of women and children." His running mate, Francis P. Blair Jr., a former Union general from Missouri who had served in Congress, was an avowed racist who wanted to "declare the reconstruction acts null and void" and withdraw all federal troops from the South. He attacked Grant for exercising military tyranny "over the eight millions of white people in the South, fixed to the earth with his bayonets." A Democrat later said that Blair's "stupid and indefensible" remarks cost Seymour a close election. Grant won all but eight states and swept the Electoral College, 214–80; but his popular majority was only a little more than 300,000 out of almost 6 million votes.

> Black votes help to elect President Grant (1868)

"LET US HAVE PEACE" In the midst of the social and political turbulence of Reconstruction, Ulysses S. Grant's slogan, "Let us have peace"—as stamped on campaign coins such as this one—struck a chord with voters.

More than 500,000 African American voters, mostly in the South, accounted for Grant's margin of victory. Although Klan violence soared during the campaign, and hundreds of freedpeople paid with their lives, the efforts of Radical Republicans to ensure voting rights for Blacks in the South had paid off.

Grant, the youngest president up to that time (he was forty-six years old when inaugurated), had said during the Civil War that he was not "a politician, never was and never hope to be." Now he was the politician-in-chief. A steadfast defender of Congressional Reconstruction and civil rights for Blacks, Grant later admitted that he thought "I could run the government of the United States as I did the staff of my army. It was my mistake, and it led me into other mistakes."

Grant followed the lead of Congress and was often blind to the political forces and self-serving influence peddlers around him. He showed poor judgment in his selection of cabinet members, often favoring friendship, family, loyalty, and military service over integrity and ability.

During Grant's two presidential terms, his seven cabinet positions changed twenty-four times. His close friend General William Tecumseh Sherman said he felt sorry for Grant because so many supposedly loyal Republicans used the president for selfish gains.

Yet Grant excelled at bringing diversity to the federal government. During his two presidential terms, he appointed more African Americans, Native Americans, Jews, and women than any of his predecessors, and he fulfilled his campaign pledge to bring peace to the divided nation.

The Battle to Enforce the Fifteenth Amendment

President Grant insisted that freedpeople be allowed to exercise their civil rights without fear of violence. In late 1870, Grant delivered a speech to Congress in which he celebrated the ratification of the Fifteenth Amendment, protecting the voting rights of African American men nationwide. "It was," he declared, ". . . the most important event that has occurred since the nation came into life . . . the realization of the Declaration of Independence."

To Frederick Douglass, the Thirteenth, Fourteenth, and Fifteenth Amendments seemed to ensure that Black people would at last gain true equality. "Never was revolution more complete," Douglass announced in 1870. To President Grant, "more than any other man, the Negro owes his enfranchisement."

> Backlash against the Fifteenth Amendment

But Douglass and others were soon bitterly disappointed. The "revolution" turned out to be incomplete, as the Fifteenth Amendment ignited a violent backlash in the South. In Georgia, White officials devised new ways to restrict Black voting, such as poll taxes and onerous registration procedures. Other states followed suit. "What is the use of talking about equality before the law," a freedman wrote as former Confederates took control of Southern society. "There is none."

Four months after the Fifteenth Amendment became the law of the land, Congress passed the Naturalization Act of 1870. For the first time, it extended the process by which immigrants had gained citizenship to include *"aliens of African nativity and to persons of African descent."* Efforts to include Asians and Indigenous Americans in the naturalization law, however, were defeated.

Asserting Women's Rights

The Fifteenth Amendment was written to protect the voting rights of men, not women. But some women's rights leaders were undeterred, such as Mary Ann Shadd Cary, a Black teacher, journalist, and the first woman to enroll in Howard University's law school. Cary argued that if women were citizens, and if voting was a right of citizenship, then women should be allowed to vote, too. It was time to test that question.

In April 1871, Cary led a group of women to the voter registration office in Washington, D.C., demanding that they be added to the voting rolls. Frederick Douglass joined them in a show of support. It was a bold move, but the women were quickly turned away. Cary called the refusal "a bitter pill to swallow."

Between 1868 and 1872, at least 700 other women attempted to vote in local, state, and national elections. Sometimes they ran for office. Victoria Woodhull, a women's rights activist, stockbroker, and journalist, declared herself a candidate for president in 1872, becoming the first woman in U.S. history to do so. Most voters, however, dismissed Woodhull as too radical to be president (not to mention that she was a woman) and did not take her campaign seriously.

When Susan B. Anthony and seventeen other women went to the polls in Rochester, New York, in 1872, a sympathetic poll worker relented and allowed them to vote. "Well I have been & gone & done it!!—positively voted the Republican ticket," Anthony wrote excitedly. But nine days later, federal marshals showed up at her door. Anthony was arrested, tried, found guilty, and fined $100 for voting. She then launched a speaking tour entitled "Is It a Crime for a Citizen of the United States to Vote?" The U.S. Constitution, she stressed, refers to "We, the people; not we, the White male citizens; nor yet we, the male citizens; but we, the whole people, who formed the Union—women as well as men." It would take nearly fifty more years for other Americans to agree and, with the Nineteenth Amendment (1920), grant women the right to vote.

MARY ANN SHADD CARY Devoted to the cause of equal rights, Cary founded the Colored Women's Progressive Franchise Association in 1880, an organization that advocated for voting rights for Black women.

Women attempt to vote in elections

"THE WOMAN WHO DARED"
This 1873 political cartoon lampooned Susan B. Anthony's attempt to vote in 1872 as a reversal of accepted gender roles. In it, Anthony is depicted in the pose of a man, while a female police officer stands nearby and a man cares for a baby.

Grant's "Peace Policy"

Policy toward Native Americans

As women were struggling for the right to vote, Native Americans were facing pressure to give up their traditional ways of life and their ancestral lands. In his 1869 inaugural address, President Grant declared that he would promote "civilization and ultimate citizenship" for Native American people. This meant requiring that Indigenous peoples first adopt aspects of American culture before they could have the rights and freedoms of American citizenship extended to them.

That same year, he appointed General Ely Parker, a Seneca chief trained as an attorney and engineer, as the new commissioner of Indian Affairs, the first Native American to hold the position. Parker had served as Grant's military secretary during the war. Now, as commissioner, Parker faced formidable challenges in creating policies for the 300,000 Indigenous people across the nation, many of whom continued to face pressure to give up their ancestral lands.

Working with Parker, Grant created a new Peace Policy toward Native Americans. "The Indians," he observed, "require as much protection from the whites as the white does from the Indians." He did not want the army "shooting these poor savages; I want to conciliate them and make them peaceful citizens."

Grant believed that lasting peace could result only from Indigenous peoples abandoning their nomadic tradition and relocating to government reservations, where federal troops would provide them "absolute protection." There they would also be pushed to learn American ways of farming and other aspects of American culture taught by Christian missionaries. Even Lieutenant General William Tecumseh Sherman, no friend of the Native Americans, acknowledged the injustice of the situation. "The poor Indians are starving," he reported to his wife in 1868. "We kill them if they attempt to hunt"; yet if they stay "within the reservation, they starve."

Indigenous leaders resisted many aspects of the reservation system. Kiowa, Apache, and Comanche people in the Southwest, for example, kept their nomadic traditions alive by continuing to hunt and raid far beyond the established reservations. "I don't want to settle there," the Kiowa chief Satanta (White Bear) wrote of the reservation he had initially agreed to in a treaty. "I love the land and the buffalo. . . . I love to roam over the wide prairie, and when I do I feel free and happy, but when we settle down we grow pale and die."

Grant tried to improve the reservation system by ending the chronic corruption practiced by licensed government traders. Many traders used their positions to swindle Native Americans out of the federally supplied food, clothing, and other provisions intended solely for the reservations. One of the accused traders was the president's brother.

To clean up the so-called Indian Ring, Grant moved the Bureau of Indian Affairs out of the control of Congress and into the War Department. He also created a Board of Indian Commissioners, a civilian agency whose mission was to oversee the operations of the Bureau of Indian Affairs. Grant then appointed Quakers as reservation traders, assuming that their honesty, humility, and pacifism would improve the distribution of government resources. "If you can make Quakers out of the Indians," Grant told them, "it will take the fight out of them. Let us have peace." Yet Quakers proved no more able than the government bureaucrats to manage policy toward the Indigenous people.

Many of the U.S. officers and soldiers sent to "pacify" Indigenous peoples in the Great Plains displayed an attitude quite different from Grant's. For example, General Philip Sheridan coined the infamous statement, "The only good Indians I know are dead." Sherman agreed. He stressed to Sheridan that "the more [Indians] we kill this year, the less we would have to kill next year." Sheridan and Sherman went on to lead American troops in a series of wars against Indigenous societies in the Great Plains that lasted into the 1890s (see Chapter 17).

Such attitudes led the abolitionist Wendell Phillips to ask why Native Americans were one of the only groups still denied citizenship. "The great poison of the age is race hatred" directed at both African Americans and Native Americans, Phillips charged. "We shall never be able to be just to other races," he continued, ". . . until we 'unlearn' contempt" for others different from us.

Scandals

President Grant's innate trust in people, especially rich people, led his administration into a cesspool of scandal. Perhaps because of his struggles as a storekeeper and farmer before the Civil War, Grant was awestruck by men of wealth. As they lavished gifts and attention on him, he was lured into their webs of self-serving deception. In the summer of 1869, two financial schemers, Jay Gould and James Fisk Jr., plotted with Abel Corbin, the president's brother-in-law, to "corner" (manipulate) the nation's gold market. They intended to create a public craze for gold by purchasing massive quantities of the precious metal to drive up its value.

The only threat to the scheme lay in the possibility that the federal Treasury would burst the bubble by selling large amounts of its gold, which would deflate the metal's market value. When Grant was seen in public with Gould and Fisk, people wrongly assumed that he supported their scheme. The value of gold soared.

> Gould-Fisk scheme to corner the gold market

On September 24, 1869—soon to be remembered as Black Friday—the Gould-Fisk scheme worked, at least for a while. Starting at $150 an ounce, the price of gold rose to $165, leading more and more investors to join the stampede.

CORNERING THE GOLD MARKET
In this political cartoon about the Black Friday gold scheme, Jay Gould attempts to manipulate the gold market, represented by caged and enraged bulls and bears. In the background, President Ulysses S. Grant dashes from the U.S. Treasury to the scene, frantically trying to bring down the soaring price of gold.

Then, around noon, Grant and his Treasury secretary realized what was happening and began selling government gold. Within fifteen minutes, the price per ounce plummeted to $138. Schemers lost fortunes amid the chaotic trading. Soon the turmoil spread to the entire stock market, claiming thousands of victims.

For weeks after the gold "bubble" collapsed, financial markets were paralyzed and business confidence was shaken. Congressman James Garfield wrote privately to a friend that Grant had compromised his office by his "indiscreet acceptance" of gifts from Fisk and Gould and that any investigation of Black Friday would lead "into the parlor of the President." One critic announced that U. S. Grant's initials actually stood for "uniquely stupid."

The plot to corner the gold market was the first of several scandals that rocked the Grant administration. The wife of the secretary of war, it turned out, had accepted bribes from merchants who traded with Indigenous people at army posts in the West. And in St. Louis, whiskey distillers bribed federal Treasury agents in an effort to avoid paying excise taxes on alcohol. Grant's personal secretary participated in the scheme, taking secret payments in exchange for confidential information. Grant urged Congress to investigate. "Let no guilty man escape," he stressed.

Liberal Republicans

Disputes over political corruption and the fate of Reconstruction helped divide Republicans into two factions: Liberals (or Conscience Republicans) and Stalwarts (or Grant Republicans).

Liberal Republicans, led by Senator Carl Schurz, embraced free enterprise capitalism and opposed government regulation of business and industry while championing gold coins as the only reliable currency. They thirsted to oust Grant from the presidency and end what Schurz called "Negro Supremacy" and the "horror" of Reconstruction.

Schurz and other Liberal Republicans also sought to lower the tariffs that were lining the pockets of big corporations and to promote "civil service reforms" to end the partisan tyranny of the patronage system, by which new presidents rewarded the "selfish greed" of political supporters with federal government jobs.

The 1872 Election

In 1872, the Liberal Republicans, many of whom were elitist newspaper editors suspicious of the working classes, held their own national convention in Cincinnati. They nominated Horace Greeley, the eccentric editor of the *New York Tribune* and a longtime champion of causes ranging from abolitionism to socialism, vegetarianism, and spiritualism (communicating with the dead).

Most Northerners were appalled by Greeley's selection. Southern Democrats, however, liked Greeley's criticism of Reconstruction. His newspaper charged that Radical Republicans' "[Black] Government" exercised "absolute political supremacy" in several states and was transferring wealth from the "most intelligent" and "influential" Southern Whites to themselves.

In the 1872 balloting, Greeley carried six states in the South and none in the North. Grant won thirty-one states and a large popular majority, gaining 56 percent of the votes. An exhausted Greeley confessed that he was "the worst beaten man who ever ran for high office." Greeley died three weeks later.

> President Grant reelected (1872)

Grant was delighted that the "soreheads and thieves who had deserted the Republican party" were defeated, and he promised to avoid the "mistakes" he had made in his first term.

The Money Supply

Complex financial issues—especially monetary policy—dominated Ulysses S. Grant's second term. Prior to the Civil War, the economy operated on a gold standard; state and private banks each issued their own paper money that could be exchanged for an equal value of gold coins. Therefore, both gold coins and thousands of different bank notes circulated as currency. **Greenbacks,** the first uniform paper currency of the United States, were issued by the federal Treasury during the Civil War to help pay for the war.

> Greenbacks vs. gold coins

When a nation's supply of money grows faster than the economy itself, prices for goods and services increase (inflation). This happened when the greenbacks were issued. After the war, the U.S. Treasury assumed that the greenbacks would be recalled from circulation so that consumer prices would decline and the nation could return to a "hard-money" currency—gold, silver, and copper coins—which had always been viewed as more reliable in value than paper currency.

The most vocal supporters of a return to hard money were eastern creditors (mostly bankers and merchants) who did not want their debtors to pay them in paper currency. Critics tended to be farmers and other debtors. These so-called soft-money advocates opposed taking greenbacks out of

greenbacks Paper money issued during the Civil War that sparked currency debates after the war.

Panic of 1873 The financial collapse triggered by President Grant's efforts to withdraw greenbacks from circulation and transition the post–Civil War economy back to hard currency.

Public Credit Act (1869)

circulation because shrinking the supply of money would bring lower prices (deflation) for their crops and livestock. In 1868, congressional supporters of such a soft-money policy—mostly Democrats—forced the Treasury to stop withdrawing greenbacks.

President Grant sided with the hard-money camp. In March 1869, he signed the Public Credit Act, which stated that investors who had purchased government bonds to help finance the war effort must now be paid back in gold. The act led to a decline in consumer prices that hurt debtors and helped creditors. It also ignited a ferocious debate over the merits of hard and soft money that would last throughout the nineteenth century—and beyond.

Financial Panic

President Grant's effort to withdraw greenbacks from circulation triggered a major economic collapse. During 1873, two dozen railroads stopped paying their bills, forcing Jay Cooke and Company, the nation's leading business lender, to go bankrupt and close its doors in September 1873.

The shocking news created a snowball effect, as other hard-pressed banks and investment companies began shutting down. A Republican senator sent Grant an urgent telegram from New York City: "Results of today indicate imminent danger of general national bank panic." The Freedmen's Bank was among the banks that closed within a year, leaving thousands of Black families devastated by the sudden loss of their life's savings.

The resulting **Panic of 1873** caused a deep economic depression. Tens of thousands of businesses closed, 3 million workers lost jobs, and those with jobs saw their wages slashed. In major cities, the unemployed and homeless crowded the streets and formed long lines at soup kitchens.

The depression signaled that the maturing industrial economy was entering a long phase of instability punctuated by periods of soaring prosperity followed by desperate panics, bankruptcies, unemployment, recessions, and even prolonged depressions.

PANIC OF 1873 The economic depression in 1873 left millions unemployed and destitute. In this contemporary woodcut, a line of somber men hugs the wall of a New York City poorhouse where they hope to get a hot meal.

The Panic of 1873 led the U.S. Treasury to reverse course and begin printing more greenbacks to increase the nation's money supply. For a time, the supporters of paper money celebrated, but in 1874, Grant vetoed a bill to issue even more greenbacks. His decision pleased the financial community but ignited a barrage of criticism. A group of merchants in Indiana charged that Grant had sold his soul to those "whose god is the dollar."

In the end, Grant's decision only prolonged what was then the worst economic depression in the nation's history. It also brought about a catastrophe for Republicans in the 1874 congressional elections. In the House, Republicans went from a 70 percent majority to a 37 percent minority. As a result, the Republican effort to reconstruct the South ground to a halt.

Republicans lose congressional majority

Domestic Terrorism

President Grant initially enforced federal efforts to reconstruct the postwar South, but White Southern resistance only increased. In Grayson County, Texas, a White man and two friends murdered three formerly enslaved people because they wanted to "thin the [Blacks] out and drive them to their holes."

Klansmen focused on intimidating prominent Republicans, both Black and White—elected officials, teachers in Black schools, state militias. In 1870 an armed mob of Whites attacked a Republican political rally in Alabama, killing four Blacks and wounding fifty-four. An Alabama Republican pleaded with Grant to intervene. "Give us poor people some guarantee of our lives," G. T. F. Boulding wrote. "We are hunted and shot down as if we were wild beasts." In South Carolina, White supremacists were especially violent. In 1871, some 500 masked men laid siege to the Union County jail and eventually lynched eight Black prisoners.

Anti-Black terrorism escalates

At Grant's urging, Republicans in Congress responded with three Enforcement Acts (1870–1871). The first imposed penalties on anyone who interfered with a citizen's right to vote. The second dispatched federal supervisors to monitor elections in Southern districts where political terrorism flourished. The third, called the Ku Klux Klan Act (1871), outlawed the main activities of the KKK—forming conspiracies, wearing disguises, resisting officers, and intimidating officials. It also allowed the president to send federal troops to any community where voting rights were being violated.

Enforcement Acts (1870–1871)

Once the legislation was approved, Grant sent Attorney General Amos Akerman, a Georgian, to recruit prosecutors and marshals to enforce it. In South Carolina alone, Akerman and federal troops and prosecutors convinced local juries to convict 1,143 Klansmen. By 1872, Grant's stern actions had effectively killed the Klan. In general, however, the Enforcement Acts were not consistently enforced. As a result, the violent efforts of Southern Whites to thwart Reconstruction escalated.

On Easter Sunday 1873 in the small Black township of Colfax, Louisiana, some 140 White vigilantes—most of them well-armed former Confederate soldiers, led by Klansmen—used a cannon, rifles, and pistols to force a group of Black Republicans holed up in the courthouse to surrender. The Whites

Colfax Massacre

then called out the names of the African Americans, told them to step forward, and either shot them, or slit their throats, or hanged them, slaughtering a total of eighty-one people.

Upon hearing of the killings, President Grant told the Senate that the Colfax Massacre was unprecedented in its "barbarity." He declared parts of Louisiana to be in a state of insurrection and imposed military rule. Federal prosecutors used the Enforcement Acts to indict seventy Whites, but only nine were put on trial and just three were convicted—but of "conspiracy," not murder, and none were sent to prison.

Southern "Redeemers"

The Klan's impact on the region's politics varied from state to state. In the Upper South, it played a modest role in helping Democrats win local elections. In the Lower South, however, Klan violence had more serious effects. In overwhelmingly Black Yazoo County, Mississippi, vengeful Whites used terrorism to reverse the political balance of power.

In the 1873 elections, Republicans cast 2,449 votes and Democrats 638; two years later, Democrats polled 4,049 votes, Republicans 7. Once Democrats regained power, they ousted Black legislators, closed public schools for Black children, and instituted poll taxes to restrict Black voting.

The activities of White supremacists disheartened Black and White Republicans alike. "We are helpless and unable to organize," wrote a Mississippi Republican. "[We] dare not attempt to canvass [campaign for candidates] or make public speeches." At the same time, Northerners displayed a growing weariness with using federal troops to reconstruct the South. "The plain truth is," noted the *New York Herald,* "the North has got tired of the Negro."

> Civil Rights Act of 1875

President Grant, however, was determined to use more federal force to preserve peace and asked Congress to pass new legislation. Congress responded with the Civil Rights Act of 1875, which stated that people of all races must be granted equal access to hotels and restaurants, railroads and stagecoaches, theaters, and other "places of public amusement."

Unfortunately for Grant, the new anti-segregation law provided little enforcement authority. Those who felt their rights were being violated had to file suit in court, and the penalties for violators were modest.

> Civil Rights Cases (1883) allow for more racial segregation measures

In 1883, the U.S. Supreme Court struck down the Civil Rights Act on the grounds that the Fourteenth Amendment focused only on the policies of state governments; it did not have authority over the actions of private businesses or individuals. Chief Justice Joseph Bradley added that it was time for Black people to assume "the rank of a mere citizen" and stop being the "special favorite of the laws." As a result, the Civil Rights Cases (1883) opened the door for a wave of racial segregation that washed over the South during the late nineteenth century.

Republican political control in the South loosened during the 1870s as all-White conservative parties mobilized the anti-Reconstruction vote. They called themselves conservatives to distinguish themselves from Northern

Democrats. Conservatives—so-called "redeemers" who supposedly "saved" the South from Republican control and "Black rule"—played on racial fear to excite the White electorate and resorted to trickery to rig the voting in their favor.

Republican political control ended in Virginia and Tennessee as early as 1869. Reconstruction lasted longer in the Lower South, where Whites abandoned Klan robes for barefaced intimidation in paramilitary groups such as the Mississippi Rifle Club and the South Carolina Red Shirts. The last Radical Republican regimes ended, however, after the elections of 1876, and the return of the old White political elite further undermined the country's commitment to Congressional Reconstruction.

The Supreme Court

Key rulings by the U.S. Supreme Court further eroded Congressional Reconstruction. The **Slaughterhouse Cases** (1873) limited the "privileges or immunities" of U.S. citizenship as outlined in the Fourteenth Amendment.

In 1869, the Louisiana legislature had granted the New Orleans livestock slaughtering business to a single company as a means of protecting public health. Competing butchers sued the state, arguing that the monopoly violated their "privileges" as U.S. citizens under the Fourteenth Amendment and deprived them of property without due process of law.

In a 5–4 decision, the Court ruled that the monopoly did not violate the Fourteenth Amendment because its "privileges and immunities" clause applied only to U.S. citizenship, not state citizenship. States, in other words, retained legal jurisdiction over their citizens, and federal protection of civil rights did not extend to the property rights of businesses.

Dissenting Justice Stephen J. Field argued that the Court's ruling rendered the Fourteenth Amendment a "vain and idle enactment" with little scope or authority. By designating the rights of state citizens as being beyond the jurisdiction of federal law, the Slaughterhouse Cases opened the door for states to discriminate against African Americans.

Three years later, in *United States v. Cruikshank* (1876), the Supreme Court further eroded the protections of individuals by overturning the convictions of William Cruikshank and two other White men who had led the Colfax Massacre. In doing so, the Court argued that the equal protection and due process clauses in the Fourteenth Amendment governed only state actions, not the behavior of individuals. The decision struck down the Enforcement Acts, ruling that the states, not the federal government, were responsible for protecting citizens from attack by other private citizens.

Taken together, the Slaughterhouse and Cruikshank cases so gutted the Fourteenth Amendment that freedpeople were left even more vulnerable to violence and discrimination. The federal government was effectively abandoning its role in enforcing Reconstruction as Northerners shifted their attention to corruption in Washington, D.C.

> Supreme Court limits federal enforcement of Reconstruction measures

Slaughterhouse Cases (1873)
A pivotal Supreme Court decision that limited the "privileges and immunities" secured by the Fourteenth Amendment and thus eroded the federal government's power to protect the citizenship rights of Black Southerners.

Seeking Restitution

After the Civil War, some resolute formerly enslaved people fought to be compensated for their years of forced labor. Henrietta Wood was one of them. She had grown up enslaved on a northern Kentucky plantation and was separated from her mother and sold several times before being legally freed in Ohio in 1848; she then worked at a boarding house, cleaning rooms. One day in 1853 the house owner, Rebecca Boyd, took her on a carriage ride to Kentucky. "I have some friends to see, and we can get back in time for supper," she assured Henrietta. Yet as they left the ferry on the Kentucky side of the river, Boyd handed her over to a slave trader who sold her to a Mississippi planter.

Eventually, Wood ended up enslaved on a Texas plantation so isolated that she did not learn of the Union victory in the Civil War until months after Robert E. Lee's surrender. Once freed, Wood returned in 1869 to Cincinnati with her young son, Arthur.

In 1870, a determined Henrietta Wood took slave trader Zebulon Ward to federal court in Cincinnati, arguing that she should be reimbursed $20,000 for the wages she had earned but never received after he re-enslaved and sold her. After numerous delays, a jury of twelve White men ruled in favor of Wood in 1878. The judge, a former slave owner himself, awarded her $2,500. It was the largest settlement of its kind, enabling her to buy a house and later send her son to college and law school. Wood's victory in court was the exception, but many other formerly enslaved people and their descendants also sought reparations for their unpaid labor when in bondage.

The Contested Election of 1876

President Grant wanted to run for an unprecedented third term in 1876, but many Republicans had lost confidence in his leadership. In the summer of 1875, he acknowledged the inevitable and announced that he would retire. The Republican convention then selected Ohio's favorite son, Rutherford B. Hayes, to succeed Grant.

Orphaned at birth and raised by a single mother, Hayes graduated first in his class at Kenyon College, then received a law degree from Harvard before becoming an anti-slavery attorney in Cincinnati. When the Civil War erupted, he joined the Union army and eventually reached the rank of major general; he was wounded four times. After the war, Hayes served three terms as governor of Ohio. His chief virtue was that, as a journalist put it, he was "obnoxious to no one."

The Democratic convention was uncharacteristically harmonious. On the second ballot, the nomination went to Samuel J. Tilden, a wealthy corporate lawyer and reform governor of New York.

The 1876 campaign avoided controversial issues. In the absence of strong ideological differences, Democrats highlighted the Republican scandals.

Republicans responded by repeatedly waving "the bloody shirt," linking the Democrats to secession, civil war, and the violence committed against Republicans in the South. As Robert G. Ingersoll, the most celebrated Republican public speaker of the time, insisted: "The man that assassinated Abraham Lincoln was a Democrat. . . . Soldiers, every scar you have on your heroic bodies was given you by a Democrat!"

Early returns pointed to a victory for Tilden. Nationwide, he outpolled Hayes by almost 300,000 votes, and by midnight following Election Day, Tilden had won 184 electoral votes, just 1 short of the total needed for victory. Republican activists realized that the election hinged on 19 disputed electoral votes from Florida, Louisiana, and South Carolina (see Map 15.2).

The Democrats needed only one of the challenged votes to claim victory; the Republicans needed all nineteen. All three states, however, were governed by Republicans who appointed the election boards, each of which reported narrow victories for Hayes. The Democrats challenged the results.

Weeks passed with no resolution. On January 29, 1877, Congress appointed an electoral commission to settle the dispute. On March 1, the commission voted 8–7 in favor of Hayes. The next day, the House of Representatives declared Hayes president by an electoral vote of 185–184.

Tilden decided not to protest the decision. His campaign manager explained that they preferred "four years of Hayes's administration to four years of civil war."

Hayes's victory hinged on the defection of key Southern Democrats, who, it turned out, had made secret deals with the Republicans. On February 26, prominent Ohio Republicans and powerful Southern Democrats had struck a private, unwritten bargain—the **Compromise of 1877**—at Wormley's Hotel in Washington, D.C. The Republicans had promised that if Hayes were named president, he would remove the last federal troops from the South.

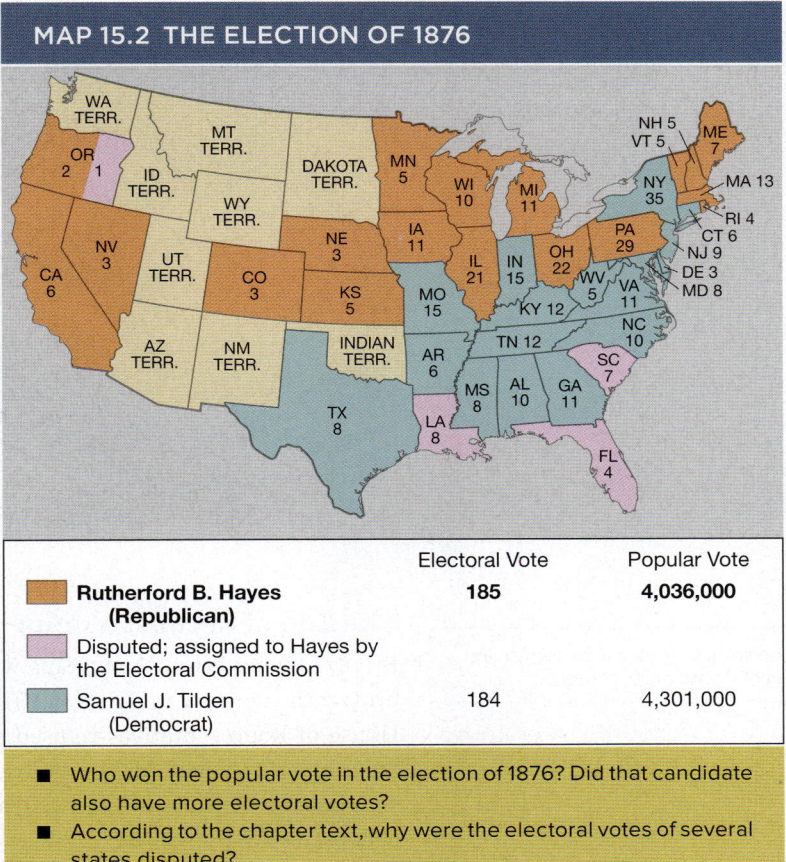

MAP 15.2 THE ELECTION OF 1876

	Electoral Vote	Popular Vote
Rutherford B. Hayes (Republican)	185	4,036,000
Disputed; assigned to Hayes by the Electoral Commission		
Samuel J. Tilden (Democrat)	184	4,301,000

- Who won the popular vote in the election of 1876? Did that candidate also have more electoral votes?
- According to the chapter text, why were the electoral votes of several states disputed?

Congress chooses Hayes; Tilden concedes

Compromise of 1877 A secret deal forged by congressional leaders to resolve the disputed election of 1876; Republican Rutherford B. Hayes, who had lost the popular vote, was declared the winner in exchange for his pledge to remove federal troops from the South, marking the end of Reconstruction.

COMPROMISE OF 1877 This illustration represents the unwritten compromise between Republicans and Southern Democrats that ended Radical Reconstruction.

> Federal troops withdrawn from civil rights enforcement

The End of Reconstruction

By 1877, many White Americans were no longer willing to pay the price to protect the newly won rights of African Americans. The Democrat-controlled House of Representatives refused to fund federal troops in the South after July, and President Hayes ordered U.S. soldiers in the South Carolina statehouse to return to their barracks. The state's Republican government collapsed soon thereafter.

In the congressional elections of 1878, Hayes admitted that the balloting in Southern states was corrupted by "violence of the most atrocious character," but he would not send federal troops again. The Democrats controlling the House went a step further and banned the use of federal troops to enforce civil rights in the former Confederacy. The news led a South Carolina African American citizen to dread his future. "I am an unprotected freedman. O God save the Colored People."

Without the sustained presence of federal troops, African Americans could not retain their newly won civil rights. New White Democratic state governments rewrote their constitutions, ousted the "carpetbaggers, scalawags, and blacks," and cut spending. As the years passed, White supremacists found various ways to prevent Black people from voting or holding office or even sharing the same railcar. State colleges and universities that had admitted Black students now reversed themselves. In short, the North had won the Civil War but lost the peace.

In an 1876 speech to the Republican National Convention, Frederick Douglass recognized that the party had won the Civil War, freed the enslaved, and passed amendments protecting their civil and voting rights. Yet, "what does it all amount to if the black man, after having been made free by the letter of your law, is unable to exercise that freedom . . . and is [again] to be subject to the slaveholder's shotgun?"

Overall, Reconstruction came to an end as the result of several factors. In the North, popular support for continuing the effort declined after the Panic of 1873, a major economic collapse that closed thousands of businesses and left millions unemployed. In the South, the election of White Democratic conservatives to state offices reversed the political gains made by Black Southerners. When Rutherford B. Hayes was elected president, the remaining federal troops in the South were withdrawn, ending Congressional Reconstruction altogether.

Reconstruction's Significance

For all its unfulfilled promises, Congressional Reconstruction did leave an enduring legacy—the Thirteenth, Fourteenth, and Fifteenth Amendments. Taken together, they represented a profound effort to extend the principle of personal and political equality to African Americans.

If Reconstruction's experiment in interracial democracy failed to provide true social equality or substantial economic opportunities for African Americans, it did create the essential constitutional foundation for future advances in the quest for equality and civil rights—and not just for African Americans, but for women and other minority groups.

Until the pivotal Reconstruction era, the states were responsible for protecting citizens' rights. Thereafter, thanks to the Fourteenth and Fifteenth Amendments, Black people had gained equal rights (in theory), and the federal government had assumed responsibility for ensuring that states treated them equally. A hundred years later, the cause of civil rights would finally be embraced again by the federal government. "With malice toward none, with charity for all, with firmness in the right," as Abraham Lincoln urged in his second inaugural address, "let us strive to finish the work we are in, to bind up a nation's wounds, to . . . cherish a just and lasting peace." His vision for a reconstructed America would retain its relevance to this day.

> **CORE OBJECTIVE**
> **5.** Explain the significance of Reconstruction to the nation's future.

Reviewing the
CORE OBJECTIVES

- **Reconstruction Challenges** With the defeat of the Confederacy and the passage of the Thirteenth Amendment, the federal government had to develop policies and procedures to address a number of difficult questions: What was the status of the defeated states, and how would they be reintegrated into the nation's political life? What would be the political status of the formerly enslaved people, and what would the federal government do to integrate them into the nation's social and economic fabric?

- **Reconstruction over Time** Abraham Lincoln and his successor, the Southerner Andrew Johnson, preferred the more lenient *Presidential Reconstruction Plan* for the states of the South. The *Freedmen's Bureau* attempted to educate and aid formerly enslaved people, negotiate labor contracts, and reunite families. Lincoln's assassination led Northerners to favor the *Radical Republicans*, who wanted a more radical plan designed to transform the South's society and economy. Southern Whites resisted and established *Black codes* to restrict the lives of formerly enslaved people. *Congressional Reconstruction* responded by stipulating that to reenter the Union, former Confederate states had to ratify the *Fourteenth* (1866) and *Fifteenth* (1870) *Amendments* to the U.S. Constitution to expand and protect the rights of African Americans.

- **Views of Reconstruction** Many formerly enslaved people found comfort in their families and the independent churches they established, but land ownership reverted to the old White elite, reducing newly freed Black farmers to *sharecropping*. African Americans enthusiastically participated in politics, with many Black men serving as elected officials. Along with White Southern Republicans (scalawags) and Northern carpetbaggers, they worked to rebuild the South's economy. Many White Southerners, however, blamed their own poverty on formerly enslaved people and Republicans, and they supported the *Ku Klux Klan*'s violent intimidation of the supporters of these Reconstruction efforts and the goal of "redemption," or White Democratic control of state governments in the South.

- **Political and Economic Developments and the End of Reconstruction** Scandals during the Grant administration involving an attempt to corner the gold market, plus the *Panic of 1873* and disagreement over whether to continue the use of *greenbacks* or return to the gold standard, eroded Northern support for Reconstruction. That same year, the Supreme Court began limiting the federal government's authority to protect citizenship rights in the *Slaughterhouse Cases*. Southern White Democrats were elected in 1874, successfully reversing the political progress of Republicans and Blacks. In the *Compromise of 1877*, Democrats agreed to the election of Republican Rutherford B. Hayes, who removed federal troops from the South.

- **The Significance of Reconstruction** Southern state governments quickly renewed long-standing patterns of discrimination against African Americans, but the Fourteenth and Fifteenth Amendments remained enshrined in the Constitution, creating the essential constitutional foundation for future advances in civil rights. These amendments give the federal government responsibility for ensuring equal treatment and political equality within the states, a role it would increasingly assume to this day.

KEY TERMS

Radical Republicans *p. 633*

Freedmen's Bureau *p. 633*

Presidential Reconstruction Plan *p. 638*

Black codes *p. 643*

Fourteenth Amendment (1866) *p. 644*

Congressional Reconstruction *p. 646*

Fifteenth Amendment (1870) *p. 648*

sharecropping *p. 654*

Ku Klux Klan *p. 656*

greenbacks *p. 663*

Panic of 1873 *p. 664*

Slaughterhouse Cases (1873) *p. 667*

Compromise of 1877 *p. 669*

CHRONOLOGY

1865 Congress establishes the Freedmen's Bureau
Lincoln is assassinated on April 14
Johnson issues Proclamation of Amnesty

1865–1866 All-White state legislatures in the South pass Black codes

1866 Ku Klux Klan is organized
Congress passes Civil Rights Act

1867 Congress passes Military Reconstruction Act
Freedmen begin participating in elections

1868 Fourteenth Amendment is ratified
Impeachment trial of President Andrew Johnson
Grant is elected president
Seven former Confederate states are readmitted to the Union

1869 Reestablishment of White Democratic rule in former Confederate states
President Grant creates Peace Policy related to Indigenous people

1870 Fifteenth Amendment is ratified
First Enforcement Acts are passed

1872 Grant wins reelection
Susan B. Anthony is arrested for voting
Victoria Woodhull runs for president

1873 Panic of 1873 triggers economic depression

1877 Compromise of 1877 ends Reconstruction

InQuizitive

Go to InQuizitive to see what you've learned—and learn what you've missed—with personalized feedback along the way.

THINKING LIKE A HISTORIAN

DEBATING Reconstruction's Demise

Understanding the causes of important events in American history is at the heart of the historian's work. Who, or what, was most responsible for bringing on significant moments of change? Historians often debate this question vigorously. Some point to multiple, long-term causes of a given event that involved the actions of many people. Others emphasize the role that one particular action, or even one person, can play in bringing about a significant moment in history. These different interpretations sometimes arise from conflicting information gathered from *primary sources*. Or historians may interpret previously examined sources in new ways by applying new methodologies and theories, or by being influenced by the values of their own society and times. For Part 4, *"A House Divided,"* the case study of debating Reconstruction's demise demonstrates how the views of historians can differ significantly on the basic question of *historical causation*.

For this exercise you have two tasks:

PART 1: Compare the two secondary sources on Reconstruction.

PART 2: Using primary sources, evaluate the arguments of the two secondary sources.

PART I Comparing and Contrasting Secondary Sources

Two *secondary sources*, the work of prominent historians who disagree about how and why Congressional (or Radical) Reconstruction ended, are included below for you to review. The first excerpt is from Eric Foner of Columbia University, whose *Reconstruction: America's Unfinished Revolution, 1863-1877*, originally published in 1988, has become a classic in the field. At the time he wrote it, Foner sought to highlight the achievements of Reconstruction—especially the advancement of citizenship rights for Black people—but he acknowledged its many problems that ultimately brought it to an end. More recently, Kidada E. Williams of Wayne State University, a leading scholar of African-American history and the author of *I Saw Death Coming: A History of Terror and Survival in the War Against Reconstruction* (2023), has placed focused attention on racial violence and on the role that White supremacists played in defeating Reconstruction.

Compare the work of these two historians by answering the following questions. Be sure to support your answers with specific examples drawn from the selections by Foner and Williams.

- Generally, how does each author portray the end of Reconstruction? What, or who, do they argue was the cause of Reconstruction's demise?
- What are the similarities in these two excerpts?
- Why does Foner refer to the end of Reconstruction as a "failure," while Williams calls it a "defeat"? What are the differences between these two characterizations of the period?

Secondary Source 1

Eric Foner, *Reconstruction: America's Unfinished Revolution*, 1988

Nonetheless, whether measured by the dreams inspired by emancipation or the more limited goals of securing blacks' rights as citizens and free laborers, and establishing an enduring Republican presence in the South, Reconstruction can only be judged a failure. Among the host of explanations for this outcome, a few seem especially significant. Events far beyond the control of Southern Republicans—the nature of the national credit and banking systems, the depression of the 1870s, the stagnation of world demand for cotton—severely limited the prospects for far-reaching economic change. The early rejection of federally sponsored land reform left in place a planter class far weaker and less affluent than before the war, but still able to bring its prestige and experience to bear against Reconstruction. Factionalism and corruption, although hardly confined to Southern Republicans, undermined their claim to legitimacy and made it difficult for them to respond effectively to attacks by resolute opponents. The failure to develop an effective long-term appeal to white voters made it increasingly difficult for Republicans to combat the racial politics of the Redeemers. None of these factors, however, would have proved decisive without the campaign of violence that turned the electoral tide in many parts of the South, and the weakening of Northern resolve, itself a consequence of social and political changes that undermined the free labor and egalitarian precepts at the heart of Reconstruction policy.

For historians, hindsight can be a treacherous ally. Enabling us to trace the hidden patterns of past events, it beguiles us with the mirage of inevitability, the assumption that different outcomes lay beyond the limits of the possible. . . . Yet one can, I think, imagine alternative scenarios and modest successes: the Republican party establishing itself as a permanent fixture on the Southern landscape, the North summoning the resolve to insist that the Constitution must be respected. . . .

Here, however, we enter the realm of the purely speculative. What remains certain is that Reconstruction failed, and that for blacks its failure was a disaster whose magnitude cannot be obscured by the genuine accomplishment that did endure.

Source: Foner, Eric. *Reconstruction: America's Unfinished Revolution*, 1863–1877. New York: Harper & Row, 1988, 603–604.

Secondary Source 2

Kidada E. Williams, *I Saw Death Coming: A History of Terror and Survival in the War against Reconstruction*, 2023

White men—like those who denied Edward Crosby his vote and rallied the Klan to punish him—mobilized around the belief that, although secessionists had surrendered the battlefield to United States forces, the war to maintain complete mastery over Black people was still on. . . .

But Confederates did not merely wait passively. Unable to reclaim political power legitimately through the ballot box and the statehouse, and unwilling to confront their individual Black adversaries man-to-man, right-wingers organized into a shadow army of paramilitary gangs and attacked African Americans directly, waging war against anyone who threatened white people's social, economic, or political power. Killing and maiming large numbers of enslaved people had been unprofitable, but doing the same to *free* Black people, especially those actively trying to act on their new rights and privileges, was, as one government agent surmised, "nobody's loss."[12]

Some Confederates' indifference to free Black people's lives was reflected in unremitting waves of extremist violence. Enslavers' refusal to release Black people from bondage rippled across the South. First they retaliated by maiming and killing Black people trying to escape or rescue their kin. Then came the raging torrent of assassinations of Black voters and officeholders. When that wasn't enough to keep men like Edward from the polls, extremists unleashed the tidal force of Klan strikes on Black southerners generally. Reporting on conditions in Texas in 1868, Secretary of War Edwin Stanton wrote that the killings of Black people were so common as to "render it impossible to keep an accurate account of them." . . .

African Americans' stories about this *other* war challenge the "failure" narrative of Reconstruction—that bold experiment that expanded freedom and democracy. Confederates and their sympathizers spun a mythic tale of white southerners needing to protect their honor after northerners placed them and their families under the thumb of ignorant and predatory Black men. This interpretation of Reconstruction formed the basis of racist "Lost Cause" ideology that justified the slaughter of thousands of Black southerners. It rationalized lynching and the establishment of the Jim Crow system, which restored many of the social, economic, and political relations of slavery. . . .

In recent years, other historians have unintentionally amplified the "Lost Cause" narrative by using the language of "failure" as a shorthand for what the historical records reveal: federal officials "failed" to aid freed people's hunger for self-sufficiency and self-determination, "failed" to redistribute land, "failed" to enforce Black people's civil and political rights, "failed" to punish whites who attacked and killed Black people. Government entities bear some responsibility for Reconstruction not living up to its promises, certainly. But this "failure" narrative erases the story Black Americans like Edward Crosby told about Reconstruction: it did not simply fail, white conservatives overthrew it.

Source: Williams, Kidada E. *I Saw Death Coming: A History of Terror and Survival in the War against Reconstruction*. New York: Bloomsbury, 2023, xvi–xxi.

PART II Using Primary Sources to Evaluate Secondary Sources

When historians are faced with competing interpretations of the past, they often look at primary source material as part of the process of evaluating the different arguments. In the following selections, you'll find *primary sources* relating to the period of Reconstruction.

Carefully read the primary sources and answer the following questions. Decide how the primary source documents support or refute Foner's and Williams's arguments about this period. You may find that some documents do both but for different parts of each historian's interpretation. Be sure to identify which specific components of each historian's argument the documents support or refute.

- What are the main problems of Reconstruction described in each of these primary source documents?

- Which of the two historians' arguments is best supported by the documents? If you find that both arguments are well supported by the evidence, why do you think the two historians produced such different interpretations?

- Based on your reading of the two arguments and the primary sources, what have you learned about the challenges involved in identifying historical causation?

Primary Source 1
Mississippi's Republican Governor Adelbert Ames to his wife, Blanche, September 5, 1875

JACKSON, MISS., *September* 5, 1875

DEAR BLANCHE: I had finished my letter to you yesterday and was looking for George to mail it when Capt. Fisher came to me out of breath and out of heart to tell me of a riot which had just taken place at Clinton . . .

There were present at a Republican barbecue about fifteen hundred colored people, men, women and children. Seeking the opportunity white men, fully prepared, fired into this crowd. Two women were reported killed, also two children. As the firing continued, the women ran away with the men in many instances, leaving their children on the ground. Today there are some forty carriages, wagons and carts which were abandoned by the colored people in their flight. Last night, this morning and today squads of white men are scouring the county killing Negroes. . . .

This is but in keeping with the programme of the Democracy at this time. They know we have a majority of some thirty thousand and to overcome it they are resorting to intimidation and murder. It is cold-blooded murder on the part of the "white liners"—but there are other cases exactly like this in other parts of the state. . . .

The "white liners" have gained their point—they have, by killing and wounding, so intimidated the poor Negroes that they can in all human probability prevail over them at the election. I shall at once try to get troops from the general government. Of course it will be a difficult thing to do.

Source: Adelbert Ames to Blanche, September 5, 1875, in *Chronicles from the Nineteenth Century: Family Letters of Blanche Butler and Adelbert Ames*. Vol. 2. Clinton, Mass., 1957, 163–164.

Primary Source 2
Committee of South Carolina Freedmen to President Andrew Johnson, 1865

Edisto Island S.C. Oct 28th 1865.

We the freedmen Of Edisto Island South Carolina have learned From you through Major General O O Howard commissioner of the Freedmans Bureau. with deep sorrow and Painful hearts of the possibility of goverment restoring These lands to the former owners. . . .

This is our home, we have made These lands what they are. we were the only true and Loyal people that were found in posession of these Lands. we have been always ready to strike for Liberty and humanity yea to fight if needs be To preserve this glorious union. Shall not we who Are freedman and have been always true to this Union have the same rights as are enjoyed by others? Have we broken any Law of these United States? Have we forfieted our rights of property In Land?— If not then! are not our rights as A free people and good citizens of these United States To be considered before the rights of those who were Found in rebellion against this good and just Goverment . . .

We are ready to pay for this land When Government calls for it. and now after What has been done will the good and just government take from us all this right and make us Subject to the will of those who have cheated and Oppressed us for many years God Forbid! We the freedmen of this Island and of the State of South Carolina—Do therefore petition to you as the President of these United States, that some provisions be made by which Every colored man can purchase land. and Hold it as his own. . . .

In behalf of the Freedmen Committee
Henry Bram.
Ishmael. Moultrie.
yates. Sampson.

676

Source: Henry Bram et al., to the President of the United States, October 28, 1865, in Steven Hahn et al., *Freedom: A Documentary History of Emancipation*, 1861–1867, Series 3, Vol. I: Land and Labor, 1865. Chapel Hill: UNC Press, 2008, 442–444.

Primary Source 3
Testimony Before Congress by R. B. Avery, Northern White Carpetbagger, 1880

WASHINGTON, *Wednesday, March* 17, 1880.

TESTIMONY OF R. B. AVERY.

Q. What is the condition of the colored people as to the comforts of living and their prosperity generally —A. I had occasion to investigate the claims of a large number of colored men in Liberty County, in Georgia. I do not say that what I saw was a fair average, but I went to the homes of perhaps one hundred and fifty different men. In all of these houses I found but two chairs—just two chairs in all of them. I do not mean two in each house, but two in all of the one hundred and fifty houses. I honestly believe that I could have put every solitary thing in sight in those houses and in and around those cabins—except the dogs—in six-mule wagon. I thought I had seen poverty in the great cities of the country and elsewhere, but I never saw anything to compare with the poverty of those negroes there. Those negroes are generally engaged in working a little rice patch and a little corn, and I found but one of them that had any horses.

Q. What were these claims for which you were investigating?—A. The claims of the colored people were for property taken in 1865. They had more in 1865 than they have had since, and I think their claims amounted to more than the entire value of the whole county now.

Q. What do they live on?—A. They live on a little rice and things of that sort, and they have their dogs with which to catch "varmints," as they call it.

Source: Testimony of R. B. Avery, March 17, 1880, Report and Testimony of the Select Committee of the U.S. Senate to Investigate the Causes of the Removal of the Negroes from the Southern States to the Northern States, Part II, 46th Congress, 2nd Session, Report 693 Pt. 2. Washington: Government Printing Office, 1880, 260–261.

Primary Source 4
Testimony Before Congress by Charlotte Fowler, South Carolina Freedwoman, 1871

SPARTANBURGH, SOUTH CAROLINA, *July* 6, 1871.

CHARLOTTE FOWLER (colored) sworn and examined....

Question. How long ago is it since your husband was killed?
Answer. It was the 1st of May.
Question. What was his name?
Answer. Wallace Fowler....
Question. How many men did you see?
Answer. I saw only one man with a mask.
Question. Which one shot Wallace?
Answer. The man with the mask.
Question. From the time they first knocked at the door until they shot was a very short time?
Answer. Yes, sir; but a very few minutes.
Question. Nothing was said but "God damn you."
Answer. Nothing; but they grabbed him, and said, "God damn you; I have got you now;" and said, " Don't you run;" and took him out, and then I heard the crack.
Question. Did you know the man who had the mask?
Answer. No, sir ...

By Mr. STEVENSON:
Question. What are these men called that go about masked in that way?
Answer. I don't know; they call them Ku-Klux.
Question. How long have they been going about in that neighborhood?
Answer. I don't know how long; they have been going a long time, but they never pestered the plantation until that night. I have heard of Ku-Klux, but they never pestered Mr. Jones before.
Question. Did your old man belong to any party?
Answer. Yes, sir.
Question. What party?
Answer. The radicals.
Question. How long had he belonged to them?
Answer. Ever since they started the voting.
Question. Was he a pretty strong radical?
Answer. Yes, sir; a pretty strong radical.
Question. Did he work for that party?
Answer. Yes, sir.
Question. What did he do?
Answer. He held up for it, and said be never would turn against the United States for anybody, as the democrats wanted him to.
Question. Did he talk to the other colored people about it?
Answer. No, sir; he never said nothing much. He was a man that never said much but just what he was going to do. He never traveled any where to visit people only when they had a meeting; then he would go there to the radical meetings, but would come back home again.
Question. Did he make speeches at those meetings?
Answer. No, sir.
Question. Did they make him president of their meetings?

Answer. I don't know about that.

Question. Did you ever go with him?

Answer. No, sir.

Question. Did they ever make him president or vice-president, or put him upon the platform?

Answer. No, sir. Several, I heard, went there and did, but he never undertook such a thing. He would go to hear what the best of them had to say, but he never did anything.

By the CHAIRMAN:

Question. Are the colored people afraid of these people that go masked?

Answer. Yes, sir; they are as 'fraid as death of them. There is now a whole procession of people that have left their houses and are lying out. You see the old man was so old, and he did no harm to anybody; he didn't believe anybody would trouble him.

By Mr. STEVENSON:

Question. Did he vote at the last election?

Answer. Yes, sir.

Source: Testimony of Charlotte Fowler, July 10, 1871, Report of the Joint Select Committee Appointed to Inquire into the Condition of Affairs in the Late Insurrectionary States Vol. 1, South Carolina (Washington: Government Printing Office, 1872), 386–392.

Glossary

abolitionism A movement that called for an immediate end to slavery throughout the United States.

affirmative action Programs designed to give preferential treatment to women and people of color as compensation for past injustices and to counterbalance systemic inequalities.

Affordable Care Act (ACA) (2010) A vast health-care-reform initiative championed by President Obama, and widely criticized by Republicans, that aimed to make health insurance more affordable and make health care accessible to everyone, regardless of income or prior medical conditions.

Agricultural Adjustment Act (1933) Legislation passed during the Great Depression that paid farmers to produce less in order to raise crop prices for all; the AAA was later declared unconstitutional by the U.S. Supreme Court in the case of *United States v. Butler* (1936).

Albany Plan of Union (1754) A failed proposal by the seven northern colonies in anticipation of the French and Indian War, urging the unification of the colonies under one Crown-appointed president.

Alien and Sedition Acts of 1798 Four measures passed during the undeclared war with France that limited the freedoms of speech and press and restricted the liberty of immigrants.

American Anti-Imperialist League A coalition of anti-imperialist groups that united in 1899 to protest American territorial expansion, especially in the Philippine Islands; its membership included prominent politicians, industrialists, labor leaders, and social reformers.

American Colonization Society (ACS) Established in 1816, an organization whose mission was to send freed, formerly enslaved people to Africa.

American Federation of Labor Founded in 1886, a national federation of trade unions made up of skilled workers.

American System The economic plan championed by Henry Clay of Kentucky that called for federal tariffs on imports, a strong national bank, and federally financed internal improvements—roads, bridges, canals—all intended to strengthen the national economy and end American economic dependence on Great Britain.

American Tobacco Company A business founded in 1890 by North Carolina's James Buchanan Duke, who combined the major tobacco manufacturers of the time, controlling 90 percent of the country's booming cigarette production.

Anaconda Plan During the Civil War, the Union's primary strategy calling for a naval blockade of major Southern seaports and then dividing the Confederacy by gaining control of the Tennessee, Cumberland, and Mississippi Rivers.

anti-Federalists Opponents of the Constitution as an infringement on individual and states' rights, whose criticism led to the addition of a Bill of Rights to the document. Many anti-Federalists later joined Thomas Jefferson's Democratic-Republican Party.

Appomattox Court House The Virginia village where Confederate general Robert E. Lee surrendered to Union general Ulysses S. Grant on April 9, 1865.

Articles of Confederation The first form of government for the United States, ratified by the original thirteen states in 1781; weak in central authority, it was replaced by the U.S. Constitution drafted in 1787.

Atlanta Compromise (1895) A speech by Booker T. Washington that called for the Black community to strive for economic prosperity before demanding political and social equality.

Atlantic Charter (1941) The joint statement crafted by Franklin D. Roosevelt and British prime minister Winston Churchill that listed the war goals of the Allied Powers.

Axis alliance A military alliance formed in 1937 by the three major fascist powers: Germany, Italy, and Japan.

baby boom A markedly high birth rate in the years following World War II, leading to the biggest demographic "bubble" in U.S. history.

Bacon's Rebellion (1676) An unsuccessful revolt led by planter Nathaniel Bacon against Virginia governor William Berkeley's administration, which, Bacon charged, had failed to protect settlers from raids by Indigenous Americans.

Bank of the United States The national bank, founded in 1791, responsible for holding and transferring federal government funds, making business loans, and issuing a national currency.

Bank War The political struggle in the early 1830s between President Jackson and financier Nicholas Biddle over the renewing of the Second Bank's charter.

Barbary pirates North Africans who waged war (1801–1805) on the United States after President Jefferson refused to pay tribute (a bribe) to protect American ships.

Battle of Antietam (1862) A turning-point battle near Sharpsburg, Maryland, leaving almost 25,000 soldiers dead or wounded, in which Union forces halted a Confederate invasion of the North.

Battle of Gettysburg (1863) A monumental three-day battle in southern Pennsylvania, widely considered a turning point in the Civil War, in which Union forces defeated Lee's Confederate army and forced it back into Virginia.

Battle of Midway (1942) A 1942 battle that proved to be the turning point in the Pacific front during World War II; it was the Japanese navy's first major defeat in 350 years.

Battle of New Orleans (1814–1815) The final major battle in the War of 1812 in which the Americans under General Andrew Jackson unexpectedly and decisively countered the British attempt to seize the port of New Orleans, Louisiana.

Battle of Tippecanoe (1811) A battle in northern Indiana between U.S. troops and Indigenous American warriors led by the prophet Tenskwatawa, the half-brother of Tecumseh.

Battle of Trenton (1776) The first decisive American victory in the Revolutionary War that proved pivotal in reviving morale and demonstrating General Washington's abilities.

Battle of Vicksburg (1863) A protracted battle in northern Mississippi in which Union forces under Ulysses S. Grant besieged the last major Confederate fortress on the Mississippi River, forcing the inhabitants into starvation and then submission on July 4, 1863.

Battle of Yorktown (1781) The last major battle of the Revolutionary War; General Cornwallis, along with over 7,000 British troops, surrendered to George Washington at Yorktown, Virginia, on October 17, 1781.

Battles of Saratoga (1777) The decisive defeat of almost 6,000 British troops under General John Burgoyne in several battles near Saratoga, New York, in October 1777; the American victory helped convince France to enter the war on the side of the Patriots.

Bay of Pigs (1961) A failed CIA operation that deployed Cuban rebels to overthrow Fidel Castro's Communist regime.

Beats A group of bohemian writers, artists, and musicians who flouted convention in favor of liberated forms of self-expression.

Berlin airlift (1948–1949) The effort by the United States and Great Britain to fly massive amounts of food and supplies into West Berlin in response to the Soviet land blockade of the city.

Berlin Wall The twenty-seven-mile-long concrete wall constructed in 1961 by East German authorities to stop the flow of East Germans fleeing to West Berlin.

Bill of Rights (1791) The first ten amendments to the U.S. Constitution, adopted in 1791 to guarantee individual rights and to help secure ratification of the Constitution by the states.

birth rate The proportion of births per 1,000 of the total population.

Black codes Laws passed in southern states to restrict the rights of formerly enslaved people.

Black Lives Matter (BLM) A sociopolitical movement in protest of police brutality toward Black people, with origins in Missouri and a growing global presence.

Black Power movement A militant form of civil rights protest focused on urban communities in the North that emerged as a response to impatience with the nonviolent tactics of Martin Luther King Jr.

Bleeding Kansas (1856) Journalists' name for a series of violent conflicts in the Kansas Territory between anti-slavery and pro-slavery factions over the status of slavery.

blitzkrieg The German "lightning war" strategy characterized by swift, well-organized attacks using infantry, tanks, and warplanes.

bonanza farms Large-scale-operation farms owned by companies and established in the western United States during the late nineteenth century to provide food to major cities.

Bonus Expeditionary Force (1932) A protest march on Washington, D.C., in 1932 by thousands of military veterans and their families, calling for immediate payment of their service bonus certificates; violence ensued when President Herbert Hoover ordered their tent villages cleared.

Boston Massacre (1770) A violent confrontation between British soldiers and a Boston mob on March 5, 1770, in which five colonists were killed.

Boston Tea Party (1773) A demonstration against the Tea Act of 1773 in which the Sons of Liberty, dressed as Native Americans, dumped hundreds of chests of British-owned tea into Boston Harbor.

bracero program The system that permitted seasonal farmworkers from Mexico to work in the United States on yearlong contracts.

***Brown v. Board of Education* (1954)** The landmark Supreme Court case that struck down racial segregation in public schools and declared "separate but equal" unconstitutional.

Bush Doctrine A national security policy initiated in 2002 by which the Bush administration claimed the right to launch preemptive military attacks against perceived enemies, particularly outlaw nations or terrorist organizations believed to possess weapons of mass destruction (WMD).

Cahokia The largest chiefdom of the Mississippian Indigenous culture located in what is present-day Illinois and the site of a sophisticated farming settlement that supported up to 15,000 inhabitants.

California gold rush (1849) A massive migration of gold hunters, mostly young men, who transformed the national economy after extensive amounts of gold were discovered in northern California.

campaign of 1828 The bitter presidential contest between Democrat Andrew Jackson and National Republican John Quincy Adams (running for reelection), resulting in Jackson's victory.

Camp David Accords (1978) The peace agreement facilitated by President Carter between Prime Minister Menachem Begin of Israel and President Anwar el-Sadat of Egypt, the first Arab head of state to officially recognize the state of Israel.

Carnegie Steel Company A corporation under the leadership of Andrew Carnegie that came to dominate the American steel industry.

Central Intelligence Agency (CIA) An intelligence-gathering government agency founded in 1947; under President Eisenhower's orders, it secretly undermined elected governments deemed susceptible to communism.

ceremonial mounds A funereal tradition, practiced in the Mississippi and Ohio valleys by the Adena-Hopewell cultures, of erecting massive mounds of earth over graves, often shaped in the designs of serpents and other animals.

chattel slavery The system of slavery that considered people a legal form of movable property. This type of enslavement included being bought and sold and forced to perform unpaid labor for life. Chattel slavery is most associated with slavery in the Americas and people of African descent.

Chicago Democratic National Convention (1968) The presidential convention in 1968 where the social unrest over the Vietnam War and civil rights movement came to a violent head between student protesters and the Chicago police. Hubert H. Humphrey was ultimately nominated as the presidential candidate for the Democratic Party.

Chinese Exclusion Act (1882) A federal law that barred Chinese laborers from immigrating to America.

Christian Right Christian conservatives with a faith-based political agenda that includes prohibiting abortion and allowing prayer in public schools.

citizen-soldiers Part-time non-professional soldiers, mostly poor farmers or recent immigrants who had been indentured servants, who played an important role in the Revolutionary War.

Civil Rights Act of 1964 Legislation that outlawed discrimination in public accommodations and employment, passed at the urging of President Lyndon B. Johnson.

civil service reform An extended effort led by political reformers to end the patronage system; the reform led to the Pendleton Act (1883), which called for government jobs to be awarded based on merit rather than party loyalty.

Clayton Anti-Trust Act (1914) Legislation that served to enhance the Sherman Anti-Trust Act (1890) by clarifying what constituted "monopolistic" activities and declaring that labor unions were not to be viewed as "monopolies in restraint of trade."

clipper ships Tall, slender ships favored over older merchant ships for their speed; they ultimately gave way to steamships because clipper ships lacked cargo space.

Coercive Acts (1774) Four parliamentary measures that required the colonies to pay for damages caused by the Boston Tea Party. The Acts closed the port of Boston, imposed a military government, disallowed colonial trials of British soldiers, and forced the quartering of troops in private homes.

Columbian Exchange The transfer of biological and social elements, such as plants, animals, people, diseases, and cultural practices, among Europe, the Americas, and Africa in the wake of Christopher Columbus's voyages to the Americas.

Comanche A Native American nomadic tribe from the southern Plains of North America. Comanche people today belong to the federally recognized Comanche Nation.

Committee of Correspondence A group of Boston colonists organized by Samuel Adams to address American grievances, assert American rights, and form a network of rebellion.

***Common Sense* (1776)** A popular pamphlet written by Thomas Paine attacking British principles of hereditary rule and monarchical government and advocating a declaration of American independence.

Compromise of 1850 A package of five bills presented to Congress by Henry Clay intended to avoid secession or civil war by reducing tensions between North and South over the status of slavery.

Compromise of 1877 A secret deal forged by congressional leaders to resolve the disputed election of 1876; Republican Rutherford B. Hayes, who had lost the popular vote, was declared the winner in exchange for his pledge to remove federal troops from the South, marking the end of Reconstruction.

Comstock Lode A mine in eastern Nevada acquired by Canadian fur trapper Henry Comstock that between 1860 and 1880 yielded almost $1 billion worth of gold and silver.

Congressional Reconstruction A phase of Reconstruction directed by Radical Republicans in Congress and based on the Military Reconstruction Act; primary goal was to protect citizenship rights of freed people.

conquistadores A term from the Spanish word for "conquerors," applied to Spanish and Portuguese soldiers who conquered lands held by Indigenous peoples in central and southern America as well as in the area that became the current states of Texas, New Mexico, Arizona, and California.

consumer culture A society in which mass production and consumption of nationally advertised products comes to dictate much of social life and status.

containment A U.S. Cold War strategy to exert political, economic, and, if necessary, military pressure on global Soviet expansion as a means of combating the spread of communism.

Continental Army The army authorized by the Continental Congress, 1755–1784, to fight the British; commanded by George Washington.

contrabands During the Civil War, freedom seekers who sought refuge in Union military camps or who lived in areas of the Confederacy under Union control.

Contract with America (1994) A list of conservative promises in response to the supposed liberalism of the Clinton administration; drafted by Speaker of the House Newt Gingrich and other congressional Republicans as a campaign tactic for the 1994 midterm elections.

"corrupt bargain" The scandal in which presidential candidate and Speaker of the House Henry Clay secured John Quincy Adams's victory over Andrew Jackson in the 1824 election, supposedly in exchange for naming Clay secretary of state.

cotton White fibers harvested from plants that made comfortable, easy-to-clean products, especially clothing; the most valuable cash crop driving the economy in nineteenth-century United States and Great Britain.

cotton gin A hand-operated machine invented by Eli Whitney that quickly removed seeds from cotton bolls, enabling the mass production of cotton in nineteenth-century America.

cotton kingdom The cotton-producing region, relying predominantly on slave labor, that extended from North Carolina west to Louisiana and reached as far north as southern Illinois.

counterculture The unorganized youth rebellion of the 1960s against mainstream institutions, values, and behavior that more often focused on cultural radicalism rather than on political activism.

COVID-19 pandemic The global pandemic resulting from the airborne and contagious coronavirus disease that took millions of lives, debilitated governments and institutions, and necessitated new cultural norms of social distancing and face masking.

crime bill (1994) The largest crime bill in the history of the United States credited with reducing overall crime, while creating the problem of mass incarceration.

Cuban missile crisis (1962) A thirteen-day U.S.-Soviet standoff sparked by the discovery of Soviet missile sites in Cuba; the closest the world has come to nuclear war since 1945.

cult of domesticity A pervasive nineteenth-century ideology urging women to celebrate their role as manager of the household and nurturer of the children.

***Dartmouth College v. Woodward* (1819)** The Supreme Court ruling that expanded the definition of *contract* to put corporations beyond the reach of the states that chartered them.

Daughters of Liberty Colonial women who protested the British government's tax policies by boycotting British products, such as clothing, and who wove their own fabric, or "homespun."

Dawes Severalty Act of 1887 Federal legislation that divided ancestral Indigenous American lands among the heads of each family in an attempt to "Americanize" Indigenous people by forcing them to become farmers working individual plots of land.

death rate The proportion of deaths per 1,000 of the total population; also called the *mortality rate*.

Declaration of Independence (1776) The formal statement, principally drafted by Thomas Jefferson and adopted by the Second Continental Congress on July 4, 1776, that officially announced the thirteen colonies' break with Great Britain.

Declaration of Rights and Sentiments (1848) A document based on the Declaration of Independence that called for gender equality, written primarily by Elizabeth Cady Stanton and signed by Seneca Falls Convention delegates.

détente A period of improving relations between the United States and Communist nations, particularly China and the Soviet Union, during the Nixon administration.

Deists Those who applied Enlightenment thought to religion, emphasizing reason, morality, and natural law rather than scriptural authority or an ever-present god intervening in the daily life of humans.

de Lôme letter (1898) Private correspondence written by the Spanish ambassador to the United States, Depuy de Lôme, that described President McKinley as "weak"; the letter was stolen by Cuban revolutionaries and published in the *New York Journal* in 1898, deepening American resentment of Spain and moving the two countries closer to war in Cuba.

Dien Bien Phu A cluster of Vietnamese villages and the site of a major Vietnamese victory over the French in the First Indochina War.

Distribution Act (1836) A law requiring distribution of the federal budget surplus to the states, creating chaos among unregulated state banks dependent on such federal funds.

Dixiecrats A breakaway faction of White southern Democrats who defected from the national Democratic Party in 1948 to protest the party's increased support for Black civil rights and to nominate their own segregationist candidates for elective office.

***Dobbs v. Jackson Women's Health Organization* (2022)** The ruling by a 6–3 conservative majority on the Supreme Court that overturned *Roe v. Wade* (1973), returning to individual states the right to determine abortion access.

dollar diplomacy The practice advocated by President Theodore Roosevelt in which the U.S. government fostered American investments in less developed nations and then used U.S. military force to protect those investments.

Dred Scott v. Sandford **(1857)** The U.S. Supreme Court ruling that enslaved people were not U.S. citizens and that Congress could not prohibit slavery in the territories.

Dust Bowl A vast area of the Midwest where windstorms blew away millions of tons of topsoil from parched farmland after a long drought in the 1930s, causing great social distress and a massive migration of farm families.

Eastern Woodland peoples Various Native American societies, particularly the Algonquian, Iroquoian, and Muskogean regional groups, who once dominated the Atlantic seaboard from Maine to Louisiana.

Economic Opportunity Act of 1964 Key legislation in President Johnson's War on Poverty that created the Office of Economic Opportunity and programs like Head Start and the work-study financial-aid program for low-income college students.

election of 1800 The presidential election involving Thomas Jefferson and John Adams that resulted in the first Democratic-Republican victory after the Federalist administrations of George Washington and John Adams.

election of 1864 Abraham Lincoln's successful reelection campaign capitalizing on Union military successes in Georgia to defeat his Democratic opponent, former general George B. McClellan, who ran on a peace platform.

Electoral College (1787) An electoral system established in Article II, Section I, of the U.S. Constitution to determine the presidential and vice-presidential selection process. Presidential candidates must win the majority of electoral votes in order to secure the presidency.

Emancipation Proclamation (1863) The military order issued by President Abraham Lincoln that freed enslaved people in areas still controlled by the Confederacy.

Embargo Act (1807) A law promoted by President Thomas Jefferson prohibiting American ships from leaving for foreign ports, in order to safeguard them from British and French attacks. This ban on American exports proved disastrous to the U.S. economy.

encomienda A land-grant system under which Spanish army officers (*conquistadores*) were awarded large parcels of land taken from Indigenous Americans.

Enlightenment A revolution in thought begun in Europe in the seventeenth century that emphasized reason and science over the authority and myths of traditional religion.

Environmental Protection Agency (EPA) A federal environmental agency created by President Nixon to appease the demands of congressional Democrats for a federal environmental watchdog agency.

Erie Canal (1825) The most important and profitable of the many barge canals built in the early nineteenth century, connecting the Great Lakes to the Hudson River and making New York City the nation's largest port.

ethnic cleansing The systematic removal of an ethnic group from a territory through violence or intimidation in order to create a homogeneous society; the term was popularized by the Yugoslav policy brutally targeting Albanian Muslims in Kosovo.

Exodusters African Americans who migrated west from the South in search of a haven from racism and poverty after the collapse of Radical Republican rule.

Fair Deal (1949) President Truman's proposals to build upon the New Deal with national health insurance, the repeal of the Taft-Hartley Act, new civil rights legislation, and other initiatives; most were rejected by the Republican-controlled Congress.

"falling-domino" theory The theory that if one country fell to communism, its neighboring countries would necessarily follow suit.

Farmers' Alliances Like the Granger movement, these organizations sought to address the issues of small farming communities; however, Alliances emphasized more political action and called for the creation of a third party to advocate for their concerns.

fascism A radical form of totalitarian government that emerged in 1920s Italy and Germany in which a dictator uses propaganda and brute force to seize control of all aspects of national life.

Federal Deposit Insurance Corporation (FDIC) (1933) An independent government agency, established to prevent bank panics, that guarantees the safety of deposits in citizens' savings accounts.

Federal Reserve Act (1913) Legislation passed by Congress to create a new national banking system in order to regulate the nation's currency supply and ensure the stability and integrity of member banks that made up the Federal Reserve System across the nation.

Federal Trade Commission (FTC) (1914) An independent agency created by the Wilson administration that replaced the Bureau of Corporations as an even more powerful tool to combat unfair trade practices and monopolies.

Federal-Aid Highway Act (1956) The largest federal project in U.S. history, the act created a national network of interstate highways.

federalism The concept of dividing governmental authority between the national government and the states.

The Federalist Papers A collection of eighty-five essays, published widely in newspapers in 1787 and 1788, written by Alexander Hamilton, James Madison, and John Jay in support of adopting the proposed U.S. Constitution.

field hands Enslaved people who toiled in the cotton or cane fields in organized work gangs.

Fifteenth Amendment (1870) An amendment to the U.S. Constitution forbidding states to deny any male citizen the right to vote on grounds of "race, color or previous condition of servitude."

First New Deal (1933–1935) Franklin D. Roosevelt's ambitious first-term cluster of economic and social programs designed to combat the Great Depression.

First Red Scare Outbreak of anti-Communist hysteria that included the arrest without warrants of thousands of suspected radicals, most of whom (especially Russian immigrants) were deported.

flappers Young women of the 1920s whose rebellion against prewar standards of femininity included wearing shorter dresses, bobbing their hair, dancing to jazz music, driving cars, smoking cigarettes, and indulging in illegal drinking and gambling.

Force Bill (1833) Legislation, sparked by the nullification crisis in South Carolina, that authorized the president's use of the army to compel states to comply with federal law.

Fourteen Points President Woodrow Wilson's proposed plan for the peace agreement after the Great War, which included the creation of a "league" of nations intended to keep the peace.

Fourteenth Amendment (1866) An amendment to the U.S. Constitution guaranteeing equal protection under the law to all U.S. citizens, including formerly enslaved people.

Freedmen's Bureau A federal Reconstruction agency established to protect the legal rights of formerly enslaved people and to assist with their education, jobs, health care, and land ownership.

Freedom Riders Activists who, beginning in 1961, traveled by bus through the South to test federal court rulings that banned segregation on buses and trains.

Free-Soil Party A political coalition created in 1848 that opposed the expansion of slavery into the new western territories.

French and Indian War (Seven Years' War) (1756–1763) The last and most important of four colonial wars between England and France for control of lands in North America east of the Mississippi River.

French Revolution (1789–1799) The revolutionary movement beginning in 1789 that overthrew the monarchy and transformed France into an unstable republic before Napoléon Bonaparte assumed power in 1799.

frontier revivals A religious revival movement within the Second Great Awakening that took place in frontier churches in western territories and states in the early nineteenth century.

Fugitive Slave Act (1850) A part of the Compromise of 1850 that authorized federal officials to help capture and then return freedom seekers to their owners without trials.

fundamentalism A movement in American Christianity that began in the early twentieth century in opposition to theological liberalism. Its followers believed in the literal truth of the Bible and embraced a return to strict Christian orthodoxy.

genocide The deliberate killing of a large number of people from a particular nation or ethnic group with the aim of destroying that nation or group.

Ghost Dance movement A spiritual and political movement among Indigenous people whose followers performed a ceremonial "ghost dance" intended to connect the living with the dead and make the Indigenous people bulletproof in battles seeking to restore their homelands.

***Gibbons v. Ogden* (1824)** The Supreme Court case that gave the federal government the power to regulate interstate commerce.

GI Bill of Rights (1944) Legislation that provided unemployment, educational, and financial benefits for World War II veterans to ease their transition back to the civilian world.

Gilded Age An era of dramatic industrial and urban growth characterized by widespread political corruption and loose government oversight of corporations.

glasnost The Russian term for "openness"; applied to the loosening of censorship in the Soviet Union under Mikhail Gorbachev.

globalization An important and controversial transformation of the world economy led by the growing number of multinational companies and the Internet, whereby an international marketplace for goods and services was created.

Glorious Revolution (1688) A successful coup, instigated by a group of English aristocrats, that overthrew King James II and instated William of Orange and Mary, his English wife, to the English throne.

Granger movement A movement that began by offering social and educational activities for isolated farmers and their families and later promoted "cooperatives" in which farmers could join together to buy, store, and sell their crops to avoid the high fees charged by brokers and other middlemen.

Great Awakening An emotional religious revival movement that swept through the thirteen colonies from the 1730s through the 1740s.

Great Depression (1929–1941) The worst economic downturn in American history; it was spurred by the stock market crash in the fall of 1929 and lasted until World War II.

Great Migration Mass exodus of African Americans from the rural South to the Northeast and Midwest during and after the Great War.

Great Recession (2007–2009) A massive, prolonged economic downturn sparked by the collapse of the housing market and the financial institutions holding unpaid mortgages; resulted in 9 million Americans losing their jobs.

Great Sioux War A conflict between Sioux and Cheyenne warriors and federal troops over lands in the Dakotas in the mid-1870s.

Great Society A term coined by President Lyndon B. Johnson in his 1965 State of the Union address, in which he proposed legislation to address problems of voting rights, poverty, diseases, education, immigration, and the environment.

greenbacks Paper money issued during the Civil War that sparked currency debates after the war.

Haitian Revolution (1791–1804) A slave rebellion on the Caribbean island of Saint-Domingue, a French colony, led by Toussaint L'Ouverture. Renamed the Republic of Haiti by the revolutionaries, it won independence from France and became the first independent Black nation.

Harlem Renaissance The nation's first self-conscious Black literary and artistic movement; centered in New York City's Harlem district, which had a largely Black population in the wake of the Great Migration from the South.

Hartford Convention (1814–1815) A series of secret meetings in December 1814 and January 1815 at which New England Federalists protested American involvement in the War of 1812 and discussed several constitutional amendments, including limiting each president to one term, designed to weaken the dominant Republican Party.

Haymarket Riot (1886) A violent uprising in Haymarket Square, Chicago, at which police clashed with labor demonstrators in the aftermath of a bombing.

headright A land-grant policy that promised fifty acres to any colonist who could afford passage to Virginia and fifty more for each accompanying servant. The headright policy was also adopted in other colonies.

Hessians German mercenary soldiers who were paid by the British royal government to fight alongside the British army during the American Revolution.

Hiroshima (1945) The Japanese port city that was the first target of the newly developed atomic bomb on August 6, 1945. The American attack killed 78,000 people immediately and destroyed most of the city.

HIV/AIDS Human immunodeficiency virus (HIV) transmitted via the bodily fluids of infected persons to cause acquired immunodeficiency syndrome (AIDS), an often-fatal disease of the immune system when it appeared in the 1980s.

holding company A corporation established to own and manage other companies' stock rather than to produce goods and services itself.

Holocaust Systematic efforts by the Nazis to exterminate the Jews of Europe, resulting in the murder of over 6 million Jews and more than a million other "undesirables."

Homestead Act (1862) Legislation granting 160 acres of government-owned land to settlers who agreed to work the land for at least five years.

Homestead Steel Strike (1892) A labor conflict at the Homestead steel mill near Pittsburgh, Pennsylvania, culminating in a battle between strikers and private security agents hired by the factory's management.

horizontal integration The process by which one firm acquires another firm operating in the same industry or producing the same line of products in an effort to reduce direct competition.

horses The animals that the Spanish introduced to the Americas, eventually transforming many Indigenous American cultures.

House Committee on Un-American Activities (HUAC) A committee of the U.S. House of Representatives that was formed in 1938; originally tasked with investigating Nazi subversion during World War II and later focused on rooting out Communists in the government and the motion-picture industry.

Immigration Act of 1924 Federal legislation intended to favor northern and western European immigrants over those from southern and eastern Europe by restricting the number of immigrants from any one European country to 2 percent of the total number of immigrants per year, with an overall limit of slightly over 150,000 new arrivals per year.

Immigration and Nationality Services Act of 1965 Legislation that abolished discriminatory quotas based upon immigrants' national origin and treated all nationalities and races equally.

imperialism The use of diplomatic or military force to extend a nation's power and enhance its economic interests, often by acquiring territory or colonies and justifying such behavior with assumptions of racial superiority.

indentured servants Settlers who signed on for a temporary period of servitude to a master in exchange for passage to the New World.

Independent Treasury Act (1840) A system created by President Martin Van Buren that moved federal funds from favored state banks to the U.S. Treasury, whose financial transactions could only be in gold or silver.

Indian Removal Act (1830) A law permitting the forced relocation of Indigenous peoples to federal lands west of the Mississippi River in exchange for the land they occupied in the East and South.

Indian wars Bloody conflicts between U.S. soldiers and Indigenous groups that raged in the West from the early 1860s to the late 1870s, sparked by American settlers moving into Indigenous ancestral lands.

Industrial Revolution A major shift in the nineteenth century from handmade manufacturing to mass production in mills and factories using water-, coal-, and steam-powered machinery.

infectious diseases Also called contagious diseases, illnesses that can pass from one person to another by way of invasive biological organisms able to reproduce in the bodily tissues of their hosts. Europeans unwittingly brought many such diseases to the Americas, devastating the Native American peoples.

The Influence of Sea Power upon History, 1660–1783 A historical work in which Rear Admiral Alfred Thayer Mahan argued that a nation's greatness and prosperity come from the power of its navy; the book helped bolster imperialist sentiment in the United States in the late nineteenth century.

Intermediate-Range Nuclear Forces (INF) Treaty (1987) An agreement signed by U.S. president Ronald Reagan and Soviet premier Mikhail Gorbachev to eliminate the deployment of intermediate-range missiles with nuclear warheads.

internal improvements Construction of roads, canals, and other projects intended to facilitate the flow of goods and people.

Interstate Commerce Commission (ICC) (1887) An independent federal agency established to oversee businesses engaged in interstate trade, especially railroads, but whose regulatory power was limited when tested in the courts.

Iran-Contra affair (1987) A Reagan administration scandal over the secret, unlawful U.S. sale of arms to Iran in partial exchange for the release of hostages in Lebanon; the arms money in turn was used illegally to aid Nicaraguan right-wing insurgents, the Contras.

Iranian hostage crisis (1979) The storming of the U.S. embassy in Tehran by Iranian revolutionaries, who held fifty-two Americans hostage for 444 days, despite President Carter's appeals for their release and a botched rescue attempt.

iron curtain A term coined by Winston Churchill to describe the Cold War divide between Western Europe and the Soviet Union's Eastern European satellite nations.

Iroquois League An alliance of the Iroquois Nations, originally formed sometime between 1450 and 1600, that used their combined strength to pressure Europeans to work with them in the fur trade and to wage war across what is today eastern North America. The League's unique constitution, the Great Law of Peace, was based on principles of peace, equity, and justice, and it gave power to all the people.

J. Pierpont Morgan and Company An investment bank under the leadership of J. Pierpont Morgan that bought or merged unrelated American companies, often using capital acquired from European investors.

Jay's Treaty (1794) A controversial agreement between Britain and the United States, negotiated by Chief Justice John Jay, that settled disputes over trade, prewar debts owed to British merchants, British-occupied forts in American territory, and the seizure of American ships and cargo.

Jazz Age A term coined by writer F. Scott Fitzgerald to characterize the spirit of rebellion and spontaneity among young Americans in the 1920s, a spirit epitomized by the hugely popular jazz music of the era.

Jeffersonian Republicans A political party founded by Thomas Jefferson in opposition to the Federalist Party led by Alexander Hamilton and John Adams; also known as the Democratic-Republican Party.

Jim Crow laws State and local statutes enacted in the late nineteenth century to enforce racial segregation and discrimination against African Americans.

joint-stock companies Businesses owned by investors, who purchase shares of stock and share the profits and losses.

Kansas-Nebraska Act (1854) Controversial legislation that created two new territories taken from Indigenous Americans, Kansas and Nebraska, where resident males would decide whether slavery would be allowed (popular sovereignty).

King Philip's War (1675–1678) A war in New England resulting from the escalation of tensions between Indigenous Americans and English settlers; the defeat of the Indigenous Americans led to broadened freedoms for the settlers and their dispossessing the region's Indigenous Americans of most of their land.

Knights of Labor A national labor organization with a broad reform platform; it reached peak membership in the 1880s.

Know-Nothings A nativist, anti-Catholic third party organized in 1854 in reaction to large-scale German and Irish immigration.

Ku Klux Klan A secret terrorist organization founded in Pulaski, Tennessee, in 1866 targeting formerly enslaved people who voted and held political offices, as well as people the KKK labeled as carpetbaggers and scalawags.

laissez-faire An economic doctrine holding that businesses and individuals should be able to pursue their economic interests without government interference.

League of Nations Organization of nations formed in the aftermath of the Great War to mediate disputes and maintain international peace; despite President Wilson's intense lobbying for the League of Nations, Congress did not ratify the Versailles Treaty and the United States failed to join.

Lend-Lease Act (1941) Legislation that allowed the president to lend or lease military equipment to any country whose own defense was deemed vital to the defense of the United States.

Lewis and Clark expedition (1804–1806) Led by Meriwether Lewis and William Clark, a mission to the Pacific coast commissioned for the purposes of scientific and geographical exploration.

Lincoln-Douglas debates (1858) In the Illinois race between Republican Abraham Lincoln and Democrat Stephen A. Douglas for a seat in the U.S. Senate, a series of seven dramatic debates focusing on the issue of slavery in the territories.

Lost Cause legend An American historical myth that claims the cause of the Confederate states during the American Civil War was just, heroic, and not centered on slavery. It would be used to extend White supremacy and discrimination against African Americans for more than a century after the Civil War.

Louisiana Purchase (1803) President Thomas Jefferson's purchase of the Louisiana Territory from France for $15 million, doubling the size of U.S. territory.

Lowell system Model New England factory communities that provided employees—mostly young women—with meals, a boardinghouse, moral discipline, and educational opportunities.

Loyalists Colonists who remained loyal to Britain before and during the Revolutionary War.

Lusitania British ocean liner torpedoed and sunk by a German U-boat; the deaths of nearly 1,200 of its civilian passengers, including many Americans, caused international outrage.

maize (corn) The primary grain crop in Mesoamerica, yielding small kernels often ground into cornmeal. Easy to grow in a broad range of conditions, it enabled a global population explosion after being brought to Europe, Africa, and Asia.

manifest destiny The widespread belief that America was "destined" by God to expand westward across the continent into lands claimed by Indigenous Americans as well as European empires.

***Marbury v. Madison* (1803)** The first Supreme Court decision to declare a federal law—the Judiciary Act of 1789—unconstitutional ("judicial review").

March on Washington (1963) A civil rights demonstration on the National Mall, where Martin Luther King Jr. gave his famous "I Have a Dream" speech.

market economy Large-scale manufacturing and commercial agriculture that emerged in America during the first half of the nineteenth century, displacing much of the premarket subsistence and barter-based economy and producing boom-and-bust cycles while raising the American standard of living.

marriage equality The legal right for gay and lesbian couples to marry; the most divisive issue in the culture wars of the early 2010s as increasing numbers of court rulings affirmed this right across the United States.

Marshall Plan (1948) Secretary of State George C. Marshall's post–World War II program providing massive U.S. financial and technical assistance to war-torn European countries.

Massachusetts Bay Colony The English colony founded by Puritans in 1630 as a haven for persecuted Congregationalists.

massive resistance A White rallying cry for disrupting federal efforts to enforce racial integration in the South.

massive retaliation A strategy that used the threat of nuclear warfare as a means of combating the global spread of communism.

Mayflower Compact (1620) A formal agreement signed by the Separatist colonists aboard the *Mayflower* to abide by laws made by leaders of their choosing.

McCarthyism Anti-Communist hysteria led by Senator Joseph McCarthy's witch hunts attacking the loyalty of politicians, federal employees, and public figures, despite a lack of evidence.

McCormick reapers The mechanical reaper invented by Cyrus Hall McCormick in 1831 that dramatically increased the production of wheat.

***McCulloch v. Maryland* (1819)** The Supreme Court ruling that prohibited states from taxing the Bank of the United States.

Medicare (1965) and Medicaid (1965) Health-care programs designed to aid the elderly and disadvantaged, respectively, as part of President Johnson's Great Society initiative.

mercantilism The policy, practiced by England and other imperial powers, of regulating colonial economies to benefit the mother country.

Mexica Otherwise known as the Aztec, a Mesoamerican people of northern Mexico who founded the vast Aztec Empire in the fourteenth century. It was later conquered by the Spanish under Hernán Cortés in 1521.

Mexica Empire The dominion established in the fourteenth century under the imperialistic Mexica, or Aztec, people in the valley of Mexico.

microprocessor An electronic circuit printed on a tiny silicon chip; a major technological breakthrough in 1971, it paved the way for the development of the personal computer.

Middle Passage The hellish and often deadly middle leg of the transatlantic "triangular trade" in which European ships carried manufactured goods to Africa, then transported enslaved Africans to the Americas and the Caribbean islands, and finally conveyed American agricultural products back to Europe.

Militia Act (1862) A congressional measure that permitted formerly enslaved people to serve as laborers or soldiers in the U.S. Army.

militias Part-time "citizen-soldiers" called out to protect their towns from foreign invasion and ravages during the American Revolution.

Mississippi Plan (1890) A series of state constitutional amendments that sought to disenfranchise Black voters; the Plan was quickly adopted by nine other southern states.

Missouri Compromise (1820) The legislative decision to admit Missouri as a slave state while prohibiting slavery in the area west of the Mississippi River and north of the parallel 36°30'.

moderate Republicanism The promise to curb federal government and restore state and local government authority, spearheaded by President Eisenhower.

modernism An early twentieth-century cultural movement that rejected traditional notions of reality and adopted radical new forms of artistic expression.

money question The late nineteenth-century national debate over the nature of U.S. currency; supporters of a fixed gold standard were generally moneylenders and thus preferred to keep the value of money high, while supporters of silver (and gold) coinage were debtors who owed money, so they wanted to keep the value of money low by increasing the currency supply (inflation).

monopoly Any corporation so large that it effectively controls the entire market for its products or services.

Monroe Doctrine (1823) The U.S. foreign policy that barred further colonization in the Western Hemisphere by European powers and pledged that there would be no American interference with any existing European colonies.

Montgomery bus boycott A boycott of the bus system in Montgomery, Alabama, organized by civil rights activists after the arrest of Rosa Parks in 1955.

Mormon Church The Church of Jesus Christ of Latter-day Saints, founded by Joseph Smith, emphasizing universal salvation and a modest lifestyle; often persecuted for its separateness and the practice of polygamy.

Morrill Land-Grant College Act (1862) A federal statute that granted federal lands to states to help fund the creation of land-grant colleges and universities, which were founded to provide technical education in agriculture, mining, and industry.

muckrakers Writers who exposed corruption and abuses in politics, business, consumer safety, working conditions, and more, spurring public interest in progressive reforms.

Mugwumps Reformers who bolted from the Republican Party in 1884 to support Democrat Grover Cleveland for president over Republican James G. Blaine, whose secret dealings on behalf of railroad companies had brought charges of corruption.

Nat Turner's Rebellion (1831) An insurrection in rural Virginia led by Black overseer Nat Turner, who killed slave owners and their families; in turn, federal troops indiscriminately killed hundreds of enslaved people in the process of putting down Turner and his rebels.

National Association for the Advancement of Colored People (NAACP) The organization founded in 1910 by Black activists and White progressives that promotes education as a means of combating social problems and focuses on legal action to secure the civil rights supposedly guaranteed by the Fourteenth and Fifteenth Amendments.

National Banking Act (1863) Legislation through which the U.S. Congress created a national banking system to finance the enormous expense of the Civil War. It enabled loans to the government and established a single national currency, including the issuance of paper money ("greenbacks").

National Recovery Administration (NRA) (1933) A controversial federal agency established during the Great Depression that brought together business and labor leaders to create "codes of fair competition" and "fair-labor" policies, including a national minimum wage.

National Security Act (1947) Congressional legislation that created the Department of Defense, the National Security Council, and the Central Intelligence Agency.

National Trades' Union An organization formed in 1834 to organize all local trade unions into a stronger national association; it dissolved amid the economic depression in the late 1830s.

nativism A reactionary conservative movement characterized by heightened nationalism, anti-immigrant sentiment, and laws setting stricter regulations on immigration.

nativists Native-born Americans who viewed immigrants as a threat to their job opportunities and way of life.

natural rights An individual's basic rights (to life, liberty, and property) that should not be violated by any government or community.

Navigation Acts (1651–1775) Restrictions passed by Parliament to control colonial trade and bolster the mercantile system.

neutrality laws A series of laws passed by Congress aimed at avoiding a second world war; these included the Neutrality Act of 1935, which banned the selling of weapons to warring nations.

New Democrats Centrist ("moderate") Democrats led by President Bill Clinton that emerged in the late 1980s and early 1990s to challenge the "liberal" direction of the party.

new economy A period of sustained economic prosperity during the 1990s marked by federal budget surpluses, the explosion of dot-com industries, low inflation, and low unemployment.

New Freedom A program championed in 1912 by the Woodrow Wilson campaign that aimed to restore competition in the economy by eliminating all trusts rather than simply regulating them.

New Frontier A proposed domestic program championed by the incoming Kennedy administration in 1961 that aimed to jump-start the economy and trigger social progress.

new immigrants The wave of newcomers from southern and eastern Europe, including many Jews, who became a majority among immigrants to America after 1890.

New Left A term coined by the Students for a Democratic Society to distinguish their efforts at grassroots democracy from those of the 1930s Old Left, which had embraced orthodox Marxism and admired the Soviet Union under Stalin.

New Mexico A region in the American Southwest originally established by the Spanish, who settled there in the sixteenth century, founded Catholic missions, and exploited the region's Indigenous peoples.

New Netherland A Dutch colony conquered by the English in 1667, out of which four new colonies were created—New York, New Jersey, Pennsylvania, and Delaware.

Nineteenth Amendment (1920) Constitutional amendment that granted women the right to vote in national elections.

nonviolent civil disobedience The tactic of defying unjust laws through peaceful actions championed by Dr. Martin Luther King Jr.

North American Free Trade Agreement (NAFTA) (1994) An agreement eliminating trade barriers that was signed in 1994 by the United States, Canada, and Mexico, making North America the largest free-trade zone in the world.

North and South Carolina English proprietary colonies, originally formed as the Carolina colonies, that were officially separated into the colonies of North and South Carolina in 1712. Their semitropical climate made them profitable centers of rice, timber, and tar production.

North Atlantic Treaty Organization (NATO) A defensive political and military alliance formed in 1949 by the United States, Canada, and ten Western European nations to deter Soviet expansion in Europe.

Northwest Ordinance (1787) The land policy for new western territories in the Ohio Valley that established the terms and conditions for self-government and statehood while also banning slavery from the region.

NSC-68 The top-secret policy paper approved by President Truman that outlined a militaristic approach to combating the spread of global communism.

nullification The right claimed by some states to veto a federal law they deemed unconstitutional.

Nuremberg Trials A series of trials of Nazi leaders by an international tribunal that exposed the full extent of Nazi atrocities and set important precedents for international law in the post–World War II era.

Old Southwest The region covering western Georgia, Alabama, Mississippi, Louisiana, Arkansas, and Texas, where low land prices and fertile soil attracted droves of settlers after the American Revolution.

Open Door policy (1899) The official U.S. assertion that Chinese trade would be open to all nations; Secretary of State John Hay unilaterally announced the policy in 1899 in hopes of protecting the Chinese market for U.S. exports.

Operation Desert Storm (1991) An assault by American-led multinational forces that quickly defeated Iraqi forces under Saddam Hussein in the First Gulf War, ending the Iraqi occupation of Kuwait.

Operation Overlord The Allies' assault on Hitler's "Atlantic Wall," a seemingly impregnable series of fortifications and minefields along the French coastline that German forces had created using captive Europeans for laborers.

Oregon Fever The lure of fertile land and economic opportunities in the Oregon Country that drew hundreds of thousands of settlers westward, beginning in the late 1830s.

Overland Trails Trail routes followed by wagon trains bearing settlers and trade goods from Missouri to the Oregon Country, California, and New Mexico, beginning in the 1840s.

Pacific Railway Act (1862) Legislation under which Congress provided funding for a transcontinental railroad from Nebraska west to California.

Panic of 1819 A financial panic that began a three-year economic crisis triggered by reduced demand in Europe for American cotton, declining land values, and reckless practices by local and state banks.

Panic of 1837 A financial calamity in the United States brought on by a dramatic slowdown in the British economy and falling cotton prices, failed crops, high inflation, and reckless state banks.

Panic of 1873 The financial collapse triggered by President Grant's efforts to withdraw greenbacks from circulation and transition the post–Civil War economy back to hard currency.

Panic of 1893 A major collapse in the national economy after several major railroad companies declared bankruptcy, leading to a severe depression and several violent clashes between workers and management.

Parliament The legislature of Great Britain, composed of the House of Commons, whose members are elected, and the House of Lords, whose members either hold hereditary positions or are appointed.

party "boss" A powerful political leader who controlled a "machine" of associates and operatives to promote both individual and party interests, often using informal tactics such as intimidation or the patronage system.

Patriots Colonists who rebelled against British authority before and during the Revolutionary War.

patronage An informal system (sometimes called the "spoils system") used by politicians to reward their supporters with government appointments or contracts.

Pearl Harbor (1941) The surprise Japanese attack on the U.S. fleet at Pearl Harbor, Hawaii, on December 7, which prompted the immediate American entry into World War II.

People's Party (Populists) A political party that formed in 1892 following the success of Farmers' Alliance candidates; Populists advocated for a variety of reforms, including free coinage of silver, a progressive income tax, postal savings banks, regulation of railroads, and direct election of U.S. senators.

perestroika The Russian term for economic restructuring; applied to Mikhail Gorbachev's series of political and economic reforms that included shifting a centrally planned Communist economy to a mixed economy allowing for capitalism.

Personal Responsibility and Work Opportunity Act of 1996 (PRWOA) A comprehensive welfare-reform measure aiming to decrease the size of the "welfare state" by limiting the amount of government unemployment aid to encourage its recipients to find jobs.

plain White folk Yeoman farmers in the South who lived and worked on their own small farms, growing food and cash crops to trade for necessities.

plantation mistress The matriarch of a planter's household, responsible for supervising the domestic aspects of the estate.

planters Owners of large farms in the South that were worked by twenty or more enslaved people and supervised by overseers.

***Plessy v. Ferguson* (1896)** A landmark U.S. Supreme Court decision ruling that racial segregation laws did not violate the U.S. Constitution as long as the facilities for each race were equal in quality, a doctrine that came to be known as "separate but equal."

political polarization The divergence of political attitudes away from the center, toward ideological extremes.

Pontiac's Rebellion (1763) A series of Indigenous American attacks on British forts and settlements after France ceded to the British its territory east of the Mississippi River as part of the Treaty of Paris without consulting France's Indigenous American allies.

popular sovereignty The legal concept by which the White male settlers in a U.S. territory would vote to decide whether to permit slavery.

Powhatan Confederacy An alliance of several powerful Algonquian societies under the leadership of Chief Powhatan, organized into thirty chiefdoms along much of the Atlantic coast in the late sixteenth and early seventeenth centuries.

Presidential Reconstruction Plan President Andrew Johnson's plan to require Southern states to ratify the Thirteenth Amendment, disqualify wealthy former Confederates from voting, and appoint a Unionist governor.

Proclamation Act of 1763 The proclamation drawing a boundary along the Appalachian Mountains from Canada to Georgia in order to minimize occurrences of violence between settlers and Indigenous Americans; colonists were forbidden to go west of the line.

professions Occupations requiring specialized knowledge of a particular field; the Industrial Revolution and its new organization of labor created an array of professions in the nineteenth century.

Progressive Party A political party founded by Theodore Roosevelt to support his bid to regain the presidency in 1912 after his split from the Taft Republicans.

Prohibition (1920–1933) A national ban on the manufacture and sale of alcohol, although the law was widely violated and proved too difficult to enforce effectively.

Protestant Reformation A sixteenth-century religious movement initiated by Martin Luther, a German monk whose public criticism of corruption in the Roman Catholic Church and whose teaching that Christians can communicate directly with God gained a wide following.

public schools Established during the 1800s, elementary and secondary schools funded by the state and free of tuition—and open to all children.

Pueblo Revolt The Pueblo Revolt of 1680, also known as Popé's Rebellion, was an uprising of most of the Indigenous Pueblo people against the Spanish colonizers in the province of Santa Fe, New Mexico.

Pullman Strike (1894) A national strike by the American Railway Union, whose members shut down major railways in sympathy with striking workers in Pullman, Illinois; ended with the intervention of federal troops.

Puritans English religious dissenters who sought to "purify" the Church of England of its Catholic practices.

racial covenants Clauses inserted into property deeds that prohibit the purchase, lease, or occupation of a property based on race, color, religion, or national origin.

racial justice protests The largest collection of multiracial and intergenerational protests across the United States in opposition to racism toward Black people, prompted by the documented murder of George Floyd, a Black man, by a Minneapolis police officer.

Radical Republicans Congressmen who identified with the abolitionist cause and sought swift emancipation of the enslaved, punishment of the Rebels, and tight controls over former Confederate states.

railroads Steam-powered vehicles that improved passenger transportation, quickened western settlement, and enabled commercial agriculture in the nineteenth century.

Reaganomics President Reagan's "supply-side" economic philosophy combining tax cuts with the goals of decreased government spending, reduced regulation of business, and a balanced budget.

Reconstruction Finance Corporation (RFC) (1932) A federal program established under President Hoover to loan money to banks and other corporations to help them avoid bankruptcy.

redeemers Postwar White Democratic leaders in the South who supposedly saved the region from political, economic, and social domination by Northerners and Blacks.

Red Power Activism by militant Indigenous American groups to protest living conditions on reservations through demonstrations, legal action, and at times, violence.

republican ideology A political belief in representative democracy in which citizens govern themselves by electing representatives, or legislators, to make key decisions on the citizens' behalf.

republican simplicity A deliberate attitude of humility and frugality, as opposed to monarchical pomp and ceremony, adopted by Thomas Jefferson during his presidency.

restrictive covenants Legal agreements that limited owners from selling their property to persons of a different race. The NAACP targeted these covenants in its effort to improve housing access for people of color.

***Roe v. Wade* (1973)** The landmark Supreme Court decision striking down state laws that banned abortions during the first trimester of pregnancy.

Roman Catholicism The Christian faith and religious practices of the Roman Catholic Church, which exerted great political, economic, and social influence on much of western Europe and, through the Spanish and Portuguese Empires, on the Americas.

Roosevelt Corollary (1904) President Theodore Roosevelt's revision (1904) of the Monroe Doctrine (1823) in which he argued that the United States could use military force in Central and South America to prevent European nations from intervening in the Western Hemisphere.

Rough Riders The First Volunteer Cavalry, led in the Spanish-American War by Theodore Roosevelt; victorious in their only engagement, the Battle of San Juan Hill.

Sacco and Vanzetti case (1921) The trial of two Italian immigrants that occurred at the height of Italian immigration and against the backdrop of numerous terror attacks by anarchists; despite a lack of clear evidence, the two defendants, both self-professed anarchists, were convicted of murder and were executed.

salutary neglect An informal British policy during the first half of the eighteenth century that allowed the American colonies freedom to pursue their economic and political interests in exchange for colonial obedience to the Crown.

Sand Creek Massacre (1864) Colonel Chivington's unprovoked slaughter of the Cheyenne and Arapaho in Colorado, initially reported as a justified battle but soon exposed for the despicable massacre it was.

Scopes Trial (1925) The highly publicized trial of a high-school teacher in Tennessee for violating a state law that prohibited the teaching of evolution; the trial was seen as the climax of the fundamentalist war on Darwinism.

Second Bank of the United States Established in 1816 after the first national bank's charter expired; it stabilized the economy by creating a sound national currency; by making loans to farmers, small manufacturers, and entrepreneurs; and by regulating the ability of state banks to issue their own paper currency.

Second Great Awakening A religious revival movement that arose in reaction to the growth of secularism and rationalist religion; it spurred the growth of the Baptist and Methodist denominations.

Second Industrial Revolution Beginning in the late nineteenth century, a wave of technological innovations, especially in iron and steel production, steam and electrical power, and telegraphic communications, all of which spurred industrial development and urban growth.

Second New Deal (1935–1938) An expansive cluster of legislation proposed by President Roosevelt that established new regulatory agencies, strengthened the rights of workers to organize unions, and laid the foundation of a federal social welfare system through the creation of Social Security.

Securities and Exchange Commission (SEC) (1934) A federal agency established in 1934 to regulate the issuance and trading of stocks and bonds in an effort to avoid financial panics and stock market crashes.

Seneca Falls Convention (1848) The convention organized by feminists Lucretia Mott and Elizabeth Cady Stanton to promote women's rights and issue the pathbreaking Declaration of Rights and Sentiments.

"separate but equal" The underlying principle behind segregation that was legitimized by the Supreme Court ruling in *Plessy v. Ferguson* (1896).

separation of powers The strict division of the powers of government among three separate branches (executive, legislative, and judicial), which in turn check and balance one another.

Seventeenth Amendment (1913) The constitutional amendment that provided for the public election of senators rather than the traditional practice of allowing state legislatures to name them.

sharecropping system A farming system developed after the Civil War by which landless workers farmed land in exchange with the landowner for farm supplies and a share of the crop.

Shays's Rebellion (1786–1787) The storming of the Massachusetts federal arsenal in 1787 by Daniel Shays and 1,200 armed farmers seeking debt relief from the state legislature through the issuance of paper currency and lower taxes.

Sherman's "March to the Sea" (1864) The Union army's devastating march through Georgia from Atlanta to Savannah led by General William T. Sherman, intended to demoralize civilians and destroy the resources the Confederate army needed to fight.

silent majority A term popularized by President Richard Nixon to describe the great majority of American voters who did not express their political opinions publicly; "the non-demonstrators."

Sixteenth Amendment (1913) The constitutional amendment that authorized the federal income tax.

Slaughterhouse Cases (1873) A pivotal Supreme Court decision that limited the "privileges and immunities" secured by the Fourteenth Amendment and thus eroded the federal government's power to protect the citizenship rights of Black Southerners.

slave codes Laws passed by each colony, and later by states, governing the treatment of enslaved people; designed to deter freedom seekers and rebellions, slave codes often included severe punishments for infractions.

social Darwinism The application of Charles Darwin's theory of evolutionary natural selection to human society; social Darwinists used the concept of "survival of the fittest" to justify class distinctions, explain poverty, and oppose government intervention in the economy.

social gospel A mostly Protestant movement that stressed the Christian obligation to address the mounting social problems caused by urbanization and industrialization.

Social Security Act (1935) Legislation enacted to provide federal assistance to retired workers through tax-funded pension payments and benefit payments to the unemployed and disabled.

Sons of Liberty First organized by Samuel Adams in the 1770s, groups of colonists dedicated to militant resistance against British control of the colonies.

Southern Christian Leadership Conference (SCLC) A civil rights organization formed by Dr. Martin Luther King Jr. that championed nonviolent direct action as a means of ending segregation.

Spanish Armada A massive Spanish fleet of 130 warships that was defeated at Plymouth, England, in 1588 by the English navy during the reign of Queen Elizabeth I.

spirituals Songs with religious messages sung by enslaved people to help ease the strain of field labor and to voice their suffering at the hands of their masters and overseers.

Square Deal Theodore Roosevelt's progressive agenda of the "Three Cs": control of corporations, conservation of natural resources, and consumer protection.

stagflation A term coined by economists during the Nixon presidency to describe the unprecedented situation of stagnant economic growth and consumer price inflation occurring at the same time.

Stamp Act (1765) An act of Parliament requiring that all printed materials in the American colonies use paper with an official tax stamp in order to pay for British military protection of the colonies.

Standard Oil Company A corporation under the leadership of John D. Rockefeller that attempted to dominate the entire oil industry through horizontal and vertical integration.

staple crops Profitable market crops, such as cotton, tobacco, and rice, that predominate in a region.

state constitutions Charters that define the relationship between the state government and local governments and individuals, while also protecting individual rights and freedoms.

steamboats Ships and boats powered by wood-fired steam engines that made two-way traffic possible in eastern river systems, creating a transcontinental market and an agricultural empire.

Stonewall Uprising (1969) Violent clashes between police and gay patrons of New York City's Stonewall Inn, seen as the starting point of the modern gay rights movement.

Stono Rebellion A 1739 slave uprising in South Carolina that was brutally quashed, leading to executions as well as a severe tightening of the slave codes.

Strategic Arms Limitation Treaty (SALT I) (1972) An agreement signed by President Nixon and Premier Leonid Brezhnev prohibiting the development of missile defense systems in the United States and the Soviet Union and limiting the quantity of nuclear warheads for both.

Strategic Defense Initiative (SDI) (1983) Ronald Reagan's proposed space-based anti-missile defense system, dubbed "Star Wars" by the media, which aroused great controversy and escalated the arms race between the United States and the Soviet Union.

Student Nonviolent Coordinating Committee (SNCC) An interracial organization formed in 1960 with the goal of intensifying the effort to end racial segregation.

suburbia Communities formed from the mass migration of middle-class Whites from urban centers.

Suez crisis (1956) A British, French, and Israeli attack on Egypt after Nasser's seizure of the Suez Canal; President Eisenhower interceded to demand the withdrawal of the British, French, and Israeli forces from the Sinai Peninsula and the strategic canal.

Taft-Hartley Labor Act (1947) Congressional legislation that banned "unfair labor practices" by unions, required union leaders to sign anti-Communist "loyalty oaths," and prohibited federal employees from going on strike.

Tariff of 1816 Taxes on various imported items, to protect America's emerging iron and textile industries from British competition.

Tariff of Abominations (1828) A tax on imported goods, including British cloth and clothing, that strengthened New England textile companies but hurt southern consumers, who experienced a decrease in British demand for raw cotton grown in the South.

tariff reform (1887) An effort led by the Democratic Party to reduce taxes on imported goods, which Republicans argued were needed to protect American industries from foreign competition.

Taylorism A labor system based on the detailed study of work tasks, championed by Frederick Winslow Taylor, intended to maximize efficiency and profits for employers.

Tea Party movement A right-wing populist movement, largely made up of middle-class, White male conservatives, that emerged as a response to the expansion of the federal government under the Obama administration.

Teapot Dome Scandal (1923) A Harding administration scandal in which Secretary of the Interior Albert B. Fall profited from secret leasing of government oil reserves in Wyoming to private oil companies.

Tecumseh's Indian Confederacy A group of Indigenous American nations under the leadership of Shawnees Tecumseh and Tenskwatawa; its mission of fighting off American expansion was thwarted at the Battle of Tippecanoe (1811), when the Indian Confederacy fell apart.

telegraph system The system of electronic communication invented by Samuel F. B. Morse that could transmit messages instantaneously across great distances.

Teller Amendment (1898) An addition to the congressional war resolution of April 20, 1898, that marked the U.S. entry into the war with Spain; the amendment declared that the United States' goal in entering the war was to ensure Cuba's independence, not to annex Cuba as a territory.

temperance A widespread reform movement led by militant Christians that focused on reducing the use of alcoholic beverages.

tenements Shabby, low-cost inner-city apartment buildings that housed the urban poor in cramped, unventilated apartments.

Tet offensive (1968) A surprise attack by Viet Cong guerrillas and the North Vietnamese army on U.S. and South Vietnamese forces that shocked the American public and led to widespread sentiment against the war.

Texas Revolution (1835–1836) A conflict between Texas colonists and the Mexican government that resulted in the creation of the separate Republic of Texas in 1836.

Thirteenth Amendment (1865) An amendment to the U.S. Constitution that ended slavery and freed all enslaved people in the United States.

tobacco A "cash crop" grown in the Caribbean as well as the Virginia and Maryland colonies, made increasingly profitable by the rapidly growing popularity of smoking in Europe after the voyages of Columbus.

Tonkin Gulf Resolution (1964) A congressional action that granted the president unlimited authority to defend U.S. forces abroad after an allegedly unprovoked attack on American warships off the coast of North Vietnam.

Townshend Acts (1767) Parliamentary measures to extract more revenue from the colonies; the Revenue Act of 1767, which taxed tea, paper, and other colonial imports, was one of the most notorious of these policies.

Trail of Tears (1838–1839) The forced, 800-mile journey of Indigenous people from the southern Appalachians to Indian Territory.

transatlantic slave trade The oceanic trade in captured African men, women, and children across the Atlantic to the Americas that took place from the sixteenth through the nineteenth centuries. It is estimated that 10 to 12 million enslaved Africans were brought to the Americas through this global system of forced removal and captivity.

transcendentalism The philosophy of New England writers and thinkers of the nineteenth century who advocated personal spirituality, self-reliance, social reform, and harmony with nature.

transcontinental railroads Railroads in the United States that were completed to connect the East Coast and the West Coast; designed to spur travel for westward expansion.

Transcontinental Treaty (1819) The treaty between Spain and the United States that clarified the boundaries of the Louisiana Purchase and arranged for the transfer of Florida to the United States in exchange for cash.

Treaty of Alliance (1778) A critical diplomatic, military, and economic alliance between France and the newly independent United States.

Treaty of Ghent (1814) The agreement between Great Britain and the United States that ended the War of 1812.

Treaty of Guadalupe Hidalgo (1848) The treaty between the United States and Mexico that ended the Mexican-American War.

Treaty of Paris (1763) The settlement between Great Britain and France that ended the French and Indian War.

Treaty of Paris (1783) The treaty that ended the Revolutionary War, recognized American independence from Britain, created the border between Canada and the United States, set the western border at the Mississippi River, and ceded Florida to Spain.

Treaty of Versailles (1919) Peace treaty that ended the Great War, forcing Germany to dismantle its military, pay immense war reparations, and give up its colonies around the world.

trench warfare A form of prolonged combat between the entrenched positions of opposing armies, often with little tactical movement.

triangular trade A network of trade in which exports from one region were sold to a second region; the second sent its exports to a third region, which exported its own goods back to the first country or colony. The term most often applies to the transatlantic slave trade of the seventeenth and early eighteenth centuries.

Triple Alliance (Central Powers) One of the two sides during the Great War, including Germany, Austria-Hungary, Bulgaria, and Turkey (the Ottoman Empire).

Triple Entente (Allied Powers) Nations fighting the Central Powers during the Great War, including France, Great Britain, and Russia; later joined by Italy and, after Russia quit the war in 1917, the United States.

Truman Doctrine (1947) President Truman's program of "containing" communism in Eastern Europe and providing economic and military aid to any nations at risk of Communist takeover.

trust Any business arrangement that gives a person or corporation (the "trustee") the legal power to manage another person's money or another company without owning those entities outright.

Tuskegee Airmen The U.S. Army Air Corps unit of African American pilots whose combat success spurred military and civilian leaders to desegregate the armed forces after the war.

two-party system The domination of national politics by two major political parties, such as the Whigs and the Democrats during the 1830s and 1840s.

U-boats German military submarines used during the Great War to attack warships as well as merchant ships of enemy and neutral nations.

Underground Railroad A secret system of routes, safe houses, and abolitionists that helped freedom seekers reach freedom in the North.

Unitarians Members of the liberal New England Congregationalist offshoot, often well educated and wealthy, who profess the oneness of God and the goodness of rational worshippers.

United Farm Workers (UFW) An organization formed in 1962 to represent the interests of Mexican American migrant workers.

Universalists Generally working-class members of a New England religious movement who believed in a merciful God and universal salvation.

USA Patriot Act (2001) Wide-reaching congressional legislation, triggered by the war on terror, that gave government agencies the right to eavesdrop on confidential conversations between prison inmates and their lawyers and permitted suspected terrorists to be tried in secret military courts.

U.S. battleship *Maine* An American warship that exploded in the Cuban port of Havana on February 15, 1898; though later discovered to be the result of an accident, the destruction of the *Maine* was initially attributed by war-hungry Americans to Spain, contributing to the onset of the Spanish-American War.

utopian communities During the nineteenth century, ideal communities that offered innovative social and economic relationships to those who were interested in achieving salvation—now.

Valley Forge (1777–1778) During the Revolutionary War, the American military encampment near Philadelphia where more than 3,500 soldiers deserted or died from cold and hunger in the winter.

vertical integration The process by which a company controls different stages along the supply chain. Instead of relying on external suppliers, the company strives to bring external processes in-house to have better control over the entire production process.

Viet Cong Communist guerrillas in South Vietnam who launched attacks on the Diem government.

Vietnamization The Nixon-era policy of equipping and training South Vietnamese forces to take over the burden of combat from U.S. troops.

Virginia Statute of Religious Freedom (1786) A Virginia law, drafted by Thomas Jefferson in 1777 and enacted in 1786, that guarantees freedom of, and from, religion.

virtual representation The idea that the American colonies, although they had no actual representative in Parliament, were "virtually" represented by all members of Parliament.

Voting Rights Act of 1965 Legislation ensuring that all Americans were able to vote; ended literacy tests and other means of restricting voting rights.

Wagner Act (1935) Legislation that guaranteed workers the right to organize unions, granted them direct bargaining power, and barred employers from interfering with union activities.

War of 1812 (1812–1815) A conflict fought in North America and at sea between Great Britain and the United States over American shipping rights and British-inspired attacks on American settlements by Indigenous groups. Canadians and Indigenous Americans also fought in the war on each side.

war on terror The global crusade launched by President George W. Bush to root out anti-Western and anti-American Islamist terrorist cells as a response to the 9/11 attacks.

War Powers Act (1973) Legislation requiring the president to inform Congress within forty-eight hours of the deployment of U.S. troops abroad and to withdraw them after sixty days unless Congress approves their continued deployment.

War Production Board A federal agency created by Roosevelt in 1942 that converted America's industrial output to war production.

war relocation camps Detention camps housing thousands of Japanese Americans from the West Coast who were forcibly interned from 1942 until the end of World War II.

Watergate (1972–1974) The scandal that exposed the criminality and corruption of the Nixon administration and ultimately led to President Nixon's resignation in 1974.

weapons of mass destruction (WMD) Lethal nuclear, radiological, chemical, or biological devices aimed at harming people, institutions, and a nation's sense of security.

Western Front Contested frontier between the Central and Allied Powers that ran along northern France and across Belgium.

Whig Party A political party founded in 1834 in opposition to the Jacksonian Democrats; supported federal funding for internal improvements, a national bank, and high tariffs on imports.

Whiskey Rebellion (1794) A violent protest by western Pennsylvania farmers against the federal excise tax on corn whiskey; the protest was put down by a federal army.

Wilmington Insurrection (1898) Led by Alfred Waddell in Wilmington, North Carolina, an uprising in which White supremacists rampaged through the Black community, overthrew the local government, and forced over 2,000 African Americans into exile.

Wilmot Proviso (1846) A proposal by Congressman David Wilmot, a Pennsylvania Democrat, to prohibit slavery in any lands acquired in the Mexican-American War.

witchcraft hysteria Cases of mass hysteria in early modern Europe and colonial America in which thousands of people were accused of being witches, many of whom were put on trial, tortured, and executed.

Women's Army Corps The women's branch of the U.S. Army; by the end of World War II, nearly 150,000 women had served in the WAC.

Women's Loyal National League (1863) An organization that was formed to campaign for an amendment to the U.S. Constitution that would abolish slavery. Petitions with almost 400,000 signatures presented to Congress contributed to passage of the Thirteenth Amendment.

Women's March on Washington The largest one-day demonstration in U.S. history, the march was a protest in support of a broad range of moderate to progressive policies such as abortion rights and immigration reform; it took place the day after President Donald Trump's inauguration.

women's movement The wave of activism sparked by Betty Friedan's *The Feminine Mystique* (1963); it argued for equal rights for women and fought against the cult of domesticity that limited women's roles to the home as wife, mother, and homemaker.

women's suffrage The movement to give women the right to vote through a constitutional amendment, spearheaded by Susan B. Anthony and Elizabeth Cady Stanton's National Woman Suffrage Association.

women's work A traditional term referring to labor in the house, garden, and fields performed by women; eventually expanded in the colonies to include medicine, shopkeeping, upholstering, and the operation of inns and taverns.

Works Progress Administration (WPA) (1935) A government agency established to manage several federal job programs created under the New Deal; it became the largest employer in the nation.

Yalta Conference (1945) A meeting of the "Big Three" Allied leaders—Franklin D. Roosevelt, Winston Churchill, and Joseph Stalin—to discuss how to divide control of postwar Germany and eastern Europe.

yellow journalism A type of news reporting, epitomized in the 1890s by the newspaper empires of William Randolph Hearst and Joseph Pulitzer, that intentionally manipulates public opinion through sensational headlines, illustrations, and articles about both real and invented events.

Zimmermann telegram Message sent by a German official to the Mexican government urging an invasion of the United States; the telegram was intercepted by British intelligence agents and angered Americans, many of whom called for war against Germany.

Appendix

The Declaration of Independence (1776)

When in the Course of human events, it becomes necessary for one people to dissolve the political bands which have connected them with another, and to assume among the powers of the earth, the separate and equal station to which the Laws of Nature and of Nature's God entitle them, a decent respect to the opinions of mankind requires that they should declare the causes which impel them to the separation.

We hold these truths to be self-evident, that all men are created equal, that they are endowed by their Creator with certain unalienable Rights, that among these are Life, Liberty and the pursuit of Happiness. —That to secure these rights, Governments are instituted among Men, deriving their just powers from the consent of the governed, —That whenever any Form of Government becomes destructive of these ends, it is the Right of the People to alter or to abolish it, and to institute new Government, laying its foundation on such principles and organizing its powers in such form, as to them shall seem most likely to effect their Safety and Happiness. Prudence, indeed, will dictate that Governments long established should not be changed for light and transient causes; and accordingly all experience hath shewn, that mankind are more disposed to suffer, while evils are sufferable, than to right themselves by abolishing the forms to which they are accustomed. But when a long train of abuses and usurpations, pursuing invariably the same Object evinces a design to reduce them under absolute Despotism, it is their right, it is their duty, to throw off such Government, and to provide new Guards for their future security.—Such has been the patient sufferance of these Colonies; and such is now the necessity which constrains them to alter their former Systems of Government. The history of the present King of Great Britain is a history of repeated injuries and usurpations, all having in direct object the establishment of an absolute Tyranny over these States. To prove this, let Facts be submitted to a candid world.

He has refused his Assent to Laws, the most wholesome and necessary for the public good.

He has forbidden his Governors to pass Laws of immediate and pressing importance, unless suspended in their operation till his Assent should be obtained; and when so suspended, he has utterly neglected to attend to them.

He has refused to pass other Laws for the accommodation of large districts of people, unless those people would relinquish the right of Representation in the Legislature, a right inestimable to them and formidable to tyrants only.

He has called together legislative bodies at places unusual, uncomfortable, and distant from the depository of their public Records, for the sole purpose of fatiguing them into compliance with his measures.

He has dissolved Representative Houses repeatedly, for opposing with manly firmness his invasions on the rights of the people.

He has refused for a long time, after such dissolutions, to cause others to be elected; whereby the Legislative powers, incapable of Annihilation, have returned to the People at large for their exercise; the State remaining in the mean time exposed to all the dangers of invasion from without, and convulsions within.

He has endeavoured to prevent the population of these States; for that purpose obstructing the Laws for Naturalization of Foreigners; refusing to pass others to encourage their migrations hither, and raising the conditions of new Appropriations of Lands.

He has obstructed the Administration of Justice, by refusing his Assent to Laws for establishing Judiciary powers.

He has made Judges dependent on his Will alone, for the tenure of their offices, and the amount and payment of their salaries.

He has erected a multitude of New Offices, and sent hither swarms of Officers to harrass our people, and eat out their substance.

He has kept among us, in times of peace, Standing Armies without the Consent of our legislatures.

He has affected to render the Military independent of and superior to the Civil power.

He has combined with others to subject us to a jurisdiction foreign to our constitution, and unacknowledged by our laws; giving his Assent to their Acts of pretended Legislation:

For quartering large bodies of armed troops among us:

For protecting them, by a mock Trial, from punishment for any Murders which they should commit on the Inhabitants of these States:

For cutting off our Trade with all parts of the world:

For imposing Taxes on us without our Consent:

For depriving us in many cases, of the benefits of Trial by Jury:

For transporting us beyond Seas to be tried for pretended offences

For abolishing the free System of English Laws in a neighbouring Province, establishing therein an Arbitrary government, and enlarging its Boundaries so as to render it at once an example and fit instrument for introducing the same absolute rule into these Colonies:

For taking away our Charters, abolishing our most valuable Laws, and altering fundamentally the Forms of our Governments:

For suspending our own Legislatures, and declaring themselves invested with power to legislate for us in all cases whatsoever.

He has abdicated Government here, by declaring us out of his Protection and waging War against us.

He has plundered our seas, ravaged our Coasts, burnt our towns, and destroyed the lives of our people.

He is at this time transporting large Armies of foreign Mercenaries to compleat the works of death, desolation and tyranny, already begun with circumstances of Cruelty & perfidy scarcely paralleled in the most barbarous ages, and totally unworthy the Head of a civilized nation.

He has constrained our fellow Citizens taken Captive on the high Seas to bear Arms against their Country, to become the executioners of their friends and Brethren, or to fall themselves by their Hands.

He has excited domestic insurrections amongst us, and has endeavoured to bring on the inhabitants of our frontiers, the merciless Indian Savages, whose known rule of warfare, is an undistinguished destruction of all ages, sexes and conditions.

In every stage of these Oppressions We have Petitioned for Redress in the most humble terms: Our repeated Petitions have been answered only by repeated injury. A Prince whose character is thus marked by every act which may define a Tyrant, is unfit to be the ruler of a free people.

Nor have We been wanting in attentions to our Brittish brethren. We have warned them from time to time of attempts by their legislature to extend an unwarrantable jurisdiction over us. We have reminded them of the circumstances of our emigration and settlement here. We have appealed to their native justice and magnanimity, and we have conjured them by the ties of our common kindred to disavow these usurpations, which, would inevitably interrupt our connections and correspondence. They too have been deaf to the voice of justice and of consanguinity. We must, therefore, acquiesce in the necessity, which denounces our Separation, and hold them, as we hold the rest of mankind, Enemies in War, in Peace Friends.

We, therefore, the Representatives of the united States of America, in General Congress, Assembled, appealing to the Supreme Judge of the world for the rectitude of our intentions, do, in the Name, and by Authority of the good People of these Colonies, solemnly publish and declare, That these United Colonies are, and of Right ought to be Free and Independent States; that they are Absolved from all Allegiance to the British Crown, and that all political connection between them and the State of Great Britain, is and ought to be totally dissolved; and that as Free and Independent States, they have full Power to levy War, conclude Peace, contract Alliances, establish Commerce, and to do all other Acts and Things which Independent States may of right do. And for the support of this Declaration, with a firm reliance on the protection of divine Providence, we mutually pledge to each other our Lives, our Fortunes and our sacred Honor.

Georgia
Button Gwinnett
Lyman Hall
George Walton

North Carolina
William Hooper
Joseph Hewes
John Penn

South Carolina
Edward Rutledge
Thomas Heyward, Jr.
Thomas Lynch, Jr.
Arthur Middleton

Massachusetts
John Hancock

Maryland
Samuel Chase
William Paca
Thomas Stone
Charles Carroll of Carrollton

Virginia
George Wythe
Richard Henry Lee
Thomas Jefferson
Benjamin Harrison

Thomas Nelson, Jr.
Francis Lightfoot Lee
Carter Braxton

Pennsylvania
Robert Morris
Benjamin Rush
Benjamin Franklin
John Morton
George Clymer
James Smith
George Taylor
James Wilson
George Ross

Delaware
Caesar Rodney
George Read
Thomas McKean

New York
William Floyd
Philip Livingston
Francis Lewis
Lewis Morris

New Jersey
Richard Stockton
John Witherspoon
Francis Hopkinson
John Hart
Abraham Clark

New Hampshire
Josiah Bartlett
William Whipple

Massachusetts
Samuel Adams
John Adams
Robert Treat Paine
Elbridge Gerry

Rhode Island
Stephen Hopkins
William Ellery

Connecticut
Roger Sherman
Samuel Huntington
William Williams
Oliver Wolcott

New Hampshire
Matthew Thornton

Articles of Confederation (1787)

To all to whom these Presents shall come, we the undersigned Delegates of the States affixed to our Names send greeting.

Whereas the Delegates of the United States of America in Congress assembled did on the fifteenth day of November in the Year of our Lord One Thousand Seven Hundred and Seventy-seven, and in the Second Year of the Independence of America agree to certain articles of Confederation and perpetual Union between the States of Newhampshire, Massachusetts-bay, Rhodeisland and Providence Plantations, Connecticut, New York, New Jersey, Pennsylvania, Delaware, Maryland, Virginia, North-Carolina, South-Carolina and Georgia in the Words following, viz.

Articles of Confederation and perpetual Union between the States of Newhampshire, Massachusetts-bay, Rhodeisland and Providence Plantations, Connecticut, New-York, New-Jersey, Pennsylvania, Delaware, Maryland, Virginia, North-Carolina, South-Carolina and Georgia.

Article I. The stile of this confederacy shall be "The United States of America."

Article II. Each State retains its sovereignty, freedom and independence, and every power, jurisdiction and right, which is not by this confederation expressly delegated to the United States, in Congress assembled.

Article III. The said States hereby severally enter into a firm league of friendship with each other, for their common defence, the security of their liberties, and their mutual and general welfare, binding themselves to assist each other, against all force offered to, or attacks made upon them, or any of them, on account of religion, sovereignty, trade or any other pretence whatever.

Article IV. The better to secure and perpetuate mutual friendship and intercourse among the people of the different States in this Union, the free inhabitants of each of these States, paupers, vagabonds and fugitives from justice excepted, shall be entitled to all privileges and immunities of free citizens in the several States; and the people of each State shall have free ingress and regress to and from any other State, and shall enjoy therein all the privileges of trade and commerce, subject to the same duties, impositions and restrictions as the inhabitants thereof respectively, provided that such restrictions shall not extend so far as to prevent the removal of property imported into any State, to any other State of which the owner is an inhabitant; provided also that no imposition, duties or restriction shall be laid by any State, on the property of the United States, or either of them.

If any person guilty of, or charged with treason, felony, or other high misdemeanor in any State, shall flee from justice, and be found in any of the United States, he shall upon demand of the Governor or Executive power, of the State from which he fled, be delivered up and removed to the State having jurisdiction of his offence.

Full faith and credit shall be given in each of these States to the records, acts and judicial proceedings of the courts and magistrates of every other State.

ARTICLE V. For the more convenient management of the general interests of the United States, delegates shall be annually appointed in such manner as the legislature of each State shall direct, to meet in Congress on the first Monday in November, in every year, with a power reserved to each State, to recall its delegates, or any of them, at any time within the year, and to send others in their stead, for the remainder of the year.

No State shall be represented in Congress by less than two, nor by more than seven members; and no person shall be capable of being a delegate for more than three years in any term of six years; nor shall any person, being a delegate, be capable of holding any office under the United States, for which he, or another for his benefit receives any salary, fees or emolument of any kind.

Each State shall maintain its own delegates in a meeting of the States, and while they act as members of the committee of the States.

In determining questions in the United States, in Congress assembled, each State shall have one vote.

Freedom of speech and debate in Congress shall not be impeached or questioned in any court, or place out of Congress, and the members of Congress shall be protected in their persons from arrests and imprisonments, during the time of their going to and from, and attendance on Congress, except for treason, felony, or breach of the peace.

ARTICLE VI. No State without the consent of the United States in Congress assembled, shall send any embassy to, or receive any embassy from, or enter into any conference, agreement, alliance or treaty with any king, prince or state; nor shall any person holding any office of profit or trust under the United States, or any of them, accept of any present, emolument, office or title of any kind whatever from any king, prince or foreign state; nor shall the United States in Congress assembled, or any of them, grant any title of nobility.

No two or more States shall enter into any treaty, confederation or alliance whatever between them, without the consent of the United States in Congress assembled, specifying accurately the purposes for which the same is to be entered into, and how long it shall continue.

No State shall lay any imposts or duties, which may interfere with any stipulations in treaties, entered into by the United States in Congress assembled, with any king, prince or state, in pursuance of any treaties already proposed by Congress, to the courts of France and Spain.

No vessels of war shall be kept up in time of peace by any State, except such number only, as shall be deemed necessary by the United States in Congress assembled, for the defence of such State, or its trade; nor shall any body of forces be kept up by any State, in time of peace, except such number only, as in the judgment of the United States, in Congress assembled, shall be deemed requisite to garrison the forts necessary for the defence of such State; but every State shall always keep up a well regulated and disciplined militia, sufficiently armed and accoutred, and shall provide and constantly have ready for use, in public stores, a due number of field pieces and tents, and a proper quantity of arms, ammunition and camp equipage.

No State shall engage in any war without the consent of the United States in Congress assembled, unless such State be actually invaded by enemies, or shall have received certain advice of a resolution being formed by some nation of Indians to invade such State, and the danger is so imminent as not to admit of a delay, till the United States in Congress assembled can be consulted: nor shall any State grant commissions to any ships or vessels of war, nor letters of marque or reprisal, except it be after a declaration of war by the United States in Congress assembled, and then only against the kingdom or state and the subjects thereof, against which war has been so declared, and under such regulations as shall be established by the United States in Congress assembled, unless such State be infested by pirates, in which case vessels of war may be fitted out for that occasion, and kept so long as the danger shall continue, or until the United States in Congress assembled shall determine otherwise.

ARTICLE VII. When land-forces are raised by any State of the common defence, all officers of or under the rank of colonel, shall be appointed by the Legislature of each State respectively by whom such forces shall be raised, or in such manner as such State shall direct, and all vacancies shall be filled up by the State which first made the appointment.

ARTICLE VIII. All charges of war, and all other expenses that shall be incurred for the common defence or general welfare, and allowed by the United States in Congress assembled, shall be defrayed out of a common treasury, which shall be supplied by the several States, in proportion to the value of all land within each State, granted to or surveyed for any person, as such land and the buildings and improvements thereon shall be estimated according to such mode as the United States in Congress assembled, shall from time to time direct and appoint.

The taxes for paying that proportion shall be laid and levied by the authority and direction of the Legislatures of the several States within the time agreed upon by the United States in Congress assembled.

ARTICLE IX. The United States in Congress assembled, shall have the sole and exclusive right and power of determining on peace and war, except in the cases mentioned in the sixth article—of sending and receiving ambassadors—entering into treaties and alliances, provided that no treaty of commerce shall be made whereby the legislative power of the respective States shall be restrained from imposing such imposts and duties on foreigners, as their own people are subjected to, or from prohibiting the exportation or importation of and species of goods or commodities whatsoever—of establishing rules for deciding in all cases, what captures on land or water shall be legal, and in what manner prizes taken by land or naval forces in the service of the United States shall be divided or appropriated—of granting letters of marque and reprisal in times of peace—appointing courts for the trial of piracies and felonies committed on the high seas and establishing courts for receiving and determining finally appeals in all cases of captures, provided that no member of Congress shall be appointed a judge of any of the said courts.

The United States in Congress assembled shall also be the last resort on appeal in all disputes and differences now subsisting or that hereafter may arise between two or more States concerning boundary, jurisdiction or any other cause whatever; which authority shall always be exercised in the manner following. Whenever the legislative or executive authority or lawful agent of any State in controversy with another shall present a petition to Congress, stating the matter in question and praying for a hearing, notice thereof shall be given by order of Congress to the legislative or executive authority of the other State in controversy, and a day assigned for the appearance of the parties by their lawful agents, who shall then be directed to appoint by joint consent, commissioners or judges to constitute a court for hearing and determining the matter in question: but if they cannot agree, Congress shall name three persons out of each of the United States, and from the list of such persons each party shall alternately strike out one, the petitioners beginning, until the number shall be reduced to thirteen; and from that number not less than seven, nor more than nine names as Congress shall direct, shall in the presence of Congress be drawn out by lot, and the persons whose names shall be so drawn or any five of them, shall be commissioners or judges, to hear and finally determine the controversy, so always as a major part of the judges who shall hear the cause shall agree in the determination: and if either party shall neglect to attend at the day appointed, without reasons, which Congress shall judge sufficient, or being present shall refuse to strike, the Congress shall proceed to nominate three persons out of each State, and the Secretary of Congress shall strike in behalf of such party absent or refusing; and the judgment and sentence of the court to be appointed, in the manner before prescribed, shall be final and conclusive; and if any of the parties shall refuse to submit to the authority of such court, or to appear or defend their claim or cause, the court shall nevertheless proceed to pronounce sentence, or judgment, which shall in like manner be final and decisive, the judgment or sentence and other proceedings being in either case transmitted to Congress, and lodged among the acts of Congress for the security of the parties concerned: provided that every commissioner, before he sits in judgment, shall take an oath to be administered by one of the judges of the supreme or superior court of the State where the case shall be tried, "well and truly to hear and determine the matter in question, according to the best of his judgment, without favour, affection or hope of reward:" provided also that no State shall be deprived of territory for the benefit of the United States.

All controversies concerning the private right of soil claimed under different grants of two or more States, whose jurisdiction as they may respect such lands, and the states which passed such grants are adjusted, the said grants or either of them being at the same time claimed to have originated antecedent to such settlement of jurisdiction, shall on the petition of either party to the Congress of the United States, be finally determined as near as may be in the same manner as is before prescribed for deciding disputes respecting territorial jurisdiction between different States.

The United States in Congress assembled shall also have the sole and exclusive right and power of regulating the alloy and value of coin struck by their own authority, or by that of the respective States—fixing the standard of weights and measures throughout the United States—regulating the trade and managing all affairs with the Indians, not members of any of the States, provided that the legislative right of any State within its own limits be not infringed or violated—establishing and regulating post-offices from one State to another, throughout all of the United States, and exacting such postage on the papers passing thro' the same as may be requisite to defray the expenses of the said office—appointing all officers of the land forces, in the service of the United States, excepting regimental officers—appointing all the officers of the naval forces, and commissioning all officers whatever in the service of the United States—making rules for the government and regulation of the said land and naval forces, and directing their operations.

The United States in Congress assembled shall have authority to appoint a committee, to sit in the recess of Congress, to be denominated "a Committee of the States," and to consist of one delegate from each State; and to appoint such other committees and civil officers as may be necessary for managing the general affairs of the United States under their direction—to appoint one of their number to preside, provided that no person be allowed to serve in the office of president more than one year in any term of three years; to ascertain the necessary sums of money to be raised for the service of the United States, and to appropriate and apply the same for defraying the public expenses—to borrow money, or emit bills on the credit of the United States, transmitting every half year to the respective States an account of the sums of money so borrowed or emitted,—to build and equip a navy—to agree upon the number of land forces, and to make requisitions from each State for its quota, in proportion to the number of white inhabitants in such State; which requisition shall be binding, and thereupon the Legislature of each State shall appoint the regimental officers, raise the men and cloath, arm and equip them in a soldier like manner, at the expense of the United States; and the officers and men so cloathed, armed and equipped shall march to the place appointed, and within the time agreed on by the United States in Congress assembled: but if the United States in Congress assembled shall, on consideration of circumstances judge proper that any State should not raise men, or should raise a smaller number of men than the quota thereof, such extra number shall be raised, officered, cloathed, armed and equipped in the same manner as the quota of such State, unless the legislature of such State shall judge that such extra number cannot be safely spared out of the same, in which case they shall raise officer, cloath, arm and equip as many of such extra number as they judge can be safely spared. And the officers and men so cloathed, armed and equipped, shall march to the place appointed, and within the time agreed on by the United States in Congress assembled.

The United States in Congress assembled shall never engage in a war, nor grant letters of marque and reprisal in time of peace, nor enter into any treaties or alliances, nor coin money, nor regulate the value thereof, nor ascertain the sums and expenses necessary for the defence and welfare of the United States, or any of them, nor emit bills, nor borrow money on the credit of the United States, nor appropriate money, nor agree upon the number of vessels to be built or purchased, or the number of land or sea forces to be raised, nor appoint a commander in chief of the army or navy, unless nine States assent to the same: nor shall a question on any other point, except for adjourning from day to day be determined, unless by the votes of a majority of the United States in Congress assembled.

The Congress of the United States shall have power to adjourn to any time within the year, and to any place within the United States, so that no period of adjournment be for a longer duration than the space of six months, and shall publish the journal of their proceedings monthly, except such parts thereof relating to treaties, alliances or military operations, as in their judgment require secresy; and the yeas and nays of the delegates of each State on any question shall be entered on the Journal, when it is desired by any delegate; and the delegates of a State, or any of them, at his or their request shall be furnished with a transcript of the said journal, except such parts as are above excepted, to lay before the Legislatures of the several States.

ARTICLE X. The committee of the States, or any nine of them, shall be authorized to execute, in the recess of Congress, such of the powers of Congress as the United States in Congress assembled, by the consent of nine States, shall from time to time think expedient to vest them with; provided that no power be delegated to the said committee, for the exercise of which, by the articles of confederation, the voice of nine States in the Congress of the United States assembled is requisite.

ARTICLE XI. Canada acceding to this confederation, and joining in the measures of the United States, shall be admitted into, and entitled to all the advantages of this Union: but no other colony shall be admitted into the same, unless such admission be agreed to by nine States.

ARTICLE XII. All bills of credit emitted, monies borrowed and debts contracted by, or under the authority of Congress, before the assembling of the United States, in pursuance of the present confederation, shall be deemed and considered as a charge against the United States, for payment and satisfaction whereof the said United States, and the public faith are hereby solemnly pledged.

Article XIII. Every State shall abide by the determinations of the United States in Congress assembled, on all questions which by this confederation are submitted to them. And the articles of this confederation shall be inviolably observed by every State, and the Union shall be perpetual; nor shall any alteration at any time hereafter be made in any of them; unless such alteration be agreed to in a Congress of the United States, and be afterwards confirmed by the Legislatures of every State.

And whereas it has pleased the Great Governor of the world to incline the hearts of the Legislatures we respectively represent in Congress, to approve of, and to authorize us to ratify the said articles of confederation and perpetual union. Know ye that we the undersigned delegates, by virtue of the power and authority to us given for that purpose, do by these presents, in the name and in behalf of our respective constituents, fully and entirely ratify and confirm each and every of the said articles of confederation and perpetual union, and all and singular the matters and things therein contained: and we do further solemnly plight and engage the faith of our respective constituents, that they shall abide by the determinations of the United States in Congress assembled, on all questions, which by the said confederation are submitted to them. And that the articles thereof shall be inviolably observed by the States we respectively represent, and that the Union shall be perpetual.

In witness thereof we have hereunto set our hands in Congress. Done at Philadelphia in the State of Pennsylvania the ninth day of July in the year of our Lord one thousand seven hundred and seventy-eight, and in the third year of the independence of America.

The Constitution of the United States (1787)

We the People of the United States, in Order to form a more perfect Union, establish Justice, insure domestic Tranquility, provide for the common defence, promote the general Welfare, and secure the Blessings of Liberty to ourselves and our Posterity, do ordain and establish this Constitution for the United States of America.

Article. I.

Section. 1. All legislative Powers herein granted shall be vested in a Congress of the United States, which shall consist of a Senate and House of Representatives.

Section. 2. The House of Representatives shall be composed of Members chosen every second Year by the People of the several States, and the Electors in each State shall have the Qualifications requisite for Electors of the most numerous Branch of the State Legislature.

No Person shall be a Representative who shall not have attained to the Age of twenty five Years, and been seven Years a Citizen of the United States, and who shall not, when elected, be an Inhabitant of that State in which he shall be chosen.

Representatives and direct Taxes shall be apportioned among the several States which may be included within this Union, according to their respective Numbers, which shall be determined by adding to the whole Number of free Persons, including those bound to Service for a Term of Years, and excluding Indians not taxed, three fifths of all other Persons. The actual Enumeration shall be made within three Years after the first Meeting of the Congress of the United States, and within every subsequent Term of ten Years, in such Manner as they shall by Law direct. The Number of Representatives shall not exceed one for every thirty Thousand, but each State shall have at Least one Representative; and until such enumeration shall be made, the State of New Hampshire shall be entitled to chuse three, Massachusetts eight, Rhode-Island and Providence Plantations one, Connecticut five, New-York six, New Jersey four, Pennsylvania eight, Delaware one, Maryland six, Virginia ten, North Carolina five, South Carolina five, and Georgia three.

When vacancies happen in the Representation from any State, the Executive Authority thereof shall issue Writs of Election to fill such Vacancies.

The House of Representatives shall chuse their Speaker and other Officers; and shall have the sole Power of Impeachment.

Section. 3. The Senate of the United States shall be composed of two Senators from each State, chosen by the Legislature thereof for six Years; and each Senator shall have one Vote.

Immediately after they shall be assembled in Consequence of the first Election, they shall be divided as equally as may be into three Classes. The Seats of the Senators of the first Class shall be vacated at the Expiration of the second Year, of the second Class at the Expiration of the fourth Year, and of the third Class at the

Expiration of the sixth Year, so that one third may be chosen every second Year; and if Vacancies happen by Resignation, or otherwise, during the Recess of the Legislature of any State, the Executive thereof may make temporary Appointments until the next Meeting of the Legislature, which shall then fill such Vacancies.

No Person shall be a Senator who shall not have attained to the Age of thirty Years, and been nine Years a Citizen of the United States, and who shall not, when elected, be an Inhabitant of that State for which he shall be chosen.

The Vice President of the United States shall be President of the Senate, but shall have no Vote, unless they be equally divided.

The Senate shall chuse their other Officers, and also a President pro tempore, in the Absence of the Vice President, or when he shall exercise the Office of President of the United States.

The Senate shall have the sole Power to try all Impeachments. When sitting for that Purpose, they shall be on Oath or Affirmation. When the President of the United States is tried, the Chief Justice shall preside: And no Person shall be convicted without the Concurrence of two thirds of the Members present.

Judgment in Cases of Impeachment shall not extend further than to removal from Office, and disqualification to hold and enjoy any Office of honor, Trust or Profit under the United States: but the Party convicted shall nevertheless be liable and subject to Indictment, Trial, Judgment and Punishment, according to Law.

Section. 4. The Times, Places and Manner of holding Elections for Senators and Representatives, shall be prescribed in each State by the Legislature thereof; but the Congress may at any time by Law make or alter such Regulations, except as to the Places of chusing Senators.

The Congress shall assemble at least once in every Year, and such Meeting shall be on the first Monday in December, unless they shall by Law appoint a different Day.

Section. 5. Each House shall be the Judge of the Elections, Returns and Qualifications of its own Members, and a Majority of each shall constitute a Quorum to do Business; but a smaller Number may adjourn from day to day, and may be authorized to compel the Attendance of absent Members, in such Manner, and under such Penalties as each House may provide.

Each House may determine the Rules of its Proceedings, punish its Members for disorderly Behaviour, and, with the Concurrence of two thirds, expel a Member.

Each House shall keep a Journal of its Proceedings, and from time to time publish the same, excepting such Parts as may in their Judgment require Secrecy; and the Yeas and Nays of the Members of either House on any question shall, at the Desire of one fifth of those Present, be entered on the Journal.

Neither House, during the Session of Congress, shall, without the Consent of the other, adjourn for more than three days, nor to any other Place than that in which the two Houses shall be sitting.

Section. 6. The Senators and Representatives shall receive a Compensation for their Services, to be ascertained by Law, and paid out of the Treasury of the United States. They shall in all Cases, except Treason, Felony and Breach of the Peace, be privileged from Arrest during their Attendance at the Session of their respective Houses, and in going to and returning from the same; and for any Speech or Debate in either House, they shall not be questioned in any other Place.

No Senator or Representative shall, during the Time for which he was elected, be appointed to any civil Office under the Authority of the United States, which shall have been created, or the Emoluments whereof shall have been encreased during such time; and no Person holding any Office under the United States, shall be a Member of either House during his Continuance in Office.

Section. 7. All Bills for raising Revenue shall originate in the House of Representatives; but the Senate may propose or concur with Amendments as on other Bills.

Every Bill which shall have passed the House of Representatives and the Senate shall, before it become a Law, be presented to the President of the United States; If he approve he shall sign it, but if not he shall return it, with his Objections to that House in which it shall have originated, who shall enter the Objections at large on their Journal, and proceed to reconsider it. If after such Reconsideration two thirds of that House shall agree to pass the Bill, it shall be sent, together with the Objections, to the other House, by which it shall likewise be reconsidered, and if approved by two thirds of that House, it shall become a Law. But in all such Cases the Votes of both Houses shall be determined by yeas and Nays, and the Names of the Persons voting for and against the Bill shall be entered on the Journal of each House respectively. If any Bill shall not be returned by the President within ten Days (Sundays excepted) after it shall have been presented to him, the Same shall be a Law, in like Manner as if he had signed it, unless the Congress by their Adjournment prevent its Return, in which Case it shall not be a Law.

Every Order, Resolution, or Vote to which the Concurrence of the Senate and House of Representatives may be necessary (except on a question of Adjournment) shall be presented to the President of the United States; and before the Same shall take Effect, shall be approved by him, or being disapproved by him, shall be repassed by two thirds of the Senate and House of Representatives, according to the Rules and Limitations prescribed in the Case of a Bill.

Section. 8. The Congress shall have Power To lay and collect Taxes, Duties, Imposts and Excises, to pay the Debts and provide for the common Defence and general Welfare of the United States; but all Duties, Imposts and Excises shall be uniform throughout the United States;

To borrow Money on the credit of the United States;

To regulate Commerce with foreign Nations, and among the several States, and with the Indian Tribes;

To establish an uniform Rule of Naturalization, and uniform Laws on the subject of Bankruptcies throughout the United States;

To coin Money, regulate the Value thereof, and of foreign Coin, and fix the Standard of Weights and Measures;

To provide for the Punishment of counterfeiting the Securities and current Coin of the United States;

To establish Post Offices and post Roads;

To promote the Progress of Science and useful Arts, by securing for limited Times to Authors and Inventors the exclusive Right to their respective Writings and Discoveries;

To constitute Tribunals inferior to the supreme Court;

To define and punish Piracies and Felonies committed on the high Seas, and Offences against the Law of Nations;

To declare War, grant Letters of Marque and Reprisal, and make Rules concerning Captures on Land and Water;

To raise and support Armies, but no Appropriation of Money to that Use shall be for a longer Term than two Years;

To provide and maintain a Navy;

To make Rules for the Government and Regulation of the land and naval Forces;

To provide for calling forth the Militia to execute the Laws of the Union, suppress Insurrections and repel Invasions;

To provide for organizing, arming, and disciplining, the Militia, and for governing such Part of them as may be employed in the Service of the United States, reserving to the States respectively, the Appointment of the Officers, and the Authority of training the Militia according to the discipline prescribed by Congress;

To exercise exclusive Legislation in all Cases whatsoever, over such District (not exceeding ten Miles square) as may, by Cession of particular States, and the Acceptance of Congress, become the Seat of the Government of the United States, and to exercise like Authority over all Places purchased by the Consent of the Legislature of the State in which the Same shall be, for the Erection of Forts, Magazines, Arsenals, dock-Yards, and other needful Buildings;—And

To make all Laws which shall be necessary and proper for carrying into Execution the foregoing Powers, and all other Powers vested by this Constitution in the Government of the United States, or in any Department or Officer thereof.

Section. 9. The Migration or Importation of such Persons as any of the States now existing shall think proper to admit, shall not be prohibited by the Congress prior to the Year one thousand eight hundred and eight, but a Tax or duty may be imposed on such Importation, not exceeding ten dollars for each Person.

The Privilege of the Writ of Habeas Corpus shall not be suspended, unless when in Cases of Rebellion or Invasion the public Safety may require it.

No Bill of Attainder or ex post facto Law shall be passed.

No Capitation, or other direct, Tax shall be laid, unless in Proportion to the Census or enumeration herein before directed to be taken.

No Tax or Duty shall be laid on Articles exported from any State.

No Preference shall be given by any Regulation of Commerce or Revenue to the Ports of one State over those of another; nor shall Vessels bound to, or from, one State, be obliged to enter, clear, or pay Duties in another.

No Money shall be drawn from the Treasury, but in Consequence of Appropriations made by Law; and a regular Statement and Account of the Receipts and Expenditures of all public Money shall be published from time to time.

No Title of Nobility shall be granted by the United States: And no Person holding any Office of Profit or Trust under them, shall, without the Consent of the Congress, accept of any present, Emolument, Office, or Title, of any kind whatever, from any King, Prince, or foreign State.

Section. 10. No State shall enter into any Treaty, Alliance, or Confederation; grant Letters of Marque and Reprisal; coin Money; emit Bills of Credit; make any Thing but gold and silver Coin a Tender in Payment of Debts; pass any Bill of Attainder, ex post facto Law, or Law impairing the Obligation of Contracts, or grant any Title of Nobility.

No State shall, without the Consent of the Congress, lay any Imposts or Duties on Imports or Exports, except what may be absolutely necessary for executing it's inspection Laws: and the net Produce of all Duties and Imposts, laid by any State on Imports or Exports, shall be for the Use of the Treasury of the United States; and all such Laws shall be subject to the Revision and Controul of the Congress.

No State shall, without the Consent of Congress, lay any Duty of Tonnage, keep Troops, or Ships of War in time of Peace, enter into any Agreement or Compact with another State, or with a foreign Power, or engage in War, unless actually invaded, or in such imminent Danger as will not admit of delay.

Article. II.

Section. 1. The executive Power shall be vested in a President of the United States of America. He shall hold his Office during the Term of four Years, and, together with the Vice President, chosen for the same Term, be elected, as follows:

Each State shall appoint, in such Manner as the Legislature thereof may direct, a Number of Electors, equal to the whole Number of Senators and Representatives to which the State may be entitled in the Congress: but no Senator or Representative, or Person holding an Office of Trust or Profit under the United States, shall be appointed an Elector.

The Electors shall meet in their respective States, and vote by Ballot for two Persons, of whom one at least shall not be an Inhabitant of the same State with themselves. And they shall make a List of all the Persons voted for, and of the Number of Votes for each; which List they shall sign and certify, and transmit sealed to the Seat of the Government of the United States, directed to the President of the Senate. The President of the Senate shall, in the Presence of the Senate and House of Representatives, open all the Certificates, and the Votes shall then be counted. The Person having the greatest Number of Votes shall be the President, if such Number be a Majority of the whole Number of Electors appointed; and if there be more than one who have such Majority, and have an equal Number of Votes, then the House of Representatives shall immediately chuse by Ballot one of them for President; and if no Person have a Majority, then from the five highest on the List the said House shall in like Manner chuse the President. But in chusing the President, the Votes shall be taken by States, the Representation from each State having one Vote; A quorum for this purpose shall consist of a Member or Members from two thirds of the States, and a Majority of all the States shall be necessary to a Choice. In every Case, after the Choice of the President, the Person having the greatest Number of Votes of the Electors shall be the Vice President. But if there should remain two or more who have equal Votes, the Senate shall chuse from them by Ballot the Vice President.

The Congress may determine the Time of chusing the Electors, and the Day on which they shall give their Votes; which Day shall be the same throughout the United States.

No Person except a natural born Citizen, or a Citizen of the United States, at the time of the Adoption of this Constitution, shall be eligible to the Office of President; neither shall any Person be eligible to that Office who shall not have attained to the Age of thirty five Years, and been fourteen Years a Resident within the United States.

In Case of the Removal of the President from Office, or of his Death, Resignation, or Inability to discharge the Powers and Duties of the said Office, the Same shall devolve on the Vice President, and the Congress may by Law provide for the Case of Removal, Death, Resignation or Inability, both of the President and Vice President, declaring what Officer shall then act as President, and such Officer shall act accordingly, until the Disability be removed, or a President shall be elected.

The President shall, at stated Times, receive for his Services, a Compensation, which shall neither be increased nor diminished during the Period for which he shall have been elected, and he shall not receive within that Period any other Emolument from the United States, or any of them.

Before he enter on the Execution of his Office, he shall take the following Oath or Affirmation:—"I do solemnly swear (or affirm) that I will faithfully execute the Office of President of the United States, and will to the best of my Ability, preserve, protect and defend the Constitution of the United States."

Section. 2. The President shall be Commander in Chief of the Army and Navy of the United States, and of the Militia of the several States, when called into the actual Service of the United States; he may require the Opinion, in writing, of the principal Officer in each of the executive Departments, upon any Subject relating to the Duties of their respective Offices, and he shall have Power to grant Reprieves and Pardons for Offences against the United States, except in Cases of Impeachment.

He shall have Power, by and with the Advice and Consent of the Senate, to make Treaties, provided two thirds of the Senators present concur; and he shall nominate, and by and with the Advice and Consent of the Senate, shall appoint Ambassadors, other public Ministers and Consuls, Judges of the supreme Court, and all other Officers of the United States, whose Appointments are not herein otherwise provided for, and which shall be established by Law: but the Congress may by Law vest the Appointment of such inferior Officers, as they think proper, in the President alone, in the Courts of Law, or in the Heads of Departments.

The President shall have Power to fill up all Vacancies that may happen during the Recess of the Senate, by granting Commissions which shall expire at the End of their next Session.

Section. 3. He shall from time to time give to the Congress Information of the State of the Union, and recommend to their Consideration such Measures as he shall judge necessary and expedient; he may, on extraordinary Occasions, convene both Houses, or either of them, and in Case of Disagreement between them, with Respect to the Time of Adjournment, he may adjourn them to such Time as he shall think proper; he shall receive Ambassadors and other public Ministers; he shall take Care that the Laws be faithfully executed, and shall Commission all the Officers of the United States.

Section. 4. The President, Vice President and all civil Officers of the United States, shall be removed from Office on Impeachment for, and Conviction of, Treason, Bribery, or other high Crimes and Misdemeanors.

Article. III.

Section. 1. The judicial Power of the United States shall be vested in one supreme Court, and in such inferior Courts as the Congress may from time to time ordain and establish. The Judges, both of the supreme and inferior Courts, shall hold their Offices during good Behaviour, and shall, at stated Times, receive for their Services a Compensation, which shall not be diminished during their Continuance in Office.

Section. 2. The judicial Power shall extend to all Cases, in Law and Equity, arising under this Constitution, the Laws of the United States, and Treaties made, or which shall be made, under their Authority;—to all Cases affecting Ambassadors, other public Ministers and Consuls;—to all Cases of admiralty and maritime Jurisdiction;—to Controversies to which the United States shall be a Party;—to Controversies between two or more States;— between a State and Citizens of another State,—between Citizens of different States,—between Citizens of the same State claiming Lands under Grants of different States, and between a State, or the Citizens thereof, and foreign States, Citizens or Subjects.

In all Cases affecting Ambassadors, other public Ministers and Consuls, and those in which a State shall be Party, the supreme Court shall have original Jurisdiction. In all the other Cases before mentioned, the supreme Court shall have appellate Jurisdiction, both as to Law and Fact, with such Exceptions, and under such Regulations as the Congress shall make.

The Trial of all Crimes, except in Cases of Impeachment, shall be by Jury; and such Trial shall be held in the State where the said Crimes shall have been committed; but when not committed within any State, the Trial shall be at such Place or Places as the Congress may by Law have directed.

Section. 3. Treason against the United States, shall consist only in levying War against them, or in adhering to their Enemies, giving them Aid and Comfort. No Person shall be convicted of Treason unless on the Testimony of two Witnesses to the same overt Act, or on Confession in open Court.

The Congress shall have Power to declare the Punishment of Treason, but no Attainder of Treason shall work Corruption of Blood, or Forfeiture except during the Life of the Person attainted.

Article. IV.

Section. 1. Full Faith and Credit shall be given in each State to the public Acts, Records, and judicial Proceedings of every other State. And the Congress may by general Laws prescribe the Manner in which such Acts, Records and Proceedings shall be proved, and the Effect thereof.

Section. 2. The Citizens of each State shall be entitled to all Privileges and Immunities of Citizens in the several States.

A Person charged in any State with Treason, Felony, or other Crime, who shall flee from Justice, and be found in another State, shall on Demand of the executive Authority of the State from which he fled, be delivered up, to be removed to the State having Jurisdiction of the Crime.

No Person held to Service or Labour in one State, under the Laws thereof, escaping into another, shall, in Consequence of any Law or Regulation therein, be discharged from such Service or Labour, but shall be delivered up on Claim of the Party to whom such Service or Labour may be due.

Section. 3. New States may be admitted by the Congress into this Union; but no new State shall be formed or erected within the Jurisdiction of any other State; nor any State be formed by the Junction of two or more States, or Parts of States, without the Consent of the Legislatures of the States concerned as well as of the Congress.

The Congress shall have Power to dispose of and make all needful Rules and Regulations respecting the Territory or other Property belonging to the United States; and nothing in this Constitution shall be so construed as to Prejudice any Claims of the United States, or of any particular States.

Section. 4. The United States shall guarantee to every State in this Union a Republican Form of Government, and shall protect each of them against Invasion; and on Application of the Legislature, or of the Executive (when the Legislature cannot be convened), against domestic Violence.

Article. V.

The Congress, whenever two thirds of both Houses shall deem it necessary, shall propose Amendments to this Constitution, or, on the Application of the Legislatures of two thirds of the several States, shall call a Convention for proposing Amendments, which, in either Case, shall be valid to all Intents and Purposes, as Part of this Constitution, when ratified by the Legislatures of three fourths of the several States, or by Conventions in three fourths thereof, as the one or the other Mode of Ratification may be proposed by the Congress; Provided that no Amendment which may be made prior to the Year One thousand eight hundred and eight shall in any Manner affect the first and fourth Clauses in the Ninth Section of the first Article; and that no State, without its Consent, shall be deprived of its equal Suffrage in the Senate.

Article. VI.

All Debts contracted and Engagements entered into, before the Adoption of this Constitution, shall be as valid against the United States under this Constitution, as under the Confederation.

This Constitution, and the Laws of the United States which shall be made in Pursuance thereof; and all Treaties made, or which shall be made, under the Authority of the United States, shall be the supreme Law of the Land; and the Judges in every State shall be bound thereby, any Thing in the Constitution or Laws of any State to the Contrary notwithstanding.

The Senators and Representatives before mentioned, and the Members of the several State Legislatures, and all executive and judicial Officers, both of the United States and of the several States, shall be bound by Oath or Affirmation, to support this Constitution; but no religious Test shall ever be required as a Qualification to any Office or public Trust under the United States.

Article. VII.

The Ratification of the Conventions of nine States, shall be sufficient for the Establishment of this Constitution between the States so ratifying the Same.

The Word, "the," being interlined between the seventh and eighth Lines of the first Page, the Word "Thirty" being partly written on an Erazure in the fifteenth Line of the first Page, The Words "is tried" being interlined between the thirty second and thirty third Lines of the first Page and the Word "the" being interlined between the forty third and forty fourth Lines of the second Page.

Attest William Jackson Secretary

Done in Convention by the Unanimous Consent of the States present the Seventeenth Day of September in the Year of our Lord one thousand seven hundred and Eighty seven and of the Independance of the United States of America the Twelfth In witness whereof We have hereunto subscribed our Names,

G°. Washington
Presidt and deputy from Virginia

Delaware	Geo: Read Gunning Bedford jun John Dickinson Richard Bassett Jaco: Broom	New Hampshire	John Langdon Nicholas Gilman
		Massachusetts	Nathaniel Gorham Rufus King
Maryland	James McHenry Dan of St Thos. Jenifer Danl. Carrol	Connecticut	Wm. Saml. Johnson Roger Sherman
		New York	Alexander Hamilton
Virginia	John Blair James Madison Jr.	New Jersey	Wil: Livingston David Brearley Wm. Paterson Jona: Dayton
North Carolina	Wm. Blount Richd. Dobbs Spaight Hu Williamson		
South Carolina	J. Rutledge Charles Cotesworth Pinckney Charles Pinckney Pierce Butler	Pennsylvania	B Franklin Thomas Mifflin Robt. Morris Geo. Clymer Thos. FitzSimons Jared Ingersoll James Wilson Gouv Morris
Georgia	William Few Abr Baldwin		

Amendments to the Constitution

The Bill of Rights: A Transcription

The Preamble to The Bill of Rights

Congress of the United States
begun and held at the City of New-York, on
Wednesday the fourth of March, one thousand seven hundred and eighty nine.

THE Conventions of a number of the States, having at the time of their adopting the Constitution, expressed a desire, in order to prevent misconstruction or abuse of its powers, that further declaratory and restrictive clauses should be added: And as extending the ground of public confidence in the Government, will best ensure the beneficent ends of its institution.

RESOLVED by the Senate and House of Representatives of the United States of America, in Congress assembled, two thirds of both Houses concurring, that the following Articles be proposed to the Legislatures of the several States, as amendments to the Constitution of the United States, all, or any of which Articles, when ratified by three fourths of the said Legislatures, to be valid to all intents and purposes, as part of the said Constitution; viz.

ARTICLES in addition to, and Amendment of the Constitution of the United States of America, proposed by Congress, and ratified by the Legislatures of the several States, pursuant to the fifth Article of the original Constitution.

Note: The first ten amendments to the Constitution were ratified December 15, 1791, and form what is known as the "Bill of Rights."

Amendment I

Congress shall make no law respecting an establishment of religion, or prohibiting the free exercise thereof; or abridging the freedom of speech, or of the press; or the right of the people peaceably to assemble, and to petition the Government for a redress of grievances.

Amendment II

A well regulated Militia, being necessary to the security of a free State, the right of the people to keep and bear Arms, shall not be infringed.

Amendment III

No Soldier shall, in time of peace be quartered in any house, without the consent of the Owner, nor in time of war, but in a manner to be prescribed by law.

Amendment IV

The right of the people to be secure in their persons, houses, papers, and effects, against unreasonable searches and seizures, shall not be violated, and no Warrants shall issue, but upon probable cause, supported by Oath or affirmation, and particularly describing the place to be searched, and the persons or things to be seized.

Amendment V

No person shall be held to answer for a capital, or otherwise infamous crime, unless on a presentment or indictment of a Grand Jury, except in cases arising in the land or naval forces, or in the Militia, when in actual service in time of War or public danger; nor shall any person be subject for the same offence to be twice put in jeopardy of life or limb; nor shall be compelled in any criminal case to be a witness against himself, nor be deprived of life, liberty, or property, without due process of law; nor shall private property be taken for public use, without just compensation.

Amendment VI

In all criminal prosecutions, the accused shall enjoy the right to a speedy and public trial, by an impartial jury of the State and district wherein the crime shall have been committed, which district shall have been previously ascertained by law, and to be informed of the nature and cause of the accusation; to be confronted with the witnesses against him; to have compulsory process for obtaining witnesses in his favor, and to have the Assistance of Counsel for his defence.

Amendment VII

In Suits at common law, where the value in controversy shall exceed twenty dollars, the right of trial by jury shall be preserved, and no fact tried by a jury, shall be otherwise re-examined in any Court of the United States, than according to the rules of the common law.

Amendment VIII

Excessive bail shall not be required, nor excessive fines imposed, nor cruel and unusual punishments inflicted.

Amendment IX

The enumeration in the Constitution, of certain rights, shall not be construed to deny or disparage others retained by the people.

Amendment X

The powers not delegated to the United States by the Constitution, nor prohibited by it to the States, are reserved to the States respectively, or to the people.

Amendment XI

Passed by Congress March 4, 1794. Ratified February 7, 1795.

Note: Article III, section 2, of the Constitution was modified by amendment 11.

The Judicial power of the United States shall not be construed to extend to any suit in law or equity, commenced or prosecuted against one of the United States by Citizens of another State, or by Citizens or Subjects of any Foreign State.

Amendment XII

Passed by Congress December 9, 1803. Ratified June 15, 1804.

Note: A portion of Article II, section 1 of the Constitution was superseded by the 12th amendment.

The Electors shall meet in their respective states and vote by ballot for President and Vice-President, one of whom, at least, shall not be an inhabitant of the same state with themselves; they shall name in their ballots the person voted for as President, and in distinct ballots the person voted for as Vice-President, and they shall make distinct lists of all persons voted for as President, and of all persons voted for as Vice-President, and of the number of votes for each, which lists they shall sign and certify, and transmit sealed to the seat of the government of the United States, directed to the President of the Senate; — the President of the Senate shall, in the presence of the Senate and House of Representatives, open all the certificates and the votes shall then be counted; — The person having the greatest number of votes for President, shall be the President, if such number be a majority of the whole number of Electors appointed; and if no person have such majority, then from the persons having the highest numbers not exceeding three on the list of those voted for as President, the House of Representatives shall choose immediately, by ballot, the President. But in choosing the President, the votes shall be taken by states, the representation from each state having one vote; a quorum for this purpose shall consist of a member or members from two-thirds of the states, and a majority of all the states shall be necessary to a choice. [And if the House of Representatives shall not choose a President whenever the right of choice shall devolve upon them, before the fourth day of March next following, then the Vice-President shall act as President, as in case of the death or other constitutional disability of the President. —]* The person having the greatest number of votes as Vice-President, shall be the Vice-President, if such number be a majority of the whole number of Electors appointed, and if no person have a majority, then from the two highest numbers on the list, the Senate shall choose the Vice-President; a quorum for the purpose shall consist of two-thirds of the whole number of Senators, and a majority of the whole number shall be necessary to a choice. But no person constitutionally ineligible to the office of President shall be eligible to that of Vice-President of the United States.

---

*Superseded by section 3 of the 20th amendment.

Amendment XIII

Passed by Congress January 31, 1865. Ratified December 6, 1865.

Note: A portion of Article IV, section 2, of the Constitution was superseded by the 13th amendment.

Section 1.
Neither slavery nor involuntary servitude, except as a punishment for crime whereof the party shall have been duly convicted, shall exist within the United States, or any place subject to their jurisdiction.

Section 2.
Congress shall have power to enforce this article by appropriate legislation.

Amendment XIV

Passed by Congress June 13, 1866. Ratified July 9, 1868.

Note: Article I, section 2, of the Constitution was modified by section 2 of the 14th amendment.

Section 1.
All persons born or naturalized in the United States, and subject to the jurisdiction thereof, are citizens of the United States and of the State wherein they reside. No State shall make or enforce any law which shall abridge the privileges or immunities of citizens of the United States; nor shall any State deprive any person of life, liberty, or property, without due process of law; nor deny to any person within its jurisdiction the equal protection of the laws.

Section 2.
Representatives shall be apportioned among the several States according to their respective numbers, counting the whole number of persons in each State, excluding Indians not taxed. But when the right to vote at any election for the choice of electors for President and Vice-President of the United States, Representatives in Congress, the Executive and Judicial officers of a State, or the members of the Legislature thereof, is denied to any of the male inhabitants of such State, being twenty-one years of age,* and citizens of the United States, or in any way abridged, except for participation in rebellion, or other crime, the basis of representation therein shall be reduced in the proportion which the number of such male citizens shall bear to the whole number of male citizens twenty-one years of age in such State.

Section 3.
No person shall be a Senator or Representative in Congress, or elector of President and Vice-President, or hold any office, civil or military, under the United States, or under any State, who, having previously taken an oath, as a member of Congress, or as an officer of the United States, or as a member of any State legislature, or as an executive or judicial officer of any State, to support the Constitution of the United States, shall have engaged in insurrection or rebellion against the same, or given aid or comfort to the enemies thereof. But Congress may by a vote of two-thirds of each House, remove such disability.

---

*Changed by section 1 of the 26th amendment.

Section 4.
The validity of the public debt of the United States, authorized by law, including debts incurred for payment of pensions and bounties for services in suppressing insurrection or rebellion, shall not be questioned. But neither the United States nor any State shall assume or pay any debt or obligation incurred in aid of insurrection or rebellion against the United States, or any claim for the loss or emancipation of any slave; but all such debts, obligations and claims shall be held illegal and void.

Section 5.
The Congress shall have the power to enforce, by appropriate legislation, the provisions of this article.

Amendment XV

Passed by Congress February 26, 1869. Ratified February 3, 1870.

Section 1.
The right of citizens of the United States to vote shall not be denied or abridged by the United States or by any State on account of race, color, or previous condition of servitude—

Section 2.
The Congress shall have the power to enforce this article by appropriate legislation.

Amendment XVI

Passed by Congress July 2, 1909. Ratified February 3, 1913.

Note: Article I, section 9, of the Constitution was modified by amendment 16.

The Congress shall have power to lay and collect taxes on incomes, from whatever source derived, without apportionment among the several States, and without regard to any census or enumeration.

Amendment XVII

Passed by Congress May 13, 1912. Ratified April 8, 1913.

Note: Article I, section 3, of the Constitution was modified by the 17th amendment.

The Senate of the United States shall be composed of two Senators from each State, elected by the people thereof, for six years; and each Senator shall have one vote. The electors in each State shall have the qualifications requisite for electors of the most numerous branch of the State legislatures.

When vacancies happen in the representation of any State in the Senate, the executive authority of such State shall issue writs of election to fill such vacancies: *Provided*, That the legislature of any State may empower the executive thereof to make temporary appointments until the people fill the vacancies by election as the legislature may direct.

This amendment shall not be so construed as to affect the election or term of any Senator chosen before it becomes valid as part of the Constitution.

Amendment XVIII

Passed by Congress December 18, 1917. Ratified January 16, 1919. Repealed by amendment 21.

Section 1.
After one year from the ratification of this article the manufacture, sale, or transportation of intoxicating liquors within, the importation thereof into, or the exportation thereof from the United States and all territory subject to the jurisdiction thereof for beverage purposes is hereby prohibited.

Section 2.
The Congress and the several States shall have concurrent power to enforce this article by appropriate legislation.

Section 3.
This article shall be inoperative unless it shall have been ratified as an amendment to the Constitution by the legislatures of the several States, as provided in the Constitution, within seven years from the date of the submission hereof to the States by the Congress.

Amendment XIX

Passed by Congress June 4, 1919. Ratified August 18, 1920.

The right of citizens of the United States to vote shall not be denied or abridged by the United States or by any State on account of sex.

Congress shall have power to enforce this article by appropriate legislation.

Amendment XX

Passed by Congress March 2, 1932. Ratified January 23, 1933.

Note: Article I, section 4, of the Constitution was modified by section 2 of this amendment. In addition, a portion of the 12th amendment was superseded by section 3.

Section 1.
The terms of the President and the Vice President shall end at noon on the 20th day of January, and the terms of Senators and Representatives at noon on the 3rd day of January, of the years in which such terms would have ended if this article had not been ratified; and the terms of their successors shall then begin.

Section 2.
The Congress shall assemble at least once in every year, and such meeting shall begin at noon on the 3d day of January, unless they shall by law appoint a different day.

Section 3.
If, at the time fixed for the beginning of the term of the President, the President elect shall have died, the Vice President elect shall become President. If a President shall not have been chosen before the time fixed for the beginning of his term, or if the

President elect shall have failed to qualify, then the Vice President elect shall act as President until a President shall have qualified; and the Congress may by law provide for the case wherein neither a President elect nor a Vice President shall have qualified, declaring who shall then act as President, or the manner in which one who is to act shall be selected, and such person shall act accordingly until a President or Vice President shall have qualified.

Section 4.
The Congress may by law provide for the case of the death of any of the persons from whom the House of Representatives may choose a President whenever the right of choice shall have devolved upon them, and for the case of the death of any of the persons from whom the Senate may choose a Vice President whenever the right of choice shall have devolved upon them.

Section 5.
Sections 1 and 2 shall take effect on the 15th day of October following the ratification of this article.

Section 6.
This article shall be inoperative unless it shall have been ratified as an amendment to the Constitution by the legislatures of three-fourths of the several States within seven years from the date of its submission.

Amendment XXI

Passed by Congress February 20, 1933. Ratified December 5, 1933.

Section 1.
The eighteenth article of amendment to the Constitution of the United States is hereby repealed.

Section 2.
The transportation or importation into any State, Territory, or Possession of the United States for delivery or use therein of intoxicating liquors, in violation of the laws thereof, is hereby prohibited.

Section 3.
This article shall be inoperative unless it shall have been ratified as an amendment to the Constitution by conventions in the several States, as provided in the Constitution, within seven years from the date of the submission hereof to the States by the Congress.

Amendment XXII

Passed by Congress March 21, 1947. Ratified February 27, 1951.

Section 1.
No person shall be elected to the office of the President more than twice, and no person who has held the office of President, or acted as President, for more than two years of a term to which some other person was elected President shall be elected to the office of President more than once. But this Article shall not apply to any

person holding the office of President when this Article was proposed by Congress, and shall not prevent any person who may be holding the office of President, or acting as President, during the term within which this Article becomes operative from holding the office of President or acting as President during the remainder of such term.

Section 2.
This article shall be inoperative unless it shall have been ratified as an amendment to the Constitution by the legislatures of three-fourths of the several States within seven years from the date of its submission to the States by the Congress.

Amendment XXIII

Passed by Congress June 16, 1960. Ratified March 29, 1961.

Section 1.
The District constituting the seat of Government of the United States shall appoint in such manner as Congress may direct:

A number of electors of President and Vice President equal to the whole number of Senators and Representatives in Congress to which the District would be entitled if it were a State, but in no event more than the least populous State; they shall be in addition to those appointed by the States, but they shall be considered, for the purposes of the election of President and Vice President, to be electors appointed by a State; and they shall meet in the District and perform such duties as provided by the twelfth article of amendment.

Section 2.
The Congress shall have power to enforce this article by appropriate legislation.

Amendment XXIV

Passed by Congress August 27, 1962. Ratified January 23, 1964.

Section 1.
The right of citizens of the United States to vote in any primary or other election for President or Vice President, for electors for President or Vice President, or for Senator or Representative in Congress, shall not be denied or abridged by the United States or any State by reason of failure to pay poll tax or other tax.

Section 2.
The Congress shall have power to enforce this article by appropriate legislation.

Amendment XXV

Passed by Congress July 6, 1965. Ratified February 10, 1967.

Note: Article II, section 1, of the Constitution was affected by the 25th amendment.

Section 1.
In case of the removal of the President from office or of his death or resignation, the Vice President shall become President.

Section 2.

Whenever there is a vacancy in the office of the Vice President, the President shall nominate a Vice President who shall take office upon confirmation by a majority vote of both Houses of Congress.

Section 3.

Whenever the President transmits to the President pro tempore of the Senate and the Speaker of the House of Representatives his written declaration that he is unable to discharge the powers and duties of his office, and until he transmits to them a written declaration to the contrary, such powers and duties shall be discharged by the Vice President as Acting President.

Section 4.

Whenever the Vice President and a majority of either the principal officers of the executive departments or of such other body as Congress may by law provide, transmit to the President pro tempore of the Senate and the Speaker of the House of Representatives their written declaration that the President is unable to discharge the powers and duties of his office, the Vice President shall immediately assume the powers and duties of the office as Acting President.

Thereafter, when the President transmits to the President pro tempore of the Senate and the Speaker of the House of Representatives his written declaration that no inability exists, he shall resume the powers and duties of his office unless the Vice President and a majority of either the principal officers of the executive department or of such other body as Congress may by law provide, transmit within four days to the President pro tempore of the Senate and the Speaker of the House of Representatives their written declaration that the President is unable to discharge the powers and duties of his office. Thereupon Congress shall decide the issue, assembling within forty-eight hours for that purpose if not in session. If the Congress, within twenty-one days after receipt of the latter written declaration, or, if Congress is not in session, within twenty-one days after Congress is required to assemble, determines by two-thirds vote of both Houses that the President is unable to discharge the powers and duties of his office, the Vice President shall continue to discharge the same as Acting President; otherwise, the President shall resume the powers and duties of his office.

Amendment XXVI

Passed by Congress March 23, 1971. Ratified July 1, 1971.

Note: Amendment 14, section 2, of the Constitution was modified by section 1 of the 26th amendment.

Section 1.

The right of citizens of the United States, who are eighteen years of age or older, to vote shall not be denied or abridged by the United States or by any State on account of age.

Section 2.

The Congress shall have power to enforce this article by appropriate legislation.

Amendment XXVI

Originally proposed Sept. 25, 1789. Ratified May 7, 1992.

No law, varying the compensation for the services of the Senators and Representatives, shall take effect, until an election of representatives shall have intervened.

PRESIDENTIAL ELECTIONS

Year	Number of States	Candidates	Parties	Popular Vote	% of Popular Vote	Electoral Vote	% Voter Participation
1789	11	**GEORGE WASHINGTON**	No party designations			69	
		John Adams				34	
		Other candidates				35	
1792	15	**GEORGE WASHINGTON**	No party designations			132	
		John Adams				77	
		George Clinton				50	
		Other candidates				5	
1796	16	**JOHN ADAMS**	Federalist			71	
		Thomas Jefferson	Democratic-Republican			68	
		Thomas Pinckney	Federalist			59	
		Aaron Burr	Democratic-Republican			30	
		Other candidates				48	
1800	16	**THOMAS JEFFERSON**	Democratic-Republican			73	
		Aaron Burr	Democratic-Republican			73	
		John Adams	Federalist			65	
		Charles C. Pinckney	Federalist			64	
		John Jay	Federalist			1	
1804	17	**THOMAS JEFFERSON**	Democratic-Republican			162	
		Charles C. Pinckney	Federalist			14	
1808	17	**JAMES MADISON**	Democratic-Republican			122	
		Charles C. Pinckney	Federalist			47	
		George Clinton	Democratic-Republican			6	
1812	18	**JAMES MADISON**	Democratic-Republican			128	
		DeWitt Clinton	Federalist			89	
1816	19	**JAMES MONROE**	Democratic-Republican			183	
		Rufus King	Federalist			34	
1820	24	**JAMES MONROE**	Democratic-Republican			231	
		John Quincy Adams	Independent			1	

Year	#	Candidate	Party	Popular Vote	%	Electoral	Turnout %
1824	24	**JOHN QUINCY ADAMS**	Democratic-Republican	108,740	30.5	84	26.9
		Andrew Jackson	Democratic-Republican	153,544	43.1	99	
		Henry Clay	Democratic-Republican	47,136	13.2	37	
		William H. Crawford	Democratic-Republican	46,618	13.1	41	
1828	24	**ANDREW JACKSON**	Democratic	647,286	56.0	178	57.6
		John Quincy Adams	National-Republican	508,064	44.0	83	
1832	24	**ANDREW JACKSON**	Democratic	688,242	54.5	219	55.4
		Henry Clay	National-Republican	473,462	37.5	49	
		William Wirt	Anti-Masonic	101,051	8.0	7	
		John Floyd	Democratic			11	
1836	26	**MARTIN VAN BUREN**	Democratic	765,483	50.9	170	57.8
		William H. Harrison	Whig			73	
		Hugh L. White	Whig	739,795	49.1	26	
		Daniel Webster	Whig			14	
		W. P. Mangum	Whig			11	
1840	26	**WILLIAM H. HARRISON**	Whig	1,274,624	53.1	234	80.2
		Martin Van Buren	Democratic	1,127,781	46.9	60	
1844	26	**JAMES K. POLK**	Democratic	1,338,464	49.6	170	78.9
		Henry Clay	Whig	1,300,097	48.1	105	
		James G. Birney	Liberty	62,300	2.3		
1848	30	**ZACHARY TAYLOR**	Whig	1,360,967	47.4	163	72.7
		Lewis Cass	Democratic	1,222,342	42.5	127	
		Martin Van Buren	Free Soil	291,263	10.1		
1852	31	**FRANKLIN PIERCE**	Democratic	1,601,117	50.9	254	69.6
		Winfield Scott	Whig	1,385,453	44.1	42	
		John P. Hale	Free Soil	155,825	5.0		

Year	Number of States	Candidates	Parties	Popular Vote	% of Popular Vote	Electoral Vote	% Voter Participation
1856	31	**JAMES BUCHANAN**	Democratic	1,832,955	45.3	174	78.9
		John C. Frémont	Republican	1,339,932	33.1	114	
		Millard Fillmore	American	871,731	21.6	8	
1860	33	**ABRAHAM LINCOLN**	Republican	1,865,593	39.8	180	81.2
		Stephen A. Douglas	Democratic	1,382,713	29.5	12	
		John C. Breckinridge	Democratic	848,356	18.1	72	
		John Bell	Constitutional Union	592,906	12.6	39	
1864	36	**ABRAHAM LINCOLN**	Republican	2,206,938	55.0	212	73.8
		George B. McClellan	Democratic	1,803,787	45.0	21	
1868	37	**ULYSSES S. GRANT**	Republican	3,013,421	52.7	214	78.1
		Horatio Seymour	Democratic	2,706,829	47.3	80	
1872	37	**ULYSSES S. GRANT**	Republican	3,596,745	55.6	286	71.3
		Horace Greeley	Democratic	2,843,446	43.9	66	
1876	38	**Rutherford B. Hayes**	Republican	4,036,572	48.0	185	81.8
		Samuel J. Tilden	Democratic	4,284,020	51.0	184	
1880	38	**JAMES A. GARFIELD**	Republican	4,453,295	48.5	214	79.4
		Winfield S. Hancock	Democratic	4,414,082	48.1	155	
		James B. Weaver	Greenback-Labor	308,578	3.4		
1884	38	**GROVER CLEVELAND**	Democratic	4,879,507	48.5	219	77.5
		James G. Blaine	Republican	4,850,293	48.2	182	
		Benjamin F. Butler	Greenback-Labor	175,370	1.8		
		John P. St. John	Prohibition	150,369	1.5		
1888	38	**BENJAMIN HARRISON**	Republican	5,477,129	47.9	233	79.3
		Grover Cleveland	Democratic	5,537,857	48.6	168	
		Clinton B. Fisk	Prohibition	249,506	2.2		
		Anson J. Streeter	Union Labor	146,935	1.3		

Year	#	Candidate	Party	Popular Vote	%	Electoral	Turnout %
1892	44	**GROVER CLEVELAND**	Democratic	5,555,426	46.1	277	74.7
		Benjamin Harrison	Republican	5,182,690	43.0	145	
		James B. Weaver	People's	1,029,846	8.5	22	
		John Bidwell	Prohibition	264,133	2.2		
1896	45	**WILLIAM MCKINLEY**	Republican	7,102,246	51.1	271	79.3
		William J. Bryan	Democratic	6,492,559	47.7	176	
1900	45	**WILLIAM MCKINLEY**	Republican	7,218,491	51.7	292	73.2
		William J. Bryan	Democratic; Populist	6,356,734	45.5	155	
		John C. Wooley	Prohibition	208,914	1.5		
1904	45	**THEODORE ROOSEVELT**	Republican	7,628,461	57.4	336	65.2
		Alton B. Parker	Democratic	5,084,223	37.6	140	
		Eugene V. Debs	Socialist	402,283	3.0		
		Silas C. Swallow	Prohibition	258,536	1.9		
1908	46	**WILLIAM H. TAFT**	Republican	7,675,320	51.6	321	65.4
		William J. Bryan	Democratic	6,412,294	43.1	162	
		Eugene V. Debs	Socialist	420,793	2.8		
		Eugene W. Chafin	Prohibition	253,840	1.7		
1912	48	**WOODROW WILSON**	Democratic	6,296,547	41.9	435	58.8
		Theodore Roosevelt	Progressive	4,118,571	27.4	88	
		William H. Taft	Republican	3,486,720	23.2	8	
		Eugene V. Debs	Socialist	900,672	6.0		
		Eugene W. Chafin	Prohibition	206,275	1.4		
1916	48	**WOODROW WILSON**	Democratic	9,127,695	49.4	277	61.6
		Charles E. Hughes	Republican	8,533,507	46.2	254	
		A. L. Benson	Socialist	585,113	3.2		
		J. Frank Hanly	Prohibition	220,506	1.2		
1920	48	**WARREN G. HARDING**	Republican	16,143,407	60.4	404	49.2
		James M. Cox	Democratic	9,130,328	34.2	127	
		Eugene V. Debs	Socialist	919,799	3.4		
		P. P. Christensen	Farmer-Labor	265,411	1.0		

Year	Number of States	Candidates	Parties	Popular Vote	% of Popular Vote	Electoral Vote	% Voter Participation
1924	48	**CALVIN COOLIDGE**	Republican	15,718,211	54.0	382	48.9
		John W. Davis	Democratic	8,385,283	28.8	136	
		Robert M. La Follette	Progressive	4,831,289	16.6	13	
1928	48	**HERBERT C. HOOVER**	Republican	21,391,993	58.2	444	56.9
		Alfred E. Smith	Democratic	15,016,169	40.9	87	
1932	48	**FRANKLIN D. ROOSEVELT**	Democratic	22,809,638	57.4	472	56.9
		Herbert C. Hoover	Republican	15,758,901	39.7	59	
		Norman Thomas	Socialist	881,951	2.2		
1936	48	**FRANKLIN D. ROOSEVELT**	Democratic	27,752,869	60.8	523	61.0
		Alfred M. Landon	Republican	16,674,665	36.5	8	
		William Lemke	Union	882,479	1.9		
1940	48	**FRANKLIN D. ROOSEVELT**	Democratic	27,307,819	54.8	449	62.5
		Wendell L. Willkie	Republican	22,321,018	44.8	82	
1944	48	**FRANKLIN D. ROOSEVELT**	Democratic	25,606,585	53.5	432	55.9
		Thomas E. Dewey	Republican	22,014,745	46.0	99	
1948	48	**HARRY S. TRUMAN**	Democratic	24,179,345	49.6	303	53.0
		Thomas E. Dewey	Republican	21,991,291	45.1	189	
		J. Strom Thurmond	States' Rights	1,176,125	2.4	39	
		Henry A. Wallace	Progressive	1,157,326	2.4		
1952	48	**DWIGHT D. EISENHOWER**	Republican	33,936,234	55.1	442	63.3
		Adlai E. Stevenson	Democratic	27,314,992	44.4	89	
1956	48	**DWIGHT D. EISENHOWER**	Republican	35,590,472	57.6	457	60.6
		Adlai E. Stevenson	Democratic	26,022,752	42.1	73	
1960	50	**JOHN F. KENNEDY**	Democratic	34,226,731	49.7	303	62.8
		Richard M. Nixon	Republican	34,108,157	49.5	219	
1964	50	**LYNDON B. JOHNSON**	Democratic	43,129,566	61.1	486	61.9
		Barry M. Goldwater	Republican	27,178,188	38.5	52	
1968	50	**RICHARD M. NIXON**	Republican	31,785,480	43.4	301	60.9
		Hubert H. Humphrey	Democratic	31,275,166	42.7	191	
		George C. Wallace	American Independent	9,906,473	13.5	46	

Year		Candidates	Party	Popular Vote	% Popular Vote	Electoral Vote	% Voter Participation
1972	50	**RICHARD M. NIXON**	Republican	47,169,911	60.7	520	55.2
		George S. McGovern	Democratic	29,170,383	37.5	17	
		John G. Schmitz	American	1,099,482	1.4		
1976	50	**James E. CARTER**	Democratic	40,830,763	50.1	297	53.5
		Gerald R. Ford	Republican	39,147,793	48.0	240	
1980	50	**RONALD REAGAN**	Republican	43,901,812	50.7	489	52.6
		James E. Carter	Democratic	35,483,820	41.0	49	
		John B. Anderson	Independent	5,719,437	6.6		
		Ed Clark	Libertarian	921,188	1.1		
1984	50	**RONALD REAGAN**	Republican	54,451,521	58.8	525	53.1
		Walter F. Mondale	Democratic	37,565,334	40.6	13	
1988	50	**GEORGE H. W. BUSH**	Republican	47,917,341	53.4	426	50.1
		Michael Dukakis	Democratic	41,013,030	45.6	111	
1992	50	**WILLIAM J. CLINTON**	Democratic	44,908,254	43.0	370	55.0
		George H. W. Bush	Republican	39,102,343	37.4	168	
		H. Ross Perot	Independent	19,741,065	18.9		
1996	50	**WILLIAM J. CLINTON**	Democratic	47,401,185	49.0	379	49.0
		Robert Dole	Republican	39,197,469	41.0	159	
		H. Ross Perot	Independent	8,085,295	8.0		
2000	50	**GEORGE W. BUSH**	Republican	50,455,156	47.9	271	50.4
		Al Gore	Democratic	50,997,335	48.4	266	
		Ralph Nader	Green	2,882,897	2.7		
2004	50	**GEORGE W. BUSH**	Republican	62,040,610	50.7	286	60.7
		John F. Kerry	Democratic	59,028,444	48.3	251	
2008	50	**BARACK OBAMA**	Democratic	69,456,897	52.9	365	63.0
		John McCain	Republican	59,934,814	45.7	173	
2012	50	**BARACK OBAMA**	Democratic	65,915,795	51.1	332	57.5
		Mitt Romney	Republican	60,933,504	47.2	206	
2016	50	**DONALD J. TRUMP**	Republican	62,979,636	46.1	304	60.2
		Hillary Rodham Clinton	Democratic	65,844,610	48.2	227	
2020	50	**JOSEPH R. BIDEN**	Democratic	81,268,924	51.31	302	66.8
		Donald J. Trump	Republican	74,216,154	46.86	232	
2024	50	**DONALD J. TRUMP**	Republican	76,722,400	50.0	312	63.68
		Kamala D. Harris	Democratic	74,169,608	48.3	226	

Candidates receiving less than 1 percent of the popular vote have been omitted. Thus the percentage of popular vote given for any election year may not total 100 percent. Before the passage of the Twelfth Amendment in 1804, the Electoral College voted for two presidential candidates; the runner-up became vice president.

ADMISSION OF STATES

Order of Admission	State	Date of Admission	Order of Admission	State	Date of Admission
1	Delaware	December 7, 1787	26	Michigan	January 26, 1837
2	Pennsylvania	December 12, 1787	27	Florida	March 3, 1845
3	New Jersey	December 18, 1787	28	Texas	December 29, 1845
4	Georgia	January 2, 1788	29	Iowa	December 28, 1846
5	Connecticut	January 9, 1788	30	Wisconsin	May 29, 1848
6	Massachusetts	February 7, 1788	31	California	September 9, 1850
7	Maryland	April 28, 1788	32	Minnesota	May 11, 1858
8	South Carolina	May 23, 1788	33	Oregon	February 14, 1859
9	New Hampshire	June 21, 1788	34	Kansas	January 29, 1861
10	Virginia	June 25, 1788	35	West Virginia	June 30, 1863
11	New York	July 26, 1788	36	Nevada	October 31, 1864
12	North Carolina	November 21, 1789	37	Nebraska	March 1, 1867
13	Rhode Island	May 29, 1790	38	Colorado	August 1, 1876
14	Vermont	March 4, 1791	39	North Dakota	November 2, 1889
15	Kentucky	June 1, 1792	40	South Dakota	November 2, 1889
16	Tennessee	June 1, 1796	41	Montana	November 8, 1889
17	Ohio	March 1, 1803	42	Washington	November 11, 1889
18	Louisiana	April 30, 1812	43	Idaho	July 3, 1890
19	Indiana	December 11, 1816	44	Wyoming	July 10, 1890
20	Mississippi	December 10, 1817	45	Utah	January 4, 1896
21	Illinois	December 3, 1818	46	Oklahoma	November 16, 1907
22	Alabama	December 14, 1819	47	New Mexico	January 6, 1912
23	Maine	March 15, 1820	48	Arizona	February 14, 1912
24	Missouri	August 10, 1821	49	Alaska	January 3, 1959
25	Arkansas	June 15, 1836	50	Hawaii	August 21, 1959

POPULATION OF THE UNITED STATES

Year	Number of States	Population	% Increase	Population per Square Mile
1790	13	3,929,214		4.5
1800	16	5,308,483	35.1	6.1
1810	17	7,239,881	36.4	4.3
1820	23	9,638,453	33.1	5.5
1830	24	12,866,020	33.5	7.4
1840	26	17,069,453	32.7	9.8
1850	31	23,191,876	35.9	7.9
1860	33	31,443,321	35.6	10.6
1870	37	39,818,449	26.6	13.4
1880	38	50,155,783	26.0	16.9
1890	44	62,947,714	25.5	21.1
1900	45	75,994,575	20.7	25.6
1910	46	91,972,266	21.0	31.0
1920	48	105,710,620	14.9	35.6
1930	48	122,775,046	16.1	41.2
1940	48	131,669,275	7.2	44.2
1950	48	150,697,361	14.5	50.7
1960	50	179,323,175	19.0	50.6
1970	50	203,235,298	13.3	57.5
1980	50	226,504,825	11.4	64.0
1985	50	237,839,000	5.0	67.2
1990	50	250,122,000	5.2	70.6
1995	50	263,411,707	5.3	74.4
2000	50	281,421,906	6.8	77.0
2005	50	296,410,404	5.3	77.9
2010	50	308,745,538	9.7	87.4
2015	50	321,931,311	4.3	91.1
2020	50	331,449,281	7.4	93.8
2024	50	337,194,721	1.7	95.4

IMMIGRATION BY REGION AND SELECTED COUNTRY OF LAST RESIDENCE, FISCAL YEARS 1820–2027

Region and country of last residence	1820 to 1829	1830 to 1839	1840 to 1849	1850 to 1859	1860 to 1869	1870 to 1879	1880 to 1889	1890 to 1899
Total	128,502	538,381	1,427,337	2,814,554	2,081,261	2,742,137	5,248,568	3,694,294
Europe	99,272	422,771	1,369,259	2,619,680	1,877,726	2,251,878	4,638,677	3,576,411
Austria-Hungary	—	—	—	—	3,375	60,127	314,787	534,059
Austria	—	—	—	—	2,700	54,529	204,805	268,218
Hungary	—	—	—	—	483	5,598	109,982	203,350
Belgium	28	20	3,996	5,765	5,785	6,991	18,738	19,642
Bulgaria	—	—	—	—	—	—	—	52
*Former Czechoslovakia	—	—	—	—	—	—	—	—
Denmark	173	927	671	3,227	13,553	29,278	85,342	56,671
Finland	—	—	—	—	—	—	—	—
France	7,694	39,330	75,300	81,778	35,938	71,901	48,193	35,616
Germany	5,753	124,726	385,434	976,072	723,734	751,769	1,445,181	579,072
Greece	17	49	17	32	51	209	1,807	12,732
Ireland	51,617	170,672	656,145	1,029,486	427,419	422,264	674,061	405,710
Italy	430	2,225	1,476	8,643	9,853	46,296	267,660	603,761
Netherlands	1,105	1,377	7,624	11,122	8,387	14,267	52,715	29,349
Norway-Sweden	91	1,149	12,389	22,202	82,937	178,823	586,441	334,058
Norway	—	—	—	—	16,068	88,644	185,111	96,810
Sweden	—	—	—	—	24,224	90,179	401,330	237,248
Poland	19	366	105	1,087	1,886	11,016	42,910	107,793
Portugal	177	820	196	1,299	2,083	13,971	15,186	25,874
Romania	—	—	—	—	—	—	5,842	6,808
Russia	86	280	520	423	1,670	35,177	182,698	450,101
Spain	2,595	2,010	1,916	8,795	6,966	5,540	3,995	9,189
Switzerland	3,148	4,430	4,819	24,423	21,124	25,212	81,151	37,020
United Kingdom	26,336	74,350	218,572	445,322	532,956	578,447	810,900	328,759
*Former Yugoslavia	—	—	—	—	—	—	—	—
Other Europe	3	40	79	4	9	590	1,070	145

Immigration to the United States, Fiscal Years 1820-2027

Asia	34	55	121	36,080	54,408	134,128	71,151	61,285
China	3	8	32	35,933	54,028	133,139	65,797	15,268
Hong Kong	—	—	—	—	—	166	247	102
India	9	38	33	42	50	166	—	102
Iran	—	—	—	—	—	—	—	—
*Israel	—	—	—	—	—	—	—	—
Japan	—	—	—	—	138	193	1,583	13,998
Jordan	—	—	—	—	—	—	—	—
*Korea	—	—	—	—	—	—	—	—
Philippines	—	—	—	—	—	—	—	—
Syria	—	—	—	—	—	—	—	—
Taiwan	—	—	—	—	—	—	—	—
Turkey	19	8	45	94	129	382	2,478	27,510
Vietnam	—	—	—	—	—	—	—	—
Other Asia	3	1	11	11	63	248	1,046	4,407
North America	9,655	31,905	50,516	84,145	130,292	345,010	524,826	37,350
Canada and Newfoundland	2,297	11,875	34,285	64,171	117,978	324,310	492,865	3,098
Mexico	3,835	7,187	3,069	3,446	1,957	5,133	2,405	734
Caribbean	3,061	11,792	11,803	12,447	8,751	14,285	27,323	31,480
Cuba	—	—	—	—	—	—	—	—
Dominican Republic	—	—	—	—	—	—	—	—
Haiti	—	—	—	—	—	—	—	—
Jamaica	—	—	—	—	—	—	—	—
Other Caribbean	3,061	11,792	11,803	12,447	8,751	14,285	27,323	31,480
Central America	57	94	297	512	70	173	279	649
Belize	—	—	—	—	—	—	—	—
Costa Rica	—	—	—	—	—	—	—	—
El Salvador	—	—	—	—	—	—	—	—
Guatemala	—	—	—	—	—	—	—	—
Honduras	—	—	—	—	—	—	—	—
Nicaragua	—	—	—	—	—	—	—	—
Panama	—	—	—	—	—	—	—	—
Other Central America	57	94	297	512	70	173	279	649

Region and country of last residence	1820 to 1829	1830 to 1839	1840 to 1849	1850 to 1859	1860 to 1869	1870 to 1879	1880 to 1889	1890 to 1899
South America	405	957	1,062	3,569	1,536	1,109	1,954	1,389
Argentina	—	—	—	—	—	—	—	—
Bolivia	—	—	—	—	—	—	—	—
Brazil	—	—	—	—	—	—	—	—
Chile	—	—	—	—	—	—	—	—
Colombia	—	—	—	—	—	—	—	—
Ecuador	—	—	—	—	—	—	—	—
Guyana	—	—	—	—	—	—	—	—
Paraguay	—	—	—	—	—	—	—	—
Peru	—	—	—	—	—	—	—	—
Suriname	—	—	—	—	—	—	—	—
Uruguay	—	—	—	—	—	—	—	—
Venezuela	—	—	—	—	—	—	—	—
Other South America	405	957	1,062	3,569	1,536	1,109	1,954	1,389
Other America	—	—	—	—	—	—	—	—
Africa	15	50	61	84	407	371	763	432
Egypt	—	—	—	—	4	29	145	51
Ethiopia	—	—	—	—	—	—	—	—
Liberia	1	8	5	7	43	52	21	9
Morocco	—	—	—	—	—	—	—	—
South Africa	—	—	—	—	35	48	23	9
Other Africa	14	42	56	77	325	242	574	363
Oceania	3	7	14	166	187	9,996	12,361	4,704
Australia	2	1	2	15	—	8,930	7,250	3,098
New Zealand	—	—	—	—	—	39	21	12
Other Oceania	1	6	12	151	187	1,027	5,090	1,594
Not Specified	19,523	83,593	7,366	74,399	18,241	754	790	14,112

Immigration to the United States, Fiscal Years 1820-2027

Region and country of last residence	1900 to 1909	1910 to 1919	1920 to 1929	1930 to 1939	1940 to 1949	1950 to 1959	1960 to 1969	1980 to 1989
Total	8,202,388	6,347,380	4,295,510	699,375	856,608	2,499,268	3,213,749	6,244,379
Europe	7,572,569	4,985,411	2,560,340	444,399	472,524	1,404,973	1,133,443	668,866
Austria-Hungary	2,001,376	1,154,727	60,891	12,531	13,574	113,015	27,590	20,437
Austria	532,416	589,174	31,392	5,307	8,393	81,354	17,571	15,374
Hungary	685,567	565,553	29,499	7,224	5,181	31,661	10,019	5,063
Belgium	37,429	32,574	21,511	4,013	12,473	18,885	9,647	7,028
Bulgaria	34,651	27,180	2,824	1,062	449	97	598	1,124
*Former Czechoslovakia	—	—	101,182	17,757	8,475	1,624	2,758	5,678
Denmark	61,227	45,830	34,406	3,470	4,549	10,918	9,797	4,847
Finland	—	—	16,922	2,438	2,230	4,923	4,310	2,569
France	67,735	60,335	54,842	13,761	36,954	50,113	46,975	32,066
Germany	328,722	174,227	386,634	119,107	119,506	576,905	209,616	85,752
Greece	145,402	198,108	60,774	10,599	8,605	45,153	74,173	37,729
Ireland	344,940	166,445	202,854	28,195	15,701	47,189	37,788	22,210
Italy	1,930,475	1,229,916	528,133	85,053	50,509	184,576	200,111	55,562
Netherlands	42,463	46,065	29,397	7,791	13,877	46,703	37,918	11,234
Norway-Sweden	426,981	192,445	170,329	13,452	17,326	44,224	36,150	13,941
Norway	182,542	79,488	70,327	6,901	8,326	22,806	17,371	3,835
Sweden	244,439	112,957	100,002	6,551	9,000	21,418	18,779	10,106
Poland	—	—	223,316	25,555	7,577	6,465	55,742	63,483
Portugal	65,154	82,489	44,829	3,518	6,765	13,928	70,568	42,685
Romania	57,322	13,566	67,810	5,264	1,254	914	2,339	24,753
Russia	1,501,301	1,106,998	61,604	2,463	605	453	2,329	33,311
Spain	24,818	53,262	47,109	3,669	2,774	6,880	40,793	22,783
Switzerland	32,541	22,839	31,772	5,990	9,904	17,577	19,193	8,316
United Kingdom	469,518	371,878	341,552	61,813	131,794	195,709	220,213	53,644
*Former Yugoslavia	—	—	49,215	6,920	2,039	6,966	17,990	16,267
Other Europe	514	6,527	22,434	9,978	5,584	11,756	6,845	3,447

A-41

Region and country of last residence	1900 to 1909	1910 to 1919	1920 to 1929	1930 to 1939	1940 to 1949	1950 to 1959	1960 to 1969	1980 to 1989
Asia	299,836	269,736	126,740	19,231	34,532	135,844	358,605	2,391,356
China	19,884	20,916	30,648	5,874	16,072	8,836	14,060	170,897
Hong Kong	—	—	—	—	—	13,781	67,047	112,132
India	3,026	3,478	2,076	554	1,692	1,850	18,638	231,649
Iran	—	—	208	198	1,144	3,195	9,059	98,141
*Israel	—	—	—	—	98	21,376	30,911	43,669
Japan	139,712	77,125	42,057	2,683	1,557	40,651	40,956	44,150
Jordan	—	—	—	—	—	4,899	9,230	28,928
*Korea	—	—	—	—	83	4,845	27,048	322,708
Philippines	—	—	—	391	4,099	17,245	70,660	502,056
Syria	—	—	5,307	2,188	1,179	1,091	2,432	14,534
Taiwan	—	—	—	—	—	721	15,657	119,051
Turkey	127,999	160,717	40,450	1,327	754	2,980	9,464	19,208
Vietnam	—	—	—	—	—	290	2,949	200,632
Other Asia	9,215	7,500	5,994	6,016	7,854	14,084	40,494	483,601
North America	277,809	1,070,539	1,591,278	230,319	328,435	921,610	1,674,172	2,695,329
Canada and Newfoundland	123,067	708,715	949,286	162,703	160,911	353,169	433,128	156,313
Mexico	31,188	185,334	498,945	32,709	56,158	273,847	441,824	1,009,586
Caribbean	100,960	120,860	83,482	18,052	46,194	115,661	427,235	790,109
Cuba	—	—	12,769	10,641	25,976	73,221	202,030	132,552
Dominican Republic	—	—	—	1,026	4,802	10,219	83,552	221,552
Haiti	—	—	—	156	823	3,787	28,992	121,406
Jamaica	—	—	—	—	—	7,397	62,218	193,874
Other Caribbean	100,960	120,860	70,713	6,229	14,593	21,037	50,443	120,725
Central America	7,341	15,692	16,511	6,840	20,135	40,201	98,560	339,376
Belize	77	40	285	193	433	1,133	4,185	14,964
Costa Rica	—	—	—	431	1,965	4,044	17,975	25,017
El Salvador	—	—	—	597	4,885	5,094	14,405	137,418
Guatemala	—	—	—	423	1,303	4,197	14,357	58,847
Honduras	—	—	—	679	1,874	5,320	15,078	39,071
Nicaragua	—	—	—	405	4,393	7,812	10,383	31,102

Region/Country								
Panama	—	—	—	1,452	5,282	12,601	22,177	32,957
Other Central America	7,264	15,652	16,226	2,660	—	—	—	—
South America	15,253	39,938	43,025	9,990	19,662	78,418	250,754	399,862
Argentina	—	—	—	1,067	3,108	16,346	49,384	23,442
Bolivia	—	—	—	50	893	2,759	6,205	9,798
Brazil	—	—	4,627	1,468	3,653	11,547	29,238	22,944
Chile	—	—	—	347	1,320	4,669	12,384	19,749
Colombia	—	—	—	1,027	3,454	15,567	68,371	105,494
Ecuador	—	—	—	244	2,207	8,574	34,107	48,015
Guyana	—	—	—	131	596	1,131	4,546	85,886
Paraguay	—	—	—	33	85	576	1,249	3,518
Peru	—	—	—	321	1,273	5,980	19,783	49,958
Suriname	—	—	—	25	130	299	612	1,357
Uruguay	—	—	—	112	754	1,026	4,089	7,235
Venezuela	—	—	—	1,155	2,182	9,927	20,758	22,405
Other South America	15,253	39,938	38,398	4,010	7	17	28	61
Other America	—	—	29	25	25,375	60,314	22,671	83
Africa	6,326	8,867	6,362	2,120	6,720	13,016	23,780	141,990
Egypt	—	—	1,063	781	1,613	1,996	5,581	26,744
Ethiopia	—	—	—	10	28	302	804	12,927
Liberia	—	—	—	35	37	289	841	6,420
Morocco	—	—	—	73	879	2,703	2,880	3,471
South Africa	—	—	—	312	1,022	2,278	4,360	15,505
Other Africa	6,326	8,867	5,299	909	3,141	5,448	9,314	76,923
Oceania	12,355	12,339	9,860	3,306	14,262	11,353	23,630	41,432
Australia	11,191	11,280	8,404	2,260	11,201	8,275	14,986	16,901
New Zealand	—	—	935	790	2,351	1,799	3,775	6,129
Other Oceania	1,164	1,059	521	256	710	1,279	4,869	18,402
Not Specified	33,493	488	930	—	135	12,472	119	305,406

Region and country of last residence	1990 to 1999	2000 to 2009	2010 to 2019
Total	9,775,398	10,299,430	9,738,948
Europe	1,348,612	1,349,609	866,874
Austria-Hungary	27,529	33,929	26,637
Austria	18,234	21,151	16,923
Hungary	9,295	12,778	9,714
Belgium	7,077	8,157	6,512
Bulgaria	16,948	40,003	22,588
*Former Czechoslovakia	8,970	18,691	9,885
Denmark	6,189	6,049	3,986
Finland	3,970	3,970	4,029
France	35,945	45,637	40,406
Germany	92,207	122,373	56,116
Greece	25,403	16,841	12,074
Ireland	65,384	15,642	15,889
Italy	75,992	28,329	32,057
Netherlands	13,345	17,351	11,638
Norway-Sweden	17,825	19,382	13,321
Norway	5,211	4,599	2,765
Sweden	12,614	14,783	10,556
Poland	172,249	117,921	63,537
Portugal	25,497	11,479	11,136
Romania	48,136	52,154	32,659
Russia	433,427	167,152	84,772
Spain	18,443	17,695	25,030
Switzerland	11,768	12,173	7,285
United Kingdom	156,182	171,979	123,645
*Former Yugoslavia	57,039	131,831	38,261
Other Europe	29,087	290,871	168,028
Asia	2,859,899	3,470,835	3,618,477
China	342,058	591,711	592,347
Hong Kong	116,894	57,583	25,396
India	352,528	590,464	552,546
Iran	76,899	76,755	87,339
*Israel	41,340	54,081	41,454
Japan	66,582	84,552	46,304
Jordan	42,755	53,550	70,679
*Korea	179,770	209,758	120,031
Philippines	534,338	545,463	471,391

Region and country of last residence	1990 to 1999	2000 to 2009	2010 to 2019
Syria	22,906	30,807	38,508
Taiwan	132,647	92,657	52,999
Turkey	38,687	48,394	70,766
Vietnam	275,379	289,616	306,352
Other Asia	637,116	745,444	956,264
North America	5,137,743	4,441,529	3,936,315
Canada and Newfoundland	194,788	236,349	105,875
Mexico	2,757,418	1,704,166	1,382,438
Caribbean	1,004,687	1,053,357	1,190,801
Cuba	159,037	271,742	428,136
Dominican Republic	359,818	291,492	457,589
Haiti	177,446	203,827	200,561
Jamaica	177,143	172,523	191,265
Other Caribbean	181,243	113,773	69,423
Central America	610,189	591,130	397,632
Belize	12,600	9,682	8,481
Costa Rica	17,054	21,571	20,704
El Salvador	273,017	251,237	194,225
Guatemala	126,043	156,992	111,961
Honduras	72,880	63,513	87,319
Nicaragua	80,446	70,015	35,590
Panama	28,149	18,120	13,004
Other Central America	—		0
South America	570,624	856,508	767,971
Argentina	30,065	47,955	38,201
Bolivia	18,111	21,921	17,124
Brazil	50,744	115,404	126,907
Chile	18,200	19,792	16,750
Colombia	137,985	236,570	187,980
Ecuador	81,358	107,977	100,470
Guyana	74,407	70,373	52,797
Paraguay	6,082	4,623	3,889
Peru	110,117	137,614	112,015
Suriname	2,285	2,363	1,606
Uruguay	6,062	9,827	10,632
Venezuela	35,180	82,087	99,596
Other South America	28	2	4
Other America	37	19	11

Region and country of last residence	1990 to 1999	2000 to 2009	2010 to 2019
Africa	346,416	759,734	955,113
Egypt	44,604	81,564	92,695
Ethiopia	40,097	87,207	120,326
Liberia	13,587	23,316	33,549
Morocco	15,768	40,844	38,874
South Africa	21,964	32,221	29,114
Other Africa	210,396	494,582	565,123
Oceania	56,800	65,793	49,110
Australia	24,288	32,728	28,327
New Zealand	8,600	12,495	8,130
Other Oceania	23,912	20,570	11,781
Not Specified	25,928	211,930	114,596

— Represents zero or not available.

*Note that (a) Korea split into North Korea and South Korea in 1945; (b) Czechoslovakia separated into the Czech Republic and the Slovak Republic in 1993; (c) Former Yugoslavia, beginning in the 1990s, broke into the six nations of Serbia, Montenegro, Slovenia, Croatia, Macedonia, and Kosovo; (d) and due to the way United States immigration statistics are recognized and collected, immigrants from the Occupied Palestinian Territories are grouped together with immigrants from Israel.

Immigration to the United States, Fiscal Years 1820–2027 | A-47

Region and country of last residence[1]	2020	2021	2022	2023	2024	2025	2026	2027
Total	707,362	740,002	1,018,349					
Europe	70,284	60,744	69,145					
Austria-Hungary[2,3]	1,144	1,108	1,140					
Austria[2,3]	415	408	395					
Hungary[2,3]	729	700	745					
Belgium	653	651	548					
Bulgaria[4]	1,084	959	1,024					
Czechoslovakia[5]	887	810	743					
Denmark	441	351	408					
Finland[6]	325	345	287					
France	4,212	4,234	4,353					
Germany[3]	4,220	4,293	4,295					
Greece	1,001	859	966					
Ireland[7]	1,019	1,421	1,407					
Italy	1,188	3,213	3,549					
Netherlands	274	1,078	953					
Norway-Sweden[8]	914	1,106	1,163					
Norway[8]	3,222	244	280					
Sweden[8]	704	862	883					
Poland[3]	1,855	2,860	2,667					
Portugal[9]	8,213	765	720					
Romania	2,826	1,726	1,450					
Russia[3,6,10]	690	5,344	7,563					
Spain	10,398	3,015	3,124					
Switzerland	3,444	698	680					
United Kingdom[11]	17,881	9,983	10,331					
Yugoslavia[12]	3,444	2,881	2,631					
Other Europe	17,881	13,044	19,143					
Asia	260,706	283,898	377,942					
China	39,642	48,072	62,022					
Hong Kong	2,143	1,602	2,564					
India	44,367	90,967	120,121					
Iran	7,915	4,978	8,011					
Israel	3,989	3,275	3,393					
Japan	4,153	4,336	4,248					
Jordan	3,334	3,283	3,830					
Korea[13]	16,021	12,352	14,899					
Philippines	24,112	24,376	27,692					
Syria[14]	2,072	1,024	2,161					

Region and country of last residence[1]	2020	2021	2022	2023	2024	2025	2026	2027
Taiwan	4,759	4,233	4,714					
Turkey[14]	5,000	4,805	6,824					
Vietnam	29,334	16,000	22,604					
Other Asia	73,865	64,595	94,859					
America	275,790	300,808	369,564					
Canada and Newfoundland[15,16,17]	11,297	12,053	13,916					
Mexico[16,17]	96,900	102,730	117,710					
Caribbean	71,422	76,076	94,672					
Cuba	15,609	22,494	31,019					
Dominican Republic	29,723	24,232	36,007					
Haiti	9,116	11,086	8,546					
Jamaica[18]	12,516	13,046	13,603					
Other Caribbean[18]	4,458	5,218	5,497					
Central America	35,931	40,891	61,869					
Belize	502	694	493					
Costa Rica	1,757	2,059	1,882					
El Salvador	15,385	15,801	25,609					
Guatemala	7,369	8,100	15,328					
Honduras	7,843	9,425	14,762					
Nicaragua	2,435	3,754	2,907					
Panama[19]	640	950	888					
Other Central America	0	0	0					
South America	60,237	69,058	81,396					
Argentina	2,902	3,152	3,392					
Bolivia	922	1,049	1,337					
Brazil	16,571	18,103	20,806					
Chile	1,572	1,803	1,615					
Colombia	11,375	14,661	16,763					
Ecuador	6,166	7,544	10,615					
Guyana	2,748	3,209	2,685					
Paraguay	237	339	261					
Peru	5,450	4,936	6,653					
Suriname	98	118	87					
Uruguay	673	833	578					
Venezuela	11,523	13,361	16,604					
Other South America	0	0	0					
Other America	3	0	1					
Africa	76,789	64,983	82,117					

Immigration to the United States, Fiscal Years 1820-2027 A-49

Region and country of last residence[1]	2020	2021	2022	2023	2024	2025	2026	2027
Egypt	6,720	4,320	7,378					
Ethiopia	6,468	3,902	5,268					
Liberia	1,600	2,284	1,874					
Morocco	2,773	3,621	4,307					
South Africa	2,927	2,774	3,573					
Other Africa	56,301	48,082	59,717					
Oceania	4,748	4,715	4,982					
Australia[20]	2,843	3,046	2,930					
New Zealand[20]	704	820	652					
Other Oceania	1,201	849	1,400					
Not Specified[21]	19,045	24,854	114,599					

[1] Prior to 1906, refers to country of origin; from 1906 onward, refers to country of last residence. Because of changes in country boundaries, data for a particular country may not necessarily refer to the same geographic area over time.
[2] Austria and Hungary not reported separately for all years during 1860 to 1869, 1890 to 1899, and 1900 to 1909.
[3] Poland included in Austria, Germany, Hungary, and Russia from 1899 to 1919.
[4] Bulgaria included Serbia and Montenegro from 1899 to 1919.
[5] Includes Czechia, Czechoslovakia (former), and Slovakia.
[6] Finland included in Russia from 1899 to 1919.
[7] Northern Ireland included in Ireland prior to 1925.
[8] Norway and Sweden not reported separately until 1861.
[9] Cape Verde included in Portugal from 1892 to 1952.
[10] Refers to the Russian Empire from 1820 to 1920. Between 1920 and 1990, refers to the Soviet Union. From 1991 to 1999, refers to Russia, Armenia, Azerbaijan, Belarus, Georgia, Kazakhstan, Kyrgyzstan, Moldova, Tajikistan, Turkmenistan, Ukraine, and Uzbekistan. Beginning in 2000, refers to Russia only.
[11] United Kingdom refers to England, Scotland, Wales, and Northern Ireland since 1925.
[12] Includes Bosnia and Herzegovina, Croatia, Kosovo, Macedonia, Montenegro, Serbia, Serbia and Montenegro (former), and Slovenia.
[13] Includes North Korea and South Korea.
[14] Syria included in Turkey from 1886 to 1923.
[15] Includes British North America and Canadian provinces.
[16] Land arrivals not completely enumerated until 1908.
[17] No data available for Canada or Mexico from 1886 to 1893.
[18] Jamaica included in British West Indies from 1892 to 1952.
[19] Panama Canal Zone included in Panama from 1932 to 1972.
[20] New Zealand included in Australia from 1892 to 1924.
[21] Includes 32,897 persons returning in 1906 to their homes in the United States.

Note: Official recording of immigration to the United States began in 1820 after the passage of the Act of March 2, 1819. From 1820 to 1867, figures represent alien passenger arrivals at seaports; from 1868 to 1891 and 1895 to 1897, immigrant alien arrivals; from 1892 to 1894 and 1898 to 2014, immigrant aliens admitted for permanent residence; from 1892 to 1903, aliens entering by cabin class were not counted as immigrants. Land arrivals were not completely enumerated until 1908. For this table, Fiscal Year 1843 covers 9 months ending September 30, 1843; Fiscal Years 1832 and 1850 cover 15 months ending December 31 of the respective years; Fiscal Year 1868 covers 6 months ending June 30, 1868; and Fiscal Year 1976 covers 15 months ending September 30, 1976.

LEGAL IMMIGRATION TO THE UNITED STATES

	Number of Legal Immigrants
2016	1,183,505
2017	1,127,167
2018	1,096,611
2019	1,031,765
2020	707,362
2021	740,002
2022	1,018,349
2023	TO BE RELEASED
2024	TO BE RELEASED
2025	TO BE RELEASED
2026	TO BE RELEASED
2027	TO BE RELEASED
Total	6,904,761

PRESIDENTS, VICE PRESIDENTS, AND SECRETARIES OF STATE

	President	Vice President	Secretary of State
1.	George Washington, Federalist 1789	John Adams, Federalist 1789	Thomas Jefferson 1789 Edmund Randolph 1794 Timothy Pickering 1795
2.	John Adams, Federalist 1797	Thomas Jefferson, Dem.-Rep. 1797	Timothy Pickering 1797 John Marshall 1800
3.	Thomas Jefferson, Dem.-Rep. 1801	Aaron Burr, Dem.-Rep. 1801 George Clinton, Dem.-Rep. 1805	James Madison 1801
4.	James Madison, Dem.-Rep. 1809	George Clinton, Dem.-Rep. 1809 Elbridge Gerry, Dem.-Rep. 1813	Robert Smith 1809 James Monroe 1811
5.	James Monroe, Dem.-Rep. 1817	Daniel D. Tompkins, Dem.-Rep. 1817	John Q. Adams 1817
6.	John Quincy Adams, Dem.-Rep. 1825	John C. Calhoun, Dem.-Rep. 1825	Henry Clay 1825
7.	Andrew Jackson, Democratic 1829	John C. Calhoun, Democratic 1829 Martin Van Buren, Democratic 1833	Martin Van Buren 1829 Edward Livingston 1831 Louis McLane 1833 John Forsyth 1834
8.	Martin Van Buren, Democratic 1837	Richard M. Johnson, Democratic 1837	John Forsyth 1837
9.	William H. Harrison, Whig 1841	John Tyler, Whig 1841	Daniel Webster 1841

	President	Vice President	Secretary of State
10.	John Tyler, Whig and Democratic 1841	None	Daniel Webster 1841 Hugh S. Legaré 1843 Abel P. Upshur 1843 John C. Calhoun 1844
11.	James K. Polk, Democratic 1845	George M. Dallas, Democratic 1845	James Buchanan 1845
12.	Zachary Taylor, Whig 1849	Millard Fillmore, Whig 1848	John M. Clayton 1849
13.	Millard Fillmore, Whig 1850	None	Daniel Webster 1850 Edward Everett 1852
14.	Franklin Pierce, Democratic 1853	William R. King, Democratic 1853	William L. Marcy 1853
15.	James Buchanan, Democratic 1857	John C. Breckinridge, Democratic 1857	Lewis Cass 1857 Jeremiah S. Black 1860
16.	Abraham Lincoln, Republican 1861	Hannibal Hamlin, Republican 1861 Andrew Johnson, Unionist 1865	William H. Seward 1861
17.	Andrew Johnson, Unionist 1865	None	William H. Seward 1865
18.	Ulysses S. Grant, Republican 1869	Schuyler Colfax, Republican 1869 Henry Wilson, Republican 1873	Elihu B. Washburne 1869 Hamilton Fish 1869
19.	Rutherford B. Hayes, Republican 1877	William A. Wheeler, Republican 1877	William M. Evarts 1877

	President	Vice President	Secretary of State
20.	James A. Garfield, Republican 1881	Chester A. Arthur, Republican 1881	James G. Blaine 1881
21.	Chester A. Arthur, Republican 1881	None	Frederick T. Frelinghuysen 1881
22.	Grover Cleveland, Democratic 1885	Thomas A. Hendricks, Democratic 1885	Thomas F. Bayard 1885
23.	Benjamin Harrison, Republican 1889	Levi P. Morton, Republican 1889	James G. Blaine 1889 John W. Foster 1892
24.	Grover Cleveland, Democratic 1893	Adlai E. Stevenson, Democratic 1893	Walter Q. Gresham 1893 Richard Olney 1895
25.	William McKinley, Republican 1897	Garret A. Hobart, Republican 1897 Theodore Roosevelt, Republican 1901	John Sherman 1897 William R. Day 1898 John Hay 1898
26.	Theodore Roosevelt, Republican 1901	Charles Fairbanks, Republican 1905	John Hay 1901 Elihu Root 1905 Robert Bacon 1909
27.	William H. Taft, Republican 1909	James S. Sherman, Republican 1909	Philander C. Knox 1909
28.	Woodrow Wilson, Democratic 1913	Thomas R. Marshall, Democratic 1913	William J. Bryan 1913 Robert Lansing 1915 Bainbridge Colby 1920
29.	Warren G. Harding, Republican 1921	Calvin Coolidge, Republican 1921	Charles E. Hughes 1921
30.	Calvin Coolidge, Republican 1923	Charles G. Dawes, Republican 1925	Charles E. Hughes 1923 Frank B. Kellogg 1925

	President	Vice President	Secretary of State
31.	Herbert Hoover, Republican 1929	Charles Curtis, Republican 1929	Henry L. Stimson 1929
32.	Franklin D. Roosevelt, Democratic 1933	John Nance Garner, Democratic 1933 Henry A. Wallace, Democratic 1941 Harry S. Truman, Democratic 1945	Cordell Hull 1933 Edward R. Stettinius Jr. 1944
33.	Harry S. Truman, Democratic 1945	Alben W. Barkley, Democratic 1949	Edward R. Stettinius Jr. 1945 James F. Byrnes 1945 George C. Marshall 1947 Dean G. Acheson 1949
34.	Dwight D. Eisenhower, Republican 1953	Richard M. Nixon, Republican 1953	John F. Dulles 1953 Christian A. Herter 1959
35.	John F. Kennedy, Democratic 1961	Lyndon B. Johnson, Democratic 1961	Dean Rusk 1961
36.	Lyndon B. Johnson, Democratic 1963	Hubert H. Humphrey, Democratic 1965	Dean Rusk 1963
37.	Richard M. Nixon, Republican 1969	Spiro T. Agnew, Republican 1969 Gerald R. Ford, Republican 1973	William P. Rogers 1969 Henry Kissinger 1973
38.	Gerald R. Ford, Republican 1974	Nelson Rockefeller, Republican 1974	Henry Kissinger 1974
39.	James E. Carter, Democratic 1977	Walter Mondale, Democratic 1977	Cyrus Vance 1977 Edmund Muskie 1980

40.	Ronald Reagan, Republican 1981	George H. W. Bush, Republican 1981	Alexander Haig 1981 George Schultz 1982
41.	George H. W. Bush, Republican 1989	J. Danforth Quayle, Republican 1989	James A. Baker 1989 Lawrence Eagleburger 1992
42.	William J. Clinton, Democratic 1993	Albert Gore Jr., Democratic 1993	Warren Christopher 1993 Madeleine Albright 1997
43.	George W. Bush, Republican 2001	Richard B. Cheney, Republican 2001	Colin L. Powell 2001 Condoleezza Rice 2005
44.	Barack Obama, Democratic 2009	Joseph R. Biden Jr., Democratic 2009	Hillary Rodham Clinton 2009 John Kerry 2013
45.	Donald J. Trump, Republican 2017	Michael R. Pence, Republican 2017	Rex W. Tillerson 2017 Michael R. Pompeo 2018
46.	Joseph R. Biden Jr., Democratic 2021	Kamala D. Harris, Democratic 2021	Antony J. Blinken 2021
47.	Donald J. Trump Republican 2025	James D. Vance Republican 2025	Marco A. Rubio 2025

Further Readings

Chapter 1

A fascinating study of pre-Columbian migration is Gavin Menzies and Ian Hudson, *Who Discovered America? The Untold Story of the Peopling of the Americas* (2014). Clarissa Confer's *Daily Life in Pre-Columbian Native America* (2007) reveals what life was like before the arrival of Europeans. Erik Wahlgren describes the Norse settlements in the North Atlantic in *The Vikings and America* (2000). Alice B. Kehoe's *North American Indians: A Comprehensive Account*, 3rd ed. (2005), provides an encyclopedic treatment of Native Americans. Equally valuable is Anton Treuer's *Atlas of Indian Nations* (2014). See also Charles Mann's *1491: New Revelations of the Americas before Columbus* (2005) and *1493: Uncovering the New World That Columbus Created* (2011), Colin G. Calloway's *One Vast Winter Count: The Native American West* (2006), Daniel K. Richter's *Before the Revolution: America's Ancient Pasts* (2011), and Peter Silver's *Our Savage Neighbors: How Indian War Transformed Early America* (2008). On North America's largest Native American city, see Timothy R. Pauketat, *Cahokia: Ancient America's Great City on the Mississippi* (2010).

The conflict between Native Americans and Europeans is the focus of James Axtell's *The Invasion Within: The Contest of Cultures in Colonial North America* (1986) and *Beyond 1492: Encounters in Colonial North America* (1992). Colin G. Calloway's *New Worlds for All: Indians, Europeans, and the Remaking of Early America* (1997) explores the ecological effects of European settlement, while Peter Mitchell's *Horse Nations: The Worldwide Impact of the Horse on Indigenous Societies Post-1492* (2015) explains the transformational impact of horses on Native Americans.

The inclusion of African kingdoms adds depth to our understanding of the collision of cultures. Work including Michael A. Gomez's *African Dominion: A New History of Empire in Early and Medieval West Africa* (2018), John Parker and Richard Rathbone's *African History: A Very Short Introduction* (2007), and Robert O. Collins's *Western African History: African History in Documents* (1990) offer rich histories of African societies that operated regionally and eventually interacted with European and Asian empires. The work of Ivan Van Sertima, *They Came before Columbus: The African Presence in Ancient America* (1976), is a classic text outlining the presence of Africans in the Americas, including explorers.

On the religious turmoil of the era, see Matthew Carr's *Blood and Faith: The Purging of Muslim Spain* (2010), Carlos M. N. Eire's *Reformations: The Early Modern World, 1450–1650* (2016), Alec Ryrie's *Protestants: The Faith That Made the Modern World* (2017), Lyndal Roper's *Martin Luther: Renegade and Prophet* (2017), and Peter H. Wilson's *Europe's Tragedy: A History of the Thirty Years' War* (2009). Benjamin Friedman's *Religion and the Rise of Capitalism* (2021) examines the relationship between Protestantism and economics.

Laurence Bergreen examines the voyages of Columbus in *Columbus: The Four Voyages* (2011). To learn about the queen who sent Columbus to the New World, see Kristin Downey's *Isabella: The Warrior Queen* (2014). For sweeping overviews of Spain's creation of a global empire, see Hugh Thomas's *Rivers of Gold: The Rise of the Spanish Empire, from Columbus to Magellan* (2004) and *World without End: Spain, Philip II, and the First Global Empire* (2016), and Robert Goodwin's *Spain: The Center of the World, 1519–1682* (2015).

The Spanish conquest of the Mexica is the focus of David M. Carballo's *Collision of Worlds: A Deep History of the Fall of Aztec Mexico and the Forging of New Spain* (2021). For a more favorable view of the Spanish invaders, see Fernando Cervantes's

Conquistadores: A New History (2021). David J. Weber examines Spanish colonization in *The Spanish Frontier in North America* (1992). For comprehensive overviews of the Hispanic influence in U.S. history, see Felipe Fernández-Armesto's *Our America: A Hispanic History of the United States* (2014), Carrie Gibson's *El Norte: The Epic and Forgotten Story of Hispanic North America* (2020), and Paul Ortiz's *An African American and Latinx History of the United States* (2018).

For the French experience in North America, see William J. Eccles's *France in America*, rev. ed. (1990). For an insightful comparison of Spanish and English modes of settlement, see J. H. Elliott's *Empires of the Atlantic World: Britain and Spain in America, 1492–1830* (2006). The Spanish settlement of what became the state of Texas is described in Donald E. Chipman's *Spanish Texas, 1519–1821* (1992).

Chapter 2

Two excellent surveys of early American history are Peter C. Hoffer's *The Brave New World: A History of Early America*, 2nd ed. (2006), and William R. Polk's *The Birth of America: From before Columbus to the Revolution* (2006). More recently, Jill Lepore published a *New York Times* bestseller, *These Truths: A History of the United States* (2018), changing the approach to American history and a national conversation about this history.

Bernard Bailyn's *The Barbarous Years: The Peopling of British North America; The Conflict of Civilizations, 1600–1675* (2013) tells the often-brutal story of British settlement in America during the seventeenth century. On the impact of the North American environment on colonial settlement, see Malcolm Gaskill's *Between Two Worlds: How the English Became Americans* (2015) and Sam White's *A Cold Welcome: The Little Ice Age and Europe's Encounter with North America* (2019). The best overview of the colonization of North America is Alan Taylor's *American Colonies: The Settling of North America* (2001). On the interactions among Indigenous American, European, and African cultures, see Andrew Lipman's *The Saltwater Frontier: Indians and the Contest for the American Coast* (2015), Gary B. Nash's *Red, White, and Black: The Peoples of Early North America*, 5th ed. (2005), and Margaret Ellen Newell's *Brethren by Nature: New England Indians, Colonists, and the Origins of American Slavery* (2016). The works by Ned Blackhawk, *The Rediscovery of America: Native Peoples and the Unmaking of U.S. History* (2023), Pekka Hamalainen, *Indigenous Continent: The Epic Contest for North America* (2022), and Roxanne Dunbar-Ortiz, *An Indigenous People's History of the United States* (2014) shaped a broader understanding of Indigenous people and their experiences in early America.

A good overview of the founding of Virginia and Maryland is Jean and Elliott Russo's *The Early Chesapeake in British North America* (2012). For information regarding the Puritan settlement of New England, see David D. Hall's two fine books, *A Reforming People: Puritanism and the Transformation of Public Life in New England* (2013) and *The Puritans: A Transatlantic History* (2019). On the pilgrims and Plymouth, see Francis J. Bremer's *One Small Candle: The Plymouth Puritans* (2020) and Martyn Whittock's *Mayflower Lives: Pilgrims in a New World and the Early American Experience* (2019). The best biography of John Winthrop is Francis J. Bremer's *John Winthrop: America's Forgotten Founding Father* (2003). On Roger Williams, see John M. Barry's *Roger Williams and the Creation of the American Soul* (2012) and James A. Warren's *God, War, and Providence: The Epic Struggle of Roger Williams and the Narragansett Indians against the Puritans of New England* (2018). Studies of colonial Georgia include Betty Wood's *Slavery in Colonial Georgia, 1730–1775* (2007) and the recent biography *James Oglethorpe, Father of Georgia: A Founder's Journey from Slave Trader to Abolitionist* by Michael Thurmond (2024).

The pattern of settlement in the middle colonies is the subject of Barry Levy's *Quakers and the American Family: British Settlement in the Delaware Valley* (1988). On the early history of New York, see Russell Shorto's *The Island at the Center of the World: The Epic Story of Dutch Manhattan and the Forgotten Colony That Shaped America* (2004). Settlement of the Chesapeake Bay region is the focus of James Horn's *Adapting to a New World: English Society in the Seventeenth-Century Chesapeake* (1994). On North Carolina, see Noeleen McIlvenna's *A Very Mutinous People: The Struggle for North Carolina, 1660–1713* (2009).

On the shifting political dynamics in England during the seventeenth century, see Peter Ackroyd's *The History of England from James I to the Glorious Revolution* (2015) and Steve Pincus's *1688: The First Modern Revolution* (2009). For a study of race and the settlement of South Carolina, see Peter H. Wood's *Black Majority: Negroes in Colonial South Carolina from 1670 through the Stono Rebellion* (1974). On the flourishing trade in captive Native Americans, see Alan Gallay's *The Indian Slave Trade: The Rise of the English Empire in the American South, 1670–1717* (2002) and Andres Resendez's *The Other Slavery: The Uncovered Story of Indian Enslavement in America* (2016). On the Yamasee War, see Steven J. Oatis's *A Colonial Complex: South Carolina's Frontiers in the Era of the Yamasee War, 1680–1730* (2004) and William L. Ramsey's *The Yamasee War: A Study of Culture, Economy, and Conflict in the Colonial South* (2010).

Chapter 3

The diversity of colonial societies is featured in David Hackett Fischer's *Albion's Seed: Four British Folkways in America* (1989). John Frederick Martin's *Profits in the Wilderness: Entrepreneurship and the Founding of New England Towns in the Seventeenth Century* (1991) demonstrates how economic concerns rather than spiritual motives were driving forces in many New England towns.

Bernard Rosenthal challenges many myths concerning the Salem witch trials in *Salem Story: Reading the Witch Trials of 1692* (1993). Mary Beth Norton's *In the Devil's Snare: The Salem Witchcraft Crisis of 1692* (2002) emphasizes the role of Native American violence, while Stacy Schiff's *The Witches: Salem, 1692* (2016) provides a riveting analysis of the many factors influencing the outbreak of anti-witch hysteria. See also Benjamin C. Ray's *Satan and Salem: The Witch-Hunt Crisis of 1692* (2015).

Colorful discussions of women in the New England colonies can be found in Laurel Thatcher Ulrich's *Good Wives: Image and Reality in the Lives of Women in Northern New England, 1650–1750* (1980) and Mary Beth Norton's *Separated by Their Sex: Women in Public and Private in the Colonial Atlantic World* (2011). On women and religion, see Susan Juster's *Disorderly Women: Sexual Politics and Evangelicalism in Revolutionary New England* (1994). John Demos describes family life in *A Little Commonwealth: Family Life in Plymouth Colony*, new ed. (2000).

For analyses of Native American wars, see Alfred A. Cave's *The Pequot War* (1996), James D. Drake's *King Philip's War: Civil War in New England* (2000), and Jill Lepore's *The Name of War: King Philip's War and the Origins of American Identity* (1998). The story of the Iroquois is told well in Daniel K. Richter's *The Ordeal of the Longhouse: The Peoples of the Iroquois League in the Era of European Colonization* (1992). Indigenous Americans in the southern colonies are the focus of James Axtell's *The Indians' New South: Cultural Change in the Colonial Southeast* (1997). On the fur trade, see Eric Jay Dolan's *Fur, Fortune, and Empire: The Epic Story of the Fur Trade in America* (2010). For insights into the Glorious Revolution in England, see Steve Pincus's *1688: The First Modern Revolution* (2009).

For the social history of the southern colonies, see Allan Kulikoff's *Tobacco and Slaves: The Development of Southern Cultures in the Chesapeake, 1680–1800* (1986). On the interaction between Blacks and Whites, see Mechal Sobel's *The World They Made Together: Black and White Values in Eighteenth-Century Virginia* (1987). On the selling of enslaved Africans, see William St. Clair's *The Door of No Return: The History of Cape Coast Castle and the Atlantic Slave Trade* (2007). African Americans during colonial settlement are the focus of Timothy H. Breen and Stephen Innes's *"Myne Owne Ground": Race and Freedom on Virginia's Eastern Shore, 1640–1676*, new ed. (2004). David W. Galenson's *White Servitude in Colonial America: An Economic Analysis* (1981) looks at the lives of indentured laborers. Herman L. Bennett's *African Kings and Black Slaves: Sovereignty and Dispossession in the Early Modern Atlantic* (2020), Stephanie E. Smallwood's *Saltwater Slavery: A Middle Passage from Africa to American Diaspora* (2008), and Marcus Rediker's *The Slave Ship: A Human History* (2008) all provide original history of the trade in African people.

Henry F. May's *The Enlightenment in America* (1976) and Donald H. Meyer's *The Democratic Enlightenment* (1976) examine intellectual trends in eighteenth-century America. See also Ritchie Robertson's *The Enlightenment: The Pursuit of Happiness, 1680–1790* (2020). On the Great Awakening, see Frank Lambert's *Inventing the "Great Awakening"* (1999) and Thomas S. Kidd's *The Great Awakening: The Roots of Evangelical Christianity in Colonial America* (2007). Excellent biographies of the key revivalists are Phillip F. Gura's *Jonathan Edwards: A Life* (2003) and Thomas S. Kidd's *George Whitefield: America's Spiritual Founding Father* (2015).

Chapter 4

A good introduction to the imperial phase of the colonial conflicts is Douglas Edward Leach's *Arms for Empire: A Military History of the British Colonies in North America, 1607–1763* (1973). Also useful is Brendan Simms's *Three Victories and a Defeat: The Rise and Fall of the First British Empire* (2008). Fred Anderson's *Crucible of War: The Seven Years' War and the Fate of Empire in British North America, 1754–1766* (2000) is the best history of the Seven Years' War. For the implications of the British victory in 1763, see Colin G. Calloway's *The Scratch of a Pen: 1763 and the Transformation of North America* (2006). On the French colonies in North America, see David W. J. Eccles's *The French in North America: 1500–1783* (2010), David Hackett Fischer's *Champlain's Dream* (2008), and Allan Greer's *The People of New France* (1997).

For a narrative survey of the events leading to the Revolution, see Nina Sankovitch's *American Rebels: How the Hancock, Adams, and Quincy Families Fanned the Flames of Revolution* (2020) and Eric Hinderaker's *Boston's Massacre* (2017). For Great Britain's perspective on the imperial conflict, see Ian R. Christie's *Crisis of Empire: Great Britain and the American Colonies, 1754–1783* (1966). Also see Jeremy Black's *George III: America's Last King* (2007), David Preston's *Braddock's Defeat: The Battle of the Monongahela and the Road to Revolution* (2015), and Nick Bunker's *An Empire on the Edge: How Britain Came to Fight America* (2015). For a social history of the Revolution, see Gary Nash's *The Unknown American Revolution: The Unruly Birth of Democracy and the Struggle to Create America* (2006) and Alan Taylor's *American Revolutions: A Continental History, 1750–1802* (2017).

The intellectual foundations of revolt are explored in Bernard Bailyn's *The Ideological Origins of the American Revolution* (1992). To understand how these views were connected to organized protest, see Jon Butler's *Becoming America: The Revolution before 1776* (2000) and Kevin Phillips's *1775: A Good Year for a Revolution* (2012). On the first major battle, see Nathaniel Philbrick's *Bunker Hill: A City, a Siege, a Revolution* (2013).

On the efforts of colonists to boycott the purchase of British goods, see T. H. Breen's *The Marketplace of Revolution: How Consumer Politics Shaped American Independence* (2004). For the critical events during the summer of 1776, see Joseph J. Ellis's *1776: The Summer the Revolution Was Born* (2013). Pauline Maier's *American Scripture: Making the Declaration of Independence* (1997) remains the best analysis of the framing of that pathbreaking document. The best analysis of why Americans supported independence is Thomas Slaughter's *Independence: The Tangled Roots of the American Revolution* (2014).

Chapter 5

Military affairs in the early phases of the Revolutionary War are the focus of John Ferling's *Almost a Miracle: The American Victory in the War for Independence* (2009). The Revolutionary War is the subject of Holger Hoock's *Scars of Independence: America's Violent Birth* (2017) and Jeremy Black's *War for America: The Fight for Independence, 1775–1783* (1991). For a splendid account of Washington's generalship, see Robert Middlekauf's *Washington's Revolution: The Making of America's First Great Leader* (2015).

On the social history of the Revolutionary War, see John W. Shy's *A People Numerous and Armed: Reflections on the Military Struggle for American Independence*, rev. ed. (1990). Colin G. Calloway tells the neglected story of the Native American experiences during the Revolution in *The American Revolution in Indian Country: Crisis and Diversity in Native American Communities* (1995). For a continental assessment of the Revolution, see Alan Taylor's *American Revolutions: A Continental History* (2016).

Why many Americans remained loyal to the Crown is the subject of Thomas B. Allen's *Tories: Fighting for the King in America's First Civil War* (2010) and Maya Jasanoff's *Liberty's Exiles: American Loyalists in the Revolutionary War* (2011). A superb study of African Americans during the Revolutionary era is Douglas R. Egerton's *Death or Liberty: African Americans and Revolutionary America* (2009). For insights into the role of Indigenous Americans in the war, see Colin G. Calloway's *The American Revolution in Indian Country* (1995), Ethan A. Schmidt's *Native Americans in the American Revolution: How the War Divided, Devastated, and Transformed the Early American Indian World* (2014), and Joseph T. Glatthaar and James Kirby Martin's *Forgotten Allies: The Oneida Indians and the American Revolution* (2007). The strategic American victory at Saratoga is the focus of Richard M. Ketchum's *Saratoga: Turning Point of America's Revolutionary War* (1999).

Carol Berkin's *Revolutionary Mothers: Women in the Struggle for America's Independence* (2005) documents the role that women played in securing independence. A superb biography of Revolutionary America's most prominent woman is Woody Holton's *Abigail Adams* (2010). A fine new biography of America's commander-in-chief is Ron Chernow's *Washington: A Life* (2010). The best analysis of the British side of the war is Andrew Jackson O'Shaughnessy's *The Men Who Lost America: British Leadership, the American Revolution, and the Fate of Empire* (2013).

Chapter 6

A good overview of the Confederation period is Richard B. Morris's *The Forging of the Union, 1781–1789* (1987). For the role played by key leaders, see Joseph J. Ellis's *The Quartet: Orchestrating the Second American Revolution, 1783–1789* (2016).

Daniel Bullen's *Daniel Shays's Honorable Rebellion: An American Story* (2021) covers that fateful incident.

An excellent overview of post-Revolutionary life is Joyce Appleby's *Inheriting the Revolution: The First Generation of Americans* (2000). For the dramatic story of the framers of the Constitution, see Richard Beeman's *Plain, Honest Men: The Making of the American Constitution* (2009). Woody Holton's *Unruly Americans and the Origins of the Constitution* (2007) emphasizes the role of taxes and monetary policies in the crafting of the Constitution. A more comprehensive study of the economic issues facing the new republic is Thomas K. McCraw's *The Founders and Finance: How Hamilton, Gallatin, and Other Immigrants Forged a New Economy* (2012). The complex story of ratification is well told in Pauline Maier's *Ratification: The People Debate the Constitution, 1787–1788* (2010). Excellent studies of James Madison's development as a political theorist are Michael Signer's *Becoming Madison: The Extraordinary Origins of the Least Likely Founding Father* (2015) and David O. Stewart's *Madison's Gift: Five Partnerships That Built America* (2015).

On attitudes toward religion in the new United States, see Jon Meacham's *American Gospel: God, the Founding Fathers, and the Making of a Nation* (2006).

The best introduction to the early Federalists remains John C. Miller's *The Federalist Era, 1789–1801* (2011). Other works analyze the ideological debates among the nation's first leaders. Richard Buel Jr.'s *Securing the Revolution: Ideology in American Politics, 1789–1815* (1972) and Stanley Elkins and Eric McKitrick's *The Age of Federalism: The Early American Republic, 1788–1800* (1993) trace the persistence and transformation of ideas first fostered during the Revolutionary crisis. The best studies of George Washington's political career are John Ferling's *The Ascent of George Washington: The Hidden Political Genius of an American Icon* (2009) and Edward Larson's *The Return of George Washington: Uniting the States, 1783–1789* (2015). Studies of enslaved women such as Ona Judge shed new light on the history of George Washington's presidency, according to Erica Armstrong Dunbar's *Never Caught: The Washingtons' Restless Pursuit of Their Runaway Slave, Ona Judge* (2017). For work on slavery during this era, see David Waldstrecher's *Slavery's Constitution: From the Revolution to Ratification* (2010) and Elizabeth Dowling Taylor's *A Slave in the White House: Paul Jennings and the Madisons* (2014).

The 1790s may also be understood through the views and behavior of national leaders. See the following biographies: Richard Brookhiser's *Founding Father: Rediscovering George Washington* (1996), *Alexander Hamilton, American* (1999), and *James Madison* (2013); and Joseph J. Ellis's *Passionate Sage: The Character and Legacy of John Adams* (1993). On social life, see Jack Larkin's *Everyday Life in America, 1790–1840* (1989). On the presidency of John Adams and his controversial crackdown on free speech, see Wendell Bird's *Criminal Dissent: Prosecutions under the Alien and Sedition Acts of 1798* (2020).

On the formation of the federal government and its economic policies, see Thomas K. McCraw's *The Founders and Finance: How Hamilton, Gallatin, and Other Immigrants Forged a New Economy* (2012). Federalist foreign policy is explored in Jerald A. Combs's *The Jay Treaty: Political Battleground of the Founding Fathers* (1970) and William Stinchcombe's *The XYZ Affair* (1980).

Chapter 7

The most comprehensive overviews of the first years of the new nation are Alan Taylor's *American Republics: A Continental History of the United States, 1783–1850* (2021) and Gordon S. Wood's *Empire of Liberty: A History of the Early Republic,*

1789–1815 (2010). The best treatment of the election of 1800 is Edward J. Larson's *A Magnificent Catastrophe: The Tumultuous Election of 1800* (2007).

The standard biography of Jefferson is Joseph J. Ellis's *American Sphinx: The Character of Thomas Jefferson* (1996). More recent analyses include John Boles's *Jefferson: Architect of American Liberty* (2017) and Andrew Burstein's *Democracy's Muse: How Thomas Jefferson Became an FDR Liberal, a Reagan Republican, and a Tea Party Fanatic, All the While Being Dead* (2015). Studies of Jefferson and slavery include Annette Gordon-Reed's work, *Thomas Jefferson and Sally Hemings: An American Controversy* (1998) and *The Hemingses of Monticello: An American Family* (2009). On the life of Jefferson's friend and successor, James Madison, see Drew R. McCoy's *The Last of the Fathers: James Madison and the Republican Legacy* (1989).

Regarding the magisterial influence of John Marshall on American legal philosophy, see Richard Brookhiser's *John Marshall: The Man Who Made the Supreme Court* (2018) and Joel Richard Paul's *Without Precedent: John Marshall and His Times* (2018). The concept of judicial review and the courts can be studied in Cliff Sloan and David McKean's *The Great Decision: Jefferson, Adams, Marshall, and the Battle for the Supreme Court* (2009). A recent biography of Jefferson's political nemesis is Nancy Isenberg's *Fallen Founder: The Life of Aaron Burr* (2008). On the duel that saw Aaron Burr kill Alexander Hamilton, see John Sedgwick's *War of Two: Alexander Hamilton, Aaron Burr, and the Duel That Stunned the Nation* (2015).

For the Louisiana Purchase, consult Jon Kukla's *A Wilderness So Immense: The Louisiana Purchase and the Destiny of America* (2003). The development of the states bordering the Gulf of Mexico is told well in Jack E. Davis's *The Gulf: The Making of an American Sea* (2017). For a captivating account of the Lewis and Clark expedition, see Stephen Ambrose's *Undaunted Courage: Meriwether Lewis, Thomas Jefferson, and the Opening of the American West* (1996).

Burton Spivak's *Jefferson's English Crisis: Commerce, Embargo, and the Republican Revolution* (1979) discusses Anglo-American relations during Jefferson's administration; Clifford L. Egan's *Neither Peace nor War: Franco-American Relations, 1803–1812* (1983) covers America's relations with France. An excellent revisionist treatment of the events that brought on war in 1812 is J. C. A. Stagg's *Mr. Madison's War: Politics, Diplomacy, and Warfare in the Early American Republic, 1783–1830* (1983). See also Paul A. Gilje's *Free Trade and Sailors' Rights in the War of 1812* (2013) and Willard Sterne Randall's *Unshackling America: How the War of 1812 Truly Ended the American Revolution* (2017). The war itself is the focus of Donald R. Hickey's *The War of 1812: A Forgotten Conflict* (1989). For the perspective of those who fought in the war, see A. J. Langguth's *Union 1812: The Americans Who Fought the Second War of Independence* (2007). See also Alan Taylor's award-winning *The Civil War of 1812: American Citizens, British Subjects, Irish Rebels, and Indian Allies* (2011).

Chapter 8

The best overview of the second quarter of the nineteenth century is Daniel Walker Howe's *What Hath God Wrought: The Transformation of America, 1815–1845* (2007). The classic study of transportation and economic growth during the early nineteenth century is George Rogers Taylor's *The Transportation Revolution, 1815–1860* (1951). A more recent treatment is Sarah H. Gordon's *Passage to Union: How the Railroads Transformed American Life, 1829–1929* (1996). On the Erie Canal, see Gerard Koeppel's *Bond of Union: Building the Erie Canal and the American Empire* (2009). On the development of clipper ships, see Stephen Ujifusa's *Barons of the Sea: The Race to Build Clipper Ships* (2018).

On the Industrial Revolution, see Charles R. Morris's *The Dawn of Innovation: The First American Industrial Revolution* (2013). The impact of technology is examined in David J. Jeremy's *Transatlantic Industrial Revolution: The Diffusion of Textile Technologies between Britain and America, 1790–1830s* (1981). On the invention of the telegraph, see Kenneth Silverman's *Lightning Man: The Accursed Life of Samuel F. B. Morse* (2003). Women inventors are discussed in Denise E. Pilato's *The Retrieval of a Legacy: Nineteenth-Century American Women Inventors* (2000).

The interconnected economies of the industrial North and the agricultural South, and the investment of northern banks and insurance companies in the southern slavery system, are well detailed in Sharon Murphy's *Banking on Slavery: Financing Southern Expansion in the Antebellum United States* (2023) and Sven Beckert and Seth Rockman, eds., *Slavery's Capitalism: A New History of American Economic Development* (2016).

The outlook of the working class during this time of transition is surveyed in Edward E. Pessen's *Most Uncommon Jacksonians: The Radical Leaders of the Early Labor Movement* (1967). See also James R. Barrett's *History from the Bottom Up and Inside Out: Ethnicity, Race, and Identity in Working-Class History* (2017). Detailed case studies of working communities include Anthony F. C. Wallace's *Rockdale: The Growth of an American Village in the Early Industrial Revolution* (1978), David R. Roediger's *The Wages of Witness: Race and the Making of the American Working Class* (2007), Seth Rockman's *Scraping By: Wage Labor, Slavery, and Survival in Early Baltimore* (2009), and Sean Wilentz's *Chants Democratic: New York and the Rise of the American Working Class, 1788–1850* (1984). Other important examinations of working-class women's labor include Thomas Dublin's *Women at Work: The Transformation of Work and Community in Lowell, Massachusetts, 1826–1860* (1979), Leslie Harris's *In the Shadow of Slavery: African Americans in New York City, 1626–1863* (2003), and Christine Stansell's *City of Women: Sex and Class in New York, 1789–1860* (1986).

For a fine treatment of urbanization, see Charles N. Glaab and A. Theodore Brown's *A History of Urban America* (1967). On immigration, see John Bodnar's *The Transplanted: A History of Immigrants in Urban America* (1987), Roger Daniels's *Coming to America: A History of Immigration and Ethnicity in American Life* (2002), Leonard Dinnerstein's *Ethnic Americans: A History of Immigration* (2009), Jay P. Dolan's *The Irish Americans: A History* (2008), and John Kelly's *The Graves Are Walking: The Great Famine and the Saga of the Irish People* (2012). For a fascinating account of two sisters who became the first female physicians in America, see Janice Nimura's *The Doctors Blackwell: How Two Pioneering Sisters Brought Medicine to Women—and Women to Medicine* (2021); and for a lively treatment of the actress Fanny Kemble, see Catherine Clinton's *Fanny Kemble's Civil Wars* (2000).

Chapter 9

The standard overview of the Era of Good Feelings remains George Dangerfield's *The Awakening of American Nationalism, 1815–1828* (1965). A classic summary of the economic trends of the period is Douglass C. North's *The Economic Growth of the United States, 1790–1860* (1961). An excellent synthesis of the era is Charles Sellers's *The Market Revolution: Jacksonian America, 1815–1846* (1991).

On Monroe, see Harlow Giles Unger's *The Last Founding Father: James Monroe and a Nation's Call to Greatness* (2010) and Tim McGrath's *James Monroe: A Life* (2020). On John Quincy Adams, see William J. Cooper's *The Lost Founding Father: John Quincy Adams and the Transformation of American Politics* (2017), Charles N. Edel's *John Quincy Adams and the Grand Strategy of the Republic* (2014), and Fred Kaplan's *John Quincy Adams: American Visionary* (2014). For diplomatic relations during James Monroe's presidency, see William Earl Weeks's *John Quincy Adams and American Global Empire* (1992).

Chapter 10

The best comprehensive surveys of politics and culture during the Jacksonian era are Daniel Walker Howe's *What Hath God Wrought: The Transformation of America, 1815–1848* (2007) and David S. Reynolds's *Waking Giant: America in the Age of Jackson* (2008). A more political focus can be found in Harry L. Watson's *Liberty and Power: The Politics of Jacksonian America* (1990). On the rise of urban political machines, see Terry Golway's *Machine Made: Tammany Hall and the Creation of Modern American Politics* (2014).

For an outstanding analysis of women in New York City during the Jacksonian period, see Christine Stansell's *City of Women: Sex and Class in New York, 1789–1860* (1986). In *Chants Democratic: New York City and the Rise of the American Working-Class, 1788–1850* (1984), Sean Wilentz analyzes the social basis of working-class politics. More recently, Wilentz has traced the democratization of politics in *The Rise of American Democracy: Jefferson to Lincoln* (2009).

The best biography of Jackson remains Robert Vincent Remini's three-volume work: *Andrew Jackson: The Course of American Empire, 1767–1821* (1977), *Andrew Jackson: The Course of American Freedom, 1822–1832* (1981), and *Andrew Jackson: The Course of American Democracy, 1833–1845* (1984). A more critical study of the seventh president is Andrew Burstein's *The Passions of Andrew Jackson* (2003). See also Jon Meacham's *American Lion: Andrew Jackson in the White House* (2009). On Jackson and the Native Americans, see Robert Remini's *Andrew Jackson and His Indian Wars* (2001). The story of the Trail of Tears is told in A. J. Langguth's *Driven West: Andrew Jackson and the Trail of Tears* (2011) and Claudio Saunt's *Unworthy Republic* (2020).

On Jackson's successor, consult Ted Widmer's *Martin Van Buren* (2005). Studies of other major figures of the period include Robert Elder's *Calhoun: American Heretic* (2021), Merrill D. Peterson's *The Great Triumvirate: Webster, Clay, and Calhoun* (1987), James C. Klotter's *Henry Clay: The Man Who Would Be President* (2018), and Robert Vincent Remini's *Daniel Webster: The Man and His Time* (1997).

The political philosophies of Jackson's opponents are treated in Michael F. Holt's *The Rise and Fall of the American Whig Party: Jacksonian Politics and the Onset of the Civil War* (1999) and Harry L. Watson's *Andrew Jackson vs. Henry Clay: Democracy and Development in Antebellum America* (1998). The outstanding book on the nullification issue remains William W. Freehling's *Prelude to Civil War: The Nullification Controversy in South Carolina, 1816–1836* (1965). John M. Belohlavek's *"Let the Eagle Soar!": The Foreign Policy of Andrew Jackson* (1985) is a thorough study of Jacksonian diplomacy.

New work on Indigenous people during this period is offered by Barbara Krauthamer's *Black Slaves, Indian Masters: Slavery, Emancipation, and Citizenship in the Native American South* (2013), Celia E. Naylor's *African Cherokees in Indian Territory: From Chattel to Citizens* (2008), and Tiya Miles's *Ties That Bind: The Story of an Afro-Cherokee Family in Slavery and Freedom* (2015).

Chapter 11

Three efforts to understand the mind of the Old South and its defense of slavery are Lacy K. Ford's *Deliver Us from Evil: The Slavery Question in the Old South* (2009), Eugene D. Genovese's *The Slaveholders' Dilemma: Freedom and Progress* in *Southern Conservative Thought, 1820–1860* (1992), William W. Freehling's *The Road to Disunion: Secessionists Triumphant, 1854–1861* (2007), and Walter Johnson's *River of Dark Dreams: Slavery and Empire in the Cotton Kingdom* (2013). Stephanie McCurry's *Masters of Small Worlds: Yeoman Households, Gender Relations, and the Political Culture of the Antebellum South Carolina Low Country* (1995) describes southern households, religion, and political culture. Erskine Clarke's *Dwelling Place: A Plantation Epic* (2005) focuses on a Georgia plantation owned by a Presbyterian minister and sustained by enslaved workers. The best recent book on the role of slavery in creating the cotton culture is Edward E. Baptist's *The Half Has Never Been Told: Slavery and the Making of American Capitalism* (2014).

Other essential works on southern culture and society include Bertram Wyatt-Brown's *Honor and Violence in the Old South* (1986), Elizabeth Fox-Genovese's *Within the Plantation Household: Black and White Women of the Old South* (1988), Joan E. Cashin's *A Family Venture: Men and Women on the Southern Frontier* (1991), and Theodore Rosengarten's *Tombee: Portrait of a Cotton Planter* (1986).

John W. Blassingame's *The Slave Community: Plantation Life in the Antebellum South*, rev. and enlarged ed. (1979), Eugene D. Genovese's *Roll, Jordan, Roll: The World the Slaves Made* (1974), and Herbert G. Gutman's *The Black Family in Slavery and Freedom, 1750–1925* (1976) all stress the theme of a persisting and identifiable culture emerging among the enslaved population. The crucial role of religion and the church in African American culture is the focus of Henry Louis Gates Jr.'s *The Black Church: This Is Our Story, This Is Our Song* (2021). The emergence of a political culture among African Americans in the northern states is the subject of Van Gosse's *The First Reconstruction: Black Politics in America from the Revolution to the Civil War* (2021) and Kate Masur's *Until Justice Be Done: America's First Civil Rights Movement* (2021).

On the question of slavery's profitability, see Sven Beckert's *Empire of Cotton: A Global History* (2014), Robert Johnson's *River of Dark Dreams: Slavery and Empire in the Cotton Kingdom* (2017), Edward E. Baptist's *The Half Has Never Been Told: Slavery and the Making of American Capitalism* (2014); and Stephanie E. Jones-Rogers's *They Were Her Property: White Women as Slave Owners in the American South* (2019). For work on freedom seekers and the Underground Railroad, see Alice L. Baumgartner's *South to Freedom: Runaway Slaves to Mexico and the Road to the Civil War* (2022). For the business aspects of selling enslaved people, see Joshua D. Rothman's *The Ledger and the Chain* (2021) and Calvin Schermerhorn's *The Business of Slavery* (2015). A massive uprising of enslaved people in Louisiana is the subject of Daniel Rasmussen's *American Uprising: The Untold Story of America's Largest Slave Revolt* (2011); and a new perspective on the Nat Turner rebellion is offered by Vanessa M. Holden in *Surviving Southampton: African American Women and Resistance in Nat Turner's Community* (2021).

Chapter 12

On the reform impulse, consult Ronald G. Walter's *American Reformers, 1815–1860*, rev. ed. (1997). Revivalist religion is treated in Nathan O. Hatch's *The Democratization of American Christianity* (1989), Christine Leigh Heyrman's *Southern Cross: The Beginnings of the Bible Belt* (1997), and Ellen Eslinger's *Citizens of Zion: The Social Origins of Camp Meeting Revivalism* (1999). On the Mormons, see Alex Beam's *American Crucifixion: The Murder of Joseph Smith and the Fate of the Mormon Church* (2014) and Benjamin E. Park's award-winning *Kingdom of Nauvoo: The Rise and Fall of a Religious Empire on the American Frontier* (2020).

The best treatment of transcendentalist thought is Robert Gross's *The Transcendentalists and Their World* (2021). On Henry D. Thoreau, see Michael Sims's

The Adventures of Henry Thoreau: A Young Man's Unlikely Path to Walden Pond (2014). Edgar Allan Poe is the subject of Jerome McGann's *The Poet Edgar Allan Poe: Alien Angel* (2015). On Margaret Fuller, see Charles Capper's *Margaret Fuller: An American Romantic Life* (2009). On Frances Wright, Frances Ellen Watkins Harper, and Maria Stewart, see Alison Parker's *Articulating Rights: Nineteenth-Century American Women on Race, Reform, and the State* (2010), as well as Martha S. Jones's sweeping account of Black women's feminism in *Vanguard: How Black Women Broke Barriers, Won the Vote, and Insisted on Equality for All* (2020). A fascinating study of Charity Bryant and Sylvia Drake is Rachel Hope Cleve's *Charity and Sylvia: A Same-Sex Marriage in Early America* (2014).

For the war against alcohol, see W. J. Rorabaugh's *The Alcoholic Republic: An American Tradition* (1979) and Barbara Leslie Epstein's *The Politics of Domesticity: Women, Evangelism, and Temperance in Nineteenth-Century America* (1981). On prison reform and other humanitarian projects, see David J. Rothman's *The Discovery of the Asylum: Social Order and Disorder in the New Republic*, rev. ed. (2002) and Thomas J. Brown's biography *Dorothea Dix: New England Reformer* (1998). On women's rights, see Louise Michele Newman's *White Women's Rights: The Racial Origins of Feminism* (1999), Martha S. Jones's *Vanguard* (see above), and Lisa Tetrault, *The Myth of Seneca Falls: Memory and the Women's Suffrage Movement, 1848–1898* (2014). On race and the rise of public education, see Hilary J. Moss's *Schooling Citizens: The Struggle for African American Education in Antebellum America* (2009). On the rise of the first civil rights movement in northern states, see Kate Masur's magisterial *Until Justice Be Done: America's First Civil Rights Movement, the Revolution to Reconstruction* (2021).

Important surveys of abolitionism include Manisha Sinha's *The Slave's Cause: A History of Abolition* (2017), James Brewer Stewart's *Holy Warriors: The Abolitionists and American Slavery*, rev. ed. (1997), and Julie Roy Jeffrey's *The Great Silent Army of Abolitionism: Ordinary Women in the Antislavery Movement* (1998). Detailed and fascinating biographies of Black abolitionist leaders include David Blight's *Frederick Douglass: Prophet of Freedom* (2018), Nell Irvin Painter's *Sojourner Truth: A Life, A Symbol* (2009), Kate Clifford Larson's *Bound for the Promised Land: Harriet Tubman, Portrait of an American Hero* (2003). For the dramatic story of the role of the Underground Railroad in freeing enslaved persons, see Eric Foner's *Gateway to Freedom: The Hidden History of the Underground Railroad* (2015).

Chapter 13

For background on Whig programs and ideas, see Michael F. Holt's *The Rise and Fall of the American Whig Party: Jacksonian Politics and the Onset of the Civil War* (1999). On John Tyler, see Edward P. Crapol's *John Tyler: The Accidental President* (2006), Richard J. Ellis's *Old Tip vs. The Sly Fox: The 1840 Election and the Making of a Partisan Nation* (2020), and Christopher Leahy's *President without a Party: The Life of John Tyler* (2020).

On American expansion and imperialism, see Walter Nugent's *Habits of Empire: A History of American Expansionism* (2008), Richard White's *"It's Your Misfortune and None of My Own": A New History of the American West* (1991), Steven E. Woodworth's *Manifest Destinies: Expansion and the Road to the Civil War* (2010), Amy S. Greenberg, *Manifest Manhood and the Antebellum American Empire* (2005), and Steven Hahn, *A Nation without Borders: The United States and Its World in an Age of Civil Wars, 1830–1910* (2016). Compelling studies of the South's imperialist visions are Matthew Karp's *This Vast Southern Empire: Slaveholders at the Helm of American Foreign Policy* (2016) and Kevin Waite's *West of Slavery: The Southern Dream of a Transcontinental Empire* (2021). On the creation of the

California missions, see Steven W. Hackel's *Junípero Serra: California's Founding Father* (2013) and Gregory Orfalea's *Journey to the Sun: Junípero Serra's Dream and the Founding of California* (2014).

On Comanche history, see Pekka Hämäläinen's *The Comanche Empire* (2008). Other important surveys of North American Indigenous history in the West are Pekka Hämäläinen's *Indigenous Continent: The Epic Contest for North America* (2022). For the impact of post offices in facilitating western expansion, see Cameron Blevins's *Paper Trails: The US Post and the Making of the American West* (2021). The movement of settlers to the West is ably documented in John Mack Faragher's *Women and Men on the Overland Trail*, 2nd ed. (2001), David Dary's *The Santa Fe Trail: Its History, Legends, and Lore* (2000), and Rinker Buck's *The Oregon Trail: A New American Journey* (2015). On the Donner Party tragedy, see Michael Wallis's *The Best Land under Heaven: The Donner Party in the Age of Manifest Destiny* (2017). The best examination of life inside the gold-mining camps is Susan Lee Johnson's *Roaring Camp: The Social World of the California Gold Rush* (2000).

Gene M. Brack's *Mexico Views Manifest Destiny, 1821–1846: An Essay on the Origins of the Mexican War* (1975) takes Mexico's viewpoint on U.S. designs on the West. For excellent overviews of the position of Mexico and Mexicans in American expansionism, see Neil Foley's *Mexicans in the Making of America* (2014) and Juan Gonzalez's *Harvest of Empire: A History of Latinos in America* (2011). Essential studies of slavery and slave resistance along the U.S-Mexico border include Alice Baumgartner's *South to Freedom: Runaway Slaves to Mexico and the Road to Civil War* (2020) and Andrew J. Torget's *Seeds of Empire: Cotton, Slavery, and the Transformation of the Texas Borderlands, 1800–1850* (2015).

For the American political perspective on Texas, see Joel H. Silbey's *Storm over Texas: The Annexation Controversy and the Road to Civil War* (2005). On the siege of the Alamo, see Bryan Burrough and Chris Tomlinson's *Forget the Alamo: The Rise and Fall of an American Myth* (2021) and William C. Davis's *Three Roads to the Alamo: The Lives and Fortunes of David Crockett, James Bowie, and William Barret Travis* (1998). An excellent biography related to the emergence of Texas is Gregg Cantrell's *Stephen F. Austin: Empresario of Texas* (1999).

On the diplomatic aspects of Mexican American relations, see David M. Pletcher's *The Diplomacy of Annexation: Texas, Oregon, and the Mexican War* (1973). On James K. Polk, see Robert W. Merry's *A Country of Vast Designs: James K. Polk, the Mexican War, and the Conquest of the American Continent* (2009). Sarah Polk's story is told in Amy S. Greenberg's *Lady First: The World of First Lady Sarah Polk* (2019). The best surveys of the conflict are John S. D. Eisenhower's *So Far from God: The U.S. War with Mexico, 1846–1848* (1989) and Amy S. Greenberg's *A Wicked War: Polk, Clay, Lincoln, and the 1846 U.S. Invasion of Mexico* (2013). The Mexican war as viewed from the perspective of the soldiers is described in Richard Bruce Winders's *Mr. Polk's Army: American Military Experience in the Mexican War* (1997).

Abraham Lincoln's early views of slavery are outlined in William W. Freehling's *Becoming Lincoln* (2019) and James Oakes's *The Crooked Path to Abolition: Abraham Lincoln and the Antislavery Constitution* (2021). The growing tensions in Congress during the 1850s are the focus of Joanne Freeman's *The Field of Blood: Violence in Congress and the Road to Civil War* (2019). Mark J. Stegmaier's *Texas, New Mexico, and the Compromise of 1850: Boundary Dispute and Sectional Crisis* (1996) probes that crucial dispute, while Michael F. Holt's *The Political Crisis of the 1850s* (1978) traces the demise of the Whigs. See also Fergus M. Bordewich's *America's Great Debate: Henry Clay, Stephen A. Douglas, and the Compromise That Preserved the Union* (2012). The role that gender played in inflaming sectional politics is described in Lauren N. Haumesser's *The Democratic Collapse: How Gender Politics Broke a Party and a Nation, 1856–1861* (2022). On the Buchanan presidency, see Jean H.

Baker's *James Buchanan* (2004). Eric Foner, in *Free Soil, Free Labor, Free Men: The Ideology of the Republican Party before the Civil War* (1970), shows how events and ideas combined in the formation of a new political party.

The best surveys of the forces and events leading to the Civil War include James M. McPherson's *Battle Cry of Freedom: The Civil War Era* (1988), Elizabeth Varon's *Disunion: The Coming of the American Civil War, 1789–1859* (2008), James Oakes's *The Scorpion's Sting: Antislavery and the Coming of the Civil War* (2015), and Bruce Levine's *Half Slave and Half Free: The Roots of Civil War* (1992). The pivotal *Dred Scott* case is assessed in Earl M. Maltz's *Dred Scott and the Politics of Slavery* (2007), and Harriet Scott's story is told in Lea VanderVelde's *Mrs. Dred Scott: A Life on Slavery's Frontier* (2009). On the role of John Brown in the sectional crisis, see Robert E. McGlone's *John Brown's War against Slavery* (2009).

A detailed study of the South's journey to secession is William W. Freehling's *The Road to Disunion*, vol. 1, *Secessionists at Bay, 1776–1854* (1990) and *The Road to Disunion*, vol. 2, *Secessionists Triumphant, 1854–1861* (2007). Robert E. Bonner traces the emergence of southern nationalism in *Mastering America: Southern Slaveholders and the Crisis of American Nationhood* (2009). An indispensable study of how slavery led the South to secede is Charles B. Dew's *Apostles of Disunion: Southern Secession Commissioners and the Cause of the Civil War* (2002). Maury Klein's *Days of Defiance: Sumter, Secession, and the Coming of the Civil War* (1997) treats the Fort Sumter controversy. An excellent collection of interpretive essays is *Why the Civil War Came* (1996), edited by Gabor S. Boritt.

Chapter 14

On the start of the Civil War, see Adam Goodheart's *1861: The Civil War Awakening* (2011). The best one-volume overviews of the Civil War period are James M. McPherson's *Battle Cry of Freedom: The Civil War Era* (1988) and Elizabeth Varon's *Armies of Deliverance: A New History of the Civil War* (2019). The best brief history is Louis Masur's *The Civil War: A Concise History* (2011). A good introduction to the military events is Herman Hattaway's *Shades of Blue and Gray: An Introductory Military History of the Civil War* (1997). The outlook and experiences of the common soldier are explored in James M. McPherson's *For Cause and Comrades: Why Men Fought in the Civil War* (1997) and Chandra Manning's *What This Cruel War Was Over: Soldiers, Slavery, and the Civil War* (2007). For the global dimensions of the conflict, see Don H. Doyle's *The Cause of All Nations: An International History of the American Civil War* (2015).

Important overviews of life in the Confederacy include Gary Gallagher's *The Confederate War* (1997), Stephanie McCurry's *Confederate Reckoning: Power and Politics in the Civil War South* (2010), Yael Sternhell's *Routes of War: The World of Movement in the Confederate South* (2012), and Drew Gilpin Faust's *Mothers of Invention: Women of the Slaveholding South in the American Civil War* (1996). On the president of the Confederacy, see James M. McPherson's *Embattled Rebel: Jefferson Davis as Commander in Chief* (2014). On two of the leading Confederate commanders, see Michael Korda's *Clouds of Glory: The Life and Legend of Robert E. Lee* (2014) and S. C. Gwynne's *Rebel Yell: Stonewall Jackson* (2014). On the key Union generals, see Michael Fellman's *Citizen Sherman: The Life of William Tecumseh Sherman* (1997) and Joan Waugh's *U.S. Grant: American Hero, American Myth* (2009). Reaction to Sherman's March to the Sea is examined in Anne Sarah Rubin's *Through the Heart of Dixie: Sherman's March and American Memory* (2014).

The history of the North during the war is surveyed in Philip Shaw Paludan's *A People's Contest: The Union and Civil War, 1861–1865*, 2nd ed. (1996), J. Matthew

Gallman's *The North Fights the Civil War: The Home Front* (1994), and Gary W. Gallagher's *The Union War* (2011). Important studies of Northern women include Nina Silber's *Daughters of the Union: Northern Women Fight the Civil War* (2005), and Judith Giesberg's *Army at Home: Women and the Civil War on the Northern Home Front* (2009). On northern politics, see Jennifer L. Weber's *Copperheads: The Rise and Fall of Lincoln's Opponents in the North* (2006). The central Northern political figure, Abraham Lincoln, is the subject of many books. See James McPherson's *Abraham Lincoln* (2009) and Ronald C. White Jr.'s *A. Lincoln: A Biography* (2009).

The Civil War's medical history is recounted in Shauna Devine's *Learning from the Wounded: The Civil War and the Rise of American Medical Science* (2015). On nurses and nursing, see Jane E. Schultz's *Women at the Front: Hospital Workers in Civil War America* (2004).

The experience of the African American soldier is surveyed in Joseph T. Glatthaar's *Forged in Battle: The Civil War Alliance of Black Soldiers and White Officers* (1990) and Ira Berlin, Joseph P. Reidy, and Leslie S. Rowland's *Freedom's Soldiers: The Black Military Experience in the Civil War* (1998). For other important overviews of the process of emancipation, including the South's refugee crisis, see James Oakes's *Freedom National: The Destruction of Slavery in the United States, 1861–1865* (2013), Thavolia Glymph's *Out of the House of Bondage: The Transformation of the Plantation Household* (2003), and Amy Murrell Taylor's *Embattled Freedom: Journeys through the Civil War's Slave Refugee Camps* (2018). On Lincoln's evolving racial views, see Eric Foner's *The Fiery Trial: Abraham Lincoln and American Slavery* (2010). On the Emancipation Proclamation, see Louis P. Masur's *Lincoln's Hundred Days: The Emancipation Proclamation and the War for the Union* (2012). On the leadership of Harriet Tubman, see Edda L. Fields-Black's *Combee: Harriet Tubman, the Combahee River Raid, and Black Freedom during the Civil War* (2024).

An excellent analysis of Fredericksburg, one of the war's crucial battles, is John Matteson's *A Worse Place than Hell: How the Civil War Battle of Fredericksburg Changed a Nation* (2021). The Union siege of Petersburg is the focus of A. Wilson Greene's *A Campaign of Giants: The Battle for Petersburg* (2018). For the efforts of the Union navy to blockade southern ports, see Gil Hahn's *Campaign for the Confederate Coast* (2021).

Additional gender and ethnic studies include Nina Silber's *Gender and the Sectional Conflict* (2008), Judith Giesberg and Randall Miller's *Women and the American Civil War: North-South Counterpoints* (2018), Amy Murrell Taylor's *The Divided Family in Civil War America* (2005), William L. Burton's *Melting Pot Soldiers: The Union's Ethnic Regiments*, 2nd ed. (1998), and Susannah J. Ural, ed., *Civil War Citizens: Race, Ethnicity, and Identity in America's Bloodiest Conflict* (2010). The story of Sarah Rosetta (Lyons) Wakeman is told in Lauren Cook Burgess, ed., *An Uncommon Soldier: The Civil War Letters of Sarah Rosetta Wakeman* (1996).

What Civil War veterans experienced after the conflict ended is the subject of Brian Matthew Jordan's *Marching Home: Union Veterans and Their Unending Civil War* (2015) and James Marten's *Sing Not War: The Lives of Union and Confederate Veterans in Gilded Age America* (2011). The emergence of new death and mourning practices is described in Drew Gilpin Faust's monumental *This Republic of Suffering: Death and the American Civil War* (2008).

Chapter 15

The most comprehensive treatments of Reconstruction are Eric Foner's *Reconstruction: America's Unfinished Revolution, 1863–1877* (1988), W.E.B. Du Bois's classic *Black Reconstruction in America, 1860–1880* (1935), and Manisha Sinha's more recent *The Rise and Fall of the Second American Republic: Reconstruction, 1860–1920* (2024). Good brief histories include Michael W. Fitzgerald's *Splendid Failure: Postwar Reconstruction in the American South* (2007) and Alan Guelzo's *Reconstruction: A Concise History* (2018). On Andrew Johnson, see Hans L. Trefousse's *Andrew Johnson: A Biography* (1989) and David D. Stewart's *Impeached: The Trial of Andrew Johnson and the Fight for Lincoln's Legacy* (2009).

A fine biography of one of the leading Radical Republicans is Bruce Levine's *Thaddeus Stevens* (2021). The ideology of the Radicals is also explored in Michael Les Benedict's *A Compromise of Principle: Congressional Republicans and Reconstruction, 1863–1869* (1974). On Black politics and political leadership, see Phillip Dray's *Capitol Men: The Epic Story of Reconstruction through the Lives of the First Black Congressmen* (2008), Stephen Hahn's *A Nation under Our Feet: Black Political Struggles in the Rural South from Slavery to the Great Migration* (2005). The important work of the freedmen's conventions is detailed in P. Gabrielle Foreman, Jim Casey, and Sarah Lynn Patterson, eds., *The Colored Conventions Movement: Black Political Organizing in the Nineteenth Century* (2021). Additional books on southern state politics during Reconstruction include Michael Perman's *The Road to Redemption: Southern Politics, 1869–1879* (1984) and Mark W. Summers's *Railroads, Reconstruction, and the Gospel of Prosperity: Aid under the Radical Republicans, 1865–1877* (1984). On the scalawags, see James Alex Bagget's *The Scalawags: Southern Dissenters in the Civil War and Reconstruction* (2003).

The intransigence of White supremacist politics is examined in Stephen Kantrowitz's *Ben Tillman and the Reconstruction of White Supremacy* (2000) and Michael Perman's *Reunion without Compromise: The South and Reconstruction, 1865–1868* (1973). The intensity of racial violence is described in Allen W. Trelease's *White Terror: The Ku Klux Klan Conspiracy and Southern Reconstruction* (1971) and Kidada Williams's *I Saw Death Coming: A History of Terror and Survival in the War against Reconstruction* (2023). On particular moments of conflict, see Charles Lane's *The Day Freedom Died: The Colfax Massacre, the Supreme Court, and the Betrayal of Reconstruction* (2008) and Beverly Greene Bond and Susan Eva O'Donovan, eds., *Remembering the Memphis Massacre: An American Story* (2020).

The Reconstruction of southern plantation regions is documented in James L. Roark's *Masters without Slaves: Southern Planters in the Civil War and Reconstruction* (1977), Leon F. Litwack's *Been in the Storm So Long: The Aftermath of Slavery* (1979), Julie Saville's *The Work of Reconstruction: From Slave to Wage Labor in South Carolina, 1860–1870* (1996), and Gregory P. Downs's *After Appomattox: Military Occupation and the Ends of War* (2015). Recent studies of churches and schools include Ronald E. Butchart's *Schooling the Freedpeople: Teaching, Learning, and the Struggle for Black Freedom, 1861–1876* (2010) and Nicole Myers Turner's *Soul Liberty: The Evolution of Black Religious Politics in Postemancipation Virginia* (2020). On the reunification of Black families, see Ira Berlin and Leslie S. Rowland, eds., *Families and Freedom: A Documentary History of African-American Kinship in the Civil War Era* (1997). The Freedmen's Bureau is explored in William S. McFeely's *Yankee Stepfather: General O. O. Howard and the Freedmen* (1968).

On gender and citizenship rights in the Reconstruction era, see Martha S. Jones, *Vanguard: How Black Women Broke Barriers, Won the Vote, and Insisted on Equality for All* (2020); also Eric Foner's *The Second Founding: How the Civil War and Reconstruction Remade the Constitution* (2020) and N.E.H. Hull's *The Woman Who Dared to Vote* (2012).

Reconstruction in the West is gaining increasing attention from historians. Among the most influential studies are Stacey Smith's *Freedom's Frontier: California and the Struggle over Unfree Labor, Emancipation, and Reconstruction* (2013), Alaina E. Roberts's *I've Been Here All the While: Black Freedom on Native Land* (2021), Colin

G. Calloway's *Our Hearts Fell to the Ground: Plains Indian Views of How the West Was Lost* (1996), Elliot West's *The Last Indian War: The Nez Perce Story* (2009), and Ari Kelman's *A Misplaced Massacre: Struggling over the Memory of Sand Creek* (2013). On the Chinese American experience in this period, see Beth Lew Williams's *The Chinese Must Go: Violence, Exclusion, and the Making of the Alien in America* (2018).

The politics of corruption outside the South is depicted in William S. McFeely's *Grant: A Biography* (1981). The best recent biography of the eighteenth president is Ron Chernow's *Grant* (2017). The political maneuvers of the election of 1876 and the resultant crisis and compromise are explained in Michael Holt's *By One Vote: The Disputed Presidential Election of 1876* (2008). For a provocative interpretation of the lasting effects of the Civil War and Reconstruction, see Heather Cox Richardson's *How the South Won the Civil War: Oligarchy, Democracy, and the Continuing Fight for the Soul of America* (2020).

Text Credits

Chapter 1
Nzinga Mbemba: From Davidson, Basil. *The African Past: Chronicles from Antiquity to Modern Times*. 1964. Boston: Little, Brown. Copyright © 1964 by The Estate of Basil Davidson. Reprinted by permission of Curtis Brown, Ltd. All rights reserved.

Chapter 3
John Reid Jr.: Indenture of apprenticeship with Robert Livingston Jr. (The Gilder Lehrman Institute of American History, GLC03107.002668). Reproduced with permission.

Chapter 4
Bernard Bailyn: From *The Ideological Origins of the American Revolution* by Bernard Bailyn, Cambridge, Mass.: The Belknap Press of Harvard University Press. Copyright © 1967, 1992 by the President and Fellows of Harvard College. Used by permission. All rights reserved.

Gary B. Nash: Excerpts from "Social Change and the Growth of Prerevolutionary Urban Radicalism," by Gary B. Nash. From *The American Revolution: Explorations in the History of American Radicalism*, by Alfred F. Young (ed.). Copyright © 1976 by Northern Illinois University Press. Used with permission of Northern Illinois University Press.

Chapter 7
Paul Finkelman: From "Jefferson and Slavery," by Paul Finkelman in *Jeffersonian Legacies*, Onuf, Peter S., ed. pp. 181–183, 210–211. © 1993 by the Rector and Visitors of the University of Virginia. Reprinted by permission of the University of Virginia Press.

Douglas L. Wilson: Excerpts from "Thomas Jefferson and the Character Issue," by Douglas L. Wilson. Originally published in *The Atlantic Monthly*, November 1992. Used by permission of the author.

Chapter 11
Map 11.2: From Schermerhorn, Calvin. 2015. *The Business of Slavery and the Rise of American Capitalism, 1815–1860*. New Haven: Yale University Press. Courtesy of the Digital Scholarship Lab, University of Richmond.

Chapter 14
Ella Gertrude Clanton Thomas: From *The Secret Eye: The Journal of Ella Gertrude Clanton Thomas, 1848–1889* edited by Virginia Ingraham Burr. Copyright © 1990 by Virginia Ingraham Burr and Gertrude T. Despeaux. Used by permission of the University of North Carolina Press.

Chapter 15
Eric Foner: From *Reconstruction: America's Unfinished Revolution 1863–1877* by Eric Foner. Copyright © 1988 by Eric Foner. Used by permission of HarperCollins Publishers.

Kidada E. Williams: Excerpt from Williams, Kidada E. 2023. *I Saw Death Coming: A History of Terror and Survival in the War against Reconstruction*. New York: Bloomsbury. Copyright © 2023 by Kidada E. Williams.

Photo Credits

Authors
(David Emory Shi): Photo by Jason Shi; (Daina Ramey Berry): Photo by Brenda Ladd; (Joseph Crespino): Photo by Caroline Crespino; (Amy Murrell Taylor): Photo by Mark Mahan.

Frontmatter
Title page: The Protected Art Archive/Alamy Stock Photo; p. xii (and in margins throughout): National Archives; p. xv: © New-York Historical Society/Bridgeman Images; p. xvi: dbimages/Alamy Stock Photo; p. xvii: Peter Newark American Pictures/Bridgeman Images; p. xviii: Library of Congress; p. xix: National Archives.

Chapter 1
Page 2 (clockwise from top left): Library of Congress; © New-York Historical Society/Bridgeman Images; Everett Collection/Shutterstock; The Picture Art Collection/Alamy Stock Photo; North Wind Picture Archives/Alamy Stock Photo; bpk, Berlin/Kunstbibliothek, Staatliche Museen/Knud Petersen/Art Resource, NY; p. 4: © The Trustees of the British Museum/Art Resource, NY; p. 4 (margin): © British Library Board. All Rights Reserved/Bridgeman Images; p. 5: akg-images/Werner Forman; p. 5 (margin): © British Library Board. All Rights Reserved/Bridgeman Images; p. 6: Photo © Derek Bayes/Bridgeman Images; p. 10: DEA/G. Dagli Orti/De Agostini via Getty Images; p. 11: Science History Images/Alamy Stock Photo; p. 14: YinYang/Getty Images; p. 15: Linck, Shirley N./Superstock; p. 17: MPI/Archive Photos/Getty Images; p. 22: Ariadne Van Zandbergen/Alamy Stock Photo; p. 23: incamerastock/Alamy Stock Photo; p. 25: Sarin Images/GRANGER; p. 27 (both): Bridgeman Images; p. 28 (and in margins throughout): Scisetti Alfio/Shutterstock; p. 31: bpk/Deutsches Historisches Museum/Sebastian Ahlers/Art Resource, NY; p. 33: Chronicle of World History/Alamy Stock Photo; p. 36: Benson Latin American Collection, LLILAS Benson Latin American Studies and Collections, The University of Texas at Austin; p. 44: Hemis/Alamy Stock Photo; p. 46: akg-images/Werner Forman; p. 51: Sarin Images/GRANGER.

Chapter 2
Page 54: © British Library Board. All Rights Reserved/Bridgeman Images; p. 59: GRANGER; p. 61: Sarin Images/GRANGER; p. 62: Sarin Images/GRANGER; p. 63: History and Art Collection/Alamy Stock Photo; p. 65: Lebrecht Music & Arts/Alamy Stock Photo; p. 71 (top): Album/Alamy Stock Photo; (bottom): Library of Congress, Rare Book and Special Collections Division; p. 72: Everett Collection Inc./Alamy Stock Photo; p. 73: Sarin Images/GRANGER; p. 74: North Wind Picture Archives/Alamy Stock Photo; p. 75: Sarin Images/GRANGER; p. 78: CBW/Alamy Stock Photo; p. 83: The New-York Historical Society/Getty Images; p. 84: Bettmann/Corbis/Getty Images; p. 88: Sarin Images/GRANGER; p. 89: From State Laws of Georgia, 1755-1860. Board of Regents of the University System of Georgia; p. 91: GRANGER; p. 94: Plate (pg. 80) from Latin translation of Thomas Harriot's A brief and true report of the new found land of Virginia (Frankfurt: Johann Wechel, 1590. 1608 edition). Copperplate engravings by Theodor de Bry after watercolors by John White/Duke University Libraries/Internet Archive; p. 95: Sarin Images/GRANGER; p. 96: GRANGER; p. 97: © The Trustees of the British Museum/Art Resource, NY.

Chapter 3
Page 102: Sarin Images/GRANGER; p. 105: Sarin Images/GRANGER; p. 106 (left): ART Collection/Alamy Stock Photo; (right): IanDagnall Computing/Alamy Stock Photo; p. 108: Connecticut Museum of Culture and History; p. 110: Courtesy of The Charleston Museum, Charleston, South Carolina, www.Charlestonmuseum.org; p. 111: Earl Gregg Swem Library, Special Collections Research Center, William & Mary Libraries; p. 113: Sarin Images/GRANGER; p. 114: North Wind Picture Archive/Alamy; p. 115: Sarin Images/GRANGER; p. 116: Germantown Historical Society/Historic Germantown; p. 121: GRANGER; p. 123: The Picture Art Collection/Alamy Stock Photo; p. 125: Sarin Images/GRANGER; p. 128: © New-York Historical Society/Bridgeman Images; p. 129: © New-York Historical Society/Bridgeman Images; p. 130: Library Company of Philadelphia; p. 132: Philadelphia Museum of Art, Gift of Mr. and Mrs. Wharton Sinkler/Bridgeman Images; p. 133: Sarin Images/GRANGER; p. 134: Bridgeman Images; p. 135: From The New York Public Library.

Chapter 4
Page 140: Library of Congress Prints and Photographs Division Washington, D.C.; p. 143: Ivy Close Images/Alamy Stock Photo; p. 145: MPI/Getty Images; p. 148: The New York Public Library/Art Resource, NY; p. 149: The Picture Art Collection/Alamy Stock Photo; p. 152: Library of Congress; p. 153: New-York Historical Society/Bridgeman Images; p. 154: GRANGER; p. 157: North Wind Picture Archives/Alamy Stock Photo; p. 159: Library of Congress; p. 160: Library of Congress; p. 161: Library of Congress; p. 163: Peter Newark American Pictures/Bridgeman Images; p. 164: Library of Congress; p. 165: North Wind Picture Archives/Alamy Stock Photo; p. 166: Sarin Images/GRANGER; p. 167: Library of Congress; p. 169: Library of Congress; p. 172: © Virginia Historical Society/Bridgeman Images; p. 174: Sarin Images/GRANGER; p. 177: ClassicStock/Alamy Stock Photo; p. 180: © Don Troiani. All Rights Reserved 2024/Bridgeman Images; p. 181: North Wind Picture Archives/Alamy Stock Photo; p. 184: IanDagnall Computing/Alamy Stock Photo.

Chapter 5
Page 192 (clockwise from top left): Photo © Christie's Images/Bridgeman Images; Sarin Images/GRANGER; Photography by Erik Arnesen © Nicholas S. West; Photo © Christie's Images/Bridgeman Images; GRANGER; © New-York Historical Society/Bridgeman Images; p. 194: Art Collection 2/Alamy Stock Photo; (margin): © British Library Board. All Rights Reserved/Bridgeman Images; p. 195: Library of Congress; (margin): © British Library Board. All Rights Reserved/Bridgeman Images; p. 196: incamerastock/Alamy Stock Photo; p. 198: Anne S.K. Brown Military Collection Brown University Library; p. 200: US Senate Collection; p. 203: Alonzo Chappel, Battle of Long Island, 1858; M1986.29.1; Brooklyn Public Library, Center for Brooklyn

C-3

History; p. 204 (left): Courtesy American Antiquarian Society; (right): GL Archive/Alamy Stock Photo; p. 207: © Don Troiani. All Rights Reserved 2024/Bridgeman Images; p. 208: IanDagnall Computing/Alamy Stock Photo; p. 211: Sarin Images/GRANGER; p. 212: Sarin Images/GRANGER; p. 215: Bravo Images/Alamy Stock Photo; p. 216: © NPL - DeA Picture Library/M. Seemuller/Bridgeman Images; p. 217: ART Collection/Alamy Stock Photo; p. 221: Library of Congress; p. 224: GRANGER; p. 226: GRANGER; p. 227 (left): Science History Images/Alamy Stock Photo; (right): Library Company of Philadelphia; p. 230: Everett/Shutterstock.

Chapter 6
Page 234: Ian Dagnall/Alamy Stock Photo; p. 238: GRANGER; p. 242: North Wind Picture Archives/Alamy Stock Photo; p. 243: MPI/Getty Images; p. 244: Library of Congress; p. 248: © Massachusetts Historical Society/Bridgeman Images; p. 249: The Picture Art Collection/Alamy Stock Photo; p. 250: History and Art Collection/Alamy Stock Photo; p. 252: Library of Congress; p. 256: © New-York Historical Society/Bridgeman Images; p. 261: Albert Knapp/Alamy Stock Photo; p. 262: The Miriam and Ira D. Wallach Division of Art, Prints and Photographs: Print Collection, The New York Public Library, Digital Collections; p. 264: Everett Collection Historical/Alamy Stock Photo; p. 266: dbimages/Alamy Stock Photo; p. 268: Library of Congress; p. 271: Sarin Images/GRANGER; p. 272: Gift of Edgar William and Bernice Chrysler/The Metropolitan Museum of Art; p. 274: Art Collection 2/Alamy Stock Photo; p. 275: National Portrait Gallery, Smithsonian Institution; p. 276: Sarin Images/GRANGER; p. 277: Sarin Images/GRANGER.

Chapter 7
Page 282: Photography by Erik Arnesen © Nicholas S. West; p. 284: Library of Congress; p. 285: Alex Wong/Getty Images; p. 287: GABRIELLA DEMCZUK/The New York Times/Redux; p. 288: Art Collection 2/Alamy Stock Photo; p. 291: © 2024 The Jacob and Gwendolyn Knight Lawrence Foundation, Seattle/Artists Rights Society (ARS), New York; Image: Courtesy of the Amistad Research Center, New Orleans, LA/Bridgeman Images; p. 292: Historic Collection/Alamy Stock Photo; p. 293: © American Philosophical Society; p. 296: "York Memorial" by Ed Hamilton, © Ed Hamilton 2003. Photo Credit: Nathaniel Spencer; p. 297: Photo by MPI/Getty Images; p. 300: Timothy H. O'Sullivan/Digital image courtesy of the Getty Museum's Open Content Program; p. 301: © New-York Historical Society/Bridgeman Images; p. 302: Library of Congress; p. 303: North Wind Picture Archives/Alamy Stock Photo; p. 304: Sarin Images/GRANGER; p. 305: Sarin Images/GRANGER; p. 306: Library of Congress; p. 308: © Courtesy, American Antiquarian Society/Bridgeman Images; p. 313: Sarin Images/GRANGER; p. 315: Library of Congress; p. 318: Library of Congress.

Chapter 8
Page 328 (clockwise from top left): National Currency Foundation/Wikimedia, public domain; Peter Newark American Pictures/Bridgeman Images; Sarin Images/GRANGER; The Protected Art Archive/Alamy Stock Photo; GRANGER; © Courtesy of Swann Auction Galleries/Bridgeman Images; p. 330 (top): © Saint Louis Art Museum/Gift of Bank of America/Bridgeman Images; (bottom): Yale University Art Gallery; (margin): © British Library Board. All Rights Reserved/Bridgeman Images; p. 331: Gift of Miss Sadie B. Feldman in memory of her brother, Samson Feldman, 1987, The Walters Art Museum, Baltimore; (margin): © British Library Board. All Rights Reserved/Bridgeman Images; p. 332: Gift of Mrs. Huttleston Rogers, Courtesy National Gallery of Art, Washington; p. 337: The Protected Art Archive/Alamy Stock Photo; p. 340: Messrs. Smith & Co. Ship Yard, 1833, by James Fulton Pringle, oil on canvas, H: 32 x W: 50.75 inches, Fenimore Art Museum, Cooperstown, New York. Gift of Stephen C. Clark. N0394.1955. Photograph by Richard Walker; p. 341: North Wind Picture Archives/Alamy Stock Photo; p. 343: Library of Congress; p. 344: The Picture Art Collection/Alamy Stock Photo; p. 345: Sarin Images/GRANGER; p. 348: from the official catalog Great Exhibition, Crystal Palace, London 1851; p. 350: Sarin Images/GRANGER; p. 354: Gift of Edgar William and Bernice Chrysler Garbisch, Courtesy National Gallery of Art, Washington; p. 355: FineArt/Alamy Stock Photo; p. 359: Sarin Images/GRANGER; p. 360: The New York Public Library/Art Resource, NY; p. 362: Penta Springs Limited/Alamy Stock Photo; p. 363: © Schlesinger Library, Radcliffe Institute, Harvard/Bridgeman Images.

Chapter 9
Page 366: Yale University Art Gallery; p. 369: Library of Congress; p. 371: Rogers Fund, 1942. Metropolitan Museum of Art; p. 372: National Currency Foundation/Wikimedia, public domain; p. 374: The History Collection/Alamy; p. 380: Sarin Images/GRANGER; p. 383: Yale University Art Gallery; p. 385: Library of Congress; p. 386: Gift of I. N. Phelps Stokes, Edward S. Hawes, Alice Mary Hawes, and Marion Augusta Hawes, 1937. The Metropolitan Museum of Art; p. 388: Library of Congress; p. 390: From The New York Public Library.

Chapter 10
Page 394: The Museum of the City of New York/Art Resource, NY; p. 397: Library of Congress; p. 399: Sarin Images/GRANGER; p. 400: Private Collection/Peter Newark American Pictures/Bridgeman Images; p. 402: Fotosearch/Getty Images; p. 403: Andrew Cribb/Alamy Stock Photo; p. 404: Sarin Images/GRANGER; p. 407: Alpha Stock/Alamy Stock Photo; p. 408 (top): George Catlin, Os-ce-o-lá, The Black Drink, a Warrior of Great Distinction, 1838, oil on canvas, 30 7/8 x 25 7/8 in. (78.4 x 65.6 cm), Smithsonian American Art Museum, Gift of Mrs. Joseph Harrison, Jr., 1985.66.301; (bottom): US Marine Corps and National Archives; p. 409: GRANGER; p. 410: Original photo from Charles Steger's booklet on the Hagerty Family. Digital photo by Paul Ridenour; p. 411 (top): Hum Images/Alamy Stock Photo; (bottom): © David H. Wright. All rights reserved 2024/Bridgeman Images; p. 413: GRANGER; p. 418: Library of Congress; p. 420: Stocktrek Images, Inc./Alamy Stock Photo; p. 421: Library of Congress; p. 423: Library of Congress.

Chapter 11
Page 428: Everett Collection/Shutterstock; p. 432: GRANGER; p. 434: Internet Archive; p. 439: Sarin Images/GRANGER; p. 440: Fotosearch/Getty Images; p. 441: North Wind Picture Archives/Alamy Stock Photo; p. 446: GL Archive/Alamy Stock Photo; p. 447: Courtesy of Swann Auction Galleries/Bridgeman Images; p. 450: Sarin Images/GRANGER; p. 454: Peter Newark American Pictures/Bridgeman Images; p. 455: GL Archive/Alamy Stock Photo; p. 457: Everett Collection Historical/Alamy Stock Photo.

Chapter 12
Page 462: The Picture Art Collection/Alamy Stock Photo; p. 466: GRANGER; p. 467 (top): Classic Image/Alamy Stock Photo; (bottom): Rogers Fund, 1942. The Metropolitan Museum of Art;

p. 468: Schomburg Center for Research in Black Culture, Manuscripts, Archives and Rare Books Division. The New York Public Library, Digital Collections; p. 470: Library of Congress; p. 472: Lordprice Collection/Alamy Stock Photo; p. 473: Gift of Mrs. Russell Sage, 1908. The Metropolitan Museum of Art; p. 474: Library of Congress; p. 475: Science History Images/Alamy Stock Photo; p. 476: Everett Collection/Shutterstock; p. 477: IanDagnall Computing/Alamy Stock Photo; p. 478: Library of Congress Prints and Photographs Division Washington, D.C.; p. 479: Gift of Miss Sadie B. Feldman in memory of her brother, Samson Feldman, 1987, The Walters Art Museum, Baltimore; p. 481: World History Archive/Alamy Stock Photo; p. 483: Cultural Archive/Alamy Stock Photo; p. 485: The New York Public Library, Digital Collections; p. 486: Library of Congress Prints and Photographs Division Washington, D.C.; p. 490: Everett/Shutterstock; p. 492 (left): National Portrait Gallery, Smithsonian Institution; (right): Library of Congress; p. 494: Library of Congress; p. 498 (both): Library of Congress.

Chapter 13
Page 508 (clockwise from top left): Library of Congress; Sarin Images/GRANGER; Library of Congress; Everett/Shutterstock; Sarin Images/GRANGER; Library of Congress; Smithsonian American Art Museum, Gift of William T. Evans; p. 510: Private Collection; Peter Newark American Pictures/Bridgeman Images; (margin): © British Library Board. All Rights Reserved/Bridgeman Images; p. 511: © Civil War Archive/The Bridgeman Art Library; (margin): © British Library Board. All Rights Reserved/Bridgeman Images; p. 512: Art Collection 3/Alamy Stock Photo; p. 516: Morris K. Jesup Fund, 1933. The Metropolitan Museum of Art; p. 518: Smithsonian American Art Museum, Gift of Mrs. Joseph Harrison, Jr., 1985.66.346; p. 519: Peter Newark American Pictures/Bridgeman Images; p. 521: Peter Newark American Pictures/Bridgeman Images; p. 522: Sarin Images/GRANGER; p. 526: MPI/Getty Images; p. 527: © Museum of Fine Arts, Houston/The Bayou Bend Collection, gift of Miss Ima Hogg/Bridgeman Images; p. 529: GRANGER; p. 530: Collection of the James K. Polk Memorial Association, Columbia, TN; p. 535: The Art Archive/Shutterstock; p. 538: © Courtesy, American Antiquarian Society/Bridgeman Images; p. 541: Art Resource, NY; p. 542: Library of Congress; p. 544: Sarin Images/GRANGER; p. 549: Look and Learn/Illustrated Papers Collection/Bridgeman Images; p. 550: Library of Congress; p. 554: INTERFOTO/Alamy Stock Photo; p. 558: Chronicle/Alamy Stock Photo; p. 559 (left): National Portrait Gallery, Smithsonian Institution; Frederick Hill Meserve Collection; (right): Library of Congress; p. 562: Everett Collection/Shutterstock; p. 565: ZUMA Press, Inc./Alamy Stock Photo.

Chapter 14
Page 570: Pictures Now/Alamy Stock Photo; p. 572: Library of Congress; p. 575: Library of Congress; p. 576: Library of Congress; p. 577: The Stapleton Collection/Bridgeman Images; p. 578: Courtesy Jackson K. Doane, Jr.; p. 580: Library of Congress; p. 581: Library of Congress Prints and Photographs Division Washington, D.C.; p. 582: Alpha Stock/Alamy Stock Photo; p. 583: Reading Room 2020/Alamy Stock Photo; p. 587: Library of Congress; p. 589: Library of Congress; p. 590: Library of Congress Prints and Photographs Division Washington, D.C.; p. 591: Library of Congress; p. 593: Library of Congress; p. 594: Library of Congress Prints and Photographs Division Washington, D.C.; p. 595: Library of Congress; p. 597: Beinecke Rare Book and Manuscript Library, Yale University/Wikimedia Commons; p. 601 (both): Library of Congress; p. 602: MPVHistory/Alamy Stock Photo; p. 604: World History Archive/Alamy Stock Photo; p. 607: Library of Congress; p. 610: Library of Congress; p. 611: Library of Congress; p. 614: Everett Collection Historical/Alamy Stock Photo; p. 617: Library of Congress; p. 621: Library of Congress.

Chapter 15
Page 628: Sarin Images/GRANGER; p. 630: The Historic New Orleans Collection Lost Friends Database, digital reproductions of the Lost Friends ads courtesy of the Louisiana State University Libraries Special Collections, Hill Memorial Library; p. 631: Library of Congress; p. 634: Collection of the Smithsonian National Museum of African American History and Culture; p. 635: Heritage Image Partnership Ltd/Alamy Stock Photo; p. 636 (top): Smithsonian Institution Archives, Acc. 11-006, Box 004, Image No. MAH-2502; (bottom): Science History Images/Alamy Stock Photo; p. 637: Library of Congress; p. 639: Sarin Images/GRANGER; p. 642: Everett Collection/Shutterstock; p. 644: Library of Congress; p. 647: Science History Images/Alamy Stock Photo; p. 648: Library of Congress; p. 650: GRANGER; p. 652: Library of Congress; p. 653: Library of Congress; p. 655: Sarin Images/GRANGER; p. 658: John Kraljevich/John Kraljevich Americana; p. 659: GRANGER; p. 660: Library of Congress; p. 662: Library of Congress; p. 664: akg-images/Fototeca Gilardi; p. 670: Library of Congress.

Index

Maps, figures, and photographs are indicated in *italics*.

AASS (American Anti-Slavery Society), 490–91, 499
abolition movement, 487. *See also* emancipation
    ACS and, 488–89
    African American leadership in, 491–93, *492*
    Appeal to the Colored Citizens of the World and, 488
    Bleeding Kansas and, 554–55
    Brown, John's, raid and, 561–62
    Fugitive Slave Act of 1850 and, 548–49
    gradualism to, 489
    in Great Britain, 489
    Industrial Revolution and, 346–47
    liberty laws and, 549
    Liberty Party and, 499–500, 530
    mail censorship and, 419
    Missouri Compromise and, 375, *378*, 378–79, 539
    newspapers for, *434*, 489–91, *490*, 493
    Pottawatomie Massacre and, 555
    reactions to, 500–501
    Senate violence over, 555
    southbound Underground Railroad and, 524
    splits within, 495, 498–99
    Thirteenth Amendment and, 500, 624–25, 643
    Uncle Tom's Cabin and, 550–51
    Underground Railroad and, 487–88, 524
    Van Buren fighting, 419
    women and, 498–99
Acadia, 152
Acoma Pueblo, 44
ACS (American Colonization Society), 488–89
Act of Supremacy, England, 33
Act to Prevent Frauds and Abuses, 149
Adams, Abigail
    on Shays's Rebellion, 242
    on women's freedoms and equality, 183, 184, *184*
Adams, John, 202–3, 256, *275*
    administration of, 275
    on American ambition, 283
    on American Revolution, 185, 222
    on Boston Tea Party, 169
    on *Common Sense*, 178
    on Confederation Congress, 236
    Convention of 1800 and, 277
    Declaration of Independence and, 179, 230
    on democracy, 286

    election of, 275
    electoral loss of, 277–78, *278*
    on First Continental Congress, 171
    France naval war and, 275–76, 278
    French Revolution and, 268
    on Jefferson's State Department resignation, 269
    Judiciary Act of 1801 and, 277
    on Senate, 246
    Stamp Act of 1765 opposed by, 162
    Townshend Acts and, 165
    Treaty of Paris (1783) and, 219
    as vice president, 255, 257
    on women and freedoms, 184
    XYZ Affair and, 276, *276*
Adams, John Quincy, 279, *386*, 500, 533
    activist government of, 386–87
    corrupt bargain and, 384–85
    election of 1824 and, 383–84, *385*
    election of 1828 and, *387*, 387–89
    electoral defeat of, 390–91
    as elitist, 389
    on Jackson, A., 383
    Monroe Doctrine and, 382
    pedigree of, 385–86
    Transcontinental Treaty and, 380–81
    Treaty of Ghent and, 316
    on Van Buren, 420
Adams, Samuel, *166*, 190
    arrest evaded by, 173
    Battle of Lexington and, 174
    Committee of Correspondence and, 168
    Gage's bribe resisted by, 172
    Patriots and, 166
    Sons of Liberty and, 166
Adena, 16
Aetna Insurance Company, 345
Africa. *See also* transatlantic slave trade
    ACS and, 489
    ancient societies of, 20–21
    discovery and exploration of, 20, 23
    transatlantic slave trade roots in, 120–21
    West African cultures and empires, 20–23, *21*
African Americans. *See also* abolition movement; enslaved people; segregation; slavery
    in abolition movement leadership, 491–93, *492*
    in American Revolution, 179–81, *180*, *181*, 184
    Black codes and, 643
    British recruitment of, 225–26, *226*
    Christianity and, 135, 455
    churches of, 649–51, *650*

    citizenship for, 644, 674–75
    Civil War service of, *581*, 581–82, *582*, 597, *597*, 600
    Colfax Massacre and, 665–66, 667
    in colonial America, *118*
    as contrabands, 581–82, *589*, 590
    convict leasing and, 643–44
    democracy denied to, 286
    domestic terrorism against, 665–67
    education and, 649–51
    Emancipation Proclamation and, *593*, 593–94
    empowering freed, 635
    enslaved people owned/protected by, 446
    Fifteenth Amendment and, 510, 648, 658–59
    Fourteenth Amendment and, 510, 643, 644, 667
    Freedman's Bank and, 635–36, *636*, 664
    Freedmen's conventions and, 638–39, *639*
    as "free persons of color," 444–46
    Great Awakening and, 135
    Irish immigrants' relations with, 357
    Jackson, A., and, 389–90, 397
    KKK violence against, *655*, 655–56, 658, 665–67
    land ownership for freed, 652–53
    liberty and, 227
    Memphis race massacre and, 642, *642*
    Military Reconstruction Act and, 645
    minstrel shows and, 355
    Naturalization Act of 1790 and, 261
    newspapers and, 340, 389–90, *390*
    New York City draft riots and, 597
    political leadership in Reconstruction of, 651–52, *652*
    poll taxes and, 658–59
    in public schools of nineteenth century, 483–84
    Reconstruction and conventions of, 640
    Reconstruction and society of, 649–57
    religion and, 454–55
    in Revolutionary War, *180*, 206–7, *207*, 221–22, 225–27, *226*
    Second Great Awakening and, *467*, 468
    Seneca Falls Convention and, 495
    sharecropping and, *653*, 653–54
    slavery and culture of, 122–23, *123*, 453
    Thirteenth Amendment and, 500, 624–25, 643
    Union League and, 651
    voting rights and, 510, 629, 642
    War of 1812 and, 312–14
    women, religion and, 110
    women's household work and, 351–52

I-1

African Methodist Episcopal (AME) Church, 468, 650
Age of Exploration. *See* discovery and exploration
Age of Reason, 131
agriculture. *See also* cotton
    Caribbean sugar plantations, 77–78, *78*
    Columbian Exchange and, 39
    commercial, 334–35, 348–49
    CSA and, 566
    English colonies and, 90
    enslaved women and, 109
    Indigenous Americans and, 70, 90
    in market economy, 334–35
    of Mexica, 12
    Midwest farming and, 345, 348–49
    in New England colonies, 115
    plain White folk and, 441
    plantation management and, 109–10
    rice, 80, 113, 124, 431
    sharecropping and, *653*, 653–54
    in South, *428*, 429–30
    staple crops, 113
    sugar, 77–78, *78*, 431
    technological advancements and, 346–49, *348*, 348–49
    tobacco, 64, 90, 431
Akerman, Amos, 665
Alabama, 240, 293
    cotton production in, 432–34, *433*
    secession of, 566
    Tecumseh in, 306
Alamance, Battle of, 166
Alamo, 146, 525–27, *526*
Albany Plan of Union, 152
Albemarle, 77
alcohol
    Industrial Revolution and, 354
    Puritans and, 114
    taverns and, *130*, 130–31
    temperance and, 480–81, *481*
    Whiskey Rebellion and, 271–72, *272*
Algonquians, 17, *17*, 94, *94*
Ali, Sonni, 23
Alien and Sedition Acts of 1798, 276, *277*
All Creation Going to the White House (Cruikshank, R.), *397*
Allen, Richard, 468
Alliance, Treaty of, 210
Ambler, Richard, 436
AME (African Methodist Episcopal) Church, 468, 650
American Anti-Slavery Society (AASS), 490–91, 499
American Bible Society, 481
American Colonization Society (ACS), 488–89
American Crisis, The (Paine), 204, *204*, 206
American Party, 358–59, 556
American Red Cross, 602
American Revenue Act of 1764, 160

American Revolution. *See also* Revolutionary War
    Adams, S., and, 166
    African Americans in, 179–81, *180*, *181*, 184
    Articles of Confederation and, 194, 223, 236, 237
    Boston Massacre and, *167*, 167–68
    Boston Tea Party and, *140*
    British military power and, 199–200
    causes of, 184–85
    Coercive Acts and, 170–71
    Committee of Correspondence and, 168
    Common Sense and, 177–78
    Continental Army and, 200–201
    debating origins of, 188–91
    debts from, 262–63
    Declaration of Independence and, 178–80, 230, 326
    divisions in, 198–99
    equality and limitations after, 181–84, 225–31
    finance and supply problems in, 201
    France and, 194
    freedom of religion and, 224, 224–25
    Gaspée incident and, 168
    ideology shaping, 188, 189
    liberty and, 224
    Loyalists and, 166, 171, 193, 198–99, *221*, 221–22
    movement toward armed conflict in, 172–73
    nationalism's emergence after, 230–31
    Patriots and, 166, 171–72, 178, 193, 199, 201
    political participation expansion after, 223–24
    republican ideology and, 222–23
    slavery and freedom contradictions in, 180–81, 225–27, *226*, 228–29
    social and political changes of, 188–90, 197–98
    state constitutions and, 222–23
    Treaty of Alliance in, 210
    Treaty of Paris (1763) and, 154–55, 157
    Treaty of Paris (1783) and, 218–20
    unified resistance of, 185
    women's equality and freedoms in, 181–84, 227, *227*, 230
American Society for the Promotion of Temperance, 480–81
American Sunday School Union, 481
American System, 372–73, 528
American Temperance Union, 481
American Tract Society, 481
Americas. *See also* Central America; Mesoamerica; North America; South America
    Columbian Exchange and, 39–40
    Dutch explorations of, *48*
    early cultures in, 9–18

early maps of, *27*
English explorations of, *48*, 50, *51*
European colonists' motives with, 4
first migrations to, 7–9
French explorations of, 47–48, *48*, 142
geographic formation of, 7
hunter-gatherer societies in, 9
Spanish explorations of, *42*
Ames, Adelbert, 654, 676
Ames, Fisher, 244
Anaconda Plan, 576–77
Anasazi, 14, *14*
Ancestral Pueblo, 14, *14*
"And Ar'n't I a Woman?" (Truth), 506
Anderson, Jourdon, 599
Anderson, Robert, 567, 619
Andros, Edmund, 148, 149
Anglican Church, 32, 34, 59, 68, 71, 224
Anthony, Susan B., 625, 659, *660*
Antietam, Battle of, *591*, 591–93
anti-Federalists, *252*, 252–53
anti-immigrant prejudice, 357
Anti-Masonic Party, 416–17
Anti-Segregation Act of 1855, 483
anti-slavery movements. *See* abolition movement
"anti-sodomy" laws, 556
Anti-Vagrancy Act, 543
Antrobus, John, *455*
Apache, 15, 516, 523, 660
Appeal to the Colored Citizens of the World (Walker, D.), 488
Arapaho, 15, 47
Arawak, 27
Arkansas state, 432–33, *433*
Arkansas Territory, 375
Armada Portrait, *33*
Armstrong, John, 313
Articles of Confederation, 194, 223, 236, 237. *See also* Confederation Congress
Asian Americans. *See* Chinese Americans
asylum reform movements, 482
Atchison, David, 554
Atlanta, Battle of, 617, *620*
Attucks, Crispus, 168
Auburn Penitentiary, 482
auctions of enslaved people, 446–50, *447*, *450*
Augsburg, Treaty of, 31
Austin, Stephen Fuller, 523–25
Austria, 267
Avery, R. B., 677
Aztec, *11*, 11–13, 36–37

Bacon, Nathaniel, 90–91
Bacon's Rebellion, 90–93, *91*
Bad Axe Massacre, 408
Bailey, Ann ("Samuel Gay"), *227*, 230
Bailyn, Bernard, 188, 189
Baker, James, 581
Ball, Charles, 443

Ballou, Sullivan, 580–81
Bank of England, 264, 421
Bank of the United States
    Bank War and rechartering of, 399–401, *400*
    First, *264*, 264–65
    Jackson, A.'s, elimination of, 417–19, 421
    Panic of 1819 and, 374–75
    Second, 319–20, 368, 372
Bank War, 399–401, *400*
Baptists
    denominational growth of, 465, 467–68
    frontier revivals and, 466–67
Barbados, 77–78
Barbary pirates, 300–301, *301*
bare-knuckle boxing, 354, *354*
Barker, Penelope, 170
Barton, Clara, *601*, 602
bathrooms, 115
Bear Flag Revolt of 1846, 535, *535*
Beauregard, Pierre G. T., 567, 575, 585
Bedford, Gunning, 245
Beecher, Catharine, 493–94, 499
Beecher, Lyman, 480, 481, 493
Bell, John, 563, *564*
Bell, Sally, 541
Benton, Thomas Hart, 372, 405, 417, 539
Bering Strait, 7–8
Berkeley, John, 85
Berkeley, William, 66, 91, 93
Bernard, Francis, 191
Berrien, John, 404
Bethune, Mary McLeod, 650–51
Bethune-Cookman University, 651
"Beyond the Search for Sisterhood" (Hewitt), 505
Biddle, Nicholas, 399–400, 417
Bierstadt, Albert, *512*
Bill of Rights, 253, 257, 258, 259
Bingham, George Caleb, *274*
Birney, James Gillespie, 499–500
birth rates, 105
birthright citizenship, 644
Black codes, 643
Blackfeet, 15
Black Friday, 661–62, *662*
Black Hawk War, 408
Blackstone, William, 182
Blackwell, Elizabeth, 362, *363*
Blair, Francis P., Jr., 657
Bleeding Kansas, 554–55
Board of Indian Commissioners, 661
Board of Trade and Plantations, 93
Boleyn, Anne, 33
Bonaparte, Napoléon, 277, 290–93, 518
Book of Mormon, The, 470
Boone, Daniel, 274, *274*
Boost, W. L., 434
Booth, John Wilkes, 562, 620, 622, 636–37
Boston, Massachusetts, *148*, 149
    Irish immigrants in, 357

Boston Gazette, 165, 168
Boston Massacre, *167*, 167–68
Boston Port Act, 170
Boston Tea Party, *140*, 169–70
Boudinot, Elias, *409*
Boulding, G. T. E., 665
boundaries in exploration and trade, 28–29
boxing, 354, *354*
Boyd, Rebecca, 668
Braddock, Edward, 153
Bradford, William, 70, 94
Bradley, Joseph, 666
Bragg, Braxton, 586, 612
Brazil, 30
bread riots, in CSA, 606
Breckinridge, John C., 563, *564*
Brewster, Mary, 68–69
British colonies. *See* English colonies
Brom and Bett v. Ashley, 248
Brooks, Preston, 555
Brown, Charles, 655
Brown, John, 500, 554–55, 561–62, *562*
Brown, Josiah, 449
Brown, William Wells, 491
Bruce, Blanche K., 651–52, *652*
Bryan, Andrew, 135, *135*
Bryant, Charity, 479
Bryant, William Cullen, 479
Buchanan, James
    background of, 556
    Dred Scott v. Sandford and, 557–58, 558
    election of, 555–56
    Kansas, Lecompton Constitution and, 558–59
    King, W. R.'s, relationship with, 556
    Panic of 1857 and, 557
    Southern secession and, 565
Buchanan-Pakenham Treaty, 531, *532*
Buell, Don Carlos, 586
Buena Vista, Battle of, 536
buffalo, 47
Bull Run
    First Battle of, *575*, 575–76
    Second Battle of, 587–89, *592*
Bunker Hill, Battle of, 176
Burdett, Clarissa, 595–96
Burdett, Elijah, 595
Bureau of Colored Troops, 597
Burgoyne, John, 208, *208*, 210
Burke, Edmund, 220
burned-over district, 469
Burns, Anthony, 549
Burnside, Ambrose E., 596
Burr, Aaron, 275, 277, *278*, 297–99
Burras, Anne, 63
Burr Conspiracy, 299
Burton, Mary, 125
Butler, Andrew Pickens, 555
Butler, Benjamin, 581

cabinet
    Jackson, A.'s, divisions of, 398
    Jackson, A.'s, new, 403–4, *404*
    of Jefferson, 287–88
    of Washington, G., 257
Cabot, John, 30
Cahokia, 17
Cajuns, 152
Calhoun, John C., 307, 335, *421*
    Compromise of 1850 and, 544–45
    compromise tariff of, 406
    First Seminole War and, 379
    internal improvements urged by, 399
    Jackson, A.'s, tensions with, 401, 403–5
    slavery defended by, 501
    Tariff of Abominations and, 401–2
    Texas annexation and, 529
    Van Buren's conflict with, 398, 403–4, *404*
    as vice president, 385, 398
    Wilmot Proviso and, 539
California
    annexation of, 533–35
    Anti-Vagrancy Act in, 543
    Bear Flag Revolt of 1846 and, 535, *535*
    Chinese immigrants in, 356, *541*, 542
    clipper ships and, 339
    Compromise of 1850 and, *544*, 544–45, *545*, 548
    Donner party in, 522–23
    Fifteenth Amendment opposed by, 649
    gold rush in, 540–43, *541*, *542*
    Indian Act of 1850 in, 543
    Overland Trails to, 515, *515*
    Pony Express Company and, 341, *341*
    settlement of, *521*, 521–23, *522*
    statehood of, 543
    Sutter's Fort in, 522, *522*
Calvert, Cecilius, 66–68
Calvert, Charles, *249*
Calvert, George, 66
Calvin, John, 32
Calvinism, 32, 71
Campbell, Alexander, 579
Campbell, David, 314
Campbell, James, 579
Canada, 30
    Buchanan-Pakenham Treaty and, 531, *532*
    freedom seekers in, 377
    French colonization of, 47–48, 142
    French loss of, 154
    Madison, J., and invasion of, 308–10, *309*
    Revolutionary War in, 201–2
    War of 1812 and, 306–7, 308–10, *309*
canals, *336*, 337–38
capitalism
    cotton, 345
    mercantilism compared to, 261
    racial, 430
    railroads and, 339

Capitol Building, *284*, 285
carbon sink phenomena, 40
Cardozo, Francis, 651
Caribbean colonies, 77–78, *78*, 124, 241
Carolina colony. *See also* North Carolina colony; South Carolina colony
   Caribbean sugar plantations and, 77–78, *78*
   governance of, 79
   immigrants and, 79
   Indigenous slavery in, 112
   map of, *77*
   profit from, 79–80
   Yamasee warfare and, 112–13
"carpetbaggers," in Reconstruction, 654–55, 677
Carteret, George, 85
Cartier, Jacques, 47–48
Cart War, 531
Cartwright, Francine Gaines, *467*
Cartwright, Peter, *467*
Cary, Mary Ann Shadd, 659, *659*
Cass, Lewis, 519, 539–40
Catherine of Aragon, 33
Catholic Church/Catholicism
   California settlement and missionaries form, *521*, 521–22
   Calvinism and, 32
   Counter-Reformation of, 32
   English Reformation and, 32–34
   French Catholics, *118*, 142
   Indigenous American conversions and, 44
   Irish immigrants and, 357
   Jesuit missionaries in New France and, 145, *145*
   Know-Nothings against, 358–59
   Lutheranism and, 31–32
   Maryland colony and, 67–68
   nativists against, 358–59
   in New Spain, 38–39
   Protestant Reformation and, 30–32
   slavery in Spanish Florida and, 123–24
   Spanish Inquisition and, 32
Cavaliers, 60
Cavelier, René-Robert, 146
Cayuga, 212
Celia, 452–53
censorship, mail, 419
Central America, *12. See also* Americas; Mesoamerica
ceremonial mounds, 14
Chamberlain, Joshua, 622
Champlain, Samuel de, 48, *142*, 142–43
Chancellorsville, Battle of, 607, *608*
Charles I, 59, *59*, 66, 71
Charles II, 84, 92–93, 148
Charleston, South Carolina, 79, 109, 129
Charter of Freedoms and Exemptions, 82
Chattanooga, Battle of, 612
chattel slavery, 123–29

Cherokee, 14, 112, 201, *407*, 527, 551–52, 583
   Battle of Taliwa and, *411*
   forced removal of, 409–10, *412*
   Indian Removal Act of 1830 and, 407, 410
   Jackson, A., and, 415
   Nanyehi, *411*, 411–12
   Supreme Court relief sought by, 409–10
   Trail of Tears and, 411–13, *412*, *413*
   Treaty of New Echota and, 410–11
   White American customs adopted by, 410
Cherokee Nation v. Georgia, 409
Cherokee Phoenix, 340, *409*
Chesapeake Bay, War of 1812 in, 312
Chesapeake incident, 302
Chesapeake region colonies, 60–68
Chestnut, Mary Boykin, 440, *440*
Cheyenne, 15, 47
Chicago Daily Tribune, 355
Chicago Tribune, 620
Chickasaw, 112, 410, 583
chiefdoms, 17, *17*
childbirth, maternal mortality in colonial life and, 105, *106*
children, as enslaved people, 447, 450, 454, *454*
Chinese Americans
   in California, 356, *541*, 542
   citizenship, voting rights and, 648–49
   Fifteenth Amendment and, 648–49
   prejudice against, *648*, 648–49
Choctaw, 410, 583
cholera, 520
Christianity/Christians, 67–68. *See also specific sects*
   African Americans and, 135, 455
   Calvinism and, 32, 71
   Congregationalists and, 71
   English Reformation and, 32–34
   in Enlightenment, 133
   evangelism and, 133–37
   Great Awakening and, 133–37
   Indigenous American conversions to, 27, 44, 91, 141, 145, *145*
   Indigenous American religions compared to worldview of, 15
   Jesuit missionaries in New France and, 145, *145*
   Lutheranism and, 31–32
   manifest destiny and, 463–64
   parish system and, 133
   Protestant Reformation and, 30–32, 34
   salvation and, 463
   Second Great Awakening and, 465–72
   Unitarianism, Universalism and, 464–65
Christy, Jacob, 600
Church of England, 32, 34, 59, 68, 71, 224
Church of Jesus Christ of Latter-day Saints (Mormon Church), 469–72, *470–72*

cities
   enslaved people in, 452
   Industrial Revolution and growth of, 352, *352*, *353*
Citizen Genêt, *268*, 268–69
citizenship
   for African Americans, 644, 674–75
   Alien and Sedition Acts of 1798 and, 276, *277*
   birthright, 644
   Chinese Americans and, 648–49
   Civil Rights Act of 1866 and, 644
   colonial life and, 105–6
   Fourteenth Amendment and, 510, 643, 644, 667
   Indigenous Americans and, 661
   Naturalization Act of 1790 and, 261
   Slaughterhouse Cases and, 667
citizen-soldiers, 200, 202
"Civil Disobedience" (Thoreau), 476
Civil Rights Act of 1866, 644
Civil Rights Cases of 1883, 666
Civil War, U.S., 458–59, 510–11. *See also* Confederate States of America; Reconstruction
   African Americans serving in, *581*, 581–82, *582*, 597, *597*, 600
   Anaconda Plan in, 576–77
   Appomattox Court House and end of, *621*, 621–22
   armies formed in, *577*, 577–78
   Battle of Antietam in, *591*, 591–93, *592*
   Battle of Atlanta in, 617, *620*
   Battle of Bull Run, First, *575*, 575–76
   Battle of Bull Run, Second, 587–89, *592*
   Battle of Chancellorsville in, 607, *608*
   Battle of Chattanooga in, 612
   Battle of Cold Harbor in, 615, *616*
   Battle of Fredericksburg in, 596
   Battle of Gettysburg in, *608*, 609–11, *610*, *611*
   Battle of New Orleans in, 586
   Battle of Perryville in, 586
   Battle of Shiloh in, 584–86
   Battle of Spotsylvania Court House in, 615, *616*
   Battle of the Wilderness in, 614–15, *616*
   Battle of Vicksburg in, 607–9
   choosing sides in, 572–74, *573*
   contrabands during, 581–82, *589*, 590
   CSA strategy for, 577
   currency during, 604, *604*
   daily life of soldiers in, 580, *580*
   desertions in, 580
   election of 1864 and, 613, 618
   emancipation and, 589–97, 600
   families divided over, 579
   finances during, 603–5
   forces mobilized in, 572
   Fort Pillow Massacre in, 614, *614*
   Fort Sumter attack and start of, 567, 571–72

Gettysburg Address in, 612, 625
government during, 603
Habeas Corpus Act of 1863 and, 605
Indigenous Americans in, 583, *583*
in Kansas, 582–83
Kentucky in, 584
medicine during, 600–601
Militia Act and, 597
as modern war, 623–24
New York City draft riots and, 597
peninsular campaign in, 587, *588*
Petersburg siege in, 615–16, *616*
Planter incident in, 582, *582*
politics during, 605–7
racism after, 632
regional advantages in, 574
Sherman, W. T.'s, "March to the Sea" in, 618–19, *620*
Sherman, W. T.'s, South Carolina campaign in, 619, *620*
South and aftermath of, *631*, 631–32
stakes of, 579
Tennessee in, 584
Texas in, 583
as transformational, 622–25
volunteering for, 578
Western campaigns in, 582–86, *585*
women in disguise in, *578*, 578–79, 602–3
women's roles in, *601*, 601–3
Claiborne, J. F. H., 606
Clark, George Rogers, 211–12, *213*
Clark, William, 293, *293*, 296–97, *298*
class
Bacon's Rebellion and, 92–93
of "poor Whites" in South, 442
in social history, 504
Clay, Henry, *372*, 422
American System and, 372–73, 528
Bank War and, 400–401
Compromise of 1850 and, 544, *544*
corrupt bargain and, 384–85
election of 1832 and, 416–17
election of 1844 and, 530
electoral defeat of, 383–84
on freedom seekers in Canada, 377
on Jackson, A., 424
Jackson, A.'s, rivalry with, 388–89
Masonic order and, 416
Maysville Road Bill and, 399
Missouri Compromise and, 378–79
Panic of 1837 and, 422
Tyler and, 528–29
War of 1812 and, 307, 316
Clemson, Thomas, 443
Clermont, 336
Clinton, Catherine, 504–5
Clinton, DeWitt, 337–38
Clinton, Henry, 212–14, 228
clipper ships, 339, *340*
coal, 349

Cobb, Thomas Reade, 442
Cobbett, William, 480
cockfighting, 354
Coercive Acts (Intolerable Acts), 170–71
Cold Harbor, Battle of, 615, *616*
Cole, Thomas, *473*
Coleto, Battle of, 527
Colfax Massacre, 665–66, 667
Collet, John, *134*
colonial economy
of English colonies compared, 113–19
indentured servitude and, *111*, 111–12
Indigenous slavery in Carolina, 112
in middle colonies, 116–19
in New England colonies, *115*, 115–16
slavery and, 123, 125, 128–29
in southern colonies, 113
staple crops and, 113
Yamasee warfare and, 112–13
colonial governance
Carolina colony and, 79
of Dutch Republic, 84
General Court of Plymouth Plantation and, 70
in Maryland colony, 66–68
in Massachusetts Bay Colony, 71–72
Mayflower Compact and, 70
Negro Act of 1740 and, 128
in Pennsylvania colony, 87
self-government in English colonies, 146–47
slave codes and, 124
in Virginia colony, 64–65
colonial life
birth rates and, 105
chattel slavery and, 123–29
in cities, 129
citizenship and, 105–6
culture and, 129–37
death rates and, 104
demographics, 104–7
divorce in, 107, 184
economy and, 110–23
in Enlightenment, 131–33
enslaved women in, 109
Great Awakening and, 133–37
immigrants and, 105–6, 116–17, *118*
mail delivery and, 131
maternal mortality in, 105, *106*
in middle colonies, 116–19
nativism and, 106–7
in New England colonies, 114–16
newspapers and, 131
plantation management and, 109–10
population growth and, 104
prostitution and, 108
religion and, 110, 133–37
slavery and, 119–23, *123*
social and political order of, 129–30
in southern colonies, 113
taverns and, *130*, 130–31

travel and, 130
women in, 107–10
colonies. *See* English colonies
Columbian Exchange, 39–40
Columbus, Christopher, 3
in Cuba, 25–26
first voyage of, 24–26
in Hispaniola, 26, 27
Indigenous Americans and, 25–26
in San Salvador, 25, *25*
second and third voyages of, 27, 30
Spain return of, 26
transatlantic slave trade and, 27
Treaty of Tordesillas and, 26
voyages of, *24*
Columbus's Landfall, *25*
Comanche, 15, 47, 516–18, *517*, *518*, 523, 660
Commentaries on the Laws of England (Blackstone), 182
Commerce Clause, 248
commercial agriculture, 334–35, 348–49
Committee of Correspondence, 168
Committee of South Carolina Freedmen, 676
Common Sense (Paine), 177–78
Commonwealth v. Hunt, 360
communication
mail delivery and, 131, 341, *341*, 419
newspapers and, 131, 340–41
telegraph system and, 341–42
transportation improvements and, 340–42
communitarians, 484
"complex marriage," 485
Compromise of 1790, 264
Compromise of 1850, 544, 544–45, *545*, 548
Compromise of 1877, 669, *670*
Concord, Battle of, *173*, 174–75
Conestogas, 520
Confederate States of America (CSA). *See also* Civil War; Reconstruction
army formed by, 577–78
army size of, 574
conscription law of, 578
Davis, J., as president of, 566
on emancipation, 595
finances of, 604–5
Fort Sumter attack by, 567, 571–72
goals of, 575
inflation and, 604–5
Johnson, A.'s, pardons and, 638
politics and states' rights in, 605–7
population of, 574
regional advantages of, 574
secession of, 547, *565*, 565–67, 571–74, *573*
slavery as foundation of, 566
surrender of, *621*, 621–22
taxation and, 604
war strategy of, 577
women in bread riots in, 606

Confederation Congress
  British tensions with, 238–39
  challenges of, 236
  currency of, 236, 241
  debts of, 241
  formation of, 223
  Land Ordinances of 1784 and 1785 and, 237–38, *238*, *239*
  Morris and, 236
  Newburgh Conspiracy and, 236–37
  Northwest Ordinance and, 238, *240*
  republicanism and, 237
  Shays's Rebellion and, 242, *242*
  Spanish tensions with, 239–40
  taxation protests against, 241–42
  trade and economy of, 240–41
  weakness of, 236–37, 242
Confessions of Nat Turner, The (Gray), 457
Congregationalists, 71, 467
Congress, in Constitution, 246. *See also* House of Representatives; Senate
Congressional Reconstruction, 646, 656–57
Connecticut colony, 76
Connecticut state
  Constitution ratification and, *253*
  War of 1812 and refusal of, 307
conquistadores, 35, 37–38
Conspiracy of 1741, 125, *128*
Constitution, of United States
  Bill of Rights and, 253, 257, 258, 259
  Commerce Clause of, 248
  drafting, 244–45
  Electoral College in, 247
  immigration and, 260
  judiciary in, 247
  legislature in, 246
  limits of, 247–51
  need for, 243
  presidency in, 246
  ratification of, 251–55, *253*
  separation of powers in, 246–47
  signing, *243*
  slavery and, 248–50
  women and, 250–51
Constitutional Convention
  call for, 243
  delegates at, 243–44
  Electoral College and, 247
  federalism and, 245
  Great Compromise at, 245
  guiding assumptions of, 244–45
  Indigenous Americans and, 247–48
  limits of, 247–51
  Madison, J., at, *244*, 244–46, 248, 250
  New Jersey Plan and, 245
  ratification and, 251–55, *253*
  separation of powers and, 246–47
  slavery and, 248–50
  Three-Fifths Compromise and, 249
  transatlantic slave trade and, 249

Virginia Plan and, 245
  Washington, G., at, *243*, 244
  women and, 250–51
Continental Army, 200–201, 226
Continental Association of 1774, 171
Continental Congress, First, 171–72
Continental Congress, Second, 175–76, 178–79, 193–94, 223, 230
Continentals, 236
contrabands, 581–82, *589*, 590
contract rights, 370
Convention of 1800, 277
Convention of 1818, 379
convict leasing, 643–44
Cooke, Lucy, 516
Cooper, Anthony Ashley, 79
Copernicus, Nicolaus, 131
Corbin, Abel, 661
Corey, Martha, 75
corn, 9, 16
Cornish, Samuel, 389–90, *390*
Cornstalk, Chief, 157
Cornwallis, Charles, 214–18
Corps of Discovery, 293, 296
corrupt bargain, 384–85
corruption
  railroads and, 339
  spoils system and, 398
Cortés, Hernán, *6*, *11*, 35–37, *36*
Cosa, Juan de la, *27*
cotton, 374
  Civil War impact on export of, 623
  collapse in global demand for, 437
  emancipation impact on, 632
  Industrial Revolution and, 343–45, *345*
  kingdom in South, 430–38, *433*
  Old Southwest production of, 432–34, *433*
  profitability of, 429–30, 431, 437–38
  racial capitalism and, 430
  slavery and, 344–45, 430
  South, population growth and production of, 436, *437*
  technology advancements and, 343–44, *345*, 431–32
Cotton, John, 107
cotton gin, 343–44, *345*, 431–32
Counter-Reformation, 32
coverture, 182–83
Cowpens, Battle of, 215
Craft, Ellen, 549, *549*
Craft, William, 549, *549*
Crawford, William, 383
Creek, 18, 112, 124, 240, 310–12, *311*, 410, 583
Creek War, 310–12, *311*
Crittenden, John J., 566
Crockett, David, 311, 525, *526*
Cromwell, Oliver, 59–60, 67, 147
Crow, 15
Cruikshank, Robert, *397*

Cruikshank, William, 667
CSA. *See* Confederate States of America
Cuba, 25–26, 35
cult of domesticity, 493–94
culture
  colonial life and, 129–37
  of enslaved people, 122–23, *123*, 453, 455
  Industrial Revolution and, 353–55
currency
  during Civil War, 604, *604*
  of Confederation Congress, 236, 241
  greenbacks and, 663–64
  Independent Treasury Act and, 422
  Second Bank of the United States and, 368
  Supreme Court on national, 370

Dale, Thomas, 113
Dale's Laws, 113
Dare, Virginia, 50
Dartmouth College v. Woodward, 370
Daughters of Liberty, 163
Davenport, John, 76
Davis, Jefferson, 544, 551, *572*, 575, 585
  Battle of Vicksburg and, 609
  capture and imprisonment of, 622
  conscription law of, 578
  as CSA president, 566
  finances and, 604–5
  Lee, Robert E.'s, resignation refused by, 612
  public frustration with, 606
  on secession, 571
  surrender resisted by, 619
Dawes, William, 173
Death of General Mercer at the Battle of Princeton, The, *196*
death rates, 104
Declaration of American Rights, 171
Declaration of Independence, 178–80, 230, 326
Declaration of Rights, England, 149
Declaration of Rights and Sentiments, 494–95, 496
Declaration of the Rights and Grievances of the Colonies, 164
Declaratory Act, 164
Deere, John, 348
Deism, 132, 464
Delany, Martin, 635, *635*
Delaware colony, *81*, 87
Delaware state
  Constitution ratification and, 253, *253*, *254*
  secession resisted by, 572
democracy
  direct, 222
  Jackson, A.'s, undemocratic impulses, 397
  Jefferson and, 286
  Massachusetts Bay Colony and, 71–72
  political, 396–97

presidential conventions and, 398
representative, 222, 246
spoils system and, 398
Democratic Party, 396
Compromise of 1877 and, 669, *670*
in election of 1868, 657–58
election of 1876 and, 668–69, *669*
first presidential convention of, 398
Irish immigrants and, 358
Reconstruction's end and, 670–71
in Union politics during Civil War, 605
Van Buren running, 397
Whig factions joining, 552
Democratic-Republican Party. *See* Republicans, Jeffersonian
denim jeans, 542
Denmark, 30
Denmark Vesey Revolt, 456–57
Deslondes, Charles, 456
Dial magazine, 475
Dickinson, Charles, 388
Dickinson, Emily, *477*, 477–78
Dickinson, John, 190–91
diplomatic nationalism, 379–82, *380*, *381*
direct democracy, 222
Discourse on Women (Mott), 506
discovery and exploration
of Africa, 20, 23
boundaries in, 28–29
Columbian Exchange and, 39–40
by Columbus, 23–27, 30
Dutch, *48*, 80–81
English, *48*, 50, *51*
French, 41–42, 47–48, *48*
global trade and, 18–34
professionals in, 30
Spanish, 35–37, 41–44, *42*, 47
technological advancements for, 19
by Vespucci, 30
disease. *See* infectious diseases
Distribution Act, 418, *418*
District of Columbia. *See* Washington, D.C.
divorce, in colonial life, 107, 184
Dix, Dorothea Lynde, 482, 601–2
dogfighting, 354
dogs, 46
domestic slave trade, 434–36, *435*, 446–50
Dominican Republic, 26
Donelson, John, 388
Donner, George, 522–23
Doolittle, Amos, *174*, *252*
Douglas, Stephen A., 342, 544, 548, 551–52, 605
election of 1860 and, 562–64, *564*
Lincoln, A., debates with, *559*, 559–61
Douglass, Frederick, 562, 567, *652*
in abolition movement, 491–93, *492*
on Emancipation Proclamation, 594
escape of, 458, 492
Fifteenth Amendment enforcement and, 658

on July 4th holiday, 497
on Lincoln, A.'s, assassination, 637
on overseers, 440
on Reconstruction's end, 670
on *Uncle Tom's Cabin*, 551
on voting rights, 648
women's rights supported by, 659
Drake, Sylvia, 479
Dred Scott v. Sandford, 557–58, *558*
drivers, 441
Drummond, Sarah, 93
Drummond, William, 93
Drunkard's Progress, The, 481
dueling, 439
Durand, John, *129*
Dutch East India Company, 80–81
Dutch Republic
Charter of Freedoms and Exemptions and, 82
English colonies seizing, 84–85, 147
global trade and, 80–85
governance of, 84
New Netherland becomes New York colony, 82, *83*
patroonship and, 82
population of, 80
slavery and, 84, *125*
tolerance and limitations of, 82–84
Dutch West India Company, *65*, 82, 84
Dyer, Mary, 86

Eastern Woodland peoples, *17*, 17–18
East Florida, 306–7. *See also* Spanish Florida
East India Company, *140*, 169
Easty, Mary, 75–76
Eaton, John, 404
economic nationalism, 368–69, 420
economy. *See also* colonial economy; Industrial Revolution; taxation; trade; transportation improvements
American System and, 372–73, 528
capitalism, 261, 339
colonial life and, 110–23
Confederation Congress and, 240–41
cotton and, 344–45
emancipation impact on, 632
Embargo Act of 1807 impact on, 302–3
Erie Canal impact on, 338
household, 334
Jefferson's policies on, 290
land grants and, 342
market, 334–35
mercantilism, 261
Panic of 1819 and, 374–75
Panic of 1837 and, *421*, 421–22
Panic of 1857 and, 557
Panic of 1873 and, *664*, 664–65
War of 1812 and independence of, 319–20

Edenton Tea Party, 170
Edict of Nantes, 79
education
of African Americans in Reconstruction, 649–51
Freedmen's Bureau and, 634, *634*
gender and, 181, 227
medical profession and, 362
public schools in nineteenth century and, 482–84, *483*
in Renaissance, 19
segregation in, 483–84
teaching profession and, 361, *362*
Edwards, Jonathan, *133*, 133–35
Edward VI, 33–34
Electoral College, in Constitution, 247
Elguézabal, Juan Bautista, 346
Elizabeth I, *33*, 33–34, 49–51, 58
emancipation. *See also* abolition movement
CSA view of, 595
early days of, 629–30
economic impact of, 632
families reuniting following, 630, *630*
Juneteenth and, *594*
Lincoln, A., and, 589–96, *593*
Massachusetts, lawsuits for, 248
reactions to, *594*, 594–96, *595*
Second Confiscation Act on, 590
Thirteenth Amendment and, 500, 624–25, 643
women's rights movements and, 624
Emancipation (Nast), *628*
Emancipation Day, *594*
Emancipation Proclamation, *593*, 593–94, 624
Embargo Act of 1807, 302–3, *303*
Emerson, Ralph Waldo, 331, 463, *474*, 474–75, 479, 486, 548, 571
Emigrants Crossing the Plains, or the Oregon Trail (Bierstadt), *512*
enclosure movement, 58
encomienda system, 38
Enforcement Acts, 665
engineering profession, 362
England. *See also* Great Britain
Act of Supremacy in, 33
Act to Prevent Frauds and Abuses and, 149
Americas and explorations of, *48*, 50, *51*
Civil War of 1640s in, 147
Coercive Acts and, 170–71
Declaration of Rights in, 149
Dutch Republic seized by, 84–85, 147
Gaspée incident and, 168
Glorious Revolution and, 60, 148–49
Iroquois League at war with, 97
mercantilism and, 147
monarchy challenged in, *59*, 59–60
Navigation Acts and, 147, 149
Proclamation Act of 1763 and, 158

England *(continued)*
   professional explorers from, 30
   Reformation in, 32–34
   religious conflict in, 58–60
   in rise of global trade, 20
   Spanish Armada defeated by, 49
   taxation in English colonies compared to, 156
   Tea Act of 1773 and, 169
   Toleration Act in, 67–68
   transatlantic slave trade and, 65
English colonies, 141. *See also* American Revolution; colonial economy; colonial life; middle colonies; New England colonies; Virginia colony
   Act to Prevent Frauds and Abuses and, 149
   agriculture and, 90
   Bacon's Rebellion and, 90–93, *91*
   British goods boycotted in, 171–72
   Carolina colony, *77*, 77–80, *78*
   in Chesapeake region, 60–68
   Coercive Acts and, 170–71
   Committee of Correspondence and, 168
   Declaratory Act and, 164
   Dutch Republic seized by, 84–85, 147
   economies compared, 113–19
   in Enlightenment, 131–33
   geography of, 56, *57*
   Georgia colony, *88*, 88–90, *89*
   Grenville's policy and, 160–62
   indentured servitude in, 58
   Indigenous Americans and, 89–97
   infectious diseases in, 70, 71
   Iroquois League at war with, 97
   as joint-stock companies, 56
   King Philip's War and, *95*, 95–96
   map of, 1713, *155*
   map of, 1763, *156*
   Maryland colony, 64, 66–68, *67*
   Mayflower Compact and, 70
   mercantilism and, 147
   Naturalization Act in, 105–6
   Navigation Acts and, 147, 149
   New France competing with, 142
   New Jersey colony, *81*, 85
   New York colony, *81*, 82–85, *83*
   Pennsylvania colony, *81*, 85–87
   Pequot War and, 94
   Pilgrims in, 59
   Plymouth, 68–70, *69*
   Pocahontas and, 62, *63*
   political traditions of, 58
   Pontiac's Rebellion and, 157, *157*
   population of, 56, 119, 129
   Proclamation Act of 1763 and, 158
   protests in, 162–66
   Puritans in, 58–59
   Quartering Act of 1765 and, 160–61
   Quartering Act of 1774 and, 170
   resentment in, 148
   salutary neglect and, 149–50
   self-government in, 146–47
   slavery in, 55–56, 65–66
   slavery in Spanish Florida compared to, 123–24
   Stamp Act of 1765 and, *161*, 161–62
   Sugar Act of 1764 and, 160
   system of, 146–50
   taverns in, 131
   taxation in England compared to, 156
   thriving, 97–99
   Townshend Acts and, 164–65, 168
   virtual representation of, 162
   witches in Salem and, *74*, 74–76, *75*
   women and religion in, 110
Enlightenment, 131–33
enslaved people. *See also* slavery
   African Americans owning/protecting, 446
   auctions of, 446–50, *447*, *450*
   breeding of, 452
   children as, 447, 450, 454, *454*
   in cities, 452
   colonial life and, 119–23, *123*
   community forged by, 453–59
   culture of, 122–23, *123*, 453, 455
   Denmark Vesey Revolt and, 456–57
   domestic trade of, 434–36, *435*, 446–50
   exploitation of, 443
   families of, 454, *454*
   as field hands, 451
   as freedom seekers, 128–29, 221–22, 250, *250*, 259, 377, 436, 458
   Gabriel's Rebellion by, 456
   German Coast Uprising by, 456
   as human capital, 443
   labor of, 451
   maroon communities and, 436
   Nat Turner's Rebellion and, *457*, 457–58
   population of, 119, 321, 442, *444*, *445*
   as property, 122
   rebellions of, 122, 128–29, 180, 455–58
   religion of, 454–55
   sexual assault and, 440, 447, 452
   in South, 442–59, *444*, *445*, *450*
   spirituals sung by, 453, 455
   Texas and emancipation of, 376
   Three-Fifths Compromise and, 249
   White supremacy and, 442–43
   women as, 109, 251, 440, 447, 450–53
enslavers, 438–39, *439*
environment
   Columbian Exchange and, 40
   Industrial Revolution reshaping, 352
   Little Ice Age and, 40
Episcopalians, 465
equality
   American Revolution and, 181–84, 225–31
   Blackstone on, 182
   "free persons of color" and, 446
   gender and, 250–51
   Industrial Revolution and desire for, 363
   women and, 181–84, 227, *227*, 230
Era of Good Feelings, 373–75, *374*, 378–79
Erie Canal, *336*, 337–38
Estevanico, 146
Ethiopia Regiment, *180*, 181, 225
Europe. *See also specific countries*
   expansion of, 19–20
   religious conflict in, 30–34
   Renaissance in, 19
   rise of global trade and, 19–20
European colonists. *See also* Columbus, Christopher; English colonies; transatlantic slave trade
   Age of Exploration and, 18–34
   Columbian Exchange and, 39–40
   environmental changes brought by, 40
   Indigenous Americans and impact of, 3, 55
   infectious diseases from, 40
   motivations of, 55, 103
   motives of, 4
evangelism/evangelists, 133–37
executive branch, 246
exploration. *See* discovery and exploration

Fairfax, Bryan, 170
Fallen Timbers, Battle of, 269
"fancy trade," in slavery, 447
Fargo, William G., 341
farmers. *See* agriculture
Farragut, David G., 586
federal circuit courts, 277, 288
federalism, 245
Federalist Papers, The, 253
Federalists, 195
   Adams, John's, election and, 275
   Alien and Sedition Acts of 1798 and, 276, *277*
   electoral loss in 1800 of, 277–78, *278*
   French Revolution and, 267
   Hartford Convention and, 318–19
   Jeffersonian Republicans compared to, 255, 266–67
   Jefferson's hatred of, 285
   on Louisiana Purchase, 293
   in ratification debate, *252*, 252–53
   on Western land policy, 272–73
Female Antislavery Society of Philadelphia, 494
Female Guide, The (Ogden, J.), 250
Ferdinand II of Aragon, 20, 26
Ferguson, Patrick, 214–15
field hands, 451
Fields, John W., 443
Fifteenth Amendment, 510, 648–49, 658–59
Filley, Lester, 586
Fillmore, Millard, 548, 551, 556
Finkelman, Paul, 325

Finney, Charles G., 469
First African Baptist Church, 135
First Amendment, 260
First Continental Congress, 171–72
First Seminole War, 379–80, *380*
fisheries, in New England colonies, *115*, 115–16
Fisk, James, Jr., 661
Fitzhugh, George, 440, 443
Five Nation League of the Iroquois, 14
Florida. *See also* South; Spanish Florida
   secession of, 566
   Spanish transfer of, 375
   Transcontinental Treaty and, 380–81, *381*
Flucker, Lucy, 198
Foner, Eric, 674–75
Force Bill of 1833, 406
Forest Leaves (Harper), 478
Forrest, Nathan Bedford, 614, *614*
Fort Clatsop, 296
Fort Duquesne, 151, 153, 157
Forten, Charlotte, 634
Fort Jackson, Treaty of, 312
Fort Mandan, 296, *298*
Fort McHenry, 314
Fort Necessity, 152
Fort Pillow Massacre, 614, *614*
Fort Pitt, 157
Fort Sumter attack, 567, 571–72
Foster, Stephen, 355
Four Soldiers, *198*
Fourteenth Amendment, 510, 643, 644, 667
Fowler, Charlotte, 677
Fox, George, 85, 86
Fox Nation, 408
France
   American Revolution and, 194
   Americas and explorations of, 41–42, 47–48, *48*, 142
   in Battle of Yorktown, 217–18, *218*
   Canada colonized by, 47–48, 142
   Canada lost by, 154
   Convention of 1800 and, 277
   Edict of Nantes and, 79
   Embargo Act of 1807 and, 302–3, *303*
   Genêt and, *268*, 268–69
   Haitian Revolution and, 268, *291*, 291–92
   Iroquois League at war with, 97
   Louisiana Purchase and, 290–93
   naval harassment by, 301–2
   naval war with, 275–76, 278
   Non-Intercourse Act of 1809 and, 303–4
   Reign of Terror in, 267
   Revolution in, 267–69
   in rise of global trade, 20
   Spanish exploration of Florida and, 41–42
   Treaty of Alliance with, 210
   Treaty of Paris (1763) and, 154–55, 157
   Treaty of Paris (1783) and, 218–20
   XYZ Affair and, 276, *276*

Franklin, Abiah Folger, 105, *106*
Franklin, Benjamin, 104, *132*
   Albany Plan of Union and, 152
   American Revolution and family divisions of, 198
   businesses and inventions of, 132–33
   on Constitution ratification, 251, 254
   Declaration of Independence and, 179
   Great Awakening and, 133
   on immigrants, 106
   political cartoon by, *152*
   on presidency, 246
   printing business of, 132
   Treaty of Paris (1783) and, 218–19
   Whitefield and, 135
Franklin, Sarah, 161
Franklin, William, 198
Frazier, Garrison, 649
Fredericksburg, Battle of, 596
"free banking era," 417
Freedman's Bank, 635–36, *636*, 664
Freedman's Village, 590, *590*
Freedmen's Bureau, 633–35, *634*
Freedmen's conventions, 638–39, *639*
freedom
   American Revolution, slavery contradicting, 180–81, 225–27, *226*, 228–29
   American Revolution, women's equality and, 181–84, 227, *227*, 230
   Bill of Rights and, 253, 257, 258, 259
   Reconstruction debate on, 633
   of religion, *224*, 224–25, 260
   slavery and, 259
Freedom, Cuff, 207, *207*
Freedom, Jube, 207, *207*
freedom seekers, 128–29, 221–22, 250, *250*, 259, 377, 436, 458
Freedom's Journal, 340, 389–90, *390*
Freeman, Elizabeth "Mum Bett," 248, *248*
"free persons of color," 444–46
Free-Soil Party, 540
freezers, 343, *343*
Frémont, John C., 534–35, 555–57
French and Indian War
   Albany Plan of Union and, 152
   Battle of Monongahela in, 153
   Battle of Quebec in, 154
   Braddock's defeat and, 153
   climax and aftermath of, 154
   major campaigns of, *151*
   origins of, 150–52
French Catholics, *118*, 142
French colonies. *See* New France
French Revolution, 267–69
frontier revivals, *466*, 466–67
Fugitive Slave Act of 1793, 250
Fugitive Slave Act of 1850, 548–49
Fugitive Slave Clause, 250
Fuller, Margaret, 475, *475*
Fuller, Timothy, 375

Fulton, Robert, 370
Fulton, Sarah Bradlee, 163
Fur Traders Descending the Missouri, 516

Gabriel's Rebellion, 456
Gadsden Purchase of 1853, 537
Gage, Thomas, 172–73
Gallatin, Albert, 288, 307
Gálvez, Bernardo de, 216–17, *217*
Garfield, James A., 622
Garner, Henry, 443
Garner, Margaret "Peggy," 549–50, *550*
Garrido, Juan, 41, 146
Garrison, William Lloyd, 489–91, *490*, 495, 498, 499, 533
Gaspée, 168
Gates, Horatio, 214
Gates, Thomas, 63–64
gender. *See also* women
   Bacon's Rebellion and, 92–93
   Declaration of Rights and Sentiments and, *494*, 494–95, 496
   education and, 181, 227
   Emerson on, 474–75
   equality and, 250–51
   household work and, 351–52
   in Iroquois culture, 18
   in New England colonies, 68
   New Harmony community and, 487
   Powhatan Confederacy and, 61
   separate spheres and, 351
   in social history, 504
   in teaching profession, 361, *362*
General Court of Plymouth Plantation, 70
Genêt, Edmond-Charles, *268*, 268–69
Genius of Universal Emancipation, The, 434
George Barrell Emerson School, 483
George I, 149
George II, 88, 149, 154
George III, 154, *154*, 155, 158, 177, 179, 218, 220
Georgia colony, *88*, 88–90, *89*
Georgia Gazette, 229
Georgia Messenger, 376
Georgia state. *See also* South
   Constitution ratification and, 253, *253*, 254
   cotton production in, 432–33, *433*
   Indigenous Americans' removal fought in, 409–10
   poll taxes and, 658–59
   in Revolutionary War, 214
   secession of, 566
   slavery in, 249
Germain, George, 214
German Coast Uprising, 456
German immigrants, 106, 116–17, *118*, 358–59
Gerry, Elbridge, 244
Gettysburg, Battle of, *608*, 609–11, *610*, *611*
Gettysburg Address, 612, 625

Ghana, *21*, 21–22
Ghent, Treaty of, 316
Gibbons, Thomas, 370–71
Gibbons v. Ogden, 370–71
Gilmer, George, 409
global trade. *See also* trade; transatlantic slave trade
  Age of Exploration and rise of, 18–34
  Atlantic routes of, 1600–1800, *117*
  boundaries in, 28–29
  clipper ships and, 339
  Dutch Republic and, 80–85
  Embargo Act of 1807 and, 302–3, *303*
  Non-Intercourse Act of 1809 and, 303–4
Glorious Revolution, 60, 148–49
"Go Down, Moses," 455
gold rush, California, 540–43, *541*, *542*
Good, Sarah, 75
Gooding, James Henry, 597
Goodyear, Charles, 343
Gordon, John B., 615
Gorges, Ferdinando, 76
Gould, Jay, 661
governance. *See* colonial governance
Gower, Elizabeth, 601
Gower, George, *33*
Gower, T. G., 601
Graduation Act of 1854, 348
Grant, Ulysses S., *607*
  administration of, 658
  Appomattox Court House and, *621*, 621–22
  Battle of Cold Harbor and, 615, *616*
  Battle of Spotsylvania Court House and, 615, *616*
  Battle of the Wilderness and, 614–15, *616*
  Battle of Vicksburg and, 607–9
  Black Friday and, 661–62, *662*
  Civil War victories and prestige of, 584
  domestic terrorism and, 665–67
  election of 1868 and, 657–58
  election of 1872 and, 663
  Enforcement Acts and, 665
  Fifteenth Amendment enforcement and, 658–59
  greenbacks and, 663–64
  Indigenous Americans and policies of, 660–61
  Johnson, A.'s, impeachment and, 647
  Ku Klux Klan Act of 1871 and, 665
  Liberal Republicans and, 622–23
  on Mexican-American War, 537
  Panic of 1873 and, *664*, 664–65
  Petersburg siege and, 615–16, *616*
  Public Credit Act of 1869 and, 664
  reservation system and, 660–61
  retirement of, 668
  Sherman, W. T., and, 614, 658
  slogan of, *658*
  sobriety of, 586
  strategy of, 613–14

tenacity of, 615
"whiskey ring" and, 622
Grasse, François Joseph Paul de, 217
Gray, Thomas R., *457*
Great Awakening
  first, 133–37
  second, 465–72
Great Britain. *See also* England; Revolutionary War; War of 1812
  abolition movement in, 489
  African Americans recruited by, 225–26, *226*
  Battle of New Orleans and, 317–18, *318*
  Buchanan-Pakenham Treaty and, 531, *532*
  Chesapeake incident and, 302
  colonial boycotts against goods from, 171–72
  Confederation Congress tensions with, 238–39
  Convention of 1818 and, 379
  diplomatic nationalism and, 379
  Embargo Act of 1807 and, 302–3, *303*
  formation of, 58
  impressment and, 302, 305, *305*
  Jay's Treaty and, 269–71, *271*
  military power of, 199–200
  naval harassment by, 301–2
  Non-Intercourse Act of 1809 and, 303–4
  population of, 193
  Revolutionary War setbacks of, 1777–1781, 208–21
  Rush-Bagot Agreement of 1817 and, 379
  staple crops and, 113
  Treaty of Ghent and, 316
  Treaty of Paris (1763) and, 154–55, 157
  Treaty of Paris (1783) and, 218–20
  Washington, D.C., burned by, 312–14, *313*
Great Compromise, 245
Great Dying, 40
Great Law of Peace, 96–97
Great Meadows, Battle of, 152
Great Plains Indigenous Americans, 15, *46*, 46–47
Great Serpent Mound, *15*
Greeley, Horace, 541, 663
greenbacks, 663–64
Greene, Catherine, 344, *344*
Greene, Nathanael, 200, 215
Greenhow, Rose O'Neal, 576
Greenland, 30
Greenville, Treaty of, 269, *270*
Gregory, James, 124, 126
Grenville, George, *160*, 160–62, *164*, 165
Grimes, Ruth A., 634
Grimké, Angelina, *498*, 498–99
Grimké, Sarah, *498*, 498–99
Griswold, Roger, 277
Guadalupe Hidalgo, Treaty of, 536–37
Guilford Courthouse, Battle of, 216
Gwyn, Hugh, 124, 126

Habeas Corpus Act of 1863, 605
Hagerty, Rebecca McIntosh Hawkins, 410, *410*
Haida, 14–15
Haiti, 26, 268, 291–92
Haitian Revolution, 268, *291*, 291–92
Hale, John P., 551
Halleck, Henry, 586, 605
Hamilton, Alexander, 235, 255, *261*
  background of, 261–62
  Bank of the United States and, *264*, 264–65
  Burr's duel with, 297–99
  Compromise of 1790 and, 264
  on Constitutional Convention, 243
  economy and, 261
  The Federalist Papers and, 253
  French Revolution and, 268
  Jefferson competing with, 266
  leadership of, 266
  manufacturing encouraged by, 265–66
  Newburgh Conspiracy and, 237
  opposition to, 264
  revenue plans of, 263
  on state debts, 263
  tariffs under, 262–63
  Treasury Department and, 257, 261, 264
  Washington, G.'s, inauguration and, 257
  Whiskey Rebellion and, 271–72
Hammond, James, 419, 437, 452, 501, 606
Hampton, Wade, III, 641
Hancock, John, 184
Harper, Frances Ellen Watkins, 478, *478*, 495, 501
Harrison, Benjamin, 179
Harrison, William Henry, 295, 306, 420
  election of, 422–23, *423*
Hartford, Treaty of, 94
Hartford Convention, 318–19
Hawthorne, Nathaniel, 474, 475, 477, 571
Hayes, Rutherford B.
  election of 1876 and, 668–69, *669*
  Reconstruction's end and, 670–71
Hayne, Robert Y., 402–3, *403*, 405
Haynes, Lemuel, *224*
headright system, 64, 79
Hemings, Sarah "Sally," 286–87, *287*
Hennes, Mathilde, 524
Henrietta Maria, 66
Henry, Patrick, 164, 172, *172*, 252
Henry VII, 30
Henry VIII, 32–34
Hessians, 199
Hewitt, Nancy A., 505
Hidalgo y Costilla, Miguel, 518
Higginson, Thomas, 594
Highland Scots, *118*
Hispaniola, 26, 27
Historical Caricature of the Cherokee Nation, *407*
historical causation, 674

historiography, 188, 504
HMS *Leopard*, 302
Hoban, James, *285*
Hohokam, 14
Holloway, Houston, 630
Holmes, Oliver Wendell, Jr., 622
Homestead Act of 1862, 603, 623
Hood, James Walker, 638
Hood, John Bell, 583, 617, 618
Hooker, Joseph, 607
Hooker, Thomas, 76
Hooper, William, 201
Hopewell, 16
Hopi, 14
horses, Spanish, *46*, 46–47
Horseshoe Bend, Battle of, 312
Horton, Albert C., 449
household economy, 334
household work, women and, 351–52
House of Burgesses, 64
House of Representatives
　in Constitution, 246
　slavery and brawl in, 561
Houston, James, 122
Houston, Sam, 525–27, *527*
Howard, Oliver O., 633–34
Howe, Elias, 343
Howe, Richard, 175, 202, 204
Howe, William, 176, 202, 206, 208
Hudson, Henry, 80
Hudson's Bay Company, 143
　map of, 1713, *155*
　map of, 1763, *156*
Hughson, John, 125
Huguenots, 79, 117, *118*
Hull, William, 308–9
human capital, enslaved people as, 443
humanism, 19
human sacrifice, 13
hunter-gatherer societies, 9
Huron, 143
Hutchinson, Anne, *73*, 73–74
Hutchinson, Thomas, 168, 171, 190
hysteria, witches in Salem and, 76

ice cream, 343, *343*
identity, regional, 330, 334
Ideological Origins of the American Revolution, The (Bailyn), 189
Ignatius of Loyola, 32. *See also* Jesuits
immigration/immigrants. *See also specific groups*
　Alien and Sedition Acts of 1798 and, 276, *277*
　Carolina colony and, 79
　Civil War enlistment of, 577
　colonial life and, 105–6, 116–17, *118*
　Constitution and, 260
　growth of, 158
　indentured servitude and, 111, 159
　independence for, 159

Mennonites, 117
in middle colonies, 116–17, *118*
nativists organizing against, 358–59
Naturalization Act of 1790 and, 261
in nineteenth century, 355–59, *356*
prejudices faced by, 333–34
rise of prejudice against, 357
in South, 429
impeachment, 246
　of Johnson, A., 646–48, *647*
impressment, 302, 305, *305*
Inca, 11, 37–38
Incidents in the Life of a Slave Girl (Jacobs), 452
indentured servitude
　colonial life and, *111*, 111–12
　in English colonies, 58
　immigration and, 111, 159
　kidnapped, 111
　in legal system by race, 126–27
　rights of, 111
　slavery compared to, 111–12
　slavery outgrowing, 124–25
　tobacco farming and, 64
Independence Day, 230–31
Independence Day Celebration (Krimmel), 374
Independent Treasury Act, 422
Indian Act of 1850, 543
Indian Confederacy, Tecumseh's, 306
Indian Removal Act of 1830, 407, 410
Indian Ring, 661
Indigenous Americans. *See also specific tribes*
　agricultural practices of, 70
　agriculture and, 90
　Anti-Vagrancy Act and, 543
　Bacon's Rebellion and, 90–93, *91*
　Bad Axe Massacre and, 408
　Battle of Horseshoe Bend and, 312
　in Battle of Monongahela, 153
　Battle of Tippecanoe and, 306, 423
　Black Hawk War and, 408
　buffalo hunting and, 47
　California Catholic missions and, *521*, 521–22
　California gold rush and, 541–42
　ceremonial mounds and, 14
　Cherokee Nation v. Georgia and, 409
　Christianity and conversions of, 27, 44, 91, 141, 145, *145*
　Christians' worldview compared to religions of, 15
　citizenship and, 661
　in Civil War, 583, *583*
　Columbian Exchange and, 39–40
　Columbus and, 25–26
　Constitution and, 247–48
　democracy denied to, 286
　Dutch Republic tolerance and limitations with, 83

Eastern Woodland peoples, *17*, 17–18
English colonies and, 89–97
European colonists' impact on, 3, 55
first migrations of, *8*, 8–9
First Seminole War and, 379–80, *380*
forced relocation of, 284, 290, 334, *412*
genocide of, 5
Grant's policies toward, 660–61
Great Law of Peace and, 96–97
of Great Plains, 15, *46*, 46–47
Inca, 11, 37–38
Indian Act of 1850 and, 543
Indian Removal Act of 1830 and, 407, 410
Iroquois League and, 96–97
Jackson, A.'s, policy on, 406–15
Kansas-Nebraska Act and, 551–52, *553*
King Philip's War and, *95*, 95–96
Land Ordinance of 1785 and, 238
Lewis and Clark expedition and, 296–97, *298*
Louisiana Purchase and, 291, 295, 297
maize and, 9, 16
Maya, 9–10, 35
Mexica/Aztec, *11*, 11–13, 36–37
Mississippians, *15*, 16–17
mound-building cultures of, *15*, 16–17
Naturalization Act of 1790 and, 261
New France relations with, 143–45
newspapers and, 340, *409*
North American societies around 1500, 13–18, *16*
of Northwest, 14–15
Northwest Ordinance and, 238
Pequot War and, 94
Pocahontas, 62, *63*
Pontiac's Rebellion and, 157, *157*
Powhatan Confederacy and, 61–62
pre-Columbian civilizations of, *12*
Proclamation Act of 1763 and, *156*, 158
Pueblo, 14, *14*, 44–46
Quakers and, 87
reservation system and, 660–61
resettlement resisted by, *408*, 408–10
in Revolutionary War, 184, 201, 212, 230
Second Seminole War and, 408, *408*
slavery of, 94, 112
smallpox and, 40, 70, 71
of Southwest, 14, *14*
Spanish horses and, *46*, 46–47
Supreme Court on removal of, 409–10
Taino, 25
Tecumseh's defeat and, 310
Tecumseh's Indian Confederacy and, 306
Trail of Tears and, 411–13, *412*, *413*
Treaty of Greenville and, 269, *270*
Treaty of New Echota and, 410–11
Treaty of Paris (1763) impact on, 157
Treaty of Paris (1783) impact on, 220
wampum belt and, *97*

Indigenous Americans *(continued)*
    War of 1812 and, 283, 305, 307–8, 310–12, 320–21
    Westward expansion and, 516–18, *517, 518*
    White America customs adopted by, 410
    Williams, Roger, supporting, 72–73
Indigenous Plains peoples, 516–18, *517, 518*
indigo, 109, 124
Industrial Revolution
    abolition movement and, 346–47
    alcohol and, 354
    coal power and, 349
    cotton and, 343–45, *345*
    environment reshaped by, 352
    equal opportunities desire in, 363
    growth of cities and, 352, *352, 353*
    labor and, 349
    Lowell system and, 350–51
    mass production and, 342, 360
    Midwest farming in, 345, 348–49
    popular culture in, 353–55
    slavery and, 345
    steam engine and, 342
    tariffs and, 349–50
    technological advancements and, 343–44, *348*
    textile manufacturers and, 349–51
    theater during, 354–55, *355*
    urban recreation during, 354, *354*
    women, household work and, 351–52
infectious diseases
    Columbian Exchange and, 40
    in English colonies, 70, 71
    Jesuit missionaries in New France and, 145
    in Revolutionary War, 202, 207
    in Virginia colony, 65
    Westward expansion and, 520
inflation, CSA and, 604–5
infrastructure, 335. *See also* transportation improvements
Ingersoll, Robert G., 669
Ingham, Samuel, 404
Inness, George, *332*
Inquiry into the Nature and Causes of the Wealth of Nations, An (Smith, Adam), 261, 349
Institutes of the Christian Religion, The (Calvin), 32
internal improvements, 369, 399
Internal Revenue Service (IRS), 604
interstate commerce
    Maysville Road Bill and, 399
    Supreme Court on, 370–71
Irish immigrants, 106, 117
    African Americans' relations with, 357
    Catholicism and, 357
    Democratic Party and, 358
    impact of, 358
    New York City draft riots and, 597
    in nineteenth century, 357
    prejudice against, 357

iron plows, 348
Iroquois, 14, 17–18, 96–97, *142*, 143, *153*, 201, 212, *212*
Iroquois League, 96–97
IRS (Internal Revenue Service), 604
Isabella I of Castile, 20, 26, 27
I Saw Death Coming (Williams, K. E.), 675

Jackson, Andrew, 316, 382, *383*
    adultery and, 388–89
    African Americans and, 389–90, 397
    anti-democratic impulses of, 397, 425
    attempted assassination of, 416
    Bank of the United States eliminated by, 417–19, 421
    Bank War and, 399–401, *400*
    Battle of New Orleans and, 317–18, *318*
    cabinet divisions of, 398
    Calhoun's tensions with, 401, 403–5
    censuring of, 417
    Cherokee and, 415
    Clay's rivalry with, 388–89
    congressional career of, 383
    corrupt bargain and, 384–85
    Creek War and, *311*, 311–12
    Distribution Act and, 418, *418*
    election of, 334, 390–91
    election of 1824 and, 383–84
    election of 1828 and, *387*, 387–89
    election of 1832 and, 416–17
    First Seminole War and, 379–80
    Force Bill of 1833 and, 406
    "free banking era" and, 417
    health of, 395–96
    inauguration of, *397*, 397–98
    Indian Removal Act of 1830 and, 407, 410
    Indigenous Americans policy of, 406–15
    as "jackass," 389
    legacy of, 424–25
    mail censorship and, 419
    Masonic order and, 416
    Maysville Road Bill and, 399, *399*
    military successes of, 318
    new cabinet of, 403–4, *404*
    as polarizing figure, 395–96
    political democracy and, 397
    presidential conventions and, 398
    re-election of, 405, 417
    in Revolutionary War, 383
    Ross, J.'s, letter to, 414
    South Carolina Nullification Ordinance and, 405–6
    Specie Circular and, *418*, 418–19, 421
    spoils system and, 398
    Texas annexation and, 528
    voting rights expansion and election of, 389
    on Webster-Hayne debate, 403
    Whig Party responding to, 423–24
Jackson, Mary, 606
Jackson, Rachel, *388*, 388–89
Jackson, Thomas "Stonewall," 576, *576*, 607

Jacobins, 267–68
Jacobs, Harriet, 452
Jamaica, colonization of, 35
James, Henry, 541
James II, 60, 148
Jamestown colony, *54*, 61–66
Jane Grey, 34
Jay, John, 219, 243
    The Federalist Papers and, 253
    Jay's Treaty and, 269–71, *271*
    as Supreme Court chief justice, 257
Jay's Treaty, 269–71, *271*
Jefferson, Thomas, 132, 170, 175, *243*, 255, 263, *266*, *304*
    Alien and Sedition Acts of 1798 countered by, 276
    Bank of the United States opposed by, 264
    Barbary pirates and, 301, *301*
    on Battle of King's Mountain, 215
    on Bonaparte, 290
    Burr Conspiracy and, 299
    cabinet of, 287–88
    Chesapeake incident and, 302
    contradictions of, 286–87
    Declaration of Independence and, 179–80, 326
    democracy and, 286
    economic policies of, 290
    election of, 195, 277–78, *278*, 283
    electoral loss of, 275
    Embargo Act of 1807 and, 302–3
    Federalists hated by, 285
    on First Amendment, 260
    French Revolution and, 268–69
    on *Gibbons v. Ogden*, 371
    Hamilton competing with, 266
    Hemings and, 286–87, *287*
    inauguration of, 279, 284–85
    Land Ordinance of 1784 and, 237–38
    legacy of, 299–300
    Louisiana Purchase and, 290–94, 297
    Marbury v. Madison and, 288–89
    at Monticello, 287, *288*
    naval harassment by Britain and France and, 301–2
    Notes on the State of Virginia by, 326–27
    on rebellions, 242
    re-election of, 298–99
    republican simplicity of, 285
    Revolution of 1800 and, 279
    slavery and, 179–80, 225, 286–87, *287*, 324–27, 373
    State Department and, 257, 264
    State Department resignation of, 269
    transatlantic slave trade ended by, 299–300
    Virginia Statute of Religious Freedom and, 225
    on War of 1812, 319
    Western expansion and, 290
    on women and Constitution, 251
    on women and freedoms, 184

"Jefferson and Slavery" (Finkelman), 325
Jeffersonian Republicans. *See* Republicans, Jeffersonian
Jeremiah, Thomas "Jerry," 225–26
Jesuits, 32, 145, *145*
João, King, 29
Johnson, Andrew, 605, 637, *637*
    Civil Rights Act of 1866 and, 644
    Committee of South Carolina Freedmen and, 676
    Confederate pardons of, 638
    convict leasing and, 644
    election of 1864 and, 613
    Fourteenth Amendment fought by, 644
    impeachment of, 646–48, *647*
    political trajectory of, 637–38
    Presidential Reconstruction Plan of, 638
    Radical Republicans and, 639, 642–45
Johnson, Nancy, 343, *343*
Johnson, Sally, 452
Johnson, Samuel, 172
Johnson, William, 446
Johnston, Albert Sydney, 584
Johnston, Frances Benjamin, *653*
Johnston, Joseph E., 587
joint-stock companies, 56, 71
Judaism/Jews
    in colonial America, *118*
    Dutch Republic tolerance and limitations with, 83–84, *84*
Judge, Ona, 250
judicial nationalism, 369, 369–71
judicial review, 289, 369
Judiciary Act of 1789, 289
Judiciary Act of 1801, 277, 288
judiciary branch, 247. *See also* Supreme Court
July 4th holiday, Douglass on, 497
Juneteenth, *594*

Kaaterskill Clove (Peale, H. C.), *462*
Kansas
    Bleeding Kansas and, 554–55
    Civil War in, 582–83
    Lecompton Constitution and, 558–59
    Pottawatomie Massacre and, 555
    Sack of Lawrence and, 554–55
Kansas-Nebraska Act, 551–54, *553*
Kant, Immanuel, 131
Kearny, Stephen, 535
Kelley, Abigail, 499
Kemble, Fanny, 354, *355*, 440
Kemble, Margaret, 173
Kentucky, 345
    in Civil War, 584
    secession and, 572–73
    State Convention of Colored Men in, 640
    Wilderness Road and, 274
Key, Francis Scott, 314, *315*
King, Martin Luther, Jr., 476
King, Rufus, 303, 373
King, William Rufus, 556

King Philip's (Metacom's) War, *95*, 95–96
Kingsley, Bathsheba, 136
King's Mountain, Battle of, 214–15, *215*
King William's War, 150
Kiowa, 47, 519, 523, 660
KKK (Ku Klux Klan), *655*, 655–56, 658, 665–67
Knight, Sarah Kemble, 130
Know-Nothings, 358–59, *359*, 552
Knox, Henry, 198, 243, 257
Kocoum, 62
Krimmel, John Lewis, *366*, *374*
Ku Klux Klan (KKK), *655*, 655–56, 658, 665–67
Ku Klux Klan Act of 1871, 665
Kwakiutl, 15

labor. *See also* indentured servitude; organized labor; slavery
    activism of women and, 351
    of enslaved people, 451
    household work of women and, 351–52
    Industrial Revolution and, 349
    Irish immigrants and, 357
    professions and, 361–62
    sharecropping and, *653*, 653–54
    of women, 107–10
    of women in textile mills, *350*, 350–51
Lackawanna Valley (Inness), *332*
Lafayette, Marquis de (Gilbert du Motier), 211
Lake Champlain, Battle of, 315–16
Lakota, 516
Lambeth, William M., 448–49
Land Act of 1796, 273
Land Act of 1800, 273
land grants, 342
Land Ordinances of 1784 and 1785, 237–38, *238*, *239*
land ownership, for freedpeople, 652–53
Lane, Harriet, 556
Las Casas, Bartolomé de, 38, 51
Latrobe, Benjamin Henry, *284*
Latrobe, John H. B., *479*
Laurens, Henry, 184, 226
Lawrence, 310
Lawrence, Amos, 549
Lawrence, Jacob, *291*
Lawrence, Richard, 416
Leaves of Grass (Whitman), 479
Lecompton Constitution, 558–59
Lee, Ann (Mother Ann), 484–85
Lee, Henry "Lighthorse Harry," 272
Lee, Jarena, 468, *468*
Lee, Richard Henry, 178–79
Lee, Robert Edward, 562, *587*
    Appomattox Court House surrender of, *621*, 621–22
    Battle of Antietam and, 591–93
    Battle of Chancellorsville and, 607
    Battle of Fredericksburg and, 596
    Battle of Gettysburg and, 609–11

    Battle of Spotsylvania Court House and, 615, *616*
    Battle of the Wilderness and, 614–15, *616*
    Davis, J., refusing resignation of, 612
    military strategy of, 587
    Petersburg siege and, 615–16, *616*
    in Second Battle of Bull Run, 587–88
legal profession, 361
Legal Tender Act of 1862, 604
legislature, in Constitution, 246
"Letter from a Farmer in Pennsylvania" (Dickinson, J.), 190–91
"Letter to the Lords of Trade" (Bernard), 191
Lewis, Meriwether, 293, *293*, 296–97, *298*
Lewis and Clark expedition, 293, *293*, 296–97, *298*
Lexington, Battle of, *173*, 173–74, *174*
LGBTQ people
    "anti-sodomy" laws and, 556
    Buchanan, J.'s, relationship with King, W. R., and, 556
    Whitman's poems and, 479
Liberator, The, 490, *490*
liberty
    African Americans and, 227
    American Revolution and, 224
    Blackstone on, 182
    women and, 227
Liberty, Pomp, 207, *207*
liberty laws, 549
Liberty Party, 499–500, 530
Liele, George, 135
Lienzo de Tlaxcala, *36*
Lincoln, Abraham, 500, 509–10, 533, 544
    African Americans serving in Civil War and, 581–82, 600
    army formed by, *577*, 577–78
    assassination of, 635–36, *636*
    Douglas debates with, *559*, 559–61
    election of 1860 and, 563–64, *564*
    election of 1864 and, 613, 618
    emancipation and, 589–96, *593*
    Gettysburg Address of, 612, 625
    Habeas Corpus Act of 1863 and, 605
    inauguration of, first, 341, 566–67
    inauguration of, second, 619–21, 671
    Kansas-Nebraska Act and, 553
    on Know-Nothings, 359
    McClellan and frustration of, 586–87, 593
    physical appearance of, *559*, 560
    Reconstruction plan of, 632–33
    in Richmond, Virginia, *570*
    Sherman, W. T.'s, "March to the Sea" and, 619
    on slavery, 546
    son's death and, 584
    Southern secession after election of, 547, *565*, 565–67, 571–72
    team surrounding, 576
    Thirteenth Amendment and, 624–25
    wartime government of, 603

Lincoln, Benjamin, 214
Lincoln, Mary Todd, 560, 579, 584
Lincoln-Douglas debates, *559*, 559–61
Lincoln's Drive through Richmond, *570*
Lipan Apache, 516, 523
literature
   in newspapers, 479–80
      Romanticism and, 476–80
      transcendentalism and, 473–76
Little Crow, 320
Little Ice Age, 40
livestock, 431
Livingston, Gilbert, 251–52
Livingston, Robert, Jr., 126–27
Livingston, Robert R., 291, 294, 336, 370
Locke, John, 79, 132, 149, *149*
Loguen, Jermain, 548
longhouses, 18
Long Island, Battle of, 202, *203*, 204, *205*
Longstreet, James, 610, 655
Loom and Spindle or Life among the Early Mill Girls (Robinson, H.), 506–7
Louisiana Purchase
   cost of, 292
   Haitian Revolution impact on, 291–92
   Indigenous Americans and, 291, 295, 297
   Lewis and Clark expedition of, 293, *293*, 296–97, *298*
   motivations for, 290
   negotiations over, 291–93
   political disagreement over, 293
   political schemes and fears of, 297–98
   significance of, 293, 294
Louisiana state, 293. *See also* New Orleans
   cotton production in, 432–33, *433*
   secession of, 566
Louisiana Territory, 146, 154
   Burr Conspiracy and, 299
   Lewis and Clark expedition of, 293, *293*, 296–97, *298*
   map of, 1713, *155*
   map of, 1763, *156*
   map of, 1783, *219*
   Spain's acquisition of, 239–40
   Transcontinental Treaty and, 380–81, *381*
Louis XV, 154
L'Ouverture, Toussaint, 268, 291, *291*
Lovejoy, Elijah P., 500
Lowell, Francis Cabot, 350
"Lowell girls," *350*, 350–51
Lowell system, 350–51
Lower Creeks, 310–12
Loyalists, 166, 171, 193, 198–99, *221*, 221–22
Luther, Martin, 30–31, *31*
Lutheranism, 31–32
Lynch, James D., 638
Lyon, Matthew, *277*

Macdonough, Thomas, 315–16
Madison, Dolley, 303

Madison, James, 266, 269
   Alien and Sedition Acts of 1798 countered by, 276
   Bank of the United States opposed by, 264
   Bill of Rights and, 257, 258
   Canada invasion and, 308–10, *309*
   Compromise of 1790 and, 264
   at Constitutional Convention, *244*, 244–46, 248, 250
   economic nationalism and, 368–69
   election of, 303
   Embargo Act of 1807 and, 302
   The Federalist Papers and, 253
   on House of Representatives, 246
   internal improvements and, 369
   Marbury v. Madison and, 288–89, 369
   Non-Intercourse Act of 1809 and, 303–4
   peaceable coercion strategy of, 303–4
   Second Bank of the United States created by, 319–20, 368
   as Secretary of State, 288
   on Senate, 246
   on slavery, 250
   on state debts, 263
   tariffs and, 320, 368–69
   Virginia Plan and, 245
   War of 1812 and, 304–5, 307–8, 313–14, 319–20
mail delivery
   colonial life and, 131
   nineteenth-century improvements in, 341, *341*
   post office expansion and, 341
   slavery and censorship in, 419
Maine colony, 76
Maine state, 375
maize (corn), 9, 16
Mali, *21–23*, 22
Malinche, 35
Mallory, Shepard, 581
Mamout, Yarrow, *446*
manifest destiny, 463–64, 514
Manigault, Judith, 79
Manigault, Louis, 542
Mann, Horace, 361, 482–83
manufacturing, Hamilton encouraging, 265–66
mappa mundi (map of the world), *27*
Marbury, William, 288–89
Marbury v. Madison, 288–89, 369
"March to the Sea," of Sherman, W. T., 618–19, *620*
Marion, Francis, 214
market economy, 334–35
maroon communities, 436
Marquette, Jacques, 146
marriage
   Comanche and, 517
   "complex," 485
   plural, 471

Marshall, John
   on Burr Conspiracy, 299
   on *Cherokee Nation v. Georgia*, 409
   Dartmouth College v. Woodward and, 370
   Gibbons v. Ogden and, 370–71
   judicial nationalism and, *369*, 369–71
   Marbury v. Madison and, 288–89, 369
   McCulloch v. Maryland and, 370
Martin, Luther, 249
Mary I, 34
Mary II, 148–49
Maryland colony
   governance in, 66–68
   map of, *67*
   population stagnation in, 66
   as proprietary colony, 66
   religion in, 67–68
   St. Mary's settlement in, 66
   tobacco farming in, 64, 113
Maryland state
   Constitution ratification and, *253*, 254
   secession resisted by, 572–73
Mason, George, 246, 252
Mason, John, 76
Masonic order, 416
Massachusetts Anti-Slavery Society, 492
Massachusetts Bay Colony
   governance in, 71–72
   infectious disease and death in, 71
   as joint-stock company, 71
   map of, *69*
   population growth of, 70
   prostitution in, 108
   rebellion in, 149
   religion in, 70–72
   women's work in, 108
Massachusetts General Court, 72
Massachusetts Government Act, 170
Massachusetts state
   Constitution ratification and, 253, *253*, *254*
   emancipation lawsuits in, 248
   Shays's Rebellion in, 242, *242*
   War of 1812 and refusal of, 307
mass production, 342, 360
maternal mortality, in colonial life, 105, *106*
Mather, Cotton, 105
Mather, Increase, 114
Maya, 9–10, *10*, 35
Mayflower, 69–70
Mayflower Compact, 70
Maysville Road Bill, 399, *399*
Mbemba, Nzinga, 29
McClellan, George B.
   Battle of Antietam and, 591–93
   election of 1864 and, 613, 618
   Lincoln, A.'s, frustration with, 586–87, 593
   peninsular campaign of, 587, *588*
McCormick, Cyrus Hall, 348–49
McCormick reapers, *348*, 349

McCulloch, James, 370
McCulloch v. Maryland, 370
McGready, James, 467
Meade, George Gordon, 533, 609–11
meals, 115
Mecca, 22, *23*
medical profession, 361–62, *363*
medicine, during Civil War, 600–601
Memphis race massacre, 642, *642*
Menendez de Aviles, Pedro, 41–42
Mennonites, 117
mental illness, 482
mercantilism, 147, 261
Mercer, Hugh, *196*
Meredith, Minerva, 606
Mesoamerica. See also Americas
    Inca in, 11, 37–38
    Maya in, 9–10, *10*, 35
    Mexica/Aztec in, *11*, 11–13, 36–37
    pre-Columbian Indigenous civilizations in, *12*
    Toltec in, 10
Mestizos, 45
Metacom's (King Philip's) War, *95*, 95–96
Methodists
    African Americans, revivalism and, *467*, 468
    denominational growth of, 465, 467–68
    frontier revivals and, 466–67
Mexica, *11*, 11–13, 36–37
Mexica Empire, *11*, 11–13, 35
Mexican Americans, California gold rush and, 541–42
Mexican-American War, 346–47
    army sizes in, 533
    Battle of Buena Vista in, 536
    California annexation and, 533–35
    fronts of, 533, *534*
    legacies of, 537–38
    Mexico City assault in, 536
    opposition to, 533
    origins of, 532–33
    Treaty of Guadalupe Hidalgo and, 536–37
    Veracruz assault in, 536
Mexico. See also Mesoamerica; New Spain
    end of slavery in, 376
    independence of, 518
    map of, 1783, *219*
    Mestizos in, 45
    southbound Underground Railroad and, 524
    Spanish conquest of, 11, 35–39
    Texas Revolution and, 524–27
    Westward expansion and, 518–19
middle colonies. See also New York colony
    Delaware colony, *81*, 87
    Dutch Republic and trade in, 80–85
    ethnic culture in, 116–17
    immigrant groups in, 116–17, *118*
    life and economy in, 116–19

New Jersey colony, *81*, 85, 116
Pennsylvania colony, *81*, 85–87, 116
Quakers in, 85–86
Middle Passage, *121*, 122
Midwest farming, in Industrial Revolution, 345, 348–49
migration, first, 7–9, *8*
Military Reconstruction Act, 645–46, *646*
Militia Act, 597
militias, 206
Minnesota, 293, 356
    statehood of, 561
minstrel shows, 355
Miranda, Francisco de, 216, *216*
missionaries
    California settlement and Catholic, *521*, 521–22
    Jesuit missionaries in New France, 145, *145*
Mississippi, 293, 345
    Black codes in, 643
    cotton production in, 432–33, *433*
    KKK violence in, 666
    secession of, 547, 566
Mississippians, *15*, 16–17
Mississippi River, 41
Missouri Compromise, 375, *378*, 378–79, 539
Missouri state
    creation of, 375, *378*, 378–79
    secession and, 572–73
Missouri Territory, 375
Mitchell, Louise, 361
Moctezuma, *6*
Moctezuma II, 36–37
Monongahela, Battle of, 153
Monroe, James, 319
    administration of, 373–74
    election of, 373
    Era of Good Feelings and, 373–74, *374*
    First Seminole War and, 379–80
    foreign policy under, 381–82
    Louisiana Purchase and, 291
    re-election of, 382
    as secretary of war, 314
Monroe, Sarah, 361
Monroe Doctrine, 381–82
Montagu, John (Lord Sandwich), 172
Montana, 293
Montgomery, Richard, 202
Monticello, 287, *288*
Moore's Creek Bridge, Battle of, 178
Morgan, Daniel, 215
Mormon Church (Church of Jesus Christ of Latter-day Saints), 469–72, *470–72*
Morrill Land Grant College Act of 1862, 603
Morris, Robert, 236
Morse, Jedidiah, 125
Morse, Samuel F. B., 341–42

Motier, Gilbert du (Marquis de Lafayette), 211
Mott, Lucretia, 494, 496, 506
mound-building cultures, *15*, 16–17
"Mulattoes," 446
Mulberry Grove plantation, 344
Murray, John, 225, 465
Murray, Judith Sargent, 251
Musa, Mansa, 22, *22*, 23
muscovado, 78
Muskogeans, 17, 18
"My Old Kentucky Home" (Foster), 355

Nanyehi, *411*, 411–12
Narragansett, 95
Narrative of the Life of Frederick Douglass (Douglass), 492
Narrative of William W. Brown (Brown, W. W.), 491
Narváez, Pánfilo, 41
Nash, Beverly, 652
Nash, Gary, 188, 189–90
Nashoba community, 486
Nast, Thomas, *628*, *644*
National Banking Act of 1863, 603
National Convention of Colored Citizens, 495
National Intelligencer, 422
nationalism
    American Revolution and emergence of, 230–31
    American System and, 372–73, 528
    diplomatic, 379–82, *380*, *381*
    economic, 368–69, 420
    Era of Good Feelings and, 374
    internal improvements and, 369
    judicial, *369*, 369–71
    sectionalism's conflict with, 367, 373
National Road, 369
National Trades' Union, 360–61
Native Americans. See Indigenous Americans
nativism
    colonial life and, 106–7
    Know-Nothings and, 358–59, *359*, 552
nativists, 358–59
Nat Turner's Rebellion, *457*, 457–58
Naturalization Act of 1740, 105–6
Naturalization Act of 1790, 261
Naturalization Act of 1870, 659
natural rights, 149
Nauvoo, Illinois, *470*, 470–71, *471*
Navajos, 15
Navigation Acts, 147, 149
Negro Act of 1740, 128
Netherlands. See also Dutch Republic
    discovery and explorations of, *48*, 80–81
    Spain and revolt of, 49
    transatlantic slave trade and, *65*
New Amsterdam, 82, *83*, *125*
Newburgh Conspiracy, 236–37

New Echota, Treaty of, 410–11
Newell, Mary Harrison, 543
Newell, William, 543
New England colonies
   agriculture in, 115
   artisans of, *102*
   Connecticut colony, 76
   economy in, *115*, 115–16
   fisheries in, *115*, 115–16
   housing in, *114*, 115
   Hutchinson, A.'s, trial and, *73*, 73–74
   life in, 114–16
   Maine colony, 76
   Massachusetts Bay Colony, *69*, 70–72, 108
   New Hampshire colony, 76
   Plymouth colony, 68–70, *69*
   Puritans in, 76–77, 114–15
   in Revolutionary War, 201
   Rhode Island colony, *69*, 72–73
   Sugar Act of 1764 and, 160
   transatlantic slave trade and, 158–59
   triangular trade and, 116, *117*
   witches in Salem and, *74*, 74–76, *75*
Newfoundland, 30
New France, 141. *See also* colonial governance; colonial life
   Canada lost by, 154
   English colonies competing with, 142
   founding of, 47–48, 142
   Indigenous American relations with, 143–45
   Indigenous conversions to Christianity in, 145, *145*
   Jesuit missionaries in, 145, *145*
   map of, *144*, *155*
   New Spain fending off, 146
   in South, 145–46
   trade and, 143
New Hampshire colony, 76
New Hampshire state, 253, *253*, *254*
New Harmony community, 486–87
New Haven Colony, 76
New Jersey colony, *81*, 85
   Battle of Princeton in, *200*, 207
   Battle of Trenton in, 206–7
   Revolutionary War and winter in, 207–8
New Jersey Plan, 245
New Jersey state, 253, *253*, *254*
New Mexico
   Acoma Pueblo revolt in, 44
   Compromise of 1850 and, *544*, 544–45, *545*, 548
   Indigenous American conversion to Christianity in, 44
   Mestizos in, 45
   Pueblo Revolt in, 45–46
   Spanish, 43–44, *44*
   statehood of, 543
New Netherland, 82, *83*, 147
New Orleans, Louisiana

   Battle of, 1814–1815, 317–18, *318*
   Battle of, in Civil War, 586
   Burr Conspiracy and, 299
   German Coast Uprising and, 456
   Louisiana Purchase and, 291, *292*
   Pinckney's Treaty of 1795 and, 272, *273*
   trade and, 291
Newport, Rhode Island, 129
New Spain, 98. *See also* colonial governance; colonial life; Mexico
   Catholic Church in, 38–39
   Columbian Exchange and, 39–40
   conquest of, 35–39
   Cortés conquest of, 35–37
   in decline, 50–51
   encomienda system in, 38
   environmental changes in, 40
   Indigenous conversions to Christianity in, 141
   map of, 1713, *155*
   map of, 1763, *156*
   Mestizos in, 45
   New France encroaching on, 146
   Pizzaro's invasion of Inca in, 37–38
   smallpox in, 40
   Transcontinental Treaty and, 380–81, *381*
newspapers
   for abolition movement, *434*, 489–91, *490*, 493
   African Americans and, 340, 389–90, *390*
   colonial life and, 131
   Indigenous Americans and, 340, *409*
   literature in, 479–80
   nineteenth-century growth of, 340–41
Newton, Isaac, 131–32
New York City
   as capital of nation, 254, 263
   Civil War draft riots in, 597
   colonial population of, 129
   Irish immigrants in, 357, 358
   Revolutionary War in, 202–4
   slavery in, 125, *128*
New York colony, 116
   Battles of Saratoga in, *208*, 210
   Dutch Republic origins of, 82–85, *83*
   formation of, 84–85
   Iroquois League and, 96–97
   map of, *81*
   Revolutionary War in, 202–4, *203*, *205*, *208*, *209*, 210
New York Herald, 666
New York state
   Burr's governor campaign in, 297
   Constitution ratification and, 253, *253*, *254*
   Erie Canal and, *336*, 337–38
New York Tailoresses' Society, 361
New York Times, 590, 595, 623, 625, 629
New York Tribune, 357, 663

Niles' Register, 377, 421
Niña, 24
Niño, Pedro Alonzo (El Negro), 24–25
Nipmuc, 95
Non-Importation Act, 301
nonimportation movement, 163
Non-Intercourse Act of 1809, 303–4
Nootka, 15
North, Lord, 167, *169*, 169–70, 218
North America. *See also* Americas; specific regions
   first migrations to, 7–9, *8*
   French explorations of, 47–48, *48*
   geographic formation of, 7
   immigrants in colonial, *118*
   Indigenous American societies in, 1500, 13–18, *16*
   map of, 1713, *155*
   map of, 1783, *219*
   Spanish in, 41–51, *42*
North Carolina colony
   Battle of Alamance and, 166
   Battle of Guilford Courthouse in, 216
   Battle of Moore's Creek Bridge and, 178
   Carolina colony and, *77*, 77–80, *78*
   Edenton Tea Party and, 170
   formation of, 77, 79
   map of, *77*
   profit of, 79–80
   Regulators, *165*, 165–66
   in Revolutionary War, 201
North Carolina state
   Battle of King's Mountain in, 214–15, *215*
   Constitution ratification and, 253, *254*
   cotton production in, 432, *433*
   Revolutionary War in, 214–16
North Dakota, 296
North Star, 493
Northup, Solomon, 447, 451
Northwest Indigenous Americans, 14–15
Northwest Ordinance, 238, *240*, 375
Northwest Territory, 238, *238*, *240*
   Treaty of Greenville and, 269, *270*
Norway, 30
Notes on the State of Virginia (Jefferson), 326–27
Noyes, John Humphrey, 485–86
nullification, *402*, 402–6
Nurse, Rebecca, 75, *114*

Obama, Barack, 413
Ogden, Aaron, 370–71
Ogden, John, 250
Oglethorpe, James E., 88
Ohio Country
   in French and Indian War, 150–52
   Treaty of Greenville and, 269, *270*
"Oh! Susanna" (Foster), 355
Oklahoma, 334
"Old Black Joe" (Foster), 355
"Old Folks at Home" (Foster), 355

Old Southwest, cotton production in, 432–34, *433*
Oliver, Andrew, 190
Olvera, Isabel de, 43–44
Oñate, Juan de, 43–44
Oneida Community, *485*, 485–86
"On the Equality of the Sexes" (Murray, Judith Sargent), 251
Order of the Star-Spangled Banner, 358
Oregon Country, 297, 519–20, 531, *532*
Oregon Fever, 520
Oregon state
    Fifteenth Amendment opposed by, 649
    statehood of, 561
organized labor
    Commonwealth v. Hunt and, 360
    mass production and, 360
    National Trades' Union and, 360–61
    in nineteenth century, 359–63
    shoemakers and, 360, *360*
    women leading strikes and, 361
Osborne, Sarah, 75, 136
Osceola, *408*
O'Sullivan, Timothy H., *611*
Otis, James, Jr., 162, 166, 180
Overland Mail Company, 341
Overland Trails, 514–16, *515*, *519*
overland transportation improvements, 335, *336*
overseers, 440, *441*
Overzee, Syman, 128
Owen, Robert, 486–87
Oxbow, The (Cole), *473*

Pacific Railway Act of 1862, 603
Page, Margaret, 108
Paine, Thomas, 177–78, 199, 204, *204*, 206, 222
Pakenham, Edward, 317
Paleo-Indians, first migrations of, *8*, 8–9
palisade, 17
Palladio, Andrea, *288*
Palmer, Phoebe Worrall, 468–69
Panic of 1819, 374–75
Panic of 1837, *421*, 421–22
Panic of 1857, 557
Panic of 1873, *664*, 664–65
Paris, Treaty of (1763), 154–55, 157
Paris, Treaty of (1783), 218–20
parish system, 133
Parker, Alice, 75
Parker, Ely, 660
Parker, John, 174
Parker, Mary, 75
Parliament, 58
Parris, Betty, 75
Parris, Samuel, 75
Patent Office, 343
Paterson, William, 245
Patriots, 166, 171–72, 178, 193, 199, 201
patroonship, 82

Patterson, Elizabeth, 606
Pawnee, 519
Peace Democrats, 605
Peale, Charles Willson, *200*
Peale, Harriet Cany, *462*
Pember, Phoebe, 602
Pemberton, John C., 609, 611–12
Penn, William, 86–87, *116*, 116–17
Pennsylvania colony, *81*, 85–87, 116
    Revolutionary War in, 208, *209*
Pennsylvania Gazette, 132, *152*, 157
Pennsylvania Journal, 161
Pennsylvania Society for the Abolition of Slavery, 488
Pennsylvania state
    Battle of Gettysburg and, *608*, 609–11, *610*, *611*
    Constitution ratification and, *253*, *254*
    Whiskey Rebellion in, 271–72, *272*
People v. Hall, 648
Pequot War, 94
Perry, Oliver Hazard, 310
Perryville, Battle of, 586
Peru, 35
Petersburg siege, 615–16, *616*
Petigru, James L., 565
Philadelphia, 129, *159*
    as capital of nation, 263
    Irish immigrants in, 357
Philadelphia, 301, *301*, *302*
Philadelphia-Lancaster Turnpike, 369
Philip, King, 34
Philip II, 49
Phillips, Wendell, 661
Pickens, Andrew, 212
Pickens, Francis, 419
Pickering, Timothy, 285
Pickett, George, *610*, 610–11
piecework, 351
Pierce, Franklin, 551
Pike, Zebulon, 310
Pilgrims, 59, 70
Pinchback, Pinckney, 651
Pinckney, Charles, 110, 249, 299, 303
Pinckney, Elizabeth Lucas, 109–10, *110*
Pinckney, Thomas, 272
Pinckney's Treaty, 1795, 272, *273*, 379
Pinta, 24
"Pit and the Pendulum, The" (Poe), 478
Pitcairn, John, 174
Pitt, William, 162, 164–65
Pizarro, Francisco, 37–38
plain White folk, 441
Plantation Burial (Antrobus), *455*
plantation management, 109–10
plantation mistress, 439–40
Planter, C.S.S., 582, *582*
planters, 438
plants, Columbian Exchange and, 39
plows, 348
plural marriage (polygamy), 471

Plymouth colony, 68–70, *69*
Pocahontas, 62, *63*
Pocumtuck, 95
Poe, Edgar Allan, 476, 478
Poems on Miscellaneous Subjects (Harper), 478
"Poet, The" (Emerson), 475
political cartoons, *152*
political democracy, 396–97
political parties, 195, 266–67. *See also specific parties*
Politics in an Oyster House, 479
Polk, James K., 476, 530
    Buchanan-Pakenham Treaty and, 531, *532*
    California annexation and, 533–35
    election of 1844 and, 530
    goals of, 531
    Mexican-American War and, 532–38
    rise of, 530
    Texas annexation and, 529–30
    Wilmot Proviso and, 539
Polk, Sarah, 530, *530*
poll taxes, 658–59
polygamy (plural marriage), 471
Poma de Ayala, Felipe Guamán, *44*
Ponce de León, Juan, 41
Pontiac's Rebellion, 157, *157*
Pony Express Company, 341, *341*
"poor Whites," 442
Pope, John, 587
popular sovereignty, 539–40
Portugal, 4, 29
    in rise of global trade, 20
    transatlantic slave trade and, 65
    Treaty of Tordesillas and, 26, 28
    Vespucci and, 30
post offices, expansion of, 341
potatoes, 39
Pottawatomie Massacre, 555
Powhatan Confederacy, 61–62
prairie schooners, 520
Preemption Act of 1830, 348
Presbyterians
    denominational growth of, 465, 467–68
    Finney and, 469
    frontier revivals and, 466–67
Presbyterian Scots, 85
presentism, 324
presidency, in Constitution, 246
presidential conventions, 398
Presidential Reconstruction Plan, 638
Preston, John, 215
primary sources, 188
    on American Revolution origins, 190–91
    on Jefferson and slavery, 326–27
    on Reconstruction's demise, 676–78
    on women and separate spheres, 506–7
Princeton, Battle of, *200*, 207
printing press, 26
prison reform movements, 482

privies, 115
Proclamation Act of 1763, *156*, 158
Proclamation of Amnesty and Reconstruction, 1863, 632–33
professions, 361–62
proprietary colony, 66
prostitution, 108, 230
Protestantism, 30–32, 34
   nativists and, 358
Protestant Reformation, 30–32, 34
Prussia, 267
Public Credit Act of 1869, 664
public schools, in nineteenth century, 482–84, *483*
Pudeator, Ann, 75
Pueblo, 14, *14*, 44–46, 516
Pueblo Revolt, 45–46
Puerto Rico, colonization of, 35, 41
Punch, John, 124, 126
Punderson, Prudence, *108*
Puritans
   alcohol and, 114
   beliefs of, 59, 114
   book of psalms of, *71*
   English monarchy challenged by, 58–59
   Hutchinson, A.'s, trial and excommunication by, *73*, 73–74
   Indigenous American conversions to Christianity by, 91
   in Maryland colony, 67–68
   in Massachusetts Bay Colony, 70–72
   membership of, 71
   in New England colonies, 76–77, 114–15
   Pequot War and, 94
   in Plymouth colony, 68–70
   Quakers banned by, 86
   in Rhode Island colony, 72–73
   Separatists, 68–70
   as "visible saints," 68
   Williams, Roger, and, *72*, 72–73
   women as, 110

Quakers, 498, 661
   beliefs of, 85–86
   Indigenous Americans and, 87
   Pennsylvania colony founding and, 85–87
Quantrill, William, 583
Quartering Act of 1765, 160–61
Quartering Act of 1774, 170
Quebec, Battle of, 154
Quetzalcoatl, 36

race
   Bacon's Rebellion and, 92–93
   chattel slavery based on, 123–29
   indentured servants in legal system by, 126–27
   Mestizos in New Spain, 45
   in Nashoba community, 486
   New Harmony community and, 487
   in social history, 504
   Westward expansion and, 514
racial capitalism, 430
racism
   against African American soldiers in Civil War, 600
   after Civil War, 632
   of Irish immigrants and African Americans, 357
   KKK violence and, *655*, 655–56, 658, 665–67
   minstrel shows and, 355
   slavery justified by, 128–29
   voting rights in Reconstruction and, 652
Radical Republicans, 633, 639, 642–45
railroads
   capitalism and, 339
   corruption around, 339
   Kansas-Nebraska Act and, *551*, *553*
   Nineteenth-century emergence of, 338–39, *339*
   Pacific Railway Act of 1862 and, 603
Rainbow, 339
Raleigh, Walter, 50
Randolph, John, 303, 434
Rapalje Children, The (Durand), *129*
Ratcliffe, Phillip, 114
rationalism, 464
"Raven, The" (Poe), 478
Reconstruction, 511
   African American churches and schools in, 649–51, *650*
   African American conventions during, 640
   African American political leadership in, 651–52, *652*
   African American society under, 649–57
   beginning of, 629–31
   Black codes and, 643
   "carpetbaggers" in, 654–55, 677
   challenges of, 630–31
   Compromise of 1877 and, 669, *670*
   Congressional, 646, 656–57
   congressional wartime plans for, 633
   convict leasing in, 643–44
   debating demise of, 674–78
   election of 1868 and, 657–58
   empowering freedpeople in, 635
   end of, 670–71
   Enforcement Acts in, 665
   Fifteenth Amendment enforcement and, 658–59
   Freedman's Bank in, 635–36, *636*, 664
   Freedmen's Bureau and, 633–35, *634*
   Freedmen's conventions in, 638–39, *639*
   freedom debated in, 633
   inequality during, 649
   Johnson, A.'s, impeachment and, 646–48, *647*
   Johnson, A.'s, Presidential Reconstruction Plan for, 638
   KKK violence during, *655*, 655–56, 658, 665–67
   land ownership for freedpeople in, 652–53
   legacy of, 656–57
   Liberal Republicans and, 622–23
   Lincoln, A.'s, assassination in, *636*, 636–37
   Lincoln, A.'s, wartime plan for, 632–33
   Military Reconstruction Act and, 645–46, *646*
   poll taxes and, 658–59
   racism against voting rights in, 652
   Radical Republicans and, 633, 639, 642–45
   restitution for slavery sought in, 668
   "scalawags" in, 654–55
   sharecropping in, *653*, 653–54
   significance of, 671
   Southern redeemers in, 666–67
   Supreme Court eroding, 666–67
   Union League and, 651
   women's rights in, 659, *659*
Reconstruction (Foner), 674–75
redeemers, Southern, 666–67
Red Sticks, 310–12
Reed, Wilmot, 75
reform movements. *See also* abolition movement
   motivations of, 480
   for prisons and asylums, 482
   public schools and, 482–84, *483*
   Seneca Falls Convention and, *494*, 494–95, 496
   as social control, 481
   temperance and, 480–81, *481*
   utopian, 484–87
   for women's rights, 487, 493–95
regional identity, 330, 334
Regulators, *165*, 165–66, 242, *242*
Reid, John, Jr., 127
Reign of Terror, in France, 267
religion. *See also specific religions*
   African Americans and, 454–55
   of Algonquians, 94, *94*
   colonial life and, 110, 133–37
   English conflict over, 58–60
   in Enlightenment, 133
   of enslaved people, 454–55
   European conflict over, 30–34
   First Amendment and, 260
   freedom of, *224*, 224–25, 260
   of German immigrants, 358
   Great Awakening and, 133–37
   of Indigenous Americans compared to Christians, 15
   in Maryland colony, 67–68
   in Massachusetts Bay Colony, 70–72
   of Maya, 9–10
   of Mexica, 13, 36
   of Northwest Indigenous Americans, 15

rationalism and, 464
reform and, 469–72
in Renaissance, 19
Second Great Awakening and, 465–72
of Sioux, 13
slavery and, 123–24
women and, 110
Renaissance, 19
representative democracy, 222, 246
republican ideology, 222–23
republicanism, 237
Republican Party, 400
   Compromise of 1877 and, 669, *670*
   in election of 1868, 657–58
   election of 1876 and, 668–69, *669*
   emergence of, 552–64
   Liberal Republicans and, 622–23
   Radical, 633, 639, 642–45
   Reconstruction's end and, 670–71
   Union League and, 651
   Whig factions joining, 552
Republicans, Jeffersonian, 195. *See also* Jefferson, Thomas
   Adams, John's, election and losses of, 275
   Alien and Sedition Acts of 1798 and, 276, *277*
   electoral victory in 1800 of, 277–78, *278*
   Federalists compared to, 255, 266–67
   formation of, 255
   French Revolution and, 267
   Genêt and, 269
   Jay's Treaty and, 271
   on Louisiana Purchase, 293
   on Western land policy, 272–73
republican simplicity, of Jefferson, 285
reservation system, Indigenous Americans and, 660–61
restitution, for slavery, 668
Revels, Hiram, 651, *652*
Revenue Act of 1767, 164–65
Revere, Paul, *95*, *167*, 173
revivalism
   African Americans and, *467*, 468
   frontier, *466*, 466–67
   Great Awakening and, 133–37
   Second Great Awakening and, 465–72
   women in leadership of, *468*, 468–69
Revolutionary War. *See also* American Revolution
   African Americans in, 181, 206–7, *207*, 221–22, 225–27, *226*
   The American Crisis on, 204, *204*, 206
   Battle of Bunker Hill and, 176
   Battle of Concord and, *173*, 174–75
   Battle of Cowpens in, 215
   Battle of Guilford Courthouse in, 216
   Battle of King's Mountain in, 214–15, *215*
   Battle of Lexington and, *173*, 173–74, *174*
   Battle of Long Island and, 202, *203*, 204, *205*

   Battle of Moore's Creek Bridge and, 178
   Battle of Princeton in, *200*, 207
   Battle of Trenton in, 206–7
   Battle of White Plains and, 202, *205*
   Battle of Yorktown in, 217–18, *218*
   Battles of Saratoga in, *208*, 210
   British military power and, 199–200
   British recruiting African Americans in, 225–26, *226*
   British setbacks in, 1777–1781, 208–21
   in Canada, 201–2
   as change engine, 221–25
   Continental Army and, 200–201
   Ethiopia Regiment in, *180*, 181, 225
   finance and supply problems in, 201
   Georgia state in, 214
   Indigenous Americans in, 184, 201, 212, 230
   infectious diseases in, 202, 207
   Jackson, A., in, 383
   lessons of, 206
   militias in, 206
   in New York City, 202–4
   in New York colony, 208, *209*, 210
   in North Carolina state, 214–16
   Patriot prisoner deaths in, 201
   in Pennsylvania colony, 208, *209*
   "runaway slave" advertisement during, 229
   social and political changes of, 197–98
   in South Carolina state, 214–16
   Southern campaigns in, 212–16, *216*
   Spain in, 216–17
   Spanish Florida after, 222, 240
   start of, 175
   state debts from, 263
   Treaty of Alliance in, 210
   Treaty of Paris (1763) and, 154–55, 157
   Treaty of Paris (1783) and, 218–20
   Valley Forge and, 210–11, *211*
   in Virginia state, 217–18, *218*
   Washington, G., and, 175–76, 202–4, 206–8, 220–21
   Western campaigns in, 211–14, *213*
   winter in New Jersey colony during, 207–8
   women in, *227*, 230
Revolution of 1800, 279
Rhode Island colony, *69*, 72–73, 129
Rhode Island state, *253*, *254*
rice, 80, 113, 124, 431
Rice, Spottswood, 630
Ridge, John, 411
Ridge, Major, 410–11
roads, new, 335–36, *336*, 369, 399
Robards, Lewis, 388
Roberts, Benjamin, 483
Roberts, Sarah, 483–84
Robinson, Harriett H., 506–7
Rockingham, Lord, 164

Rolfe, John, 62, *63*
Roman Catholicism, 30. *See also* Catholic Church
Romanticism
   Emerson and, *474*, 474–75
   Fuller, M., and, 475, *475*
   literature and, 476–80
   origins of, 472
   Thoreau and, 475–76, *476*
   transcendentalism and, 473–76
Rosecrans, William, 612
Ross, Edmund G., 648
Ross, John, 410–14, *411*
Rossiter, Thomas Pritchard, *243*
royal admiralty courts, 149
rubber, vulcanized, 343
Ruffin, Edmund, 622–23
Ruffin v. Commonwealth, 643
rum, 89
"runaway slave" advertisement, 229
Rush, Benjamin, 193
Rush-Bagot Agreement of 1817, 379
Russwurm, John, 389–90, *390*
Rutledge, Edward, 226

Sacagawea, 296, *297*
Sack of Lawrence, 554–55
Saint-Domingue. *See* Haiti
Salcedo, Nemesio, 346
Salem, Peter, *226*
Salem, witches in, *74*, 74–76, *75*
salutary neglect, 149–50
salvation, 463
Sampson, Deborah, *227*
Sandwich, Lord (John Montagu), 172
Sandys, Edwin, 64
San Jacinto, Battle of, 527
Sankore mosque, *22*
San Patricios, 536
San Salvador (Guanahani), 25, *25*
Santa Anna, Antonio López de, 525–27, 535–37
Santa María, 24
Saratoga, Battles of, *208*, 210
Sassacus, 94
Sassamon, John, 95
Satanta (White Bear), 660
Sauk, 408
Savage, Samuel, 171
Savannah, Georgia, 88, *88*
"scalawags," in Reconstruction, 654–55
Scandinavia, 30
Scandinavian immigrants, 356
Schurz, Carl, 622–23
Scots-Irish, 106, 117, *118*
Scott, Dred, 557–58, *558*
Scott, Harriet, 557–58, *558*
Scott, Margaret, 75
Scott, Winfield, 536, 551, 576

secondary sources
    on American Revolution origins, 189–90
    on Jefferson and slavery, 324–25
    on Reconstruction's demise, 674–75
    on women and separate spheres, 504–5
Second Bank of the United States, 319–20, 368, 372
Second Confiscation Act, 590
Second Continental Congress, 175–76, 178–79, 193–94, 223, 230
Second Great Awakening
    African Americans and, 467, 468
    burned-over district in, 469
    denominational growth and, 467–68
    Finney and, 469
    frontier revivals and, 466, 466–67
    Mormon Church and, 469–72, 470–72
    rise of, 465–66
    women in leadership of, 468, 468–69
Second Seminole War, 408, 408
sectionalism
    American System conflicts with, 372–73
    Missouri Compromise and, 378–79
    nationalism's conflict with, 367, 373
secularism, 19
segregation
    Civil Rights Cases of 1883 as precursor to, 666
    in education, 483–84
Seguín, Juan, 525–26
self-government, in English colonies, 146–47
seminaries, 483
Seminoles, 124, 379–80, 380, 408, 408, 583
Seminole War
    First, 379–80, 380
    Second, 408, 408
Senate
    in Constitution, 246
    slavery and violence in, 555
Seneca, 212
Seneca Falls Convention, 494, 494–95, 496
separate spheres, 351, 504–7
separation of powers, 246–47
Seven Years' War. See French and Indian War
Seward, William H., 544, 545, 551, 591
sewer systems, 343
sewing machines, 343
sex, in Oneida Community, 485–86
sexual assault, in slavery, 440, 447, 452
sexuality. See LGBTQ people
Seymour, Horatio, 657
Shakers, 484–85
sharecropping, 653, 653–54
Shawnee, 157
Shays, Daniel, 242
Shays's Rebellion, 242, 242
Shelby, Joseph, 622
Sheridan, Philip, 621, 656, 661
Sherman, John, 623

Sherman, Roger, 245
Sherman, William Tecumseh
    Battle of Atlanta and, 617
    Battle of Shiloh and, 584–86
    election of 1864 and victories of, 618
    Grant and, 614, 658
    Indigenous Americans and, 660–61
    "March to the Sea" of, 618–19, 620
    South Carolina campaign of, 619, 620
Shiloh, Battle of, 584–86
shoemakers, 360, 360
Sickles, Daniel, 567
Sidney, Allen, 451
Singer, Isaac Merritt, 343
Singer Sewing Machine Company, 343
Sioux, 13, 15, 47, 296
Sixth Connecticut Regiment, 207, 207
Slaughterhouse Cases, 667
"Slave Auction, The" (Harper), 478
slave codes, 124, 442–43, 453
slavery. See also abolition movement; emancipation; enslaved people; transatlantic slave trade
    Africans as property in, 122
    American Revolution and paradox of, 180–81, 225–27, 226, 228–29
    American System and future of, 373
    auctions in, 446–50, 447, 450
    Bleeding Kansas and, 554–55
    breeding in, 452
    Brown, John's, raid on, 561–62
    business of, 125, 128–29, 446–49, 447
    Caribbean colonies and, 77–78, 78, 124
    chattel, 123–29
    children in, 447, 450, 454, 454
    Civil War stakes for, 579
    colonial economy and, 123, 125, 128–29
    colonial life and, 119–23, 123
    Compromise of 1850 and, 544, 544–45, 545, 548
    Conspiracy of 1741 and, 125, 128
    Constitution and, 248–50
    Cortés and, 35
    cotton and, 344–45, 430
    as CSA foundation, 566
    defenders of, 500–501
    Denmark Vesey Revolt and, 456–57
    domestic slave trade, 434, 434–36, 435, 446–50
    Dred Scott v. Sandford and, 557–58, 558
    drivers in, 441
    Dutch Republic and, 84, 125
    Emancipation Proclamation and, 593, 593–94
    end of, 510
    in English colonies, 55–56, 65–66
    enslavers in, 438–39, 439
    "fancy trade" in, 447
    freedoms and rights under, 259
    Free-Soil Party and, 540
    Fugitive Slave Act of 1793 and, 250

    Fugitive Slave Act of 1850 and, 548–49
    Gabriel's Rebellion and, 456
    Georgia colony and, 87, 89
    in Georgia state, 249
    German Coast Uprising and, 456
    Haitian Revolution and, 268, 291, 291–92
    House of Representatives brawl over, 561
    indentured servitude compared to, 111–12
    indentured servitude slowing with increased, 124–25
    of Indigenous Americans, 94, 112
    Industrial Revolution and, 345
    Jackson, A.'s, anti-democratic impulses and, 397
    Jefferson and, 179–80, 225, 286–87, 287, 324–27, 373
    Kansas, Lecompton Constitution and, 558–59
    Kansas-Nebraska Act and, 551–54, 553
    Know-Nothings and, 359
    languages and, 120
    Lewis and Clark expedition and, 296, 296
    liberty laws and, 549
    Lincoln, A., on, 546
    Lincoln-Douglas debates on, 559–61
    livestock and, 431
    mail censorship and, 419
    maroon communities and, 436
    Mexico ending, 376
    Missouri Compromise and, 375, 378, 378–79, 539
    Missouri Territory and, 375
    Nat Turner's Rebellion and, 457, 457–58
    in New York City, 125, 128
    Northwest Ordinance and, 238, 375
    overseers in, 440, 441
    plantation management and, 109–10
    plantation mistress and, 439–40
    planters and, 438
    popular sovereignty and, 539–40
    Pottawatomie Massacre and, 555
    profits from, 436, 443
    racial capitalism and, 430
    racism justifying, 128–29
    rebellions against, 122, 128–29, 180, 455–58
    regional variations of, 119–20, 123–25
    religion and, 123–24
    restitution for, 668
    "runaway slave" advertisement, 229
    Senate violence over, 555
    sexual assault in, 440, 447, 452
    in South Carolina colony, 80, 113, 158
    in South Carolina state, 226, 249, 300
    Southern secession over, 571–72
    Southwest Ordinance and, 375
    "The Star-Spangled Banner" and, 314, 315

Stono Rebellion and, 128
Taylor, Z., and, 540
Texas and, 528
Thirteenth Amendment ending, 500, 624–25, 643
Thoreau on, 476
Three-Fifths Compromise and, 249
tobacco farming and, 64
Uncle Tom's Cabin and, 550–51
urban, 452
violence in, 124, 451
War of 1812's impact on, 317
in Washington, D.C., 285, *285*
Washington, G., and, 181, 225
Wilmot Proviso and, *538*, 538–39
women in, 109, 251, 440, 447, 450–53
as "worse than death," 549–50, *550*
slave ships, *121*, 121–22
smallpox, 40, 70, 71, 202, 207
Smalls, Robert, 582, *582*, 652
Smith, Adam, 261, 349
Smith, Edmund Kirby, 586
Smith, Hyrum, 471
Smith, John, *54*, 61–63, *62*, 90
Smith, Joseph, Jr., 469–71
"Social Change and the Growth of Prerevolutionary Urban Radicalism" (Nash, G.), 189–90
social history, 504–7
Society of Friends, 85, 498
Songhai, *21*, 23
Sons of Liberty, 162–63, *163*, 166
Soto, Hernando de, 41, 123
South. *See also* Civil War; Confederate States of America; Reconstruction; slavery
agriculture in, *428*, 429–30
Black codes in, 643
Civil War aftermath in, *631*, 631–32
Compromise of 1850 and, *544*, 544–45, *545*, 548
as cotton kingdom, 430–38, *433*
domestic slave trade in, *434*, 434–36, *435*, 446–50
drivers in, 441
dueling in, 439
enslaved people forging community in, 453–59
enslaved people in, 442–59, *444*, *445*, *450*
enslavers in, 438–39, *439*
"free persons of color" in, 444–46, *446*
immigrants in, 429
as minority, 561
New France in, 145–46
Old Southwest cotton production, 432–34, *433*
overseers in, 440, *441*
plain White folk in, 441
plantation mistress in, 439–40
"poor Whites" in, 442

population growth in, 436, *437*
racial capitalism in, 430
secession of, 547, *565*, 565–67, 571–74, *573*
slave codes in, 442–43, 453
slavery profits in, 436
tobacco, rice, sugar, livestock in, 431
Whites in, 438–42
South America. *See also* Americas; *specific countries*
first migrations to, 7–9, *8*
geographic formation of, 7
pre-Columbian Indigenous civilizations in, *12*
Vespucci in, 30
southbound Underground Railroad, 524
South Carolina colony
Carolina colony and, *77*, 77–80, *78*
Charleston, 79, 109, 129
formation of, 77, 79
map of, *77*
profit of, 79–80
Regulators, 165–66
in Revolutionary War, 201
rice in, 80, 113
slave codes in, 124
slavery in, 80, 113, 158
Stono Rebellion in, 128
South Carolina Declaration on the Immediate Causes of Secession, 571
South Carolina Exposition and Protest (Calhoun), 402
South Carolina state
Battle of Cowpens in, 215
Black codes in, 643
Calhoun's compromise tariff and, 406
Constitution ratification and, *253*, 254
cotton production in, *433*, 433
Denmark Vesey Revolt in, 456–57
"free persons of color" and, 444
nullification and, *402*, 402–6
Revolutionary War in, 214–16
secession of, *565*, 565, 571
Sherman, W. T.'s, campaign in, 619, *620*
slavery in, 226, 249, *300*, 458
Tariff of Abominations and, 401–2
Southeast, Spanish, 41–43
southern colonies, life and economy in, 113
Southern Cultivator, 431
Southern redeemers, 666–67
Southwest
Indigenous Americans of, 14, *14*
Ordinance, 375
Spanish, 43
Spain, 4. *See also* Columbus, Christopher
California settlement and Catholic missionaries from, *521*, 521–22
challenges to empire of, 47–49, *48*
colonial empire of, 34–39
Columbian Exchange and, 39–40
Columbus' return to, 26

Confederation Congress tensions with, 239–40
conquistadores and, 35, 37–38
discovery and explorations of, 35–37, 41–44, *42*, 47
Dutch revolt and, 49
encomienda system of, 38
Florida transferred by, 375
Great Plains and horses from, *46*, 46–47
Inquisition in, 32
Louisiana Territory acquisition by, 239–40
Mexico conquest of, 11, 35–39
in New Mexico, 43–44, *44*
in North America, 41–51, *42*
Pinckney's Treaty of 1795 and, 272, *273*, 379
Pueblo Revolt against, 45–46
in Revolutionary War, 216–17
in rise of global trade, 20
in Southeast, 41–43
in Southwest, 43
Spanish Armada defeated by England, 49
Transcontinental Treaty and, 380–81, *381*
Treaty of Tordesillas and, 26, 28
Spanish Armada, 49
Spanish colonies. *See* New Spain
Spanish Florida, 154
exploration of, 41–43
First Seminole War in, 379–80, *380*
Pinckney's Treaty of 1795 and, 272, *273*, 379
after Revolutionary War, 222, 240
slavery in English colonies compared to, 123–24
Spanish transfer of, 375
Transcontinental Treaty and, 380–81, *381*
War of 1812 and, 306–7
Spanish Texas, 346
Specie Circular, *418*, 418–19, 421
speech, First Amendment and, 260
spinning bees, 163
spirituals, 453, 455
spoils system, 398
Spotsylvania Court House, Battle of, 615, *616*
Sprigs, Elizabeth, 111
Squanto (Tisquantum), 70
stagecoaches, 335, 341
Stamp Act of 1765
colonial unity against, 163–64
nonimportation movement and, 163
opposition to, *161*, 162
passage of, 161
protests against, 162–63
repeal of, 164, *164*
Stanton, Edwin M., 605, 647
Stanton, Elizabeth Cady, 494, *494*, 496, 624
staple crops, 113

Staples Act, 147
Star of the West, 565
"Star-Spangled Banner, The" (Key), 314, *315*
state constitutions, 222–23
State Department, 257, 264, 269, 288
steamboats, 336–37, *337*, 371
steam engine, 342
Stearns, Junius Brutus, *234*
steel plow, 348
Steinweg, Heinrich, 358
Stephens, Alexander H., 566, 571–72, 629
Steuben, Frederick Wilhelm, Baron von, 211, *211*
Stevens, Thaddeus, 605, 633, 639, 646
Stewart, Alexander T., 358
Stewart, Maria Miller, 495
Stewart, William, 644
Still, William, 488
St. Mary's settlement, 66
Stockton, Robert F., 535
Stone, Lucy, 499
Stono Rebellion, 128
Stowe, Harriet Beecher, 550–51
Strauss, Levi, 542
strikes, women leading labor, 361
Strong, Anna, 227
Stuart, J. E. B., 609
Stuyvesant, Peter, 83–84
sugar, 77–78, *78*, 431, 632
Sugar Act of 1764, 160
Sullivan, John, 212
Sumner, Charles, 346–47, 605, 624, 633, 639, 642–43
    Brooks's attack on, 555
Sumter, Thomas, 214
Supreme Court. *See also specific cases*
    on Burr Conspiracy, 299
    Cherokee seeking relief in, 409–10
    Civil Rights Cases of 1883 and, 666
    on contract rights, 370
    in *Dred Scott* case, 557–58, *558*
    first law overruled by, 288–89, 369
    on Indigenous Americans' removal, 409–10
    on interstate commerce, 370–71
    Jay as chief justice of, 257
    judicial nationalism and, *369*, 369–71
    judicial review and, 289
    Judiciary Act of 1801 and, 277, 288
    on national currency, 370
    Reconstruction eroded by, 666–67
    Slaughterhouse Cases and, 667
Surratt, Mary, 637
Susquehannock, *54*
Sutter, John A., 522, 540
Svinin, Pavel Petrovich, *371*
Sweden, 30
Swedes, in colonial America, 116, *118*

Taino, 25
Taliwa, Battle of, *411*
Tallmadge, James, Jr., 375

Taney, Roger B., 558, 605
Tappan, Arthur and Lewis, 490
tar, in North Carolina, 79–80
Tariff of Abominations (Tariff of 1828), 401–2
tariffs
    Calhoun's compromise, 406
    of 1816, 349–50, 369
    of 1828, 401–2
    under Hamilton, 262–63
    Industrial Revolution and, 349–50
    Madison, J., and, 320, 368–69
Tarleton, Banastre, 215
taverns, *130*, 130–31
taxation. *See also* economy
    colonial resistance to, 165–66, 172
    Confederation Congress and protests over, 241–42
    CSA and, 604
    in England compared to English colonies, 156
    Grenville and, 160–62, 165
    representation and, 172
    Stamp Act of 1765 and, *161*, 161–64, *164*
    Townshend Acts and, 164–65, 168
    Whiskey Rebellion against, 271–72, *272*
Taxation No Tyranny (Johnson, Samuel), 172
Tayloe, John, III, 446
Taylor, Mary Ann, 433
Taylor, Susie King, *601*
Taylor, Zachary
    death of, 548
    election of, 540
    Mexican-American War and, 532, 533, 535–36
    slavery and, 540
    Wilmot Proviso and, *538*
Tea Act of 1773, 169
teaching profession, 361, *362*
technological advancements. *See also specific inventions*
    agriculture and, *348*, 348–49
    cotton gin, 343–44, *345*, 431–32
    for discovery and exploration, 19
    Industrial Revolution and, 343–44, 346–49, *348*
    in Spanish Texas, 346
Tecumseh, 295, 305–6, *306*, 310
Tecumseh's Indian Confederacy, 306
telegraph system, 341–42
"Tell-Tale Heart, The" (Poe), 478
temperance, 480–81, *481*
Tennessee, 379, 383
    in Civil War, 584
    Memphis race massacre in, 642, *642*
Tenochtitlán, 11, *11*, 36–37
Tenskwatawa, 305–6
Tenth Amendment, 257
Tenure of Office Act, 647
Texas

American settlements in, 518, 523–24
    annexation of, 528–31, 537
    Cart War and, 531
    in Civil War, 583
    Compromise of 1850 and, *545*, 548
    cotton production in, 433, *433*
    emancipation of enslaved people in, 376
    Mexican-American War and, 346–47
    population growth in, 529
    Revolution, 524–27
    secession of, 566
    slavery and, 528
    Transcontinental Treaty and, 380–81, *381*
    Underground Railroad and, 524
Texas–New Mexico Act, *545*, 548
textile manufacturers, 349–51, 374
theater, 354–55, *355*
third parties, 416–17
Thirteenth Amendment, 500, 624–25, 643
Thomas, Ella Gertrude Clanton, 598
Thomas, George, 618
Thomas, Jesse, 375
"Thomas Jefferson and the Character Issue" (Wilson, D.), 324–25
Thoreau, Henry David, 331, 473–76, *476*, 479–80, 520
Three-Fifths Compromise, 249
Three Sisters, 17
"Ties That Bind, The" (Clinton, C.), 504–5
Tilden, Samuel J., 668–69, *669*
Timbuktu, Mali, 22, *22*
Tippecanoe, Battle of, 306, 423
Tituba, *74*, 74–75
tobacco, 64, 90, 113, 124, 431, 632
Tocqueville, Alexis de, 396
Toleration Act, England, 67–68
Toltec, 10
Tordesillas, Treaty of, 26, 28
Totonac, 35
Townsend, William, 581
Townshend, Charles, 165
Townshend Acts, 164–65, 168
trade. *See also* global trade; transatlantic slave trade; transportation improvements
    Confederation Congress and, 240–41
    Embargo Act of 1807 and, 302–3, *303*
    New France and, 143
    New Orleans and, 291
    Non-Intercourse Act of 1809 and, 303–4
    triangular, 116, *117*
Trail of Tears, 411–13, *412*, *413*
transatlantic slave trade, 4. *See also* slavery
    African roots of, 120–21
    Caribbean colonies and, 78
    Columbus and, 27
    Constitutional Convention and, 249
    destinations of, 119, *120*
    Dutch and, 65
    England and, 65

growth of, 158
Jefferson ending, 299–300
Middle Passage and, *121*, 122, 249
New England colonies and, 158–59
Portugal and, 65
size of, 119, *120*
triangular trade and, 116, *117*
Transcendental Club, 475
transcendentalism, 473–76
Transcontinental Treaty, 380–81, *381*
transportation improvements
canals and, *336*, 337–38
clipper ships and oceanic, 339, *340*
communication and, 340–42
economic nationalism and, 369
government's role in, 342
land grants and, 342
new roads and, 335–36, *336*, 369, 399
overland, 335, *336*
Panic of 1837 halting, 421
railroads and, 338–39, *339*
stagecoaches and, 335, 341
steamboats and, 336–37, *337*
water, *336*, 336–38, *337*
travel, colonial life and, 130
Travis, William B., 525–26
Treasury Department, 257, 261, 264, 288, 422
Treatise on Domestic Economy, A (Beecher, C.), 493
Trenton, Battle of, 206–7
triangular trade, 116, *117*
Tripoli, 300–301, *301*
Truth, Sojourner, *492*, 493, 506, 653
Tryon, William, 166
Tubman, Harriet, 488, *602*, 602–3
Turkey, 20
Turner, Nat, *457*, 457–58
turnpikes, 369
Tuscarora, 112
Twelfth Amendment, 298
Twice-Told Tales (Hawthorne), 477
two-party system, 420
Two Treatises on Government (Locke), 149
Tyler, John, 423
Clay and, 528–29
Texas annexation and, 529, 530

Uncle Tom's Cabin (Stowe), 550–51
Underground Railroad, 487–88, 524
Union League, 651
unions. *See* organized labor
Unitarianism, 464–65
United States Journal, 330
United States v. Cruikshank, 667
Universalism, 464–65
Upper Creeks, 310–12
urban recreation, in Industrial Revolution, 354, *354*
urban slavery, 452
Utah state, 472

Utah Territory, *471*, 472, 523, *545*, 548
utopian communities, 484–87

Valley Forge, 210–11, *211*
Van Buren, Martin, *420*
abolition movement fought by, 419
background and principles of, 420
Calhoun's conflict with, 398, 403–4, *404*
Democratic Party run by, 397
election of 1832 and, 416–17
election of 1836 and, 420
election of 1840 and, 423, *423*
Free-Soil Party and, 540
inauguration of, 420–21
Independent Treasury Act and, 422
Panic of 1837 and, *421*, 421–22
Texas annexation and, 528
Trail of Tears and, 411–13, *412*, *413*
Van Rensselaer, Stephen, 310
Vázquez de Coronado, Francisco, 41
Velazquez, Loretta Jean, 602
Vermont, 242
Verrazano, Giovanni da, 47
Vesey, Denmark, 456–57
Vespucci, Amerigo, 30
Vicksburg, Battle of, 607–9
Views of Society and Manners in America (Wright, F.), 486
Vikings, 30
Virginia colony
Bacon's Rebellion and, 90–93, *91*
governance in, 64–65
headright system and, 64
infectious diseases in, 65
Jamestown, *54*, 61–66
map of, *54*, *67*
Pocahontas and, 62, *63*
population growth in, 63–64
Powhatan Confederacy and, 61–62
Roanoke colony in, 50, *51*
slave codes in, 124
starvation in, 62–64
tobacco farming in, 64, 90, 113
women's work in, 107–10
Virginia Company, 60–61, *61*, 63–65
Virginia Gazette, 111
Virginia Plan, 245
Virginia Resolves, 163–64
Virginia state
Anglican Church and, 224
Battle of Yorktown in, 217–18, *218*
after Civil War, 631
Constitution ratification and, 253, *253*, 254
cotton production in, 432–33, *433*
early political strength of, 284
first legislature of, 197
Gabriel's Rebellion in, 456
Lincoln, A., in, *570*
Revolutionary War in, 217–18, *218*
Virginia Statute of Religious Freedom, 225

virtual representation, 162
voting rights
African Americans and, 510, 629, 642
Chinese Americans and, 648–49
Fifteenth Amendment and, 510, 648
Jackson, A.'s, election and expansion of, 389
land ownership and, 514
Military Reconstruction Act and, 645
poll taxes and, 658–59
racism in Reconstruction against, 652
Union League and, 651
women and, 494–95, 648, 659
vulcanized rubber, 343

Waddell, Joseph, 579
Wade, Benjamin, 576
Wade-Davis Bill, 633
Wade-Davis Manifesto, 633
Wahunsunacock (Chief Powhatan), 61–62, *62*
Wakeman, Sarah Rosetta (Lyons), *578*, 578–79
Walden (Thoreau), 476
Walden Pond, 476
Waldseemüller, Martin, *27*
Walker, David, 488
Walker, Mary Edwards, 603
Walker, Quock, 248
Walker, Robert J., 559
Walker, William, 513
Walpole, Robert, 149–50
Wampanoag, 95
wampum belt, *97*
Ward, Zebulon, 668
War Democrats, 605
Wardwell, Samuel, 75
warfare. *See also specific battles*
Bacon's Rebellion, 90–93, *91*
Iroquois League and, 97
King Philip's War and, *95*, 95–96
of Mexica, 13
Pequot War and, 94
Pontiac's Rebellion and, 157, *157*
Washington, G.'s, lessons from, 206
Yamasee, 112–13
Warmoth, Henry Clay, 656
War of 1812, *282*
African Americans and, 312–14
aftermath of, 316–21
Battle of Horseshoe Bend and, 312
Battle of Lake Champlain and, 315–16
Battle of New Orleans and, 317–18, *318*
Canada and, 306–7, 308–10, *309*
in Chesapeake Bay, 312
Congress vote on, 304
Creek War and, 310–12, *311*
economic independence from, 319–20
fronts of, 308
Hartford Convention and, 318–19
hawks for, 307

War of 1812, 282 (continued)
  Hull's surrender in, 309
  Indigenous Americans and, 283, 305, 307–8, 310–12, 320–21
  legacies of, 319–21
  motivations for, 305
  naval battles in, 308, 308
  preparation for, 307–8
  slavery and impact of, 317
  soldiers for, 307
  Spanish Florida and, 306–7
  Tecumseh's defeat in, 310
  Treaty of Fort Jackson and, 312
  Washington, D.C., burned in, 312–14, 313
Warren, Mercy Otis, 180
Washington, D.C.
  Compromise of 1790 and, 264
  first inauguration in, 284–85
  slavery in, 285, 285
  War of 1812 and burning of, 312–14, 313
Washington, George, 105, 196, 304
  on African American enlistment, 226
  The American Crisis ordered by, 206
  Bank of the United States and, 264–65
  Battle of Long Island and, 202, 203, 204, 205
  Battle of Princeton and, 200
  Battle of Trenton and, 206–7
  Battle of Yorktown and, 217
  cabinet of, 257
  on citizen-soldiers, 200, 202
  on *Common Sense*, 178
  on Confederation Congress, 236
  at Constitutional Convention, 243, 244
  Continental Army and, 200–201, 226
  Continental Congress and, 193
  election of, 255–56
  Fairfax and, 170
  farewell address of, 275
  in French and Indian War, 150–52, 153
  French Revolution and, 268–69
  Fugitive Slave Act of 1793 and, 250
  on future of United States of America, 231
  Genêt and, 268
  on Hamilton and Jefferson feud, 266
  inauguration of, 256, 257
  Jay's Treaty and, 270–71
  Jefferson's State Department resignation and, 269
  Naturalization Act of 1790 and, 261
  Newburgh Conspiracy and, 236–37
  Proclamation Act of 1763 and, 158
  re-election of, 268
  Revolutionary War and, 175–76, 202–4, 206–8, 220–21
  slavery and, 181, 225
  smallpox and mass inoculation by, 207
  soldier's wives and, 230
  on Spanish alliance, 216
  Steuben and, 211, 211

  success of, 220–21
  transfer of power by, 274–75
  Valley Forge and, 210–11, 211
  warfare lessons of, 206
  Whiskey Rebellion and, 271–72, 272
Washington, Martha Custis, 105, 106, 109, 176, 250, 256
water transportation improvements, 336, 336–38, 337
Watie, Stand, 583, 583
Watkins, Sam, 585
Watson, Henry, 432
Wayne, "Mad" Anthony, 269
Wealth of Nations, The (Smith, Adam), 261, 349
Webster, Daniel, 343, 397, 400–401, 420, 529
  Compromise of 1850 and, 544–45
  on nullification, 402–3, 403
Webster-Hayne debate, 402–3, 403
Weetamoo, 95
Welles, Gideon, 647
Wells, Henry, 341
Wells Fargo stagecoaches, 341
Welsh, in colonial America, 117, 118
We Owe Allegiance to No Crown (Woodside), 282
West, Benjamin, 132
West, Thomas (Lord De La Warr), 87
West Africa. *See also* transatlantic slave trade
  Ghana, 21, 21–22
  Mali, 21–23, 22
  rice cultivation in, 80
  Songhai, 21, 23
Western land policy debates, 272–73
West Indies, 241
Westward expansion. *See also* Mexican-American War
  Buchanan-Pakenham Treaty and, 531, 532
  California annexation and, 533–35
  California gold rush and, 540–43, 541, 542
  California settlement and, 521, 521–23, 522
  California statehood and, 543
  Compromise of 1850 and, 544, 544–45, 545, 548
  Donner party and, 522–23
  goals of, 513–14
  Indigenous Plains peoples and, 516–18, 517, 518
  infectious diseases and, 520
  Kansas-Nebraska Act and, 551–54, 553
  manifest destiny and, 514
  Mexico and, 518–19
  New Mexico statehood and, 543
  Oregon Country and, 519–20, 531, 532
  Overland Trails in, 514–16, 515, 519
  popular sovereignty and, 539–40
  race and, 514

  southbound Underground Railroad and, 524
  Sutter's Fort and, 522, 522
  Texas annexation and, 528–31, 537
  Texas Revolution and, 524–27
  Texas settlements and, 518, 523–24
  Wilmot Proviso and, 538, 538–39
"What to the Slave Is the Fourth of July?" (Douglass), 497
Wheatley, Phillis, 181, 181
Whig Party
  economic nationalism and, 420
  election of 1844 and, 529, 530
  formation of, 419–20
  Jackson, A., and response of, 423–24
  split of, 552
Whigs
  on Grenville's policies, 162
  nonimportation movement and, 163
  Sons of Liberty and, 162–63, 163, 166
Whiskey Rebellion, 271–72, 272
"whiskey ring," 622
White, Hugh, 167–68, 420
White, John, 17, 50
White, William, 366
White Bear (Satanta), 660
Whitefield, George, 134, 135
White House, slave labor and, 285, 285
White Lion, 65
White Plains, Battle of, 202–3, 205
Whitesides, D. B., 655
Whites in South, 438–42
White supremacy, 442–43, 675. *See also* Ku Klux Klan; slavery
Whitman, Walt, 479, 560
Whitmire, Eliza, 412
Whitney, Eli, 343–44, 345, 431–32
Wickliffe, C. A., 377
wigwams, 17
"wildcat" banks, 417
Wilderness, Battle of the, 614–15, 616
Wilderness Road, 274
William III, 148–49
Williams, Abigail, 75
Williams, Kidada E., 675
Williams, Roger, 72, 72–73
Williamson, Hugh, 185
Wilmot, David, 538–39
Wilmot Proviso, 538, 538–39
Wilson, Douglas L., 324–25
Wilson, James, 245
Winthrop, John, 71, 71, 73–74, 107, 115
Wisconsin, 356
witches in Salem, 74, 74–76, 75
Withers, Thomas Jefferson, 565
Woman in the Nineteenth Century (Fuller, M.), 475
women. *See also* gender
  abolition movement and, 498–99
  American Revolution, freedoms and equality of, 181–84, 227, 227, 230

in bread riots in CSA, 606
California gold rush and, 543
in Civil War in disguise, *578*, 578–79, 602–3
Civil War roles of, *601*, 601–3
in colonial life, 107–10
Comanche and, 517
Constitution and, 250–51
cotton production in Old Southwest and, 433–34
coverture and, 182–83
cult of domesticity and, 493–94
Declaration of Rights and Sentiments and, *494*, 494–95, 496
democracy denied to, 286
divorce and, 107, 184
Edenton Tea Party and, 170
Emerson on, 474–75
as enslaved people, 109, 251, 440, 447, 450–53
Fifteenth Amendment and, 648
Great Awakening and, 136
Industrial Revolution and household work of, 351–52
as inventors, 343, *343*
in Iroquois culture, 18

labor activism of, 351
liberty and, 227
in medical profession, 362, *363*
Military Reconstruction Act and, 645
in New Harmony community, 487
organized labor and strikes led by, 361
plantation management and, 109–10
as plantation mistress, 439–40
political democracy and, 396–97
Powhatan Confederacy and, 61
in professional workforce, 362
prostitution and, 108, 230
as Puritans, 110
religion and, 110
in Revolutionary War, *227*, 230
in Second Great Awakening leadership, *468*, 468–69
Seneca Falls Convention and, *494*, 494–95, 496
separate spheres and, 504–7
in teaching profession, 361, *362*
in textile mills, *350*, 350–51
in theater, 354, *355*
voting rights and, 494–95, 648, 659
witches in Salem, *74*, 74–76, *75*
work and colonial, 107–10

Women's Loyal National League, 624
women's rights movements, 487, 493–95
  Douglass supporting, 659
  emancipation and, 624
  in Reconstruction, 659, *659*
women's work, 107–10
Wood, Henrietta, 668
Woodhull, Victoria, 659
Woodside, John Archibald, *282*
Worcester v. Georgia, 409–10
work, colonial women and, 107–10
world maps, early, *27*
Wright, Frances, *486*, 486–87
writs of assistance, 149

XYZ Affair, 276, *276*

Yamasee, 112–13
Yancey, William L., 561
Yates, Richard, 644, 648
Yeager, Joseph, *366*
York, Lewis and Clark expedition and, 296, *296*
Young, Brigham, 471–72, *472*

Zuni, 14

160°W 140°W 120°W 100°W 80°W 60°W 40°W 20°W 0°
80°N
60°N
40°N
20°N
0°
20°S
40°S
Beaufort Sea
Bering Strait
Bering Sea
Aleutian Islands
Gulf of Alaska
Haida Gwaii (Queen Charlotte Is.)
Victoria Island
Ellesmere Island
Baffin Island
Baffin Bay
Greenland (Den.)
Nuuk (Godthåb)
Reykjavík
Arctic Circle
ICELAND
UNITED KINGDOM
IRELAND
London
FRANCE
PORTUGAL
SPAIN
Rabat
MOROCCO
Hudson Bay
Labrador Sea
CANADA
Ottawa
UNITED STATES
Washington, D.C.
Azores (Port.)
Bermuda (U.K.)
ATLANTIC OCEAN
Canary Islands (Sp.)
Western Sahara (Morocco)
MEXICO
Gulf of Mexico
Havana
Tropic of Cancer
Mexico City
BAHAMAS
JAMAICA
HAITI
CUBA
DOMINICAN REPUBLIC
ST. KITTS AND NEVIS
ANTIGUA AND BARBUDA
DOMINICA
BARBADOS
GRENADA
TRINIDAD AND TOBAGO
ST. LUCIA
Caribbean Sea
MAURITANIA
CAPE VERDE
SENEGAL
MALI
GAMBIA
GUINEA-BISSAU
GUINEA
SIERRA LEONE
LIBERIA
CÔTE D'IVOIRE
BURKINA FASO
GHANA
BELIZE
GUATEMALA
EL SALVADOR
HONDURAS
NICARAGUA
COSTA RICA
PANAMA
Caracas
VENEZUELA
GUYANA
SURINAME
French Guiana (Fr.)
Bogotá
COLOMBIA
Quito
ECUADOR
Equator
Galápagos Islands (Ecuador)
Phoenix Islands
Marquesas Islands (Fr.)
PACIFIC OCEAN
SAMOA
Apia
PERU
Lima
BRAZIL
BOLIVIA
La Paz
Sucre
Brasília
Tahiti
French Polynesia (Fr.)
Cook Islands (N.Z.)
Nuku'alofa
TONGA
Tropic of Capricorn
Pitcairn Islands (U.K.)
Easter Island (Chile)
PARAGUAY
Asunción
São Paulo
CHILE
Santiago
URUGUAY
Buenos Aires
Montevideo
ARGENTINA
ATLANTIC OCEAN
Prime Meridian
0 1,000 2,000 Miles
0 1,000 2,000 Kilometers
Falkland Islands (U.K.)
South Georgia (U.K.)
Scotia Sea

0 200 400 Miles
0 200 400 Kilometers
Shetland Islands (U.K.)
NORWAY
Oslo
FINLAND
Gulf of Bothnia
Helsinki
Tallinn
St. Petersburg
Stockholm
SWEDEN
North Sea
Northern Ireland
Scotland
Belfast
IRELAND
Dublin
UNITED KINGDOM
Wales
England
London
Celtic Sea
ESTONIA
LATVIA
Riga
RUSSIAN FEDERATION
Moscow
Baltic Sea
DENMARK
Copenhagen
Kaliningrad
RUSSIA
LITHUANIA
Vilnius
Minsk
BELARUS
Dnieper R.
NETHERLANDS
Amsterdam
Berlin
POLAND
Warsaw
ATLANTIC OCEAN
English Channel
Brussels
BELGIUM
GERMANY
Luxembourg
LUXEMBOURG
Paris
Prague
CZECH REP.
UKRAINE
Kiev
FRANCE
LIECHTENSTEIN
SLOVAKIA
Vienna
Bratislava
Rostov-na-Donu
Bay of Biscay
Bern
SWITZERLAND
AUSTRIA
Budapest
HUNGARY
MOLDOVA
Chisinau
Ljubljana
SLOVENIA
Sea of Azov
Crimea
ROMANIA
Venice
Zagreb
CROATIA
BOS. & HERZ.
Belgrade
SERBIA
Bucharest
PORTUGAL
ANDORRA
Andorra la Vella
SAN MARINO
MONACO
Sarajevo
Danube R.
Black Sea
Lisbon
Madrid
Barcelona
Corsica (FRANCE)
ITALY
Adriatic Sea
MONT.
KOS.
Sofia
BULGARIA
Skopje
SPAIN
VATICAN CITY
Rome
Tirana
ALBANIA
MACEDONIA
Istanbul
ASIA
Sardinia (ITALY)
Ankara
TURKEY
Strait of Gibraltar
BALEARIC ISLANDS (SPAIN)
Tyrrhenian Sea
Mediterranean Sea
Aegean Sea
GREECE
Athens
Sicily
Ionian Sea
MOROCCO
AFRICA
TUNISIA
Valletta
MALTA
ALGERIA
Sea of Crete
Nicosia
CYPRUS

20°E
40°E
60°E
80°E
100°E
120°E
140°E
160°E
Svalbard (Norway)
Franz Josef Land
Barents Sea
Novaya Zemlya
Kara Sea
Laptev Sea
New Siberian Islands
80°N
East Siberian Sea
ARCTIC OCEAN
NORWAY
SWEDEN
FINLAND
ESTONIA
LATVIA
LITHUANIA
BELARUS
North Sea
DEN.
NETH.
POLAND
GERMANY
Paris
UKRAINE
Moscow
RUSSIAN FEDERATION
Sea of Okhotsk
60°N
Bering Sea
Aleutian Islands
Lake Baikal
Caspian Sea
Astana
KAZAKHSTAN
Ulaanbaatar
MONGOLIA
ROMANIA
BULGARIA
ITALY
Black Sea
GEORGIA
ARMENIA
AZERBAIJAN
UZBEKISTAN
KYRGYZSTAN
TURKMENISTAN
TAJIKISTAN
Mediterranean Sea
GREECE
TURKEY
Beijing
N. KOREA
Pyongyang
Seoul
S. KOREA
Tokyo
JAPAN
40°N
TUNISIA
CYPRUS
LEBANON
ISRAEL
SYRIA
IRAQ
Tehran
IRAN
AFGHANISTAN
CHINA
PACIFIC OCEAN
Tripoli
Cairo
BAHRAIN
PAKISTAN
New Delhi
NEPAL
BHUTAN
Shanghai
LIBYA
EGYPT
JORDAN
KUWAIT
QATAR
Red Sea
U.A.E.
OMAN
SAUDI ARABIA
INDIA
MYANMAR (BURMA)
BANGLADESH
Bay of Bengal
Taipei
TAIWAN
Northern Mariana Islands (U.S.)
ALGERIA
NIGER
Khartoum
CHAD
SUDAN
ERITREA
YEMEN
Mumbai
Arabian Sea
Hanoi
LAOS
VIETNAM
THAILAND
Bangkok
CAMBODIA
South China Sea
Philippine Sea
Manila
PHILIPPINES
Guam (U.S.)
20°N
NIGERIA
N'Djamena
DJIBOUTI
Addis Ababa
ETHIOPIA
SRI LANKA
BRUNEI
PALAU
MARSHALL IS.
BENIN
TOGO
CENT. AFR. REP.
SOUTH SUDAN
CAMEROON
EQ. GUINEA
GABON
Juba
UGANDA
SOMALIA
Mogadishu
MALDIVES
Kuala Lumpur
MALAYSIA
Celebes Sea
FEDERATED STATES OF MICRONESIA
CONGO
RWANDA
BURUNDI
KENYA
Nairobi
DEM. REP. OF THE CONGO
SINGAPORE
Sumatra
INDONESIA
Java Sea
Jakarta
Java
NAURU
KIRIBATI
0°
PAPUA NEW GUINEA
SOLOMON IS.
SEYCHELLES
TANZANIA
Dar es Salaam
Luanda
MALAWI
COMOROS
Diego Garcia (U.K.)
Dili
TIMOR LESTE
Arafura Sea
Port Moresby
TUVALU
ANGOLA
ZAMBIA
Lusaka
MOZAMBIQUE
MADAGASCAR
Antananarivo
Coral Sea
VANUATU
FIJI
NAMIBIA
ZIMBABWE
Harare
MAURITIUS
Réunion (Fr.)
20°S
Windhoek
BOTSWANA
Gaborone
Pretoria
INDIAN OCEAN
AUSTRALIA
New Caledonia (Fr.)
Bloemfontein
SWAZILAND
LESOTHO
SOUTH AFRICA
Cape Town
North Island
Great Australian Bight
Canberra
NEW ZEALAND
Tasman Sea
40°S
Wellington
Tasmania
South Island
60°S
Antarctic Circle
ANTARCTICA

0
500
1,000 Miles
0
500
1,000 Kilometers
RUSSIAN FEDERATION
ASIA
Moscow
EUROPE
Volga R.
Astana
Kiev
UKRAINE
Irtysh R.
KAZAKHSTAN
Caspian Sea
Lake Balkhash
Black Sea
UZBEKISTAN
Bishkek
KYRGYZSTAN
GEORGIA
Tbilisi
ARMENIA
AZERBAIJAN
Tashkent
Ankara
Yerevan
Baku
TURKMENISTAN
TAJIKISTAN
TURKEY
Ashgabat
Dushanbe
CYPRUS
Nicosia
SYRIA
Tehran
CHINA
Kabul
LEBANON
Beirut
Damascus
Baghdad
AFGHANISTAN
Islamabad
ISRAEL
Amman
IRAQ
IRAN
Indus R.
Jerusalem
Persian Gulf
Cairo
JORDAN
New Delhi
BHUTAN
EGYPT
KUWAIT
Kuwait City
PAKISTAN
NEPAL
Manama
Kathmandu
Thimphu
BAHRAIN
Doha
Abu Dhabi
INDIA
Ganges R.
Riyadh
Red Sea
Dhaka
QATAR
U.A.E.
Muscat
Arabian Sea
AFRICA
SAUDI ARABIA
OMAN
BANGLADESH